MW01631041

Art | Basel

YEAR 45

jrp|ringier

A–M

- Hong Kong (green)
- Basel (blue)
- Miami Beach (red)

The images in the Galleries sections (Exhibitors Lists) were supplied in response to the question "Where do you work best?"

Table of Contents

Tour d'horizon 5
Sarah Thornton
Introduction 8
Marc Spiegler
Maps 12
Partners Pages 19

#

14 Rooms 36 (Basel)
Klaus Biesenbach
and Hans Ulrich Obrist
Exhibitors List 46
Focus 49
303 Gallery

A

α (alpha) pulse 52 (Hong Kong)
Carsten Nicolai
Nadim Abbas 60 (Hong Kong)
Exhibitors List 68
Focus 79
Galería Juana de Aizpuru

B

Basel 82 (Basel)
Portfolio
Biennales 2015 121
Okwui Enwezor
RoseLee Goldberg
Eungie Joo
Ralph Rugoff
Exhibitors List 128
Focus 143
von Bartha

C

Cultural Sponsorship 146
András Szántó
Curators' Choices 154
Hou Hanru (Hong Kong)
Jessica Morgan (Hong Kong)
Bice Curiger (Basel)
Massimiliano Gioni (Basel)
Stuart Comer (Miami Beach)
Taiyana Pimentel (Miami Beach)
Exhibitors List 192
Focus 206
Galerie Gisela Capitain

D

Discoveries 208 (Hong Kong)
Prize Winner:
Nadia Kaabi-Linke
Exhibitors List 220
Focus 227
Massimo De Carlo

E

Encounters 230 (Hong Kong)
Yuko Hasegawa
Edition 246
Emi Eu
Exhibitors List 256
Focus 261
Eslite Gallery

F

Feature 264 (Basel)
Douglas Fogle
Film 280 (Basel)
Jane & Louise Wilson
Exhibitors List 286
Focus 293
Foksal Gallery Foundation

G

Giving Back: Art Basel Crowdfunding Initiative 296
Exhibitors List 302
Focus 314
Galerie Karsten Greve

H

Hong Kong 316 (Hong Kong)
Portfolio
Exhibitors List 354
Focus 362
Galerie Max Hetzler

I

Insights 364 (Hong Kong)
Cosmin Costinas
Exhibitors List 376
Focus 380
Taka Ishii Gallery

J

Joan Jonas 382 (Basel)
Exhibitors List 386
Focus 390
Jablonka Galerie

K

Kabinett 392 (Miami Beach)
Pablo León de la Barra
Exhibitors List 402
Focus 415
David Kordansky Gallery

L

Life Like 418
Portfolio
Exhibitors List 430
Focus 440
Yvon Lambert

M

Magazines 442
Miami Beach 446 (Miami Beach)
Portfolio
MEƎM 4 MIAMI 474 (Miami Beach)
Ryan McNamara
Exhibitors List 488
Focus 508
Mendes Wood DM

N–Z

Hong Kong
Basel
Miami Beach

The images in the Galleries sections (Exhibitors Lists) were supplied in response to the question "Where do you work best?"

N

Next 2015 510
Nova 514
Alex Gartenfeld
Exhibitors List 524
Focus 531
Richard Nagy Ltd.

O

Ovations 534
Harry Bellet
Exhibitors List 544
Focus 548
One and J. Gallery

P

Parcours 550
Portfolio
Positions 562
Ruba Katrib
Public 570
Portfolio
Exhibitors List 582
Focus 593
P.P.O.W

Q

R

Retrospective 596
Paula Cooper
Exhibitors List 606
Focus 614
Anthony Reynolds Gallery

S

Statements 616
Chus Martinez
Survey 626
Portfolio
Exhibitors List 638
Focus 658
Sfeir-Semler Gallery

T

Top Tens 660
Claire Hsu
Gregor Muir
Rudy Tseng
Anne Pasternak
Tony Salamé
Wolfgang Tillmans
Shelley Fox Aarons & Philip Aarons
Mario García Torres
Ella Fontanals-Cisneros
Exhibitors List 680
Focus 688
Tornabuoni Art

U

Unlimited 690
Portfolio
Exhibitors List 718
Focus 719
Upstream Gallery

V

Virtual Visual 722
Chrissie Iles with
Rachel Rose and Tabor Robak
Exhibitors List 726
Focus 730
Annemarie Verna Galerie

W

Kurt Wyss 732
Portfolio
Exhibitors List 744
Focus 750
Waddington Custot Galleries

X

Xu Zhen 752
Exhibitors List 758
Focus 759
XVA Gallery

Y

Exhibitors List 762
Focus 764
Y++ Wada Gallery

Z

Exhibitors List 766
Focus 768
Zeno X Gallery

Index

Index 769

Imprint 780

The Changing Face of Artistic Success

Sarah Thornton

Sarah Thornton is the author of *Seven Days in the Art World* (2009) and *33 Artists in 3 Acts* (2014). She has a BA in Art History and a PhD in Sociology and was chief writer on contemporary art for *The Economist*. She lives in San Francisco.

The chief currency of the art world is not dollars, pounds, Swiss francs, rubles, or Chinese yuan. It is an elusive and often contested value called "credibility." At once a social sphere and a professional network, the art world is also an orbit of belief. Not everyone has faith in contemporary art; some think that art ended with the Impressionists, others believe in science and distrust what they see as pretentious cultural experiments. But soaring museum attendance figures and global sales volumes attest to a growing contingent of believers in the relevance of recently made art.

Acceptance of contemporary art does not lead to confidence in *all* living artists. On the contrary, one of the key pleasures in visiting art fairs and biennials is judgment—distinguishing between the cool and the derivative, the ever emergent and imminently blue chip, the authentic and ersatz, the art that matters and stuff that simply "looks like art," as John Baldessari sometimes describes student work.

Instrumental to viewers' decisions about where to invest their faith, is knowledge of who conceived of the work. The answer is essential to making sense of a piece. Although some art world insiders insist that the artwork takes precedence over its maker, it is really a double act. After all, artists are the people who have the authority to designate a found object as "art." They have all the ambition, intention, and discipline that an inanimate object does not.

Artists' integrity is a guarantor of their work and, as such, always under interrogation. While innovative painters such as Courbet, Manet, and Turner faced diverse credibility issues, Marcel Duchamp, the grandfather of contemporary art, made belief a central artistic theme. When he signed a urinal and declared it an artwork titled *Fountain* in 1917, he made it both easier and harder for artists to be taken seriously. He decisively liberated art from craft, transforming artists into ideas people who could happily delegate the manual labor of art making to others. Their intelligence and integrity no longer resided in their hand, but in their distinctive way of thinking, and this heightened intellectual status contributed to their rise up the cultural ranks. However, in claiming a godlike power for artists to designate anything they choose as art, Duchamp put great pressure on their individual authority, contributing to the fraught distinction between "real artists" and the rest (who are nowadays variously dismissed as pretenders, unoriginal wannabes, and cynical manufacturers). It is no accident that Duchamp crafted identities as well as ideas, presenting himself as a confidence man or con artist and a vaguely upper-middle-class woman called Rrose Sélavy, two social types that were unlikely to inspire conviction in artwork at the time. Isn't it the case that the best way to counter prejudice is to spoof it very specifically?

For much of the 20th century, "genuine" artists were male artists. When researching my book *33 Artists in 3 Acts*, I heard a lot about the extra hurdles women encountered.

Feminist issues were considered too frivolous for art, explained Martha Rosler, who learned early on that she had to adopt "hard-edged, fast-talking, wisecracking, heavy-drinking" behavior to gain the respect of her male peers. In the 1970s, Marina Abramović said, a love of fashion "made you a bad artist." Even personal physical beauty could disrupt the process of being taken seriously, so Cindy Sherman felt the need to "experiment with being as ugly as possible." Motherhood was a major can of worms. Laurie Simmons told me that you knew you weren't supposed to mention your kids in an artist talk (even if she did). Although women artists under the age of 45 still experience gender bias, having children is no longer a credibility-killer.

Another change in the expectations that befall professional artists relates to self-expression, particularly the cathartic outpouring of emotion associated with Abstract Expressionism. The purely expressive function of art has been reassigned to the untrained, inmates of prisons and psychiatric hospitals, and creative people with disabilities. It is celebrated within the world of Outsider art, but considered cliché in the insider art world. Only artists from older generations can pull off the art-as-therapy trope in ways that command respect. Yayoi Kusama, for example, sleeps in an asylum around the corner from her studio, but her white "Infinity Net" paintings from the late 1950s didn't just protect her from being obliterated by an immeasurable void, they bridged the gap between Abstract Expressionism and Minimalism.

More than ever, globalization is a driver of change in the style and substance of credibility. "Local artist" has become synonymous with unambitious artist. It used to be that national recognition was the first step on the ladder toward the real deal of international appreciation, but today "support," as it is called, is almost as likely to come from abroad. Artists have long congregated in cities like Paris, Berlin, and New York. Emigration helps them escape the burdens of their cultural heritage and embrace identities that they might otherwise feel inhibited in assuming. But, increasingly, the art world expects artists to be sophisticated, globalized selves—familiar with a broad range of venues and audiences, networked with curators and dealers in cities on several continents, able to rise swiftly to the occasion of a site specific work in New Orleans, Sante Fe, Kassel, or Kabul. If art is what you can get away with, clearly you can get away with different things in different parts of the world.

When I asked Ai Weiwei one of my favorite questions—what is an artist?—he told me the story of his father, Ai Qing, who was perceived as an enemy of successive governments, including being deemed a "rightist" by the Maoists and sentenced to hard labor in the remote province of Xinjiang for 18 years. According to Ai, his father's crime was that "he thought that the garden should have variety—all kinds of ideas and expressions—rather than just a single beauty." When Ai finished recounting this history, I returned to the question that had prompted it. So, is an artist, or at least a significant one, an enemy of the state? Ai lifted his eyebrows with half-surprise then said, "The artist is an enemy of general sensibilities." His response was an attenuation of a romantic, avant-garde position, which maintains that aesthetic advancement goes hand in hand with political progress. Living in a non-democracy with no human right to freedom of speech, Ai can credibly enliven this mythic role, whereas an American or German would likely be accused of trite delusion.

The chief currency of the art world is not dollars, pounds, Swiss francs, rubles, or Chinese yuan. It is an elusive and often contested value called "credibility."

At the moment, the factor affecting the perception of artists' credibility more than any other is their relation to the market. In the wake of the financial crisis, a booming art market, and the widening gap between the rich and the poor, the art world has become more polarized. What was decorous class antagonism has become a full-fledged culture war. "Curators are steering away from showing artists with markets. They want power and the only way they can have any is to keep the gates locked," said one young American artist who spoke on the condition of anonymity. "Artists are not supposed to talk about the market. We are supposed to be innocent victims of our own success," he added.

Damien Hirst is the definitive test case. He challenged the art world's belief in him in at least two ways that were so extreme that even a large solo exhibition with record-breaking attendance at Tate Modern hasn't dispelled the doubt. First, he auctioned off over two hundred newly made artworks at Sotheby's for £111 million ($198 million) in September 2008. Many people regarded the sale—a landmark in the commoditization of art, with the ironic title *Beautiful Inside My Head Forever*—as a conceptual event, marking a moment of unprecedented artistic empowerment and a fulfillment of Warhol's idea of the "business artist." The elusive cult-artist Cady Noland, for example, told me that she wished that more artists had such control. But many others declared that, with this act, Hirst had ceased to be an artist. Artists are supposed to have goals more profound than profit, and the auction was openly mercenary. Hirst, they thought, had mutated into a designer of luxury goods.

Then a year later, Hirst appeared to have a midlife crisis when he abandoned making the style of work for which he was known (spin, spot, and butterfly paintings, cabinets filled with pills, zircons, and other things) in favor of making paintings with his own hand in the manner of Francis Bacon. This dramatic departure from his previous work seemed to renounce it. At the time, he told me, "I'd undergone some big changes in myself, which hadn't come through in the work. Maybe if I hadn't changed so much, I could have carried on making that work forever." The statement sounds fair enough, except that such about-faces are subject to critical scrutiny and the new paintings were unable to bear it.

An artist's apparent relationship to the market tends to have more impact on their credibility than their actual financial position. "Art is one of the few fields where creating the illusion that you are less successful is a benefit to your reputation," says a UCLA graduate, who works for an artist who lives in fear of being labeled "commercial." Although this artist concentrates on museum shows and rarely does gallery exhibitions, he makes a high volume of work, which is sold out of the studio and his galleries' backrooms. "Overproduction looks bad," adds the assistant. "It looks like the artist is pandering to the market, mindlessly feeding demand, laughing all the way to the bank." But, many artists enjoy being prolific and trying out lots of versions and ideas for their own sake. So the prevailing prejudices of the art world sometimes compel artists, paradoxically, to behave in disingenuous ways in order to maintain their credibility.

Although critics are said to have lost their influence over the fate of artists' careers, the media (a sprawling combination of mass, niche, and social) have arguably more impact than ever. Indeed, the perceptual power of the market results in part from the fact that high prices command headlines. But a record price at auction is just as likely to discredit as validate an artist (especially a young one) in the minds of all but the most gullible of neophyte collectors. As Walter Robinson wrote last year in a much-quoted article titled "Flipping and the Rise of Zombie Formalism," money talks, so the real question is: "What is it saying?" Underneath the diverse loud-mouthed declarations of money, I hear a ceaseless whisper, confessing, "I don't believe in anything but myself"—an admission that undermines its ability to endorse.

It is intriguing to note that Giorgio Vasari's Renaissance tome, *Lives of the Artists*, is littered with references to the fame of his artist subjects. Fame was the unqualified marker of success at a time when museums, not to mention solo retrospectives, did not exist. Vasari didn't distinguish between celebrity and recognition. Today, art world insiders disdain celebrity as vapid notoriety, whereas they revere recognition, which is a tribute to achievement and acknowledges who you really are. In our global, pluralistic times, recognition often comes hand in hand with what feels to artists like misrecognition (being loved for the wrong reasons, described in inaccurate ways, valued by a social group adjacent to their actual target audience). Whatever the outcome, artists today need to perform in ways that yield a faithful following. Although it is often said that they must accrue a "consensus of belief" to succeed, unanimity is rare. Artists should feel free to appreciate the tenacious conviction of a faction.

Marc Spiegler
Director
Art Basel

Dear Reader,

You hold in your hands the second edition of Art Basel's annual book, which captures our wide-ranging activities and those of the art world that we inhabit. When the first edition appeared last year, many people mistakenly assumed it was a one-off, simply due its imposing weight and extensive content. But from the beginning we felt every year deserves to be so thoroughly documented.

In entirely rethinking our approach to publishing, we shifted from a neutral stance to one in which great efforts and remarkable moments are spotlighted. For this edition, we have once again asked curators, critics, and collectors to share their highlights; their wide-ranging choices embody the pluralism of tastes that drive today's art world.

For Art Basel, 2014 was marked by our staging major events at all three fairs. First, Carsten Nicolai's *α (alpha) pulse* took over the entire 484-meter facade of Kowloon's ICC Tower—an artwork of unprecedented height, visible to literally a million people. Next was Basel's *14 Rooms* project in collaboration with the Fondation Beyeler and the Theater Basel, curated by Hans Ulrich Obrist and Klaus Biesenbach—a landmark moment for live art. Finally came *MEƎM 4 Miami*, a spellbinding piece by artist Ryan McNamara, commissioned by Performa, in which many forms of dance were interwoven within an experience driven by the neurology of this digital native. Just as importantly, we have launched a collaboration with Kickstarter that has increased funding and lifted the profile for non-profits worldwide.

Space constraints do not allow a detailed thank-you to the galleries, cultural allies, corporate sponsors, and team members who make Art Basel's year-round activities possible. But I would like to thank those who have made this book so vibrant in evoking all of these activities worldwide: Lionel Bovier and his team at JRP|Ringier.

Wishing you many delights and discoveries over Year 45's 776 pages,

Marc Spiegler
Director, Art Basel

Liebe Leserinnen, Liebe Leser,

In Ihren Händen halten Sie die zweite Ausgabe des Jahrbuchs der Art Basel, eine Veröffentlichung, die unser breites Spektrum an Aktivitäten und die Welt der Kunst, in der wir leben, darstellen möchte. Als letztes Jahr die erste Ausgabe erschien, gingen viele Menschen aufgrund des beachtlichen Gewichts und des umfassenden Inhalts irrtümlicherweise von einer einmaligen Veröffentlichung aus. Wir finden jedoch, dass jedes Jahr es verdient, ausführlich dokumentiert zu werden.

Unsere Vorgehensweise bei der Herausgabe haben wir komplett überdacht und sind dabei von einem neutralen Ansatz dazu übergegangen, die grossen Bemühungen und außergewöhnliche Augenblicke in den Vordergrund zu stellen. Für diese Ausgabe haben wir erneut Kuratoren, Kritiker und Sammler gebeten, uns von ihren Highlights zu erzählen.

Für die Art Basel war das Jahr 2014 geprägt durch unsere Großveranstaltungen auf allen drei Messen. Zunächst bedeckte Carsten Nicolais mit *α (alpha) pulse* die gesamte 484 Meter hohe Fassade des ICC Tower in Kowloon – ein Kunstwerk, das für sage und schreibe eine Million Menschen sichtbar war. Darauf folgte das Basler Projekt *14 Rooms* in Zusammenarbeit mit der Fondation Beyeler und dem Theater Basel, kuratiert von Hans Ulrich Obrist und Klaus Biesenbach – ein Meilenstein in der lebendigen Kunst. Und schliesslich wurde *MEƎM 4 Miami* aufgeführt, ein bezauberndes, von Performa in Auftrag gegebenes Werk des Künstlers Ryan McNamara, bei dem viele Tanzarten aufeinander trafen, durch die das Erleben und die Denkweise dieses Künstlers der digitalen Generation zum Ausdruck kommen. Gleichermassen von Bedeutung war unsere mit Kickstarter ins Leben gerufene Zusammenarbeit, durch die weitere Mittel für Projekte zur Verfügung gestellt werden konnten.

Für eine detaillierte Danksagung an alle Gallerien, Kulturpartner, Sponsoren und Teammitglieder, welche die ganzjährige Tätigkeit der Art Basel ermöglichen, fehlt hier der Platz, aber nennen möchte ich Lionel Bovier und sein Team bei JRP|Ringier.

Ich wünsche Ihnen viel Freude und zahlreiche Entdeckungen auf den 775 Seiten des Year 45,

Marc Spiegler
Direktor, Art Basel

Caro lettore,

Quella che tiene in mano è la seconda edizione dell'annuario di Art Basel, una pubblicazione che mira ad abbracciare le nostre molteplici attività ed il mondo artistico di cui facciamo parte. Quando l'anno scorso è apparsa la prima edizione, molte persone hanno pensato che l'esperienza non si sarebbe ripetuta, tenendo conto dell'enorme peso del catalogo e dell'estensione del contenuto. Per quanto ci riguarda, siamo profondamente convinti che ogni anno meriti di essere documentato in maniera approfondita.

Ripensando completamente il nostro approccio alla pubblicazione, ci siamo spostati da una posizione neutrale a mettere in primo piano gli sforzi ed i momenti di maggiore rilievo. In quest'edizione abbiamo nuovamente chiesto ai curatori, ai critici ed ai collezionisti di condividere i loro punti forti e le loro scelte di ampio respiro.

Per Art Basel, il 2014 è stato caratterizzato dai nostri maggiori eventi, che hanno interessato tutte le tre fiere. Cominciamo con *α (alpha) pulse* di Carsten Nicolai, che ha preso possesso dell'intera facciata di 484 metri della torre del Centro Internazionale della Finanza di Kowloon ad Hong Kong - un'opera d'arte, visibile, letteralmente, ad un milione di persone. Poi, in collaborazione con la Fondation Beyeler ed il Theater Basel, è arrivato il progetto *14 Rooms* a cura di Hans Ulrich Obrist e Klaus Biesenbach— una vera e propria esperienza di riferimento per l'arte dal vivo. Infine, è stata la volta di *MEƎM 4 Miami*, un pezzo di grande fascino dell'artista Ryan McNamara, commissionato da Performa, in cui molte forme di danza si sono intrecciate all'interno di una personale esperienza neurologica di questo nativo digitale. Un altro fatto molto importante è stato l'avvio di una collaborazione con Kickstarter, che ha portato ad un incremento dei fondi per progetti vari.

Per motivi di spazio non possiamo ringraziare in maniera esaustiva tutte le gallerie, tutti i soci culturali, gli sponsor associati ed i membri delle varie squadre che rendono possibili le varie attività di Art Basel durante tutto l'arco dell'anno, ma ci tengo a ringraziare Lionel Bovier e la sua squadra presso JRP|Ringier.

A questo punto, non mi resta che augurare di fare piacevoli sorprese ed interessanti scoperte nelle 775 pagine dedicate al 45° anno di Art Basel.

Marc Spiegler
Direttore Art Basel

Estimado lector,

Tiene en sus manos la segunda edición del anuario de Art Basel, una publicación que pretende recogerla amplia diversidad de nuestras actividades y el mundo del arte que habitamos. Cuando se publicó la primera edición el año pasado, muchas personas supusieron que se trataba de algo excepcional, debido principalmente a su imponente peso y su extenso contenido. No obstante, consideramos que cada año merece ser contado con la misma minuciosidad.

Replanteándonos por completo nuestro enfoque respecto a la publicación, hemos pasado de adoptar una postura neutral a situar en primer plano los grandes esfuerzos y los momentos inolvidables. De nuevo en esta edición hemos pedido a conservadores, críticos y coleccionistas que compartan lo más destacado desde su punto de vista y sus múltiples elecciones.

Para Art Basel, 2014 estuvo marcado por nuestros grandes acontecimientos en las tres ferias. En primer lugar, *α (alpha) pulse*, de Carsten Nicolai, se apoderó de la fachada completa de 484 metros de la torre ICC de Kowloon (Hong Kong), una obra de arte, a la vista de, literalmente, un millón de personas. Le siguió el proyecto de Art Basel *14 Rooms* en colaboración con la Fondation Beyeler y el Theater Basel, comisariado por Hans Ulrich Obrist y Klaus Biesenbach, un momento histórico para el arte en vivo. Finalmente llegó *MEƎM 4 Miami*, una pieza fascinante obra del artista Ryan McNamara y encargada por Performa, en la que se entrelazaron muchas formas de danza dentro de una experiencia guiada por la neurología de este nativo del mundo digital. Otro hecho no menos importante es que hemos puesto en marcha una colaboración con Kickstarter que ha incrementado la financiación de proyectos y ha elevado el perfil sin ánimo de lucro por todo el mundo.

Las limitaciones de espacio no permiten un agradecimiento pormenorizado a las galerías, instituciónes culturales, patrocinadores corporativos y miembros del equipo que hacen que las actividades de Art Basel a lo largo de todo el año sean posibles, pero me gustaría dar las gracias a Lionel Bovier y su equipo de JRP|Ringier.

Les deseamos que disfruten y hagan nuevos descubrimientos dentro de las más de 774 páginas de Year 45,

Marc Spiegler
Director Art Basel

Chère lectrice, Cher lecteur,

Vous tenez entre vos mains la deuxième édition du livre annuel d'Art Basel, une publication qui vise à rendre compte de notre large éventail d'activités et du monde de l'art dans lequel nous vivons. Lorsque le premier ouvrage est paru, l'année dernière, beaucoup ont cru que cela resterait une publication isolée, simplement en raison de son imposant format et de la richesse de son contenu. En réalité, nous pensons que chaque année mérite d'être aussi bien documentée que la précédente !

En repensant entièrement notre approche de la publication, nous sommes passés d'une position de neutralité à une autre qui tend à mettre au premier plan les efforts particuliers et les moments les plus remarquables. Dans cette édition, nous avons à nouveau demandé à de nombreux curateurs, critiques et collectionneurs de partager leurs coups de cœur et leurs choix.

Pour Art Basel, 2014 a été marquée par des événements majeurs dans chacune des trois foires. D'abord, avec *α (alpha) pulse*, Carsten Nicolai s'est approprié les 484 mètres de hauteur de la tour ICC de Kowloon – une œuvre d'art d'une dimension sans précédent et visible par littéralement un million de personnes. Ensuite, le projet *14 Rooms* d'Art Basel, réalisé en collaboration avec la Fondation Beyeler et le Theater Basel et organisé par Hans Ulrich Obrist et Klaus Biesenbach, a été un moment historique pour l'art de la performance. Enfin, *MEƎM 4 Miami*, une pièce envoûtante de l'artiste Ryan McNamara, commissionnée par Performa, entremêlaient de nombreuses formes de danse au sein d'une expérience pilotée par la neurologie de ce « digital native ». Tout aussi important, nous avons lancé une collaboration avec Kickstarter qui a accru le financement de projets dans le monde entier.

La place manque ici pour remercier individuellement toutes les galeries, tous les partenaires culturels, sponsors et membres des équipes qui rendent possibles les activités d'Art Basel tout au long de l'année, mais je tiens à remercier Lionel Bovier et son équipe chez JRP|Ringier.

Je vous souhaite beaucoup de plaisir et de découvertes à la lecture des 774 pages de cet ouvrage,

Marc Spiegler
Directeur, Art Basel

各位读者：

您手中的是巴塞尔艺术展年刊第二，年刊旨在记录多元化的活动和我们所身处的艺术世界。"Art Basel | Year 44" 于去年问世，内容多采多姿，份量十足，因此很多人以为那是一次性出版的刊物。然而，我们深信每年都应该作如此深入详尽的记录。

我们重新构思出版方向，一改以往中立的角度，以求突出各个精心准备的非凡时刻。我们再次邀请策展人、评论家及收藏家分享重要心得及多元化的选择，兼容并蓄各种带领当代艺术世界的品味。

对巴塞尔艺术展而言, 2014 年的特别之处在于三个展会中的主要活动。首先是 Carsten Nicolai 创作的 *α (alpha) pulse*, 作品展现于楼高 484 米的九龙环球贸易广场外墙，覆盖范围之广乃是前所未见，多达一百万人都可欣赏得到。另外，由巴塞尔艺术展、Fondation Beyeler、Theater Basel 联手合作，Hans Ulrich Obrist 及 Klaus Biesenbach 策划的 "14房间" 展览为临场艺术树立了重要的里程碑。最后是 Performa 委托著名当代艺术家 Ryan McNamara 创作的 *MEƎM 4 Miami*, 这位数码原生代的神经网络体验与多种不同风格的舞蹈相互交织，内涵丰富，引人入胜。同样重要的是，我们已经与 Kickstarter 展开合作，增加计划拨款，提升非营利视觉艺术机构的国际地位。

巴塞尔艺术展的全年活动得以顺利举行，实在有赖各方倾力支持，但碍于篇幅有限，无法向所有艺廊、文化盟友、企业赞助商、及团队成员一一道谢。谨借此机会感谢 Lionel Bovier 及其 JRP|Ringier 团队为本书注入无穷活力，带动全球相关的艺术活动。

衷心希望 773 页的 "Art Basel | Year 45" 会为各位带来无尽喜悦及精彩发现。

巴塞尔艺术展总监
Marc Spiegler

各位讀者：

您手中的是巴塞爾藝術展年刊第二冊，年刊旨在記錄多元化的活動和我們所身處的藝術世界。"Art Basel | Year 44" 於去年問世，內容多采多姿，份量十足，因此很多人以為那是一次性出版的刊物。然而，我們深信每年都應該作如此深入詳盡的記錄。

我們重新構思出版方向，一改以往中立的角度，以求突出各個精心準備的非凡時刻。我們再次邀請策展人、評論家及收藏家分享重要心得及多元化的選擇，兼容並蓄各種帶領當代藝術世界的品味。

對巴塞爾藝術展而言，2014年的特別之處在於三個展覽中的主要活動。首先是 Carsten Nicolai 創作的 *α (alpha) pulse*, 作品展現於樓高 484 米的九龍環球貿易廣場外牆，覆蓋範圍之廣乃是前所未見，多達一百萬人都可欣賞得到。另外，由巴塞爾藝術展、Fondation Beyeler、Theater Basel 聯手合作，Hans Ulrich Obrist 及 Klaus Biesenbach 策劃的 "14房間" 展覽為臨場藝術樹立了重要的里程碑。最後是 Performa 委託著名當代藝術家 Ryan McNamara 創作的 *MEƎM 4 Miami*, 這位數碼原生代的神經網絡體驗與多種不同風格的舞蹈相互交織，內涵豐富，引人入勝。同樣重要的是，我們已經與 Kickstarter 展開合作，增加計劃撥款，提升非營利視覺藝術機構的國際地位。

巴塞爾藝術展的全年活動得以順利舉行，實在有賴各方傾力支持，但礙於篇幅有限，無法向所有藝廊、文化盟友、企業贊助商、及團隊成員一一道謝。謹藉此機會感謝 Lionel Bovier 及其 JRP|Ringier 團隊為本書注入無窮活力，帶動全球相關的藝術活動。

衷心希望 773 頁的 "Art Basel | Year 45" 會為各位帶來無盡喜悅及精彩發現。

巴塞爾藝術展總監
Marc Spiegler

Galleries by City

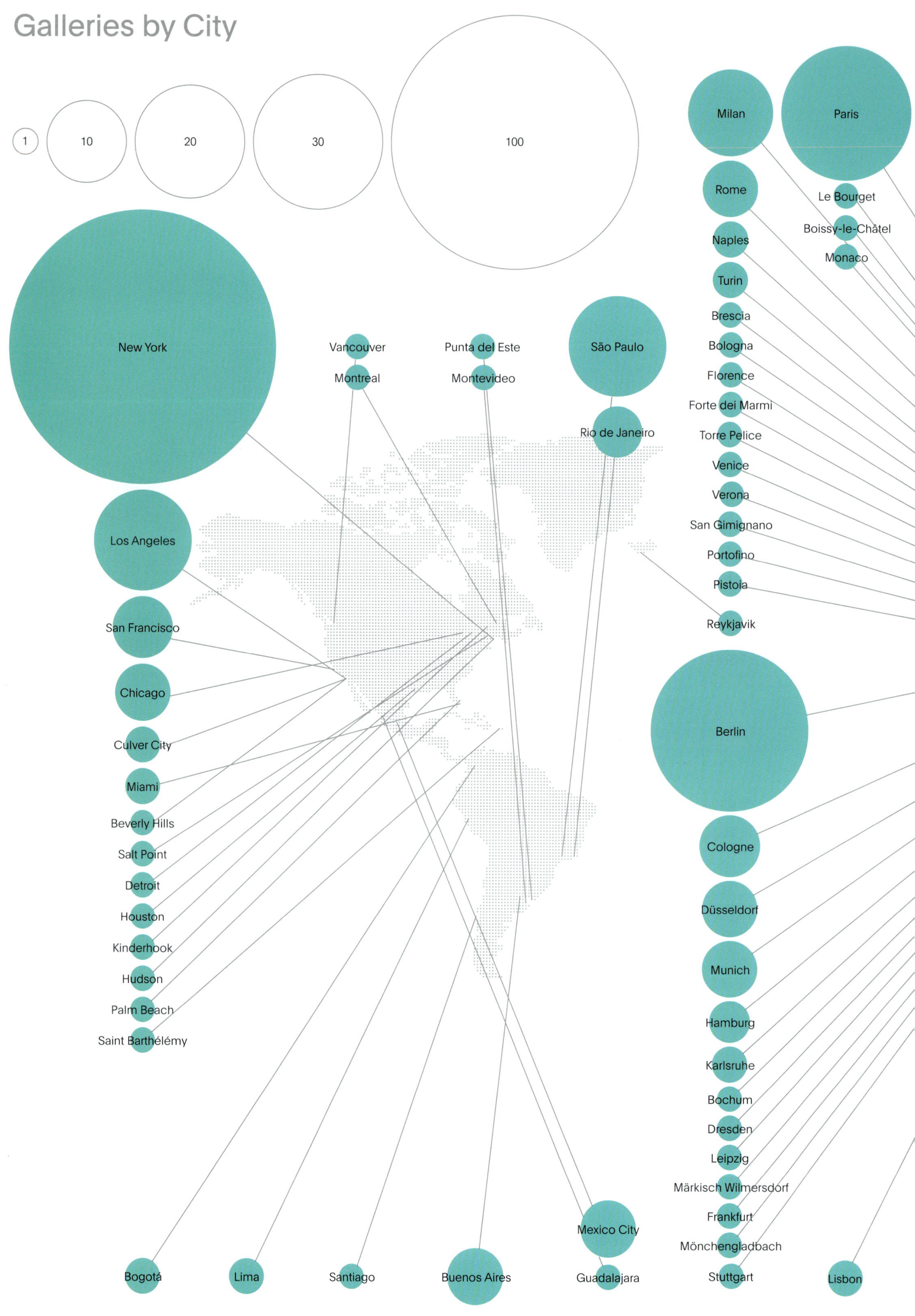

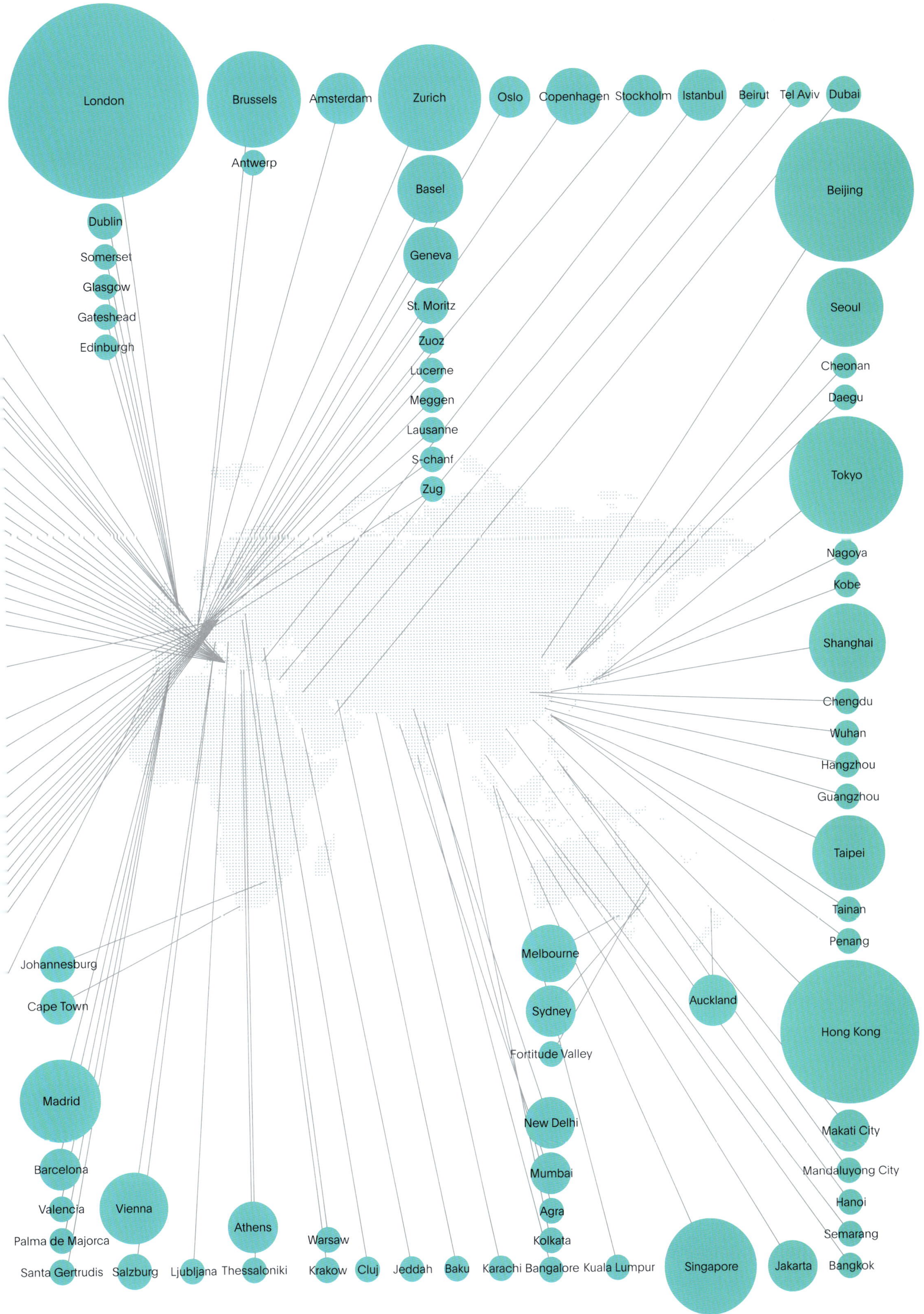
London
Brussels
Amsterdam
Zurich
Oslo
Copenhagen
Stockholm
Istanbul
Beirut
Tel Aviv
Dubai
Antwerp
Basel
Beijing
Dublin
Somerset
Glasgow
Gateshead
Edinburgh
Geneva
St. Moritz
Zuoz
Lucerne
Meggen
Lausanne
S-chanf
Zug
Seoul
Cheonan
Daegu
Tokyo
Nagoya
Kobe
Shanghai
Chengdu
Wuhan
Hangzhou
Guangzhou
Taipei
Tainan
Penang
Johannesburg
Cape Town
Melbourne
Sydney
Fortitude Valley
Auckland
Hong Kong
Madrid
New Delhi
Makati City
Barcelona
Mumbai
Mandaluyong City
Valencia
Vienna
Athens
Agra
Hanoi
Palma de Majorca
Warsaw
Kolkata
Semarang
Santa Gertrudis
Salzburg
Ljubljana
Thessaloniki
Krakow
Cluj
Jeddah
Baku
Karachi
Bangalore
Kuala Lumpur
Singapore
Jakarta
Bangkok

Average Gallery Size in Square Meters

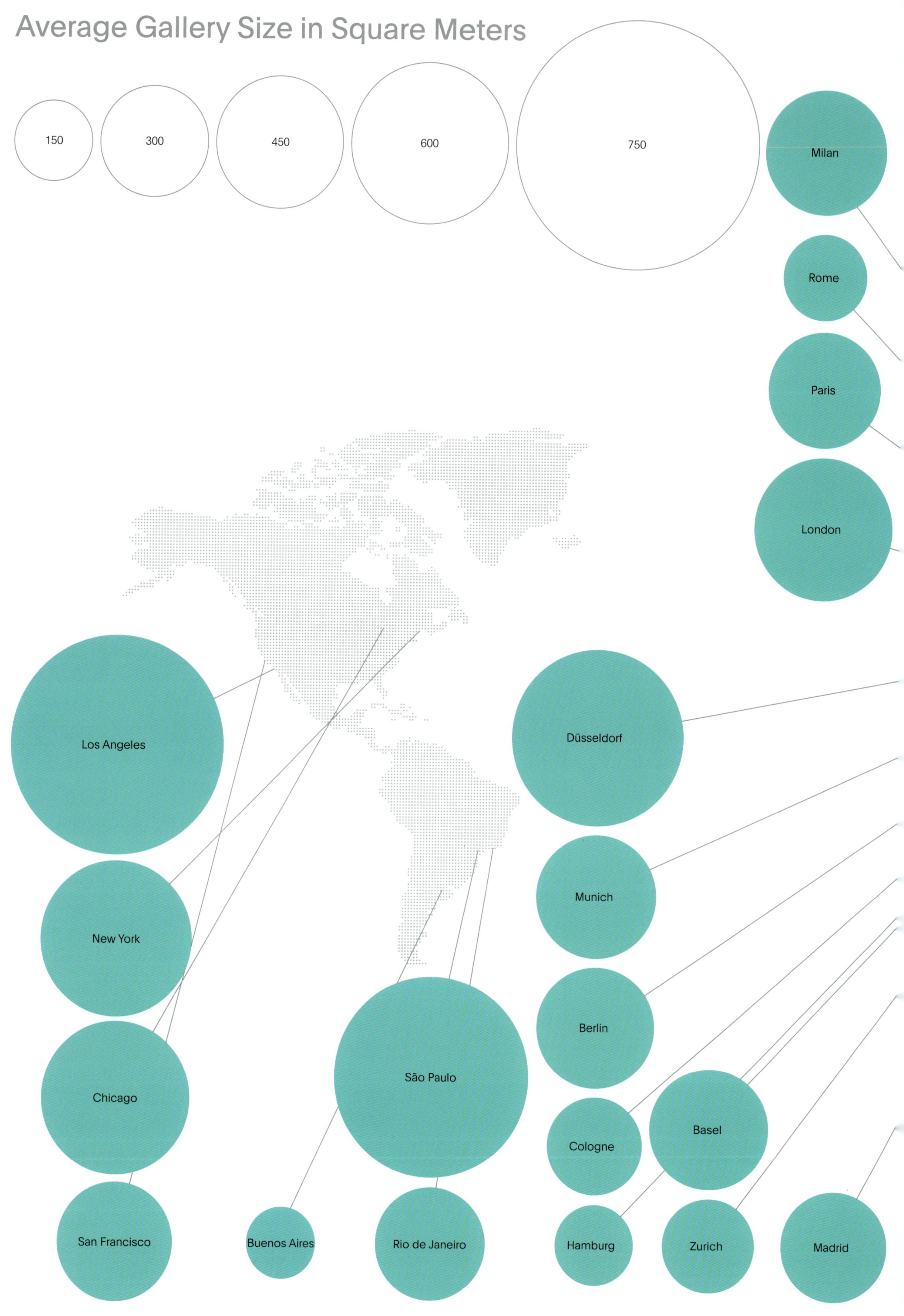

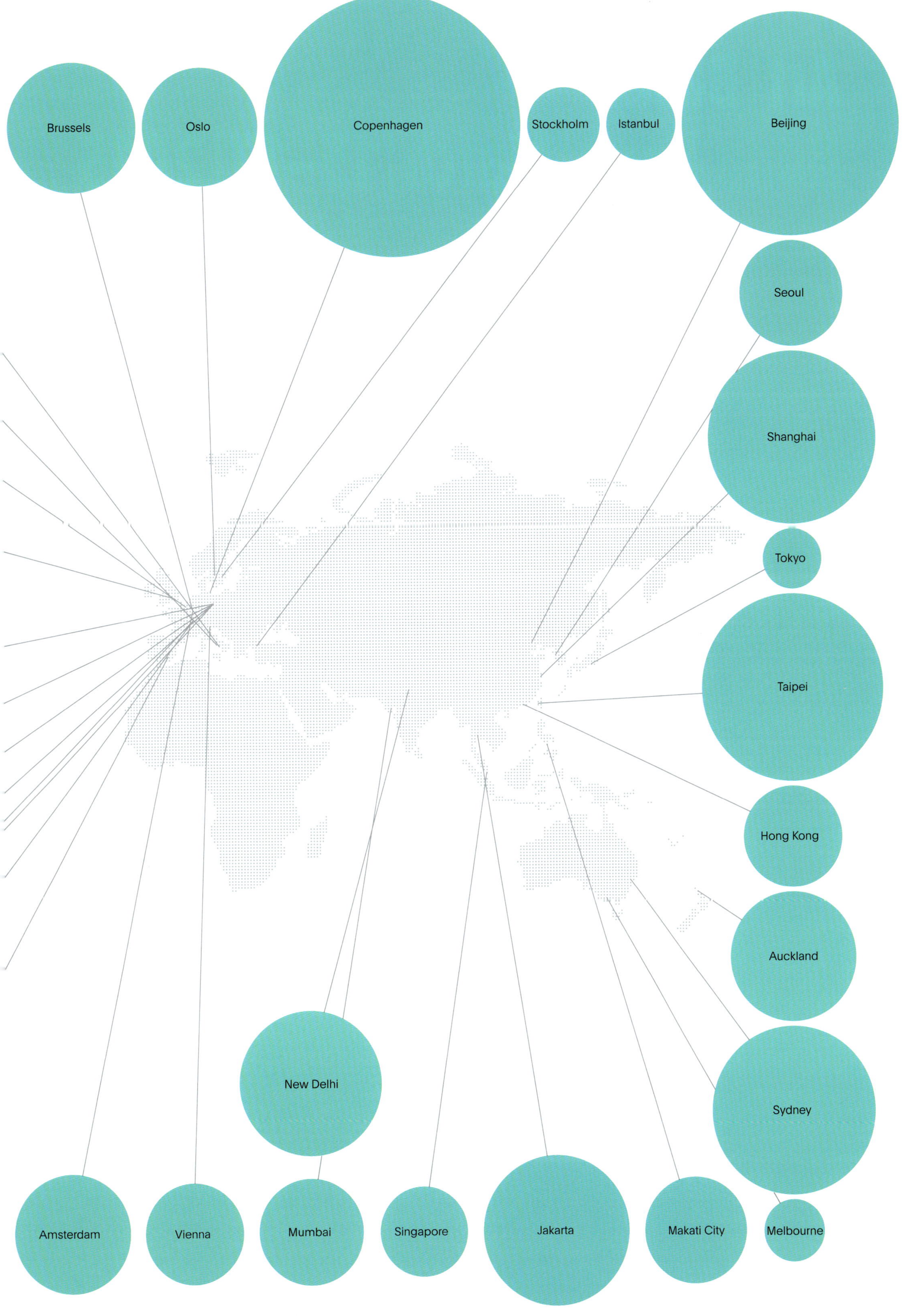

AVERAGE GALLERY SIZE IN SQUARE METERS

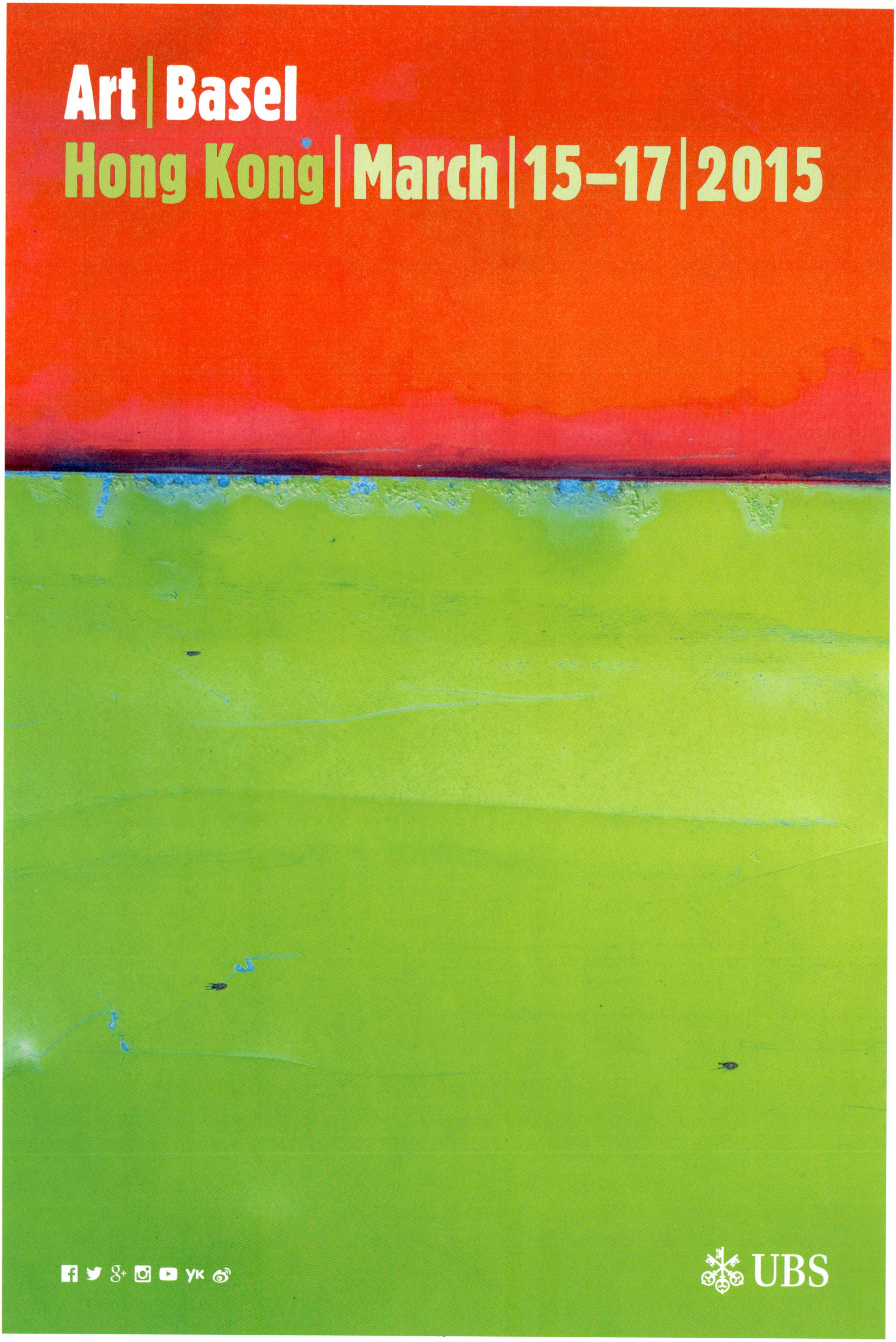

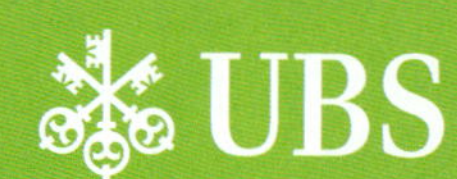
UBS

Art | Basel

Basel | June | 18–21 | 2015

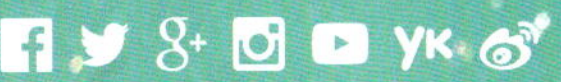

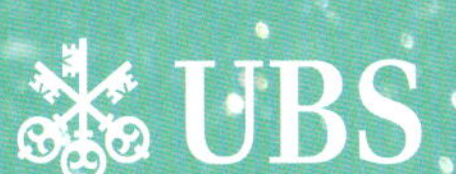

Global Partners

Lead Partner

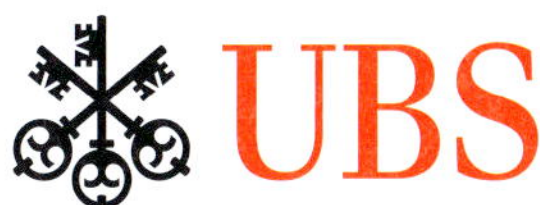

Associate Partner

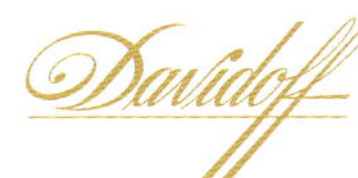

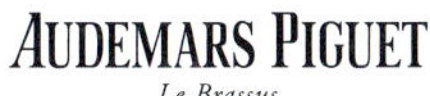

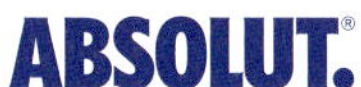

NETJETS

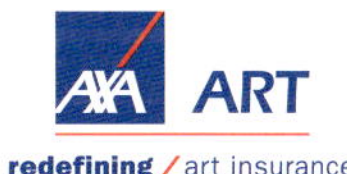

Lounge Host

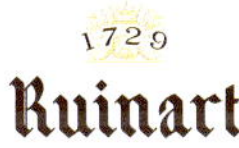

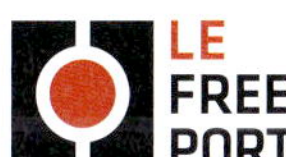

Official Partner

Automotive

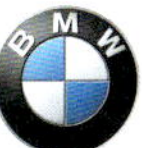

Digital

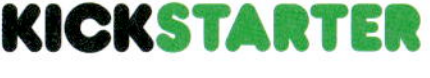

Local Partners

Hong Kong

Official Hotel

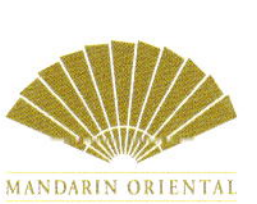

Official Carrier

SWISS

Official Concierge

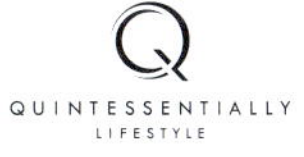

Basel

Show Partner

Baloise Group

Lounge Host

VIENNA
NOW OR NEVER

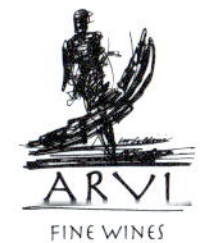

Miami Beach

Official Furniture and Interiors

MOROSO

Official Hotel

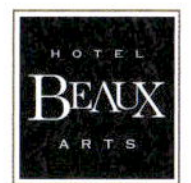

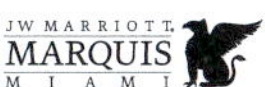

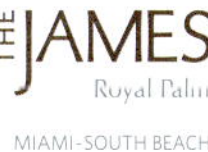

Media Partners

Global

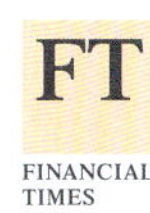

Hong Kong

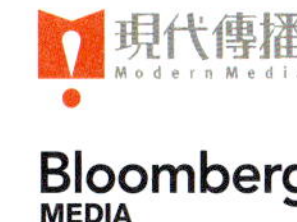

Bloomberg MEDIA

PRESTIGE

Basel

Neue Zürcher Zeitung

LE TEMPS

Miami Beach

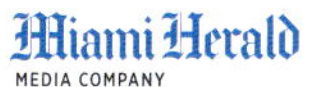

Statement by Sergio P. Ermotti
Group Chief Executive Officer
UBS

UBS is proud of its longstanding, global support of Art Basel, as a core component of our broader involvement with contemporary art. Our art initiatives, including our work with the renowned UBS Art Collection, are integral to our corporate culture, inspiring and challenging us while encouraging the innovative thinking that is indispensable to success in business. These are the reasons why we are committed to Art Basel, the world's premier event for art collectors, and why we look forward again in 2015 to participating in all of its shows.

Many of our clients have shown us time and time again that they share our passion for collecting contemporary art, and that they recognize UBS as a trusted partner in this endeavor. They look to us to provide them with information, insights, and a very high level of access to the best in contemporary art.

As the most recent expression of our commitment to offering access to vital art resources, we have introduced the first version of "Planet Art," a free new app available for iPad. Planet Art distills global news about contemporary art from dozens of media sources, both mainstream and niche, and breaks down the information according to the needs and interests of the individual, helping to give a full and usable picture of the art world in real time. We think of Planet Art as a logical extension of the way we do business, by providing clients with the clarity and direction they need to navigate today's complex financial world.

Like so many of our clients, UBS wants to be wherever the art world gathers, contributing meaningfully to the dialogue about contemporary art. That is why we collaborate with several museums internationally, most notably with the Solomon R. Guggenheim Museum on the Guggenheim UBS MAP Global Art Initiative. It is why we offer our valued clients the insights of services such as the UBS Art Competence Center and the UBS Arts Forum. And it is why we are pleased to be the global Lead Partner of Art Basel in Basel, Miami Beach, and Hong Kong.

We congratulate Art Basel on its ongoing success and look forward to meeting again with our clients and friends, arts professionals, and fellow collectors at one of the great cultural gatherings in the world.

Mitteilung von Sergio P. Ermotti
Group Chief Executive Officer UBS

UBS ist stolz auf ihr langjähriges und globales Engagement für Art Basel, einen der Eckpfeiler unserer Aktivitäten im Kunstbereich. All unsere Kunstinitiativen, wozu auch die anerkannte UBS Art Collection zählt, sind wichtiger Bestandteil unserer Unternehmenskultur. Sie sind für uns Anregung und Herausforderung zugleich und fördern eine innovative Denkweise, die auch für geschäftlichen Erfolg unverzichtbar ist. Dies sind gute Gründe, weshalb wir uns für Art Basel, die weltweit führende Veranstaltung für Kunstsammler, auch in Zukunft engagieren. Wir freuen uns, auch 2015 an all ihren Anlässen teilzunehmen.

Viele unserer Kunden haben uns immer wieder gezeigt, dass sie unsere Leidenschaft für das Sammeln zeitgenössischer Kunst teilen und UBS in dieser Hinsicht als zuverlässigen Partner erachten. Unsere Experten bieten ihnen jederzeit Fachwissen, Marktkenntnisse und Zugang zu erstklassiger zeitgenössischer Kunst.

Ein weiteres Beispiel für unser umfassendes Kunstengagement ist «Planet Art», eine von UBS neu entwickelte iPad-App. Planet Art filtert globale News über zeitgenössische Kunst aus zahlreichen traditionellen und Nischen-Medienquellen. Die Informationen können auf die individuellen Bedürfnisse und Interessen der Benutzer zugeschnitten werden und bieten so ein aktuelles Bild des Geschehens in der Kunstwelt. So, wie Planet Art dem Leser hilft, die komplexe Kunstwelt von heute besser zu verstehen, so verstehen wir auch unsere Aufgabe als Bank: unseren Kunden Klarheit und Orientierung für das Navigieren in der ebenso komplexen Finanzwelt zu bieten.

UBS teilt den Wunsch vieler ihrer kunstinteressierten Kunden, nicht nur überall dort zu sein, wo die Kunstwelt zusammentrifft, sondern auch etwas Sinnvolles zum Dialog über zeitgenössische Kunst beizutragen. Deshalb arbeitet UBS mit mehreren Museen weltweit zusammen, allen voran mit dem Solomon R. Guggenheim Museum im Rahmen der Guggenheim UBS MAP Global Art Initiative. Aus demselben Grund bieten wir unseren geschätzten Kunden ebenfalls vertiefte Einblicke in Kunst über Dienstleistungen wie das UBS Art Competence Center und das UBS Arts Forum. Und insbesondere deshalb sind wir gerne globaler Lead Partner der Art Basel in Basel, Miami Beach und Hongkong.

Wir gratulieren Art Basel zu ihrem fortdauernden Erfolg. Gleichzeitig freuen wir uns, unsere Kunden, Freunde, Kunstexperten und Sammler an einer dieser weltweit bedeutenden Kulturveranstaltungen zu treffen.

Comunicado de Sergio P. Ermotti
Group Chief Executive Officer
UBS

En UBS estamos orgullosos del apoyo global que desde hace mucho tiempo brindamos a Art Basel, uno de los componentes básicos de nuestro amplio compromiso con el arte contemporáneo. Nuestras iniciativas en el mundo del arte, que incluyen nuestro trabajo con la renombrada UBS Art Collection, son una parte integral de nuestra cultura corporativa y nos inspiran y desafían, a la vez que motivan el pensamiento innovador indispensable para el éxito en los negocios. Estos son los motivos de nuestro compromiso con Art Basel, el evento más importante del mundo para los coleccionistas de arte, y también lo que nos hace alegrarnos de participar de nuevo en 2015 en todas sus exhibiciones.

Muchos de nuestros clientes nos han demostrado una y otra vez que comparten nuestra pasión por coleccionar arte contemporáneo y que reconocen a UBS como un socio de confianza en este empeño. Nos piden que les proporcionemos información, conocimientos y un muy alto grado de acceso al mejor arte contemporáneo.

La expresión más reciente de nuestro esfuerzo por ofrecer acceso a los recursos vitales del arte es la primera versión de «Planet Art», una nueva aplicación gratuita disponible para el iPad. Planet Art filtra las noticias globales acerca del arte contemporáneo de docenas de fuentes informativas, tanto convencionales como especializadas, y desglosa esa información de conformidad con las necesidades e intereses del usuario, contribuyendo así a brindar un panorama completo y útil del mundo del arte en tiempo real. Pensamos que Planet Art es una extensión lógica de la forma en que hacemos negocios, basada en proporcionar a nuestros clientes la orientación y claridad que necesitan para navegar por el complejo mundo financiero actual.

Al igual que muchos de nuestros clientes, UBS desea estar presente donde quiera que se reúna el mundo del arte, contribuyendo significativamente al diálogo acerca del arte contemporáneo. Es por eso que colaboramos con muchos museos a nivel internacional, principalmente con el Solomon R. Guggenheim Museum a través de la iniciativa de arte Guggenheim UBS MAP Global Art Initiative. Y es por eso que ofrecemos a nuestros apreciados clientes los conocimientos de servicios para clientes como el UBS Art Competence Center y el UBS Arts Forum. Y es también por eso que estamos orgullosos de ser el principal socio mundial de Art Basel, participando en sus festivales en Basilea, Miami Beach y Hong Kong.

Queremos felicitar a Art Basel por su exitosa trayectoria y expresar nuestro deseo de volver a encontrarnos con nuestros clientes y amigos, profesionales del arte y coleccionistas como nosotros en uno de los mayores encuentros culturales del mundo.

瑞銀集團行政總裁 Sergio P. Ermotti 的話

瑞銀一直以來為巴塞爾藝術展提供全球支持，以作為集團對當代藝術的廣泛參與的核心部分，並對此引以自豪。我們的藝術行動（包括知名的瑞銀藝術藏品）是我們的企業文化中一個關鍵部分，不單為我們帶來啟發與挑戰，還推動對業務成功不可或缺的創新思維。正因如此，我們一直致力支持巴塞爾藝術展這項藝術品收藏家的世界級盛事，亦再次期待於 2015 年參與其所有展覽。

我們不少客戶一再向我們展示他們對收藏當代藝術品的熱誠，並認同瑞銀在藝術工作中付出的努力，是個值得信賴的合作夥伴。他們倚靠我們提供資訊和見解，讓他們涉獵最優秀的當代藝術品。

為致力讓客戶接觸寶貴的藝術資源，我們最近推出第一版的 iPad 全新免費應用程式「Planet Art」。Planet Art 從大量主流及小眾媒體來源中過濾出有關當代藝術的全球消息，並根據個人的需要及興趣分析有關資訊，以助實時瞭解全面而實用的藝術世界面貌。我們認為 Planet Art 是我們的營商方式的合理延伸，為客戶提供駕馭當今複雜的金融世界所需的清晰度和方向。

正如我們很多客戶一樣，瑞銀希望進軍藝術世界匯聚的地方，為當代藝術的對話作出重要貢獻。因此，我們與數間博物館進行國際性合作，最佳例子是與古根漢美術館合作舉辦古根漢美術館瑞銀 MAP 全球藝術行動。因此，我們為尊貴客戶提供服務卓見，例如瑞銀藝術諮詢服務中心及瑞銀藝術論壇。亦因此，我們欣然成為巴塞爾藝術展的巴塞爾、邁阿密海灘及香港三大展會的全球主要合作夥伴。

我們為巴塞爾藝術展一直以來的成功感到高興，並期望在這世界最頂尖的文化聚會之一，再次與我們的客戶友好、藝術專家及各收藏家聚首一堂。

One location for art intelligence distilled

14,000 new articles analyzed

45,000 artists and galleries tagged

9,000,000 keywords scanned

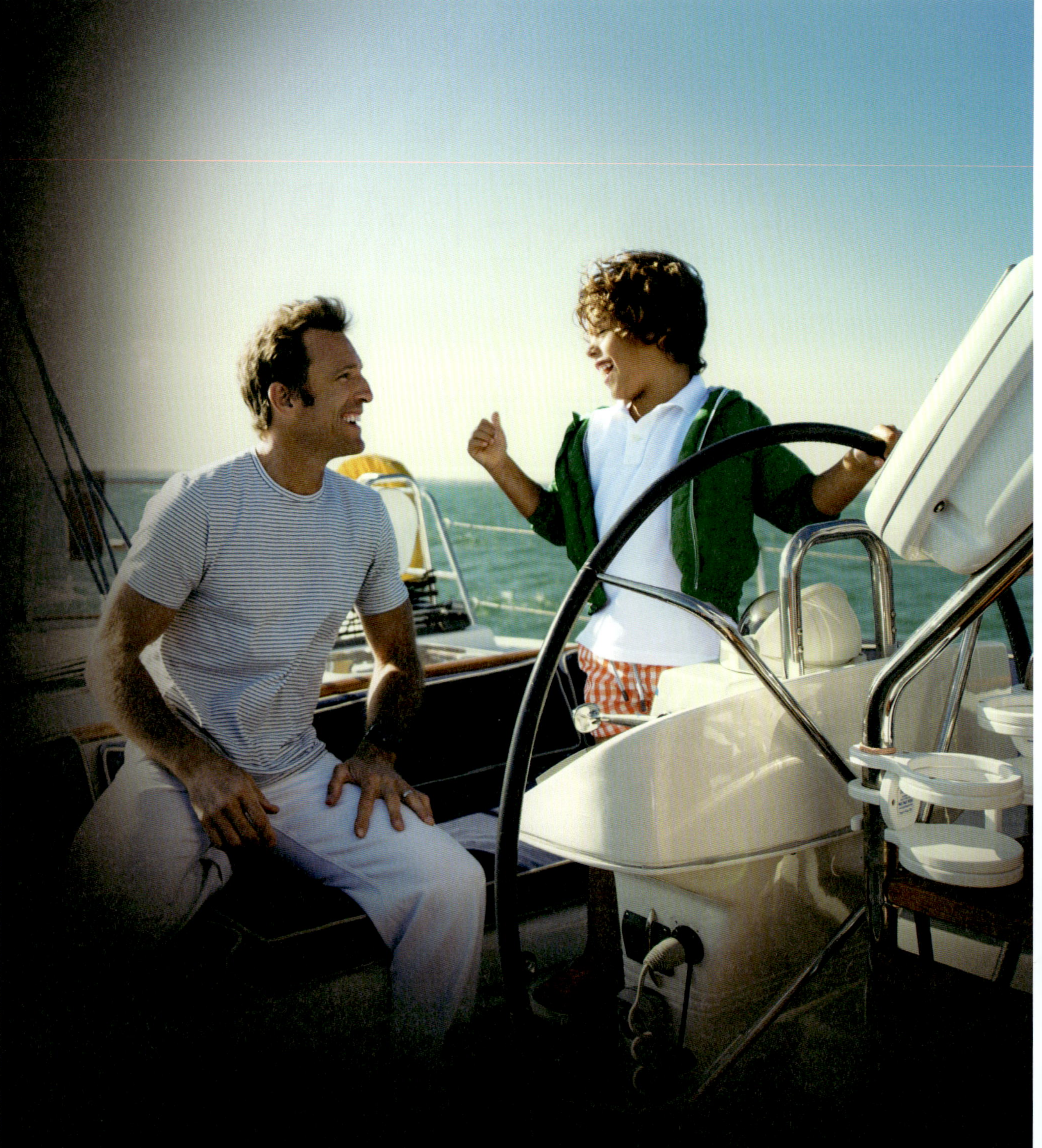

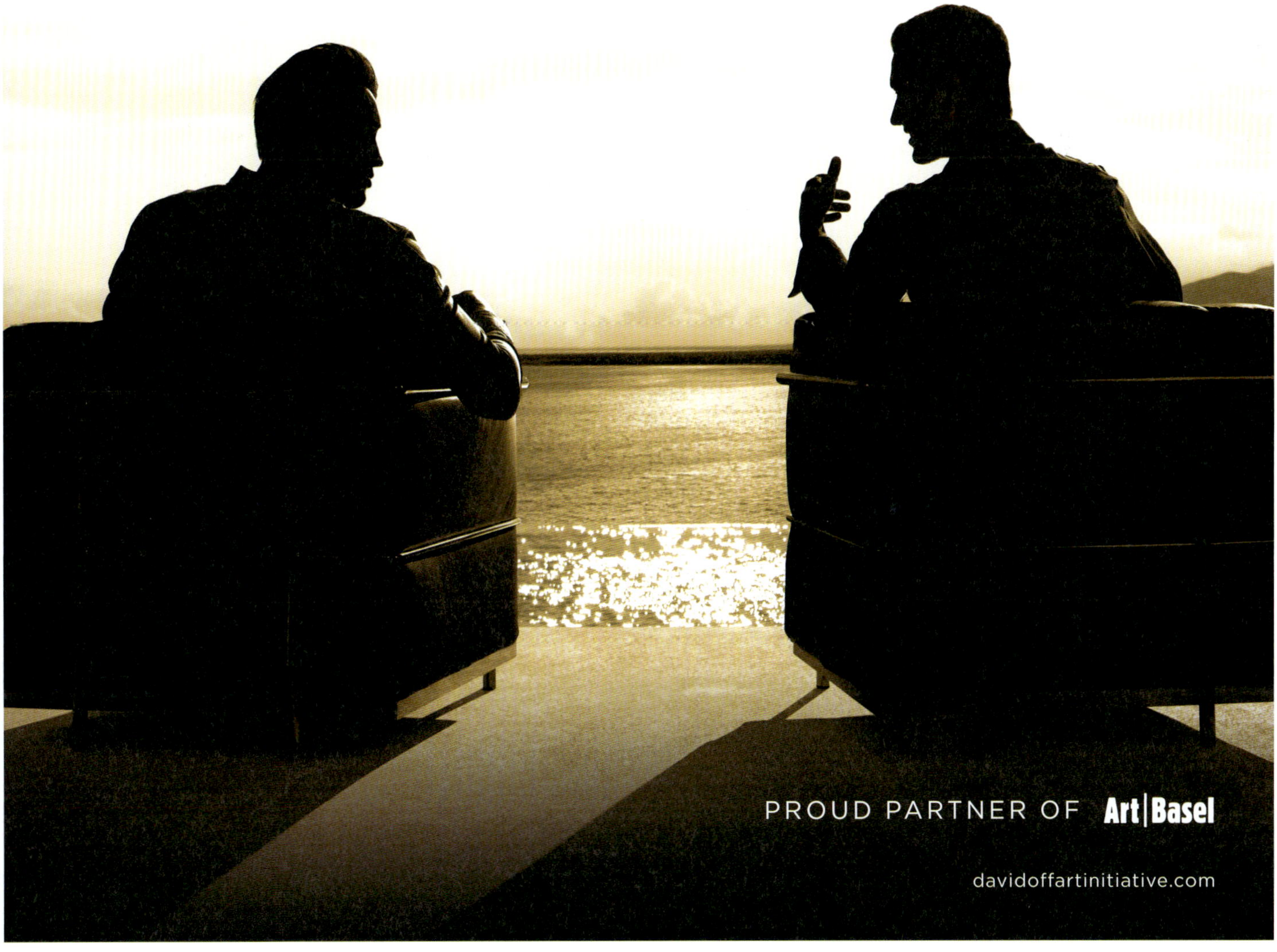

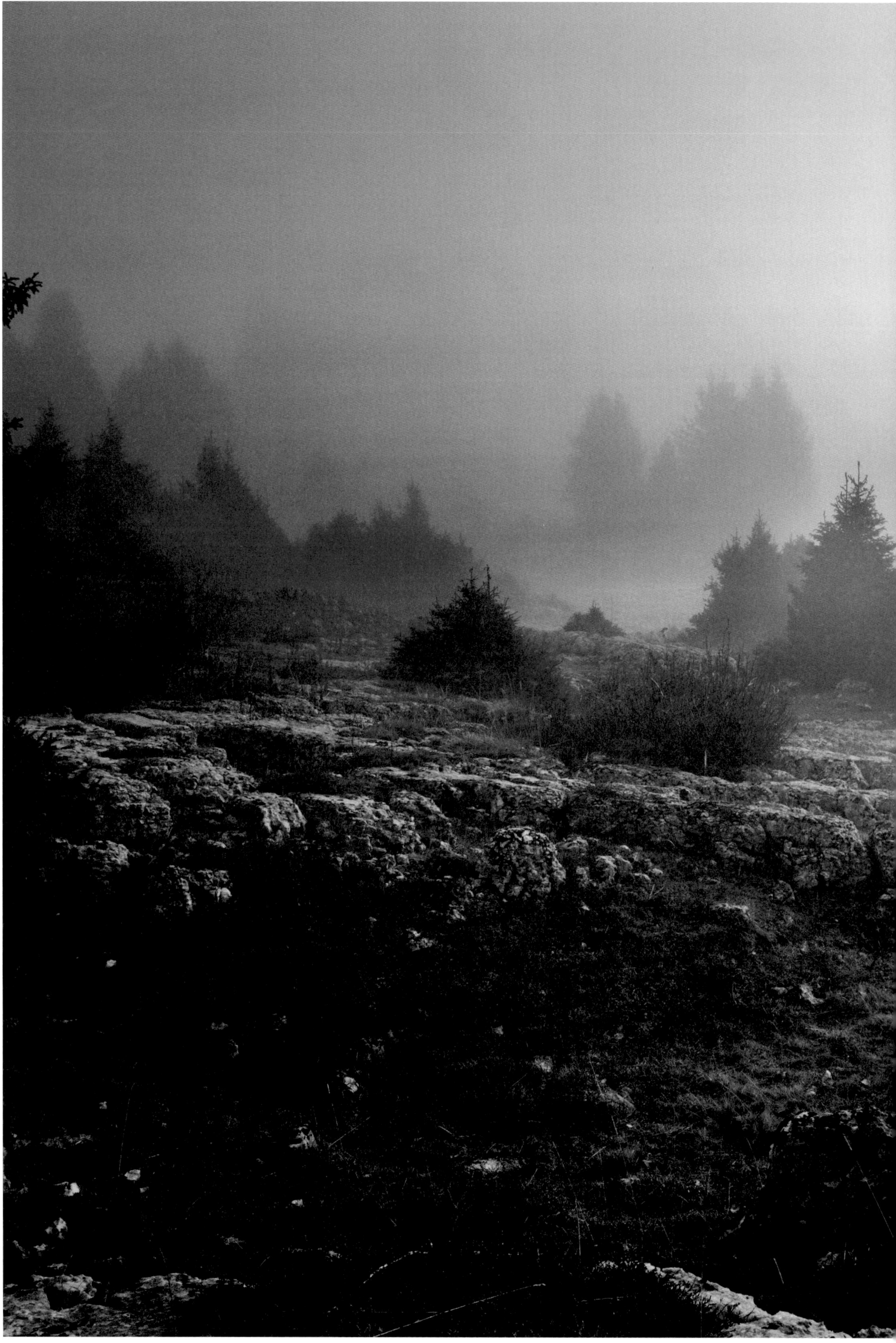

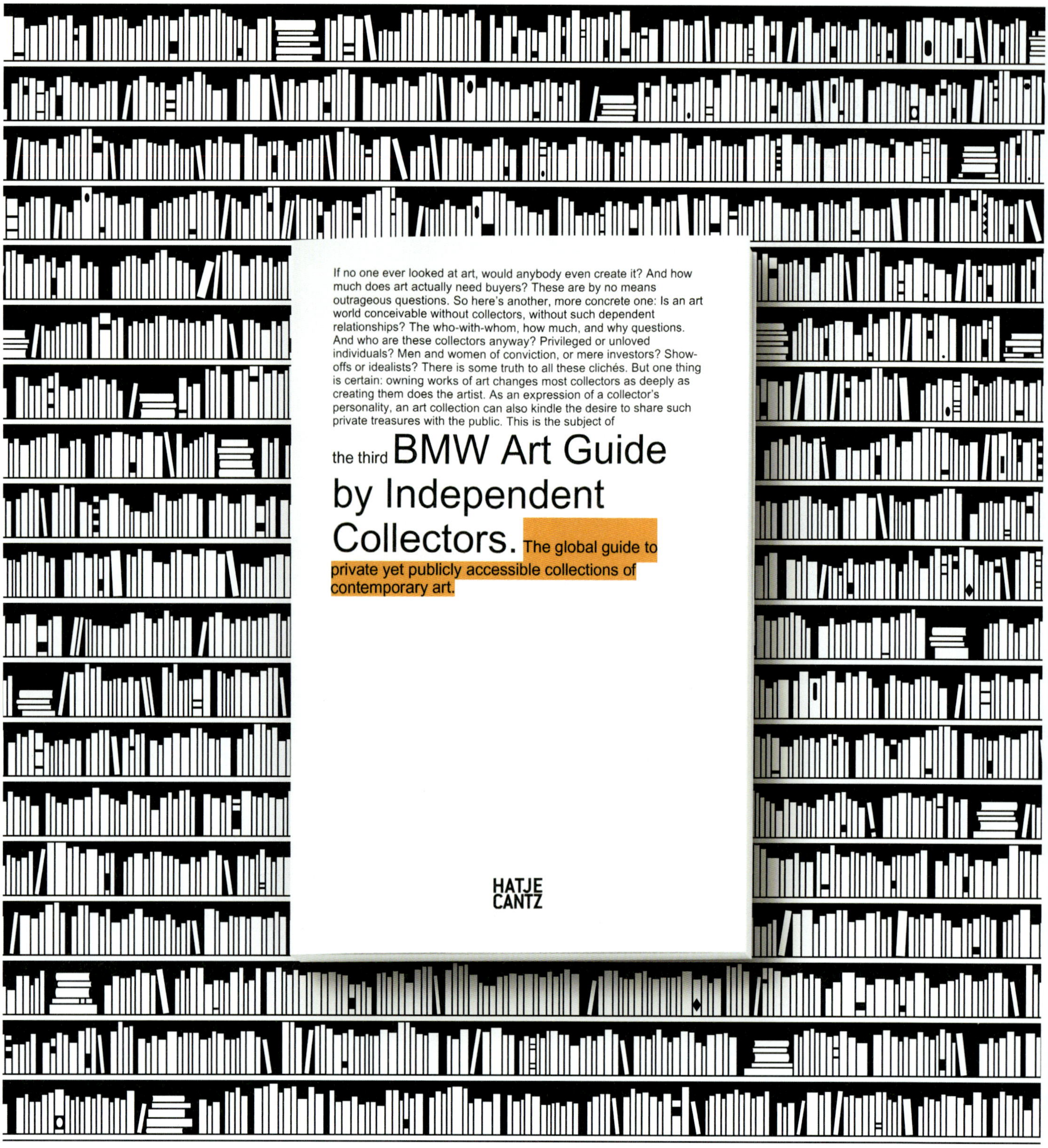

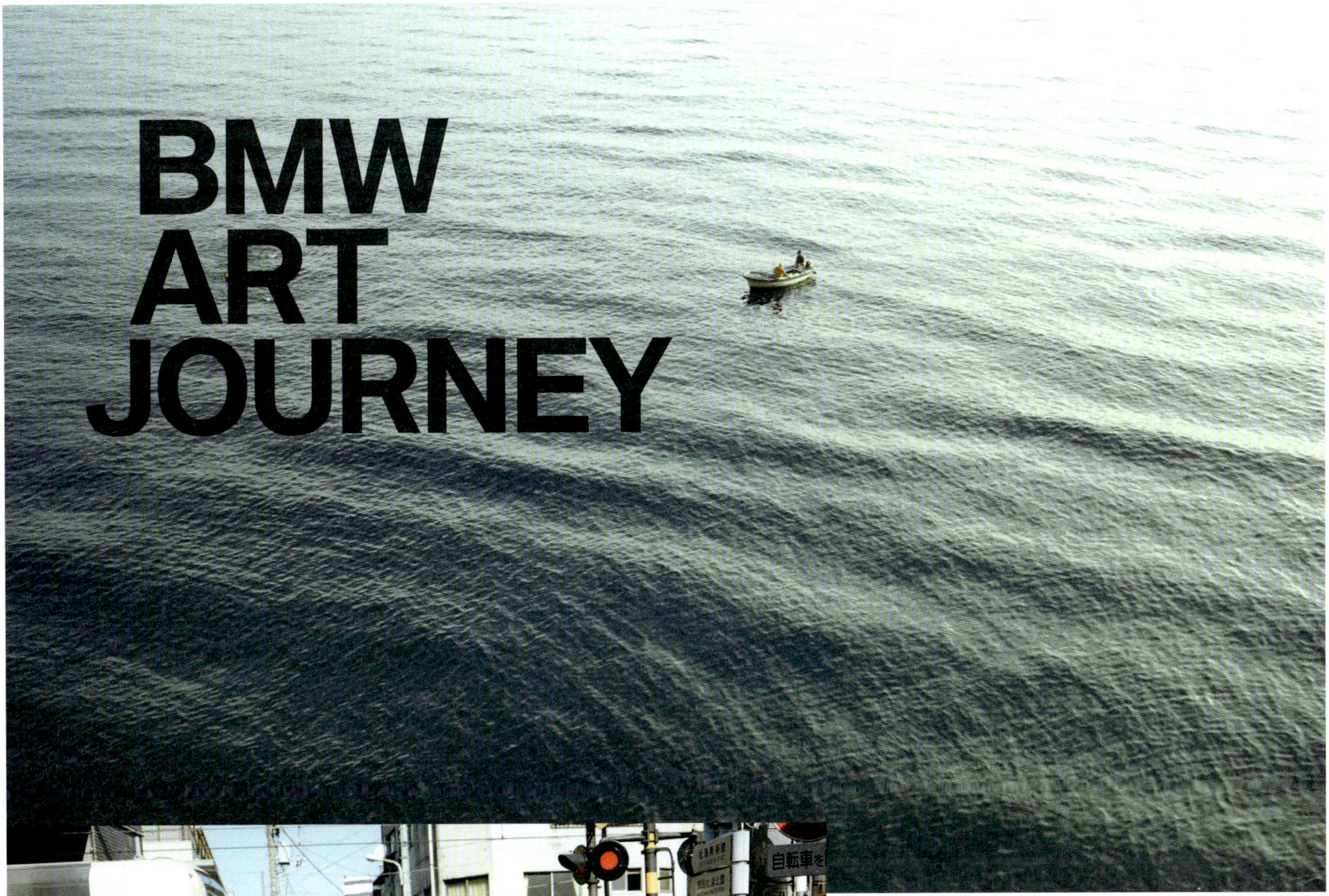

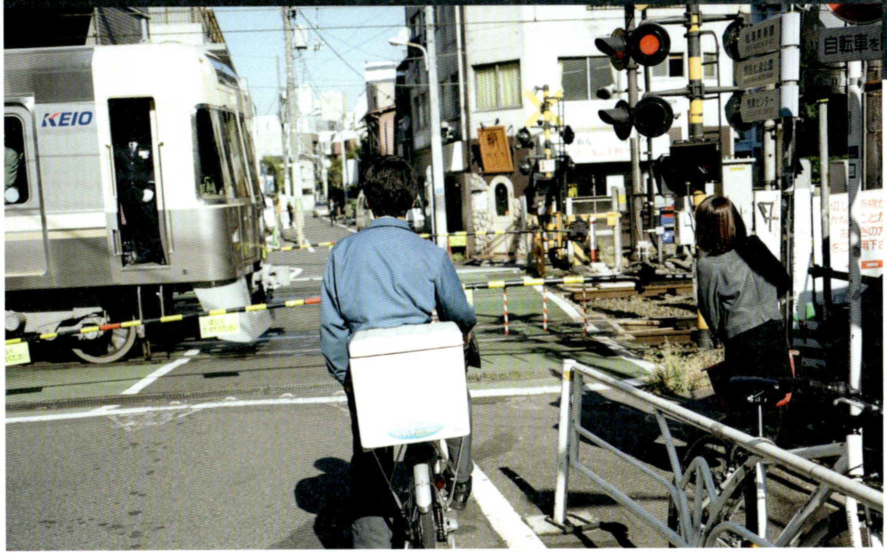

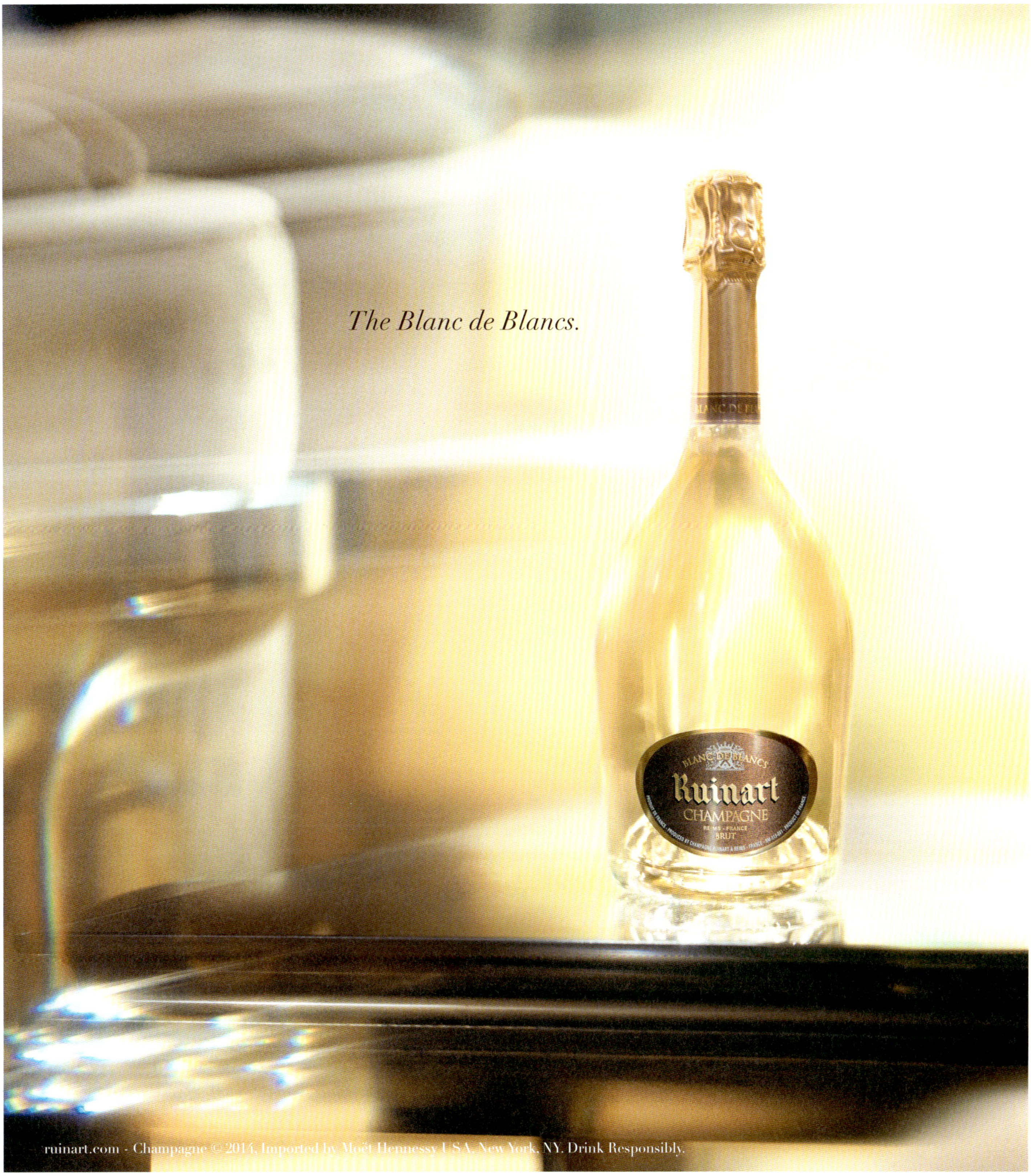

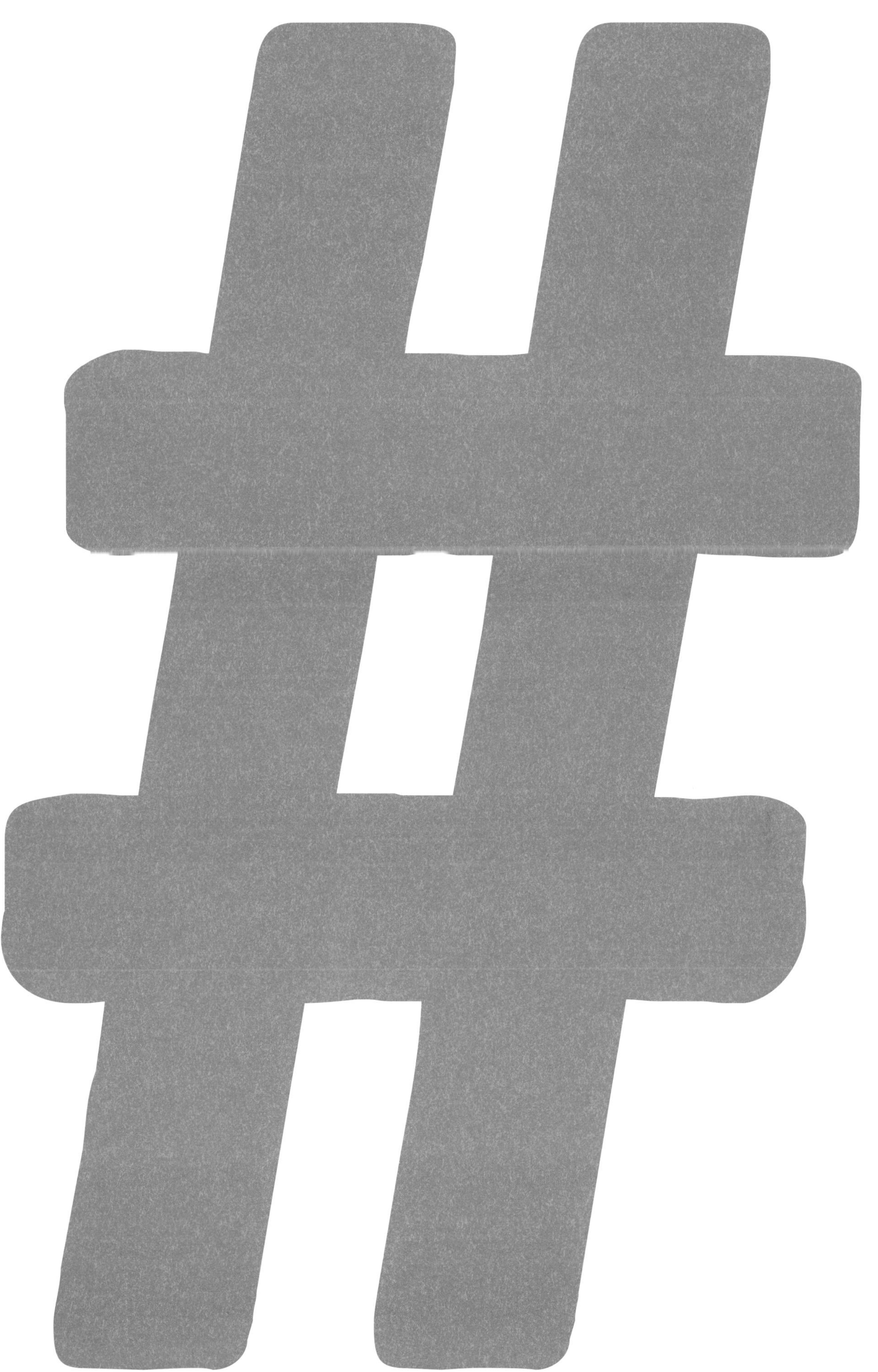

#

In 2014, Fondation Beyeler, Art Basel, and Theater Basel staged *14 Rooms*, a singular live-art exhibition adjacent to Messeplatz. Curated by Klaus Biesenbach and Hans Ulrich Obrist, the exhibition featured performative works by renowned artists in an architectural environment conceived by Herzog & de Meuron. Each work challenged the very notions of live art and human experience.

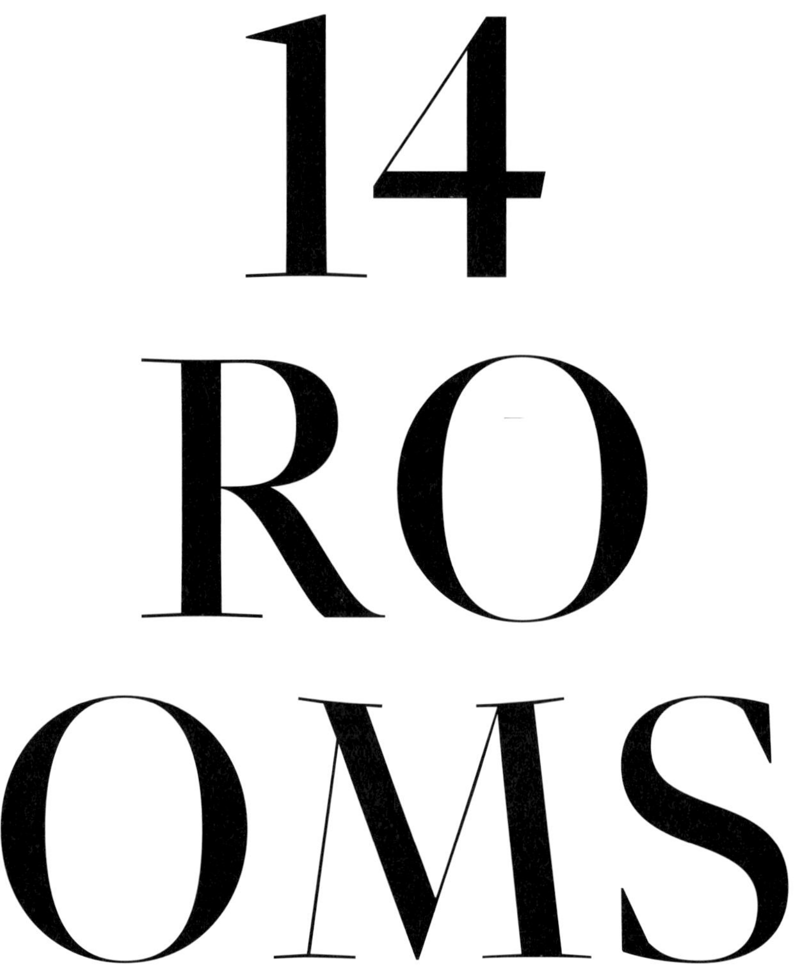

Participating artists

Marina Abramović
Allora & Calzadilla
Ed Atkins
John Baldessari
Dominique Gonzalez-Foerster
Damien Hirst
Joan Jonas
Laura Lima
Bruce Nauman
Otobong Nkanga
Roman Ondák
Yoko Ono
Tino Sehgal
Santiago Sierra
Jordan Wolfson
Xu Zhen

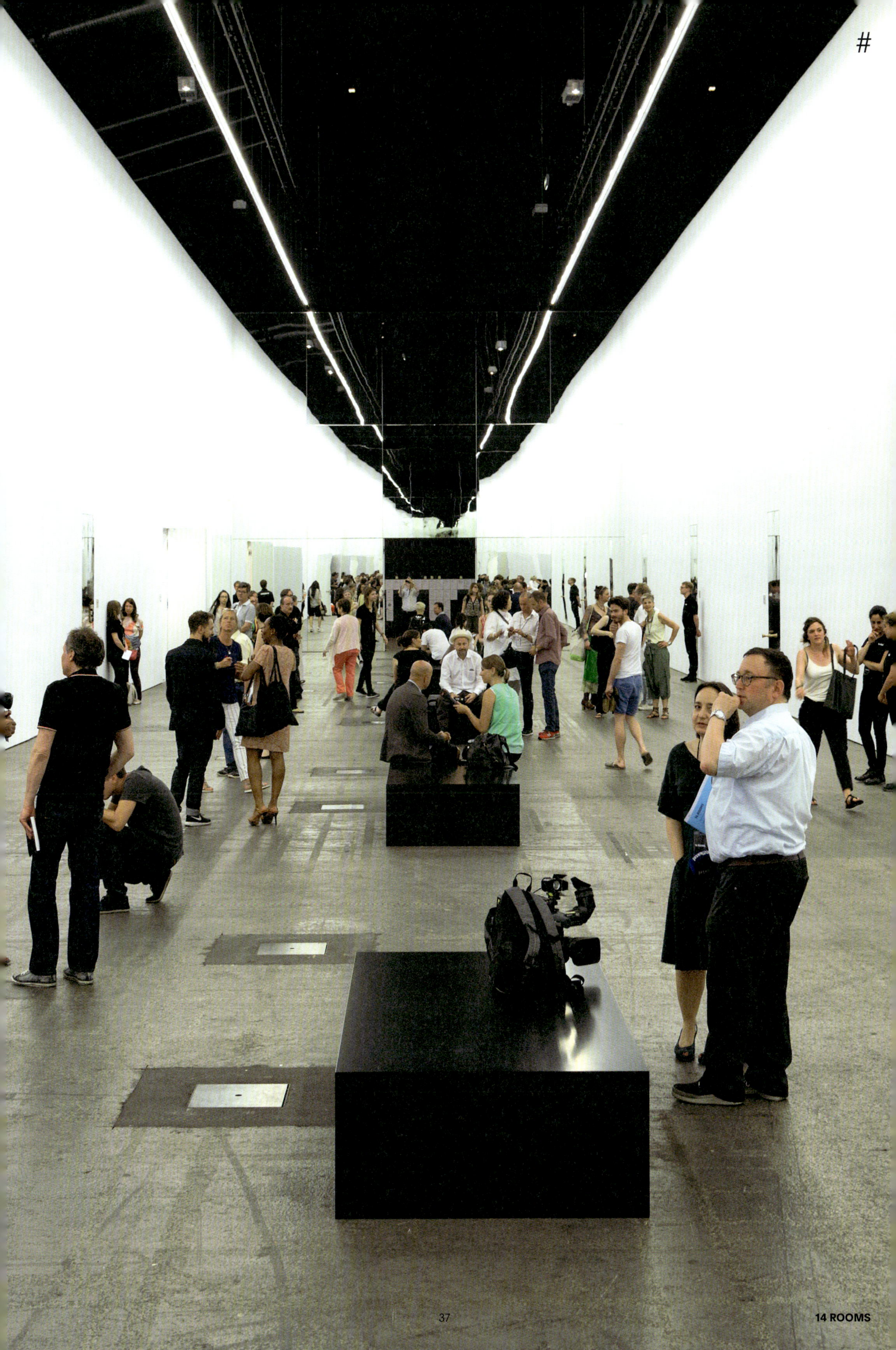

#

14 Rooms

Klaus Biesenbach and Hans Ulrich Obrist in conversation*

HANS ULRICH OBRIST A lot of the inspiration for this show has come from the idea that live art can also be sculpture and have a duration similar to a physical object—that is, from morning to night, throughout the opening hours of a gallery. But when the last visitors leave, and the gallery closes its doors for the evening, the sculptures will all walk out as well ... We also liked the possibility of creating an exhibition that could be restaged later. We were interested in this idea because, like music, it could become part of a catalogue of works that can be performed again in different contexts. This idea of repeatability—the idea that an exhibition can be opened up and restaged like Duchamp's *Boîte-en-valise*—is something that Philippe Parreno and I certainly sought to achieve with *Il Tempo del Postino* at the Manchester International Festival in 2007. There we sought to rethink the idea of the exhibition as a way of occupying time rather than simply occupying space ... We wanted to rethink the exhibition and all of its elements as something like a generative, evolving open score ... *13 Rooms* [realized in Sydney in 2013] stemmed from this idea ...

Slowness is important not only for the curatorial process, but also for the experience of the *13 Rooms* exhibition. It's surprising, but normally people don't actually spend much time in front of artworks in museums. The Louvre once analyzed it: even in front of the Mona Lisa, on average visitors only spend a few seconds. The experience of *13 Rooms* creates the opposite of this acceleration: it's a deceleration. Movement is slowed down by the fact that you have to open the door—it's like entering somebody's house. It's an intimate encounter.

It can be an encounter in a dark or light space. With Marina Abramović it's painfully bright. With an artist like Tino Sehgal it's a conversation. With Santiago Sierra it's the opposite: total silence. With Roman Ondák it's the basic experience of exchange ... So there are all kinds of different interactions that can happen; they take time and slow things down. Exhibitions are fundamentally a medium of social encounter ...

KLAUS BIESENBACH I think that exhibitions are sometimes like plots, like recurrent stories. You have an idea of the story, you have the draft of a story, you have a summary of a story, you have the long version of a story, you have the version with added chapters. I think that an exhibition is always a combination of certain stories and plots. For example, Hans Ulrich is well known for the exhibition *Do It* (1993–), which is a show that's only instructions. It's very conceptual; it's not objects, it's just instructions, which I think in today's market-driven economy is very important. Then there are other exhibitions that are considered "live art" exhibitions or "live exhibitions" or "performance exhibitions" or whatever you want to call them.

We found that there are many artists working with instruction pieces that involve labor, performance, reinterpretation, dance, or acting. Then we thought we could propose the idea of art as an instruction even

*This discussion is excerpted from the exhibition catalogue *14 Rooms*, produced by Fondation Beyeler, Art Basel, and Theater Basel, Hatje Cantz, 2014. The first part of the conversation was originally published in the exhibition catalogue *13 Rooms*, the 27th Kaldor Public Art Project, presented in Sydney in April 2013. *11 Rooms* was presented at the Manchester Art Gallery, July 9–17, 2011, during the Manchester International Festival, and included Marina Abramović, John Baldessari, Allora & Calzadilla, Simon Fujiwara, Joan Jonas, Laura Lima, Roman Ondák, Lucy Raven, Tino Sehgal, Santiago Sierra, and Xu Zhen. *12 Rooms* was shown during the International Arts Festival Ruhrtriennale at the Folkwang Museum, August 17–26, 2012, and added Xavier Le Roy to the list of artists. *13 Rooms* took place at Pier 2/3, Hickson Road, Walsh Bay, April 11–21, 2013, as part of Kaldor Public Art Projects, with the additional participation of Clark Beaumont.

to artists who hadn't worked that way, because it's an important artistic practice. So you bring the motif of the instruction exhibition together with the motif of the performance exhibition and there you have, together with the domestic scale and the doors, the exhibition experience of *13 Rooms*. The exhibition provides situations for experience and participation and the possibility of direct involvement, however you define this.

HUO A year after Sydney and three years after the first project in Manchester, we are presenting *14 Rooms* here in Basel. At the same time, it still feels as if everything has only just begun!

KB … It's also important to note that we learned and took a lot from the previous projects. From the example of Sydney we learned how it is possible for an exhibition to spread out in the urban context: we were at a pier in the harbor, near the museum and the opera. A long line formed in front of the exhibition every day. As a result of this line, the exhibition spread out toward the city in an organic way and got people talking about it. Wherever large crowds of people gather, a new public and urban space is created, initiating new levels of dialogue. This idea of public space in connection with the exhibition is something that we want to take with us to Basel.

HUO For *14 Rooms* it's not only the exhibition architecture that is important, but also the particular urban architectural environment where the exhibition takes place.

We invited Herzog & de Meuron to create a structure once again that, importantly, not only focuses on what happens in the exhibition, but also on how what occurs around an exhibition is woven into the urban fabric. Even though Herzog & de Meuron built the amazing new exhibition hall with the oculus for Messe Basel, they proposed that the project take place in one of the old exhibition halls that is a bit removed from the big fair hubbub and is therefore also inscribed in the urban context in a very different way …

KB It will be a public space where nothing will be sold, but instead—inspired by Tony Bennett—it will be place that is simply social, where people go, where they don't have to buy anything, but deal with in verbal matters, ideas, and emotions …

HUO The concept comes not only from Tony Bennett but also from Richard Sennett, who discusses the disappearance of public space in his books. What interests us as well is this idea of opening toward the outside, the creation of public spaces, and how it is possible to create such spaces. The new concept of the mirrored corridor also contributes to this: visitors stroll between the rooms, and through their reflected images, themselves become part of *14 Rooms*. We are also showing the documentation of an early work by John Baldessari, which he proposed to MoMA in 1970, throughout the exhibition. In *Unrealized Proposal for Cadaver Piece*, Baldessari wanted to exhibit a cadaver in order to address how death is dealt with in art and in society. It's not surprising that it still hasn't been possible to realize this project, although we attempted to do so in Manchester. The archive presents our endless communication with local and global bureaucracy and authorities …

When the last visitors leave, and the gallery closes its doors for the evening, the sculptures will all walk out as well …
—Hans Ulrich Obrist

Normally exhibitions have a very limited lifespan. They come, they go, there is a tour, it is arranged logically and pragmatically, it goes to two or three cities and costs are reduced as a result. Normally exhibitions are disbanded, and it would be highly complex and very costly to reconstruct them at a later moment in time …

Our exhibition, however, functions according to another logic. It will never die because it continues to exist in the form of instructions. It may well be the case that a curator-student or a museum director will bring this exhibition back to life again in a hundred years …

After three years, developing from *11 Rooms* to *14 Rooms*, it's possible to gauge whether it's slowly coming to an end or not. During the preparations for this exhibition, Klaus and I had many ideas for who might occupy the 14 rooms here in Basel. We would have liked to invite more artists, but the Fondation Beyeler and Art Basel told us that 40 rooms would be a bit too much … although it was painful, we had to limit ourselves. However, as previously in Sydney, we are certain that we could continue our project for years, if not for decades. What an optimistic prospect!

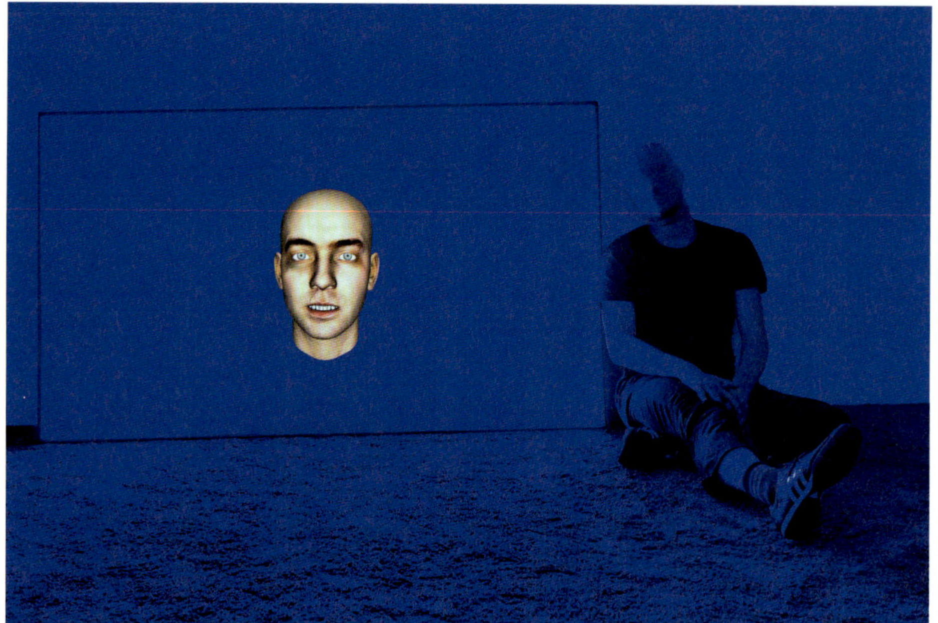

Ed Atkins
No-one is more "work" than me, 2014

On a large unadorned flat screen a 1:1 3D head, shaved and tattooed, makes a bid for his humanity. A real-life person is present, performing according to the directive to "bear witness to" the avatar's six-hour pitch to be a convincing person.

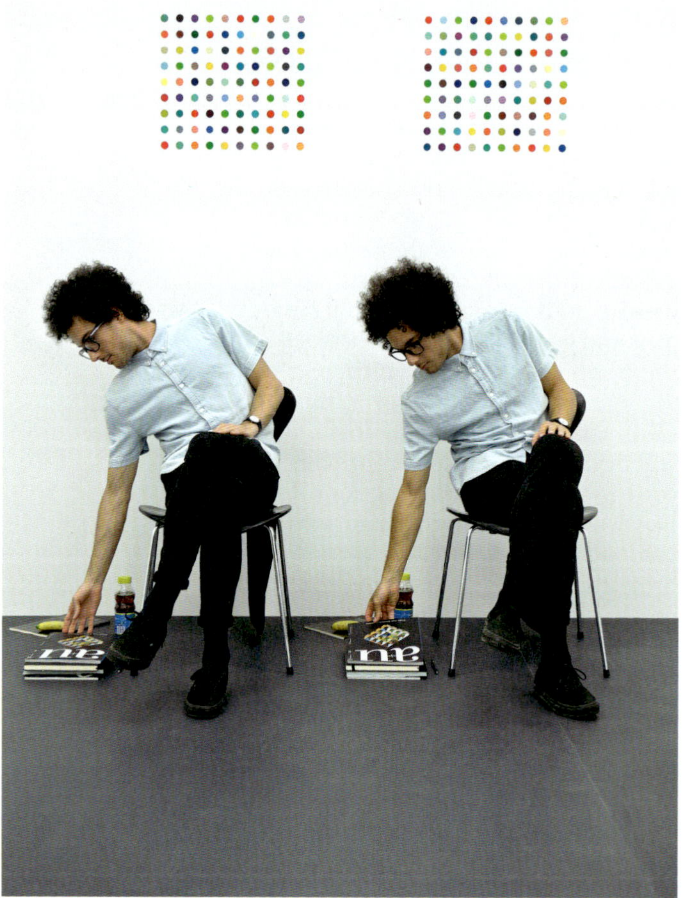

Damien Hirst
Leonard, Raphael, 2014

The installation consists of identical twins, seated in front of a pair of spot paintings applied directly onto the wall behind. The work's title changes according to the names of the participating twins: when first exhibited in 1992 it was variously titled *Marianne, Hildegard* and *Ingo, Torsten*.

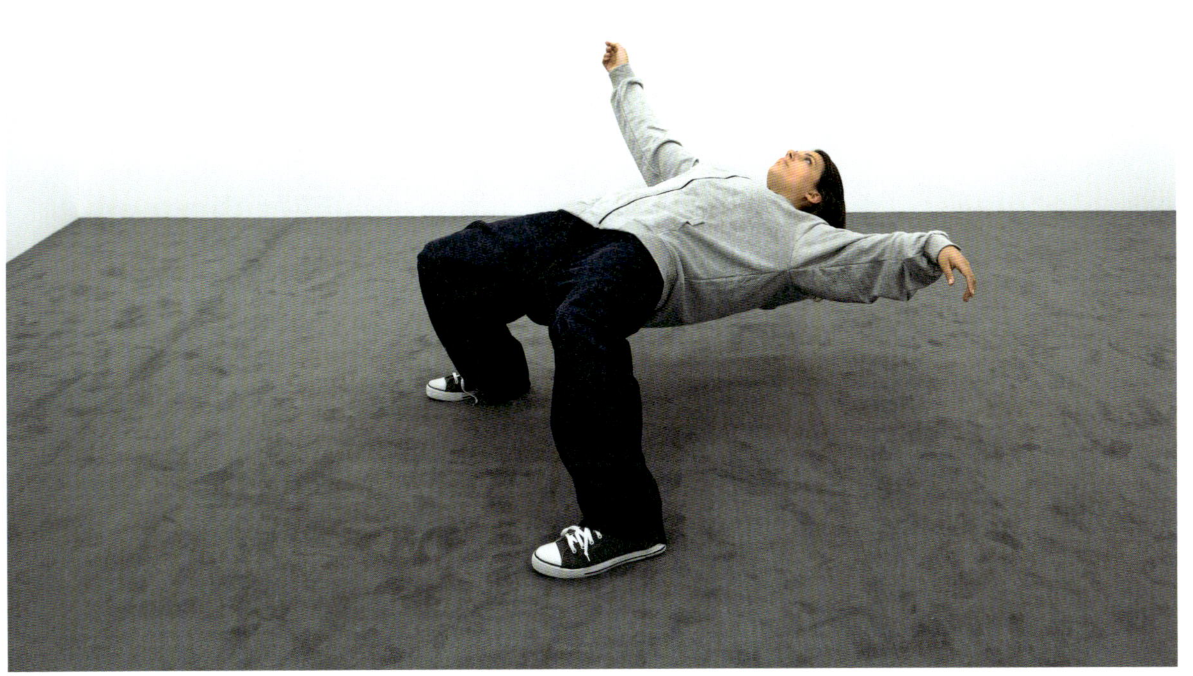

Xu Zhen
In just a blink of an eye, 2005

A person floats mysteriously in mid-air, frozen in time and space as if defying the constraints of physics. The work engages with the notions of the body as material and the materiality of the body, testing the limits of physical and cognitive possibilities as we try to comprehend what we see.

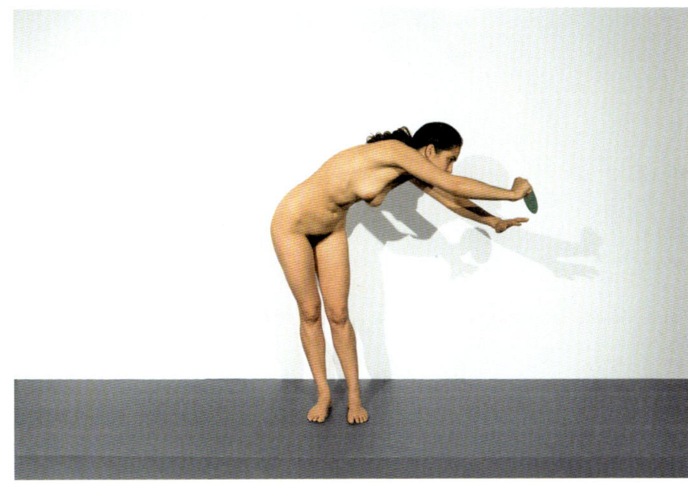

Joan Jonas
Mirror Check, 1970/2014

The performer observes and examines her own naked body with a small, round, hand-held mirror. The mirror serves as a symbol of self-portraiture, but also as a device of fragmentation, reflecting parts of the body but not the whole.

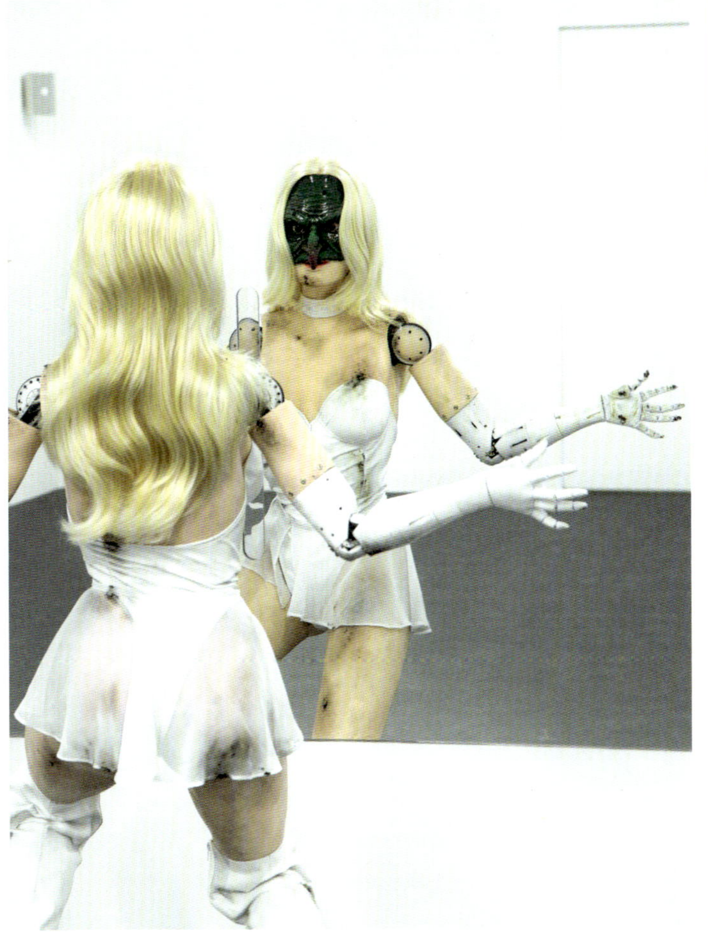

Jordan Wolfson
(Female figure) 2014, 2014

An animatronic dancer moves lasciviously in front of a large mirror. She tries to catch the eye of the spectator while at the same time watching herself, much in the way that viewers are confronted with their own mirror images.

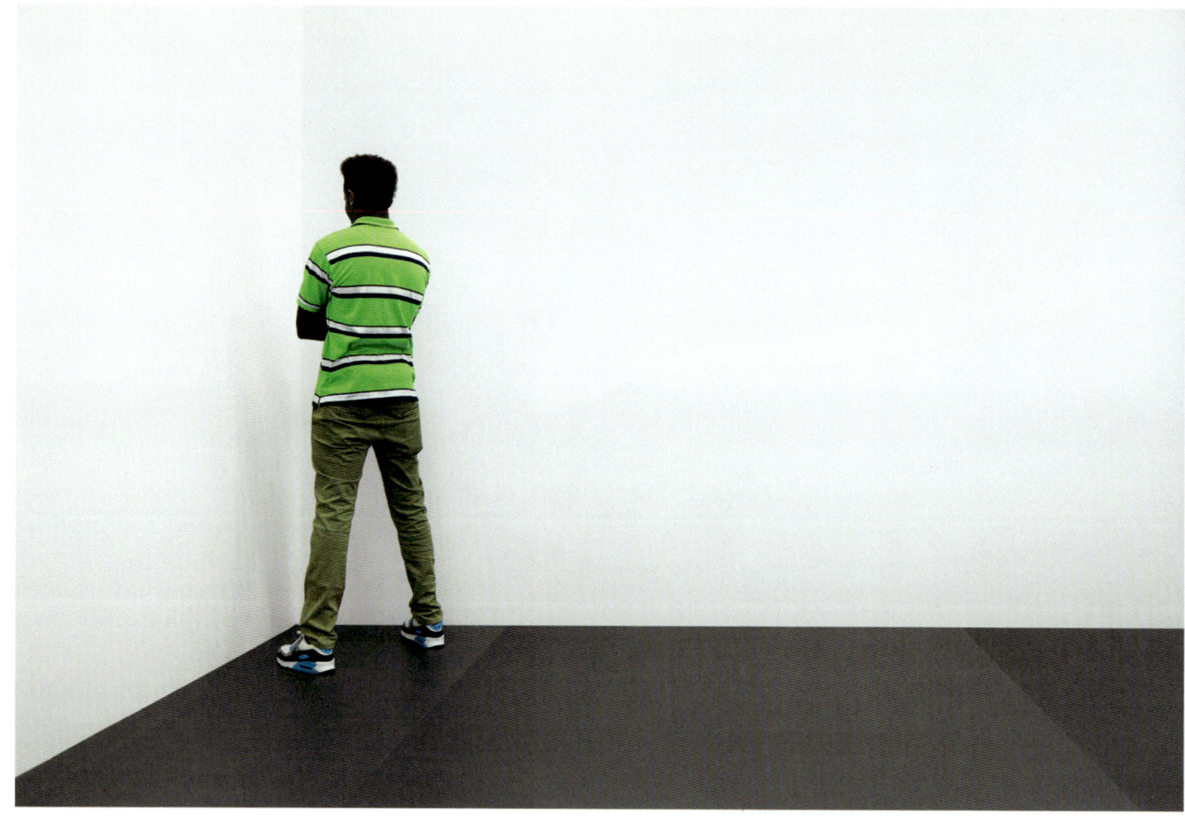

Santiago Sierra
Veterans of the Wars of Eritrea, Kosovo, and Togo Facing the Corner, 2014

A war veteran faces the corner and neither responds nor reacts to the audience. This creates a profoundly disquieting experience for the visitor, as the pertinent question of how veterans should or should not be treated within society is raised.

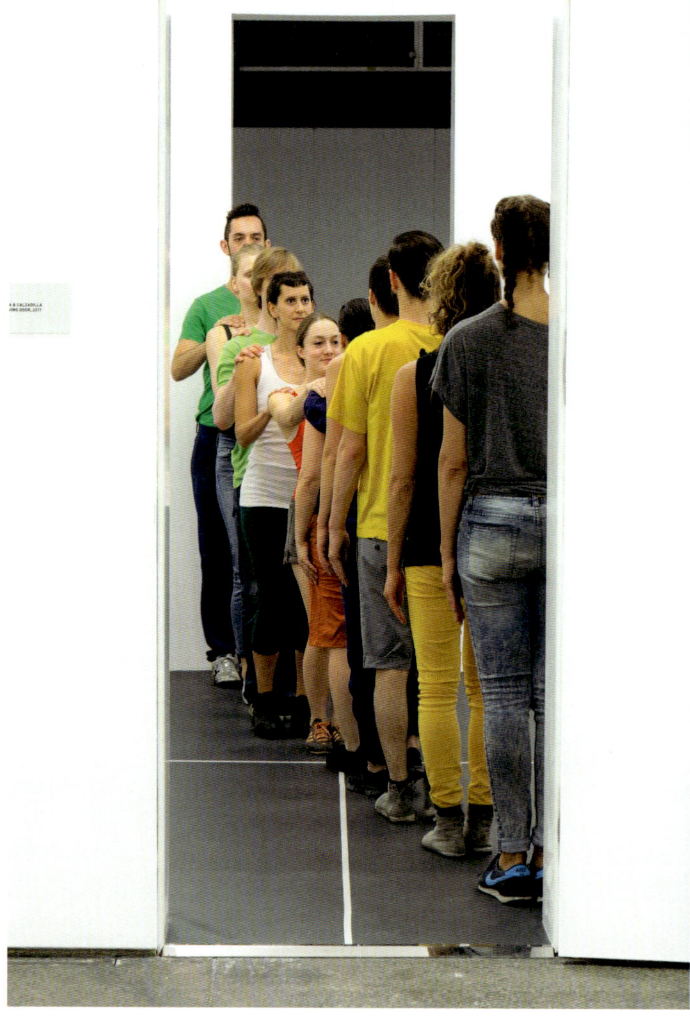

Allora & Calzadilla
Revolving Door, 2011

A group of dancers is lined up from wall to wall, blocking the visitor's path. Their movements are based on political protests, military marches, and chorus lines, among others. The line slowly rotates, obliging the public to move from one side of the room to the other as if passing through a revolving door.

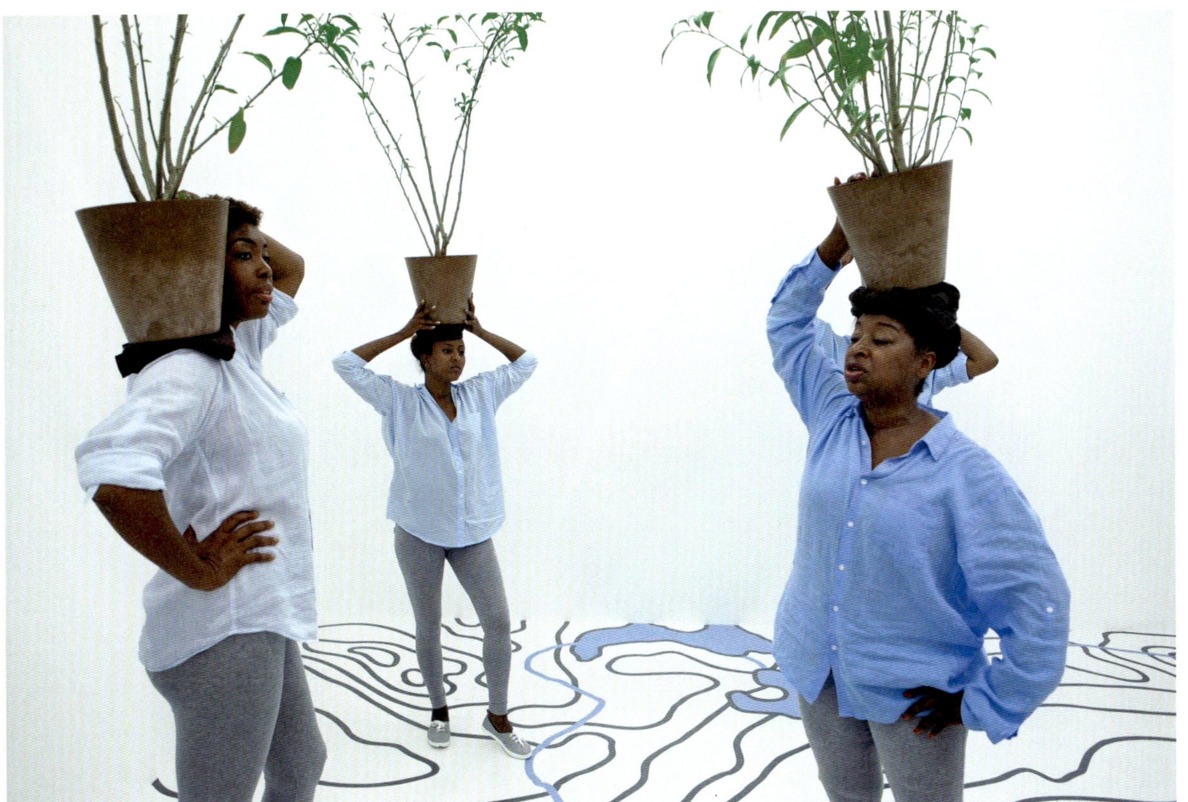

Otobong Nkanga
Diaspore, 2014

The performance consists of between one and three women carrying a *Cestrum Nocturnum*, a plant also known as "Queen of the Night." These women navigate through a topographical map on the floor, guiding their movements together with the plant through different territories.

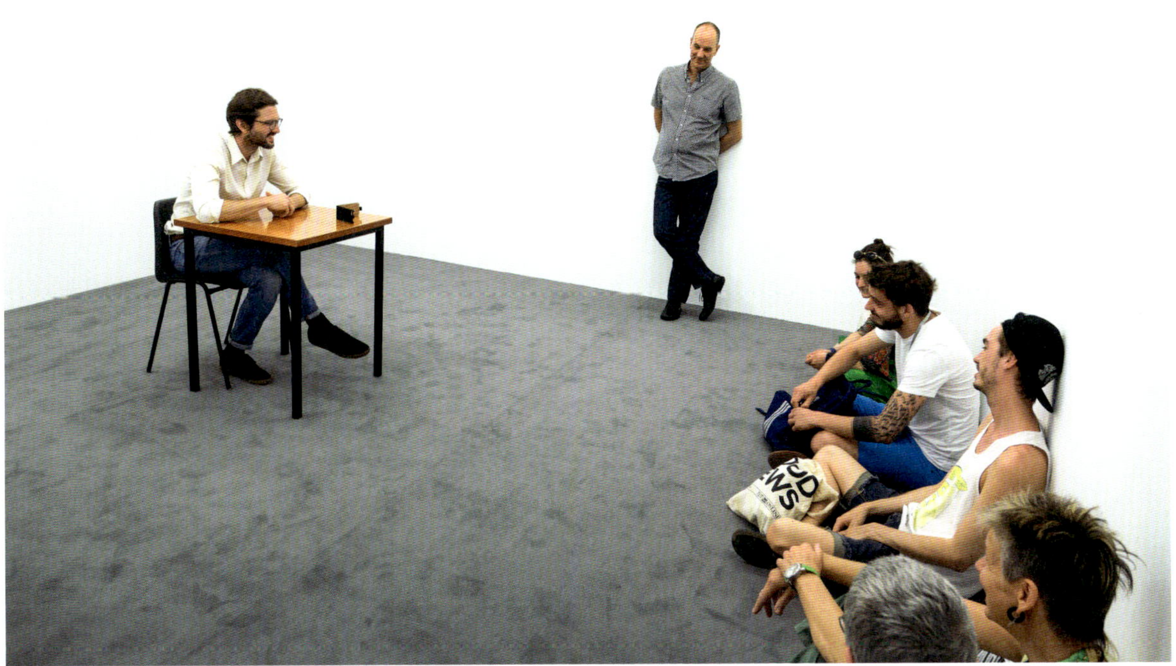

Roman Ondák
Swap, 2011

A performer sits behind a table like a vendor, with an object he has brought along. Once the first visitor enters the room, the performer tries to swap his object with any object the visitor might be carrying with them and which they are willing to give up in exchange for the performer's object. This sets in motion an endless chain of barter and communication which will go on for the entire duration of the exhibition.

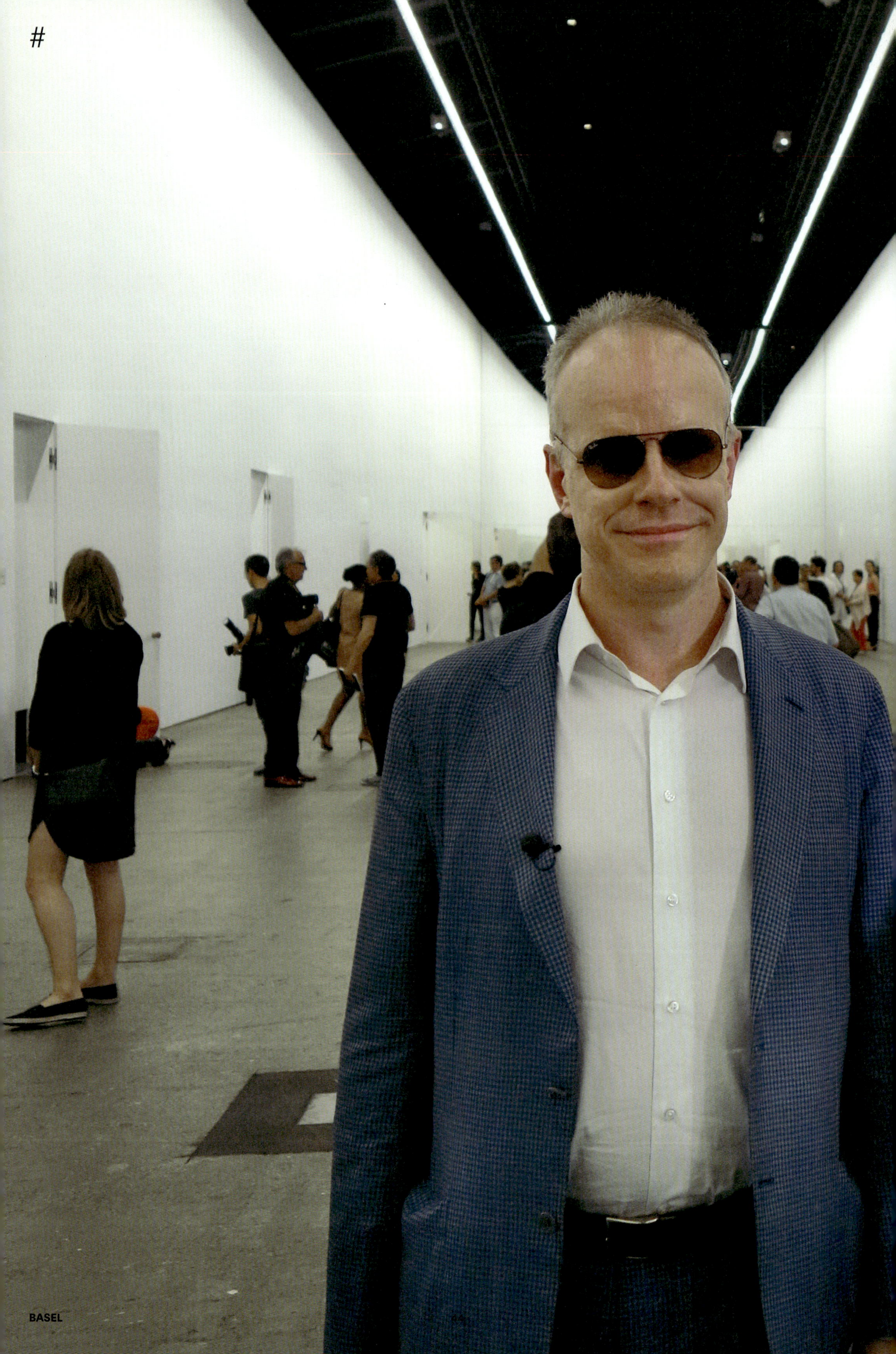

Hans Ulrich Obrist & Klaus Biesenbach
14 Rooms curators

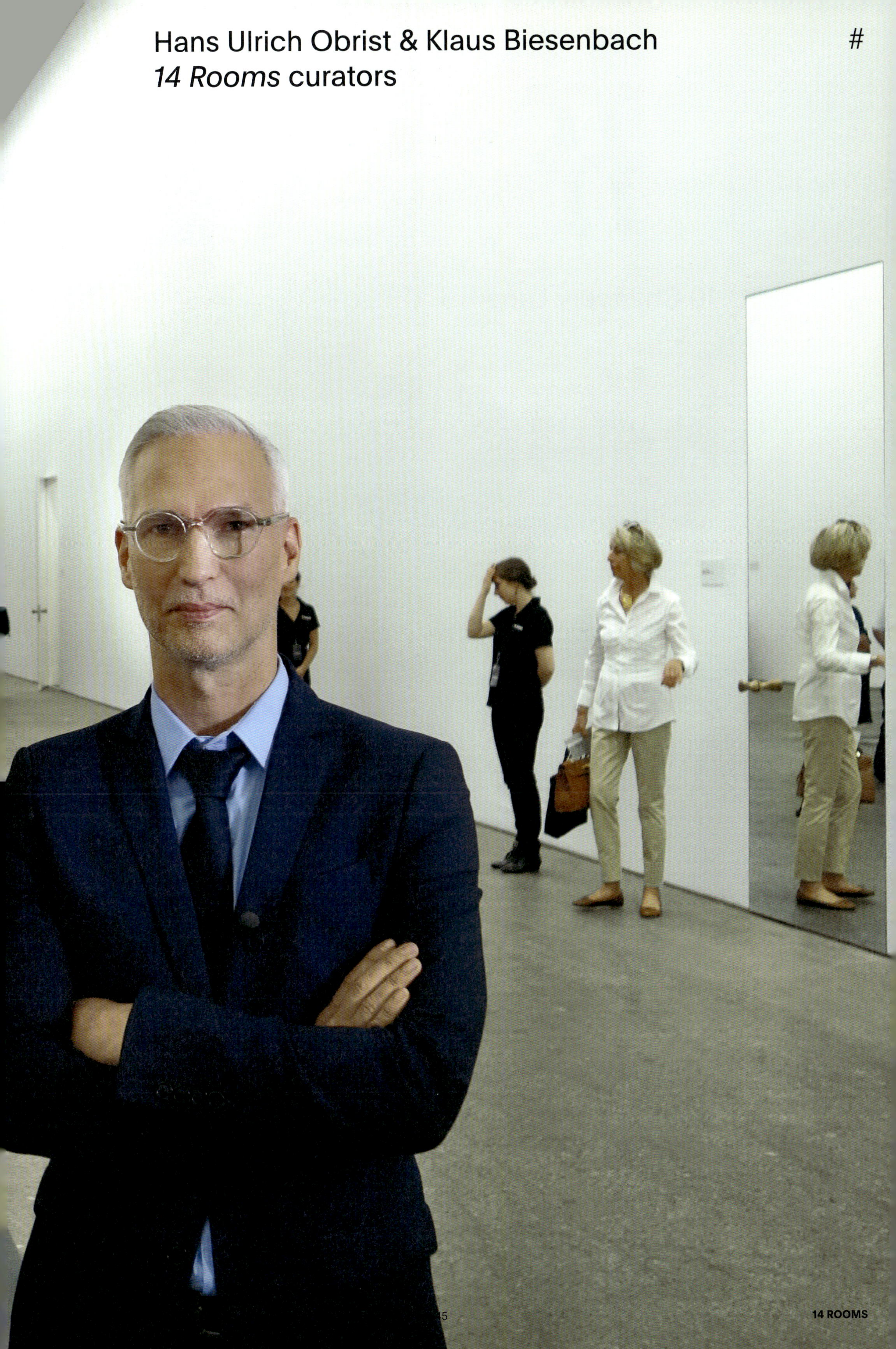

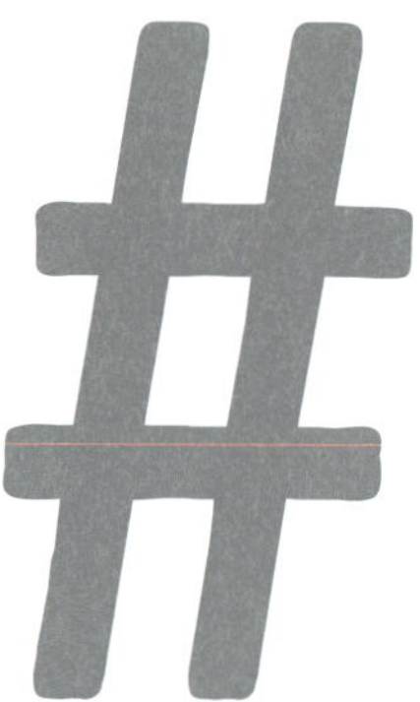

10 Chancery Lane

Hong Kong  Galleries

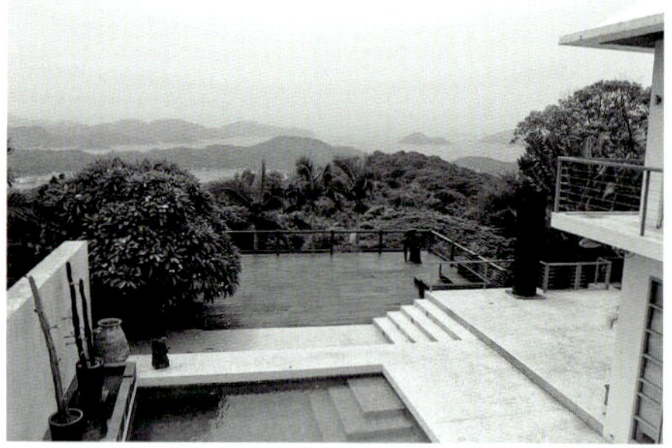

What is your favorite aspect of running a gallery?

Spending time talking with the artists and communicating their vision to collectors, as well as being part of the creation of the exhibition from its inception until it comes to fruition.

How do you choose the artists you work with?

I choose artists who inspire me, who I feel are relevant to our time, and whose minds are very interesting. The quality of the artwork is also important in my decision.

If you weren't running a gallery what else would you do?

I think I would like to teach and inspire. I also enjoy writing.

- **Contact** 10 Chancery Lane Gallery
Katie de Tilly
katie@10chancerylanegallery.com
- **Established** 2001
- **Owner(s) / Partner(s)** Katie de Tilly
- **Team** 9
- **Space(s)** 700 m²
- **Artists at Art Basel** Dinh Q. Lê
Huang Rui
Wang Keping
- **Further artists represented** Konstantin Bessmertny
Hannah Bertram
Bui Cong Khanh
Cai Yuan & Jian Jun Xi (Mad For Real)
Cang Xin
Carol Lee
Chan Dany
Atul Dodiya
Frog King
Maya Hewitt
Hung Liu
Ko Siu Lan
Sutee Kunavichayont
Lindy Lee
Pan Jian
The Propeller Group
Ren Jing
Shao Yinong and Mu Chen
Michael Shaowanasai
Shi Guorui
Manit Sriwanichpoom
Tuan Andrew Nguyen
Xiao Lu
Xiao Zheluo
Yang Zhichao
John Young
Zhao Gang

Galerie 1900-2000

Paris 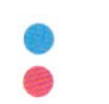 Galleries
Galleries Kabinett

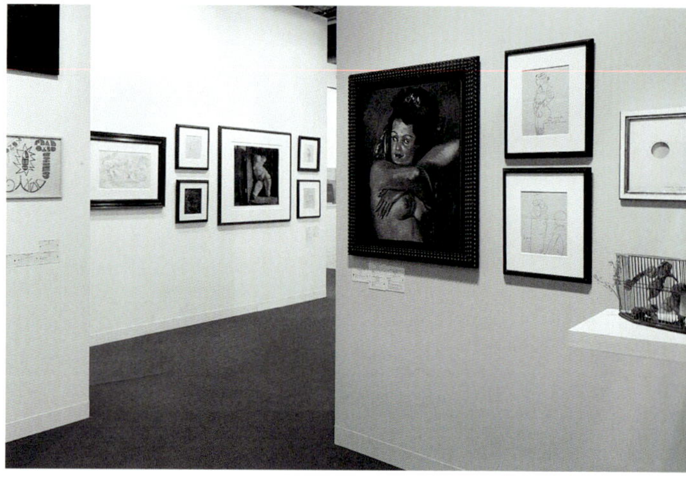

What is your favorite aspect of running a gallery?

I really like buying artworks, exhibiting them at fairs, and meeting new people, showing them different kind of works.

How do you choose the artists you work with?

We specialize in artists from different avant-garde movements like Dada, Surrealism, Lettrism, Fluxus. We mainly deal with works by artists who took parts in these movements.

If you weren't running a gallery what else would you do?

I have always wanted to run a gallery like my father, and have never thought of doing anything else.

- **Contact** Galerie 1900-2000
David Fleiss
dfleiss@galerie1900-2000.com
- **Established** 1981
- **Owner(s) / Partner(s)** David & Marcel Fleiss
- **Team** 7
- **Space(s)** 120 m²
- **Artists at Art Basel** Hans Bellmer
André Breton
Claude Cahun
Bill Copley
Óscar Domínguez
Jean Dubuffet
Marcel Duchamp
Aube Elléouët
Max Ernst
Al Hansen
Jacques Hérold
Georges Hugnet
Ray Johnson
Tetsumi Kudo
Wifredo Lam
Jean-Jacques Lebel
Man Ray
André Masson
Roberto Matta
Wolfgang Paalen
Francis Picabia
Edda Renouf
Pierre Roy
Ed Ruscha
Ivan Serpa
Yves Tanguy
James Waring
Robert Whitman
- **Further artists represented** Gaston Bertin
Xavier Escriba
Isidore Isou
Philippe Jusforgues
Frédéric Léglise
Maurice Lemaître
Gabriel Pomerand

303 Gallery

New York

- Galleries
- Galleries Unlimited
- Galleries

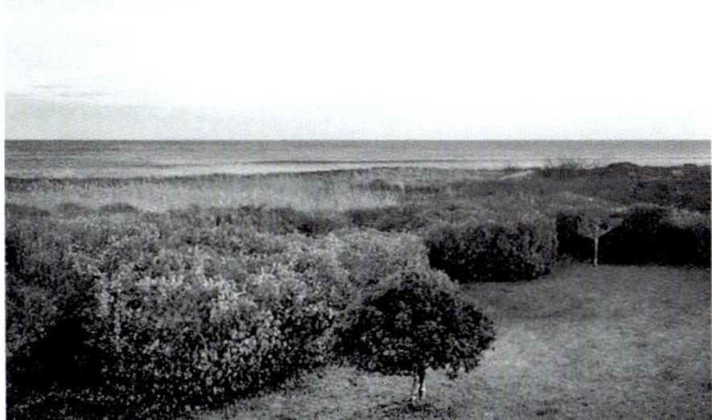

What is your favorite aspect of running a gallery?
I have never viewed the act of putting together a gallery as a creative act in itself, but I do still hold to the belief that I can, when all the right ingredients are there, provide a structure in which creative acts can take place.

How do you choose the artists you work with?
Over the years I have built very close relationships with most of the artists represented by the gallery. I look at a lot of works and usually just go with my instincts, but it is important for the works in the gallery to have a dialogue with each other. The program needs to be cohesive to provide a historical context for the artists.

If you weren't running a gallery what else would you do?
I would travel, and maybe surf a little.

- **Contact** 303 Gallery
Erika Weiss
erika@303gallery.com
- **Established** 1984
- **Owner(s) / Partner(s)** Lisa Spellman
- **Team** 16
- **Artists at Art Basel** Doug Aitken
Valentin Carron
Hans-Peter Feldmann
Ceal Floyer
Karel Funk
Maureen Gallace
Tim Gardner
Dominique Gonzalez-Foerster
Kim Gordon
Rodney Graham
Mary Heilmann
Jeppe Hein
Larry Johnson
Matt Johnson
Jacob Kassay
Karen Kilimnik
Alicja Kwade
Elad Lassry
Florian Maier-Aichen
Nick Mauss
Mike Nelson
Kristin Oppenheim
Eva Rothschild
Collier Schorr
Stephen Shore
Sue Williams
Jane and Louise Wilson

47 Canal

New York

- Nova

- **Contact** 47 Canal
Oliver Newton
info@47canal.us
- **Established** 2011
- **Owner(s) / Partner(s)** Margaret Lee
Oliver Newton
- **Team** 4
- **Space(s)** 251 m²
- **Artists at Art Basel** Michele Abeles
Ajay Kurian
- **Further artists represented** Alisa Baremboym
Martin Beck
Antoine Catala
Gregory Edwards
John Finneran
Josh Kline
Amy Lien & Enzo Camacho
Trevor Shimizu
Nolan Simon
Stewart Uoo
Amy Yao
Anicka Yi

55

Shanghai

- Discoveries

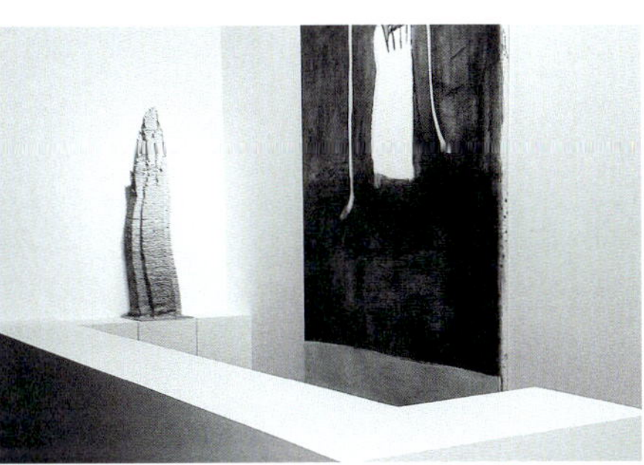

What is your favorite aspect of running a gallery?
Meeting people with different ideas.

How do you choose the artists you work with?
Based on individual concepts.

If you weren't running a gallery what else would you do?
Perhaps run a hotel.

- **Contact** 55
Ferdie Ju
ferdieju@gallery55.cn
- **Established** 2005
- **Owner(s) / Partner(s)** Ferdie Ju
- **Team** 3
- **Space(s)** 210 m²
- **Artists at Art Basel** Noritoshi Hirakawa
Qingtai Hu
- **Further artists represented** Bridegroom Xu
Li Binyuan
Liu Weiwei
Lv Houjian
Su Xiangpan
Xue Tao
Xie Caomin
Yang Maoyuan
Ye Xianyan
Wang Jun
Zeng Hong

80m2

Lima  Nova

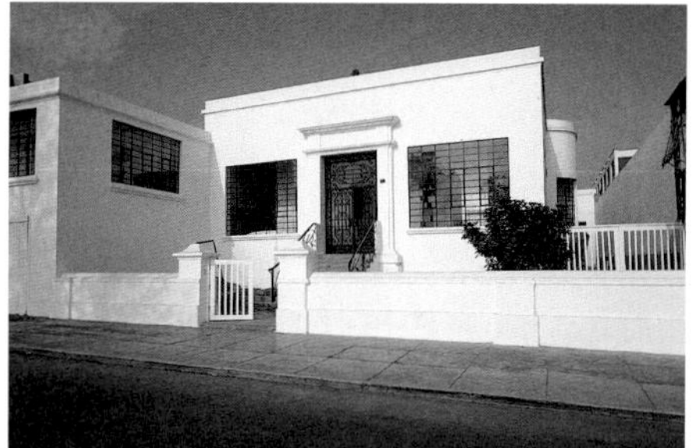

- **Contact** 80m2 Livia Benavides
  Marleny Rivera
  galeria80m2@gmail.com
- **Established** 2011
- **Owner(s) / Partner(s)** Livia Benavides Du Bois
- **Team** 3
- **Space(s)** 500 m²
- **Artists at Art Basel** Gabriel Acevedo
  Rita Ponce de León
  Maya Watanabe
  David Zink Yi
- **Further artists represented** Miguel Andrade Valdez
  Iosu Aramburu
  Ximena Garrido-Lecca
  Nancy La Rosa
  Claudia Martínez
  Raura Oblitas
  Daniela Ortiz
  Eliana Otta
  Marco Pando
  Gianfranco Piazzini
  Santiago Roose
  Juan Javier Salazar
  Juan Diego Tobalina
  Adán Vallecillo
  Sergio Zevallos

303 Gallery
Interview with Lisa Spellman

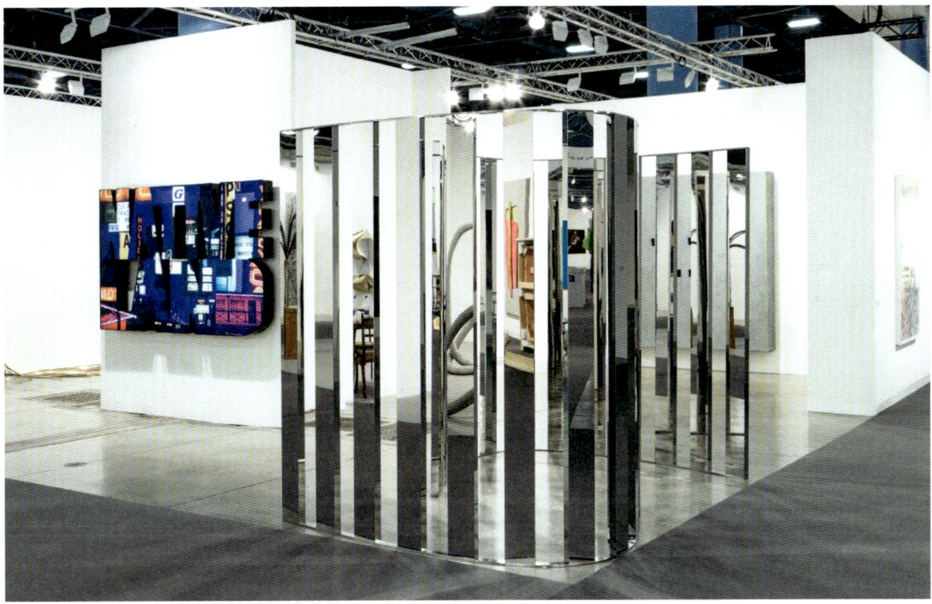

Art Basel in Miami Beach, 2014

How did you come up with the name "303"?

I started preparing for the gallery in 1983 and I opened in 1984. At the time there was a heavy presence of East village galleries with names like Civilian Warfare, Fun House, and International With Monument. I didn't identify with these creative names. I was interested in the Pictures Generation and conceptual artworks, so I was looking for something more factual. The number was literally the address of the gallery, which is not that interesting. But the thing that made me decide on it, rather than my name, was that I was obsessed with the history and the legacy of Stieglitz's gallery on 291 Fifth Avenue—which actually was not that far from were I was—even if it was a hundred years before. The back door of 291 was called 303: it was a special entrance that he used for artists and artists' projects. That was a good place to start from.

Who were the first artists you exhibited in the mid-1980s?

The first year was a lot of experimenting: we showed Larry Johnson, Liz Larner, Richard Prince … Richard collaborated with David Robbins on an exhibition in 1985 about "entertainers." I also showed Allen Ruppersberg and Jeff Koons in group shows. I was basically figuring out a program. I went to LA a lot for studio visits, because it was a fantastic period of CalArts.

I had never worked in a gallery before. When I met Colin de Land he was also in the process of opening a gallery. We thought it might be interesting to become partners, so we tried that for a year. But we had different aesthetics. The only person that worked at the gallery was Collier Schorr, then still a student and much younger than me, so she was a kind of intern/director—it was just me, her, and Colin.

Your started in the East Village, moved to SoHo, and were one of the first to open in Chelsea. What is your take on the way the New York scene has evolved in the last 25 years?

I was probably the last gallery to move into the East Village, but the situation collapsed rapidly because of the riots and the economic crash. We were already looking to go to SoHo. I was there for eight or nine years and then moved to Chelsea in 1995. I'm still there and in the process of building a new gallery on 21st Street, a two-story space in a building designed by Norman Forster. We'll move in 2016.

That's a big shift. Remembering the galleries in SoHo, yours as well as a lot of your colleagues', they weren't buildings, they were just an available wooden-floor space that was rented before it became too expensive.

It was amazing. I found a second-floor space on Greene Street because I wanted to be more central. SoHo was actually very interesting in the early 1990s: there were so many American artists coming up, such as Karen Kilimnik, Cady Noland, and Felix Gonzalez-Torres; a lot of artists were still living there and a lot of fashion designers and musicians too. We had a recording studio above us, and agnès b., Marc Jacobs, and other young designers who were located in SoHo were at the gallery all the time. It was a really nice intersection. Now, with Chelsea it is purely …

… it is segregated in a sense.

Yes, segregated, a kind of monoculture.

If we look at your list of artists now, you have a mix of Europeans and Americans from different generations. How did you continue to build your program?

In the early 1990s I started to work with artists like Sue Williams, Doug Aitken, and Rirkrit Tiravanija, but it was very important for me to build a connection between generations. The obvious twist was Hans-Peter Feldmann, who had a clear influence on the Pictures Generation and a lot of artists that I was showing. At the time he was not showing art anymore. I met him in Cologne when I came for the "Unfair." He asked for my passport because he didn't believe how old I was and asked me what I was doing in the art world, saying that I could make a perfectly good living doing something else. Something serious. [*Laughs*] We bonded immediately and I've been showing him ever since.

A few years later I felt Stephen Shore needed to be recontextualized because I was showing German photographers like Gursky and Ruff, and I knew that they were influenced by him. I was a little nervous about showing Stephen because I was a contemporary art gallery and he was in the photography world, but I though it was important to make that move, to state that he didn't just belong to photography.

You have participated in Art Basel since 2002, and you always create a special mise-en-scène in the booth; you don't just hang the works, but stage the booth.

Yes, we work on booths the whole year. You try to find areas where artists can enter into a dialogue and you try to curate it so that they reinforce each other. We always have a little "special room" in the booth, with quiet or tense works. In certain fairs we have done one-person shows: I remember doing Basel with a Hans-Peter Feldmann booth, six years ago, a booth that was like a café full of postcards.

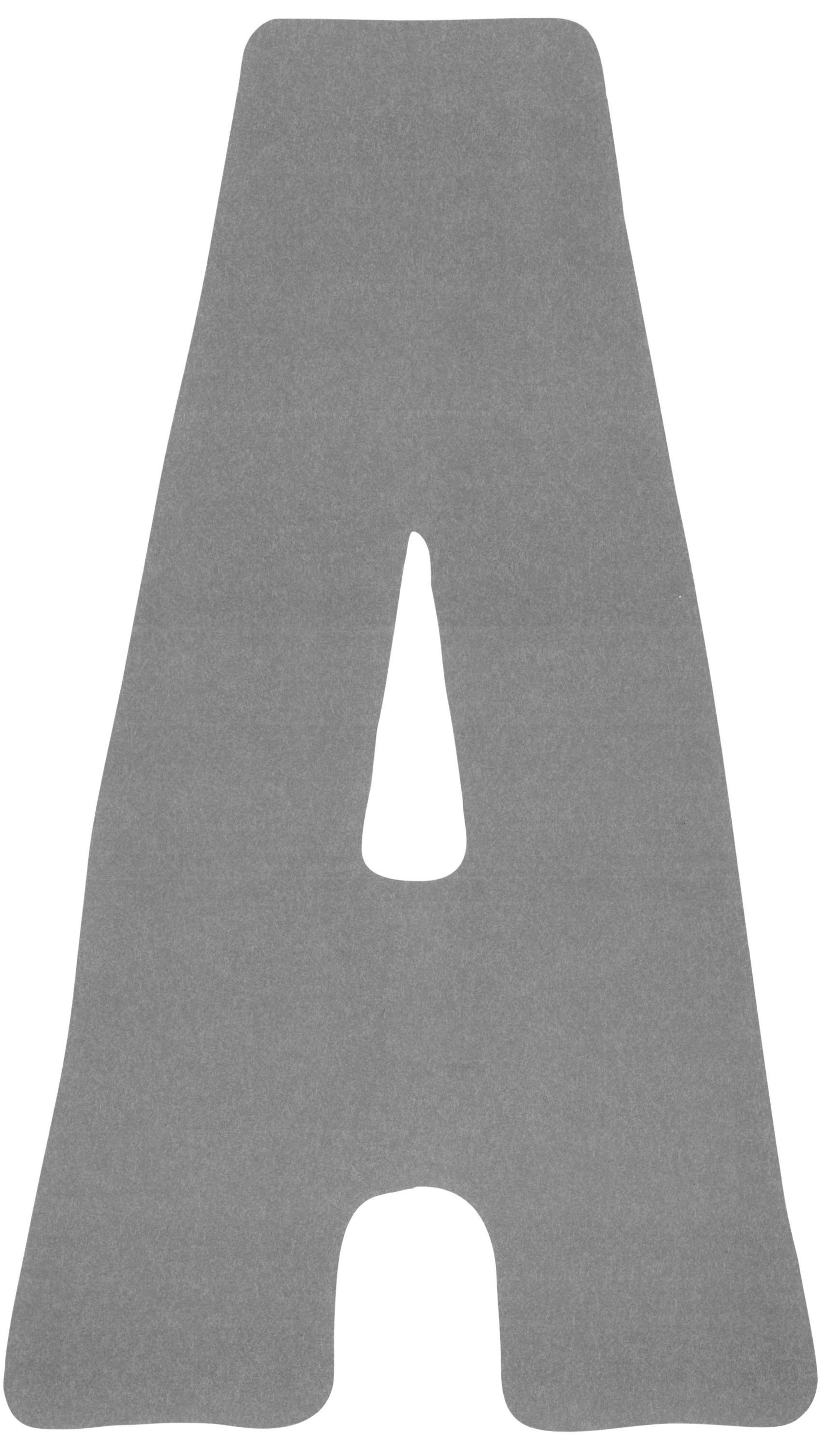

α (ALPHA) PULSE

Carsten Nicolai

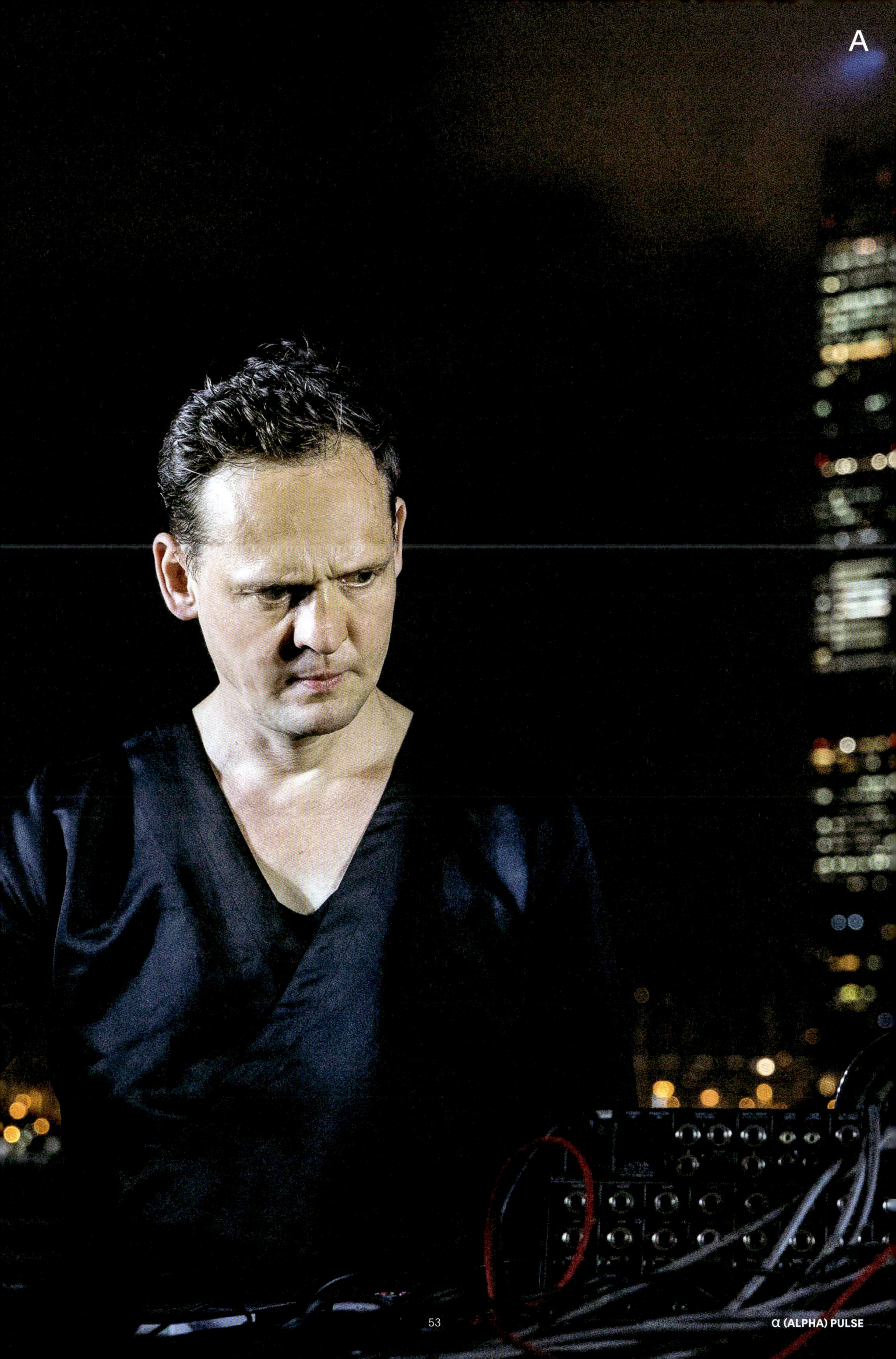

A

Acclaimed artist Carsten Nicolai created *α (alpha) pulse* for Art Basel in Hong Kong show: a generated light pattern pulsating in a synchronized frequency across the entire facade of Hong Kong's iconic 484-meter-high ICC building. The tower sent its pulses into the city like a lighthouse, reaching out to Hong Kong residents and visitors. An accompanying mobile phone application allowed audiences to synchronize their phones with the light installation.

Salon | Artist's Talk

May 16, 2014, at Art Basel in Hong Kong

Carsten Nicolai, Artist, Berlin, in conversation with Nikolaus Hirsch, Curator and Architect, Frankfurt

NIKOLAUS HIRSCH Carsten Nicolai is not only a widely exhibited visual artist, he also has a career as a musician—or music performer—under the name Alva Noto, and is the founder of the distribution label Raster-Noton. I'd like to talk about his spectacular new work, *α (alpha) pulse*, which premiered last night on the Kowloon harbor front. It is a very large work, with a great urban impact: in the performance you gave last night, you synchronized the light pattern with the International Commerce Centre (the tallest building in Hong Kong), and through a specially designed app you offered the audience the possibility to do so as well. Is this your biggest work so far? And how did you deal with the notion of scale in this project?

CARSTEN NICOLAI In terms of dimension and reach into the city, it's probably the biggest work I've ever done. Many journalists have asked me that question and every time I was surprised: I didn't think so much about the scale when I was working on it. When you plan such a project you don't work in a *real* situation: you imagine how the situation is. You build a model or have plans, but the working process is similar to smaller works, or works that may not have such a great visual presence. I realized the real dimension only yesterday, during the performance. Even then I couldn't really pay attention to it, because when I'm performing I'm involved in such a way that I cannot really *see*—so I had to look at photographs to realize it fully.

NH From the audience viewpoint, seeing you performing with this 484-meter building in the background, the contrast in scale was striking. There was also the digital dimension. How did you synchronize these elements? And how did you synchronize the different scales?

CN My first studies were in architecture, and in architecture there are measurement systems: Le Corbusier made the Modulor, in Japan there is the tatami. There's always a kind of modular grid and this grid (and how it relates to the human body) is very important in my research. I think that artworks should have a human scale. In *α (alpha) pulse*, you have this 484-meter tower, but you also have the application on your mobile device. There's a kind of micro-macro situation. This levels the scale, because the small device, the big skyscraper, the additional screens installed yesterday for the performance, all have different dimensions, but are part of the performance, with equal power. It's not only the tower. Otherwise it would have just been monumental.

NH Did you actually have direct access into the telecommunication system of the building? When we talk about the synchronization, how literal was it?

CN That was one of the first ideas: to break into the system of the building and work directly and interactively with the tower. But the system of the tower is not built for such a situation; so to synchronize everything was a long process. In the end we synchronized

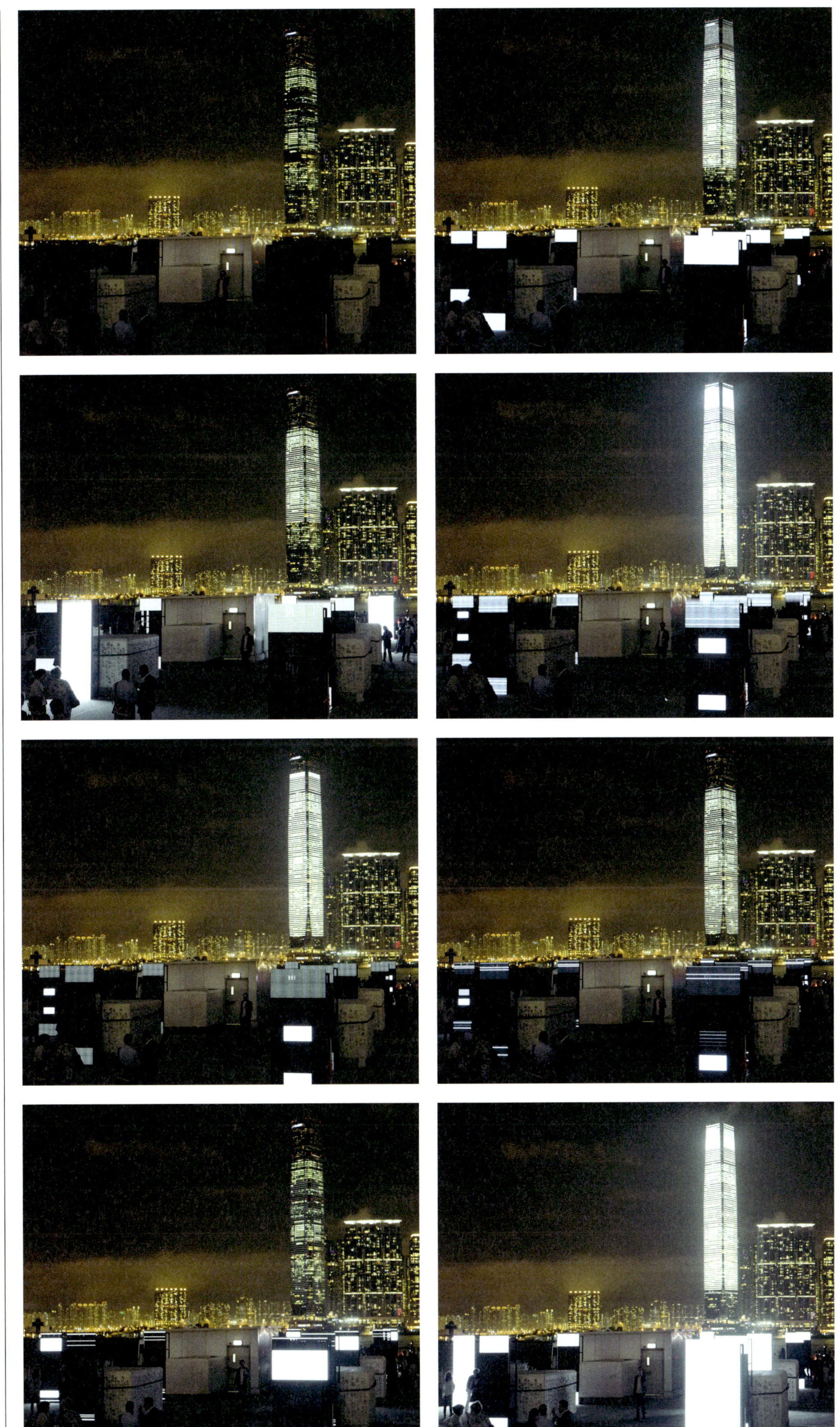

α *(alpha) pulse*
Views of the ICC Tower from the Central Waterfront Promenade, Hong Kong
Opening performance, May 15, 2014

with the iPhone app, which scans the rhythm of the light impulses. In electronic music we use the term "master-slave," which is related to music technology: here the tower is the master; everything else is basically synchronized to its visual pulse. There is no direct digital Wi-Fi or IP, or any other communications happening. It's really based on the visual impact of the tower itself, which actually works better because there are no time-delays, no cable problems. It really goes straight into what's happening.

NH What does the idea of pulse mean for you? Is there a relationship for you between the idea of pulse, alpha waves, and the urban landscape?

CN Well, the pulse is the pulse of your blood pressure, your heart beat—our body is defined by a pulse. Then the sound has a pulse and the light source has a pulse as well, and these three elements can basically interact. We are stimulated by light and sound, we "synchronize." This is actually happening all the time—our body is adjusting to its environment and is influenced by light-sources and sounds.

When I visited Tokyo straight after Fukushima, the policy was to cut off power to everything that was not essential. So all advertisements, air conditioners, etc., had been switched off. Walking through Shibuya—Shibuya is probably the most colorful, vibrant place I know—the city looked completely different. The buildings looked different, the lights on the street ... it was very dark actually. I realized that today the architecture and the impression of a city are very much defined by lights that are not installed by architects, such as advertisements or additional light sources. A classical city like Florence was defined by architects and can still be experienced the way it was designed.

Carsten Nicolai in front of Hong Kong's harbor

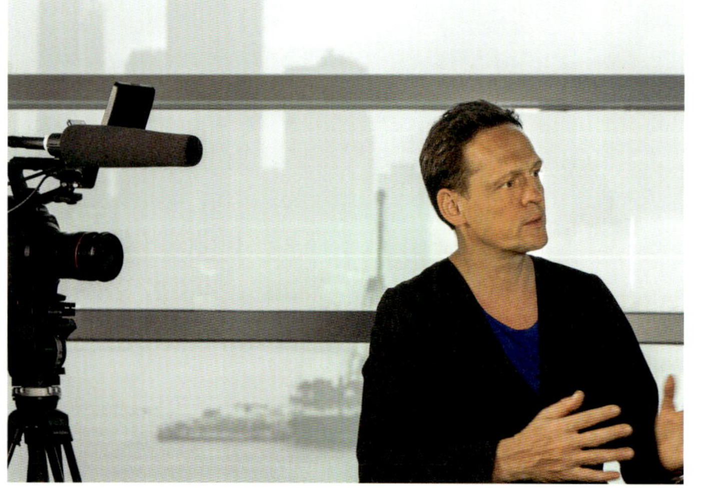

If you go to modern cities, they vary and evolve constantly.

NH In your practice, I think you cover a lot of different aspects of what we could call "distribution." On the one hand, you make artworks that can be collected, exhibited in galleries and museums; on the other there is your practice as Alva Noto, a musician, and your role as a distributor with the label Raster-Noton. Could you reflect on the notion of distribution as something that triggers your work?

CN We all know that the art world produces a lot of "unique" pieces. For instance, it's very unusual that artists' groups are composed of numerous people, or even that artists work together in the long run, but this is very common in the music sector. That's one aspect. In art you produce a single art piece, while in music it's much more about multiplying and distribution, you're not very interested in making only one CD. You're more interested in the CDs going out and reaching as many people as possible. It's a very different way of distributing or reaching out.

NH I believe that in your work these differences are made very clear. What is happening today in museums seems different to me: it's as if they try to blur traditional boundaries. Collecting time-based formats is a new direction in museum practice, visible at MoMA or Tate, for instance. What do you think of this hybridization of different formats?

CN Ten years ago, I believed that we were going to move into a situation where the borders would blur more and more and eventually there would be not much difference between these art forms. Then I had a conversation with Christian Marclay, someone who also works simultaneously in music and the visual arts: he told me that you always have to think about the context first and place things in the right one; that you cannot expect things to blur as much as you might want or try. This helped me a lot, because museums are not concert halls and concert halls are not museums. There are maybe some spaces that can work in-between, flexible artist-run spaces, but if you move to a bigger scale you really have to be careful about what you place where. And it starts with very basic questions of acoustics. We call it the white cube and the black cube, and they are really different.

Carsten Nicolai
α (alpha) pulse

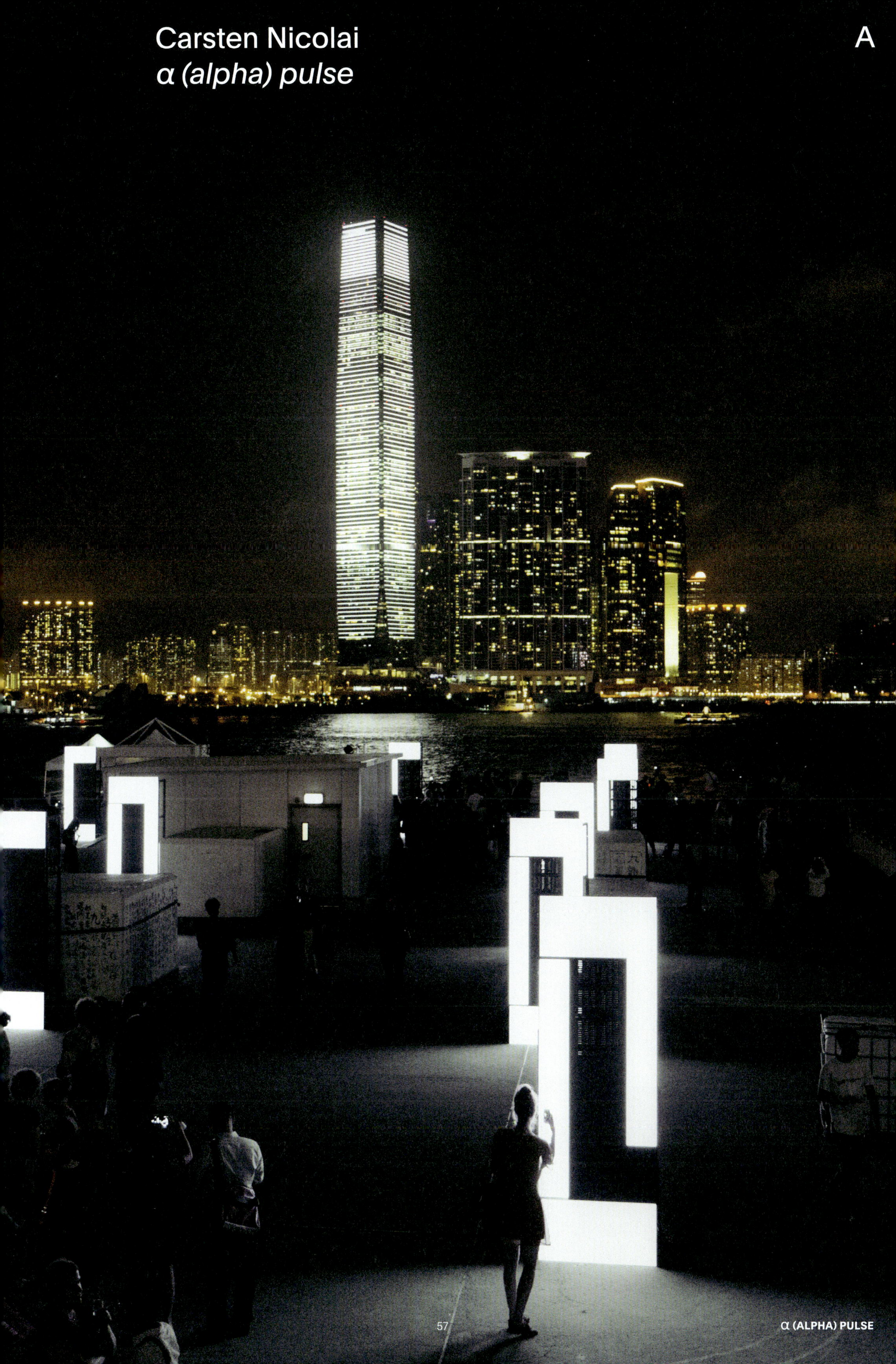

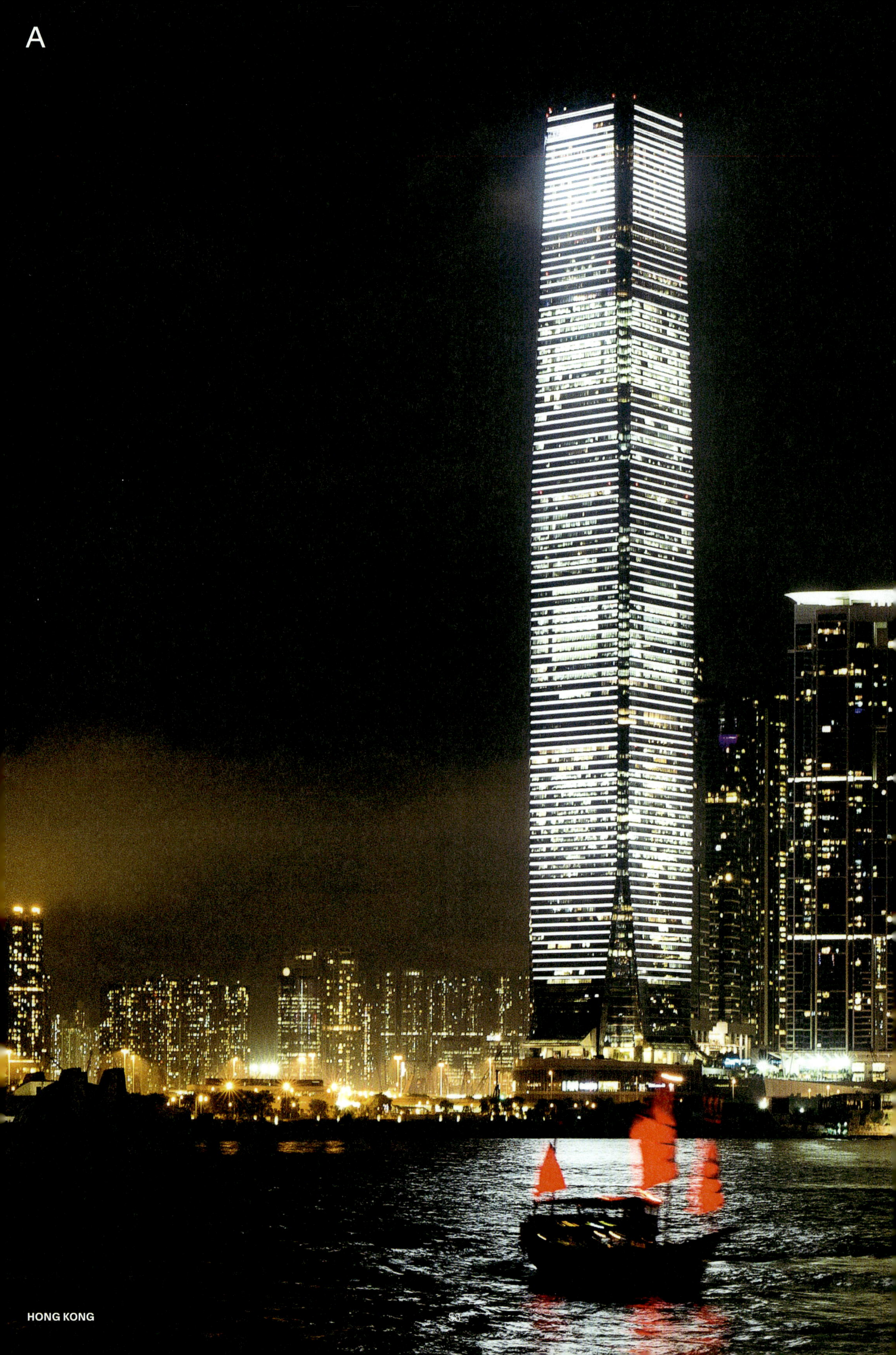

A

HONG KONG

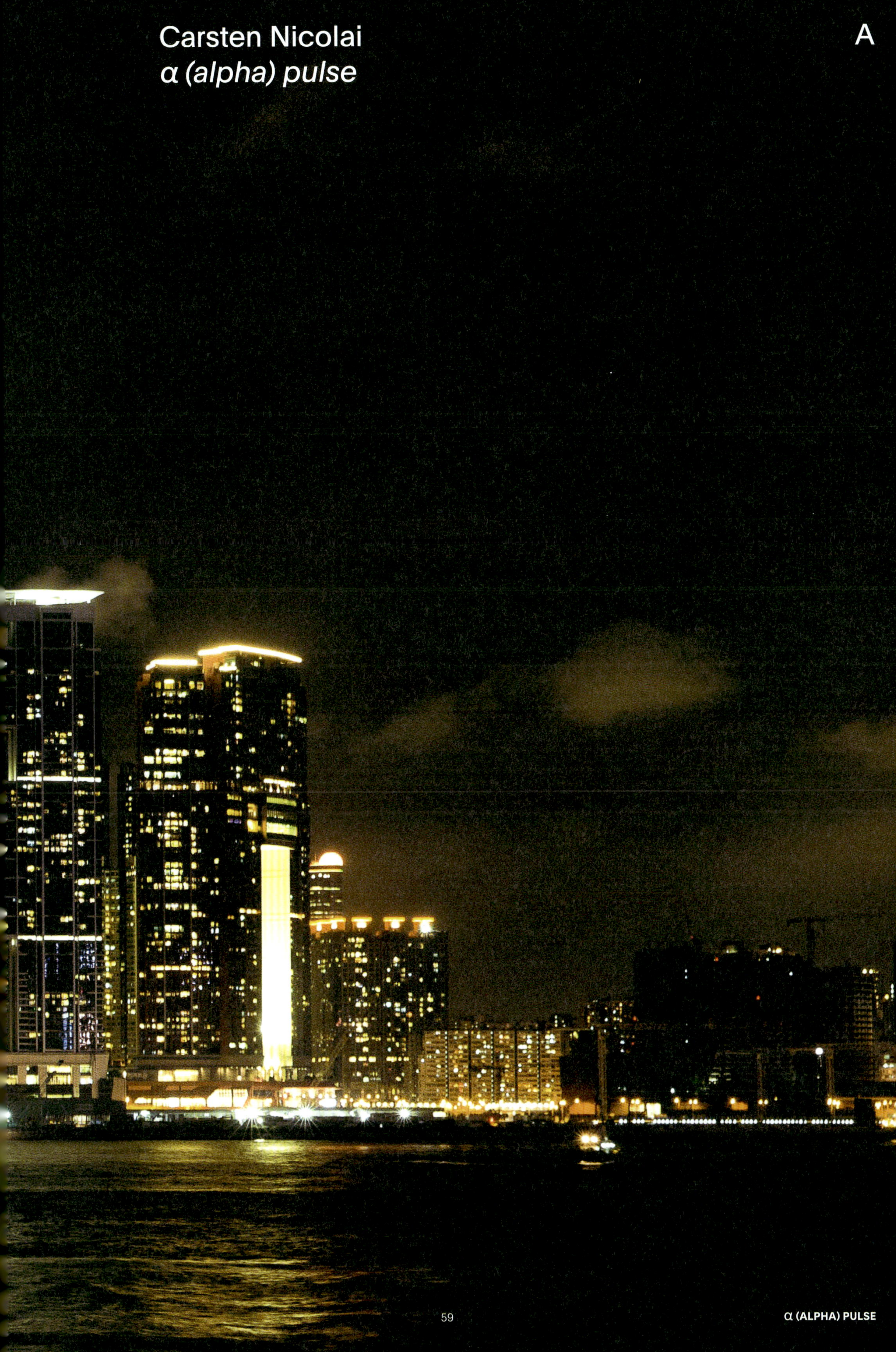

Carsten Nicolai
α (alpha) pulse

NADIM ABBAS

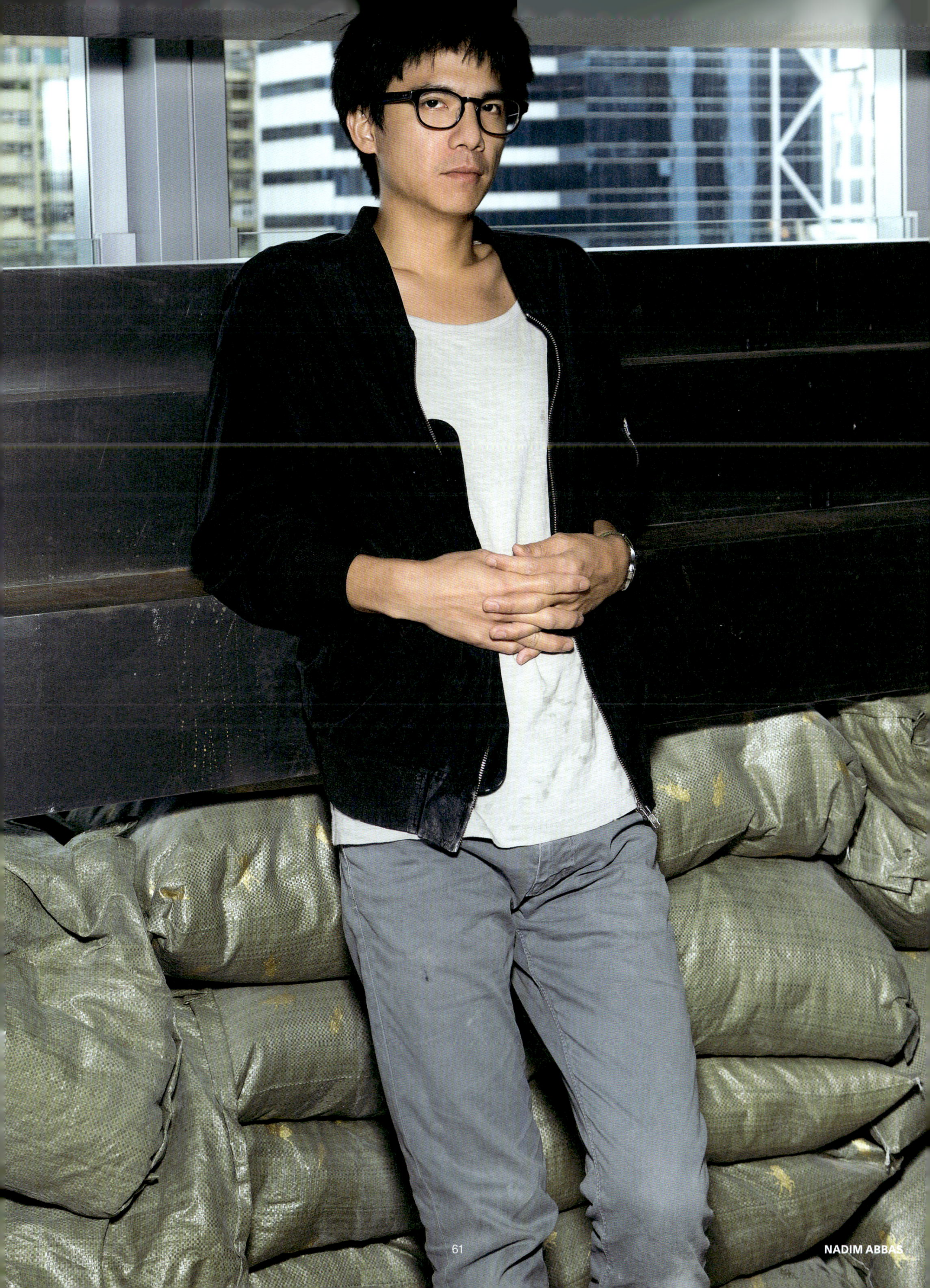

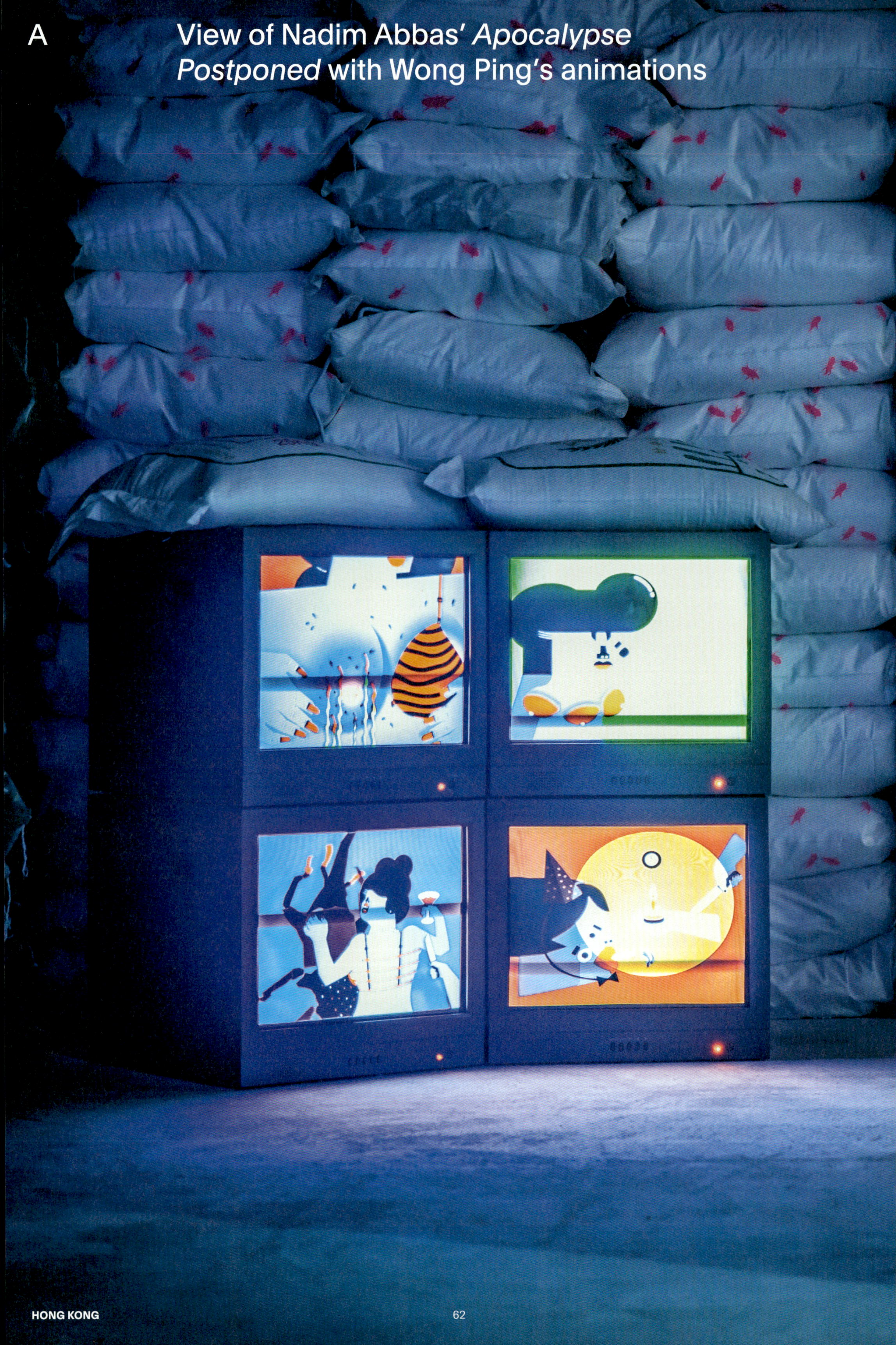

A View of Nadim Abbas' *Apocalypse Postponed* with Wong Ping's animations

Conversation with Nadim Abbas on his *Apocalypse Postponed* Absolut Art Bar, Art Basel in Hong Kong, May 2014

CLÉMENT DIRIÉ How did the collaboration with Absolut start?

NADIM ABBAS They approached me last year, at Adrian Wong's Absolut Bar during Art Basel in Hong Kong. I saw what was possible and agreed to do their next Art Bar.

LIONEL BOVIER There is something very narrative in the way you constructed your project. Did you conceive it as a script, with different characters and different atmospheres?

NA It was indeed a cinematic kind of thinking: the first image that came to my mind was this famous scene from *A Clockwork Orange*, the psychedelic milk bar. The aesthetic of this film, with its 1960s science-fiction flair that's dated in terms of style, stuck in my mind. I tried to think about what it meant—basically a meditation on violence and the social contradictions inherent in its control—and developed this "war theme," which is also related to my own practice. Recently I started to make works that deal with the relationship between domesticity and warfare, embedded in Modernist design and art. A lot of the elements that you see in this space are borrowed from 20th century fortification architecture and bunker design. Probably this is best illustrated by the slit windows, which were borrowed from the bunkers in the Atlantic Wall.

The design of the space was done in collaboration with the architect Sébastien Saint-Jean. We thought a lot about the strict utilitarian dimension of a bunker. There's a violent and dark side to it, but also a certain kind of Modernist purity. Every element of the bunker has a functional reason to exist; it's the epitome of Modernist design.

CD What is peculiar in your installation is that we feel as if we're in a basement when actually we are on the 17th floor …

NA Exactly. It was quite difficult to find the location we are in. It is a space for pop-up projects, within a new and half-occupied building. The space was raw, empty, but with windows all around. How can one turn a 17th floor into a bunker in the sky? We decided to block the view of the bay—an idea that lots of people would think of as crazy (in Hong Kong a view like that is worth millions!). The sand bags were a very practical way of emphasizing a divide between the inside and the outside, setting up a thick wall and creating a "sacred" vacuum, a sort of parallel space. This idea of "parallel reality" came out of the sci-fi influence as well.

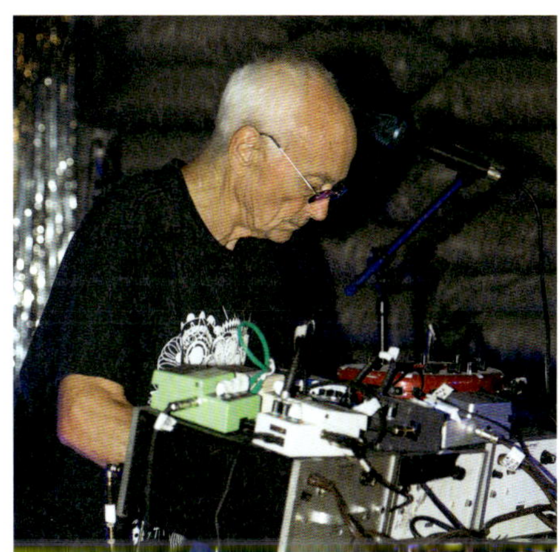

Silver Apples performance in Nadim Abbas' *Apocalypse Postponed*, May 13, 2014

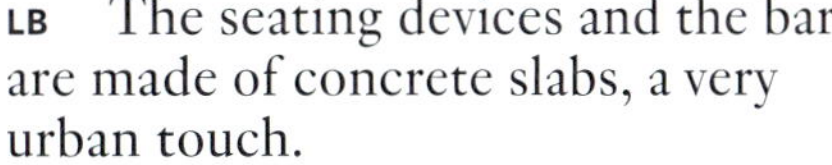

LB The seating devices and the bar are made of concrete slabs, a very urban touch.

NA Yes, they are actually road curbing that we repurposed and turned into seating and the bar. It was very important for us to make sure that all these things would work properly, that the bar would be efficient. For me, it's half a design project and half an art project. There were a lot of design issues, which is why it was very important to work with an architect and a good fabricator (LAAB), which consulted on the material and on the fabrication process.

Another element of the project is the soundtrack. I asked musician Steve Hui to compose a piece specifically for the bar, to set up a different kind of ambiance in the space. I felt it was very important to treat sound as part of the structure. I have a strong connection with the music scene, so I was able to invite a lot of local

A

musicians. Every night was different. Ming Wong did a fantastic performance in this sort of anime costume, lip-synching to Vocaloid music. We also had a couple of professional dancers: they were stationed at the "blood bags bar" during a choreographed mime act. They didn't speak to anyone, but they would come out to the floor and interact with people. Those are little details that I thought were important to the project.

Apocalypse Postponed is a play on the notion of the post-apocalyptic. It's also an obvious reference to Coppola's *Apocalypse Now*.
—Nadim Abbas

LB It's quiet a complex project with multiple collaborations.

NA Yes, it's very complex, involving a lot of people, a lot of conversations, a lot of managing and directing. It's probably the biggest project I've done so far. I don't usually work on this sort of scale. I do massive installation works, but it's more hands on. This is more about planning and working out details. The process is slightly different but the thinking was quite similar in many ways.

LB Down to the design of the cocktails. You supplemented people in calcium and evoked blood transfusions …

NA That was, of course, part of the brief. I worked with Andres Basile Leon, the Absolut mixologist, to develop the cocktails—it was really fun. I added this extra layer of ideas about modes of consumption: it wasn't only about the ingredients, but also about the vessel, the "bag," inspired by space packs and pharmaceutical supplements. All of the drinks have something to do with consuming beverages in an extreme situation—during war, in a hospital, or in space.

CD What was the thinking behind the title—it seems to tell us that the apocalypse has happened and we are the only survivors …

NA It's quite an open title. I had this basic structure in mind and the idea of a safe haven in a post-apocalyptic situation. A classic of sci-fi survival movies …

LB There are a lot of those at the moment on the cinema screens.

NA There are, because people are anxious: everyone knows that there are a lot of problems with the way that the world is functioning right now. It's very possible that we are driving ourselves into oblivion … Everyone goes to the movies to watch disasters, to witness the end of the world, as a catharsis—and to forget about it. So it's like an escape on the one hand and a sublimation of the knowledge of these problems on the other.

Apocalypse Postponed is a play on the notion of post-apocalyptic. It's also an obvious reference to Francis Ford Coppola's *Apocalypse Now*. But it's intimately connected to disaster films and these notions of catharsis and escape. In a way, this installation provides that kind of escape too. In a way I'm not exempt from that consumption mode. The term "postponed" was a nice way to emphasize the idea of repetition: the apocalypse is not this final thing; it is something that is constantly happening, again and again and again, eternally. I don't know what could be worse … [*Laughs*]

CD My last question is about Art Basel week and the art community in Hong Kong. How do you see it now, two years after the start of Art Basel in Hong Kong?

NA It's changing constantly. There are a lot of new institutions, Art Basel of course, as well as government institutions—M+, and the Central Police Station. This is contributing to interest in the scene and bringing opportunities for people like me. My generation is very fortunate to get the chance to do things and to have this kind of exposure. But younger artists are still struggling: these developments are located on an institutional level and in the more grassroots sense there's less support. You still have to deal with high rents, bureaucratic procedures for government funding, and commercial galleries find it difficult to sustain themselves, so they focus on a kind of made-for-galleries art.

LB Can you think of something that could be a potential game changer?

NA I don't know … a Communist Revolution? [*Laughs*] It's really a core infrastructure problem, which has to do with real estate, the government collusion with property development, and the fact that money is driven by big and powerful structures.

A waiter serving the *2666: A Space Cocktail*, May 14, 2014 →

View of Nadim Abbas' *Apocalypse Postponed*, May 13–17, 2014 →

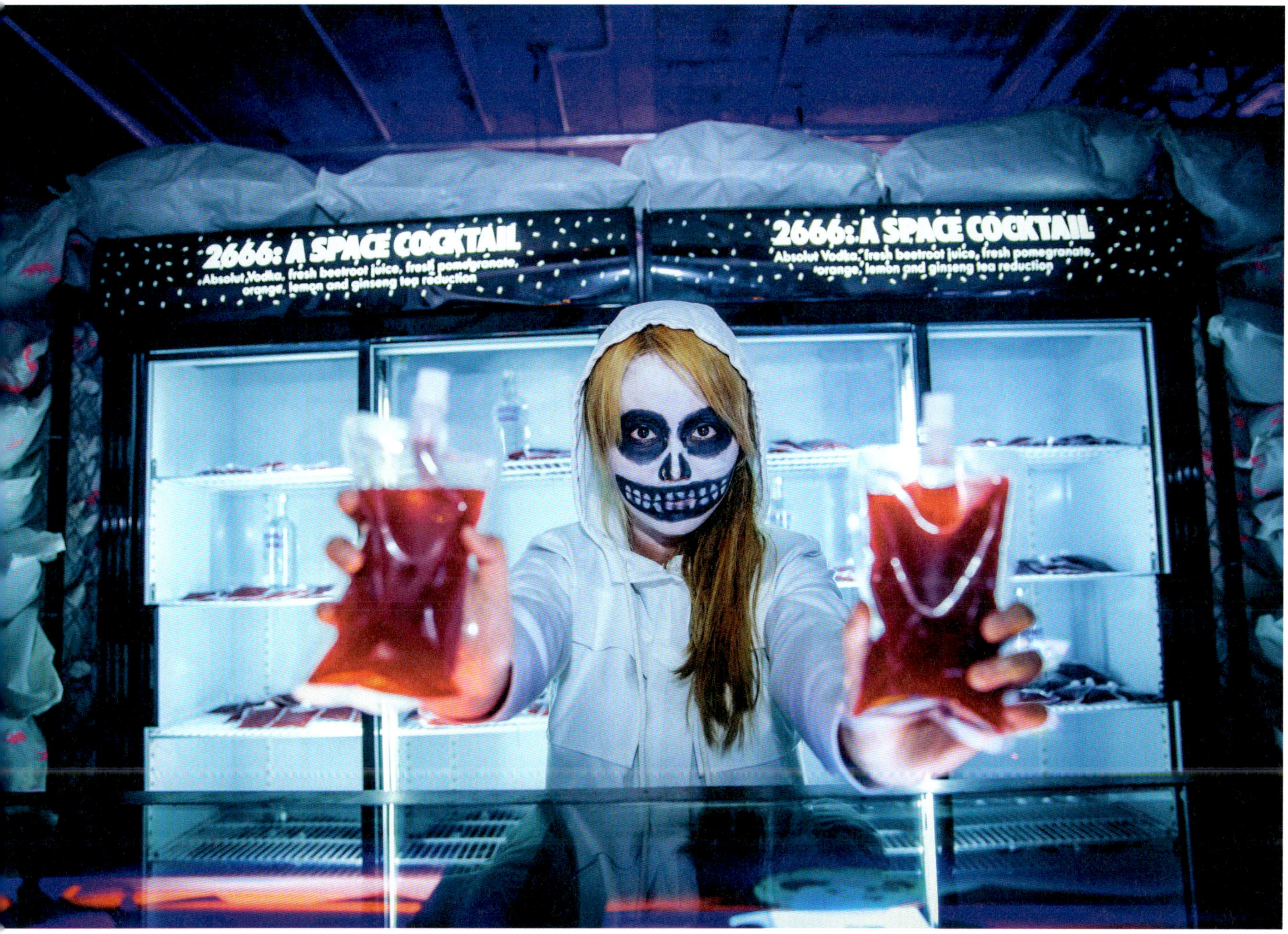

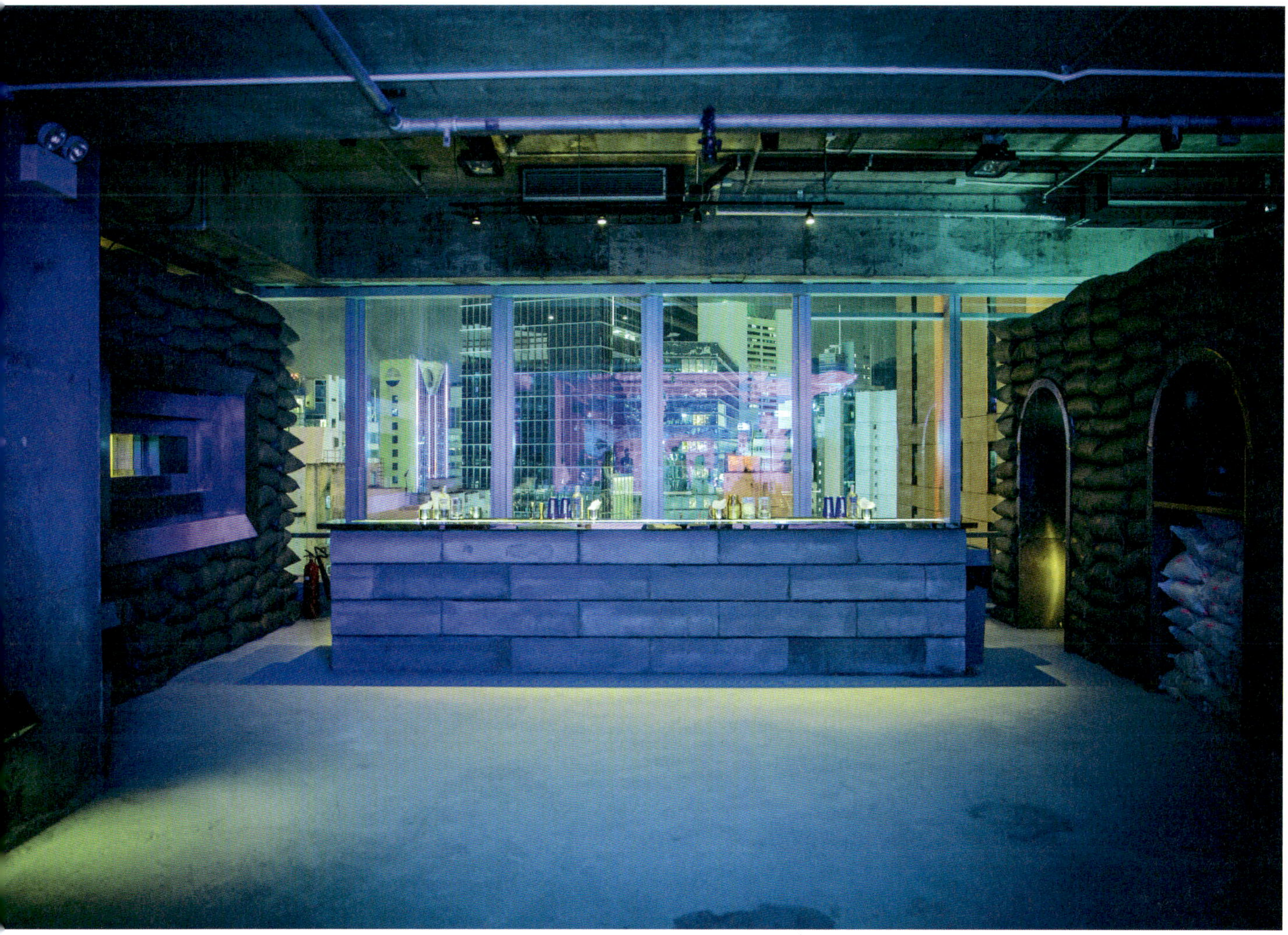

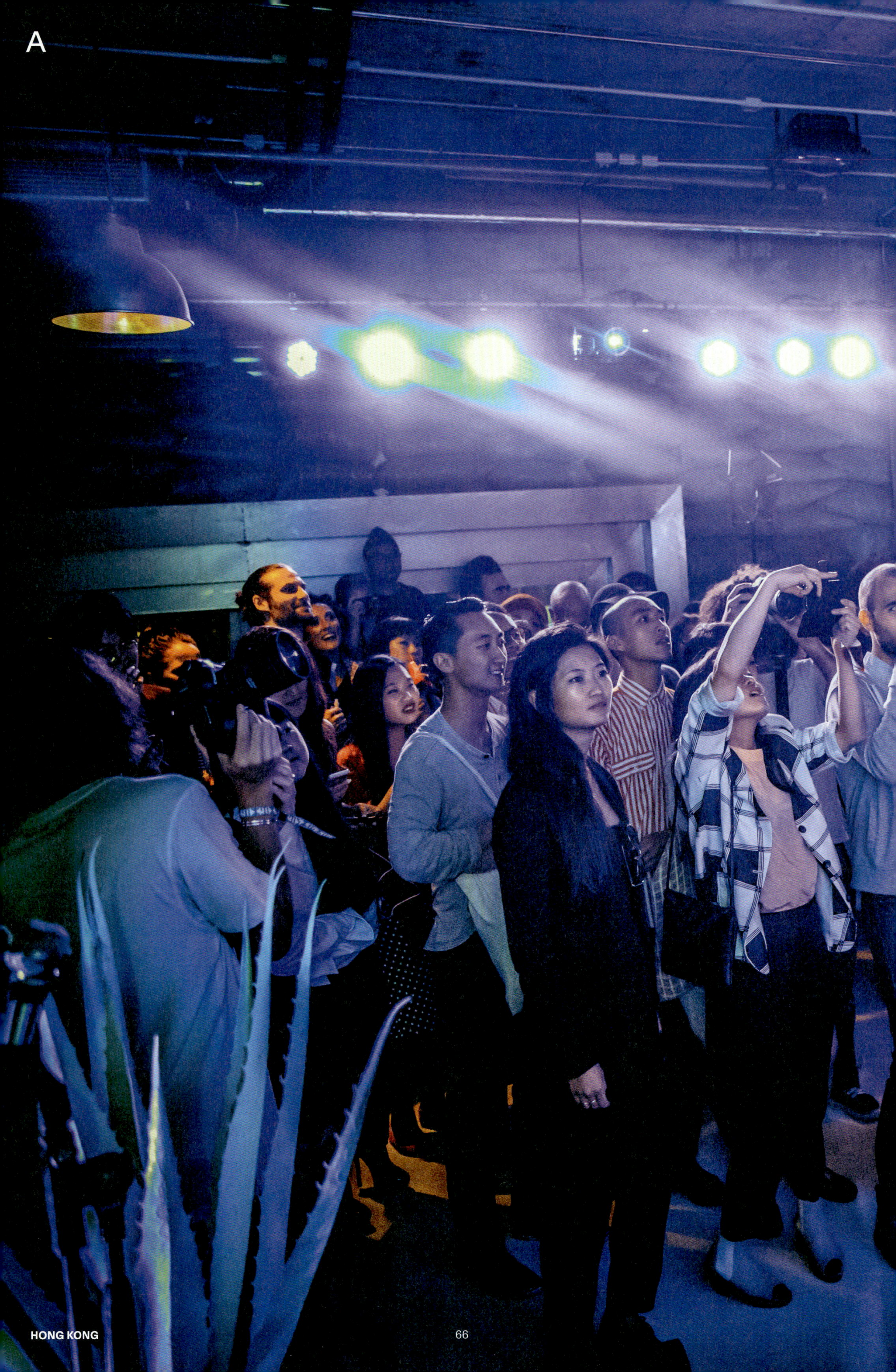
A

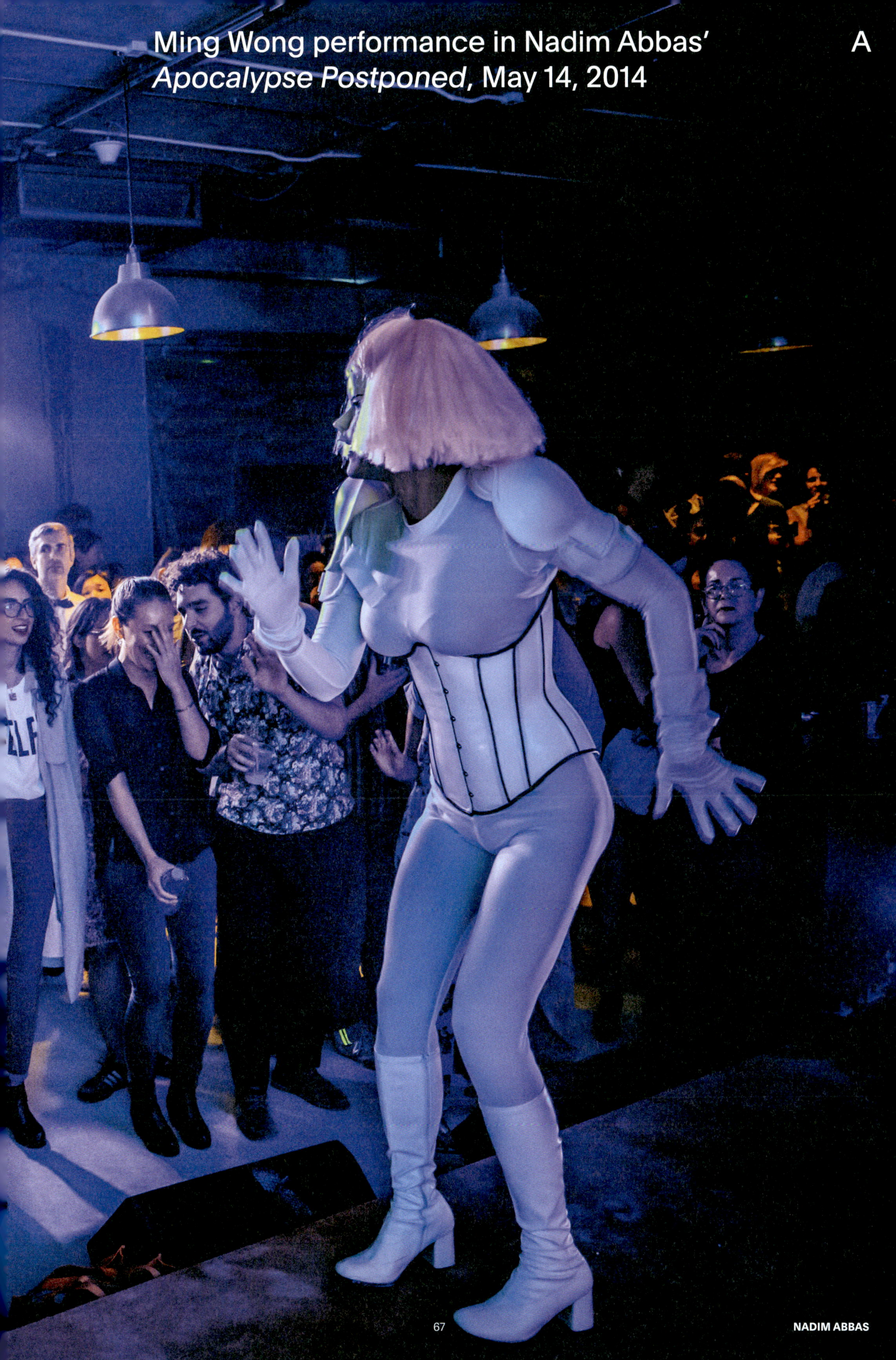

Ming Wong performance in Nadim Abbas' *Apocalypse Postponed*, May 14, 2014

A

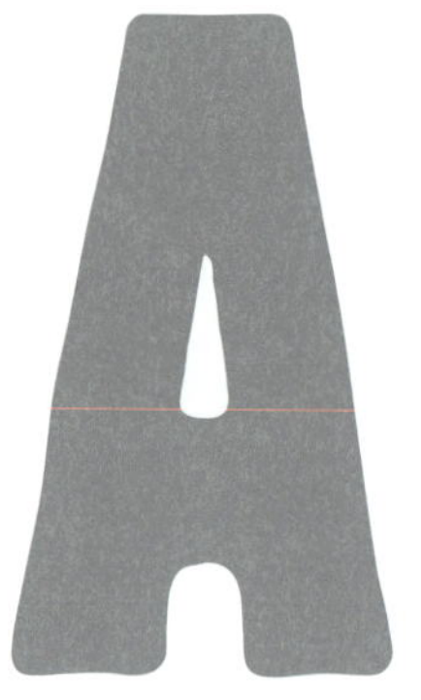

A Gentil Carioca

Rio de Janeiro

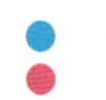

Galleries
Galleries

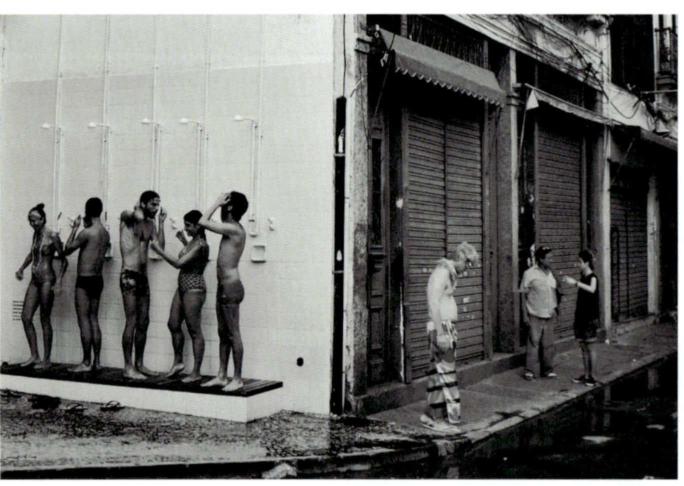

What is your favorite aspect of running a gallery?

I believe that a work of art is a "cultural bomb" able to irradiate culture anywhere this piece of art is found: on the streets, in a museum, or in a private collection.

A continuous collaboration with the artists allows for a constant and intense exchange, essential for the ability to modify a person's mind, a person's day, or even an entire life.

How do you choose the artists you work with?

I usually say that before seeing the works, I listen to the artists. And try to understand if the artist's thoughts are complete and flowing.

If you weren't running a gallery what else would you do?

Thinking about Brazil and its roots, I would say, "may nature now be culture and may culture yet be nature." If we understand more about our aboriginal roots we can have a better understanding of "modernity." A season with the Indians in the forest is an important learning experience; it combines art, culture, and nature!

- **Contact** A Gentil Carioca
Cecilia Tanure
cecilia@agentilcarioca.com.br
- **Established** 2003
- **Owner(s) / Partner(s)** Marcio Botner
Laura Lima
Ernesto Neto
- **Team** 11
- **Space(s)** 214.5 m²
- **Artists at Art Basel** José Bento
Laura Lima
Jarbas Lopes
Renata Lucas
Maria Nepomuceno
Thiago Rocha Pitta
- **Further artists represented** Ricardo Basbaum
Botner e Pedro
Cabelo
Carlos Contente
Cosmococa: Programa In Progress (Hélio Oiticica + Neville D'Almeida)
Guga Ferraz
Fabiano Gonper
Maria Laet
Evandro Machado
Matias Mesquita
Simone Michelin
João Modé
Paulo Nenflídio
Opavivará!
Bernardo Ramalho
Rodrigo Torres
Pedro Varela
Alexandre Vogler

Abreu

New York

Galleries
Galleries

What is your favorite aspect of running a gallery?

The exhibitions' installation periods during which exchanges with artists and gallery colleagues tend to reach their peak and are tested to the highest degree. The moment of truth, in other words. A close second would be the precious times when I am in a position to effectively redirect a bit of wealth from one value system to another.

How do you choose the artists you work with?

There is really no answer to this most crucial question. Every encounter with an artist I end up working with was produced by a unique set of circumstances. But it always takes a long time for the decision to come to fruition.

If you weren't running a gallery what else would you do?

I would go back to making films, which is what I learned to do and did before starting the gallery—and starve! Or I would continue to publish books, and starve more …

- **Contact** Miguel Abreu Gallery
Katherine Chan
kchan@miguelabreugallery.com
- **Established** 2007
- **Owner(s) / Partner(s)** Miguel Abreu
- **Team** 8
- **Space(s)** 497 m²
- **Artists at Art Basel** Rey Akdogan
Liz Deschenes
Sam Lewitt
Scott Lyall
Jean-Luc Moulène
Florian Pumhösl
R. H. Quaytman
Eileen Quinlan
Raha Raissnia
Jimmy Raskin
Blake Rayne
Pamela Rosenkranz
Pieter Schoolwerth
- **Further artists represented** Hans Bellmer

Acquavella

New York — Galleries / Galleries / Galleries

- **Contact** Acquavella Galleries
  William Acquavella
  info@aquavellagalleries.com
- **Established** 1921
- **Owner(s) / Partner(s)** William Acquavella
  Nicholas Acquavella
  Eleanor Acquavella Dejoux
  Alexander Acquavella

Aike-Dellarco

Shanghai — Discoveries

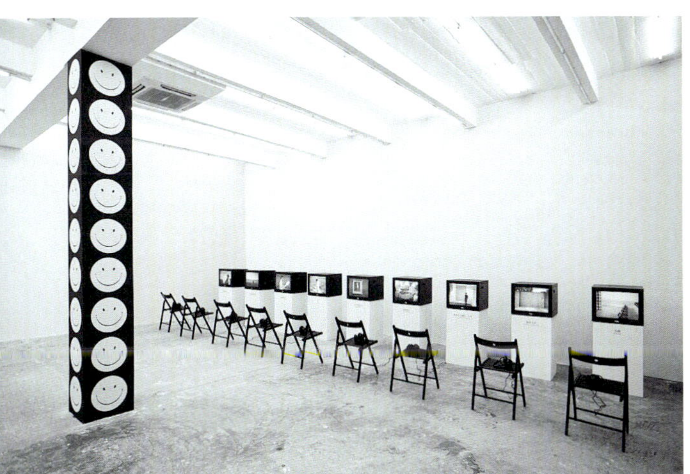

What is your favorite aspect of running a gallery?
Being involved and interacting with artists make this job special and unique.

How do you choose the artists you work with?
Once I like the work, I give all my attention to the character and personality of the artist. I think that this is what makes the difference.

If you weren't running a gallery what else would you do?
Probably be involved with music, my first and true passion.

- **Contact** Aike-Dellarco
  Roberto Ceresia
  roberto@aikedellarco.com
- **Established** 2005
- **Owner(s) / Partner(s)** Roberto Ceresia
- **Team** 5
- **Space(s)** 300 m²
- **Artists at Art Basel** Hu Yun
- **Further artists represented** Chen Jie
  Chen Zhou
  Ettore Favini
  Jiang Pengyi
  Jin Shan
  Lee Kit
  Li Ran
  Li Shurui
  Liu Xinyi
  Lui Chun Kwong
  Tang Dixin
  Zhou Siwei

Air de Paris

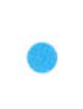

Paris — Galleries

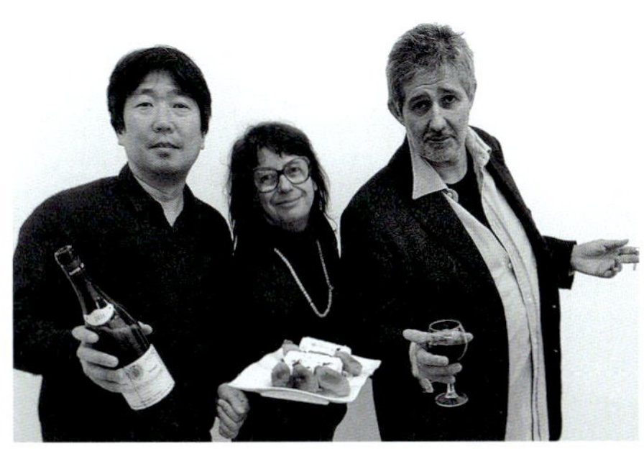

What is your favorite aspect of running a gallery?
Spending time with the artists.

How do you choose the artists you work with?
We need to like both the work and the person. We meet one or the other often by chance.

If you weren't running a gallery what else would you do?
We would be artists or curators.

- **Contact** Air de Paris
  Géraldine Convert
  geraldine@airdeparis.com
- **Established** 1990
- **Owner(s) / Partner(s)** Florence Bonnefous
  Edouard Merino
- **Team** 7
- **Space(s)** 300 m²
- **Artists at Art Basel** Leonor Antunes
  Guy de Cointet
  François Curlet
  Trisha Donnelly
  Claire Fontaine
  Guyton\Walker
  Jef Geys
  Liam Gillick
  Dorothy Iannone
  Pierre Joseph
  Adriana Lara
  Ingrid Luche
  Monica Majoli
  Philippe Parreno
  Jean-Luc Verna
- **Further artists represented** Thomas Bayrle
  Stéphane Dafflon
  Brice Dellsperger
  Joseph Grigely
  Carsten Höller
  Aaron Flint Jamison
  Ben Kinmont
  Mïrka Lugosi
  M/M (Paris)
  Sarah Morris
  Mrzyk & Moriceau
  Bruno Pelassy
  Rob Pruitt
  Sarah Pucci
  Torbjørn Rødland
  Allen Ruppersberg
  Bruno Serralongue
  Shimabuku
  Lily van der Stokker
  Sturtevant

Aizpuru

Madrid

Galleries Unlimited

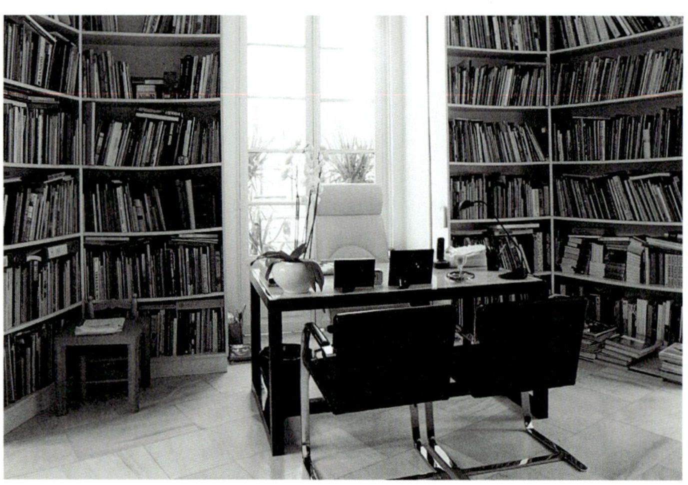

What is your favorite aspect of running a gallery?
The most interesting thing is my relationship with all the artists, which is a very close one. Since I started, 44 years ago, I have always been close to them, visiting their studios and listening to them. This is actually a way to be there sometimes at the moment of creation, which is something quite exciting.

How do you choose the artists you work with?
After so many years being in the presence of art and trying to understand each artist's language, there comes a moment when I can also understand the language of works I have never seen before and sense what is most important content-wise. Obviously there is also a kind of fascination, of falling in love with certain artworks. And, mostly, it is important that I have no artists doing similar work at my gallery.

If you weren't running a gallery what else would you do?
I would be an ecologist. Defending the Earth and animals is for me a beautiful way of living.

- **Contact** Galería Juana de Aizpuru
  Juana de Aizpuru
  juanadeaizpuru@juanadeaizpuru.es
- **Established** 1970
- **Owner(s) / Partner(s)** Juana De Aizpuru
- **Team** 7
- **Space(s)** 350 m²
- **Artists at Art Basel** Art & Language
  Elena Asins
  Mirosław Bałka
  Jean-Marc Bustamante
  Pedro Cabrita Reis
  Jiri Dokoupil
  Phillip Fröhlich
  Sandra Gamarra
  Alberto García Alix
  Pierre Gonnord
  Yasumasa Morimura
  Markus Oehlen
  Tim Parchikov
  Wolfgang Tillmans
  Heimo Zobernig
- **Further artists represented** Eric Baudelaire
  Tania Bruguera
  Luis Claramunt
  Jordi Colomer
  Alicia Framis
  Dora García
  Cristina García Rodero
  Georg Herold
  Rogelio López Cuenca
  Cristina Lucas
  Fernando Sánchez Castillo
  Andrés Serrano
  Montserrat Soto
  Franz West

Alexander

New York

Edition

- **Contact** Brooke Alexander Inc.
  Barbara Baruch
  bbaruch@baeditions.com
- **Established** 1968
- **Owner(s) / Partner(s)** Brooke Alexander
- **Team** 4
- **Space(s)** 669 m²
- **Artists at Art Basel** Josef Albers
  Richard Artschwager
  John Baldessari
  Donald Judd
  Ellsworth Kelly
  Sol LeWitt
  Robert Mangold
  Bruce Nauman
  Barnett Newman
  Raymond Pettibon
  Ken Price
  Andy Warhol
  Rémy Zaugg
- **Further artists represented** Philip Guston
  Jenny Holzer
  Jasper Johns
  Richard Long
  Robert Longo
  Allan McCollum
  Matt Mullican
  Claes Oldenburg
  Robert Rauschenberg
  Allen Ruppersberg
  Ed Ruscha
  Fred Sandback
  Richard Tuttle
  Luc Tuymans
  Lawrence Weiner
  Franz West

Alexander and Bonin

New York

Galleries
Galleries

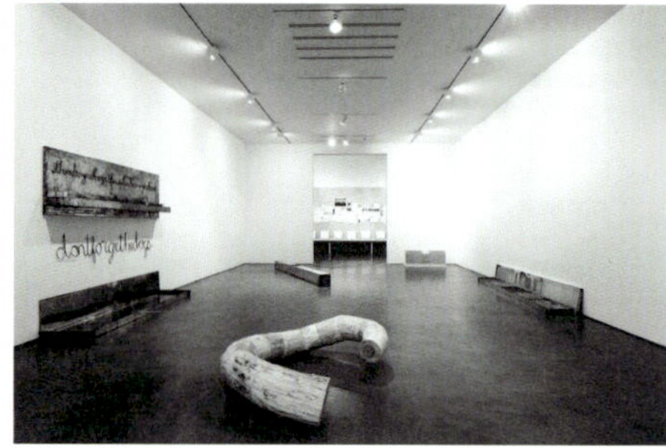

What is your favorite aspect of running a gallery?
Working closely with our artists on their exhibitions.

How do you choose the artists you work with?
They come to our attention in a variety of ways, including discussions with the artists we exhibit, the curators we have worked with, and exhibitions that we see.

If you weren't running a gallery what else would you do?
Work for a museum or a publishing house.

- **Contact** Alexander and Bonin
  Kathryn Gile
  kg@alexanderandbonin.com
- **Established** 1995
- **Owner(s) / Partner(s)** Carolyn Alexander & Ted Bonin
- **Team** 8
- **Space(s)** 371.5 m²
- **Artists at Art Basel** John Ahearn
  Jonathas de Andrade
  Matthew Benedict
  Robert Bordo
  Fernando Bryce

- **Further artists represented**
  Michael Buthe
  Willie Cole
  Eugenio Dittborn
  Willie Doherty
  Victor Grippo
  Mona Hatoum
  Diango Hernández
  Emily Jacir
  Robert Kinmont
  Stefan Kürten
  Jorge Macchi
  Rita McBride
  Ree Morton
  Sylvia Plimack Mangold
  Doris Salcedo
  Paul Thek
  Peter Hujar
  Sean Scully

Alisan

Hong Kong 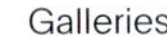 Galleries

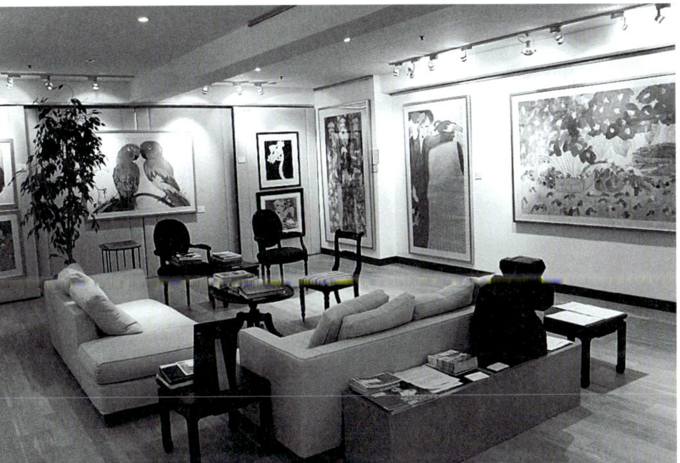

What is your favorite aspect of running a gallery?

As a pioneer in the field of contemporary Chinese art and New Ink art, the gallery focuses on promoting and presenting Chinese artists from the mainland, as well as established Hong Kong artists and artists from the Chinese diaspora living in Europe and the United States of America. In 1987 the landmark exhibition *A State of Transition, Contemporary Paintings from Shanghai* included Chen Jialing, Li Shan, Zhang Guiming at Hong Kong Arts Centre. The first solo exhibition for Zao Wou-Ki in Hong Kong in 1993 was also memorable. While introducing contemporary Chinese art to the West, Alisan Fine Arts has also staged exhibitions for Western artists, and has collaborated with galleries in Europe and the United States.

- **Contact**
  Alisan Fine Arts
  Kathleen Mak
  kmak@alisan.com.hk
- **Established**
  1981
- **Owner(s) / Partner(s)**
  Alice King
  Daphne King
- **Team**
  5
- **Space(s)**
  279 m²
- **Artists at Art Basel**
  Cai Guo-Qiang
  Gao Xingjian
  Qiu Deshu
  Wang Tiande
  Wei Ligang
  Yang Jiechang
  Zhang Yirong
- **Further artists represented**
  Chao Chung-hsiang
  Chinyee
  Chu Teh-Chun
  Chuang Che
  Ding Yang Yong
  Fang Zhaoling
  Hsiao Chin
  John Way
  Ju Ming
  Li Huasheng
  Li Shan
  Lui Shou-Kwan
  Luo Qi
  Man Fung-Yi
  Ming Fay
  T'ang Haywen
  Tseng Yuho
  Walasse Ting
  Wang Chuan
  Zao Wou-Ki

Altman Siegel

San Francisco 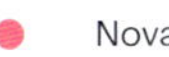 Nova

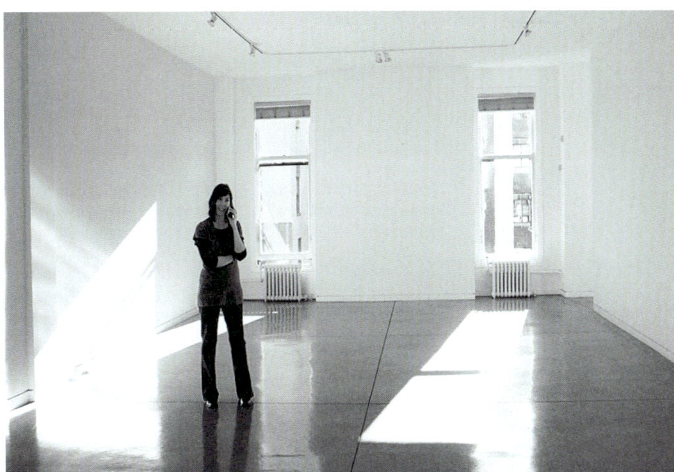

What is your favorite aspect of running a gallery?

Creative freedom and the process of making a conceptual idea a physical reality.

How do you choose the artists you work with?

When I see their work I get a buzz, my heart starts beating faster, and my mind starts spinning.

If you weren't running a gallery what else would you do?

Get a real job and be unhappy.

- **Contact**
  Altman Siegel
  Claudia Altman-Siegel
  info@altmansiegel.com
- **Established**
  2009
- **Owner(s) / Partner(s)**
  Claudia Altman-Siegel
- **Team**
  4
- **Space(s)**
  186 m²
- **Artists at Art Basel**
  Liam Everett
  Trevor Paglen
- **Further artists represented**
  Zarouhie Abdalian
  Nate Boyce
  Jessica Dickinson
  Shannon Ebner
  Laeh Glenn
  Fran Herndon
  Chris Johanson
  Matt Keegan
  Shinpei Kusanagi
  Devin Leonardi
  Will Rogan
  Sara Vanderbeek
  Emily Wardill
  Garth Weiser

American Contemporary

New York 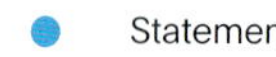 Statements

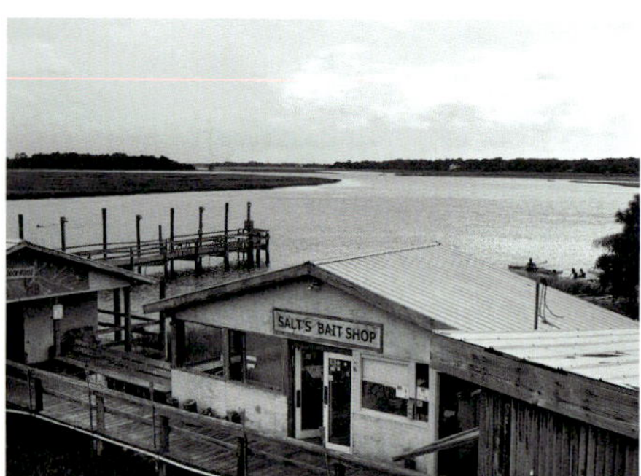

What is your favorite aspect of running a gallery?
Installing the shows with the artists. It's amazing. Everything slows down to moments of rich consideration and revelatory decision making. I love it.

How do you choose the artists you work with?
They don't need me, I need them.

If you weren't running a gallery what else would you do?
Dance.

- **Contact** American Contemporary
Matthew Dipple
matthew@americancontemporary.biz
- **Established** 2011
- **Owner(s) / Partner(s)** Matthew Dipple
- **Team** 3
- **Space(s)** 232 m²
- **Artists at Art Basel** David Brooks
- **Further artists represented** Jean-Baptiste Bernadet
Sarah Braman
Ethan Cook
Daphne Fitzpatrick
Julia Goldman
Joel Holmberg
Shara Hughes
Mariah Robertson
Jacob Robichaux
Stefan Sandner
Frank Selby
Stephen Vitiello

Ameringer McEnery Yohe

New York  Galleries
Galleries

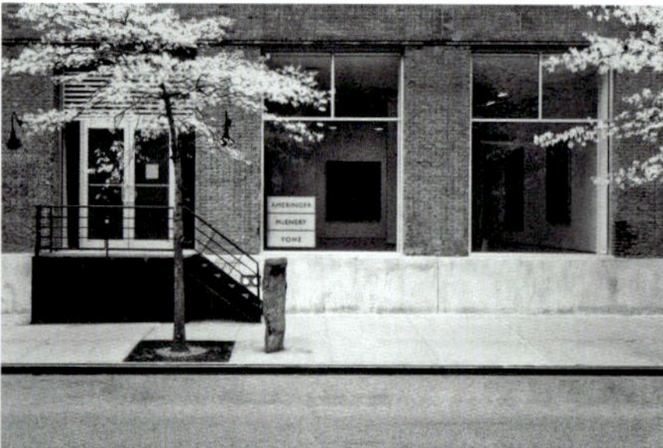

What is your favorite aspect of running a gallery?
The privilege of working closely with exceptionally gifted and awe-inspiring artists combined with the close friendships that blossom from professional relationships.

How do you choose the artists you work with?
Intuition, mind, and heart.

If you weren't running a gallery what else would you do?
Inconceivable.

- **Contact** Ameringer/McEnery/Yohe
Miles Mcenery
mm@amy-nyc.com
- **Established** 1999
- **Owner(s) / Partner(s)** Will Ameringer
Miles McEnery
James Yohe
- **Team** 12
- **Space(s)** 465 m²
- **Artists at Art Basel** Brian Alfred
Kevin Appel
Oliver Arms
Bo Bartlett
Thomas Burke
Nuno de Campos
Suzanne Caporael
Rosana Castrillo Diaz
Steven Charles
Davis Cone
Gene Davis
Stephen Dean
Franklin Evans
Helen Frankenthaler
Monique van Genderen
Iva Gueorguieva
Frederick Hammersley
Todd Hebert
Hans Hofmann
Wolf Kahn
Julio Larraz
Patrick Lee
Markus Linnenbrink
Morris Louis
George McNeil
John M. Miller
Robert Motherwell
Kenneth Noland
Rod Penner
David Allan Peters
Michael Reafsnyder
Sandra Mendelsohn Rubin
Tam Van Tran
Esteban Vicente
Partick Wilson
Guy Yanai
Liat Yossifor

Ammann

Zurich 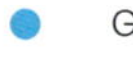 Galleries

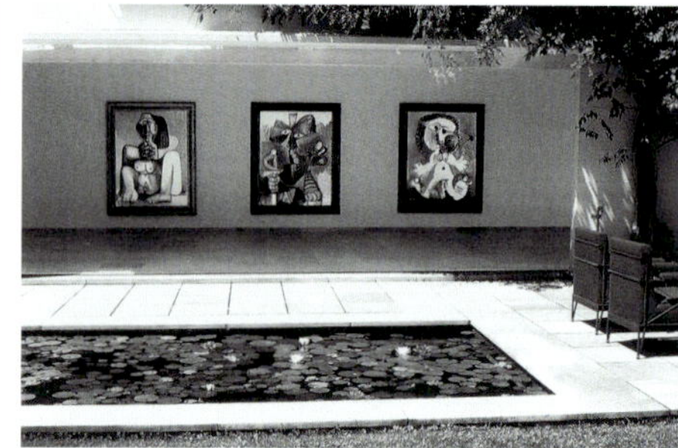

- **Contact** Thomas Ammann Fine Art AG
da@ammannfineart.com
- **Established** 1977
- **Owner(s) / Partner(s)** Doris Ammann
Georg Frei
- **Team** 6
- **Space(s)** 180 m²
- **Artists at Art Basel** The Bruce High Quality Foundation
Alexander Calder
Francesco Clemente
Willem de Kooning
Eric Fischl
Alberto Giacometti
Martin Kippenberger
Paul Klee
Gregor Lanz
Fernand Léger
Brice Marden
Agnes Martin
Andrew Masullo
Henri Matisse
Joan Miró
Albert Oehlen
Enoc Perez
Pablo Picasso
Sigmar Polke
Robert Ryman
Philip Taaffe

Marc Tansey
Cy Twombly
Andy Warhol

Andersen's

Copenhagen — Galleries

- **Contact** Andersen's Contemporary
  Scot Surdez
  info@andersen-s.dk
- **Established** 2005
- **Owner(s) / Partner(s)** Claus Andersen

Andréhn-Schiptjenko

Stockholm — Galleries, Galleries

What is your favorite aspect of running a gallery?

The long-term relationship with the artists, being able to follow and support them, developing their project and assisting in their growth. I also very much enjoy making exhibitions, being hands on with how they are installed in the space. I think a good exhibition is always something beyond the sum of the individual works that are in it. I enjoy the generosity of having a gallery, being able to show people what we think is important, and having this platform for contemporary culture.

How do you choose the artists you work with?

There is no single answer to that, but Marina Schiptjenko and myself are in constant dialogue about what we see, what we read about, and what we think. In the end it comes down to what we think is relevant in contemporary creation, coupled with our own interests and what place an artist can take in our program, nationally and internationally. I'd like to think it is a mix of gut feeling and critical thinking.

If you weren't running a gallery what else would you do?

I would be either a lawyer or a politician. Maybe a lawyer turned politician. Either way I would try and influence how people see the world, much as I try to do at the gallery.

- **Contact** Andréhn-Schiptjenko
  Ciléne Andréhn
  info@andrehn-schiptjenko.com
- **Established** 1991
- **Owner(s) / Partner(s)** Ciléne Andréhn
  Marina Schiptjenko
- **Team** 5
- **Space(s)** 330 m²
- **Artists at Art Basel** Uta Barth
  Siobhan Hapaska
  Annika von Hausswolff
  Ridley Howard
  Martin Jacobson
  Nandipha Mntambo
- **Further artists represented** Tobias Bernstrup
  José León Cerrillo
  Jacob Dahlgren
  Omid Delafrouz
  Maya Eizin Öijer
  Carin Ellberg
  Peter Hagdahl
  Katrine Helmersson
  Kristina Jansson
  Lena Johansson
  Brad Kahlhamer
  Annika Larsson
  Matts Leiderstam
  Katarina Löfström
  Tony Matelli
  Julie Roberts
  Per B Sundberg
  Xavier Veilhan
  Gunnel Wåhlstrand
  Cajsa von Zeipel
  Johan Zetterquist

Aninat

Santiago — Statements

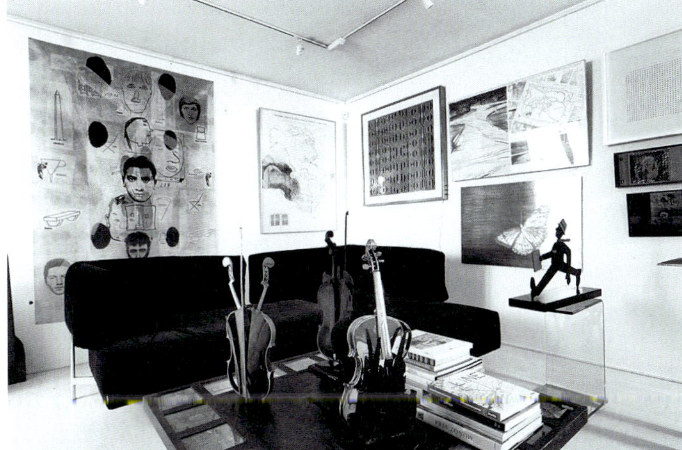

What is your favorite aspect of running a gallery?

The gallery is a space of research, experimentation, and exchange between local and international artists. Our program focuses on showcasing original projects by young and historical artists from the Latin American scene, establishing a dialogue between generations. Our aim is to project artists to the international scene and connect them with institutions, curators, collectors, and the general public.

How do you choose the artists you work with?

We periodically perform a historical review, promoting artists whose bold and innovative vision marked momentous changes, but which have only been partially recognized in historical accounts of the arts in their country. We also review artists' portfolios.

If you weren't running a gallery what else would you do?

Establishing a platform to ask the audience questions is one of the most interesting aspects of running a gallery. The university, where I taught for a few years, is another area of interest to me and I think I could have developed there as well.

- **Contact** Galería Isabel Aninat
  Isabel Aninat
  contacto@galeriaisabelaninat.cl
- **Established** 1983
- **Owner(s) / Partner(s)** Isabel Aninat
- **Team** 6
- **Space(s)** 500 m²
- **Artists at Art Basel** Paula de Solminihac
- **Further artists represented** Colectivo C.A.D.A.
  Mónica Bengoa
  Iván Contreras-Brunet
  Fernando De Szyszlo
  María I. Edwards
  Voluspa Jarpa
  Carlos Leppe
  Cecilia Paredes
  Francisco Peró
  Lotty Rosenfeld
  Pedro Tyler
  Valentina Valladares
  Manuela Viera-Gallo

Applicat-Prazan

Paris 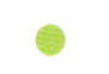 Galleries

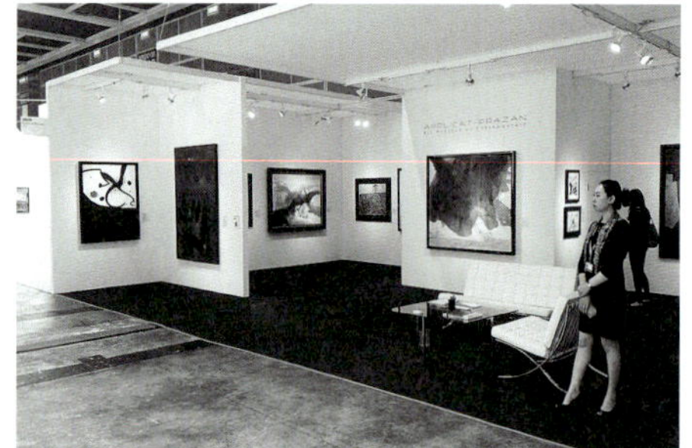

What is your favorite aspect of running a gallery?
Art! Art! Art!

How do you choose the artists you work with?
We are dedicated to the main painters from the postwar School of Paris. We know this period well; we love it. You do well what you know well!

If you weren't running a gallery what else would you do?
Cry!

- **Contact** Applicat-Prazan
Franck Prazan
franck.prazan@applicat-prazan.com
- **Established** 1993
- **Owner(s) / Partner(s)** Franck Prazan
- **Team** 5
- **Space(s)** 130 m²
- **Artists at Art Basel** Jean Dubuffet
Jean Fautrier
Hans Hartung
Georges Mathieu
Joan Miró
Serge Poliakoff
Pierre Soulages
Maria Helena Vieira Da Silva
Zao Wou-ki
- **Further artists represented** Karel Appel
Jean-Michel Atlan
Jean René Bazaine
Roger Bissière
Camille Bryen
Serge Charchoune
Chu Teh-Chun
Corneille
Olivier Debré
Maurice Estève
Jean Hélion
Auguste Herbin
Asger Jorn
Wifredo Lam
André Lanskoy
Alberto Magnelli
Alfred Manessier
André Masson
Jean-Paul Riopelle
Gérard Schneider
Nicolas de Staël
Victor Vasarely
Bram van Velde
Geer van Velde

Approach

London

Galleries Unlimited
Galleries

What is your favorite aspect of running a gallery?
Having the freedom to evolve the program alongside working with artists on a long-term basis.

How do you choose the artists you work with?
We follow our taste and instincts.

If you weren't running a gallery what else would you do?
Open an art foundation with a beautifully furnished bar, vineyard, lavish wildflower garden, peacocks, and a vintage clothes emporium somewhere sunny.

- **Contact** The Approach
Nora Heidorn
nora@theapproach.co.uk
- **Established** 1997
- **Owner(s) / Partner(s)** Jake Miller
Emma Robertson
- **Team** 6
- **Space(s)** 100 m²
- **Further artists represented** Phillip Allen
Helene Appel
Cris Brodahl
Heidi Bucher
Sophie Bueno-Boutellier
Alice Channer
Stuart Cumberland
Peter Davies
Patrick Hill
Evan Holloway
Germaine Kruip
Rezi van Lankveld
Jack Lavender
Edward Lipski
Dave Muller
Lisa Oppenheim
Magali Reus
Amanda Ross-Ho
John Stezaker
Evren Tekinoktay
Sara Vanderbeek
Gary Webb
Sam Windett

Arario

Cheonan
Seoul
Shanghai

Galleries

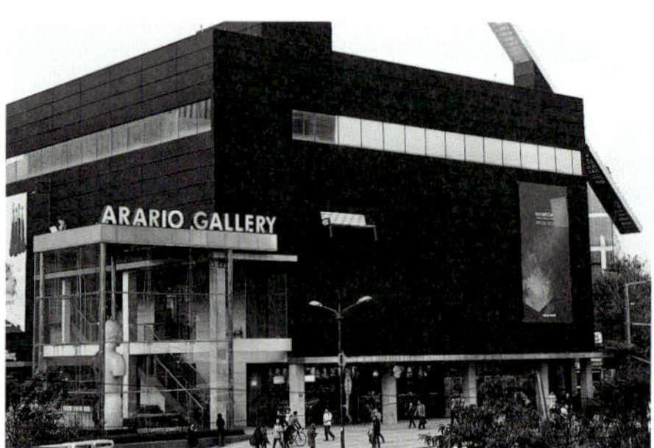

What is your favorite aspect of running a gallery?
Good artists and good exhibitions! We put enormous efforts into young and emerging artists and expect a bright future for them.

How do you choose the artists you work with?
We look for artists who have their own artistic language as well as a good personality.

- **Contact** Arario Gallery
Henna Joo
info@arariogallery.com
- **Established** 2002
- **Owner(s) / Partner(s)** Changil Kim
- **Team** 12
- **Space(s)** 750 m² (Cheonan)
450 m² (Seoul)
350 m² (Shanghai)
- **Artists at Art Basel** Aono Fumiaki
Byoung-So Choi
Gao Lei
Subodh Gupta
Osang Gwon
Hyung Koo Kang
Kohei Nawa
Li Hui
Yan Heng
Yoon Myung-Ro
- **Further artists represented** Byoungho Kim
Leslie de Chavez
Eko Nugroho
Dongwook Lee
Han Sungpil
Insane Park
Geraldine Javier
Kim Hanna
Kim Kulim
Inbai Kim

Lee Jinju
Li Fan
Nalini Malani
Shine Kong
Sung Hun Kong
L.N. Tallur
Keiji Uematsu
Won Seoung Won

ARATANIURANO

Tokyo 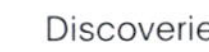 Discoveries

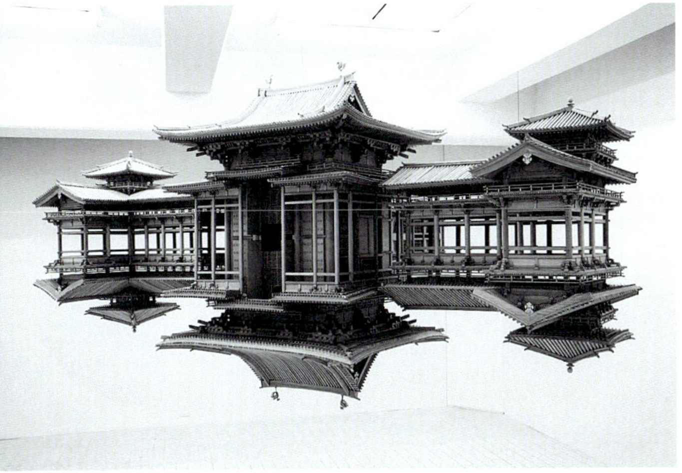

What is your favorite aspect of running a gallery?
When I can share goals, overcome difficulties, and progress together with our artists and supporters.

How do you choose the artists you work with?
I like to work with artists who have a big impact on our contemporary society.

If you weren't running a gallery what else would you do?
I might have worked for the movie industry as I'm a film enthusiast.

- **Contact** ARATANIURANO
  Mutsumi Urano
  u@arataniurano.com
- **Established** 2007
- **Owner(s) / Partner(s)** Mutsumi Urano
- **Team** 3
- **Space(s)** 45 m²
- **Artists at Art Basel** Toshiyuki Konishi
- **Further artists represented** Akiko Kinugawa
  Go Watanabe
  Hiroyuki Oki
  Keiji Izumi
  Krissakorn Thinthupthai
  Mana Konishi
  Motonao Takasaki
  Natsuko Sakamoto
  Tadasu Takamine
  Takahiro Iwasaki
  Tatzu Nishi
  Youichi Umetsu
  Yuichi Yokoyama
  Yusuke Asai

Arnaud

São Paulo 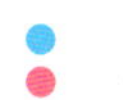 Feature
Galleries

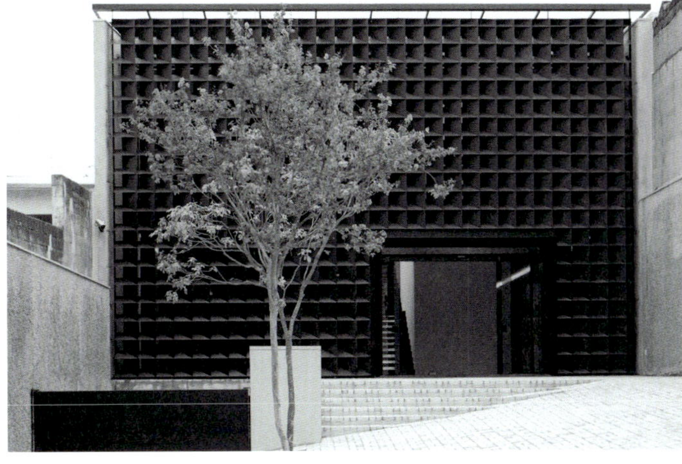

What is your favorite aspect of running a gallery?
My favorite aspect of running a gallery is to maintain a friendly contact with my artists and collectors.

How do you choose the artists you work with?
We relate to the artists we work with mainly based on affinity, both aesthetically—if the work dialogues with a geometric, concrete, kinetic language that we have specialized in—and personally. The consistency and importance of an artist is a result of the maturation and development of their ideas and research. The history of Galeria Raquel Arnaud is characterized by incisive visual choices and by the endeavor of putting into perspective the trends that it represents.

If you weren't running a gallery what else would you do?
I love architecture.

- **Contact** Galeria Raquel Arnaud
  Myra Arnaud Babenco
  myra@raquelarnaud.com
- **Established** 1973
- **Owner(s) / Partner(s)** Raquel Arnaud
  Myra Arnaud Babenco
- **Team** 12
- **Space(s)** 1,000 m²
- **Artists at Art Basel** Waltercio Caldas
  Iole de Freitas
  Carlos Fajardo
  José Resende
  Carlos Zilio
- **Further artists represented** Frida Baranek
  Elisa Bracher
  Waltercio Caldas
  Sergio Camargo
  Carla Chaim
  Elias Crespin
  Carlos Cruz-Diez
  Sérvulo Esmeraldo
  Célia Euvaldo
  Daniel Feingold
  Romulo Fialdini
  Iole de Freitas
  Marco Giannotti
  Carlos Fajardo
  Elizabeth Jobim
  Geórgia Kyriakakis
  Alberto Martins
  Cassio Michalany
  Silvia Mecozzi
  Jorge Molder
  Ding Musa
  Carlos Nunes
  Maria-Carmen Perlingeiro
  Arthur Luiz Piza
  José Resende
  Tuneu
  Wolfram Ullrich
  Julio Villani
  Carlos Zilio

Arndt

Berlin
Singapore

Galleries

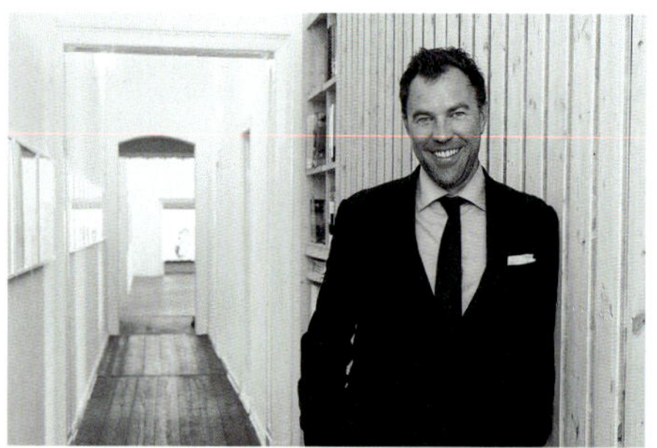

What is your favorite aspect of running a gallery?

The gallery is an independent forum to present and experiment with art of all kinds, from all parts of the world, established or emerging. There are no restrictions. I can create and anticipate new artistic trends through my selection and close collaboration with artists. The gallery space is often (and nowadays shares this status with the art fairs) the first public venue for new works. I love the proximity of working with the artists and interacting with the audience.

How do you choose the artists you work with?

I try to identify the strongest and most outstanding, sometimes extreme, artistic positions within each geographic area or genre. Then I approach artists and suggest precise mandates for our collaboration: this can be being the representative for a region or a specific body of work or taking the role of a strategic advisor. I work with a network of curators, artists, collectors, and fellow gallerists, exchanging views, sharing artists, and developing projects together.

If you weren't running a gallery what else would you do?

In my most romantic dreams, I see myself retired, as a wine- or cheesemaker in one of the many beautiful areas in France. But from the start, opening my first gallery 27 years ago and then running Arndt for 20 years now, I have never wanted to do anything other than work with art, identifying new talents, and being in direct and close interaction both with artists and audience.

- **Contact** — Arndt; Matthias Arndt; info@arndtberlin.com
- **Established** — 1994
- **Owner(s) / Partner(s)** — Matthias Arndt
- **Team** — 12
- **Space(s)** — 1,000 m²
- **Artists at Art Basel** — Sophie Calle; Jigger Cruz; Arin Dwihartanto Sunaryo; Gilbert & George; Hahan (Uji Handoko); Indieguerillas; Geraldine Javier; Yang Jiechang; Jitish Kallat; Heinz Mack; Vik Muniz; Eko Nugroho; Chiharu Shiota; Rodel Tapaya; Entang Wiharso; Qiu Zhijie
- **Further artists represented** — Erik Bulatov; FX Harsono; Mike Parr; Otto Piene; Julian Rosefeldt; Agus Suwage

Arratia Beer

Berlin

Statements

What is your favorite aspect of running a gallery?

The discussions and exchange with the artists that lead to the exhibitions.

How do you choose the artists you work with?

You know it when you see it.

- **Contact** — Arratia Beer; Euridice Arratia; euridice@arratiabeer.com
- **Established** — 2006
- **Owner(s) / Partner(s)** — Euridice Arratia; Elizabeth Beer
- **Team** — 4
- **Space(s)** — 200 m²
- **Artists at Art Basel** — Pablo Rasgado
- **Further artists represented** — Gabriel Acevedo Velarde; Maria Anwander; Patty Chang; Omer Fast; Fernanda Fragateiro; Jennie C. Jones; Matthew Metzger; Haleh Redjaian; Kateřina Šedá; Friedrich Teepe; Javier Téllez

Art : Concept

Paris

Galleries
Parcours
Galleries

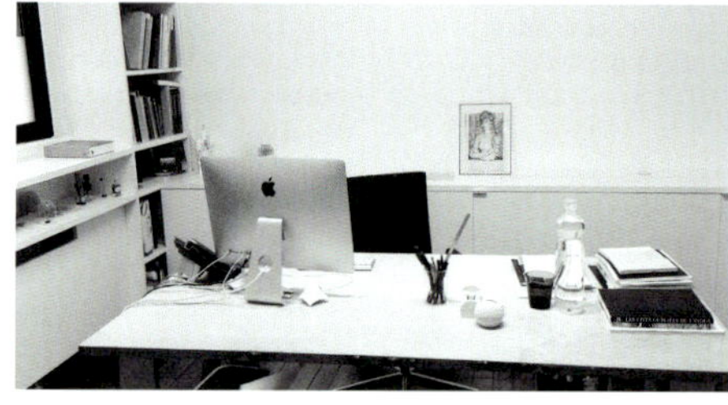

What is your favorite aspect of running a gallery?

Proposing some new concepts, different ideas, allowing artists to explore their own creative processes.

How do you choose the artists you work with?

It's a question of encounters, and the exchange of ideas.

If you weren't running a gallery what else would you do?

Nothing else.

- **Contact** — Art : Concept; Olivier Antoine; olivier@galerieartconcept.com
- **Established** — 1992
- **Owner** — Olivier Antoine
- **Team** — 6
- **Space(s)** — 150 m²
- **Artists at Art Basel** — Geert Goiris; Ulla von Brandenburg; Nathan Hylden; Jacob Kassay; Adam McEwen; Roman Signer; Francis Baudevin; Jeremy Deller; Lothar Hempel; Pierre-Olivier Arnaud; Hubert Duprat; Richard Fauguet; Julien Audebert; Vidya Gastaldon
- **Further artists represented** — Martine Aballéa; Michel Blazy; Whitney Bedford; Andrew Lewis; Philippe Perrot; Pietro Roccasalva; Alexandre Singh

Artiaco

Naples

● Galleries Unlimited
● Galleries

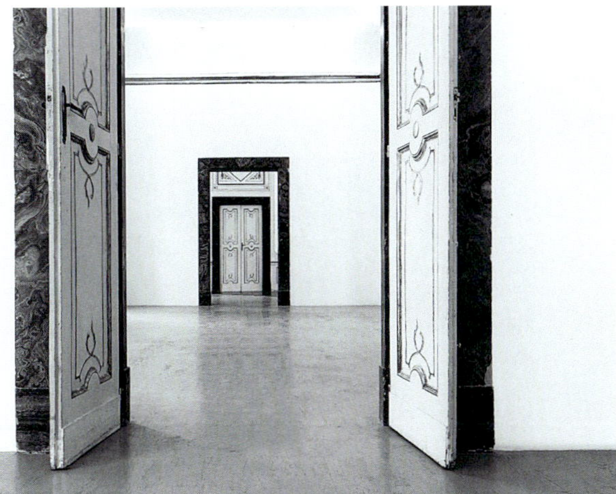

What is your favorite aspect of running a gallery?
The most exciting and rewarding aspect of running the gallery is, of course, working together with the artists: participating in the production of artworks, shows, and specific projects that allow me to be their "operating arm."

How do you choose the artists you work with?
The artists are chosen on the basis of their artistic practice and my personal research in relation to the specific insight on the contemporary art scene I am committed to promoting.

If you weren't running a gallery what else would you do?
I've been running the gallery for 28 years, so I'm not able to imagine another career for myself now! But, most probably, I would be teaching. This is another very exciting and rewarding field of work.

- **Contact** Alfonso Artiaco, Barbara Crespigni, info@alfonsoartiaco.com
- **Established** 1986
- **Owner(s) / Partner(s)** Alfonso Artiaco
- **Team** 3
- **Space(s)** 360 m²
- **Artists at Art Basel** Darren Almond, Carl Andre, Giovanni Anselmo, Robert Barry, Botto & Bruno, Alan Charlton, Victoria Civera, Gilbert & George, Liam Gillick, Gioberto Noro, Laurent Grasso, Thomas Hirschhorn, Craigie Horsfield, Ann Veronica Janssens, Jannis Kounellis, Melissa Kretschmer, Wolfgang Laib, Sol LeWitt, Lello Lopez, Raffaele Luongo, Vera Lutter, Rita McBride, Gerhard Merz, Marco Neri, Giulio Paolini, Giuseppe Penone, Perino & Vele, Anne & Patrick Poirier, Sergio Prego, Glen Rubsamen, Ulrich Rückriem, Anri Sala, Niele Toroni, David Tremlett, Juan Uslè, Lawrence Weiner

Artinformal

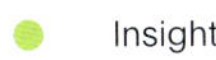

Mandaluyong City

● Insights

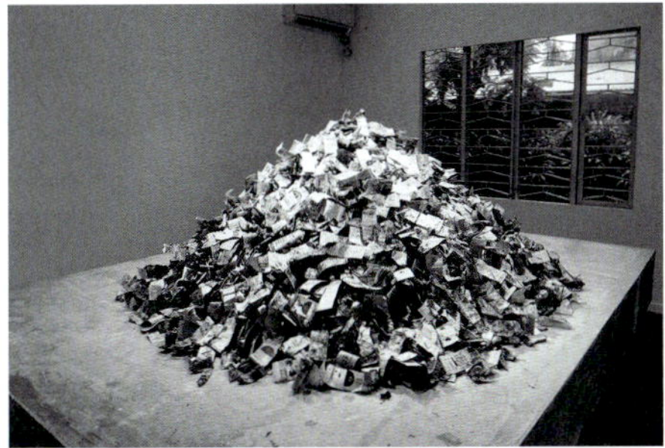

What is your favorite aspect of running a gallery?
Planning the exhibition program, exchanging ideas with artists, and seeing their career take shape. I also like to be able to educate collectors and assist them in building their collection.

How do you choose the artists you work with?
My choices are based on my taste and their attitude toward work.

If you weren't running a gallery what else would you do?
I would open a lifestyle and design store with one-of-a-kind artistic pieces.

- **Contact** Artinformal, Tina Fernandez, tinafernandez.ai@gmail.com
- **Established** 2006
- **Owner(s) / Partner(s)** Tina Fernandez
- **Team** 5
- **Space(s)** 136 m²
- **Artists at Art Basel** Nilo Ilarde
- **Further artists represented** Eugenia Alcaide, Salvador Joel Alonday, Zean Cabangis, Lui Medina, Maya Muñoz, Christina Quisumbing Ramilo, José Santos III, Mark Valenzuela, Pam Yan-Santos

Athr

Jeddah

● Insights

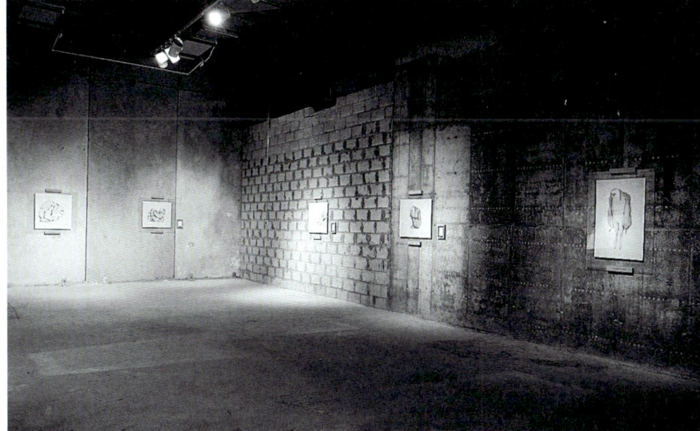

What is your favorite aspect of running a gallery?
Mohammed A. Hafiz: Working closely with the artists, through the ups and downs, and getting that call from a museum confirming an acquisition … then seeing the artist's reaction to it.

How do you choose the artists you work with?
Based on shared views and ideologies; it is very difficult to work with artists who have a completely different perception of what is "ethical."

If you weren't running a gallery what else would you do?
Possibly an architect.

- **Contact** Athr Gallery
  Jumana Ghouth
  jumana@athrart.com
- **Established** 2009
- **Owner(s) / Partner(s)** Hamza Serafi
  Mohammed A. Hafiz
- **Team** 11
- **Space(s)** 1,800 m²
- **Artists at Art Basel** Nasser Al Salem
  Dana Awartani
  Ayman Yossri Daydban
  Ahmed Mater
- **Further artists represented** Sara Abdu
  Ibrahim Abumsmar
  Musaed Al Hulis
  Arwa Al Neami
  Daniah Al Saleh
  Jowhara Al Saud
  Sami Al Turki
  Shadia Alem
  Basmah Felemban
  Aya Haidar
  Hazem Harb
  Eyad Maghazil
  Saddek Wasil

Atlas

London — Galleries

- **Contact** Atlas Gallery
  Ben Burdett
  ben@atlasgallery.com
- **Established** 1994
- **Owner(s) / Partner(s)** Ben Burdett
- **Team** 5
- **Artists at Art Basel** Nick Brandt
  René Burri
  Robert Capa
  Frauke Eigen
  Elliott Erwitt
  Mario Giacomelli
  Ernst Haas
  Philippe Halsman
  Nathan Harger
  Thomas Hoepker
  Frank Hurley
  Adam Jeppesen
  William Klein
  Michael Light
  Steve Macleod
  Jimmy Nelson
  Floris Neusüss
  Trent Parke
  Herbert G. Ponting
  Leni Riefenstahl
  Dennis Stock
  Paul Strand
  Dominique Tarlé
  Paolo Ventura

Aye

Beijing — Galleries, Feature

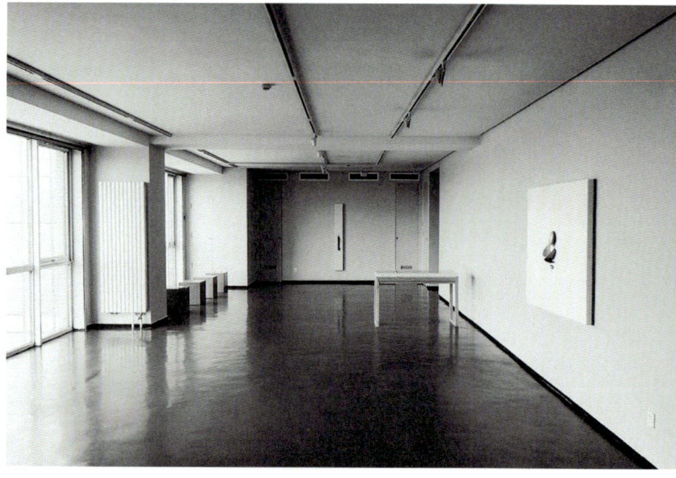

What is your favorite aspect of running a gallery?

There are always new artists, new artworks, and new collectors. Everyday your work is different. That makes things exciting. And I go to many great places to enjoy art.

How do you choose the artists you work with?

There are many aspects that enter into the choice of an artist: educational background, technique, ideas, personality, etc.

If you weren't running a gallery what else would you do?

I think I would be a full-time collector.

- **Contact** Aye Gallery
  Ziyan Meng
  juliameng2003@gmail.com
- **Established** 2005
- **Owner(s) / Partner(s)** Yan Qing
- **Team** 6
- **Space(s)** 300 m²
- **Artists at Art Basel** Chen Wenji
  Chen Yufan
  Ji Dachun
  Li Dazhi
  Mu Boyan
  Wang Mai
  Wang Yabin
  Yang Qiong
  Zhao Gang
- **Further artists represented** Hoo Mojong
  Jiang Fang
  Liu Wei
  Sheng Tianhong
  Shi Xinji
  Xia Xiaowan

Galería Juana de Aizpuru

Interview with Juana de Aizpuru

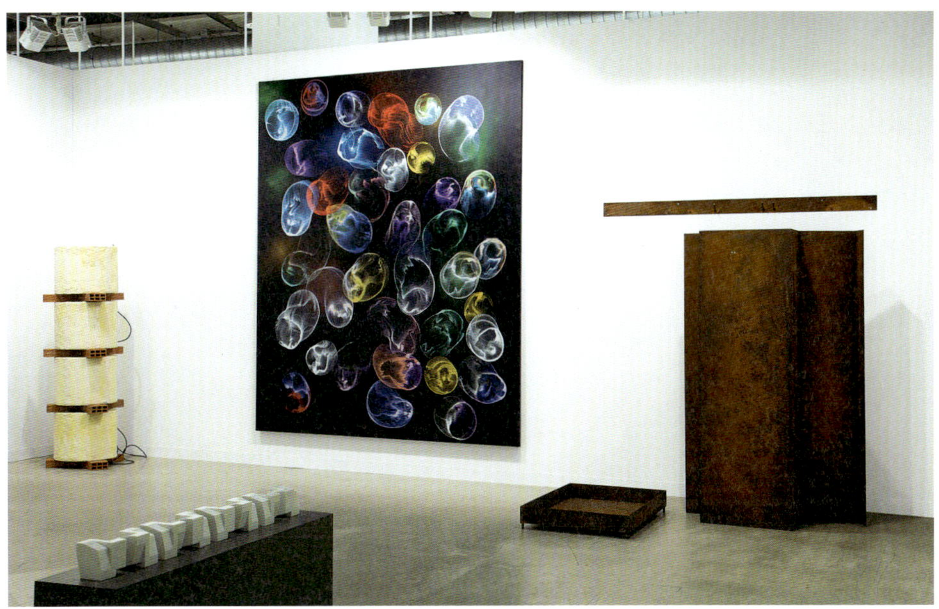

Art Basel in Basel, 2014

You opened your gallery in 1970, in Seville, in a complex political and cultural context. Could you tell us why you opened it and who were the first artists you showed?

I entered the art world as a discrete collector. In the mid-1960s I had contacts with a group of young Sevillian artists who had started to work within the new international tendencies (mostly North American then), breaking with the strong academic traditions of Spanish art. But things weren't easy for them, so they suggested that I open a gallery. It had never crossed my mind before, but I thought it was a wonderful idea when I heard it! Five months later the gallery opened and I started working with this group of artists. From the beginning I understood that this was a path I would walk for the rest of my life, and not just a temporary experience. I knew I was going to make a vital project of it; it was very important for me and for promoting Spanish artists, especially the Sevillian ones.

During the 1960s and early 1970s, when Franco was still alive, it was very difficult to have international contacts, but there was a serious interest in Spanish art and even a specific market. Miró and Dalí were the undisputed international figures. Galleries in Madrid, Barcelona, and Valencia were selling quite well and, in Seville, I was successful in awakening the interest of many people who later became passionate collectors.

Spanish artists were working in different art fields: Conceptual art (Francesc Torres, Antoni Muntadas, Francesc Abad, etc.); Minimal art (Elena Asíns, Soledad Sevilla, Manolo Barbadillo, etc.); Informal art (Manolo Millares, Antoni Tàpies, Antonio Saura, Luis Gordillo, etc.); Constructivist art (Gerardo Rueda, Eusebio Sempere, Gustavo Torner, Pablo Palazuelo, etc.). There was also a special kind of Pop art: its most important representatives were Equipo Crónica (Manolo Valdés and Rafael Solves), Equipo Realidad (J.A. Aguirre), and Eduardo Arroyo. Sculpture was quite well represented by Eduardo Chillida, Miquel Navarro … There was also an intimate form of realism, represented in Seville mostly by Carmen Laffón and Teresa Duclós, and in Madrid by Antonio López, Julio López Hernández, Amalia Avia. These artists were successful and their works sold well, although they never got international recognition. This is a very basic outline of the artists that were working in Spain when I opened my gallery—and I worked with every one of them!

How did the gallery expand its activities and program, and open up to international artists? And why did you decide to open in Madrid in 1983?

As I was saying, international contacts were difficult, because practically the borders were closed. However, through the Ministry, the Embassies, and personal contacts, I was able to host exhibitions with international artists such as David Hockney (1973), Richard Hamilton (1974), Man Ray (1974), Rauschenberg and Frank Stella (1975), among others, even under the dictatorship.

When democracy arrived (in November 1975), I started to travel frequently, mostly to visit the existing international art fairs (Cologne and Basel). There I understood the enormous rift that separated us from our international colleagues, and how it was indispensable to make great efforts to get to their level. It is for this reason that I thought of creating ARCO, the Madrid art fair. I quickly realized that it would be the best way to make this path shorter. I dedicated myself to this task with true enthusiasm from 1979 to 1982, when the first edition was celebrated. I was named director of the fair, a position I occupied until 1987, when I resigned to fully concentrate on my two galleries.

When I was directing ARCO, I used to spend more time in Madrid than in Seville and, in Madrid, a special atmosphere was emerging, later called the Movida Madrileña. I opened a gallery there in order to contribute to this cultural development and to work abroad more easily. I kept working with both galleries until 2006.

In 1982 I started to participate in Cologne and Basel art fairs and both of them helped me to develop international contacts and alter my program, and soon afterward I started working with foreign artists (the first one was Julião Sarmento). My international contacts kept increasing so I started to represent (and still represent) many well-known international artists.

In the 1990s, you became maybe the major Spanish gallery, notably showing Martin Kippenberger, Mike Kelley, etc. What memories do you have of that time?

There was a very important event in the history of my gallery: Martin Kippenberger and Albert Oehlen came to live in Seville for two years. Then they moved to Madrid and Martin stayed for almost a whole year more, while Albert has kept his contacts in Spain alive until today. Through them—especially Martin—I further expanded my contacts with the international art world. I got to know the German and Austrian art scenes well, and I held exhibitions of Franz West and Heimo Zobernig, in addition to a show by Mike Kelley and Sol LeWitt. A deep friendship arose between Martin and myself and lasted until he passed away. He started to do his first self-portraits and twisted lamps in Spain, and I had the great chance of being the first to show these paintings and sculptures, in both my galleries.

You have been taking part in Art Basel since 1982. Do you remember the atmosphere of the first years?

Art Basel has always been the most important fair, the best organized, and the one that attracts the most international collectors. Of course Art Basel—or any other fair for that matter—weren't what they are now. Back then, art fairs were not only about the art market, but also a meeting point of the different sectors of the art world. It was very common to see international artists walking through the hallways (Beuys was at Art Cologne almost every day, that's where I actually met him), and the best curators and museum directors from around the world met in a relaxed atmosphere, and exchanged ideas and opinions …

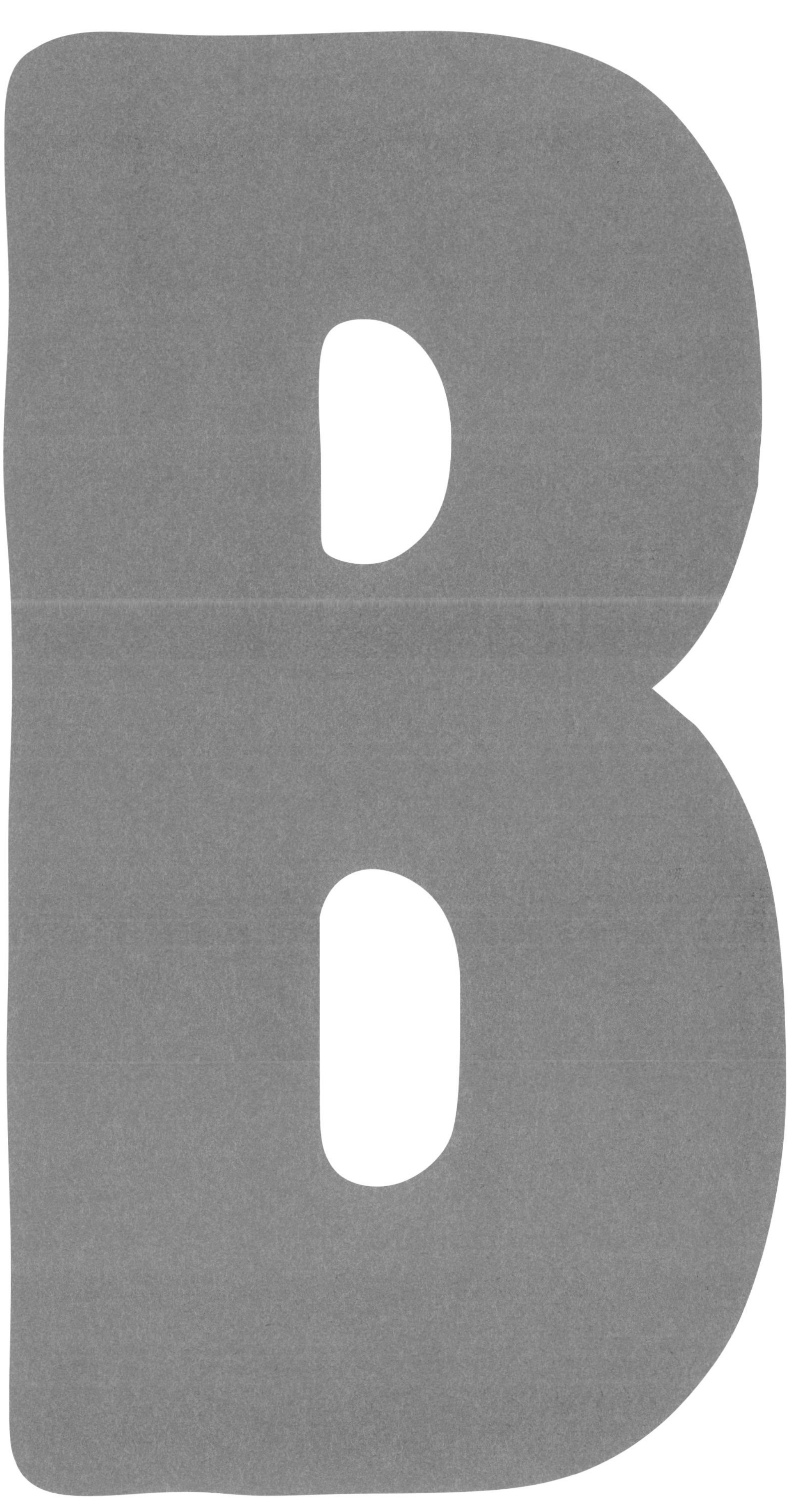

City population
211,200 (including Riehen and Bettingen)

Population density
7,640 inhabitants per square kilometer

Fair founded in
1970

Visitors in 2014
92,000

Number of exhibitors in 2014
285

Number of artists exhibited in 2014
over 4,000

BASEL

Exhibition Partners: Museums & Cultural Institutions

Antikenmuseum
Roma Eterna

Fondation Beyeler
Gerhard Richter

Bundesamt für Kultur (Messe Basel)
Swiss Art & Design Awards 2014

Haus für elektronische Kunst
Electrical Walks Basel

Hof des Basler Rathauses
Thomas Schütte: *United Enemies*

Museum der Kulturen
Make-up: Shaped for Life?; Semiwild—or Unlimited Desire

Kunsthalle
Julia Rometti and Victor Costales; Nevin Aladag

Kunstmuseum
Kazimir Malevich: *The World as Objectlessness;* Charles Ray

Kunstmuseum—Museum für Gegenwartskunst
Marcel Broodthaers: *Le Corbeau et le Renard—Revolt of Language with Marcel Broodthaers*

Kunsthaus Baselland
Ariel Schlesinger; Sarah Oppenheimer

Schaulager
Paul Chan: *Selected Works*

Museum Tinguely
Krištof Kintera: *I Am Not You*

Vitra Design Museum
Konstantin Grcic: *Panorama;* Álvaro Siza: *The Alhambra Project*

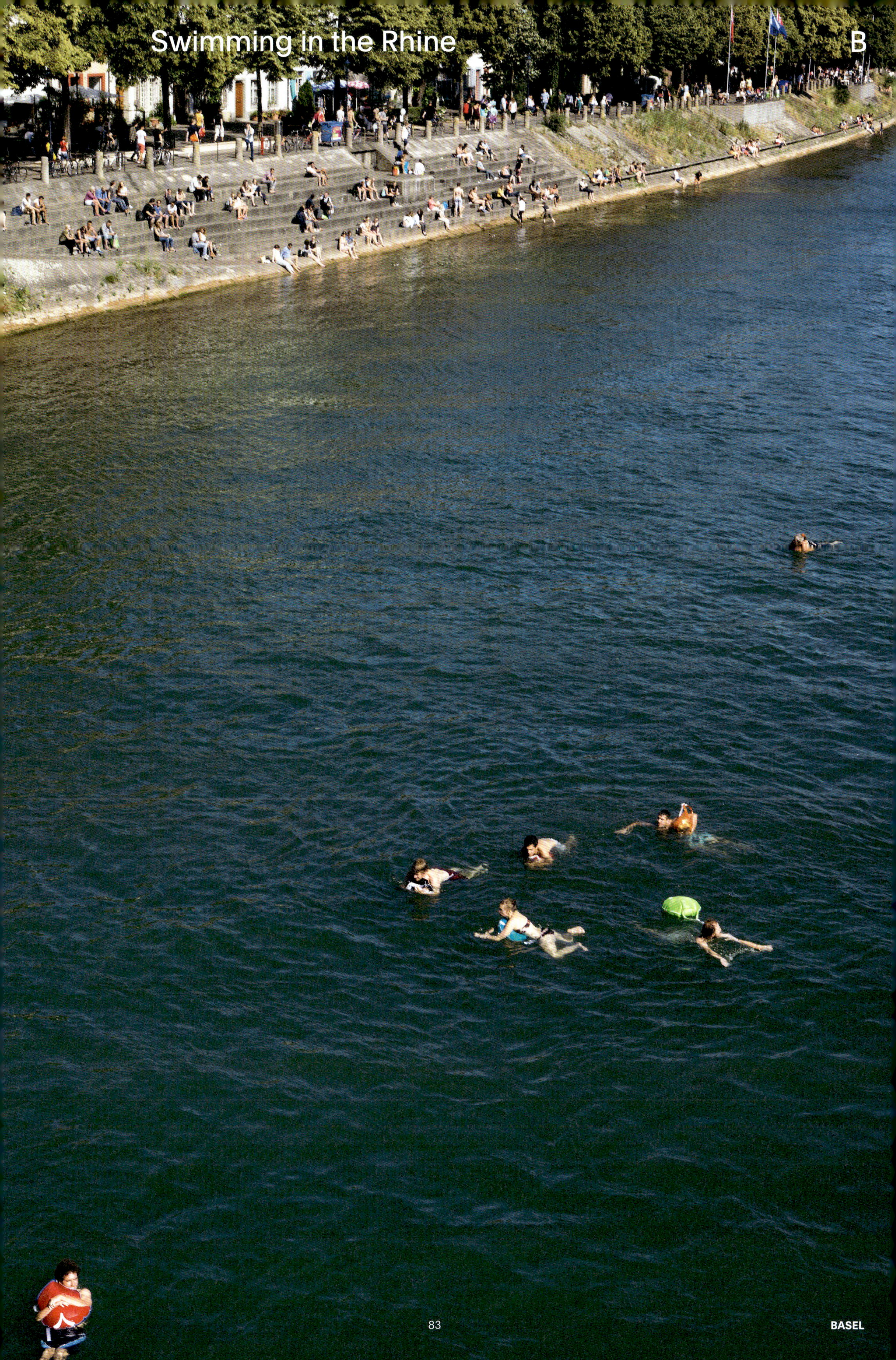

B

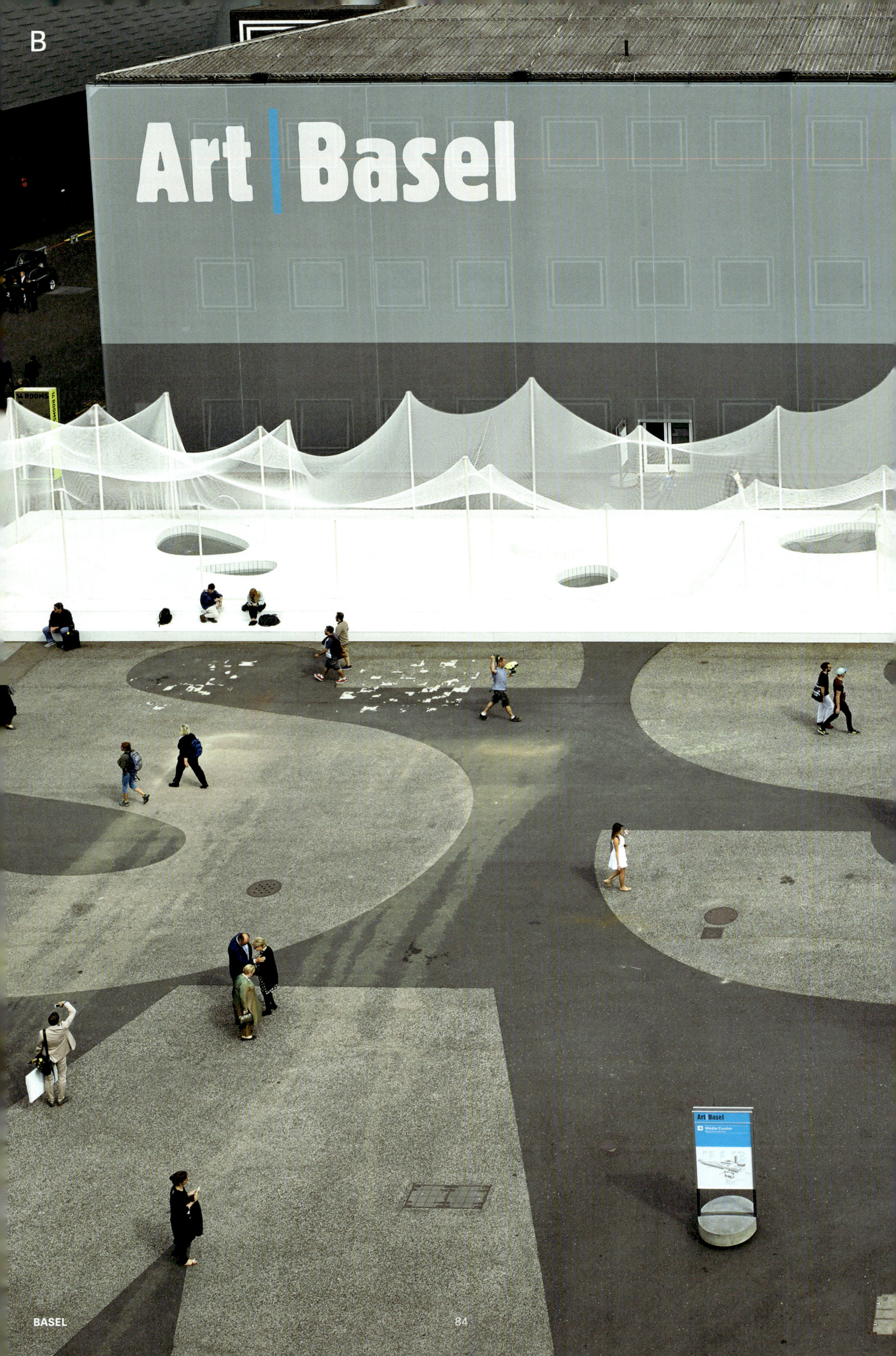

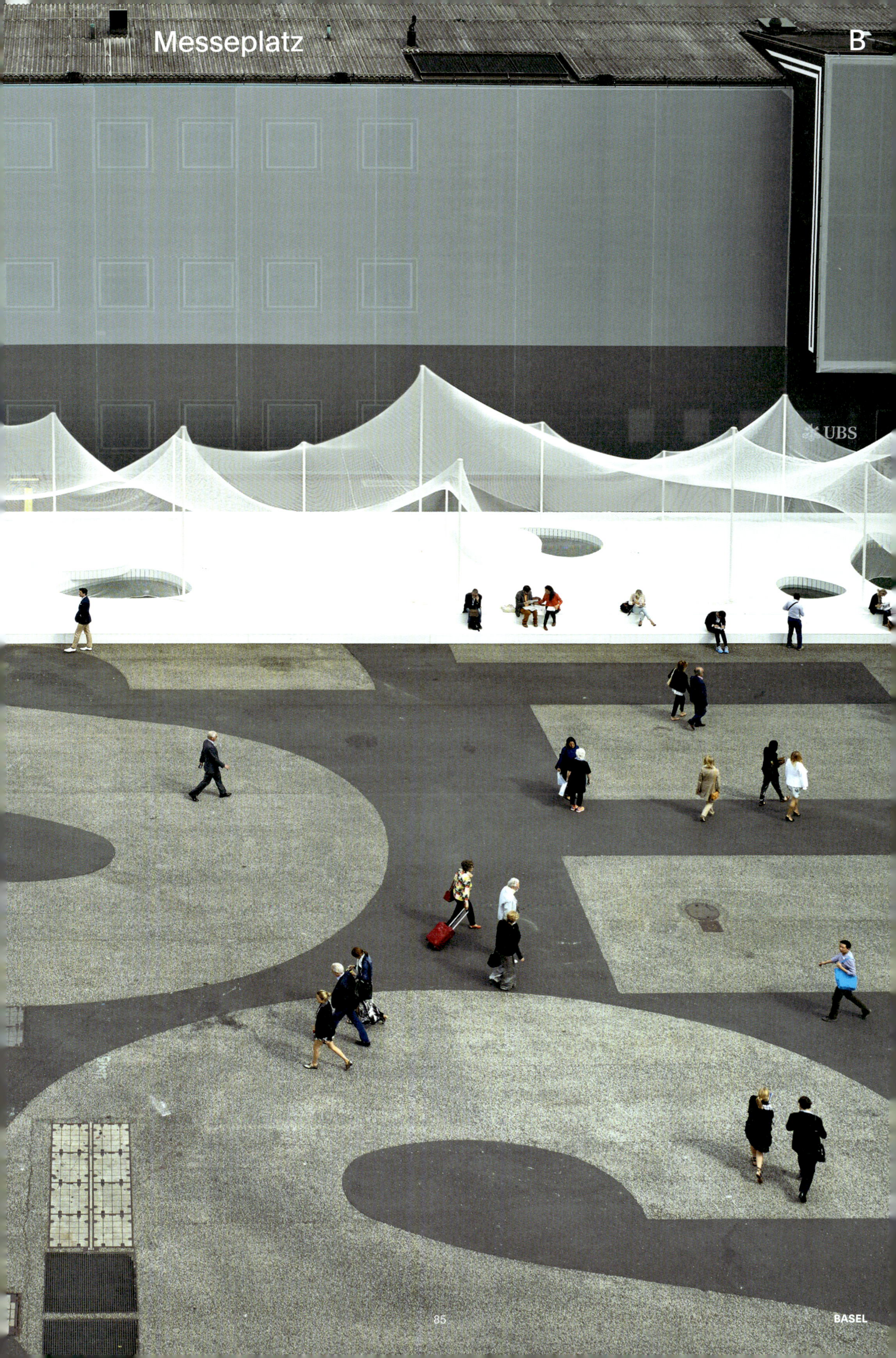
UBS

Cabinet

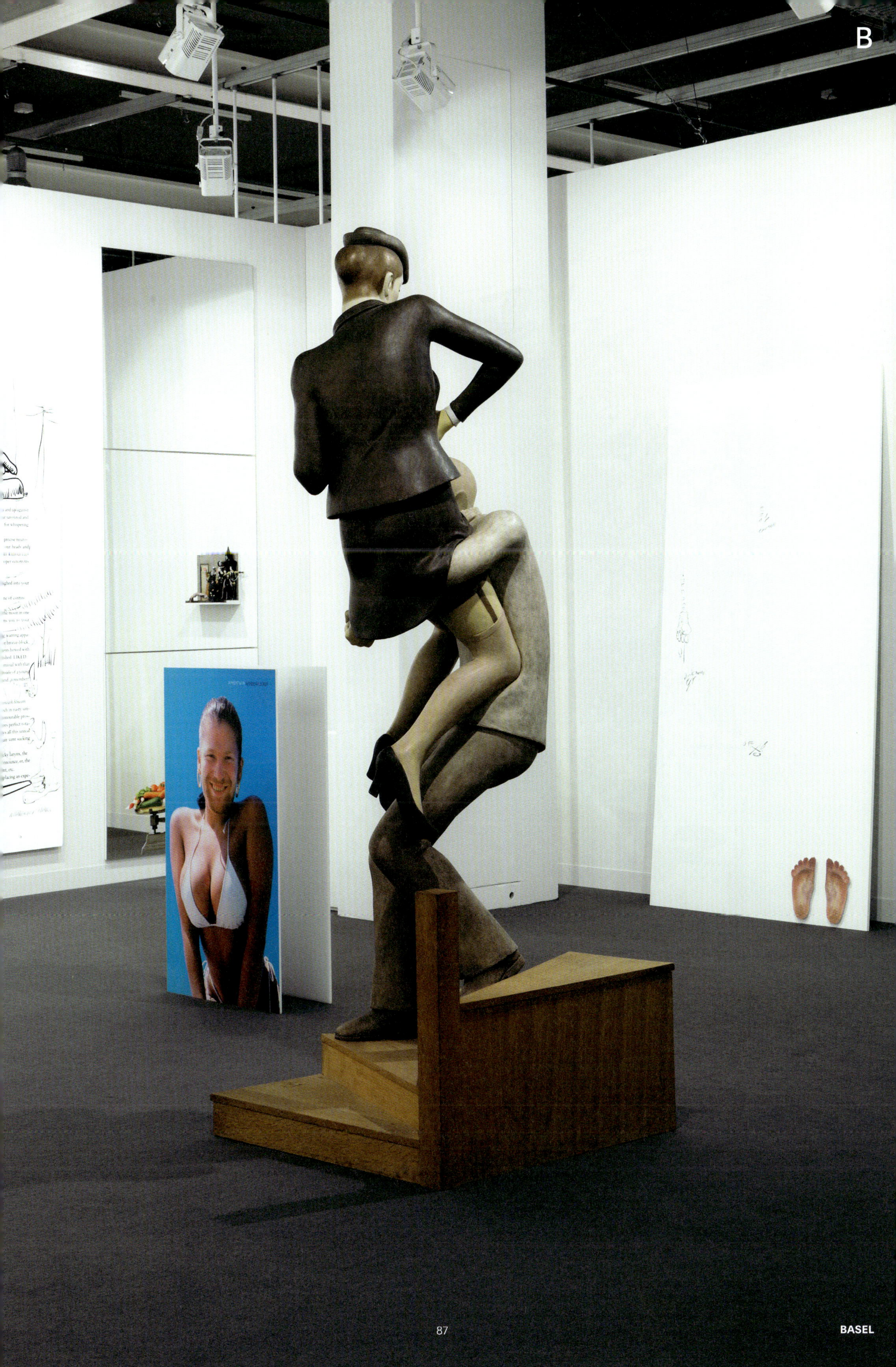

Skarstedt Gallery

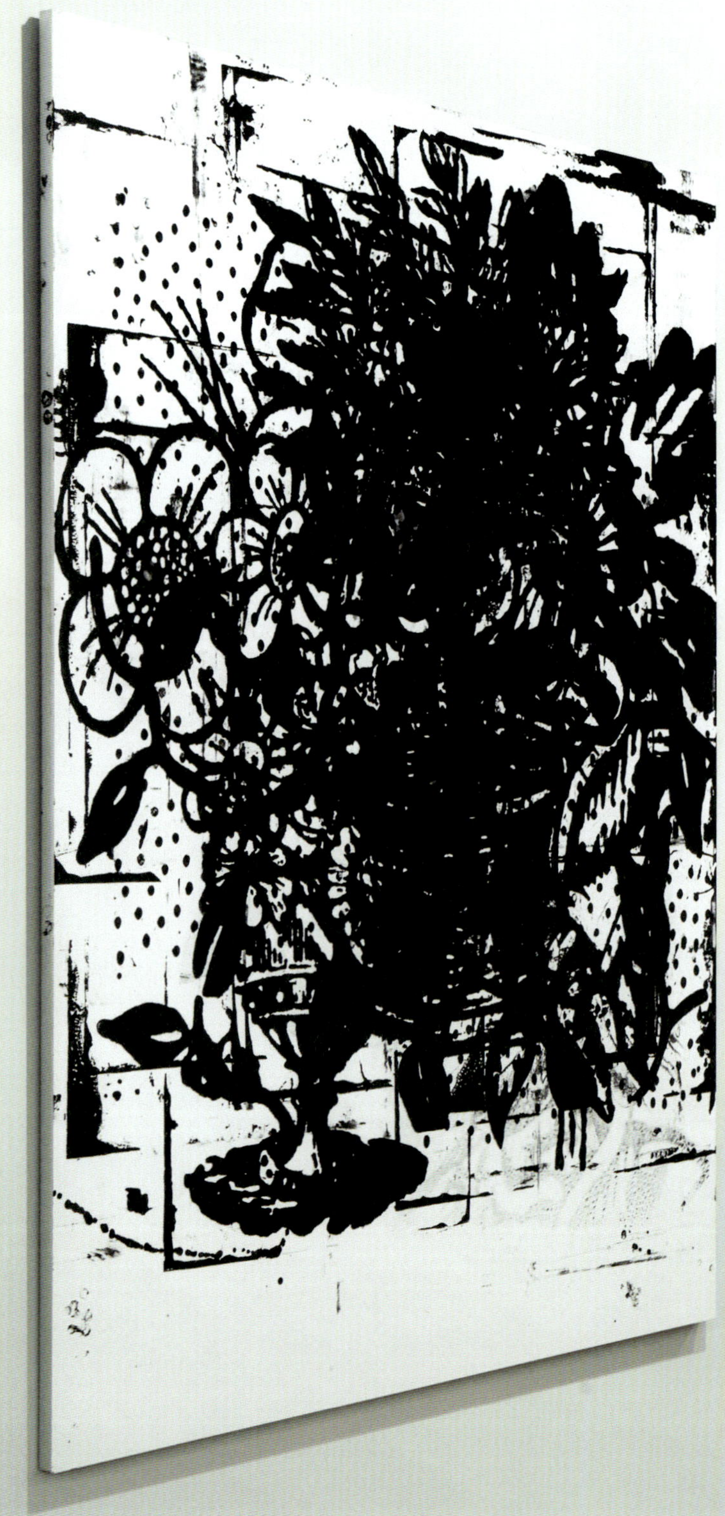

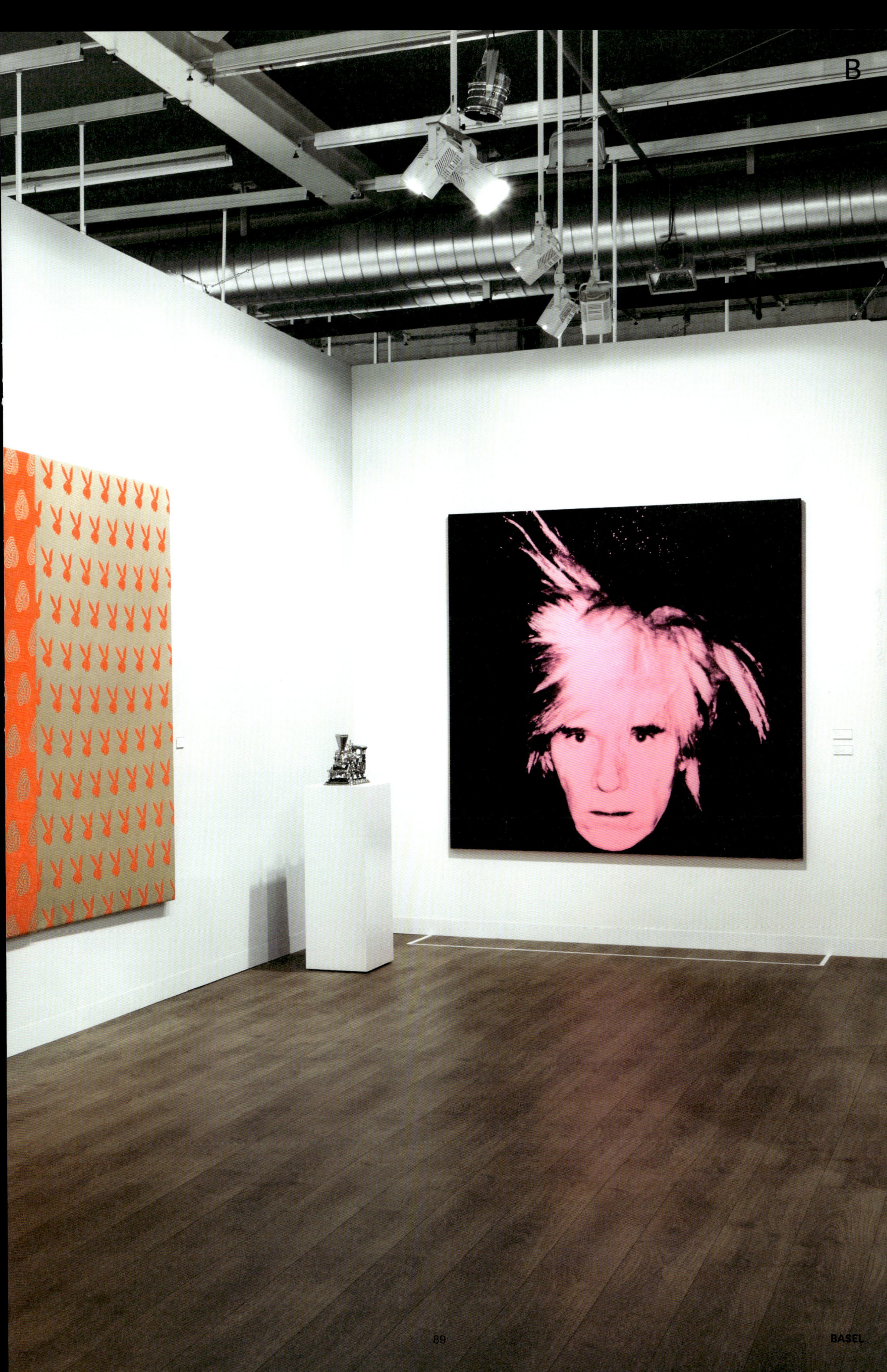

Blondeau & Cie

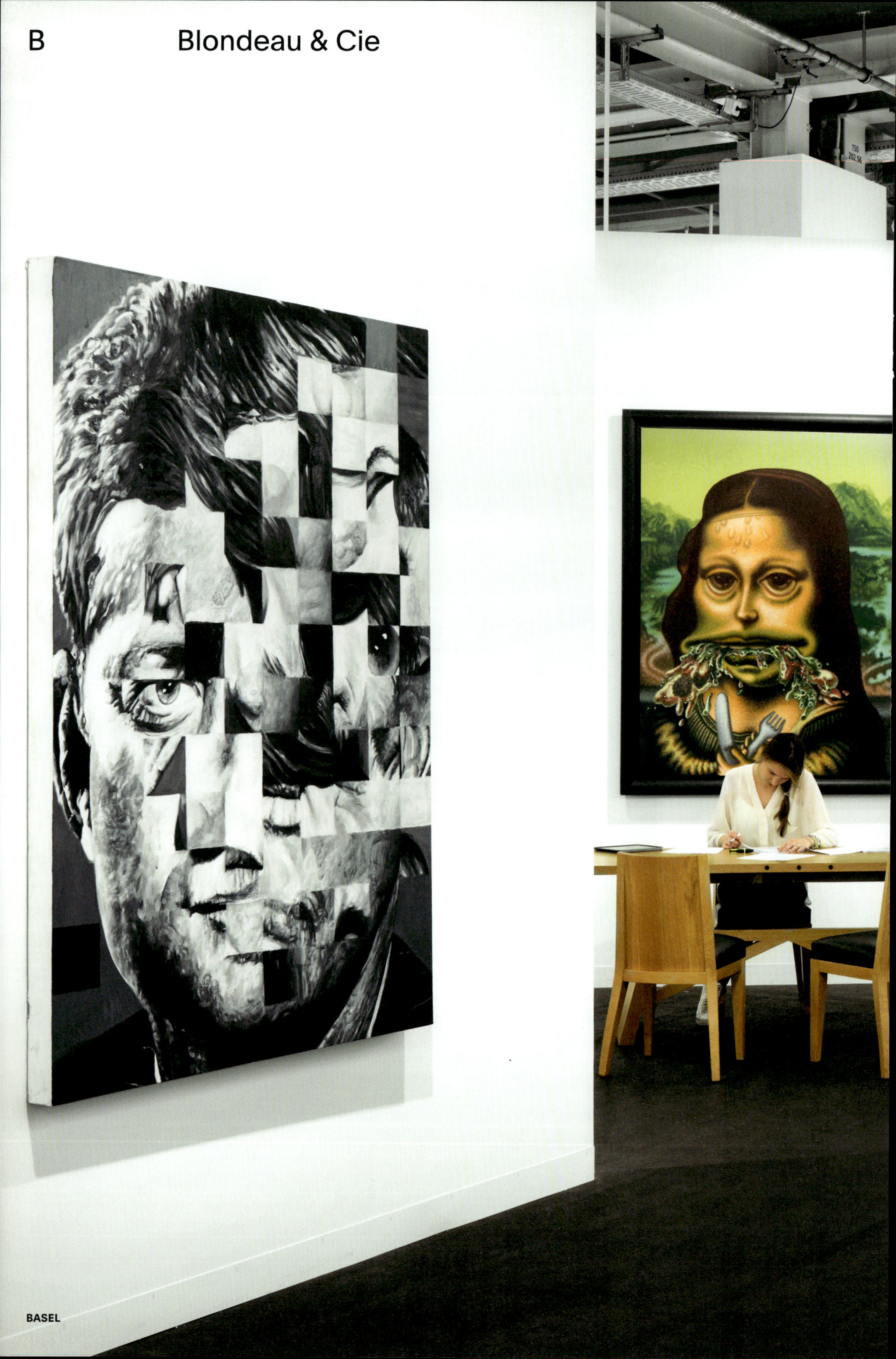

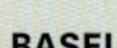

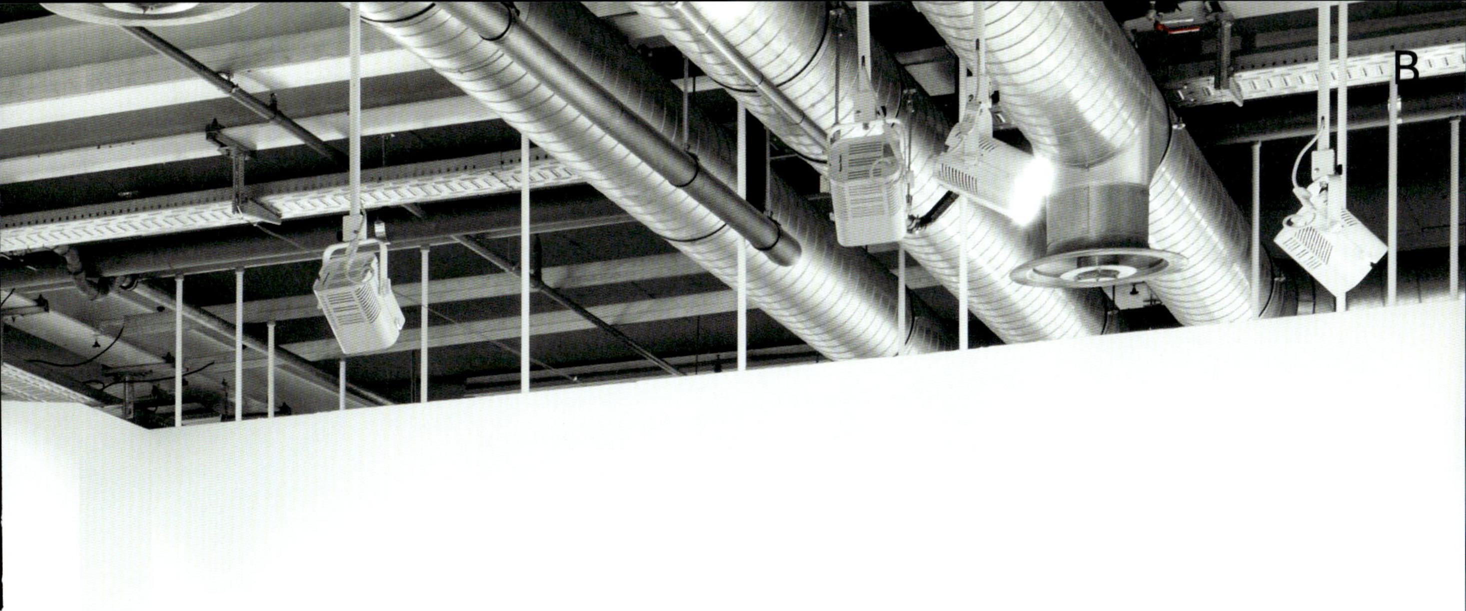

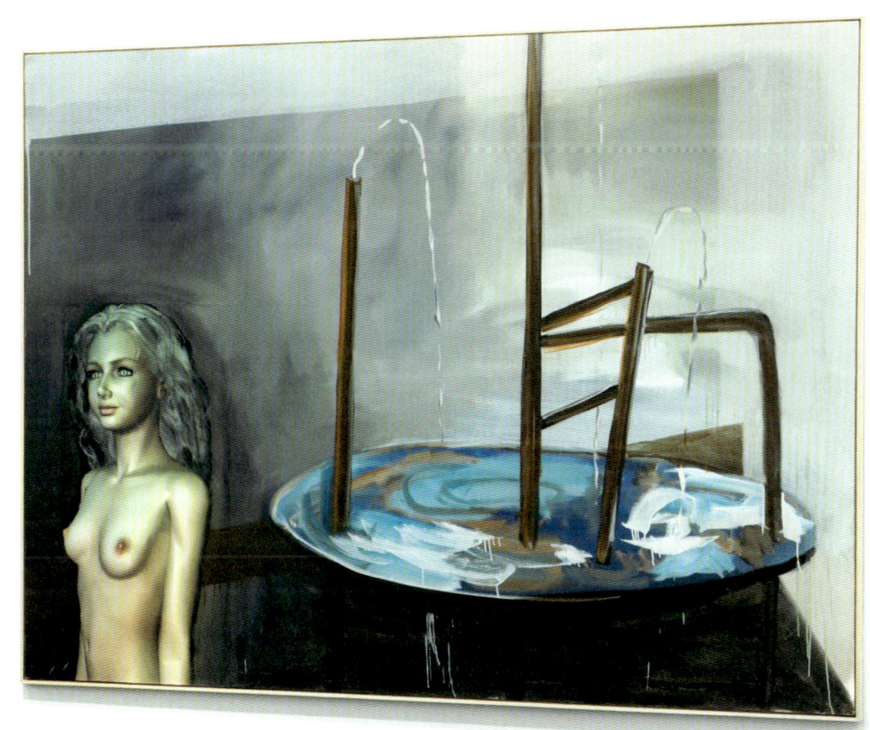

Air de Paris

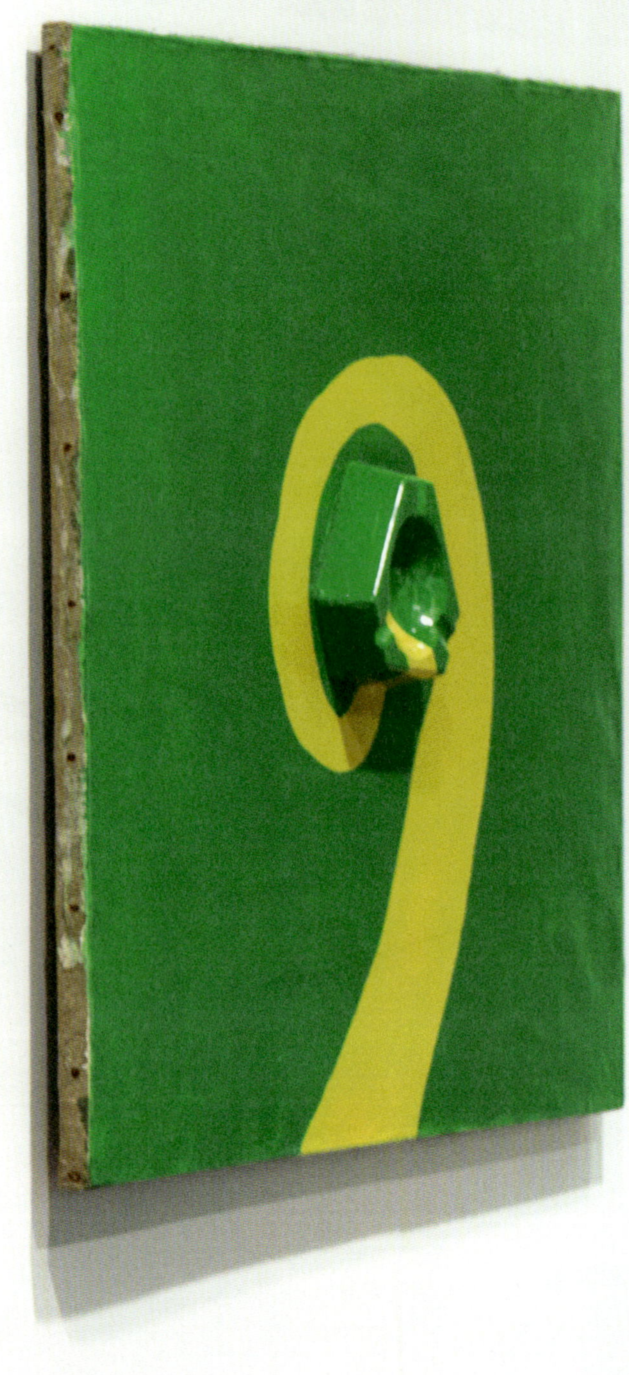

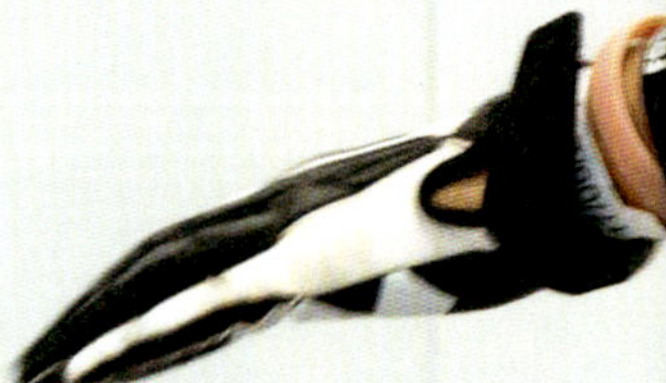

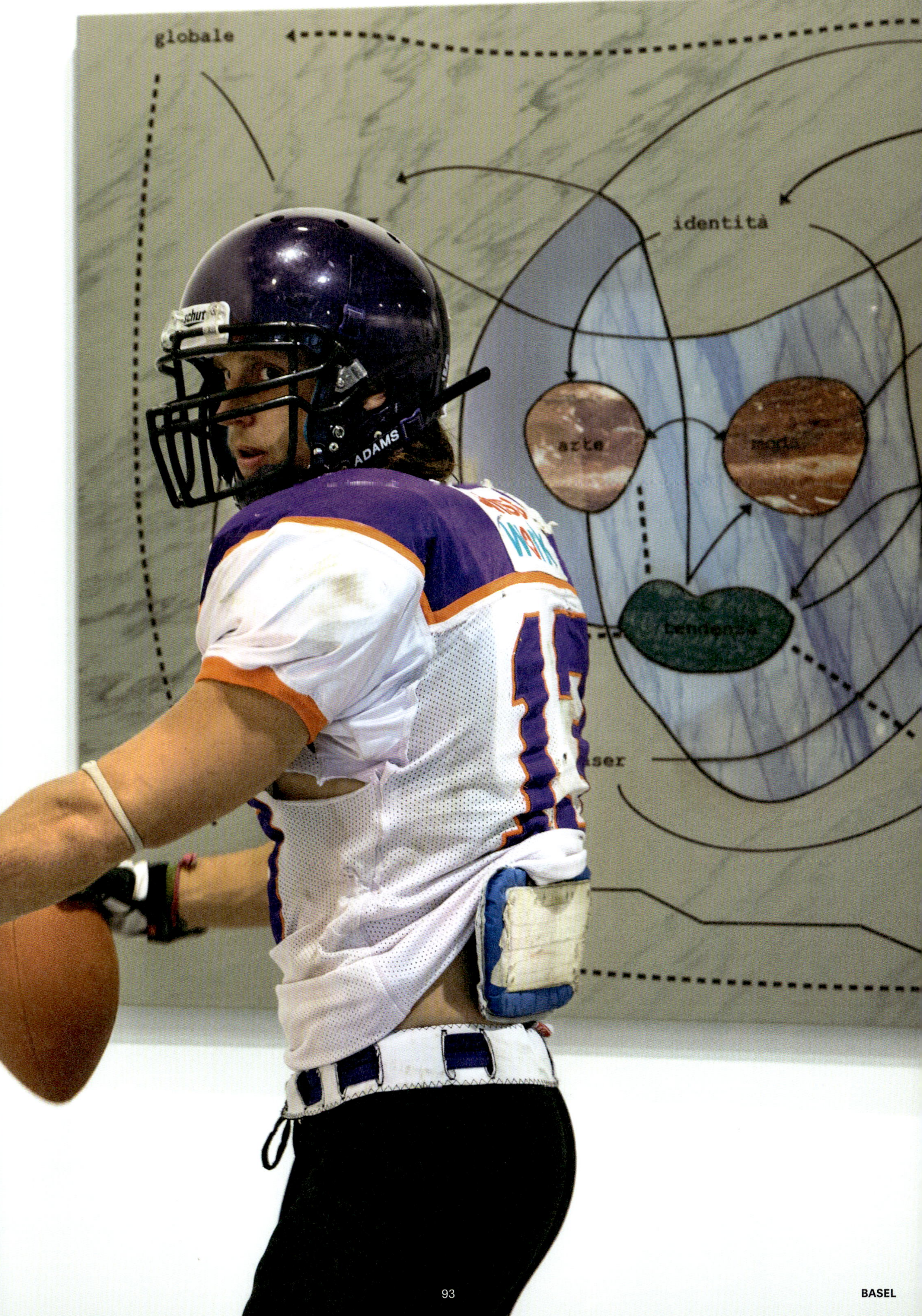
globale
identità
arte
moda
tendenze
ADAMS

B Yvon Lambert

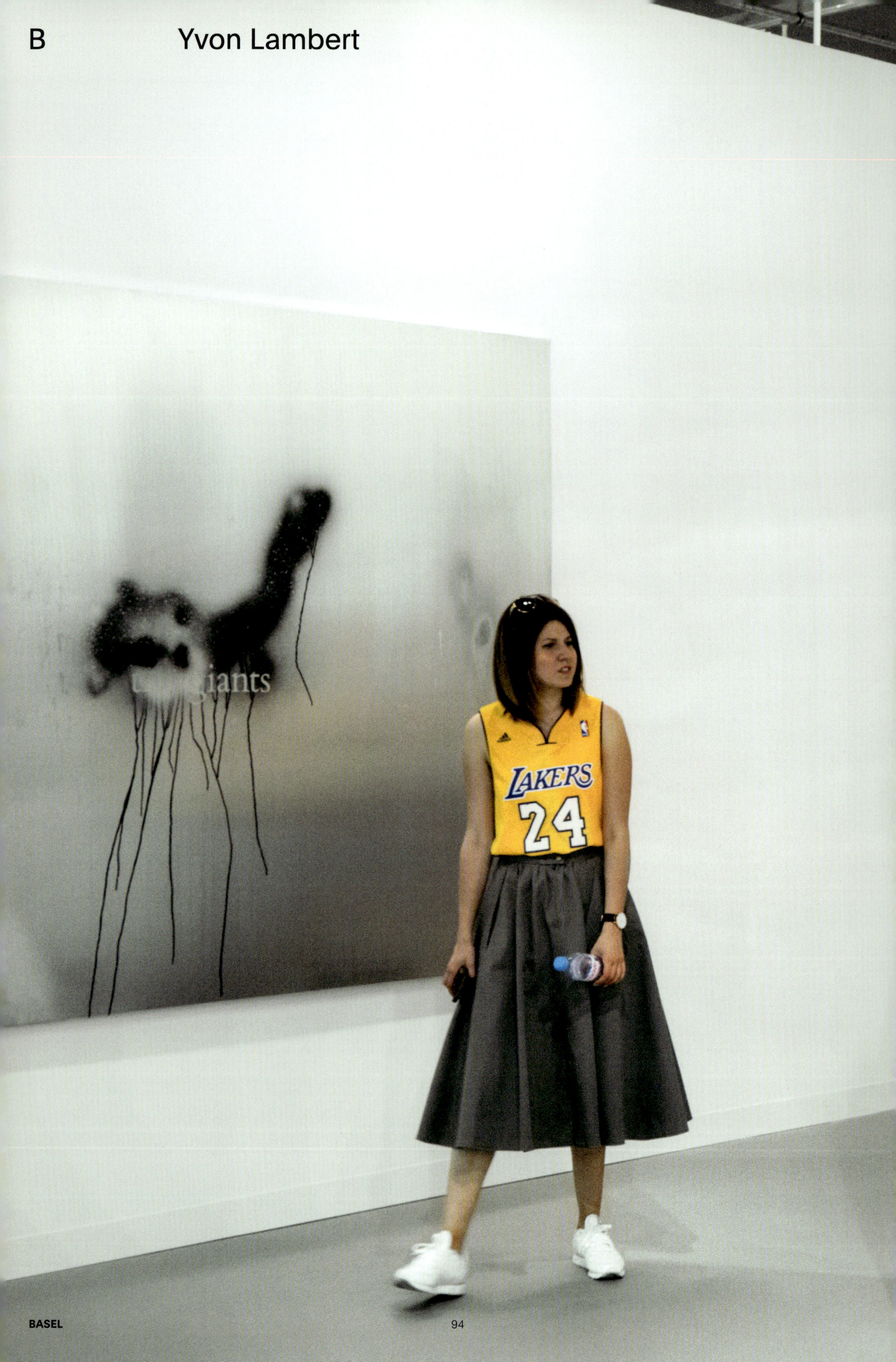

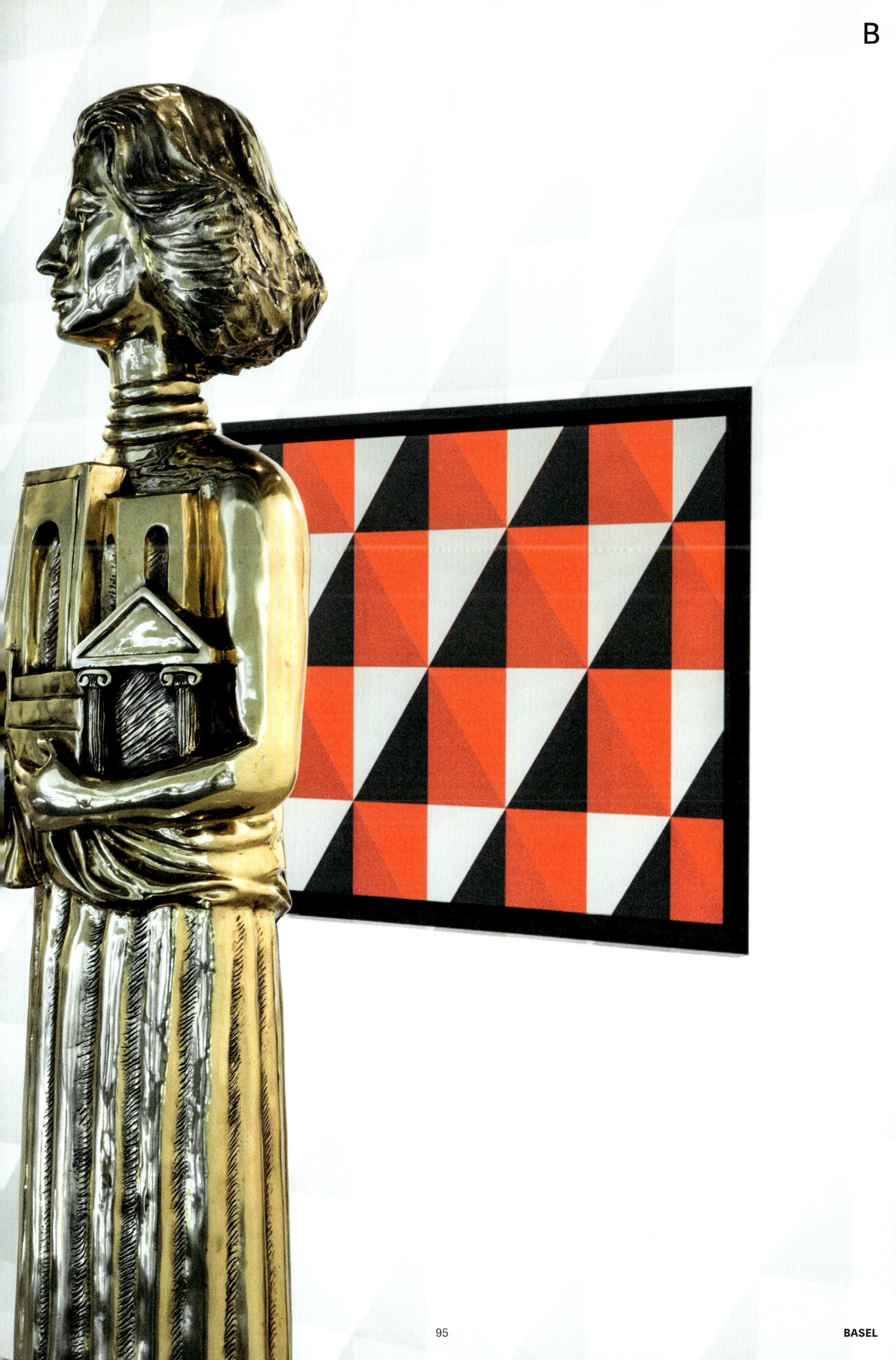

Esther Schipper

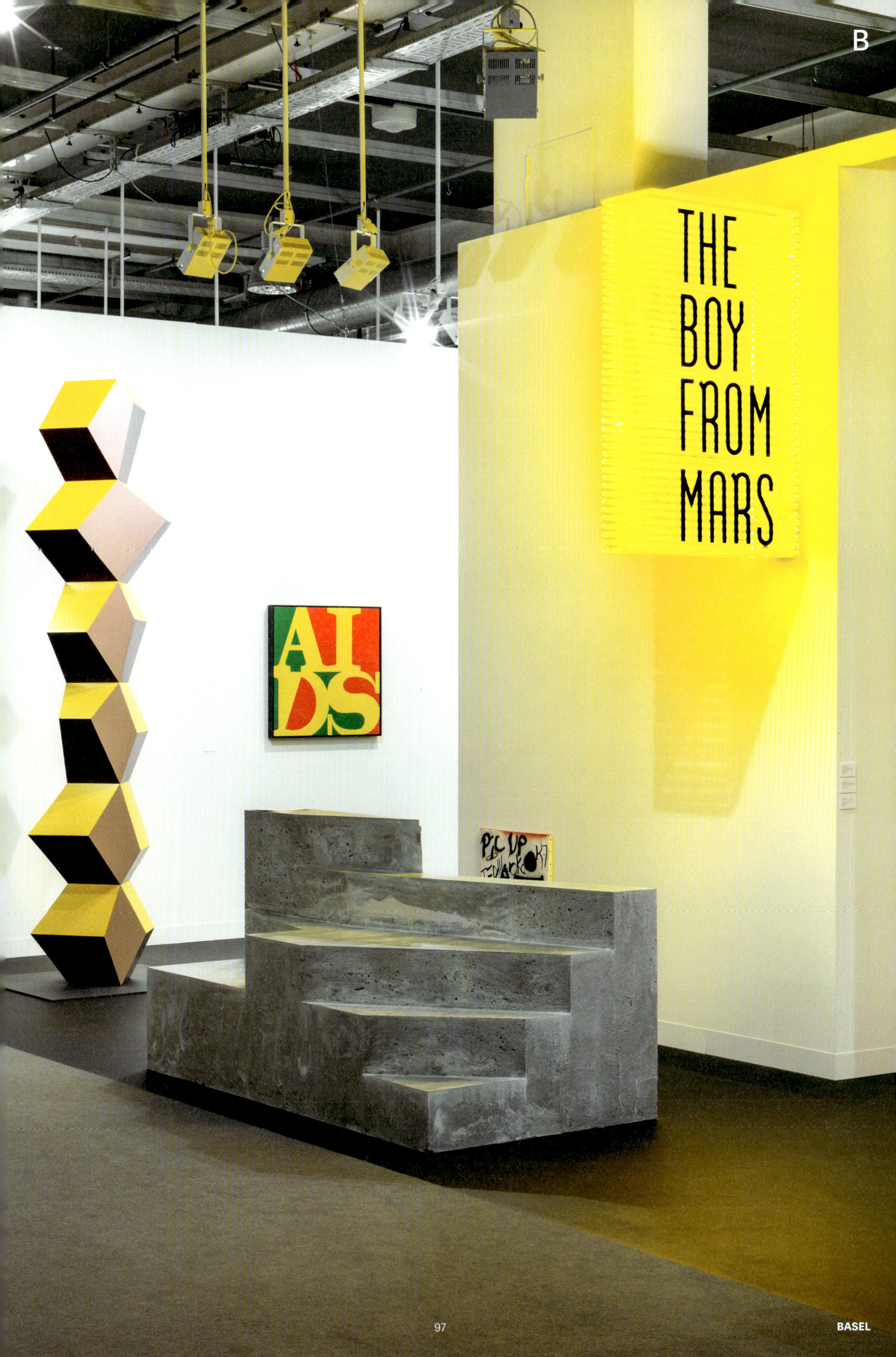
THE
BOY
FROM
MARS
AIDS

Galerie Daniel Blau
Andy Warhol

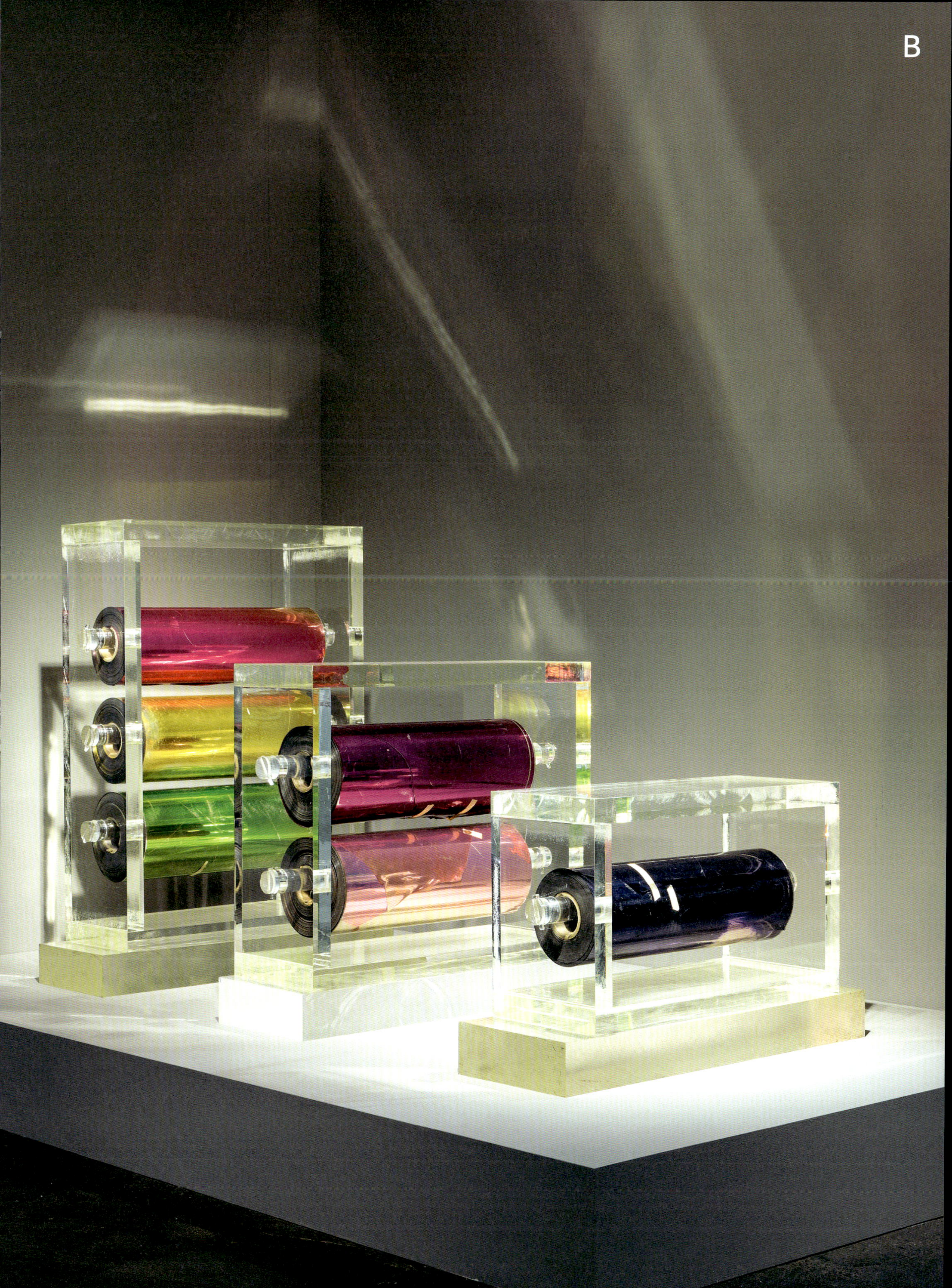
B

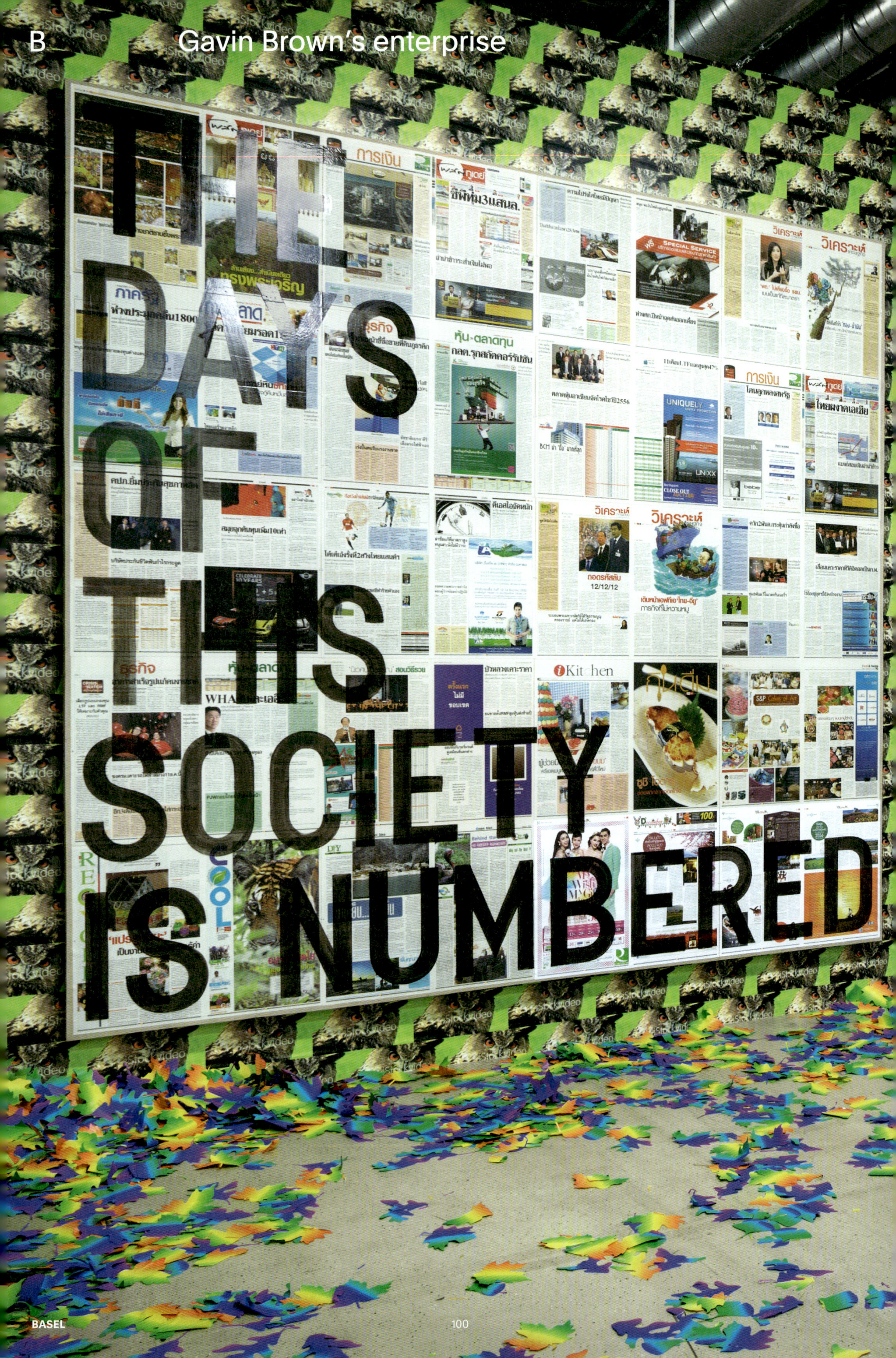
THE DAYS OF THIS SOCIETY IS NUMBERED

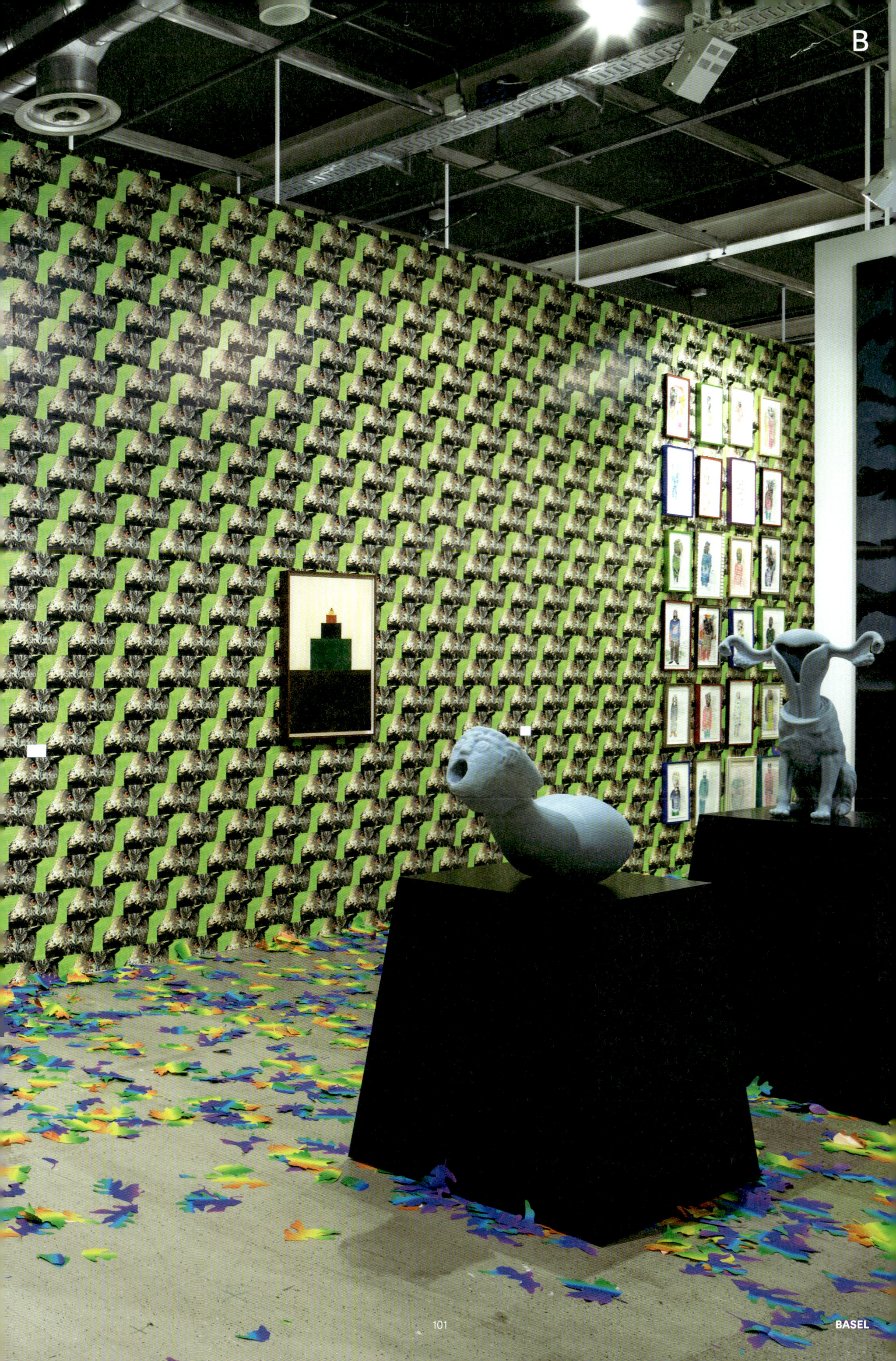

B Standard (Oslo)
Matias Faldbakken

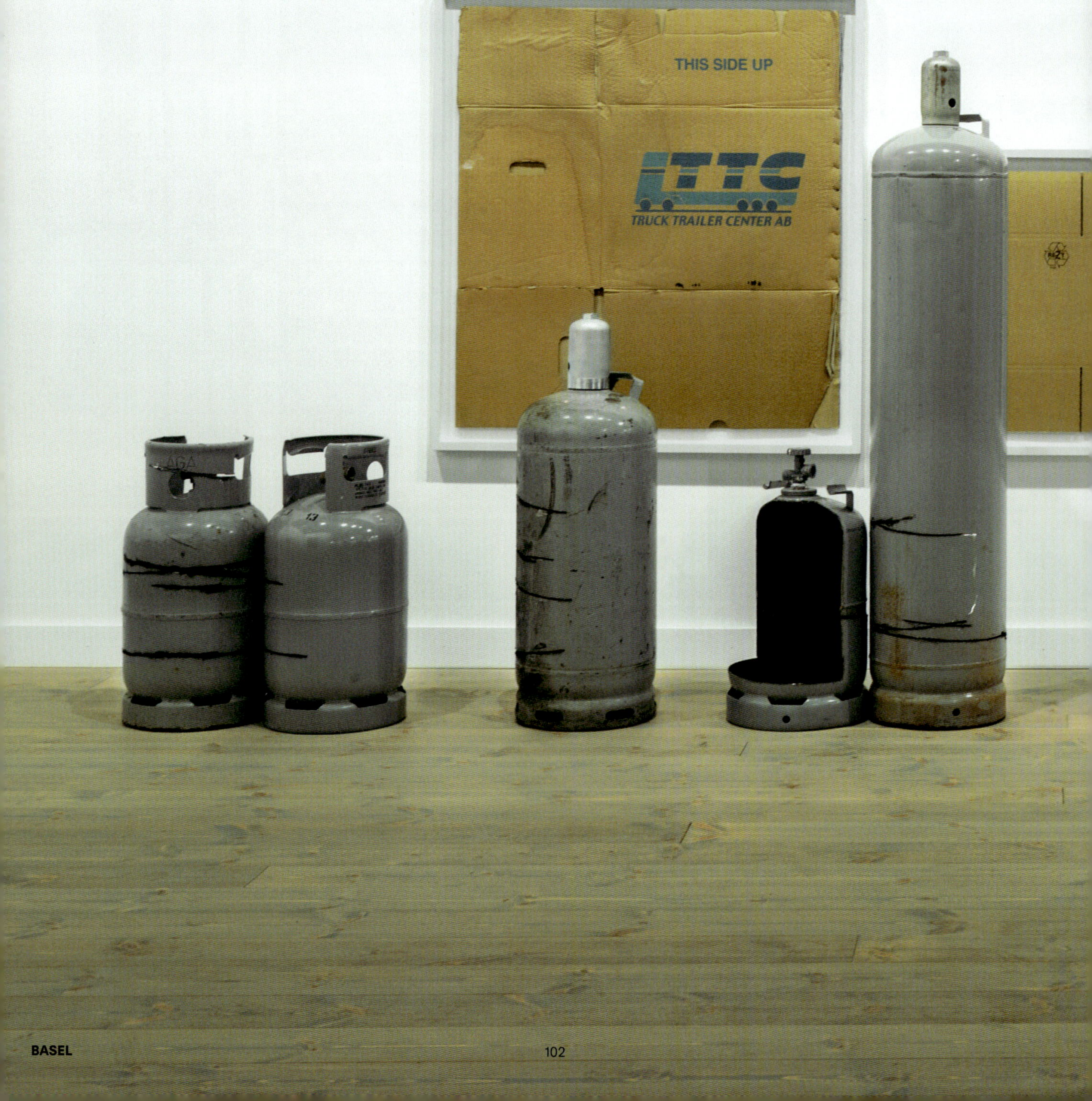

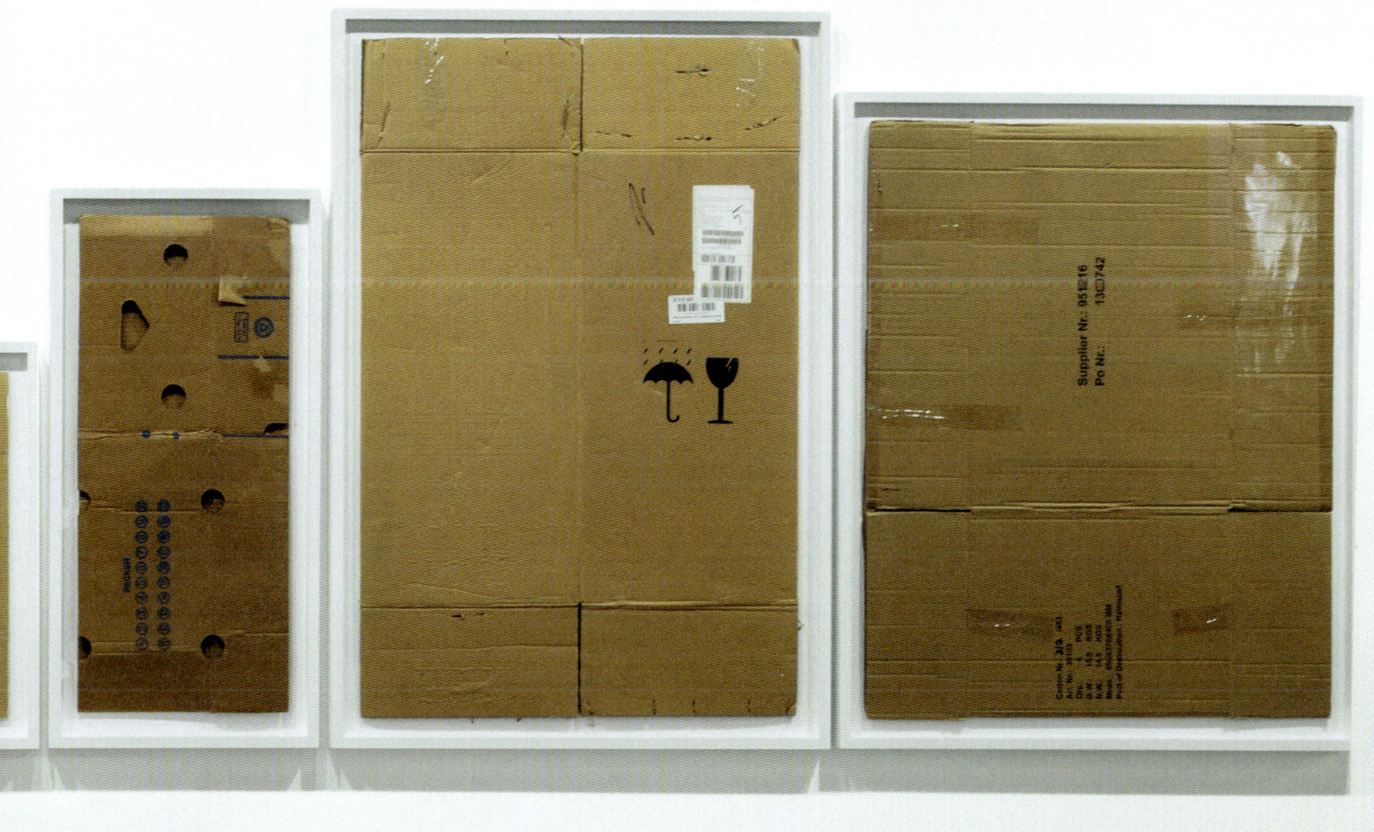

kurimanzutto

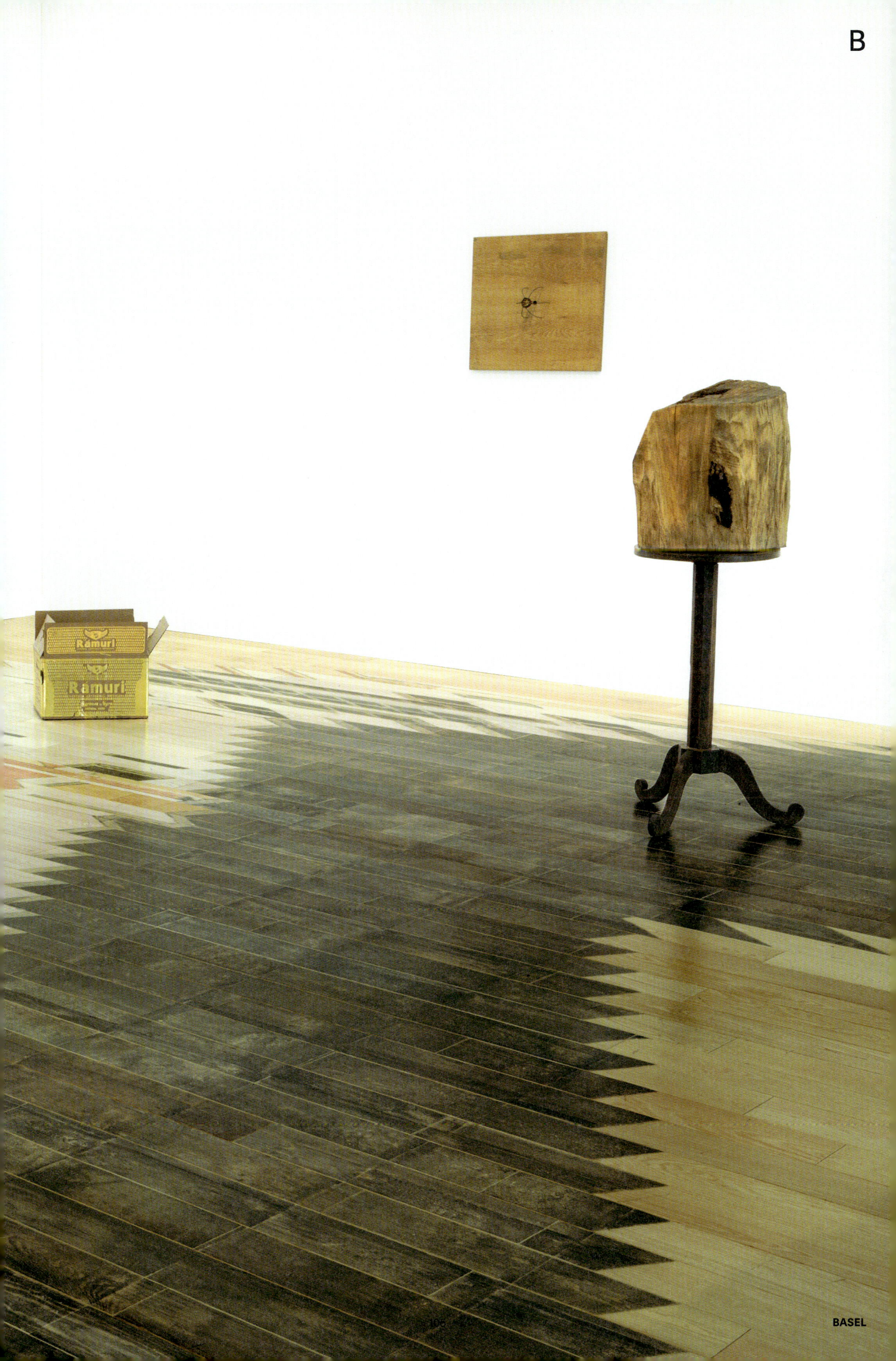

Ramuri
Ramuri

Sadie Coles HQ

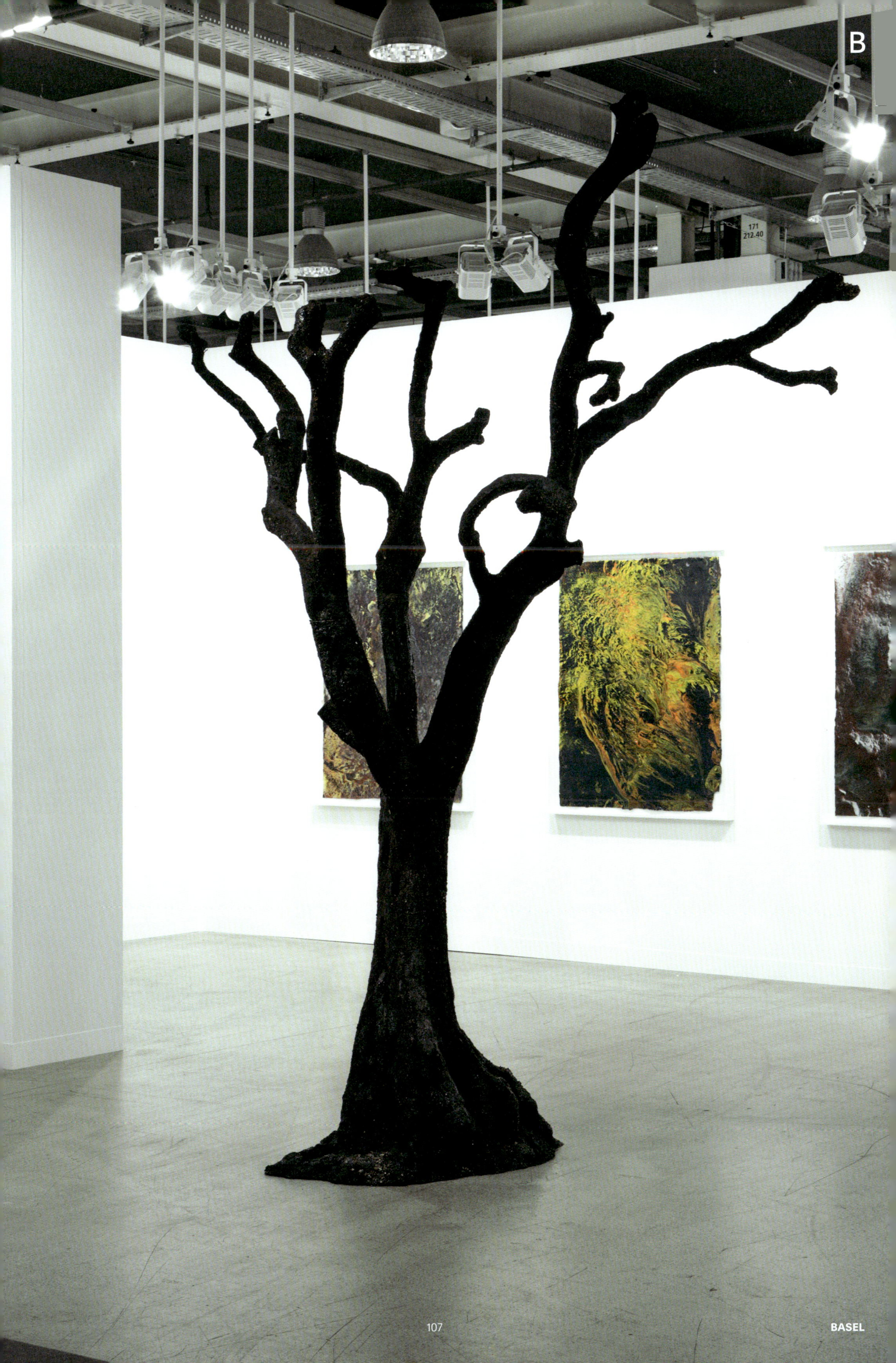
171
212.40

B

Peter Blum Gallery, Blumarts Inc.
Alex Katz

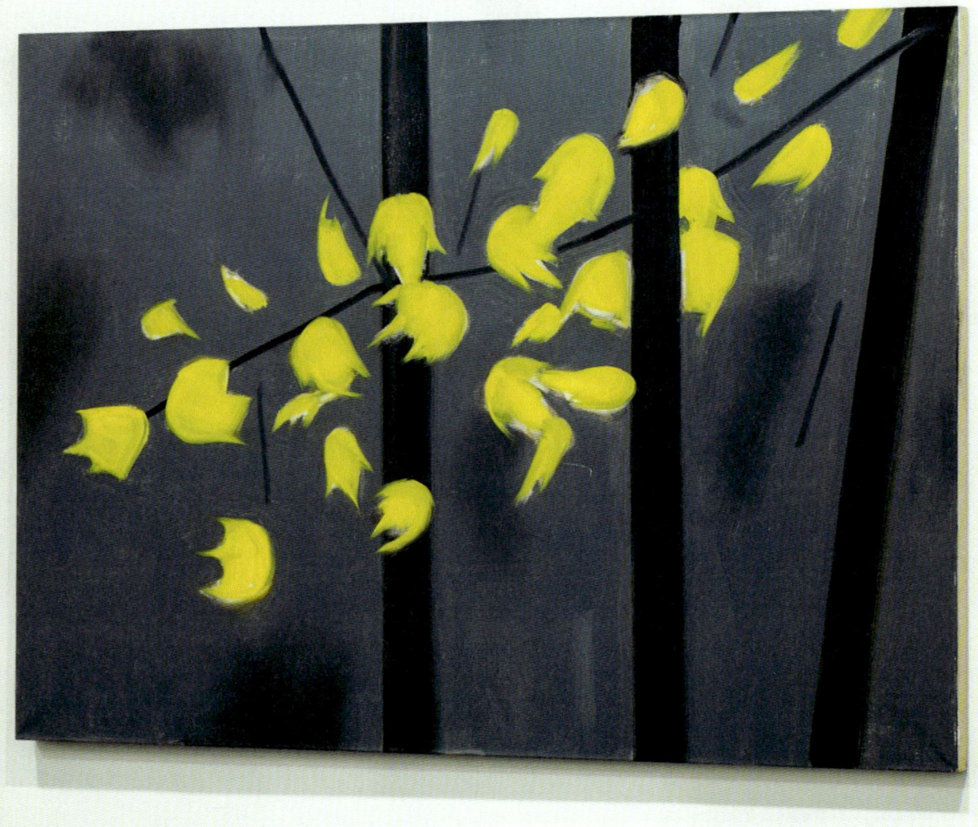

ALEX KATZ

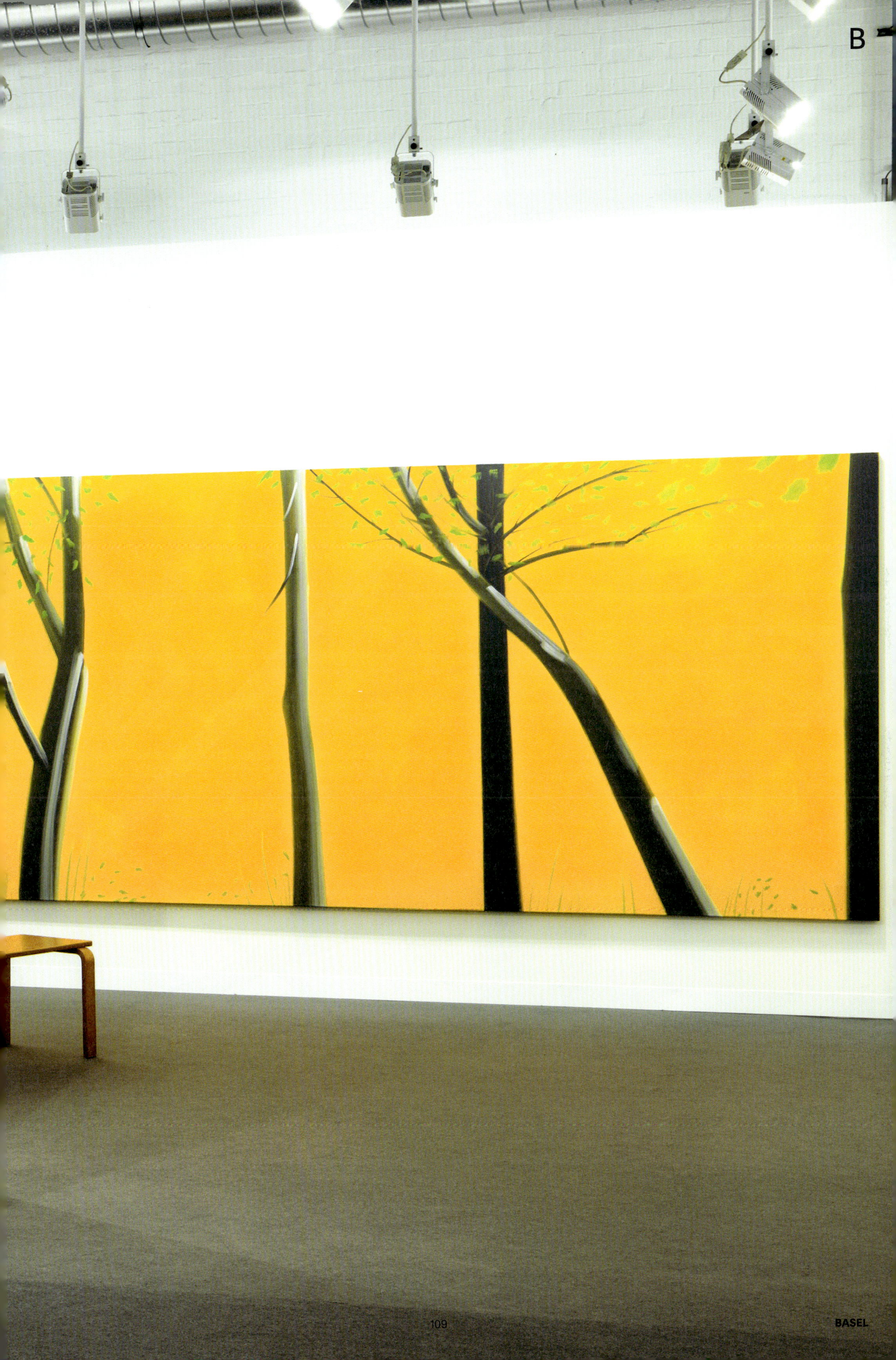
B

The Modern Institute

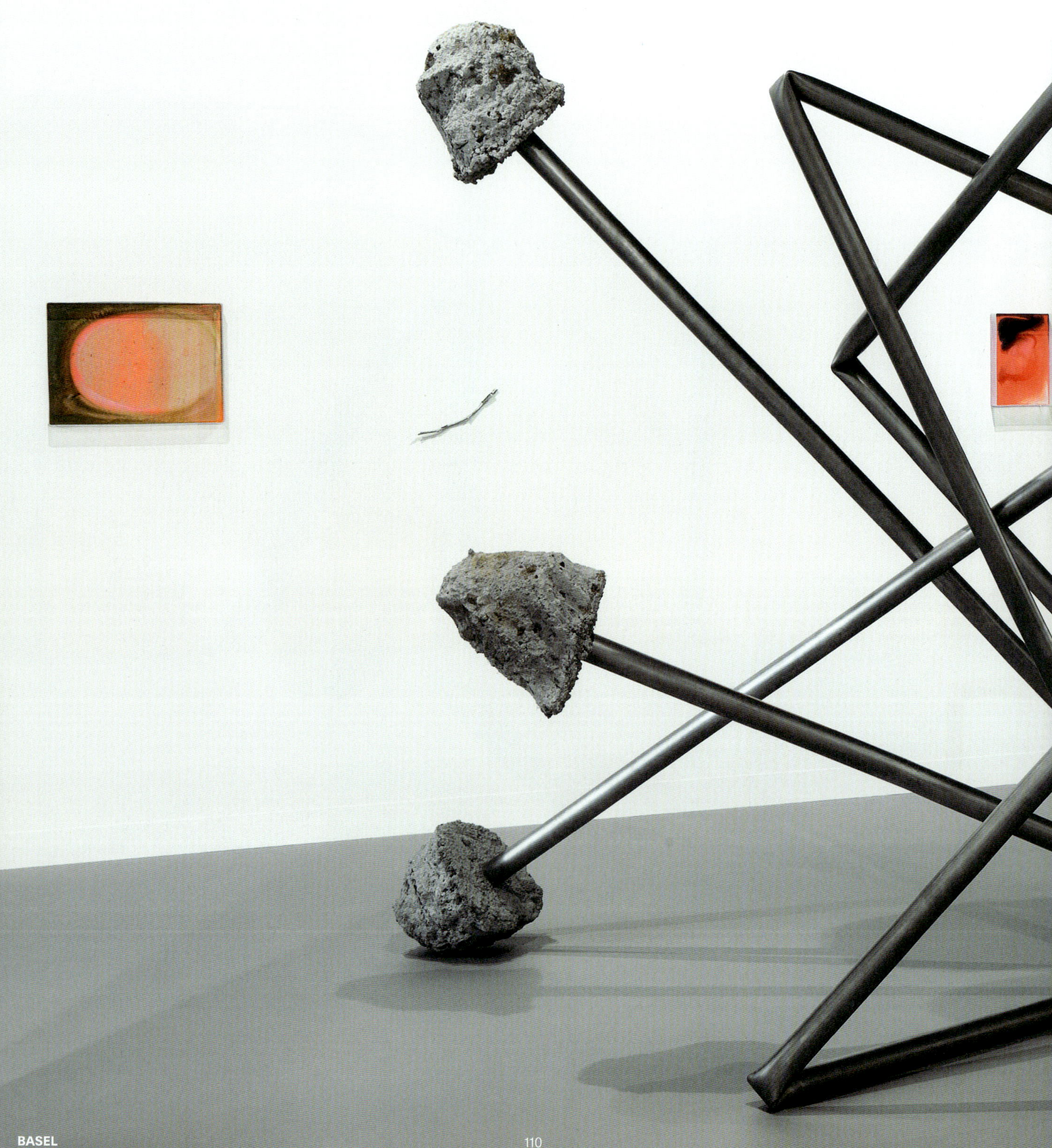

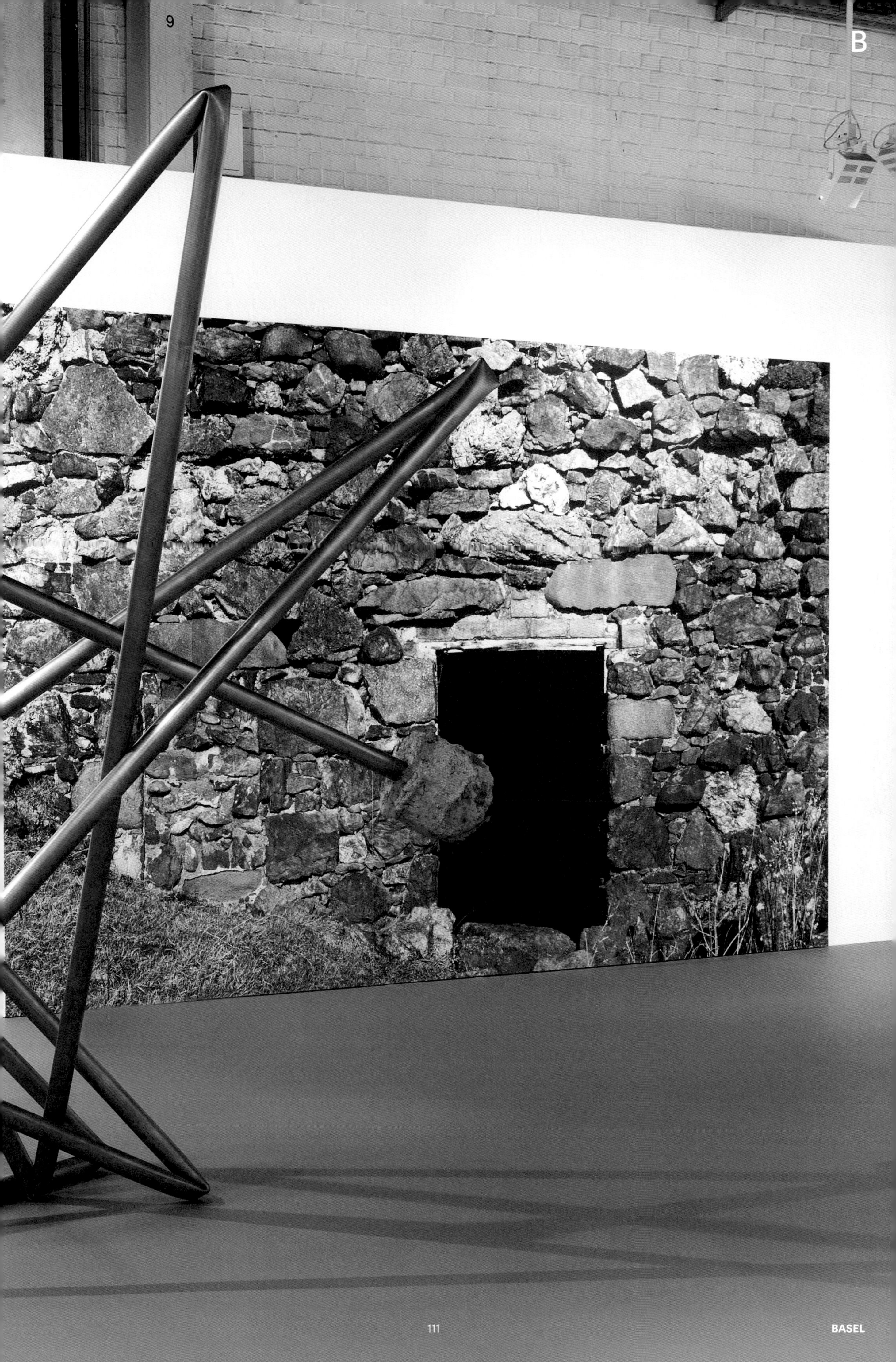
9
B

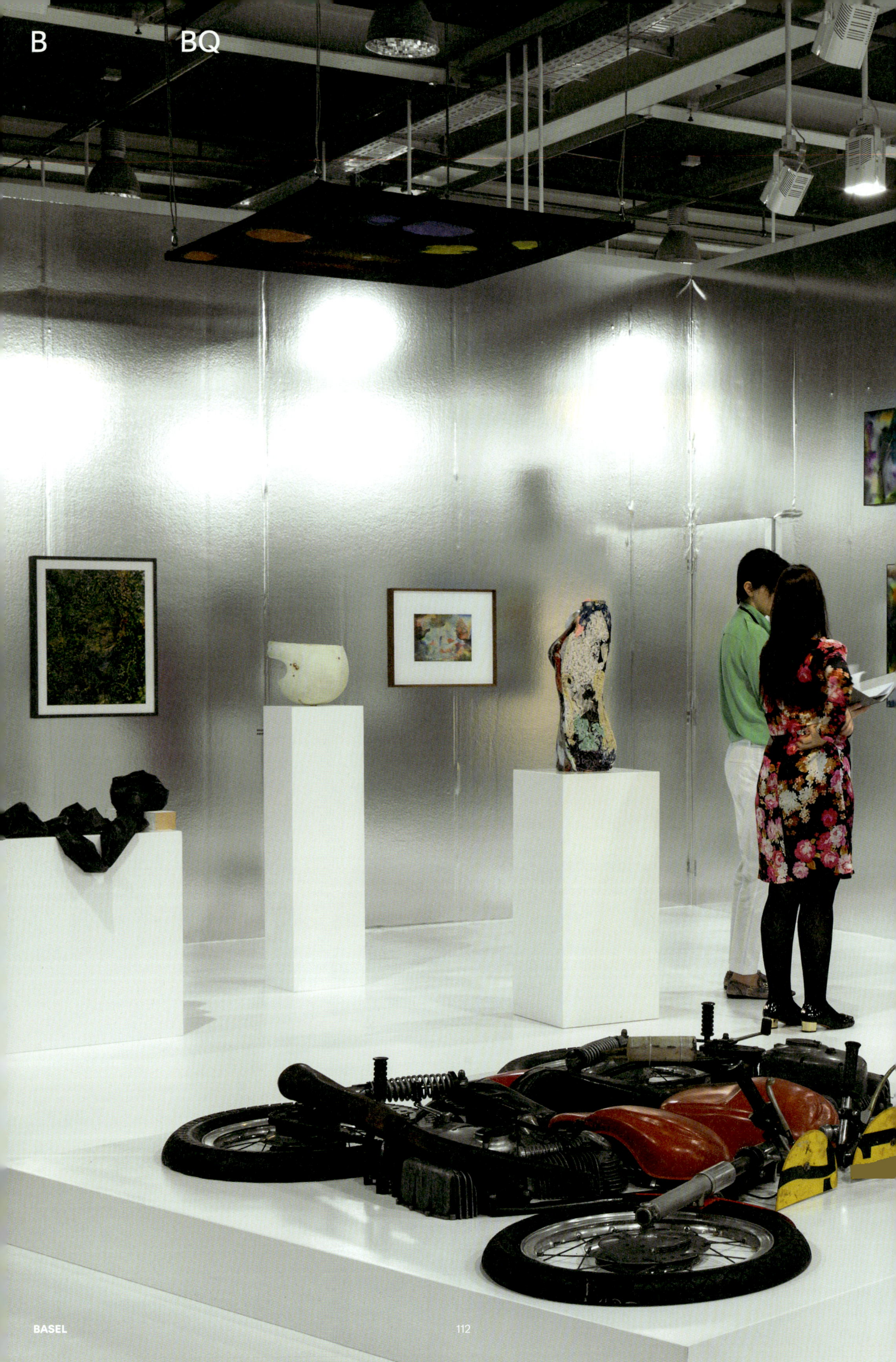

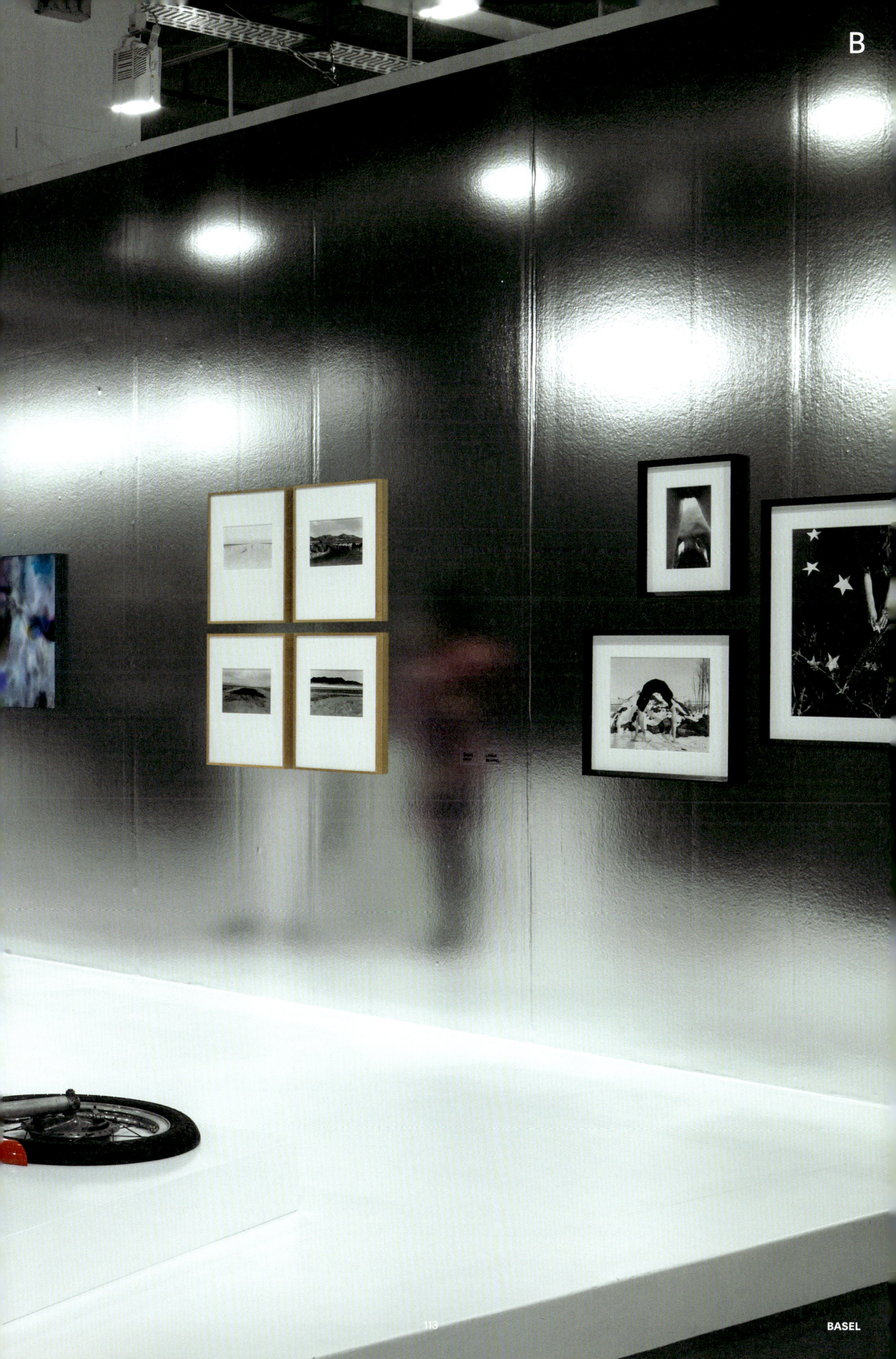

Hauser & Wirth

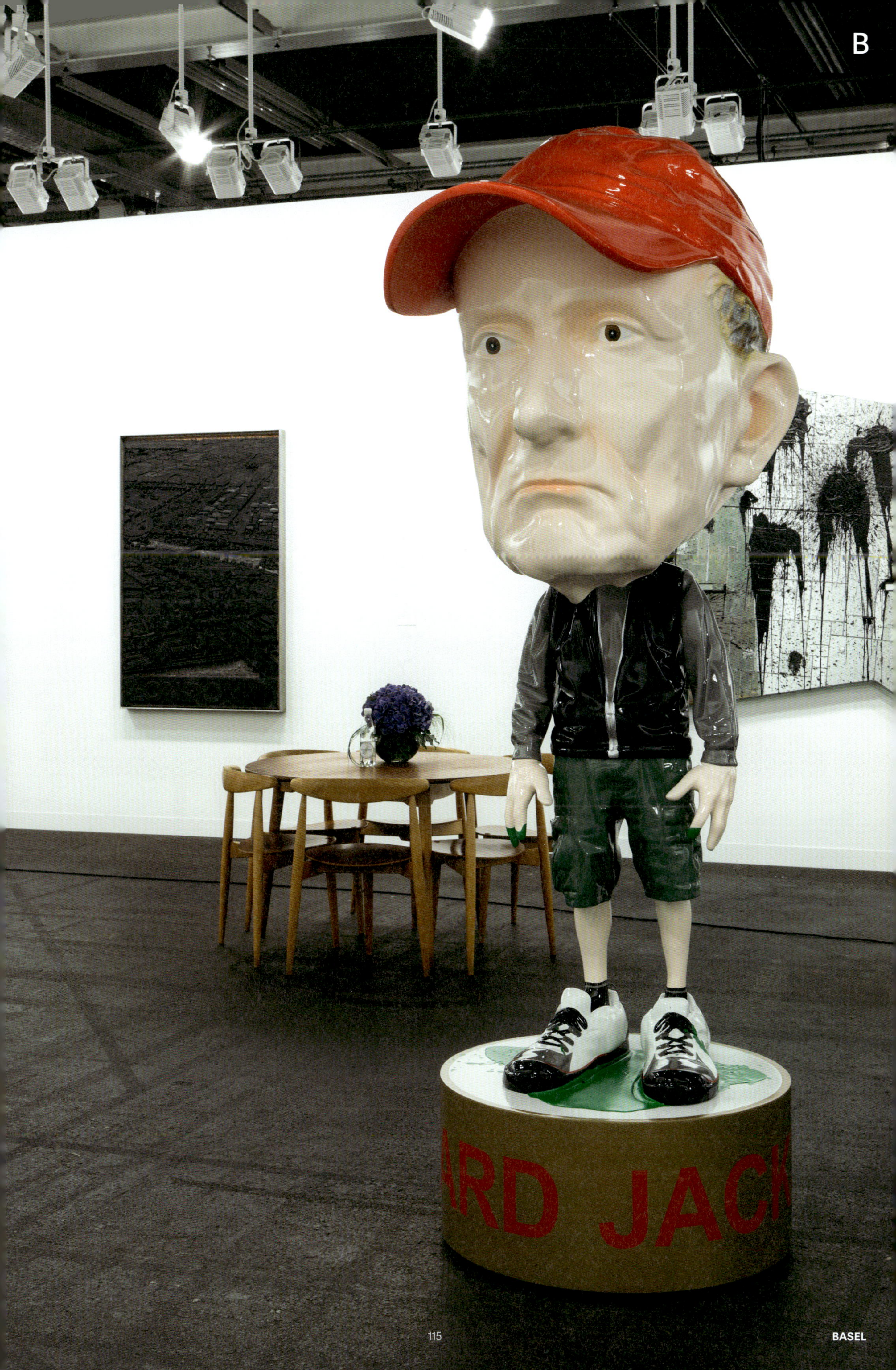
ARD JACK

Kerlin Gallery

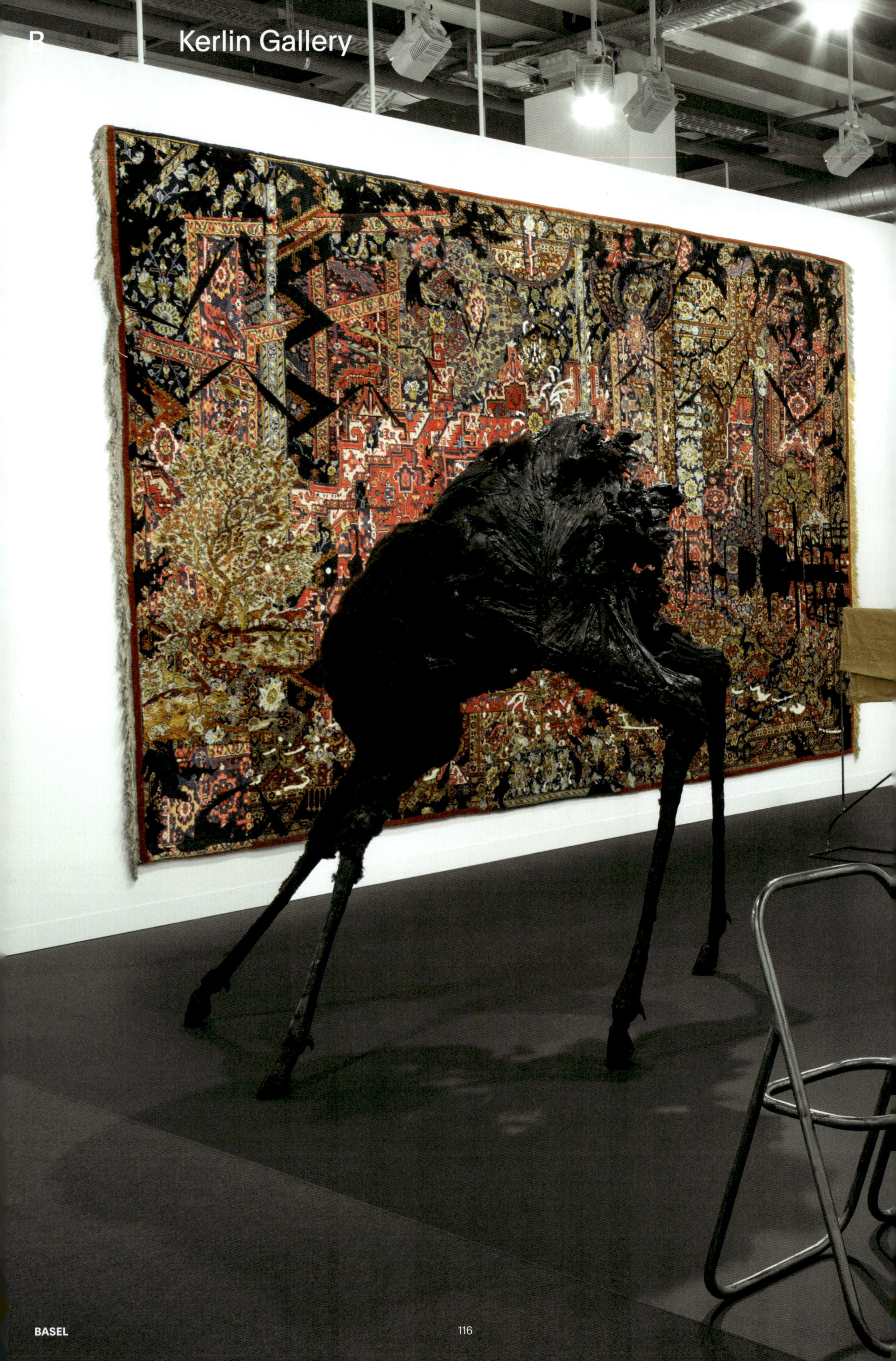

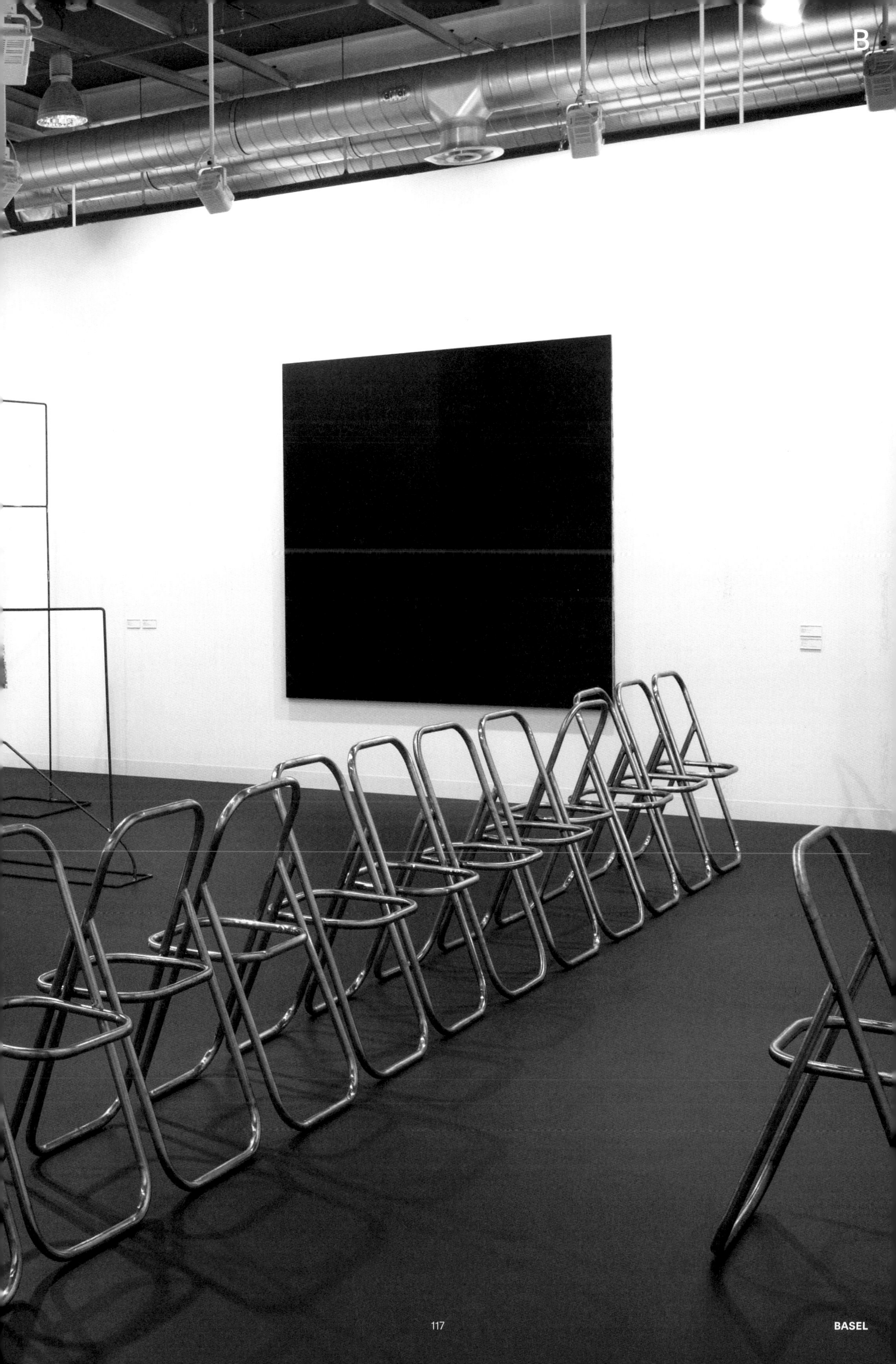

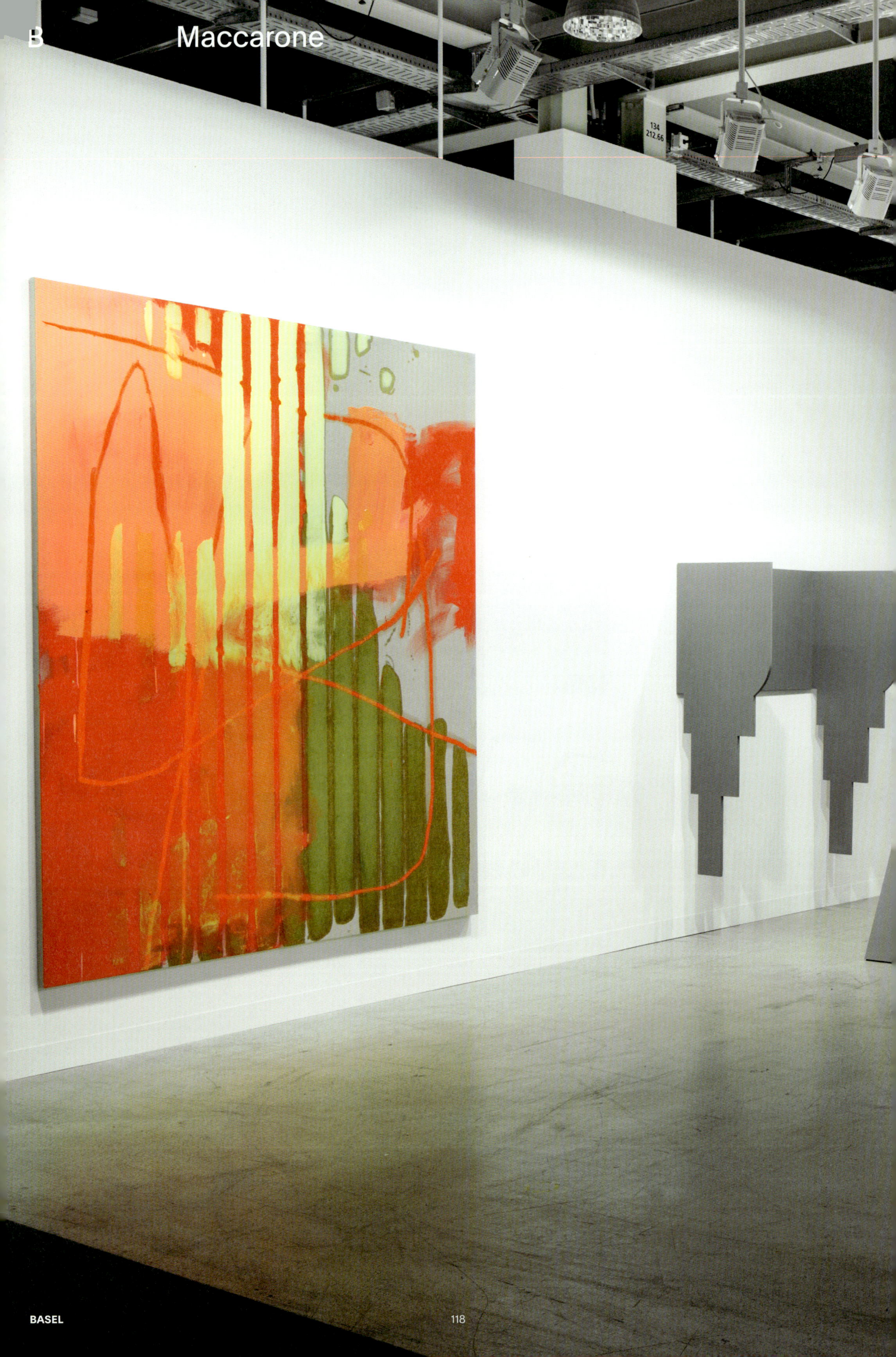
134
212.66

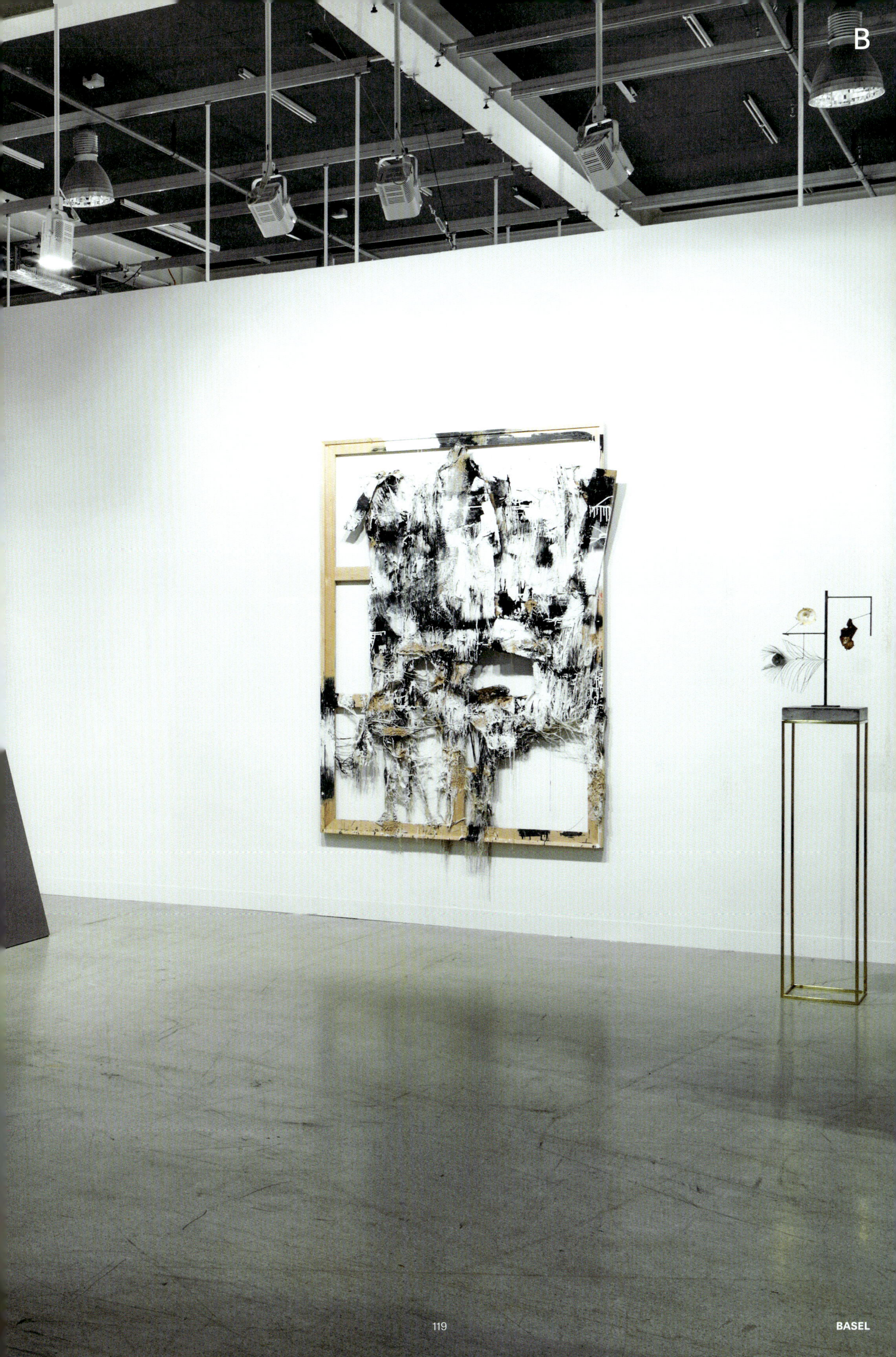

Galería Elvira González

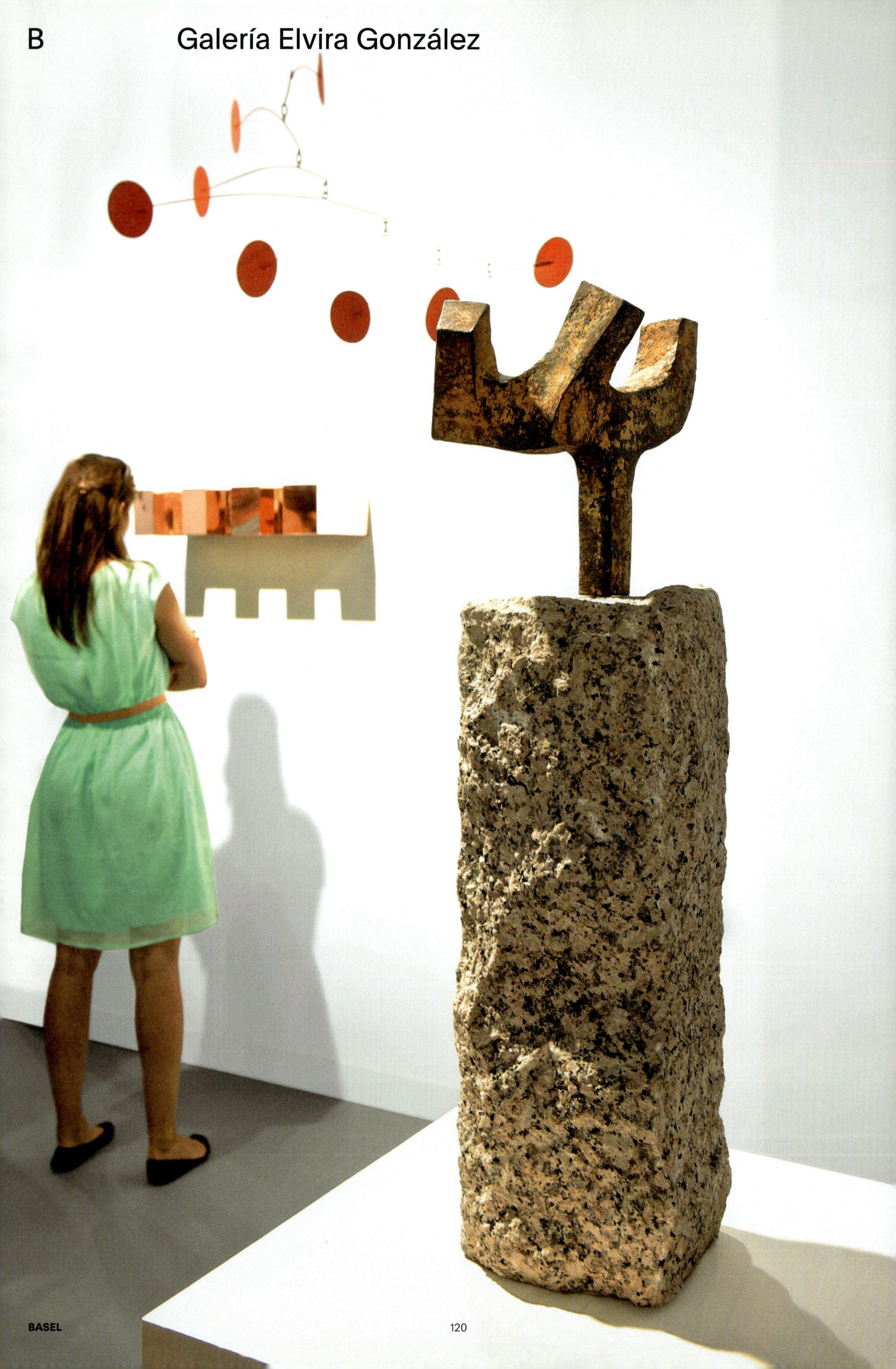

BIEN NALES 2015

Lyon
New York
Sharjah
Venice

B

13th Lyon Biennale: *La Vie moderne* September 10, 2015–January 3, 2016

Artistic Director: Ralph Rugoff

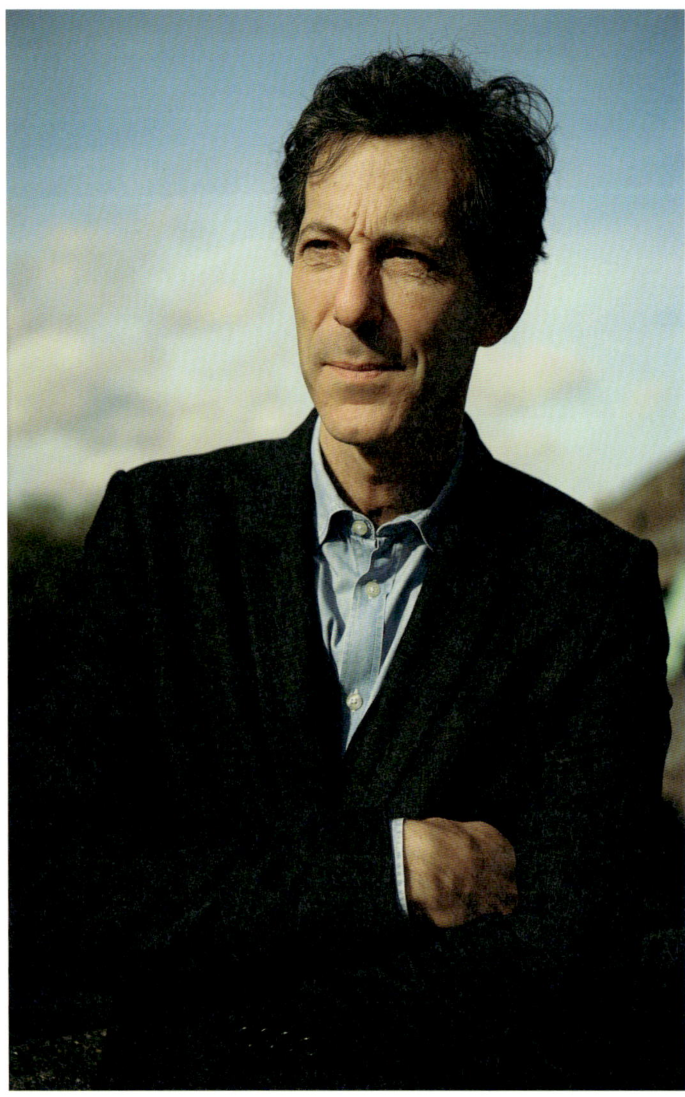

Ralph Rugoff

Introduction

The Lyon Biennale of Contemporary Art was created in 1991 with the aim of becoming one of the best-known European platforms to promote and discover contemporary art and artists, while building a long-term bond with its host territory. In even years, Lyon hosts the Lyon Dance Biennale.

The first three Biennales were curated by Thierry Raspail, Director since 1995 of the Lyon Museum of Contemporary Art—the institution that has commissioned many of the Biennale's artists. He is now the Biennale Artistic Director and invites different guest curators for each edition: Harald Szeemann (1997), Jean-Hubert Martin (2000), Xavier Douroux, Franck Gautherot, Eric Troncy, Robert Nickas, and Anne Pontégnie (2003), Nicolas Bourriaud and Jérôme Sans (2005), Stéphanie Moisdon and Hans Ulrich Obrist (2007), Hou Hanru (2009), Victoria Noorthoorn (2011), and Gunnar B. Kvaran (2013). Their projects have transformed the Lyon Biennale into a laboratory in which to debate and question contemporary art practices, issues of history, globalization, the Other, interdisciplinarity, transmission and learning, temporality, and the biennale format as an exhibition language.

What are the main topics you are addressing in your project as far as you can tell by December 2014?

Titled *La Vie moderne*, the 2015 Lyon Biennale will bring together artists who explore the contradictory and contingent character of "modern life" as it is unfolding in different parts of the world. There is (unavoidably) an ironic dimension to this title because the word "modern" has come to seem slightly anachronistic. The notion of "modern life" is now something of a period piece, a historical relic from another century. In common parlance, of course, the word "modern" is still used to denote "new," but it now carries with it the shadow of other meanings, as we are more and more conscious of a long and complex history of various "modern" traditions. So to say something is "modern," at this point, imbues it with an aura of uncertainty in terms of its temporal framework—it suggests something haunted by history even when it is forward looking. It seems to me this captures something of our current relationships to time and history, which marks a departure from classic modernism's pretense of making a clean break from, or even suppressing, the past, or disguising its links and debts to the premodern and the contradictions they embodied. At this moment, I think we have collectively realized that there is no escape from history; instead our only choice is to work with, and through, its legacies.

Under this deliberately broad umbrella of *La Vie moderne*, the Biennale can develop in ways that (hopefully) will reflect many key concerns and experiences of contemporary life in various scenarios across the globe. Among others, these would include the growing inequality of wealth across the planet, and the spiraling development of massive slums; immigration and the highly charged and divisive politics that arise from the debt of "first world" countries to those they have colonized in the past or continue to exploit economically; the precarious position of rational thought in contemporary social and economic life; the fuzzy line between an information society and a surveillance society; the merging of physical and virtual modes of experience; and the psycho-social effects of the growing crisis of global warming, a situation where seven billion people are being held hostage, their future ransomed off to pseudo-exigencies of the present. I'm also very interested in the way that the Web has created a worldwide platform for the distribution of amateur cultural productions. As we saw with the 2013 Venice Biennale, art institutions may be ready to acknowledge the canon of outsider artists, but I think the creative output of amateurs—which can be completely brilliant and at its best is less circumscribed by convention than much contemporary art—is still problematic for the so-called art world. And as always a key concern for me as a curator is presenting art in ways that encourages the public to fully assume and play their role as collaborators. I have always taken very seriously Duchamp's assertion that the viewer is responsible for half the content of any work of art, and I am partial to artists whose approach also highlights this understanding. It's crucial for me that visitors to the Biennale experience it as a jumping off point for conversations, rather than a conclusion. In this regard, James Lee Byars' notion of a "Question Lab" seems relevant—though not in the same format he created. A biennale should be a factory for generating questions. Indeed, one of the legacies that I value most about "modern life" is the impulse, and freedom, to question things, to look askance at whatever "new normal" is being presented to us.

I also think it's crucial to find ways to mitigate the somewhat inhuman scale of biennales, and the accompanying fatigue factor that can brutally curtail our capacity to actively and creatively engage with their contents. Few Biennales in my experience seem to be designed with an idea as to how visitors can best engage with large numbers of artworks. So I am trying to think about how one might go about incorporating energizing "rest stops" and quiet spaces for recovery and reflection, so that the path through a Biennale is less like a conveyor belt.

What is the context of the Biennale you are curating in 2015?

It makes sense to me to begin by considering: who is this Biennale for? Who are its different users? And in this case, it is the residents of Lyon and the surrounding region who make up the overwhelming majority of Biennale visitors. But of course, Lyon does not exist in a vacuum: the concerns I mentioned above are issues that impact this region as they do most of France, Europe, and the other "advanced" economies. It's interesting to me that Lyon's history includes key events in the evolution of some of these above-mentioned concerns: the Lumière Brothers' first film, *Workers Leaving the Lumière Factory* (1895), already hinted at how film could modify and manipulate our perceptions of reality, while the 1981 protests in Les Minguettes, a deprived housing estate in Lyon's suburbs occupied mainly by first- and second-generation immigrants from the former colonies of the Maghreb, was a major event in the politics of immigration in France. There may be artists in the Biennale who make reference to these and other local historical events, but the larger issues at stake are hardly local. In terms of immediate context, though, it is worth mentioning that the Lyon Biennale has an exemplary ongoing parallel program, Veduta, that engages a very diverse range of local stakeholders, and I will be collaborating with its director Abdelkader Damani (one of the co-curators of the 2014 Dakar Biennale) to find various direct and often intimate ways in which artists in the Biennale can contribute works designed to be shown in different areas around the city, including in flats in housing estates.

How would you phrase its differences, its singularities, both in terms of structure and contents?

The two main venues for the Lyon Biennale are the MAC—a pristine museum designed by Renzo Piano—and La Sucrière, a former sugar factory that retains an industrial scale and look. Since our experience of artworks is inseparable from the spaces in which they are shown, I think it is important to use these very different spaces in different ways; to take advantage of the varying display strategies that each can best accommodate. So I imagine that the 2015 Lyon Biennale will be structured in a somewhat schizoid manner, comprising two separate and fairly distinct exhibitions that nevertheless reflect on similar concerns, albeit in quite different ways.

At the same time, I think the structure of a Biennale needs to deliberately incorporate space for its own moments of failure. As the Italian philosopher Nicola Abbagnano has observed (in a very different context), "Reason itself is fallible, and this fallibility must find a place in our logic." Similarly, exhibitions with the unwieldy size and dimensions of a Biennale need to account in interesting ways for the inevitable holes in their logic. A Biennale is a very particular class of exhibition—one driven, in part, by extra-artistic factors—and it inevitably defies many of the "normal" parameters and approaches that I usually value in gallery exhibition making. Rather than ignore its character, and strive to create a coherent, tightly-themed exhibition, I think it's better to deal with its particular qualities, and to see if it's possible to make a virtue—a kind of positive error—of its drawbacks.

Could you give us some details about specific projects, some of the artists invited, etc. that would exemplify the specificities and topics of your Biennale?

I will only mention two participants whose concerns are very important for me. Kader Attia's work, and particularly his investigation into notions of "repair" and the idea that present cultural production, rather than constituting something new, is a reconstruction and repair of past projects, offers a crucial alternate take on our perception of the character of "modern life." Marinella Senatore, meanwhile, will undertake a massive public production project in which residents from one of Lyon's richest suburbs and from one of its poorest suburbs will collaborate; this will not be a feel-good project, but an exploration of extreme social difference that I hope will reveal something about our social relations that we do not yet know.

At this moment, I think we have collectively realized that there is no escape from history; instead our only choice is to work with, and through, its legacies.
—Ralph Rugoff

What kind of conclusions do you draw from the current multiplication of biennales in the world and how could/would yours be an answer to this situation?

On one level, the multiplication of Biennales in the world suggests a growing interest in international contemporary art, as well as (which is not the same thing) a desire among regional cities to be seen as participating in the production of international culture. To some degree, and not unlike its 19th-century precursor, the international or "universal" *exposition*, the Biennale often aspires to be a temporary global center—and judging from the multiplication of biennales, this seems to be a symbolic positioning—and a means of leveraging a certain kind of international recognition (even if this occurs only within a small yet increasingly global arts sector)—that cultural groups operating in many kinds of cities now find desirable. (I think it's telling that neither London nor New York, arguably the two global capitals of contemporary art, put on international biennales). The fact that Biennales are generally organized by cities, rather than nations, also points to the growing role, within globalism, of the city as the generator of cultural and economic change.

For curators, this proliferation poses a dilemma and a challenge, as the endless succession of biennales inevitably increases the risk of repetition and redundancy; a relatively small group of artists seems to end up appearing in biennales around the globe, while a relatively small pool of curatorial ideas are similarly circulated. This makes a strong argument for Biennales with a specific regional focus, such as those in Havana, Dakar, and Fukuoka. Ideally the particular local-global mix of a given Biennale generates some diversity in terms of content, but this can happen only when curators and artists engage with the specific resources and concerns of a given location. That is one possible answer to the challenge posed by the global Biennale epidemic. Another answer was offered by a project in the early 1990s, the Death Valley Centennial, which took place in different sites in California's Mohave Desert. This project clearly took aim at the reassuring regularity of biennales, which recur like seasonal festivals, offering some sense of enduring structure and stability to the secular calendar. The tag line for the Death Valley Centennial? "Hope to see you at the next one!"

B

Performa 15, New York November 1–22, 2015

Founding Director and Curator: RoseLee Goldberg

Performa 15's curatorial team includes RoseLee Goldberg, Adrienne Edwards, Charles Aubin; curators-at-large Mark Beasley, Defne Ayas, and Lana Wilson; and Performa Consortium partners, including The Kitchen, PS122, Danspace Project, Roulette, The Apollo Theater, Pioneer Works Times Square, The High Line, MoMA, Bowery Ballroom, The New Museum, Abrons Arts Center, and Anthology Film Archives, among others.

Introduction

Performa, an entirely new kind of biennial for visual art and performance, was launched in New York City ten years ago, in 2005. It was to be different from other biennials in its mission to focus on the importance of live performance by visual artists throughout the history of 20th-century art, to bring performance from the sidelines into the spotlight as it were, as a way of understanding the changing landscape of contemporary art of the past hundred years from around the world. That century had been nothing less than multi-disciplinary; avant-garde artists since the early 1900s had broken new ground in filmmaking, bookmaking, poetry, choreography, performances, installations, and actions of all sorts, and these in turn would shape the direction of painting and sculpture in the decades following. Performa was established to reveal a neglected history and to make it public in the most vibrant, innovative, and highly visible ways.

Performa would not simply present an overarching survey of performance every two years, but rather would instigate new possibilities for a form perfectly poised to translate the media-saturated world of the new century. For a public not yet realizing how much they would crave active engagement as complement and antidote to lives lived on-line, the Performa Commission would both captivate and be the engine driving the overall vision of Performa. It would also be a means for showing off artists' imagination at their most innovative and experimental, outside of art market forces. Providing unparalleled support, financial and curatorial as well as production expertise and dramaturgy, Performa invited artists, many of whom had not worked with performance before, to think differently: in this new idiom they would add time and "the live" as ingredients to their work, and they would experience the unfolding of untried ideas in the presence of an audience. Encouraged to think boldly and ambitiously, each Performa Commission would be assigned a venue, both frame and container, appropriate to its content and atmosphere; tantamount to a solo exhibition, each commission used the city as urban staging ground, discovering a new neighborhood with each work.

Unlike other biennials, whose administration selects a new artistic director for each new edition, Performa has an ongoing team of curators, art historians, researchers, and producers, which has, over the decade, accrued specialized knowledge about performance, its place in art history, its contemporary forms across continents and around the globe. In other words, each Performa biennial is an extension of the last, an accumulation of scholarship and expertise built on the one before. Even as we prepare for the current biennial, long-term research is in motion for a future one. The Performa biennial is always in process.

It begins with an historical research anchor that grounds contemporary performance in the rich history that came before. For Performa 09, it was Italian Futurism, with its radical manifestos to take art out of the studio, the academy, and the museum, and into the streets, public squares, and variety theaters; for Performa 11, Russian Constructivism and its utopian impetus was a touchstone for considering how performance was used in 1920s Russia to communicate shifts in political and economic tides to a broad public; and with Performa 13, Surrealism unleashed ideas from that movement, exploring the psyche, *exquisite corps* poetry, and the pursuit of "the marvelous," with a diasporic overview from Paris to Havana and Dakar. With Performa 15 we reach back in time to the Renaissance for an extraordinary precedent to today's performance, when the social and cultural role of artists as makers of live works, of pageants and triumphal processions, court fetes and revelries, royal marriages and allegorical tableaux, was the expected order of the day. Collaborative, interdisciplinary, and site specific, such activities might include after-banquet entertainment in the form of performance paintings, royal ballets, or fireworks, which also frequently communicated unveiled messages of the politics and philosophy of the patrons who sponsored them, and their sovereign worlds.

Performa 15

Looking back to the Renaissance, and forward to a new decade with performance now firmly positioned in museums and within academia as a viable form and multi-tiered discipline to engage audiences of contemporary art and media culture, we celebrate a decade of Performa, its influence and impact. We look at the results of the innovative commissioning program that has changed the public view of what constitutes visual art performance, and that has consistently produced new markers in the history of artists' performance, and we return to some of those commissioned artists. In addition, we build on the solid structures within our curatorial pantheon; the Performa Hub, a temporary architectural commission that serves as Performa's headquarters during the three weeks of the Performa biennial, and that provides a meeting place for visitors and a venue for morning to night programming, exhibitions, and screenings; the Performa Institute that realizes a comprehensive vision for performance education and history, interfacing daily with artists, curators, and the public, with workshops, lessons by artists, and process-driven residencies, and where ideas being posited by artists in the biennial program across the city are cross-referenced and discussed; and Pavilions Without Walls, a unique curatorial program that investigates the cultural landscape of a particular country, explored and developed over a two-year period with curators, artists, and cultural institutions in that country, including visits by our curators to theirs, and a curatorial residency from that country with Performa in New York in the six-month lead-up to the biennial.

With Performa 15, the Performa biennial will once again be a lively investigative platform across disciplines, exploring not only the visual arts, but also dance, film, radio, sound, fashion, food, and architecture. Subject matter will cover a broad range of topics that do not fit under a single headline: rather, like the pages of an international newspaper, with its sections on metropolitan life, political affairs, cinema, science, literature, or sports, Performa ranges across cultural sub-sets. Performa also ranges across the city and curatorial perspectives, for the Performa biennial is the sum of many parts: presented in close collaboration with the Biennial Consortium, a selective network of New York City's most adventurous cultural institutions, Performa will once again reaffirm New York City as the performance capital of the world.

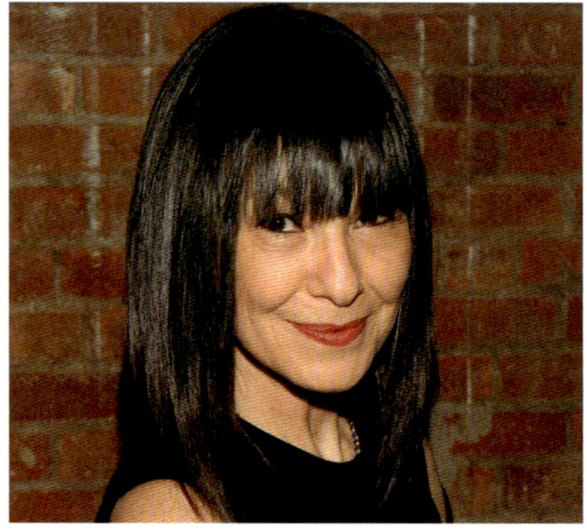

RoseLee Goldberg

Sharjah Biennial 12: *The Past, The Present, The Possible*

March 5–June 5, 2015

Artistic Director: Eungie Joo

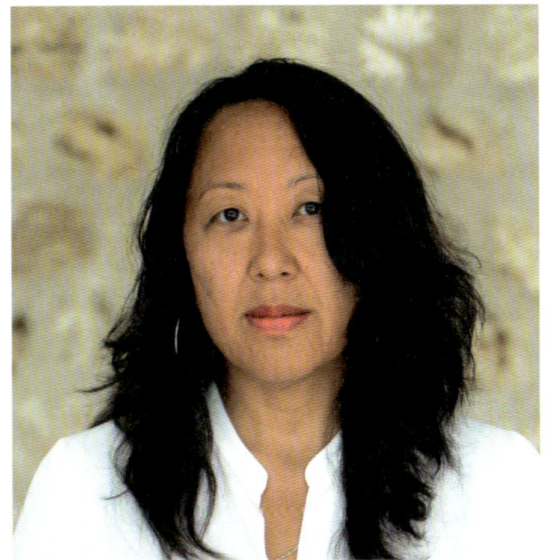

Eungie Joo

For the past two decades the Sharjah Biennial has enriched the cultural landscape of the Gulf by commissioning, producing, and presenting innovative and challenging art experiences while offering an internationally recognized platform for artists from the region.

Founded in 1993, the Sharjah Biennial has grown from a traditional and regionally focused exhibition into the global event it has become today. Originally modeled on a classic biennial format with artists chosen to officially represent each participating country, the Biennial provided a rare glimpse into the world of artistic practice. A Biennial Prize is awarded on each occasion by a jury of prominent art world figures.

In 2003, the Biennial saw a marked shift in direction as Sheikha Hoor Al Qasimi took on the role of co-curator with artist and curator Peter Lewis. With two artists at the helm, the focus turned more directly toward the art and the individual artists themselves, thereby establishing what has proven to be an enduring theme in the Biennial's future manifestations.

What are the main topics you are addressing in your project, as far as you can tell by December 2014?

Topics … A recurring yet difficult question for me, as the project—like most of my projects—rejects thematic approaches to exhibitions and also the isolation of content from formal and situational approaches to location and time. The title *The Past, The Present, The Possible* aspires to describe and evoke what little I can articulate as a conceptual thread to unite the artists, the works, the institution, and the curatorial approach. I am thinking about the present and combating hopelessness.

What is the context of the Biennial you are curating in 2015? How much does it reference the history of previous ones (locations, scope, etc.) or is it rather intended as a rupture from prior editions? How would you phrase its differences, its singularities, both in terms of structure and content?

I have only seen the past two Sharjah Biennials, and while I was interested in both editions, they were very different in terms of approach, curatorial ambition, and structure. While I think it is important to be aware of the previous Biennials and the artists, works, programs, and sites included, I don't think curatorial work is that reactionary. Instead it might be a lot about one's own head and how the curator considers contemporary art production and artists in relation to a place or time—and in this case a limited but engaged comprehension of a situation. Ultimately, Sharjah Biennial 12 will stand alone as an exhibition and series of events. What I have said in the past few months is that the Sharjah Art Foundation is one of the rare foundations in the world to offer such care and support for artists, curators, and other cultural practitioners. My goal is to share this opportunity with artists and works that make sense in this context.

I have perhaps chosen to spend a disproportionate amount of attention on the annual March Meetings, which are not necessarily organized by the Biennial curators in the non-Biennial years. I organized the panels, conversations, correspondents' open call, and structure for the March Meetings 2014 as a departure point for Sharjah Biennial 12. Almost half of the artists who are participating in the Biennial were invited to be present at that time, and were divided into group site visits prior to and following the March Meeting. The March Meeting 2015 will take place May 11–15 (away from the opening of the Biennial), and will be organized by an artist, a researcher, a curator, and a writer. They will each organize one to two days of panels and presentations related to their practice. There will be some performance and workshops nearby. The intention is to invite all the Sharjah Biennial's 12 participating artists to return to Sharjah for the March Meeting 2015 so they can experience the exhibition with some distance and share ideas with each other.

> From its inception the Sharjah Biennial has focused on commissioning artists to create new work.
> —Sheikha Hoor Al Qasimi

Could you give us some details about specific projects, some of the artists invited, etc. that would exemplify the specificities and topics of your Biennial?

You will have to wait until March 2015! Since things may change, and we are trying to accommodate what needs to happen. But work by the following artists will be presented: Basel Abbas, Ruanne Abou-Rahme, Etel Adnan, Babak Afrassiabi, Abdullah Al Saadi, Rheim Alkadhi, Ayreen Anastas, Leonor Antunes, Uriel Barthélémi, Eric Baudelaire, Mark Bradford, Unnikrishnan Chimurenga, Nikhil Chopra, Saloua Raouda Choucair, Chung Chang-Sup, Abraham Cruzvillegas, Jimmie Durham, Rene Gabri, Ahmad Ghossein, Im Heung Soon, Iman Issa, Michael Joo, Maryam Kashani, Mohammed Kazem, Hassan Khan, Kristine Khouri, Kim Beom, Byron Kim, Lee Kit, Jac Leirner, Faustin Linyekula, Jawshing Arthur Liou, Cinthia Marcelle, Rodney McMillian, Julie Mehretu, mixrice, Asunción Molinos Gordo, Eduardo Navarro, Papy Ebotani Ngoy, Damián Ortega, Lala Rukh, Rasha Salti, Hassan Sharif, Taro Shinoda, Gary Simmons, Nasrin Tabatabai, Rayyane Tabet, Rirkrit Tiravanija, Adrián Villar Rojas, Danh Vo, Xu Tan, Haegue Yang, Lynette Yiadom-Boakye, Abdul Hay Mosallam Zarara, and Fahrelnissa Zeid.

What kind of conclusions do you draw from the current multiplication of biennials in the world and how could/would yours be an answer to this situation?

Biennials serve a very important purpose, offering experimental platforms for artists and experiential/institutional platforms for publics, especially where contemporary art institutions do not exist. Some organizations are unique in the possibilities they afford and the vision of their leadership, and the Sharjah Biennial 12 embraces the opportunity to work together closely with participating artists for all these reasons and more.

56th Venice Biennale: *All the World's Futures* May 9–November 22, 2015

Artistic Director: Okwui Enwezor

In May 2015, 120 years after its first art exhibition, the International Art Exhibition of the Venice Biennale will unfold once again in the Giardini, the historical grounds where the first event took place in 1895. When that first exhibition was inaugurated there were no national pavilions. The only permanent exhibition building that existed at the time was the sepulchral structure of the Central Pavilion, with its neo-classical columns and towering winged victory perched atop the pediment. National pavilions would arrive 12 years later with the Belgian Pavilion in 1907, followed by several others in successive years, until today, standing at nearly 95 pavilions. The expansion of the pavilions in the Giardini to 30 exhibition buildings designed in various architectural styles, and the overspill of those pavilions unable to secure a plot in the Giardini itself into different areas of the city and the Arsenale area, testify to the unquestionable allure of this most anachronistic of exhibition models dedicated to national representation. Adjacent to the bourgeoning national pavilions is the non-national international exhibition in the Giardini and Arsenale.

Since its first edition, the Venice Biennale has existed at the confluence of many socio-political changes and radical historical ruptures across the fields of art, culture, politics, technology, and economics. Founded in 1893, the institution of the Venice Biennale arrived on the world stage at a significant historic period, at a point when forces of industrial modernity, capital, emergent technologies, urbanization, and colonial regimes were remaking the global map and rewriting the rules of sovereignty.

Accompanying these developments were several mass movements: from workers' to women's movements; anti-colonial to civil rights movements, etc. One hundred years after the first shots of the First World War were fired, and 75 years after the beginning of the Second World War, the global landscape again lies shattered and in disarray, scarred by violent turmoil, panicked by specters of economic crisis and viral pandemonium, secessionist politics and a humanitarian catastrophe on the high seas, in deserts, and in borderlands, as immigrants, refugees, and desperate peoples seek refuge in seemingly calmer and more prosperous lands. Everywhere one turns, new crises, uncertainty, and deepening insecurity across all regions of the world seem to leap into view.

Surveying these epic events from the vantage point of the current disquiet that pervades our time, one feels as if summoned by Paul Klee's painting *Angelus Novus*. Thanks to the philosopher and cultural critic Walter Benjamin who bought the work in 1921, the painting has acquired a kind of cult status of clairvoyance beyond its actual representation. Benjamin saw in Klee's picture what in fact was not registered nor even painted in it. Instead he read *Angelus Novus* allegorically, seeing the picture with clear historical eyes, while facing another catastrophe unfolding in Europe at a time of immense crisis. By excavating the painting as the very reality happening before him, with the state of the world he knew being dismantled right before his very own eyes, Benjamin compels us to revision the representational capacity of art. His novel interpretation of the animated stick figure standing in the middle of Klee's composition with a shocked expression in its eyes, as the "angel of history" at whose feet the wreckage of modern destruction reaches new summits, remains a vivid image. If not necessarily for what the picture actually contains and the image it registers, but for the way Benjamin brought a focus to how the work of art can challenge us to see much further and beyond the prosaic appearance of things.

The ruptures that surround and abound in and around every corner of the global landscape today recall the evanescent debris of previous catastrophes piled at the feet of the angel of history in *Angelus Novus*. How can the current disquiet of our time be properly grasped, made comprehensible, examined, and articulated? Over the course of the last two centuries, radical changes have made fascinating subject matter for artists, writers, filmmakers, performers, composers, musicians, etc. This situation is no less palpable today. It is with this recognition that in 2015 the 56th International Exhibition of the Venice Biennale proposes *All the World's Futures*, a project devoted to a fresh appraisal of the relationship of art and artists to the current state of things.

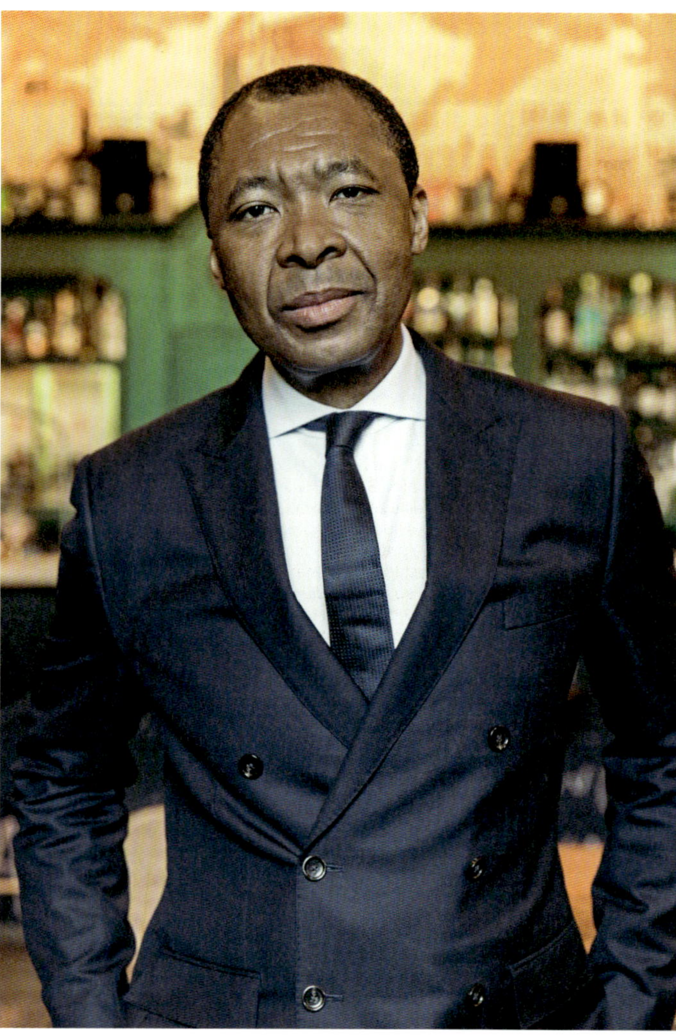

Okwui Enwezor

The Exhibition: Parliament of Forms

Rather than one overarching theme that gathers together and encapsulates diverse forms and practices into one unified field of vision, *All the World's Futures* is informed by a layer of intersecting "filters": these "filters" are a constellation of parameters that circumscribe multiple ideas, which will be touched upon to both imagine and realize a diversity of practices. In 2015, the Venice Biennial will employ the historical trajectory of the Biennale itself, over the course of its 120-year existence, as a filter through which to reflect on both the current "state of things" and the "appearance of things." *All the World's Futures* will take the present "state of things" as the ground for its dense, restless, and exploratory project that will be located in a dialectical field of references and artistic disciplines. The principal question the exhibition will pose is this: How can artists, thinkers, writers, composers, choreographers, singers, and musicians, through images, objects, words, movement, actions, lyrics, and sound bring together publics in acts of looking, listening, responding, engaging, speaking in order to make sense of the current upheaval? What material, symbolic or aesthetic, political or social acts will be produced in this dialectical field of references to give shape to an exhibition which refuses confinement within the boundaries of conventional display models? In *All the World's Futures* the curator himself, along with artists, activists, the public, and contributors of all kinds will appear as the central protagonist in the open orchestration of the project.

Over the course of the last two centuries, radical changes have made fascinating subject matter for artists, writers, filmmakers, performers, composers, musicians, etc. This situation is no less palpable today. —Okwui Enwezor

With each "filter" superimposed on another, the 56th Venice Biennale will delve into contemporary global reality as one of constant realignment, adjustment, recalibration, motility, shape-shifting. Given this fact, the presentation of *All the World's Futures* will play host to a Parliament of Forms whose orchestration and episodic unfolding will be broadly global in scope. At the core of the project is the notion of the exhibition as a stage where historical and counter-historical projects will be explored. Within this framework, aspects of the 56th Exhibition will solicit and privilege new proposals and works conceived specifically by invited artists, filmmakers, choreographers, performers, composers, and writers to work either individually or in collaboration. These projects, works, and voices, like an orchestra will occupy the spaces of the Biennale and preoccupy the time and thinking of the public.

Liveness: On Epic Duration

In the search for a language and method for the exhibition we have settled on its nature as fundamentally a visual, somatic, aural, and narrative event. In so doing, we ask how an exhibition of this scale and scope can address its format and refresh it through the potential of its temporal capacity. In this search, the concept of liveness and epic duration serve two complementary purposes: they suggest the idea that *All the World's Futures* is both a spatial and temporal manifestation that is relentlessly incomplete, structured by a logic of unfolding, a program of events that can be experienced at the intersection of liveness and display. It will be a dramatization of the space of the exhibition as a continuous, unfolding, and unceasing live event. In so doing, *All the World's Futures* will activate works that already exit, but also invite contributions that will be realized especially for the event.

Garden of Disorder

This filter, located in the Giardini, the Central Pavilion, the Arsenale, and selected areas in Venice, takes the historical ground of the Biennale in the Giardini as a metaphor through which to explore the current "state of things," namely the pervasive structure of disorder in global geopolitics, the environment, and economics. The original concept of the garden derives from Persian antiquity. It conceives of the dimension of the garden as paradise, an enclosed space of tranquility and pleasure, which over several millennia has been transformed into an allegory for the search for a space of order and purity. The 2015 Biennale returns to the ancient ground of this ideal to explore changes in the global environment, to read the Giardini with its ramshackle assemblage of pavilions as the ultimate site of a disordered world, of national conflicts, as well as territorial and geopolitical disfigurations. The artists have been invited to develop proposals that take the concept of the garden as a point of departure to realize new sculptures, films, performances, and installations.

Capital: A Live Reading

Beyond the distemper and disorder in the current "state of things," there is one pervasive preoccupation that has been at the heart of our time and modernity. Since the publication of Karl Marx's massive *Capital: Critique of Political Economy* in 1867, the structure and nature of capital has captivated thinkers and artists, as well as inspired political theorists, economists, and ideological structures across the world. *Capital* is the great drama of our age. In *All the World's Futures* the aura, effects, affects, and specters of *Capital* will be felt in one of the most ambitious explorations of this concept and term. A core part of this program of live readings is "Das Kapital," a massive meticulously researched bibliographic project, conceived for the Central Pavilion by the artistic director, starting with a live reading of the four volumes of Marx's *Das Kapital* and gradually expanding into recitals of work songs, librettos, readings of scripts, discussions, and film screenings devoted to diverse theories and explorations of *Capital*.

From this outlook, *All the World's Futures*, through its constellation of filters, will delve into the "state of things" and question "the appearance of things," shifting from the guttural enunciation of the voice to the visual and physical manifestations of the relationship between the artworks and the public.

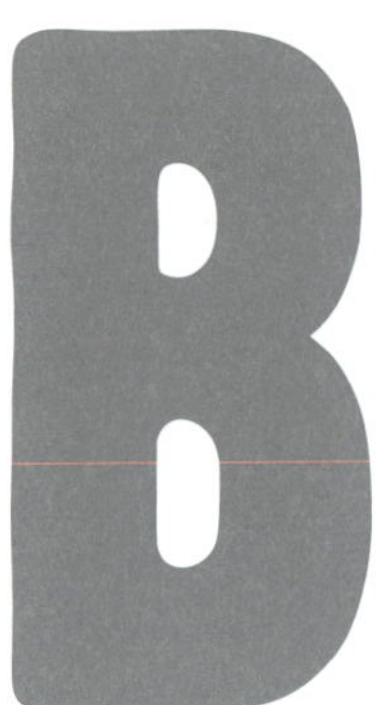

Balice Hertling

Paris
New York

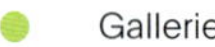 Galleries

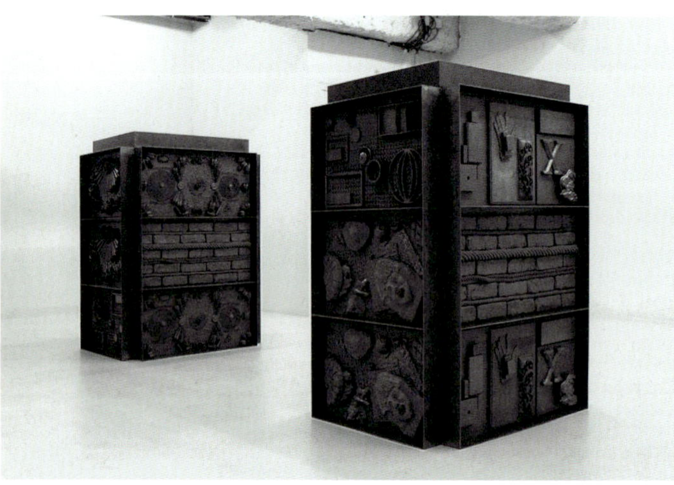

What is your favorite aspect of running a gallery?
I like to think I am able to be a mediator between the artist and the public and channel their vision to a larger public (curators, collectors, artists, art lovers, art students). I also truly enjoy spending time with artists.

How do you choose the artists you work with?
I choose artists that I think are relevant on a historical level, artists I believe are mirroring the times they live in.

If you weren't running a gallery what else would you do?
I would love to run an art magazine or an art fair.

- **Contact** — Balice Hertling, Daniele Balice, daniele@balicehertling.com
- **Established** — 2008
- **Owner(s) / Partner(s)** — Daniele Balice, Alexander Hertling
- **Team** — 4
- **Space(s)** — 100 m²
- **Artists at Art Basel** — Julie Beaufils, Neïl Beloufa, Will Benedict, Sebastian Black, Camille Blatrix, Kerstin Brätsch, Isabelle Cornaro, Mary Beth Edelson, Sam Falls, Luca Frei, Nikolas Gambaroff, Eloise Hawser, Alexander May, Greg Parma Smith, Reto Pulfer, Jon Rafman, Oscar Tuazon, Stephen Willats
- **Further artists represented** — Samuel Richardot

Baronian

Brussels

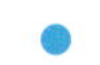 Galleries

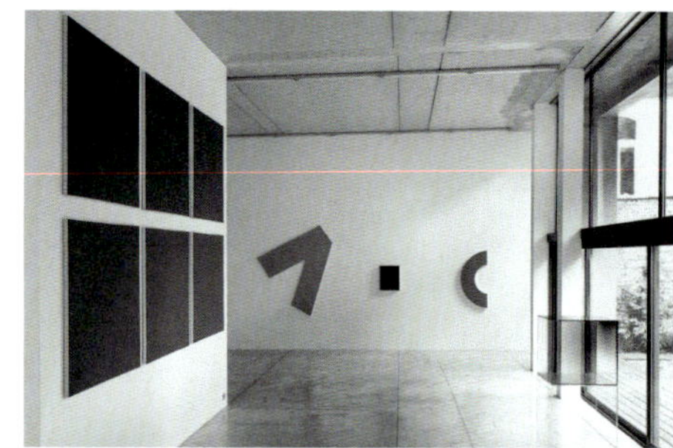

What is your favorite aspect of running a gallery?
The excitement that precedes an exhibition, or when you discover a new artist and s/he agrees to enter into the gallery's program.

How do you choose the artists you work with?
Intuitively, and through personal taste. There is an attraction toward artists whom I do not immediately understand and whose work encourages questions.

If you weren't running a gallery what else would you do?
Either a racing cyclist, professional cook, or clown.

- **Contact** — Albert Baronian, Laurence Dujardyn, laurence@albertbaronian.com
- **Established** — 1973
- **Owner(s) / Partner(s)** — Albert Baronian
- **Team** — 6
- **Space(s)** — 230 m²
- **Artists at Art Basel** — Thomas Bogaert, David Brognon & Stéphanie Rollin, Lionel Estève, Mekhitar Garabedian, Olaf Holzapfel, Florian Maier-Aichen, Tony Oursler, Benoit Platéus, David Brian Smith, Stanley Whitney, Thomas Zipp
- **Further artists represented** — Marie José Burki, Robert Devriendt, Michel Frère, Gilbert & George, Chris Johanson, Fiona Mackay, Joseph Marioni, Xavier Mary, Eric Poitevin, Ry Rocklen, Yvan Salomone, Charles Sandison, Alain Séchas, Bruno Serralongue, Helmut Stallaerts, Achraf Touloub, Marc Trivier, Wang Du, Robert Wilson, Gilberto Zorio

Barry

London ● Discoveries

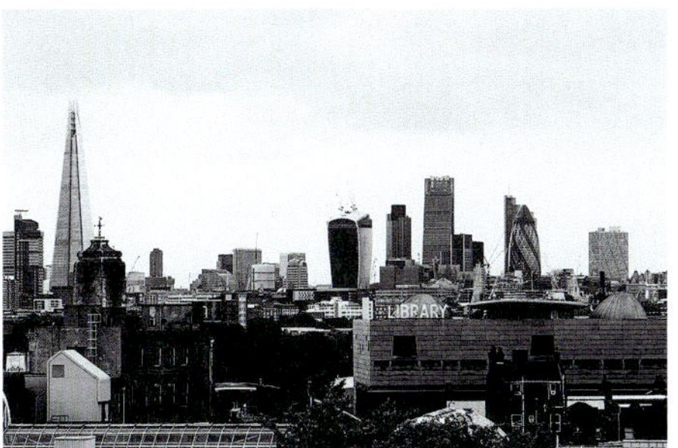

What is your favorite aspect of running a gallery?
The responsibility to artist and audience: to build knowledge and understanding of the work and continuous progress of an artist; and to feed the curiosity and enthusiasm of the audience.

How do you choose the artists you work with?
Intuition ...

- **Contact** Hannah Barry Gallery
  Hannah Barry
  hannah@hannahbarry.com
- **Established** 2008
- **Owner** Hannah Barry
- **Team** 3
- **Space(s)** 418 m²
- **Artists at Art Basel** James Capper
- **Further artists represented** Mohammed Qasim Ashfaq
  James Balmforth
  Tom Barnett
  Gareth Cadwallader
  Nathan Cash Davidson
  Bobby Dowler
  Oliver Eales
  Christopher Green
  Oliver Griffin
  Nick Jeffrey
  Marcus Kleinfeld
  Shaun McDowell
  Rob Sherwood
  Anton Zolotov

von Bartha

Basel
S-chanf ● Galleries

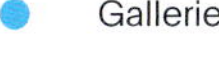

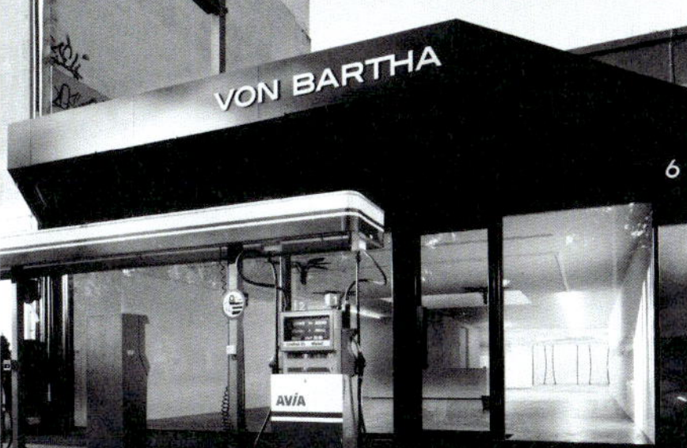

What is your favorite aspect of running a gallery?
Visiting artists' studios and preparing interesting and exciting exhibitions that will attract the public to visit the gallery.

How do you choose the artists you work with?
From the viewpoint of their compatibility with and enrichment of the gallery program.

If you weren't running a gallery what else would you do?
Despair!

- **Contact** von Bartha
  Stefan von Bartha
  stefan@vonbartha.com
- **Established** 1970
- **Owner(s) / Partner(s)** Stefan von Bartha
  Margareta von Bartha
  Miklos von Bartha
- **Team** 8
- **Space(s)** 1,100 m²
- **Artists at Art Basel** Christian Andersson
  Olle Baertling
  Andrew Bick
  Camille Graeser
  Gerhard von Graevenitz
  Terry Haggerty
  Daniel Robert Hunziker
  Imi Knoebel
  Bernhard Luginbühl
  Karim Noureldin
  Sarah Oppenheimer
  Boris Rebetez
  Bob & Roberta Smith
  Bernar Venet
  John Wood & Paul Harrison
  Beat Zoderer

Bartlett

London ● Statements

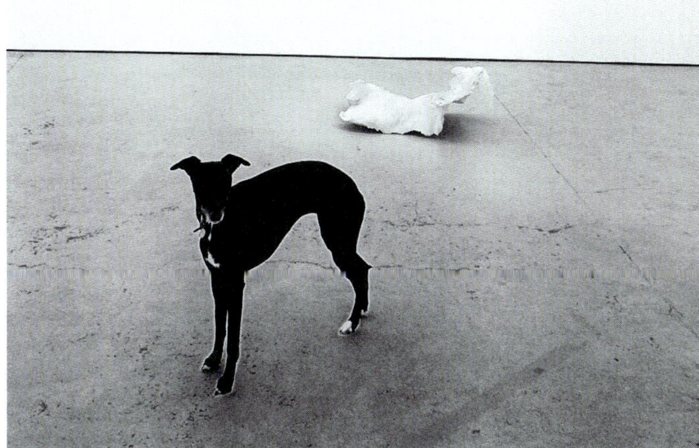

What is your favorite aspect of running a gallery?
Arriving to install an exhibition where you can just focus on the artist, the work, and the space. It's an encounter that is ultimately very personal and human. I enjoy this moment of potential and discovery. The works unfold as they begin to form an exhibition and the conversation draws out new readings.

How do you choose the artists you work with?
A conversation starts that I want to continue. There's a connection with the work, an admiration of its pursuit, and a depth of character and intellect that appeals. It's a feeling that there's something there that is important to show and help develop.

If you weren't running a gallery what else would you do?
I'd be a sheep farmer in Wales.

- **Contact** Laura Bartlett Gallery
  Laura Bartlett
  info@laurabartlettgallery.com
- **Established** 2006
- **Owner(s) / Partner(s)** Laura Bartlett
- **Team** 6
- **Space(s)** 220 m²
- **Artists at Art Basel** Marie Lund
- **Further artists represented** Becky Beasley
  Nina Beier
  Sol Calero
  John Divola
  Simon Dybbroe Møller
  Harrell Fletcher
  Cyprien Gaillard
  Beatrice Gibson
  Lydia Gifford
  Ian Law
  Elizabeth McAlpine
  Alex Olson
  Martin Skauen
  Nina Beier & Marie Lund

B

Baudach

Berlin

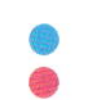

Galleries
Galleries

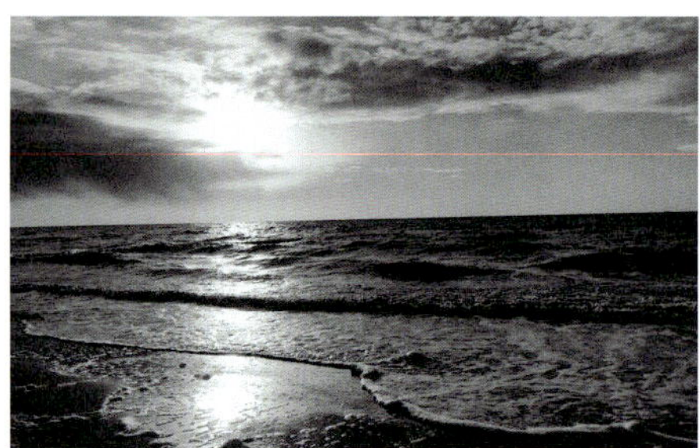

What is your favorite aspect of running a gallery?
Working with artists.

If you weren't running a gallery what else would you do?
Study and teach.

How do you choose the artists you work with?
By the quality of the work.

- **Contact** Galerie Guido W. Baudach
Guido W. Baudach
galerie@guidowbaudach.com
- **Established** 2001
- **Owner(s) / Partner(s)** Guido W. Baudach
- **Team** 6
- **Space(s)** 400 m²
- **Artists at Art Basel** Björn Dahlem
Thilo Heinzmann
Thomas Helbig
Andy Hope 1930
Erwin Kneihsl
Erik van Lieshout
Bjarne Melgaard
Aïda Ruilova
Markus Selg
Thomas Zipp
- **Further artists represented** Rashid Johnson
Jürgen Klauke

Beck & Eggeling

Düsseldorf

Galleries

What is your favorite aspect of running a gallery?
To make art emotionally visible in a historic context.

How do you choose the artists you work with?
By the quality of their oeuvre.

If you weren't running a gallery what else would you do?
Write and edit books.

- **Contact** Beck & Eggeling
Michael Beck
michael@beck-eggeling.de
- **Established** 1994
- **Owner(s) / Partner(s)** Ute Eggeling
Michael Beck
- **Team** 12
- **Space(s)** 300 m²
- **Artists at Art Basel** Marc Chagall
Gehard Demetz
Max Ernst
Katsura Funakoshi
Leiko Ikemura
Heinz Mack
Fausto Melotti
Pablo Picasso
Otto Piene
Günther Uecker
Manolo Valdés
- **Further artists represented** Magdalena Abakanowicz
Aljoscha
Nikos Aslanidis
Bertozzi & Casoni
Joachim Brohm
Wolf Hamm
Alexej Jawlensky
Ernst Ludwig Kirchner
Paul Klee
Susanne Kühn
Xavier Mascaró
Hartmut Neumann
Emil Nolde
Heribert Ottersbach
Apostolos Palavrakis
Thomas Wrede

Beijing Art Now

Beijing

Galleries

- **Contact** Beijing Art Now Gallery
Yudi Zhang
398662@qq.com
- **Established** 2004
- **Owner(s) / Partner(s)** Huang Liaoyuan

Beijing Commune

Beijing

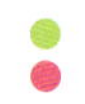

Galleries
Nova

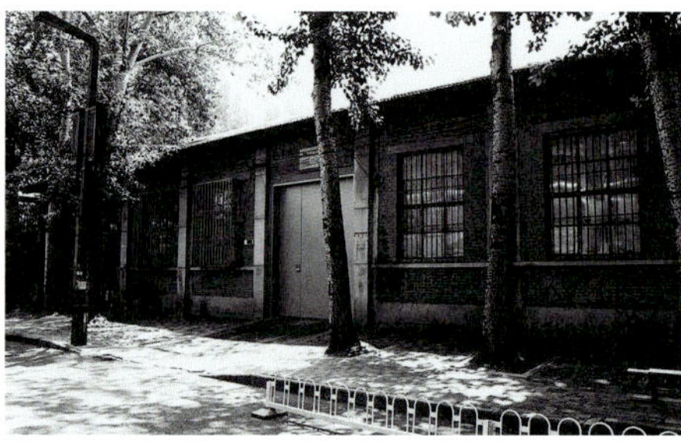

What is your favorite aspect of running a gallery?
Communicating with artists.

How do you choose the artists you work with?
I combine the trend with my understanding of the arts.

If you weren't running a gallery what else would you do?
Be an artist.

- **Contact** Beijing Commune
Jingjing Lu
lujingjing@beijingcommune.com
- **Established** 2004
- **Owner(s) / Partner(s)** Leng Lin
Lu Jingjing
- **Team** 5
- **Space(s)** 600 m²
- **Artists at Art Basel** Hu Xiaoyuan
Hong Hao
Liang Yuanwei
Ma Qiusha
Qiu Xiaofei
Song Kun
Wang Guangle
Xie Molin
Zhao Yao
Zhang Xiaogang

Benítez

Madrid 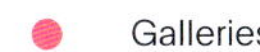 Galleries

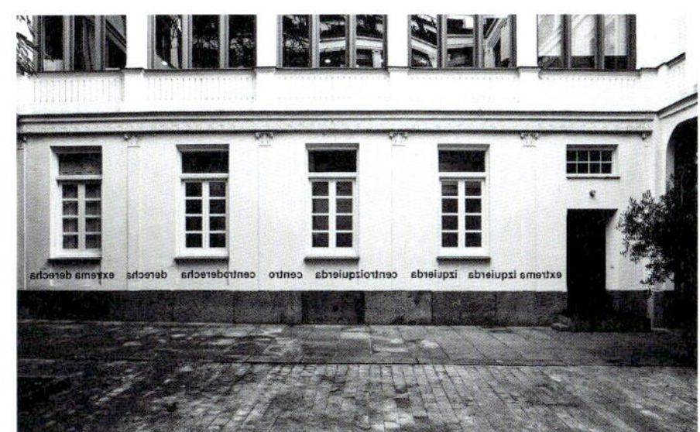

What is your favorite aspect of running a gallery?
Out of all the diverse activities a contemporary art gallery performs, it is the continuous relationship with the artists that interests me the most: conceiving a project with them, designing strategies for their career, discussing the concept that is behind their work, and, above all, learning from them.

How do you choose the artists you work with?
Initially I choose artists whose works fit inside a frame, which is the gallery's program. Since the gallery opened, this program has focused on artistic production in Latin America and artists for whom, in one way or another, architecture is a reference. I select artists whose artworks give shape to a fully developed intellectual discourse—without this condition artworks have a more decorative function.

If you weren't running a gallery what else would you do?
I would love to work in theater.

- **Contact** Galería Elba Benítez
  Pamela Cañizo
  pamela.canizo@elbabenitez.com
- **Established** 1990
- **Owner(s) / Partner(s)** Elba Benítez
- **Team** 7
- **Space(s)** 143 m²
- **Artists at Art Basel** Armando Andrade Tudela
  Carlos Bunga
  Fernanda Fragateiro
  Carlos Garaicoa
  David Goldblatt
  Cristina Iglesias
- **Further artists represented** Ignasi Aballí
  Miriam Bäckström
  Cabello/Carceller
  Juan Cruz
  Gintaras Didžiapetris
  Hreinn Fridfinnsson
  Vik Muniz
  Ernesto Neto
  Francisco Ruiz de Infante
  Francesc Torres

Benzacar

Buenos Aires  Galleries Kabinett

What is your favorite aspect of running a gallery?
In general, being able to relate to such different and interesting worlds as that of artists and that of collectors and art enthusiasts. And in particular, after 50 years, being the third generation of women to run this gallery, realizing that the core of the project maintains the same important values.

How do you choose the artists you work with?
We make a big effort to try to keep up with all the events going on in the Buenos Aires art scene and to follow the artists we find interesting. It is a lot of work, but we love visiting alternative spaces and studios. Another possible way of finding new artists we might choose to work with is hearing what the artists in our program have to say about their peers or students.

If you weren't running a gallery what else would you do?
I would probably be a doctor. I studied medicine for a few years, I do not miss it, but I loved it!

- **Contact** Ruth Benzacar Galería de Arte
  Mora Bacal
  mora@ruthbenzacar.com
- **Established** 1965
- **Owner(s) / Partner(s)** Orly Benzacar
  Mora Bacal
- **Team** 7
- **Space(s)** 700 m²
- **Artists at Art Basel** Eduardo Basualdo
  Leandro Erlich
  Sebastián Gordin
  Carlos Huffmann
  Valentina Liernur
  Jorge Macchi
  Liliana Porter
  Mariana Telleria
- **Further artists represented** Flavia Da Rin
  Marina De Caro
  Max Gomez Canle
  Carlos Herrera
  Fabio Kacero
  Luciana Lamothe
  Jazmín López
  Pablo Reinoso
  Florencia Rodriguez Giles
  Miguel Rothschild
  Mariano Sardon
  Pablo Siquier
  Adrián Villar Rojas

Bergamin

São Paulo 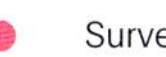 Survey

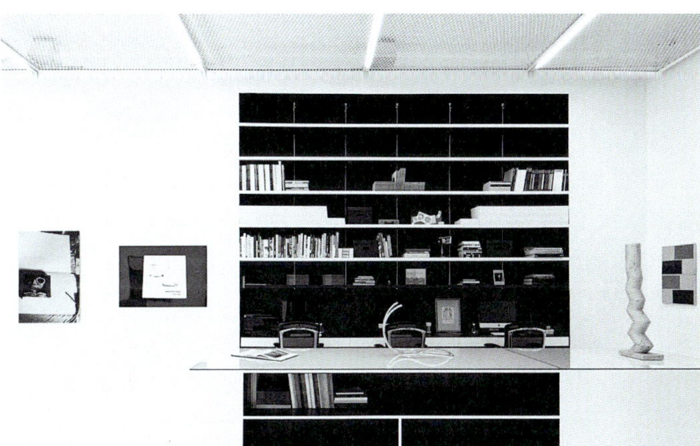

What is your favorite aspect of running a gallery?
For us our favorite aspect of running a gallery is the opportunity for a continuous learning process and a fruitful relationship with all the individuals that share the same passion, including artists, curators, collectors, advisors, and the general public. We also find it is a way to experience ideas and beliefs in a different and uniquely dedicated context. And of course, we love to spend our mornings and afternoons surrounded by great art.

How do you choose the artists you work with?
We work with artists who have made an impact on their environment—either politically, socially, or purely visually—and who have strongly influenced younger generations. We look for artists who have developed long-lasting conceptual engagements and universal languages that transcend their own cultural or political boundaries. Cildo Meireles, Lygia Pape, and Hélio Oiticica are among the artists we cherish.

If you weren't running a gallery what else would you do?
Thiago Gomide: I would be a politician.
Antonia Bergamin: If I already had enough money to support myself I think I would love to have an institute to show private collections that deserve to be available to the public.

- **Contact** Galeria Bergamin
  Antonia Bergamin
  antonia@galeriabergamin.com.br
- **Established** 2013
- **Owner(s) / Partner(s)** Antonia Bergamin
  Thiago Gomide
- **Team** 6
- **Space(s)** 150 m²

- **Artists at Art Basel** Alfredo Volpi
- **Further artists represented** Waltercio Caldas, Sergio Camargo, Aluísio Carvão, Lygia Clark, Antonio Dias, León Ferrari, Anna Maria Maiolino, Antonio Manuel, Cildo Meireles, Hélio Oiticica, Mira Schendel, Ivan Serpa, Tunga

Berggruen

San Francisco — Galleries

- **Contact** John Berggruen Gallery, Eric Lendl, eric@berggruen.com
- **Established** 1970
- **Owner(s) / Partner(s)** Gretchen Berggruen, John Berggruen

Berinson

Berlin — Galleries

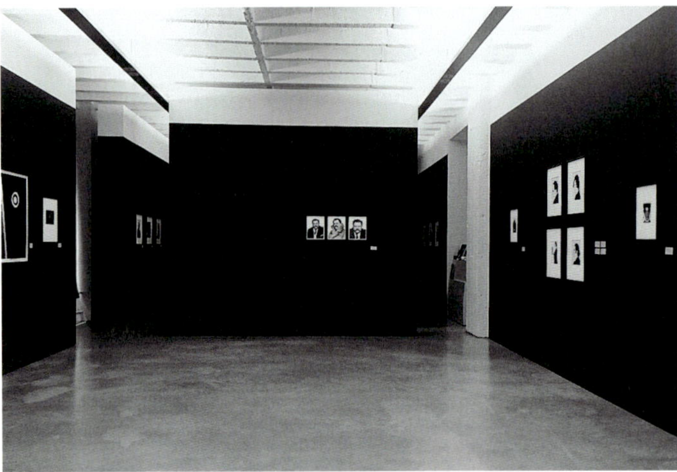

What is your favorite aspect of running a gallery?
Everything is connected.

How do you choose the artists you work with?
Everything is connected.

If you weren't running a gallery what else would you do?
Collect.

- **Contact** Galerie Berinson, Natalia Kazmierczak, info@berinson.de
- **Established** 1988
- **Owner(s) / Partner(s)** Hendrik A. Berinson
- **Team** 4
- **Space(s)** 170 m²
- **Artists at Art Basel** Alexander Archipenko, Hans Arp, Hans Bellmer, Aenne Biermann, Carl Buchheister, Erich Buchholz, Erich Comeriner, Max Ernst, Raoul Hausmann, Florence Henri, Hannah Höch, Frederick I. Kann, Almir Mavignier, Helmut Newton, Meret Oppenheim, Francis Picabia, Larry Rivers, Georg Schrimpf, Kurt Schwitters, Alina Szapocznikow, Waclaw Karol Szpakowski, Raoul Ubac, Nikolai Wassilieff, Gert Heinrich Wollheim, Andrzej Wróblewski, Unica Zürn
- **Further artists represented** Willi Baumeister, Karl Blossfeldt, Marianne Brandt, Claude Cahun, Walter Dexel, Otto Dix, Hugo Erfurth, Otto Freundlich, Carl Grossberg, George Grosz, John Heartfield, Auguste Herbin, Kurt Kranz, Alfred Kubin, Helmar Lerski, El Lissitzky, Man Ray, Moriz Melzer, Pierre Molinier, Johannes Molzahn, Georg Muche, Oskar Nerlinger, Richard Oelze, Hans Richter, Alexander Rodchenko, Franz Roh, Werner Rohde, August Sander, Oskar Schlemmer, Rudolf Schlichter, Arthur Segal, Samuel Szczekacz, Friedrich Vordemberge-Gildewart, Weegee, Wols

Bernier/Eliades

Athens — Galleries, Galleries, Galleries

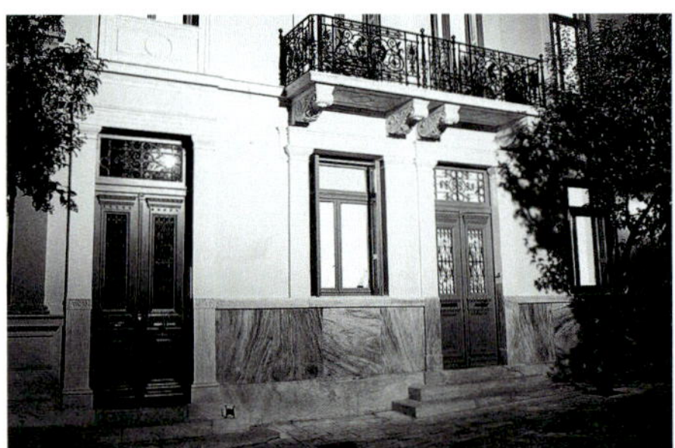

- **Contact** Bernier/Eliades, Marina Eliades, bernier@bernier-eliades.gr
- **Established** 1977
- **Owner(s) / Partner(s)** Jean Bernier, Marina Eliades
- **Team** 4
- **Artists at Art Basel** Giovanni Anselmo, Pier Paolo Calzolari, Wim Delvoye, Lionel Estève, Edy Ferguson, Gilbert & George, Hannah Greely, Zhang Hui, Cameron Jamie, Dionisis Kavallieratos, Jannis Kounellis, Moshekwa Langa, Justin Lieberman, Christiane Löhr, Richard Long, Valérie Mannaerts, Jonathan Meese, Mario Merz, Marisa Merz, Annette Messager, Tony Oursler

Lari Pittman
Daniel Richter
Susan Rothenberg
Ulrich Rückriem
Charles Sandison
Thomas Schütte
Jim Shaw
Keith Sonnier
Christiana Soulou
Liang Wei
Entang Wiharso
Sue Williams
Robert Wilson
Zhu Yu

- **Further artists represented** Stéphane Calais
Alan Charlton
Tony Cragg
Juan Muñoz
Nikos Navridis
Ed Ruscha
Marnie Weber

Fondation Beyeler

Riehen/Basel

Galleries
Galleries

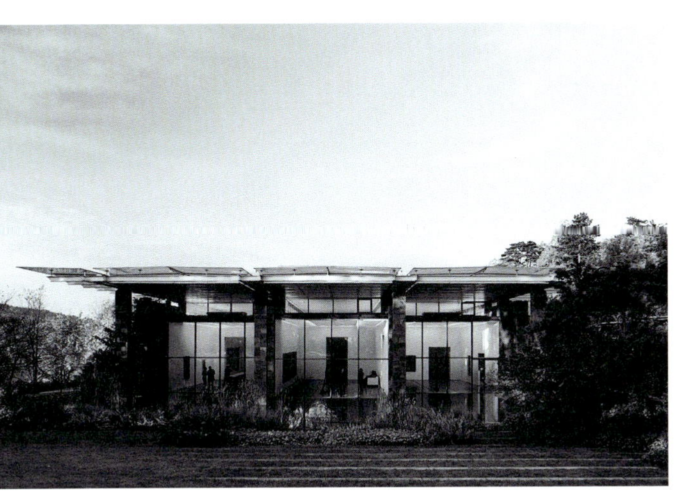

- **Contact** Fondation Beyeler
www.fondationbeyeler.ch
- **Director** Sam Keller
- **Exhibitions at Art Basel** *14 Rooms*, Georg Baselitz, Marina Abramović Institute

---

bitforms

New York

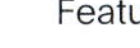

Feature

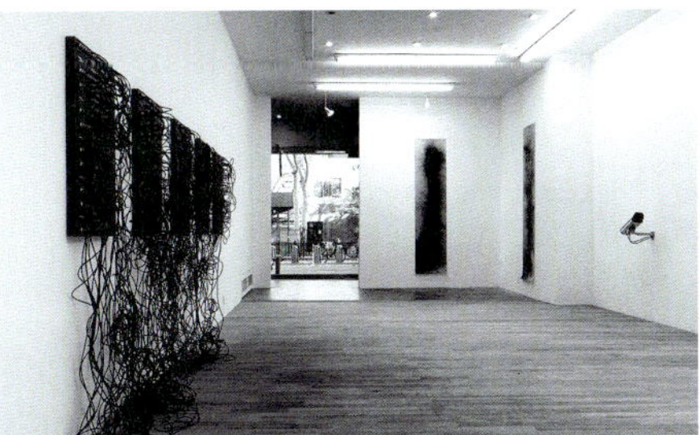

What is your favorite aspect of running a gallery?

Interaction with a wide range of innovative thinkers.

How do you choose the artists you work with?

The gallery specializes in the visual discourse of new media culture. We draw upon a diverse range of disciplines and intellectual perspectives while maintaining a clear progressive thread. The artists in our program must match these criteria.

If you weren't running a gallery what else would you do?

I enjoy design and architecture.

- **Contact** bitforms gallery
Steven Sacks
steve@bitforms.com
- **Established** 2001
- **Owner(s) / Partner(s)** Steven Sacks
- **Team** 5
- **Space(s)** 167.5 m²
- **Artists at Art Basel** Beryl Korot
- **Further artists represented** Daniel Canogar
R. Luke DuBois
Claudia Hart
Yael Kanarek
Rafael Lozano-Hemmer
Manfred Mohr
Quayola
Casey Reas
Erwin Redl
Daniel Rozin
Björn Schülke
Addie Wagenknecht
Zimoun
Marina Zurkow

Bjerggaard

Copenhagen

Survey

What is your favorite aspect of running a gallery?

Building a bridge between an artist's work and the public is key and our reason for being.

How do you choose the artists you work with?

Chemistry is crucial! Every collaboration has its own story and own way of functioning.

If you weren't running a gallery what else would you do?

No clue! When a gallerist you must live and breathe for art!

- **Contact** Galleri Bo Bjerggaard
Bibi Saugman
bibi@bjerggaard.com
- **Established** 1999
- **Owner(s) / Partner(s)** Bo Bjerggaard
Britt Bjerggaard
Morten Korsgaard
- **Team** 10
- **Space(s)** 1,087 m²
- **Artists at Art Basel** Poul Gernes
- **Further artists represented** Darren Almond
Ivan Andersen
Anna Barriball
Georg Baselitz
Per Inge Bjørlo
A K Dolven
Poul Gernes
Federico Herrero
Per Bak Jensen
Per Kirkeby
John Kørner
Jannis Kounellis
Bo Christian Larsson
Peter Linde Busk
Jonathan Meese
Tal R
Daniel Richter
Eva Schlegel
Erik Steffensen
Eve Sussman
Janaina Tschäpe
Marcel van Eeden
Brigitte Waldach
Erwin Wurm

Blau

Munich
London  Galleries

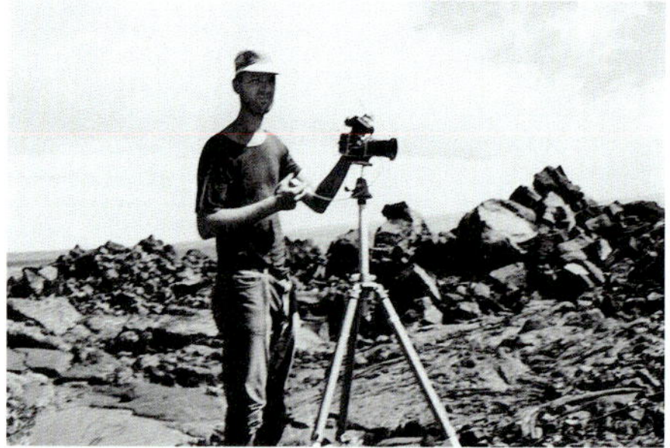

What is your favorite aspect of running a gallery?
Running a gallery allows me to look in so many drawers, under so many beds, and behind so many doors.

How do you choose the artists you work with?
In retrospect it seems as if I have been chosen by the artists, which is interesting because most of our artists are long dead.

If you weren't running a gallery what else would you do?
"Beam me up, Scotty," or I would be accompanying James Cook; but it seems as if I was born in the wrong time.

- **Contact** Daniel Blau
  Laura Seiler
  contact@danielblau.com
- **Established** 1990
- **Owner(s) / Partner(s)** Daniel Blau
- **Team** 10
- **Space(s)** 300 m²
- **Artists at Art Basel** Andy Warhol
- **Further artists represented** Georg Baselitz
  Glen Baxter
  Jake & Dinos Chapman
  Chuck Close
  Christa Dichgans
  Barry Flanagan
  Neal Fox
  Lucian Freud
  Poul Gernes
  George Grosz
  Antonius Höckelmann
  Anselm Kiefer
  Per Kirkeby
  Rachel Kneebone
  LE GUN Collective
  Eugène Leroy
  Markus Lüpertz
  Matt Mullican
  A.R. Penck
  Marc Quinn
  Stephanie von Reiswitz
  Robert Rubbish
  Don Van Vliet

Blindspot

Hong Kong 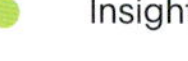 Insights

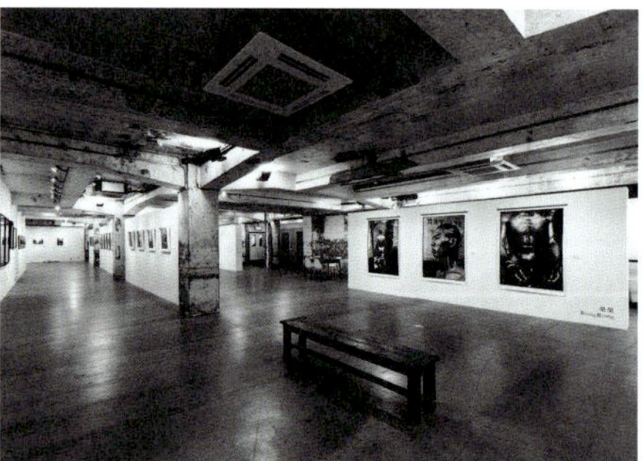

What is your favorite aspect of running a gallery?
My favorite aspect of running a gallery is being able to work with artists. It gives me an opportunity to learn more about their work and to create exhibitions together. It is also extremely rewarding when I can connect the artists with collectors and help artists grow.

How do you choose the artists you work with?
I choose the artists I work with mainly through research and sometimes introduction by curators. I always take a long time to observe the development of an artist, but there are also times when I choose young artists by instinct.

- **Contact** Blindspot Gallery
  Mimi Chun
  mimi@blindspotgallery.com
- **Established** 2010
- **Owner(s) / Partner(s)** Mimi Chun
- **Team** 3
- **Space(s)** 750 m²
- **Artists at Art Basel** Trevor Yeung
- **Further artists represented** Anothermountainman (Stanley Wong)
  Jiang Pengyi
  Nadav Kander
  Ken Kitano
  Martin Parr
  Ren Hang
  Rongrong
  Wong Wobik
  Zhang Xiao

Blondeau

Geneva  Galleries

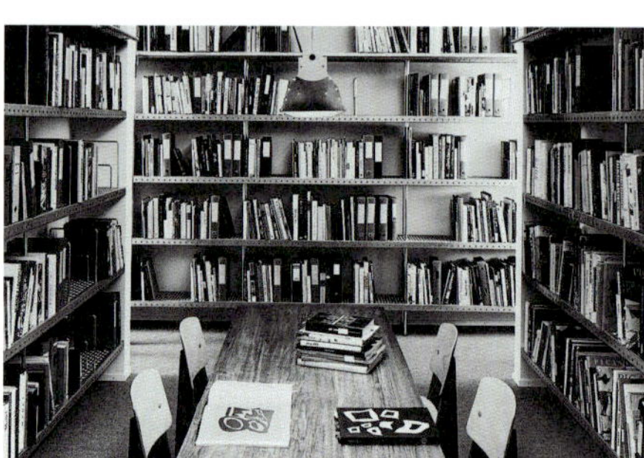

What is your favorite aspect of running a gallery?
The pleasure of setting up a challenging exhibition project.

How do you choose the artists you work with?
In reference to my partner's and my own sensibility.

If you weren't running a gallery what else would you do?
I would devote my time to putting together tailor-made collections.

- **Contact** Blondeau & Cie
  Philippe Davet
  muse@blondeau.ch
- **Established** 2000
- **Owner(s) / Partner(s)** Marc Blondeau
  Philippe Davet
- **Team** 5
- **Space(s)** 1,000 m²
- **Artists at Art Basel** Jean Arp
  Jean Dubuffet
  Mike Kelley
  Martin Kippenberger
  Louise Lawler
  Sol LeWitt
  David Maljkovic
  Henri Matisse
  Albert Oehlen
  Raymond Pettibon
  Jim Shaw
  Alessandro Twombly

Blum

New York

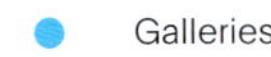

Galleries

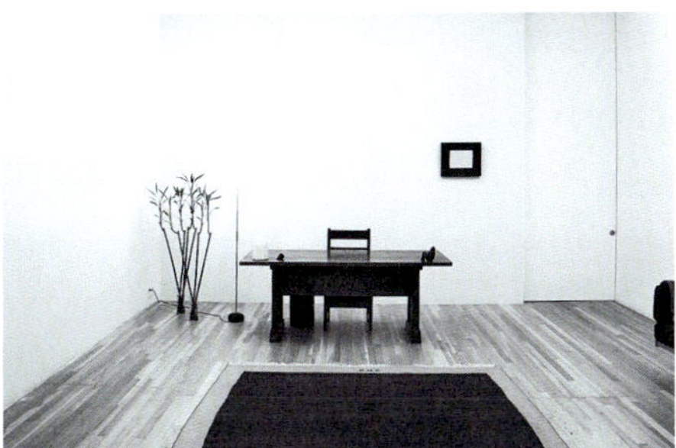

What is your favorite aspect of running a gallery?

My favorite aspect of running a gallery is the production of an exhibition—from the initial visit to the artist's studio to see the works, to discussing ideas for the exhibition, and ending with the installation and the opening at the gallery. The gallery is a place for communication between artist, client, and gallerist.

How do you choose the artists you work with?

For me, the most important discovery of new artists is through other artists. If an artist I show and respect recommends I see an artist, I never neglect to do so. Of course there are exceptions to this, such as when I see an exhibition and discover among the artists a talent I would like to pursue. I have also been pointed in the direction of new artists by curators whose vision I respect.

If you weren't running a gallery what else would you do?

It is difficult for me to imagine not running a gallery, but with my love of books I would probably choose to open a bookshop.

- **Contact** Peter Blum Gallery
David Blum
art@peterblumgallery.com
- **Established** 1993
- **Owner(s) / Partner(s)** Peter Blum
- **Team** 6
- **Artists at Art Basel** Louise Bourgeois
Alex Katz
Yves Klein
Yayoi Kusama
Agnes Martin
Robert Ryman
Robert Zandvliet
John Zurier
- **Further artists represented** John Beech
Huma Bhabha
Helmut Federle
Rosy Keyser
Esther Kläs
Chris Marker
Richard Allen Morris
Luisa Rabbia
David Rabinowitch
David Reed
Daniel Rich
Su-Mei Tse

Blum & Poe

Los Angeles
New York
Tokyo

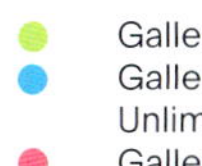

Galleries
Galleries
Unlimited
Galleries

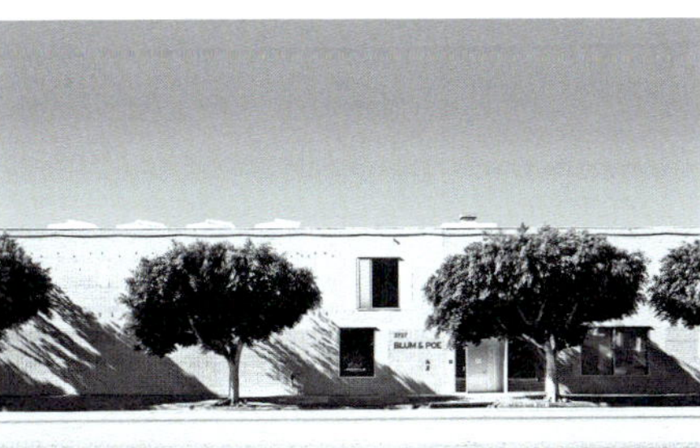

What is your favorite aspect of running a gallery?

Organizing exhibitions and working with artists.

How do you choose the artists you work with?

Very carefully.

If you weren't running a gallery what else would you do?

Movie star.

- **Contact** Blum & Poe
Sarvia Jasso
sarvia@blumandpoe.com
- **Established** 1994
- **Owner(s) / Partner(s)** Tim Blum
Jeff Poe
- **Team** 20
- **Space(s)** 2,415.5 m²
- **Artists at Art Basel** Alma Allen
Karel Appel
Sam Durant
Anya Gallaccio
Mark Grotjahn
Julian Hoeber
Matt Johnson
Gavin Kenyon
Friedrich Kunath
Linder
Florian Maier-Aichen
Dave Muller
Takashi Murakami
Yoshitomo Nara
Matt Saunders
Hugh Scott-Douglas
Jim Shaw
Penny Slinger
Kishio Suga
Henry Taylor
Michael Wilkinson
- **Further artists represented** Chico Aoshima
Darren Bader
J.B. Blunk
Slater Bradley
Chuck Close
Nigel Cooke
Carroll Dunham
Kōji Enokura
Tim Hawkinson
Drew Heitzler
Susumo Koshimizu
Shio Kusaka
Lee Ufan
Sharon Lockhart
Victor Man
Nobuo Sekine
Dirk Skreber
Keith Tyson
Chris Vasell
Zhang Huan
Zhu Jinshi

Boers-Li

Beijing

Galleries

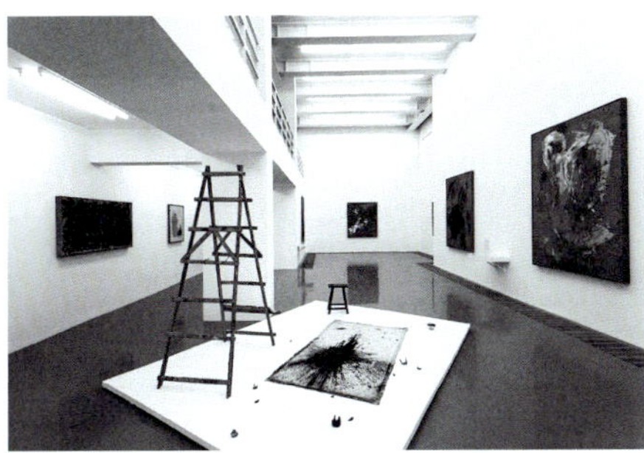

What is your favorite aspect of running a gallery?

Getting to know and appreciate artworks in the most direct and comprehensive way.

How do you choose the artists you work with?

Browsing through and filtering all sorts of resources, as well as discussions with artists.

If you weren't running a gallery what else would you do?

I would open an art gallery.

- **Contact** Boers-Li Gallery
Waling Boers
w.boers@boersligallery.com
- **Established** 2005
- **Owner(s) / Partner(s)** Waling Boers
- **Team** 10
- **Space(s)** 1,700 m²
- **Artists at Art Basel** Chen Yujun
Feng Guodong
Huang Rui
Liao Guohe
Li Shan
Ma Kelu
MAP Office
Song Kun
Xue Feng
Yang Xinguang
Zhang Peili
Zhang Wei
- **Further artists represented** Chen Shaoxiong
Fang Lu
Gade
Gong Jian
Ji Lei
Kang Wanhua
Lei Benben
Liu Heung Shing
Ma Yanhong
Qiu Anxiong
Tang Song
Xie Zhengli
Wang Wei
Zeng Hong
Zhan Rui

Boesky

New York — Galleries; Galleries Public

What is your favorite aspect of running a gallery?

I love that no two days are ever the same.

How do you choose the artists you work with?

Nineteen years into having my gallery, this process has changed a lot and is driven more and more by the artists in the program already; a conversation with myself and my team as to who and what will be additive to the incredible artists we already work with.

If you weren't running a gallery what else would you do?

I am not terribly qualified to do anything else! And I love what I do. Though in my fantasy life, real estate developer might make the top of my list.

- **Contact** Marianne Boesky Gallery
Adrian Turner
adrian@marianneboeskygallery.com
- **Established** 1996
- **Owner(s) / Partner(s)** Marianne Boesky
- **Team** 16
- **Artists at Art Basel** Diana Al-Hadid
Andisheh Avini
Pier Paolo Calzolari
Julia Dault
Barnaby Furnas
Jay Heikes
Donald Moffett
William O'Brien
Hans Op de Beeck
Roxy Paine
Anthony Pearson
Frank Stella
Kon Trubkovich
Claudia Wieser
- **Further artists represented** Matthias Bitzer
Sue de Beer
Svenja Deininger
Robert Elfgen
Rachel Feinstein
Melissa Gordon
Adam Helms
Yuichi Higashionna
Jessica Jackson
Hutchins
Dean Levin
Serge Alain Nitegeka
Jacco Olivier
Thiago Rocha Pitta
Mindy Shapero
Hannah van Bart
John Waters

BolteLang

Zurich — Discoveries

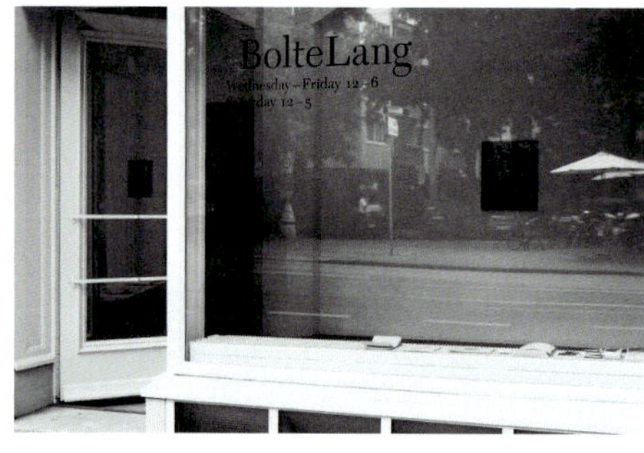

What is your favorite aspect of running a gallery?

We get to work closely with all kinds of people, to develop ideas and projects, and to travel.

How do you choose the artists you work with?

The work needs to speak to both of us, and we need to get along with the artist.

If you weren't running a gallery what else would you do?

We would be running a deli—breakfast and good coffee in the morning, freshly made food for lunch, and excellent cocktails in the evening.

- **Contact** BolteLang
Anna Bolte
anna@boltelang.com
- **Established** 2008
- **Owner(s) / Partner(s)** Anna Bolte
Chaja Lang
- **Team** 3
- **Space(s)** 115 m²
- **Artists at Art Basel** Daniel Gustav Cramer
- **Further artists represented** Vanessa Billy
Bianca Brunner
Claudia Comte
Patrick Hari
Dagmar Heppner
Benjamin Senior
Jill Spector

Bonakdar

New York — Galleries; Galleries Public

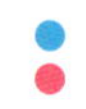

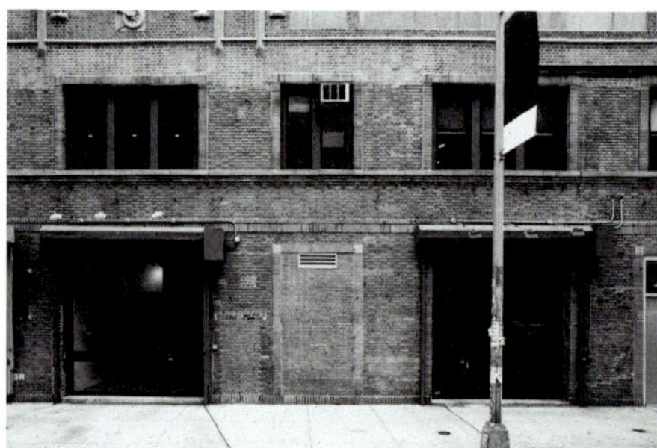

- **Contact** Tanya Bonakdar Gallery
Ethan Sklar
mail@tanyabonakdargallery.com
- **Established** 1994
- **Owner(s) / Partner(s)** Tanya Bonakdar
- **Team** 12
- **Space(s)** 512 m²
- **Artists at Art Basel** Uta Barth
Martin Boyce
Sandra Cinto
Phil Collins
Mat Collishaw
Mark Dion

Olafur Eliasson
Meschac Gaba
Siobhán Hapaska
Sabine Hornig
T. Hubbard/A. Birchler
Carla Klein
Agnieszka Kurant
Liz Larner
Charles Long
Rita Lundqvist
Mark Manders
Jason Meadows
Ernesto Neto
Rivane Neuenschwander
Susan Philipsz
Peggy Preheim
Analia Saban
Tomás Saraceno
Thomas Scheibitz
Hannah Starkey
Haim Steinbach
Dirk Stewen
Jack Strange
Sarah Sze
Neal Tait
Jeffrey Vallance
Gillian Wearing
Nicole Wermers
Michael Wilkinson

Boone

New York 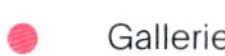 Galleries

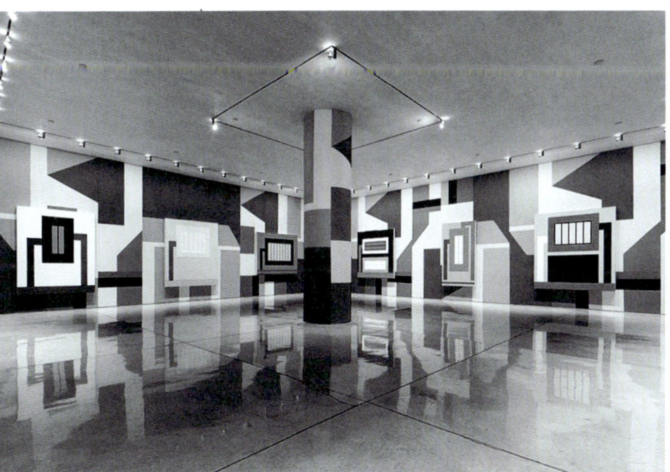

- **Contact** — Mary Boone Gallery, Mary Boone, info@maryboonegallery.com
- **Established** — 1977
- **Owner(s) / Partner(s)** — Mary Boone, Ron Warren
- **Space(s)** — 372 m^2
- **Artists at Art Basel** — Ai Weiwei, Ross Bleckner, Francesco Clemente, Will Cotton, Eric Fischl, Tomoo Gokita, Peter Halley, Hilary Harkness, Jacob Hashimoto, Kaws, Barbara Kruger, Liu Xiaodong, Peter Saul, Joe Zucker

Borch Jensen

Copenhagen
Berlin 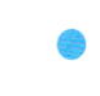 Edition Unlimited

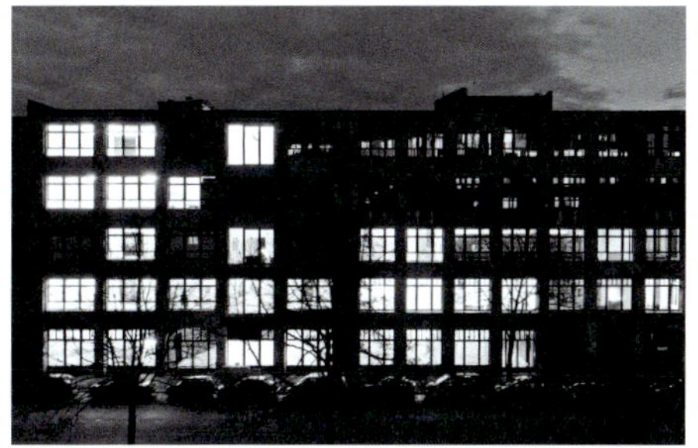

What is your favorite aspect of running a gallery?

Selling works I love to people who love them.

How do you choose the artists you work with?

I listen a lot to the artists I already work with, but in the end it comes down to personal gut reaction.

If you weren't running a gallery what else would you do?

I actually already do other things than running a gallery.

- **Contact** — Niels Borch Jensen Gallery and Editions, Lone Weigelt, lone@nielsborchjensen.com
- **Established** — 1979
- **Owner** — Niels Borch Jensen
- **Team** — 12
- **Space(s)** — 985 m^2
- **Artists at Art Basel** — Lewis Baltz, Anna Barriball, Georg Baselitz, Iñaki Bonillas, Peter Linde Busk, Tacita Dean, Thomas Demand, Olafur Eliasson, Michael Elmgreen & Ingar Dragset, Douglas Gordon, Rodney Graham, Anton Henning, Carsten Höller, Olav Christopher Jenssen, Adam Jeppesen, Clay Ketter, Martin Kippenberger, Hubert Kiecol, Per Kirkeby, Takehito Koganezawa, Bjarne Melgaard, Boris Mikhailov, Albert Oehlen, João Penalva, Tal R, Robin Rhode, Tomas Saraceno, Matt Saunders, Thaddeus Strode, Superflex, Al Taylor, Rosemarie Trockel, Alan Uglow, Sandra Vasquez de la Horra, Danh Vo
- **Further artists represented** — William Anastasi, Per Arnoldi, Per Bak Jensen, Huma Bhabha, Jens Birkemose, Lise Blomberg, Peter Bonde, Max M. Book, Jes Brinch, Janet Cardiff & George Bures Miller, Claus Carstensen, Peter Doig, A K Dolven, Stephen Ellis, Jeffrey Eugenides, Kirsten Everberg, Ceal Floyer, Erik A. Frandsen, Günther Förg, Nils Erik Gjerdevik

Joachim Grommek
Marianne Grønnow
Mathew Hale
Keith Haring
Stefan Hirsig
Damien Hirst
Peter Holst Henckel
Adi Holzer
Preben Hornung
Frans Jacobi
Linda Karshan
Eske Kath
Walter Kranz
Elke Krystufek
John Kørner
Sean Landers
Toni Larsen
Christian Lemmerz
Eva Löfdahl
Michel Majerus
H. M. Queen Margrethe II
Søren Martinsen
John Miller
Bjørn Nørgaard
Knud Odde
Chris Ofili
A. R. Penck
Lars Bent Petersen
Lars Ravn
Niels Reumert
Daniel Richter
Peter Rössell
Jørgen Rømer
Tom Sandberg
Morten Schelde
David Shrigley
Stephanie Snider
Simon Starling
Jan Svenungsson
Trine Søndergaard
& Nicolai Howalt
Nicholas Taylor
Alexander Tovborg
Katrin Von Maltzahn
Mark Wallinger
Rachel Whiteread
Troels Wörsel
Michel Würthle
Karen Yama

Bortolami

New York

- Galleries Unlimited
- Galleries

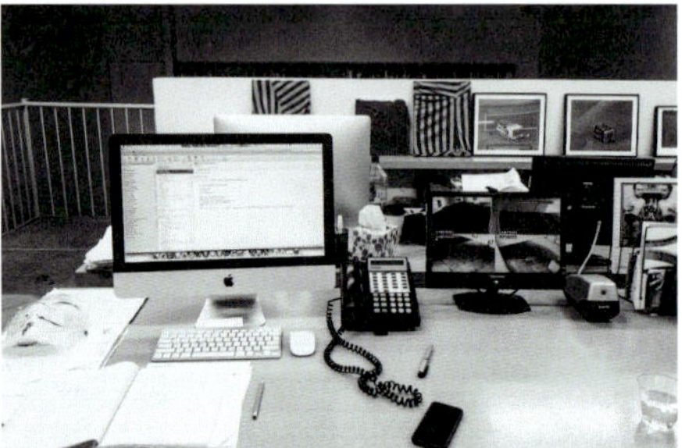

What is your favorite aspect of running a gallery?
Furthering the careers of artists that I believe in.

How do you choose the artists you work with?
I become interested in artists when they surprise me.

If you weren't running a gallery what else would you do?
Had I the financial means, I would be a collector.

- **Contact** Bortolami
Stefania Bortolami
stefania@bortolamigallery.com
- **Established** 2005
- **Owner(s) / Partner(s)** Stefania Bortolami
Christine Messineo
- **Team** 10
- **Space(s)** 464 m²
- **Artists at Art Basel** Richard Aldrich
Will Benedict
Daniel Buren
Tom Burr
Morgan Fisher
Barbara Kasten
Jutta Koether
Anna Ostoya
- **Further artists represented** Avner Ben-Gal
Michel François
Piero Golia
Nicolás Guagnini
Thilo Heinzmann
Scott King
Jonathan Meese
Ben Schumacher
Gary Webb
Eric Wesley

Bortolozzi

Berlin

- Galleries Unlimited

- **Contact** Galerie Isabella Bortolozzi
Saehee Hwang
info@bortolozzi.com
- **Established** 2004
- **Owner(s) / Partner(s)** Isabella Bortolozzi
- **Team** 6
- **Space(s)** 140 m² (main space)
220 m² (Eden Eden)
- **Artists at Art Basel** Leonor Antunes
Jos De Gruyter & Harald Thys
Oscar Murillo
Susan Philipsz
Carol Rama
Stephen G. Rhodes
Wu Tsang
- **Further artists represented** Yuri Ancarani
Ibon Aranberri
Ed Atkins
Juliette Blightman
Andrea Branzi
Jay Chung & Q Takeki Maeda
Pierre Klossowski
Maria Lai
Danny McDonald
Seth Price
Nora Schultz
Danh Vo
Betty Woodman

BQ

Berlin

- Galleries
- Galleries

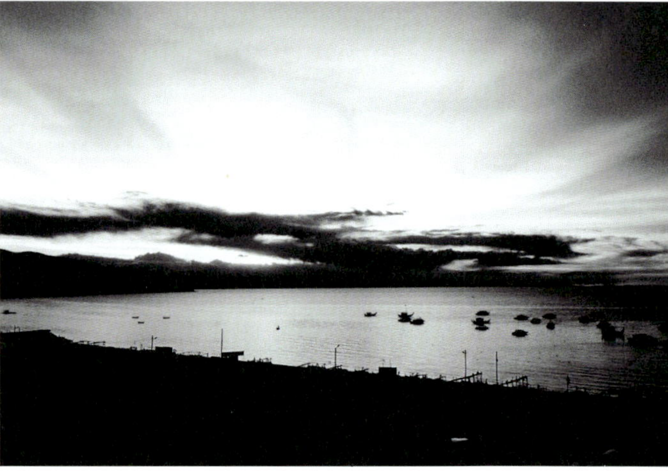

What is your favorite aspect of running a gallery?
The moment when new artworks arrive and fill the space, physically and intellectually.

How do you choose the artists you work with?
When we think about new artists for our gallery, we ask ourselves if they could become friends. As we run our gallery with our artists like a family business we have to trust each other in good and

bad times. If you share only the success, problems are inevitable.

If you weren't running a gallery what else would you do?
We would work in a zoo.

- **Contact** BQ
  Jörn Bötnagel
  info@bqberlin.de
- **Established** 1998
- **Owner(s) / Partner(s)** Jörn Bötnagel
  Yvonne Quirmbach
- **Team** 3
- **Space(s)** 200 m²
- **Artists at Art Basel** Dirk Bell
  Alexandra Bircken
  Carina Brandes
  Kriwet
  Friedrich Kunath
  Ruth Nemet
  David Shrigley
- **Further artists represented** Matti Braun
  Owen Gump
  Andrew Kerr
  Bojan Šarčević
  Marcus Steinweg
  Reinhard Voigt
  Richard Wright

Brame & Lorenceau

Paris 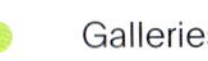 Galleries

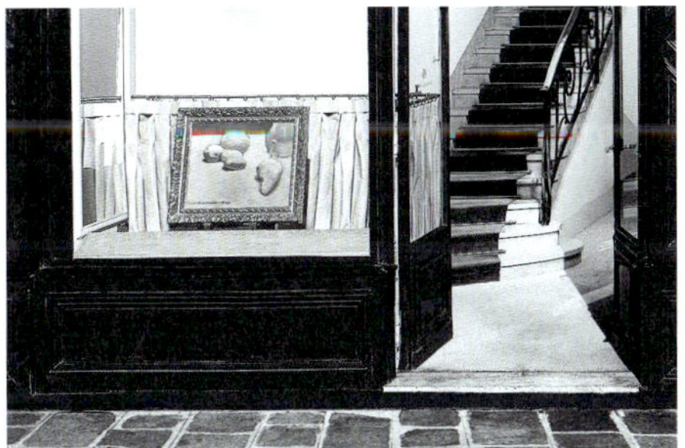

What is your favorite aspect of running a gallery?
As art dealers, we appreciate participating in the elaboration of both private and institutional collections and seeing the evolution and the meaning they give to their art quest over the years.

How do you choose the artists you work with?
Our selection is concentrated on the secondary market; we represent internationally recognized artists. We try to select qualitative works that we find emblematic of the artist's spirit.

If you weren't running a gallery what else would you do?
Since the gallery has been run by our families for the past 150 years, it felt natural to pursue this activity.

- **Contact** Brame & Lorenceau
  Thomas Lorenceau
  contact@gbl.fr
- **Established** 1864
- **Owner(s) / Partner(s)** François Lorenceau
- **Team** 12
- **Space(s)** 500 m²
- **Artists at Art Basel** Hans Arp
  Victor Brauner
  Alexander Calder
  Marc Chagall
  Olivier Debré
  Edgar Degas
  Sonia Delaunay
  Jean Dubuffet
  Max Ernst
  Sam Francis
  Hans Hartung
  Henri Matisse
  Joan Miró
  Amedeo Modigliani
  Pablo Picasso
  Serge Poliakoff
  Sayed Haider Raza
  Nicolas de Staël
  Kees van Dongen
  Bernar Venet
  Maria-Helena Vieira da Silva
  Zao Wou-Ki
- **Further artists represented** Georges Braque
  Maurice Estève
  Jean Fautrier
  Alberto Giacometti
  Yves Klein
  Roger de La Fresnaye
  Fernand Léger
  Henry Moore
  Niki de Saint Phalle
  Georges Seurat
  Pierre Soulages
  Henri Toulouse Lautrec
  Manolo Valdés
  Tom Wesselmann

Breeder

Athens 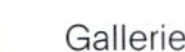 Galleries

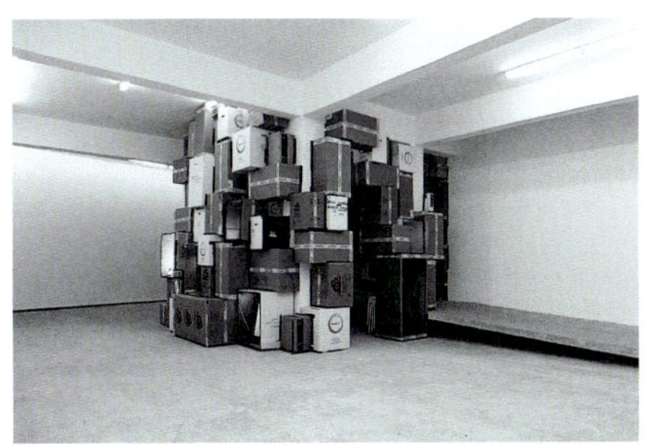

What is your favorite aspect of running a gallery?
Getting to interact with the artists and their work! We are fascinated every time we see an exhibition coming to life, watching the artist realizing their vision while transforming the space. It is a priceless experience. Even in the simplest installation, it is enchanting to feel the osmosis between the artworks and the gallery space.

How do you choose the artists you work with?
The relation with the artist is like a marriage, it's meant to be a commitment for life. You need to believe in a great future and loads of potential. And because the journey can be rocky at times, one must be sure to be in love with the work.

If you weren't running a gallery what else would you do?
We'd be beach bums.

- **Contact** The Breeder
  Nadia Gerazouni
  nadia@thebreedersystem.com
- **Established** 2002
- **Owner(s) / Partner(s)** Stathis Panagoulis
  George Vamvakidis
- **Team** 6
- **Space(s)** 650 m²
- **Artists at Art Basel** Andreas Angelidakis
  Stelios Faitakis
- **Further artists represented** Markus Amm
  Marc Bijl
  Vlassis Caniaris
  Antonis Donef
  Dora Economou
  Zoi Gaitanidou
  Marianna Gioka
  Uwe Henneken
  Hope
  Kalup Linzy
  Andreas Lolis
  Ryan McGinley
  Scott Myles
  Angelos Papadimitriou
  Chryssa Romanos
  Jennifer Rubell
  Vanessa Safavi
  Shirana Shahbazi
  Mindy Shapero
  Daniel Sinsel
  Socratis Socratous
  Gert & Uwe Tobias
  Jannis Varelas
  Allyson Vieira
  Gabriel Vormstein

Brito

São Paulo ● Galleries

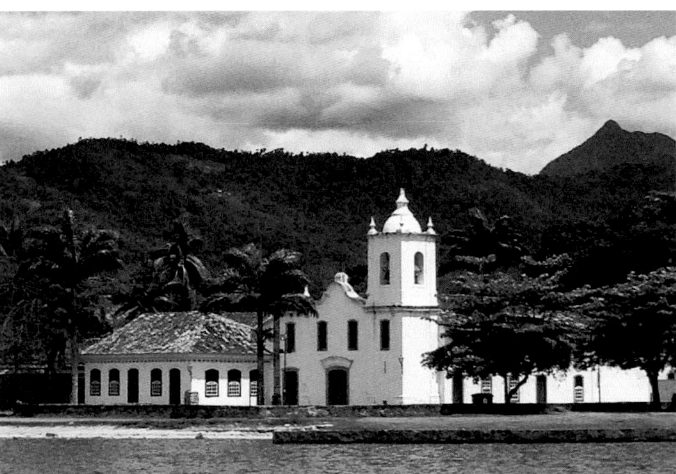

What is your favorite aspect of running a gallery?

Running a gallery is both witnessing the artists' creative process closely and making it possible by fostering their role in market. I am truly glad to see recognition of Brazilian artists growing internationally and I enjoy making key foreign artists more known in my own country.

How do you choose the artists you work with?

I prefer to think of our role as representative of a relevant sample of contemporary production. So I mostly follow my intuition and select names from previous research, keeping an attentive eye to what is exciting or important to show. Running a gallery is a cultural commitment, so my radar is open to track what brings any sort of relevant contribution to understanding our times and enhancing our sensibility.

If you weren't running a gallery what else would you do?

I have been involved with art and culture for my entire professional and academic life, so it is hard to imagine myself doing anything else. If I was not running a gallery, I would definitely be involved with arts in some possible way, maybe curating or taking part in some museum or institution. Running an independent non-commercial project aimed at supporting artistic research and education also sounds appealing to me.

- **Contact** Luciana Brito Galeria
Julia Brito
juliabrito@lucianabritogaleria.com.br
- **Established** 1997
- **Owner(s) / Partner(s)** Luciana Brito
- **Team** 14
- **Space(s)** 1,000 m²
- **Artists at Art Basel** Tiago Tebet
Tobias Putrih
- **Further artists represented** Marina Abramović
Lucas Bambozzi
Fabiana de Barros & Michel Favre
Geraldo de Barros
Ricardo Basbaum
Rafael Carneiro
Saint Clair Cemin
Waldemar Cordeiro
Rochelle Costi
Leandro Erlich
Thomaz Farkas
Paula Garcia
Gaspar Gasparian
Alex Katz
Pablo Lobato
Anthony McCall
Allan McCollum
João Luiz Musa
Mônica Nador
Fyodor Pavlov-Andreevich
Liliana Porter
Caio Reisewitz
Eder Santos
Regina Silveira
Héctor Zamora
Fernando Zarif
Raphaël Zarka

Broadway 1602

New York ● Survey

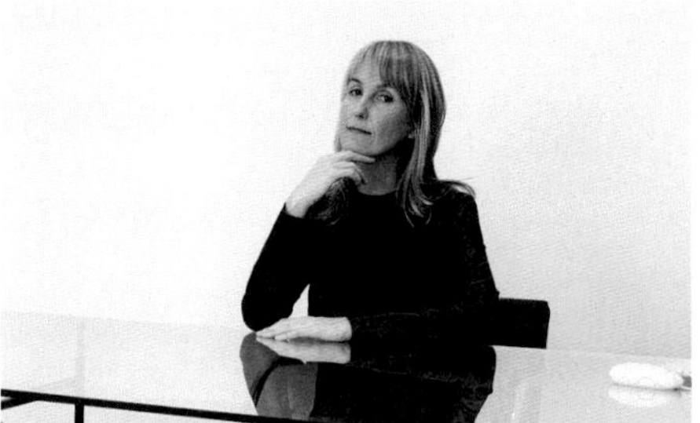

What is your favorite aspect of running a gallery?

We have a strong curatorial focus in our program on women artists from the 1960s and 1970s. Evelyne Axell, Rosemarie Castoro, Gina Pane, Sylvia Palacios Whitman, Lenora de Barros, Penny Slinger, and Lydia Okumura are outstanding pioneers of the avant-garde. My favorite aspect of being a gallerist is that I have the highest degree of independence I can think of in the art world. I am the "creative director" in my own space moving in directions and with a pace that I consider adequate.

How do you choose the artists you work with?

A lot of our work is deeply rooted in art historical research and networking in a milieu of protagonists and witnesses of the 1960s and 1970s avant-garde. After ten years of expertise in this field we also get approached regularly now by artists and Estates, who trust and respect our original approach to a scholarly, curatorial, and commercially competent gallery work.

If you weren't running a gallery what else would you do?

I would live in the country, write books, ride on horseback, and grow vegetables. But I basically already do what I love.

- **Contact** Broadway 1602
Aniko Erdosi
aniko@broadway1602.com
- **Established** 2005
- **Owner(s) / Partner(s)** Anke Kempkes
- **Team** 6
- **Space(s)** 167.5 m²
- **Artists at Art Basel** Evelyne Axell
Lenora de Barros
Rosemarie Castoro
Gina Pane
Lydia Okumura
- **Further artists represented** Mark Alexander
Laura Cottingham
Experiments in Art and Technology (E.A.T.) Archive
Zvi Goldstein
Margarete Jakschik
Devin Leonardi
Babette Mangolte
Anna Molska
Barbro Östlihn
Paul P.
Sylvia Palacios Whitman
Xanti Schawinsky
Penny Slinger

Ben Brown

Hong Kong
London

● Galleries

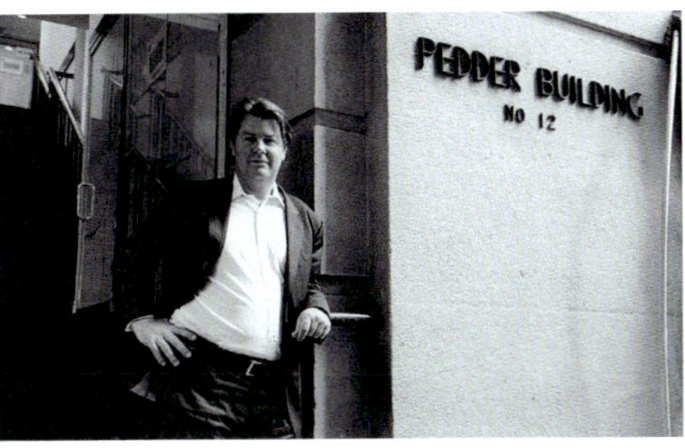

What is your favorite aspect of running a gallery?
The social element of running a gallery is undoubtedly the most enjoyable. This includes meeting and developing relationships with artists as well as helping clients to build their collections. I also find it extremely rewarding to be able to realize seminal exhibitions in both galleries with artists whose work I admire, sometimes since childhood.

How do you choose the artists you work with?
There are various ways I come to work with the artists we represent and exhibit. These include, but are not limited to, relationships built up over many years, my own personal collection, numerous visits to artist's studios, galleries, and art fairs, as well as recommendations by other artists or clients.

If you weren't running a gallery what else would you do?
I would run a vineyard, combined with a cooking school and delicious restaurant somewhere in Italy or France—perfect for spending time with my wonderful family and friends!

- **Contact** Ben Brown Fine Arts
Emilie Ortolan
emilie@benbrownfinearts.com
- **Established** 2004
- **Owner(s) / Partner(s)** Ben Brown
- **Team** 13
- **Space(s)** 300 m²
- **Artists at Art Basel** Ron Arad
Miquel Barceló
Tony Bevan
Simon Birch
Kitty Chou
Candida Höfer
Wang Keping
Claude & François-Xavier Lalanne
Vik Muniz
Nabil Nahas
Frank Stella
Tseng Kwong Chi
Gavin Turk
Not Vital
Ye Linghan
Yunizar
- **Further artists represented** Yoan Capote
Caio Fonseca
Heinz Mack
Jan Worst

Gavin Brown

New York
Los Angeles

● Galleries
Unlimited
Parcours
● Galleries

- **Contact** Gavin Brown's enterprise
Thor Shannon
thor@gavinbrown.biz
- **Established** 1994
- **Owner(s) / Partner(s)** Gavin Brown
- **Team** 17
- **Space(s)** 929 m²
- **Artists at Art Basel** Franz Ackermann
James Angus
Uri Aran
Ed Atkins
Thomas Bayrle
Dirk Bell
Jennifer Bornstein
Joe Bradley
Kerstin Brätsch
Martin Creed
Verne Dawson
Jeremy Deller
Peter Doig
Urs Fischer
Dara Friedman
Mark Handforth
Jonathan Horowitz
Alex Israel
Joan Jonas
Alex Katz
Christopher Knowles
Udomsak Krisanamis
Ella Kruglyanskaya
Mark Leckey
Bjarne Melgaard
Silke Otto Knapp
Laura Owens
Oliver Payne
Steven Pippin
Rob Pruitt
Nick Relph
Steven Shearer
Frances Stark
Sturtevant
Spencer Sweeney
Rirkrit Tiravanija

Buchholz

Cologne
Berlin

● Galleries
● Galleries

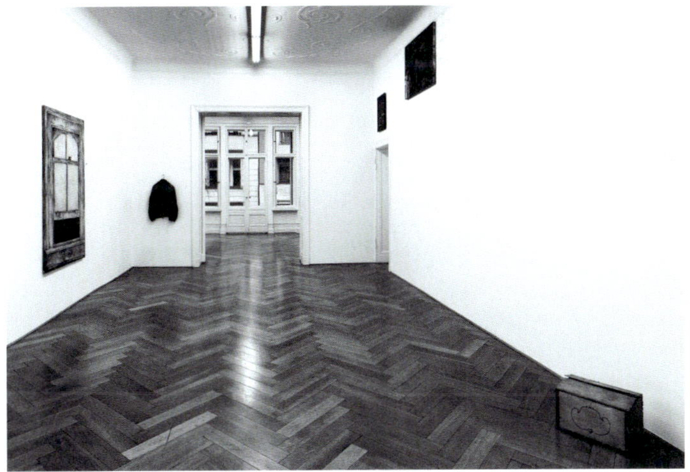

- **Contact** Galerie Buchholz
Daniel Buchholz
Christopher Müller
post@galeriebuchholz.de
- **Established** 1986
- **Team** 15
- **Space(s)** 380 m²
- **Artists at Art Basel** Tomma Abts
Lutz Bacher
Nairy Baghramian
Cosima von Bonin
Tony Conrad
Simon Denny
Liz Deschenes
Lukas Duwenhögger
Thomas Eggerer
Cerith Wyn Evans
Loretta Fahrenholz
Vincent Fecteau
Morgan Fisher
Isa Genzken
Jack Goldstein
Julian Göthe
Richard Hawkins
Cameron Jamie
John Kelsey
Jochen Klein
Jutta Koether
Michael Krebber
Mark Leckey
Sam Lewitt
Lucy McKenzie
Henrik Olesen

Paulina Olowska
Silke Otto-Knapp
Mathias Poledna
Florian Pumhösl
R.H. Quaytman
Willem de Rooij
de Rijke/de Rooij
Frances Stark
Josef Strau
Stefan Thater
Cheyney Thompson
Wolfgang Tillmans
Stewart Uoo
Danh Vo
Martin Wong
Katharina Wulff

Buchmann

Agra/Lugano —  Galleries
Berlin — Galleries

What is your favorite aspect of running a gallery?
Direct contact with the artist and art, seeing how a work is developed and created.

How do you choose the artists you work with?
By the uniqueness of the artist's expression.

- **Contact** — Buchmann Galerie
Andre Buchmann
info@buchmanngalerie.com
- **Established** — 1975
- **Owner(s) / Partner(s)** — Andre Buchmann
Elena Buchmann
- **Team** — 7
- **Space(s)** — 430 m²
- **Artists at Art Basel** — Anna & Bernhard Blume
Daniel Buren
Lawrence Carroll
John Chamberlain
Tony Cragg
Sean Dawson
Zaha Hadid
Des Hughes
Raffi Kalenderian
Wolfgang Laib
Mario Merz
Tatsuo Miyajima
Wilhelm Mundt
Arnold Odermatt
Bettina Pousttchi
Fiona Rae
Joel Sternfeld
William Tucker
Lawrence Weiner
Clare Woods

Bugada & Cargnel

Paris — 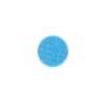 Feature
Unlimited
Parcours

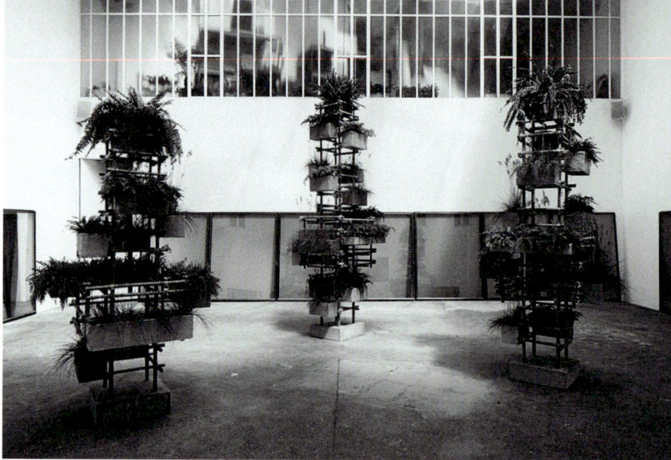

What is your favorite aspect of running a gallery?
Modestly participating in shaping artists' careers and consequently being part of the art world.

How do you choose the artists you work with?
Through affinity with people and works.

If you weren't running a gallery what else would you do?
Travel the world, visit artists' studios, galleries, museums, collect.

- **Contact** — Bugada & Cargnel
Claudia Cargnel
ccargnel@bugadacargnel.com
- **Established** — 2002
- **Owner(s) / Partner(s)** — Frédéric Bugada
Claudia Cargnel
- **Team** — 6
- **Space(s)** — 750 m²
- **Artists at Art Basel** — Julio Le Parc
Pierre Bismuth
- **Further artists represented** — Alfredo Aceto
Wilfrid Almendra
Étienne Chambaud
Julian Charrière
Mat Collishaw
Nick Devereux
Ryan Estep
Cyprien Gaillard
Piero Golia
Annika Larsson
Adrien Missika
Claire Tabouret
Iris van Dongen
Nico Vascellari

Bureau

New York —  Statements
Nova

- **Contact** — Bureau
Gabrielle Giattino
giattino@bureau-inc.com
office@bureau-inc.com
- **Established** — 2010
- **Owner(s) / Partner(s)** — Gabrielle Giattino

von Bartha
Interview with Stefan and Miklos von Bartha

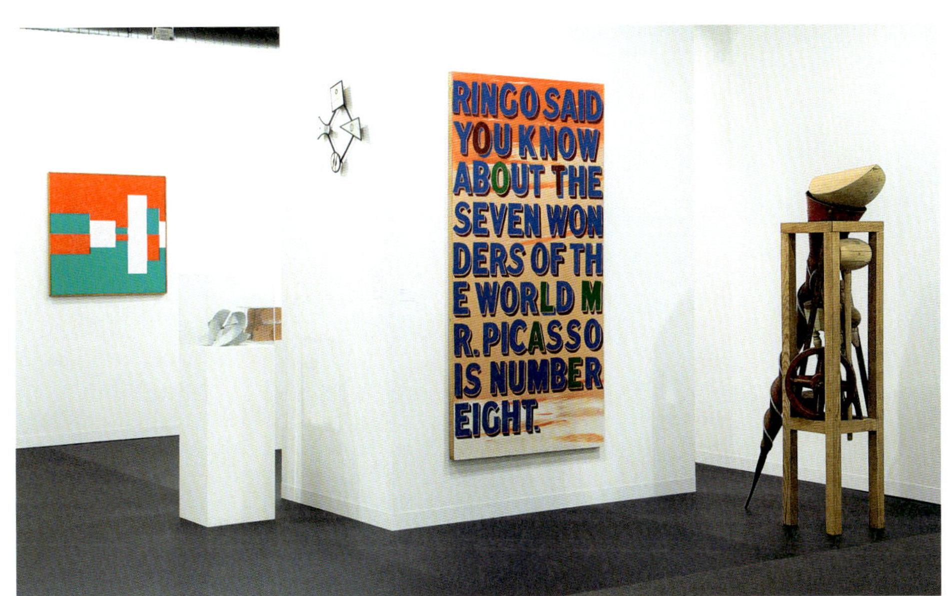

Art Basel in Basel, 2014

We'd like to know more about the beginnings of the gallery. You opened in 1970, I mean your father and your mother opened it ...

Stefan von Bartha: Exactly, my parents founded the gallery. They wanted to be graphic designers, but my father said that it was a very unsuccessful career. Their project was supported by Carl Laszlo, a famous collector and one of the founders of Art Basel.

Was the idea at the beginning to show mostly Swiss artists?

Stefan von Bartha: No, there was a profound interest in Concrete art and, as my father was Hungarian, the Hungarian avant-garde was also very important. Swedish glass was also a big focus because my mother was Swedish. In the first few years the gallery did not have a clear program; it depended more on things my parents had access to, and on design. In the past 20–25 years the program became clearer and clearer, because the gallery was growing and so they were able to approach artists they couldn't approach in the 1970s.

Since the 1980s you have been organizing shows with Latin-American artists. How did this happen?

Stefan von Bartha: One idea was to find artists known historically, but not so much in Switzerland. The Hungarian avant-garde, Latin-American Neo-Concrete, etc. In our booth this year at Art Basel we are showing Swedish artist Olle Baertling; our intention is to show something people know, but that they don't see any longer. Also Aurélie Nemours, who I would say is "la grande dame" of Minimal art in France.

As the second generation, what is your relationship with Concrete art?

Stefan von Bartha: You know, I grew up with it, so there's two ways you can go: you can hate it or like it. I decided to like it. [*Laughs*] I feel so close to Concrete art because it has to do with my education, with the fact my parents always took my brother and me to all the studios. When I started to work for my parents, let's say officially eight or nine years ago, I said that we had to bring in a new generation. The gallery has always shown a lot of contemporary artists, but not as many as we do today.

The gallery is based in Basel and you have participated in the fair every year since it opened. What is it like to have a permanent gallery in Basel?

Stefan von Bartha: Basel is a fantastic location. During the year it's good, but during one week it's insane! You have events and a lot of really good museum shows. The space we have in Basel is rather outstanding by Swiss standards (it's 850 square meters) and our program is very attractive, so it draws a lot of people. If we had a gallery in Zurich, we would be just one of many!

Do you remember the fair's early years?

Miklos von Bartha: I've been at Art Basel since the very first year, because at the time I was working for a well-known dealer, Carl Laszlo, who unfortunately died in 2013. He was one of the founders of Art Basel. Today people mainly mention Ernst Beyeler and Trudi Brucker—it's probably more stylish to attribute the fair to two local Basel figures. But the first meetings to launch and organize the event took place in Laszlo's home. He was there at the beginning, the very beginning, of this fair.

Nowadays the market is obviously very different from what it was back then. I clearly remember the 1970 fair when the Marlborough Gallery from London showed dozens of paintings by Francis Bacon, each one priced at nearly 100,000 Swiss francs. Being young at the time, I couldn't imagine anyone spending so much money on a work of art—which today would be worth 60 to 80 million francs! Which just shows how things have changed. I'm a little troubled nowadays, because most of the original collectors have passed away and even museums can often no longer buy unless they find a patron who donates the needed funds. Of course they can still acquire some things, but in general museum directors and curators who attend the show have their eye on works that already cost millions, instead of buying work by young artists. Which is obviously risky, because 20 of those would probably wind up in the storeroom, but at least there's a chance of finding—of discovering—something.

I'm also troubled by the fact that people almost never talk about the quality of a work anymore. In the daily paper, for instance, the reporter doesn't say " I saw a wonderful painting at Marlborough's," but rather, "There's a Jeff Koons worth six million, and a Warhol portrait going for 35 million." It seems like the sole criterion of a work's quality has become its price. Which isn't true! The first Basquiats I saw in Bruno Bischofberger's gallery in Zurich—large-scale works—cost $20,000, despite the fact that Bischofberger was already a very expensive dealer at the time. But he was also the best dealer in the world and a great collector, right? Nowadays, not only do people talk only of prices, but those prices are in the millions.

The atmosphere has changed considerably—your son has told us how, in the 1970s, you drove directly onto Messeplatz with the truck, and that the fair was very relaxed and friendly.

Miklos von Bartha: You could even drive your car right up to the stand! The cars were right there, people unloaded stuff, placed it on the stands, and then even left the car there because it was cheaper than paying for a parking place. All that has changed. Today people are concerned about different aspects of the job, such as security which constantly needs strengthening—which are perfectly valid arguments. Art Basel is not only the world's best art fair, it's also extremely well organized. When you go to Maastricht, for example, you have to spend one or two days with the works in the Stand Building—things are poorly organized. Here you arrive, you set up your stand, you tell the organizers you're ready, a technician arrives to adjust the lighting, and that's it! I never get annoyed here, whereas I usually get annoyed pretty fast.

CULTURAL Sponsorship

Cally Spooner
And You Were Wonderful, On Stage
2014
BMW Tate Live, Tate Britain, London

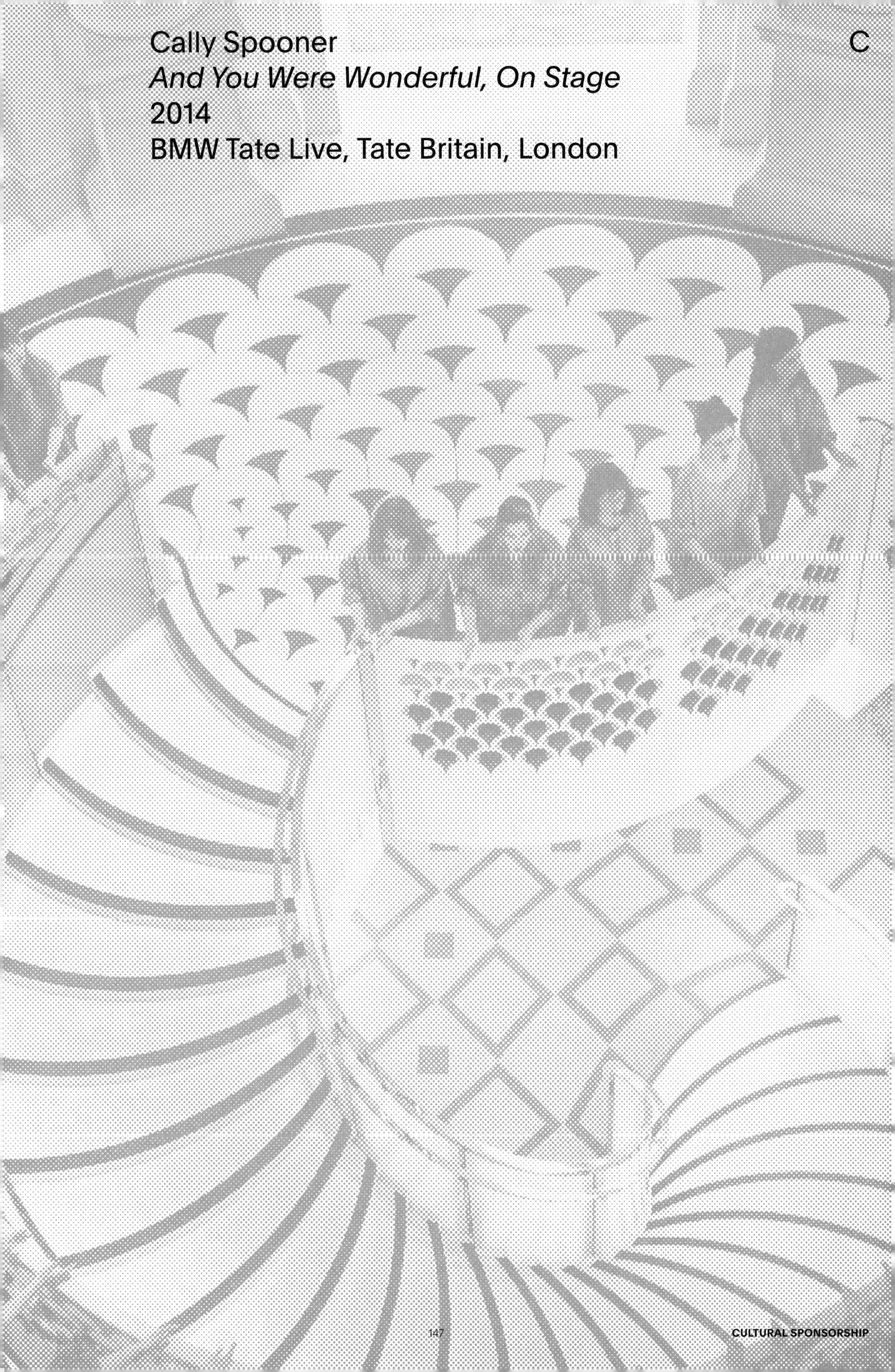

C

András Szántó talks with Thomas Girst, Head of Cultural Engagement at the BMW Group, about cultural initiatives and BMW

Launched in 2012, BMW Tate Live is a four-year partnership between Tate and the BMW Group that features a series of innovative live performances and events including live web broadcasts, in-gallery performances, seminars, and workshops.

Thomas Girst is Head of Cultural Engagement at the BMW Group. For more information on the BMW Art Journey, as well as numerous art initiatives, visit bmw.group.com/culture.

András Szántó, art market analyst and advisor to museums, foundations, and international corporations on cultural strategies, is strategic advisor to the BMW Art Journey.

ANDRÁS SZÁNTÓ You have a scholarly interest in Marcel Duchamp and have published several books about him. What would Duchamp make of a BMW Art Car?

THOMAS GIRST Duchamp never had a driver's license. He had his first and second wives drive him around. But he had a huge fascination with cars, and that was of course of particular interest to me. In an interview with John Cage, Duchamp spoke about cars. He said it would be more convenient if cars didn't have a single owner, but were shared. According to Cage, he said that early in the last century. How amazing that a hundred years later there are car-sharing initiatives all over the world.

AS You have worked closely on the BMW Art Car, which could be seen as a kind of readymade.

TG Duchamp never declared his readymades to be art, whereas the art cars are, by definition, artworks. Once again, Duchamp's idea is more complex than anything that came after. That said, he put to use a lot of car metaphors, all evolving around the mechanomorphical and desire, including in his major work, the *Large Glass*. One of his last readymades was the signed license plate of his Volkswagen.

AS So how does someone like you end up working at the intersection of art and business?

TG At the age of 19, along with some friends, I founded an art movement, which we called NPAM, or "Nonprofit Art Movement." For a decade we published an annual international anthology of art and literature in a cardboard box. It had no advertisements and it was sold at the cost of production. I wrote manifestos that railed against any infiltration of the arts by business. It's precisely such people who end up with jobs like mine in the end.

The great thing about working with the arts on the business side is that you are not tied to any single entity within culture. In our case, the core business is premium automobiles and mobility; we have no vested interest whatsoever in the art world. Our company has been active in the arts for almost five decades. Besides our focus on the arts, we have initiated manifold projects in the fields of design and architecture, music and jazz. When you can move between genres, they hold each other in check. You see the beauty of the heterogeneous culture we live in.

AS In a nutshell, how would you explain why a brand like BMW devotes significant resources to culture?

TG First, we understand BMW to be a cultured brand. People who are friends of the brand are interested in culture—that's a good starting point. Then, when it comes to international events like Art Basel, it's about visibility beyond branding, about being where your potential clients are, about storytelling and creating meaningful experiences. It is no longer about bringing them into our world, but being a trustworthy player in a world they are involved in.

Long-term commitment is important to us. It has been almost 40 years since we commissioned Gerhard Richter to create what were at the time the largest paintings he had ever painted, for the lobby of our Munich headquarters. They are now considered some of the most important works ever commissioned by a corporation.

Another aspect is corporate citizenship: returning something to the society in which we do successful business. We don't shy away from controversy. We believe in creative freedom and making creativity possible through our initiatives all over the world, honoring the vision of curators and artists.

AS BMW is a company of engineers. How do you make the case to your colleagues about what you do?

TG It's great when you have to explain what you are doing. Any successful business enterprise is looking at many options when it comes to social engagement. There is a competition within, so you need to make the case.

One point I make often is that in pre-Socratic times there was no difference between technology and art—it all fell under the notion of "technê." We have common roots. That is something engineers can appreciate. When Olafur Eliasson was working on the 16th art car, he was eager to have a dialogue with our engineers, and it was mutually beneficial. Artists are some of the most creative minds on the planet. They have a lot for sister disciplines to learn from.

AS Some of your designers are working on products that will roll off production lines in 15 to 20 years time and will still be in use in 2050. Can artists help imagine the future?

TG Yes. But we do not treat our art engagement as an outsourced think tank, with a return on investment. The strength of artists is precisely to come up with visions that are less constrained by the daily grind of the core business. Still, our company understands the importance of innovation. We thrive on it. We benefit, for example, from a dialogue about the future, like the one we had in the BMW Guggenheim Lab, which explored the challenges of megacities. It's great when disciplines come together to tackle big issues.

AS The BMW Group now calls itself a mobility company. That is a big shift in how it perceives itself and wants to be perceived. What implications does this have for cultural engagement?

TG In everything we do, we have to look ahead. Our Art Car this year celebrates its 40th anniversary, and the series will continue. At the same time, we are taking this idea one step further with a new initiative, morphing from the BMW Art Car to the BMW Art Journey. The winners of this award can go on a journey of creative discovery, which we are happy to enable in collaboration with Art Basel, and which they themselves will envision and design. Every one of us knows what it feels like to get onto a plane, into car, or onto a bicycle, and how that frees up the mind. If you have an artist on a journey, who may translate that journey into new work by means of exploration, that can be a great way of supporting art and also of advancing our own vision of cultural engagement.

AS What makes a company a good partner in culture?

Gerhard Richter, *Rot, Gelb, Blau* (detail), 1973
BMW Headquarters, Munich

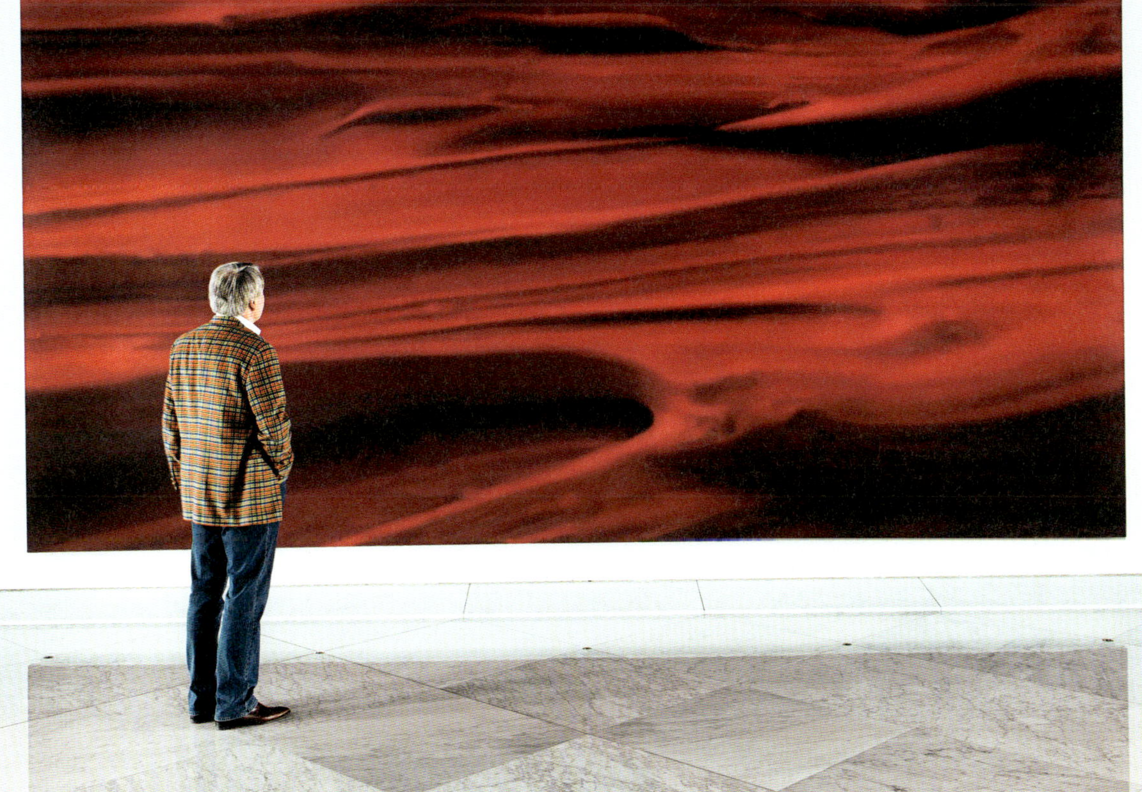

C

TG I have a few golden rules. First, never interfere with the creative freedom of artists or the institutions they work with. Second, realize that the subtler the brand positioning, the more sophisticated the company. Third, a museum is not an event location; you need to be aware of your partner's sensibilities. Fourth, don't shy away from controversy. Fifth, be honest and transparent about your goals, so everything is crystal clear on both sides.

AS With your historian's hat back on, what do you find the most distinctive about our present cultural moment?

TG Let me get back to Marcel Duchamp. He spoke of the "solitary explosion of man facing himself alone." No matter how big a business, no matter how much interest there is in an artist, in the end it is all about individuals and what they want to achieve in life, how they seek to realize their vision. This should never be compromised.

What I think is a crucial concern at the present time is the distinction between knowledge and information. We have more information at our fingertips than at any point in the history of humankind. But knowledge, I feel, is what is often missing. We are deluged with information, yet we are no wiser.

Duchamp said that the great artists of tomorrow will go underground. It's quite possible that a hundred years from now people may not even recognize the names of the artists we revere today.

Olafur Eliasson, *BMW H2R Project*, 2007

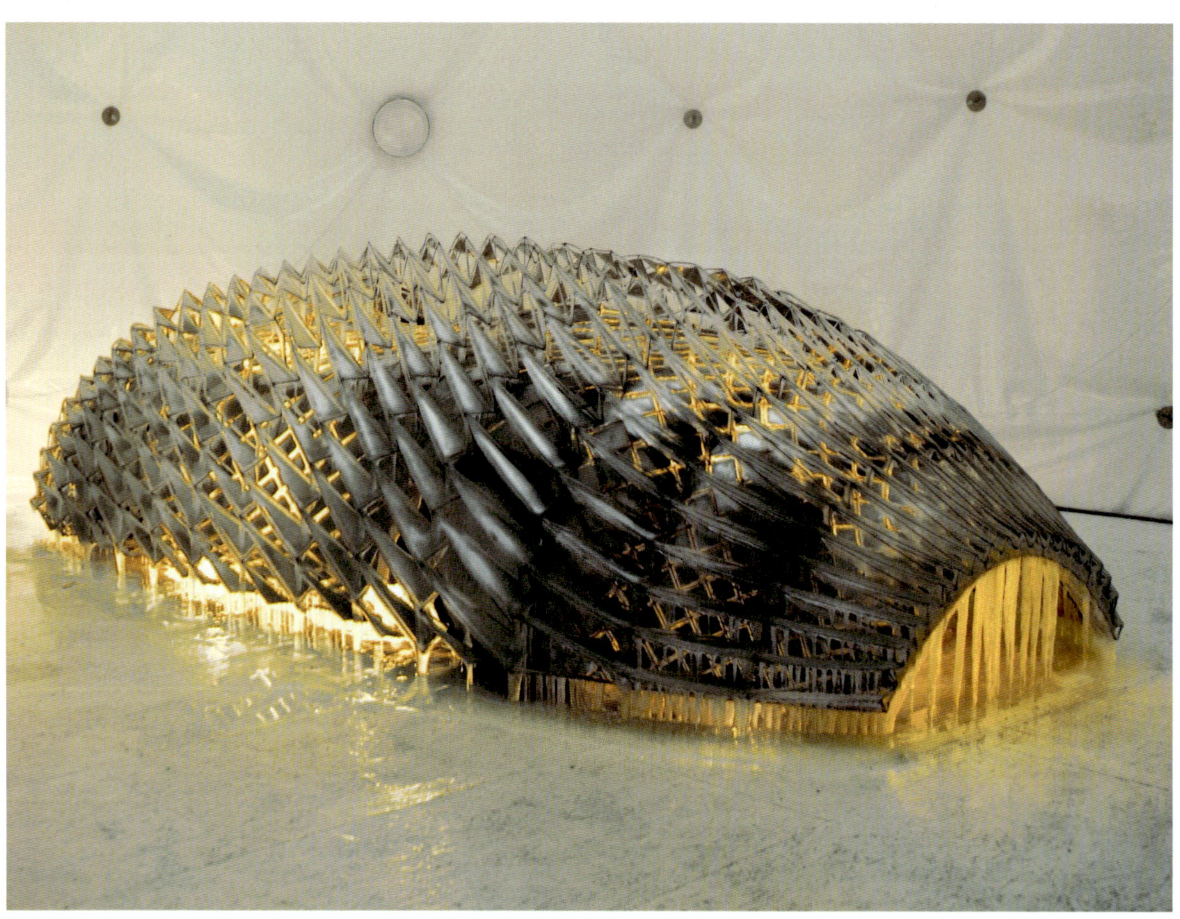

András Szántó talks with Hans-Kristian Hoejsgaard, CEO of Oettinger Davidoff, about cultural sponsorship and the Davidoff Art Initiative

C

n 2012, under Hans-Kristian Hoejsgaard's eadership, Oettinger Davidoff became an Associate Partner of Art Basel for its shows in Basel, Miami Beach, and Hong Kong, and launched the Davidoff Art Initiative. The Davidoff Art Initiative includes four global program areas: the Davidoff Art Residency, Davidoff Art Dialogues, Davidoff Art Grants, and Davidoff Art Editions. For more information visit davidoffartinitiative.com

András Szántó, art market analyst and advisor to museums, foundations, and international corporations on cultural strategies, is Chief Consultant to the Davidoff Art Initiative.

ANDRÁS SZÁNTÓ Art is somewhat of a personal passion and interest for you. How did you first get involved? When you buy art for yourself, what do you look for?

HANS-KRISTIAN HOEJSGAARD When I went to university, in Copenhagen in Denmark, I happened to find myself lodging in a private home. The landlady was very much into the art world and I met many interesting artists in her home. I became so excited that when I received my first salary from a student job, I bought a painting from a Faroe Islands painter, Joannis Kristiansson. Then as now, I buy what I like, not what experts say is hot. I happened to collect Cobra artists for a while. As I lived and worked around the world, I expanded to Chinese and American artists, and video art. Of course in the last couple of years Caribbean art has found its way onto my walls as well.

AS You have spent much of your career in the luxury sector, building brands. How did that experience influence your view of the link between companies and the arts?

HKH At the heart of luxury is craftsmanship, and in several of the luxury companies for which I had the privilege to work, I always thought of our people as artists: a watchmaker, a silversmith, a jeweler, a cognac or champagne master blender. Early on I developed the view that craftsmanship extends the notion of art, and therefore the link between luxury and art is a natural one. Furthermore, I would argue that apart from time, collecting art is probably the ultimate luxury.

AS When you arrived at Davidoff, the company didn't have much of a history in the art field. Where did you see the connection and the opportunity?

HKH Correction: we had *no* history in the art field. We happened to have a

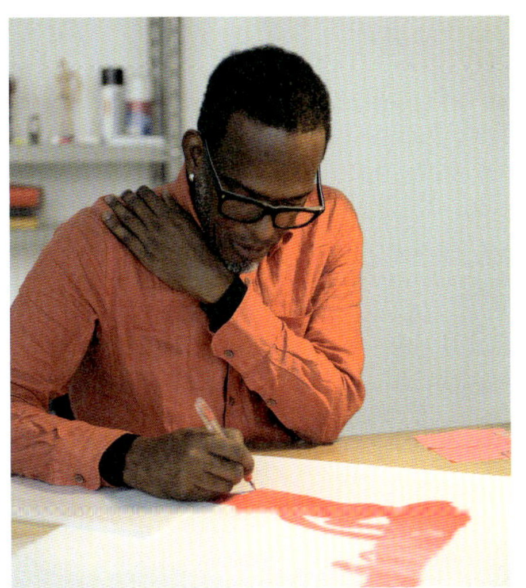

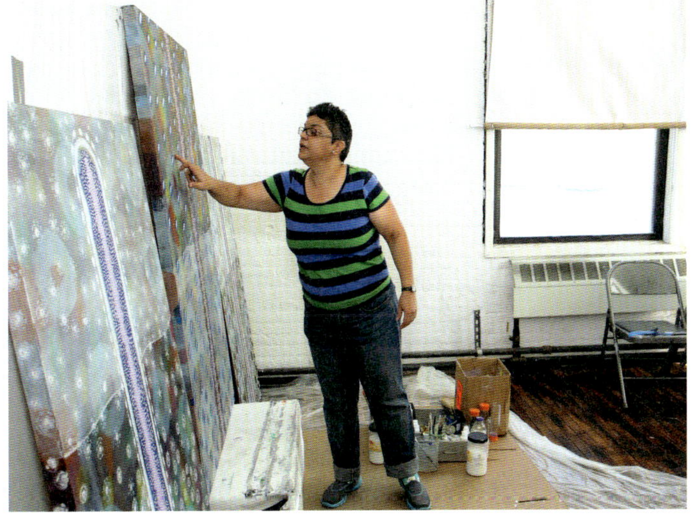

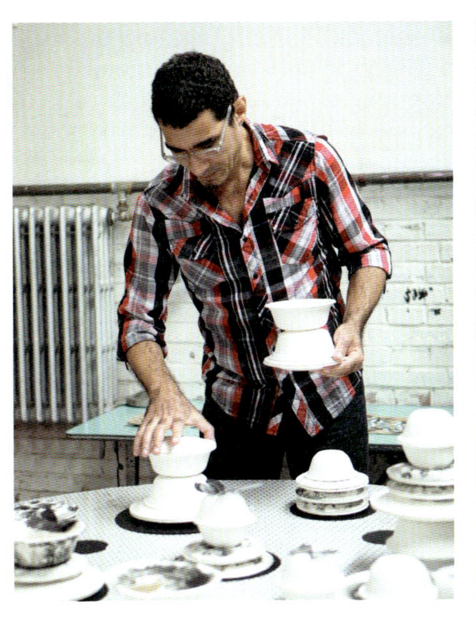

Jorge Pineda in residency at Künstlerhaus Berthanien, Berlin, 2014

Monica Ferreras de la Maza in residency at the International Studio & Curatorial Program, New York 2013

Pascal Meccariello in residency at Red Gate Gallery Residency, Beijing, 2014

C

cigar lounge at Art Basel in Miami, but I think it was fair to say that was an event-driven rather than an art-driven engagement. Because everything Davidoff Cigars does is about art and craft—the art of growing, the art of blending, the art of rolling—I saw a connection, as I described earlier. I also saw an opportunity in the combination of two Basel-based companies—Art Basel and Oettinger Davidoff—which shared a similar global strategic focus in the Americas and in Asia. I thought this would be a perfect match.

AS Davidoff's art initiative is singularly focused on Caribbean art and artists—not exactly the "usual suspects." Was there ever a temptation to do something more aligned with the art world mainstream?

HKH I think any company looking to engage in art is tempted initially to go with famous artists. But that seemed to me like a "me too" approach. It would present a risk of being perceived as a marketing ploy rather than a genuine engagement. In our early conversations with you, when you were advising us on how to establish our art engagement, you were also quite compelling in saying that going with the already-famous artists would make us one of many who chose that route. I am glad we went down this road. It gave us a more distinctive mission and approach in a crowded field of art initiatives. I am happy to see that the wider art world is now increasingly aware of the contributions of Caribbean artists—maybe we had a little bit to do with that.

AS Davidoff-supported Caribbean artists are going on residencies in New York, Berlin, and Beijing. Residencies for international artists will start in 2015 in the Dominican Republic at the Altos de Chavón School. What will these international artists find there?

HKH Five international artists from Chile, France, Kuwait, Mexico, and the USA will arrive at the Davidoff Art Residency in mid-January 2015, when we open our doors for the first time on the campus of the Altos de Chavón Art and Design school in the Dominican Republic. We are excited and feel incredibly privileged to have partnered with Altos. Our international artists will find five brand new studios, built by Oettinger Davidoff and designed by a local architect who happened to have attended the school. The studios are interconnected, providing an opportunity for the artists to interact. When they walk out of their studios, they will be in the middle of an incredibly talented student body, in the region's leading art school, headed by the tireless Dean, Stephen Kaplan.

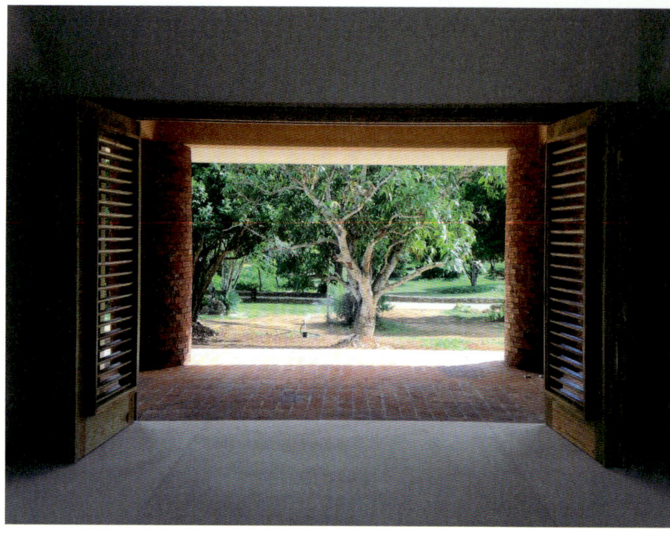

Davidoff Studios, Altos de Chavón, Dominican Republic

AS What has surprised you the most in how the initiative has played out so far?

HKH Two things. Firstly, that almost no one had previous focused on the vibrant Caribbean art scene, and therefore there was a space wide open for us to explore and engage with. Secondly, the incredibly warm welcome that we have received for the Davidoff Art Initiative and what we are trying to do.

AS What has the Davidoff Art Initiative brought to the brand and your customers in your view?

HKH A partnership that resonates with our customers, many of whom are art enthusiasts and collectors. Our customers perceive this initiative as a credible link between art and Davidoff. They realize that not only is it an art initiative, but it is a very different way of supporting a country and community to which we owe much and where most of our employees live and work.

AS Art sponsorships are sometimes viewed with a measure of suspicion in the art world. Why do you think that is the case?

HKH As I said, we have been warmly welcomed, so as Davidoff's CEO, I have yet to encounter this suspicion. However, when there is suspicion about the corporate world engaging with the art world, I think it boils down to questions of authenticity: is this genuine or just a marketing ploy? I think this attitude is generally unfair, though. Even if brands are getting a marketing advantage from these engagements over the longer term, in the meantime they are helping the art community to thrive. This is particularly the case in times when government support for the arts in many countries has been slashed.

AS What is the distinction between marketing and sponsorship? How would you explain to another CEO why you are investing resources in this area?

HKH I would first explain to another CEO why art makes sense for my brand, Davidoff. It might not make sense for his or her brand, and that brings me to the first part of your question: deciding on a sponsorship is a big decision, because it defines your brand. Brand equity and brand personality, tone and voice, are defined and protected by the Chief Marketing Officer, and therefore the connection between marketing and sponsorships is as close as it gets.

AS Can the results of art sponsorship be measured, and how?

HKH Yes, but only over the longer term. If you are not into a sponsorship for the long haul, stay away, because you cannot prove to your shareholders a return on investment in the short term. In the long run, you can measure consumer engagement with your brand and ultimately therefore sales. Also, it is important not to forget your employee engagement. Employees are excited about being proud of the company they work for, proud of what the company stands for beyond the actual products and services the company offers.

AS We are seeing a high moment of brand involvement in art. Why art now? And what mark will it leave on the arts in general?

HKH I think it is a trend that will continue. The art world is so multifaceted that many brands can find a niche or a platform that makes sense to them. The diversity of opportunities is incredible. The Davidoff Art Initiative took the place of Fondation Cartier as the sponsor of Art Basel. Cartier were all about a massive art collection, while we are about donating a cement floor in a rustic sculpture hall in an art school in the Caribbean, or sending a talented young or mid-career artist to Berlin or Beijing. The range of engagement approaches is endless, and it can leave a lasting positive impact on culture, particularly where resources are scarce.

AS For you personally, what has the experience of being involved in art through the Davidoff Art Initiative meant?

HKH Personally, it has been tremendously fulfilling. With my own eyes I have seen what a difference our modest grants and residency programs can make in an artist's life, or in an art institution's daily operations. And all the wonderful, diverse, crazy, talented, brilliant people you meet in the art world—this is just a gift.

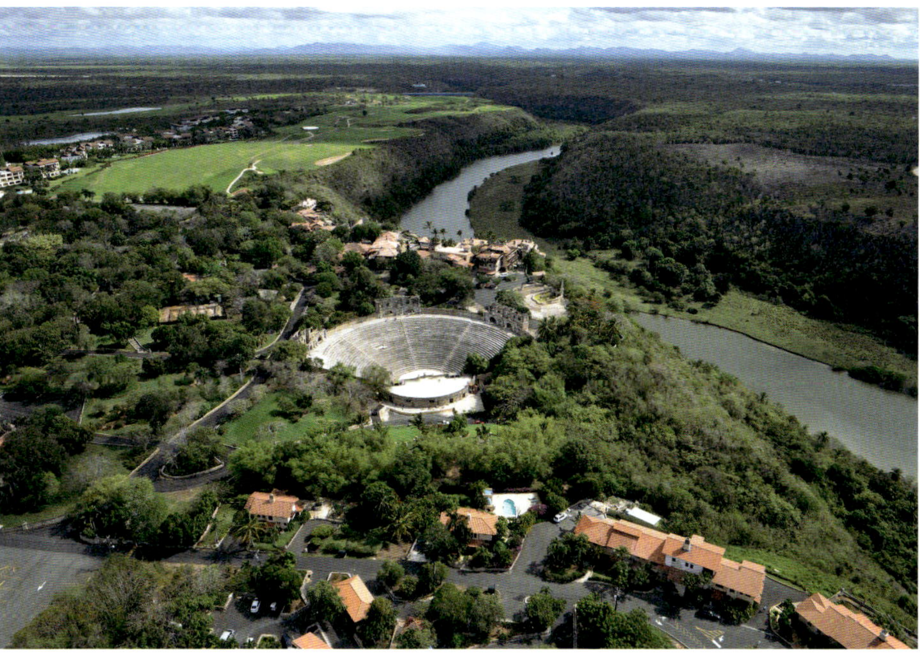

Aerial view, Altos de Chavón, Dominican Republic

Stuart Comer
Bice Curiger
Massimiliano Gioni
Hou Hanru
Jessica Morgan
Taiyana Pimentel

CURA TORS' CHOI CES

C

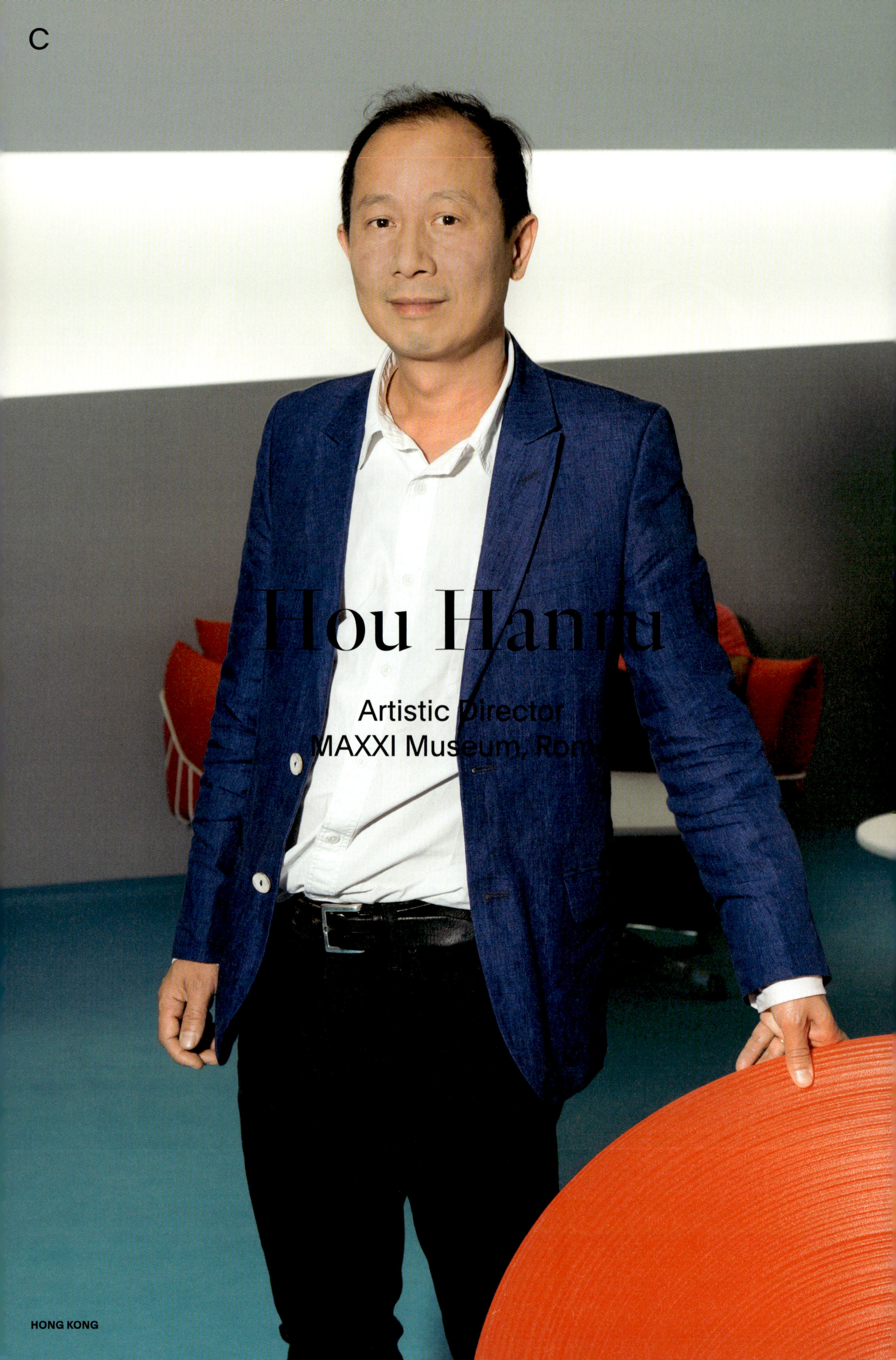

Hou Hanru

Artistic Director
MAXXI Museum, Rom

Koki Tanaka

A Behavioral Statement (or An Unconscious Protest), 2013

Vitamin Creative Space

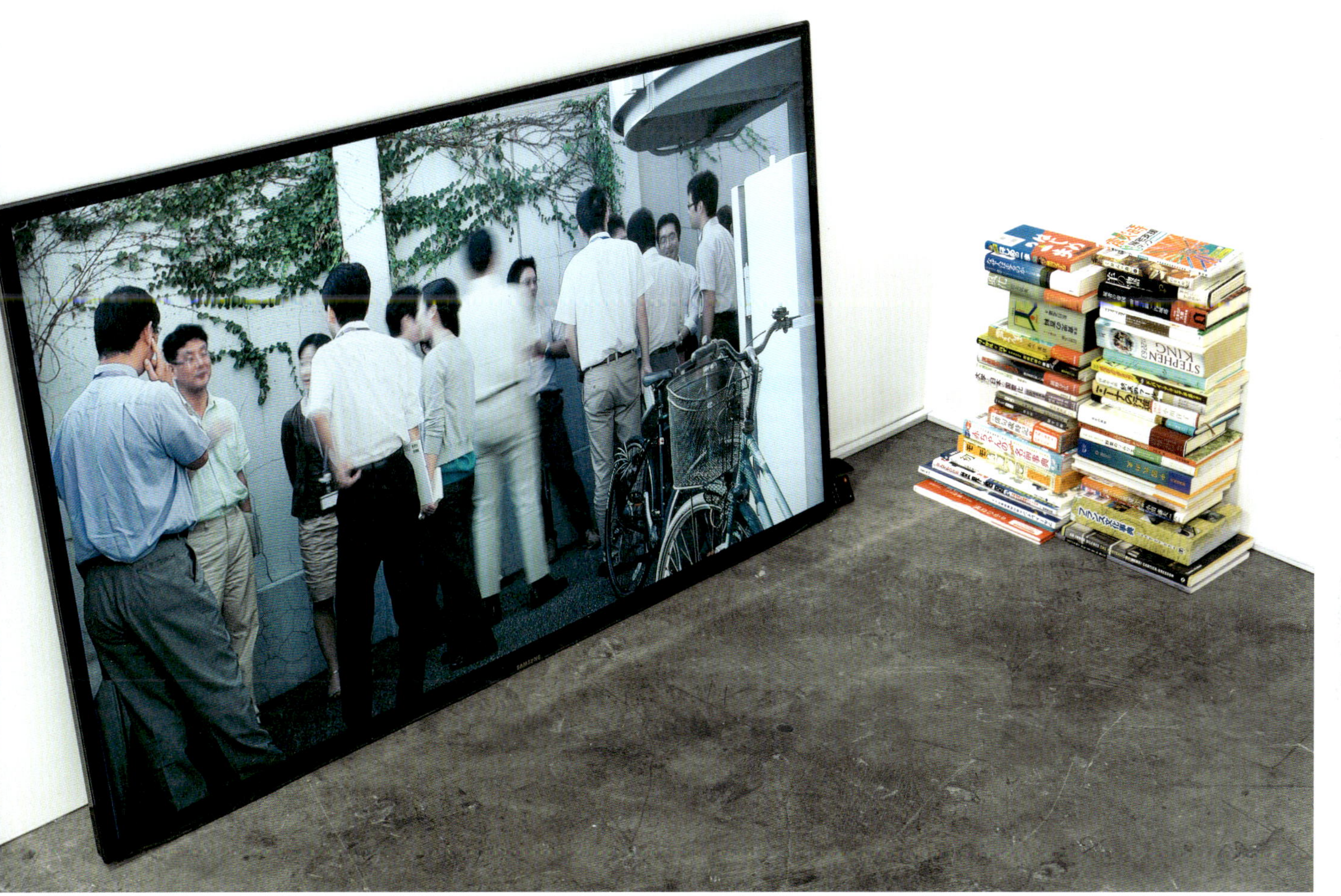

"A highly intelligent and playful gesture to express political concerns and social psychology through collective mobilization at a time of profound crisis."

C

Ahmed Mater

Desert of Pharan series, 2013

Athr Gallery (Insights)

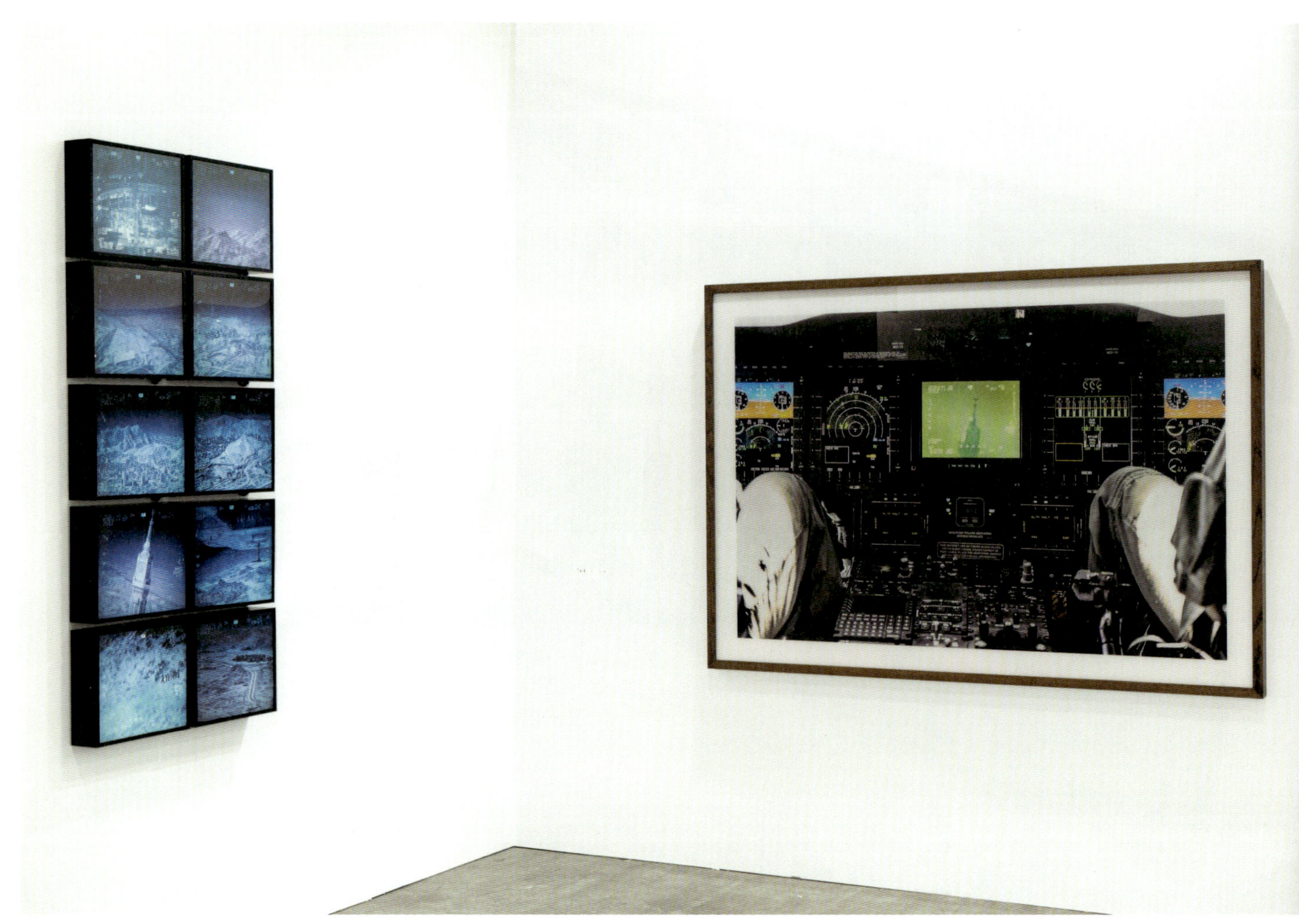

"A fresh insight into an emerging scene with ambition in a 'closed' society longing enthusiastically but critically for an opening onto the world."

Cheng Ran

Leo Xu Projects (Discoveries)

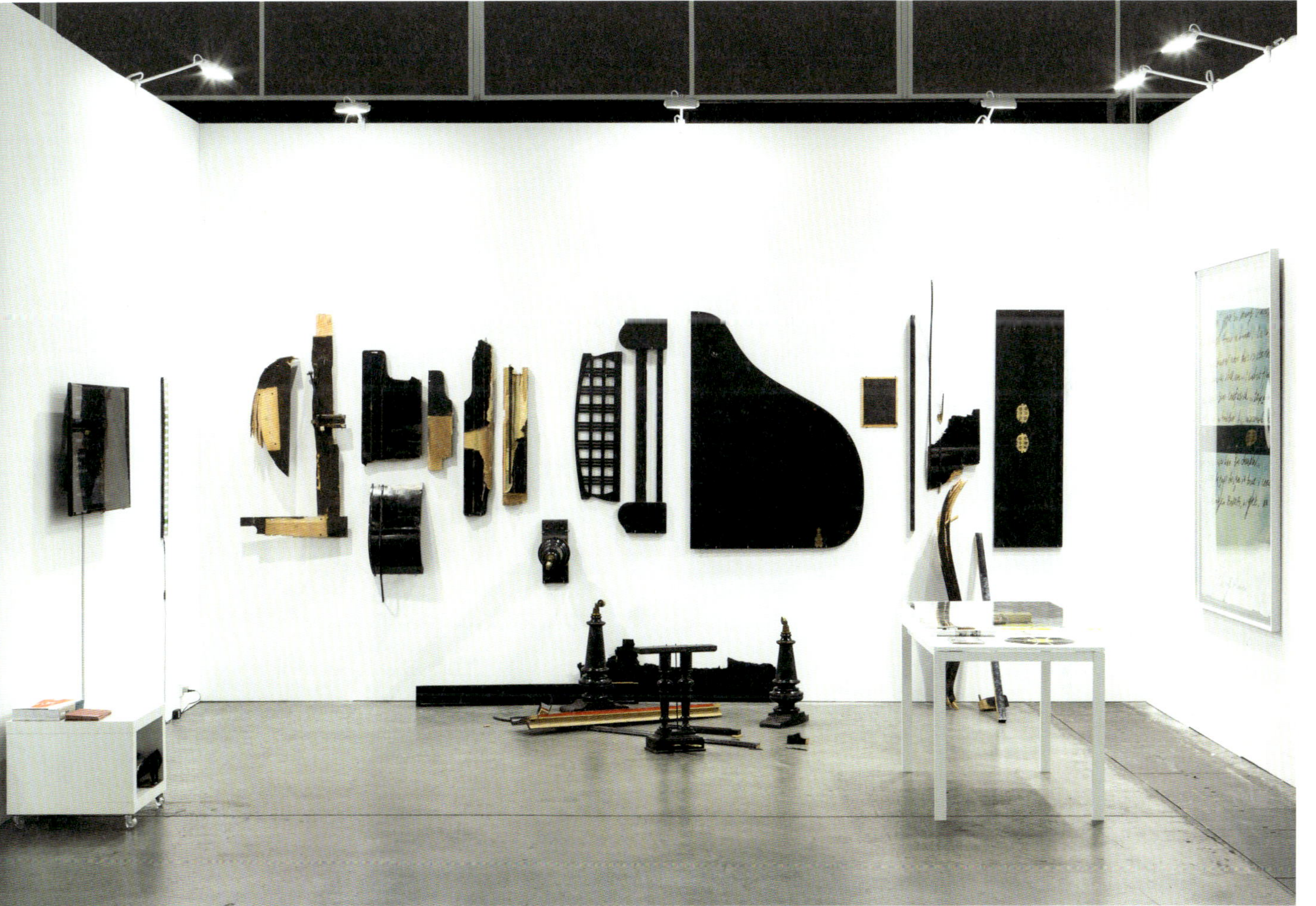

"Quite a smart exploration of today's modes of communication (about love?) via social media … with doubts."

C

Tsuyoshi Ozawa

The Return of Dr. N, 2013

Misa Shin Gallery (Insights)

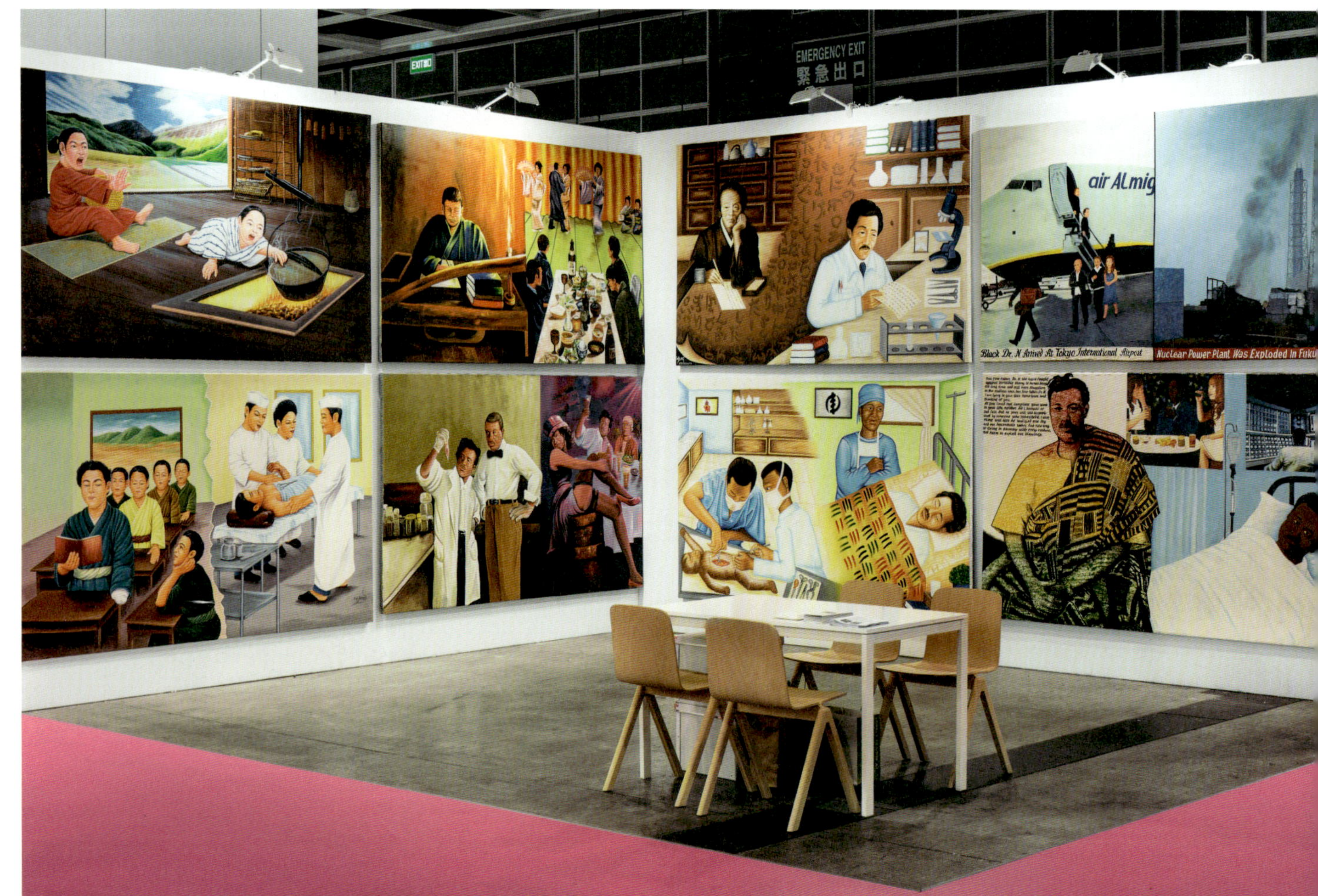

"An incredibly exciting and amusing work, with both satire and humor, presenting a widely forgotten but highly significant 'cultural exchange' case from the history of modernization outside of the Western world."

Wu Dayu
Tina Keng Gallery

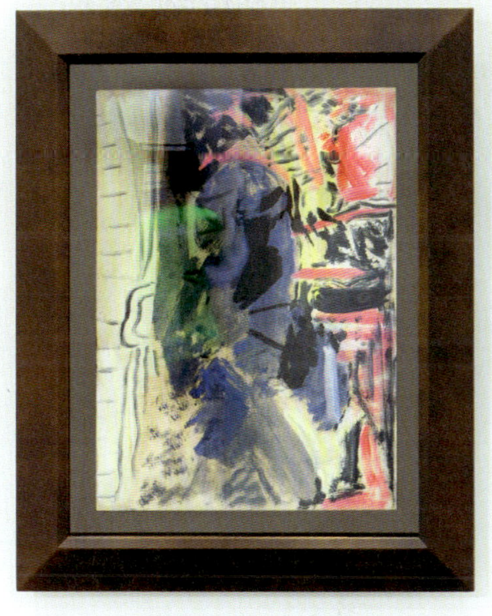

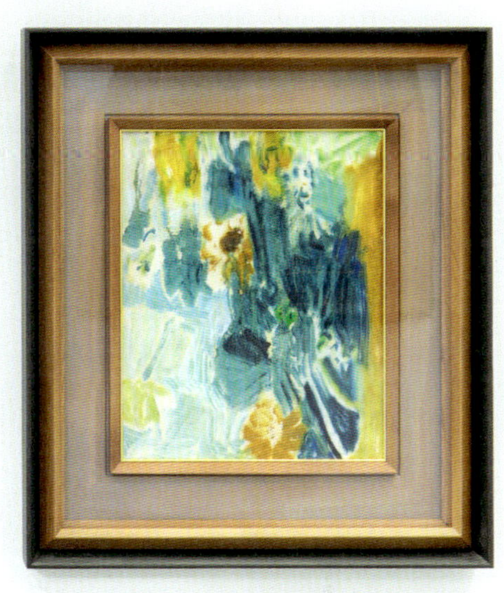

"Wu Dayu's paintings are an important revelation of a pioneer of Chinese modern art. Working during the 1920s and 1930s, he was an early avant-garde artist and a tutor for now-famous masters like Zao Wou-ki."

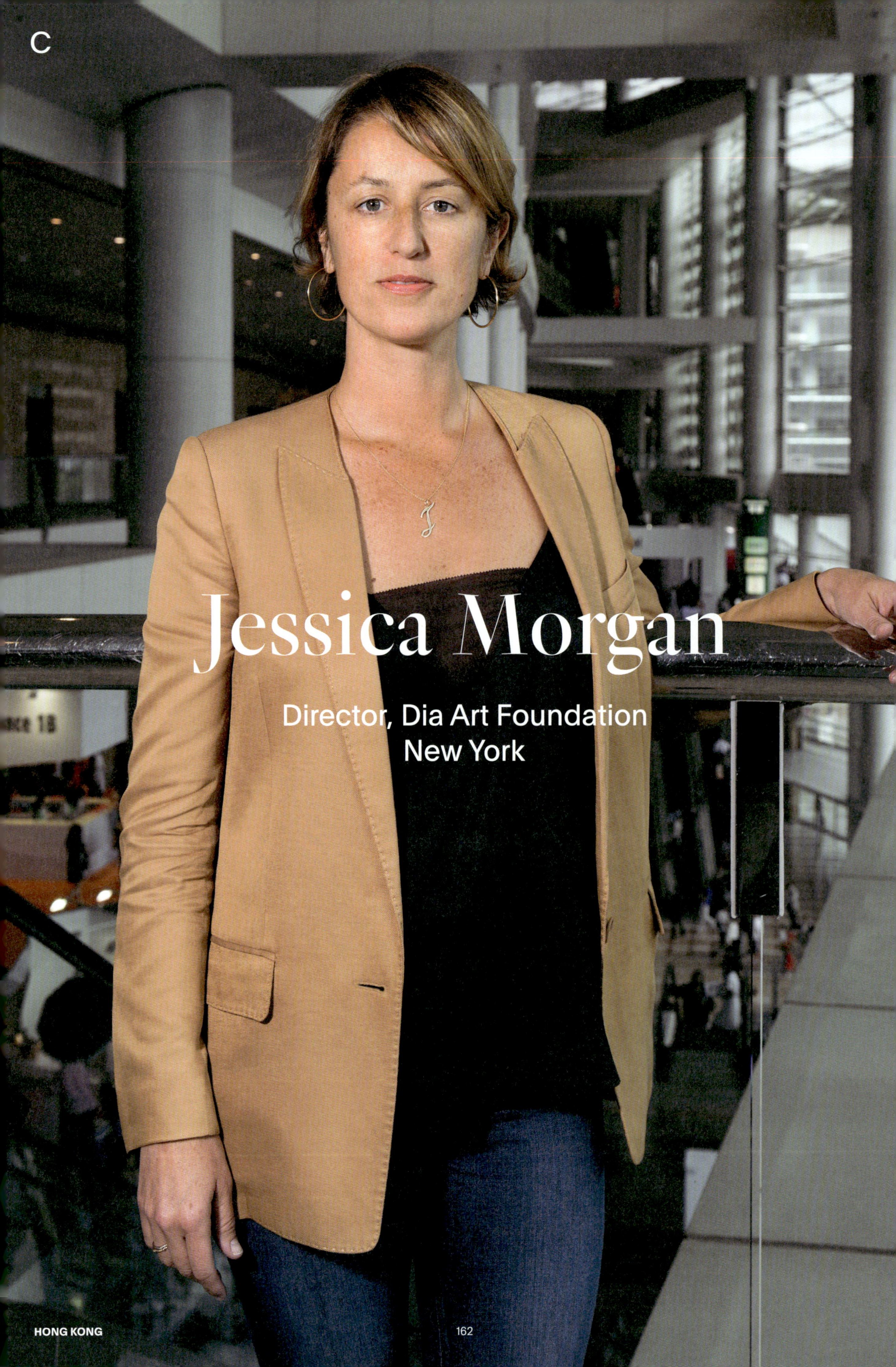

Jessica Morgan

Director, Dia Art Foundation
New York

Cheng Ran
Leo Xu Projects (Discoveries)

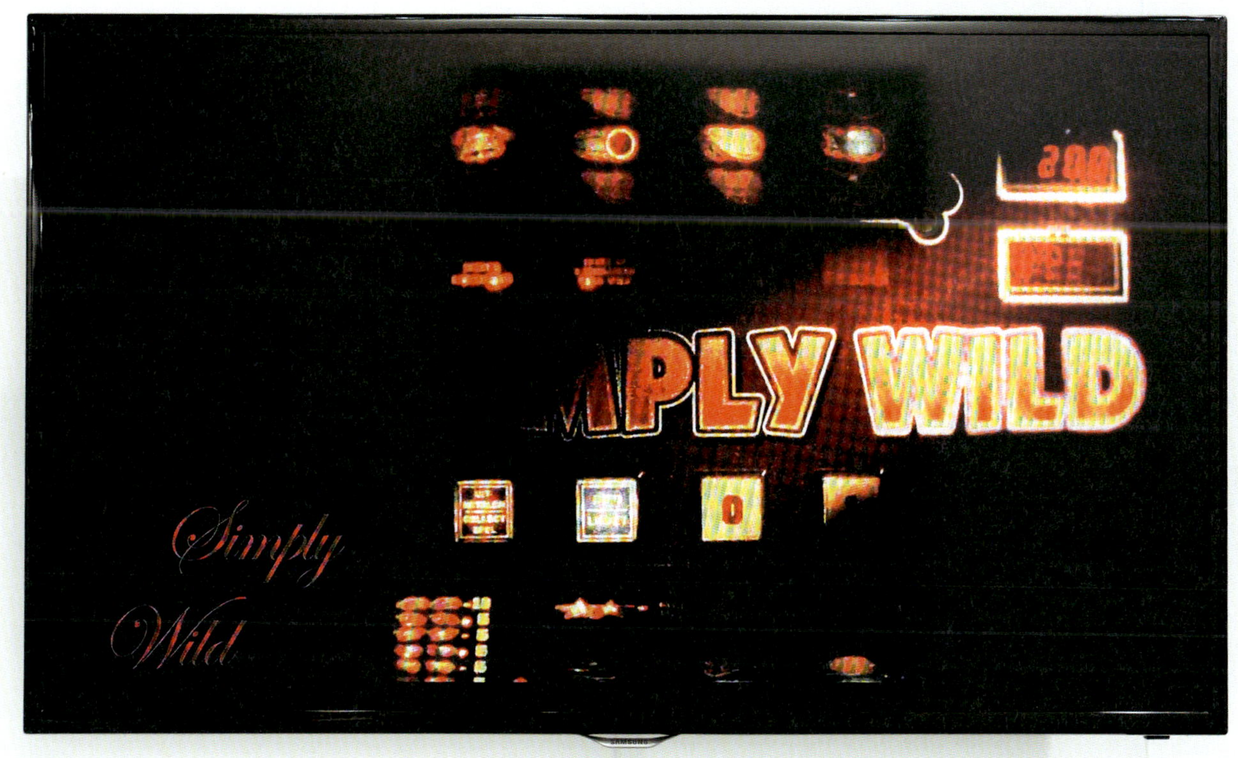

"An absurdly complex romantic tale was extracted from the unpromising beginnings of a spam email. The resulting film and installation speak of the mistranslations of our connected lives."

C

Hassan Sharif

Cardboard and Glue, 2005
Gallery Isabelle van den Eynde (Insights)

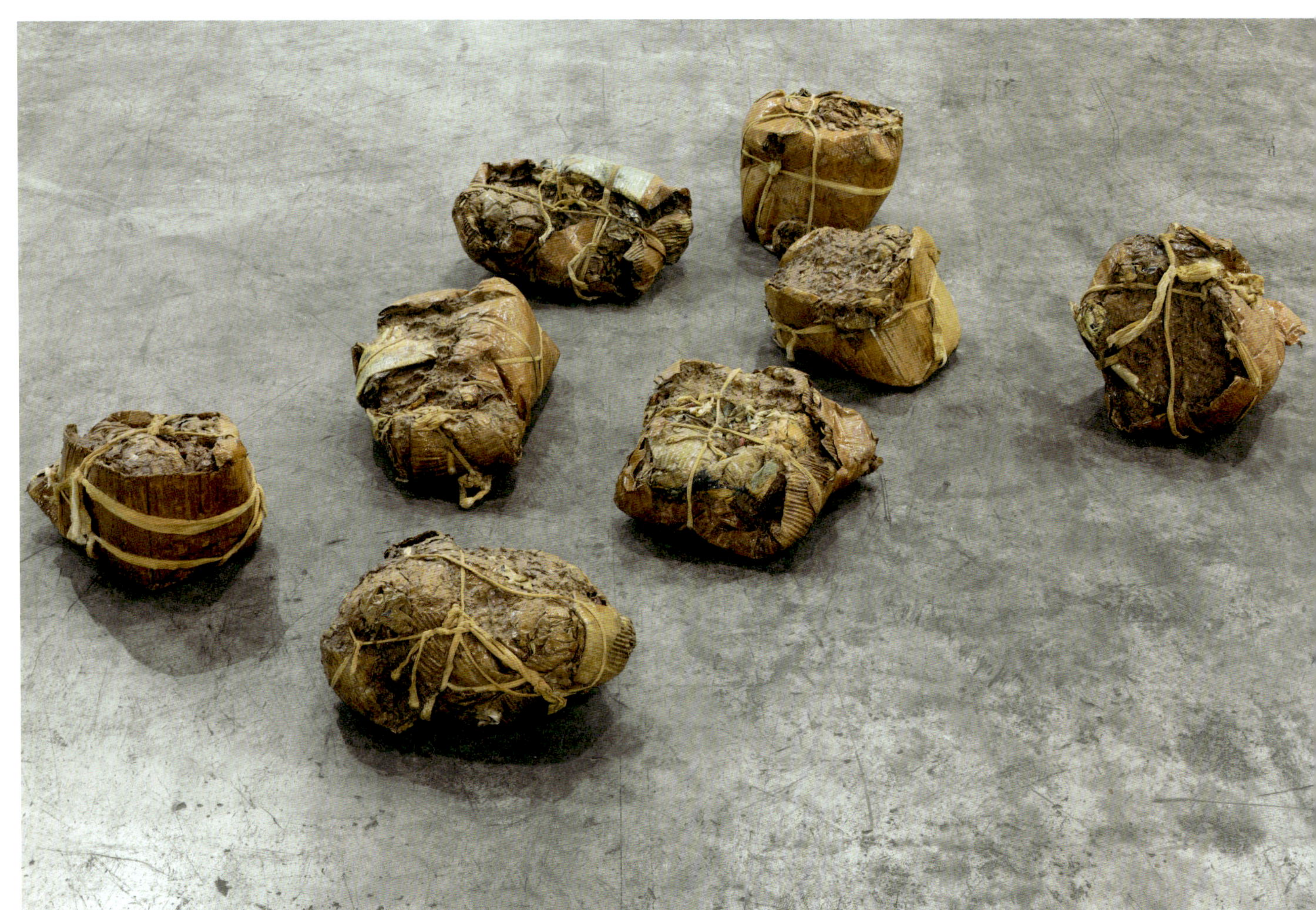

"Accumulations of materiality, Hassan Sharif's sculptures return the evidence of labor to the excess of matter that is part of our daily existence."

Koo Jeong-A

Tempos de Gossura, 2012

Pilar Corrias

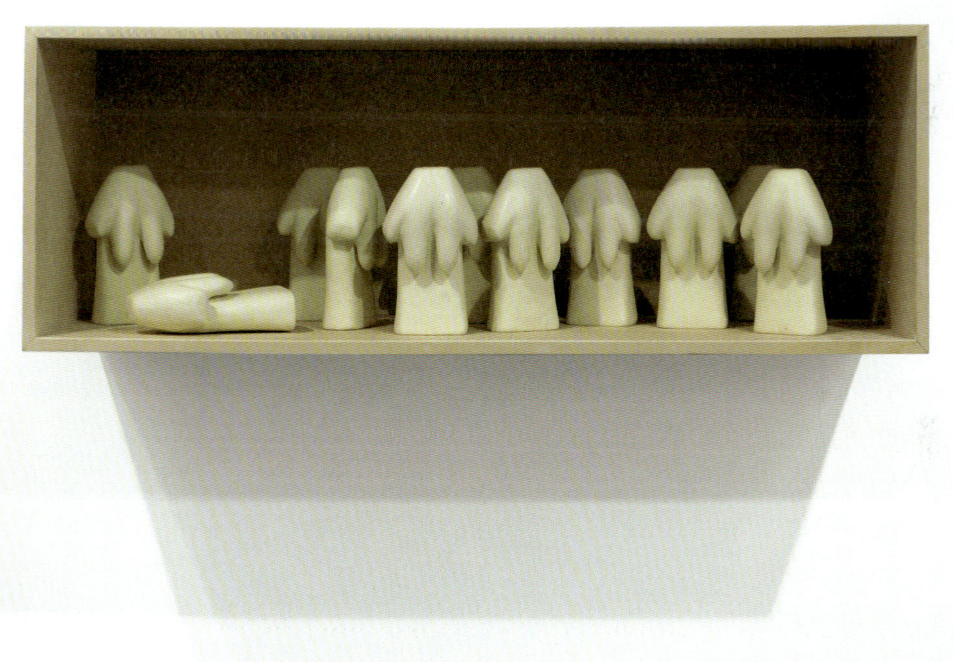

"These fluoro-painted, saggy-breasted figurines are like minions of an ancient comic culture. Reproduced from a small idol figure encountered in the home of the Italian/Brazilian architect Lina Bo Bardi, Koo Jeong-A transforms the small figurine into an army that glows in the dark."

C

Shooshie Sulaiman

Fresh Vegetable #1 and *Fresh Vegetable #2*, 2013

Tomio Koyama Gallery

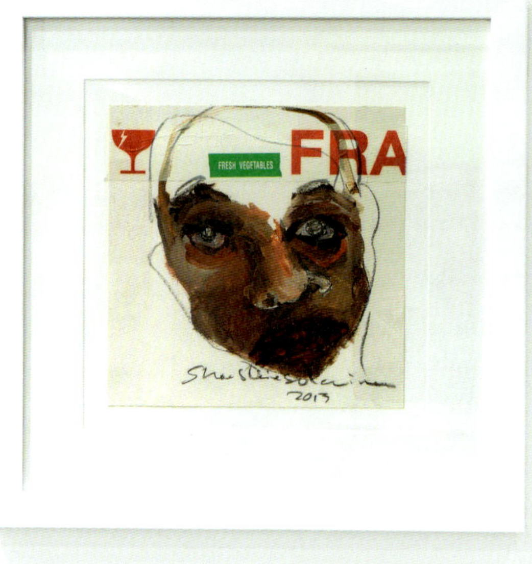

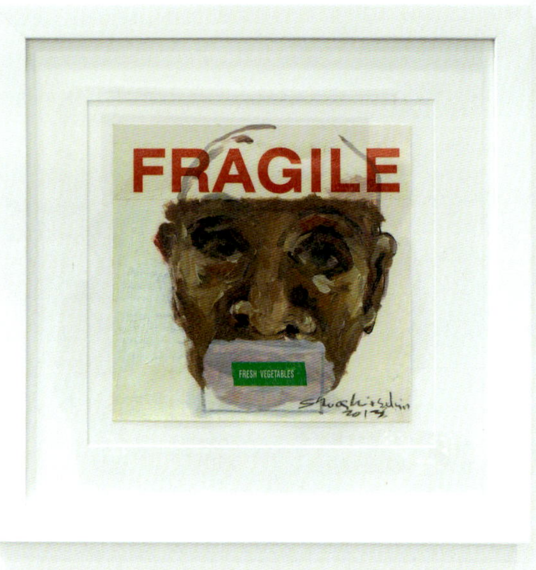

"Shooshie Sulaiman's intense series of Malay faces, painted and drawn with great facility, are stamped and categorized to suggest a pseudo-anthropology or ethnographic study."

Vivan Sundaram

Re-Take of Amrita series, 2001–2002
Chemould Prescott Road

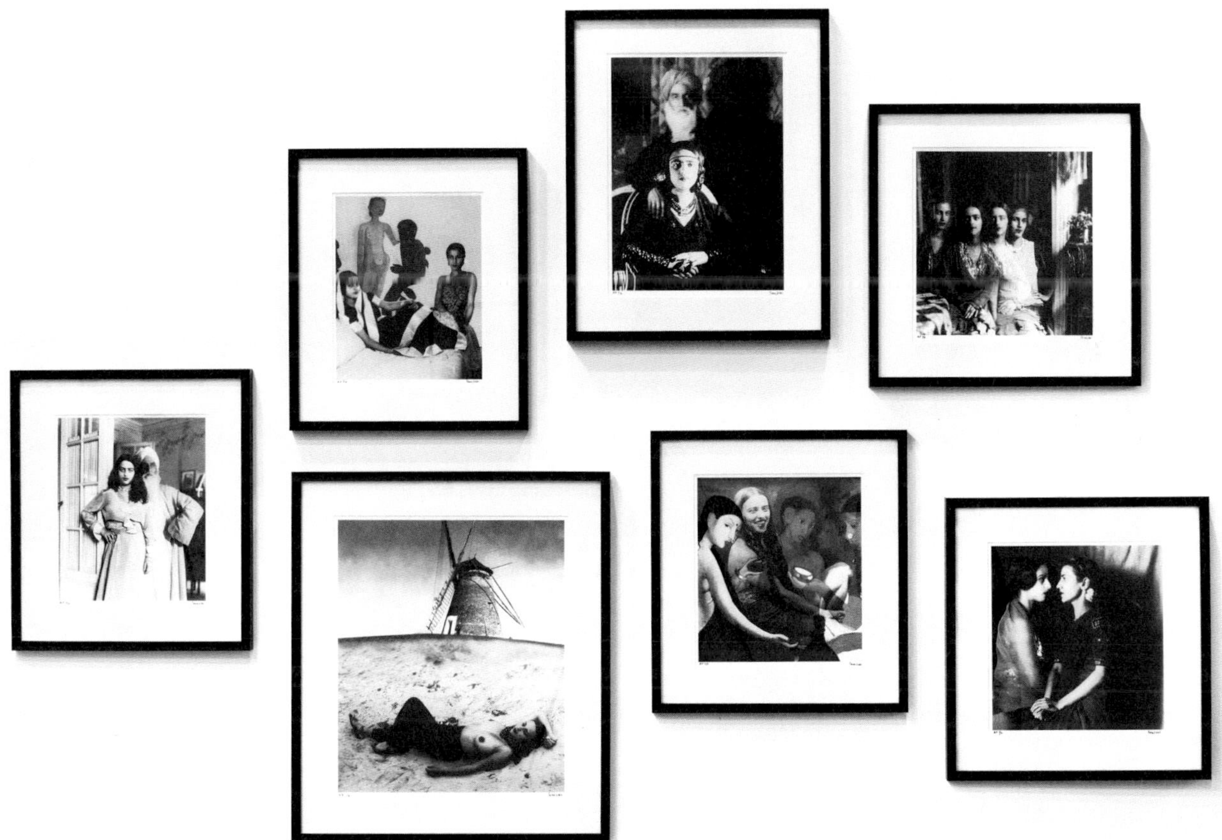

"Vivan Sundaram's ghostly photographs merge his own work with that of his illustrious artistic lineage. The already fluid roles employed by his aunt Amrita Sher-Gil and her father Umrao Singh Sher-Gil Majithia in their own portraiture are blended into a fictitious layering of history."

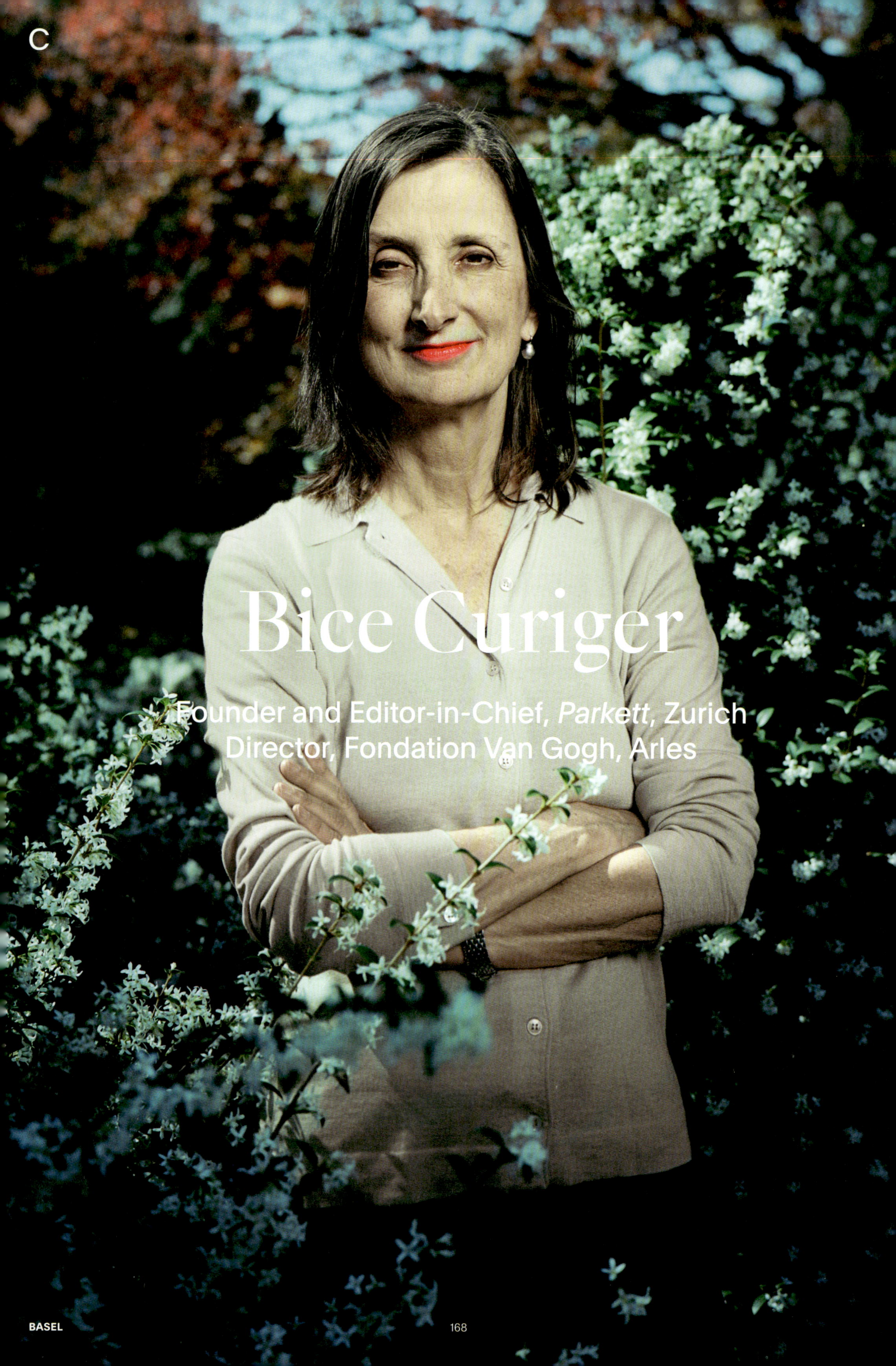

Bice Curiger

Founder and Editor-in-Chief, *Parkett*, Zurich
Director, Fondation Van Gogh, Arles

Lily van der Stokker

Blue Blob Drip Wallpainting, 2014

kaufmann repetto

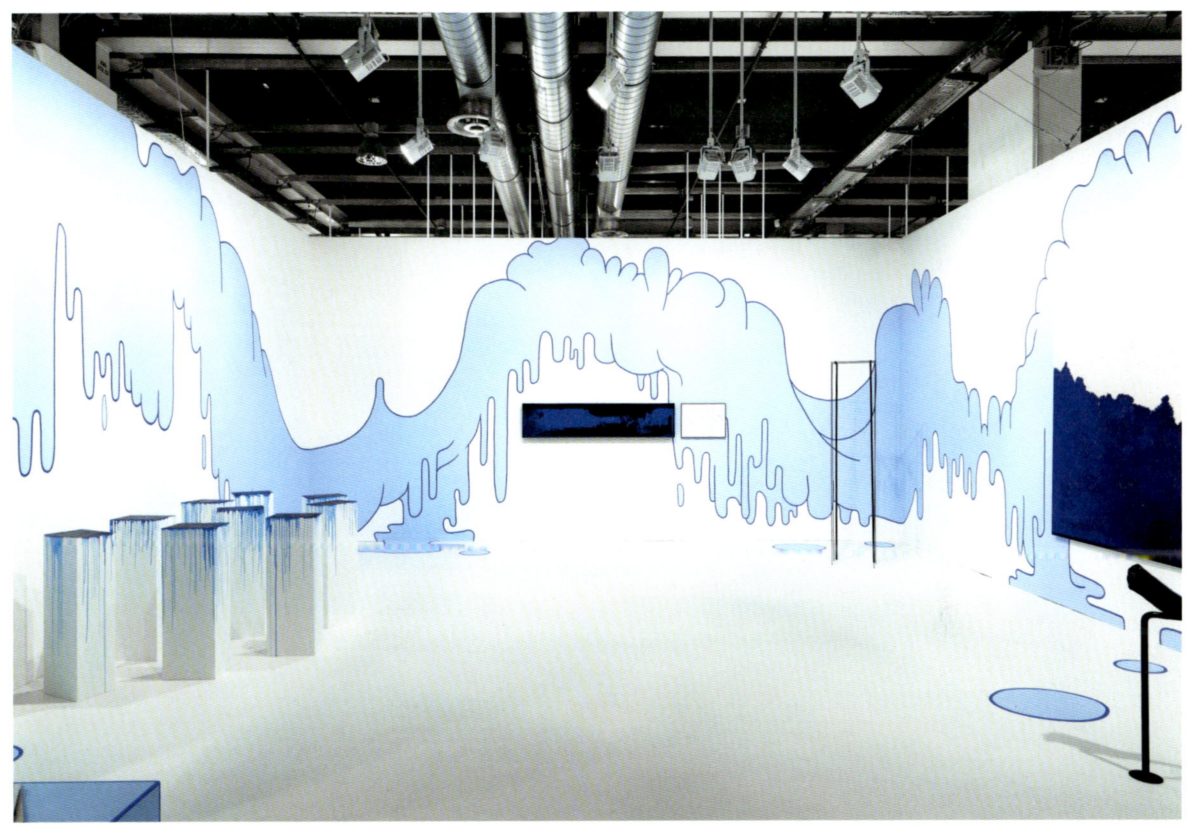

"Does the word 'subversive' mean anything anymore? Looking at Lily van der Stokker's interventions, I am full of admiration for how smart these seemingly 'silly' and 'childish' forms come across, dismantling the lofty, the pompous, the pretentious. In the context of art, these cartoon-like interventions are evocations of liquid, of splashing about in colors, of torrential rain, yet they are also signs of tenderness and of a freedom-loving sense of humor. At this booth, the work also acts as a cheerful connecting element between the monochrome blue works of the other artists Judith Hopf and Latifa Echakhch."

C

Christian Marclay

Shake Rattle and Roll (Fluxmix), 2004

Paula Cooper Gallery (Unlimited)

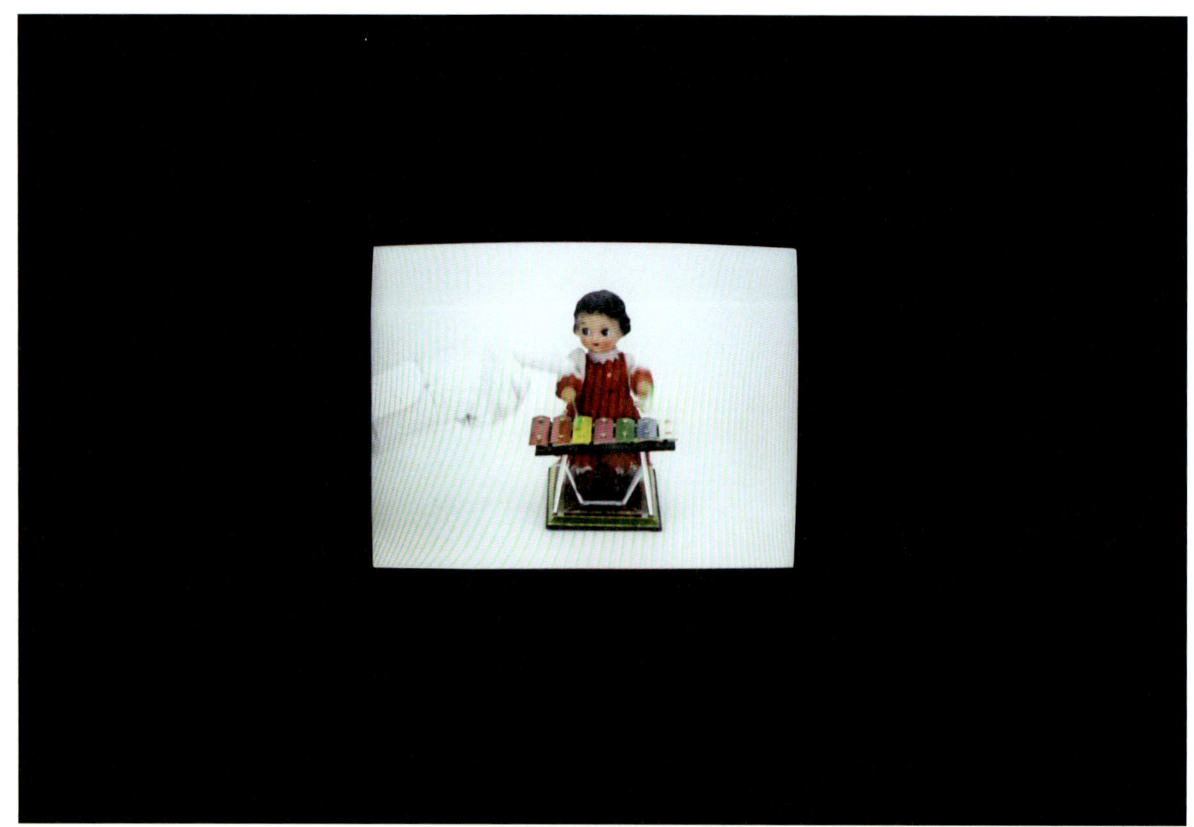

"Christian Marclay made this wonderful video piece during his residency at the Walker Art Center in Minneapolis, which houses a large Fluxus collection. The objects, neatly filed in folders and boxes, are literally brought to life. On 16 monitors, arranged in a circle, one can see hands in white gloves testing the items for their 'sonority,' for the sounds that a 'shake, rattle, and roll' can elicit. Fluxus, the influential art movement of the 1960s, has in its name 'flux,' the flow of things, of life. Once more Marclay proves himself to be Fluxus' worthiest heir."

Antonio Calderara

Annemarie Verna Galerie and Galleria Massimo Minini

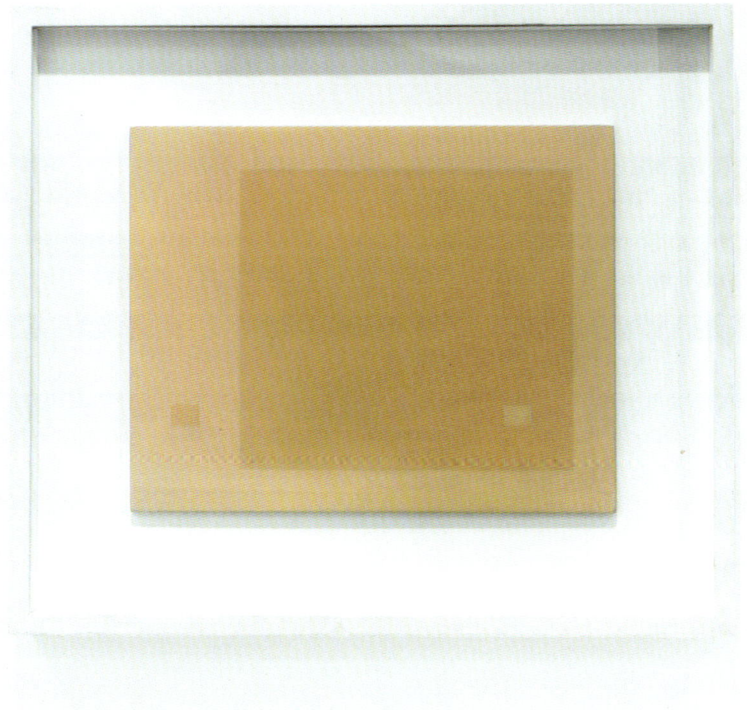

"An unexpected encounter with Antonio Calderara's early works is one of those serendipitous moments that make visiting Art Basel worthwhile. It brought back memories of how, way back when, I saw the lyrical-abstract-geometrical works of this Italian artist at the then small but radical Galerie Verna in Zurich, in the context of American Minimal art. The few examples shown here were works previously unknown to me, notably from the 1920s and 1930s, opening up an intensely atmospheric universe of silence."

C

Tacita Dean
c/o Jolyon, 2012–2013
Frith Street Gallery

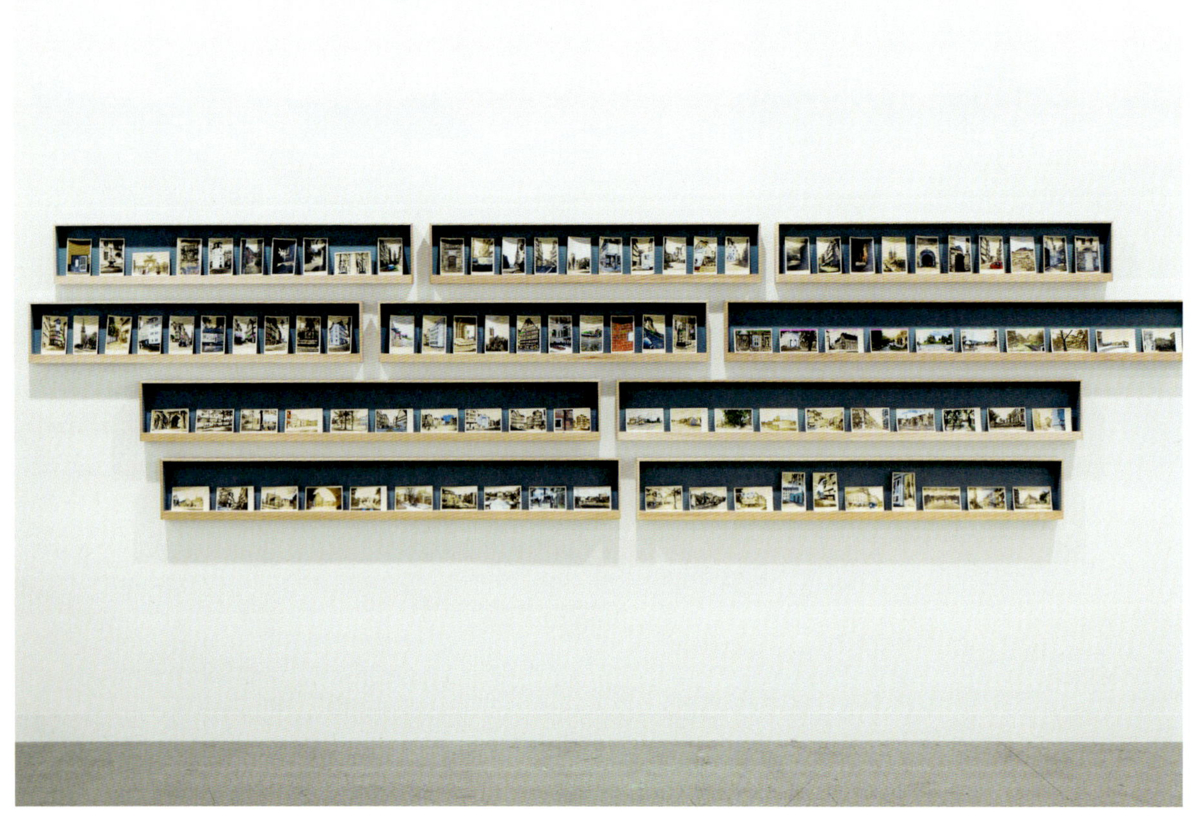

"Old postcards from the city of Kassel, sepia brown views of streets, churches, the town hall, half-timbered houses … prewar scenes, 100 pieces in neat rows. On closer examination, one notices small drawn-on interventions, for which Tacita Dean used gouache and a fine brush. These wild little *aperçus* add cartoon-like glimpses of the present day. This work, titled *c/o Jolyon*, was developed in the context of the last documenta. The artist sent the postcards to Jolyon Leslie, Cultural Attaché in Kabul, Kassel's 'twin city,' during documenta. Is there any need for more explanation on how so little can trigger so much?"

Teppei Kaneuji
ShugoArts

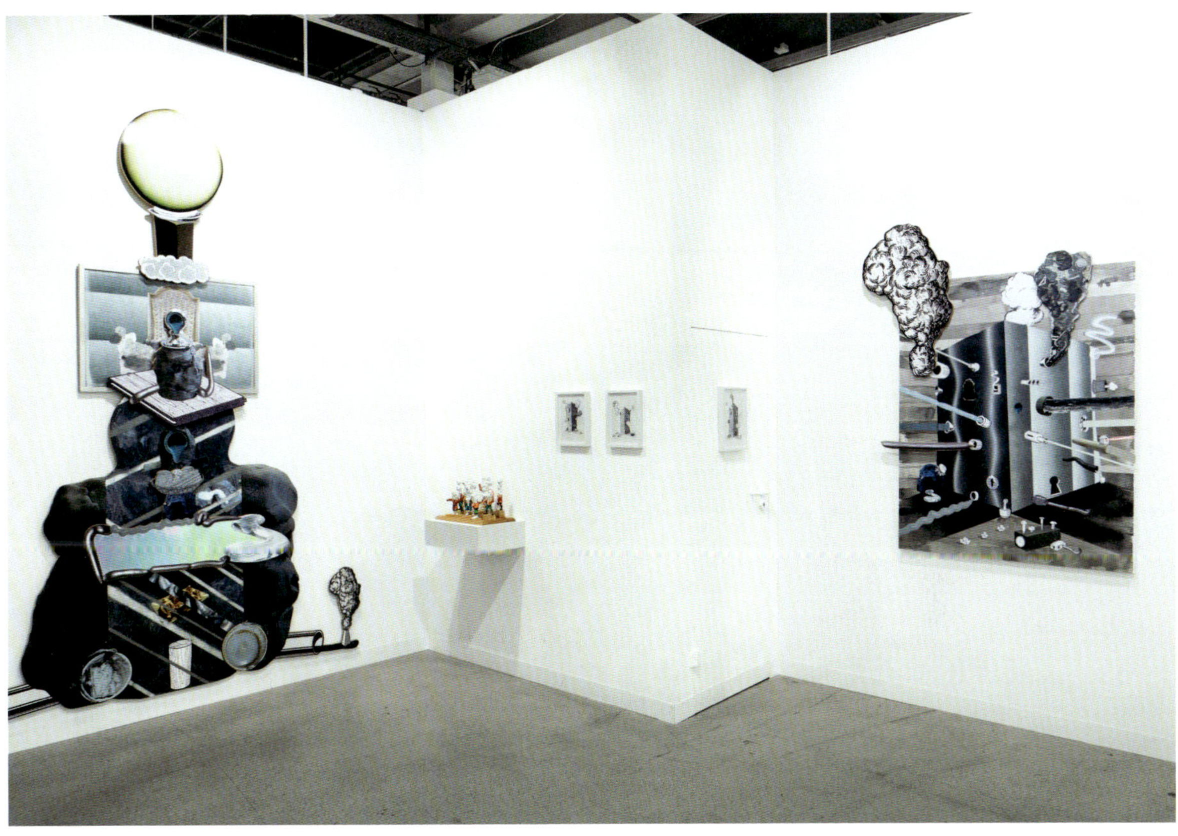

"I did not know the young Japanese artist Teppei Kaneuji (born 1978), yet somehow his works immediately captivated me. The way in which he creates art from the world of objects surrounding and sometimes overpowering us drew me in directly. His assemblages, idiosyncratically ordered conglomerations of objects, are like sweet anarchic mirror images of the gigantic hodgepodge that is our industrial manufacturing system. They seem to be just as meaningless as their source, yet possess a mesmeric force of attraction."

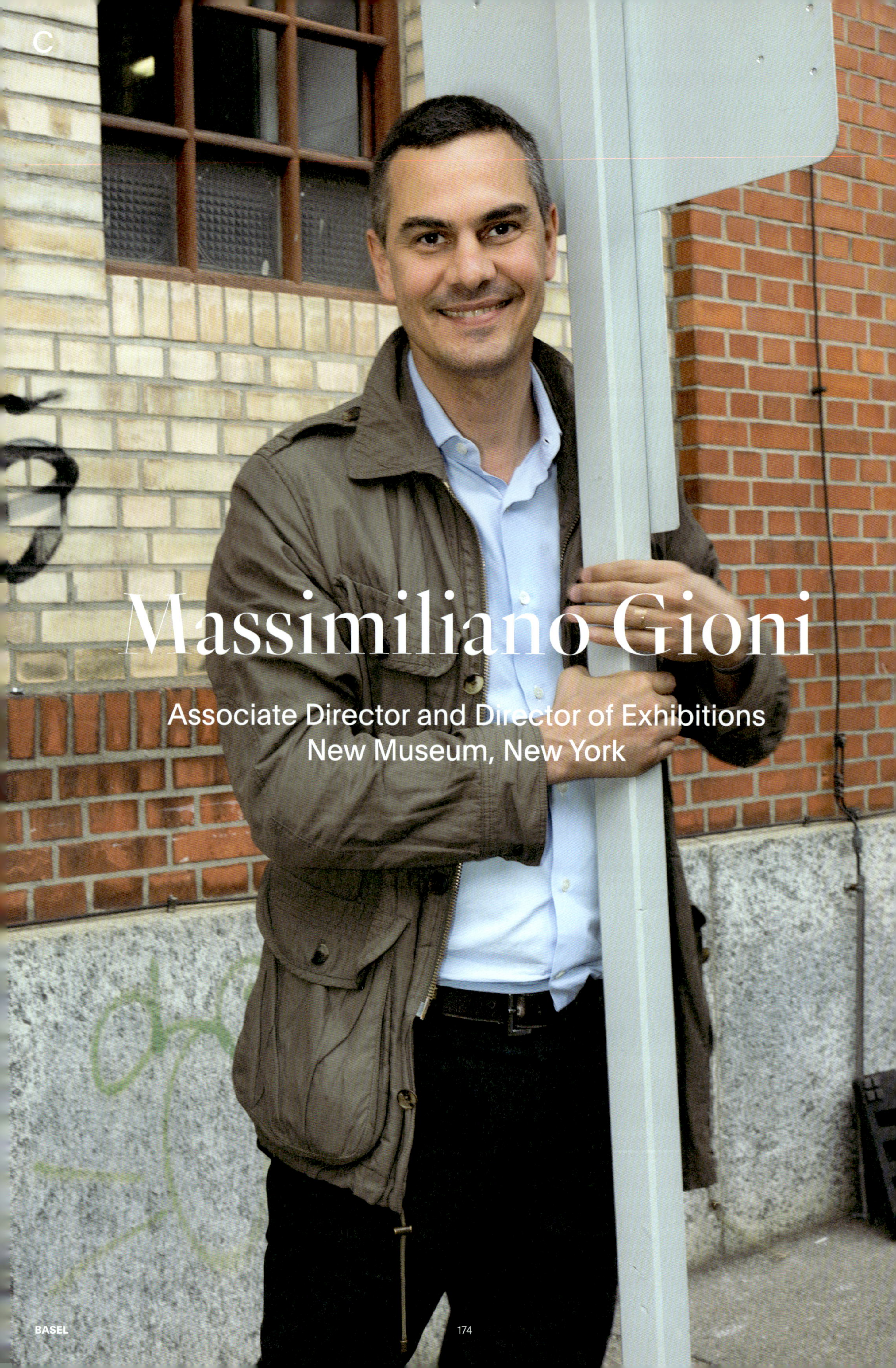

Massimiliano Gioni

Associate Director and Director of Exhibitions
New Museum, New York

Hanne Darboven

Kinder dieser Welt (Children of this World), 1990–1996
Konrad Fischer Galerie and Sprüth Magers
Berlin London (Unlimited)

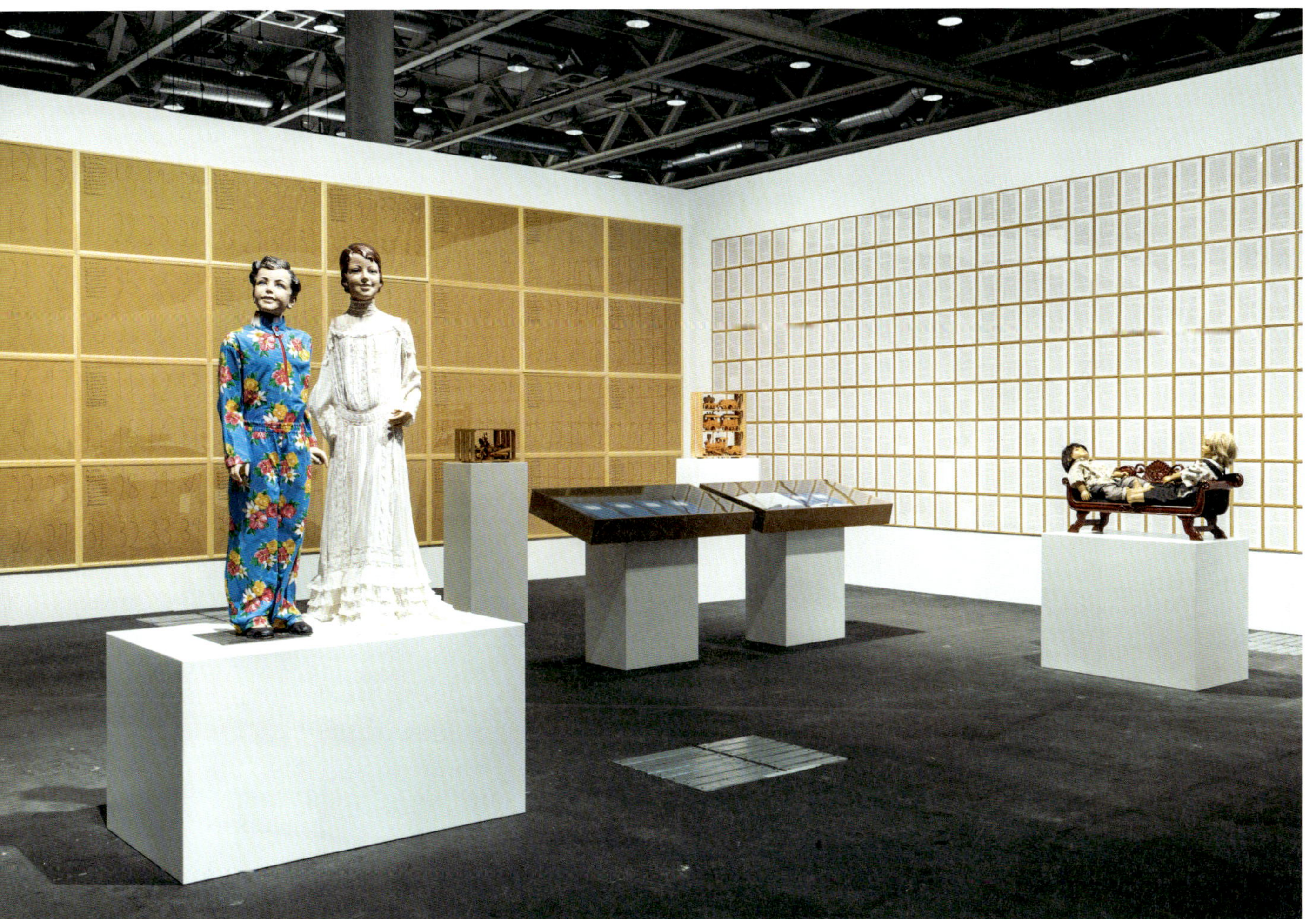

"Do I really need to say anything? This was an absolute masterpiece by a great artist and a devastating reflection on the basic human need to create effigies of ourselves."

C

Andra Ursuta

Orthodoctrinator, 2014
Massimo De Carlo and
Ramiken Crucible (Unlimited)

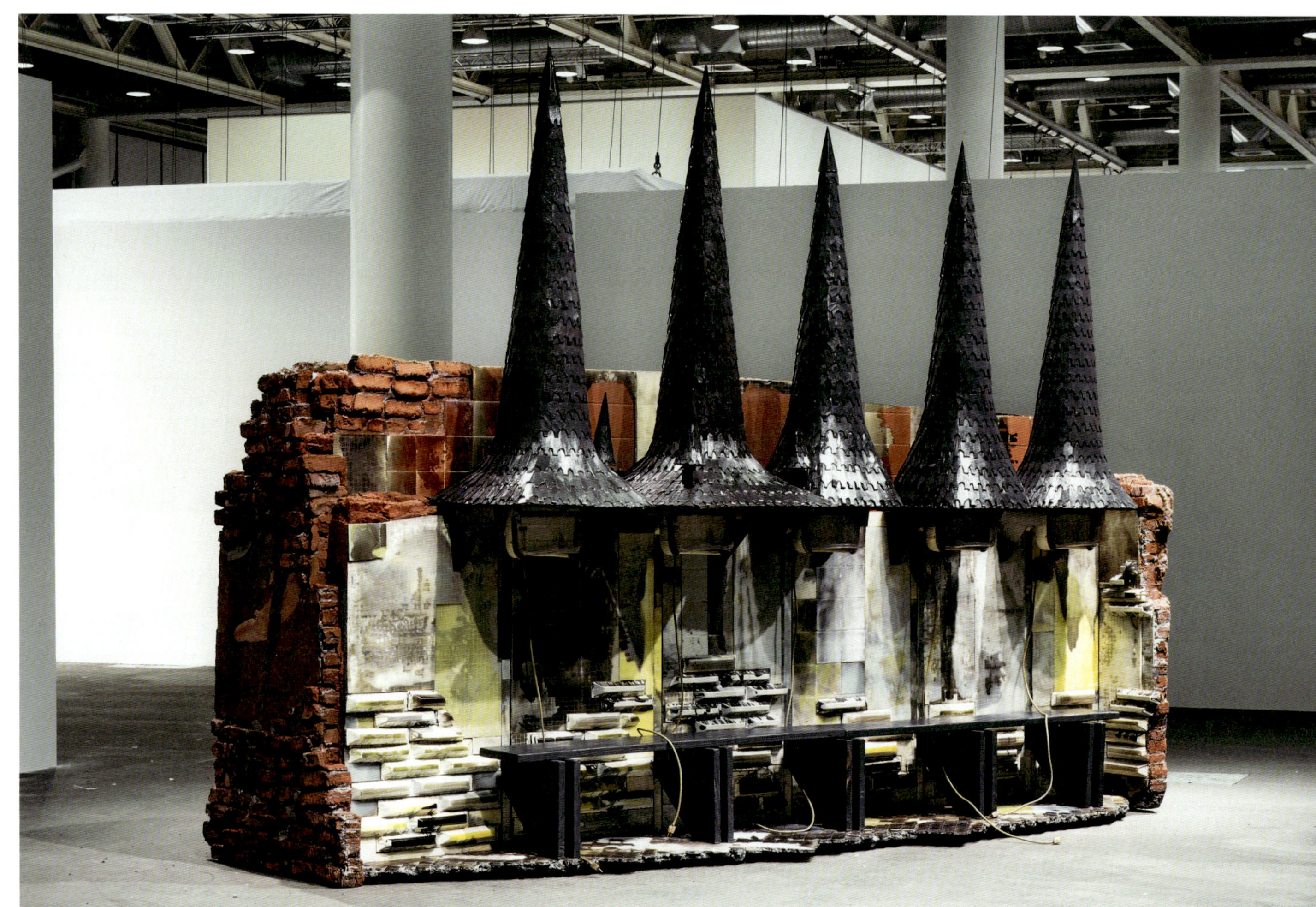

"Andra Ursuta and her turbo folk sculptures are among the most interesting works being made in New York today. Her vernacular architecture is part Gordon Matta-Clark and part hair-dressing salon."

Christian Schad

Anna Gabbioneta, 1927

Richard Nagy Ltd.

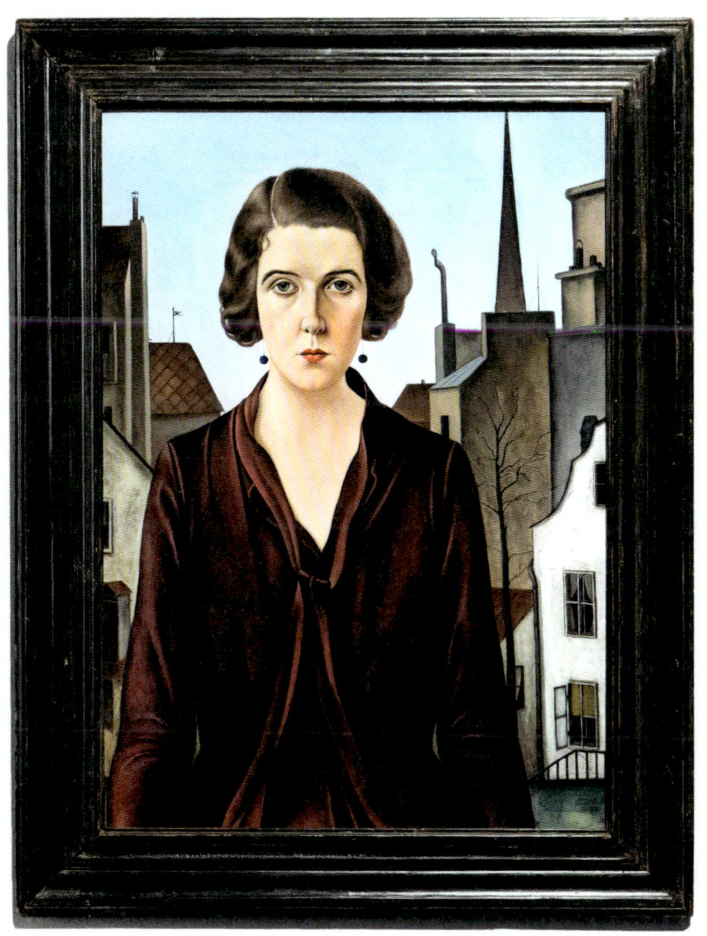

"This is exactly how I would paint, if I could and if I had the patience—with the technique and inexhaustible eye of Christian Schad."

C

Konrad Klapheck
Die Rechthaberin, 1967
Galerie Michael Haas

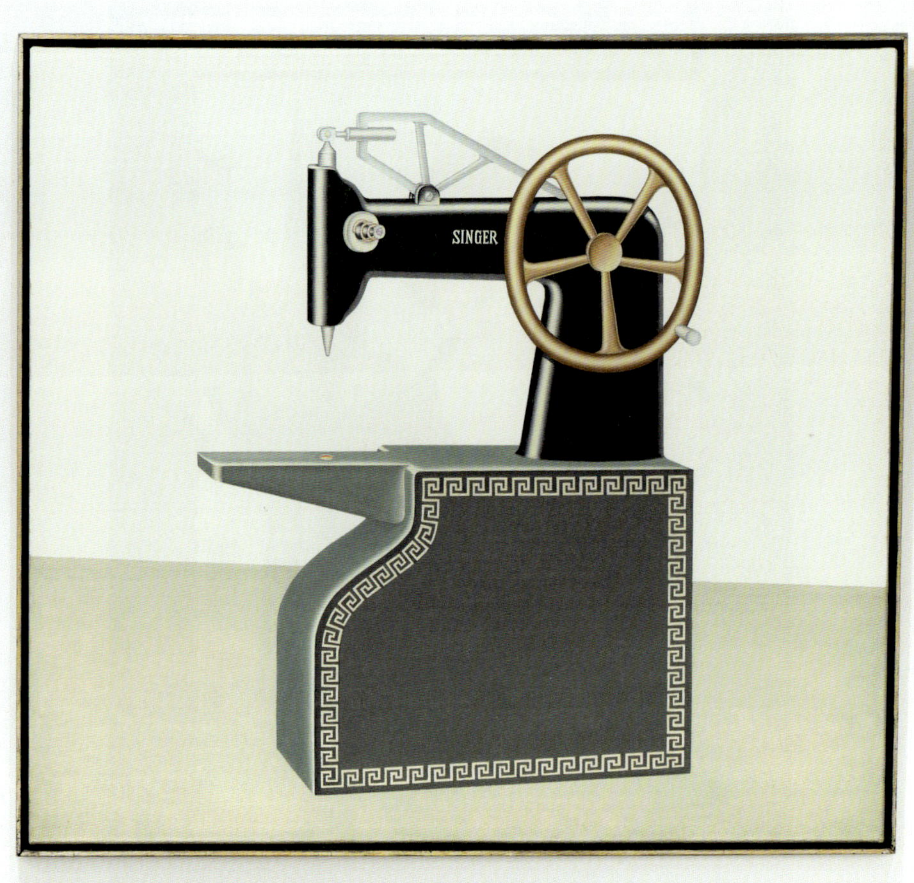

"There is so much that I admire in his work, particularly in his mechanomorphic years. If anything, he must be the only living artist who can proudly say that his work has been championed by André Breton himself: it really doesn't get much cooler than that. Well, actually it does: Christopher Williams loves his work too."

Jakub Julian Ziolkowski

Foksal Gallery Foundation

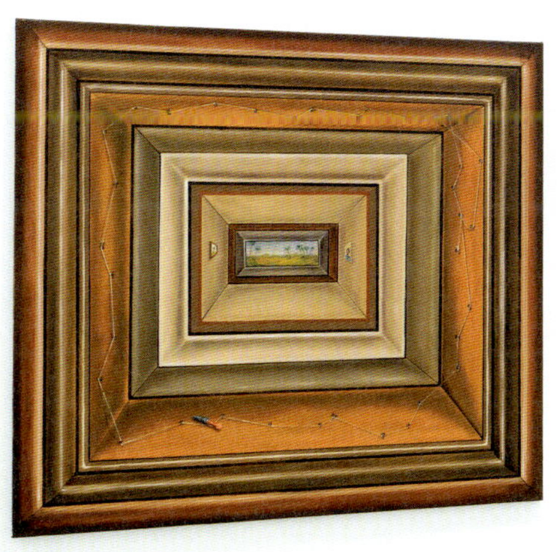

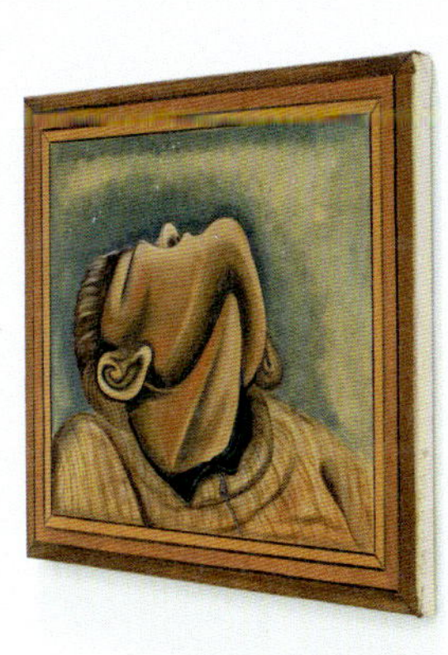

"Ziolkowski paints the mess that is in his head and the mess that is in our bodies. Sometimes I feel like his paintings, and believe me it's not a good feeling at all. Avoid his work completely if you are in the middle of a terrible hangover or during any moment of moderate depression."

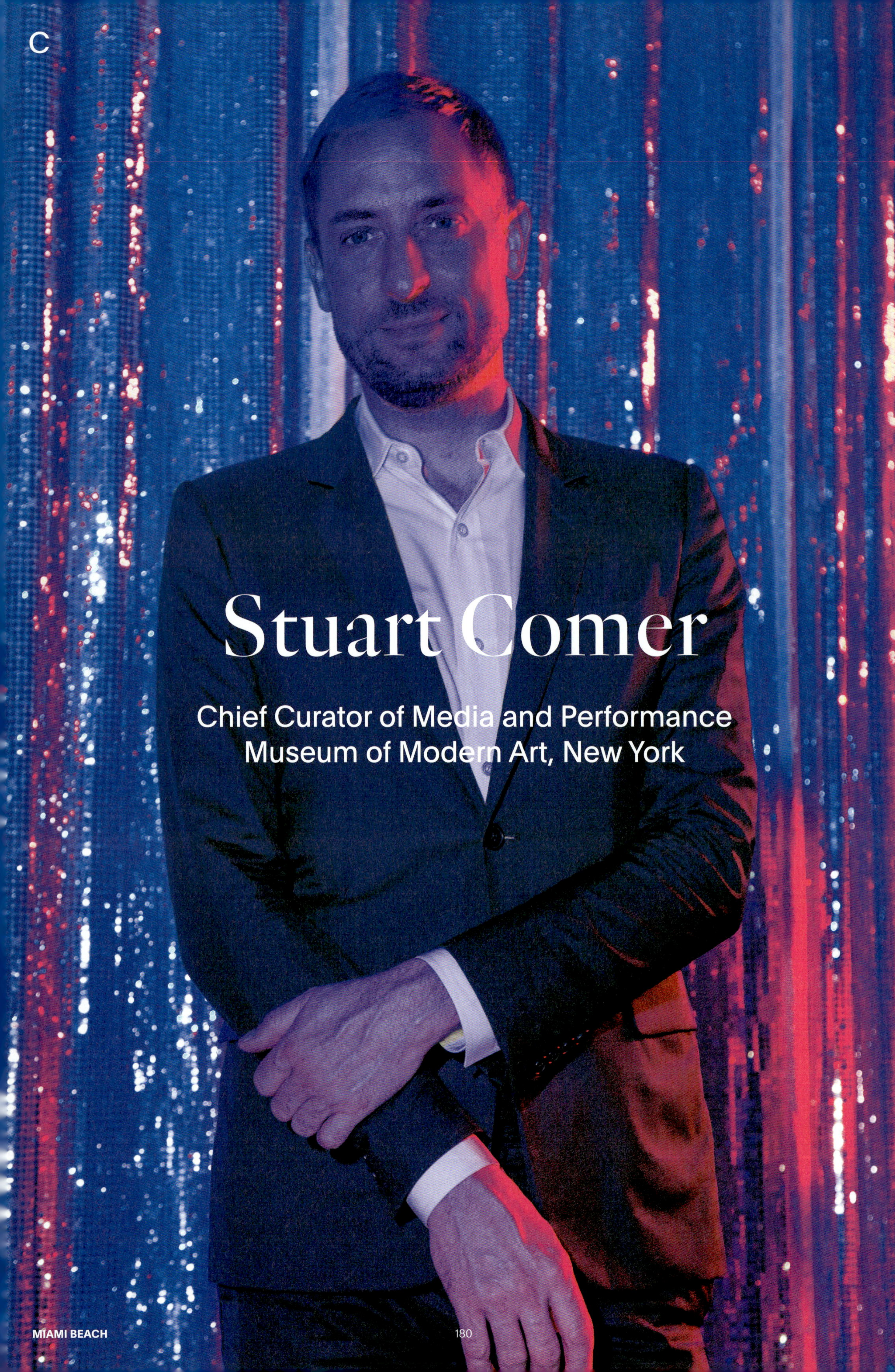

Stuart Comer

Chief Curator of Media and Performance
Museum of Modern Art, New York

Tabor Robak
Drinking Bird, 2014
Team (gallery, inc.)

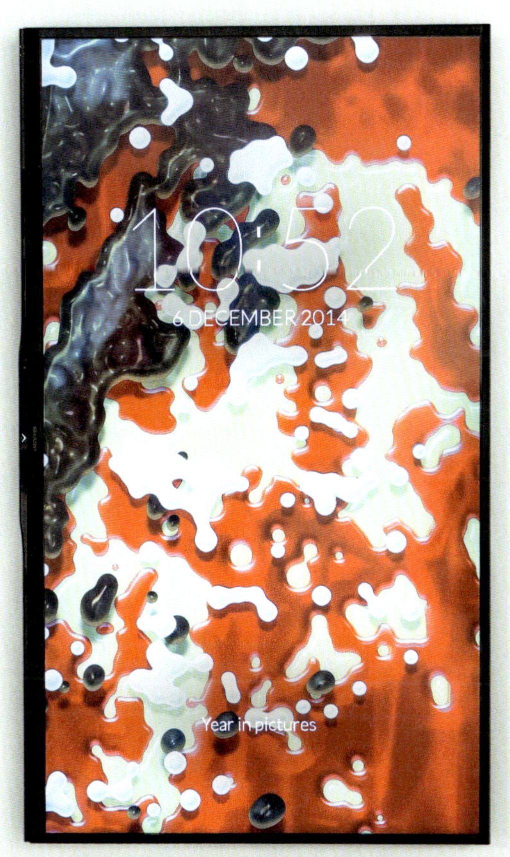

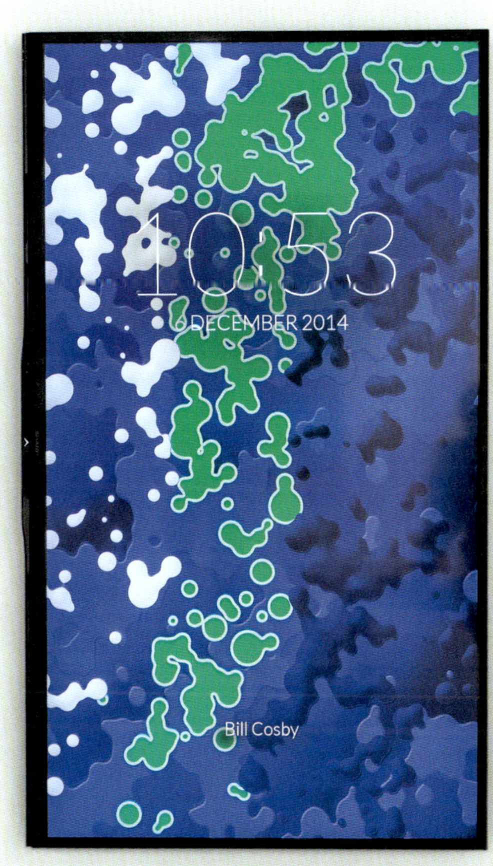

"Tabor Robak's unabashed embrace of digital culture frequently results in baroque, multiple screen works animated by video games, CGI imagery, and 3D virtual environments. *Drinking Bird* is a more pared down single-screen distillation of the strange interzone between the virtual and the real."

C

Alison Knowles
The Boat Book, 1966–2014
James Fuentes (Survey)

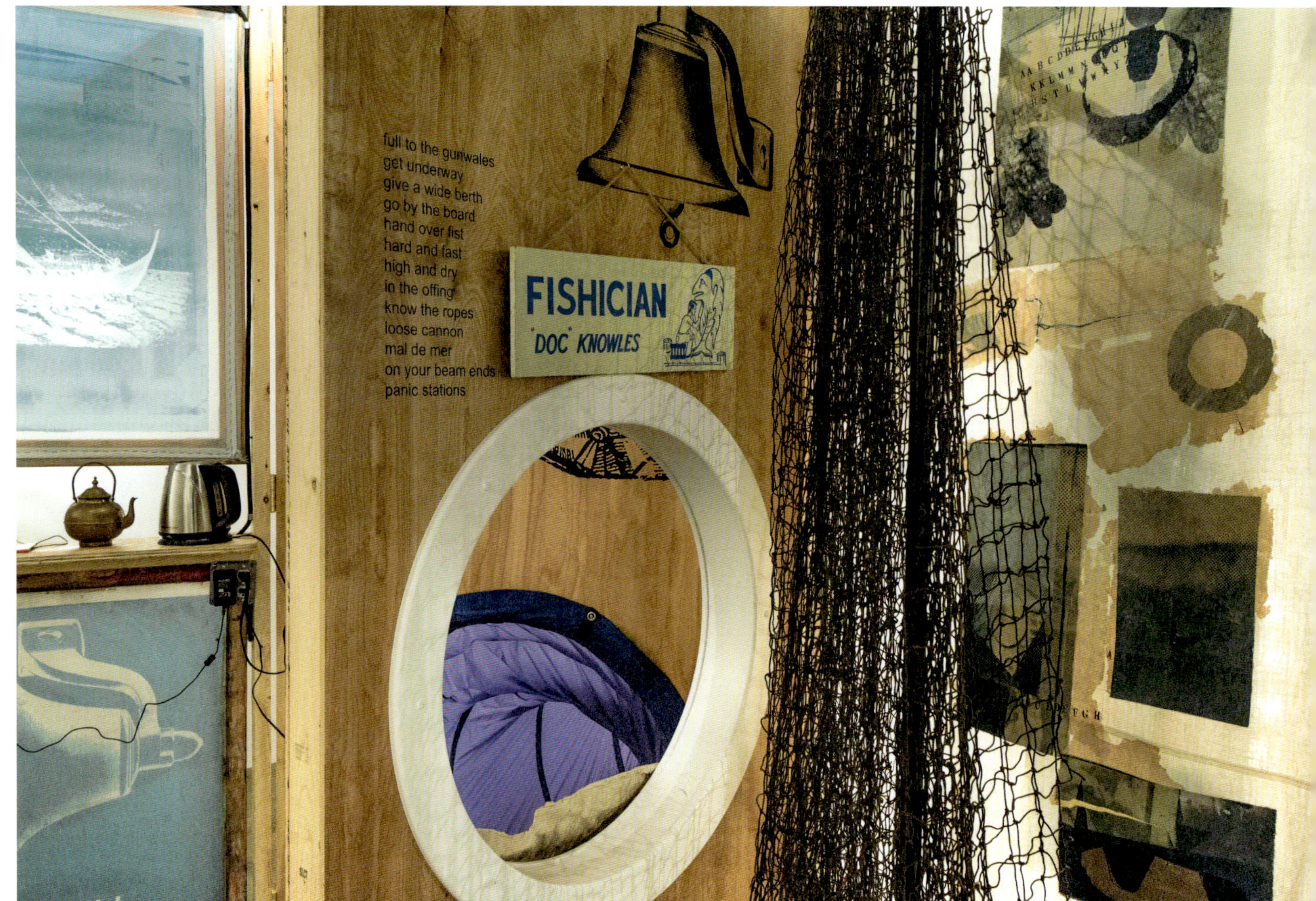

"*The Boat Book* by Fluxus pioneer Alison Knowles revisits her landmark 1966 project, *The Big Book*. Dedicated to her brother, a fisherman in East Hampton, New York, this new installation extends Knowles' many innovations in developing books as objects and language as action."

Martin Wong
Esmeralda: Songs for the Hearing Impaired, 1982
P.P.O.W

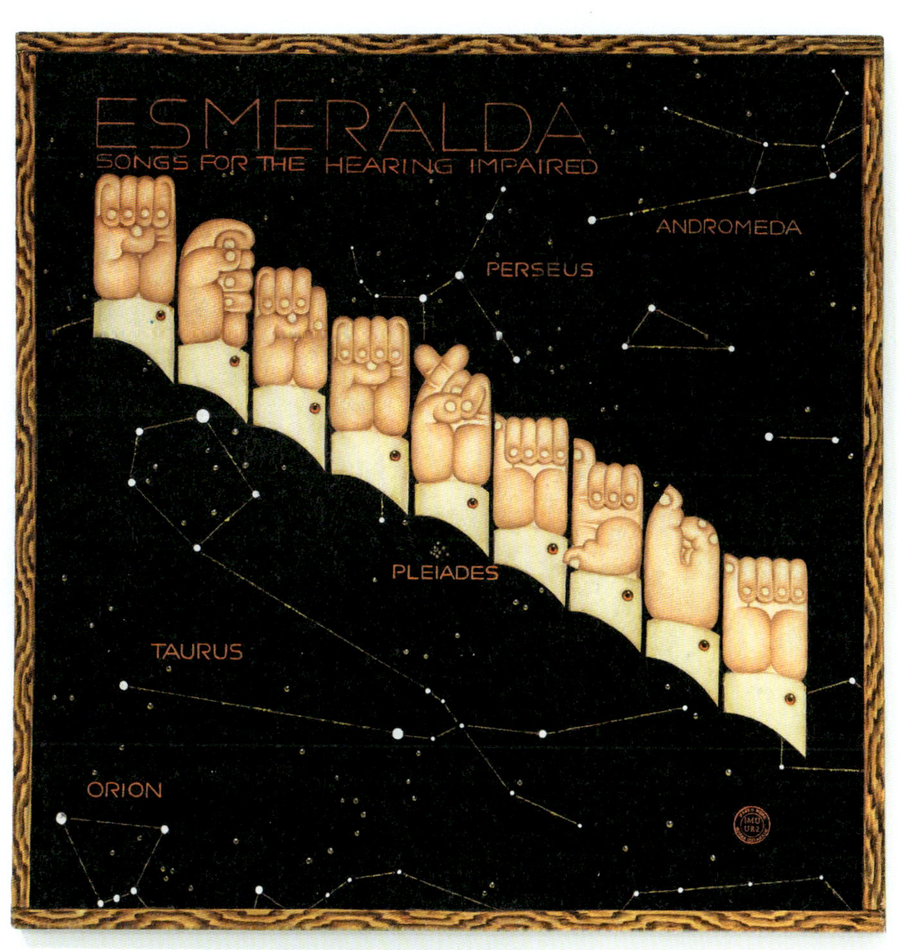

"Raised in San Francisco, Wong relocated to the Lower East Side of New York in the late 1970s. His paintings remain iconic representations of the gritty urban landscape that marked the city at that time. Wong was also active as a writer and collector. One major focus of his collection was work by graffiti artists, which led to collaborations with several of them."

C

Lotty Rosenfeld
Acciones de Arte, 1979–1999
espaivisor (Survey)

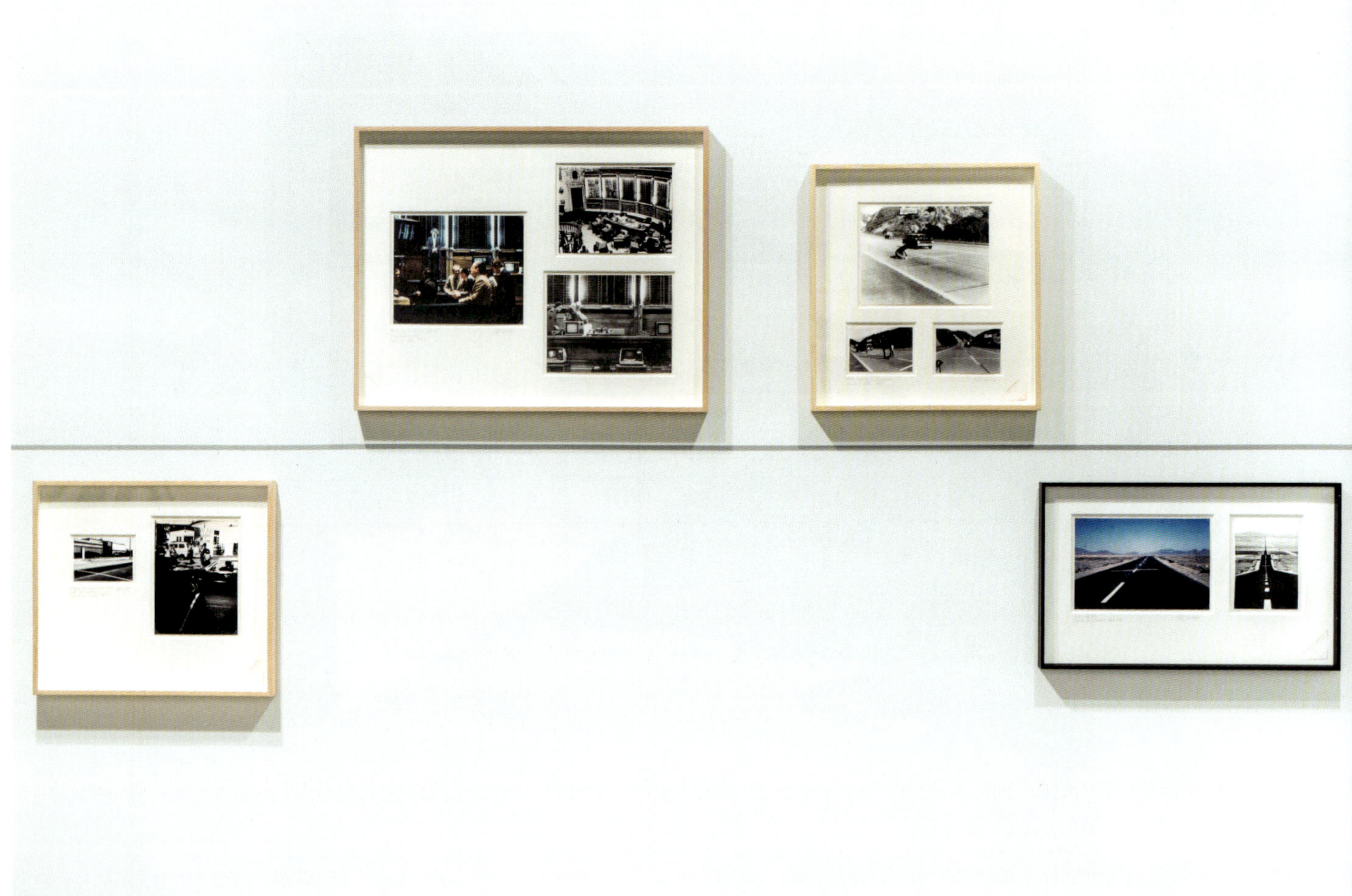

"Produced against the backdrop of military dictatorship in Chile, Lotty Rosenfeld's work in performance, video, and photography, and her interventions in public space questioned the social and political order and reflected on possibilities for art and activism."

Paulina Olowska

Raba Niżna, 2014

Foksal Gallery Foundation

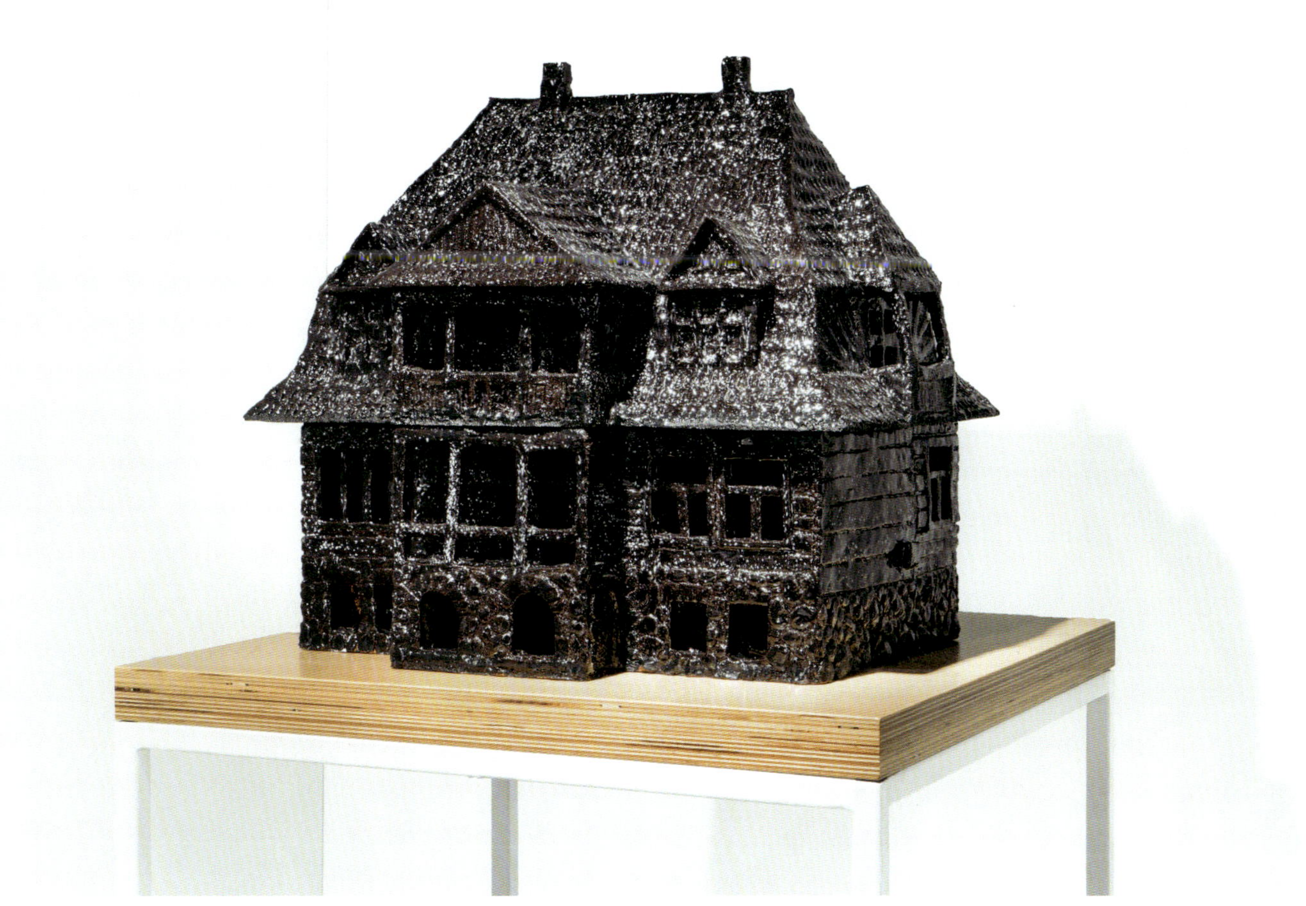

"Paulina Olowska has a longstanding interest in architectural structures, freestanding pavilions, theater sets, tableaux, and props that provide imaginary settings rooted in historical locations. These structures allow her to situate speculative acts within a matrix of historical fact, linking the past to dreamlike possibilities for the future."

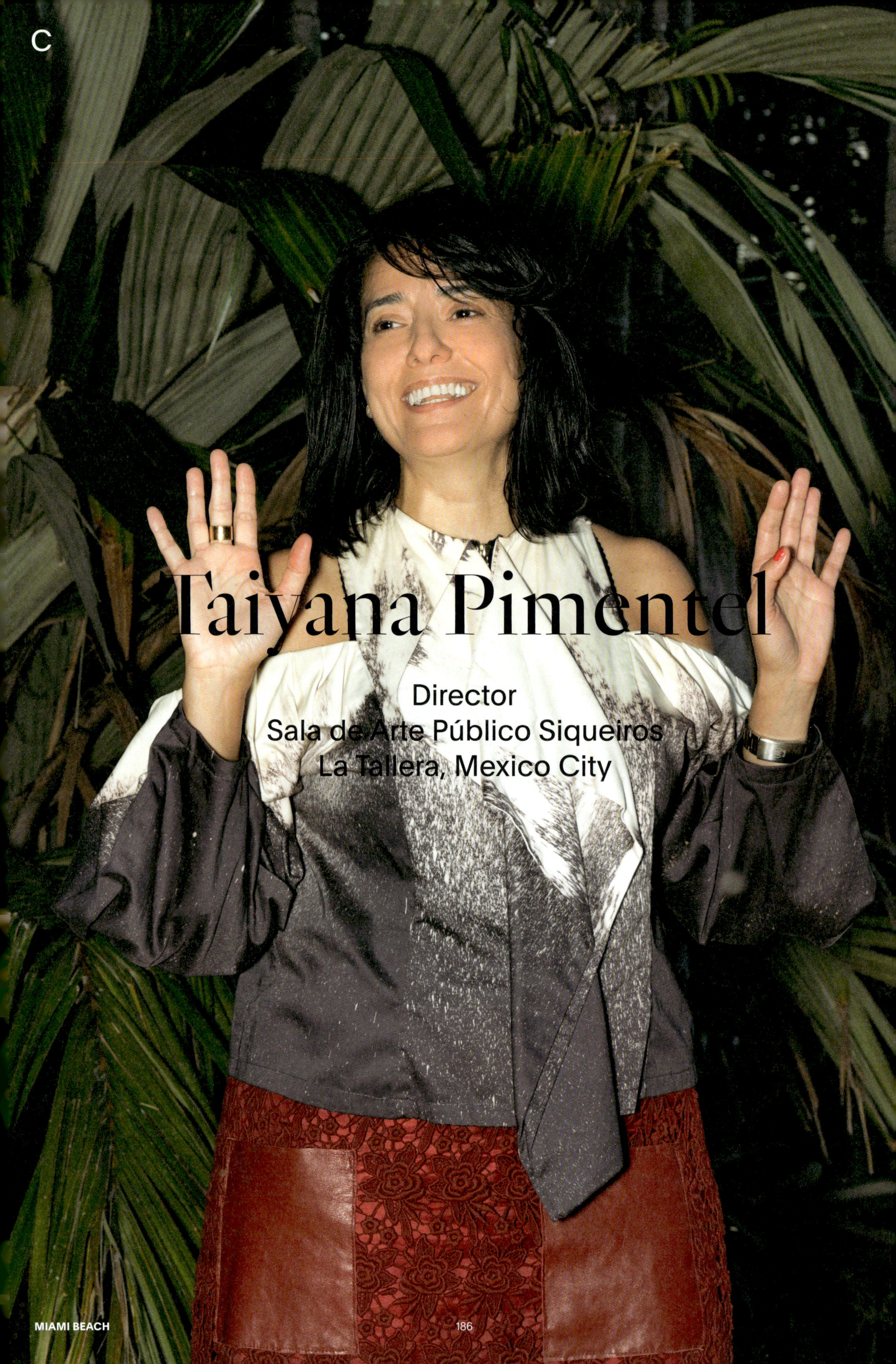

Taiyana Pimentel

Director
Sala de Arte Público Siqueiros
La Tallera, Mexico City

José Carlos Martinat

Manifiestos, 2014

Revolver Galería (Public)

C

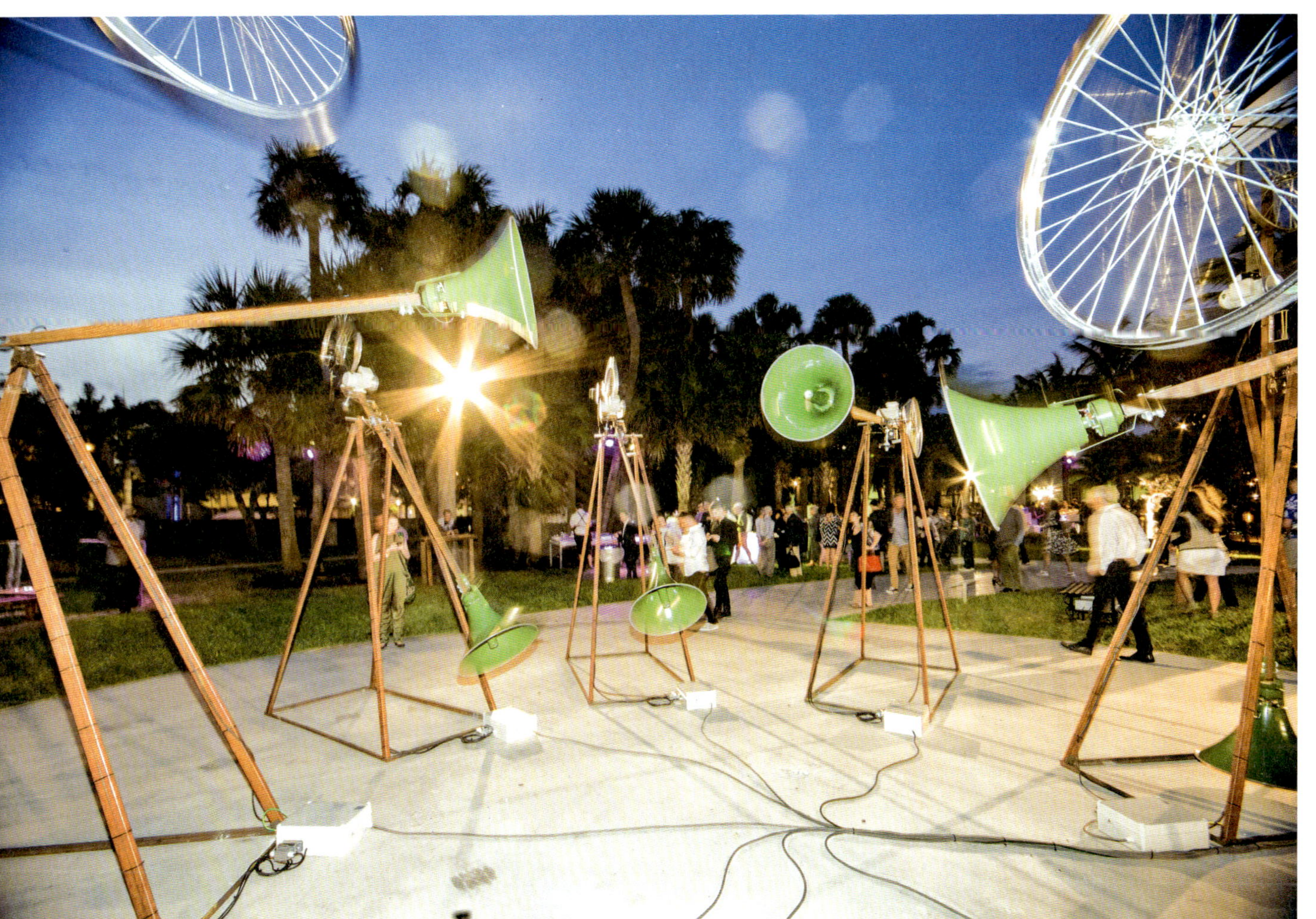

"The spirit of five commercial proposals coming from Latin American (Mexico, Peru, Colombia), interrupting the global system of contemporary art with a fresh sense of market, and positioning themselves beyond any nationalism."

Rita Ponce de León, David Zink Yi

80m2 Livia Benavides (Nova)

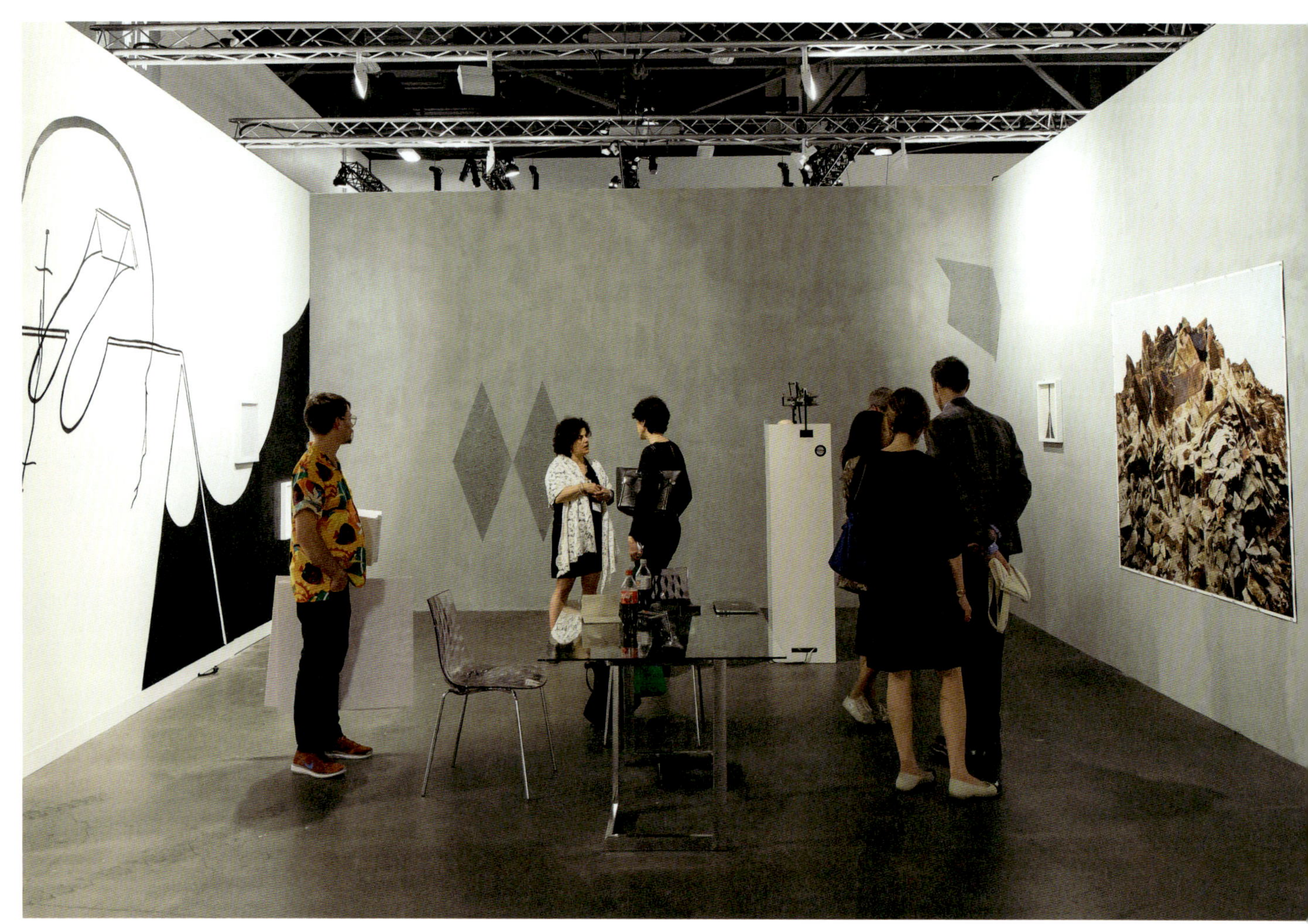

Pedro Reyes

Estatua de Karl Marx, 2014
Estatua de Leon Trotsky, 2014
Visual Bibliography I & II (Sanatorium), 2014
Labor (Nova)

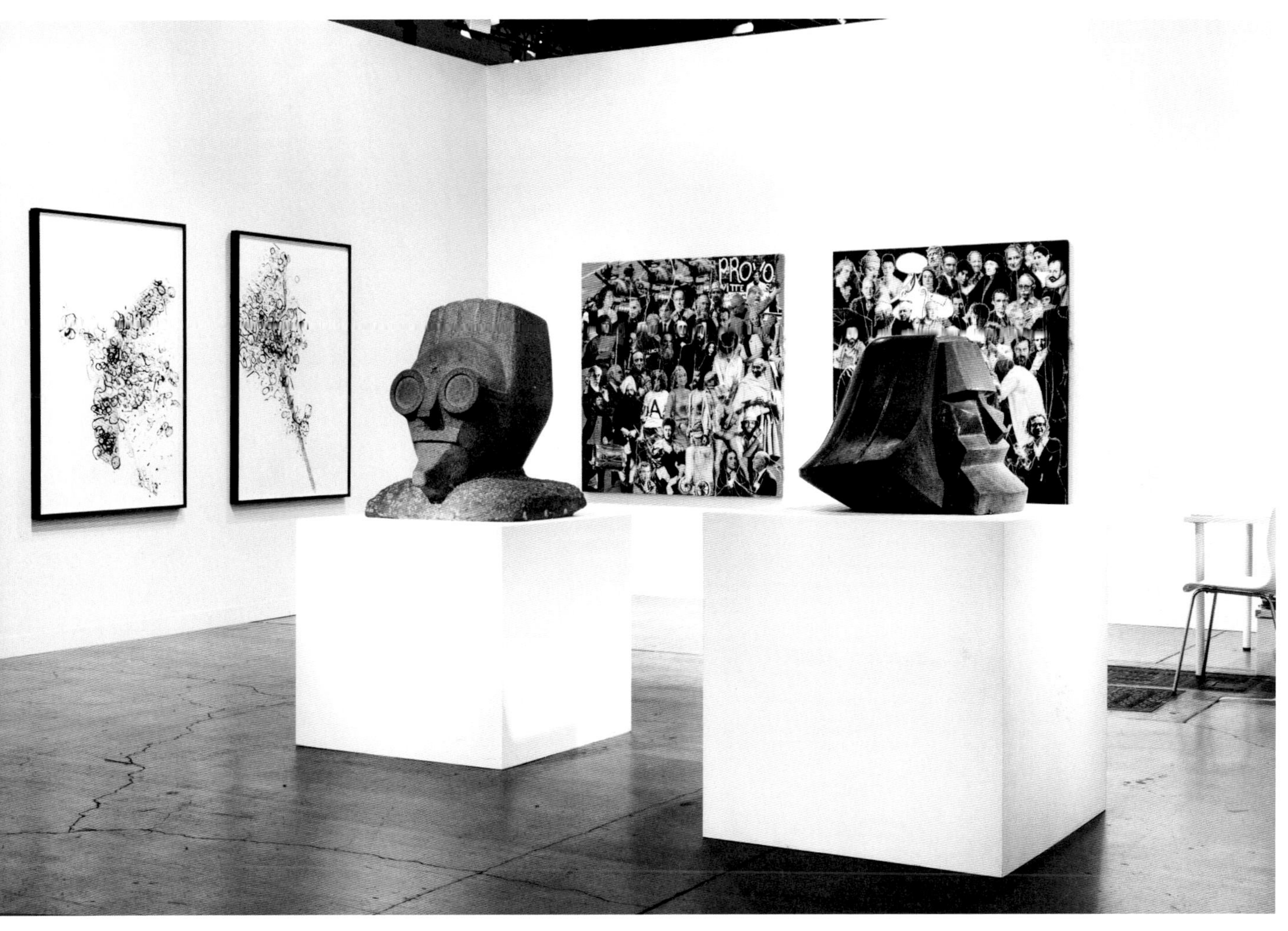

Tania Candiani
Telar, 2011–2014
Instituto de visión (Nova)

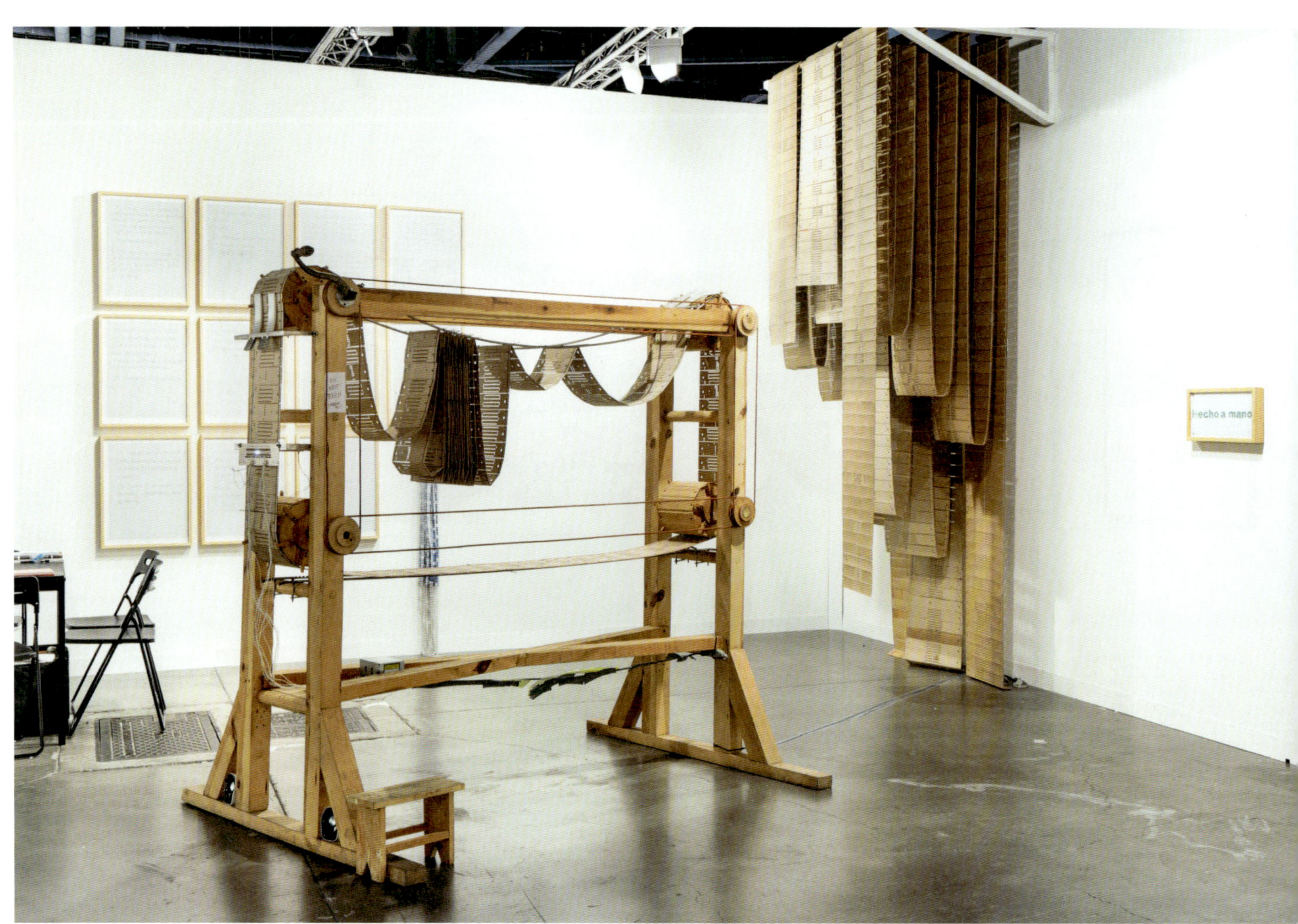

Mario García Torres, Christian Jankowski

Proyectos Monclova

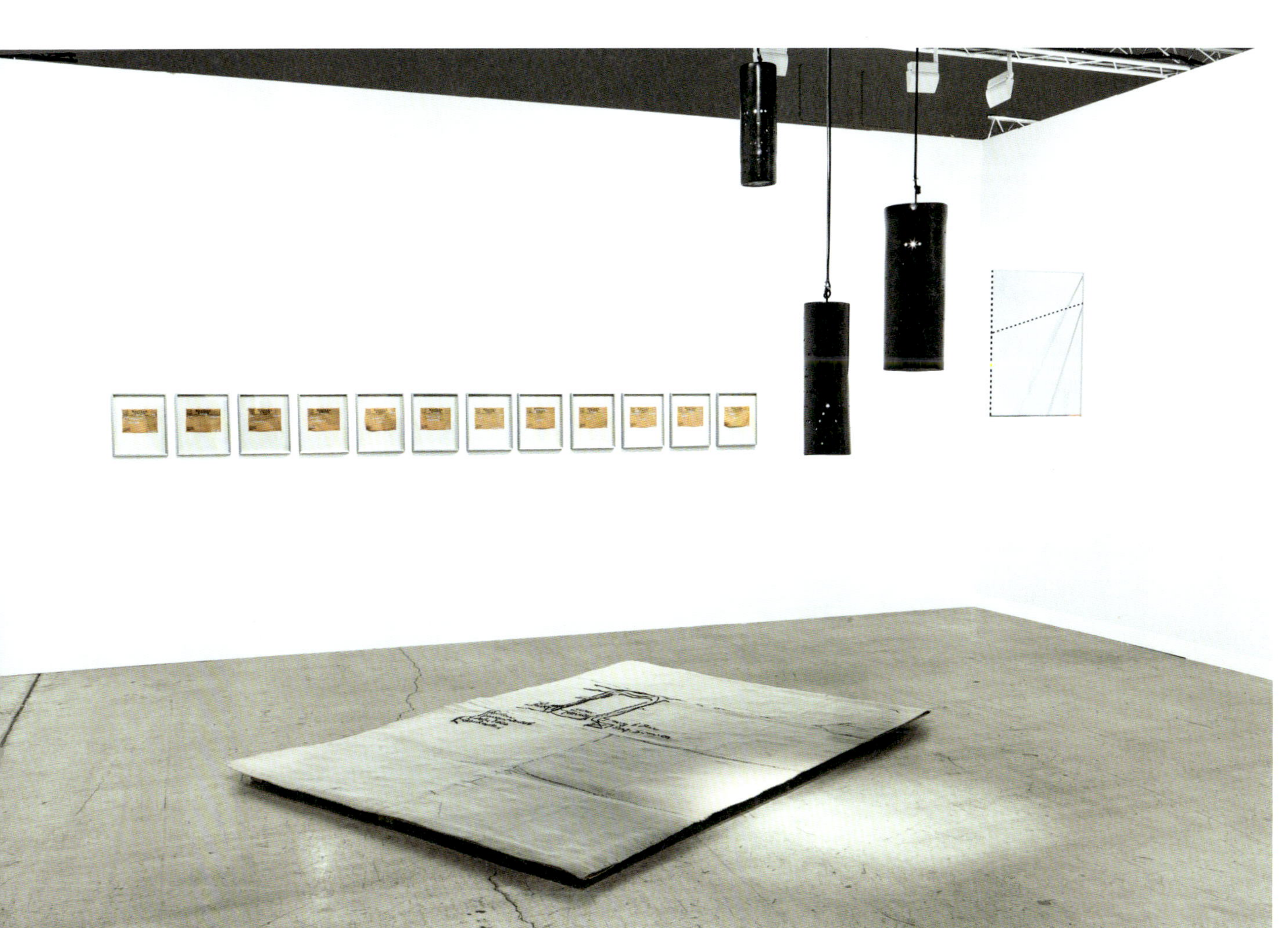

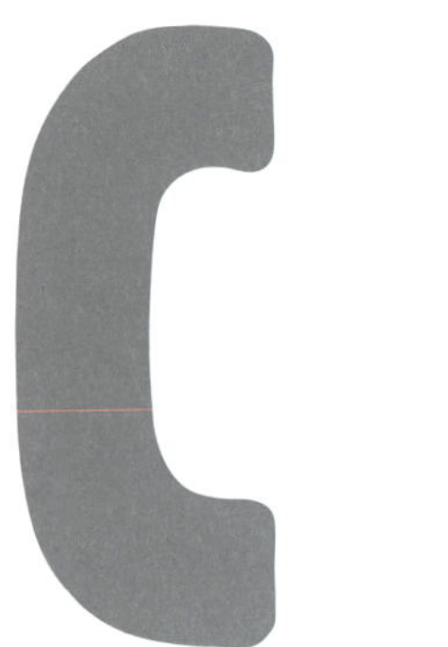

Cabinet

London  Galleries

- **Contact** Cabinet
  Martin McGeown
  art@cabinetltd.demon.co.uk
- **Established** 1991
- **Owner(s) / Partner(s)** Martin McGeown
  Andrew Wheatley

Campoli Presti

London
Paris

Galleries

What is your favorite aspect of running a gallery?
The dialogue with the artists and seeing their exhibitions come to life.

How do you choose the artists you work with?
Since the beginning we have been interested in working with a distinct group of American and European artists who share mutual concerns and affinities. While exploring the historical and material condition of their medium, the gallery's artists share an ongoing critical engagement with modes of display, notions of authorship, the digital economy of images, and the art market. This has defined the gallery program since 2003.

If you weren't running a gallery what else would you do?
Emanuela: I'd be sailing the seas.

- **Contact** Campoli Presti
  Cora Muennich
  cora@campolipresti.com
- **Established** 2003
- **Owner(s) / Partner(s)** Emanuela Campoli
  Gil Presti
- **Team** 9
- **Space(s)** 300 m² (London)/100 m² (Paris)
- **Artists at Art Basel** Liz Deschenes
  Daniel Lefcourt
  Valentina Liernur
  Eileen Quinlan
  Blake Rayne
  Nora Schultz
  Reena Spaulings
  Cheyney Thompson
- **Further artists represented** Roe Ethridge
  Jutta Koether
  Jason Loebs
  Scott Lyall
  Nick Mauss
  Charles Mayton
  John Miller
  Olivier Mosset
  Sean Paul
  Pavel Pepperstein
  Clément Rodzielski
  Christoph Ruckhäberle
  Amy Sillman
  Joanne Tatham & Tom O'Sullivan

Canna

Jakarta
Insights

- **Contact** Galeri Canna
  Inge Santoso
  info@galeri-canna.com
- **Established** 2001
- **Owner(s) / Partner(s)** Inge Santoso

Capitain

Cologne
Berlin

Galleries
Parcours

- **Contact** Galerie Gisela Capitain
  Dorothee Sorge
  sorge@galeriecapitain.de
- **Established** 1986
- **Owner(s) / Partner(s)** Gisela Capitain
  Regina Fiorito
- **Artists at Art Basel** Karla Black
  Barbara Bloom
  Maria Brunner
  Gillian Carnegie
  Günther Förg
  Luke Fowler
  Anna Gaskell
  Wade Guyton
  Uwe Henneken
  Charline von Heyl
  Margarete Jakschik
  Rachel Khedoori
  Martin Kippenberger
  Zoe Leonard
  Meuser
  Marcel Odenbach
  Albert Oehlen
  Laura Owens
  Jorge Pardo
  Ascan Pinckernelle
  Seth Price
  Stephen Prina
  Sam Samore
  Elfie Semotan
  Monika Sosnowska
  John Stezaker
  Kelley Walker
  Franz West
  Christopher Williams
  Johannes Wohnseifer
  Christopher Wool
  Katsuhiro Yamaguchi

Carberry

Chicago  Galleries
Kabinett

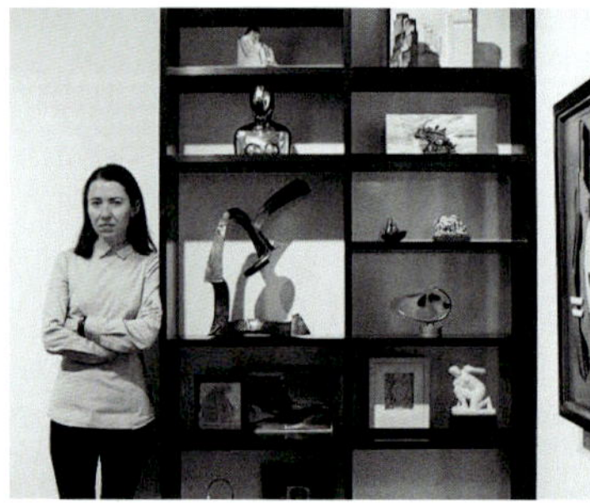

What is your favorite aspect of running a gallery?
Presenting the exhibition program. I am most proud of the quality of viewing experience we offer to all visitors, from students to experienced collectors and museum curators.

How do you choose the artists you work with?
The gallery artists inspire and inform so many of the choices we make.

If you weren't running a gallery what else would you do?
I'd cook!

- **Contact** Valerie Carberry Gallery
  Valerie Carberry
  val@valeriecarberry.com
- **Established** 2002
- **Owner(s) / Partner(s)** Valerie Carberry
- **Team** 4
- **Space(s)** 223 m²
- **Artists at Art Basel** James Brooks
  Alexander Calder
  Burgoyne Diller
  Adolph Gottlieb
  Philip Guston
  Hans Hofmann
  Alex Katz
  Willem de Kooning
  Knud Merrild
  Judith Rothschild
  John Storrs
  Jack Tworkov
- **Further artists represented** Judith Belzer
  Susanna Coffey
  Ellen Lanyon
  Laura Letinsky
  Jim Lutes
  Evelyn Statsinger
  Scott Wolniak

carlier gebauer

Berlin

Galleries
Galleries Unlimited

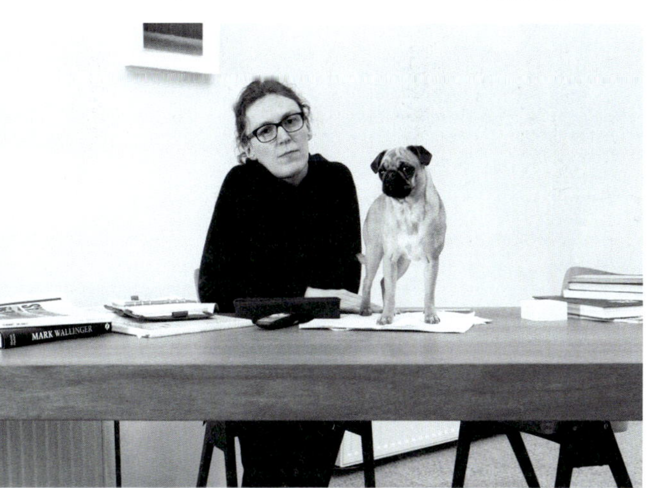

What is your favorite aspect of running a gallery?

Ulrich Gebauer & Marie-Blanche Carlier: Conversing with the artists.

How do you choose the artists you work with?

UG & MB: By finding a uniqueness of language that simultaneously seeks to express crucial aspects of our time.

If you weren't running a gallery what else would you do?

MB: I would be an artist with a collection. UG: I would be a chef.

- **Contact** carlier gebauer
  Sarah Miltenberger
  sm@carliergebauer.com
- **Established** 1991
- **Owner(s) / Partner(s)** Ulrich Gebauer
  Marie-Blanche Carlier
- **Team** 8
- **Artists at Art Basel** Sara Barker
  Sebastian Diaz Morales
  A K Dolven
  Michel François
  Paul Graham
  Asta Gröting
  Dor Guez
  Tomasz Kowalski
  Marcellvs L.
  Przemek Matecki
  Julie Mehretu
  Aernout Mik
  Kirsi Mikkola
  Richard Mosse
  Andreas Mühe
  Paul Pfeiffer
  Jessica Rankin
  Erik Schmidt
  Thomas Schütte
  Peter Stauss
  Maria Taniguchi
  Fred Tomaselli
  Janaina Tschäpe
  Marianna Uutinen
  Mark Wallinger
  Emily Wardill
  Ming Wong
  Kailiang Yang

Carroll / Fletcher

London

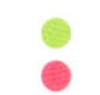

Discoveries
Positions

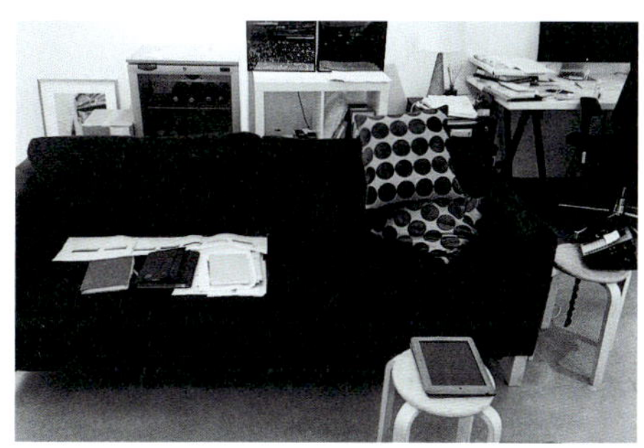

What is your favorite aspect of running a gallery?

Interaction with the artists. Mainly studio visits where I can get the first look at new works or works in progress.

How do you choose the artists you work with?

It is quite a lengthy process—firstly I need to greatly admire the work, and it also has to be consistent with the gallery program. However, it's also important for me to get to know the artist, within and outside of their art environment. I am interested in long-term relationships and collaborations. I believe it is important that the artist and the gallerist really know each other: what they care about, as well as what their expectations and ambitions are. This takes time.

If you weren't running a gallery what else would you do?

Collecting and supporting the artistic practice and production of young artists, as I was prior to opening the gallery.

- **Contact** Carroll / Fletcher
  Jonathon Carroll
  jonathon@carrollfletcher.com
- **Established** 2012
- **Owner(s) / Partner(s)** Jonathon Carroll
  Steve Fletcher
- **Team** 10
- **Space(s)** 474 m²
- **Artists at Art Basel** Constant Dullaart
- **Further artists represented** Basel Abbas and Ruanne Abou-Rahme
  John Akomfrah
  Karmelo Bermejo
  James Clar
  Michael Joaquin Grey
  Mishka Henner
  Justin Hibbs
  Rafael Lozano-Hemmer
  Eva and Franco Mattes
  Manfred Mohr
  Natascha Sadr Haghighian
  Christine Sun Kim
  Thomson & Craighead
  UBERMORGEN
  Eulalia Valldosera
  Richard I. Walker
  John Wood & Paul Harrison

C

Carzaniga

Basel

 Galleries

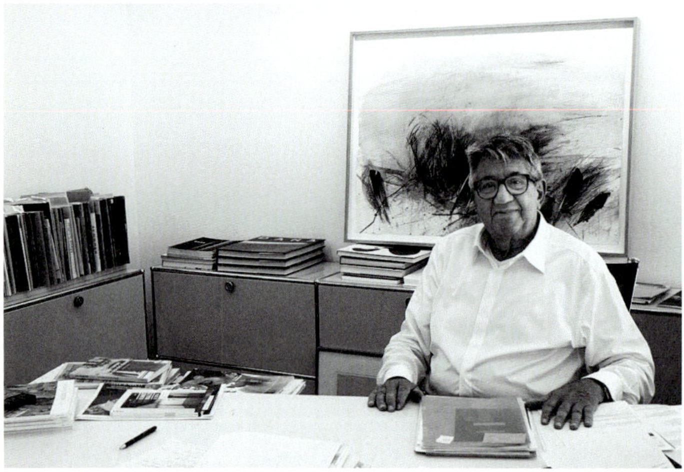

What is your favorite aspect of running a gallery?
Arnaldo Carzaniga: My favorite aspect of this very lively business is being in contact with artists and customers from all over the world.

How do you choose the artists you work with?
The most important thing for a collaboration with artists is that we are able to identify ourselves with the works. If we are not completely convinced we are also not able to convince our customers.

If you weren't running a gallery what else would you do?
Art is a very important part of my life, so if I did not run a gallery I would probably invest my time in collecting art.

- **Contact** Galerie Carzaniga
Markus Rück
markus.rueck@carzaniga.ch
- **Established** 1975/2004
- **Owner(s) / Partner(s)** Arnaldo Carzaniga
Philipp Hediger
Markus Rück
- **Team** 7
- **Space(s)** 400 m²
- **Artists at Art Basel** Julius Bissier
Walter Bodmer
Serge Brignoni
Samuel Buri
Paul Camenisch
Yves Dana
Sam Francis
Rolf Iseli
Lenz Klotz
Wilfrid Moser
Albert Müller
Robert Müller
Meret Oppenheim
Flavio Paolucci
Gianriccardo Piccoli
Marcel Schaffner
Hermann Scherer
Lorenz Spring
Albert Steiner
Niklaus Stoecklin
Mark Tobey
Varlin
Walter Kurt Wiemken
- **Further artists represented** Paolo Bellini
William S. Burroughs
Luca Caccioni
Frédéric Clot
Catherine Gfeller
Hermann Hesse
Christopher Lehmpfuhl
Luca Serra
Ludwig Stocker
Bruno Suter
Irène Zurkinden

Casa Triângulo

São Paulo

Galleries
Galleries

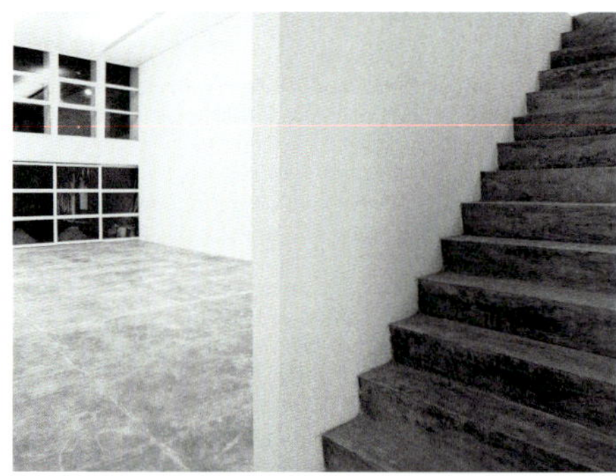

What is your favorite aspect of running a gallery?
We are very pleased to build and to consolidate the career of our artists, giving them the impulse and encouragement to materialize challenges and ideas into inspiring projects.

How do you choose the artists you work with?
Through empathy and emotion, which awaken us conceptually, aesthetically, and personally.

If you weren't running a gallery what else would you do?
After running the gallery for over 25 years, I can't imagine doing anything else.

- **Contact** Casa Triângulo
Rodrigo Editore
info@casatriangulo.com
- **Established** 1988
- **Owner(s) / Partner(s)** Ricardo Trevisan
- **Team** 8
- **Space(s)** 300 m²
- **Artists at Art Basel** Assume Vivid Astro Focus
Eduardo Berliner
Sandra Cinto
Yuri Firmeza
Vânia Mignone
Mariana Palma
Manuela Ribadeneira
Joana Vasconcelos
- **Further artists represented** Daniel Acosta
Albano Afonso
Flávio Cerqueira
Juliana Cerqueira Leite
Alex Cerveny
Max Gómez Canle
Stephen Dean
Valdirlei Dias Nunes
Yuri Firmeza
Guillermo Mora
Nazareth Pacheco
Reginaldo Pereira
Camila Sposati
Pier Stockholm
Jack Strange
Rommulo Vieira Conceição
Marcia Xavier
Tony Camargo

Casas Riegner

Bogotá

 Feature
Galleries
Kabinett

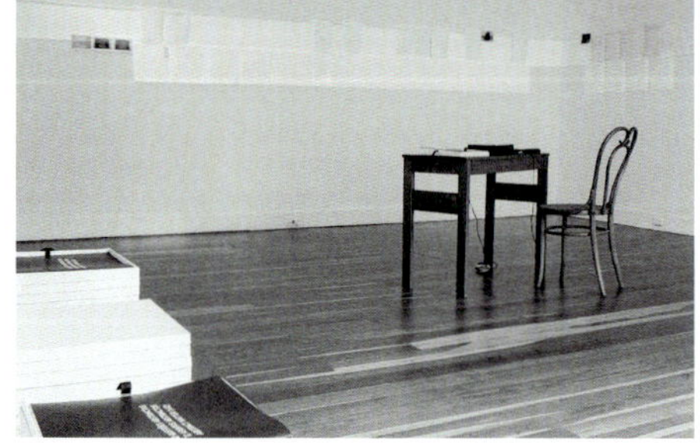

What is your favorite aspect of running a gallery?

Supporting the artists we represent, projecting their careers beyond the local scene, and introducing them to international audiences. The Colombian art scene developed for many years in a rather isolated way, so it has been my goal to accomplish this not only with the younger generations of artists, but also with the pioneers, those who paved the way. What has given me the most satisfaction is seeing their works enter the most important museums, and engaging with curators all over the world.

How do you choose the artists you work with?

Whether it is a younger or more mature artist we look for a strong and clear conceptual base. Our artists also have an experimental approach to their craft, whether they are a painter installation, or performance artist. We look for a defined language that reflects the reflective process behind it.

If you weren't running a gallery what else would you do?

I love archives, whether it is a library and its different collections or an artist's assortment of books and objects. Being submerged in those spaces, doing research, and figuring them out is something I really enjoy. We have actually had the opportunity to work on some of those projects, notably when we were put in charge of the archive of the late artist María Teresa Hincapié, as well as with the recent opening of a library within the gallery. So I guess I would be a librarian or an archive conservator.

- **Contact** — Casas Riegner
Paula Bossa
paula@casasriegner.com
- **Established** — 2001
- **Owner(s) / Partner(s)** — Catalina Casas
Alberto Casas Santamaría
- **Team** — 7
- **Space(s)** — 600 m²
- **Artists at Art Basel** — Johanna Calle
Leyla Cárdenas
Beatriz González
María Teresa Hincapié
Mateo López
Bernardo Ortiz
Gabriel Sierra
José Antonio Suárez Londoño
Icaro Zorbar
- **Further artists represented** — María Fernanda Cardoso
Antonio Caro
Cesar González
María Fernanda Plata
Alex Rodríguez
Miguel Ángel Rojas
Luis Roldán
Liliana Sánchez
Rosemberg Sandoval
Wilger Sotelo
Angélica Teuta

Castelli

New York

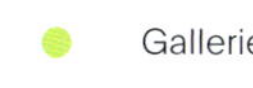

Galleries

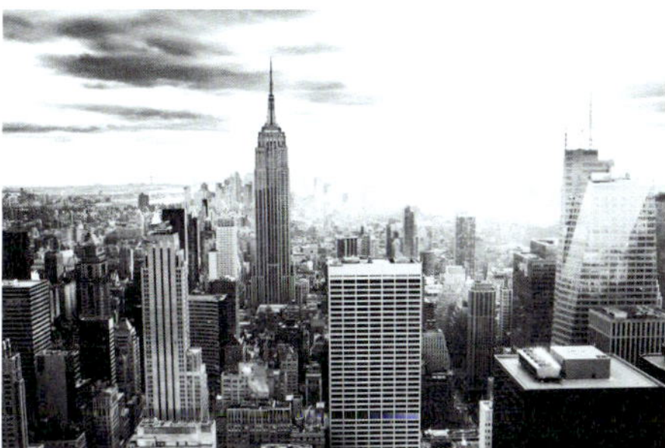

What is your favorite aspect of running a gallery?

The opportunity to meet and speak with intelligent and interesting people.

How do you choose the artists you work with?

The artists were with the gallery before I joined, and it was their work that made working at the gallery so wonderful.

If you weren't running a gallery what else would you do?

I would be an art historian.

- **Contact** — Castelli Gallery
Barbara Bertozzi Castelli
cece@castelligallery.com
- **Established** — 1957
- **Artists at Art Basel** — Richard Pettibone
- **Further artists represented** — Noriko Ambe
Jasper Johns
Roy Lichtenstein
Diana Kingsley
Joseph Kosuth
Robert Morris
Keith Sonnier
Doug and Mike Starn

Central

São Paulo ● Positions

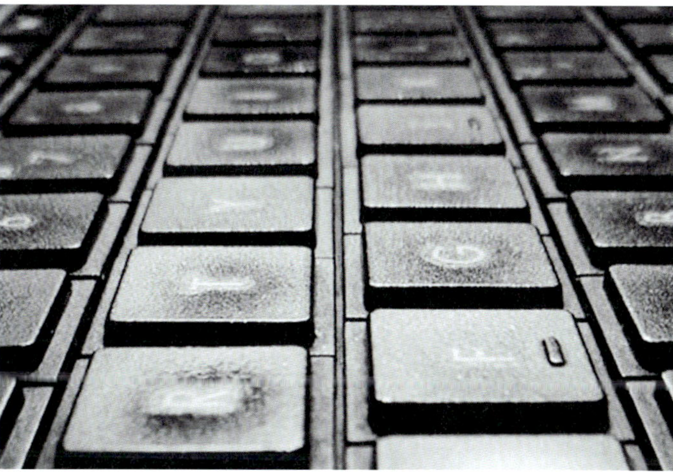

What is your favorite aspect of running a gallery?

It is like making a statement about the time we are living, about our values, the way and the direction in which they are changing.

How do you choose the artists you work with?

I like those who can expand our view about the world, those paving new territories in our symbolic vocabulary.

If you weren't running a gallery what else would you do?

Research in the philosophy of knowledge.

- **Contact** — Central Galeria de Arte
Tathiane Oberleitner
tathiane@centralgaleriadearte.com
- **Established** — 2010
- **Owner(s) / Partner(s)** — Wagner Lungov
- **Team** — 5
- **Space(s)** — 700 m²
- **Artists at Art Basel** — Nino Cais
- **Further artists represented** — Sidney Amaral
Stela Barbieri
Ricardo Barcellos
Pedro Cappeletti
Edith Derdyk
Hélio Fervenza
Pedro França
Bartolomeo Gelpi
Felipe Góes
Tiago Judas
Fernando Lindote
Ícaro Lira
Gordana Manic
Nydia Negromonte
Fernanda Rappa
Mayra Redin
José Rufino
Marcela Tiboni

C

Cera

Lisbon

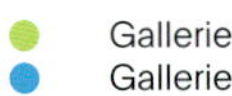

Galleries
Galleries

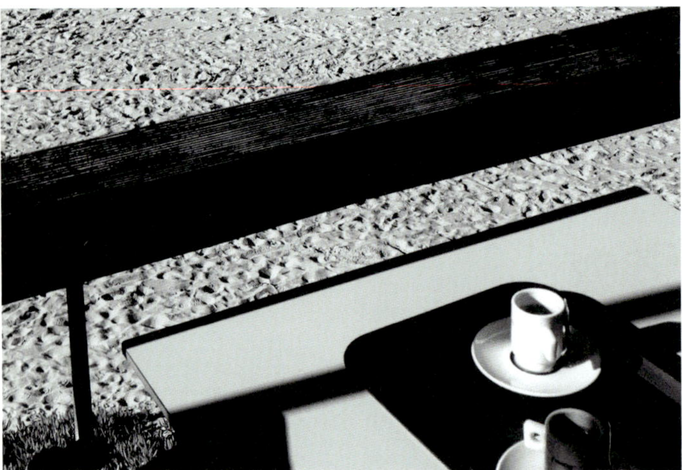

What is your favorite aspect of running a gallery?
The continuous working relation established with artists.

How do you choose the artists you work with?
Concept and aesthetics are the main aspects that are important to the choice.

If you weren't running a gallery what else would you do?
I would probably work as a lawyer. I always wanted to be a neurosurgeon, but never had the skill to do it.

- **Contact** Galeria Pedro Cera
  Vitória Guerra
  vguerra@pedrocera.com
- **Established** 1998
- **Owner(s) / Partner(s)** Pedro Cera
- **Team** 6
- **Space(s)** 350 m^2
- **Artists at Art Basel** Antonio Ballester Moreno
  Gil Heitor Cortesão
  Matt Keegan
  Ana Manso
  Adam Pendleton
  Ricardo Valentim
  Gilberto Zorio
- **Further artists represented** Diogo Evangelista
  Pedro Neves Marques
  Frank Nitsche
  Yves Oppenheim
  Vítor Pomar
  Tobias Rehberger

Cervera

Madrid

Nova
Public

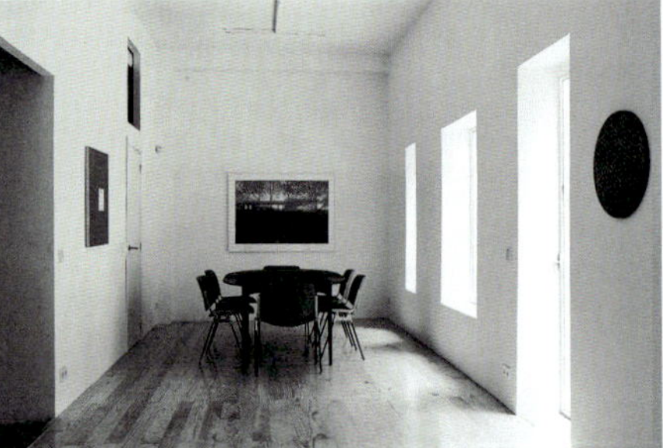

What is your favorite aspect of running a gallery?
The seduction and emotion of art gives meaning to life. Making it possible for the artists to reach the audience and the collections. Contributing to making ideas, questions, and dialogues emerge in our society through the visual arts. Helping artists to live from their work. The contact and collaboration with everyone who makes art possible, and the exchange of ideas.

How do you choose the artists you work with?
Through many of the people and institutions that give artists a platform and an audience: art centers, universities, curators, and artists. Taking into account the artists' input to the arts. Considering the depth of their investigations and interest in relation to existing art, and their talent to express this.

If you weren't running a gallery what else would you do?
I could picture being a curator, an art consultant, a publisher, or a cook.

- **Contact** Galería Marta Cervera
  Marta Cervera
  info@galeriamartacervera.com
- **Established** 2008
- **Owner(s) / Partner(s)** Marta Cervera
- **Team** 3
- **Space(s)** 200 m^2
- **Artists at Art Basel** David Diao
  Nuria Fuster
- **Further artists represented** Alex Bag
  Brian Bress
  Sam Falls
  Adam Fuss
  Begoña Goyenetxea
  Nicolás Guagnini
  Federico Guzmán
  Mark Hagen
  Patrick Hamilton
  Changha Hwang
  Francesco Jodice
  Laida Lertxundi
  Zak Prekop
  Raha Raissnia
  David Reed
  Ruth Root
  Leonor Serrano Rivas
  Ángel Vergara
  James Welling

Chambers

New York
Beijing
Salt Point

Insights

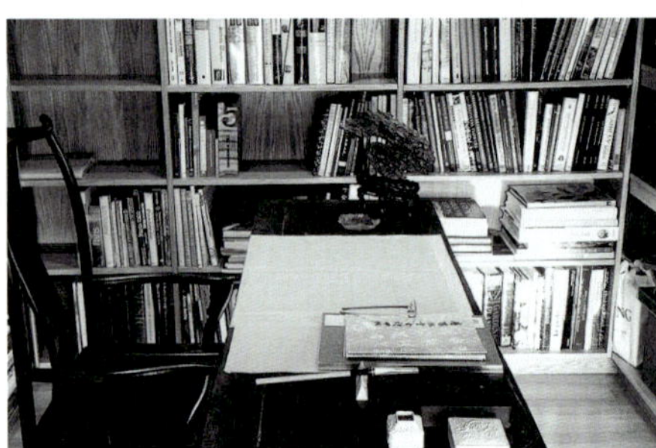

What is your favorite aspect of running a gallery?
Working with artists over an extended period of time, providing assistance and guidance in the development of their careers.

How do you choose the artists you work with?
Usually an artist is recommended to us by an artist we are already working with.

If you weren't running a gallery what else would you do?
I would be a collector. But that is easier if you happen to be an art dealer!

- **Contact** Chambers Fine Art
  David Clements
  dclements@chambersfineart.com
- **Established** 1999
- **Owner** Christophe Mao
- **Team** 8
- **Space(s)** 1,500 m^2
- **Artists at Art Basel** Zhao Zhao
- **Further artists represented** Ai Weiwei
  Cai Jin
  Chi Peng
  Feng Mengbo
  Guo Hongwei
  He Yunchang

Hong Hao
Hong Lei
Lu Shengzhong
Qiu Zhijie
Rong Rong
Shi Jinsong
Song Dong
Tan Dun
Taca Sui
Wang Tiande
Wu Jian'an
Xie Xiaoze
Yang Jiechang
Yin Xiuzhen
Zhan Wang
Zhang Dun
Zhang Huan

Charim

Vienna

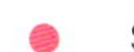

Survey

What is your favorite aspect of running a gallery?

Running a gallery is one of the most exciting professions I can think of: I can support artists and artworks, ideas and creative thinking—especially in relation to feminist political positions—I like to curate shows, deal with our collectors, advise them … and so much more!

How do you choose the artists you work with?

It all started with my first shows: Viennese Actionism and Valie Export. I am also very interested in conceptual painting. My program shows all of this.

If you weren't running a gallery what else would you do?

I would love to be a psychoanalyst. I already started studies and "Lehranalyse" in Vienna 20 years ago, after my economics and art history studies at the University of Vienna …

- **Contact** Charim Galerie
  Miryam Charim
  charim@charimgalerie.at
- **Established** 1998
- **Owner(s) / Partner(s)** Miryam Charim
- **Team** 3
- **Space(s)** 300 m²
- **Artists at Art Basel** Valie Export
  Andrei Monastyrski
  Alfons Schilling
- **Further artists represented** Maja Bajević
  Erwin Bohatsch
  Heinz Frank
  Katharina Gruzei
  Dorothee Golz
  Stephan Huber
  Moussa Kone
  Roberta Lima
  Robert Muntean
  Daniel Pitin
  Lisl Ponger
  Hubert Scheibl
  Tamuna Sirbiladze
  Milica Tomic
  Ralf Ziervogel

Cheim & Read

New York

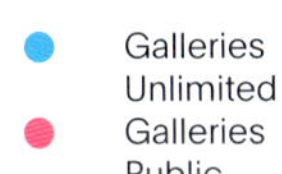

Galleries
Unlimited
Galleries
Public

What is your favorite aspect of running a gallery?

Having both gone to the Rhode Island School of Design to become visual artists, it is most gratifying to immerse ourselves in the art that we both most admire.

How do you choose the artists you work with?

We gravitate toward work with a beautiful and exciting formal resolution, and a conceptual underpinning. You cannot have one without the other.

If you weren't running a gallery what else would you do?

We would most likely be practicing artists—and still may yet be!

- **Contact** Cheim & Read
  Maria Bueno
  maria@cheimread.com
- **Established** 1997
- **Owner(s) / Partner(s)** John Cheim
  Howard Read
  Mary Gail Parr
  Adam Sheffer
- **Team** 17
- **Space(s)** 557.5 m²
- **Artists at Art Basel** Lynda Benglis
  Louise Bourgeois
  Ron Gorchov
  Jenny Holzer
  Joan Mitchell
  Jack Pierson
  Sean Scully
- **Further artists represented** Ghada Amer
  Don Bachardy
  Donald Baechler
  William Eggleston
  Louise Fishman
  Adam Fuss
  Hans Hartung
  Al Held
  Bill Jensen
  Chantal Joffe
  Jannis Kounellis
  Jonathan Lasker
  McDermott & McGough
  Barry McGee
  Tal R
  Milton Resnick
  Pat Steir
  Juan Uslé

Chemould

Mumbai

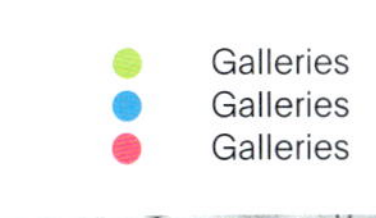

Galleries
Galleries
Galleries

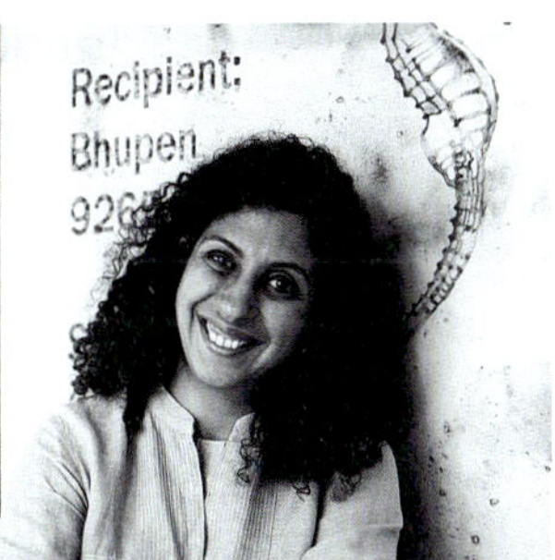

What is your favorite aspect of running a gallery?

I am process driven—I love seeing things midway … Studio visits to artists while they are not quite finished, nearly there, confused, needing input, draws me closer to a work especially in understanding where it comes from. The sense of anticipation when the doors open are also moments I cherish.

How do you choose the artists you work with?

I am drawn to artists who have a vision that is expressed through process and I like taking risks in choosing an artist at that moment. I admit to the fact that sometimes those choices might have flopped! I also choose artists based on the fact that there remains a certain homogeneity in my program—however different the artists might be from one another—one artist must have the ability to play off the other.

If you weren't running a gallery what else would you do?

Join politics!

- **Contact** Chemould Prescott Road
  Sandra Khare
  gallerychemould@gmail.com
- **Established** 1963
- **Owner(s) / Partner(s)** Shireen Gandhy

- **Team** 10
- **Space(s)** 464.5 m²
- **Artists at Art Basel** Atul Dodiya, Pushpamala N., Rashid Rana, Mithu Sen, Hema Upadhyay
- **Further artists represented** Dhruvi Acharya, Shezad Dawood, Anju Dodiya, Mehlli Gobhai, Shilpa Gupta, Archana Hande, Tushar Joag, Jitish Kallat, Reena Saini Kallat, Suhasini Kejriwal, Bhupen Khakhar, Shakuntala Kulkarni, Desmond Lazaro, Lavanya Mani, N.S. Harsha, Gigi Scaria, Nilima Sheikh, Aditi Singh, Vivan Sundaram, Surekha, Tallur L.N.

Cherry and Martin

Los Angeles

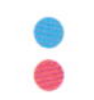
Feature
Nova

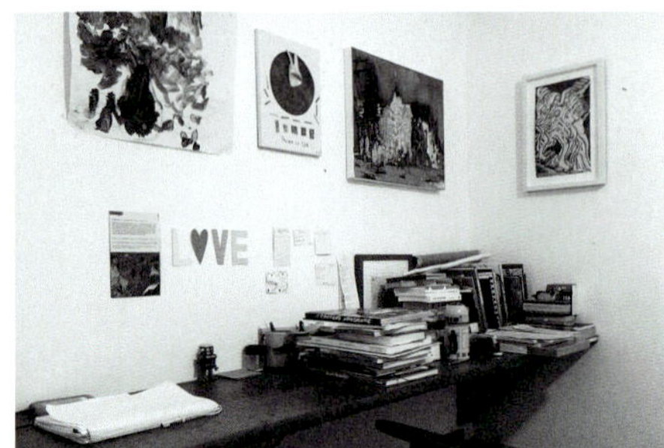

What is your favorite aspect of running a gallery?
The people that I have met. I have spent time with amazing artists, curators, collectors, and gallerists. People who are so much smarter than me, have very different experiences, and have introduced me to so many new ideas. I am genuinely thankful for it.

How do you choose the artists you work with?
I look for people who have set up studio problems they're not likely to solve any time soon. Good artists have structures—material, intellectual, emotional, and otherwise—that define their work. If they are honest in the studio, very quickly they find themselves violating these structures, and learning more about their characteristics and their deeper meaning. This makes for idiosyncratic work that reflects the individuality of a given person, their explorations, and is a true body of art.

If you weren't running a gallery what else would you do?
I have this idea that I would make a good stand-up comedian. Probably not. I also tell myself that I would be a great organic farmer. Most likely I would be still thinking about art, collecting it, and organizing shows for whoever would have me. Art is vital to me and hard to get away from.

- **Contact** Cherry and Martin, Philip Martin, philip@cherryandmartin.com
- **Established** 2006
- **Owner(s) / Partner(s)** Mary Leigh Cherry, Philip Martin
- **Team** 4
- **Space(s)** 390 m²
- **Artists at Art Basel** Brian Bress, T. Kelly Mason
- **Further artists represented** Ericka Beckman, Jennifer Boysen, Matt Connors, Holly Coulis, Katy Cowan, Mari Eastman, Hal Fischer, Robert Heinecken, Nathan Mabry, Florian Morlat, Pat O'Neill, Robert Overby, Bernard Piffaretti, Michael Rey, Alan Shields, Lew Thomas

Chi-Wen

Taipei

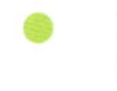
Galleries
Encounters

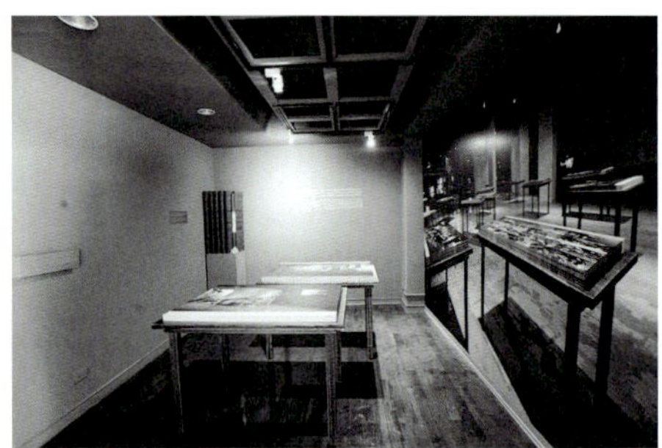

What is your favorite aspect of running a gallery?
As a gallerist you work with art—how much better can it get?!

How do you choose the artists you work with?
For me finding new artists is largely instinctive. My gallery's focus is mainly moving image and photography, which are relatively new media in artistic expression, but in my opinion firmly rooted in art history.

If you weren't running a gallery what else would you do?
Museum director.

- **Contact** Chi-Wen Gallery, Chi-Wen Huang, chiwen.huang@chi-wen.com
- **Established** 2004
- **Owner(s) / Partner(s)** Chi-Wen Huang
- **Team** 5
- **Space(s)** 90 m²
- **Artists at Art Basel** Chang Chien-Chi, Chen Chieh-Jen, Jawshing Arthur Liou, Hsieh Chun-Te, Yeh Wei-Li, Yu Cheng-Ta
- **Further artists represented** Chen Shun-Chu, Chen Yin-Ju, James T. Hung, Lee Kit, Niu Chun-Chiang, Tou Yun-Fei, Yao Jui-Chung, Yuan Goang-Ming

Chouakri

Berlin

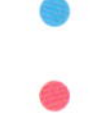
Galleries
Unlimited
Galleries

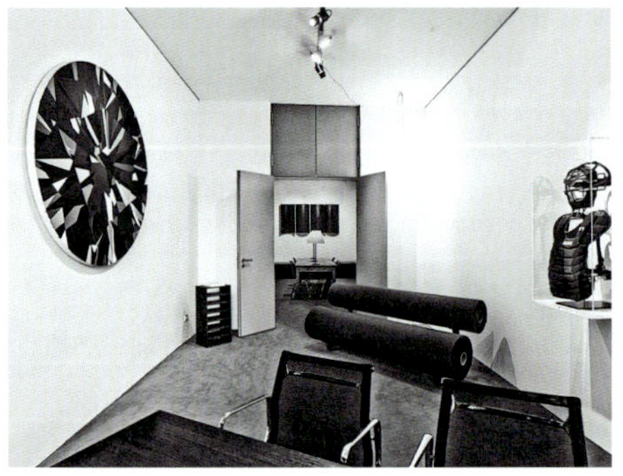

What is your favorite aspect of running a gallery?
Organizing good shows.

How do you choose the artists you work with?
Quality and affinity are priorities.

If you weren't running a gallery what else would you do?
Bake meringues.

- **Contact** Mehdi Chouakri, Alexandra Alexopoulou, galerie@mehdi-chouakri.com
- **Established** 1996
- **Owner(s) / Partner(s)** Mehdi Chouakri
- **Team** 6
- **Space(s)** 300 m²
- **Artists at Art Basel** Saâdane Afif, John M Armleder, N. Dash, Hans-Peter Feldmann, Sylvie Fleury, Mathieu Mercier, Gerold Miller, Charlotte Posenenske, Gerwald Rockenschaub, Peter Roehr, Gitte Schäfer, Luca Trevisani
- **Further artists represented** Claude Closky, Isabell Heimerdinger

Cintra + Box 4

Rio de Janeiro  Nova

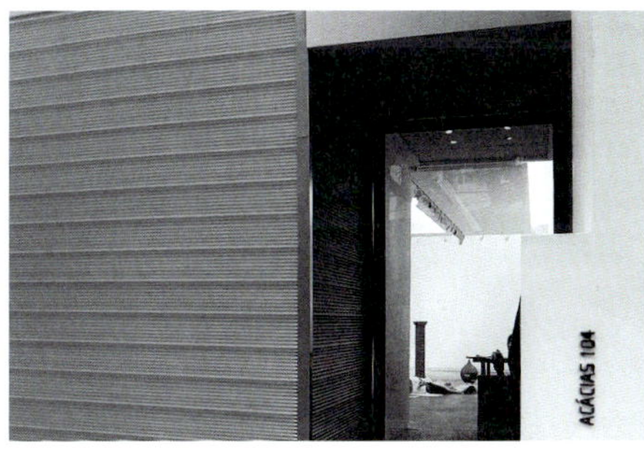

What is your favorite aspect of running a gallery?
Being permanently surrounded by the art world is what I like the most about running a gallery.

How do you choose the artists you work with?
When I started 35 years ago I had a more Constructivist take. After a while I started enhancing my taste for conceptual works and photography. The artists I represent deal with these three areas and I end up choosing them by attending the main exhibitions and discussing art with other artists and curators that are close to me.

If you weren't running a gallery what else would you do?
I would be somehow connected to art, I can't imagine doing anything else. I have been working in the art world since my early 20s and opened up my first gallery when I was 27 years old.

- **Contact** Silvia Cintra + Box 4, Juliana Cintra, galeria@silviacintra.com.br
- **Established** 1992
- **Owner(s) / Partner(s)** Silvia Cintra, Juliana Cintra
- **Team** 9
- **Space(s)** 400 m²
- **Artists at Art Basel** Cristina Canale, Maria Klabin, Pedro Motta
- **Further artists represented** Chiara Banfi, Carlito Carvalhosa, Amílcar de Castro, Leda Catunda, Marilá Dardot, Luiz Ernesto, Iole de Freitas, Marcius Galan, Mariana Galender, Renata Har, Nelson Leirner, Cinthia Marcelle, Rodrigo Matheus, Henrique Oliveira, Mayana Redin, Laercio Redondo, Miguel Rio Branco, Omar Salomão, Daniel Senise, Ana Maria Tavares

Clifton Benevento

New York ● Positions

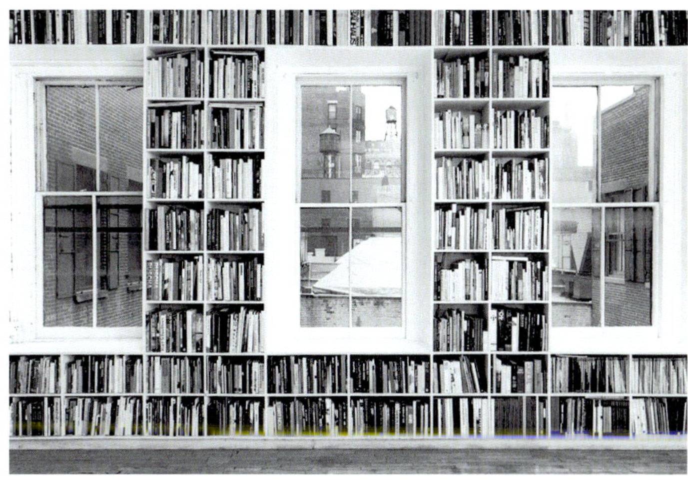

- **Contact** Clifton Benevento, Michael Clifton, mc@cliftonbenevento.com
- **Established** 2010
- **Owner(s) / Partner(s)** Michael Benevento, Michael Clifton
- **Team** 3
- **Space(s)** 167.5 m²
- **Artists at Art Basel** Zak Kitnick
- **Further artists represented** Polly Apfelbaum, Gina Beavers, Paul Cowan, D'Ette Nogle, Martin Soto Climent, Michael E. Smith, Wu Tsang, Miller Updegraff

Cohan

New York, Shanghai

● Galleries
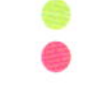 Galleries
Public

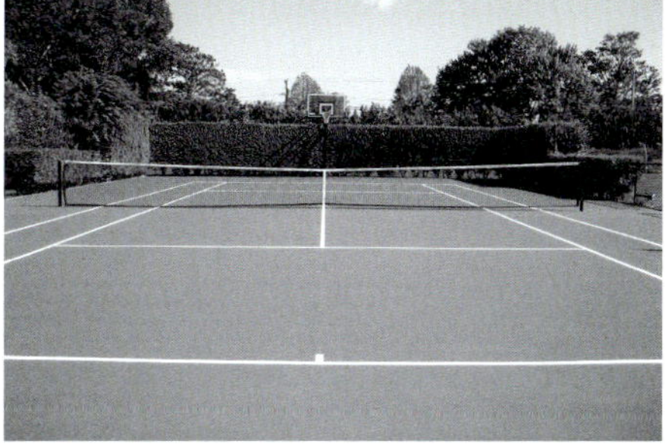

What is your favorite aspect of running a gallery?
The gallery is a laboratory and every show is an experiment. We learn from all the successes and failures equally. Each day comes with the expectation of the unexpected and I am never disappointed.

How do you choose the artists you work with?
Intuition and 32 years of experience.

If you weren't running a gallery what else would you do?
Mohel.

- **Contact** James Cohan Gallery
James Cohan
jcohan@jamescohan.com
- **Established** 1999
- **Owner(s) / Partner(s)** James Cohan
Jane Cohan
- **Team** 18
- **Space(s)** 650.5 m²
- **Artists at Art Basel** Helene Appel
Simon Evans
Spencer Finch
Michelle Grabner
Trenton Doyle Hancock
Byron Kim
Beatriz Milhazes
Alan Saret
Yinka Shonibare MBE
Shinique Smith
Alison Elizabeth Taylor
Fred Tomaselli
Bill Viola
Xu Zhen
Shi Zhiying
- **Further artists represented** Ingrid Calame
Folkert de Jong
Yun-Fei Ji
Jesper Just
Richard Long
Katie Paterson
Hiraki Sawa
Estate of Robert Smithson
Erick Swenson
Tabaimo

Sadie Coles

London

Galleries
Galleries
Unlimited
Parcours
Galleries

What is your favorite aspect of running a gallery?

I was always a bit starstruck by artists, so working with them is a dream come true. They are demanding, rigorous, and stimulating, but there is always a sense that something I hadn't thought about or hadn't imagined is being revealed.

How do you choose the artists you work with?

I often take the advice of artists I already work with, or curators whose work I admire. I keep my ears and eyes open, and I get a fluttery kind of excitement in my stomach.

If you weren't running a gallery what else would you do?

I'm not sure. At university I was very interested in film production; the organizational side of things and in making a framework for the creative people. Not so very different I suppose.

- **Contact** Sadie Coles HQ
Lieselotte Seaton
lieselotte@sadiecoles.com
- **Established** 1997
- **Owner(s) / Partner(s)** Sadie Coles
- **Team** 20
- **Space(s)** 557.5 m²
- **Artists at Art Basel** Uri Aran
William N. Copley
Steven Claydon
Adriano Costa
John Currin
Sam Durant
Shannon Ebner
Angus Fairhurst
Urs Fischer
Jonathan Horowitz
David Korty
Gabriel Kuri
Sarah Lucas
Elizabeth Peyton
Ugo Rondinone
Wilhelm Sasnal
Daniel Sinsel
Andreas Slominski
Christiana Soulou
Rudolf Stingel
Ryan Sullivan
Paloma Varga Weisz

T.J. Wilcox
Jordan Wolfson
Andrea Zittel

- **Further artists represented** Michele Abeles
Carl Andre
Darren Bader
Matthew Barney
Dirk Bell
Avner Ben-Gal
Frank Benson
John Bock
Don Brown
Marvin Gaye Chetwynd
Florian Hecker
Georg Herold
Jim Lambie
Hilary Lloyd
Helen Marten
Victoria Morton
Laura Owens
Simon Periton
Raymond Pettibon
Richard Prince
Gregor Schneider
Nicola Tyson

Contemporary Fine Arts

Berlin

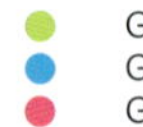

Galleries
Galleries
Galleries

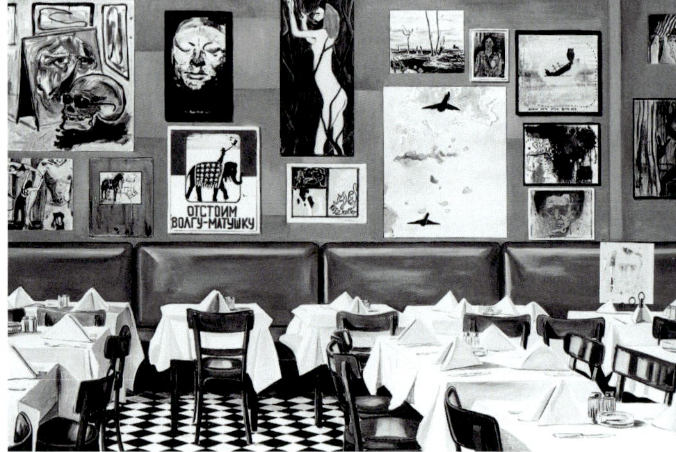

What is your favorite aspect of running a gallery?

Happiness. To share the great moments in life with our artists and audience. [Chorus:] Because I'm happy Clap along if you feel like a room without a roof Because I'm happy Clap along if you feel like happiness is the truth Because I'm happy Clap along if you know what happiness is to you Because I'm happy Clap along if you feel like that's what you wanna do.

How do you choose the artists you work with?

Looking—talking—thinking—talking—looking—thinking—deciding.

If you weren't running a gallery what else would you do?

Be the director of the CIRCUS KNIE during Art Basel fair.

- **Contact** Contemporary Fine Arts
Philipp Haverkampf
gallery@cfa-berlin.de
- **Established** 1994
- **Owner(s) / Partner(s)** Nicole Hackert
Bruno Brunnet
Philipp Haverkampf
- **Team** 13
- **Space(s)** 600 m²
- **Artists at Art Basel** Markus Bacher
Georg Baselitz
Avner Ben-Gal
Peter Böhnisch
Marc Brandenburg
Cecily Brown
Bruce High Quality Foundation
Borden Capalino
Peter Doig

Max Frisinger
Georg Herold
Thomas Kiesewetter
Michael Kunze
Sarah Lucas
Chris Ofili
Raymond Pettibon
Walter Pichler
Tal R
Anselm Reyle
Daniel Richter
Christian Rosa
Julian Schnabel
Dana Schutz
Norbert Schwontkowski
Dash Snow
Katja Strunz
Gert & Uwe Tobias

Continua

San Gimignano
Beijing
Boissy-le-Châtel

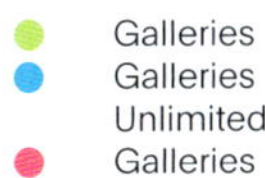

Galleries
Galleries
Unlimited
Galleries

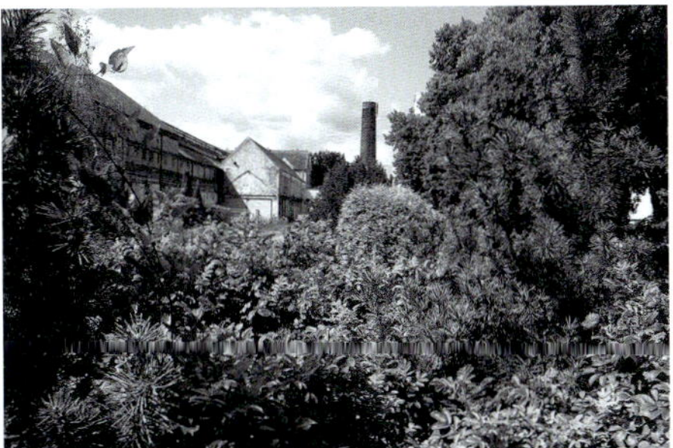

What is your favorite aspect of running a gallery?
The ability to plan, the unknown, the challenge, the poetry, and emotion conveyed by a work of art, the firm belief that art can be a means to know ourselves better, to build a better world through the vision of artists.

How do you choose the artists you work with?
We do not choose an artist through a predetermined process. It is rather a matter of crossing paths, of kindred sensitivities. We invest all our energy in each event and exhibition, for the creation and realization of new projects, giving shape to dreams and ideas. We work with artists from all over the world. Each one is the expression of a different culture and what we do is offer them the tools to express their artistic sensitivity.

If you weren't running a gallery what else would you do?
We are a group of old friends who have known each other since secondary school. The gallery has been a way for us to share our common passion for contemporary art. If we had not founded Continua, we would probably have followed paths suited to our educational background (Lorenzo Fiaschi studied at the Academy of Fine Arts, Mario Cristiani at the Faculty of Political Science, and Maurizio Rigillo at the Faculty of Informatics), but we would have nonetheless found a dynamic way to grow together.

- **Contact** Galleria Continua
Veronica Tronnolone
info@galleriacontinua.com
- **Established** 1990
- **Owner(s) / Partner(s)** Mario Cristiani
Lorenzo Fiaschi
Maurizio Rigillo
- **Team** 40
- **Space(s)** 2,500 m² (San Gimignano)
1,000 m² (Beijing)
10,000 m² (Le Moulin de Boissy)
20,000 m² (Le Moulin de Sainte-Marie)
200 m² (Le Salon-Centquatre Paris)
- **Artists at Art Basel** Ai Weiwei
Kader Attia
Daniel Buren
Loris Cecchini
Chen Zhen
Berlinde De Bruyckere
Carlos Garaicoa
Shilpa Gupta
Mona Hatoum
Anish Kapoor
Moataz Nasr
Hans Op De Beeck
Giovanni Ozzola
Michelangelo Pistoletto
Nedko Solakov
Pascale Marthine Tayou
- **Further artists represented** Etel Adnan
Jonathas de Andrade
Cai Guo-Qiang
Nikhil Chopra
Marcelo Cidade
Leandro Erlich
Meschac Gaba
Kendell Geers
Antony Gormley
Gu Dexin
Subodh Gupta
Ilya & Emilia Kabakov
Zhanna Kadyrova
Kan Xuan
André Komatsu
Jorge Macchi
Sabrina Mezzaqui
Margherita Morgantin
Ornaghi & Prestinari
Qiu Zhijie
Arcangelo Sassolino
Manuela Sedmach
Serse
Kiki Smith
Sun Yuan & Peng Yu
Nari Ward
Sophie Whettnall
Sislej Xhafa

Cooper

New York

Galleries
Unlimited
Galleries
Public

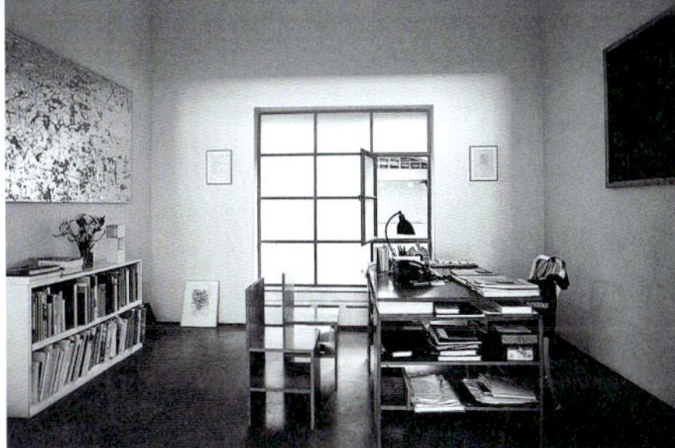

What is your favorite aspect of running a gallery?
Installing shows, having a special sense of intimacy with the work, and planning and working with artists.

How do you choose the artists you work with?
Experience and intuition

If you weren't running a gallery what else would you do?
I would run a bookstore.

- **Contact** Paula Cooper Gallery
Alexis Johnson
alexis@paulacoopergallery.com
- **Established** 1968
- **Owner(s) / Partner(s)** Paula Cooper
- **Team** 15
- **Space(s)** 850 m²
- **Artists at Art Basel** Carl Andre
Tauba Auerbach
Céleste Boursier-Mougenot
Sophie Calle
Beatrice Caracciolo
Bruce Conner
Sam Durant
Matias Faldbakken
Dan Flavin
Charles Gaines
Liz Glynn
Wayne Gonzales
Robert Grosvenor

Douglas Huebler
Donald Judd
Julian Lethbridge
Sherrie Levine
Sol LeWitt
Christian Marclay
Justin Matherly
Claes Oldenburg
& Coosje van Bruggen
Paul Pfeiffer
Walid Raad
Jan Schoonhoven
Rudolf Stingel
Mark di Suvero
Atsuko Tanaka
Kelley Walker
Dan Walsh
Meg Webster
Robert Wilson
Bing Wright
Carey Young

- **Further artists represented** Hans Haacke
Michael Hurson
Jackie Winsor

Corbett vs. Dempsey

Chicago — Galleries

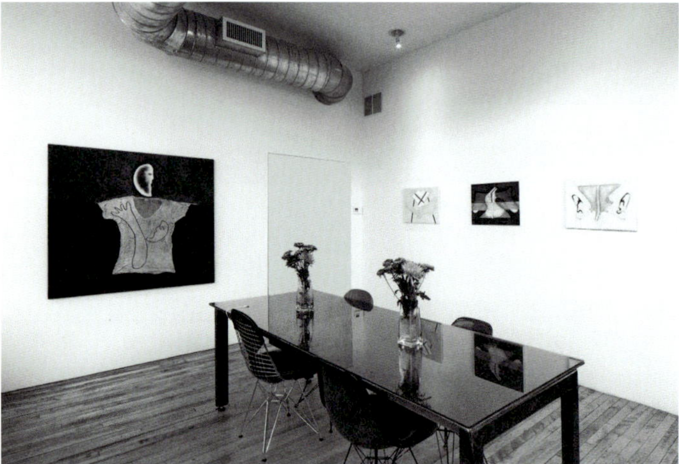

What is your favorite aspect of running a gallery?
Our favorite aspect of running a gallery is the challenge and thrill of putting together exhibitions and catalogues, particularly in collaboration with artists.

How do you choose the artists you work with?
There is no single method we use to chose the artists with whom we work; however, we only work with artists whom we like and respect.

If you weren't running a gallery what else would you do?
If we weren't running a gallery we would likely be curating films and live music events.

- **Contact** Corbett vs. Dempsey
Ben Chaffee
ben@corbettvsdempsey.com
- **Established** 2004
- **Owner(s) / Partner(s)** John Corbett
Jim Dempsey
- **Team** 7
- **Space(s)** 232.5 m²
- **Artists at Art Basel** Brian Calvin
Ed Flood
Philip Hanson
David Hartt
Robert Lostutter
Josiah McElheny
Rebecca Morris
Joyce Pensato
Jackie Saccoccio
Diane Simpson
- **Further artists represented** Morris Barazani
Margot Bergman
Peter Brötzmann
Dominick Di Meo
Robert Donley
Hedwig Eberle
Art Green
Walter Hamady
Arturo Herrera
Charline von Heyl
Dick Higgins
Thomas Kapsalis
Gina Litherland
Albert Oehlen
Christina Ramberg Estate
Seymour Rosofsky Estate
Rebecca Shore
John Sparagana
Karl Wirsum
Christopher Wool
Jimmy Wright
Molly Zuckerman-Hartung

Corrias

London — Galleries, Statements

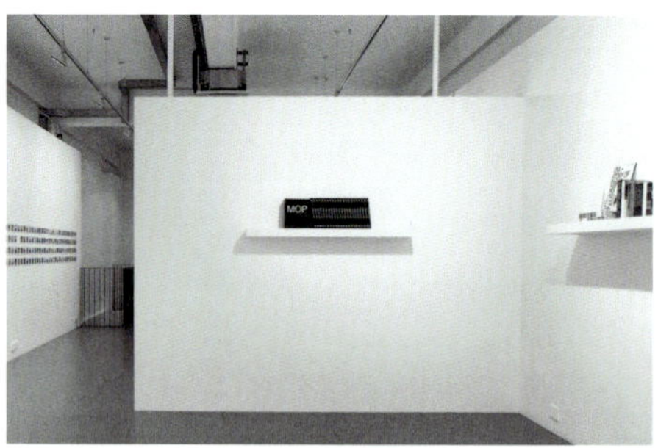
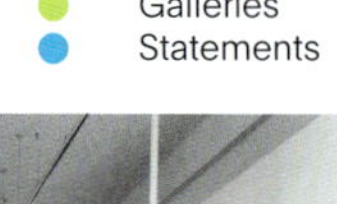

- **Contact** Pilar Corrias
Irina Stark
irina@pilarcorrias.com
- **Established** 2008
- **Owner(s) / Partner(s)** Pilar Corrias
- **Team** 6
- **Space(s)** 353 m²
- **Artists at Art Basel** Charles Avery
Koo Jeong-A
Tala Madani
Elizabeth Neel
Ken Okiishi
Philippe Parreno
Tobias Rehberger
Shahzia Sikander
John Skoog
Rirkrit Tiravanija
- **Further artists represented** Ulla von Brandenburg
Keren Cytter
Mary Reid Kelley
Leigh Ledare
Mary Ramsden
Julião Sarmento
Alice Theobald
Tunga

Cortese

Milan — Feature, Unlimited

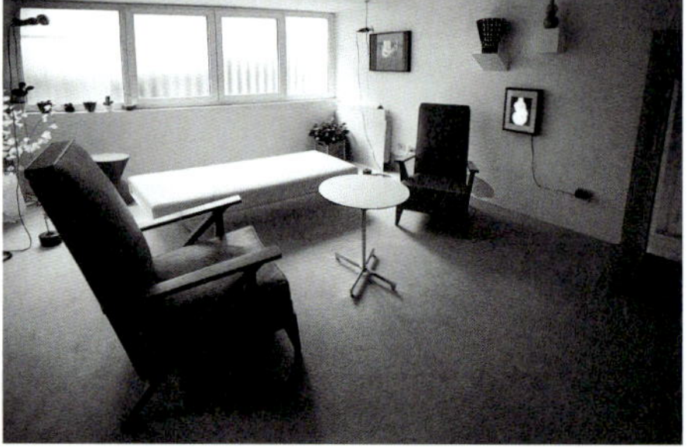

What is your favorite aspect of running a gallery?
I love planning and devising significant exhibitions with the artists, following their careers, and contributing to the

growth of distinctive collections, in a permanent dialogue with curators, museum directors, and people at large.

How do you choose the artists you work with?
The selection of artists basically follows my sensibility and deep passion for their work, and takes shape from a cultural landscape that moves between the sensual and the conceptual.

If you weren't running a gallery what else would you do?
A gardener or a collector.

- **Contact** Galleria Raffaella Cortese
  Raffaella Cortese
  info@galleriaraffaellacortese.com
- **Established** 1995
- **Owner(s) / Partner(s)** Raffaella Cortese
- **Team** 6
- **Space(s)** 420 m²
- **Artists at Art Basel** Ana Mendieta
  Martha Rosler
  Silvia Bächli
- **Further artists represented** Mirosław Bałka
  Yael Bartana
  Karla Black
  Barbara Bloom
  Alejandro Cesarco
  Keren Cytter
  Michael Fliri
  Jitka Hanzlovà
  Roni Horn
  Joan Jonas
  William E. Jones
  Kimsooja
  Zoe Leonard
  Anna Maria Maiolino
  Marcello Maloberti
  Helen Mirra
  Mathilde Rosier
  Kiki Smith
  Jana Sterbak
  Jessica Stockholder
  James Welling
  T.J. Wilcox

Crèvecoeur

Paris — Positions

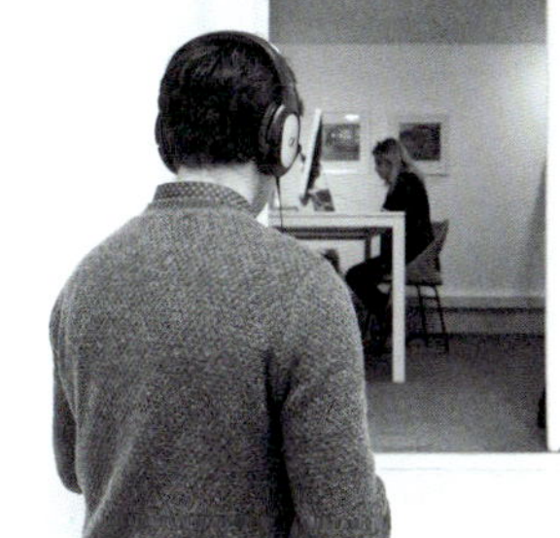

What is your favorite aspect of running a gallery?
The uninterrupted dialogue with the artists.

How do you choose the artists you work with?
Watching, listening, smelling, touching, tasting.

If you weren't running a gallery what else would you do?
We would publish books.

- **Contact** Crèvecoeur
  Alix Dionot-Morani
  alix@galeriecrevecoeur.com
- **Established** 2008
- **Owner(s)** Axel Dibie & Alix Dionot-Morani
- **Team** 2
- **Space(s)** 60 m²
- **Artists at Art Basel** Julien Carreyn
- **Further artists represented** Xavier Antin
  Erica Baum
  Jochen Dehn
  Renaud Jerez
  Shana Moulton
  Jorge Pedro Nuñez
  Mick Peter
  Florian & Michael Quistrebert

CRG

New York — Galleries

- **Contact** CRG Gallery
  Carla Chammas
  carla@crggallery.com
- **Established** 1990
- **Owner(s) / Partner(s)** Carla Chammas
  Richard Desroche
  Glenn McMillan
- **Team** 7
- **Artists at Art Basel** Efrain Almeida
  Robert Buck
  Alexandre da Cunha
  Tomory Dodge
  Ori Gersht
  Tom LaDuke
  Jumana Manna
- **Further artists represented** Eva Berendes
  Steven Bindernagel
  Russell Crotty
  Angela Dufresne
  Pia Fries
  Joana Hadjithomas & Khalil Joreige
  Butt Johnson
  Tonico Lemos Auad
  Siobhan Liddell
  O Zhang
  Melissa McGill
  Sam Reveles
  Steve Roden
  Lisa Sanditz
  Brian Tolle

Cristea

London

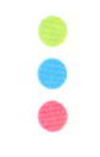

Galleries
Edition
Edition

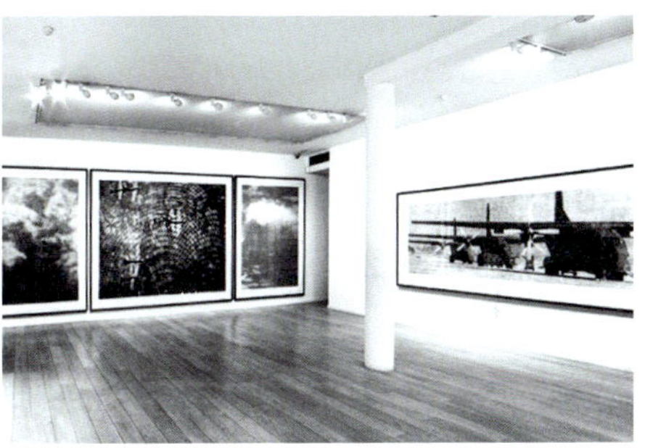

What is your favorite aspect of running a gallery?
I enjoy working directly with the artists and acting as a catalyst for the production of new work.

How do you choose the artists you work with?
So many different ways. Word of mouth, approaching artists whose work I've seen elsewhere, degree shows for the younger artists.

If you weren't running a gallery what else would you do?
I haven't the slightest idea. I'm just glad I have been lucky enough to spend my life doing this.

- **Contact** Alan Cristea Gallery
  Alan Cristea
  info@alancristea.com
- **Established** 1995
- **Owner(s) / Partner(s)** Alan Cristea
  Paul Chellgren
- **Team** 13
- **Artists at Art Basel** Josef and Anni Albers Foundation
  Christiane Baumgartner
  Gordon Cheung
  Michael Craig-Martin
  Edmund de Waal
  Jim Dine
  Naum Gabo Estate
  Richard Hamilton Estate
  Marie Harnett
  Howard Hodgkin
  Richard Long
  Julian Opie
  Lisa Ruyter
  Tom Wesselmann Estate

Paul Winstanley
Richard Woods

- **Further artists represented**: Gillian Ayres, Patrick Caulfield, Dexter Dalwood, Jan Dibbets, Ben Johnson, Allen Jones, Vicken Parsons, Joe Tilson

Crousel

Paris

- Galleries
- Galleries Unlimited
- Galleries

What is your favorite aspect of running a gallery?
Discovering, sharing, and transmitting beauty.

How do you choose the artists you work with?
The artist's language has to be profound, formally new, and internationally appreciable.

If you weren't running a gallery what else would you do?
Open a gallery.

- **Contact**: Galerie Chantal Crousel, Jeremy Dessaint, jeremy@crousel.com
- **Established**: 1980
- **Owner(s) / Partner(s)**: Chantal Crousel, Niklas Svennung
- **Team**: 14
- **Space(s)**: 950 m²
- **Artists at Art Basel**: Jennifer Allora & Guillermo Calzadilla, Abraham Cruzvillegas, Claire Fontaine, Isa Genzken, Wade Guyton, Mona Hatoum, Thomas Hirschhorn, Hassan Khan, Jean-Luc Moulène, Melik Ohanian, Gabriel Orozco, Seth Price, Clément Rodzielski, Willem de Rooij, Anri Sala, Alain Séchas, Reena Spaulings, Wolfgang Tillmans, Rirkrit Tiravanija, Danh Vo, Haegue Yang, Heimo Zobernig
- **Further artists represented**: Fikret Atay, Tarek Atoui, Wang Bing, David Douard, Fabrice Gygi, Pierre Huyghe, Michael Krebber, Moshe Ninio, José Maria Sicilia, Sean Snyder, Tim Rollins & K.O.S., Andy Warhol

Crown Point

San Francisco

- Edition

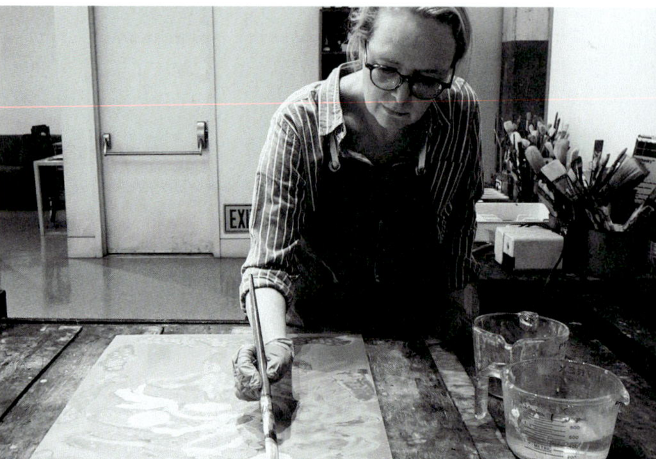

What is your favorite aspect of running a gallery?
The best thing about running a gallery, for us, is that it also means running a studio. Crown Point Press shows etchings made on our premises. Artists fly to San Francisco, usually from New York or Europe, and work with our printers for a week or two, using hands-on processes that involve copper plates instead of paper or canvas. We love having them here working, and we love seeing gallery visitors being amazed at the art. The artists are often amazed, too, at what they've been able to do.

- **Contact**: Crown Point Press, Valerie Wade, valerie@crownpoint.com
- **Established**: 1962
- **Owner(s) / Partner(s)**: Kathan Brown, Valerie Wade
- **Team**: 10
- **Space(s)**: 900 m²
- **Artists at Art Basel**: Mamma Andersson, Darren Almond, Robert Bechtle, Al Held, Sol LeWitt, Jockum Nordström, Chris Ofili, Laura Owens, Ed Ruscha, Alyson Shotz, Amy Sillman, Pat Steir, Wayne Thiebaud, Richard Tuttle, Charline von Heyl
- **Further artists represented**: Tomma Abts, John Cage, Richard Diebenkorn, Pia Fries, Mary Heilmann, Joan Jonas, Anish Kapoor, Per Kirkeby, Tom Marioni, Julie Mehretu, Markus Raetz, Shahzia Sikander, Fred Wilson

Cuc

Hanoi ● Insights

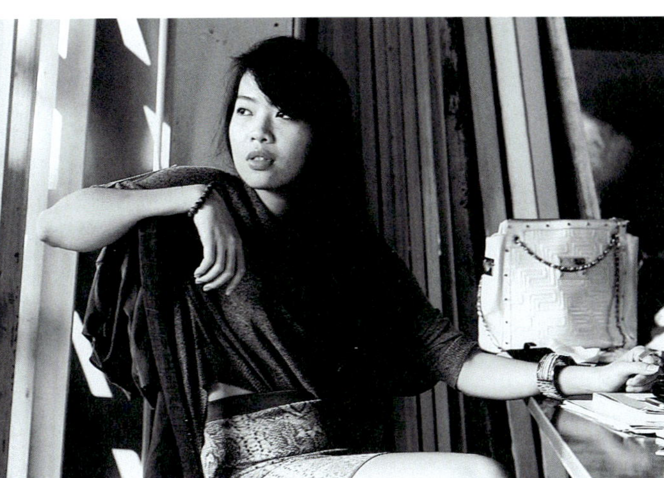

What is your favorite aspect of running a gallery?

Art makes the impossible possible—this is what I love the most about art. The most exciting part of running a gallery is that I can envision and be a part of the process making all these impossible things come to life. I feel my mind is being challenged all the time. I meet with so many extraordinary people. Meeting with artists, listening to their ideas, and becoming part of a creation are just pure joy.

How do you choose the artists you work with?

We are from Southeast Asia, so we definitely want someone authentic, and representative of our region. We are very interested in working with young artists with exciting new projects. Above all, we have to see a future together, between artists and ourselves. It is like when you date someone: first you try a few dates, you see if it works, then comes the dating and if still works, it surely is a relationship and maybe marriage after all?

If you weren't running a gallery what else would you do?

I studied Health Administration and Business as my major in college. Health information used to be my interest so I would be working in a health information organization in the US now. I chose to change my career three years ago as I wanted to be back home in Hanoi and be outside of the box and crazy at times …

- **Contact** Cuc Gallery
Cuc Pham
cuc@cucgallery.vn
- **Established** 2012
- **Owner(s) / Partner(s)** Pham Phuong Cuc
- **Team** 6
- **Space(s)** 370 m²
- **Artists at Art Basel** Nguyen Trung
- **Further artists represented** Dinh Y Nhi
Do Hoang Tuong
Ly Tran Quynh Giang
Ngoc Nau
Nguyen Bach Dan
Nguyen Son

Galerie Gisela Capitain
Interview with Gisela Capitain

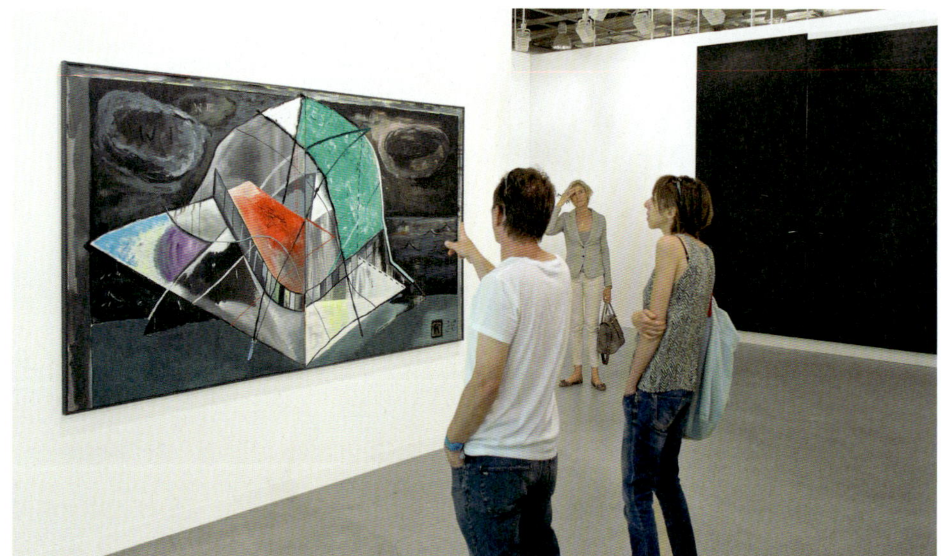

Art Basel in Basel, 2014

The first question is about how the gallery began: I read that you started because of Martin Kippenberger—maybe one of the best reasons to start a gallery!

Yes, that's why I am where I am. He taught me how to look at art, to somehow understand an artist. It was 1977, and we had just started his famous "Kippenbergers Büro." It was not a real office, but a huge loft in a beautiful Bauhaus building in Berlin, close to the Oranienplatz. He was organizing exhibitions, lectures, concerts, and all kinds of flyers for the punk club SO36. I learned how to hand-produce things like magazines, prepare exhibitions, and I witnessed what an artist's life looks like …

For him, printed matter was very important. He dedicated a lot of attention to any poster, invitation card, book …

Always. He loved any kind of printed matter and he was very fast. He had this amazing confidence in his ideas and in how to transform them from ideas into products. Flyers were literally done in a day, as fast as the printer could manage. The magazine *Sehr Gut / Very Good* was done in less than a week. He had this motto, which is also the title of a painting: "Heute denken, morgen fertig" (Think today, done tomorrow).

What was your background before meeting Kippenberger?

I moved to Berlin in 1971 and started studying philosophy and sociology at the Freie Universität in Berlin. It was a very political time with all variations of socialist and communist parties at the university including the SEW, the affiliate of the SED (the East German state's party). The studies were more a political than a scientific education … This made me nervous I have to admit [*laughs*] and in the end it became very irritating … It sent me in a more pragmatic direction and I became a teacher for five years.

Your first gallery was dedicated to multiples and prints. Was it a continuation of your experience with Kippenberger, or a choice to be working on something that was a bit less of a dealership?

Through Kippenberger I got to know Max Hetzler. In 1983 I moved from Berlin to Cologne because Max opened his gallery there and asked me to assist him. Hetzler's program was radical and he had rigorous ideas on how to present them.

In 1986 I wanted to start my own business, but I also didn't want to lose contact with all these great artists I had met through Martin and through Hetzler. So I opened a gallery for prints, drawings, and multiples and continued to work with them. I learnt how many interesting possibilities there are in this area: you can work with collages, drawings, an enormous range of print techniques including silkscreen, which was Kippenberger's favorite. Georg Herold created the most interesting multiples at that time. Toward the end of the 1980s, when this serious crisis happened in the art market, I had to stop, as this business requires a lot of investment for production. Quite a number of galleries closed in 1989–1990, especially in New York, and Cologne also started to slow down. But it was as well the time when the Wall fell, Germany reunified, so the first move of galleries to Berlin started. The situation felt unstable.

Your first participation in Art Basel was in 1987?

Yes, my first gallery was named Borgmann Capitain: Mr Borgmann had had his business for many years, which helped to get entrance to the fair. After three rounds I had to stop for three years I think, and then I started again with the first Statements sector in 1996 presenting Sam Samore. Since then I have participated every year.

You have opened different galleries with different people, and now with Friedrich Petzel in Berlin. It is not that frequent in your field. How do you explain this taste for collaboration?

I enjoy having discussions with people with whom I share ways of thinking. Friedrich Petzel was my first assistant in Cologne, when he was still studying art history. In 1989 he moved to New York; since then we have always kept an intense contact. It's important today to have international cooperation in order to build the best platform possible for the artists.

How would you define the program of the gallery?

At the beginning it was somewhat defined by artists I met through Kippenberger and Hetzler: Albert Oehlen, Werner Büttner, Georg Herold, Günther Förg. Through colleagues such as Peter Pakesch in Vienna I was introduced to Heimo Zobernig with whom I opened my gallery in 1986. Luhring Augustine in New York introduced me to Christopher Wool, and then I met Zoe Leonard, Robert Gober, Stephen Prina, Christopher Williams. In the mid-1980s Cologne had this amazing exchange with New York. Cologne and New York were the main centers for contemporary art and all these American artists visited Cologne. A great time to get to know them! Because of Zoe Leonard, who was an active feminist activist in the late 1980s, I became aware of the strength of women artists, and over the last two decades consequently asked artists such as Charline von Heyl, Laura Owens, Monika Sosnowska, and Karla Black to join the gallery. Through Friedrich Petzel, who started his own gallery in 1993, I have met a new generation of artists, like Wade Guyton and Seth Price. The program has grown organically.

How would you define your approach to art fairs? Are fairs a good platform for showcasing artists?

Always as a market platform! Cologne, as I said, lost some of its international reputation, and Germany in general is not such a vibrant marketplace as New York or London. So you have to present your artists also in this international context. You have to reassure your collectors that you are still one of the "important galleries," that you still work with the artists you have shown or sold to them. It's a way to prove that these artists have been successful, that they develop, that their prices remain stable or go up. It's a home truth to say that the market today is global. But this is why I am doing all these international fairs.

D

The Discoveries sector, Art Basel in Hong Kong's global platform for emerging contemporary artists from all over the world, allows galleries to show pieces by one or two artists from their program. In 2014, the Discoveries prize winner was Nadia Kaabi-Linke for her project *In confinement my desolate mind desires* presented by Experimenter.

DISCO VERIES

2014 participants

Neïl Beloufa/Sayre Gomez
Ghebaly

Bettina Buck
Rokeby

Hugo Canoilas
Workplace

James Capper
Barry

Daniel Gustav Cramer
BolteLang

Nicola Farquhar
Hopkinson Mossman

Giulio Frigo
Francesca Minini

David Haines
Upstream

David Hominal/Pamela Rosenkranz
Karma International

Qingtai Hu
55

Taro Izumi
Take Ninagawa

Nadia Kaabi-Linke
Experimenter

Nadia Khawaja
Erben

Christine Sun Kim
Carroll / Fletcher

Toshiyuki Konishi
ARATANIURANO

Noel McKenna
mother's tankstation

Dane Mitchell
RaebervonStenglin

Ciprian Muresan/Serban Savu
Plan B

Tom Price & Omar Ba
Hales

Saad Qureshi
Gazelli

Cheng Ran
Xu

Maeghan Reid/Sascha Pohle
Weingrüll

Ivan Seal
Freedman

Ian Tweedy
Monitor

Ryohei Usui/Yukihiro Taguchi
Mujin-to

Jake Walker
Utopian Slumps

Hu Yun
Aike-Dellarco

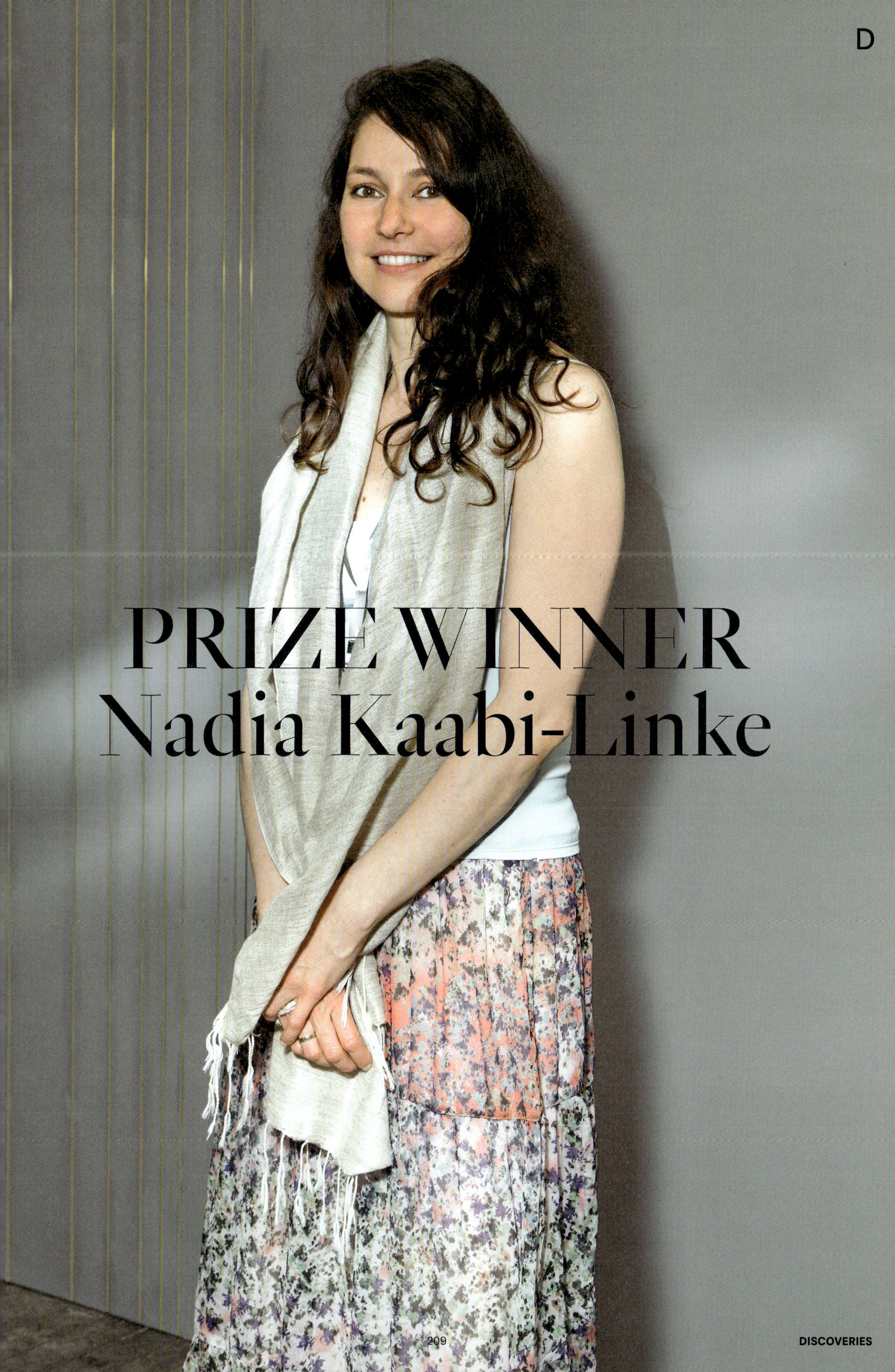

PRIZE WINNER
Nadia Kaabi-Linke

D

Nadia Kaabi-Linke
Experimenter

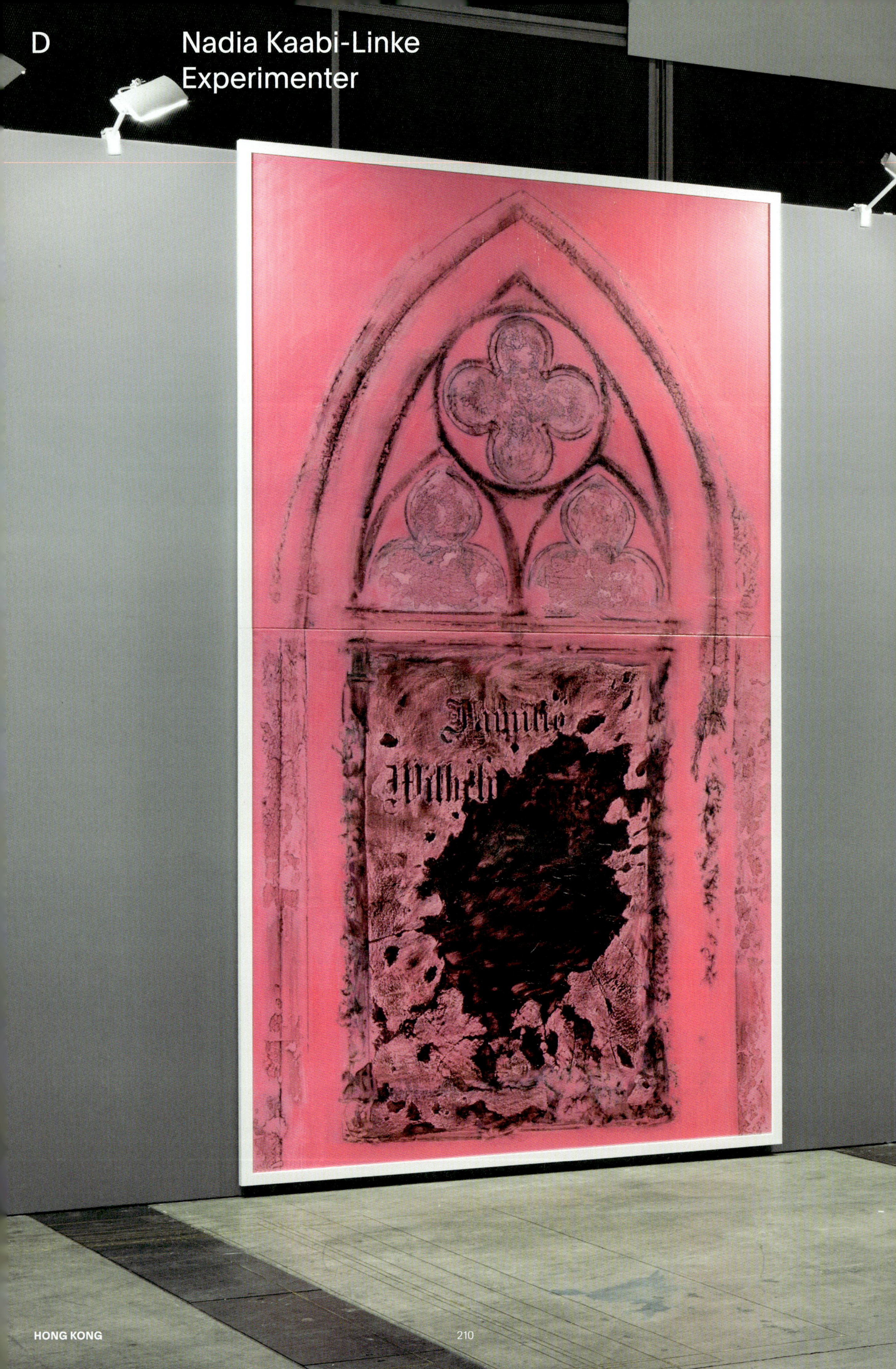

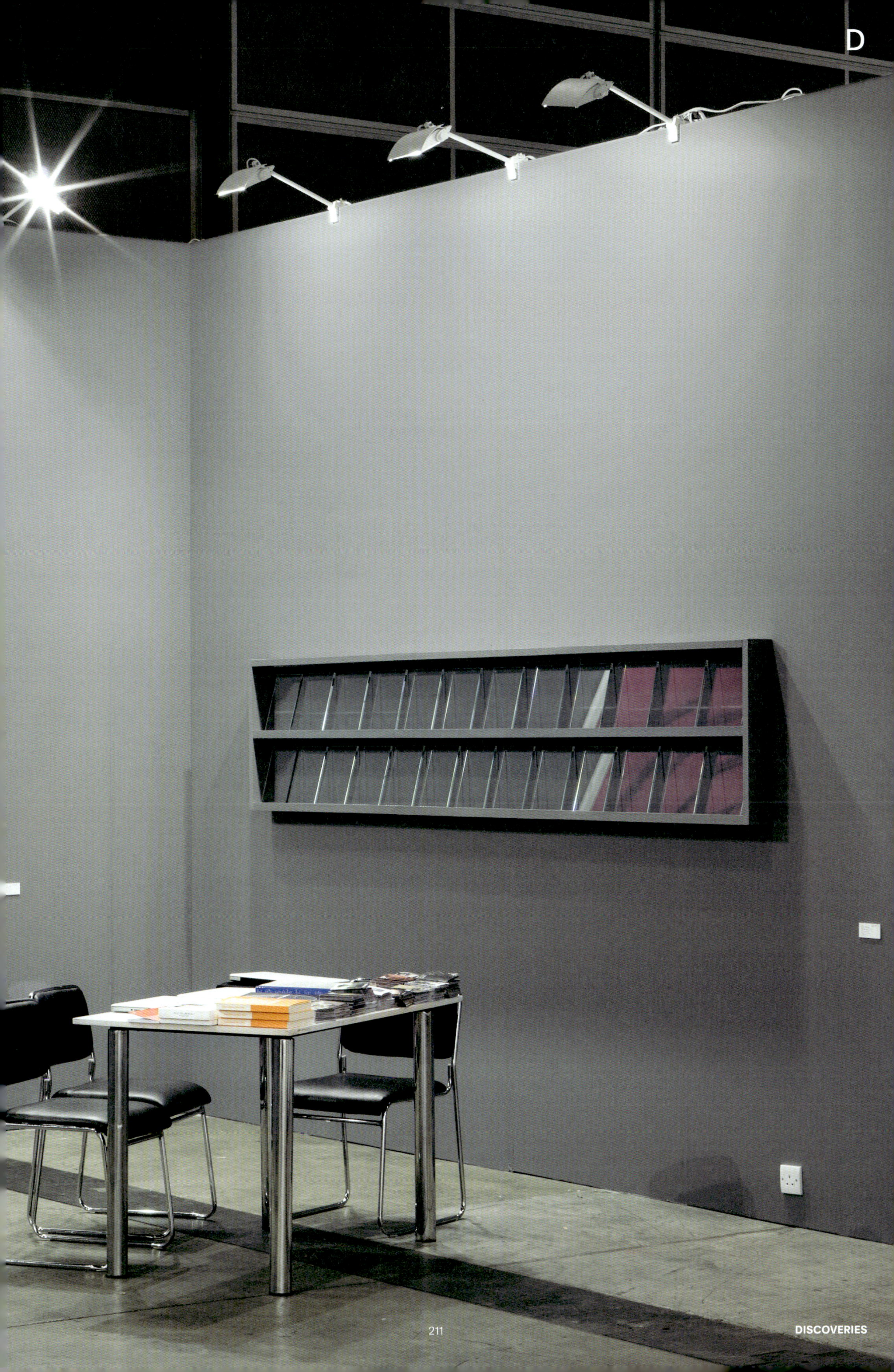

"Questions We Have to Think about *Together*"

A conversation in Hong Kong with Nadia Kaabi-Linke, winner of the 2014 Discoveries Award

The prize consists of 25,000 US$. The artist was chosen by an expert panel of judges.

After finishing secondary school in Dubai, Nadia Kaabi-Linke studied at the School of Fine Arts in Tunis, before completing a PhD in the aesthetics and theory of art from the Sorbonne in Paris. She was awarded the 2014 Discoveries Prize for work shown by the Experimenter gallery of Kolkata. She currently lives Berlin.

NADIA KAABI-LINKE The theme linking all the works on Experimenter's stand is the idea of confinement, of physically experienced enclosure, as in the case of my *Modulor* installation (2014), where I overlapped the "outlines" of 13 different prison cells. The work's title references French architect Le Corbusier and his Convent of La Tourette (1959), where the monk's cells are almost the same size as prison cells. It's a piece that raises questions about Modernist building plans: although Modernist plans are based on anthropological measurements—which is exactly what Le Corbusier was trying to do—maybe we are now losing our humanity by shutting ourselves up, enclosing each individual in an increasingly reduced space. I also wonder how architects could have been so comfortable at their drawing tables—or, today, at their computers—while designing spaces that border on the horrible.

CLÉMENT DIRIÉ I've slept at the Convent of La Tourette—if you stretch out your arm, you can touch the opposite wall. Which may be fine for meditation, but after two nights you can't avoid a certain feeling of confinement.

NKL Precisely. In Paris I lived at the Cité Internationale Universitaire, which has two dorm buildings that were designed by Le Corbusier. I'd always say to my friends that I'd pay them a visit in their "cells." For the measurements of the prison cells in *Modulor* I had to work from personal accounts. These are individual cells, designed for punishment. This version of *Modulor* includes 13 different prisons, but it's a work that is expanding as my research continues. At the moment I've collected accurate dimensions for 20 cells, but they're difficult to obtain because prisons obviously don't want to reveal this information, and even organizations like Amnesty International and Human Rights Watch don't have it. Often it comes from people who have spent time in prison and who made the measurements themselves. What's funny is that I met someone here in Hong Kong—I won't reveal the exact context—who had been in prison in a European country, and who gave me its name and dimensions. So this is really a work in progress that may resurface in the most unexpected contexts.

CD Why did you decide to materialize the measurements in bronze?

NKL Since I'm working on the Modern period, I wanted to use a material emblematic of that period. Bronze is often used on stairs, doors, etc. The allusion is nearly imperceptible, though. My work is based on layers of allusions. But I don't specialize in any given medium—the components always come together on the basis of the context.

CD What about the other works you're showing here?

NKL In particular there's a fairly large painting, *Sepulchre* (2014), which has no specific dimensions but which follows a protocol—it's an imprint of a grave in a cemetery in Berlin not far from where I live, a place where I often walk with my son. I particularly noticed a certain set of graves because they showed visible marks of blasts, traces of World War II. I'd already worked on walls and vestiges of war in Berlin, making rubbings [*frottages*] "from life." But since this was really monumental in size, we worked with scaffolding, cutting it into several pieces, and so on. In fact it's like a jigsaw puzzle.

Sepulchre is typical of my method. I see myself as a criminologist or archaeologist who tries to reconstruct an overall drawing or series of acts based on various elements, in order to understand things better. The grave in question was left unattended, so I said to myself that probably all

For me, the approach entails salvaging objects, elements, and putting them together in order to create a new grammar, a new language, to help us understand our own times. —Nadia Kaabi-Linke

the members of the family had died during the war. Then, suddenly, I saw it as an emblematic image of what total war might be like, where even the dead aren't spared. I didn't want to use only a white ground, so I chose pink, partly in reference to the war between Russia and Ukraine—I have Russian ancestry myself—and partly because we're living in a society of "the dictatorship of fun." Pink is part of the visual language of advertising—you see a lot of pink and white posters, for example, for cell phones. I wanted to force these two incompatible aspects together, to reveal the incompatibility that we all experience today.

CD How do you perceive the artist's role in today's society? Is it a question of bearing witness, of being a critic, of revealing things that have been obscured?

NKL For me, the approach entails salvaging objects, elements, and putting them together in order to create a new grammar, a new language, to help us understand our own times. What I want to do is to allow the beholder to stop and think—my approach involves raising questions that we have to think about *together*. My work uses imagery to reflect on our times.

Nadia Kaabi-Linke, *Modulor*, 2014 (details)

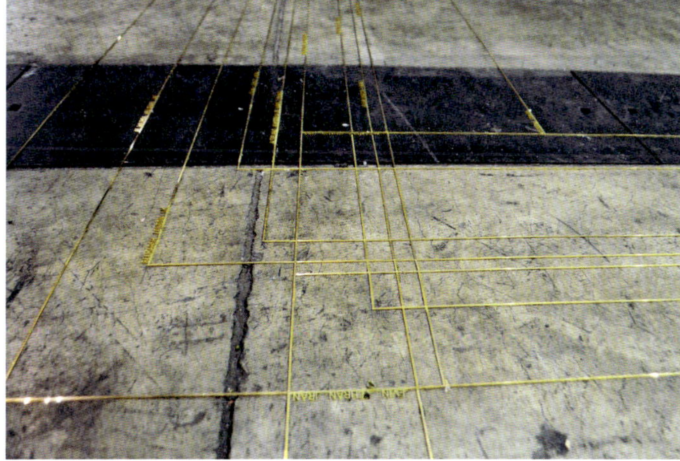

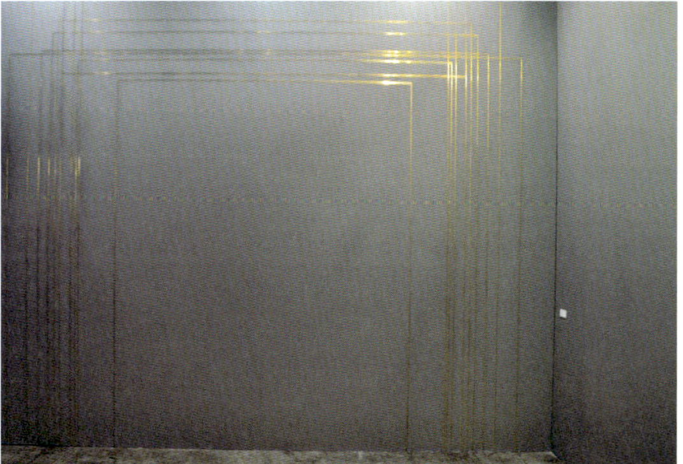

Hugo Canoilas
Workplace Gallery

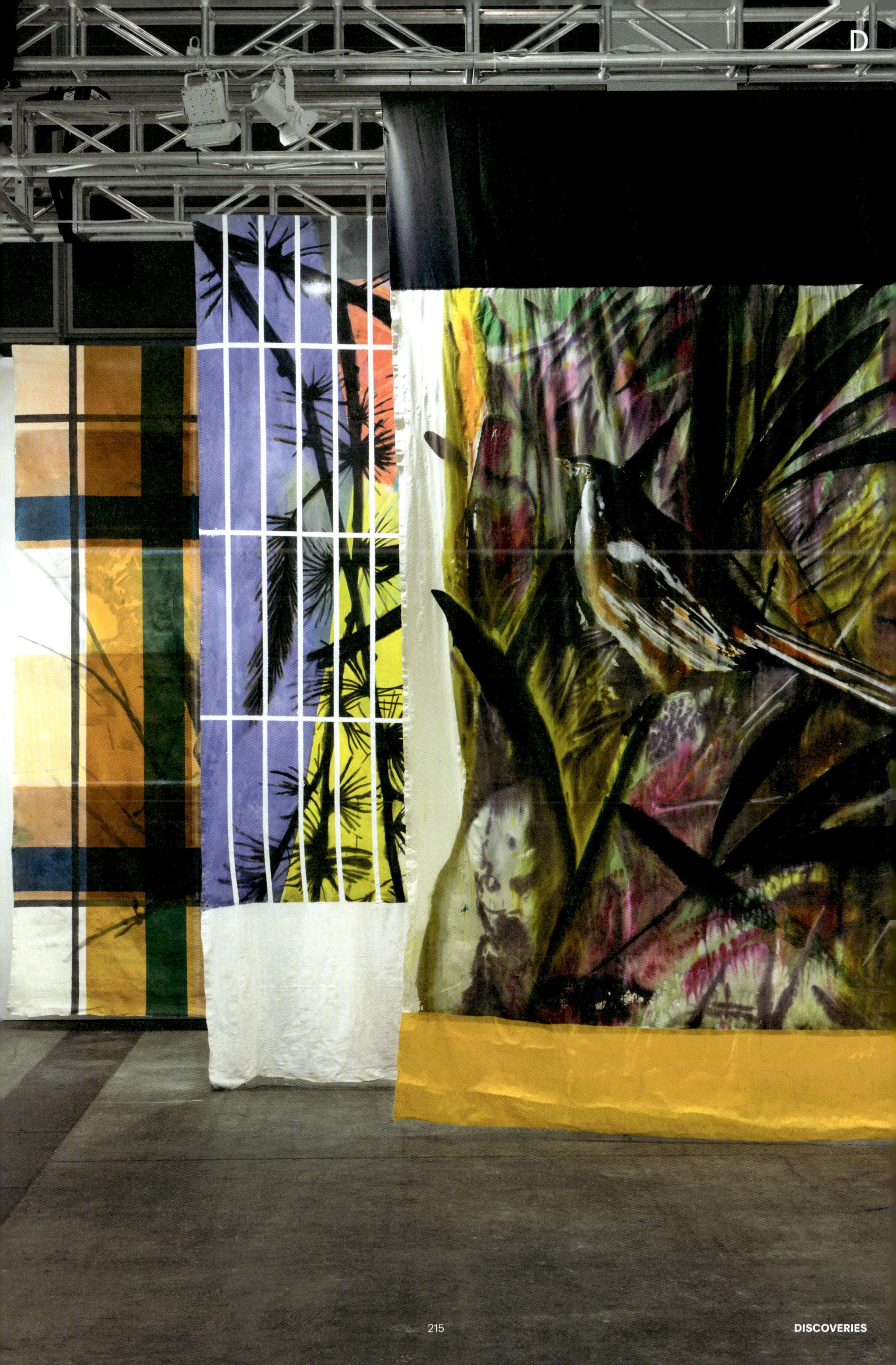

D

Maeghan Reid/Sascha Pohle
Weingrüll

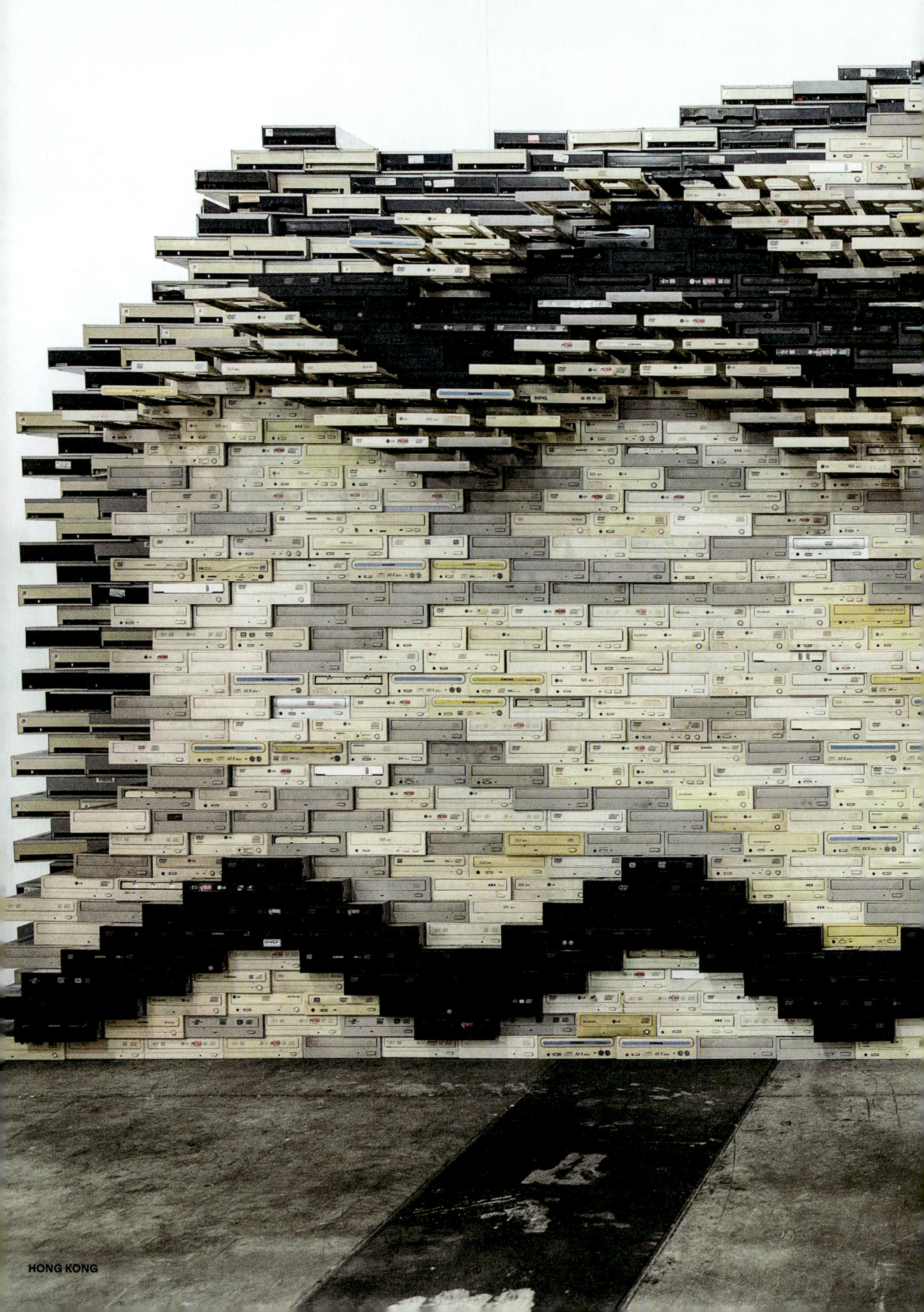

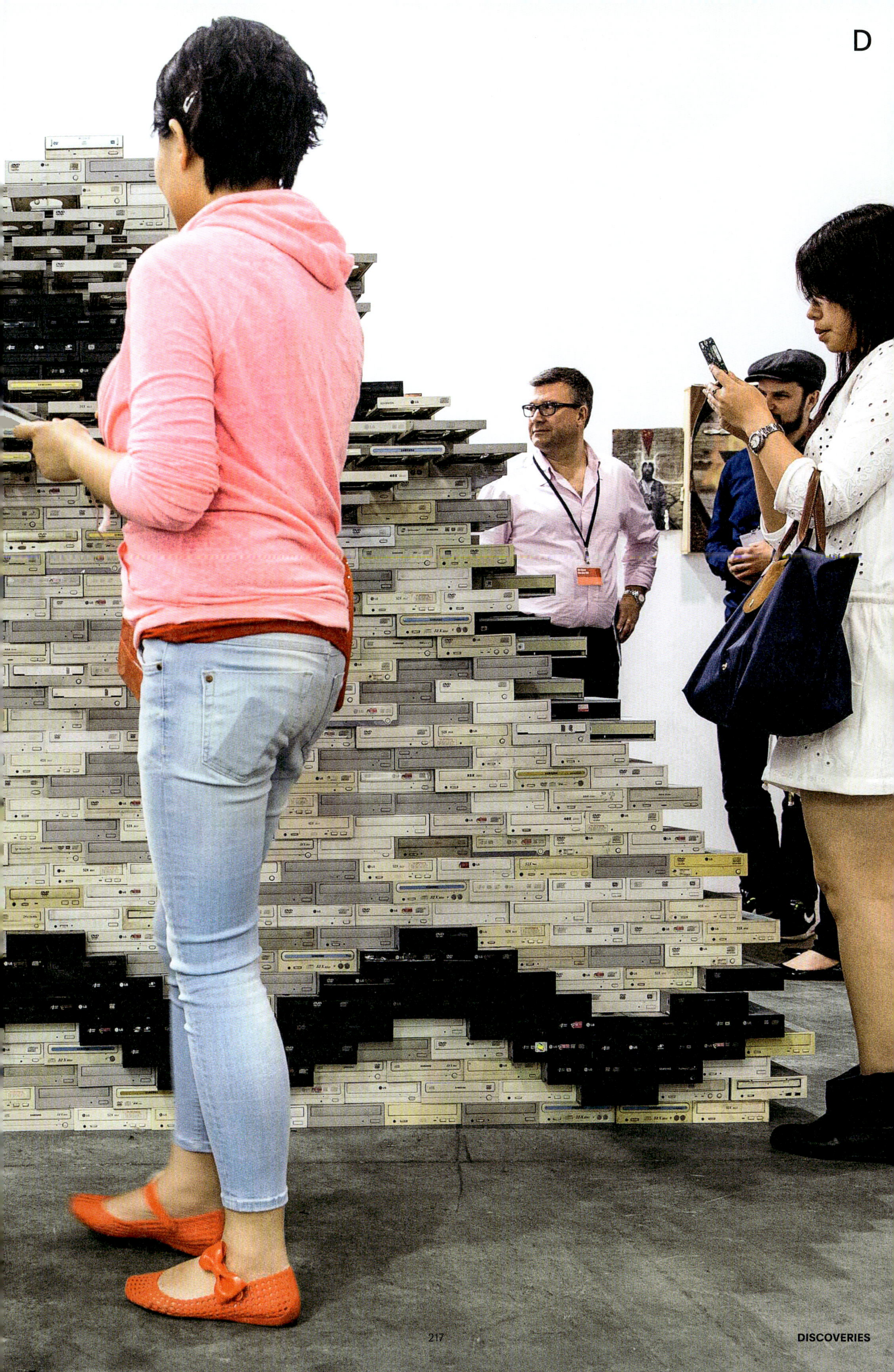

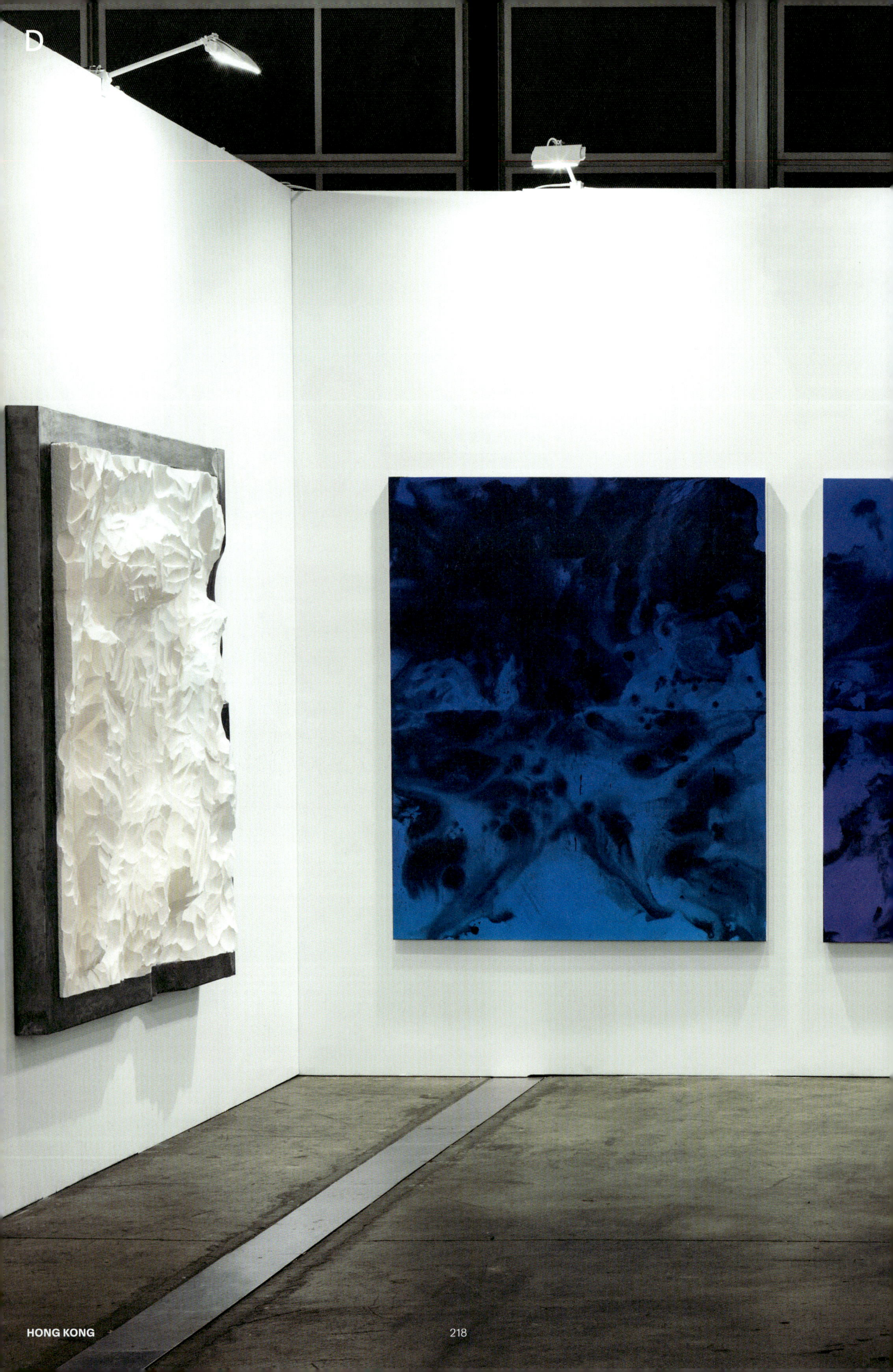

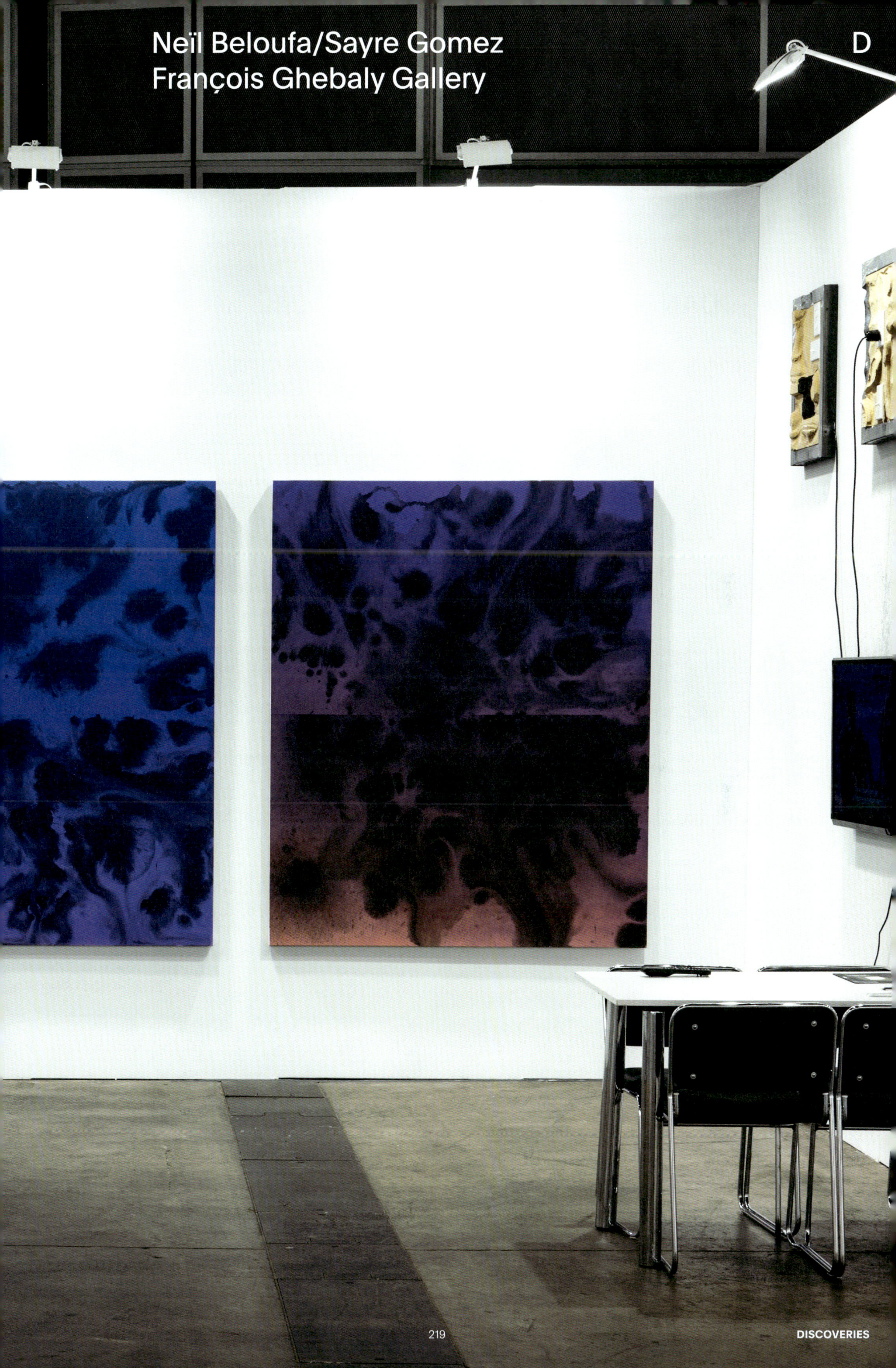

Neïl Beloufa/Sayre Gomez
François Ghebaly Gallery

D

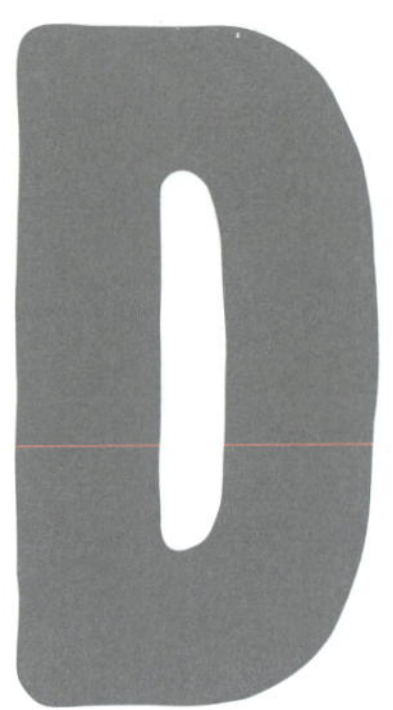
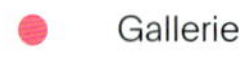

DAN

São Paulo ● Galleries

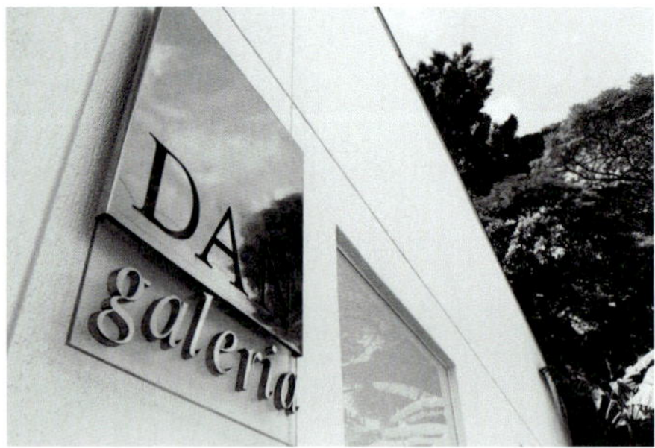

What is your favorite aspect of running a gallery?
My favorite aspect of running a gallery is the challenge of linking the artists and their works to the best collections. It is a job that combines intuition, a passion for art, and dedication. Time and patience are key elements to achieve the results we expect, with the confidence that our work is an important element of the art world chain.

How do you choose the artists you work with?
There are several conditions, but the main element is a true belief and confidence that each artist I work with has as an original and unique expression and that these qualities will remain over time.

If you weren't running a gallery what else would you do?
I really don't know now, but I think that I would like to study to be a chef.

- **Contact** DAN Galería
Flavio Cohn
flaviocohn@dangaleria.com.br
- **Established** 1972
- **Owner(s) / Partner(s)** Jozsef Peter Cohn
Glaucia Cohn
Flavio Cohn
Ulisses Cohn
- **Team** 14
- **Space(s)** 800 m²
- **Artists at Art Basel** Josef Albers
Ascânio MMM
Hércules Barsotti
Max Bill
Sérgio Camargo
Lothar Charoux
Lygia Clark
Carlos Cruz-Diez
Geraldo de Barros
Willys de Castro
Hermelindo Fiaminghi
Stephen Gilbert
Anthony Hill
José de Oliveira Macaparana
Mary Martin
Almir Mavignier
Jesús Soto
Alexandre Wollner
- **Further artists represented** José Manuel Ballester
Christian Cravo
Bill Culbert
Ian Davenport
Norman Dilworth
Dionisio Del Santo
Adolfo Estrada
Sérgio Fingermann
Cristiano Mascaro
Laura Miranda
César Paternosto
Luis Sacilotto
José Spaniol
Amélia Toledo

Dane

London ● Galleries ● Galleries

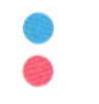
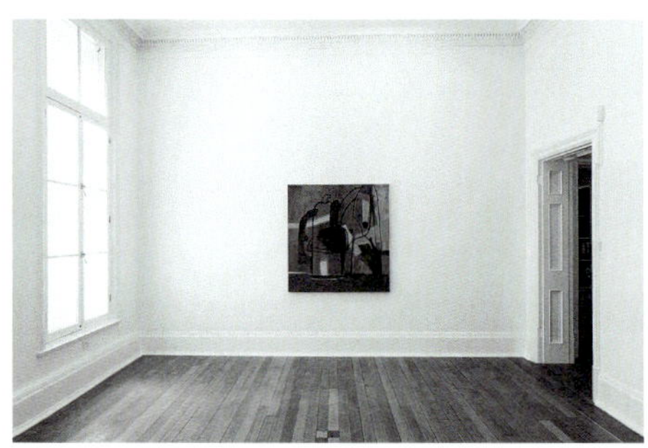

- **Contact** Thomas Dane Gallery
Elli Resvanis
elli@thomasdane.com
- **Established** 2004
- **Owner(s) / Partner(s)** Thomas Dane
Martine d'Anglejan-Chatillon
François Chatala
- **Team** 15
- **Space(s)** 350 m²
- **Artists at Art Basel** Hurvin Anderson
Lynda Benglis
Walead Beshty
Abraham Cruzvillegas
Alexandre da Cunha
José Damasceno
Michel François
Anya Gallaccio
John Gerrard
Arturo Herrera
Phillip King
Luisa Lambri
Michael Landy
Bob Law
Glenn Ligon
Steve McQueen
Tony Morgan
Jean-Luc Moulène
Paul Pfeiffer
Lari Pittman
Amy Sillman
Caragh Thuring
Kelley Walker
Akram Zaatari

Davidson

New York ● Galleries

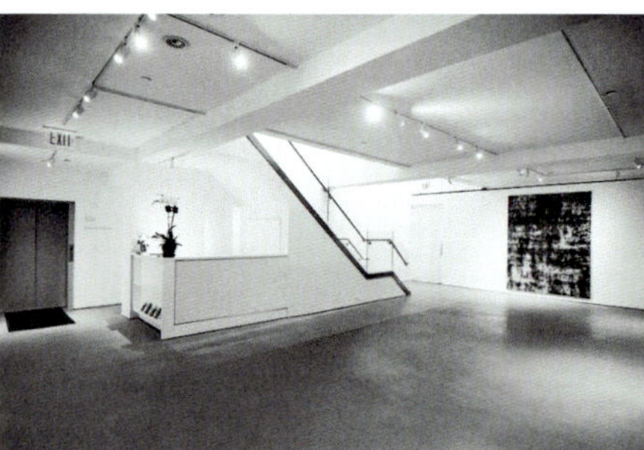

What is your favorite aspect of running a gallery?
Mounting and curating exhibitions that further introduce and expand on optical and kinetic art. I also very much enjoy that our gallery is a family business.

How do you choose the artists you work with?
They obviously have to fit into our program, but more importantly there has to be a bond with either the artist or the Estate that goes beyond the typical artist/dealer relationship. We pride ourselves on the relationships

we have forged over the years.

If you weren't running a gallery what else would you do?
Architect, film industry, and writer.

- **Contact** Maxwell Davidson Gallery
  Maxwell Davidson IV
  md4@davidsongallery.com
- **Established** 1968
- **Owner(s) / Partner(s)** Maxwell Davidson III
  Maxwell Davidson IV
  E. Mary C. Davidson
  Charles C. Davidson
- **Team** 7
- **Space(s)** 669 m²
- **Artists at Art Basel** Yaacov Agam
  Carlos Cruz-Diez
  Pedro S. de Movellan
  Kevin Osmond
  Tim Prentice
  Jesús-Rafael Soto
  George Rickey
  Victor Vasarely
- **Further artists represented** Harry Bertoia
  Estate of Mary Ann Unger
  Estate of Tom Wesselmann

de Alvear

Madrid ● Galleries

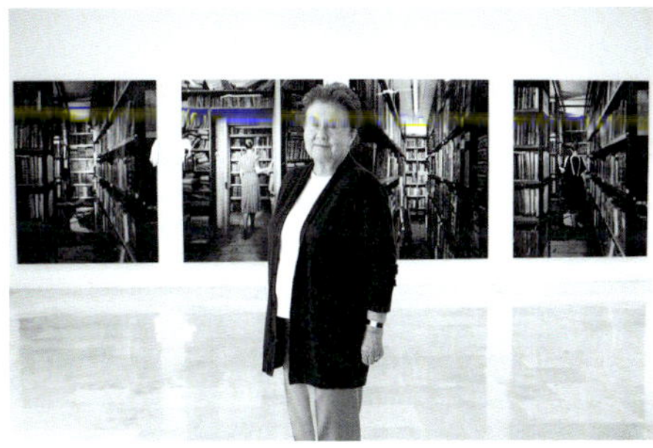

What is your favorite aspect of running a gallery?
Art is my passion and I could not conceive my life without being in direct contact with it. Proof of this is that I own a large art collection, which includes more than 2,500 works that will be donated to the region of Extremadura in Spain.

How do you choose the artists you work with?
I am lucky to work with artists who are among the best on the current art scene. That is the main reason why I follow their work and propose that they collaborate with the gallery.

If you weren't running a gallery what else would you do?
When I was young my dream was to be a pianist. Unfortunately this was not possible, but I found in the art world a perfect place to develop myself.

- **Contact** Galería Helga de Alvear
  Helga de Alvear
  violeta@helgadealvear.com
- **Established** 1984 (Galería Juana Mordó)
  1995 (Helga de Alvear)
- **Owner(s) /** Helga de Alvear
- **Team** 6
- **Space(s)** 900 m²
- **Artists at Art Basel** Santiago Sierra
- **Further artists represented** Helena Almeida
  Slater Bradley
  José Pedro Croft
  Ángela de la Cruz
  Marcel Dzama
  Elmgreen & Dragset
  Jorge Galindo
  Katharina Grosse
  Axel Hütte
  Prudencio Irazabal
  Isaac Julien
  Jürgen Klauke
  Thomas Locher
  Dan Perjovschi
  Ana Prada
  Thomas Ruff

Adrian Sauer
Santiago Sierra
DJ Simpson
Ettore Spalletti
Jane and Louise Wilson

De Carlo

Milan ● Galleries
London ● Galleries Unlimited ● Galleries

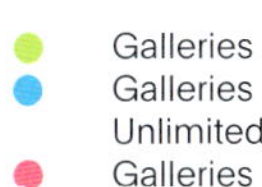

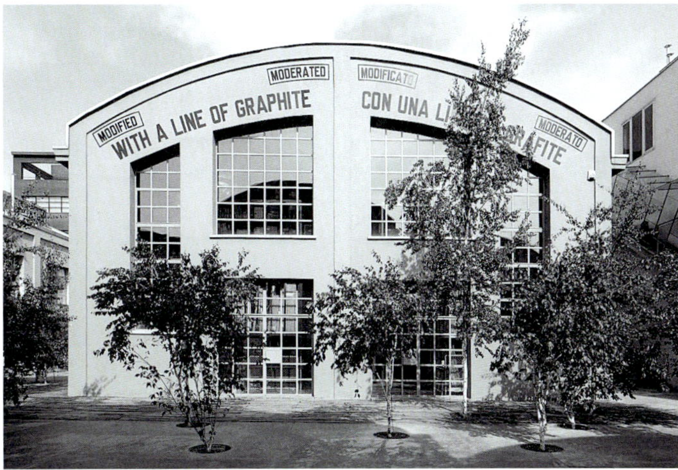

What is your favorite aspect of running a gallery?
I always thought the most important aspect would be to build special relationships with the artists. Travel, logistics, finance: these are only side effects. The relationship between artist and gallerist is based on mutual respect and trust. This is what my work is based on, and what fascinates me the most.

How do you choose the artists you work with?
In the art world today you need to process a lot of information, there's always more to look at and more to think about. And my choices are always driven by a voracious and insatiable research for quality.

If you weren't running a gallery what else would you do?
My two great passions, beyond art, are music and food. If I had not worked in the art world I definitely could have opened a bakery. I love cooking at home for my friends. It is funny to think about this as my profession.

- **Contact** Massimo De Carlo
  Massimo De Carlo
  milano@massimodecarlo.com
- **Established** 1987
- **Owner(s) / Partner(s)** Massimo De Carlo
- **Team** 30
- **Space(s)** 800 m²
- **Artists at Art Basel** John M Armleder
  Massimo Bartolini
  Marvin Gaye Chetwynd
  Steven Claydon
  Dan Colen
  George Condo
  Elmgreen & Dragset
  Gelitin
  Carsten Höller
  Christian Holstad
  Rashid Johnson
  Elad Lassry
  Tony Lewis
  Liu Xiaodong
  Nate Lowman
  Matthew Monahan
  Diego Perrone
  Paola Pivi
  Rob Pruitt
  Rudolf Stingel
  Piotr Uklański
  Kaari Upson
  Andra Ursuta
  Yan Pei-Ming
  Aaron Young

- **Further artists represented**
  Sanford Biggers
  Chris Burden
  Roland Flexner
  Thomas Grünfeld
  Sol LeWitt
  Olivier Mosset
  Matt Mullican
  Steven Parrino
  Jim Shaw
  Josh Smith
  Ettore Spalletti
  Kelley Walker
  Andrea Zittel

de Montferrand

Beijing
Hangzhou

 Insights

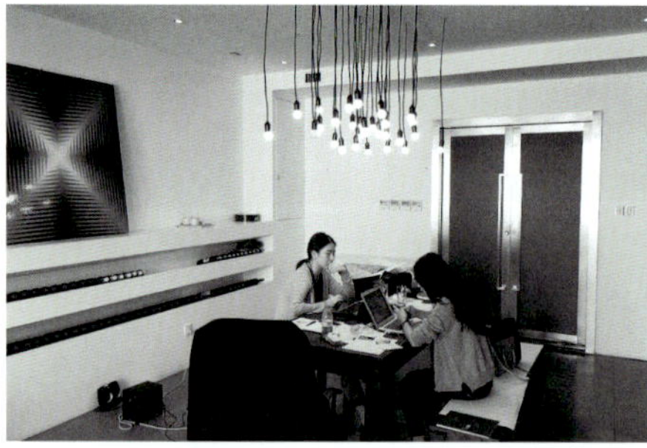

What is your favorite aspect of running a gallery?
Meeting and working with people from different backgrounds and cultures.

How do you choose the artists you work with?
We choose artists according to their current production, the evolution over the years of their creativity, and, most importantly, for the meticulousness with which they approach their craft.

If you weren't running a gallery what else would you do?
We would be working in auction houses.

- **Contact**: Hadrien de Montferrand Gallery
  Olivier Hervet
  o@hdemontferrand.com
- **Established**: 2009
- **Owner(s) / Partner(s)**: Hadrien de Montferrand
  Olivier Hervet
  Laurent Dassault
- **Team**: 9
- **Space(s)**: 290 m²
- **Artists at Art Basel**: Lu Chao
- **Further artists represented**
  Cai Jin
  Cao Yu
  Chen Han
  Ding Yi
  Guo Hongwei
  Guo Wei
  Hao Shiming
  Hou Yong
  Huang Dan
  Ling Jian
  Liu Bolin
  Liu Xiaodong
  Mao Yan
  Pan Xiaorong
  Pan Yingguo
  Song Ren
  Barthélémy Toguo
  Wang Du
  Wang Yi
  Xu Hualing
  Yu Jidong
  Zeng Hao
  Zhang Shujian
  Zhu Xinyu

de Osma

Madrid

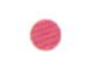 Galleries

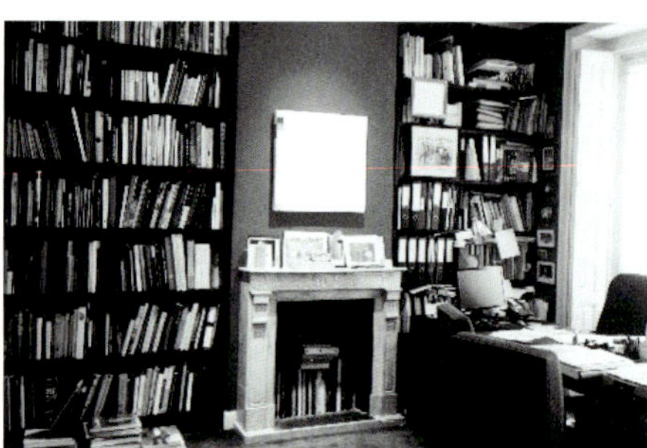

What is your favorite aspect of running a gallery?
Producing exhibitions and publishing catalogues.

How do you choose the artists you work with?
As you may know, we have a historical vision. I show artists up to the generation of the 1980s. They correspond to my personal taste, art historical interest, and intellectual challenge. We occasionally show artists who are not yet well known.

If you weren't running a gallery what else would you do?
Museum curator.

- **Contact**: Galería Guillermo de Osma
  Jose Ignacio Abeijón
  info@guillermodeosma.com
- **Established**: 1991
- **Owner(s) / Partner(s)**: Guillermo de Osma
- **Team**: 4
- **Space(s)**: 200 m²
- **Artists at Art Basel**: Josef Albers
  Waldo Balart
  Antonio Bandeira
  Washington Barcala
  Hércules Barsotti
  Alexander Calder
  Agustín Cárdenas
  Lothar Charoux
  Carlos Cruz-Diez
  Germán Cueto
  Dadamaino
  Samson Flexor
  José Gurvich
  Esteban Lisa
  Rubem Ludolf
  Juan Melé
  César Paternosto
  Mira Schendel
  Ivan Serpa
  Francisco Sobrino
  Jesús Rafael Soto
  Luis Tomasello
  Joaquín Torres- García
  Gregorio Vardanega
  Victor Vasarely
  Décio Viera
- **Further artists represented**: José Alemany
  Eduardo Chillida
  Dis Berlin
  Óscar Domínguez
  Sarah Grilo
  Esteban Lisa
  Maruja Mallo

de Sarthe

Hong Kong ● Galleries

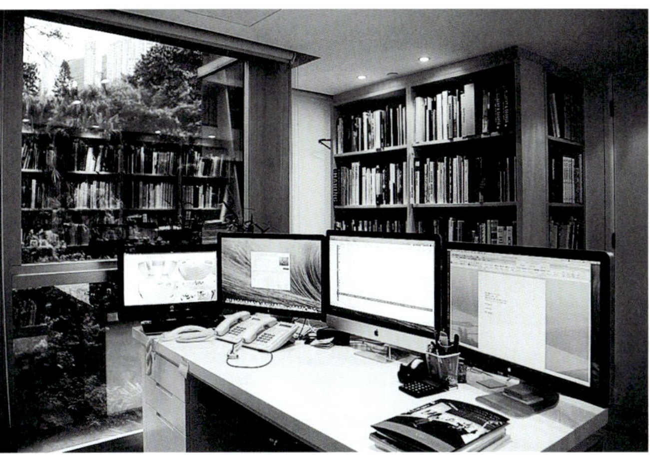

What is your favorite aspect of running a gallery?

Curating exhibitions.

How do you choose the artists you work with?

We believe that art history matters. We choose artists that have a strong place in history. When it comes to choosing a younger artist, it is important to understand where their work comes from. The work should be a response to art that was created previously, as well as a reflection on all of the aspects of their culture, such as the place and time, social life, technologies, political system, and environmental concerns.

If you weren't running a gallery what else would you do?

We started very young and have done it our entire adult lives, so we cannot see ourselves doing anything else. However, if we were not running a gallery we would definitely be doing something art related.

- **Contact** de Sarthe Gallery, Carlotta Conca, hongkong@desarthe.com
- **Established** 1977
- **Owner(s) / Partner(s)** Pascal de Sarthe, Sylvie de Sarthe
- **Team** 11
- **Space(s)** 200 m²
- **Artists at Art Basel** Chu Teh-Chun, Yayoi Kusama, Lin Jingjing, Kazuo Shiraga, T'ang Haywen, Wang Guofeng, Zao Wou-Ki, Zhao Jinhe, Zhou Wendou
- **Further artists represented** Francis Bacon, Chen Zhen, Joan Miró, Claude Monet, Mariko Mori, Pablo Picasso, Auguste Rodin, Bernar Venet

de Torres

New York ● Galleries, Encounters ● Survey

What is your favorite aspect of running a gallery?

Forging relationships with our artists and watching as they evolve in their career and artistic expression.

How do you choose the artists you work with?

Cecilia de Torres, Ltd. exhibits the work of Joaquín Torres-García and the artists associated with his "School of the South," the Taller Torres-García. The gallery also works with younger artists from Latin America who carry on the tradition of abstraction in their contemporary artistic production.

- **Contact** Cecilia de Torres Ltd., Dan Pollock, mail@ceciliadetorres.com
- **Established** 1993
- **Owner(s) / Partner(s)** Cecilia de Torres, Dan Pollock
- **Team** 5
- **Space(s)** 121 m²
- **Artists at Art Basel** Inés Bancalari, Antonio Berni, Gustavo Bonevardi, Marcelo Boullosa, Lidya Buzio, Catalina Chervin, Marta Chilindron, José Pedro Costigliolo, Elias Crespin, Carlos Cruz-Diez, León Ferrari, Julio Le Parc, César Paternosto, Luis Tomasello, Augusto Torres, Horacio Torres, Joaquín Torres-García
- **Further artists represented** Eduardo Costa, Mariano Dal Verme, Linda Kohen, Gerd Leufert, Antonio Llorens, Rogelio Polesello, Julián Terán

Dee

New York ● Galleries

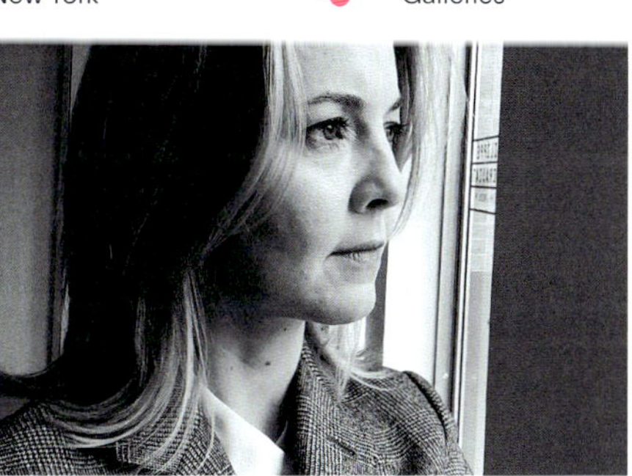

What is your favorite aspect of running a gallery?

Working with artists and developing a program (and a economy for it) is very exciting. The most inspiring aspect is the potential for innovating the profile and public awareness of artists, and to deliver opportunities that were previously out of reach. I feel great satisfaction when an artist grows from one level to another with representation and advocacy by the gallery. This is why the gallery is so important today. I also love the cultural production side of building our program.

How do you choose the artists you work with?

Choosing artists is for me about reflecting on this moment that we are living in and discovering a surprising clarity when I come across an artist that speaks to me on a level that is beyond the visual and intellectual, where I can see the work equally in the moment and 20 years from now. It is as much instinct as analysis, and I listen to factors that are less rational and perhaps more intuitive. We choose artists, but they also must choose us.

If you weren't running a gallery what else would you do?

Most likely, more of the things that I do now, with more time to devote to each: writing, reading, collecting, seeing shows, traveling, visiting friends, spending time with my family, doing yoga, going on more walks and bike rides …

- **Contact** Elizabeth Dee, Nora Orallo, nora@elizabethdee.com
- **Established** 2002
- **Owner(s) / Partner(s)** Elizabeth Dee
- **Artists at Art Basel** Mac Adams, Mark Barrow, Gabriele Beveridge, Miriam Cahn

Philippe Decrauzat
Leo Gabin
John Giorno
Joel Otterson
Julia Wachtel

Delhi Art Gallery

New Delhi
Mumbai

Galleries

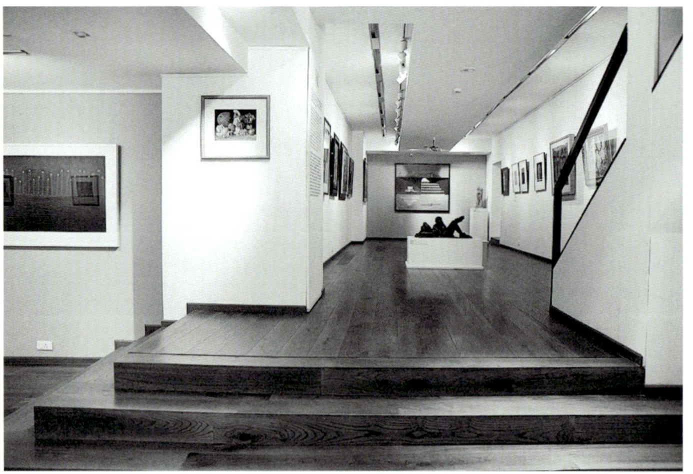

What is your favorite aspect of running a gallery?

A gallery gives you a perspective not just on the art of a country but also its socio-political narrative and environment.

How do you choose the artists you work with?

Delhi Art Gallery deals with Indian masters who assess the national engagement with its art history.

If you weren't running a gallery what else would you do?

I cannot imagine anything else. Art is my only and abiding passion.

- **Contact** Delhi Art Gallery
  Deepika Chhikara
  deepika@delhiartgallery.com
- **Established** 1993
- **Owner(s) / Partner(s)** Ashish Anand
- **Team** 70
- **Space(s)** 317.5 m² (Hauz Khas Village New Delhi)
  81 m² (DLF Emporio New Delhi)
  470.5 m² (Mumbai)
- **Artists at Art Basel** K. H. Ara
  Avinash Chandra
  M. F. Husain
  Akbar Padamsee
  Sohan Qadri
  S. H. Raza
  G. R. Santosh
  Jehangir Sabavala
  F. N. Souza
  J. Swaminathan
- **Further artists represented** J. Sultan Ali
  Nandalal Bose
  Amitava Das
  K. Laxma Goud
  Rabin Mondal
  Gogi Saroj Pal
  Jamini Roy
  Rabindranath Tagore
  Raja Ravi Varma

didier

Brussels
Paris

Edition

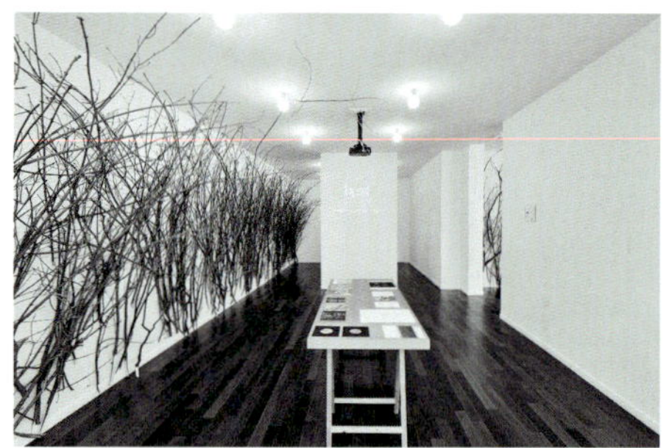

What is your favorite aspect of running a gallery?

For me, the best thing about running a gallery is that I get to work in close collaboration with the artists.

How do you choose the artists you work with?

One by one, each artist becomes a part of a set of cubes that I try to put together to create a balanced structure.

If you weren't running a gallery what else would you do?

I would probably be writing novels.

- **Contact** mfc - michèle didier
  Michèle Didier
  info@micheledidier.com
- **Established** 1987
- **Owner(s) / Partner(s)** Michèle Didier
- **Team** 3
- **Space(s)** 80 m²
- **Artists at Art Basel** Carl Andre
  Robert Barry
  Samuel Bianchini
  AA Bronson
  Claude Closky
  Braco Dimitrijević
  Yona Friedman
  Paul-Armand Gette
  Liam Gillick
  Joseph Grigely
  On Kawara
  Leigh Ledare
  Christian Marclay
  Allan McCollum
  Annette Messager
  John Miller
  Jonathan Monk
  Antonio Muntadas
  Maurizio Nannucci
  Philippe Parreno
  Raymond Pettibon
  Allen Ruppersberg
  Jim Shaw
  Josh Smith
  Klaus Scherübel
  Untel
  Christopher Wool
- **Further artists represented** Dennis Adams
  Stanley Brouwn
  Philippe Cazal
  Hannah Collins
  David Cunningham
  Charles de Meaux
  Peter Downsbrough
  Carsten Höller
  Pierre Huyghe
  Matt Keegan
  Jutta Koether
  Robert Morris
  Michelangelo Pistoletto
  Joe Scanlan
  Lawrence Weiner

Dirimart

Istanbul ● Galleries

What is your favorite aspect of running a gallery?
One of the many reasons is the dynamism and growth of the art scene in our country.

How do you choose the artists you work with?
If the artists' background—intellectual and professional—is suitable to the characteristics of Dirimart, we discuss our mutual expectations with them and proceed accordingly.

- **Contact** Dirimart
  Burcu Fikretoglu
  burcu@dirimart.com
- **Established** 2002
- **Owner(s) / Partner(s)** Hazer Ozil
- **Team** 6
- **Space(s)** 120 m²
- **Artists at Art Basel** Franz Ackermann
  Yeşim Akdeniz
  Ghada Amer
  Yüksel Arslan
  Suzan Batu
  Thomas Bayrle
  Sabine Boehl
  Doğan Doğan
  Katharina Grosse
  Özlem Günyol & Mustafa Kunt
  Özcan Kaplan
  Peter Kogler
  Fabian Marcaccio
  Bjorn Melhus
  Sarah Morris
  Paul Morrison
  Shirin Neshat
  Hermann Nitsch
  Ebru Uygun
  Ekrem Yalçındağ
  Necmi Zeka
  O Zhang
  Peter Zimmermann

Drawing Room

Makati City
Singapore 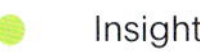 Insights

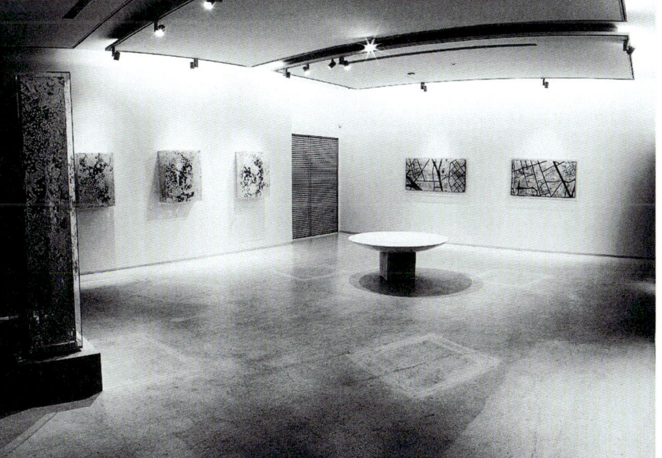

What is your favorite aspect of running a gallery?
It is a pleasure to talk about art and culture with people who are equally enthusiastic, and to form relationships and collaborations with them. Likewise, it gives so much gratification to be with artists—to be close to their practice, to access and safeguard the development of their work, and to be able to expose and promote them.

How do you choose the artists you work with?
We choose artists whose practices are honest and thoughtful enquiries into their contexts. They are often interdisciplinary and the content projects certain personal synchronicity between histories we inherit and histories we are shaping. As the gallery focuses on strategic career management, the artists that we choose also possess a commitment to developing their practice with us.

If you weren't running a gallery what else would you do?
I would still be doing marketing and business in another industry.

- **Contact** The Drawing Room
  Cesar Jr. Villalon
  contact@drawingroomgallery.com
- **Established** 1998
- **Owner(s) / Partner(s)** Cesar Villalon Jr.
- **Team** 8
- **Space(s)** 200 m² (Makati City)
  200 m² (Singapore)
- **Artists at Art Basel** Gaston Damag
  Mark Justiniani
- **Further artists represented** Alfredo and Isabel Aquilizan
  Miguel Aquilizan
  Vermont Coronel Jr.
  Kawayan de Guia
  Kiko Escora
  Roberto Feleo
  Alvin Gregorio
  Riel Hilario
  Troy Ignacio
  Diokno Pasilan
  John Frank Sabado
  Lirio Salvador
  Mark Salvatus

du Monde

Hong Kong  Insights

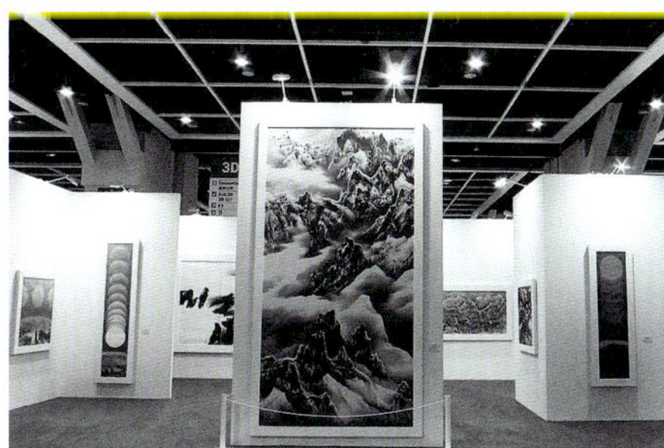

What is your favorite aspect of running a gallery?
Promoting talented young artists.

How do you choose the artists you work with?
Talent, attitude, inspired creativity.

If you weren't running a gallery what else would you do?
Make documentaries on artists.

- **Contact** Galerie du Monde
  Kelvin Yang
  kelvin.yang@galeriedumonde.com
- **Established** 1974
- **Owner(s) / Partner(s)** Fred Scholle
- **Team** 10
- **Space(s)** 220 m²
- **Artists at Art Basel** Liu Kuo-Sung
- **Further artists represented** Jiang Chuan
  Li Gang
  Li Hao
  Lu Yanpeng
  Qin Chong
  Qin Feng
  Qin Wen
  Shi Jinsong
  Zhu Yiyong

Dvir

Tel Aviv ● Galleries

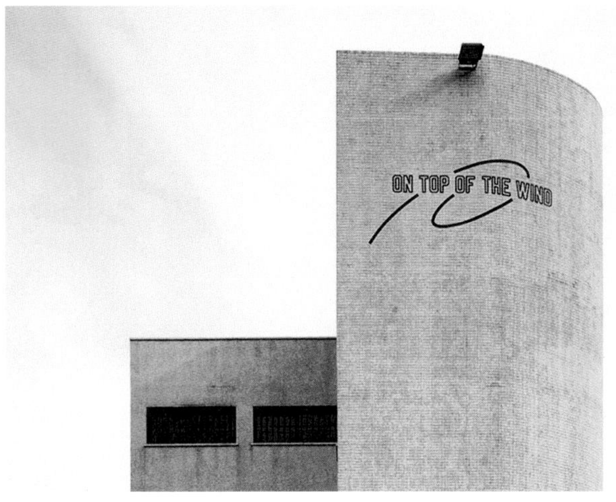

- **Contact** Dvir Gallery
  Emmanuelle Lamy
  international@dvirgallery.com
- **Established** 1982
- **Owner(s) / Partner(s)** Dvir Intrator
  Shifra Shalit
- **Team** 5
- **Space(s)** 1,000 m²
- **Artists at Art Basel** Adel Abdessemed
  Mirosław Bałka
  Mircea Cantor
  Latifa Echakhch
  Simon Fujiwara
  Douglas Gordon
  Shilpa Gupta
  Jonathan Monk
  Ariel Schlesinger
  Miri Segal
- **Further artists represented** Etty Abergel
  Nelly Agassi
  Yossi Breger
  Omer Fast
  Hans-Peter Feldmann
  Claire Fontaine
  Dor Guez
  Yudith Levin
  Moshe Ninio
  Sarah Ortmeyer
  Barak Ravitz
  Karen Russo
  Nedko Solakov
  Haim Steinbach
  Naama Tsabar
  Lawrence Weiner
  Pavel Wolberg

Massimo De Carlo
Advertisement series

In 1987.

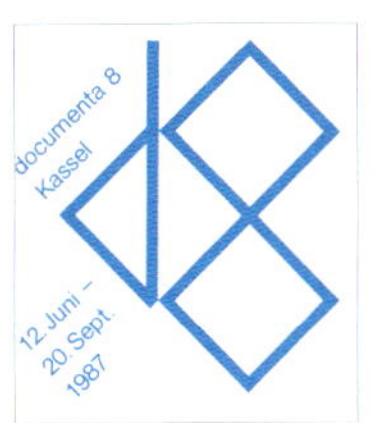

June.
Manfred Schneckenburger curates Documenta 8. The exhibition was originally to be curated by Harald Szeemann and Edy de Wilde but both resigned.
(Photo by Dietmar Walberg)

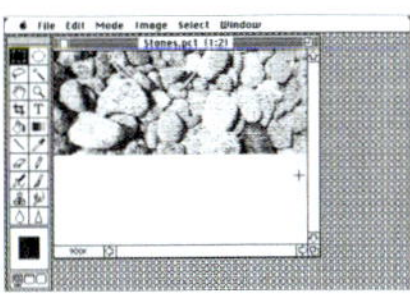

October.
Thomas and John Knoll develop the first version of Photoshop. Massimo De Carlo buys his first telefax machine.

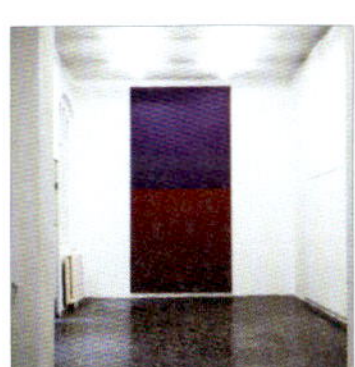

November.
The first exhibition of Massimo De Carlo Gallery is Olivier Mosset.

In 1988.

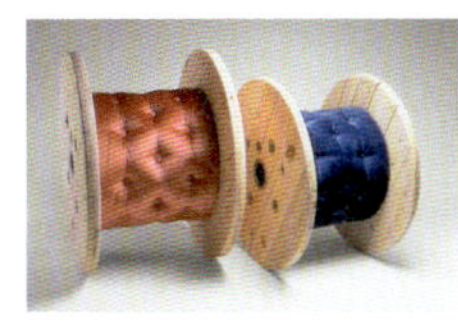

January.
Maurizio Cattelan produces DIY furniture. He believes he can make his living as a designer.

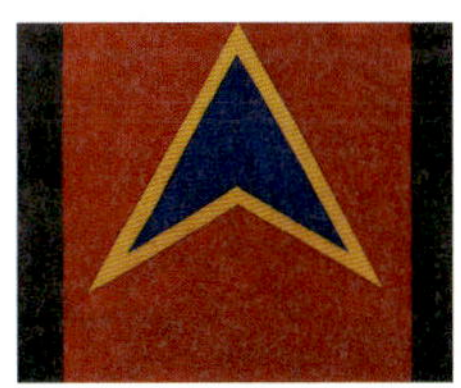

June.
Sol LeWitt participates in the Venice Biennale, and donates the ten preparatory drawings to their archive. The Biennale is thankful and in response asks the artist to refund part of the expenses for his stay: he brought his wife with him to Venice.

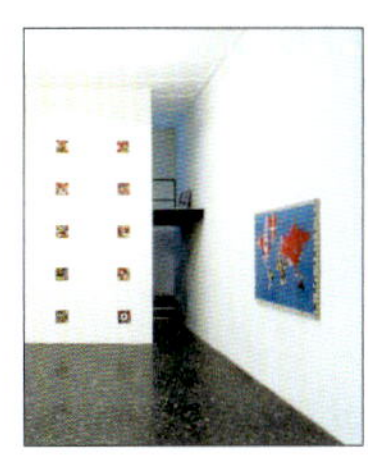

March
Alighiero Boetti's first exhibition at Galleria Massimo De Carlo in Milano. Massimo strongly tries to sell the map in the show for $14.000: unsold.

In 1991.

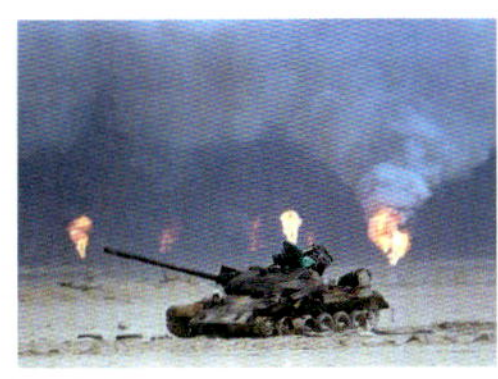

February
Because of the Gulf War, the contemporary art market falls into a very heavy crisis. Will it happen again?

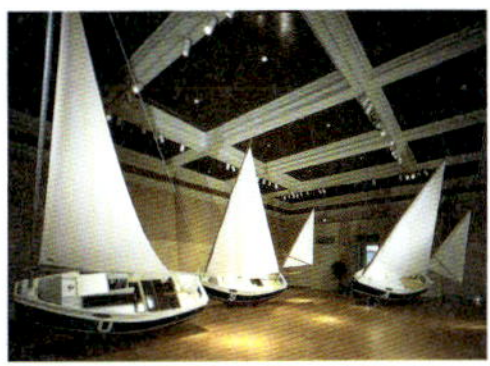

May
One of the most intriguing site-specific contemporary art exhibitions opens in Charleston, USA: Places with a Past. Among 23 different artists, it features *Three Ghost Ships* by Chris Burden.

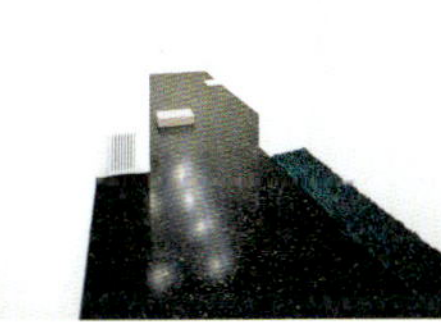

September
Massimo De Carlo shows Félix González-Torres. It was the same year that he realized the billboard project *Untitled* with a photograph of his bed, one of the icons of the XX century.

In 1993.

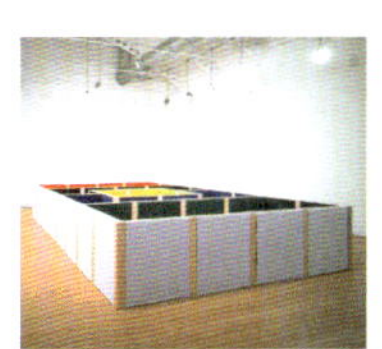

April
Matt Mullican participates in Documenta IX, and in the same year shows at Massimo De Carlo in Milan.

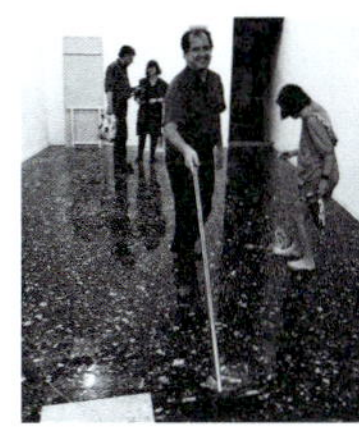

July
Massimo De Carlo moves space. His last exhibition in Via Panfilo Castaldi is with Roman Signer. The artist installs the work (flooding the space), and the gallerist deals with it.

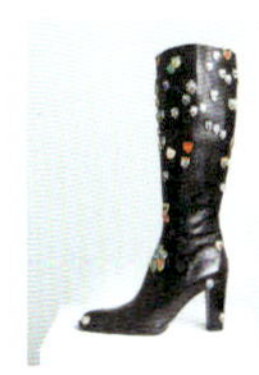

November
The Maastricht Treaty becomes law and the European Union is formally born. Goods and people can circulate freely within the European states, and the art world becomes even more global.

E

Dedicated to large-scale sculpture and installation works by leading artists from around the world, Encounters provides Art Basel in Hong Kong visitors with the opportunity to see works that transcend the traditional art fair stand. The sector presented these works in prominent locations throughout the exhibition halls. In 2014, 17 projects were chosen by Yuko Hasegawa, Chief Curator of the Tokyo Museum of Contemporary Art.

EN COUNT ERS

2014 participants

Miyanaga Aiko
Mizuma

Rebecca Baumann
Starkwhite

Marta Chilindron
de Torres

Yu Cheng-Ta
Chi-Wen

Wang Jianwei
Long March

Michael Lin
Eslite

Xu Qu
Tang

Tobias Rehberger
Meile
neugerriemschneider

Shen Shaomin
Osage

Kishio Suga
Koyama

Atelier Van Lieshout
Krinzinger
Grimm

Lee Wen
iPreciation

Gu Wenda
Hanart TZ

Morgan Wong
Lam

Sun Xun
STPI
ShanghART

Yang Xinguang
Exit

Yeesookyung
Kukje/Kim

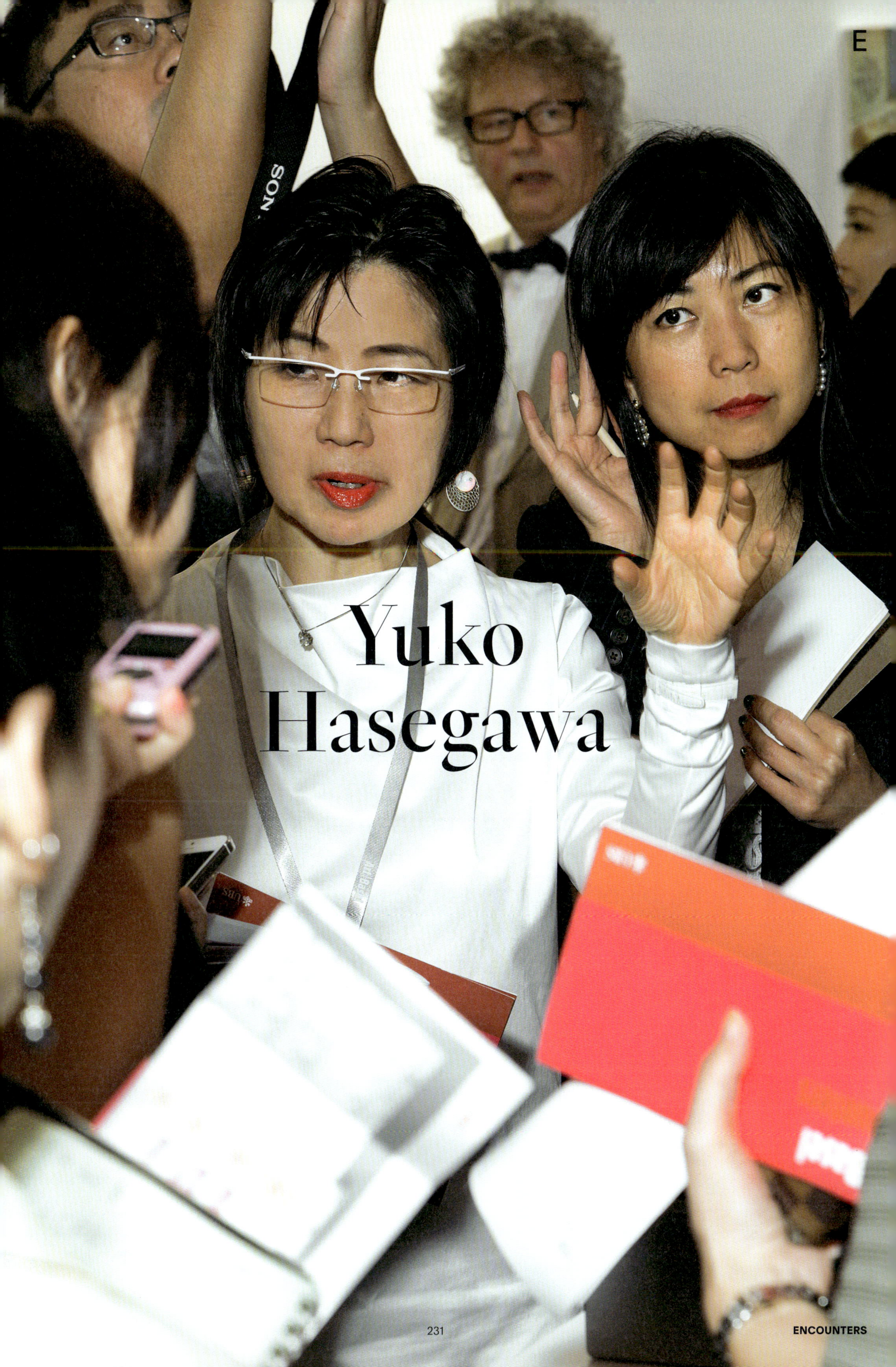

Yuko Hasegawa

E

The 2014 edition of Encounters reconsidered social memories and relationships, notions undergoing a process of complex diversification in face of globalization and new ways of relating to each other through social media. Encounters gathered together works that critically reflect this situation, whether proposing to engage these fundamental shifts or trying to resist them. The projects were divided into two types according to their proclivities: one being "participatory," that is inviting viewers' involvement as central players, as in *Homeaway* by Tobias Rehberger who recreated a favorite Frankfurt bar, or Michael Lin's *Point* which converted a meeting place into a sculpture that visitors could climb, thus reversing the relationship between the viewer and the viewed. The second means of expression chosen by artists in relation to this topic was to add many layers of meaning to the memory of objects and the nature of material. The work *Thousand* by Yeesookyung, which combined fragments of old, broken ceramics to create and regenerate new objects, is a perfect example of this attitude.

Point consists of a grandstand with an illuminated rotating sign at the top. The seating area becomes a place to view from and a place to be viewed, a stage and a catalyst for social interaction. The sign publicizes a form of rendezvous where the spectator's position is reversed, where the borders between the viewer and the viewed, the spectator and the performer, the audience and the artwork blur.

Michael Lin
Point
2014

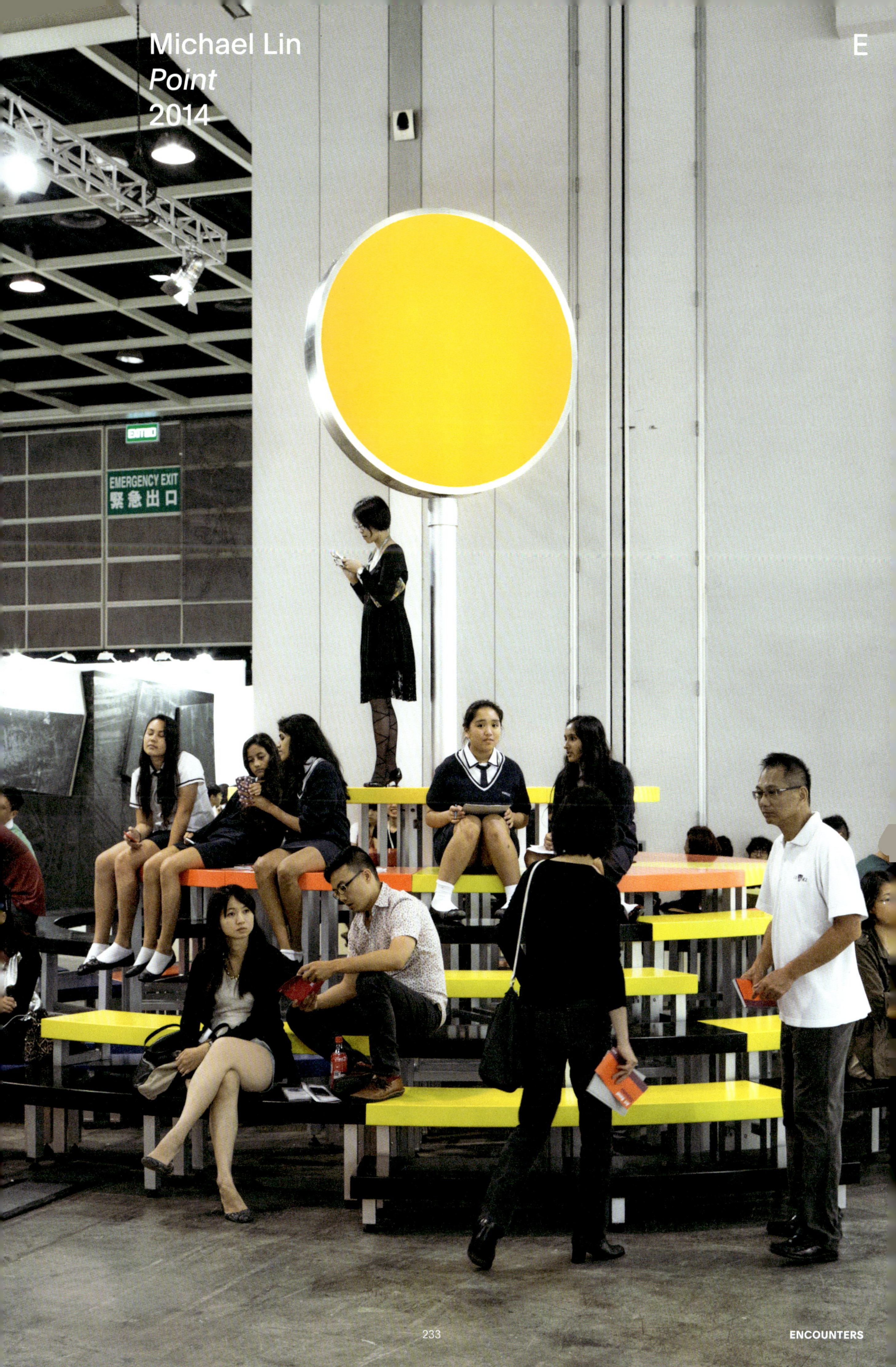

E

Sun Xun
Jing Bang: A Country Based on Whale
2014

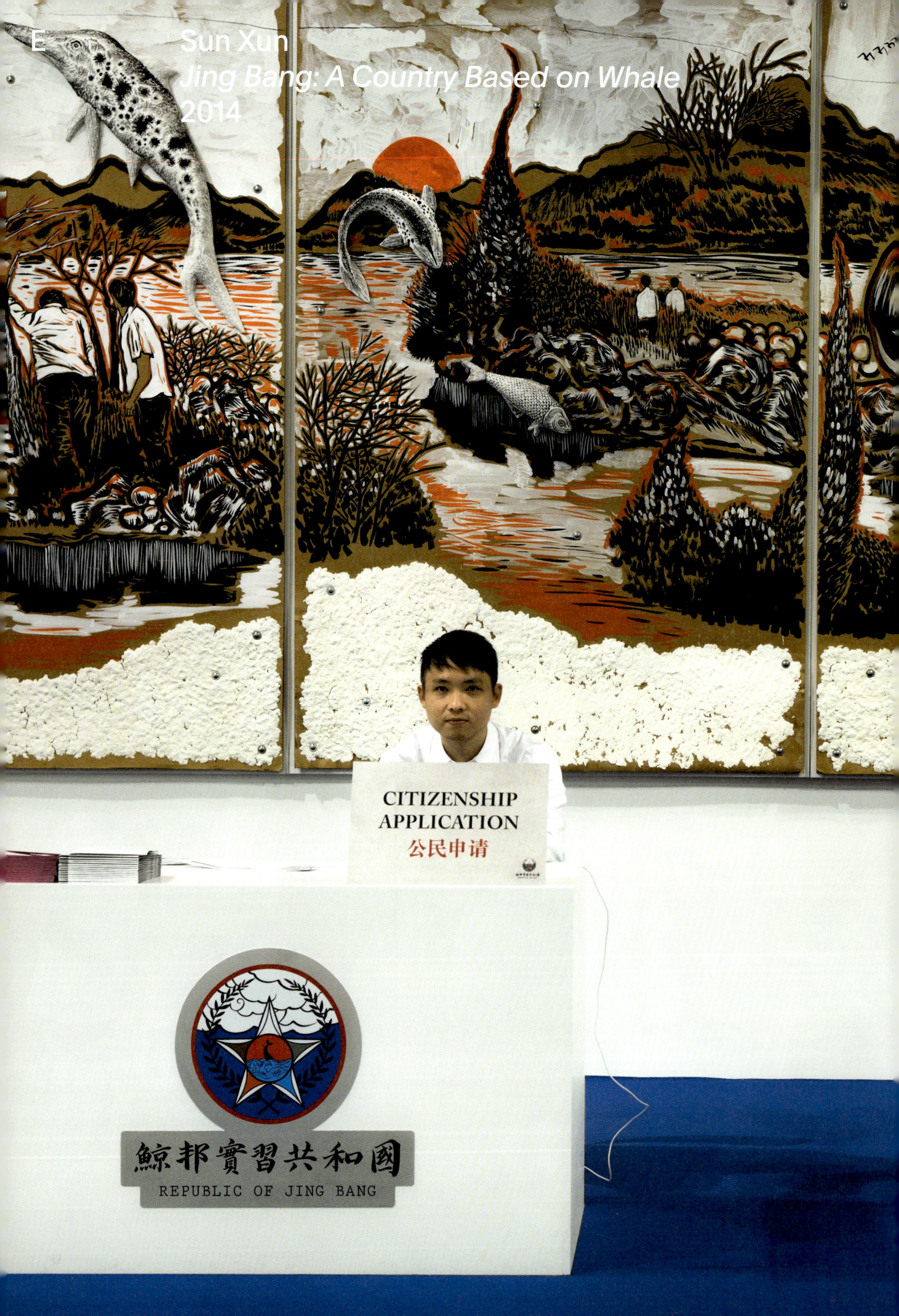

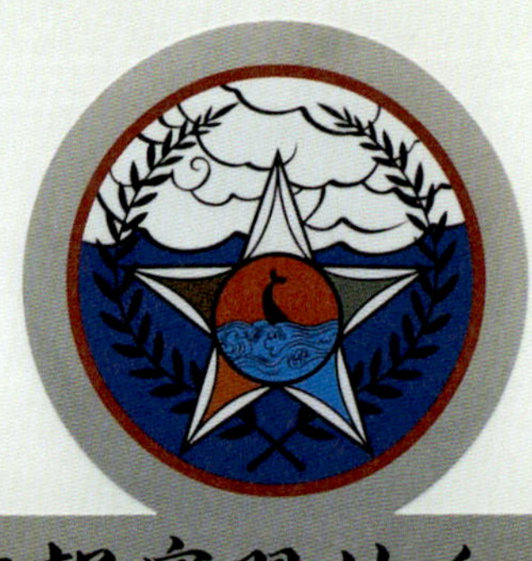

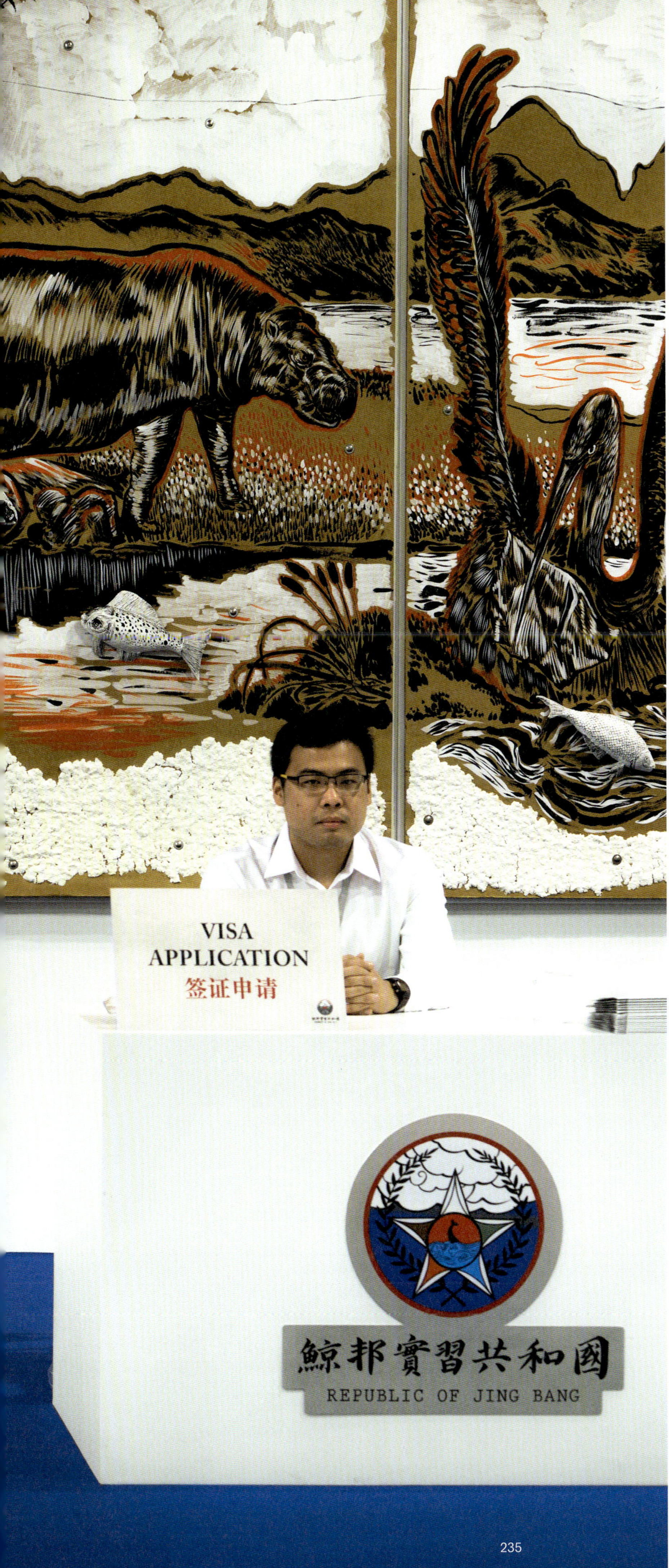

Established in 2014, *Jing Bang: A Country Based on Whale* is an independent and provisional country founded by the artist Sun Xun. In his installation and performance conceived specially for Encounters, and which includes paintings, flags, posters, and objects, he shapes a basic definition of this country, proposing an immigration office where people can apply for citizenship of this imaginary country.

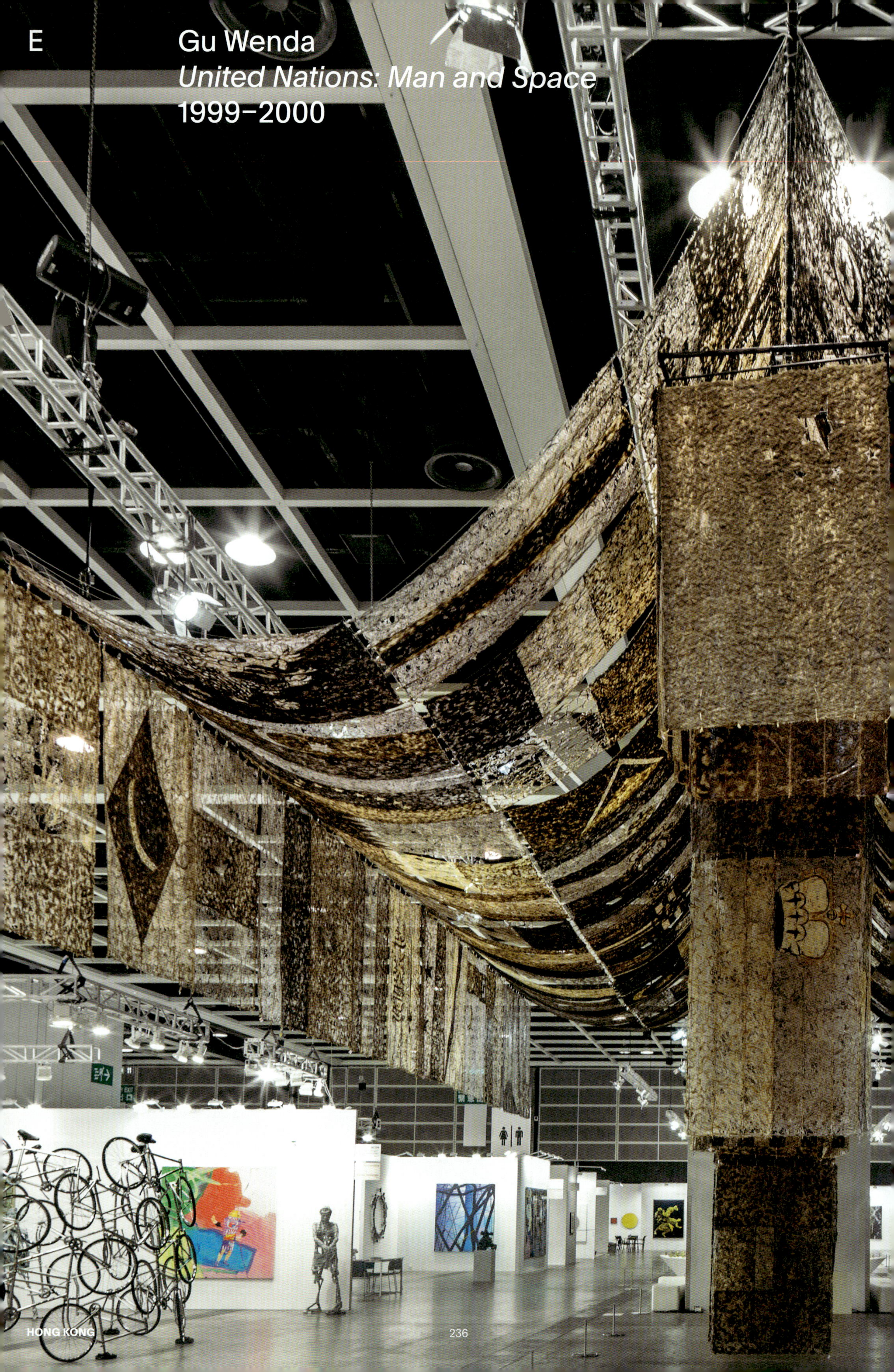

E

Gu Wenda
United Nations: Man and Space
1999–2000

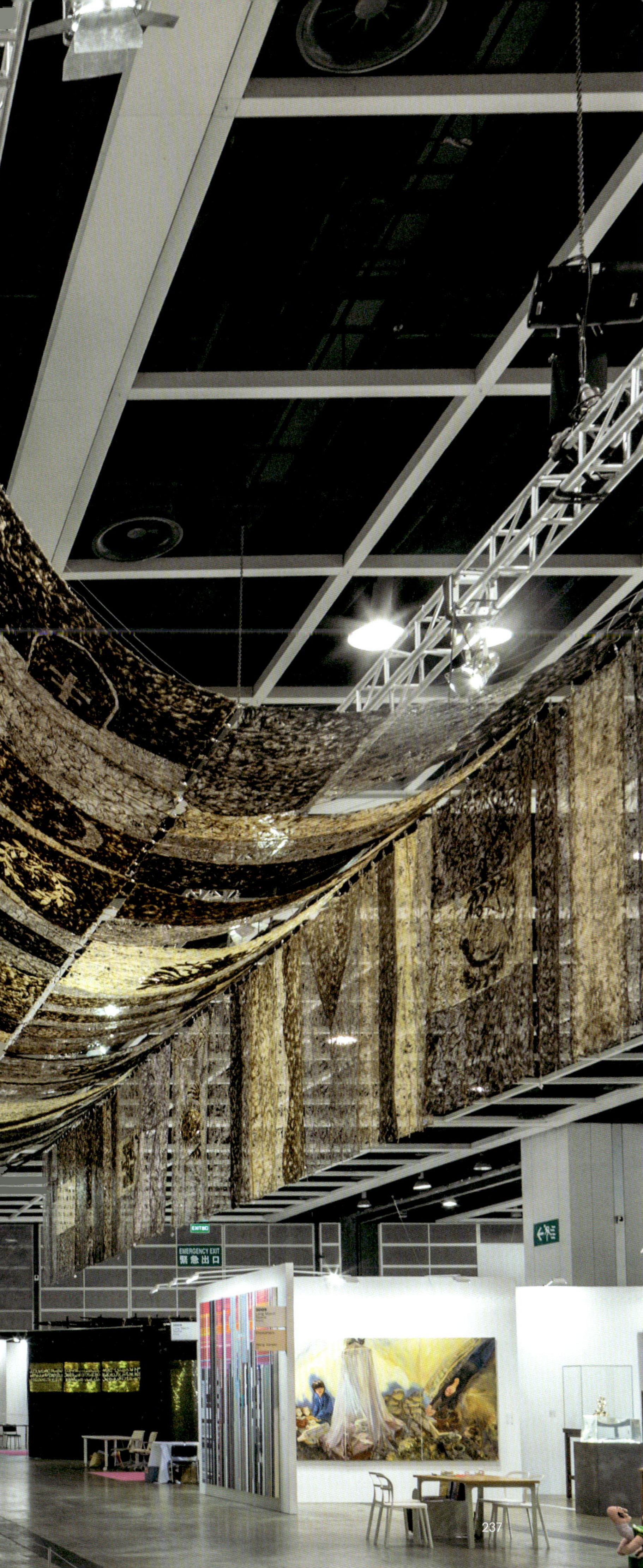

An ongoing project initiated in 1992 and exhibited in approximately 20 countries, the *United Nations* project is a body of monumental installations that captures the "identity" of countries by utilizing hair from local populations. It explores notions such as transculturalism, transnationalism, and hybridization, and provokes a paradoxical dialogue between the material, the viewers, and cultural and national pride.

E

Yeesookyung
Thousand
2014

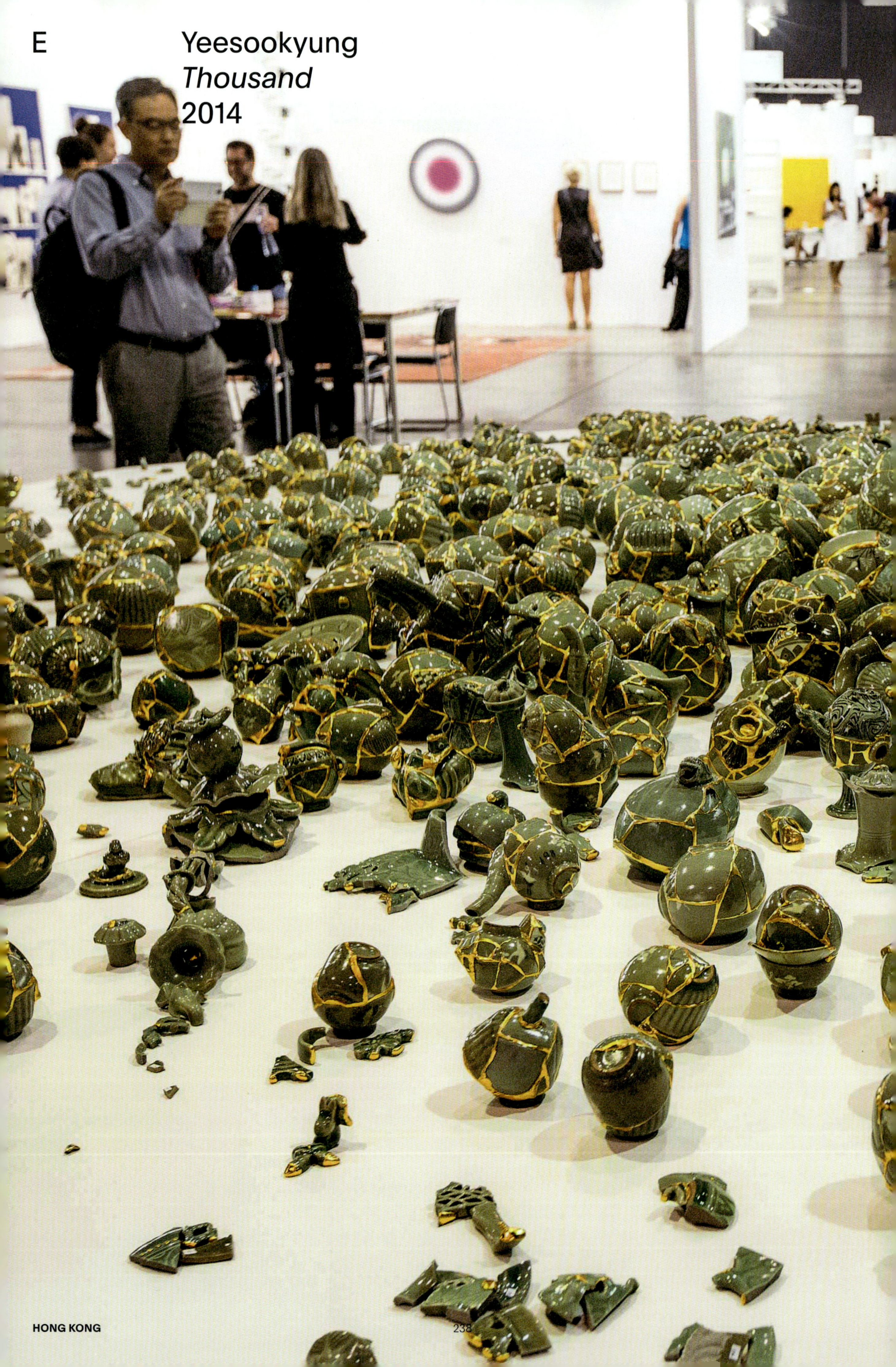

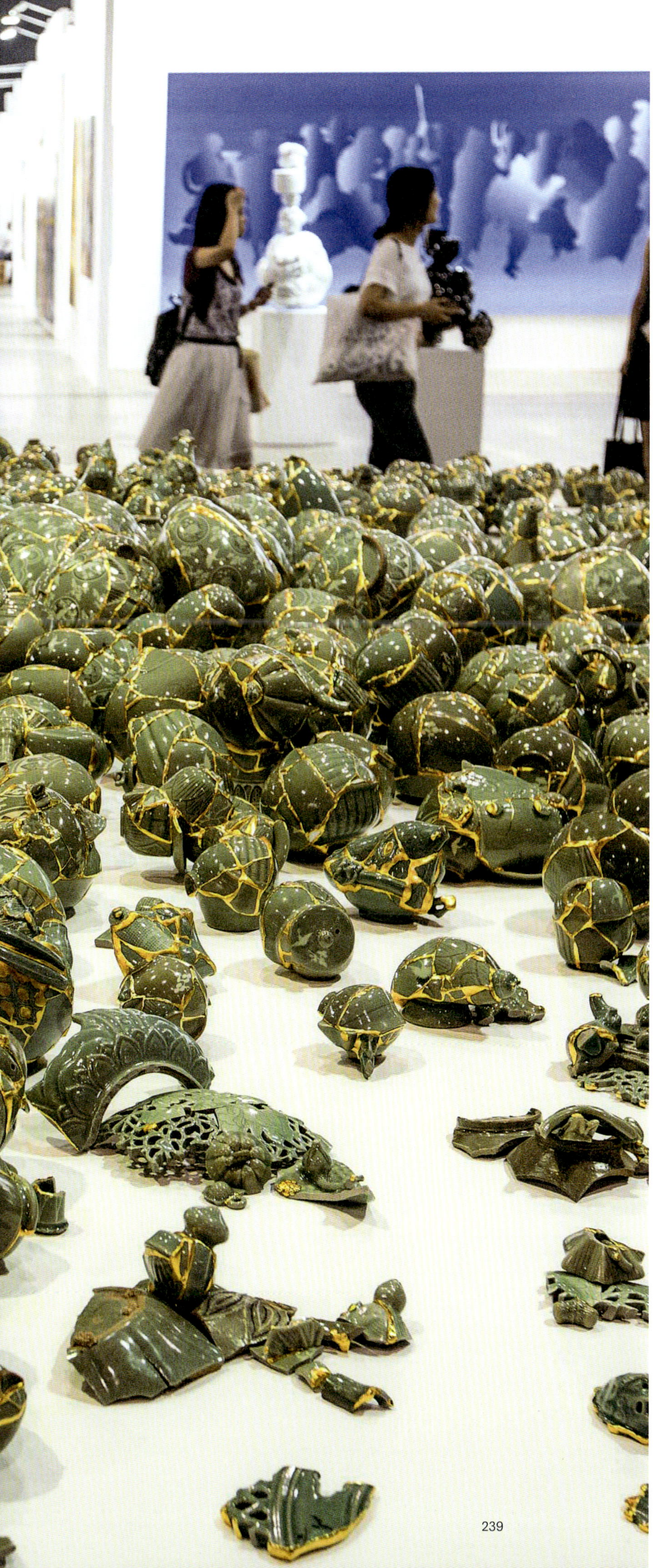

Thousand consists of one thousand ceramic sculptures displayed on a white platform, which stem from the artist's ongoing series *Translated Vase* in which she reconfigures broken pieces collected from Korean ceramic masters into new biomorphic forms. The artist instigates new connections between disparate, unrelated pieces, interlaced in waves, thus creating a new object as well as representing the history of the original.

E

In this ever-changing world, loaded with so many various thoughts, how far will our letters to the next age be carried? Such is the question asked by this series of evolutionary sculptures made of naphthalene and enclosed in transparent resin.

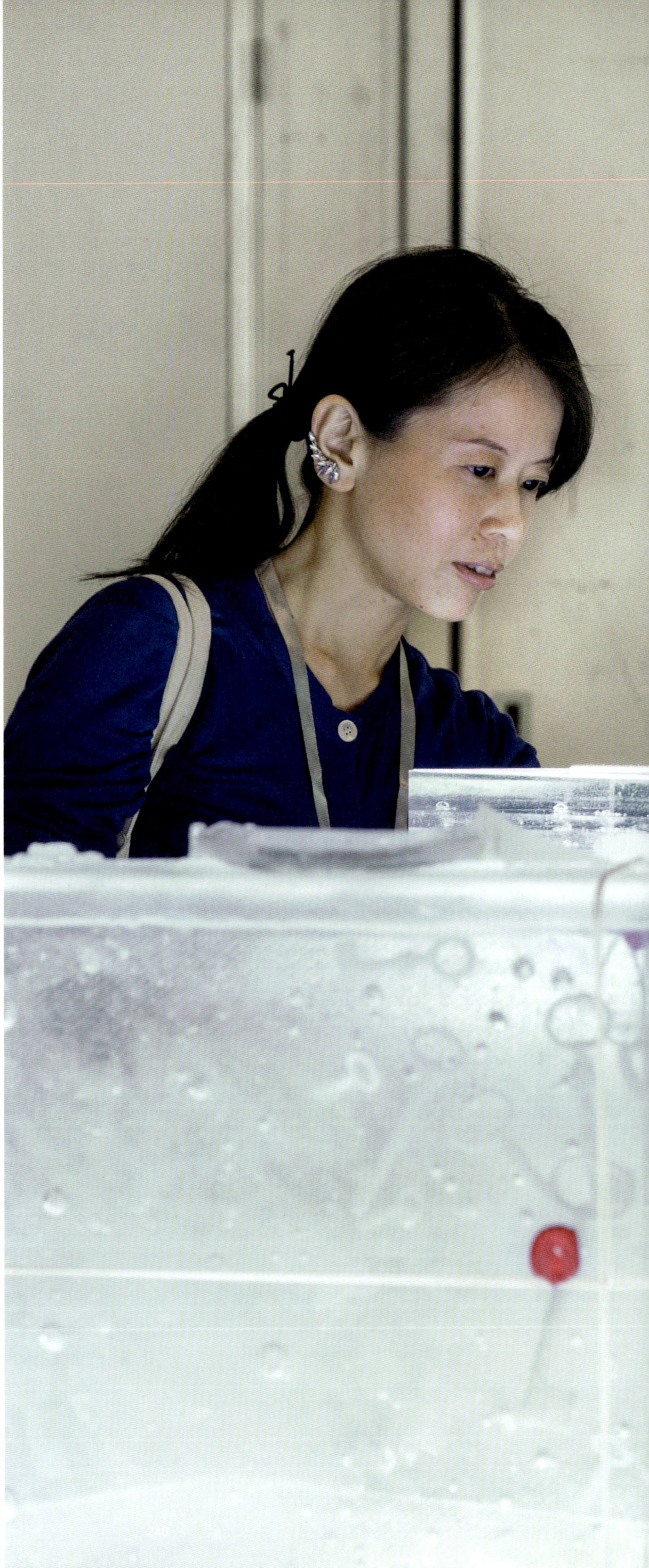

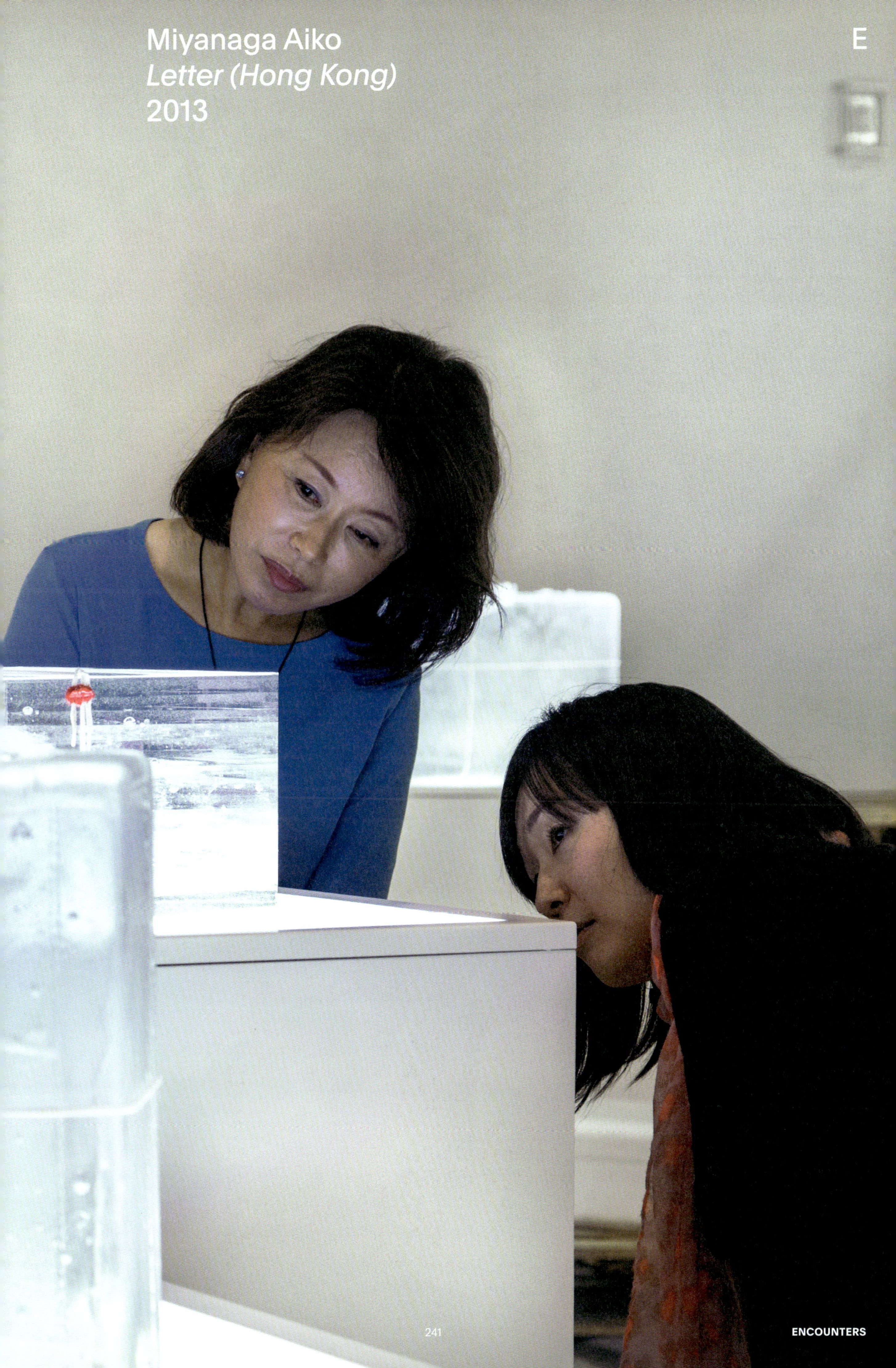

Miyanaga Aiko
Letter (Hong Kong)
2013

E

Reaching nine meters in height and eight meters in width, the installation is made up of seven panels screen-printed with an aquatic scene and bound together with ropes and chains. Explicitly made for the context of an art fair, *Conquer* draws parallels between the automobile show, very popular in China, and the art fair, whose developments could have only existed under the ultra-progressive consumer culture in modern China.

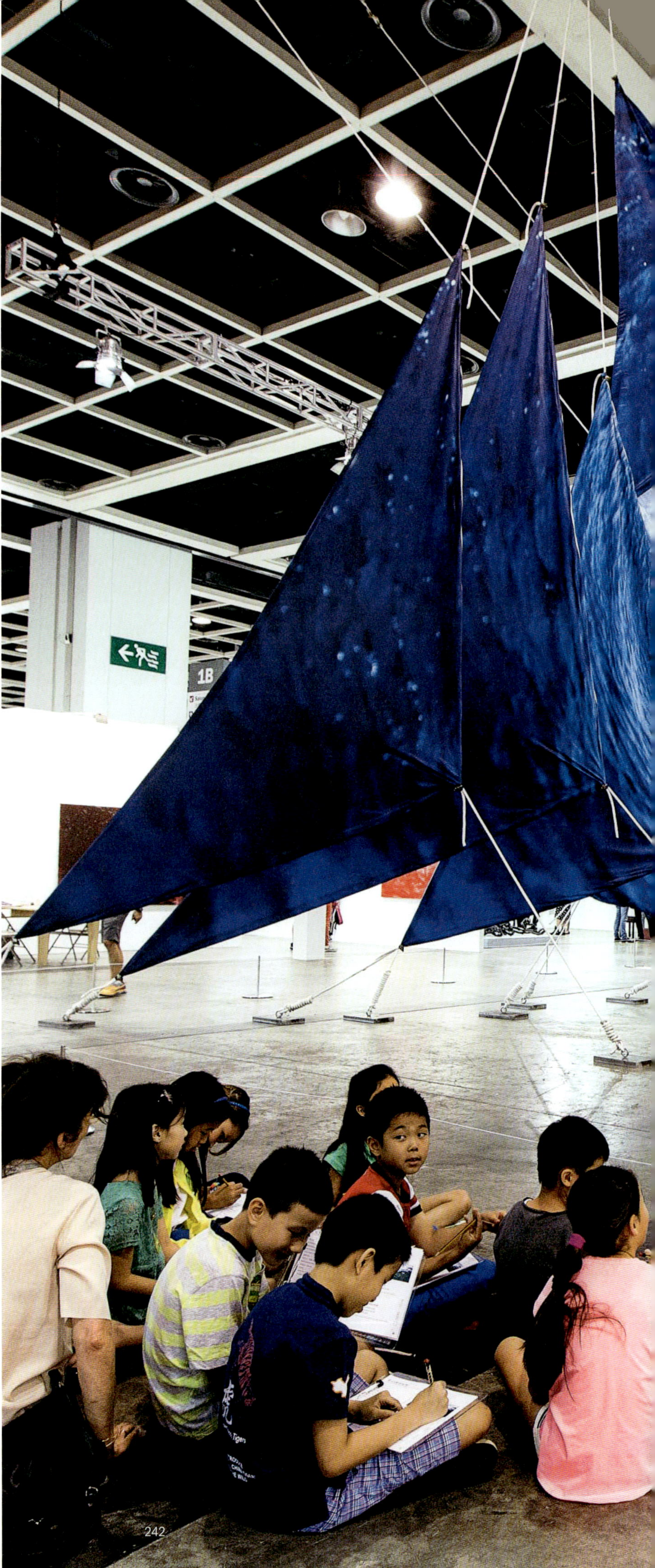

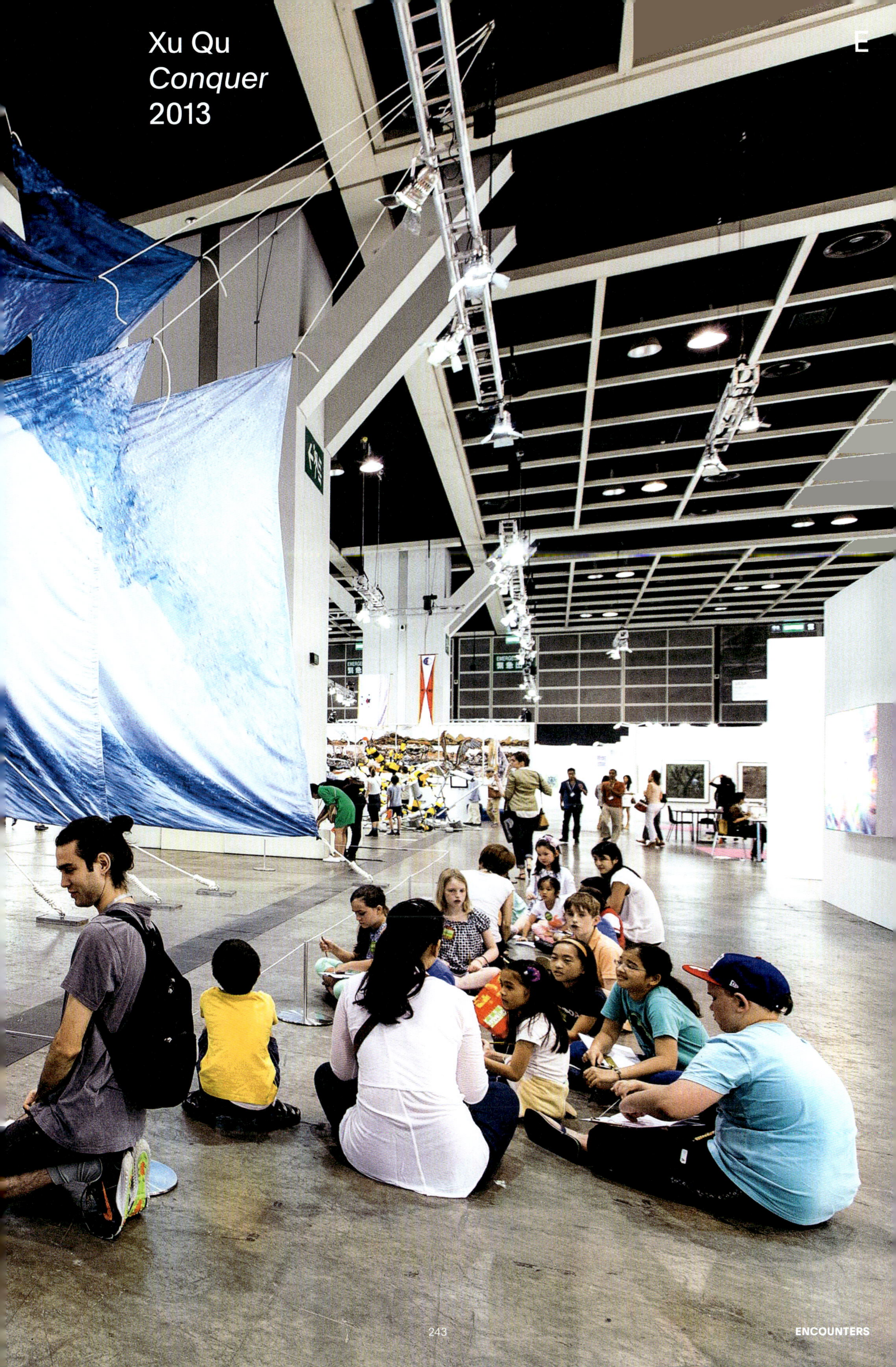

Xu Qu
Conquer
2013

E

E

Homeaway is a recreation and appropriation of Bar Oppenheimer, Tobias Rehberger's favorite bar in Frankfurt. Made entirely out of unglazed, open-pored bone china, the bar consists of walls covered with a pattern executed in a traditional watercolor technique, shelves, a counter with overhead structure and lights, and traditional Chinese stools. It is simultaneously a sculptural work and a functioning bar.

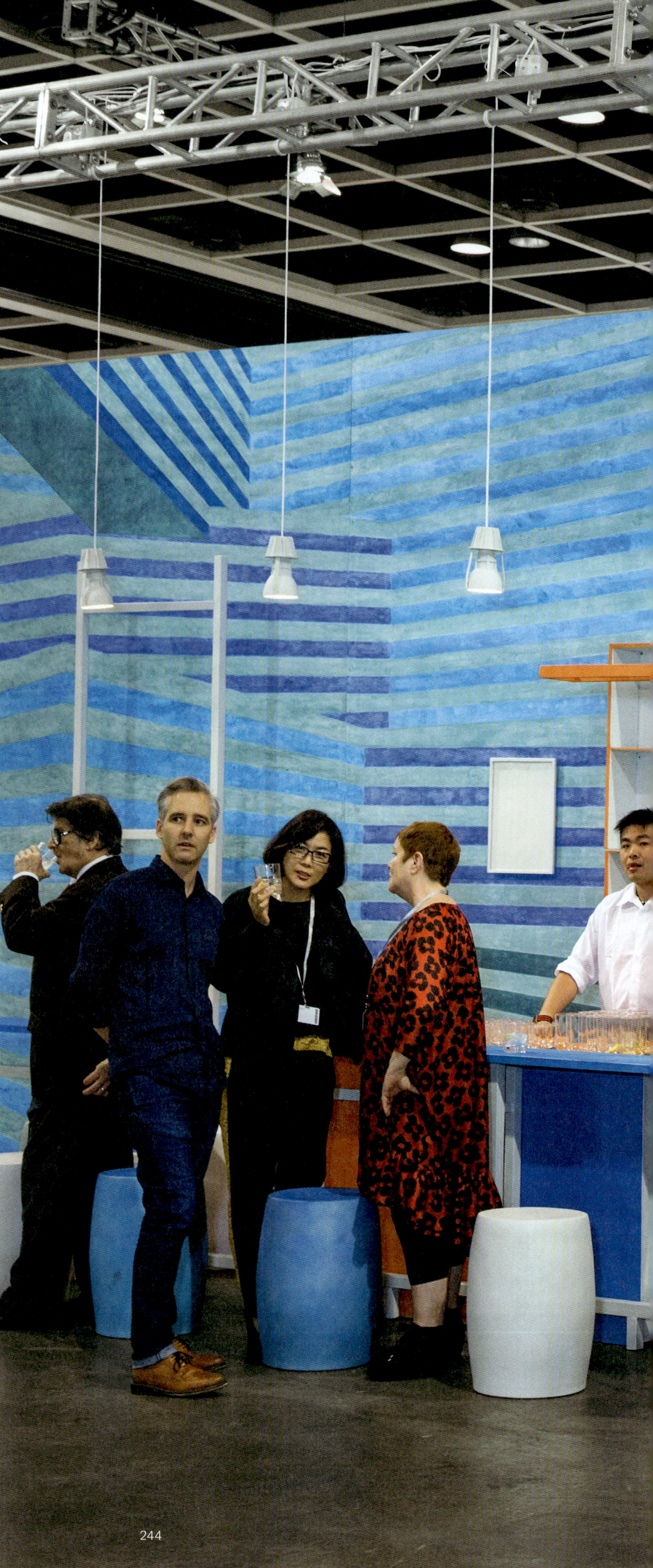

Tobias Rehberger
Homeaway
2014

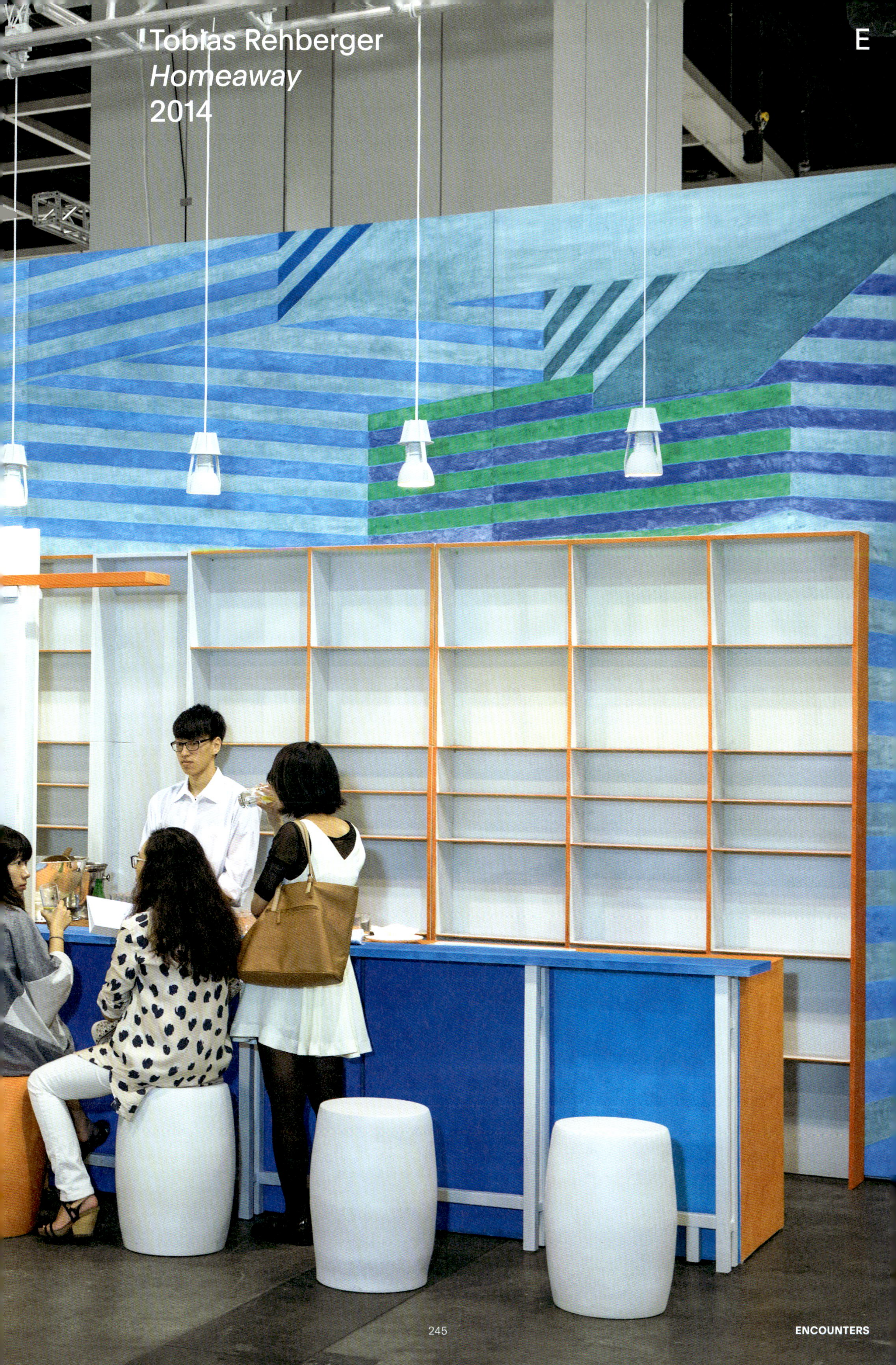

E

A strong program since it launched in 1993, the Edition sector held in Basel and Miami Beach features leading publishers of editioned works, prints, and multiples.

EDIT ION

2014 participants

Basel

Alexander
Borch Jensen
Cristea
didier
Fanal
Gemini G.E.L.
Klosterfelde Edition
Knust
Nitsch
Pace Prints
Paragon
Poligrafa
STPI
Three Star
Two Palms

Miami Beach

Cristea
Crown Point
GDM
Gemini G.E.L.
Knust
Nitsch
Pace Prints
Paragon
Polígrafa
Stolper
STPI
Two Palms

Mel Bochner
Two Palms

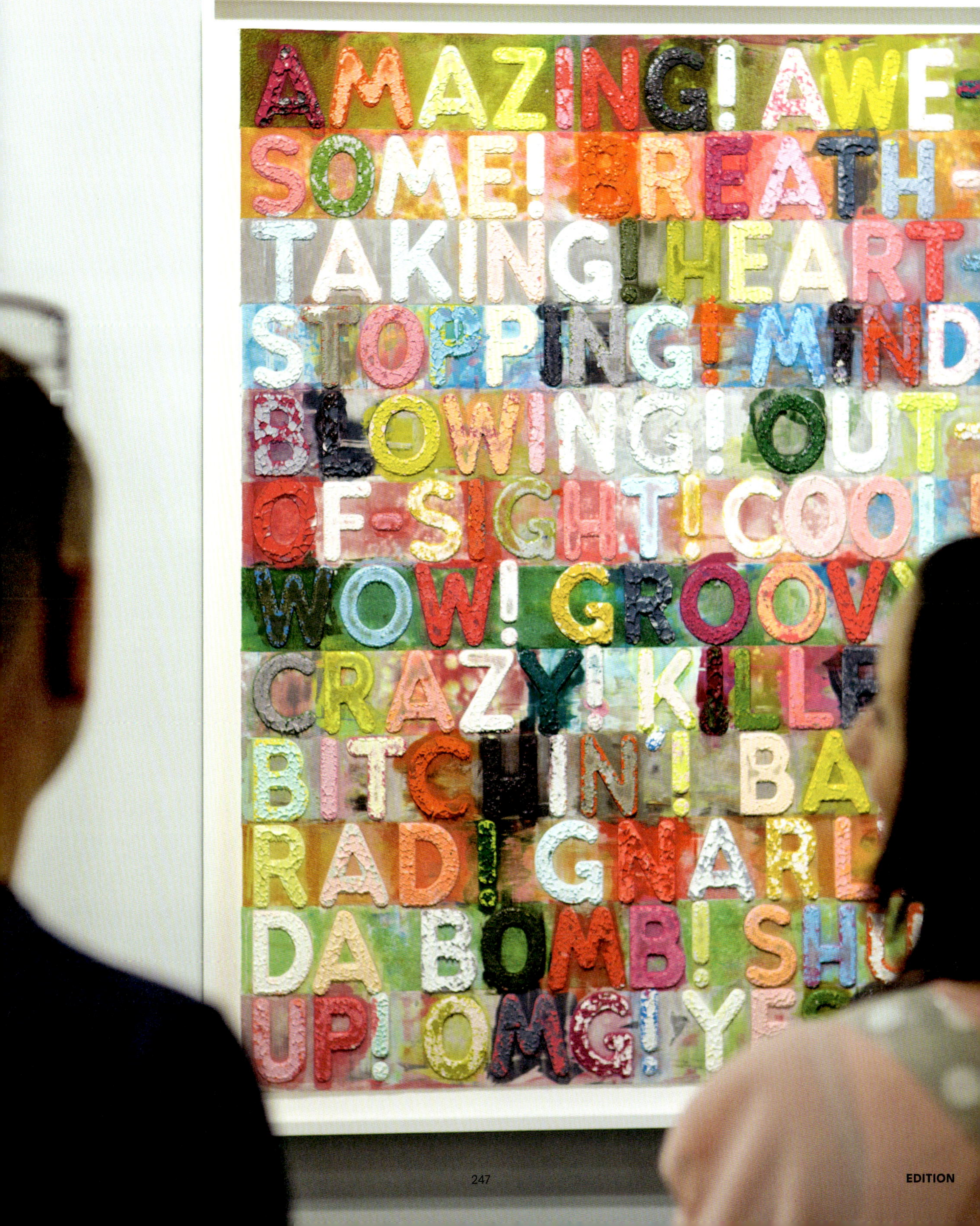

E

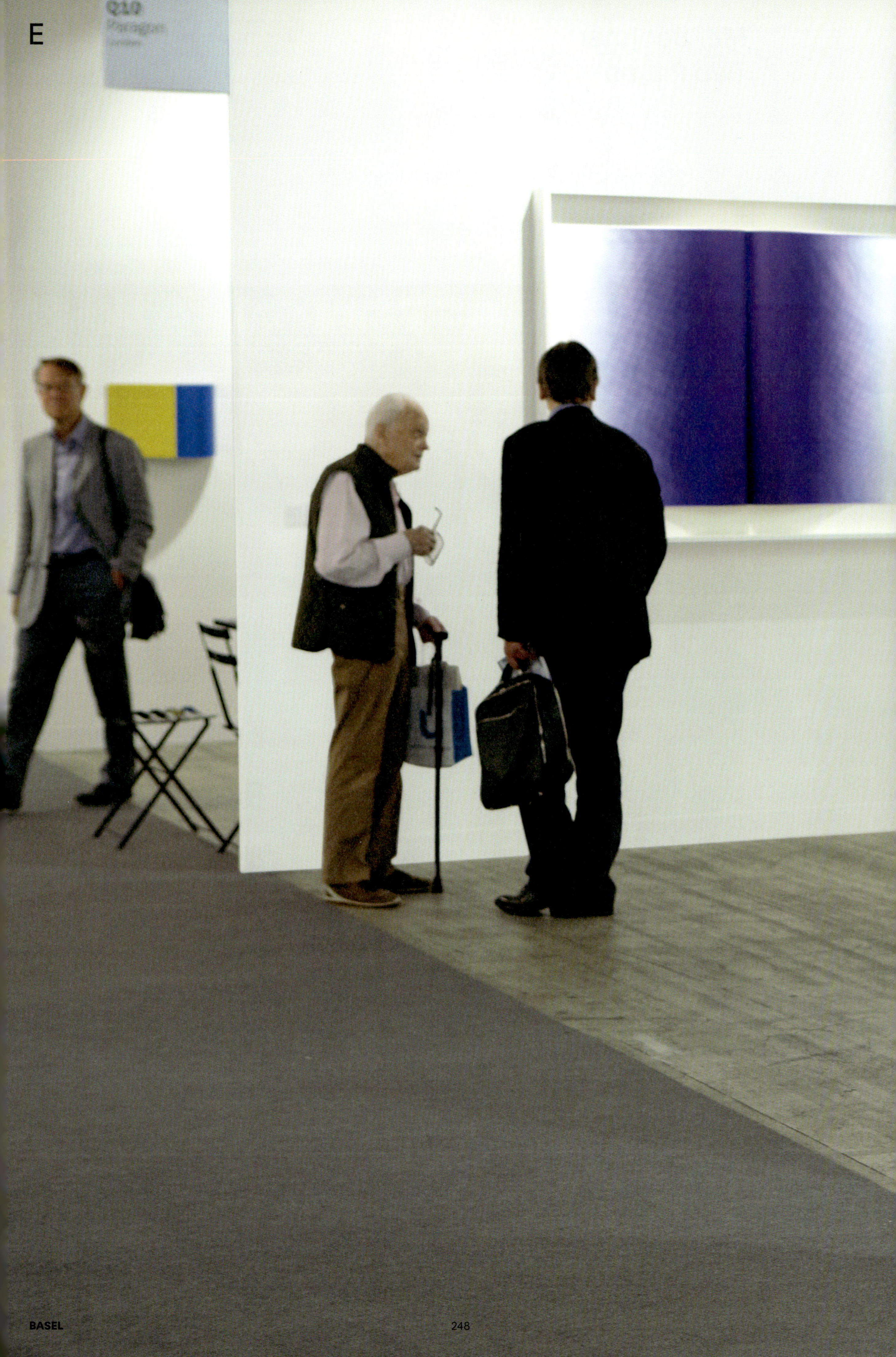

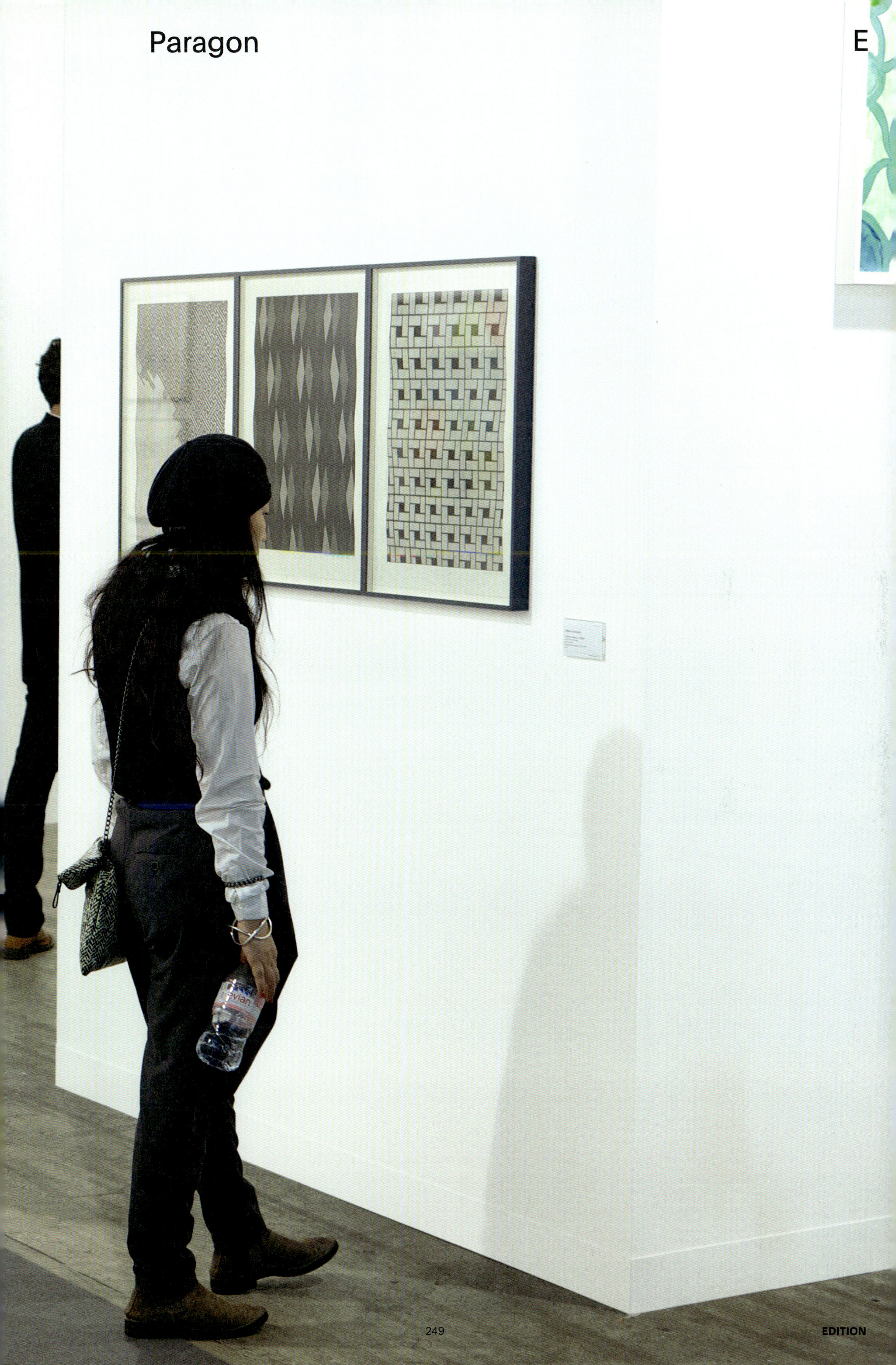
evian

E Alan Cristea Gallery

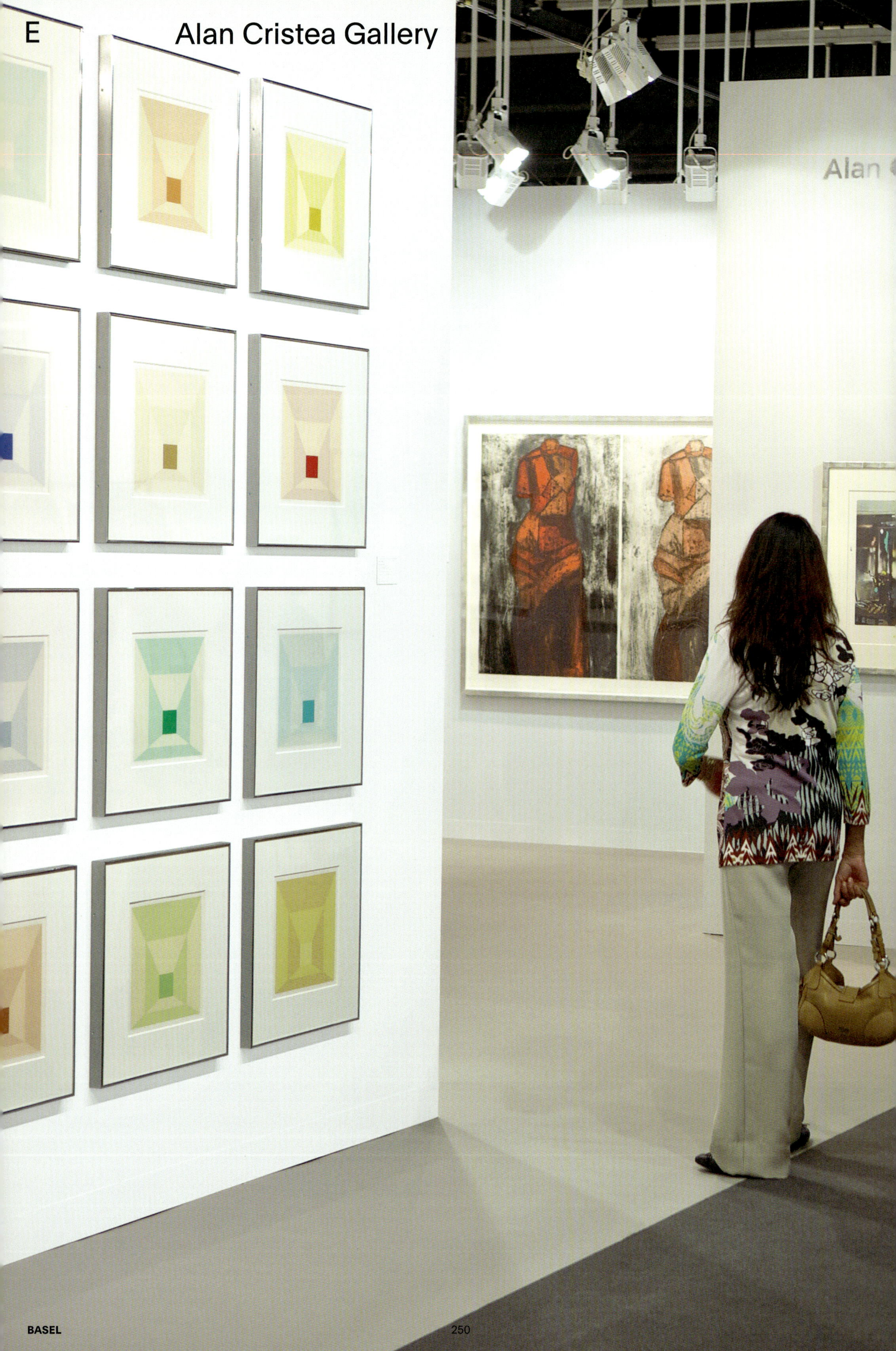

Lionel Bovier and Clément Dirié talk with STPI – Creative Workshop & Gallery (Singapore) director Emi Eu about multiples and prints in Asia

E

CLÉMENT DIRIÉ STPI was established in 2002. How did it come into being and how did the relationship with Kenneth Tyler develop?

EMI EU STPI is a very unique organization. It stems from a government initiative to catalyze the contemporary art landscape in Singapore. Singapore is only 50 years old and much of its history—almost three decades—has been spent building up a country that has no natural resources whatsoever. The government used manpower as the country's principal resource. Looking at the cultural realm, they realized that contemporary art could be as important as heritage. There was a connection with Kenneth Tyler, a very well-known American print maker, who didn't have anyone in line to continue his practice and wanted to sell his workshop and expertise. So the government put it together. The discussion started much earlier than 2002, as the Singapore government does very thorough preparatory studies for everything that they do.

Kenneth Tyler is a passionate person and his career is colossal: he has worked with the best-known artists of our time and his vision, I would say his strength, is to take this medium beyond the simple potential of reproduction techniques. That's the legacy that STPI carries.

We focus on our more immediate region as well as Asia in general. As you might know, works on paper are not so appreciated in the contemporary art world in Asia. They are seen as an inferior type of work and a lot of artists in fact do not make print works because they are referred to as reproductions. We are trying very hard to change that perception. The interest shown in prints or limited editions in Asia is a very new idea.

LIONEL BOVIER This is despite the historical importance of, say, traditional Japanese prints?

Emi Eu with Rirkrit Tiravanija at STPI – Creative Workshop & Gallery, Singapore

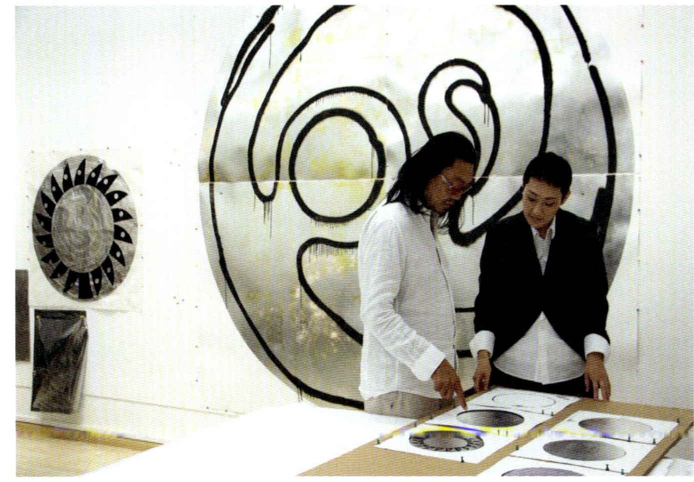

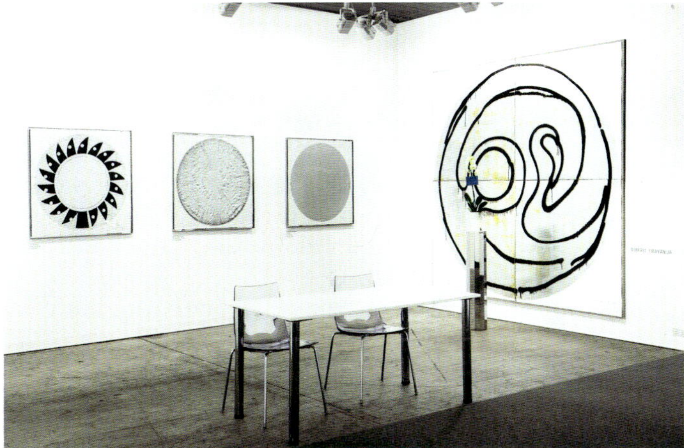

Rirkrit Tiravanija limited editions, STPI booth, Art Basel in Basel, June 2014

EE Japanese Ukiyo-e prints from the 17th and 18th centuries are a very important historical precedent, but despite the success of this particular type of print technique, limited editions by contemporary artists is a fairly recent idea to both Asian artists and collectors. And if wood block printing has been associated with China for many years, it concerns books and manuscripts more than art.

CD What kind of techniques does the workshop offer?

EE We can do lithography, etching, screen-printing, aquatint, intaglio, etc. We also have a dark room. We are working with very large presses. The workshop is about 1,100 square meters and the gallery about 650 square meters. We also have four apartments,

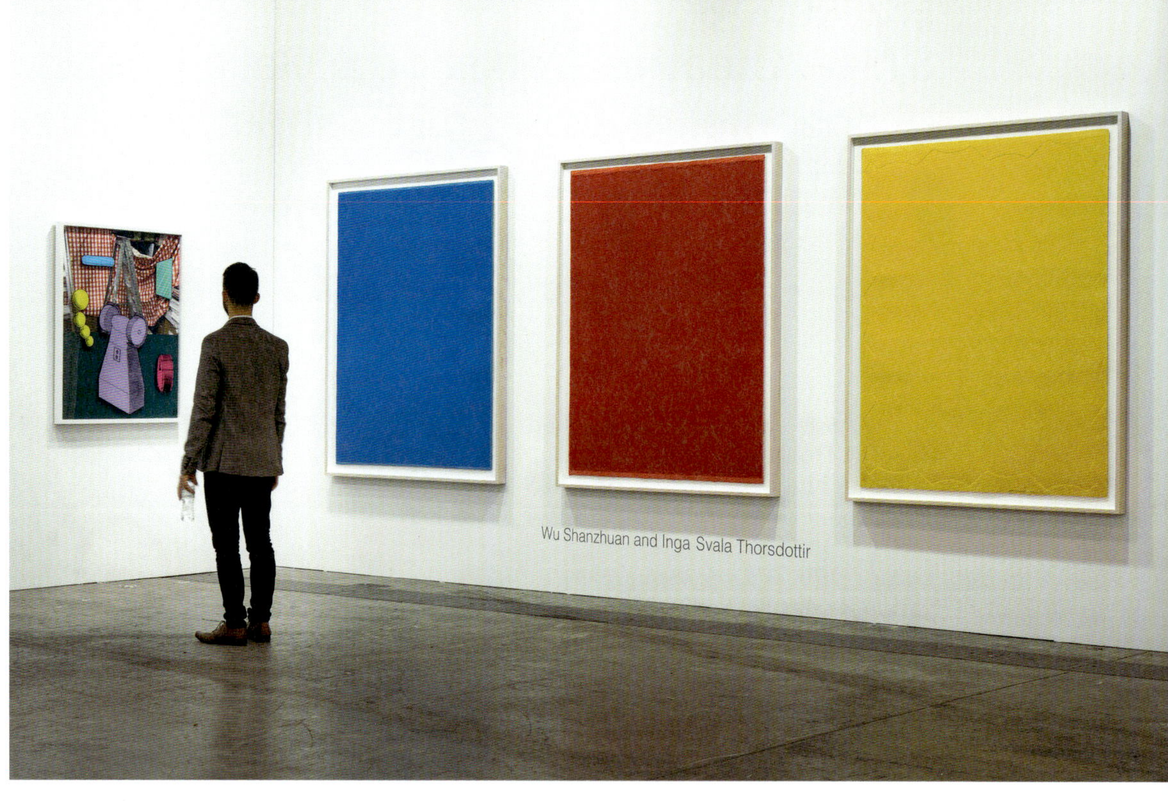

Editions by Teppei Kaneuji and Ing Svala Thorsdottir & Wu Shanzhuan, STPI booth, Art Basel in Hong Kong, May 2014

and offices. It occupies an entire heritage building, which used to be a spice warehouse, next to the river in the center of town. But we are not a traditional print publisher: we have created a residency program. We work with artists who would like to use the techniques that we can provide, we have our own paper mill (which is a really unique aspect), and my team of 12 people is the most resourceful, most important part of the workshop.

LB Do you collaborate with both Asian and Western artists?

EE Yes. Our aim is to challenge the artists and ourselves to discover new ways of using materials like paper. Also, as contemporary artists have busy schedules and often rely on being able to delegate production, they somehow lose touch with the studio practice. The residency offers this intimate and experimental situation. I call it a clinic or a rehab, where you can decelerate, chill out, and have some time to think about what will come next. It's basically an R&D environment.

CD There is a piece in your booth by Haegue Yang that seems emblematic of possibilities offered by having your own paper mill.

EE Haegue Yang works mostly with readymade, manmade, manufactured materials. She didn't really know about Singapore, so she did a lot of research and visited all the historical and tourist sites. In Little India she saw spices and got the idea of using them to represent South-East Asia as a trading hub. She brought the spices and mixed them in the paper; that's what we have here, literally "spice sheets." I don't even call them "prints": I can only refer to them as works. This set of 20 spice sheets, bearing inscriptions reproduced from their original packages, is a snapshot of trading history and the world's civilizations. "Garam masala," for instance, says "product of United Kingdom." As we know, garam masala is a mixture of different spices whose origin is here in Asia and in the Indian subcontinent, but "garam masala" itself is a product of the UK, which brings to the fore issues of globalization.

Haegue Yang, STPI booth, Art Basel in Hong Kong, May 2014

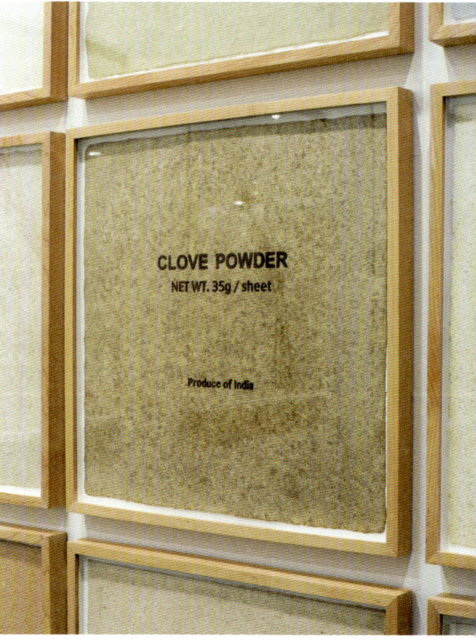

CD STPI organized the first show by Frank Stella in Asia, but you have also hosted Picasso exhibitions and collaborated with museums; there seems to be a real didactic dimension to the project.

EE Because we are in Singapore and this medium is relatively new, we wanted

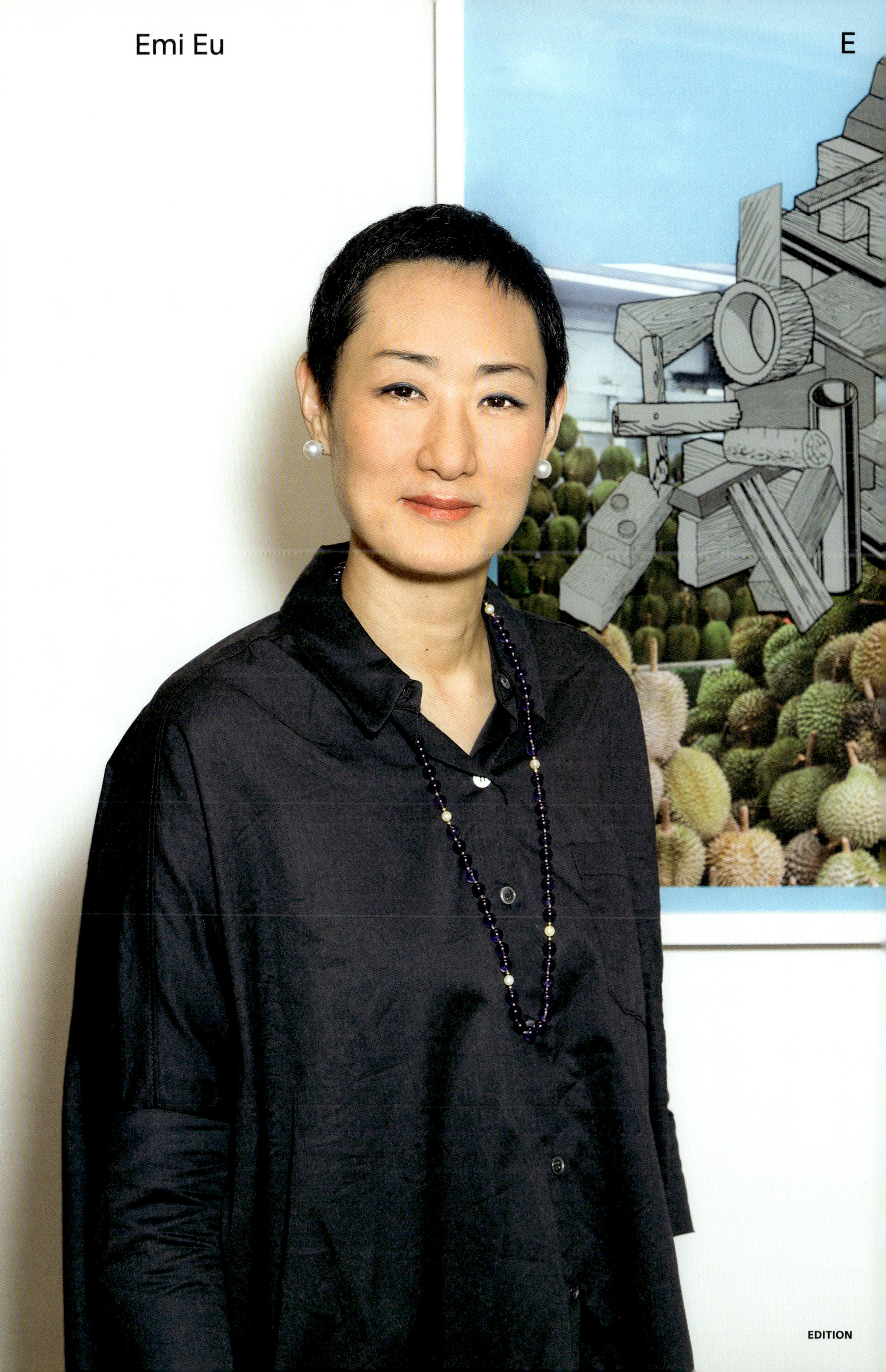

E

to have a fully developed educational side to inform the public that great artists like Picasso, Miró, the French Impressionists, have all done prints. Prints are not an inferior medium; in fact prints are much more challenging than painting or drawing. So once a year we organize an educational exhibition for the public, most often by a modern master. This year we will be working with the Minneapolis Institute of Arts and their Japanese Ukiyo-e woodblock series: *Edo Pop* will show how contemporary artists were influenced by this technique. STPI has also a very rich archive of Ken Tyler's productions with artists such as Frank Stella, David Hockney, Rosenquist, Joan Mitchell, etc., that we regularly present.

Our aim is to challenge the artists and ourselves to discover new ways of using materials like paper.
—Emi Eu

LB Do you think your activities have changed the way collectors in the Asia-Pacific region see the print market?

EE Definitely, yes. When we did our first show with Donald Sultan, one of our very first print projects in 2004, people were saying "here it's too humid, it's on paper, how do you collect this?" Now they come and buy.

LB Do you always choose the artists, or do artists sometimes apply to do the residency?

EE It's by invitation only. We do have a lot of requests, but through experience I have found that it's better that we choose. It's a big commitment on the artist's side as well as on ours (we pay for all the production costs and we share the works), so I have to make sure that the artists who come to our workshop will really benefit from what we can offer. It has to be a very good marriage. It's like a successful marriage, with children, and then you ...

LB ... sell them?! [*Laughs*]

EE [*Laughs*] ... part amicably!

CD Do you remember any collaboration in particular with an artist, or a special project that would epitomize this relationship?

EE Every project is challenging. Our current project, presented in the Encounters sector, with Chinese artist Sun Xun, in collaboration with ShanghArt (*Jing Bang: A Country Based on Whale*), is maybe a little bit more challenging than usual ... It really is a big project: we are creating a new country, an idyllic one, and we are recruiting people who agree to pay to become citizens.

CD Is the citizenship expensive?

EE Actually, no ... With 10,000 USD you get the whole package: a beautifully manufactured steel briefcase, a passport, an ID card, the book about the country and its laws. Visas start at 25 USD, a lithograph signed by the artist; the same version as an etching goes up to 150 USD.

STPI print workshop, Singapore

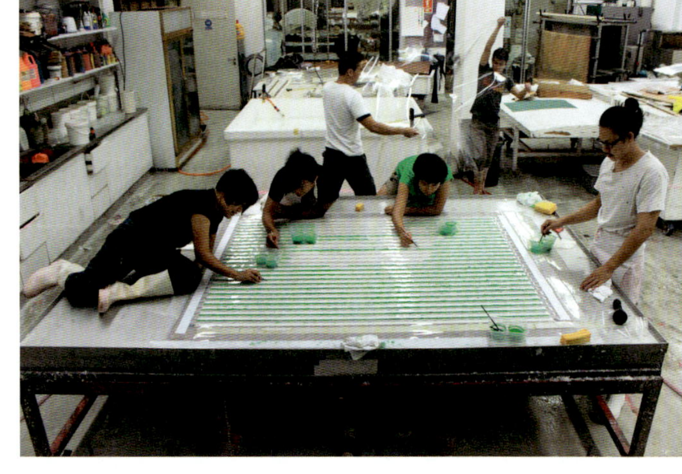

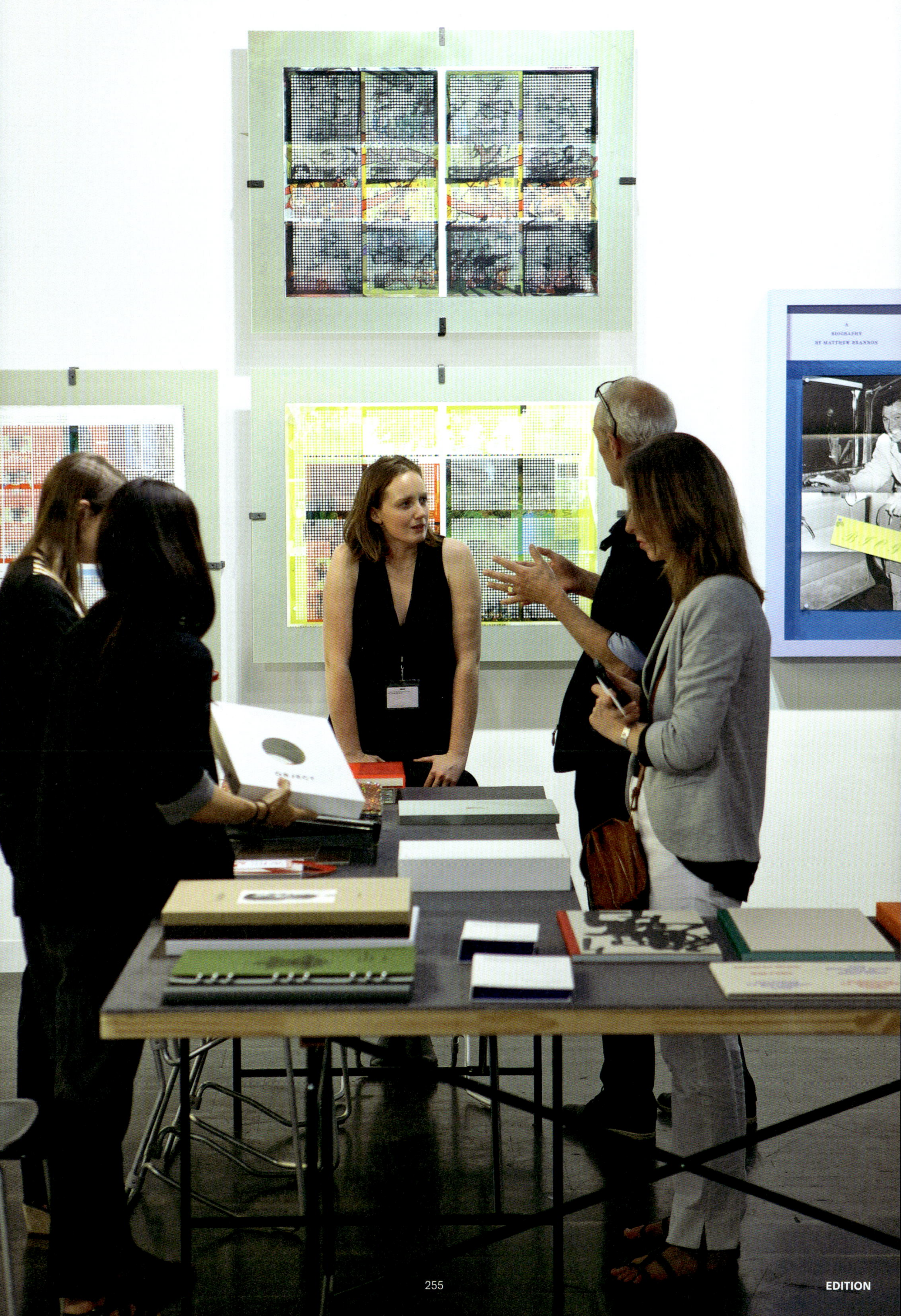
A
BIOGRAPHY
BY MATTHEW BRANNON

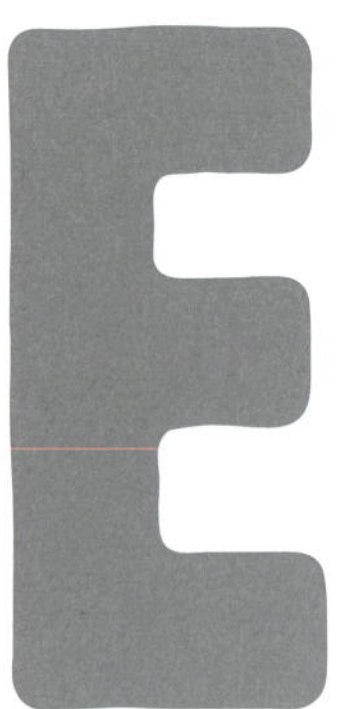

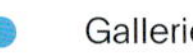

Ecart

Geneva ● Galleries

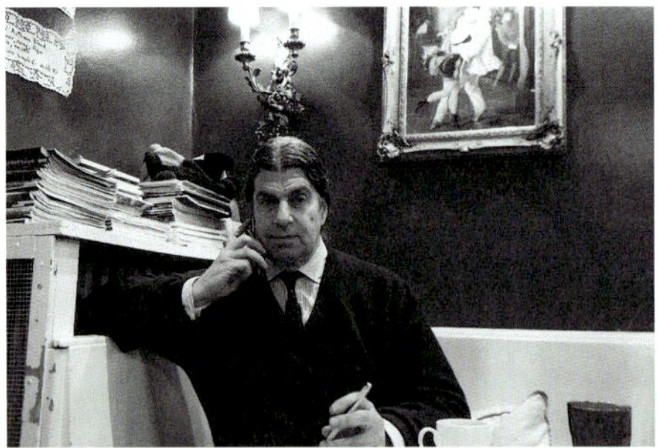

What is your favorite aspect of running a gallery?
Having a good time.

If you weren't running a gallery what else would you do?
Not much.

How do you choose the artists you work with?
I do not choose; they might.

- **Contact** Ecart
  John Armleder
  john.armleder@bluewin.ch
- **Established** 1972
- **Owner(s) / Partner(s)** John Armleder
- **Team** 1 to many (or too many)
- **Artists at Art Basel** Ralph Rumney
- **Further artists represented** Genesis B. P-Orridge
  Vern Blosum
  Poul Gernes
  Helene Lustig Cohen

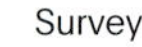

Edlin

New York ● Survey

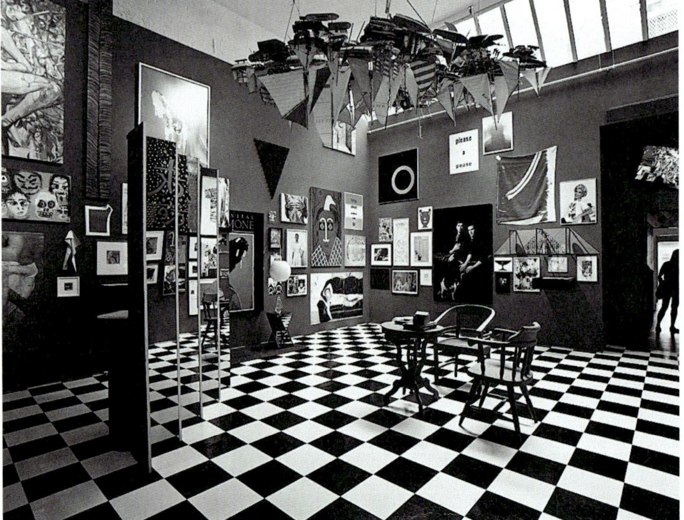

What is your favorite aspect of running a gallery?
Leveling the playing field for artists who have not been acculturated into the art system.

How do you choose the artists you work with?
Eenie, meenie, miney, mo …

If you weren't running a gallery what else would you do?
A rock 'n' roll band.

- **Contact** Andrew Edlin Gallery
  Andrew Edlin
  info@edlingallery.com
- **Established** 2001
- **Owner(s) / Partner(s)** Andrew Edlin
- **Team** 5
- **Space(s)** 186 m²
- **Artists at Art Basel** Henry Darger
  Marcel Storr
- **Further artists represented** John Byam
  Frank Calloway
  Thornton Dial
  Brian Adam Douglas
  Chris Doyle
  Tom Duncan
  Paul Edlin
  Ralph Fasanella
  Brent Green
  Albert Hoffman
  Hans Krüsi
  Gene Mann
  Mehrdad Rashidi
  Linda Carmella Sibio
  Soviet Propaganda Posters
  Charles Steffen
  Agatha Wojciechowsky
  Domenico Zindato

Edwin's

Jakarta ● Insights

What is your favorite aspect of running a gallery?
First, you get to meet different people all the time: artists, new prospective clients, etc. Then there is also the constant need to search for new emerging artists, promoting them, then convincing people about the artists that you believe in. You have to be creative and intuitive in analyzing artworks and artists. To produce good exhibitions constantly, and always to be ahead of other galleries—it is definitely most fulfilling to discover good new artists before other people discover them!

How do you choose the artists you work with?
I rely on my instincts and intuition, my gut feeling. The intensity and strength of the artists, the quality of work. Does the work speak to me, etc.; this is the one aspect that is rather non-quantifiable. However, art business has become more complicated (in Indonesia at least) over the last few years. Besides creating good artworks, artists must now possess good character, ethics, and discipline, and understand marketing and strategi, and their importance. It is not just about selling artworks; it is about common understanding, trust, and mutual respect. Both parties have to appreciate each other's accomplishments. We must be passionate about our profession, about what we do.

If you weren't running a gallery what else would you do?
I love art and design, always have. If it had not been a gallery, I would have most likely worked as a designer: furniture or lighting designer (I have sound knowledge of lighting and photography), or indeed a professional photographer (which I used to be). However, lately I have been having great fun combining my interests in mechanics with art and design and have been creating some pieces of kinetic art. I can imagine myself being a kinetic artist.

- **Contact** Edwin's Gallery
  Edwin Rahardjo
  edwins_gallery@yahoo.com
- **Established** 1984
- **Owner(s) / Partner(s)** Edwin Rahardjo
- **Team** 35

- **Space(s)** 600 m²
- **Artists at Art Basel** Jumaldi Alfi, Heri Dono
- **Further artists represented** Nasirun

EIGEN + ART

Berlin
Leipzig

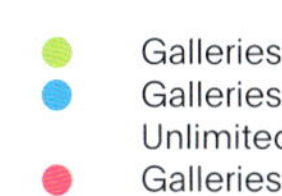

Galleries
Galleries Unlimited
Galleries

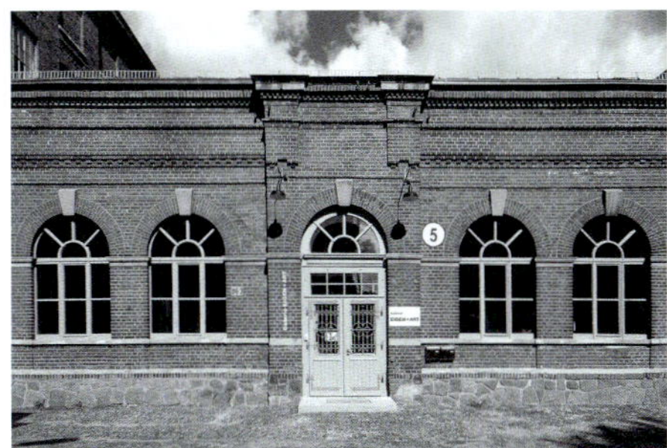

What is your favorite aspect of running a gallery?
The collaboration with our artists is one of the most important aspects in my work.

How do you choose the artists you work with?
It takes three to five years before we chose to represent someone. It is important to take time to get to know each other. I don't choose an artist because of their current style or works; I like to get to know the person. In 2012 we created the EIGEN + ART Lab to show new positions in Germany, or present them in a new context. This space gives us the possibility to work with artists that are not yet part of the gallery's program.

If you weren't running a gallery what else would you do?
I would found a gallery.

- **Contact** Galerie EIGEN + ART
Gerd Harry Lybke
berlin@eigen-art.com
- **Established** 1983 (Leipzig)/1992 (Berlin)
- **Owner(s) / Partner(s)** Gerd Harry Lybke
Kerstin Wahala
- **Team** 20
- **Artists at Art Basel** Akos Birkas
Birgit Brenner
Marc Desgrandchamps
Martin Eder
Tim Eitel
Nina Fischer/Maroan el Sani
Stella Hamberg
Jörg Herold
Christine Hill
Uwe Kowski
Melora Kuhn
Rémy Markowitsch
Maix Mayer
Ryan Mosley
Carsten Nicolai
Olaf Nicolai
Neo Rauch
Ricarda Roggan
Yehudit Sasportas
David Schnell
Annelies Štrba
Despina Stokou

elbaz

Paris — Galleries

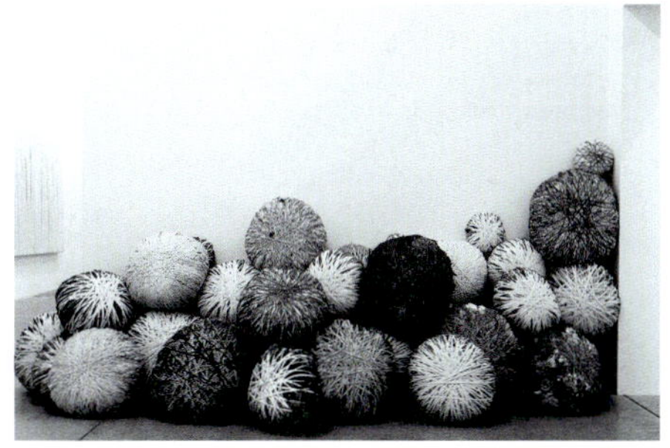

What is your favorite aspect of running a gallery?
Having fun with my artists.

How do you choose the artists you work with?
I trust my eyes.

If you weren't running a gallery what else would you do?
Professional surfer.

- **Contact** galerie frank elbaz
Frank Elbaz
frank@galeriefrankelbaz.com
- **Established** 2002
- **Owner(s) / Partner(s)** Frank Elbaz
- **Team** 6
- **Space(s)** 200 m²
- **Artists at Art Basel** Davide Balula
Mungo Thomson
- **Further artists represented** Blair Thurman
Wallace Berman
Mladen Bizumic
Greg Bogin
Tomislav Gotovac
Sheila Hicks
Julije Knifer
Rainier Lericolais
Mangelos
Kaz Oshiro
Bernard Piffaretti
Mladen Stilinović

EM

Seoul

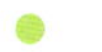

Insights

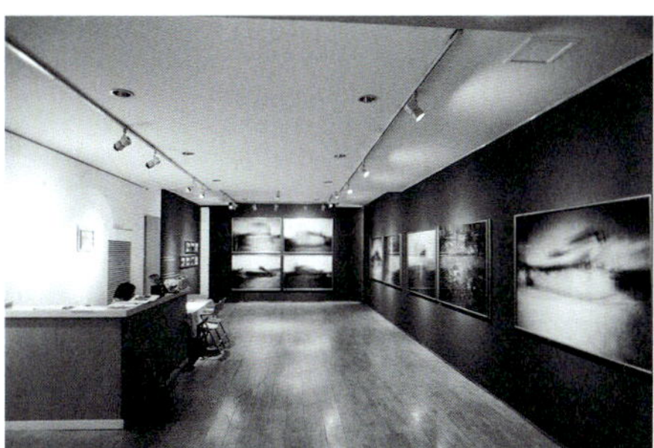

What is your favorite aspect of running a gallery?
My favorite aspect of running a gallery is meeting people from across the world who appreciate the work of the artists I represent.

How do you choose the artists you work with?
I usually receive referrals from artists, curators, and critics. If I feel the connection when seeing the works in person, then I go for them.

If you weren't running a gallery what else would you do?
Well, that's something that I haven't really thought about. Even if I were not running a gallery, I think I would still be somehow doing something in this field.

- **Contact** Gallery EM
Emma Son
emma@galleryem.co.kr
- **Established** 2007

- **Owner(s) / Partner(s)** Emma Son
- **Team** 4
- **Space(s)** 79.4 m²
- **Artists at Art Basel** Jae Yong Rhee
- **Further artists represented** Si Yeon Kim, Hyemin Lee, Hyoungsun Chang, Jeanie Lee, Jimin Chae, Jon Widman, Nakhee Sung, Jörg Obergfell, Siwoo Lee

Erben

New York

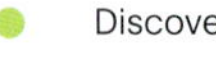

Discoveries

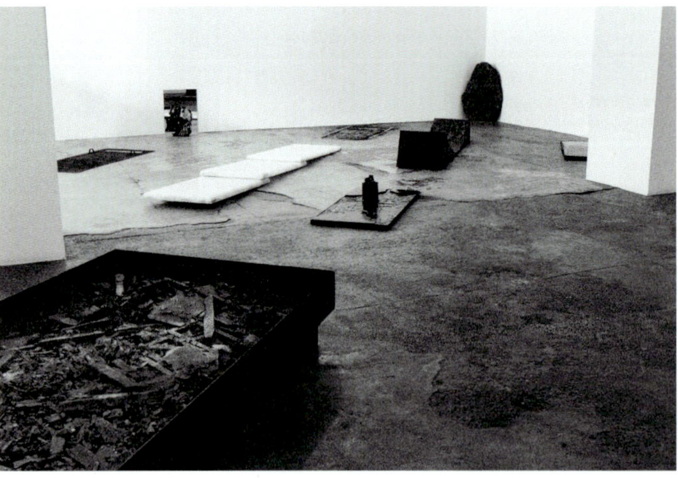

What is your favorite aspect of running a gallery?

One of the most interesting aspects of running a gallery—as enervating and erratic as it might be—is the unrelenting fluctuation of all people, events, prospects, exhibitions, and potentials, for which the gallery serves as something of a coordination point. It keeps things unpredictable, but also fresh and full of surprises.

How do you choose the artists you work with?

I like complexity in an artist's work, which I would define by several parameters: skill (or in case of deficiencies, an inventive circumvention thereof); formal innovation in regards to the chosen medium; content saturated with a broad scope of human experience; in short, work that allows for a transformational experience—visually, mentally, and emotionally.

If you weren't running a gallery what else would you do?

As a child I dreamed of becoming a marine biologist, as I imagined mankind's future being dependent on our relationship with the oceans.

- **Contact** Thomas Erben Gallery, Thomas Erben, info@thomaserben.com
- **Established** 1996
- **Owner(s) / Partner(s)** Thomas Erben
- **Team** 3
- **Space(s)** 111.5 m²
- **Artists at Art Basel** Nadia Khawaja
- **Further artists represented** Mike Cloud, Roza El-Hassan, Gauri Gill, Barbad Golshiri, Matthias Müller, Yamini Nayar, Dona Nelson, Senga Nengudi, Elaine Stocki, Newsha Tavakolian, Shanna Waddell, Tom Wood, Rose Wylie, Haeri Yoo

Eslite

Taipei

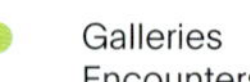

Galleries
Encounters

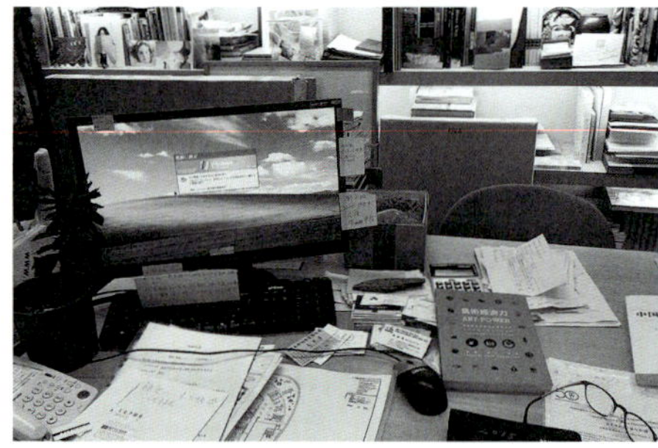

What is your favorite aspect of running a gallery?

I most enjoy talking to artists about their exhibitions, work, ideas, and creative ways of presentation. Right before the opening, I like to look at the exhibition. Another stimulant comes from competition in the art market, which is largely people-oriented and thus unpredictable by nature. The challenge is to have the ability to analyze the market in order to stay three to five years ahead.

How do you choose the artists you work with?

Based on 30 years of experience, I have come to realize that a blueprint is the key to navigating a gallery on a steady course. This blueprint is composed of different areas that represent various categories of art. You can call it a puzzle if you will, and artists are pieces that make up the bigger picture. I select artists that are at the top of their category. The most dangerous way to run a gallery is to blindly look for artists and blindly place their works in collectors' hands.

If you weren't running a gallery what else would you do?

What a silly question. I would not do anything else besides running a gallery. That is the only thing I can and want to do.

- **Contact** Eslite Gallery, Jenning King, gallery@eslite.com
- **Established** 1989
- **Owner(s) / Partner(s)** Robert Wu, Emily Li Chao
- **Team** 9
- **Space(s)** 1,000 m²
- **Artists at Art Basel** Xu Bing
- **Further artists represented** Cai Guo-Qiang, Chi Ming, Jeng Jundian, Szeto Keung, Kuo Chwen, Shida Kuo, Lai Chih-Sheng, Aichen Lee, Lee Ji-Hong, Lien Chien Hsing, Michael Lin, Lin Yen Wei, Liu Xiaodong, Lu Liang, Su Wong-Shen, Su-Mei Tse, Kuang-Yu Tsui, Wang Yuping, Wong Hoy Cheong, Tzu-Chi Yeh, Zhan Wang

espaivisor

Valencia

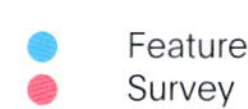

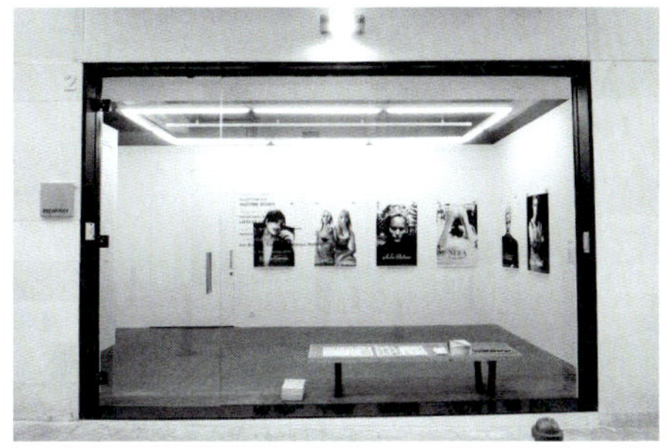

What is your favorite aspect of running a gallery?

Both gallery directors are artists, and it is for that reason that we try to take advantage of our work at the gallery to invite artists who influenced us when we were students.

How do you choose the artists you work with?

Influence is not our only reason to select an artist. We really want to make a selection of artworks that we have dreamt of seeing together in our space. We want to link very established international artists, who have been forgotten for decades, with young artists.

If you weren't running a gallery what else would you do?

We would like to work as artists only.

- **Contact** espaivisor
  Mira Bernabeu
  info@espaivisor.com
- **Established** 1982/2007
- **Owner(s) / Partner(s)** Miriam Lozano
  Mira Bernabeu
- **Team** 4
- **Space(s)** 210 m²
- **Artists at Art Basel** Sanja Iveković
  Lotty Rosenfeld
- **Further artists represented** Daniel G. Andújar
  Alberto Baraya
  Bleda Y Rosa
  Graciela Carnevale
  Lynne Cohen
  Braco Dimitrijević
  David Ferrando Giraut
  Esther Ferrer
  Joan Fontcuberta
  Hamish Fulton
  Patricia Gómez
  & Maria Jesús González
  Tomislav Gotovac
  Renée Green
  Françoise Janicot
  Carlos Leppe
  Lea Lublin
  Oswaldo Maciá
  Humberto Rivas
  Miguel Ángel Rojas
  Mladen Stilinović
  Eulàlia Valldosera
  Nil Yalter
  Sergio Zevallos

Exhibit 320

New Delhi

Insights

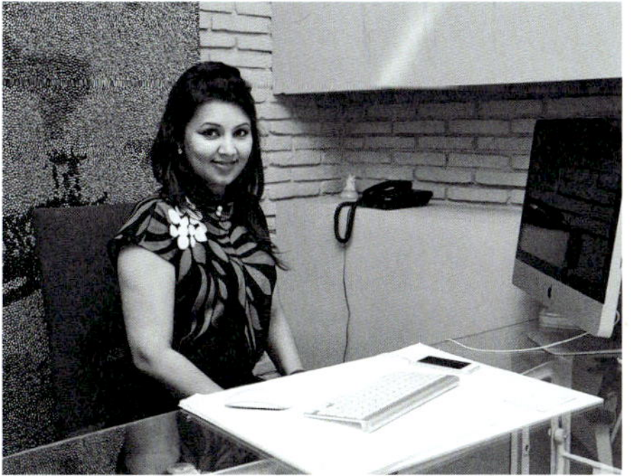

What is your favorite aspect of running a gallery?

Running a gallery gives you the opportunity to meet very different people, from the artists to eccentric art collectors. This leads to immense learning and growth …

How do you choose the artists you work with?

Choosing an artist is a lengthy process: from an initial gut feeling, to slowly understanding the thought process and what is behind it, to assessing its execution and the skills involved.

If you weren't running a gallery what else would you do?

I would be an art and design consultant.

- **Contact** Exhibit 320
  Rasika Kajaria
  rasikakajaria@gmail.com
- **Established** 2008
- **Owner(s) / Partner(s)** Rasika Kajaria
- **Team** 6
- **Space(s)** 279 m²
- **Artists at Art Basel** Vibha Galhotra
  Nandan Ghiya
  Pooja Iranna
  Bose Krishnamachari
  Muktinath Mondal
  Princess Pea
  Sachin George Sebastian
  Sumakshi Singh
  Sunoj D
- **Further artists represented** Ritesh Ajmeri
  Sonia Mehra Chawla
  Remen Chopra
  Probir Gupta
  Riddhi Shah

Exit

Hong Kong

Galleries
Encounters

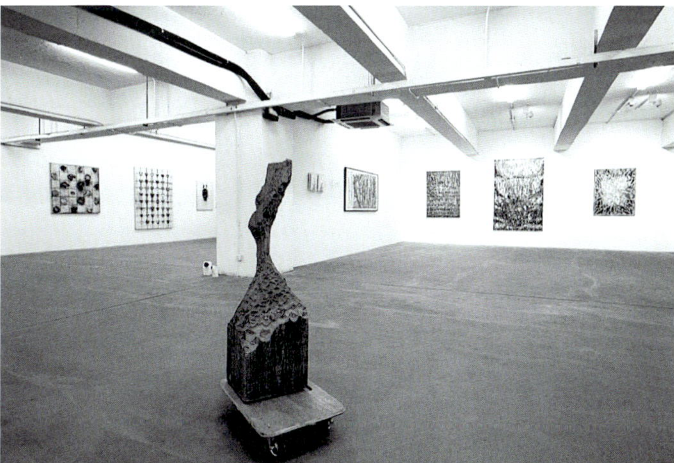

What is your favorite aspect of running a gallery?

Connecting with art lovers, working with artists, setting up exhibitions, participating in international art fairs.

How do you choose the artists you work with?

Personality and drive as an artist, edginess, intellectual depth.

If you weren't running a gallery what else would you do?

Writing, curating …

- **Contact** Gallery EXIT
  Anthony Iao
  anthonytao@galleryexit.com
- **Established** 2008
- **Owner(s) / Partner(s)** Aenon Loo
  Anthony Tao
- **Team** 6
- **Space(s)** 332 m²
- **Artists at Art Basel** Angela Su
  Chen Wei
  Chihoi
  Chris Huen
  Christine NG Mien Yin
  Makoto Fujimura

Genevieve Chua
Kong Chun Hei
Kwan Sheung Chi
Gabriel Leung
Lewis Lau
Lin Xue
Luke Ching
Lulu Ngie
Tang Kwok Hin
Wong Wai Yin
Yang Xinguang

- **Further artists represented** Nadim Abbas
Silas Fong
Hsu Yinling
Ko Sin Tung
Ivy Ma
Trevor Yeung

Experimenter

Kolkata ● Discoveries

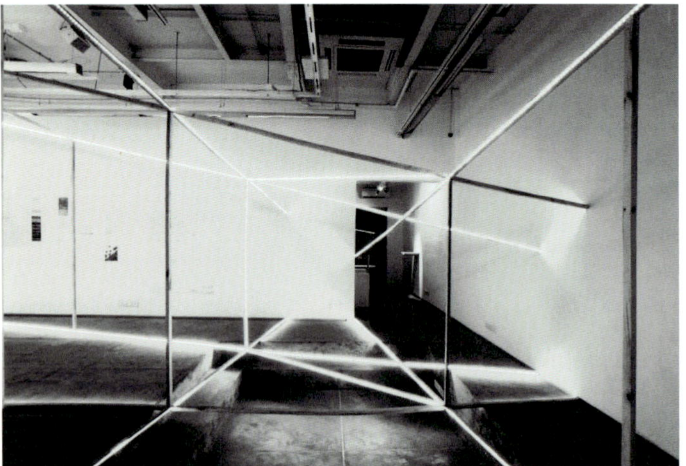

What is your favorite aspect of running a gallery?

The minds of the artists we represent are fascinating to us. We love the way they think of the world and how their creative minds are able to hold up a mirror to the world we live in. To facilitate an idea to be brought to frutition is the most rewarding experience of running a gallery. We also love to interact with the audience who sees our shows, learn what they think of the works they see. Finally, being part of a creative contemporary world.

How do you choose the artists you work with?

We feel artist-gallery relationships are like long-term marriages, where there is a period of mutual admiration and attraction toward each other's work and then a natural coming together of the two. Once established we work with our artists pretty much like all relationships need to be worked on, with care, mutual respect, and close understanding of their practice. The most basic need remains the same: to fit into our program and to show the most contemporary art out there.

If you weren't running a gallery what else would you do?

Prateek would go back to school to study architecture and be a practicing architect. The corporate world is not something that he found conducive to being in. He found the creative industry to be more compelling and rewarding. Architecture would be a natural choice. Priyanka would possibly continue in the corporate world and become an even more successful strategist than she already was when she quit and decided to work with Prateek.

- **Contact** Experimenter
Prateek Raja
prateek@experimenter.in
- **Established** 2009
- **Owner(s) / Partner(s)** Prateek & Priyanka Raja
- **Team** 5
- **Space(s)** 186 m²
- **Artists at Art Basel** Nadia Kaabi-Linke
- **Further artists represented** Bani Abidi
Rathin Barman
CAMP
Adip Dutta
Sanchayan Ghosh
Naeem Mohaiemen
Mehreen Murtaza
Prabhakar Pachpute
Raqs Media Collective
Ayesha Sultana
Hajra Waheed

Eslite Gallery
Interview with Emily Chao

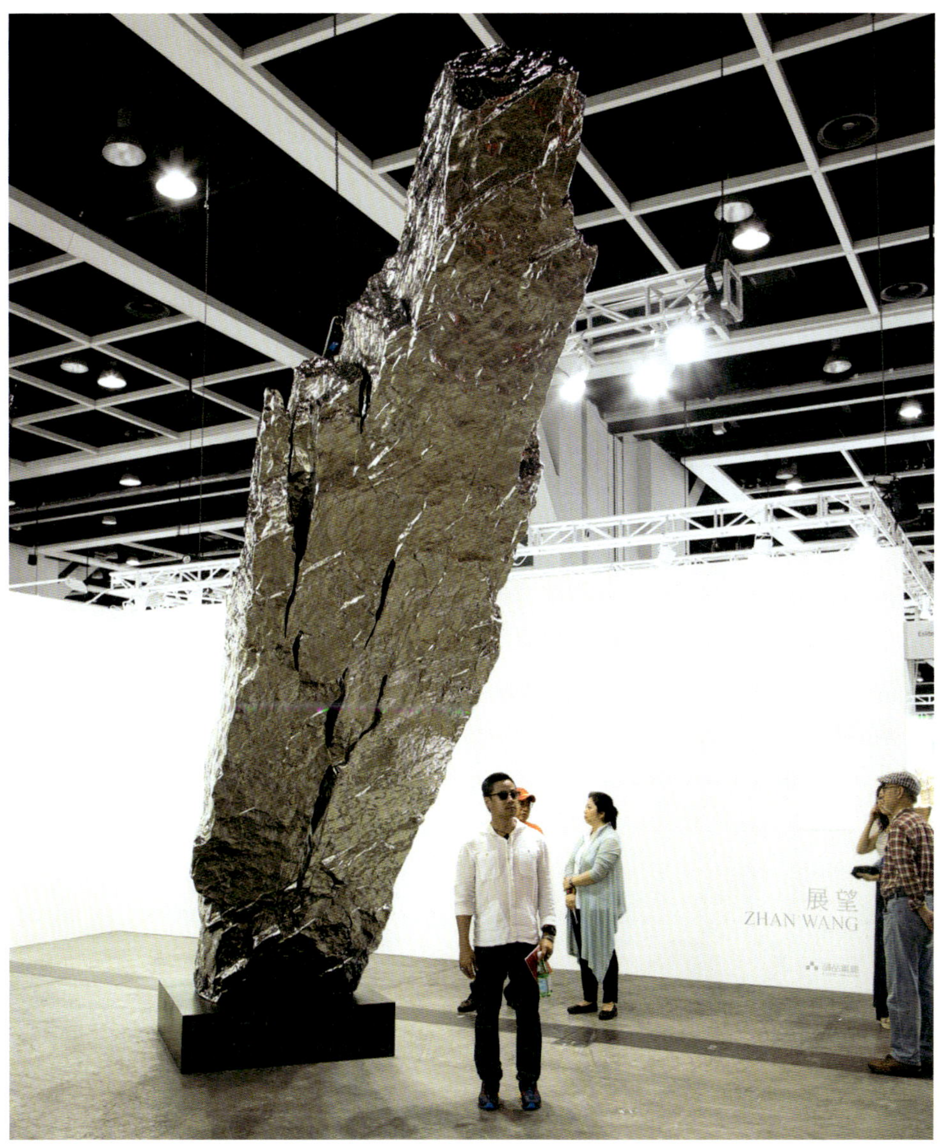

Art Basel in Hong Kong, 2014

How did Eslite Gallery start?

Eslite Gallery's founder, Robert Wu, started by founding a bookstore two months before the gallery, which opened in May 1989. In that year, Taiwan was experiencing an economic boom and financial resources were abundant, but the cultural scene was not so developed. At the beginning the gallery specialized in modern Asian masters, mostly artists who had been educated in Western Modernism.

What was the art scene in Taipei like at that time and how has it evolved?

In the 1980s and 1990s most of the galleries were concentrated on post-Second World War Taiwanese artists who where educated in the Japanese or Western tradition, as well as a few Western Modernist artists. Now Taiwan has to compete on the international level, so the galleries have had to evolve: some concentrate on old masters and some are more focused on contemporary.

What is the specificity of your gallery?

We focus on Chinese artists from all over the world, regardless of where they live (Taiwan, Malaysia, America, Europe). We always work with contemporary artists, but as the gallery is now 25 years old, artists who used to be contemporary are sometimes established ... But we continue to look for young international artists.

Could we talk about Zhan Wang's project *45 Degree Artificial Rock*, presented in 2014 at Art Basel in Hong Kong?

Eslite had been thinking about doing a solo exhibition at the Hong Kong art fair for some years. Zhan Wang decided to show a single, large piece. Most sculptures are either upright or horizontal, but this one stands at a 45 degree angle, which is dangerous as it could easily fall. It could be seen as the artist's perception of Chinese society: it is at a tipping point ...

What do you think about the current Asia-Pacific art scene and Art Basel in Hong Kong? How are things evolving now with the fair's increasing number of visitors, new institutions starting to open, etc.

The biggest and most influential market in Asia-Pacific today is China. When Western galleries come to Hong Kong, they are aiming for China; but because there are so many restrictions in China, they are waiting for the good moment to go in. Asia-Pacific's market is doing increasingly well because it was neglected for so long. Before China entered the art scene, we actually had more mature Asian markets in Japan, Taiwan, and South Korea. With a population of more than a billion in China, there are only about 1,000 serious collectors; the Western world counts 50,000 serious collectors, so in ratio with the full population, there is a lot of space for the market to grow.

This was our second participation in Art Basel in Hong Kong, and before we participated in ART HK. Since Art Basel took over, the fair has become better. But while there is a lot we can learn from Art Basel's experience, the fair in Hong Kong should become an Asian Art Basel and not a replication of Art Basel in Basel or in Miami Beach. It should remain a fair specific to Asia.

F

Focused on precisely curated projects, the Feature sector at Art Basel in Basel includes thoughtfully developed solo presentations, as well as thematic exhibits built around a range of artists across diverse cultural, generational, or artistic approaches. For the 2014 edition, we invited Los Angeles-based independent curator Douglas Fogle to choose his seven favorite booths.

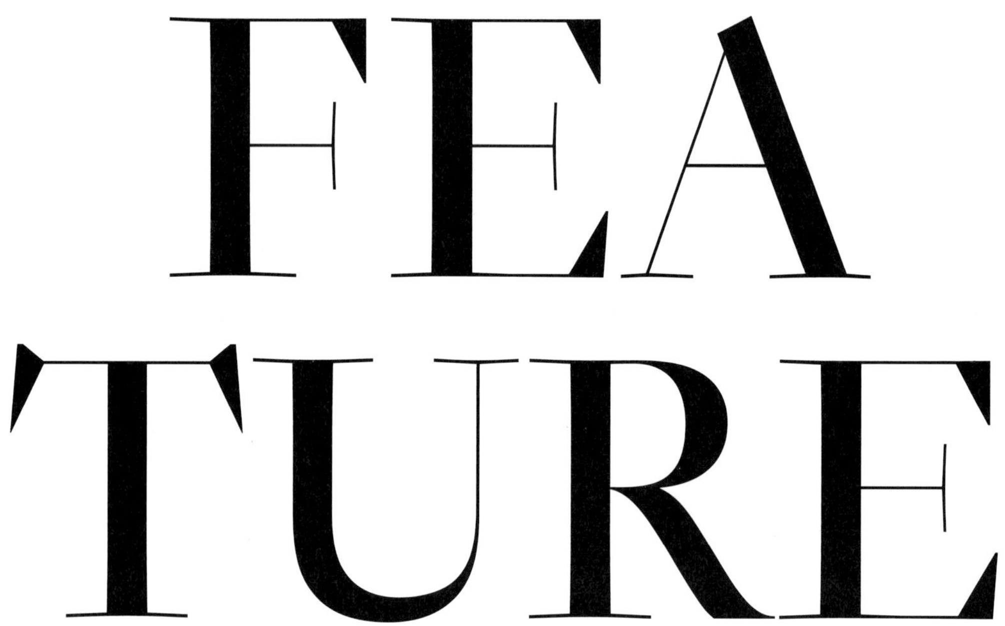

2014 participants

Art & Language
Kadel Willborn

Willi Baumeister
Friese

Dara Birnbaum
Wilkinson

Waltercio Caldas
Arnaud

Henri Chopin/ Michael Dean
Supportico Lopez

Nicole Eisenman
Vielmetter

Haris Epaminonda
Rodeo

Beatriz González/ Johanna Calle
Casas Riegner

Domenico Gnoli
Luxembourg & Dayan

Sanja Iveković
espaivisor

Dachun Ji
Aye

Mary Kelly
Houldsworth

Beryl Korot
bitforms

Julio Le Parc
Bugada & Cargnel

T. Kelly Mason
Cherry and Martin

Ana Mendieta/ Martha Rosler
Cortese

Shinro Ohtake
Take Ninagawa

Luigi Ontani
O'Neill

Dennis Oppenheim
MOT International

Alessandro Pessoli
Foxx

Santiago Sierra
KOW

Betty Tompkins
Rodolphe Janssen

David Wojnarowicz
P.P.O.W

Qiu Zhijie
Hanart TZ

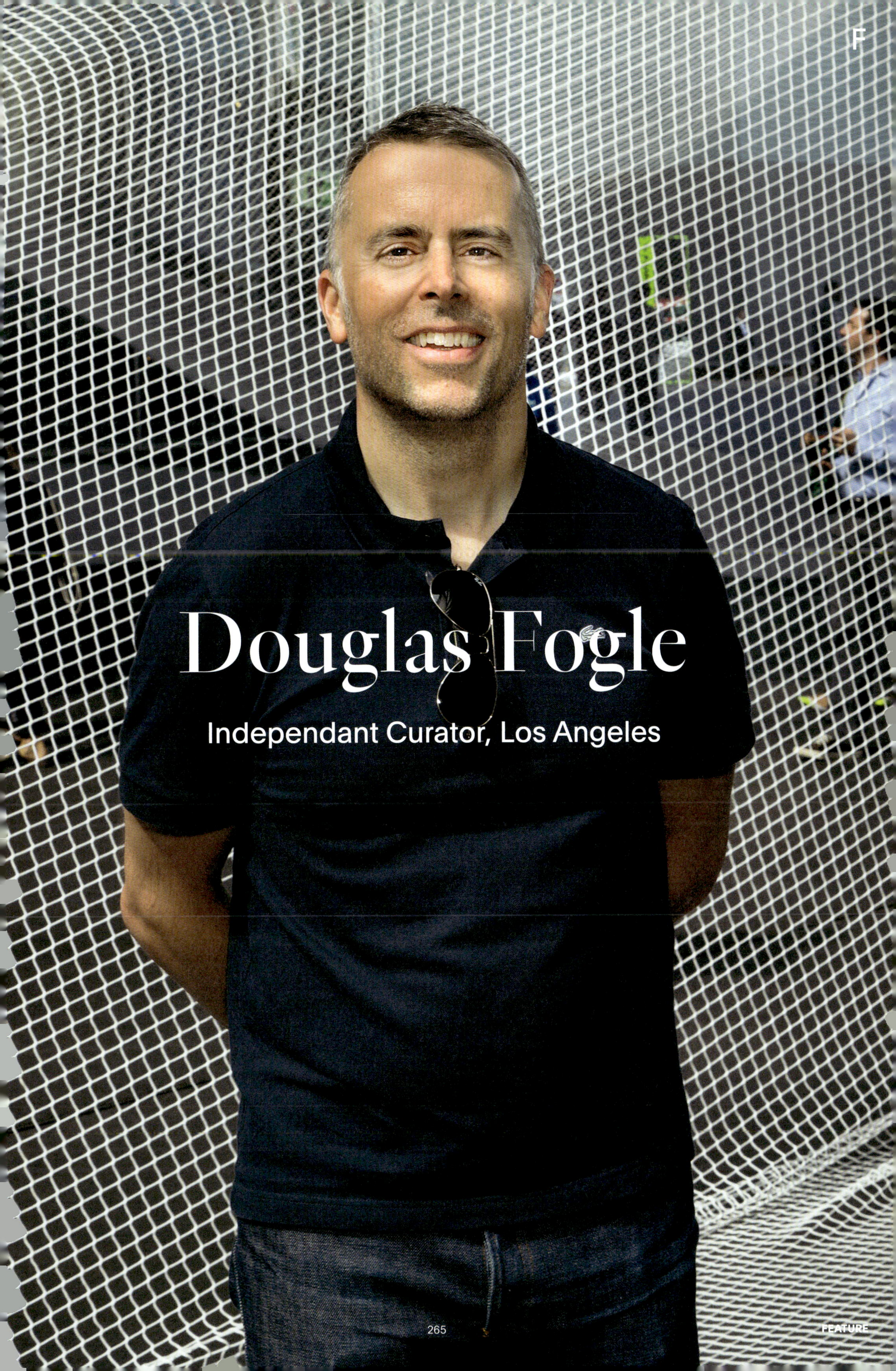

Douglas Fogle

Independant Curator, Los Angeles

Michael Dean/Henri Chopin
Supportico Lopez

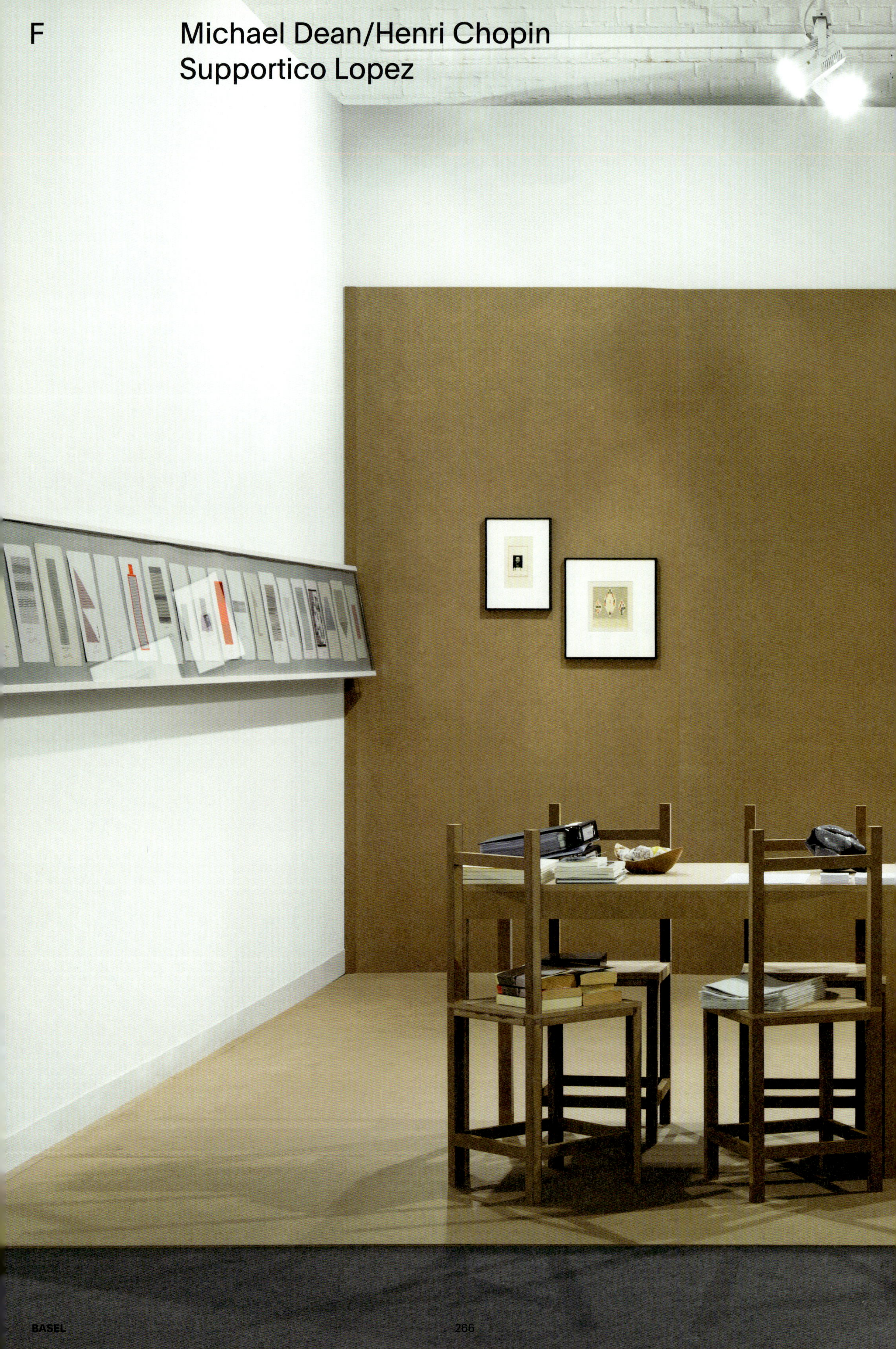

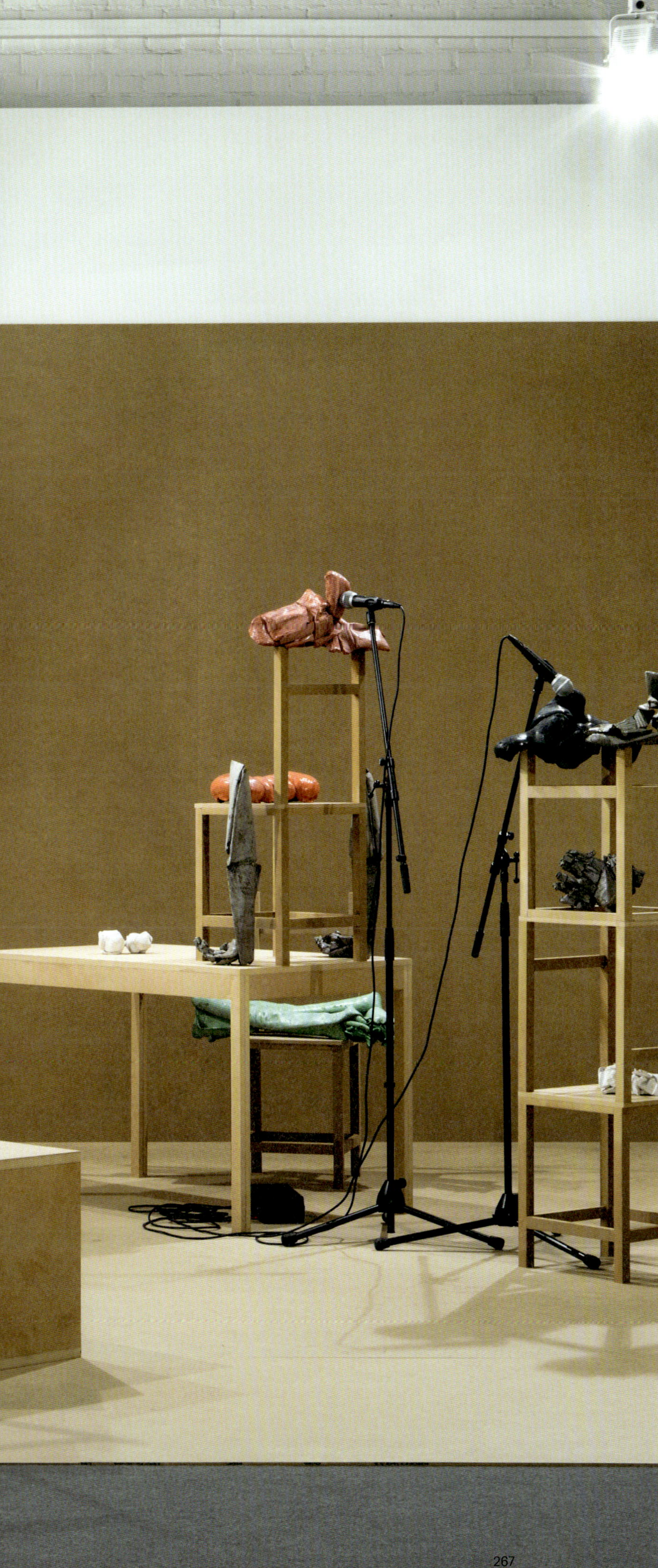

The generational gulf between artists Henri Chopin and Michael Dean was overcome in this co-presentation of their work by a focus on their mutual interest in language in their exploration of typography and sound. Typewriters and sculpted figures speak to the concrete, primordial components of language, while microphones placed near Dean's sculptures evoke a soundtrack of Chopin's experimental utterances. The birth of language was never as sexy as in this motionless choreography between these works.

F

Dara Birnbaum
Wilkinson

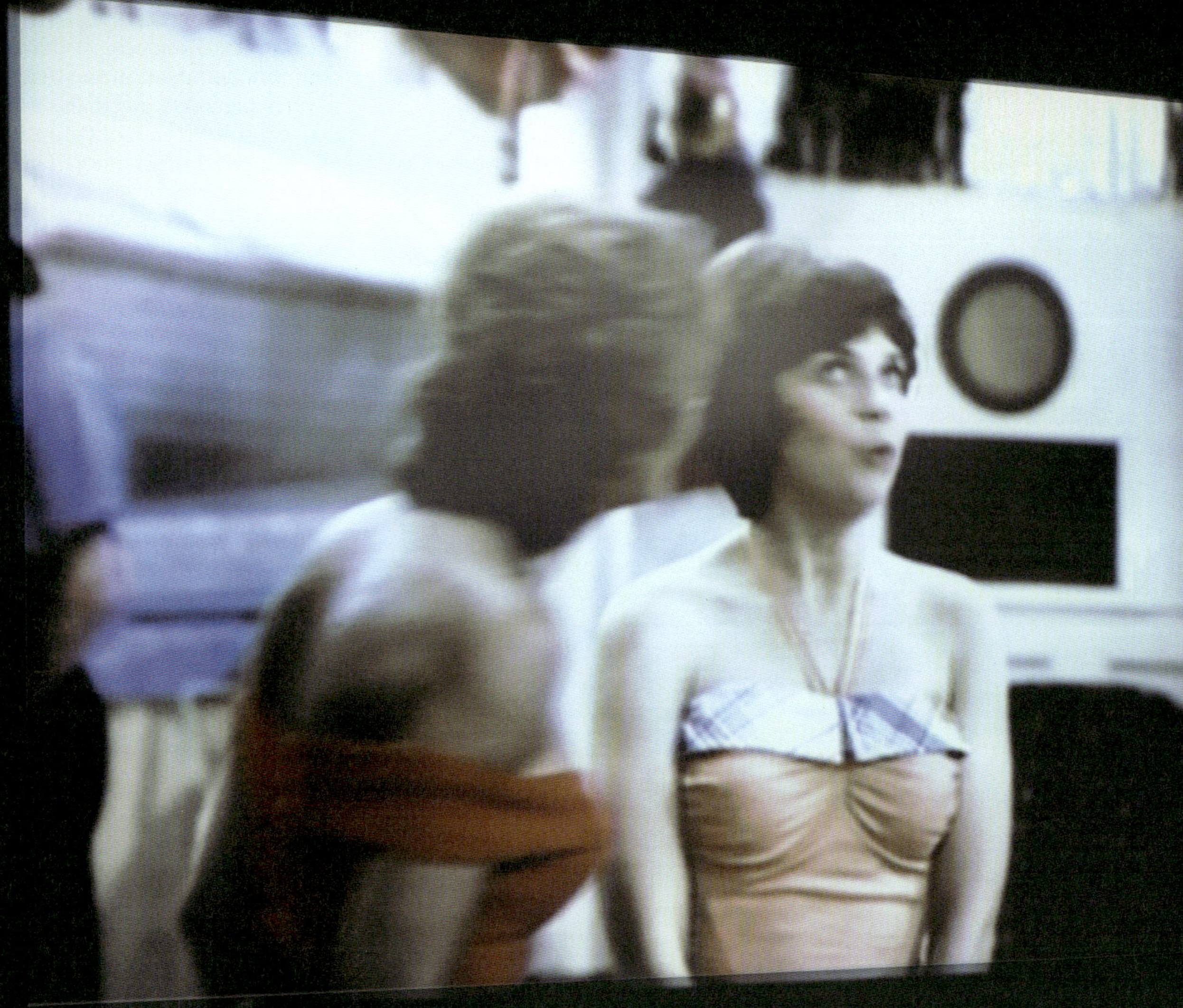

We sometimes forget that Dara Birnbaum helped invent video art in the 1970s. Seeing her 1978 installation *(A)Drift of Politics: Two Women Are Active in a Space*, which recuts an episode of the popular sitcom *Laverne and Shirley*, helps us remember that the 1980s really started in the 1970s and that appropriation in the defense of artistic liberty is no sin.

F

Approaching the figure with the knowing, soulful insights that reside beneath the outward irreverence of the figure of the clown, Alessandro Pessoli's presentation of unglazed ceramic paintings of cartoonish figureheads could be read as a meditation on the fragile inner state of the human condition. Confronted with an existential abyss? Then send in the clowns.

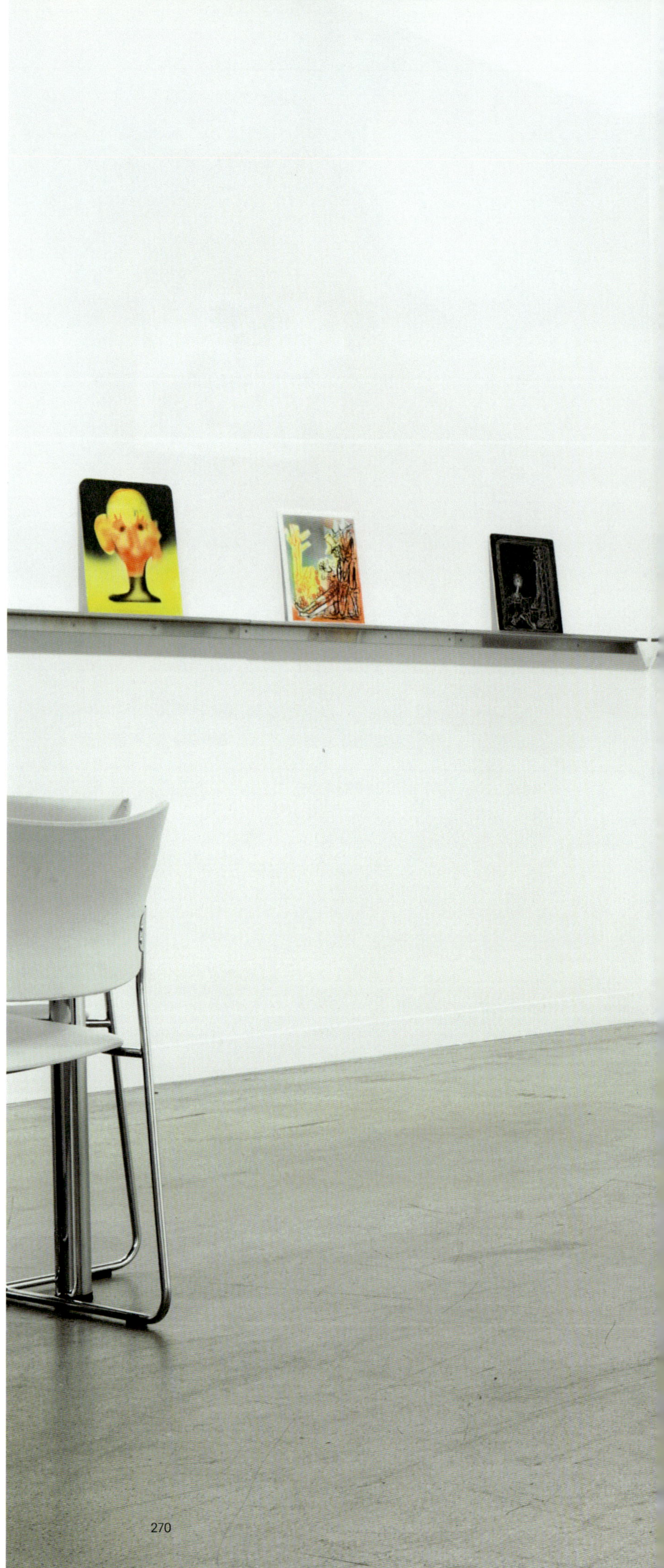

Alessandro Pessoli
Marc Foxx Gallery

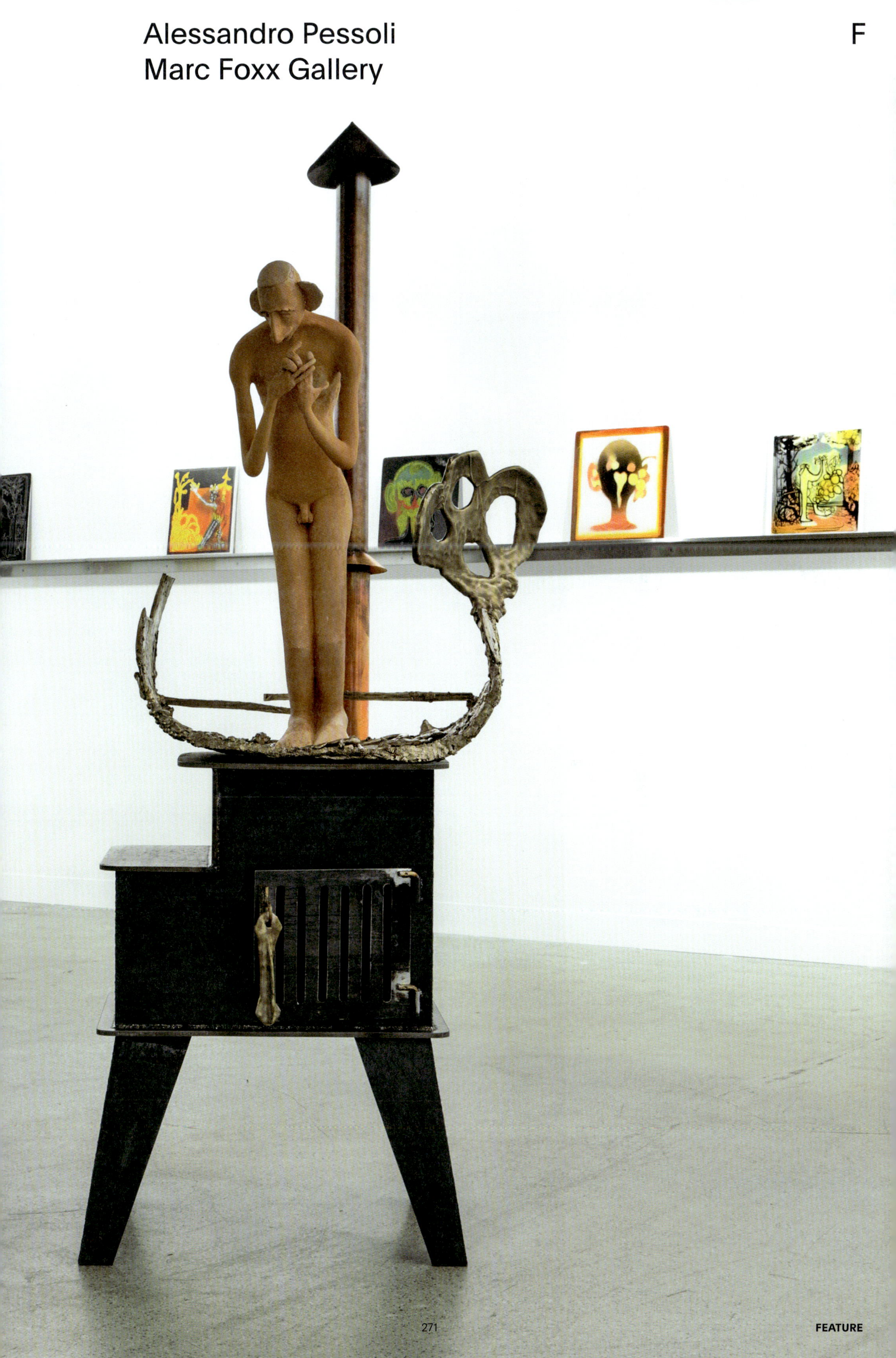

F

There was something incredibly refreshing about the presentation of video and photo works from Dennis Oppenheim's *Whirlpool (Eye of the Storm)* (1973). The impermanence and humility of this skywriting performance acts as an antidote to the hubris that has attached itself to the more monolithic status of the works of Oppenheim's Land art peers. Ghostwriters in the sky indeed.

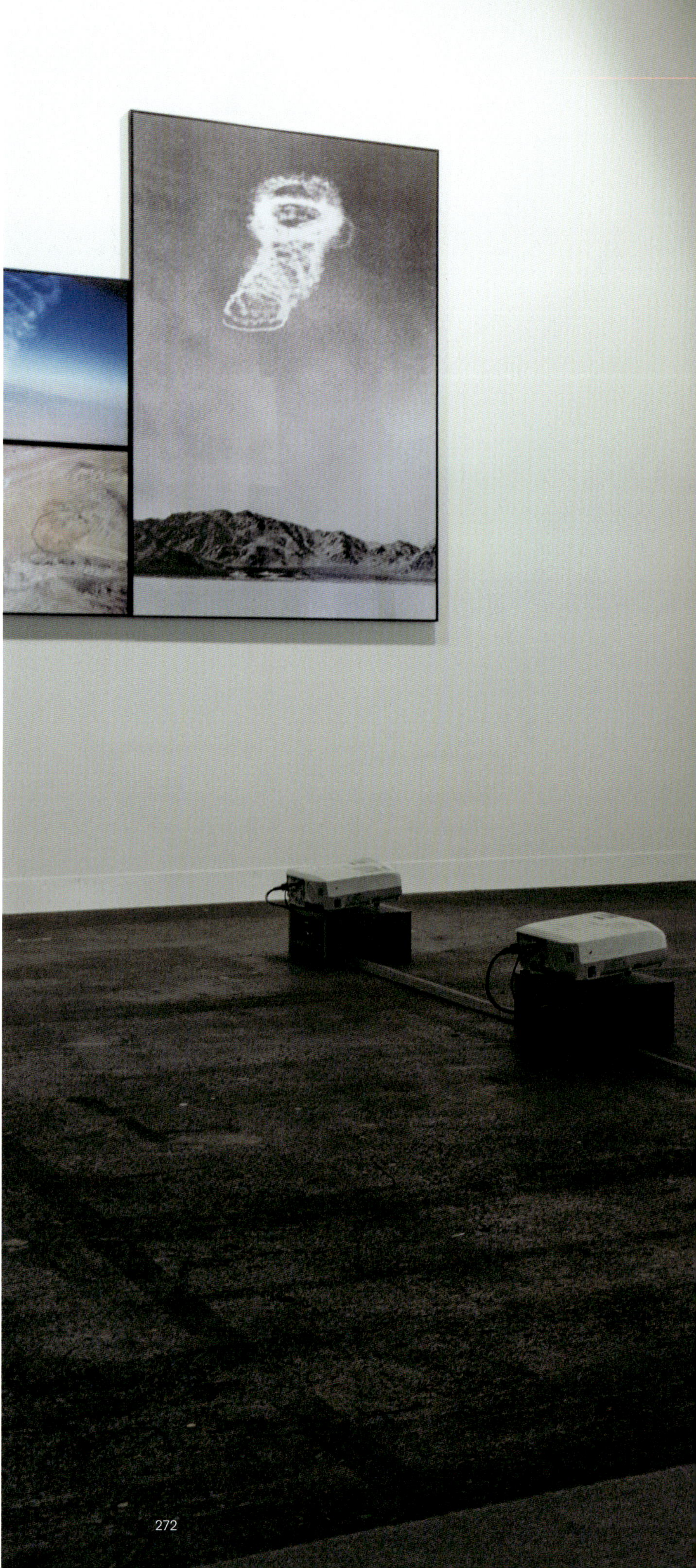

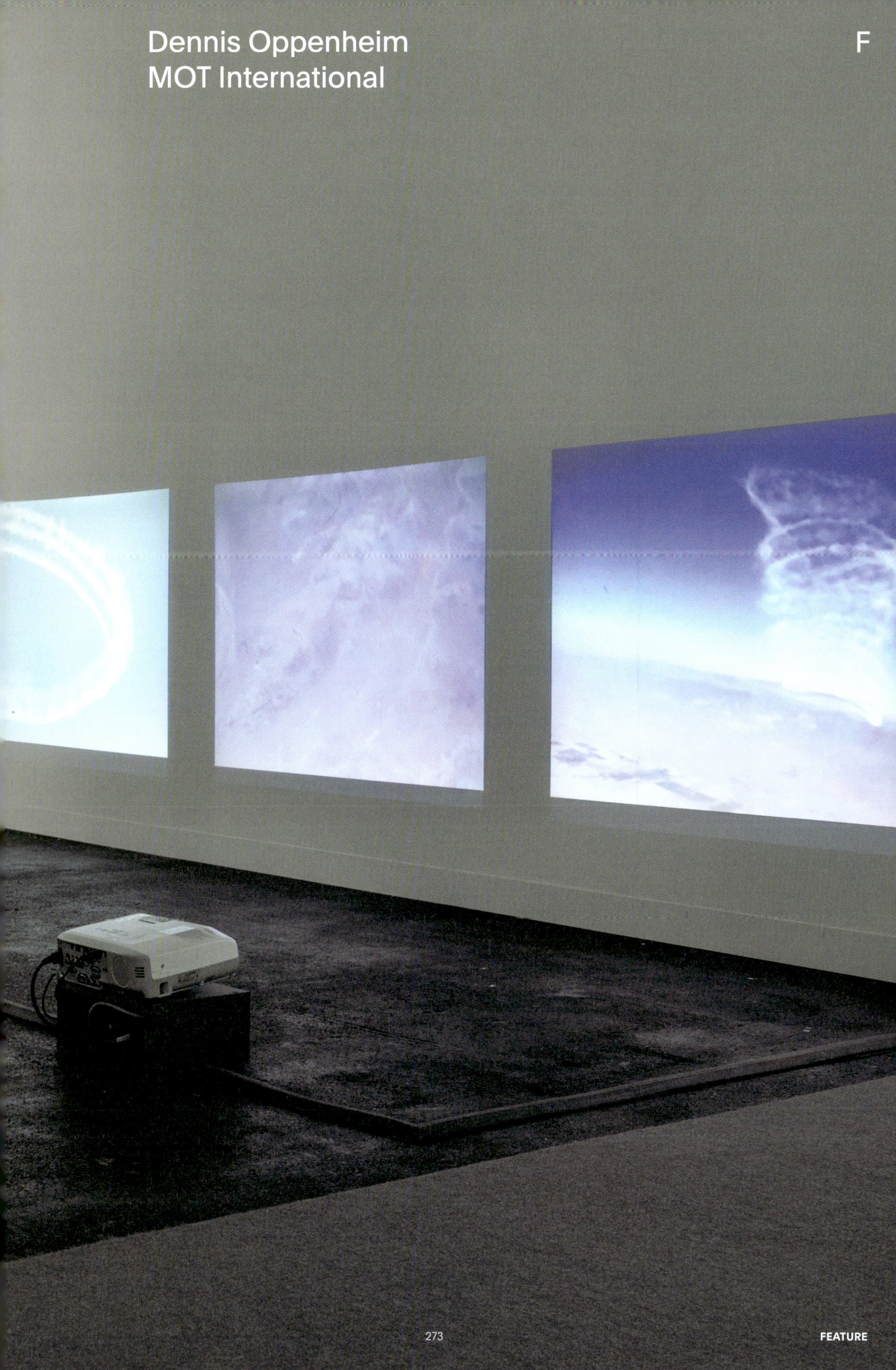

Dennis Oppenheim
MOT International

F

Art & Language
Kadel Willborn

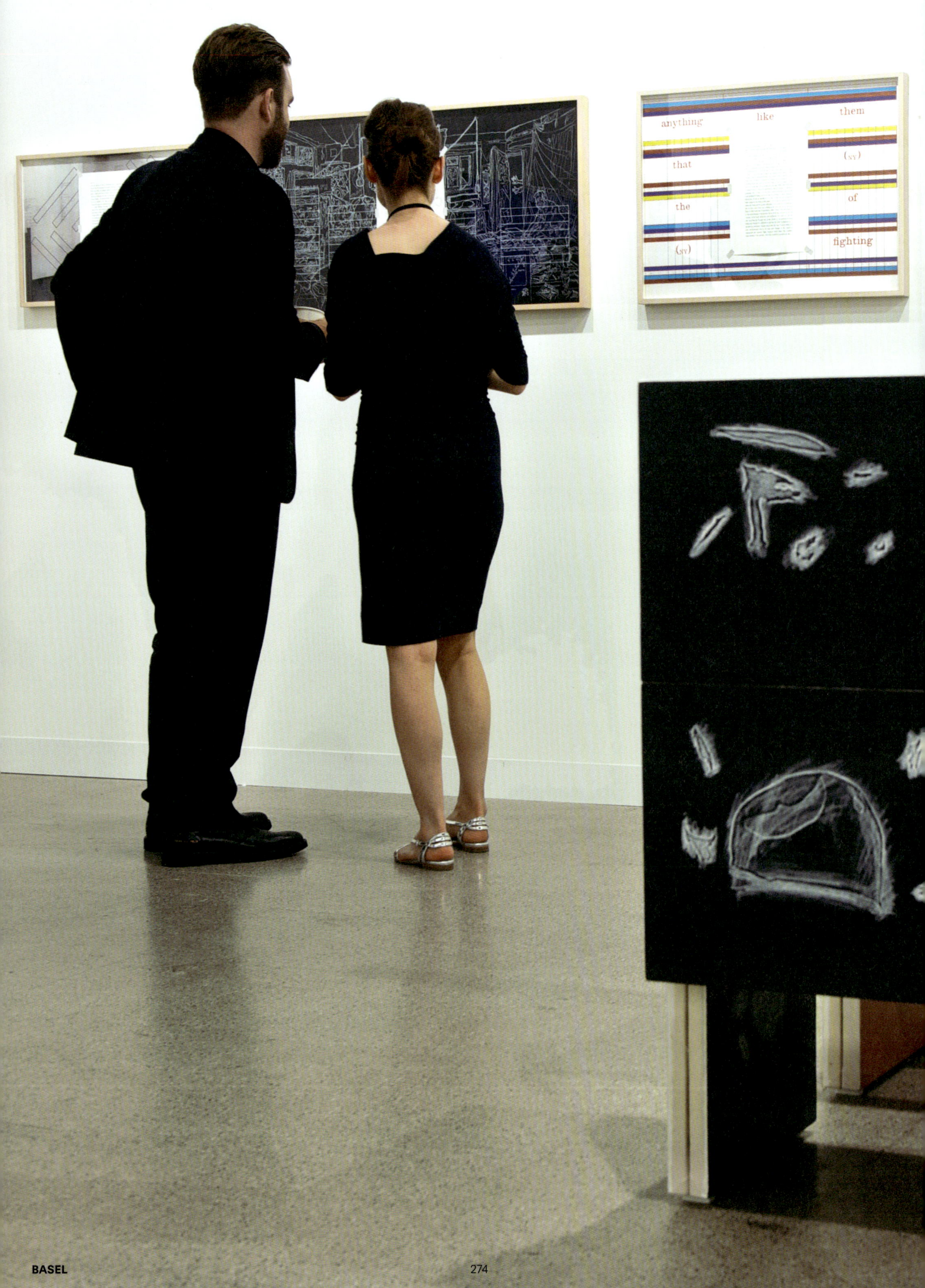

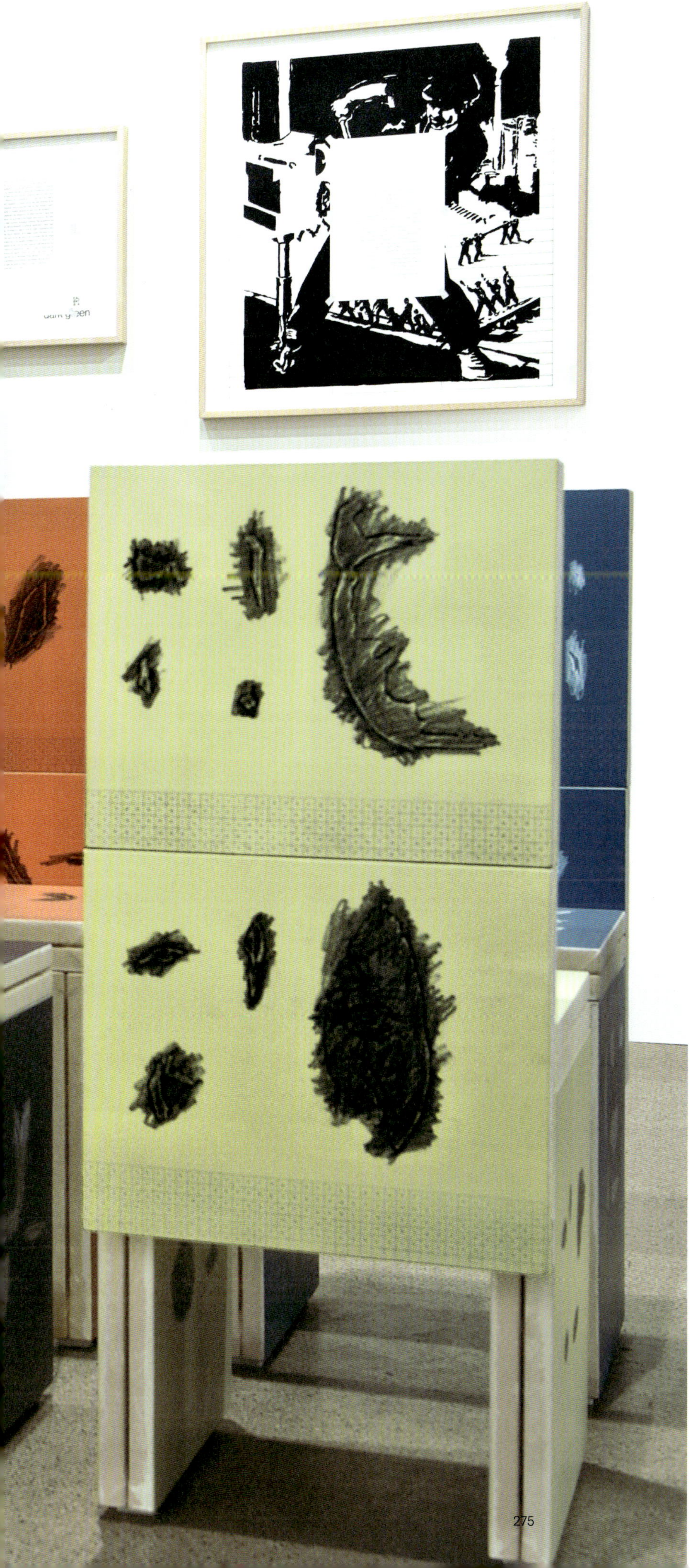

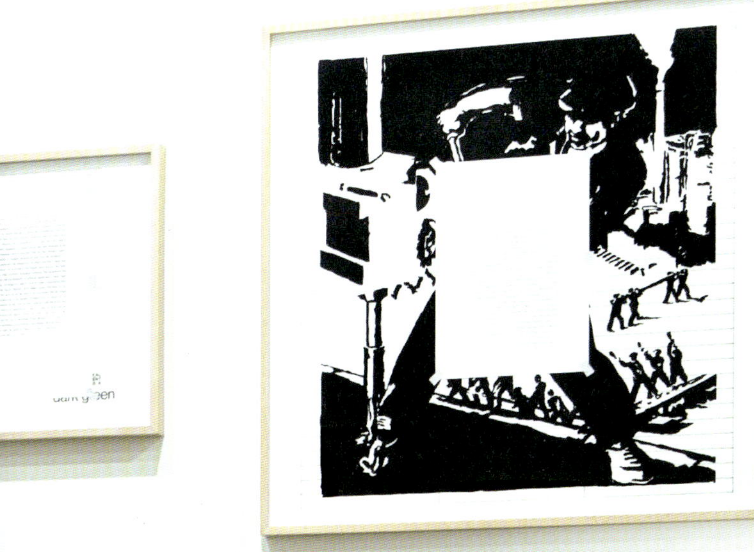

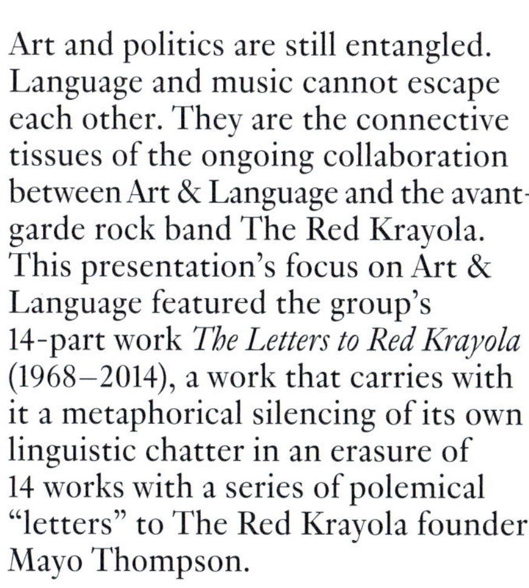

Art and politics are still entangled. Language and music cannot escape each other. They are the connective tissues of the ongoing collaboration between Art & Language and the avant-garde rock band The Red Krayola. This presentation's focus on Art & Language featured the group's 14-part work *The Letters to Red Krayola* (1968–2014), a work that carries with it a metaphorical silencing of its own linguistic chatter in an erasure of 14 works with a series of polemical "letters" to The Red Krayola founder Mayo Thompson.

F

Nicole Eisenman
Susanne Vielmetter Los Angeles Projects

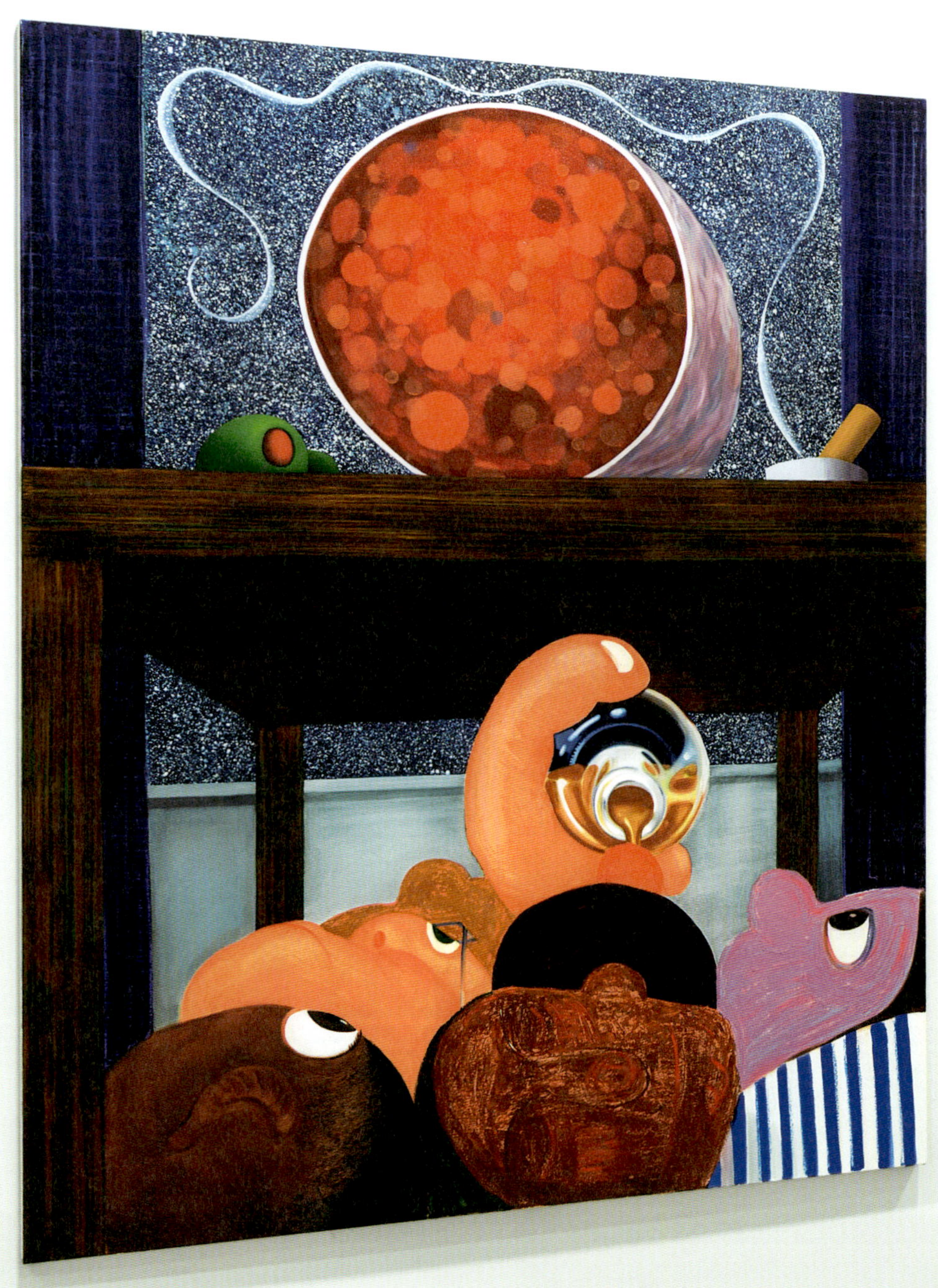

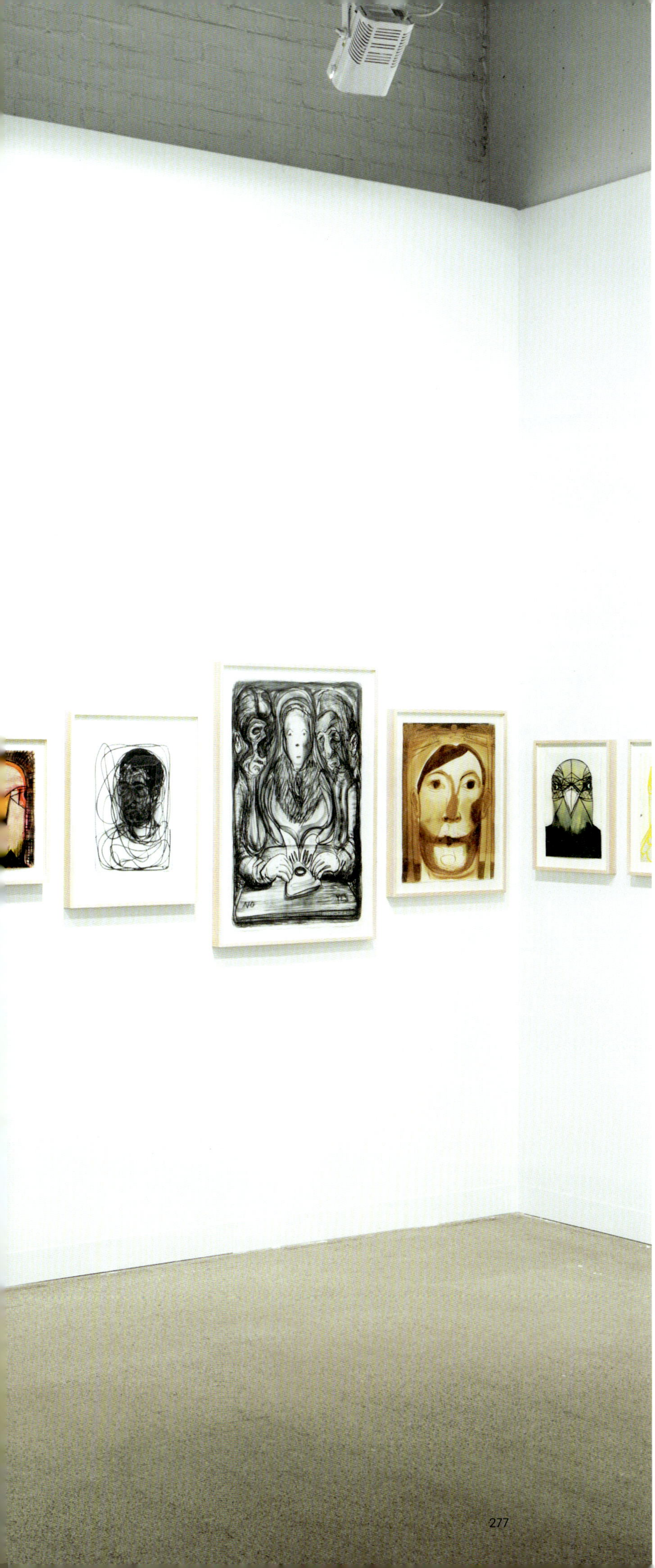

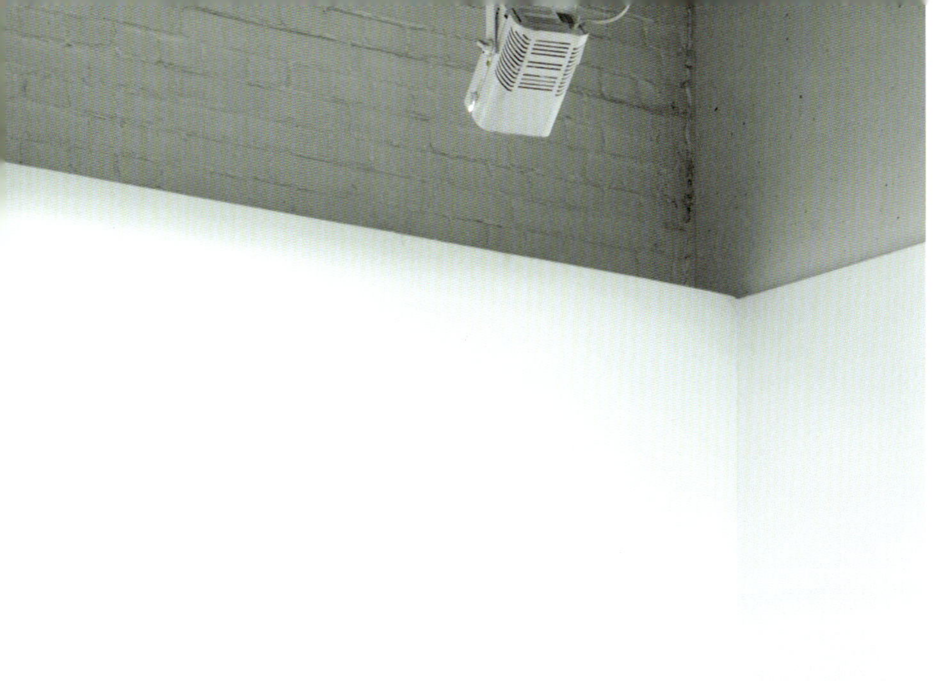

On the heels of her Carnegie Award-winning installation in the 2013 Carnegie International, this presentation of paintings and works on paper by Nicole Eisenman demonstrated why we should continue pay attention to her work. The human figure continues to haunt us even in its dissolution.

F

Sanja Iveković
espaivisor

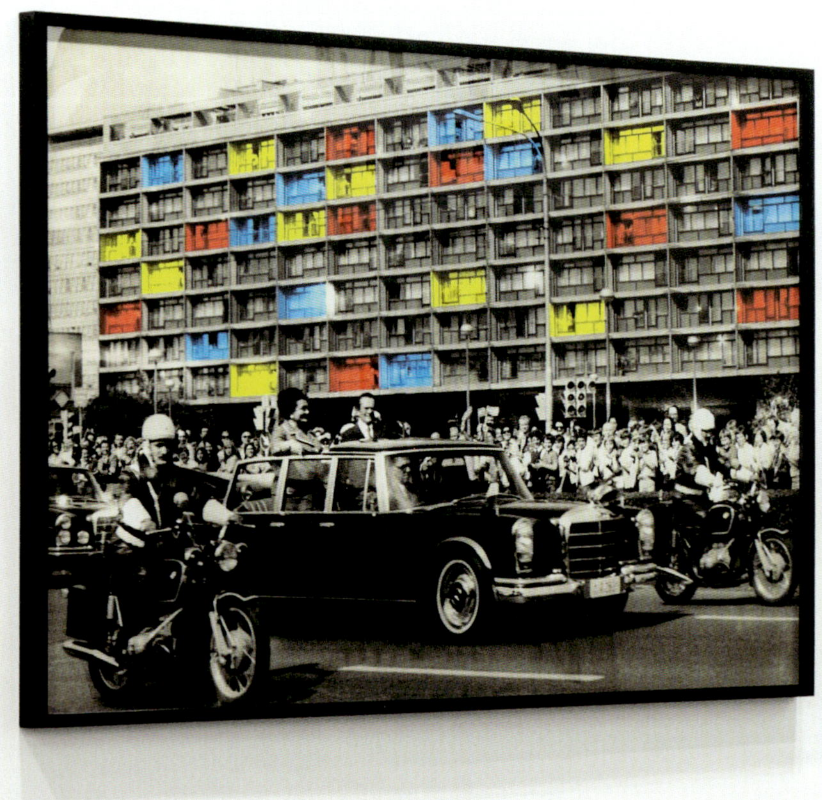

F

The artist's solo presentation at MoMA in 2012 brought renewed attention to this pioneer of feminist-inspired Conceptual art from Yugoslavia. Notable in this group of works was her photographic piece *Women in Art, Women in Yugoslavian Art* (1975). The artist coupled a page ripped from a feature in *Flash Art* of so-called "important" women in art at the time with her own simple line drawings of their unknown equivalents in the Yugoslavian art scene. Center and periphery are inverted and the authority of the art world establishment is questioned. A socialist Guerrilla Girls *avant la lettre*? In this case one questioning the geopolitical situation as well as a simple feminist critique of patriarchy.

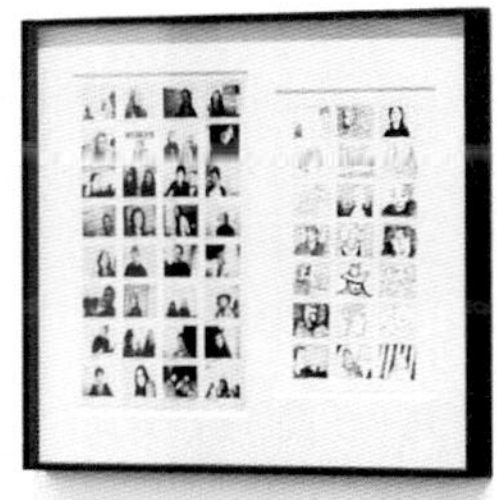

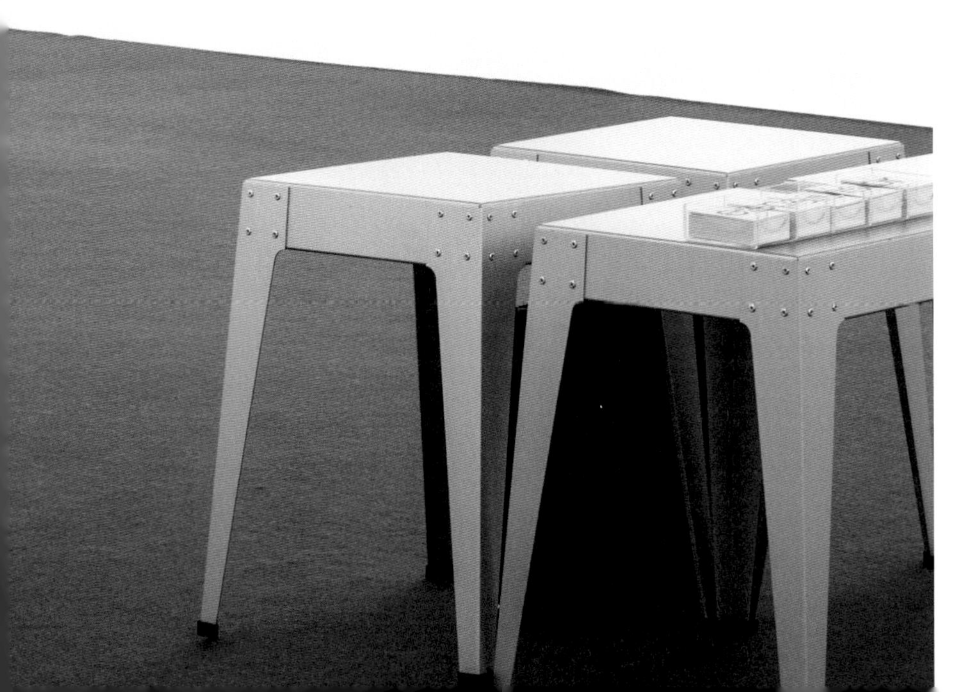

Art Basel's week-long programs of films by and about artists is curated in Basel by Berlin film scholar Marc Glöde. In Miami Beach the Film sector is organized by David Gryn, Founder of Artprojx, London, and mainly takes place in the outdoor setting of SoundScape Park, where works are shown on the 7,000-square-foot outdoor projection wall of the Frank Gehry-designed New World Center. In Basel and Miami, Zurich Film connoisseur This Brunner also curates one feature-film evening. In Hong Kong, the Film sector is curated by Li Zhenhua, Director and Founder of Beijing Art Lab, at the agnès b. cinema in the Hong Kong Arts Centre.

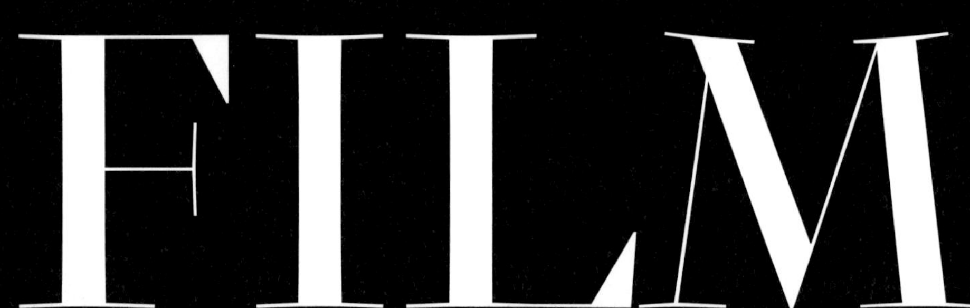

2014 participants

Hong Kong
Brian Alfred
Sookoon Ang
Andreas Angelidakis
Bill Balaskas
Polly Borland
Bettina Buck
Chien-Chi Chang
Wu Chang-Jung
Kwan Sheung Chi
Joaquín Cociña & Cristobal León
Christopher Doyle
Diogo Evangelista
Dominique Gonzalez-Foerster & Tristan Bera
Ishu Han
Paul Harrison & John Wood
Youki Hirakawa
Chen Sai Hua Kuan
Takashi Ishida
Tsubasa Kato
Naiza Khan
John Latham
Dinh Q. Lê
Cristobal León
Liao Li
Ye Linghan
Jun Nguyen-Hatsushiba
Tameka Norris
Hiroyuki Oki
Tu Pei-Shih
Chim↑Pom
Roman Signer
SHIMURAbros
Sriwhana Spong
Yukihiro Taguchi
Haiyang Wang
Guan Xiao
Miao Xiaochun
Nina Yuen
Chen Zhou

Basel
Maria Anwander
Sue de Beer
Manon de Boer
Étienne Chambaud
Harun Farocki
Nina Fischer & Maroan el Sani
Anna Gaskell
Andrea Geyer
Jan Peter Hammer
David Hartt
Rashid Johnson
Ilja Karilampi
Sung Hwan Kim
Manfred Mohr
Pat O'Neill
Elizabeth Price
Cheng Ran
Sterling Ruby
Aïda Ruilova
David Shrigley
John Smith
Superflex
Jane & Louise Wilson

Miami Beach
Larry Achiampong*
Pilar Albarracín
Charles Atlas
Vartan Avakian
Brian Alfred
Bill Balaskas
Rania Bellou
Nate Boyce
Brian Bress
Olaf Breuning
CAR (Conceptual Artists Research/Michelle Grabner and Brad Killam)
Liu Chuang
Martin Creed
Jose Dávila
Tim Davis
Chris Doyle
Marcel Dzama
Harun Farocki
Dara Friedman
Leo Gabin
Tomislav Gotovac
Brent Green
Frank Heath
Camille Henrot
Susan Hiller
Parker Ito
Taro Izumi
Jennie C. Jones*
Atsushi Kaga
Oliver Laric
Mark Leckey
Wagner Malta Tavares
Babette Mangolte
Dashiell Manley
Florian Meisenberg
Theo Michael
Takeshi Murata
Ciprian Mureşan
Jayson Musson
Rashaad Newsome
Hans Op de Beeck
Hayal Pozanti
Alex Prager
Elizabeth Price
Laure Prouvost
Jon Rafman
Clunie Reid
Charlie Richardson
Alex Rodríguez
Robin Rhode
Tabor Robak
Ana Roldán
Rachel Rose
Hiraki Sawa
David Shrigley
Stephen Vitiello*
Mark Wallinger
Maya Watanabe
Marnie Weber
Wood & Harrison
Saya Woolfalk
Raed Yassin*

*sound work

Stadtkino Basel

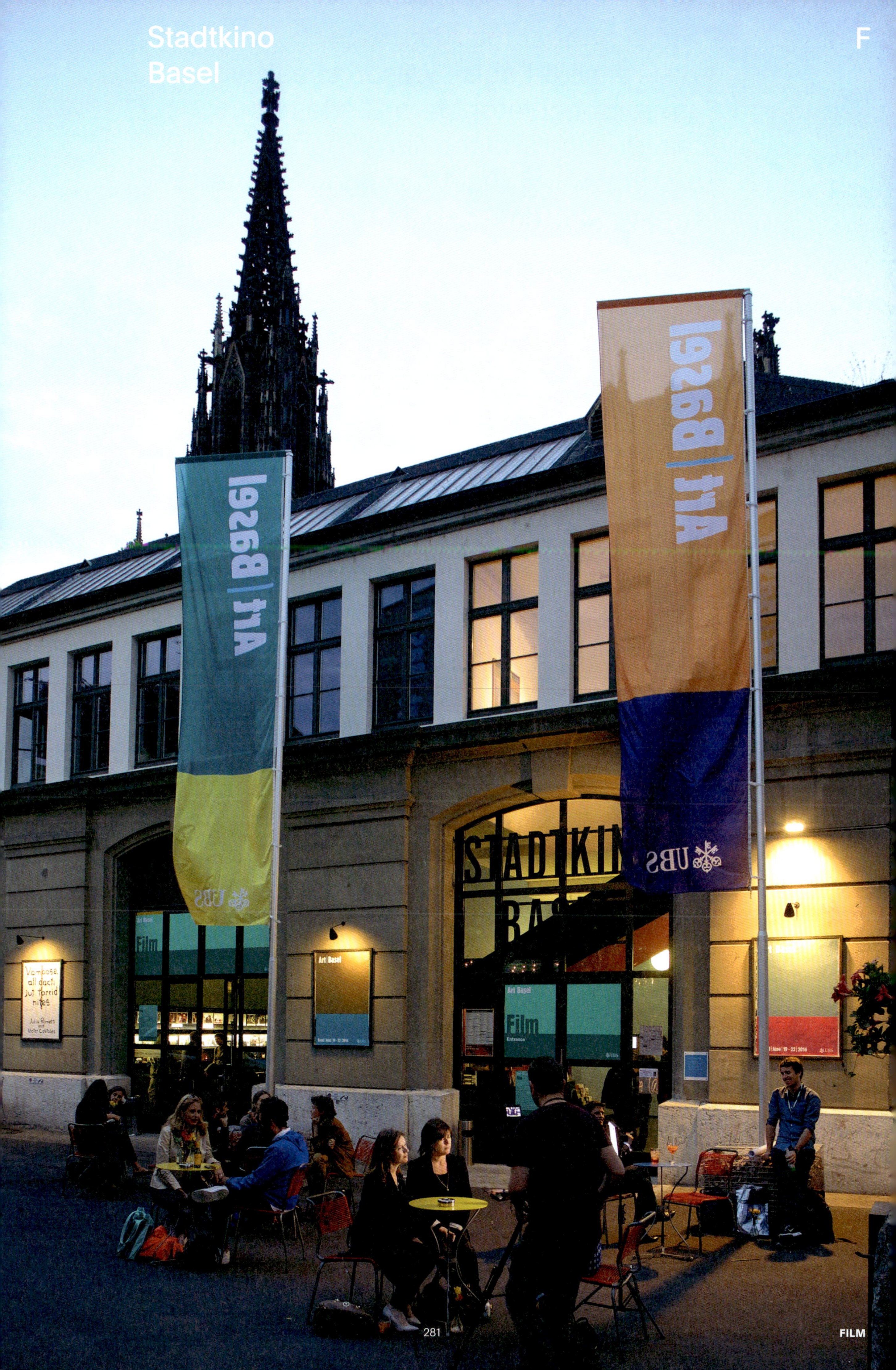

Thinking About the Aftermath

Artists Jane & Louise Wilson speak with Film sector curator Marc Glöde about their practice and the film program *Thinking About the Aftermath* screened on June 17, 2014.

CLÉMENT DIRIÉ How did you build the film program *Thinking About the Aftermath*, in which Jane & Louise Wilson's work *The Toxic Camera* (2012) is included?

MARC GLÖDE In the applications this year, coincidently both Nina Fischer & Maroan el Sani and Jane & Louise Wilson submitted material that dealt with nuclear fall-out, and how to address this topic. For me it was the perfect fit for thinking about the questions raised by Chernobyl—the main topic of the Wilsons'movie—and Fukushima—as addressed by Nina Fischer & Maroan el Sani. And we have a third position with Dominique Gonzalez-Foerster's *Atomic Park* (2004), which focuses on the Trinity site, where nuclear tests took place in the US in the 1950s. One of the ideas behind this selection of films is to see how artists are dealing with disaster, the catastrophic, but it also says something about a change from political to ecological concerns. For me, film is a way of thinking.

CD Maybe we could start with the movie that is screening tonight, *The Toxic Camera*.

JANE & LOUISE WILSON I think what is curious about this piece is that it looks very much to the materiality of the film and the effects of radioactivity on the material. The film is inspired by *The Chronicle of Difficult Weeks*, shot in 1996 by the filmmaker Vladimir Shevchenko. It was the first time someone captured radioactivity on celluloid, so it became famous as a documentary.

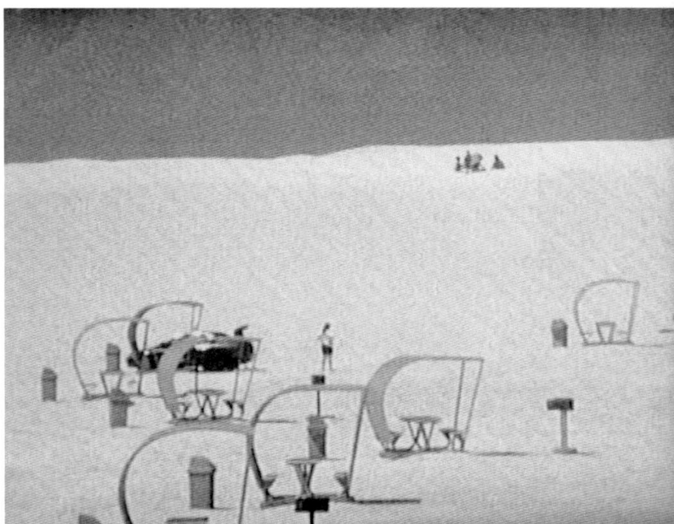

Dominique Gonzalez-Foerster, *Atomic Park*, 2003, film still

CD Three weeks after the accident, Vladimir Shevchenko flew over the Chernobyl plant ...

J&LW Yes, he filmed it, and died eight months later. We went to Kiev and interviewed the film crew that had worked with him, the three surviving members. They told us not just about the radioactivity he "captured" on celluloid, but that the camera he used (a Russian Konvas camera that continued to be used in the film school for two more years after his death ...) had levels of radioactivity so toxic that they had to bury it outside of Kiev. So we became very interested to visit, rather than Chernobyl, the burial site of the "toxic camera." That's the story. I suppose there isn't any digital record in Fukushima, because the digital tapes were wiped, while on analog film the effect of radioactivity is actually captured.

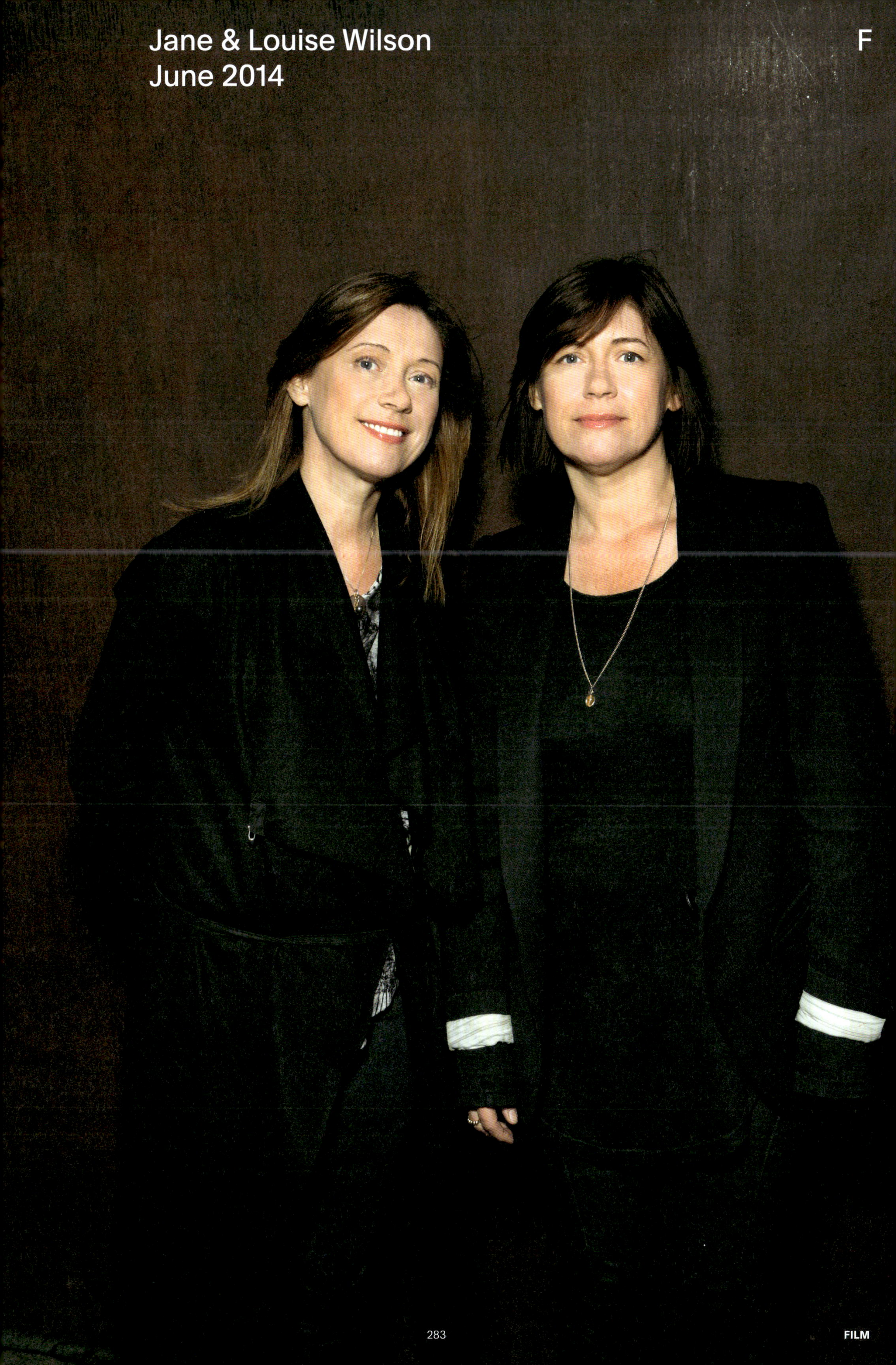
Jane & Louise Wilson
June 2014

F

There is something very powerful about the relationship between the two films, because Fukushima happened in 2011, exactly 25 years after Chernobyl. It is a key point to look at these sites in terms of the future: rather than documenting the aftermath, the films say something about the becoming of the future as a ruin.

The Toxic Camera is a non-fiction narrative. It is about a reconstruction, based on true events and on interviews, so there is an element of narration. The documentary had already been made. It was already there and what's amazing was that it chronicles the effect of radiation for the first time. The film is a document of an event, but it actually becomes an event at the same time.

CD *The Toxic Camera* could be also a metaphor for the way you make films, because you are always trying to revisit things and to go somewhere not everybody can go to.

MG It's about the desire to view. *The Toxic Camera* is almost a question: is it a desire to document or a desire to be a voyeur?

CD But what is your desire? Is it to testify, to document?

J&LW It is to actively reflect on this question.

Jane & Louise Wilson, *The Toxic Camera*, 2012, film stills

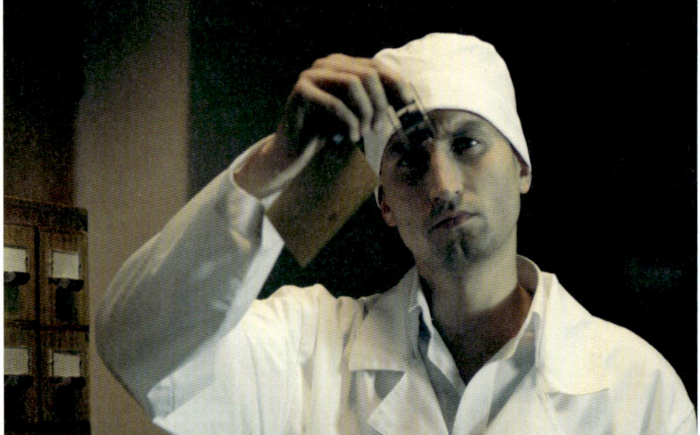

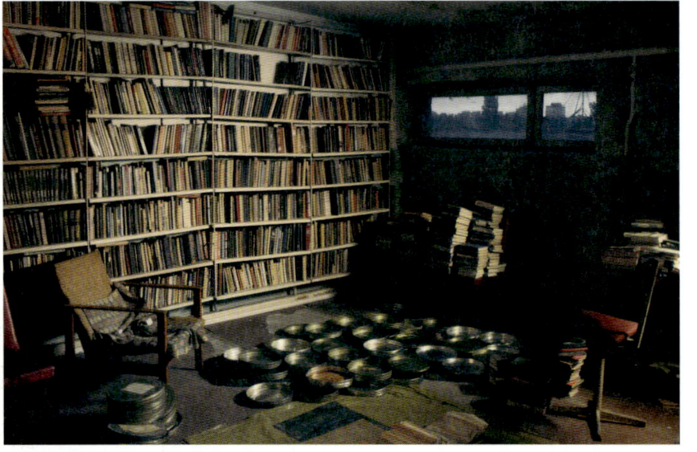

CD I have a last question for Marc. How do you build the screening program for the Film sector in general?

MG Well, at the end of each year, the galleries submit new films from their artists. I go through the submissions, and usually I don't give any kind of theme or topic in advance. Over the last seven years that I've been running this film program, it has always been very interesting to see how topics have emerged out of the submissions. It says something about what the artists are working on at the moment and the kind of topics they address. I bring this into a program. I can also add films from outside, from galleries who are not participating in the fair, in order to complete the program.

CD What other highlights of the week could you mention?

MG I'm very excited to host a screening of films by Pat O'Neill. He is very well known in the independent cinema scene—he started making amazing works on the West Coast in the 1960s—but not so much in the art world. He was picked up recently by a young gallery in Los Angeles, and we are showing some of his classics as well as his most recent works, including one he just finished; so we have a world premiere!

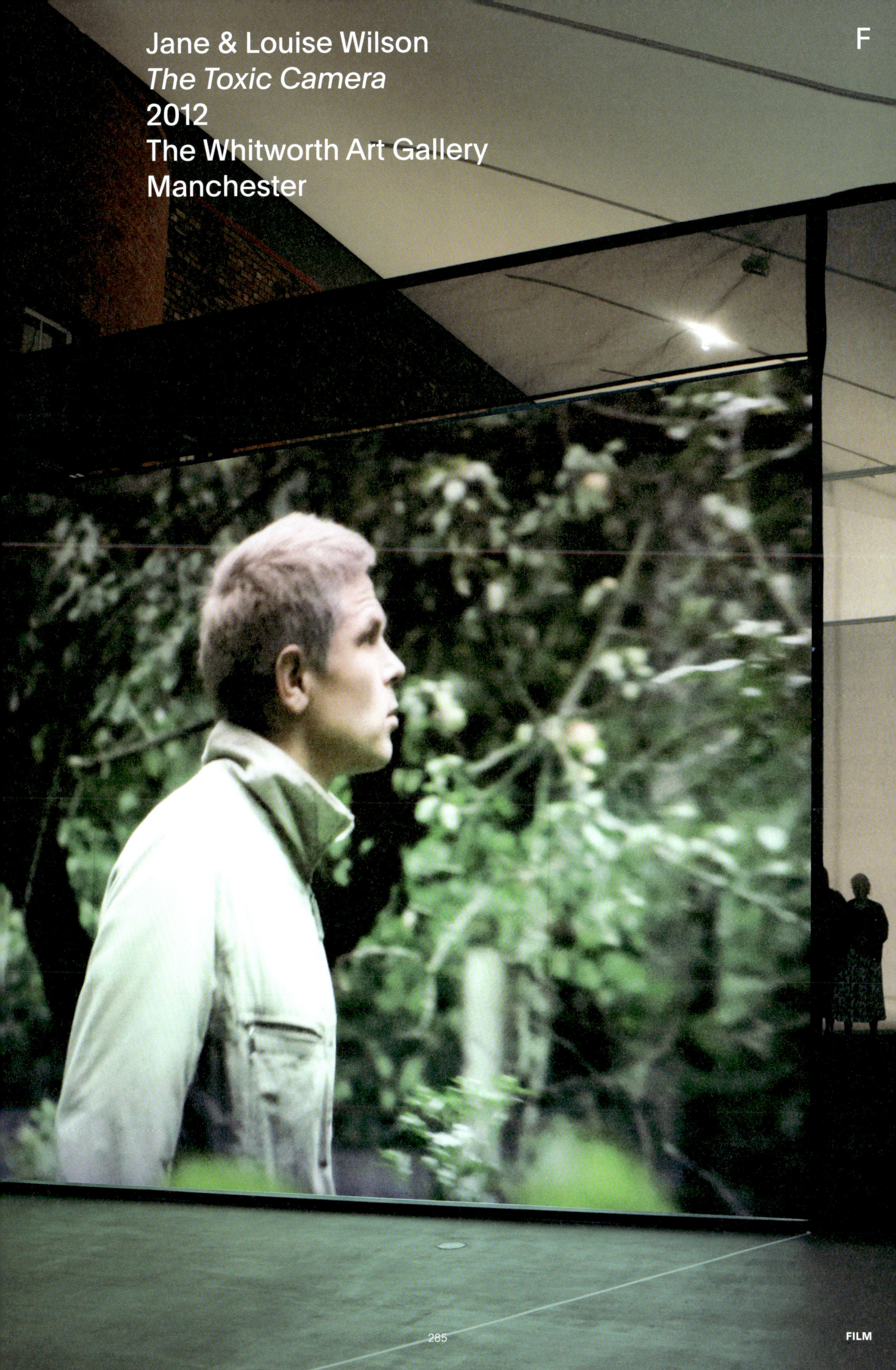

Jane & Louise Wilson
The Toxic Camera
2012
The Whitworth Art Gallery
Manchester

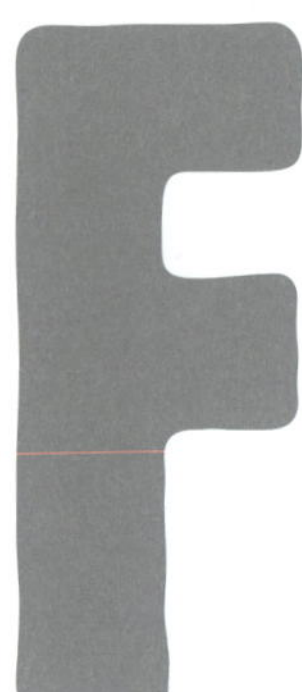
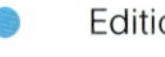

Fanal

Basel · Edition

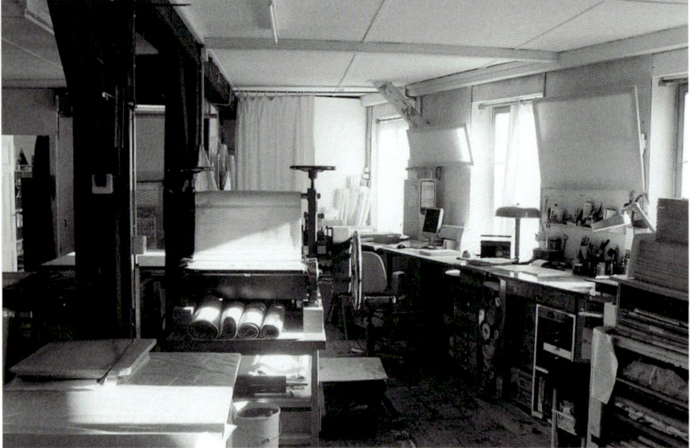

What is your favorite aspect of running a gallery?
Being both a printing studio and an art edition house, it is the dialogue and the collaboration with the artists in the process of transposing their work through one of our techniques: silkscreen and etching.

How do you choose the artists you work with?
Our line is constructive art. It is in this field that we have been collaborating over many years with internationally recognized artists. We look also for young talent by visiting ateliers, art fairs, and by following art publications.

- **Contact** Atelier-Editions Fanal
  Danielle Harder
  fanal@vtxmail.ch
- **Established** 1966
- **Owner(s) / Partner(s)** Marie-Thérèse Vacossin
  Danielle Harder
- **Team** 6
- **Space(s)** 500 m²
- **Artists at Art Basel** Ode Bertrand
  Andreas Brandt
  Geneviève Claisse
  Carlos Cruz-Diez
  Gerhard Doehler
  Gerhard Frömel
  Jean-Michel Gasquet
  Gottfried Honegger
  Stefanie Lampert
  Horst Linn
  Vera Molnar
  Aurélie Nemours
  Yves Popet
  Karin Radoy
  Nelly Rudin
  Sigurd Rompza
  Jocelyne Santos
  Klaus Staudt
  Sylvestre
  Marie-Thérèse Vacossin
  Shizuko Yoshikawa
- **Further artists represented** Serena Amrein
  Frank Badur
  Waldo Balart
  Charles Bézie
  Hartmut Böhm
  Jean Brault
  Marischa Burckhardt
  Pol Bury
  John Carter
  Max Cole
  Helmut Dirnaichner
  Rita Ernst
  Christoph Freimann
  Karl Gerstner
  Hansjörg Glattfelder
  István Haász
  Renate Kasper
  Julije Knifer
  Adalberto Mecarelli
  Christian Megert
  Manfred Mohr
  François Morellet
  Werner von Mutzenbecher
  Susanna Niederer
  Marta Pan
  François Perrodin
  Axel Rohlfs
  Vera Röhm
  Michael Rouillard
  Sato Satoru
  Maya Stange
  Erwin Steller
  Haruhiko Sunagawa
  Takashi Suzuki
  Geert van Fastenhout
  Thomas Vinson
  Jean-Pierre Viot

Faria

New York
Buenos Aires · Galleries
Kabinett

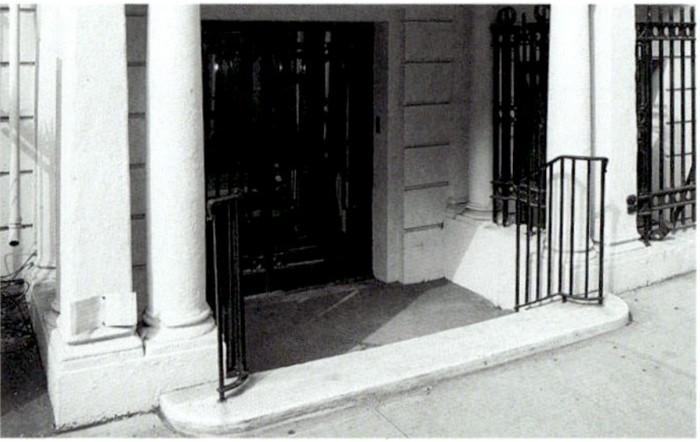

What is your favorite aspect of running a gallery?
Discovering new artists, helping them to develop their career and contextualize their works properly within museums and art history.

How do you choose the artists you work with?
Traveling around the world.

If you weren't running a gallery what else would you do?
I'd probably be running a foundation.

- **Contact** Henrique Faria Fine Art
  Eugenia Sucre
  eugenia@henriquefaria.com
- **Established** 2009
- **Owner(s) / Partner(s)** Henrique Faria
- **Team** 7
- **Space(s)** 230 m²
- **Artists at Art Basel** Alessandro Balteo Yazbeck
  Emilio Chapela
  Carlos Castillo
  Eduardo Costa
  Jaime Davidovich
  José Gabriel Fernández
  Rafael Ferrer
  Anna Bella Geiger
  Carlos Ginzburg
  Leandro Katz
  Marta Minujín
  Luis Molina-Pantin
  Alejandro Puente
  Osvaldo Romberg
  Yeni & Nan
  Horacio Zabala
- **Further artists represented** Emilia Azcárate
  Álvaro Barrios
  Mercedes Elena González
  Terence Gower
  Oswaldo Maciá
  Luis Roldán
  Eduardo Santiere
  Pedro Terán

Feigen

New York — Galleries

- **Contact** Richard L. Feigen & Co.
  John McGill
  jmcgill@rlfeigen.com
- **Established** 1958
- **Owner(s) / Partner(s)** Richard L. Feigen
- **Team** 7

Feuer

New York — Galleries

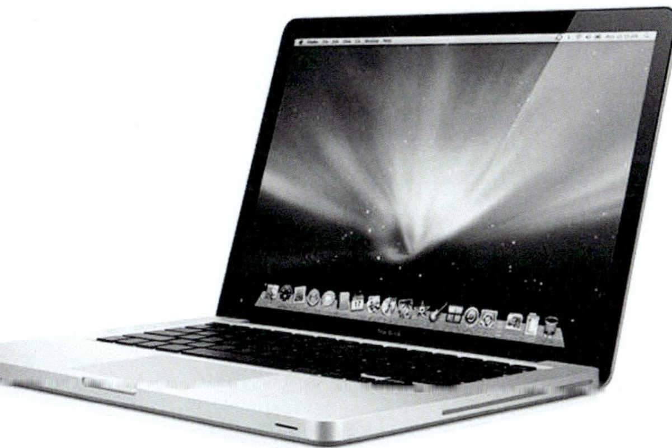

What is your favorite aspect of running a gallery?
Helping artists to realize and present their ideas to a broader public.

If you weren't running a gallery what else would you do?
I would like to be a full-time collector.

- **Contact** Zach Feuer Gallery
  Zach Feuer
  info@zachfeuer.com
- **Established** 2000
- **Owner(s) / Partner(s)** Zach Feuer
- **Team** 5
- **Space(s)** 650.5 m²
- **Artists at Art Basel** Ethan Cook
  Matt Chambers
  N. Dash
  Jeremy Deprez
  Mark Flood
  Zach Harris
  Brad Troemel
  Artie Veirkant
- **Further artists represented** Tamy Ben-Tor
  Sister Corita
  Keren Cytter
  Alistair Frost
  Stuart Hawkins
  Kristen Morgin
  Jon Rafman
  Elaine Reichek
  Kianja Strobert
  Johannes Vanderbeek
  Marianne Vitale
  Phoebe Washburn

Finale

Makati City — Insights

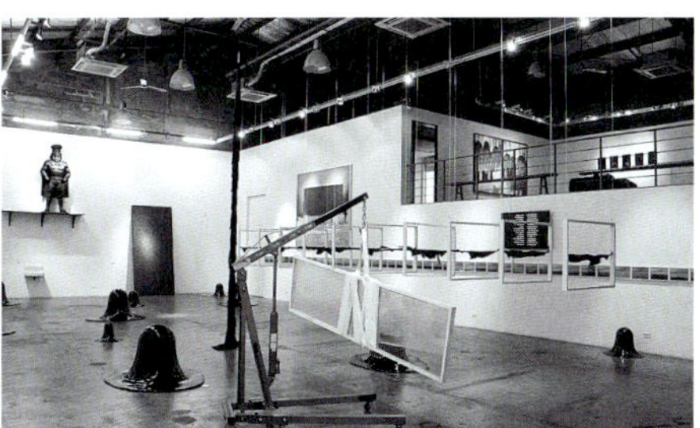

What is your favorite aspect of running a gallery?
The passion and enjoyment of being in the art business and having artists as friends that have kept the gallery going all these years.

How do you choose the artists you work with?
Foremost, we have to like the style of the artist. Then we also look to see if they are promising and have integrity and professionalism.

- **Contact** Finale Art File
  Evita Sarenas
  finaleartfileinc@gmail.com
- **Established** 1983
- **Owner(s) / Partner(s)** Evita Sarenas
- **Team** 12
- **Space(s)** 450 m²
- **Artists at Art Basel** Bembol dela Cruz
- **Further artists represented** Annie Cabigting
  Ranelle Dial
  Carlo Gabuco
  Lyra Garcellano
  Robert Langenegger
  Keiye Miranda
  Redd Nacpil
  Nikki Ocean
  Kim Oliveros
  Ian Quirante
  Wire Tuazon
  Liv Vinluan
  Paulo Vinluan

Fine Arts Literature

Wuhan  Insights

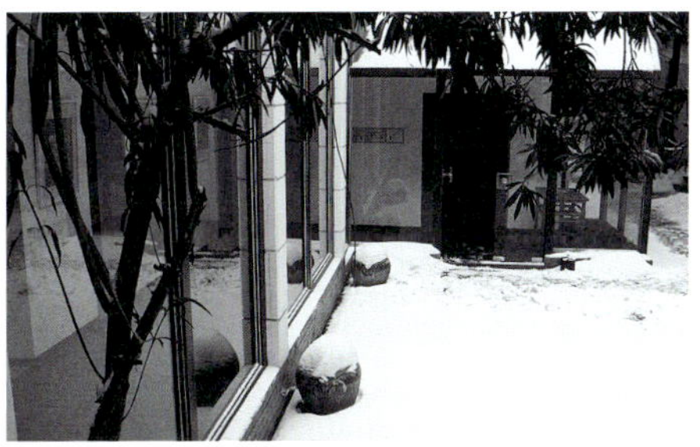

What is your favorite aspect of running a gallery?
As one of the pioneering galleries on Mainland China, we have seen the entire development of Chinese contemporary art. Our favorite aspects are the experiences, resources, and judgments given by history.

How do you choose the artists you work with?
Located in the city of Wuhan, where artists such as Zeng Fanzhi, Wang Qingsong, and a lot of younger artists come from, the gallery has fostered artists who have dominant positions and international influences, and who are also recognized as pioneers for their independent character.

If you weren't running a gallery what else would you do?
When there was no art museum in Wuhan, our gallery played that role. We held exhibitions and published an art magazine, collected artworks, stored documents and archives, and planned public projects, such as lectures on art and art collecting.

F

- **Contact** Fine Arts Literature Art Center
  Shuli Yan
  meishuwenxian@163.com
- **Established** 2003
- **Owner(s) / Partner(s)** Liu Ming
- **Team** 10
- **Space(s)** 800 m²
- **Artists at Art Basel** Hao Shiming
  Liang Quan
  Shi Jinsong
  Zhang Quan
- **Further artists represented** Chen Bo
  Fan Anxiang
  Fu Zhongwang
  Gong Jian
  Jiang Zhilong
  Li Jikai
  Waza Art Group
  Zhu Yamei

Fischer

Düsseldorf
Berlin

Galleries
Unlimited

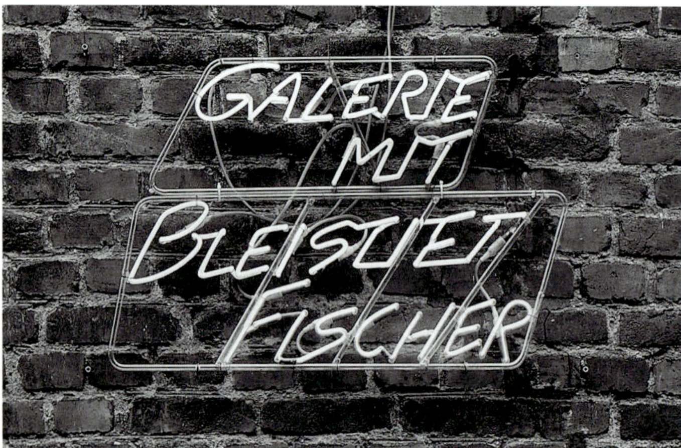

- **Contact** Konrad Fischer Galerie
  Claudia Pasko
  claudia.pasko
  @konradfischergalerie.de
- **Established** 1967
- **Owner(s) / Partner(s)** Dorothee Fischer
- **Team** 6
- **Space(s)** 900 m²
- **Artists at Art Basel** Carl Andre
  Bernd & Hilla Becher
  Stanley Brouwn
  Peter Buggenhout
  Daniel Buren
  Alan Charlton
  Tony Cragg
  Hanne Darboven
  Ilse D'Hollander
  Jan Dibbets
  Hans-Peter Feldmann
  Sofia Hultén
  On Kawara
  Harald Klingelhöller
  Wolfgang Laib
  Richard Long
  Robert Mangold
  Rita McBride
  Mario Merz
  Bruce Nauman
  Giuseppe Penone
  Manfred Pernice
  Wolfgang Plöger
  Charlotte Posenenske
  Thomas Ruff
  Robert Ryman
  Gregor Schneider
  Thomas Schütte
  Juergen Staack
  Paloma Varga Weisz
  Johannes Wald
  Lawrence Weiner
  Jerry Zeniuk
- **Further artists represented** Giovanni Anselmo
  Stephen Antonakos
  Guy Ben-Ner
  Matthew Buckingham
  Gilbert & George
  Zon Ito
  Stephen Klassenbuch
  Melissa Kretschamer
  Jim Lambie
  Sol LeWitt
  Max Neuhaus
  Maria Nordman
  Claes Oldenburg
  & Coosje van Bruggen
  Magnus Plessen
  Yuji Takeoka
  Tatjana Valsang
  Petra Wunderlich

Foksal

Warsaw

Galleries
Galleries

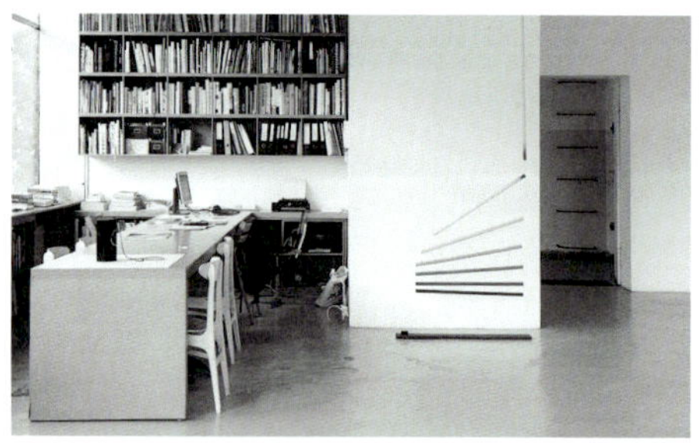

What is your favorite aspect of running a gallery?
Being part of the creative process of executing works and conceiving exhibitions. I especially like the moment just before the opening of a show when everything is done and I can look at the show alone.

How do you choose the artists you work with?
I met most of them in Warsaw in the 1990s and I wanted to help them realize their visions.

If you weren't running a gallery what else would you do?
I would be a Sherpa in the Himalayas.

- **Contact** Foksal Gallery Foundation
  Andrzej Przywara
  mail@fgf.com.pl
- **Established** 1997
- **Owner(s) / Partner(s)** Andrzej Przywara
- **Team** 5
- **Space(s)** 240 m²
- **Artists at Art Basel** Paweł Althamer
  Cezary Bodzianowski
  Piotr Janas
  Katarzyna Józefowicz
  Robert Kuśmirowski
  Edward Krasiński
  Anna Molska
  Anna Niesterowicz
  Paulina Olowska
  Wilhelm Sasnal
  Monika Sosnowska
  Jakub Julian Ziolkowski
  Artur Zmijewski

Fortes Vilaça

São Paulo

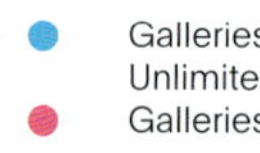

Galleries
Unlimited
Galleries

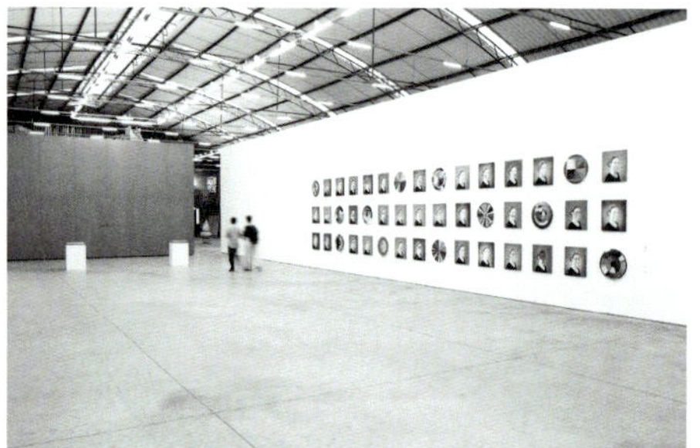

What is your favorite aspect of running a gallery?
Whenever I am in an artist's studio and encounter a work of art that moves me, I feel great pleasure in doing what I do.

How do you choose the artists you work with?
When I sense potential and recognize an unrecognized talent.

If you weren't running a gallery what else would you do?
I would be reading and writing books.

- **Contact** Galeria Fortes Vilaça
Marcia Fortes
galeria@fortesvilaca.com.br
- **Established** 2001
- **Owner(s) / Partner(s)** Marcia Fortes
Alessandra d'Aloia
- **Team** 27
- **Space(s)** 500 m²
- **Artists at Art Basel** Franz Ackermann
Efrain Almeida
Armando Andrade Tudela
Barrão
Carlos Bevilacqua
Leda Catunda
Tiago Carneiro da Cunha
Los Carpinteros
Rodrigo Cass
José Damasceno
Iran do Espírito Santo
Tamar Guimarães
João Maria Gusmão + Pedro Paiva
Marine Hugonnier
Sergej Jensen
Agnieszka Kurant
Lucia Laguna
Jac Leirner
Cristiano Lenhardt
Gabriel Lima
Ivens Machado
Rodrigo Matheus
Beatriz Milhazes
Gerben Mulder
Ernesto Neto
Rivane Neuenschwander
Damián Ortega
Osgemeos
Sara Ramo
Nuno Ramos
Mauro Restiffe
Marina Rheingantz
Michael Sailstorfer
Julião Sarmento
Valeska Soares
Janaina Tschäpe
Adriana Varejão
Erika Verzutti
Cerith Wyn Evans
Luiz Zerbini

Fost

Singapore

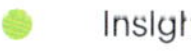 Insights

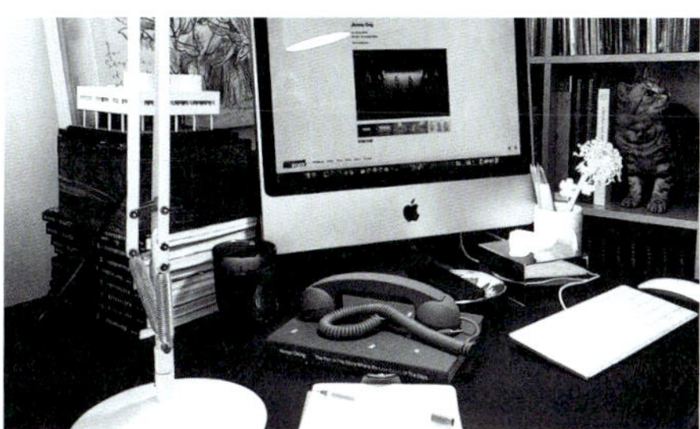

What is your favorite aspect of running a gallery?
I really enjoy visiting my artists' studios. I get a sneak preview of what they have been up to, we discuss and debate new ideas, plan for their next exhibitions. I learn so much from my artists. They are all extremely intelligent and emotive people, and I get to see the world from their perspectives.

How do you choose the artists you work with?
Intuition.

If you weren't running a gallery what else would you do?
I would most likely have been an architect.

- **Contact** Fost Gallery
Stephanie Fong
info@fostgallery.com
- **Established** 2006
- **Owner(s) / Partner(s)** Stephanie Fong
- **Space(s)** 158 m²
- **Artists at Art Basel** Sookoon Ang
- **Further artists represented** Song-Ming Ang
Chun Kaifeng
Heman Chong
Adeel Uz Zafar
Rodney Smith
Jimmy Ong
Phi Phi Oanh
Grace Tan
Wyn-Lyn Tan

Foxx

Los Angeles

Feature
Unlimited
Parcours

What is your favorite aspect of running a gallery?
Marc Foxx: It always has been and always will be making exhibitions with artists. An exhibition is a thing unto itself and can only be truly experienced in person. There is a kind of magic created in a beautifully realized exhibition installation that is not possible to translate.

How do you choose the artists you work with?
There is normally a slow and enjoyable conversation that happens over time and I trust my intuition. There can be a wonderful and special relationship that can exist between an artist and gallery that can make both entities better.

If you weren't running a gallery what else would you do?
I was able to work in many interesting creative places before working in a gallery in 1984, so when I began to work in the art world I knew I was home. I have had to develop so many different skills over my time in the art world I could pretty much do anything at this point.

- **Contact** Marc Foxx Gallery
Katie Tilford
katie@marcfoxx.com
- **Established** 1994
- **Owner(s) / Partner(s)** Marc Foxx
Rodney Nonaka-Hill
- **Team** 4
- **Space(s)** 139.5 m²
- **Artists at Art Basel** Alessandro Pessoli
Guido van der Werve
- **Further artists represented** Leonor Antunes
Cris Brodahl
Anne Collier
Andy Collins
William Daniels
Stef Driesen
Roger Hiorns
Sanya Kantarovsky
Annette Kelm
Makiko Kudo
Luisa Lambri
Kris Martin
Jason Meadows
Carter Mull
David Musgrave
Amalia Pica
Richard Rezac
Matthew Ronay
Maaike Schoorel
Frances Stark
Hiroshi Sugito
Mateo Tannatt
Michael van Ofen
Sophie von Hellermann
Jennifer West
Sam Windett

Fraenkel

San Francisco 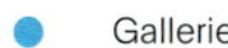 Galleries

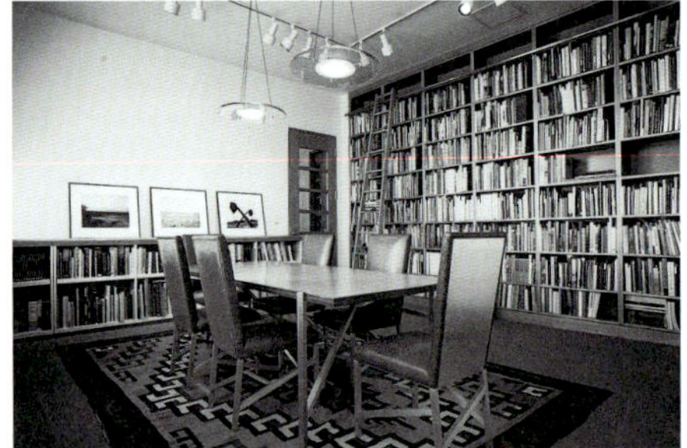

What is your favorite aspect of running a gallery?
Living with great work and helping others do the same.

How do you choose the artists you work with?
"OK Cupid"? No actually. However it is an ineffable process, not unlike choosing one's family …

If you weren't running a gallery what else would you do?
Magic.

- **Contact** Fraenkel Gallery
  Jennifer Larsen
  jlarsen@fraenkelgallery.com
- **Established** 1979
- **Owner(s) / Partner(s)** Jeffrey Fraenkel
  Frish Brandt
- **Team** 19
- **Space(s)** 125.5 m^2
- **Artists at Art Basel** Robert Adams
  Diane Arbus
  Mel Bochner
  Lee Friedlander
  Adam Fuss
  Nan Goldin
  Katy Grannan
  Peter Hujar
  Idris Khan
  Richard Learoyd
  Sol LeWitt
  Christian Marclay
  Ralph Eugene Meatyard
  Richard Misrach
  Nicholas Nixon
  Alec Soth
  Hiroshi Sugimoto
  Garry Winogrand

Fraser

Los Angeles 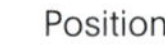 Positions

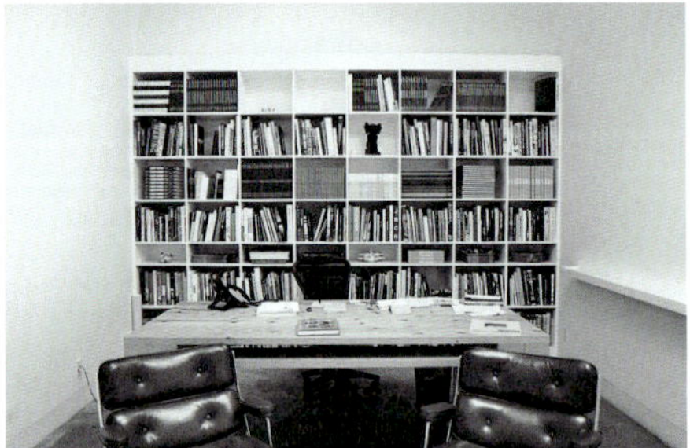

What is your favorite aspect of running a gallery?
I opened a gallery because I wanted to provide a framework within which artists can experiment and present their best work. My favorite thing is that I get to help artists make breakthroughs in their work.

How do you choose the artists you work with?
I try to see as much art as I can in museums, galleries, and studios, as well as at art fairs. I receive recommendations from artists, collectors, and other gallerists, but in the end, I forge long-term relationships with artists who have strong convictions and whose work stays in my thoughts.

If you weren't running a gallery what else would you do?
I can't imagine doing anything else. The artists and the art I work with mean the world to me.

- **Contact** Honor Fraser
  Eden Phair
  eden@honorfraser.com
- **Established** 2006
- **Owner(s) / Partner(s)** Honor Fraser
- **Team** 7
- **Space(s)** 427.5 m^2
- **Artists at Art Basel** Meleko Mokgosi
- **Further artists represented** Jeremy Blake
  Sarah Cain
  Rosson Crow
  Gustavo Godoy
  Tomoo Gokita
  Glenn Kaino
  Tillman Kaiser
  KAWS
  Annie Lapin
  Robert Lazzarini
  Kaz Oshiro
  Erik Parker
  David Ratcliff
  Kenny Scharf
  Alexis Smith
  Phoebe Unwin
  Mario Ybarra Jr.
  Brenna Youngblood

Freedman

London Discoveries

- **Contact** Carl Freedman Gallery
  Robert Diament
  robert@carlfreedman.com
- **Established** 2003
- **Owner** Carl Freedman
- **Team** 5
- **Space(s)** 135 m^2
- **Artists at Art Basel** Billy Childish
  Edith Dekyndt
  Thilo Heinzmann
  Ann Cathrin November Høibo
  John McAllister
  Ivan Seal
  Pieter Vermeersch
- **Further artists represented** Nel Aerts
  Armando Andrade Tudela
  Jessie Flood-Paddock
  Michael Fullerton
  David Brian Smith
  Fergal Stapleton
  Catherine Story
  Sebastian Stöhrer

Freedman Fitzpatrick

Los Angeles Positions

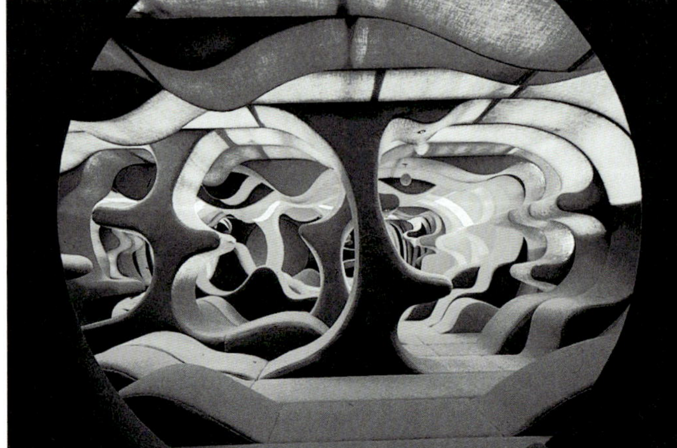

What is your favorite aspect of running a gallery?
Creative liberty.

How do you choose the artists you work with?
Community and passion.

If you weren't running a gallery what else would you do?
Run a bar.

- **Contact** Freedman Fitzpatrick
  Robbie Fitzpatrick
  r@freedmanfitzpatrick.com
- **Established** 2013
- **Owner(s) / Partner(s)** Robbie Fitzpatrick
  Alex Freedman
- **Team** 4
- **Space(s)** 74.5 m²
- **Artists at Art Basel** Lucie Stahl
- **Further artists represented** Mathis Altmann
  Vittorio Brodmann
  Karl Holmqvist
  Matthew Lutz-Kinoy
  Tobias Madison
  Lucie Stahl
  Shimabuku
  Stefan Tcherepnin
  Amelie von Wulffen
  Hannah Weinberger

Freeman

New York
Paris

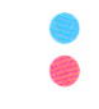

Galleries
Galleries

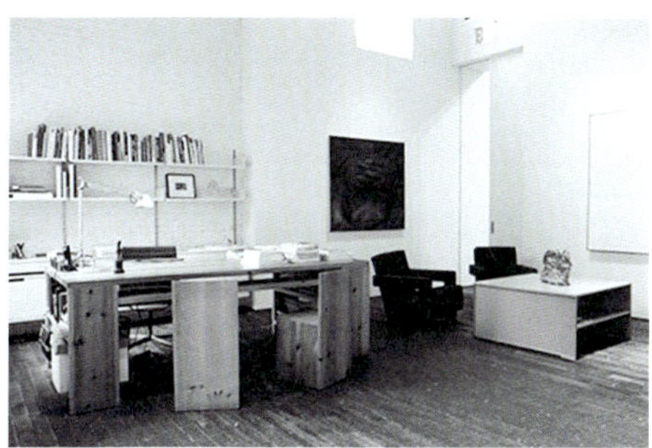

What is your favorite aspect of running a gallery?
The very public activity of making shows, which challenges and adds to a greater dialogue and understanding of what art is, or what history still relates, pushing the understanding of what is possible—all equally as true when presenting shows of new work by gallery artists as when we make historical exhibitions.

How do you choose the artists you work with?
The artists represented by the gallery were always chosen from a belief in their unique voices, that each has a vision that adds something. It then must become our job to support those voices in a meaningful way.

If you weren't running a gallery what else would you do?
Running the gallery brings together a perfect combination of creativity and intellectual challenge that would seem hard to find in most other situations. I would like to believe that the best of what we do makes a difference in the culture and has a meaningful impact on the community—as I am not a scientist or a doctor, I cannot imagine doing anything else that both personally satisfies in the same way and gives back as I hope our activities do.

- **Contact** Peter Freeman Inc.
  Suzanne Imber
  suzanne@peterfreemaninc.com
- **Established** 1990
- **Owner(s) / Partner(s)** Peter Freeman
- **Team** 18
- **Space(s)** 450 m²
- **Artists at Art Basel** David Adamo
  Dove Allouche
  Silvia Bächli
  Mel Bochner
  Pedro Cabrita Reis
  James Castle
  Jan Dibbets
  Robert Filliou
  Josephine Halvorson
  Alex Hay
  Mangelos
  Helen Mirra
  Matt Mullican
  Catherine Murphy
  Charlotte Posenenske
  Thomas Schütte
  Lucy Skaer
  Franz Erhard Walther
  James Welling
  Richard Wentworth

Friedman

London

Galleries
Galleries

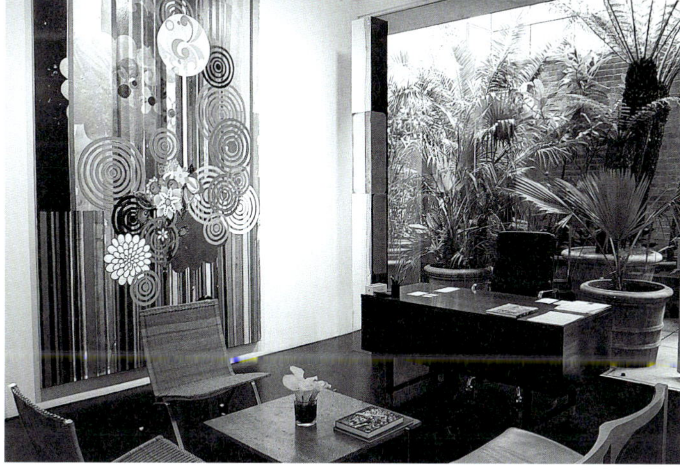

What is your favorite aspect of running a gallery?
We are celebrating our 20-year anniversary next year and many of the artists we represent today have been with us almost from the beginning. It is a joy to watch our artists and their careers evolve and flourish over the years. I am constantly astonished and impressed by the work they produce and in their ability to push boundaries. For me, guiding and supporting each artist through this process is the most gratifying aspect of running a gallery.

How do you choose the artists you work with?
I do not have specific criteria when choosing artists to work with, which explains the diversity of our program. The work has to appeal to me instinctively. I then discuss the artist with my gallery directors and discerning colleagues. For each artist or estate I decide to work with, there is an extremely considered approach, which usually takes place over some time. I also need to have a personal engagement with that artist; a good dynamic is essential in forming a fruitful relationship.

If you weren't running a gallery what else would you do?
Art is my first and foremost passion. Food follows close behind. I enjoy recommending restaurants to friends and colleagues and hosting small dinners. Each of these meals entails detailed consideration of the food and atmosphere. And there is always, always a seating plan. I think my friends would suggest I become a food critic.

- **Contact** Stephen Friedman Gallery
  info@stephenfriedman.com
- **Established** 1995
- **Owner(s) / Partner(s)** Stephen Friedman
- **Team** 20
- **Space(s)** 327 m²
- **Artists at Art Basel** Mamma Andersson
  Juan Araujo
  Tonico Lemos Auad
  Stephan Balkenhol
  Claire Barclay
  Huma Bhabha
  Robert Buck
  Melvin Edwards
  Andreas Eriksson

Manuel Espinosa
Tom Friedman
Kendell Geers
Wayne Gonzales
Daniel Guzmán
Thomas Hirschhorn
Jim Hodges
Judith Lauand
Li Tianbing
Paul McDevitt
Beatriz Milhazes
Yoshitomo Nara
Rivane Neuenschwander
Thomas Nozkowski
Catherine Opie
Cornelius Quabeck
Ged Quinn
Jennifer Rubell
Yinka Shonibare MBE
David Shrigley
Jiro Takamatsu
Anne Truitt
Kehinde Wiley

Friese

Stuttgart ● Feature

- **Contact** Galerie Klaus Gerrit Friese
  Klaus Gerrit Friese
  kunst@galeriefriese.de
- **Owner(s) / Partner(s)** Klaus Gerrit Friese

Frith Street

London ● Galleries

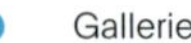

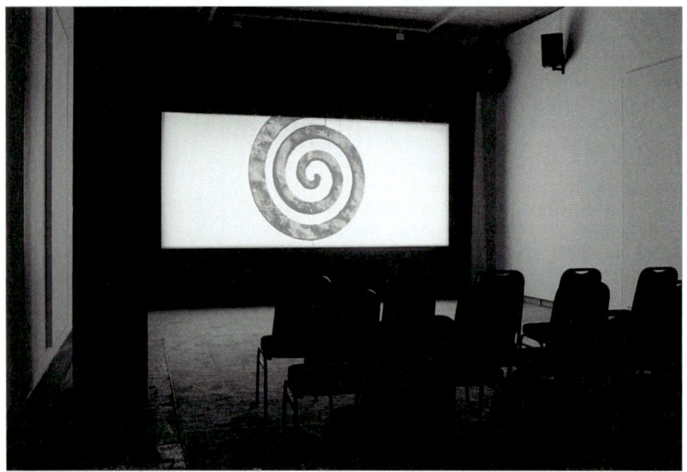

- **Contact** Frith Street Gallery
  Cornelia Behr
  cornelia@frithstreetgallery.com
- **Established** 1989
- **Owner(s) / Partner(s)** Jane Hamlyn
- **Team** 13
- **Space(s)** 324.7 m²
- **Artists at Art Basel** Polly Apfelbaum
  Fiona Banner
  Anna Barriball
  Massimo Bartolini
  Ingrid Calame
  Dorothy Cross
  Tacita Dean
  Marlene Dumas
  Callum Innes
  Jaki Irvine
  Cornelia Parker
  Raqs Media Collective
  John Riddy
  Thomas Schütte
  Dayanita Singh
  Bridget Smith
  Fiona Tan
  Juan Uslé
  Daphne Wright

Fuentes

New York ● Survey

- **Contact** James Fuentes
  James Michael Shaeffer
  jms@jamesfuentes.com
- **Established** 2007
- **Owner(s) / Partner(s)** James Fuentes
- **Team** 3
- **Space(s)** 214 m²
- **Artists at Art Basel** Alison Knowles
  Amalia Ulman
- **Further artists represented** Joshua Abelow
  Jonathan Allmaier
  Lizzi Bougatsos
  Brian Degraw
  Jessica Dickinson
  Berta Fischer
  Lonnie Holley
  John McAllister
  Jonas Mekas
  Landon Metz
  Noam Rappaport
  Benjamin Senior
  William Stone
  Daniel Subkoff

Foksal Gallery Foundation
Interview with Andrzej Przywara

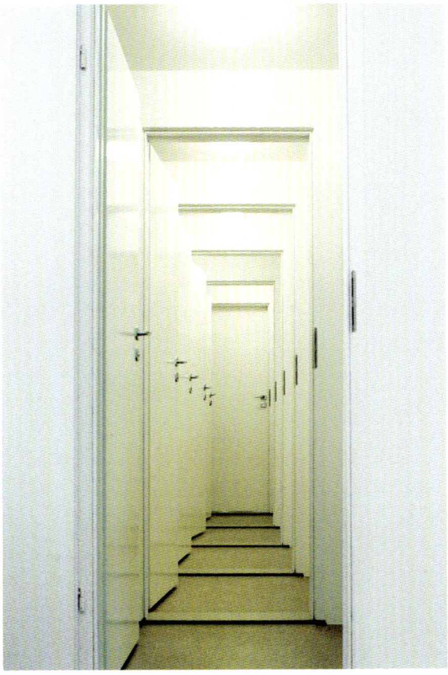

Monika Sosnowska, *Entrance*, 2003, Art Statement, Art Basel, 2003

Foksal Gallery in Warsaw has a long history, beginning in the 1960s. Could you retrace it?

I would like to start by making an important distinction between Foksal Gallery, which is an established non-commercial institution, and Foksal Gallery Foundation, which has a commercial activity. Foksal Gallery was founded in 1966 by a group of artists and art critics on a similar model to Western European galleries, but without the idea of a market. One can compare it to off-spaces today. The founders were Henryk Stażewski, a Constructivist painter, who in 1927 had co-organized the first Malevich show in Warsaw, and a group of young critics—Wiesław Borowski, Anka Ptaszkowska, and Mariusz Tchorek—as well as other artists: Edward Krasiński, Zbigniew Gostomski, and later Tadeusz Kantor. They established channels of exchange with many artists in Western Europe and later also in America. During Communism, Poland was relatively well connected. There was freedom—up to a certain point that was never clearly defined. Communists didn't really care about the visual arts: censorship was much tougher in literature, cinema, and theater.

One of the landmarks in the history of the gallery was when Foksal was invited to Lausanne to participate in the Salon des galeries-pilotes in 1969, and which was repeated a year later in Paris. It resulted in the breakup of the founding group, as Anka Ptaszkowska stayed in Paris and continued to work there. The breakup was also due to a difference of opinion about how the gallery should function: Anka was proposing to move in the direction of Situationism, transforming the gallery into a space of pure information exchange, while Kantor wanted to go on inviting artists to make exhibitions.

So the second period of the gallery started in the 1970s, with exhibitions by Lawrence Weiner, Christian Boltanski, Annette Messager. There was an important focus on environment, installation works, and unique publications. I started to work there at the end of the 1980s; it was a time of transformation, from Socialism to market economy, and in the 1990s, together with Joanna Mytkowska and Adam Szymczyk, I became active as a curator. We introduced new artists, such as Mirosław Bałka, Franz West, Luc Tuymans. Later also Gregor Schneider, Tom Friedman, and Douglas Gordon. At the end of the 1990s, a new generation emerged in Poland, with Paweł Althamer, Wilhelm Sasnal, Monika Sosnowska, Paulina Ołowska, etc. In 1997 we decided to establish the Foksal Gallery Foundation. At the end of the 1990s, there were two structures operating at the original location: the old Foksal Gallery and the Foundation. At the beginning, we tried to support the activities of the gallery through the Foundation. Step by step we started to act independently. In 2000 the Foksal Gallery Foundation began participating in art fairs, the first one being Liste in Basel. In 2001 the Foundation moved to a new space and parted ways with the Foksal Gallery.

Your first participation in Art Basel was with Monika Sosnowska in 2003.

It was at Art Statement and we got the Baloise Art Prize. That year Adam Szymczyk left the gallery to work as Director of the Kunsthalle Basel. Soon Joanna Mytkowska also left the gallery to work as curator for the Centre Georges Pompidou. I continued the program, focused on a group of Polish artists with whom we started in the 1990s. We also began to work with estates, including the studio of Edward Krasiński, to which we added a glass pavilion extension. There we established the Avant-garde Institute with a regular program of exhibitions and lectures open to the public.

In your booth in Art Basel in 2014 you exhibited early sculptures by Krasiński from the 1960s. Could you tell us more about them?

They were a recent and completely unexpected discovery. Three years ago, the artist's daughter, who lives in a house Krasiński used to live in the 1960s, renovated the roof and found some early sculptures in the attic. After carrying out research and restoration, I presented the whole set in the gallery, and MoMA acquired a number of important pieces. Krasiński's family wishes that his work be represented in good museums in Poland and introduced into prominent collections abroad. These works are from the period when he moved from the Surrealist paintings and drawings into abstraction and the spatial constructions he called *Interventions*. These objects expanded the notion of painting and addressed the site through the use of his trademark blue tape, marking both his works and the locations where they were installed resulting in a total *mise-en-scène*.

How would you define the Polish art scene today?

It's strong and dynamic on the institutional level—we have very prominent institutions like the Muzeum Sztuki in Łódź, founded in the 1930s, with a great collection of Modern art. In Warsaw there is the Zachęta National Gallery of Art, a Kunsthalle with a very good program; the Center for Contemporary Art founded at the end of the 1980s; and the Museum of Modern Art—a new institution still under construction.

So, in Poland, there is a strong institutional scene. What about the commercial one?

It has only just begun. In the 1990s there were some galleries, but to represent artists, build a career, sell works, is still something new. In Warsaw, originally, we were not dealers, we started as art critics or curators, and we saw the international art market as a way to get visibility for the artists. We used to operate locally with a very small market. But over the years it grew and now it's a different situation. It's almost in fashion to open a gallery now! There are two Polish galleries in the main fair in Basel and three in Liste. The art scene in Poland has potential. The economy is growing and in recent years Warsaw has developed a lot, the public infrastructure has improved, and new investment keeps flowing in. There is energy and a very special kind of attraction that makes many people move to Warsaw and work here.

Art Basel in Basel, 2014

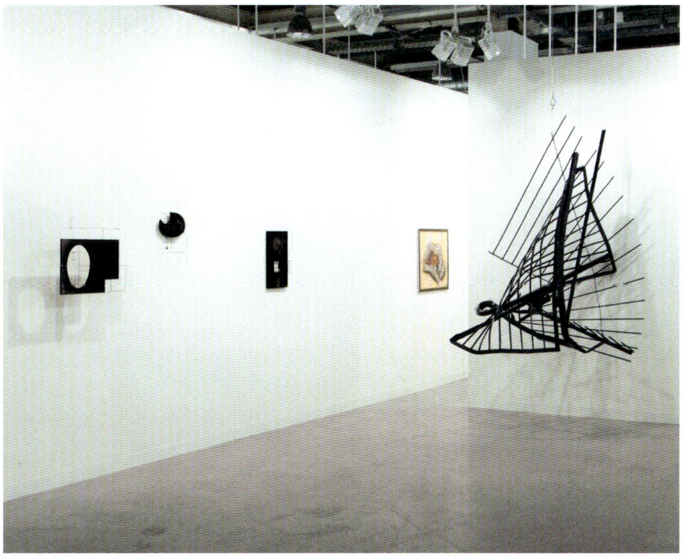

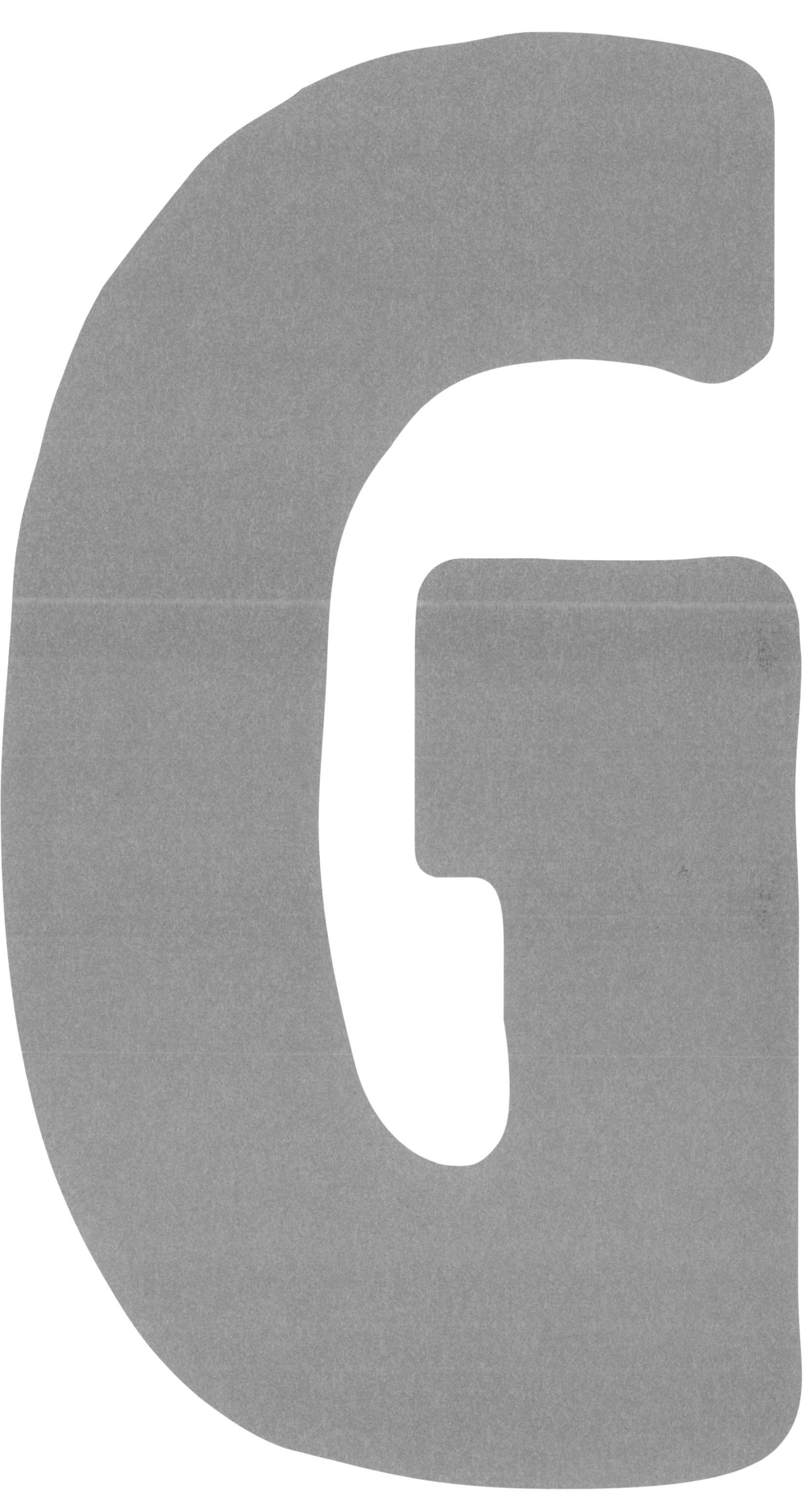

GIVING

Art Basel Crowdfunding Initiative

BACK

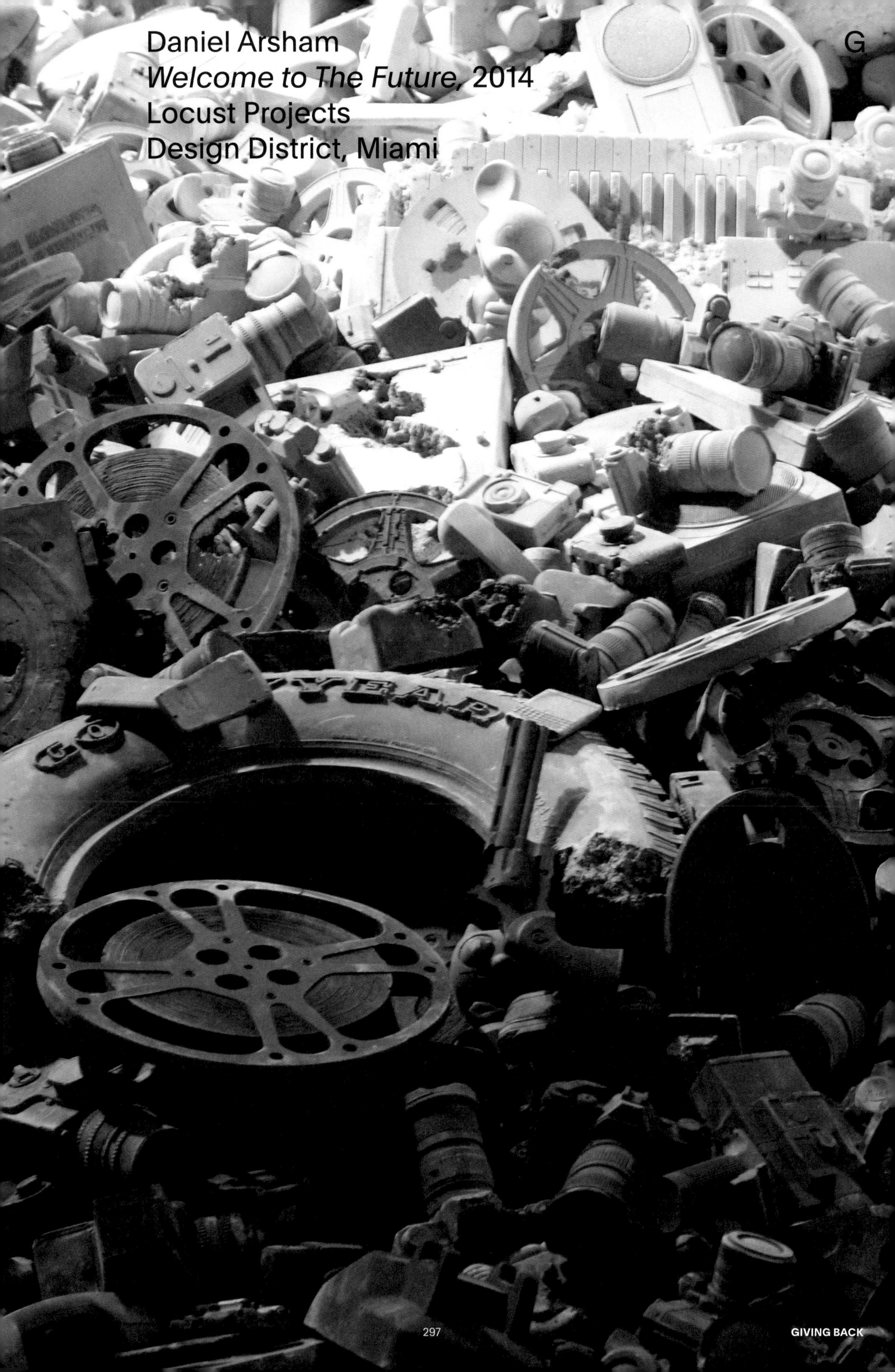

Daniel Arsham
Welcome to The Future, 2014
Locust Projects
Design District, Miami

G

In September 2014, Art Basel launched a new digital initiative in partnership with Kickstarter, the fundraising platform for creative projects. Designed specifically for non-profit visual arts organizations from around the world, the initiative offers visibility and support to a wide variety of artistic projects, selected by an independent jury. In the first few months of its existence, 8 projects selected for Art Basel's Crowdfunding Initiative have been successfully funded and have raised a total of USD 191,272 from over 969 backers (as December 15, 2014).

For updated information and to support projects from the global art community, visit artbasel.com/crowdfunding and kickstarter.com/artbasel.

The following quotes are excerpted from the Conversation held at Art Basel in Miami Beach, December 4, 2014, moderated by András Szántó and with the participation of: Glenn Phillips; Mary Ceruti, Executive Director and Chief Curator, SculptureCenter, New York; Mari Spirito; Chana Bugdazad Sheldon, Executive Director at Locust Projects, Miami; Aaron Cezar, Director of Delfina Foundation, London; and Stephanie Pereira, International Partnerships, Lead at Kickstarter, New York.

Art Basel and Kickstarter have joined forces to catalyze much-needed support for outstanding non-commercial art projects. This new initiative presents jury-selected art projects to a global community of potential benefactors, including Art Basel's audience and Kickstarter's community, who have pledged over $1 billion to creative projects to date. The goal is to support non-profit visual arts organizations—at a time when public funding for the arts has been dwindling—by sharing their stories, generating contributions, and reaching out to new audiences. Along with art galleries, non-profit visual arts organizations such as museums, Kunsthallen, art schools, and digital art platforms drive the art world forward by nurturing and supporting artists. Many of these organizations are small and struggle to obtain both funding and visibility. By tapping into a global network, crowdfunding can provide valuable exposure for the non-profit visual arts organizations by sharing experiences, generating support, and building a community.

The Art Basel Crowdfunding Initiative is designed for projects that strengthen the ecology of contemporary art practice, including artists' residencies, educational programs, publications, public art projects, and other initiatives that art organizations undertake in conjunction with their programming. Selected projects in the field of visual arts have artistic merit and are capable of attracting the interest of other artists, critics, curators, and the broader audience for contemporary art.

Each organization applying to Art Basel's Crowfunding Initiative is reviewed and selected by an independent jury comprised of the following experts: Hammad Nasar, Curator, Writer and Head of Research and Programmes at Asia Art Archive, Hong Kong; Glenn Phillips, Acting Head of the Department of Architecture and Contemporary Art at the Getty Research Institute, Los Angeles; Mari Spirito, Founding Director of Protocinema, Istanbul and New York.

Everyone is looking everywhere for alternative ways to engage, to raise support, awareness, and funding.
—Glenn Phillips

Projects are selected for their overall quality, innovation, creativity, and viability, representing the strength and diversity of non-profit arts organizations worldwide. Applications must be from the field of the visual arts, endorsed by a non-profit organization, and not be aimed at the art market.

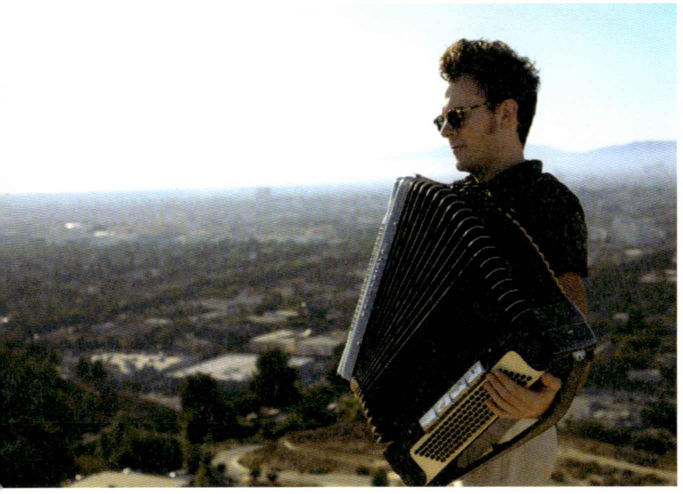

SASSAS

The SASSAS (Society for the Activation of Social Space through Art and Sound) is an organization that produces concerts recontextualizing sound and place in the greater Los Angeles area. Their successful campaign enabled them to host a concert of contemporary sound works in the hills of Greater Los Angeles.

Art Basel's Crowdfunding Initiative creates a huge amount of exposure and dialogue and will create other opportunies for other fundraising for the non-profit organizations thanks to the visibility you get for the brand, for the project.
—Mari Spirito

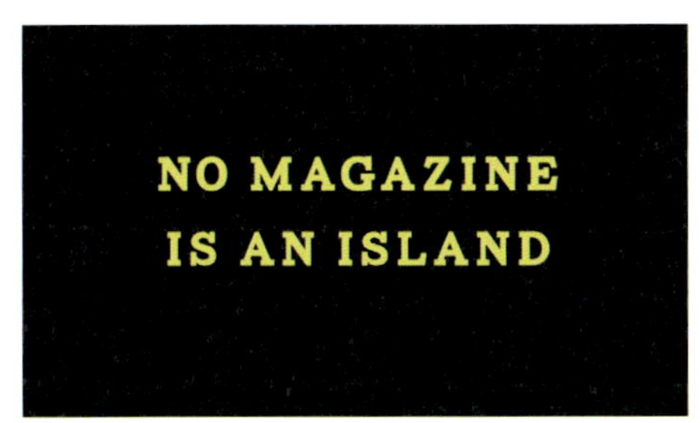

East of Borneo

After being operational for five years, this online magazine of contemporary art and its history from a Los Angeles perspective is planning a highly anticipated relaunch that will enhance user experience, add features, and increase access. Its Art Basel Crowdfunding Initiative is making this possible.

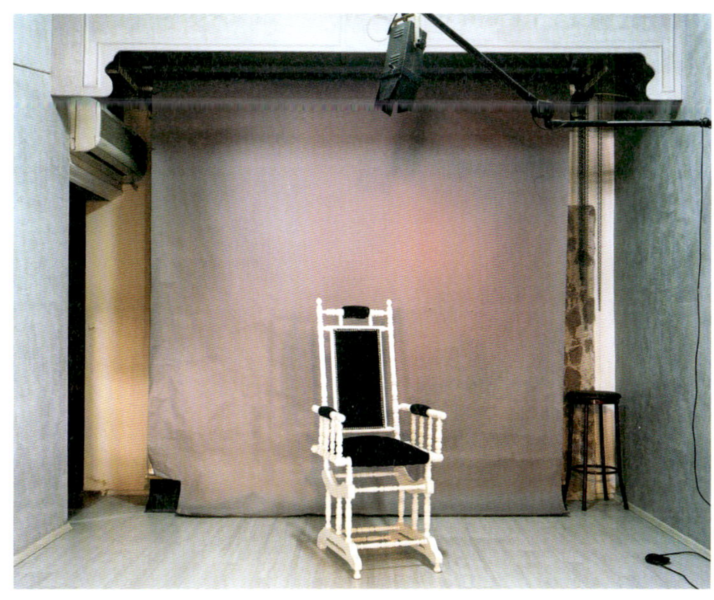

The Mosaic Rooms

The London-based cultural space presents contemporary culture from the Arab world and successfully launched a campaign to publish a book by Syrian artist Hrair Sarkissian that reflects on the disappearing tradition of studio portraiture in the Middle East.

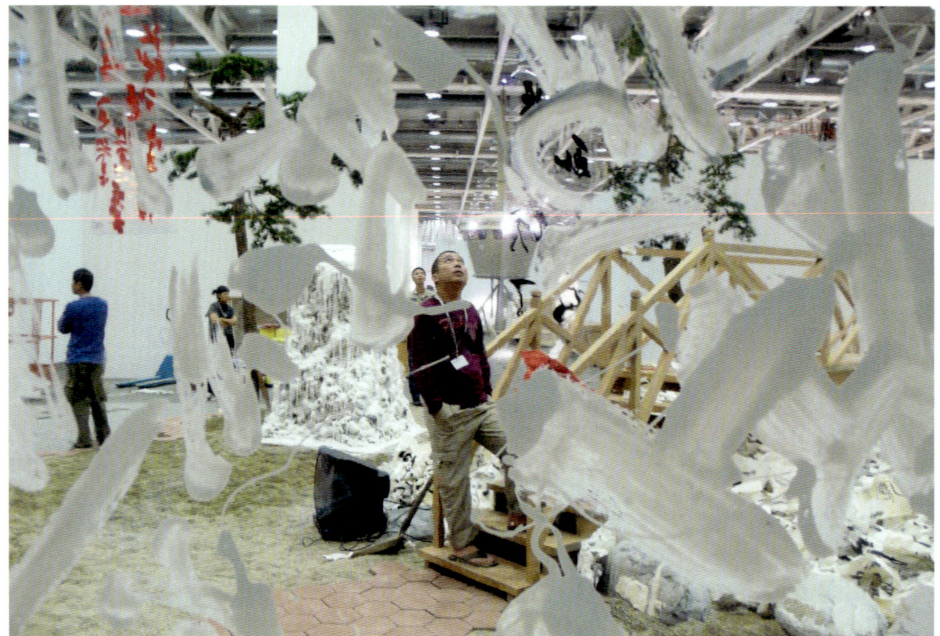

4A Centre for Contemporary Asian Art

An organization dedicated to Asian-Australian contemporary art, based in Sydney's Chinatown, 4A offers artistic programs that contribute to critical curatorial discussion through the internationalization of the Asian art discourse. Thanks to the Crowdfunding Initiative, 4A staged *Actions for Tomorrow* by the Chinese art collective Yangjiang Group in the city's Chinatown neighborhood. The project pushes the boundaries of traditional Chinese calligraphy by exploring ideas of collective action through large-scale architectural constructions, video projections, and public performances.

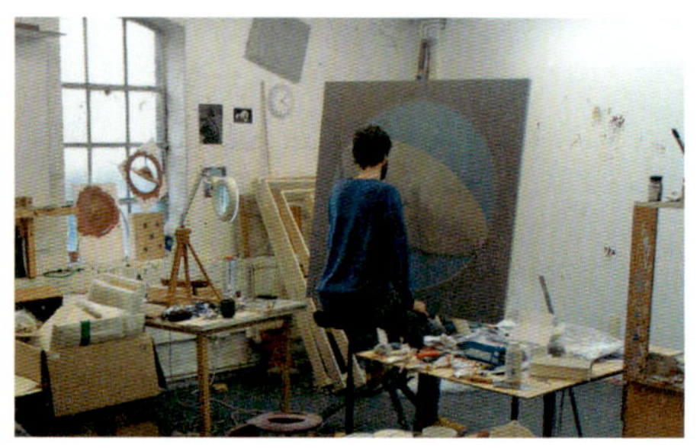

Gasworks

A London-based organization that promotes the exchange of ideas between international and local artists through exhibitions and residencies in London and at partner organizations in Cuba, China, South Africa, Kenya, and India. Thanks to its Art Basel Crowdfunding Initiative, they will be constructing additional studios for emerging artists in South London.

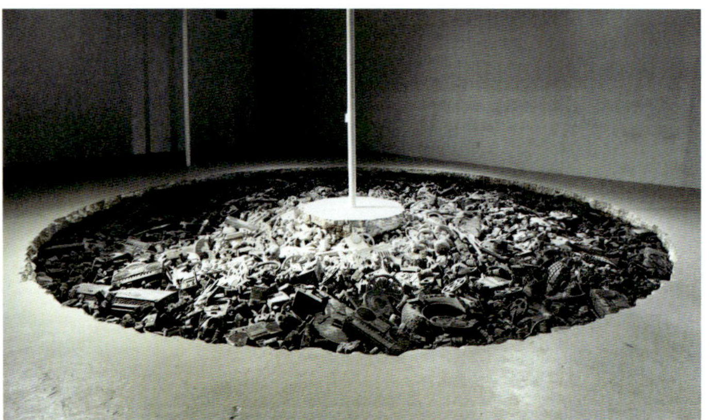

Locust Projects

Founded in 1998, Miami's longest-running alternative art space has a mission to provide contemporary visual artists the freedom to experiment with new ideas. Thanks to its Art Basel Crowdfunding Initiative, Locust Projects produced a major installation with acclaimed sculptor Daniel Arsham that was on view in the space in Miami's Design District during Art Basel in Miami Beach 2014.

Non-profit art organizations are the life blood of the art world. No artist, no gallery, no museum person, no collector who is here would be here if there was not this much wider world of quite small, good non-profit art initiatives.
—András Szántó

Every single artist showing at Art Basel can name a small non-profit that has been very important for his/her career, giving him/her support at a crucial time.
—Glenn Phillips

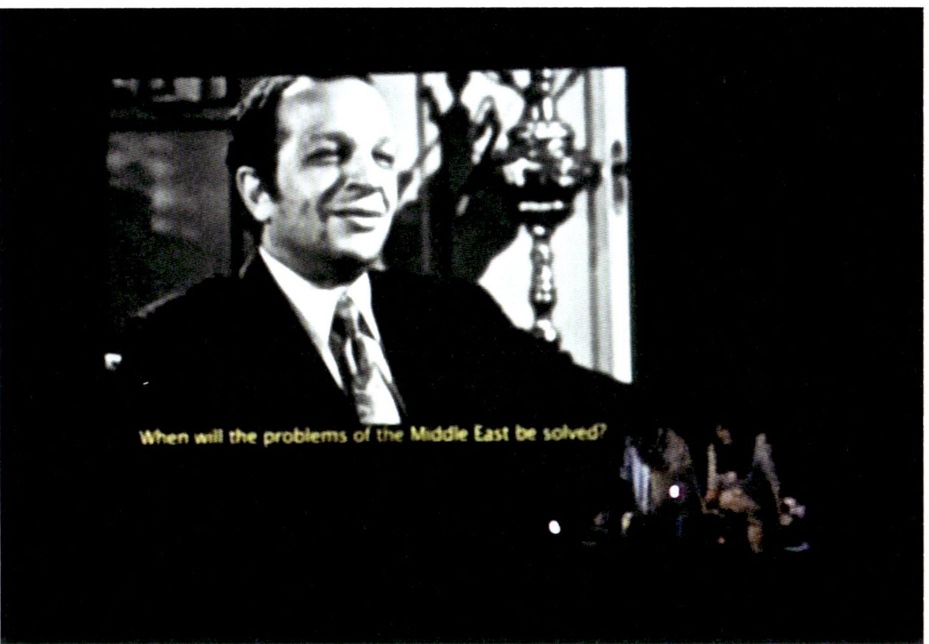

Delfina Foundation

An independent organization that facilitates artistic exchange and develops creative practice through residencies, partnerships, and public programming, Delfina has been working with the Arab region through its renowned residency program for the last seven years. Thanks to its Art Basel Crowdfunding Initiative, it is now staging a groundbreaking exhibition on the little-known history of performance art in the Arab world through rare archives and new contemporary artworks.

Is it a transaction? It is a relationship? That is the question. And when does a transaction become a relationship? We hope it is a long-term relationship and people who gave will come to the show.
—Mary Ceruti

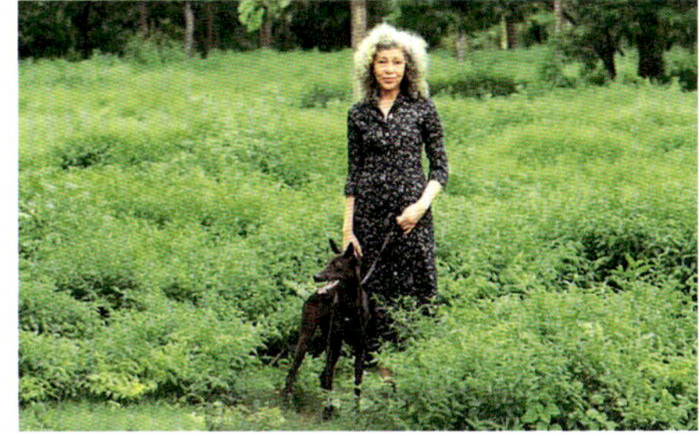

SculptureCenter

New York City's only contemporary art museum dedicated to sculpture, as well as New York's oldest artist-run space, SculptureCenter has provided thousands of artists with outstanding opportunities, including production support and wide-reaching recognition. Thanks to its Art Basel Crowdfunding Initiative, SculptureCenter will restore and present video works by Thai artist Araya Rasdjarmrearnsook for public view in 2015, during her first United States museum survey.

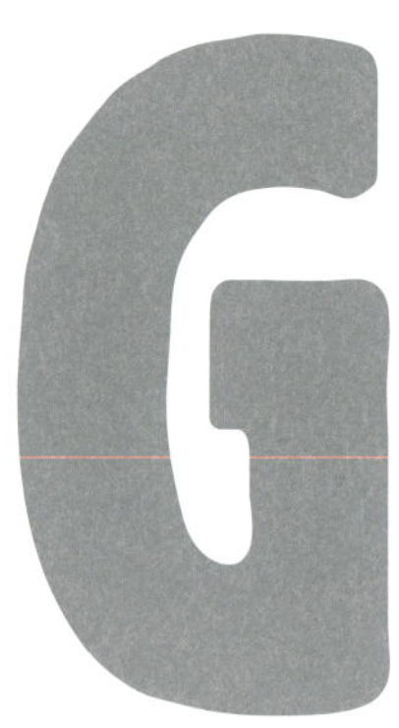

Gagosian

New York
Beverly Hills
London
Paris
Rome
Athens
Geneva
Hong Kong
Le Bourget

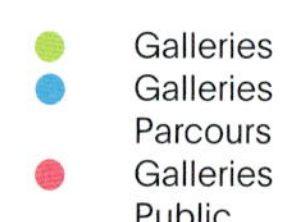

Galleries
Galleries
Parcours
Galleries
Public

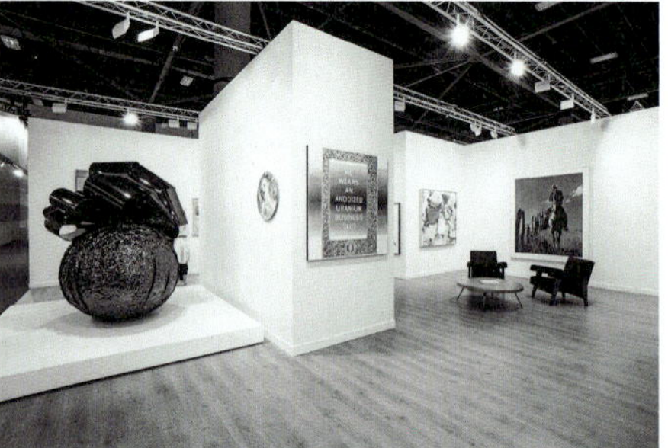

- **Contact** Gagosian Gallery
  newyork@gagosian.com
- **Established** 1979
- **Owner(s) / Partner(s)** Larry Gagosian
- **Team** Approx. 200
- **Space(s)** 14,400 m²

Gajah

Singapore  Galleries

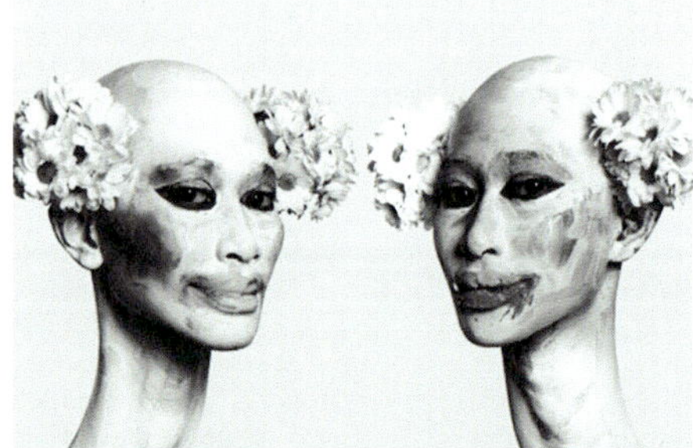

What is your favorite aspect of running a gallery?

First, it would be working with artists to develop their practice and their repertoire.

Second, participating in art fairs and showcasing both veteran and emerging artists. It's hard work, but at the end of the day, it's worth it.

How do you choose the artists you work with?

Basically, if I can connect with their work on various levels, intellectually and emotionally. On certain occasions, when a relationship or friendship can be established. Lastly, when I see potential for their work to be collected locally and internationally.

If you weren't running a gallery what else would you do?

Open a prata shop or be a farmer in Indonesia.

- **Contact** Gajah Gallery
  Tessa Wong
  tessa@gajahgallery.com
- **Established** 1996
- **Owner(s) / Partner(s)** Jasdeep Sandhu
- **Team** 4
- **Space(s)** 176.5 m²
- **Artists at Art Basel** Ahmad Zakii Anwar
  Ashley Bickerton
  Gu Gan
  Gu Wenda
  Handiwirman Saputra
  Jumaldi Alfi
  Li Jin
  Jason Lim
  Mangu Putra
  Qiu Deshu
  Teng Nee Cheong
  Ugo Untoro
  Wang Tiande
  Wei Ligang
  Yunizar
  Yusra Martunus

Galleria dello Scudo

Verona  Galleries

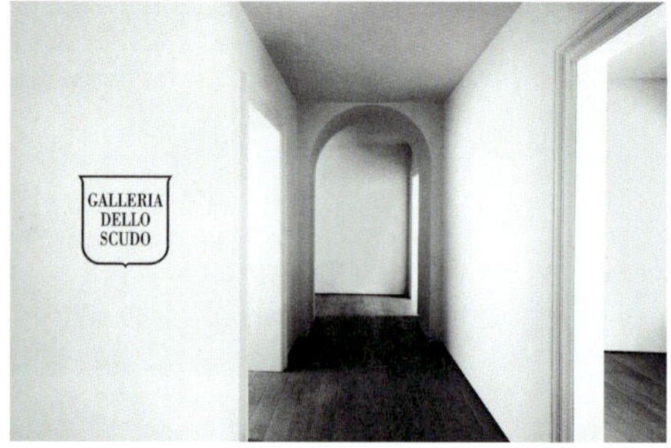

What is your favorite aspect of running a gallery?

Knowing we can help to shape the taste of collectors who are increasingly sensitive to those historical-cultural and aesthetic dynamics that are the basis of the values of the artists the gallery believes in.

How do you choose the artists you work with?

The artists are chosen because they follow the classical line of Italian art.

If you weren't running a gallery what else would you do?

Be a lawyer.

- **Contact** Galleria dello Scudo
  Massimo Di Carlo
  info@galleriadelloscudo.com
- **Established** 1968
- **Owner(s) / Partner(s)** Massimo Di Carlo
  Ettore Kovarich
  Laura Lorenzoni
- **Team** 5
- **Space(s)** 300 m²
- **Artists at Art Basel** Afro
  Alberto Burri
  Pietro Consagra
  Giorgio de Chirico
  Piero Dorazio
  Lucio Fontana
  Leoncillo
  Piero Manzoni
  Fausto Melotti
  Giorgio Morandi
  Gastone Novelli
  Antonio Sanfilippo
  Salvatore Scarpitta
  Toti Scialoja
  Tancredi
  Emilio Vedova
- **Further artists represented** Giacomo Balla
  Umberto Boccioni
  Giuseppe Capogrossi
  Carlo Carrà
  Marino Marini
  Amedeo Modigliani
  Giuseppe Santomaso
  Alberto Savinio
  Gino Severini

Gandhara

Hong Kong
Karachi

Galleries

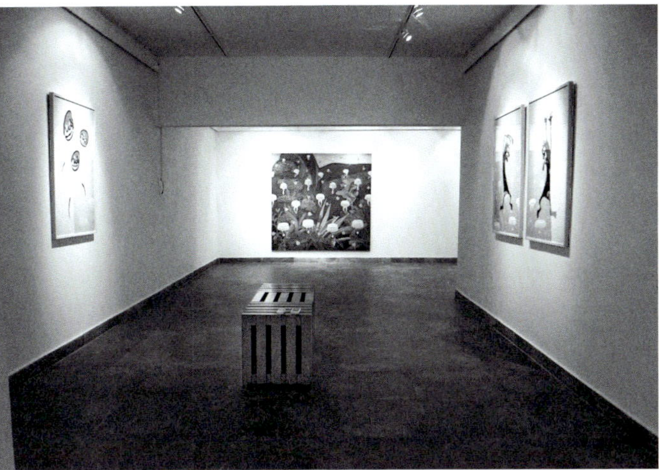

What is your favorite aspect of running a gallery?

I think working with artists is my favorite aspect of running a gallery. Artists are hardwired in a distinct manner and I am privileged to be working with them and seeing the process toward the creation of a work of art.

How do you choose the artists you work with?

The artwork is what draws me to a particular artist. It has been "blink" decisions until now, but I have not been disappointed.

If you weren't running a gallery what else would you do?

I would have been an archaeologist or an investment banker.

- **Contact** Gandhara-Art
  Amna Naqvi
  amna.naqvi@gandhara-art.com
- **Established** 2005
- **Owner(s) / Partner(s)** Amna Naqvi
- **Team** 6
- **Space(s)** 279 m²
- **Artists at Art Basel** Khadim Ali
  Noor Ali Chaghani
  Aisha Khalid
  Imran Qureshi
  Adeel Uz Zafar
- **Further artists represented** Atif Khan
  Attiya Shaukat
  Saira Wasim

Gavlak

Los Angeles
Palm Beach

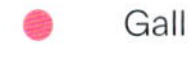

Galleries

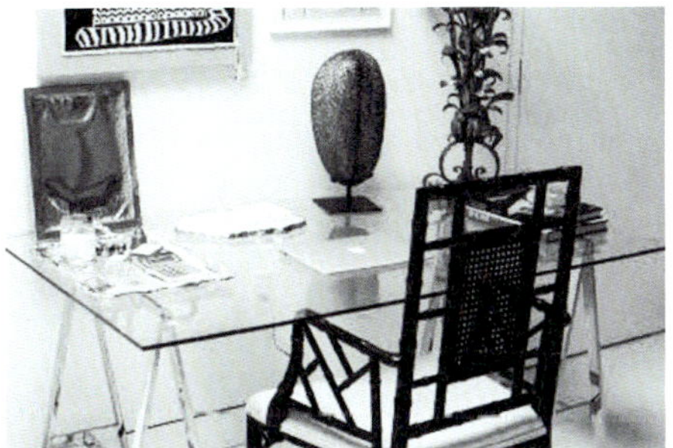

What is your favorite aspect of running a gallery?

Working with the artists.

How do you choose the artists you work with?

All of the artists I work with have an interest in the actual "craft" of what they are creating, be it a painting, photograph, ceramic, film, or sculpture. That the work is well made is as important to them as the ideas behind the work. There is also an interest in beauty, pleasure, desire, art history, and enlightenment.

If you weren't running a gallery what else would you do?

I would be a curator of 18th-century decorative arts or Old Masters works on paper.

- **Contact** Gavlak Gallery
  Sarah Gavlak
  sarah@gavlakgallery.com
- **Established** 2005
- **Owner(s) / Partner(s)** Sarah Gavlak
- **Team** 5
- **Space(s)** 604 m²
- **Artists at Art Basel** Jose Alvarez
  Lisa Anne Auerbach
  Andrew Brischler
  Lecia Dole-Recio
  Judith Eisler
  David Haxton
  Michael John Kelly
  Bovey Lee
  Simone Leigh
  Aaron Sandnes
  Vincent Szarek
  Betty Tompkins
  Brian Wills
  T.J. Wilcox
  Rob Wynne
  Bunny Yeager
- **Further artists represented** Judy Bamber
  Florence Derive
  Phillip Estlund
  Elisabeth Kley
  Marilyn Minter
  David McDermott & Peter McGough
  Jack Pierson
  Scott Reeder
  Alexis Teplin

Gazelli

London
Baku

Discoveries

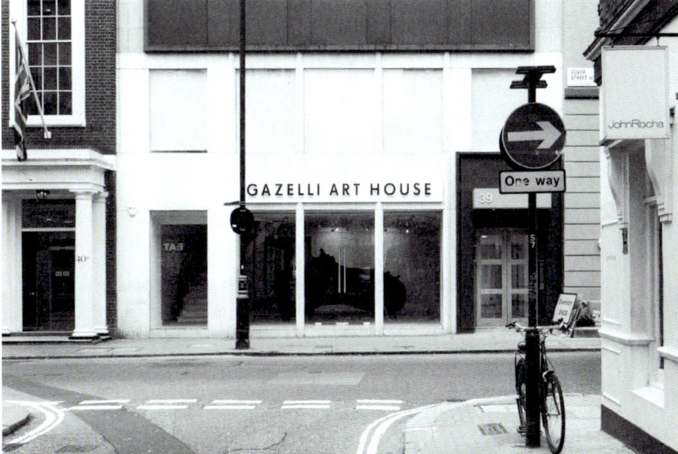

What is your favorite aspect of running a gallery?

It is a creative hub—a constant learning environment. The artists we work with, the audience interacting with the exhibitions, and each member of the gallery team all provide their own input, feeding into this platform that inspires us in turn to grow both on an individual level and collectively.

How do you choose the artists you work with?

It is a combination of instinctive decision-making and a rational thought-process that ties either a specific body of work or an artist's whole oeuvre to a curatorial direction of the gallery (no matter how general it is).

If you weren't running a gallery what else would you do?

Think of how I could be running a gallery. There is no backup plan and never has been!

- **Contact** Gazelli Art House
Sydney Townsend
sydney@gazelliarthouse.com
- **Established** 2003
- **Owner(s) / Partner(s)** Mila Askarova
- **Artists at Art Basel** Walter Hugo & Zoniel
- **Further artists represented** Aron Demetz
Aziz + Cucher
Giovanni Ozzola
Jane McAdam Freud
Khanlar Gasimov
Niyaz Najafov
Saad Qureshi
Shan Hur
Stanley Casselman

gb agency

Paris

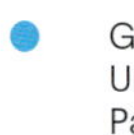

Galleries
Unlimited
Parcours

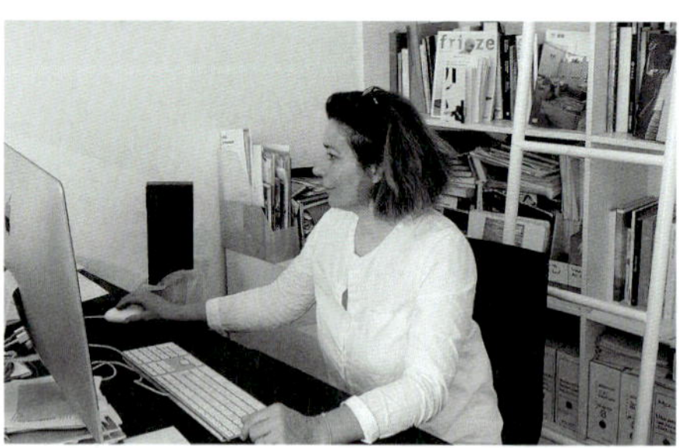

What is your favorite aspect of running a gallery?

We love the freedom offered by running a gallery, allowing us to follow artists in a long-term relationship, as well as imagining projects, shows, and events related to them. A gallery is the ideal place for meeting people passionate about art, sharing ideas with curators, dreaming with artists, and welcoming audiences.

How do you choose the artists you work with?

We always fall in love with works of art first, and then comes the time to research and engage with the artist. Choosing an artist is based on a strong relationship, trust, and mutual respect. We do not care about medium, age, nationality, but rather about singularity, a free mind, and creative exploration.

If you weren't running a gallery what else would you do?

Creating a gallery was not predestined: we would have loved to be curators in museum. Having experienced working in galleries, it gave us desire to develop a structure where we could attempt to develop other potential working forms: playing with format and temporality. Therefore we represent a small number of artists and commit time and effort to each. Our understanding of art is to go back and forth between the artistic questions of the last decades and the most contemporary and experimental forms.

- **Contact** gb agency
Guillier Solene
gb@gbagency.fr
- **Established** 2001
- **Owner(s) / Partner(s)** Guillier Solene
Boutin Nathalie
- **Team** 5
- **Space(s)** 300 m²
- **Artists at Art Basel** Nikhil Chopra
Ryan Gander
Jiří Kovanda
Roman Ondák
Pratchaya Phinthong
Hassan Sharif
- **Further artists represented** Mac Adams
Robert Breer
Elina Brotherus
Omer Fast
Mark Geffriaud
Július Koller
Deimantas Narkevicius
Dominique Petitgand
Pia Rönicke
Yann Sérandour

GDM

Paris

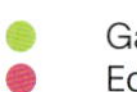

Galleries
Edition

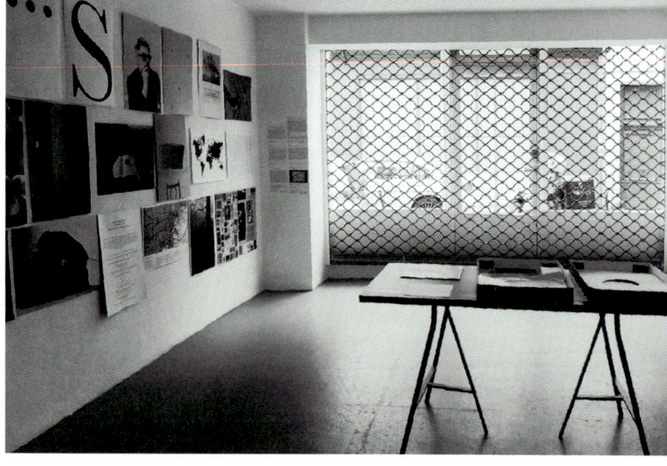

What is your favorite aspect of running a gallery?

There are three moments when I most love my job as a gallery owner. First, the moment when an artist approaches me for the first time to discuss a project, when the precise shape of the work is yet undefined. The second is the hanging: I love the thought and design process behind shaping an exhibition more than anything else. And finally, the precious hours when artists come to chat at the gallery, independently of any strategy or exhibition, just to talk about art.

How do you choose the artists you work with?

Often, I encounter a piece or series of work that astonishes me and the memory sticks in my mind for a long time. When I meet the artist behind such a piece in an exhibition or at a fair or perhaps when seeing mutual acquaintances, I propose a partnership for a project or multiple. In a way, I choose the work before the artist, even if the ties made during production of a multiple mean we will often collaborate again.

If you weren't running a gallery what else would you do?

I firmly believe I would have written about art. But published or not, my writing would not have been enough to live by, so I would have worked in event communications. I would have used my knowledge about contemporary art to recommend bowdlerized, but often more glowing versions of works of art, more accessible to the general public, more spontaneously appealing. By plundering art this way, I could have lived from art, rather than for art.

- **Contact** GDM
Magali Taureilles
galeriedemultiples@wanadoo.fr
- **Established** 2005
- **Owner(s) / Partner(s)** Gilles Drouault
- **Team** 2
- **Space(s)** 60 m²
- **Artists at Art Basel** Marcos Àvila Forero
Stéphane Calais
Claude Closky
Peter Downsbrough
Dorothy Iannone
William Kentridge
Robert Longo
Stefan Nikolaev
Matthew McCaslin
Julio Le Parc
Yan Pei-Ming
Maxime Rossi
Hans Schabus
Vincent Szarek
- **Further artists represented** Boris Achour
Saâdane Afif
Lewis Baltz
Neïl Beloufa
Monica Bonvicini
Daniel Buren
Stéphane Calais
Viriya Chotpanyavisut
Claude Closky
Peter Downsbrough

Jason Dodge
Dorothy Iannone
Regine Kolle
Alix Lambert
Julio Le Parc
Didier Marcel
Jonathan Monk
Olivier Mosset
Jean-Luc Moulène
Bruno Peinado
Clément Rodzielski
Maxime Rossi
Lei Saito
Bojan Šarčević
Hans Schabus
Nedko Solakov
Morgane Tschiember
Felice Varini
Xavier Veilhan
Jean-Luc Vilmouth

Gelink

Amsterdam 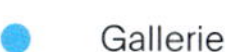 Galleries

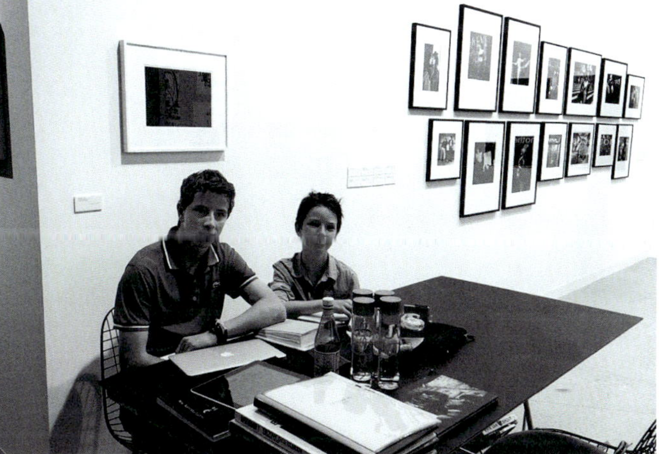

How do you choose the artists you work with?
It's all intuition.

If you weren't running a gallery what else would you do?
Cry all day.

- **Contact** Annet Gelink Gallery
Floor Wullems
info@annetgelink.com
- **Established** 2000
- **Owner(s) / Partner(s)** Annet Gelink
- **Team** 6
- **Space(s)** 1,000 m²
- **Artists at Art Basel** Yael Bartana
Carla Klein
Meiro Koizumi
Erik van Lieshout
David Maljkovic
Antonis Pittas
Wilfredo Prieto
Ed van Der Elsken
Marijke Van Warmerdam
Roger Hiorns
Glenn Sorensen
- **Further artists represented** Alicia Framis
Keith Edmier
Anya Gallaccio
Ryan Gander
Dan McCarthy
Muzi Quawson
Sarah Van Sonsbeeck
Dick Verdult
Barbara Visser

Gemini G.E.L.

Los Angeles 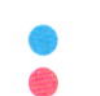 Edition
New York Edition

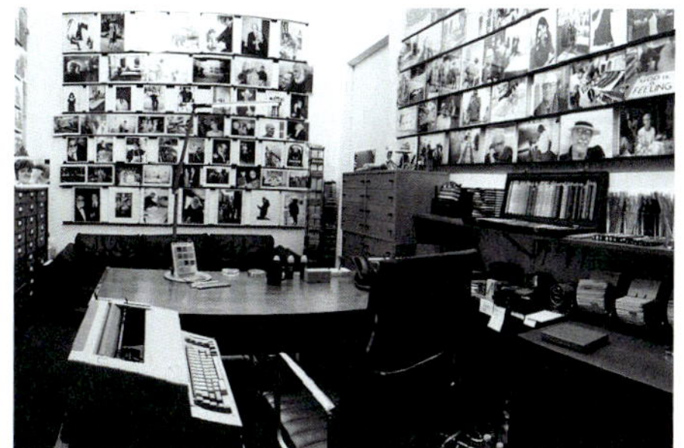

- **Contact** Gemini G.E.L. LLC
Sidney B. Felsen
editions@geminigel.com
- **Established** 1966
- **Owner(s) / Partner(s)** Sidney B. Felsen
Rosamund Felsen
Suzanne Felsen
Ayn Grinstein
Ellen Grinstein
Elyse Grinstein
Joni Weyl
- **Team** 20
- **Space(s)** 232.5 m²
- **Artists at Art Basel** John Baldessari
Jonathan Borofsky
Sophie Calle
Ann Hamilton
Michael Heizer
Ellsworth Kelly
Julie Mehretu
James Rosenquist
Richard Serra
Joel Shapiro
Richard Tuttle
Terry Winters
- **Further artists represented** David Hockney
Jasper Johns
Roy Lichtenstein
Claes Oldenburg
Bruce Nauman
Robert Rauschenberg
Susan Rothenberg
Ed Ruscha

Gerhardsen Gerner

Berlin  Galleries
Oslo Galleries

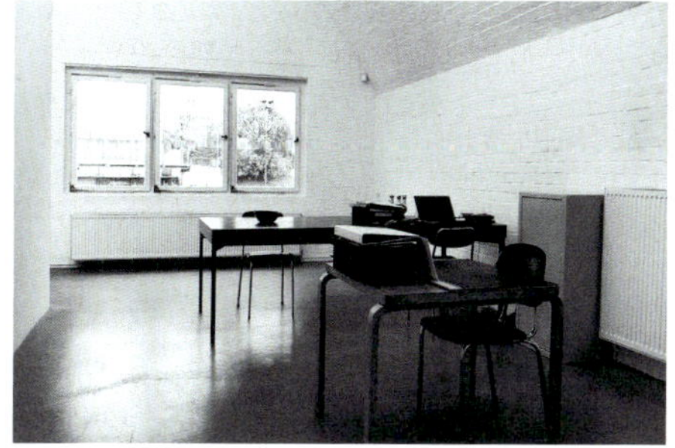

What is your favorite aspect of running a gallery?
Working with artists and clients!

How do you choose the artists you work with?
Being out there; it is a constant process of research.

If you weren't running a gallery what else would you do?
Rocket scientist.

- **Contact** Gerhardsen Gerner
Maike Fries
office@gerhardsengerner.com
- **Established** 1995 (Oslo)
2001 (Berlin)
2007 (with Nicolai-Gerner-Mathisen)

- **Owner(s) / Partner(s)** Atle Gerhardsen (Berlin, Oslo)
Nicolai Gerner-Mathisen (Berlin Oslo)
Marina Gerner-Mathisen (Oslo)
- **Team** 2
- **Space(s)** 310 m²
- **Artists at Art Basel** Amy Adler
Edgar Bryan
Jan Christensen
Carroll Dunham
Olafur Eliasson
Lothar Hempel
Georg Herold
Jim Lambie
Shintaro Miyake
Markus Oehlen
Julian Opie
Seth Pick
Tal R
Ingegerd Råman
Matthew Ritchie
David Salle
Dirk Stewen
Thaddeus Strode
Annika Ström
James White
Andrea Winkler

Ghebaly

Los Angeles 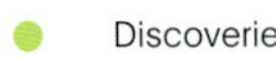 Discoveries

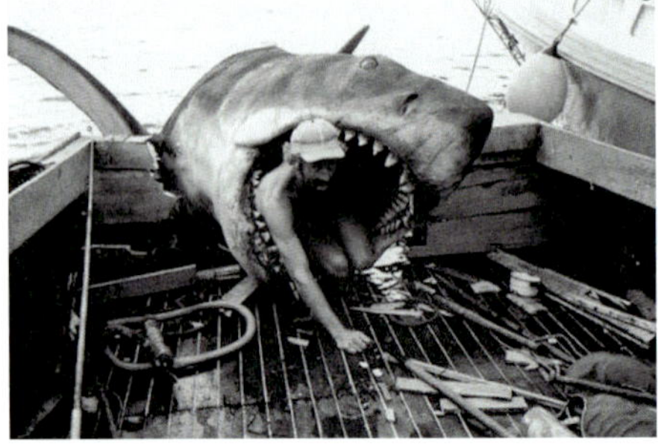

What is your favorite aspect of running a gallery?
The diversity of the people we get to interact with.

How do you choose the artists you work with?
I choose artists whose skills and intelligence allow them to thrive in any environment, but who choose art as it is the only career that will continue to challenge them. Beyond the work, which needs to be appealing to my intellect and to my eye, I choose persons that, despite all the difficulties, will continue to make art, even if no one pays attention to their work.

If you weren't running a gallery what else would you do?
I worked in a previous life doing French voice-over for Hollywood B movies and TV shows. Maybe work to become the first heavily-French-accented Hollywood movie star?

- **Contact** François Ghebaly Gallery
François Ghebaly
francois@ghebaly.com
- **Established** 2009
- **Owner(s) / Partner(s)** François Ghebaly
- **Team** 4
- **Space(s)** 650.5 m²
- **Artists at Art Basel** Neïl Beloufa
Sayre Gomez
- **Further artists represented** Davide Balula
Dan Bayles
Channa Horwitz
Patrick Jackson
Mike Kuchar
Joel Kyack
Gina Osterloh
Candice Lin
Andra Ursuta

Gladstone

New York
Brussels

- Galleries Unlimited
- Galleries Public

- **Contact** Gladstone Gallery
Mollie White
mwhite@gladstonegallery.com
- **Established** 1980
- **Owner(s) / Partner(s)** Barbara Gladstone

Gmurzynska

Zurich
St. Moritz
Zug

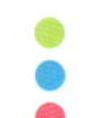

- Galleries
- Galleries
- Galleries

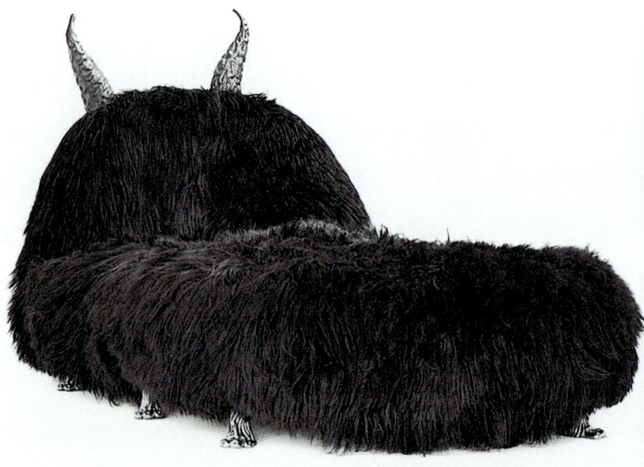

What is your favorite aspect of running a gallery?
Presenting exhibitions that will be remembered and have influence far into the future.

How do you choose the artists you work with?
We look for someone with the potential to impact art history, or who has already impacted it but without the credit they deserve.

If you weren't running a gallery what else would you do?
Dream of running a gallery.

- **Contact** Galerie Gmurzynska
Mitchell Anderson
mitchell.anderson@gmurzynska.com
- **Established** 1965
- **Owner(s) / Partner(s)** Krystyna Gmurzynska
Mathias Rastorfer
Isabelle Bscher
- **Artists at Art Basel** Fernando Botero
Alexander Calder
Adolf Luther
Scott Campbell
Marc Chagall
Ronnie Cutrone
Robert Delaunay
Sonia Delaunay
Lyonel Feininger
Lucio Fontana
Natalia Goncharova
Ferdinand Hodler
Robert Indiana
Wassily Kandinsky
Yves Klein
Robert Klippel
Karl Lagerfeld
Wifredo Lam
Mikhail Larionov
Henri Laurens
Fernand Léger
Jani Leinonen
- **Further artists represented** Dan Basen
El Lissitzky
Kazimir Malevich
Henri Matisse
Joan Miró

László Moholy-Nagy
Louise Nevelson
Pablo Picasso
Liubov Popova
Mel Ramos
Alexander Rodchenko
Karl Peter Röhl
Kurt Schwitters
David Smith
Chaim Soutine
Sylvester Stallone
Varvara Stepanova
Nikolai Suetin
Joaquín Torres-García
Theo van Doesburg
Georges Vantongerloo
Tom Wesselmann

González

Madrid

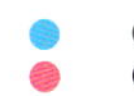

Galleries
Galleries

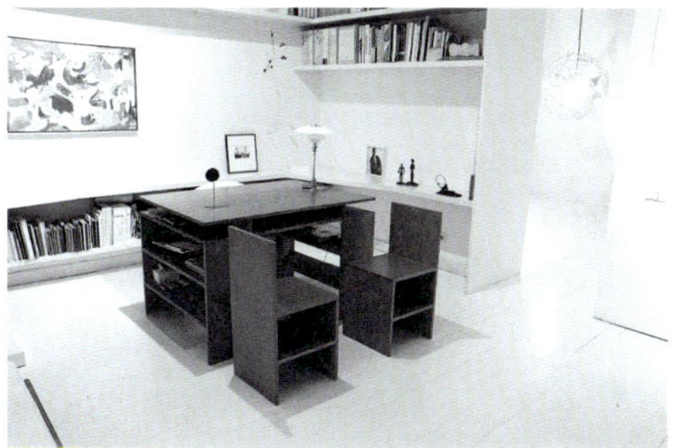

What is your favorite aspect of running a gallery?
Working with the artists.

How do you choose the artists you work with?
Deep knowledge of the artist's work and seeing the possibility of developing a career together.

If you weren't running a gallery what else would you do?
Run a bookshop.

- **Contact** Galería Elvira González
  Isabel Mignoni
  imignoni@galeriaelviragonzalez.com
- **Established** 1994
- **Owner(s) / Partner(s)** Elvira González
  Elvira Mignoni
  Isabel Mignoni
  Fernando Mignoni
- **Team** 7
- **Space(s)** 500 m²
- **Artists at Art Basel** Josef Albers
  Miquel Barceló
  Alexander Calder
  John Chamberlain
  Lucio Fontana
  Dan Flavin
  Adolph Gottlieb
  Donald Judd
  Sol LeWitt
  Robert Mangold
  Robert Mapplethorpe
  Fausto Melotti
  Rudolf Stingel
  Lee Ufan
- **Further artists represented** Juan Asensio
  Waltercio Caldas
  Eduardo Chillida
  Chema Madoz
  Elena del Rivero
  Adolfo Schlosser
  Yoshihiro Suda
  Esteban Vicente
  Dan Walsh

Goodman Gallery

Johannesburg
Cape Town

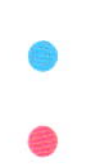

Galleries Unlimited
Galleries Public

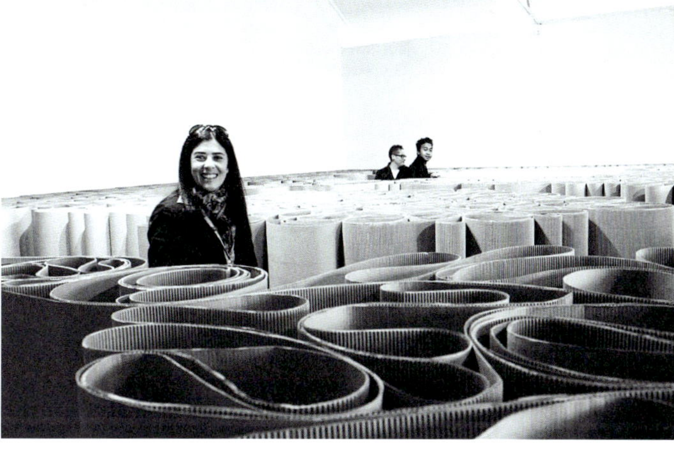

What is your favorite aspect of running a gallery?
That it is never just a "business" or an "industry"—the art world is always infinitely more than that.

How do you choose the artists you work with?
We look out for artists working within the context of a geopolitical South, who are challenging the preconceived idea of knowledge always flowing southward.

If you weren't running a gallery what else would you do?
Find another platform that allows me to work with artists.

- **Contact** Goodman Gallery
  Kirsty Wesson
  kirsty@goodman-gallery.com
- **Established** 1966
- **Owner(s) / Partner(s)** Liza Essers
- **Team** 24
- **Space(s)** 600 m²
- **Artists at Art Basel** Ghada Amer
  Willem Boshoff
  Candice Breitz
  Lisa Brice
  Carla Busuttil
  Kudzanai Chiurai
  Hasan & Husain Essop
  Mounir Fatmi
  Kendell Geers
  David Goldblatt
  Frances Goodman
  Haroon Gunn-Salie
  William Kentridge
  David Koloane
  Moshekwa Langa
  Liza Lou
  Gerald Machona
  Gerhard Marx
  Brett Murray
  Sam Nhlengethwa
  Walter Oltmann
  Rademeyer Stephanus
  Mikhael Subotzky
  Hank Willis Thomas
  Clive van den Berg
  Minnette Vári
  Diane Victor
  Jeremy Wafer
  Sue Williamson
  Nelisiwe Xaba

Marian Goodman

New York
London
Paris

Galleries
Galleries
Unlimited
Galleries

- **Contact** Marian Goodman Gallery
  Marian Goodman
  goodman@mariangoodman.com
- **Established** 1977
- **Owner(s) / Partner(s)** Marian Goodman
- **Team** 36
- **Artists at Art Basel** Eija-Liisa Ahtila
  Chantal Akerman
  Giovanni Anselmo
  John Baldessari
  Lothar Baumgarten
  Dara Birnbaum
  Christian Boltanski
  Marcel Broodthaers
  James Coleman
  Tony Cragg
  Richard Deacon
  Tacita Dean
  Rineke Dijkstra
  Pierre Huyghe
  Cristina Iglesias
  Amar Kanwar
  William Kentridge
  Steve McQueen
  Julie Mehretu
  Annette Messager
  Juan Muñoz
  Gabriel Orozco
  Giulio Paolini
  Giuseppe Penone
  Gerhard Richter
  Anri Sala
  Matt Saunders
  Tino Sehgal
  Thomas Struth
  Niele Toroni
  Adrián Villar Rojas
  Danh Vo
  Jeff Wall
  Lawrence Weiner
  Francesca Woodman
  Yang Fudong

Grässlin

Frankfurt am Main

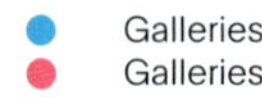

Galleries
Galleries

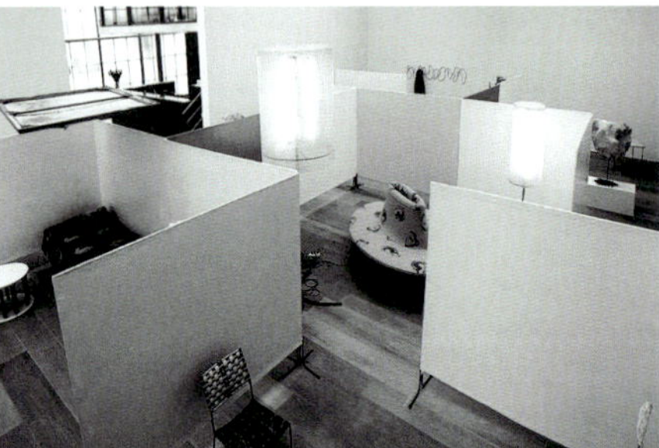

What is your favorite aspect of running a gallery?

The close cooperation with the artists and having the opportunity to participate in current art production. To place the artists I represent on the market.

How do you choose the artists you work with?

Very subjective—first of all, I must be fully convinced by the artist's oeuvre. Personality and character are also decisive criteria.

If you weren't running a gallery what else would you do?

When I was a child, I wanted to be a temple dancer in India. Since my youth I have never considered another profession. Should I decide to retire from professional life, I would look after the family collection.

- **Contact** Galerie Bärbel Grässlin
  Bärbel Grässlin
  mail@galerie-graesslin.de
- **Established** 1985
- **Owner(s) / Partner(s)** Bärbel Grässlin
- **Team** 3
- **Space(s)** 350 m²
- **Artists at Art Basel** Michael Beutler
  Jean-Marc Bustamante
  Herbert Brandl
  Werner Büttner
  Helmut Dorner
  Günther Förg
  Secundino Hernández
  Georg Herold
  Hubert Kiecol
  Martin Kippenberger
  Imi Knoebel
  Meuser
  Reinhard Mucha
  Stefan Müller
  Christa Näher
  Manuel Ocampo
  Markus Oehlen
  Tobias Rehberger
  Andreas Slominski
  Thomas Werner
  Franz West
  Heimo Zobernig

Alexander Gray

New York

Galleries

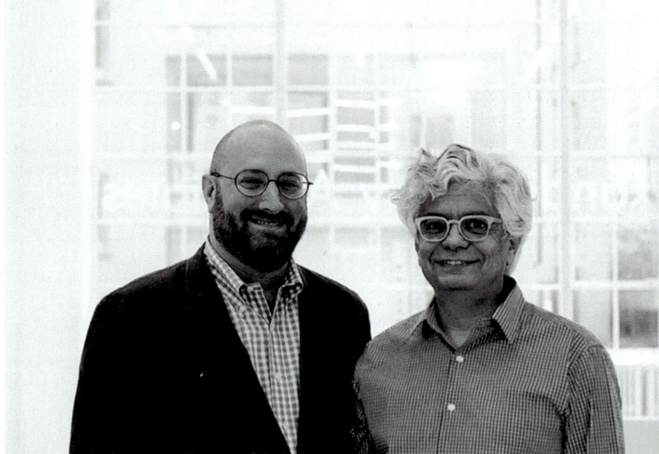

What is your favorite aspect of running a gallery?

Solo exhibitions with the gallery artists. Months of preparation—studio visits, research, logistics, publication, and exhibition design—engage the entire team. The "ah-ha!" moment comes when the show is installed, before the opening reception, when we walk through the exhibition with the artist, and see how the works engage with one another and their physical presence in the space. A solo exhibition reinforces the true power of experiencing art in person.

How do you choose the artists you work with?

Our focus is on artists who emerged in the 1960s, 1970s, and 1980s, artists who have influenced directions of contemporary artistic practice. We are interested in the achievements of artists in their late careers, especially when a spirit of experimentation is reinforced by the gravitas of an extended career.

If you weren't running a gallery what else would you do?

Partners David Cabrera and Alexander Gray bring a set of values that guides the gallery's program. The core value carries over to animal rights and vegan advocacy. Cabrera is Board President for the Woodstock Farm Animal Sanctuary and Gray is involved with Our Hen House, an animal rights organization. We would use our skills to serve animals. We certainly notice a wide gap in the market for an upscale, vegan restaurant and hotel in the Hudson Valley (New York)!

- **Contact** Alexander Gray Associates
  John Kunemund
  john@alexandergray.com

- **Established** 2006
- **Owner(s) / Partner(s)** Alexander Gray, David Cabrera
- **Team** 11
- **Space(s)** 371.5 m²
- **Artists at Art Basel** Siah Armajani, Melvin Edwards, Jack Whitten
- **Further artists represented** Luis Camnitzer, Coco Fusco, Tomislav Gotovac, Harmony Hammond, Vera Neumann, Lorraine O'Grady, Joan Semmel, Hassan Sharif, Regina Silveira, Hugh Steers

Richard Gray

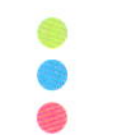

Chicago	●	Galleries
New York	●	Galleries
	●	Galleries

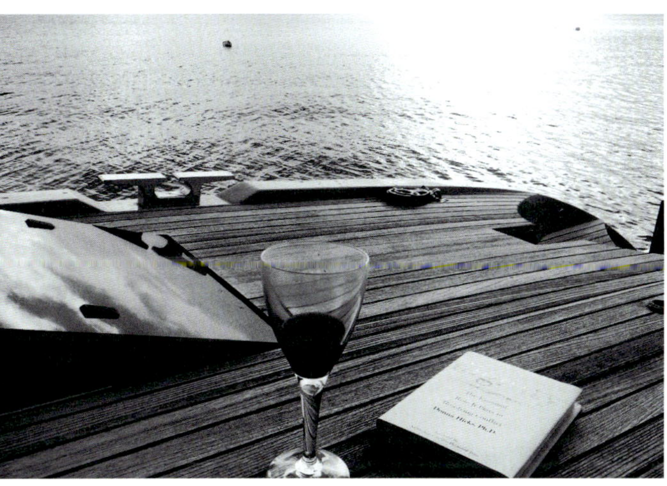

How do you choose the artists you work with?
From the gallery's beginnings in 1963, it has striven to combine connoisseurship and the building of collections with passionate advocacy for artists, both in the primary market and through the resales of historical works. Among our early exhibitions were Bob Thompson, Milton Avery, Alexander Calder, Robert Rauschenberg, Claes Oldenburg, Roy Lichtenstein, Willem de Kooning, and Jim Dine. Every one of those artists remains within the purview of the gallery 50 years later. Also in those early years, the gallery mounted exhibitions of Fernand Léger, Picasso, Surrealism, and modern master drawings by Matisse, Gorky, and Miró. Choosing artists with whom to work is largely a matter of personal conviction. We aim to be disciplined about it, but just like collectors, sometimes we are simply bowled over by artworks and by artists whose talent cannot be denied. We try to ask ourselves these questions: is the work compelling? Is it original? Is the artist sincere? Would we be delighted to have the work back someday, down the road, when the collector decides to sell? Will the work, and just as importantly, the quality of the personal relationship with the artist, sustain the sort of extended commitment needed to advocate for, invest in, exhibit, publish it, and devote hundreds of hours each year to it?

- **Contact** Richard Gray Gallery, Paul Gray, pg@richardgraygallery.com
- **Established** 1963
- **Owner(s) / Partner(s)** Richard Gray, Paul Gray, Andrew Fabricant
- **Team** 12
- **Artists at Art Basel** Carl Andre, Francis Bacon, Olivia Berckemeyer, Alexander Calder, Suzanne Caporael, Bethany Collins, Joseph Cornell, Richard Diebenkorn, Mark di Suvero, Jean Dubuffet, Sam Francis, Alberto Giacometti, Ewan Gibbs, Arshile Gorky, Adolph Gottlieb, Mark Grotjahn, Philip Guston, David Hockney, Hans Hofmann, Jasper Johns, Alex Katz, Anselm Kiefer, David Klamen, Franz Kline, Willem de Kooning, Fernand Léger, Roy Lichtenstein, Henri Matisse, Joan Miró, Henry Moore, Robert Motherwell, Claes Oldenburg, Pablo Picasso, Jack Pierson, Jaume Plensa, Richard Prince, James Rosenquist, Mark Rothko, Ed Ruscha, Richard Serra, David Smith, Mitchell Squire, Frank Stella, Cy Twombly, Andy Warhol, Tom Wesselmann, Brenna Youngblood

Greenan

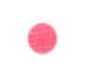

New York	●	Survey

- **Contact** Garth Greenan Gallery, Garth Greenan, garth@garthgreenan.com
- **Established** 2011
- **Owner(s) / Partner(s)** Bryan Davidson Blue, Garth Greenan
- **Team** 4
- **Space(s)** 279 m²
- **Artists at Art Basel** Paul Feeley
- **Further artists represented** Rosalyn Drexler, Audrey Flack, Victoria Gitman, Art Green, Ralph Humphrey, Nicholas Krushenick, Al Loving, Gladys Nilsson, Matthew Palladino, Howardena Pindell, Norbert Prangenberg, Patrick Strzelec, George Sugarman, Richard Van Buren

Greenberg

New York

Galleries
Galleries

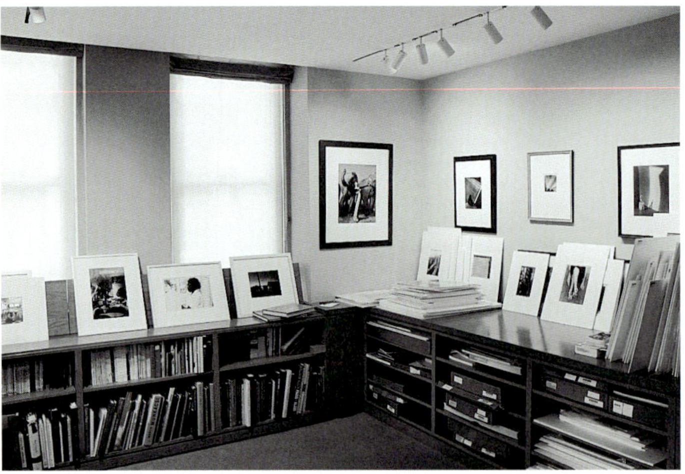

What is your favorite aspect of running a gallery?
My favorite aspect of running the gallery is curating exhibitions.

How do you choose the artists you work with?
I do not have a set formula. Choosing the artists I work with has become a complicated process as we already represent a lot of great artists and estates. Therefore, it is only very selectively and only occasionally that we do take on new artists. The criteria is that they need to both complement what the gallery is about and enhance the gallery's program.

If you weren't running a gallery what else would you do?
I would be a professional golfer (except that I am not good at it).

- **Contact** — Howard Greenberg Gallery
  Karen Marks
  karen@howardgreenberg.com
- **Established** — 1981
- **Owner(s) / Partner(s)** — Howard Greenberg
- **Team** — 16
- **Space(s)** — 600 m²
- **Artists at Art Basel** — Berenice Abbott
  Robert Adams
  Richard Avedon
  Gay Block
  Erwin Blumenfeld
  Bill Brandt
  Brassaï
  Frédéric Brenner
  Edward Burtynsky
  Henri Cartier-Bresson
  Bruce Davidson
  František Drtikol
  Robert Frank
  Jaromír Funke
  André Kertész
  William Klein
  Rudolf Koppitz
  Jacques-Henri Lartigue
  Saul Leiter
  Vivian Maier
  Joel Meyerowitz
  Barbara Morgan
  Arnold Newman
  Ruth Orkin
  Irving Penn
  George Platt Lynes
  Man Ray
  Cindy Sherman
  Edward Steichen
  Alfred Stieglitz
  Dennis Stock
  Josef Sudek
  Weegee
  Clarence H. White
- **Further artists represented** — Eugène Atget
  Walker Evans
  William Gedney
  Allen Ginsberg
  Frank Gohlke
  David Goldblatt
  Dave Heath
  Eikoh Hosoe
  Kenro Izu
  Charles Jones
  László Moholy-Nagy
  Sarah Moon
  Martin Munkácsi
  Gordon Parks
  Paul Strand
  Peter Sekaer
  Roman Vishniac
  Edward Weston
  Minor White

Greene Naftali

New York

Galleries Unlimited
Galleries

- **Contact** — Greene Naftali Gallery
  Carol Greene
  info@greenenaftaligallery.com
- **Established** — 1995
- **Owner** — Carol Greene

greengrassi

London — Galleries

- **Contact** — greengrassi
  Cornelia Grassi
  Info@greengrassi.com
- **Established** — 1997
- **Owner(s) / Partner(s)** — Cornelia Grassi
- **Team** — 4
- **Space(s)** — 120 m²
- **Artists at Art Basel** — Tomma Abts
  Roe Ethridge
  Ellen Gronemeyer
  Frances Stark
- **Further artists represented** — Stefano Arienti
  Jennifer Bornstein
  Moyra Davey
  Gretchen Faust
  Vincent Fecteau
  Giuseppe Gabellone
  Joanne Greenbaum
  Janice Kerbel
  Shio Kusaka
  Sean Landers
  Simon Ling
  Margherita Manzelli
  David Musgrave
  Kristin Oppenheim
  Silke Otto-Knapp
  Jennifer Pastor
  Alessandro Pessoli
  Karin Ruggaber
  Allen Ruppersberg
  Anne Ryan
  Jennifer Steinkamp
  Pae White
  Lisa Yuskavage

Greve

St. Moritz
Paris
Cologne

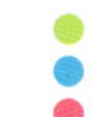

Galleries
Galleries
Galleries

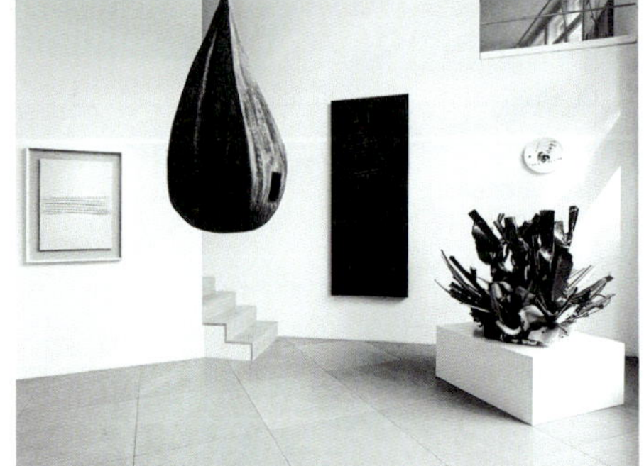

What is your favorite aspect of running a gallery?
ART! Living and working with ART.

How do you choose the artists you work with?
Observing and reflecting for a while, not spontaneously.

If you weren't running a gallery what else would you do?
Philosopher, gardener.

- **Contact** Galerie Karsten Greve AG
Karsten Greve
info@galerie-karsten-greve.ch
- **Established** 1969/1973
- **Owner(s) / Partner(s)** Karsten Greve
- **Team** 15
- **Space(s)** 1,220 m²
- **Artists at Art Basel** Josef Albers
Pierrette Bloch
Louise Bourgeois
Alexander Calder
Lawrence Carroll
John Chamberlain
Joseph Cornell
Ding Yi
Lucio Fontana
Jannis Kounellis
Piero Manzoni
Fausto Melotti
Claire Morgan
Jean-Michel Othoniel
Robert Polidori
Gideon Rubin
Georgia Russell
Joel Shapiro
Pierre Soulages
Louis Soutter
Cy Twombly
Wols
- **Further artists represented** Eugène Atget
Roger Ballen
Ilse Bing
Brassaï
Thomas Brummett
Lynn Davis
Willem de Kooning
Jean Dubuffet
Gotthard Graubner
Leiko Ikemura
Mimmo Jodice
Paco Knöller
Yiorgos Kordakis
Catherine Lee
Sally Mann
Norbert Prangenberg
Luise Unger
Sergio Vega

Grieder

Zurich — Galleries

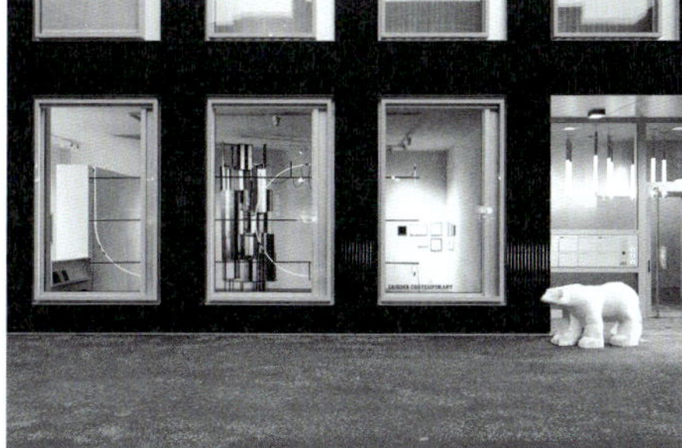

What is your favorite aspect of running a gallery?
My favorite aspect of running a gallery is meeting personalities you would not meet in any other regular profession.

How do you choose the artists you work with?
Ask my own artists! They usually have the straightest eye to judge their own competitors. Otherwise, I use my art market network and, last but not least, my hopefully experienced eye over the last 20 years.

If you weren't running a gallery what else would you do?
Run a gallery...

- **Contact** Grieder Contemporary
Melanie Dankbar
melanie@grieder-contemporary.com
- **Established** 2006
- **Owner(s) / Partner(s)** Damian Grieder
- **Team** 5
- **Space(s)** 150 m²
- **Artists at Art Basel** Nic Hess
Melli Ink
Thomas Kiesewetter
Kesang Lamdark
Thomas Kiesewetter
Dieter Meier
Michael Sailstorfer
Jorinde Voigt
- **Further artists represented** Ross Chisholm
Gregor Hildebrandt
Christian Jankowski
Alicja Kwade
Daniel Pflumm
Kerim Seiler
Richard Woods

Grimm

Amsterdam — Galleries, Encounters

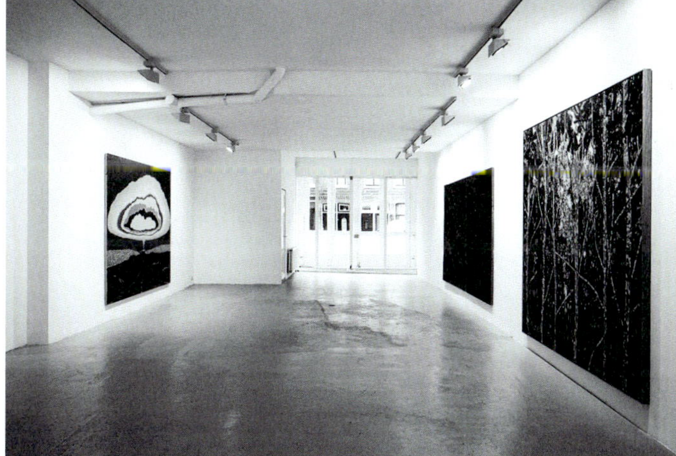

What is your favorite aspect of running a gallery?
To work directly with the various artists we represent and actively promote their work in an international context.

How do you choose the artists you work with?
We base our choices on the quality and integrity of the work.

If you weren't running a gallery what else would you do?
Film producer!

- **Contact** Grimm
Jorg Grimm
jorg@grimmgallery.com
- **Established** 2005
- **Owner(s) / Partner(s)** Jorg Grimm
Hannah Reefhuis
- **Team** 4
- **Space(s)** 320 m²
- **Artists at Art Basel** Atelier Van Lieshout
Matthias Weischer
- **Further artists** Charles Avery
Larry Bamburg
Gwenneth Boelens
Desiree Dolron
Alex Dordoy
Ger van Elk
Adam Helms
Gregor Hildebrandt
Volker Hüller
Matthew Day Jackson
Jonathan Marshall
Dave McDermott
William Monk
Ciarán Murphy
Mick Peter
Daniel Richter
Nick van Woert
Miguel Ybáñez

G

Grotto

Hong Kong — Galleries

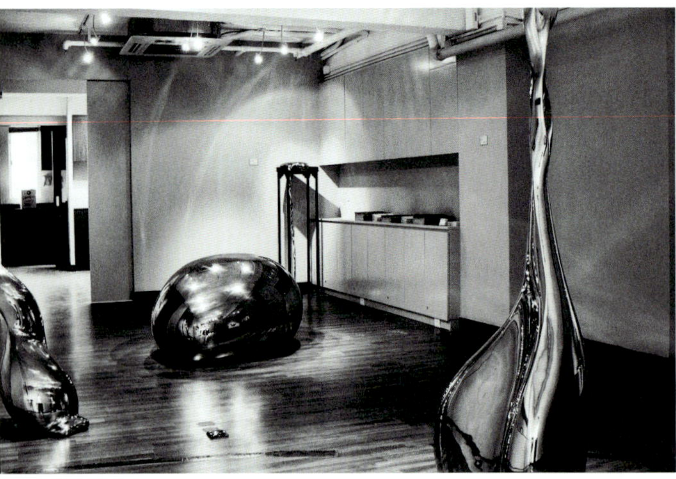

What is your favorite aspect of running a gallery?
First-hand contact with, and view of, emerging artists' work.

How do you choose the artists you work with?
Select from all local fine arts programs at universities.

If you weren't running a gallery what else would you do?
Art historian.

- **Contact** Grotto Fine Art Limited
Henry Au-yeung
henry@grottofineart.com
- **Established** 2001
- **Owner(s) / Partner(s)** Henry Au-yeung
- **Team** 3
- **Space(s)** 1,000 m²
- **Artists at Art Basel** Bovey Lee
Fai Hung
Joey Leung
Koon Wai-bong
Wai Pong-Yu

Guerra

Lisbon — Galleries Unlimited, Galleries

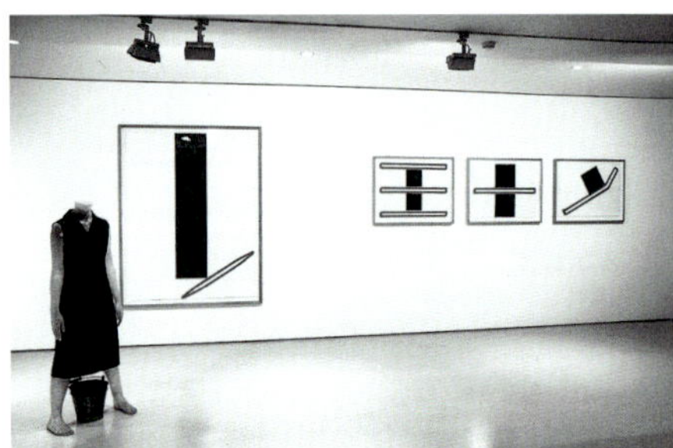

What is your favorite aspect of running a gallery?
Conceiving and accomplishing a project.

How do you choose the artists you work with?
First the work has to captivate my interest, then I try to understand and contextualize it, and finally I get to know the artist and try to understand his motivations.

If you weren't running a gallery what else would you do?
I guess I haven't thought much about it yet; I'm quite sure it would be art related.

- **Contact** Cristina Guerra Contemporary Art
Cristina Guerra
cguerra@cristinaguerra.com
- **Established** 2001
- **Owner(s) / Partner(s)** Cristina Guerra
- **Team** 5
- **Space(s)** 450 m²
- **Artists at Art Basel** Christian Andersson
Juan Araujo
Michael Biberstein
Luís Paulo Costa
Sabine Hornig
José Loureiro
João Louro
Edgar Martins
Matt Mullican
João Onofre
Julião Sarmento
Rui Toscano
Lawrence Weiner
Erwin Wurm
Yonamine
- **Further artists represented** John Baldessari
Adriana Barreto
Angela Bulloch
Filipa César
Tatjana Doll
João Paulo Feliciano
Lucia Laguna
Daniel Malhão
Diogo Pimentão
Rosângela Rennó

Gunn

Berlin — Positions

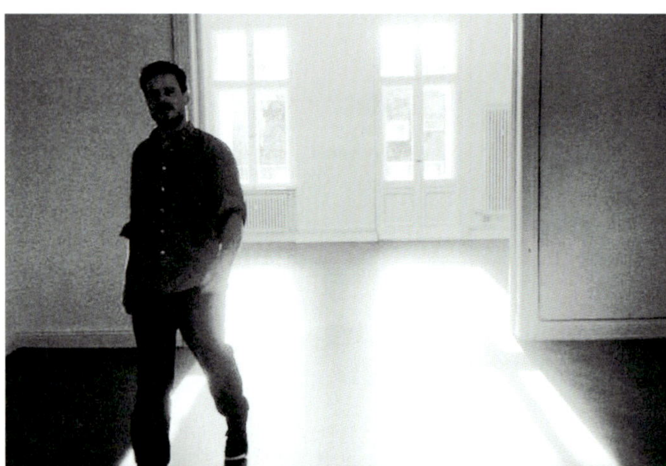

- **Contact** Dan Gunn
info@dangunn.de
- **Established** 2012
- **Owner(s) / Partner(s)** Dan Gunn
- **Team** 1
- **Space(s)** 135 m²
- **Artists at Art Basel** Tracey Rose
- **Further artists represented** Alessio delli Castelli
Ingrid Furre
Adrià Julià
Musa Paradisiaca
Alexandra Navratil
Michael Smith

Gupta

Chicago
Berlin

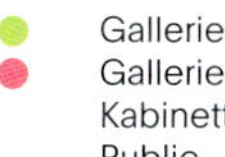

Galleries
Galleries
Kabinett
Public

What is your favorite aspect of running a gallery?
Getting to work with so many creative and passionate people from artists and curators to writers and others, and watching great ideas take form.

How do you choose the artists you work with?
I have an amazing team and, together, we're always seeking out artists with a unique vision that gets us all excited.

If you weren't running a gallery what else would you do?
It is hard to imagine doing anything other than something in art, but whatever it would be, it would definitely be in a creative field.

- **Contact** Kavi Gupta Chicago | Berlin
  Julia Fischbach
  julia@kavigupta.com
- **Established** 2002
- **Owner(s) / Partner(s)** Kavi Gupta
- **Team** 10
- **Space(s)** 1,951 m²
- **Artists at Art Basel** McArthur Binion
  Theaster Gates
  Antonia Gurkovska
  Glenn Kaino
  James Krone
  Jose Lerma
  Curtis Mann
  Angel Otero
  Roxy Paine
  Scott Reeder
  Clare Rojas
  Melanie Schiff
  Claire Sherman
  Tavares Stratchan
  Tony Tasset
- **Further artists represented** Johanna Billing
  Ari Marcopoulos
  Jessica Stockholder
  Mickalene Thomas

Galerie Karsten Greve

Interview with Karsten Greve

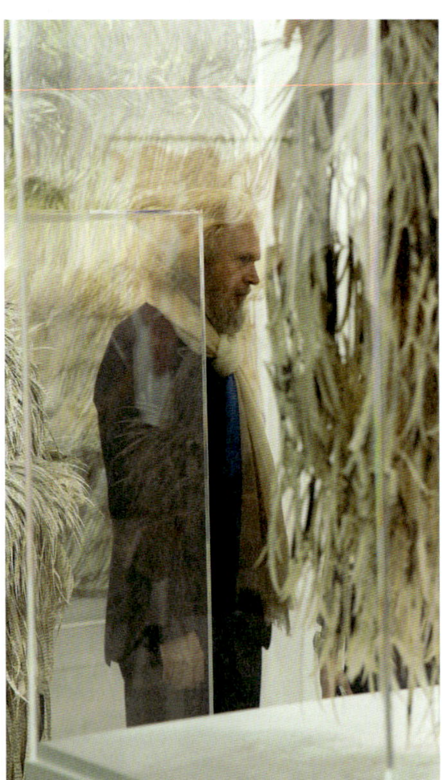

Karsten Greve at Art Basel in Hong Kong, 2014

You have participated in Art Basel almost since it started. How do you see its successful path and its specificities?

I think Basel was always a good fair because of its different sectors: classic, modern, and contemporary. Everybody could go to Basel and find his/her dream works, walk around, and discover something else. We witnessed the disaster of art fairs focused on one sector only: Cologne went to Berlin to do a young fair—they were bankrupt in 48 hours. Frieze might have been a success for some years—on a social basis at least, as it was something very new for London—but, in a way, Frieze was in trouble until they started Frieze Masters.

Art Basel was immediately successful because there were galleries showing Miró, Léger, Kandinsky, etc., including Mr. Beyeler. Over time, the problem was that, when prices surged crazily, no gallery could afford to do a Miró show every year with first class works. But some other exhibitors came in with 20, 40 works, ranging from very good to very bad, all just bought at auction. This is exactly what we did not accept in the 1980s. We did not accept somebody saying, "I want 500 square meters, because I have enough money in my bag." Now this power game has started again, but in a different way: the auctions are now dividing the market between an elite private customers base and the public museums or "normal" collectors on the other side. Besides, as an American colleague joked the other day, "There are no more auctions!" So many things belong to the auction houses today and so many guarantees are given that it is hardly auctioneering.

What is difficult today is that there is a growing demand from people who want to participate. In guise of an answer, the fair got more and more expensive; it's an inflation system. Aren't we loosing our ground, our roots, through this expansion? It's a general question in today's art world. If you go to the opening of the Venice Biennale it's not about art anymore: it's about people who think they are the kings and queens of the art world … There are some good curators, but if it's true they have power they should rather be modest in using it. If you look at the Biennale catalogues of the last 20 years, at least two thirds of the artists do not exist anymore, so the question is, how good were those curators really?

You were part of the Art Basel committee in the 1980s. How did it evolve and how was the idea of national representatives abandoned?

It was abandoned because we had a crisis. There was a big discussion about what to do. A few people were saying that we had to get rid of this national representation system; in the end we were left with three people against the old system—and three people instead of 22 in the committee! Pierre Huber from Geneva, Felix Buchmann from Basel, and me. It was an interesting combination because each of us was different and represented the diversity of approaches reflected in the fair's sectors. We had very nice, straightforward, and positive discussions. I was defending Krugier and the classic. I also like 13th century art, but who can show something important from that time or from the Renaissance? Even in Maastricht it's very hard to find this at the top level. My idea was simply to fight for the best gallerists and dealers. Dealers were not seen like gallerists in Basel, and in some periods there was even the desire to expel them. When things were difficult for Art Basel at the end of the 1970s and in the early 1980s, I proposed opening Basel to the American market. At that time most galleries were from Germany—something like 55 to only 15 Americans. There was a very good group of galleries like Leo Castelli, Sonnabend, and then also Barbara Gladstone, but there were also pure dealers, at a very high level. The question I asked the committee was very simple: do you think Mr. Beyeler is able to do a show by Kandinsky, and masterpieces by Picasso, and two others of this quality every year? So we included American dealers like Acquavella, Mnuchin, etc., and this resulted in 80% more galleries. We got so many more American collectors to Basel. I think this was one of the most important things I did during this period: to open to the American market.

And how do you see the move to open in Hong Kong?

I did a lot of business in Japan, South Korea, etc., and I have been in the area for 20 years. I am wondering what it would be like to be located here, in Asia. I am also wondering about the situation here in Hong Kong. I do not see it as a really established one. It is very interesting and positive, but I wonder whether, if we had such a fair in Mainland China, a place like Shanghai, with a free port, with government agreement to do an art fair with a special VAT system, if that wouldn't be the end of the Hong Kong fair. There can only be one winner and it will be Mainland China!

So you don't believe in Singapore as a competitor?

No, Singapore stands no chance. I was in Singapore 25 years ago just to assess the local situation. It is too isolated. The decision to do something in Hong Kong was perfectly right because you can't do it in Shanghai or Beijing at the moment, with a 32% VAT regime and the political situation, there's no way.

Taipei is very local and the quality is not good. Ten years ago Singapore started a fair that only lasted a year, built a bit like Maastricht; it didn't work, but there were people from Kuala Lumpur and from Brunei with unlimited resources. At this time, such buyers were ready to acquire a Modigliani or a Picasso, but they were not going further. So it was perfect for Art Basel to think first about America and to open there. Unfortunately, they did not buy the Chicago fair in the early 1980s—that was a big mistake. But Miami is interesting too, especially if you look at it from a South-American perspective. Although if you imagine that South-American countries would become more democratic and less heavy on taxes, you could very well see a strong fair in Venezuela or in Brazil. This would certainly be a success and Miami would die. So if you imagine 30 years from now, there is a risk for Miami. Hong Kong could also be under threat in the long run, because it's not China. At the moment, it's an entrance, a doorway to China, but it's not a future place. Or it still has to become it.

Which are the dangers do you think are threatening your work?

I have seen two, three big crises. I hope it won't, but a lot of my colleagues have been in that business for 45 years, and we are wondering when the next one will come—obviously this will be a bigger disaster. In 1973–1974, when we had the oil crisis, in Basel there were maybe 30 exhibitors. 1988 was a big drop, but we learned that a financial crisis is not a crisis for art. We learned that it's actually the opposite: if people do not trust the banks anymore, it is good for art. We learned again in 1991 that if something happens with natural resources, especially oil, then you are in a big trouble. With the current political situation in the Middle-East on one side and Russia on the other, such a crisis could come, soon.

City population
7,235,043

Population density
66,500 inhabitants per square kilometer

Fair founded in
2013 (predecessor, ART HK, founded in 2008)

Visitors in 2014
65,000

Number of exhibitors in 2014
245

Number of artists exhibited in 2013
over 3,000

HONG KONG

Exhibition Partners: Museums & Cultural Institutions

1a Space
Out of the Art Room

Art Museum, The Chinese University of Hong Kong
The Bei Shan Tang Legacy: Chinese Caligraphy;
Two Generations, and One Vision for Modern Chinese Painting

Asia Society Hong Kong Center
Xu Bing: *It Begins with Metamorphosis*

City University of Hong Kong School of Creative Media
City University 30th Anniversary Cultural Festival;
Leung Chi Wo: *I don't really know sometimes if it is because of culture*

Dr Sun Yat-sen Museum
History in Prints—The 1911 Revolution in Guangdong

Flagstaff House Museum of Tea Ware
Gems of Yixing Tea Ware from Nanjing Museums;
2013 Tea Ware by Hong Kong Potters

Goethe-Institut Hongkong
Marc Schmitz and Kingsley Ng: *Heights and Hills of Hong Kong*

Hong Kong Arts Centre
Second Annual Collectors' Contemporary Collaboration

Hong Kong Heritage Museum
Studio Ghibli Layout Designs: Understanding the Secrets of Takahata and Miyazaki Animation;
Bruce Lee: *Kung Fu. Art. Life*

Hong Kong Maritime Museum
Permanent Collection

Hong Kong Museum of Art
Ju Ming: *Sculpting the Living World*

Hong Kong Museum of Coastal Defense
Unsung Bravery: History of the Hong Kong Military Service Corps

Hong Kong Museum of History
At the Height of Imperialism: The New Territories of Hong Kong and Weihaiwei

K11 Art Foundation
Pop-up Space: *Space Painting* by Zhang Enli

K11 Art Foundation and Chinese Contemporary Art Promotion Centre
Art Nova 100 Hong Kong Station

Le French May Arts Festival
Andrée Putman: *Ambassador of Style;*
Fabienne Verdier: *Crossing Signs;*
The Essential Accessories of the Little Black Dress;
Jean-Marie Fiori: *The Monument for A Horse*

Macao Museum of Art
Macao Scenario—Animamix Biennale 2013–2014

OCT Contemporary Art Terminal Shenzhen
The 8th Shenzhen Sculpture Biennale, 2014: We Have Never Participated:Social Research, Post-participation

Oi!
Reflection!

Osage Art Foundation and City University of Hong Kong
Market Forces—Erasure From Conceptualism to Abstraction

Para Site
Ten Million Rooms of Yearning: Sex in Hong Kong

SCAD Hong Kong
Michael Joo: *Transparency Engine*

University Museum and Art Gallery, The University of Hong Kong
Chinese Art from the University's Collections

Videotage and Zen Foto Gallery
Hong Kong Obscura—Absorption and Explosion

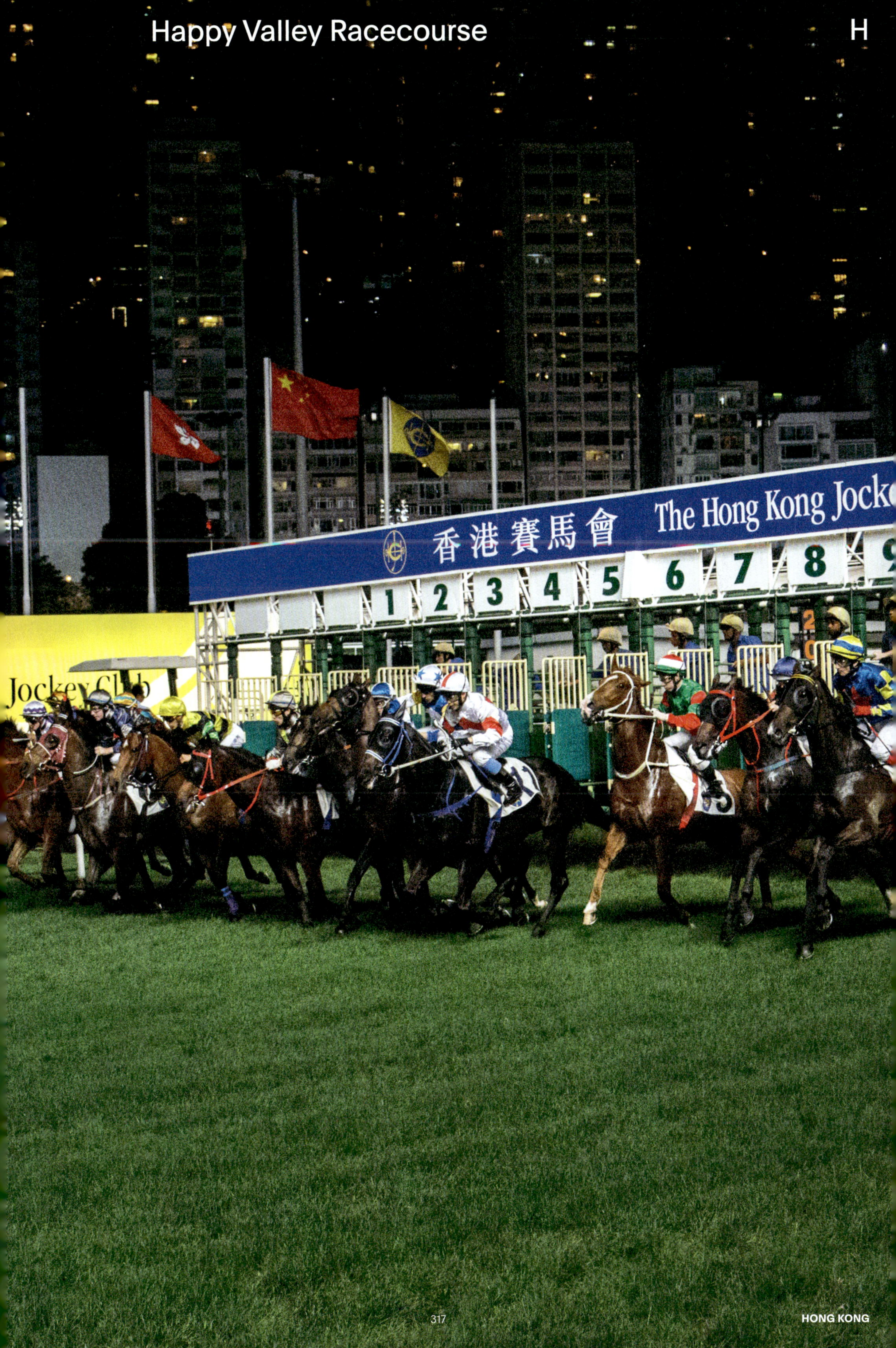
香港賽馬會
The Hong Kong
1 2 3 4 5 6 7 8

Hong Kong at night

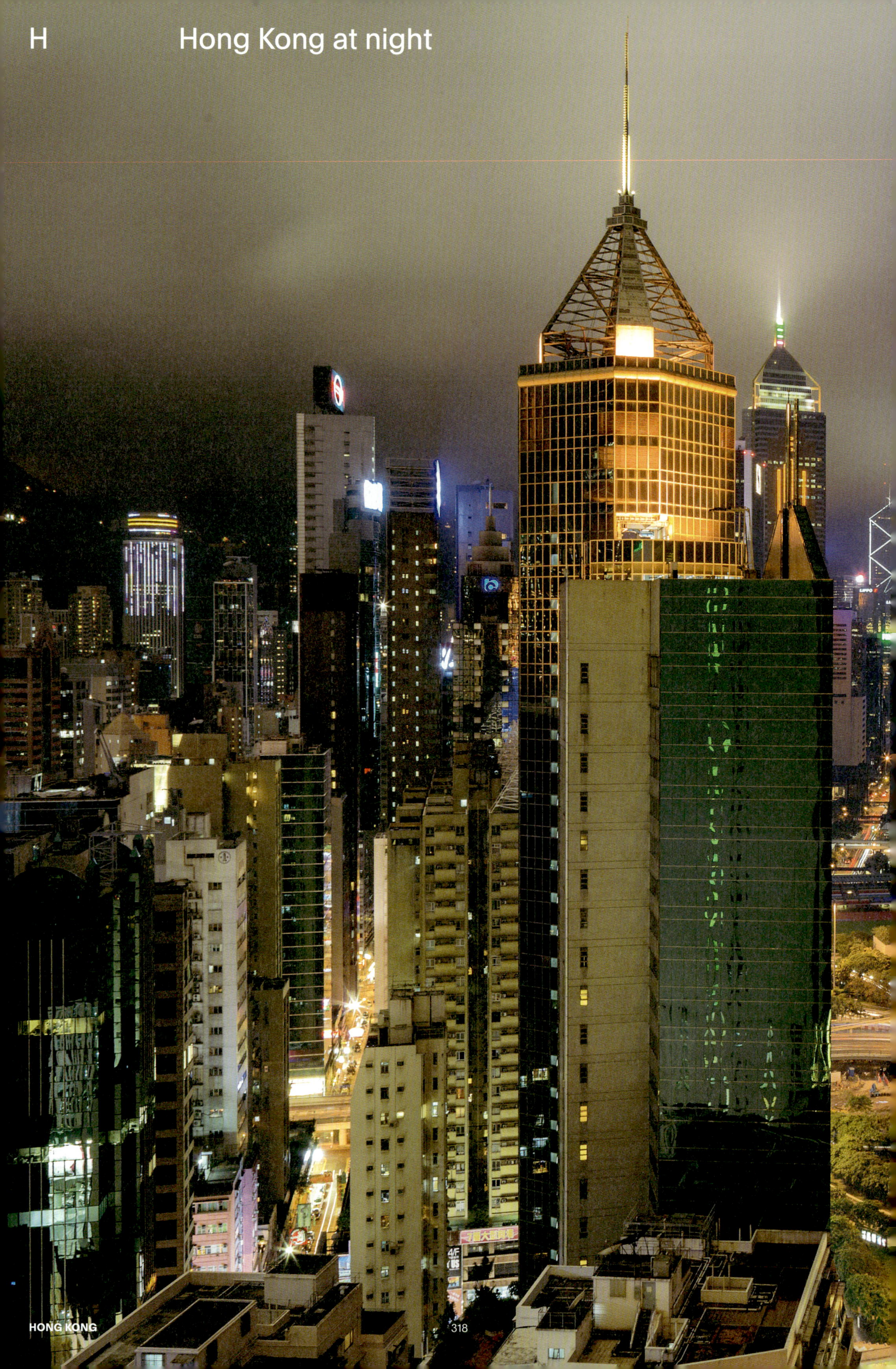

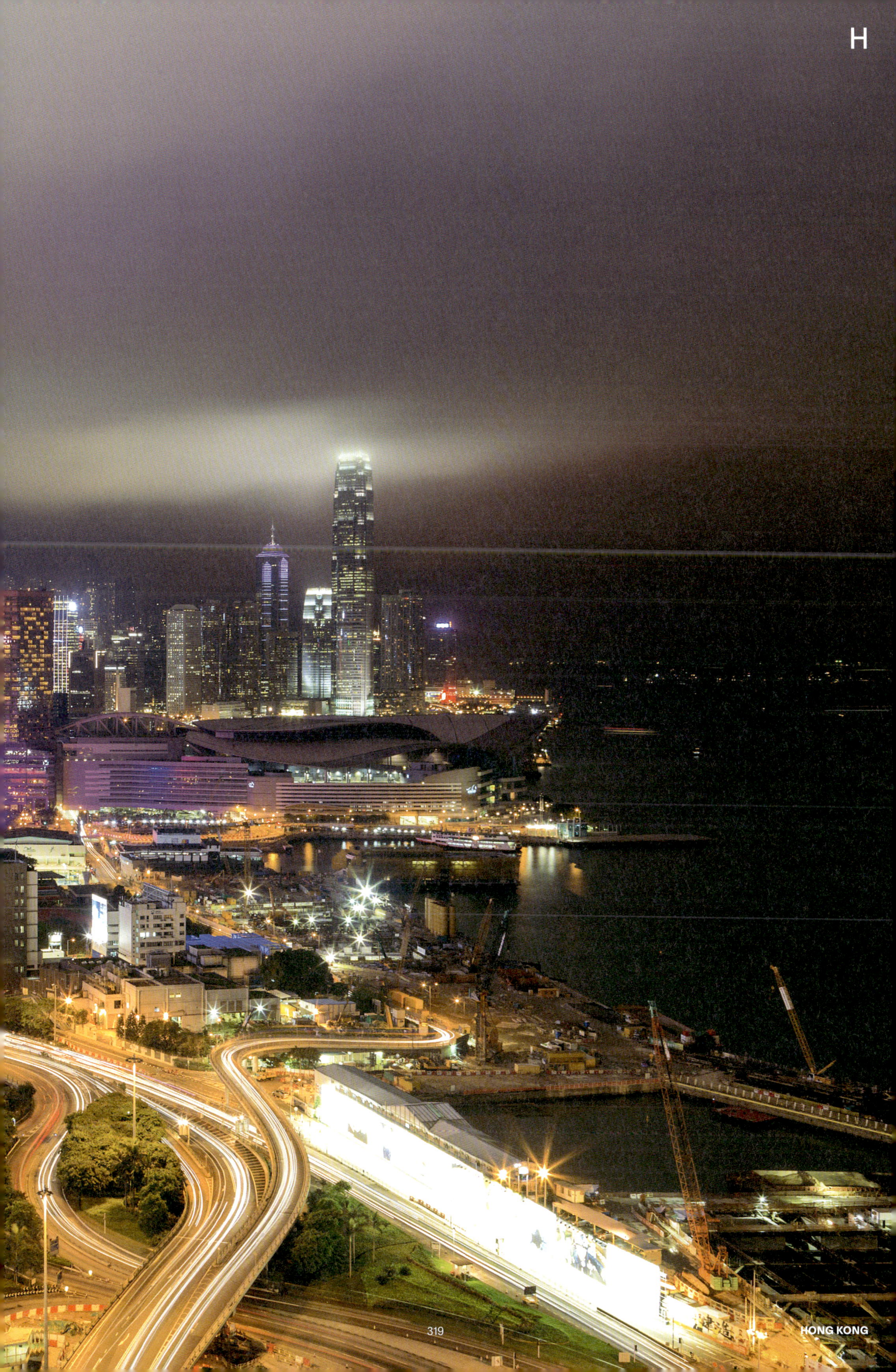

Art Basel's tram

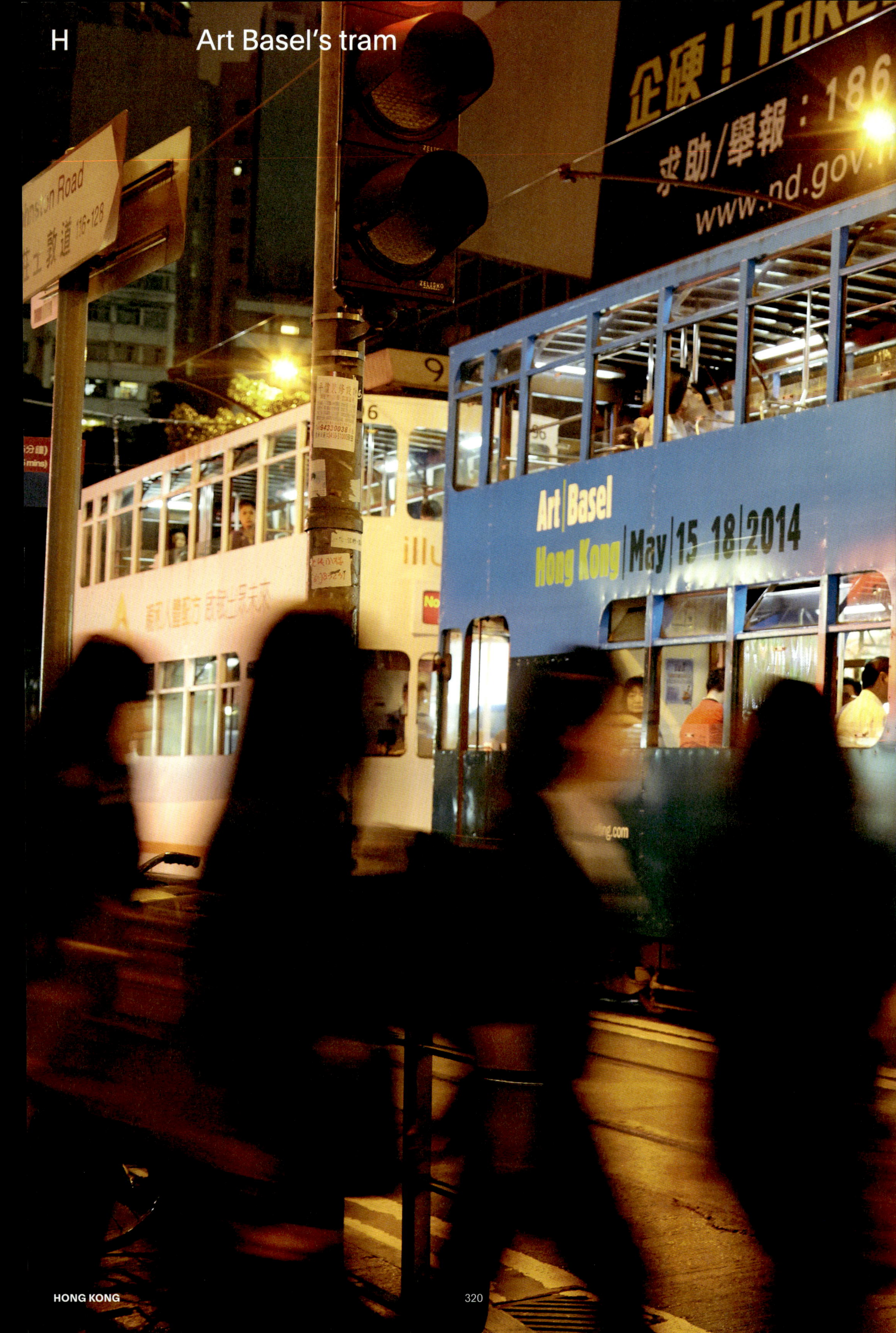

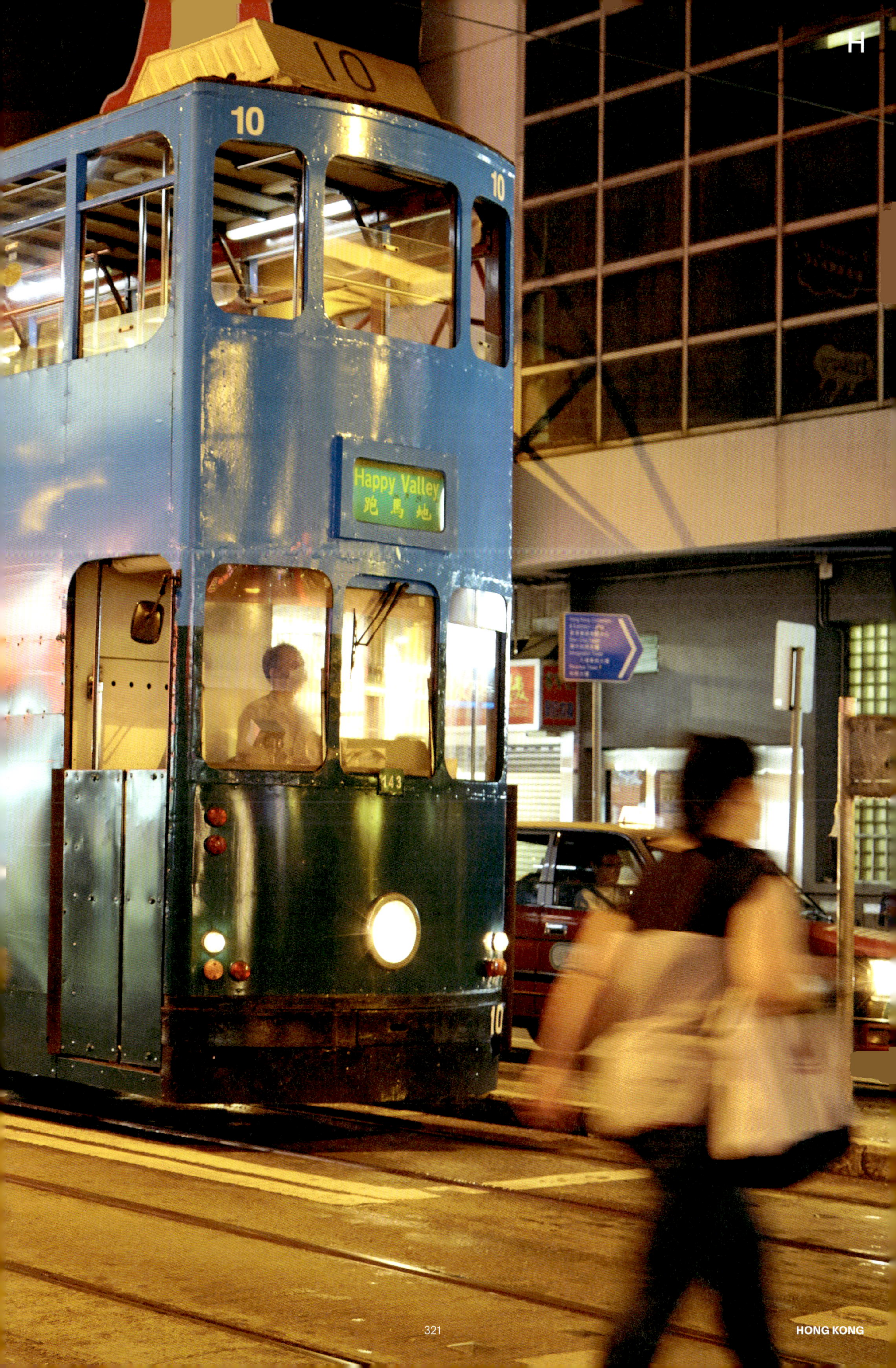
10
10
10
Happy Valley
跑馬地
143
10

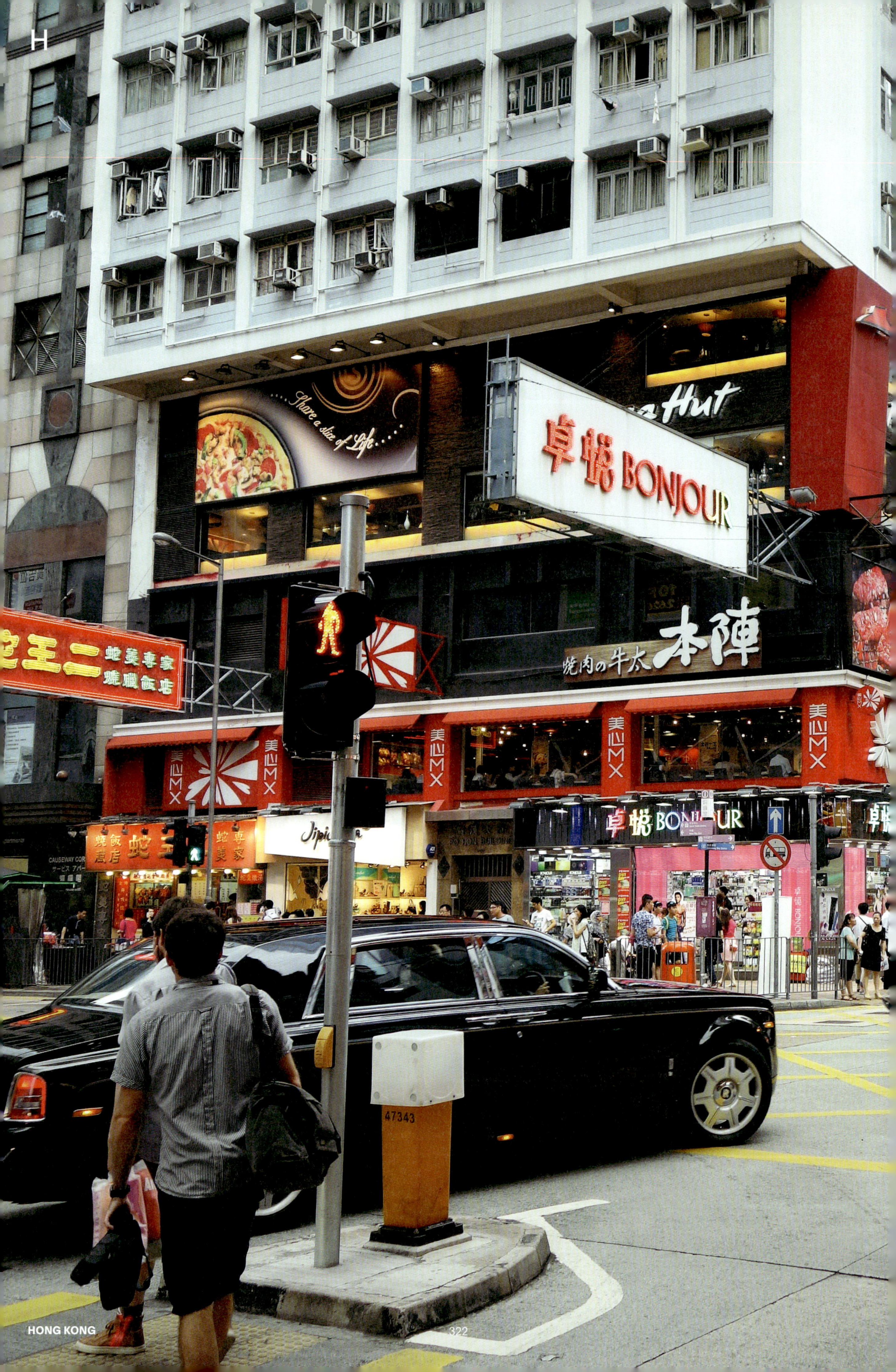
Share a slice of Life......
卓悦 BONJOUR
本陣
焼肉の牛太
蛇王二
蛇羹專家
燒臘飯店
美心MX
卓悦 BONJOUR
47343

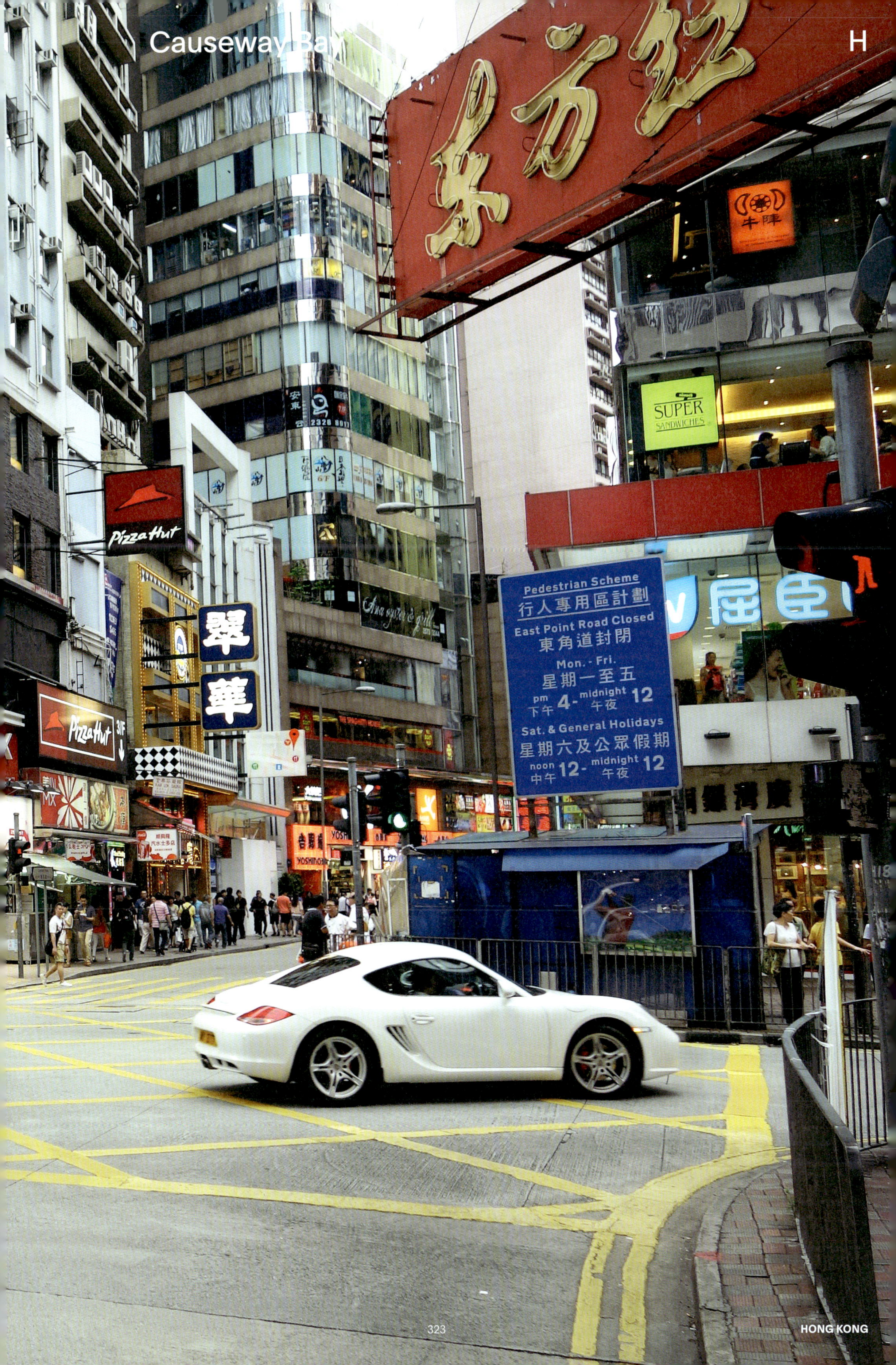
Pedestrian Scheme
行人專用區計劃
East Point Road Closed
東角道封閉
Mon. - Fri.
星期一至五
pm 下午 4- midnight 午夜 12
Sat. & General Holidays
星期六及公眾假期
noon 中午 12- midnight 午夜 12
SUPER SANDWICHES
Pizza Hut
翠
華

H

iPreciation
Lee Wen

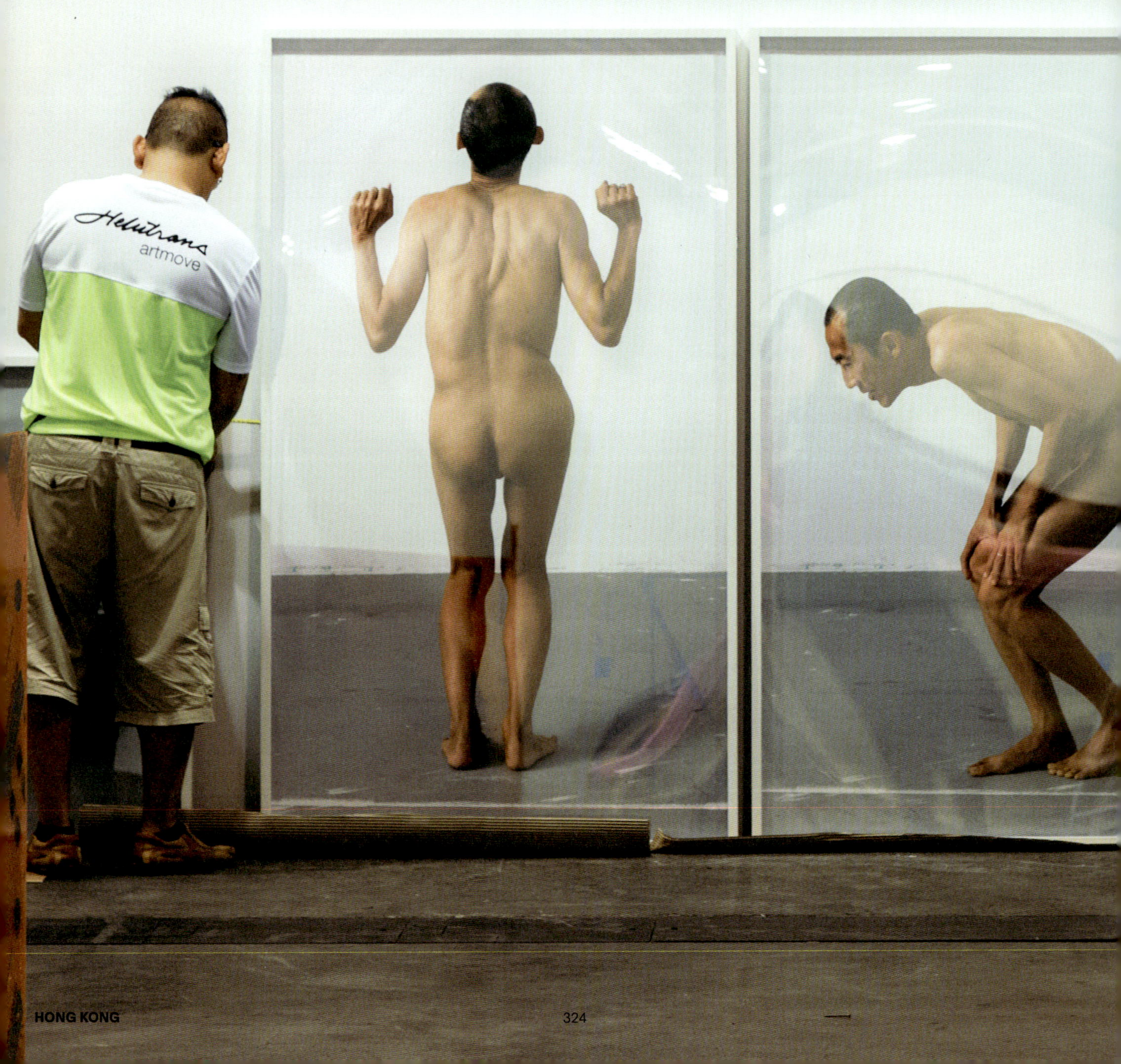

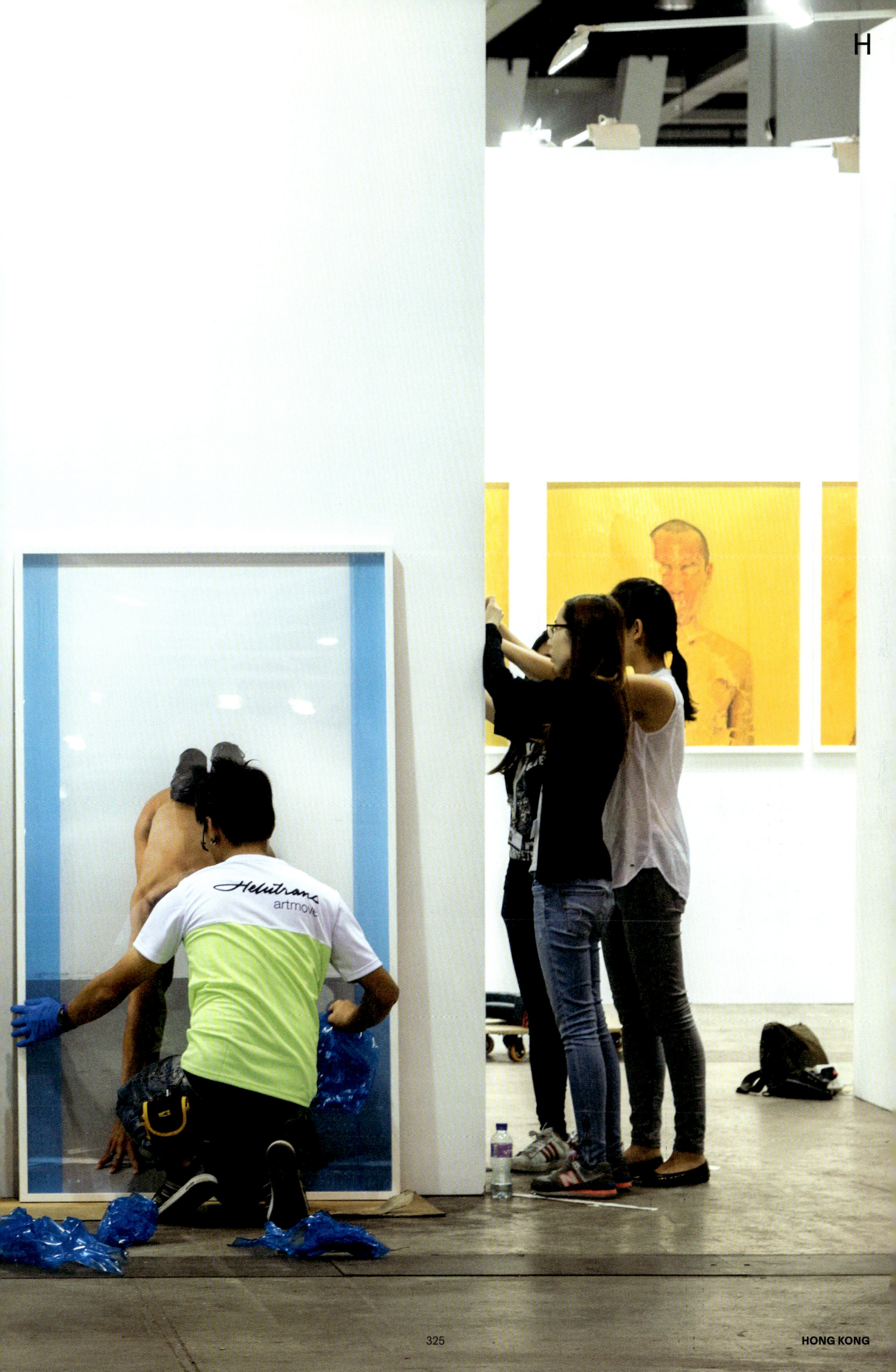
Helutrans
artmove

Edouard Malingue Gallery

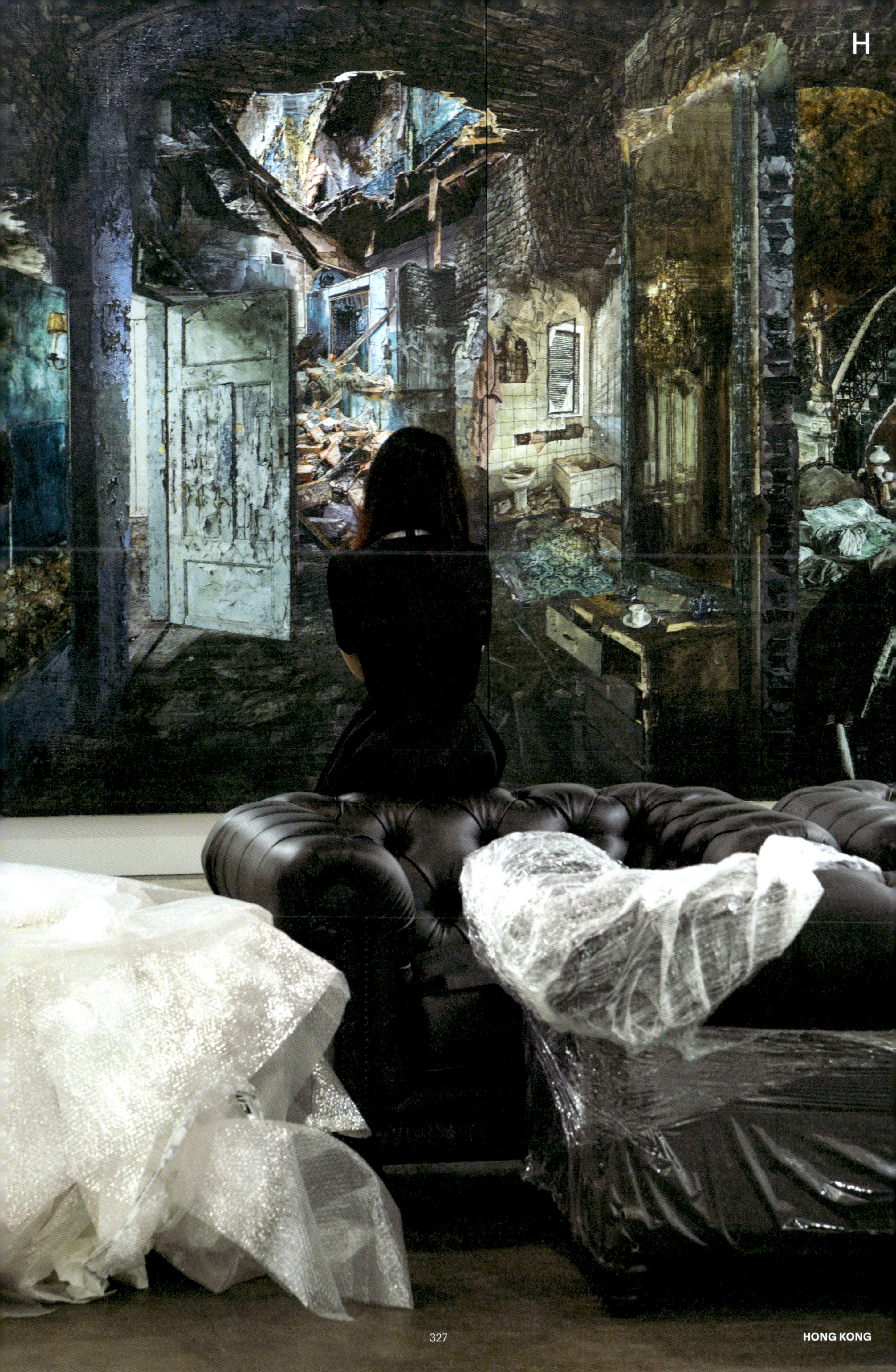

Lisson Gallery
Ryan Gander

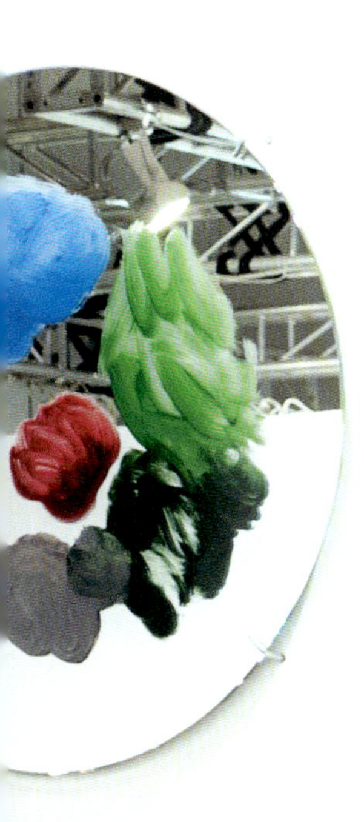
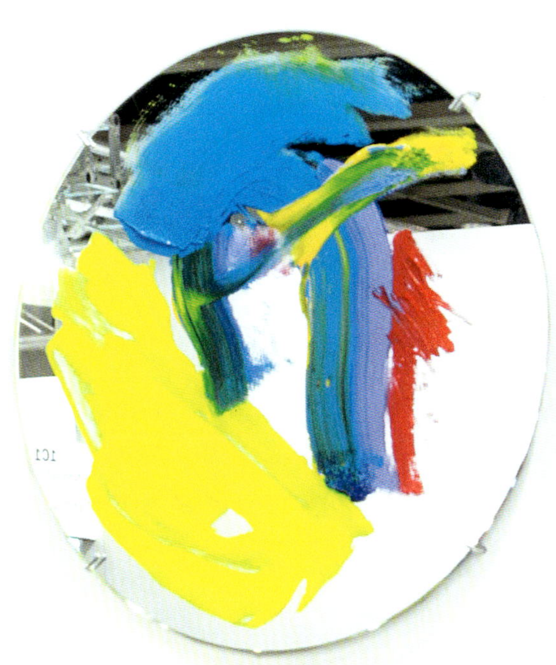
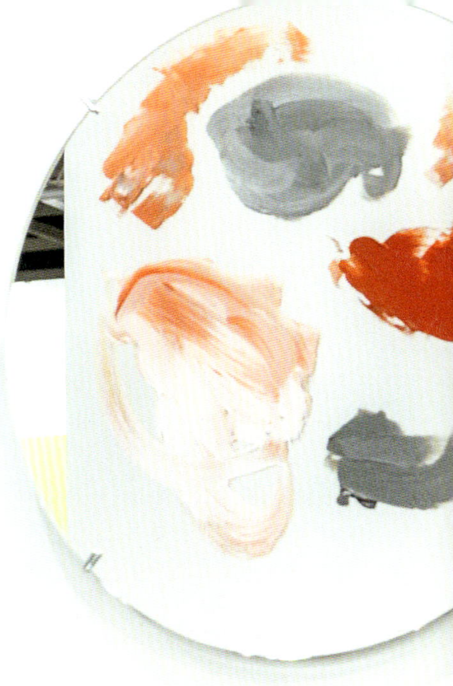
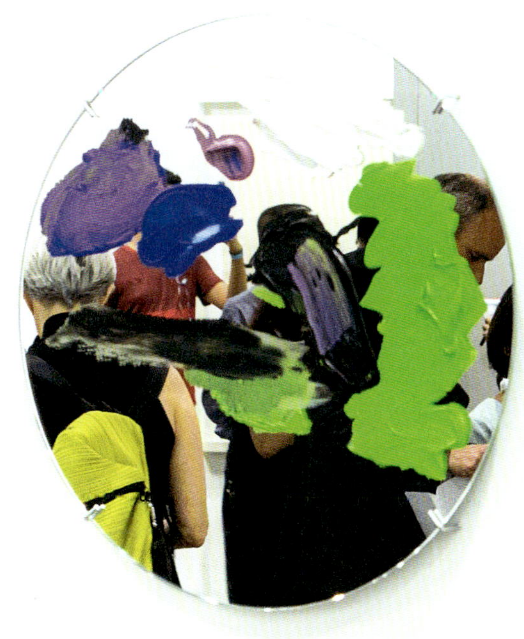
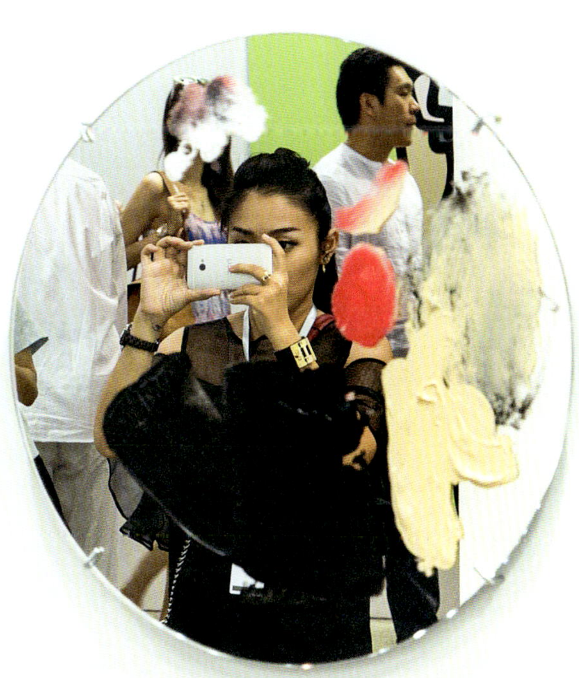
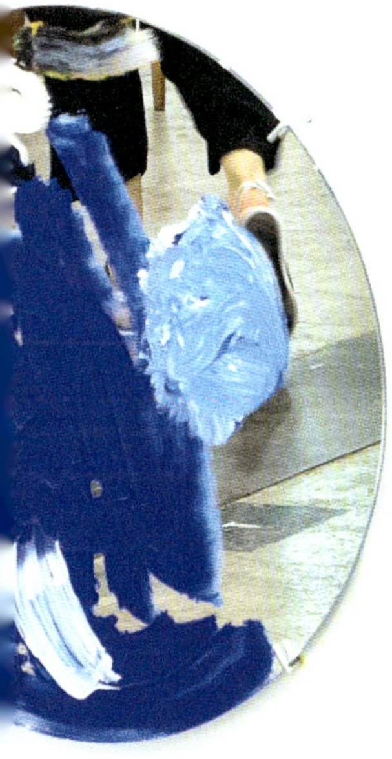
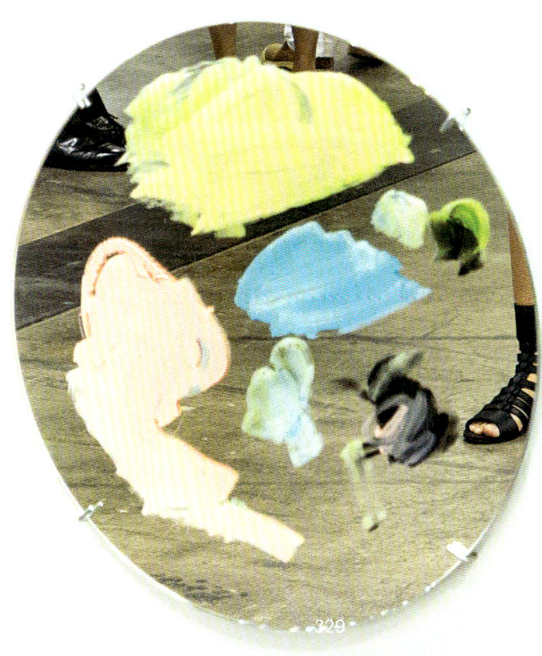
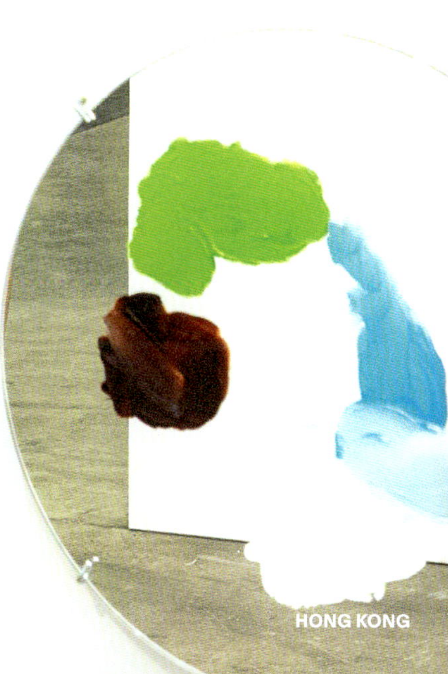

Arndt
Indieguerillas

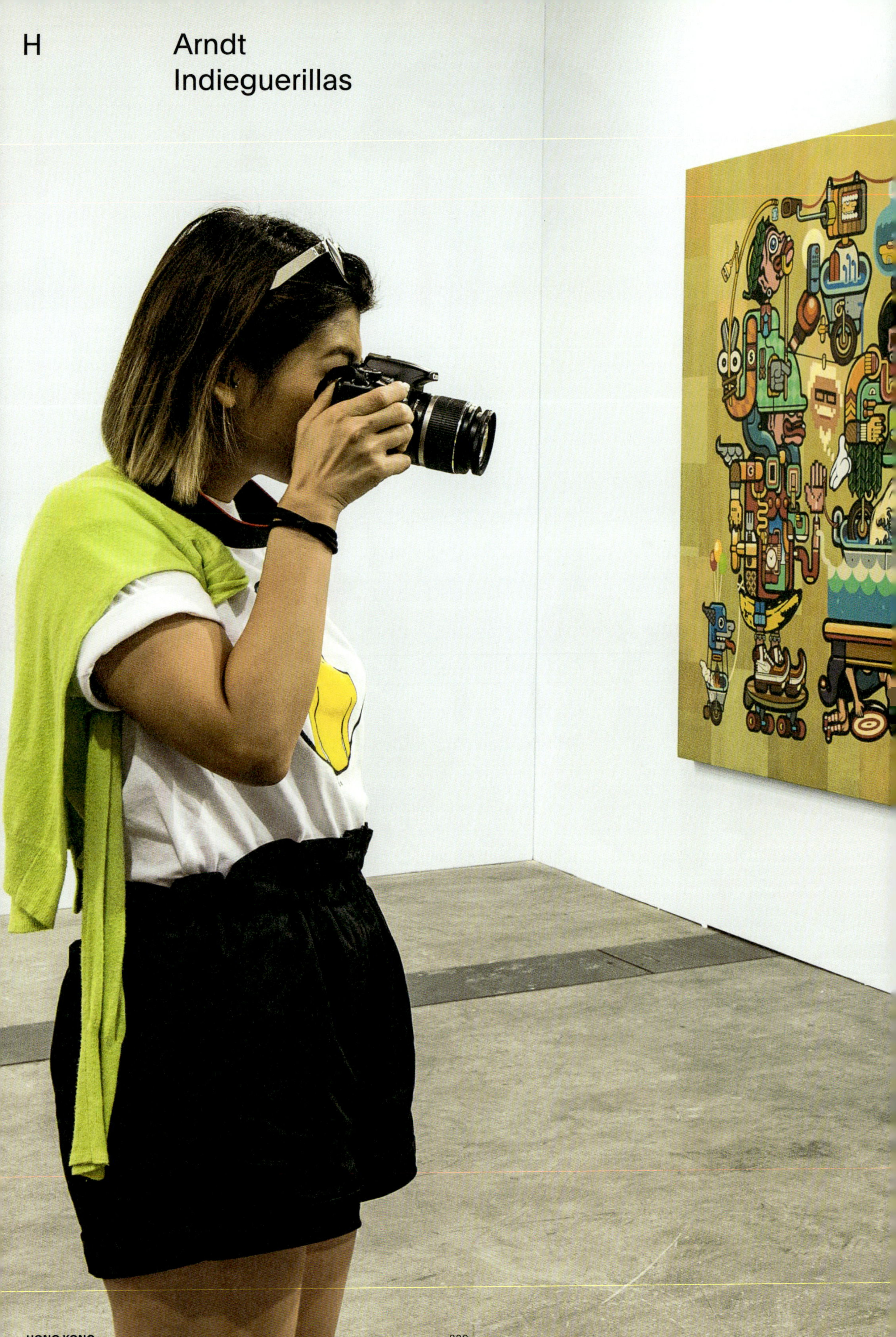

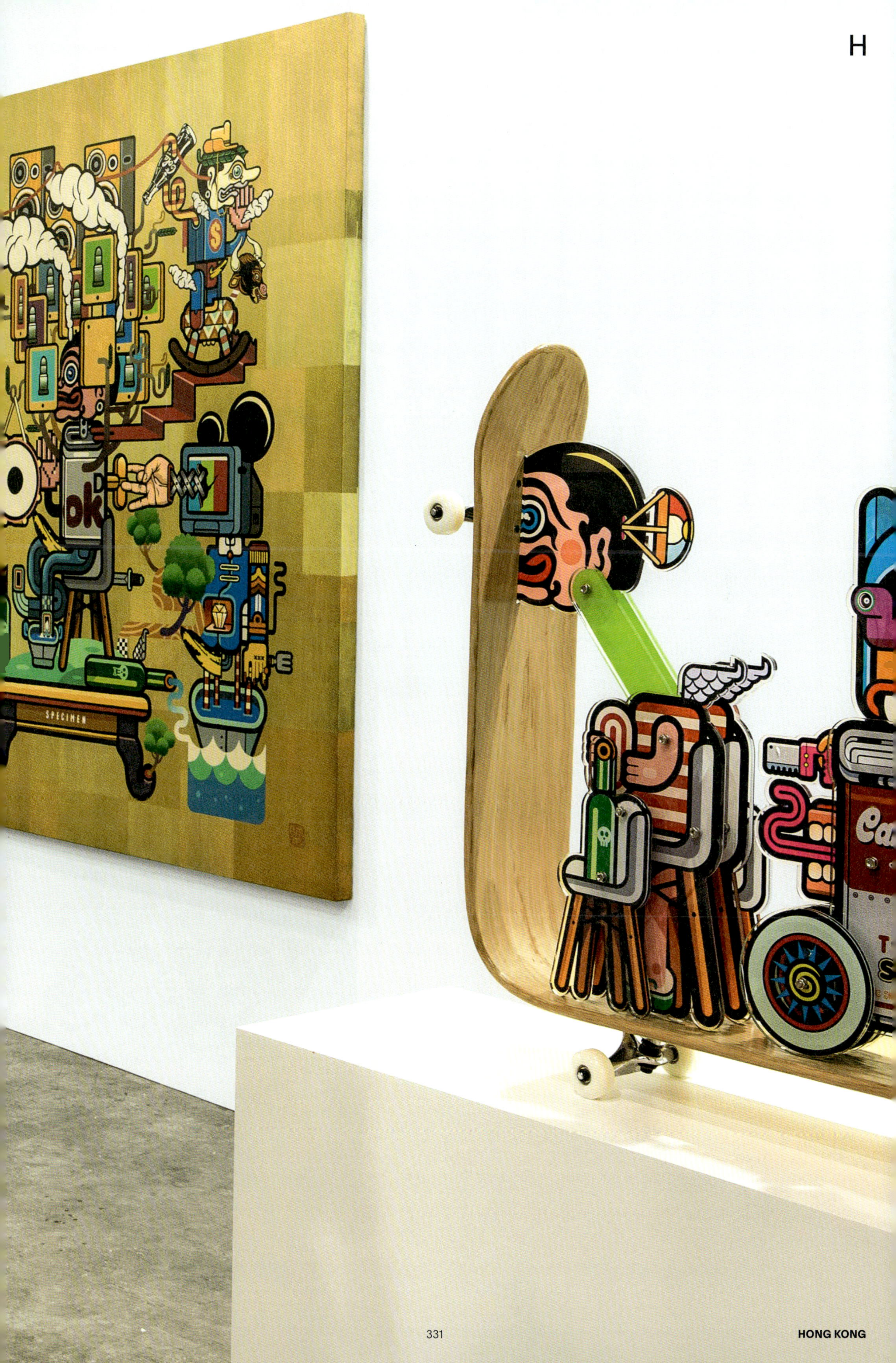
SPECIMEN

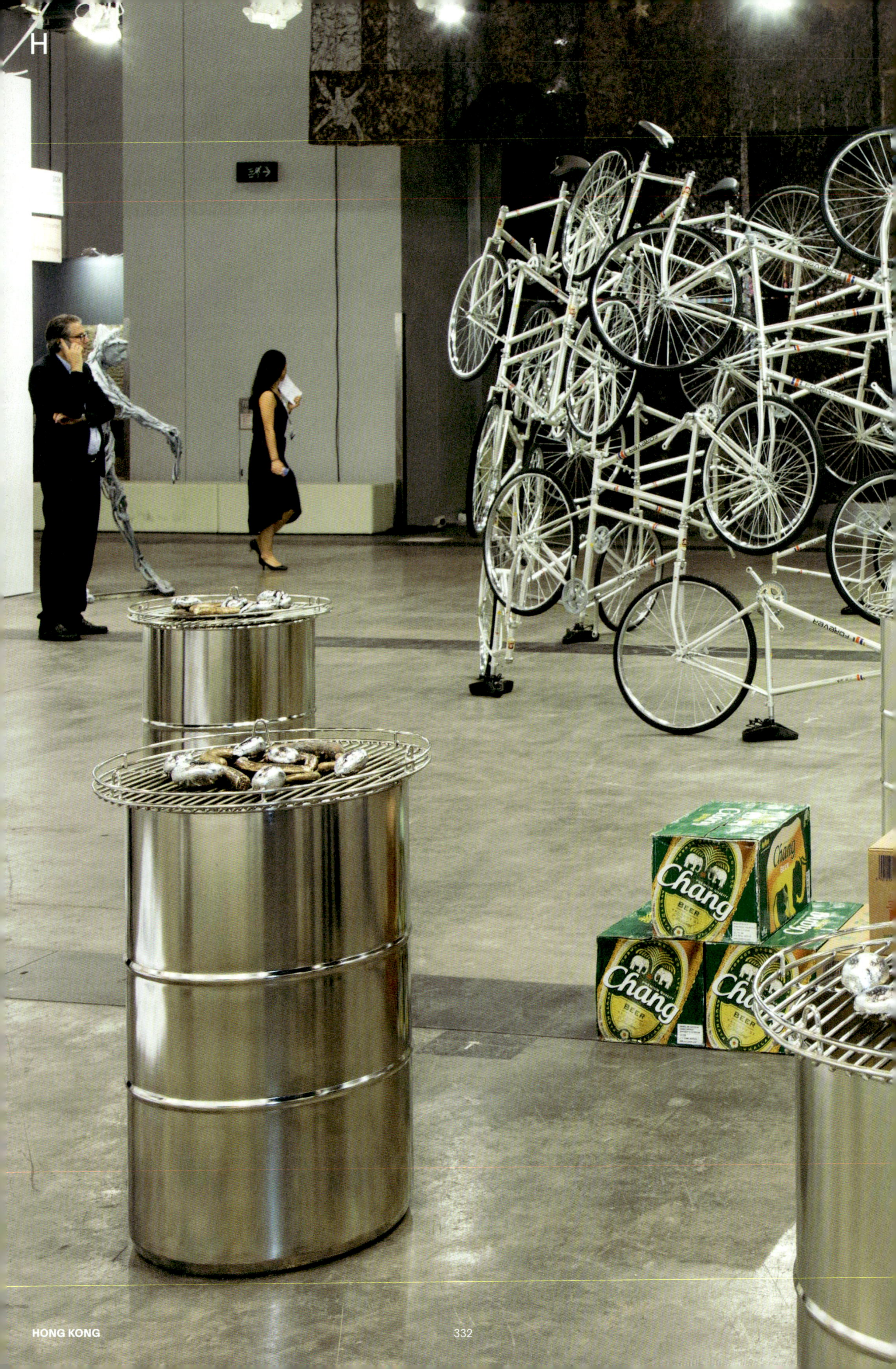
Chang
BEER
Chang
BEER
Chang
FOREVER

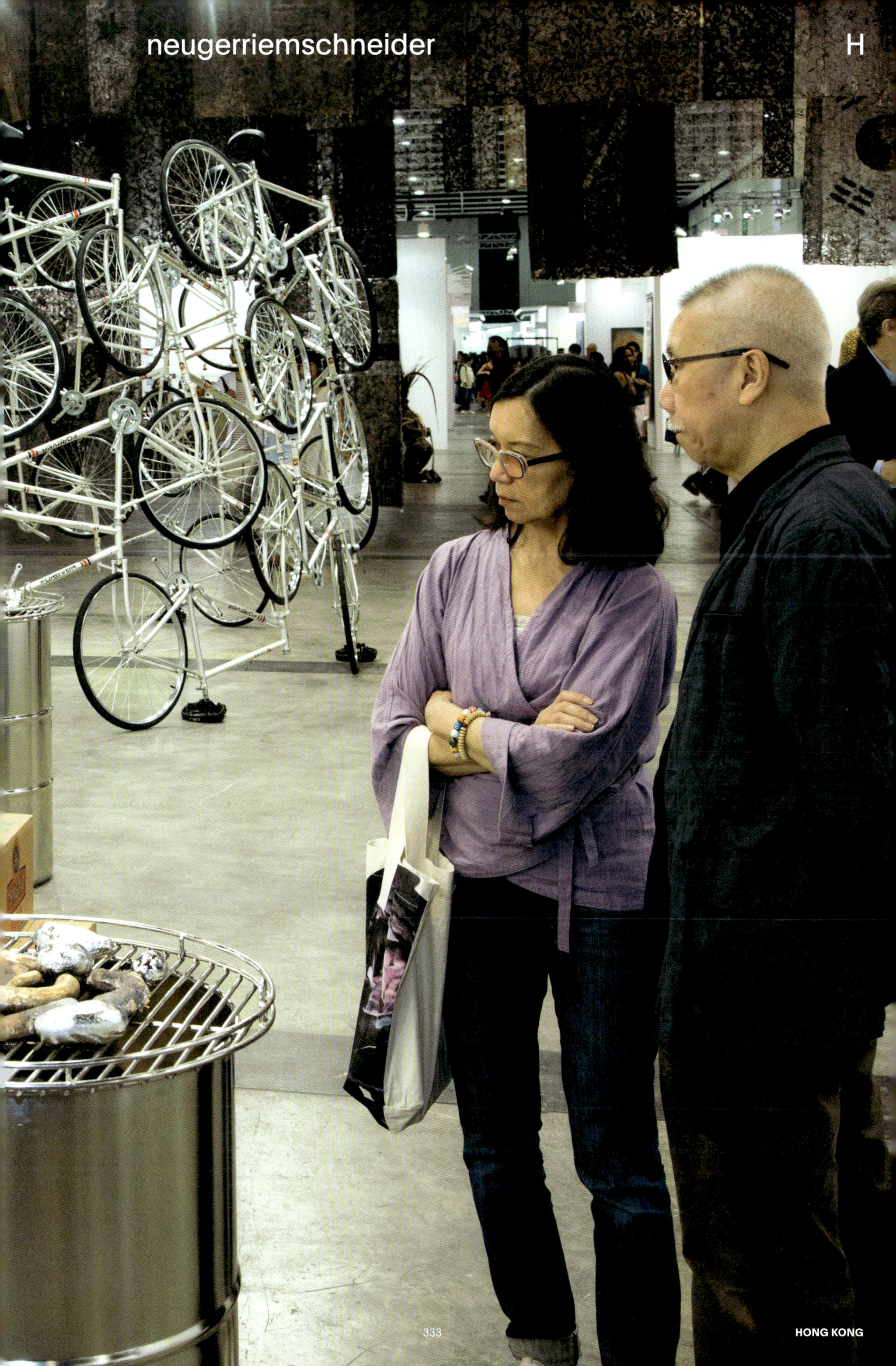

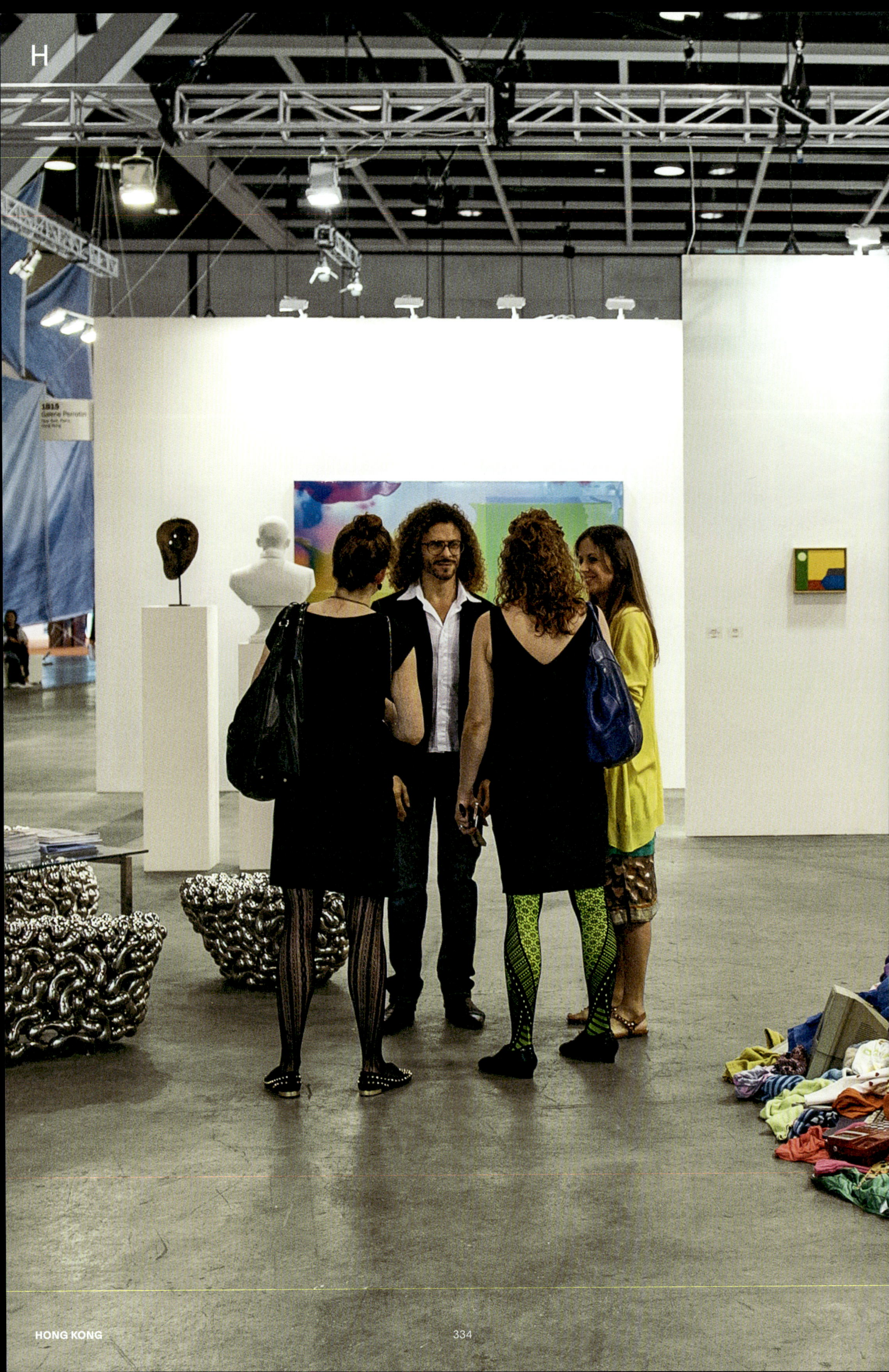

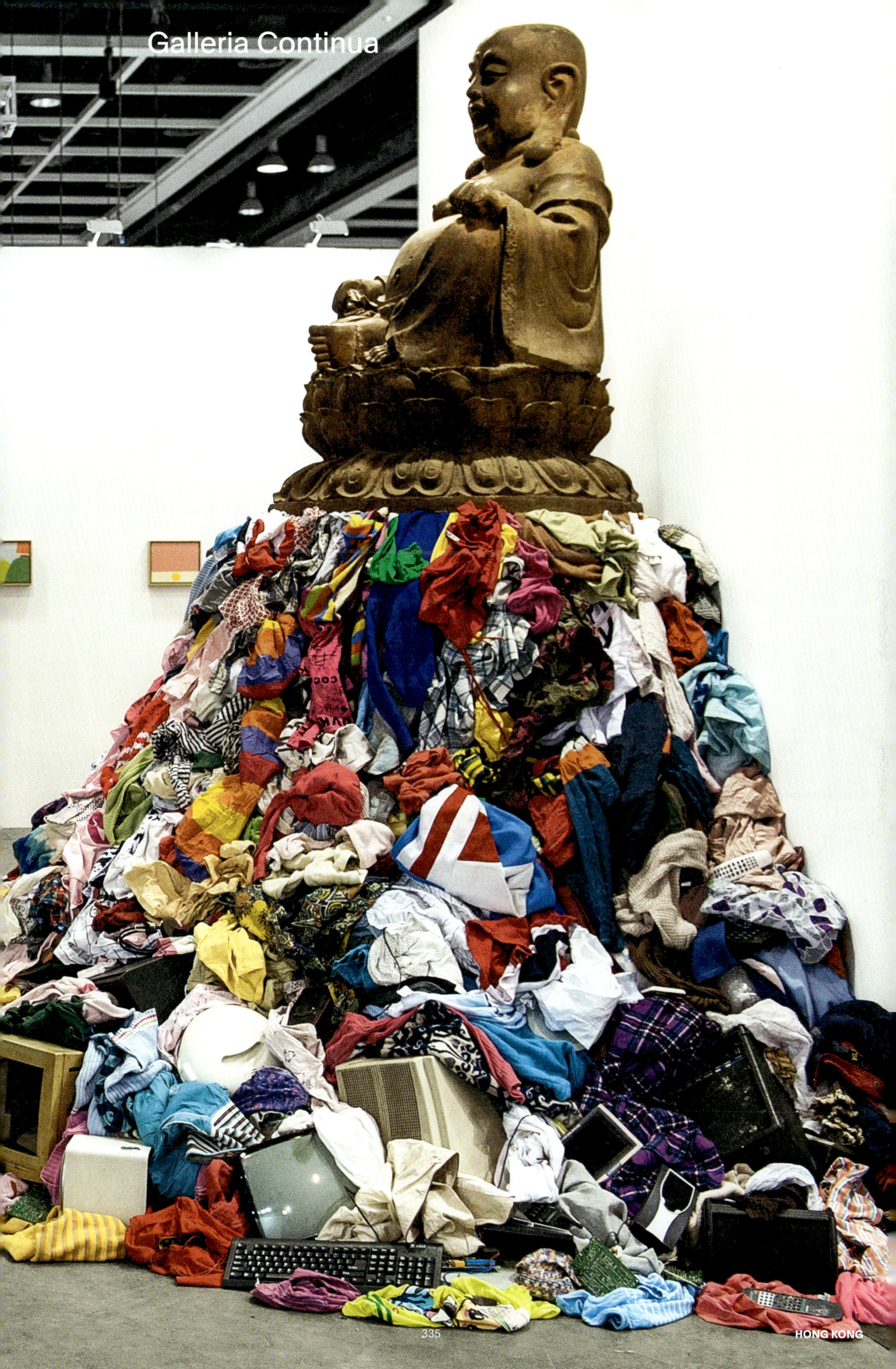
Galleria Continua

Instagram wall at Art Basel in Hong Kong

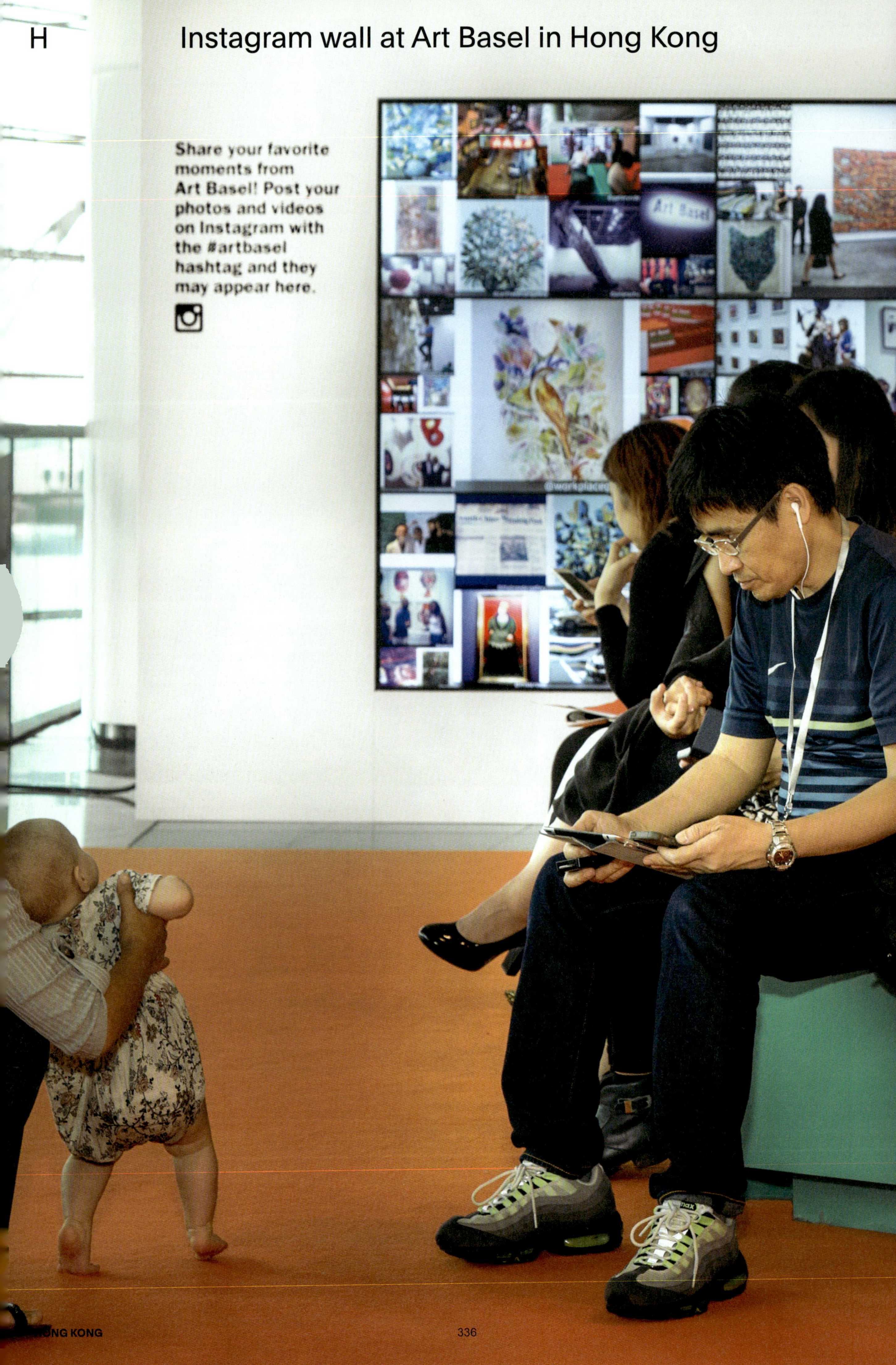

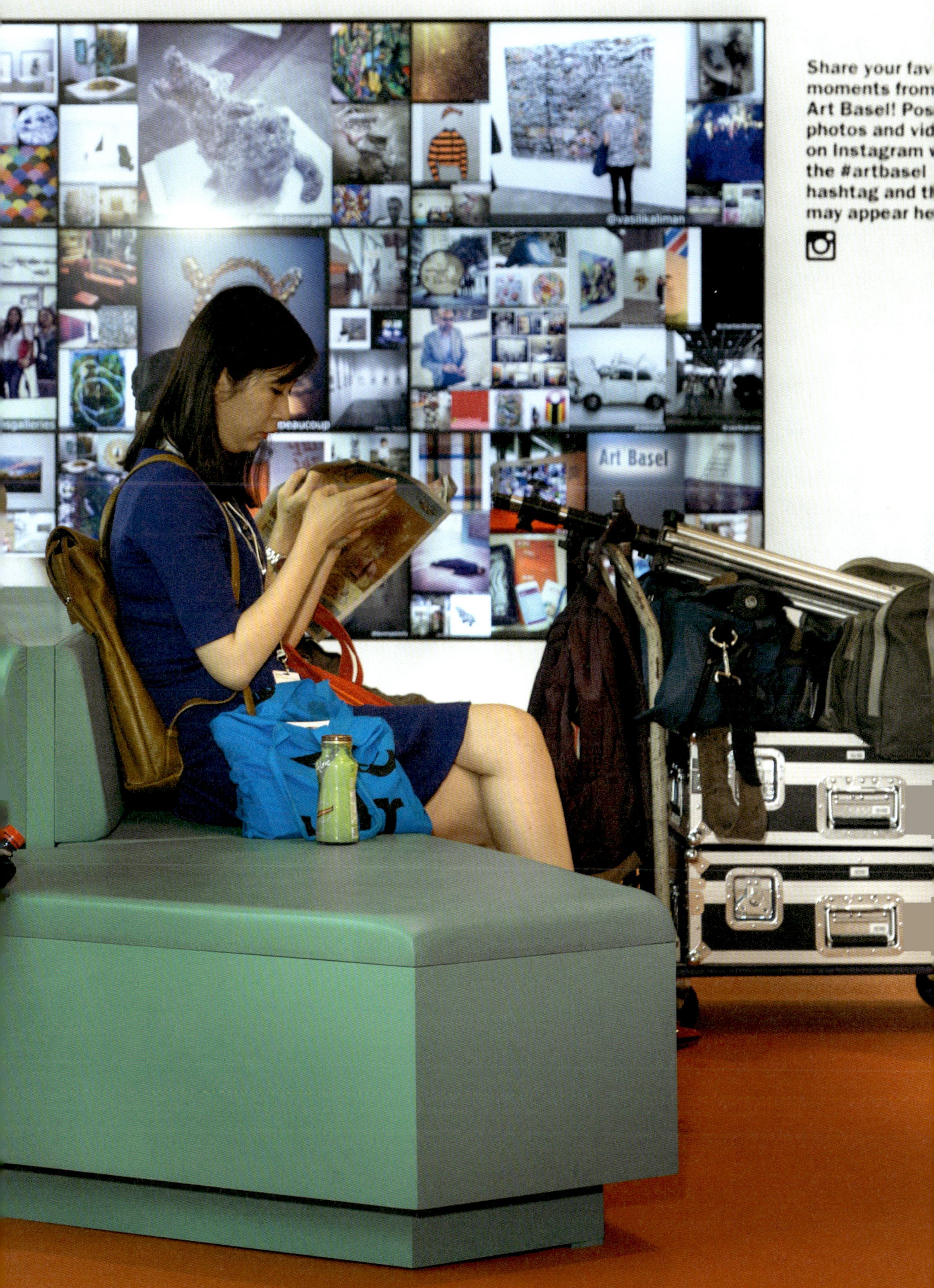
rtbasel
H
Share your fav
moments from
Art Basel! Pos
photos and vid
on Instagram w
the #artbasel
hashtag and th
may appear he
Art Basel

Rhona Hoffman Gallery
Adrian Wong

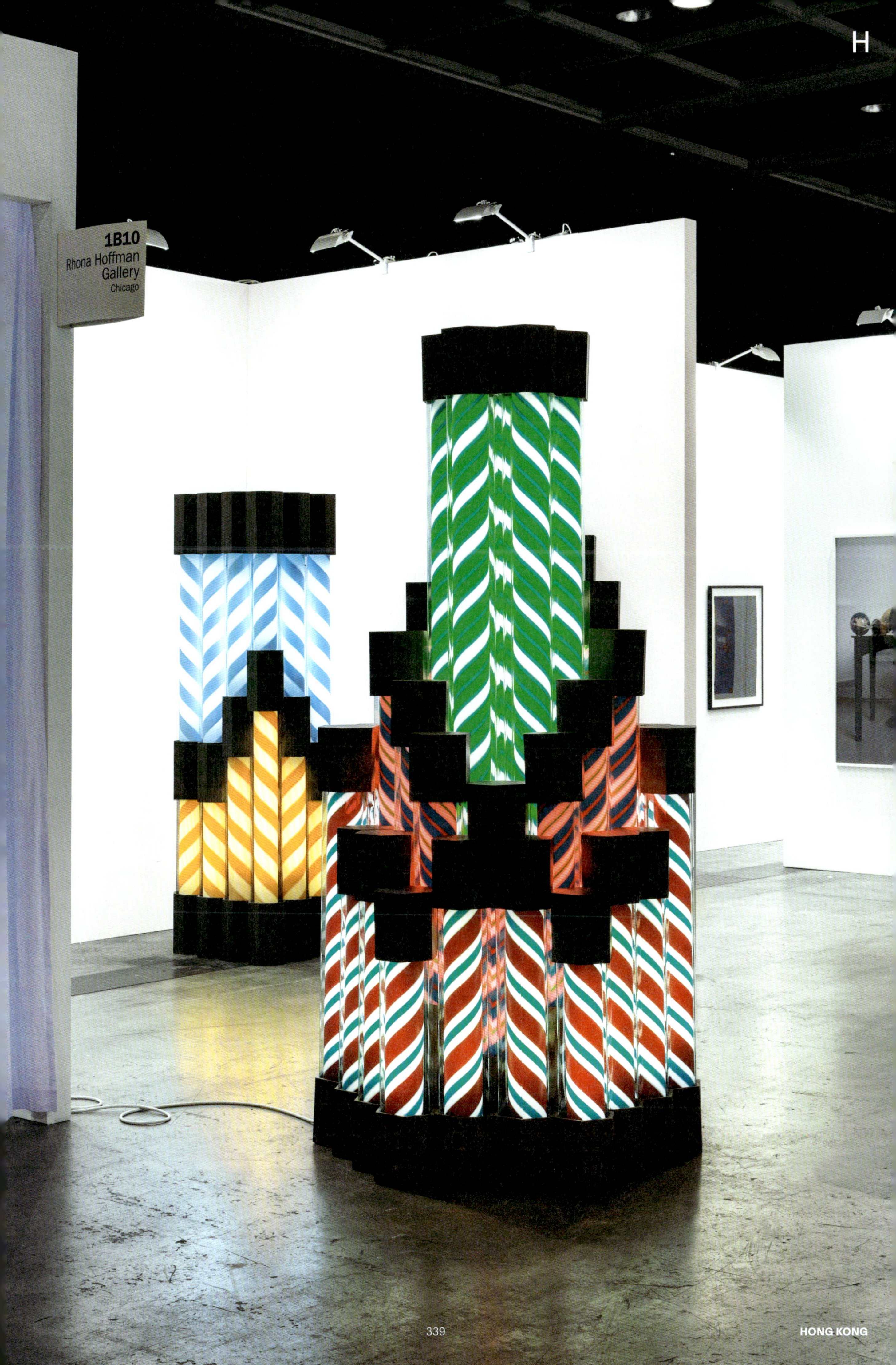
1B10
Rhona Hoffman
Gallery
Chicago

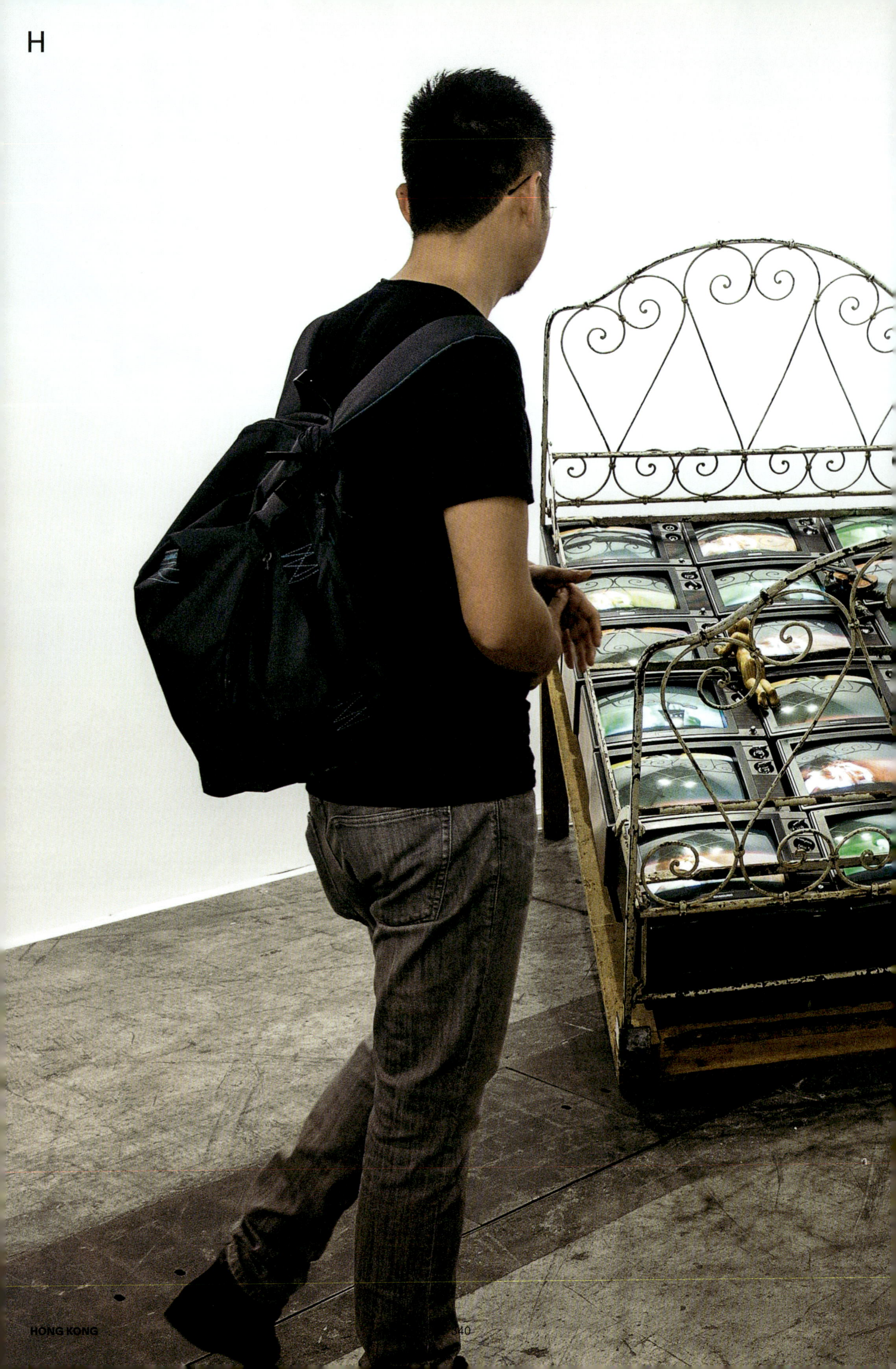

James Cohan Gallery
Nam June Paik

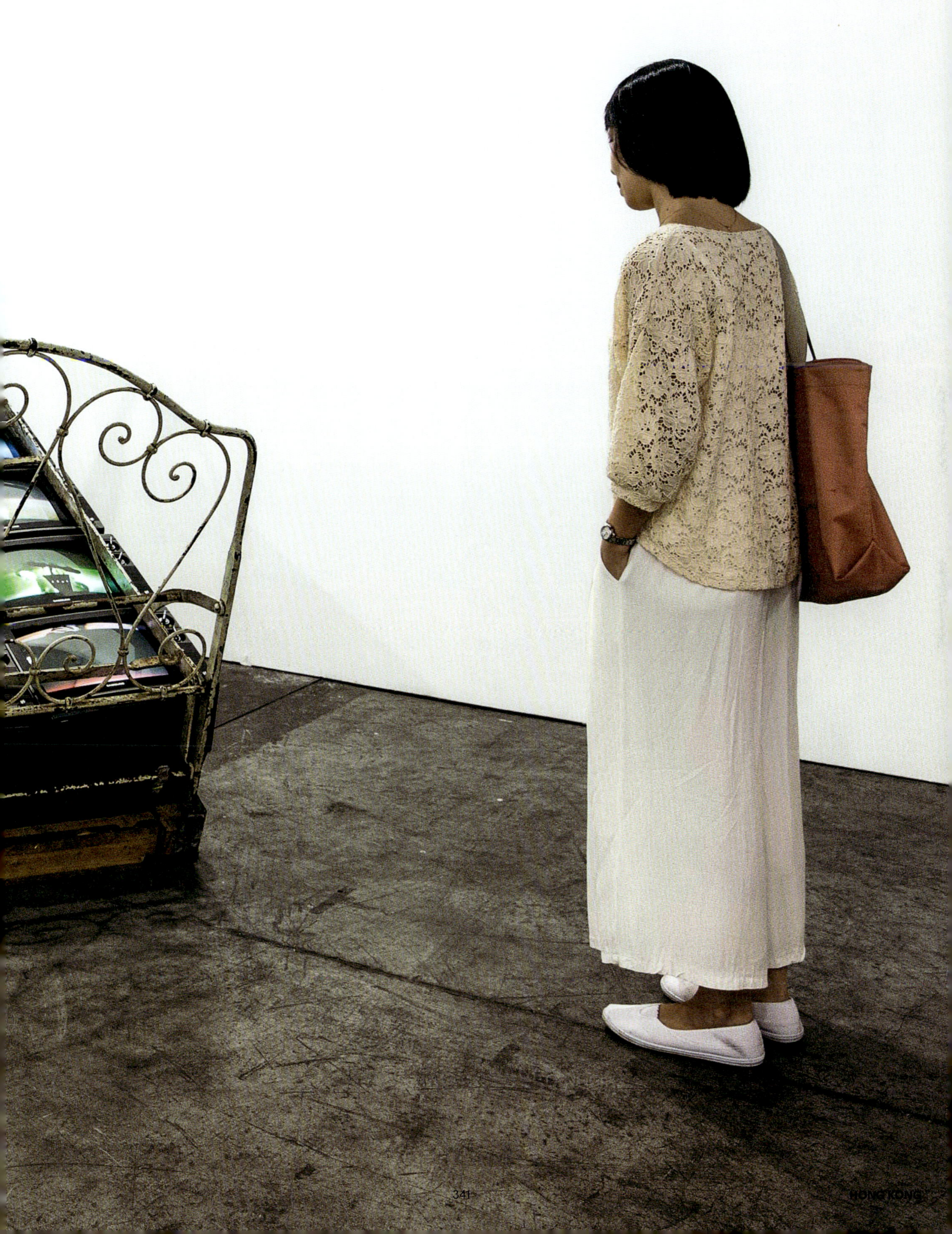

Galleria Franco Noero

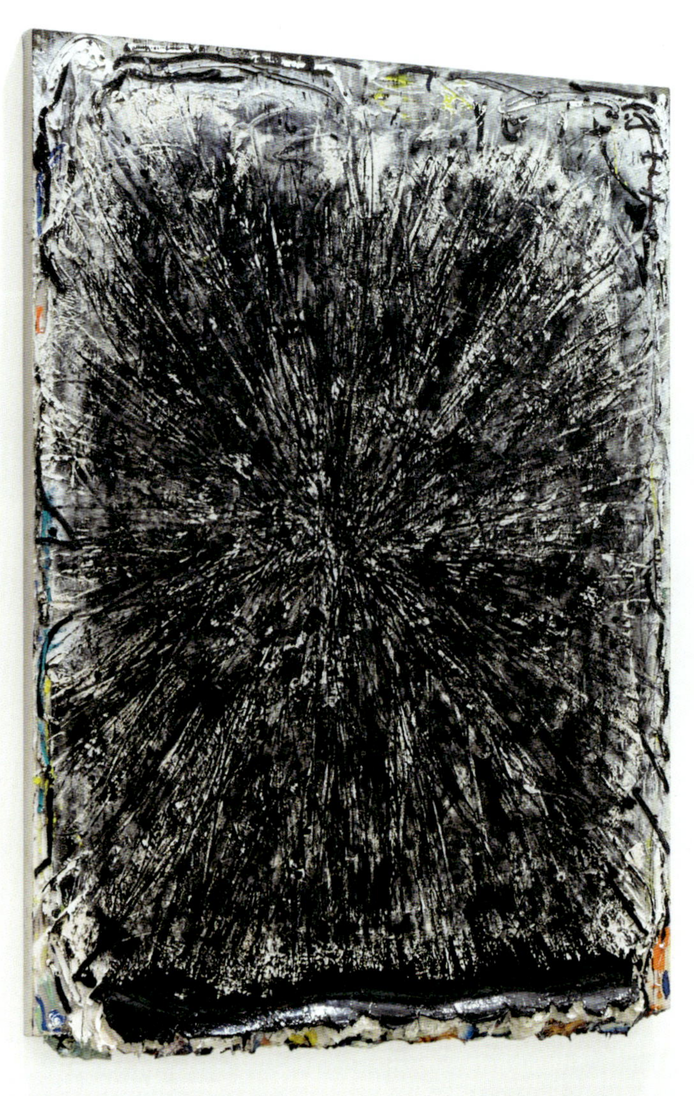

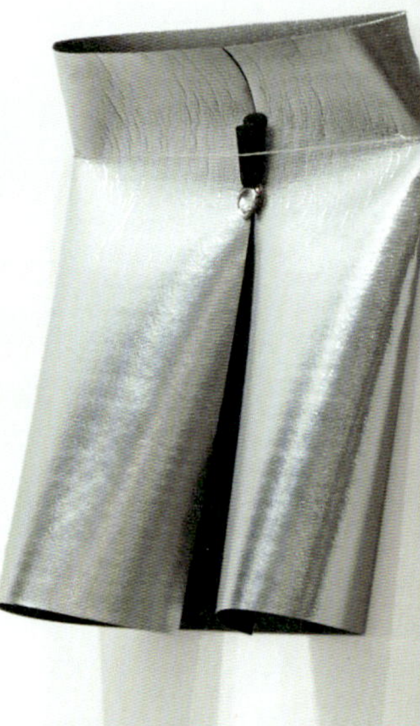

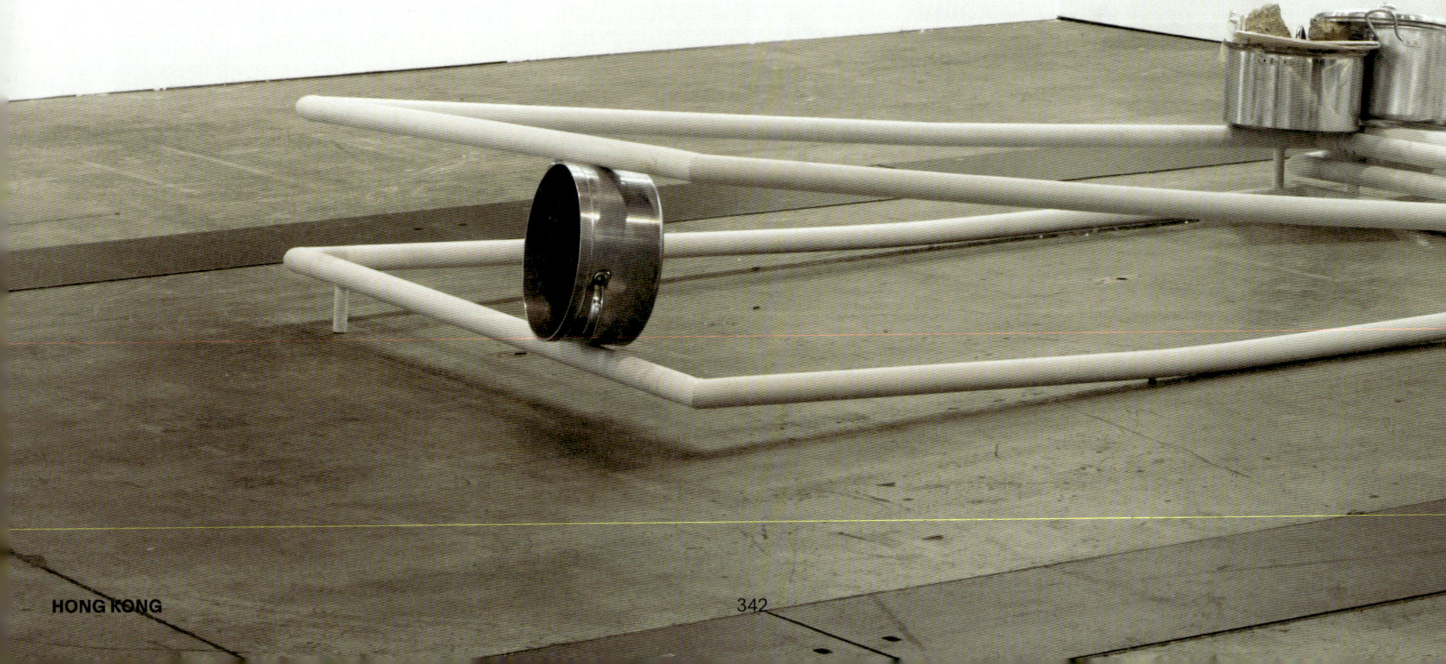

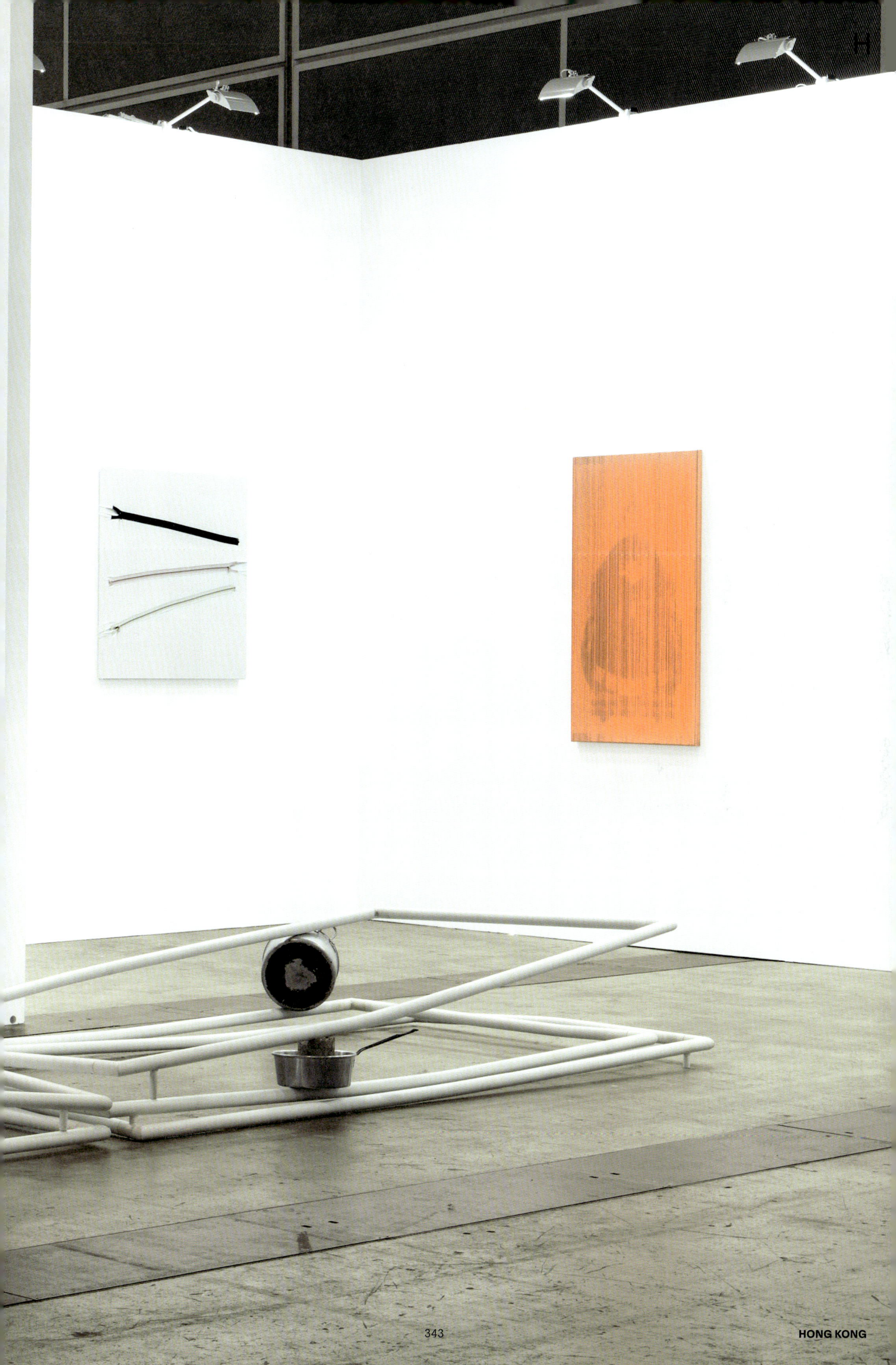

Galerie Eva Presenhuber
Douglas Gordon

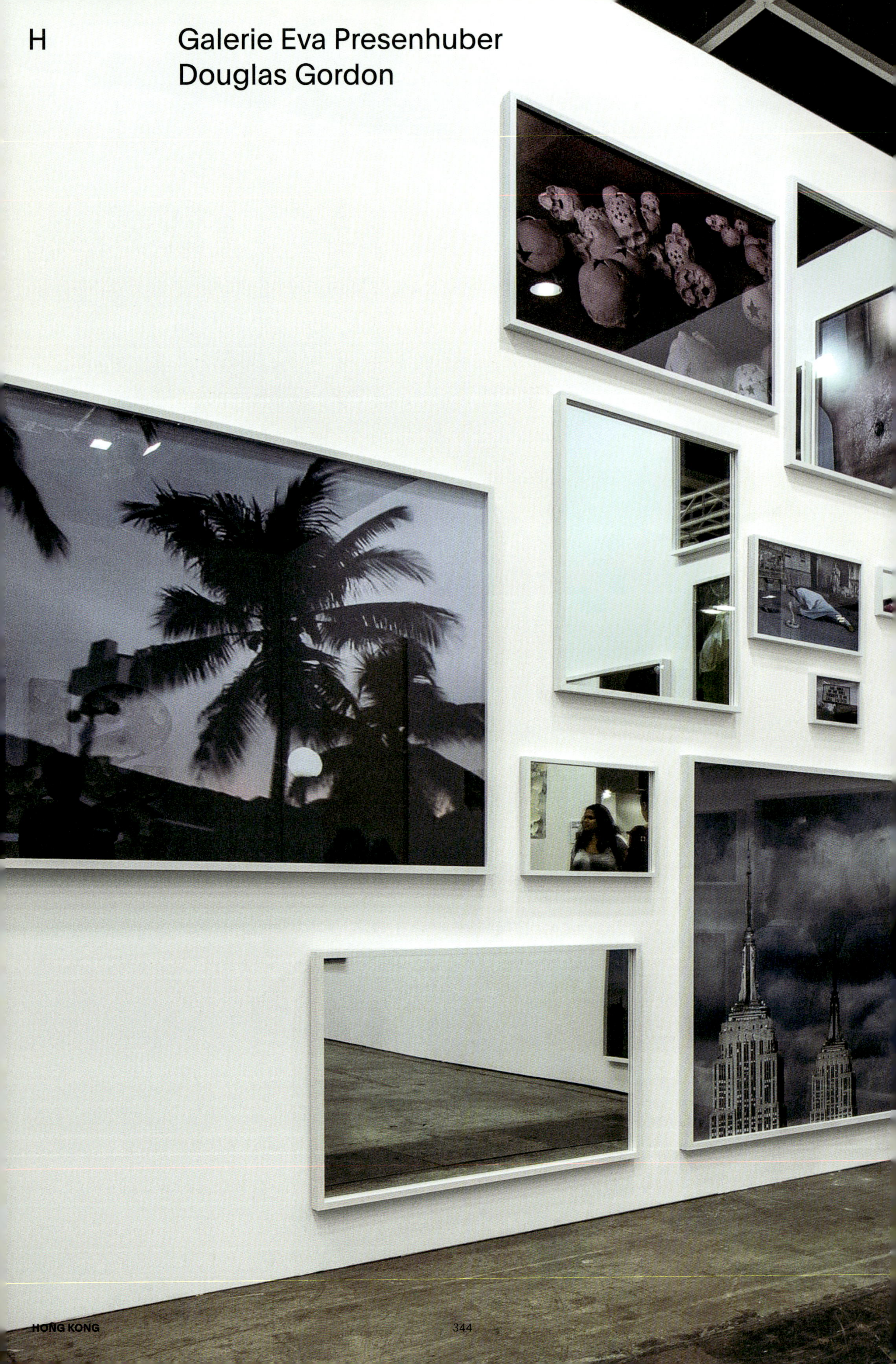

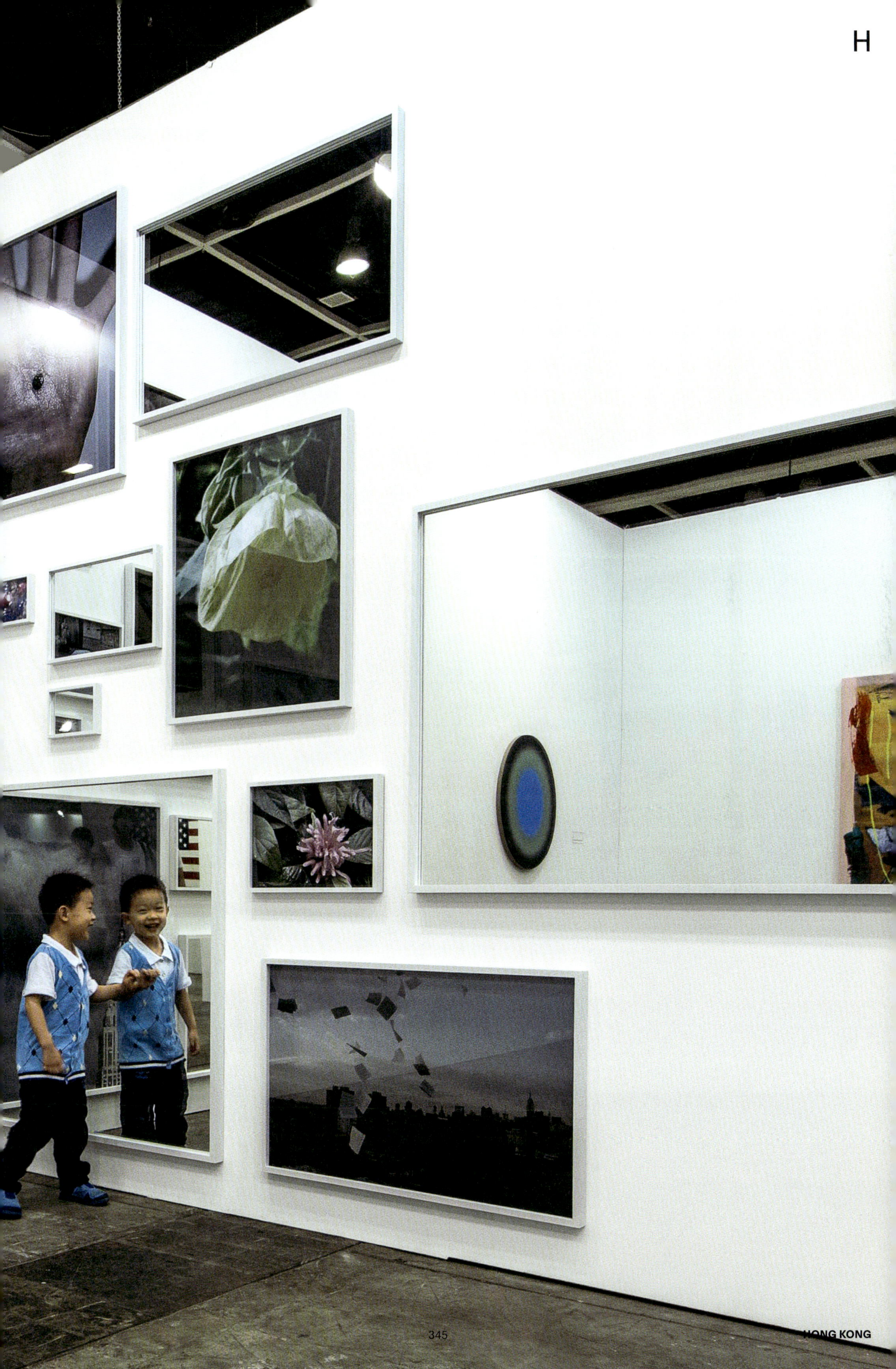

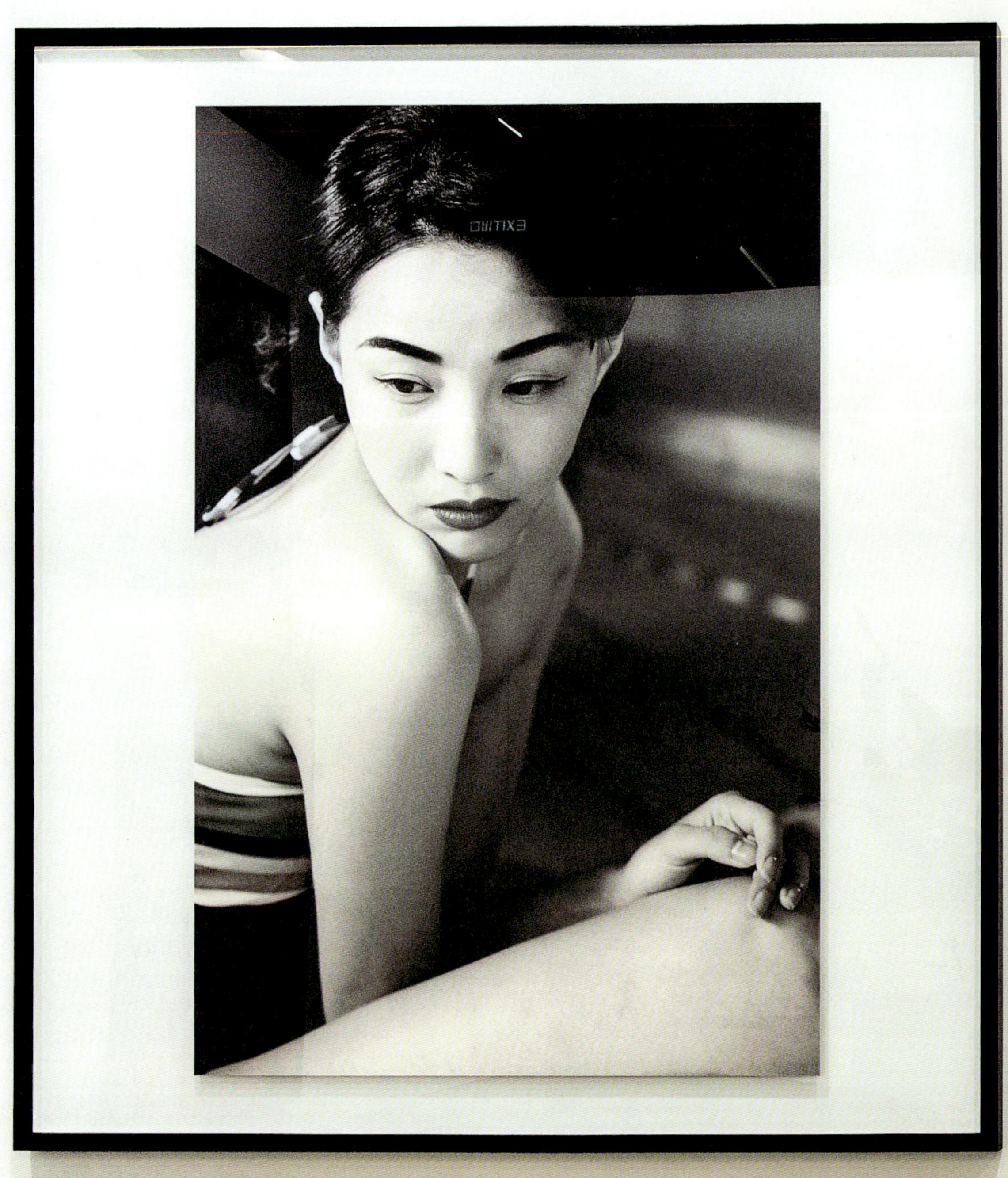

Marian Goodman Gallery
Yang Fudong

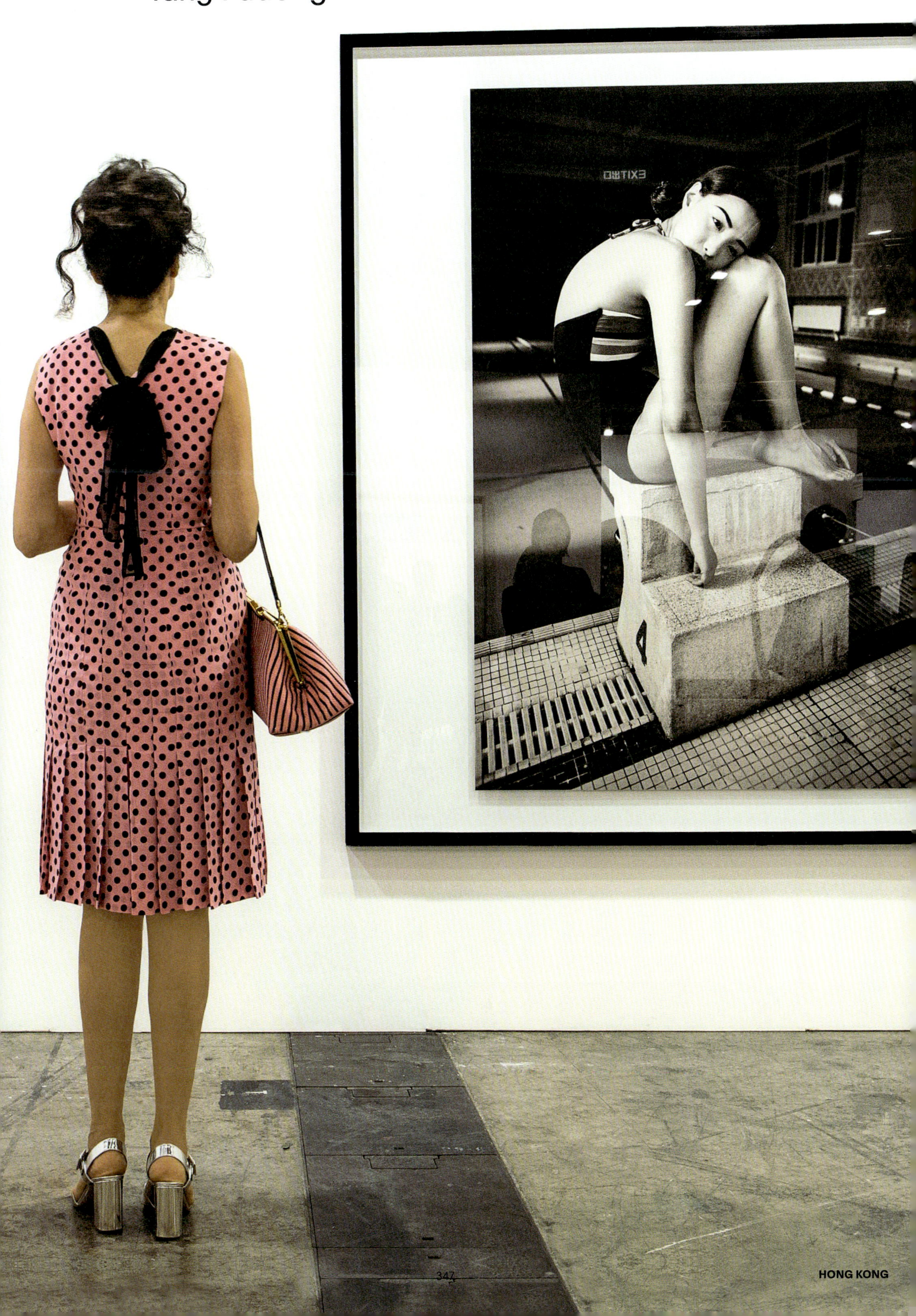

Stuart Shave/Modern Art
David Noonan

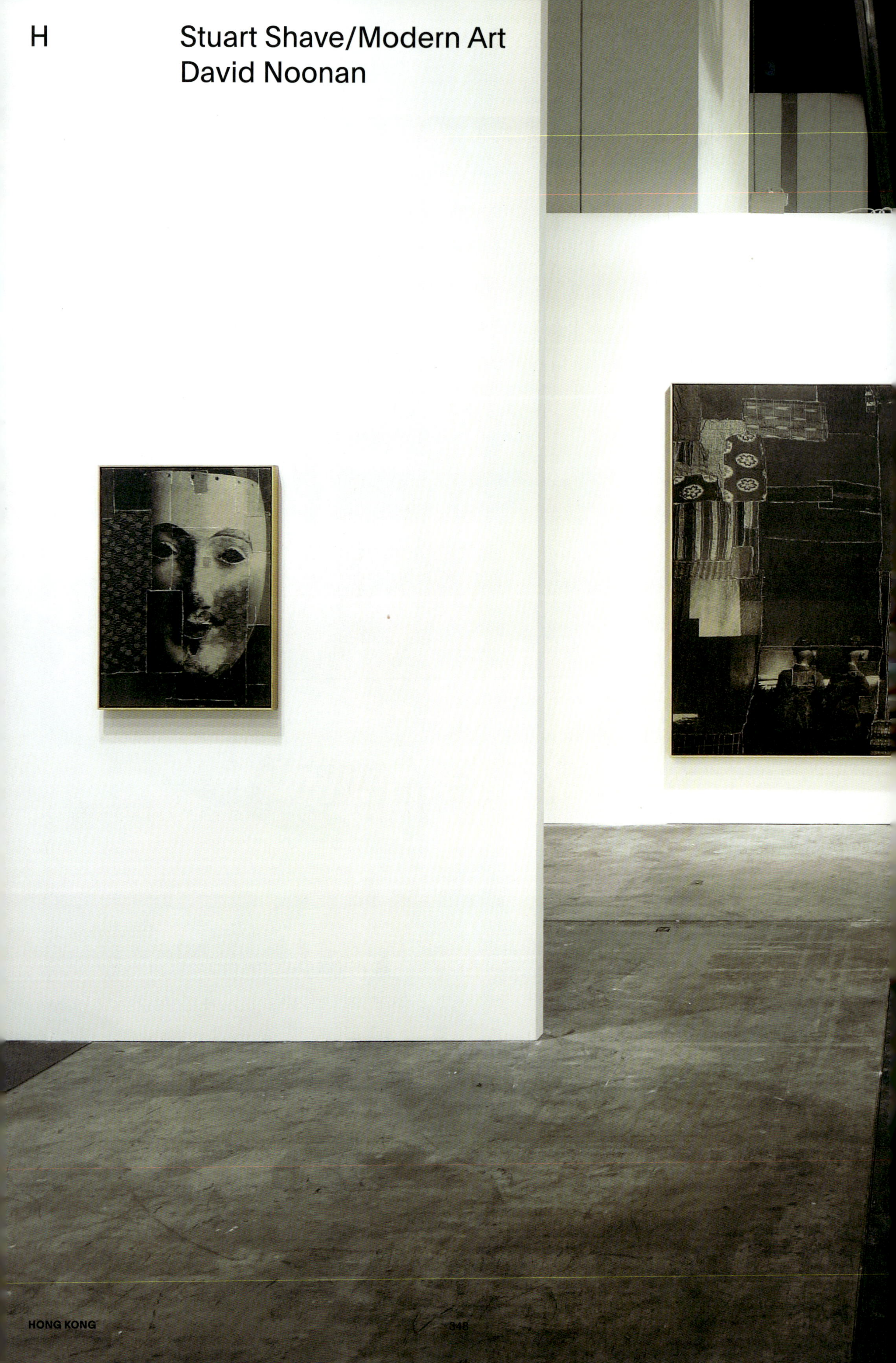

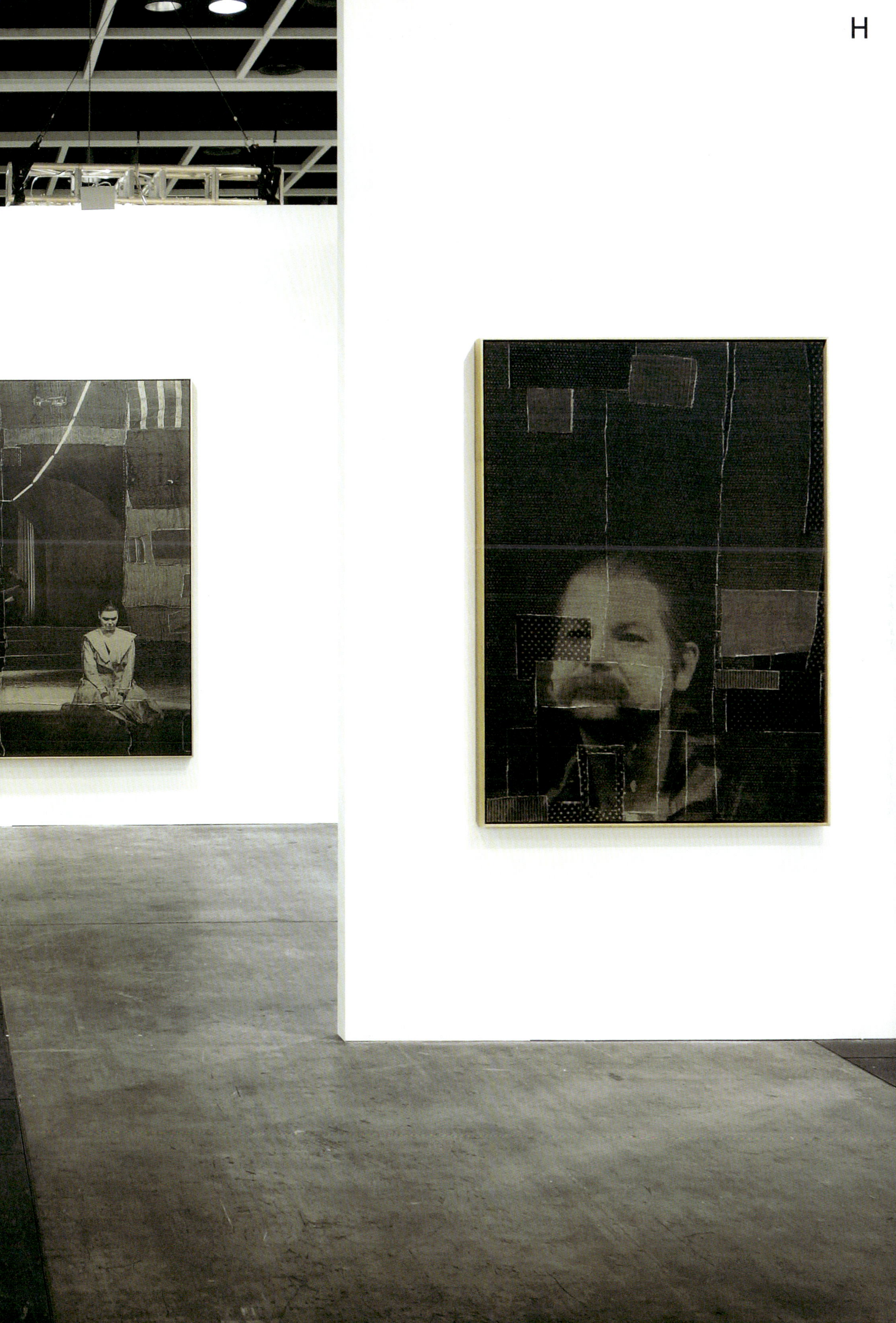
H

H

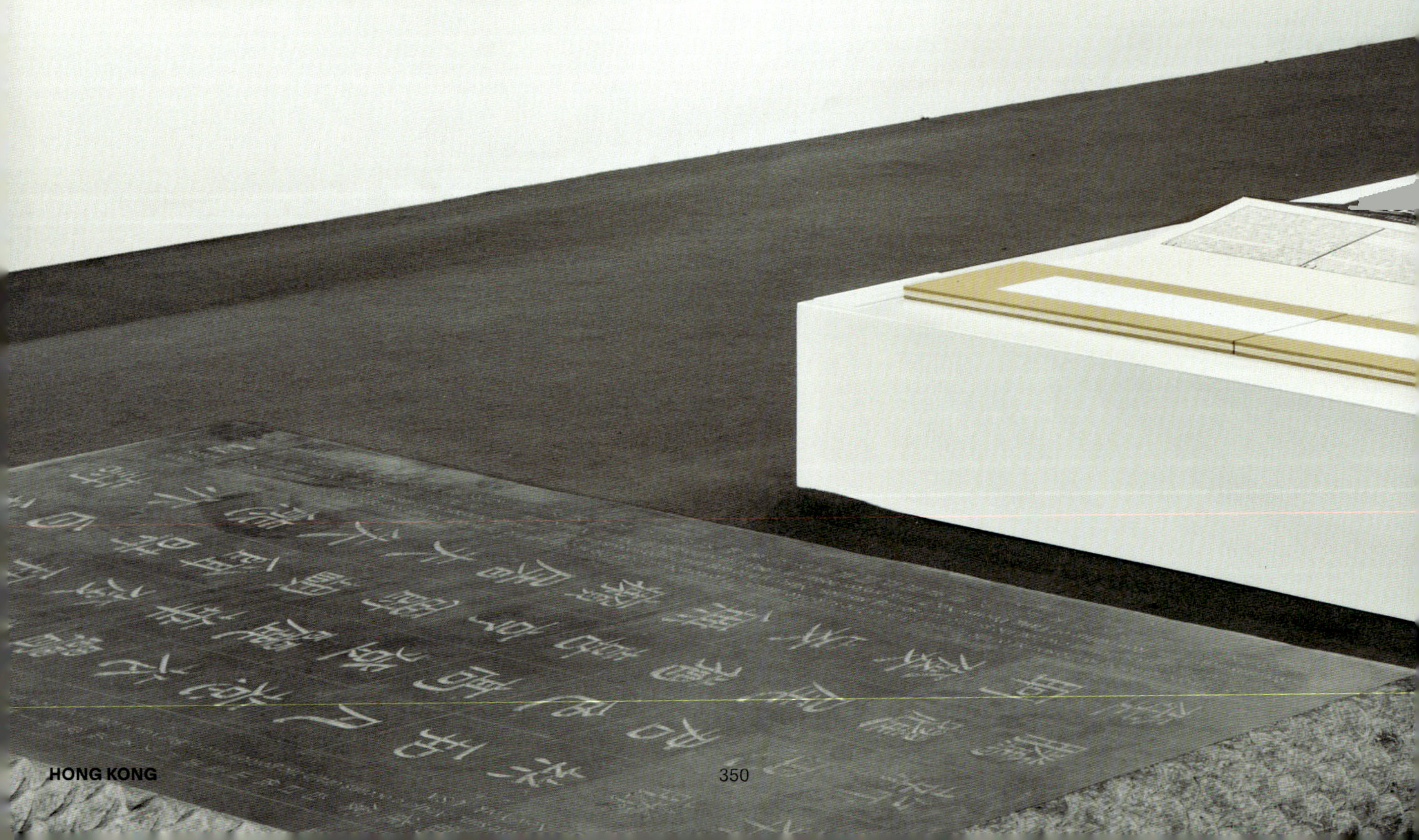

Hanart TZ Gallery
Gu Wenda

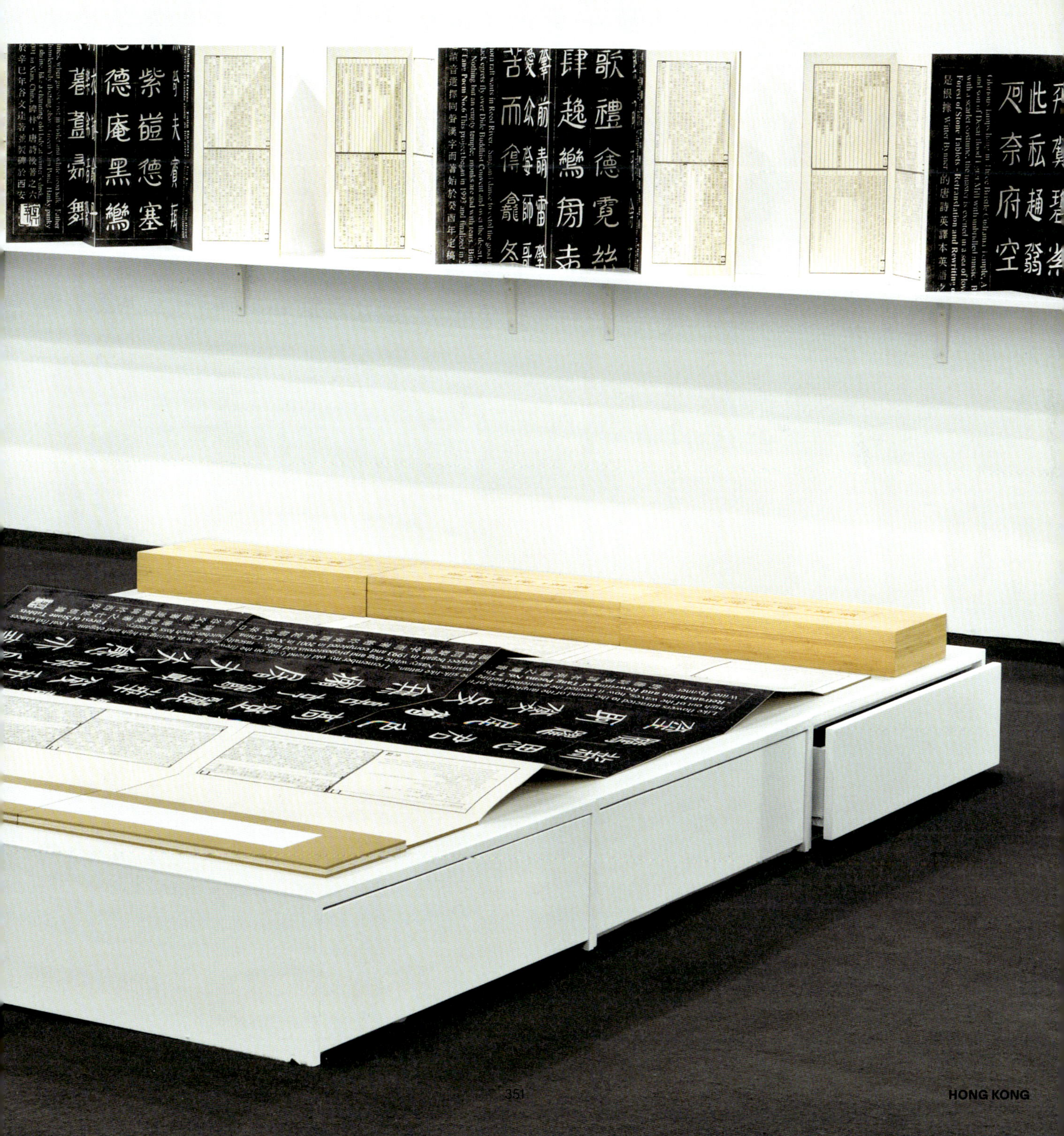

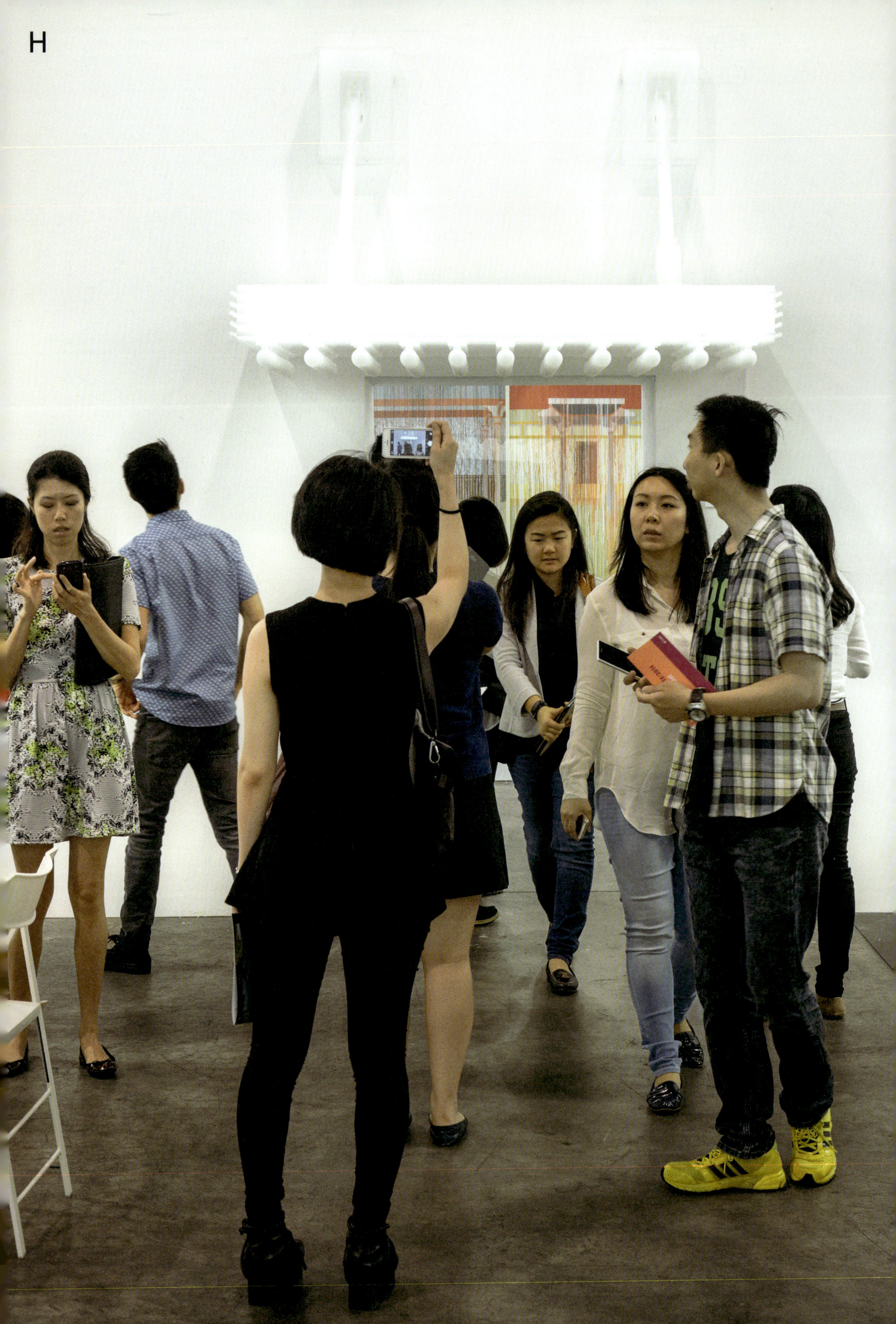

Pilar Corrias
Philippe Parreno

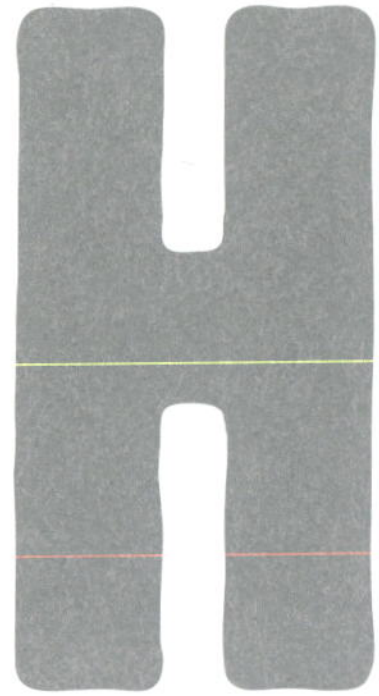

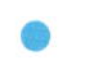

Haas

Berlin

Galleries

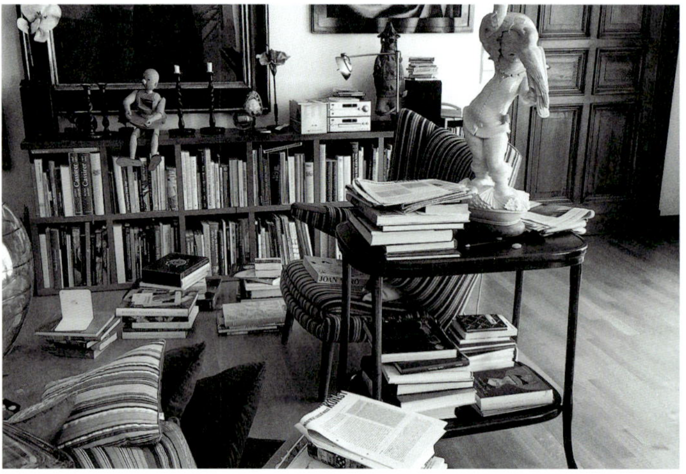

What is your favorite aspect of running a gallery?
The daily engagement with art and artists is my favorite part of the job.

How do you choose the artists you work with?
I work with the artists whose art fascinates me.

If you weren't running a gallery what else would you do?
This is a question that never came up.

- **Contact** Galerie Michael Haas
Michael Haas
contact@galeriemichaelhaas.de
- **Established** 1978
- **Owner(s) / Partner(s)** Michael Haas
- **Team** 8
- **Space(s)** 1,000 m²
- **Artists at Art Basel** Hans Arp
Georg Baselitz
Jiří Georg Dokoupil
Jean Fautrier
Marianna Gartner
Franz Gertsch
Kerstin Grimm
Almut Heise
Ferdinand Hodler
Leiko Ikemura
John Isaacs
Anselm Kiefer
Konrad Klapheck
Paul Klee
Astrid Klein
Gary Kuehn
Dirk Lange
Wolfe von Lenkiewicz
Joan Miró
A.R. Penck
Francis Picabia
Pablo Picasso
Markus Raetz
Arnulf Rainer
Odilon Redon
Carolein Smit
Louis Soutter
Antoni Tàpies
Hans Uhlmann
Félix Vallotton
René Wirths
- **Further artists represented** Nicole Bianchet
Max Beckmann
Peter Blake
George Braque
George Condo
Joseph Cornell
Giorgio De Chirico
Abraham David Christian
André Derain
Marianna Gartner
Julius Grünewald
George Grosz
Richard Jordan
Ernst Ludwig Kirchner
Fernand Léger
Anton Räderscheidt
Carol Rama
Georges Rouault
Pia Stadtbäumer
Dimitris Tzamouranis
Andy Warhol

Hakgojae

Seoul
Shanghai

Galleries

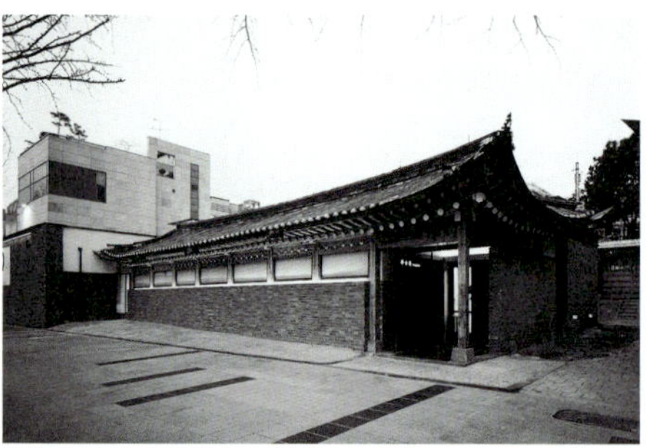

How do you choose the artists you work with?
I seek artists who could remain in art history. I am also looking for artists who criticize contemporary society and suggest directions for human development in the future, who could play the role of precursors.

If you weren't running a gallery what else would you do?
I am sure I would still be in the art field: I would publish books on art, architecture, archaeology, and history. In fact, besides running the gallery, I have also been managing Hakgojae Publishing Company since 1990, and it has produced about 350 books on art and the humanities.

- **Contact** Hakgojae Gallery
Chan-Kyu Woo
info@hakgojae.com
- **Established** 1988
- **Owner(s) / Partner(s)** Woo Chan-Kyu
- **Team** 16
- **Space(s)** 430 m² (Seoul)
230 m² (Shanghai)
- **Artists at Art Basel** Boomoon
Tim Eitel
Hong Kyoung Tack
Jin Meyerson
Jin Yangping
Lee Bae
Lee Seahyun
Lee Ufan
Lee Yongbaek
Ma Liuming
Zhang Huan
- **Further artists represented** Atta Kim
Chen Wenji
Cho Hwan
Choong Sup Lim
Chung Hyun
Chung Sang-hwa
Ian Davenport
Tim Eitel
Bernard Frize
Giuseppe Penone
Heo Suyoung
Jia Youfu

Kang Yo-bae
Kim Ho-deuk
Lee Dong-youb
Lee Jong-gu
Lee Lee Nam
Lee Myoungho
Lee Youngbin
Noh Suntag
Oh Yun
Roman Opalka
Jean-Pierre Raynaud
Shin Hak-chul
Song Hyun-Sook
Suh Yongsun
Günther Uecker
Yangachi
Yin Qi
You Hyeonkyeong
Yun Suk-nam

Hales

London 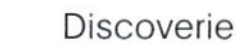 Discoveries

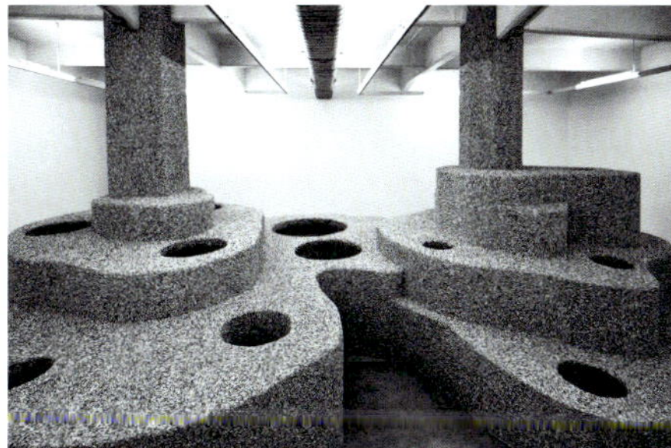

What is your favorite aspect of running a gallery?

I enjoy finding artists whose work I love, trying to figure out how they could fit into a marketplace and how I could be instrumental in developing their career. I especially enjoy finding artists that have been overlooked and whose work has become increasingly important with the years. It is the equivalent of finding a ruby in the dust, having it set properly and then presenting it to the world.

How do you choose the artists you work with?

Our gallery program is loosely based on several key radical movements and creative ideas of the 1960s and 1970s. Feminist ideas, Civil Rights, working-class emancipation, and ideas based around the land and ecological issues. A number of the artists we show have careers that began in this period and other younger artists have taken up their legacy.

If you weren't running a gallery what else would you do?

I can't think of anything else I would do. I love it and I am completely engaged with it.

- **Contact** — Hales Gallery
  Paul Hedge
  paulhedge@halesgallery.com
- **Established** — 1992
- **Owner(s) / Partner(s)** — Paul Hedge
  Paul Maslin
- **Team** — 6
- **Space(s)** — 110 m²
- **Artists at Art Basel** — Omar Ba
  Tom Price
- **Further artists represented** — Derrick Adams
  Basil Beattie
  Andrew Bick
  Frank Bowling
  Sebastiaan Bremer
  Rachael Champion
  Adam Dant
  Trenton Doyle Hancock
  Richard Galpin
  Hew Locke
  Adam Ross
  Carolee Schneemann
  Richard Slee
  Michael Smith
  Jane Wilbraham
  Martin Wilner

Hammer

New York 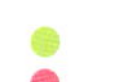 Galleries
Galleries

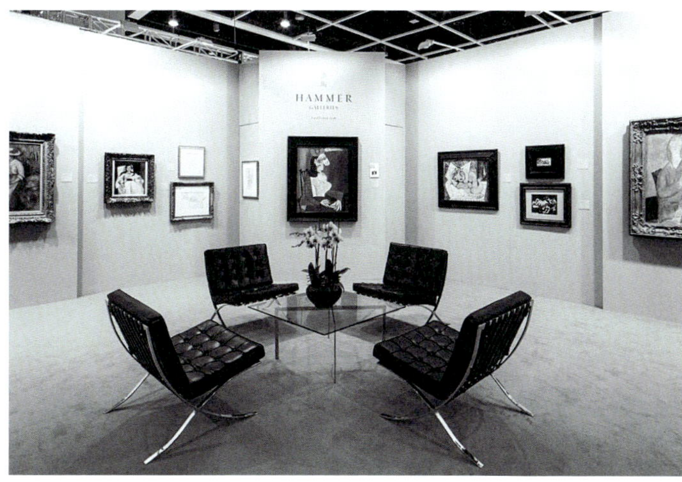

What is your favorite aspect of running a gallery?

Working with extraordinary works of art and extraordinary collectors.

How do you choose the artists you work with?

We are a secondary market gallery, specializing in Impressionist, Modern, and Postwar masters.

If you weren't running a gallery what else would you do?

After over 30 years in the art world, it is hard to imagine doing anything else.

- **Contact** — Hammer Galleries
  Howard Shaw
  info@hammergalleries.com
- **Established** — 1928
- **Owner(s) / Partner(s)** — Howard Shaw
- **Team** — 7
- **Space(s)** — 225 m²
- **Artists at Art Basel** — Alexander Calder
  Marc Chagall
  Jean Dubuffet
  Max Ernst
  Lucio Fontana
  Sam Francis
  Robert Indiana
  Wassily Kandinsky
  Fernand Léger
  Henri Matisse
  Joan Miró
  Pablo Picasso
  Chaïm Soutine
  Andy Warhol
  Tom Wesselmann
- **Further artists represented** — Pierre Bonnard
  Fernando Botero
  Georges Braque
  Paul Cézanne
  Chen Yifei
  Salvador Dalí
  Edgar Degas
  Kees van Dongen
  Paul Gauguin
  Vincent van Gogh
  Réne Magritte
  Amedeo Modigliani
  Claude Monet
  Berthe Morisot
  Camille Pissarro
  Pierre-Auguste Renoir
  Alfred Sisley
  Yves Tanguy
  Henri de Toulouse-Lautrec

Hanart TZ

Hong Kong

Galleries
Encounters
Feature

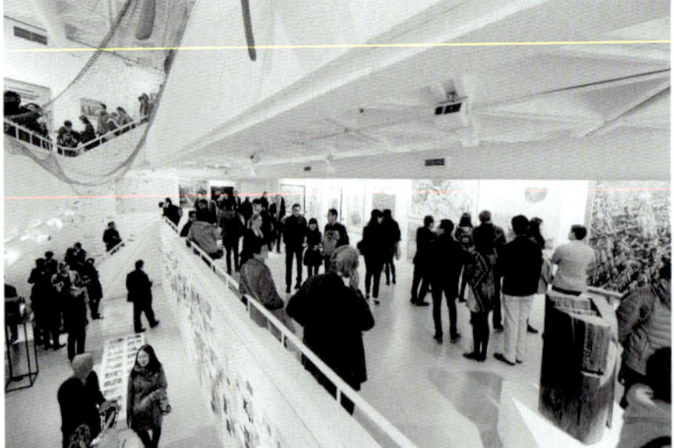

What is your favorite aspect of running a gallery?

When I started 30 years ago, I tried to create a platform in Hong Kong for art and other things I was interested in. After 30 years, the gallery remains one of my stable platforms, but "other things" have gone in diverse ways: academic research, archive, rites and rituals etc. Hanart TZ gallery is the locus of the multiple platforms I operate on; apart from art exhibitions, our gallery is a site for academic conversation, art experimentation, and intercultural exchange.

How do you choose the artists you work with?

I work with artists I believe in and on special projects I want to develop. In the market, quite a few significant artists are still under-appreciated, such as Wu Shanzhuan, Qiu Zhijie, Liu Dahong from Mainland China, and Chen Chieh-Jen, Yeh Wei-li from Taiwan. They are all my favourite artists. I am developing a selection of "calligraphy-painting," in order to investigate China's pictorial art in the context of contemporary times: Leung Kui-Ting, Yuan Jai, and Hsu Yu-Jen, etc.

If you weren't running a gallery what else would you do?

I suppose cultural practice in general. I am now working with Tsinghua University, the City University, and China Academy of Art (Hangzhou) on traditional Chinese rites ("Li"). Out of this research comes a new study of the Chinese modern body from the angle of the Confucian body, the classical Chinese ritual body. I am also keen on material culture: craft and the living space.

- **Contact** Hanart TZ Gallery
  Arman Lam
  hanart@hanart.com
- **Established** 1983
- **Owner(s) / Partner(s)** Chang Tsong-zung (Johnson Chang)
- **Team** 14
- **Space(s)** 100 m² (Hanart TZ Gallery)
  380 m² (Hanart Square)
- **Artists at Art Basel** Cao Xiaoyang
  Luis Chan Estate
  Chen Chieh-Jen
  Chow Chun Fai
  Emily Cheng
  Feng Mengbo
  Gu Wenda
  Ho Sin Tung
  Lee Michael
  Leung Kui Ting
  Liu Dahong
  Liu Guosong
  Mao Xuhui
  Qiu Shihua
  Qiu Zhijie
  Wong Chung-yu
  Wu Shanzhuan
  & Inga Svala Thorsdottir
  Xu Longsen
  Yang Jiechang
  Yao Jui-Chung
  Yeh Wei-Li

Hauser & Wirth

Zurich
New York
London
Somerset

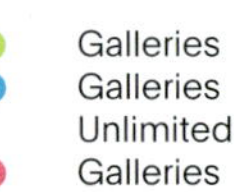

Galleries
Galleries
Unlimited
Galleries

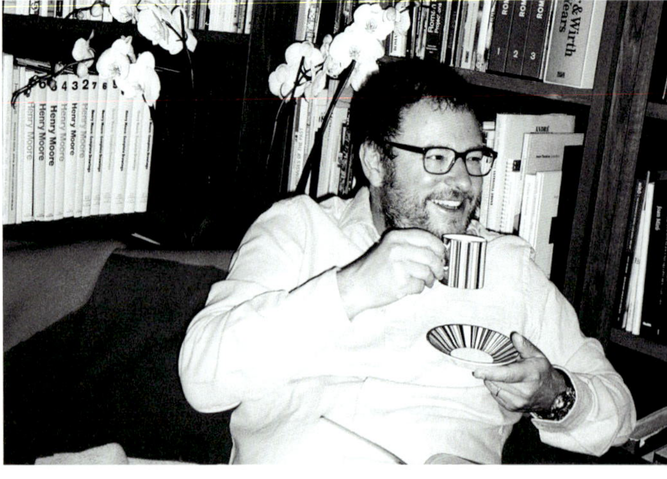

What is your favorite aspect of running a gallery?

The dialogue and conversations with the artists, and studio visits.

How do you choose the artists you work with?

I believe in love at first sight.

If you weren't running a gallery what else would you do?

Farm.

- **Contact** Hauser & Wirth
  Vanessa Rubinick
  vanessa@hauserwirth.com
- **Established** 1992
- **Owner(s) / Partner(s)** Iwan & Manuela Wirth
  Ursula Hauser
  Marc Payot
  Paul Schimmel
- **Artists at Art Basel** Rita Ackermann
  Ida Applebroog
  Phyllida Barlow
  Louise Bourgeois
  Mark Bradford
  Christoph Büchel
  Martin Creed
  Berlinde De Bruyckere
  Martin Eder
  Ellen Gallagher
  Isa Genzken
  Leon Golub
  Dan Graham
  Rodney Graham
  Subodh Gupta
  Mary Heilmann
  Eva Hesse
  Andy Hope 1930
  Roni Horn
  Thomas Houseago
  Pierre Huyghe
  Matthew Day Jackson
  Richard Jackson
  Rashid Johnson
  Josephsohn
  Allan Kaprow
  Rachel Khedoori
  Bharti Kher
  Guillermo Kuitca
  Maria Lassnig
  Lee Lozano
  Anna Maria Maiolino
  Takesada Matsutani
  Paul McCarthy
  Joan Mitchell
  Henry Moore
  Ron Mueck
  Caro Niederer
  Christopher Orr
  Djordje Ozbolt
  Michael Raedecker
  Jason Rhoades
  Pipilotti Rist
  Dieter Roth
  Sterling Ruby
  Anri Sala
  Wilhelm Sasnal

Mira Schendel
Christoph Schlingensief
Roman Signer
Anj Smith
Monika Sosnowska
Diana Thater
André Thomkins
Philippe Vandenberg
Ian Wallace
Mark Wallinger
Zhang Enli
David Zink Yi
Jakub Julian Ziolkowski

Hazlitt Holland-Hibbert

London
New York

● Galleries

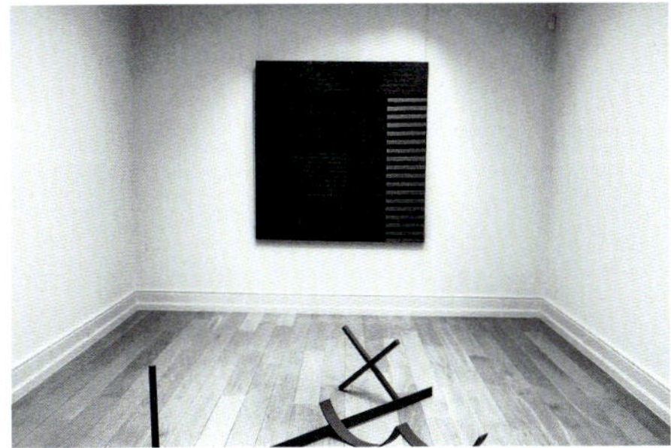

- **Contact** Hazlitt Holland-Hibbert
info@hh-h.com
- **Established** 2001
- **Owner(s) / Partner(s)** James Holland-Hibbert
- **Artists at Art Basel** Frank Auerbach
Francis Bacon
Anthony Caro
Lucian Freud
Naum Gabo
Gilbert & George
Barbara Hepworth
David Hockney
Howard Hodgkin
Leon Kossoff
Henry Moore
Ben Nicholson
Bridget Riley
Sean Scully
Stanley Spencer

Herald St

London

● Galleries
Unlimited
● Galleries

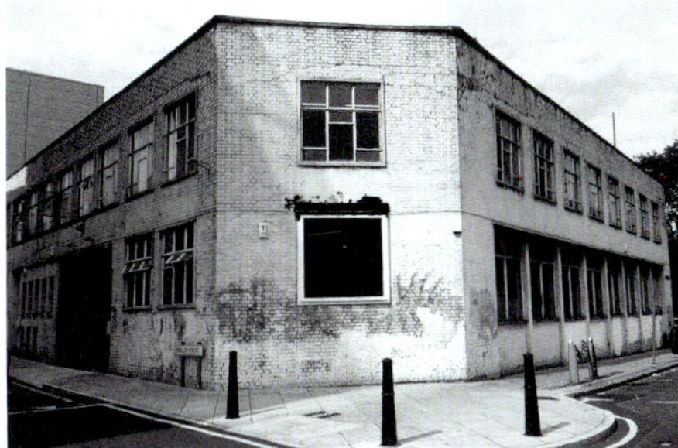

What is your favorite aspect of running a gallery?
The pleasure of getting to work with the wonderful artists we represent.

How do you choose the artists you work with?
There are many factors involved in choosing and working with an artist and each situation is always different.

If you weren't running a gallery what else would you do?
We are still running the gallery, thankfully.

- **Contact** Herald St
mail@heraldst.com
- **Established** 2005
- **Owner(s) / Partner(s)** Ash L'Ange
Nicky Verber
- **Team** 6
- **Space(s)** 200 m²
- **Artists at Art Basel** Markus Amm
Alexandra Bircken
Pablo Bronstein
Matt Connors
Matthew Darbyshire
Michael Dean
Ida Ekblad
Christina Mackie
Amalia Pica
Nick Relph
Klaus Weber
- **Further artists represented** Josh Brand
Peter Coffin
Annette Kelm
Scott King
Cary Kwok
Djordje Ozbolt
Oliver Payne
Oliver Payne & Nick Relph
Tony Swain
Donald Urquhart
Nicole Wermers

Hetzler

Berlin
Paris

● Galleries
● Galleries

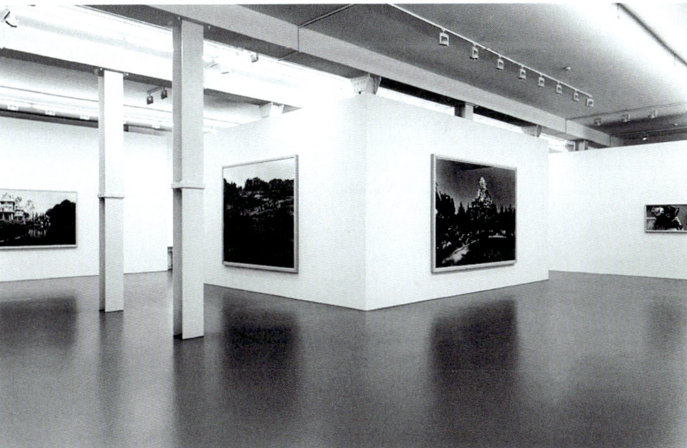

- **Contact** Galerie Max Hetzler
Wolfram Aue
wolfram.aue@maxhetzler.com
- **Established** 1974
- **Owner(s) / Partner(s)** Max Hetzler
Samia Saouma
- **Team** 10
- **Space(s)** 1,800 m²
- **Artists at Art Basel** Darren Almond
Glenn Brown
André Butzer
Rineke Dijkstra
Jeff Elrod
Günther Förg
Robert Grosvenor
Raymond Hains
Mona Hatoum
Robert Holyhead
Jeff Koons
Vera Lutter
Marepe
Beatriz Milhazes
Joan Mitchell
Ernesto Neto
Christoph Niemann
Frank Nitsche
Navid Nuur
Albert Oehlen
Yves Oppenheim
Michael Raedecker
Bridget Riley
Thomas Struth
Edmund de Waal
Rebecca Warren
Christopher Wool
Toby Ziegler

Hirschl & Adler

New York

Galleries Kabinett

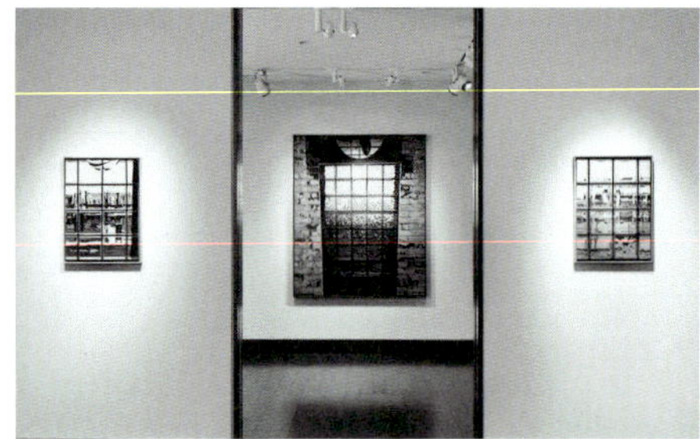

What is your favorite aspect of running a gallery?
The connoisseurship.

How do you choose the artists you work with?
Referrals, as well as our own research.

If you weren't running a gallery what else would you do?
Marine biology/run an art museum/tour Europe on a bicycle/calligraphy/travel the world as a food critic, specializing in street food/learn how to hit a golf ball/general contracting/be a ballerina/run a brothel/collect/TBD (2×)/professional photography/get the band back together/not answer this questionnaire/attend graduate school/(on safari)/stay at home and knit.

- **Contact** Hirschl & Adler Modern
  Elizabeth Feld
  elizabethf@hirschlandadler.com
- **Established** 1981
- **Owner(s) / Partner(s)** Stuart Feld
  Elizabeth Feld
- **Team** 18
- **Space(s)** 1,022 m²
- **Artists at Art Basel** Josef Albers
  Milton Avery
  George Bellows
  Oscar Bluemner
  Charles Burchfield
  Stuart Davis
  Charles Demuth
  Preston Dickinson
  John Ferren
  Charles Howard
  Walt Kuhn
  John Marin
  Fairfield Porter
  Winold Reiss
  Theodore Roszak
  Kay Sage
  Charles Sheeler
  Joseph Stella
  Henry Fitch Taylor
  Bill Traylor
- **Further artists represented** Lily Cox-Richards
  James Edward Deeds
  David Ligare
  Richard Lonsdale-Hands
  John Moore
  Stone Roberts
  Elizabeth Turk
  Stanley Twardowicz

Hoffman

Chicago

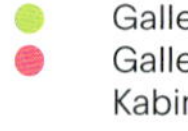

Galleries
Galleries Kabinett

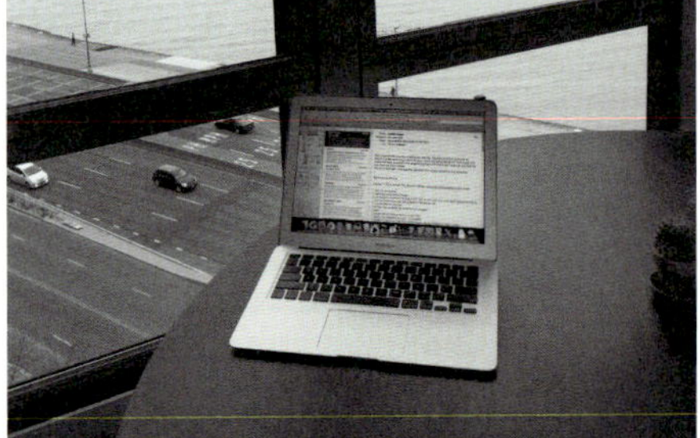

What is your favorite aspect of running a gallery?
Curating and installing exhibitions. I think the best part of running a gallery is getting to know and understand art through being with artists.

How do you choose the artists you work with?
I choose what my eyes and intellect agree on.

If you weren't running a gallery what else would you do?
Travel more for the sheer pleasure of traveling, write, spend more time with family and friends, and look at art.

- **Contact** Rhona Hoffman Gallery
  Cara Lewis
  cara@rhoffmangallery.com
- **Established** 1976
- **Owner(s) / Partner(s)** Rhona Hoffman
- **Team** 6
- **Space(s)** 260 m²
- **Artists at Art Basel** Vito Acconci
  Derrick Adams
  Pier Paolo Calzolari
  Spencer Finch
  Natalie Frank
  Chris Garofalo
  Luis Gispert
  Jacob Hashimoto
  Susan Hefuna
  Robert Heinecken
  Deana Lawson
  Sol LeWitt
  Michael Rakowitz
  Richard Rezac
  Siebren Versteeg
  Anne Wilson
- **Further artists represented** New Catalogue
  Todd Chilton
  Julia Fish
  Judy Ledgerwood
  Fred Sandback
  David Schutter
  Nancy Spero

Hopkins

Paris

Galleries

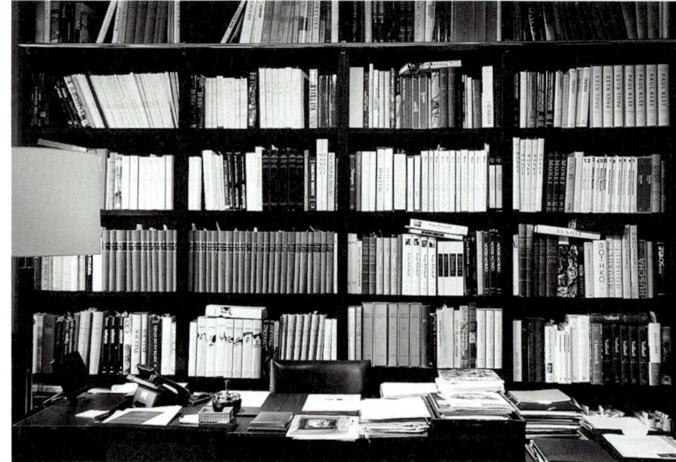

What is your favorite aspect of running a gallery?
Buying exceptional paintings.

If you weren't running a gallery what else would you do?
Museum work.

- **Contact** Galerie Hopkins
  Caroline van Herpen
  hopkins@galeriehopkins.com
- **Established** 1984
- **Owner(s) / Partner(s)** Waring Hopkins
- **Team** 6
- **Space(s)** 250 m²
- **Artists at Art Basel** Victor Brauner
  Jean Dubuffet
  Max Ernst
  Julio González

Hans Hartung
René Magritte
Henri Matisse
Giorgio Morandi
Robert Motherwell
Pablo Picasso
Pierre Soulages
Nicolas de Staël
Maria Helena Vieira da Silva
Zao Wou-Ki

Hopkinson Mossman

Auckland ● Discoveries

- **Contact** Hopkinson Mossman
Danae Mossman
danae@hopkinsonmossman.com
- **Established** 2010
- **Owner(s) / Partner(s)** Sarah Hopkinson
Danae Mossman
- **Team** 2
- **Space(s)** 200 m²
- **Artists at Art Basel** Nicola Farquhar
- **Further artists represented** Nick Austin
Andrew Barber
Ruth Buchanan
Fiona Connor
Bill Culbert
Oscar Enberg
Milli Jannides
Daniel Malone
Nicholas Mangan
Dane Mitchell
Tahi Moore
Kate Newby
Peter Robinson
Luke Willis Thompson

Hoppen

London ● Galleries

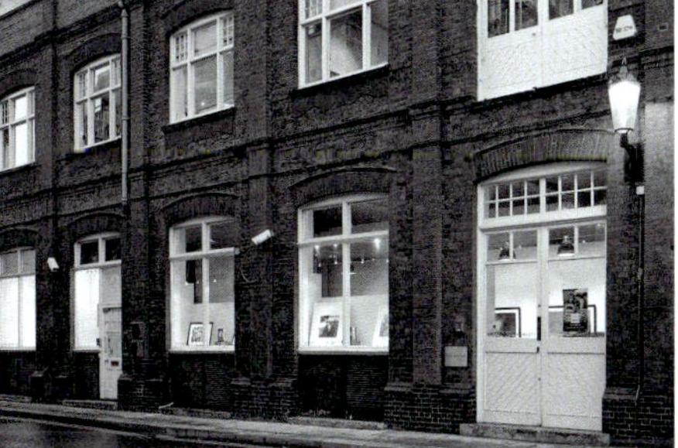

What is your favorite aspect of running a gallery?
Meeting everyone who comes to the gallery and the art fairs, and also working closely with artists and their collectors.

How do you choose the artists you work with?
Would I hang their work in my home? If yes, then we would represent their work.

If you weren't running a gallery what else would you do?
Fishing in the Indian Ocean Mondays, Wednesdays, and Fridays.

- **Contact** Michael Hoppen Gallery
Michael Hoppen
michael
@michaelhoppengallery.com
- **Established** 1992
- **Owner(s) / Partner(s)** Michael Hoppen
- **Team** 10
- **Space(s)** 464.5 m²
- **Artists at Art Basel** William Klein
Chema Madoz
Hiroshi Sugimoto

Houk

New York ● Galleries
Zurich ● Galleries

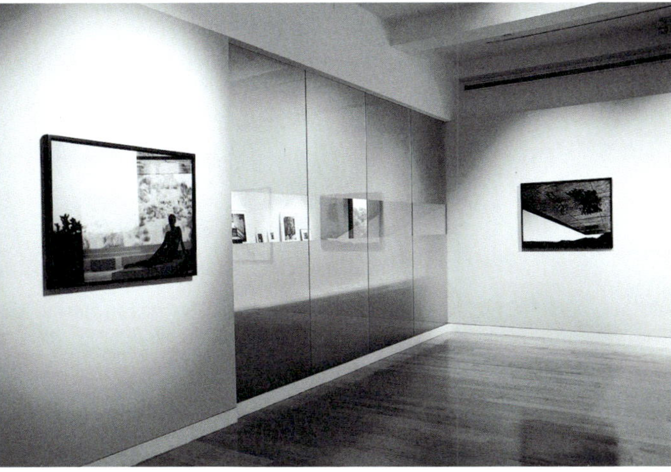

What is your favorite aspect of running a gallery?
Living with art.

If you weren't running a gallery what else would you do?
Teach.

How do you choose the artists you work with?
Carefully.

- **Contact** Edwynn Houk Gallery
Edwynn Houk
info@houkgallery.com
- **Established** 1980
- **Owner(s) / Partner(s)** Edwynn Houk
- **Team** 9
- **Space(s)** 1,115 m²
- **Artists at Art Basel** Valérie Belin
Sebastiaan Bremer
Bill Brandt
Brassaï
Manuel Álvarez Bravo
Michael Eastman
Elliott Erwitt
Lalla Essaydi
Sissi Farassat
Robert Frank
André Kertész
Gail Albert Halaban
Mona Kuhn
Vera Lutter
Danny Lyon
Sally Mann
László Moholy-Nagy
Abelardo Morell
Vik Muniz
Cathleen Naundorf
Robert Polidori
Man Ray
Herb Ritts
Stephen Shore
Edward Weston
- **Further artists represented** Ilse Bing
Erwin Blumenfeld
Henri Cartier-Bresson
Walker Evans
Dorothea Lange
Jacques-Henri Lartigue
El Lissitzky
Danny Lyon
Alexander Rodchenko
August Sander
Alfred Stieglitz

Houldsworth

London  Feature

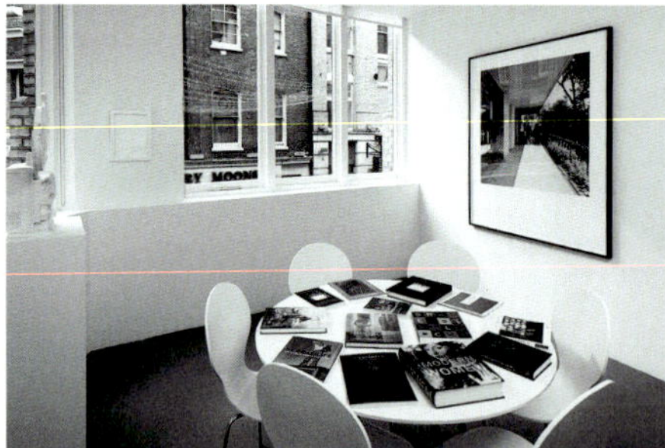

What is your favorite aspect of running a gallery?
Seeing the new works when they arrive in the gallery after months of working closely with an artist is always immensely exciting.

How do you choose the artists you work with?
I like artists who not only display a combination of talent, originality, and intellect, but also respect the past, make a difference to the present, and look to the future.

If you weren't running a gallery what else would you do?
I would spend more time with my children and less time worrying.

- **Contact** Pippy Houldsworth Gallery
  Pippy Houldsworth
  pippy@houldsworth.co.uk
- **Established** 1999
- **Owner(s) / Partner(s)** Pippy Houldsworth
- **Team** 6
- **Space(s)** 172 m²
- **Artists at Art Basel** Mary Kelly
- **Further artists represented** Daniel Arsham
  Ruth Claxton
  Clem Crosby
  Francesca Dimattio
  Neil Farber
  Rachel Goodyear
  Dan Holdsworth
  Martin Kobe
  Yuken Teruya

Hufkens

Brussels  Galleries Unlimited
Galleries

What is your favorite aspect of running a gallery?
Working with artists is the greatest privilege of running a gallery. When a studio feels like a second home, and an artist shows you his/her work for the first time, it's very special. What often begins as an intimate conversation between you and the artist deepens into something richer and more meaningful in the gallery space. In other words, when you share it with others. That's what I love about running a gallery—it is a platform for conversation and for a genuine exchange of ideas.

How do you choose the artists you work with?
I would like to say instinctively and, perhaps at the beginning, I relied on my gut feelings to a certain extent. But when you have been working in the art world for almost 30 years, your decisions are also influenced by your visual memory. I travel a lot, attend art fairs, visit studios, and I often see things before anyone else. I choose artists with whom I feel an affinity and, in that sense, it is incredibly personal: you have to believe in an artist to be able to show their work.

If you weren't running a gallery what else would you do?
If I didn't run a gallery I would be making wine. Winemaking is a creative craft, much like painting, or any other form of art.

- **Contact** Xavier Hufkens
  Elisabeth Van Caelenberge
  elisabeth.vancaelenberge@xavierhufkens.com
- **Established** 1987
- **Owner(s) / Partner(s)** Xavier Hufkens
- **Team** 15
- **Space(s)** 800 m²
- **Artists at Art Basel** Harold Ancart
  David Altmejd
  Evan Holloway
  Thomas Houseago
  Sterling Ruby
- **Further artists represented** Saâdane Afif
  Richard Artschwager
  Louise Bourgeois
  Cris Brodahl
  Daniel Buren
  Jean-Marc Bustamante
  John Chamberlain
  George Condo
  Thierry De Cordier
  William Eggleston
  Michel François
  Adam Fuss
  Antony Gormley
  Roni Horn
  Jonathan Horowitz
  Pierre Huyghe
  Jacob Kassay
  Willem de Kooning
  Bertrand Lavier
  Robert Mapplethorpe
  Malcolm Morley
  David Noonan
  Alessandro Pessoli
  Jack Pierson
  Ken Price
  Tim Rollins & K.O.S.
  Robert Ryman
  Walter Swennen
  Padraig Timoney
  Lesley Vance
  Jan Vercruysse
  Danh Vo
  Cathy Wilkes
  Erwin Wurm

Hutton

New York  Galleries

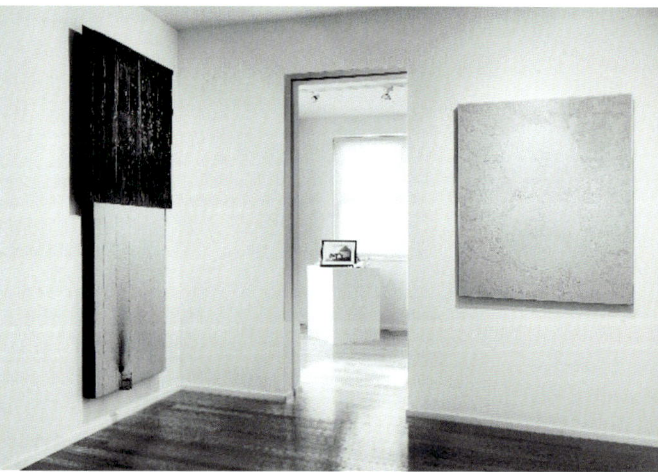

What is your favorite aspect of running a gallery?
Creating interesting and thought-provoking exhibitions.

How do you choose the artists you work with?
I don't necessarily choose an artist as much as I choose quality artworks that speak to me.

If you weren't running a gallery what else would you do?
There is nothing I would rather do.

- **Contact** Leonard Hutton Galleries
  Ingrid Hutton
  art@leonardhuttongalleries.com

- **Established** 1957
- **Owner(s) / Partner(s)** Ingrid Hutton
- **Team** 4
- **Space(s)** 139.5 m²
- **Artists at Art Basel** Josef Albers
Hans Arp
James Brooks
Salvador Dalí
Sonia Delaunay
Jean Dubuffet
Max Ernst
Lucio Fontana
Alberto Giacometti
Adolph Gottlieb
Jacob Hashimoto
Alexej Jawlensky
Paul Klee
Lee Krasner
Henri Laurens
Joan Miró
Joan Mitchell
Robert Motherwell
Kenneth Noland
Sophie Taeuber-Arp
Yves Tanguy
- **Further artists represented** Alexander Calder
Pierpaolo Calzolari
Anthony Caro
Niki de Saint Phalle
Robert Delaunay
Sam Francis
Helen Frankenthaler
Natalia Goncharova
Al Held
Wassily Kandinsky
Fernand Léger
Kazimir Malevich
Fausto Melotti
David Nash
Giulio Paolini
Pablo Picasso
Richard Pousette-Dart
Robert Rauschenberg
James Rosenquist
Oskar Schlemmer
Jack Tworkov
Nadezhda Udaltsova
Andy Warhol
Tom Wesselmann

Galerie Max Hetzler

Interview with Max Hetzler & Samia Saouma

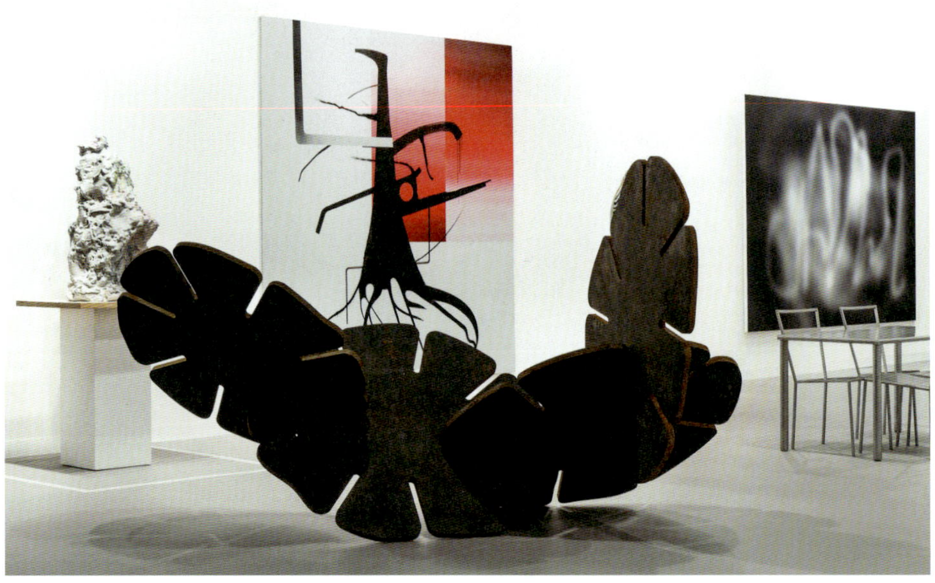

Art Basel in Miami Beach, 2014

What was your background before opening the gallery?

Max Hetzler: I had none. I always wanted to become a gallerist and art dealer, but I didn't know what it meant, so I started to work in galleries after school. Coming from Stuttgart, I always thought it was best to start there. I opened the gallery in September 1974, with German artists Ulrich Rückriem and Klaus Rinke, but also Mario Merz and David Rabinowitch, John Hilliard and Victor Burgin. It was an international program from the very beginning. In the early 1980s, when Martin Kippenberger and Günther Förg joined the gallery, it became obvious that Stuttgart was not the most important place in the art world, so I moved to Cologne in 1983.

You organized some ambitious group shows, such as *Junge Kunst aus Westdeutschland* (1981), which tried to map the young German art scene, while also showing the American art scene of the 1980s.

MH: Absolutely. There was always the intention to be international. The competition in Cologne was very intense. We showed Jeff Koons' *Banality* in 1988 and his *Made in Heaven* series in 1991. Christopher Wool had his first solo exhibition at the gallery in 1989. We also showed Robert Gober, Cady Noland, etc.

How did you meet these American artists?

MH: I used to travel to New York a lot, and it became a sort of two-way exchange for artists of this generation: American artists showed in Cologne and German artists in New York. It was the time—it was still West Germany—when the Cologne Art Fair was very important. There were very important dealers like Michael Werner and Rudolf Zwirner. There were big art collectors also, like Peter Ludwig. That made a scene.

Speaking about this German-American relationship, you also had a gallery in Santa Monica, California.

MH: We opened this space with Luhring Augustine in the late 1980s and it lasted for only three years. We did some remarkable shows with Felix Gonzalez-Torres and Cady Noland. We also showed Los Angeles-based artists like Christopher Williams, Stephen Prina, Mike Kelley. Then the crisis hit us in the early 1990s.

You moved to Berlin in 1993, five years after the fall of the Berlin Wall.

M: Yes, at the end of 1993, when Samia lived with me more regularly—she was in Paris before, running her own gallery.

Were you working together at that time?

Samia Saouma: Not really, but we had some artists in common. I was showing Kippenberger and later Günther Förg, Christopher Wool, and Albert Oehlen. That's why it was important for us to open the new gallery in Paris (in May 2014) with Oehlen, 33 years after his first exhibition at the Galerie Max Hetzler. Actually, we first met because I wanted to show Albert …

When you opened in Berlin, how different was the scene from the Cologne one?

MH: You could feel it was the only place where something *could* happen, but there was basically nothing! In the early 1990s there the economic crisis hit the art world hard. I though it might be interesting to reinvent myself, to rethink what I was doing when I moved to Berlin. It took me almost 10 years … The program became even more international, even if we continued working with a number of artists we started with (like Thomas Struth and Günther Förg, as well as some of the American artists I mentioned). We also worked with international artists who lived and worked in Berlin through the DAAD exchange program, like Mona Hatoum.

In 2013 you organized *Remember Everything*, an exhibition dedicated to the 40th year of the gallery. It was the last show in your former Berlin space, before moving to Charlottenburg.

SS: All the artists were present and made new works, and we simultaneously organized a retrospective of Joan Mitchell in one of our new spaces, as well as a sound performance by Tarek Atoui in the other one. The two new spaces are really different: one is a typical Charlottenburg apartment; the other is a former post office, more like a loft. It gives us the possibility of doing very different types of exhibitions.

MH: We were showing both artists for the first time! We like to establish encounters between older and younger artists in our program. We also show a lot of painters, a lot of female painters, like Bridget Riley. Joan Mitchell's work seemed also very contemporary—it made sense.

Why did you open in Paris? Will the program reflect the Berlin one?

MH: We realized many of our artists didn't have a gallery there. And Paris is very appealing for artists.

SS: The artists we show in Berlin will also be shown in Paris, as well as new ones, like Navid Nuur for example. It's an opportunity to broaden the program. We've started to represent the Estate of Raymond Hains as well; his work feels so contemporary, and is a big influence on artists today.

Insights hosts projects developed specifically for the Hong Kong show. Participating galleries must be based in the broader Asia-Pacific region and present works exclusively by artists from that region. In 2014, the sector featured solo shows, art historical material, and thematic exhibitions. Cosmin Costinas, Executive Director and Curator of Hong Kong's Para Site, reveals his five favorite booths.

2014 participants

Sookoon Ang
Fost

Jumaldi Alfi
Edwin's

Xu Bacheng
L-Art

Natasha Bieniek
tanzer

Burçak Bingöl
Zilberman

Brian Brake
Koru

Vermont Coronel Jr./Troy Ignacio
Drawing Room

Bembol Dela Cruz
Finale

eX de Medici/Tony Albert/Sam Leach/Alex Seton
Sullivan+Strumpf

Wang Fujui/Luxury Logico/Wang Chung-Kun
Project Fulfill

Vibha Galhotra
Exhibit 320

Syaiful Aulia Garibaldi
ROH

Takeo Hanazawa/Fumito Urabe/Masaru Tatsuki
Side 2

FX Harsono
Canna

Susan Hefuna/Tayeba Begum Lipi/Gulay Semercioglu
Pi

Youki Hirakawa
Standing Pine

UnKyung Hur
Leeahn

Chia-En Jao
TKG+

Wu Jian'an
Chambers

Qiu Jiongjiong
Star

Halim al Karim/Faiza Butt
XVA

Tatsuo Kawaguchi
Yamaki

Si Yeon Kim
EM

Ahmed Mater
Athr

Danie Mellor
Murphy

Tsuyoshi Ozawa
Shin

Jiang Pengyi/Nadav Kander/Noh Suntag
Blindspot

Liang Quan/Zhang Quan/Hao Shiming
Fine Arts Literature

José Santos III
Artinformal

Hassan Sharif
van den Eynde

Jakkai Siributr
Yavuz

Hisako Sugiyama
Y++ Wada

Bae Joonsung
IHN

Liu Kuo Sung
du Monde

Aiko Tezuka
Michael Janssen

Nguyen Trung
Cuc

Peng Wei
Ora-Ora

Lee Wen
iPreciation

Yabin Wang/Gong Guo
Nuoart

Choy Chun Wei
Wei-Ling

Sun Xun/Wang Yi/Chu Teh-Chun/Xiao Feng/Song Ren
de Montferrand

Takahiro Yamamoto
Kogure

Chiu Ya-Tsai
Ming

Kim Tschang Yeul
Park Ryu Sook

Yang Yongliang
Galerie Paris-Beijing

Dong Yuan
Yang

Yuan Yuan
Malingue

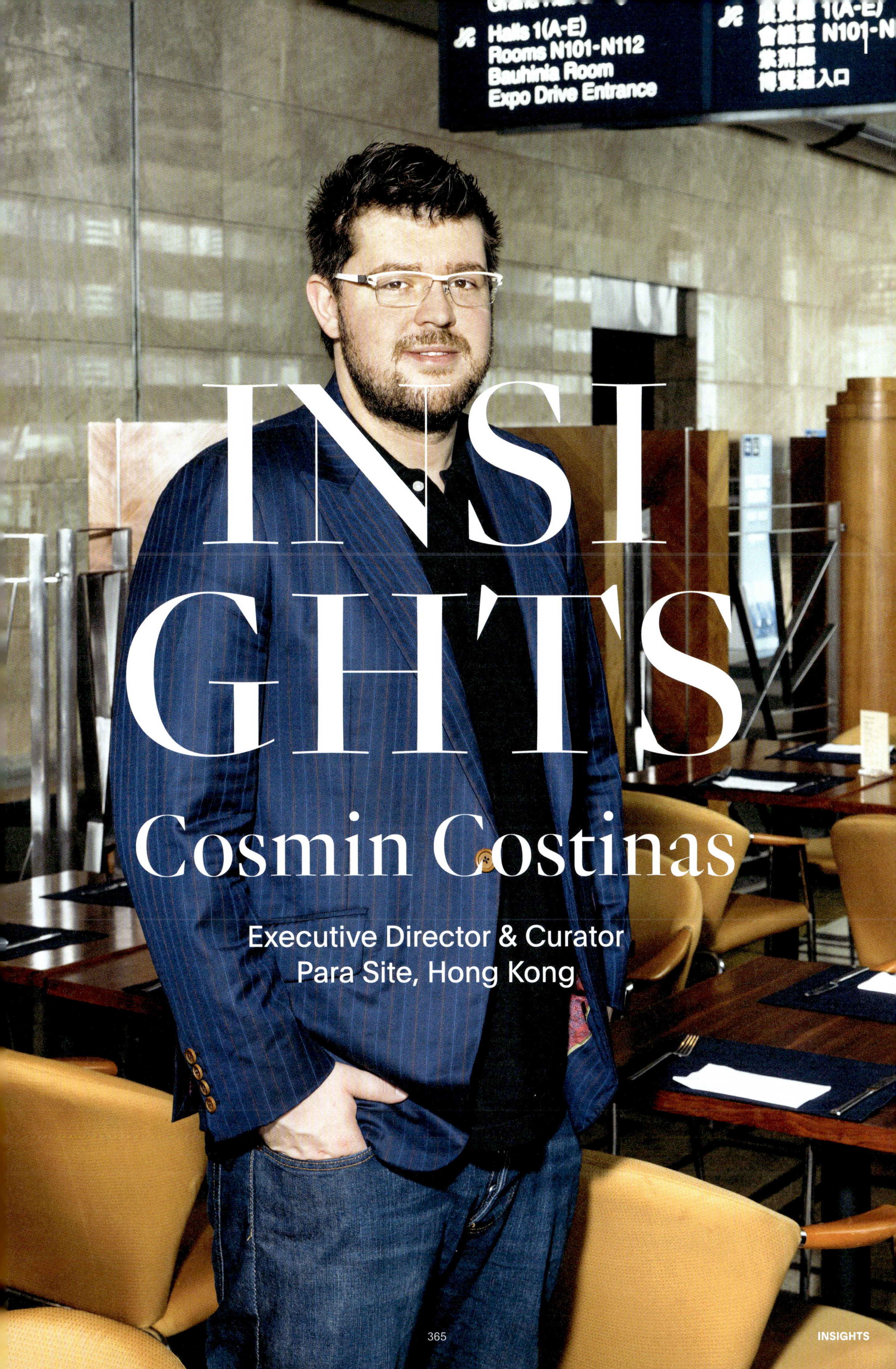

INSIGHTS

Cosmin Costinas

Executive Director & Curator
Para Site, Hong Kong

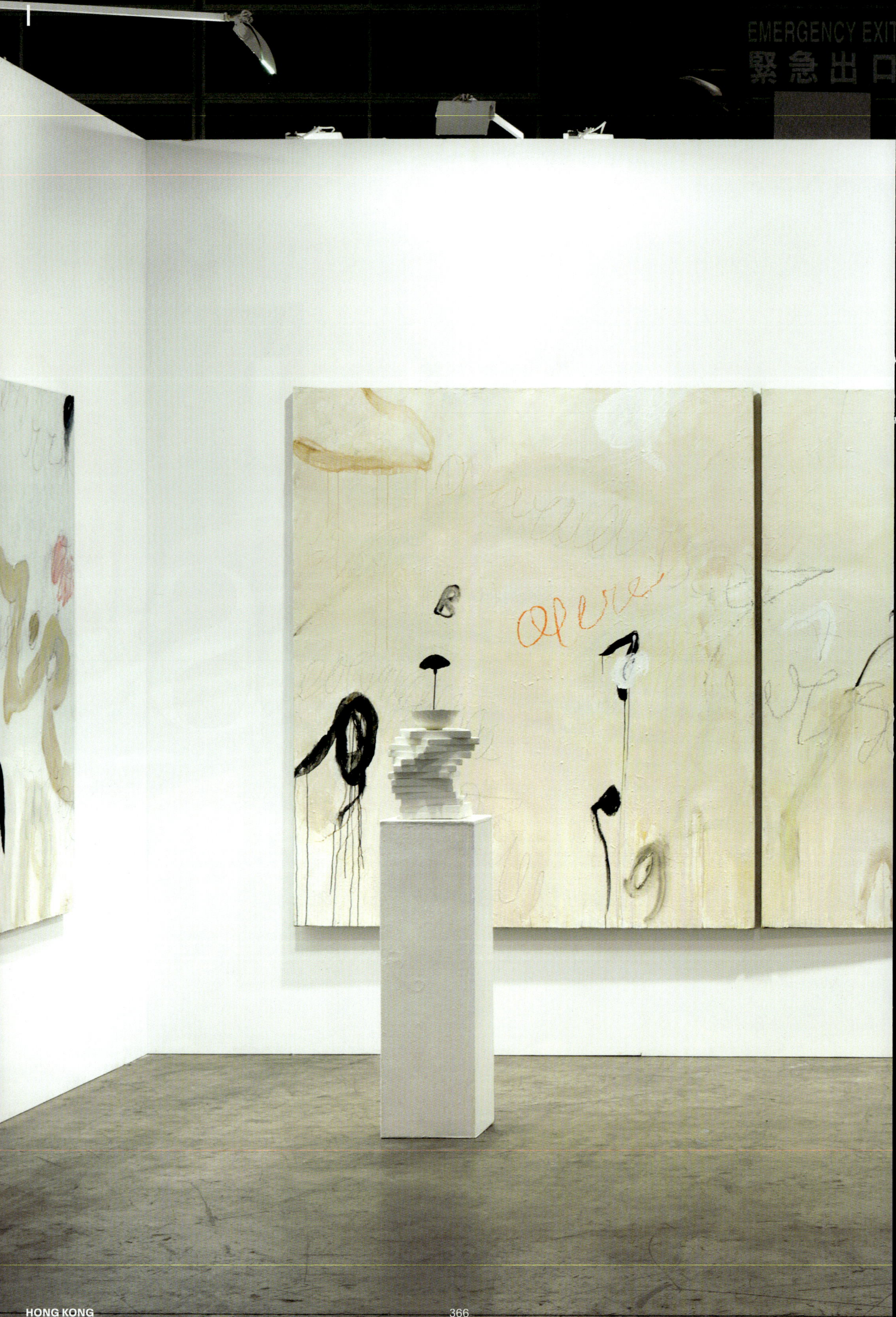
EMERGENCY EXIT
緊急出口

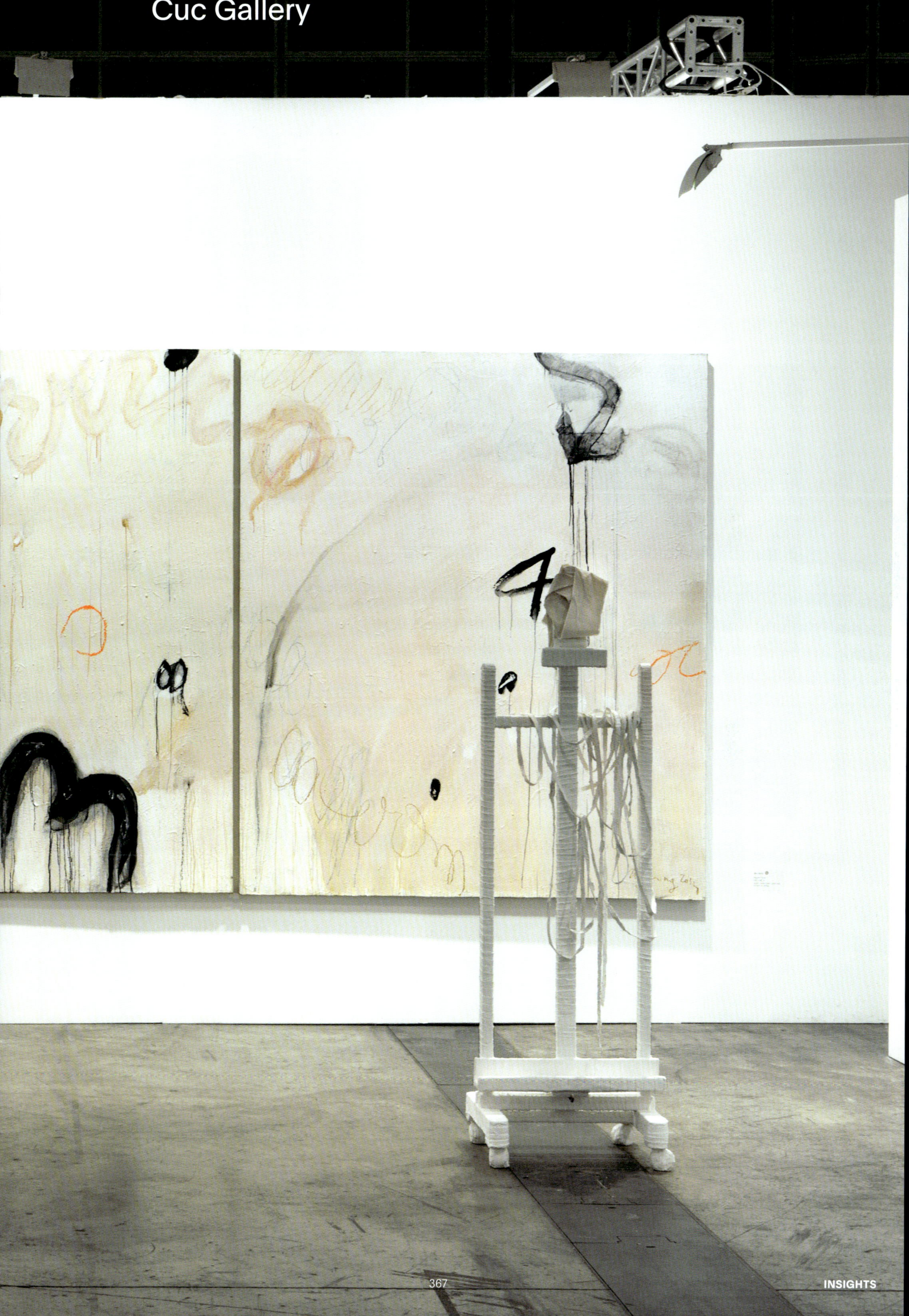

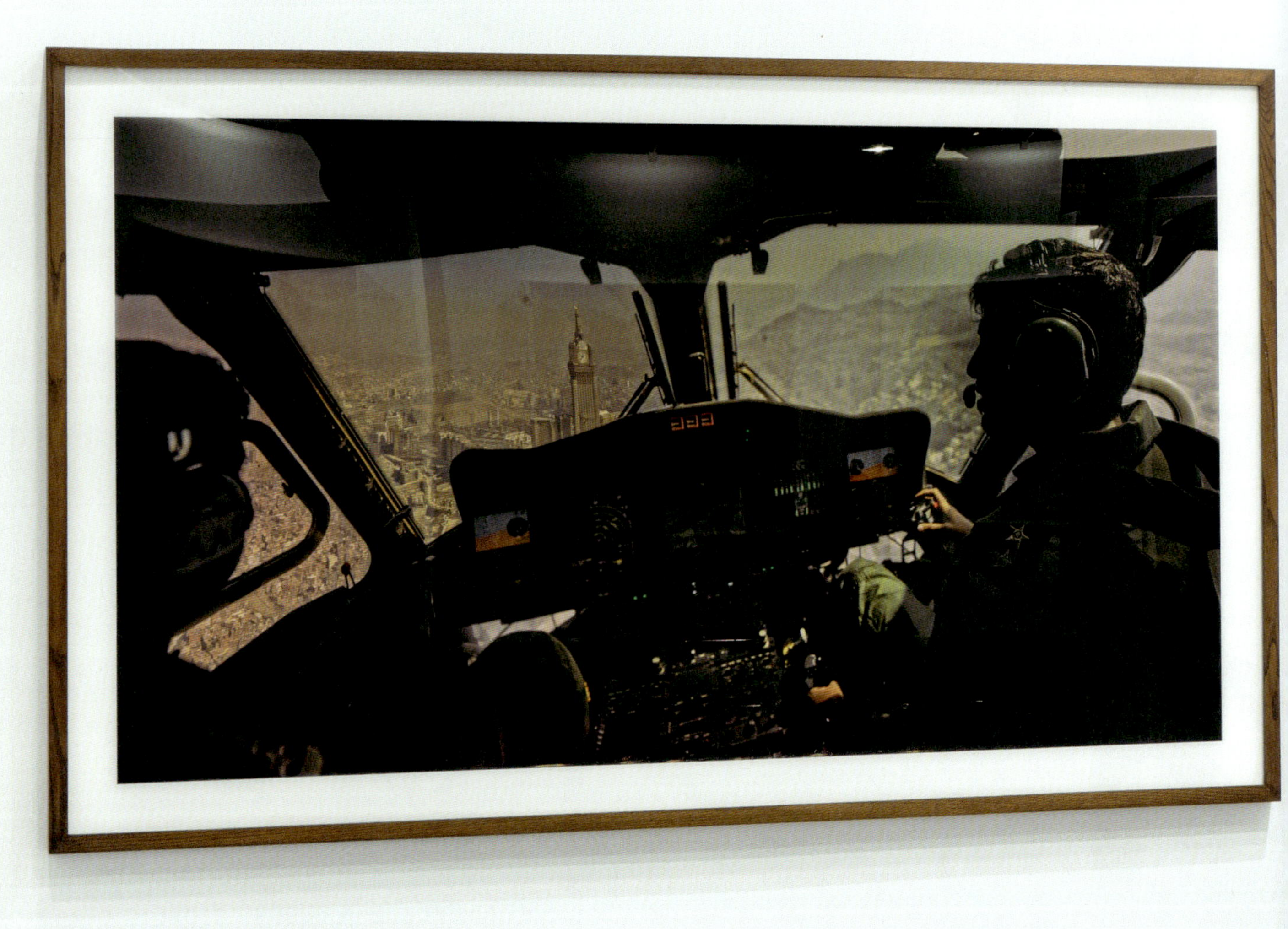

Ahmed Mater
Athr Gallery

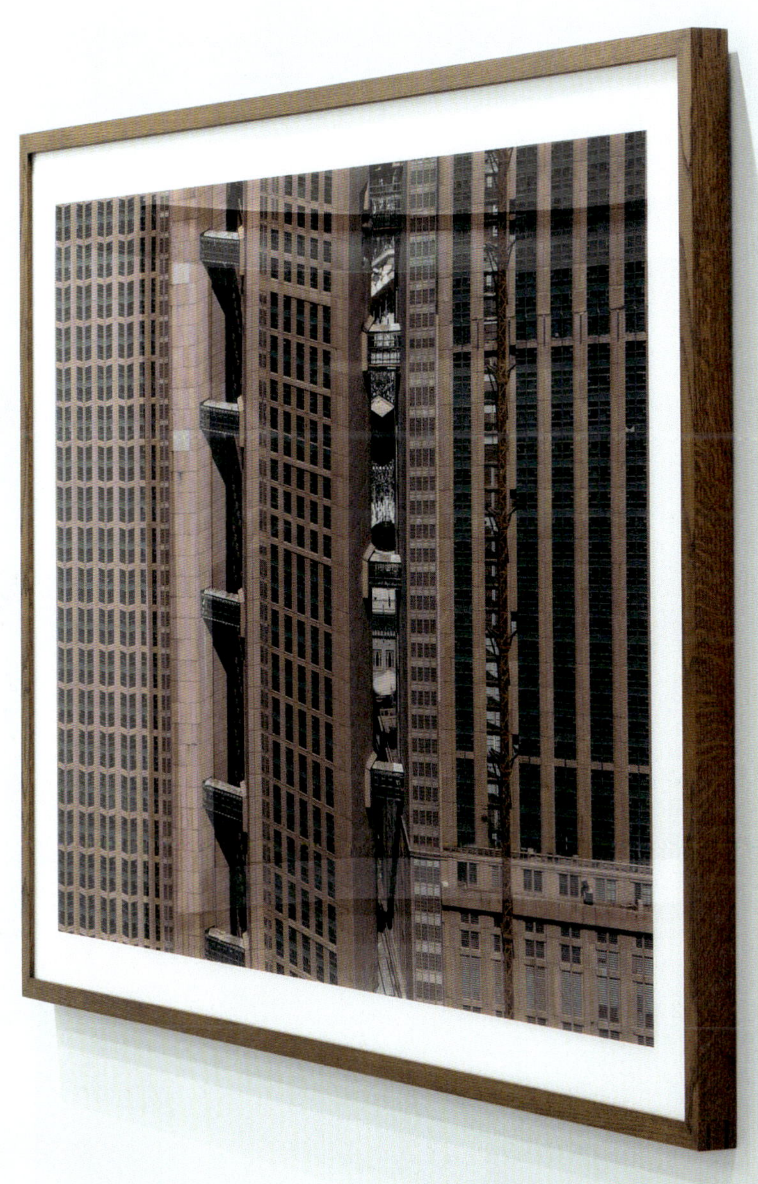

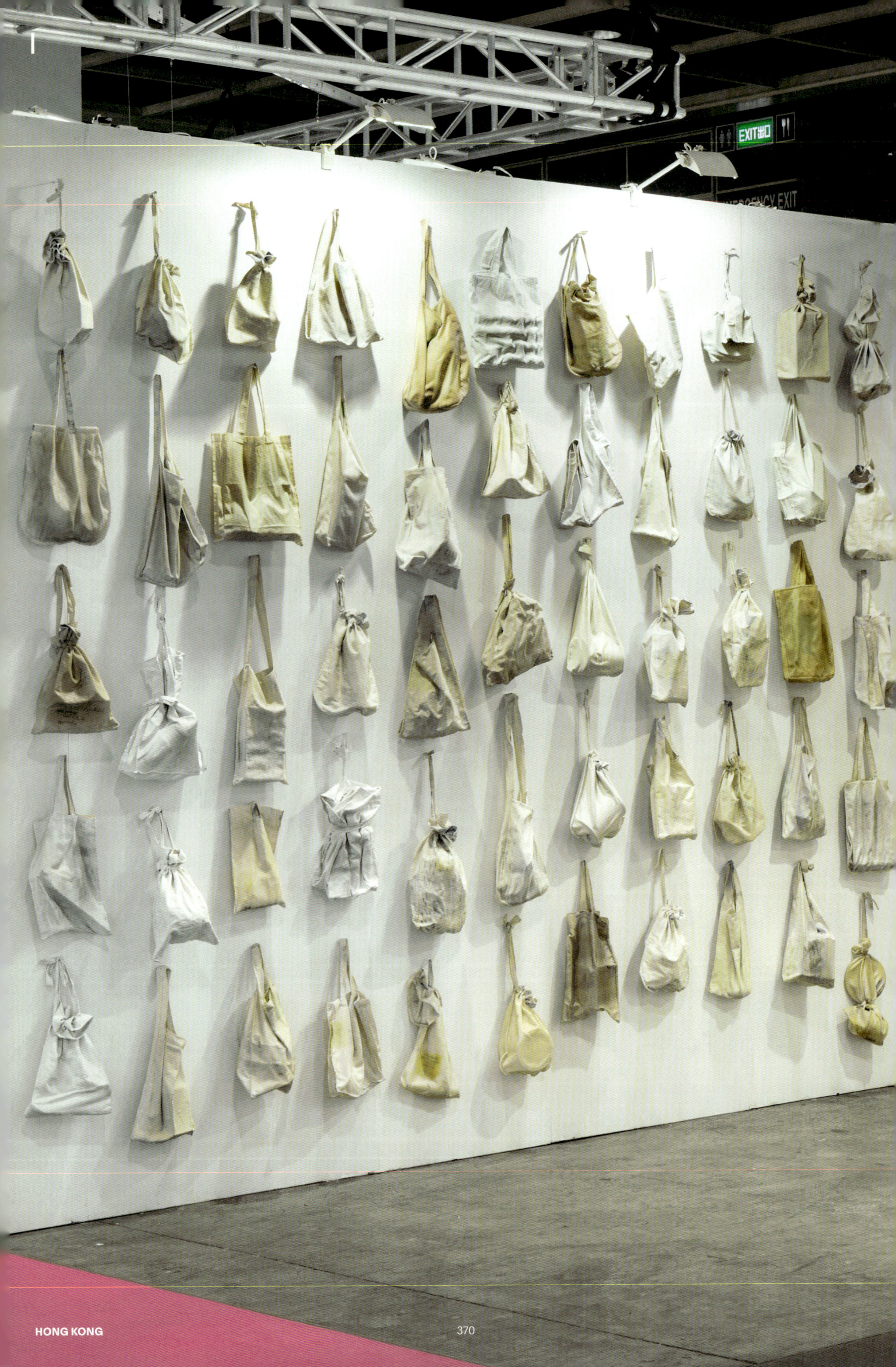
EXIT出口
EMERGENCY EXIT

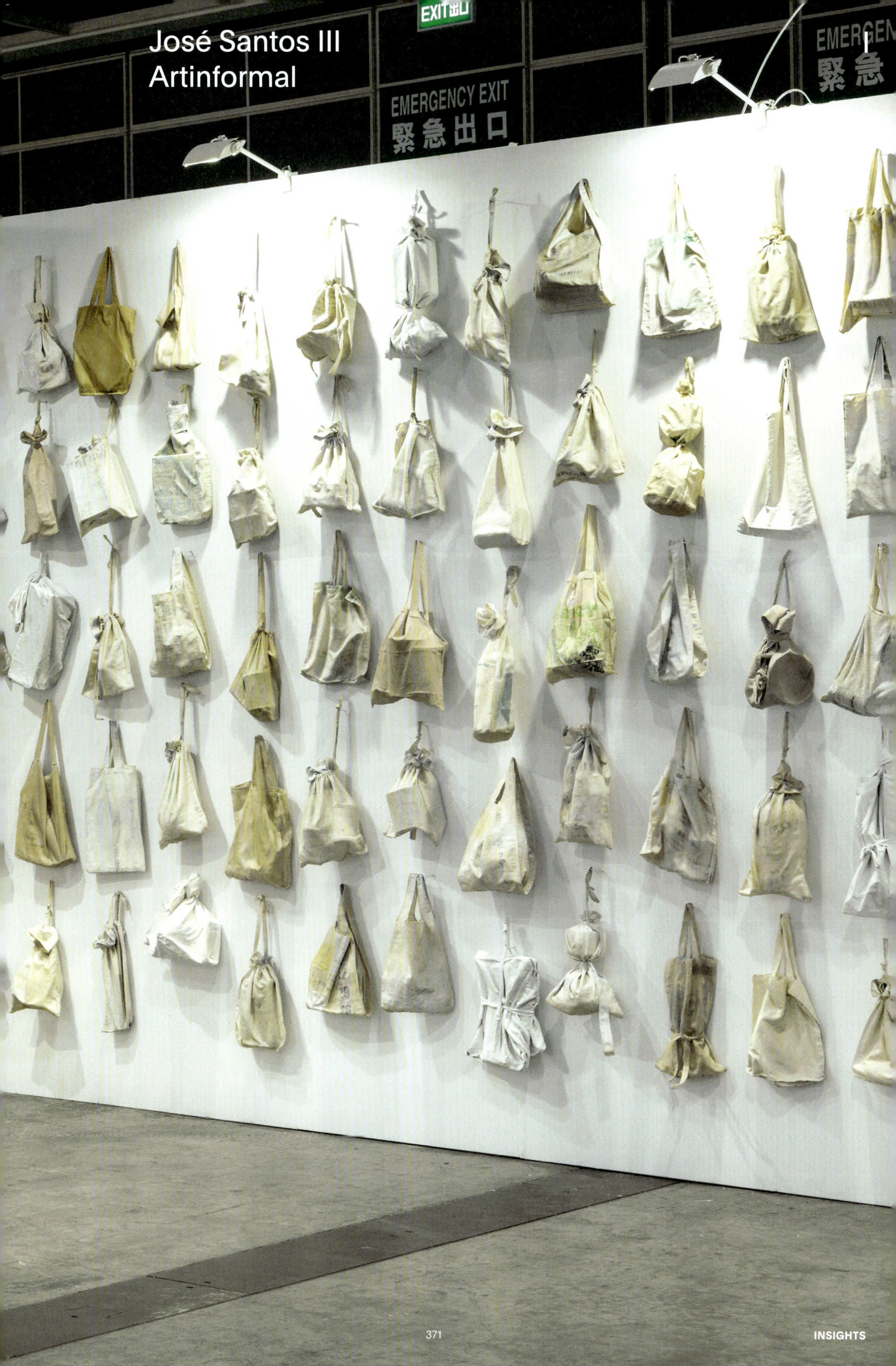

José Santos III
Artinformal

I

Wang Fujui/Luxury Logico/ Wang Chung-Kun Project Fulfill Art Space

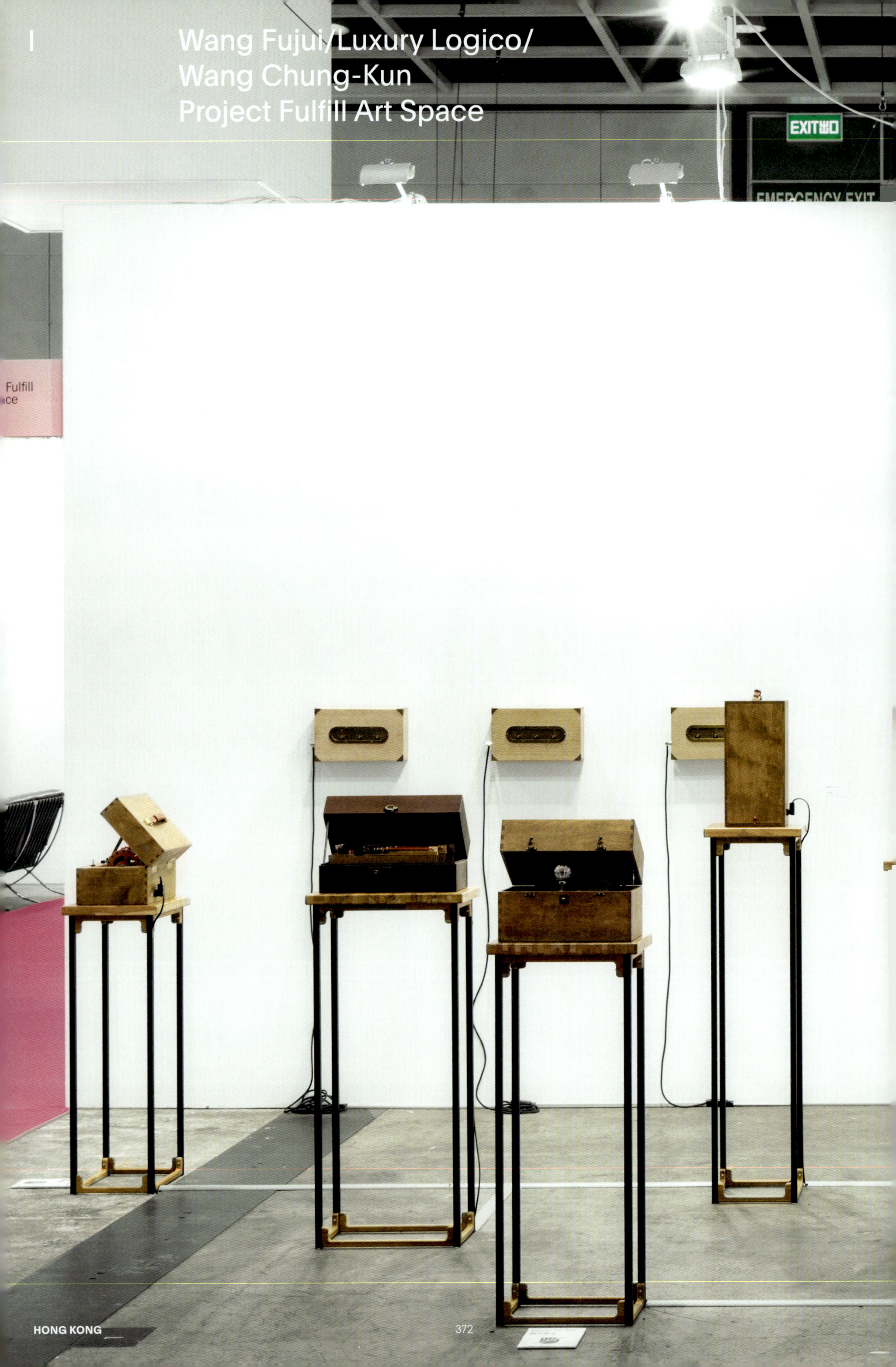

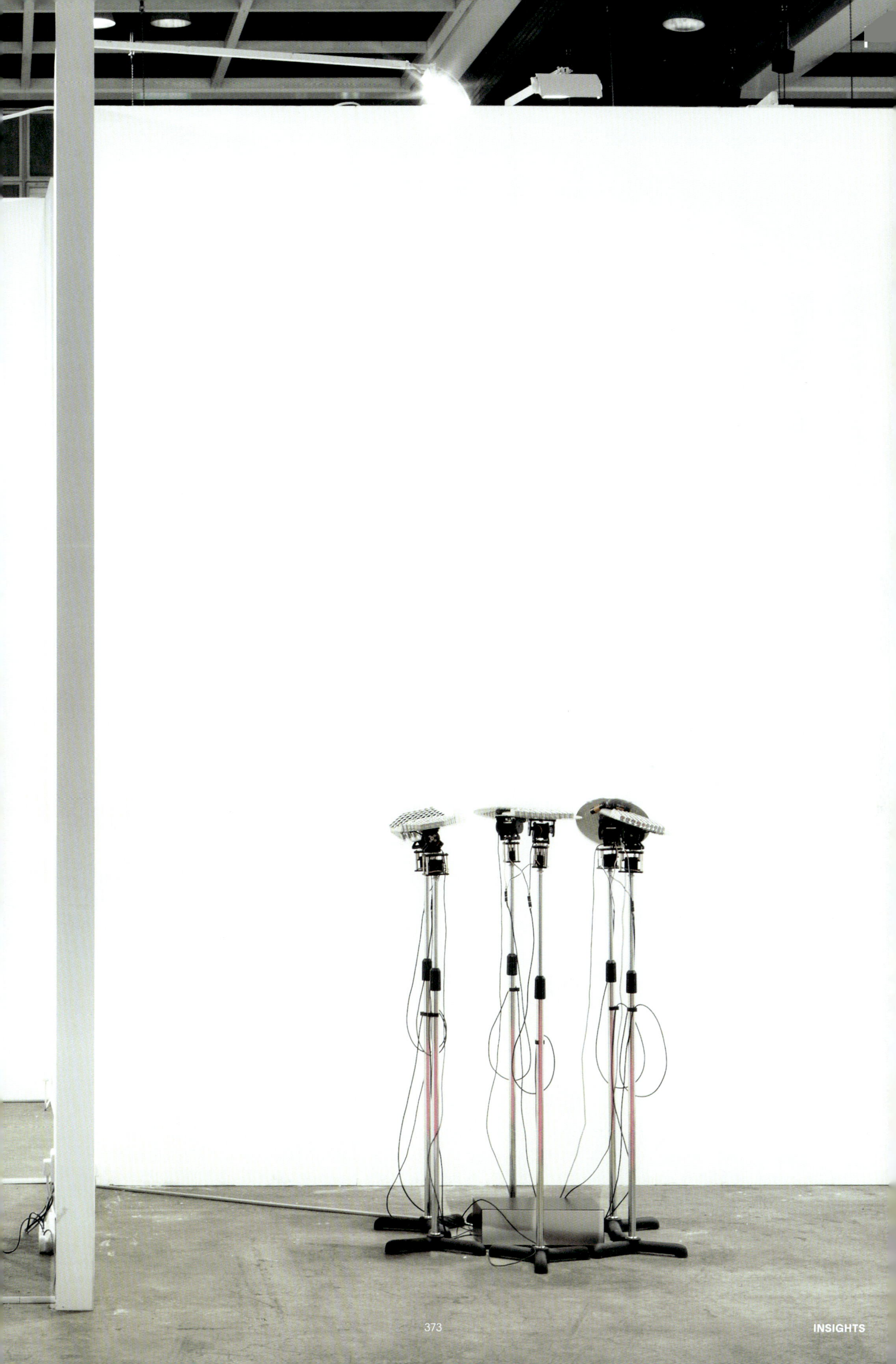

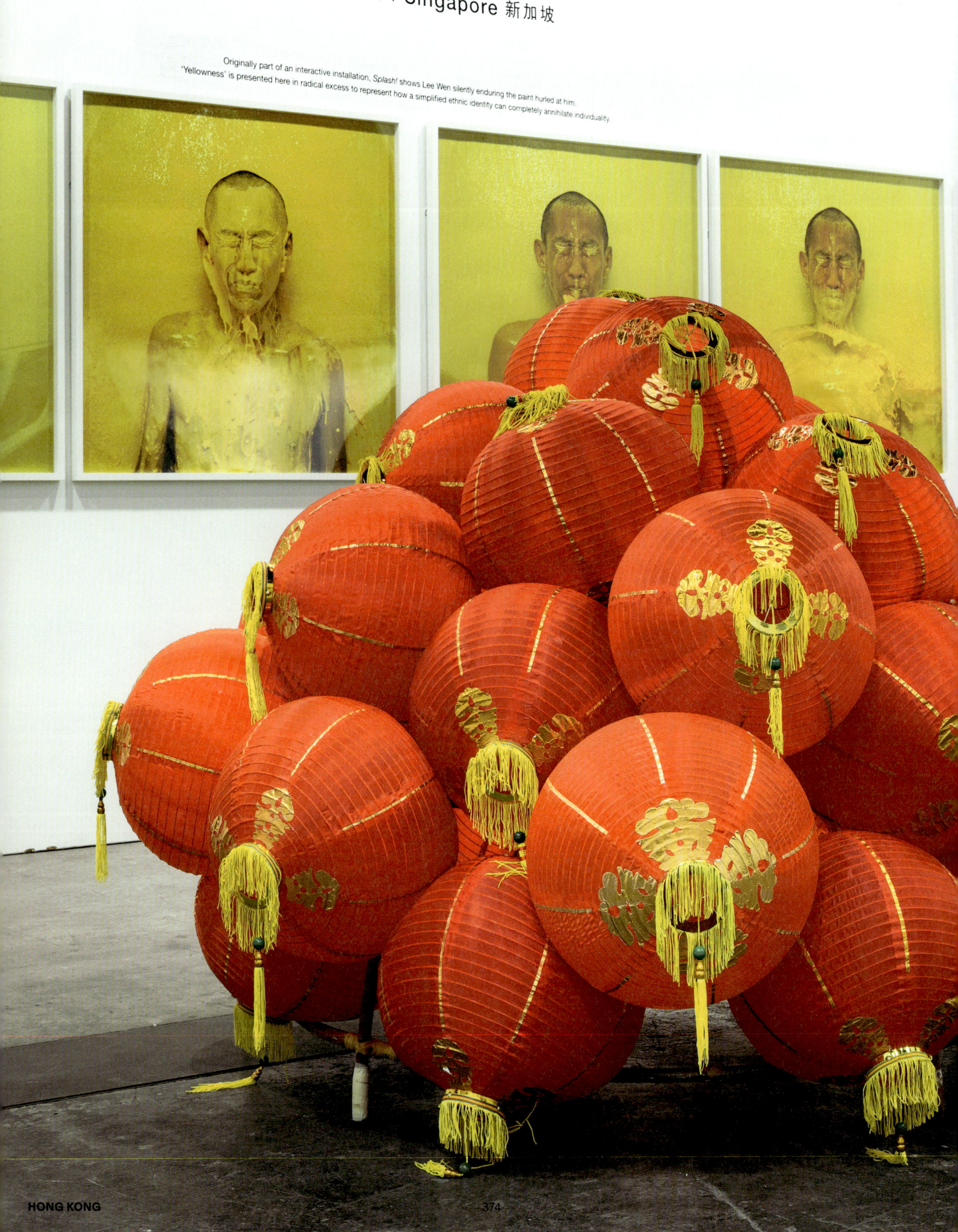
Lee Wen 李文 | Singapore 新加坡
Originally part of an interactive installation, Splash! shows Lee Wen silently enduring the paint hurled at him.
'Yellowness' is presented here in radical excess to represent how a simplified ethnic identity can completely annihilate individuality.

Lee Wen
iPreciation

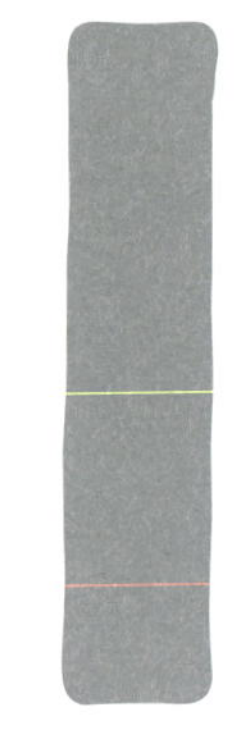
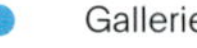

i8

Reykjavik

Galleries

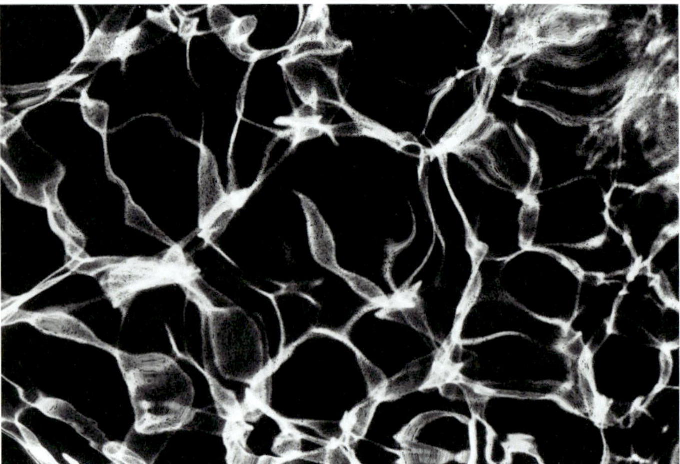

What is your favorite aspect of running a gallery?
Being among those who make great works and those who desire them.

How do you choose the artists you work with?
We look them in the eye, and we look at their work with our eyes.

If you weren't running a gallery what else would you do?
Farmer.

- **Contact** — i8 Gallery, Borkur Arnarson, borkur@i8.is
- **Established** — 1995
- **Owner(s) / Partner(s)** — Börkur Arnarson, Edda Jónsdóttir, Sigurður Gísli Pálmason
- **Team** — 6
- **Space(s)** — 150 m²
- **Artists at Art Basel** — Hreinn Fridfinnsson, Kristján Gudmundsson, Sigurdur Gudmundsson
- **Further artists represented** — Birgir Andrésson, Ingólfur Arnarsson, Margrét H. Blöndal, Olafur Eliasson, Elín Hansdóttir, Roni Horn, Janice Kerbel, Ragnar Kjartansson, Ernesto Neto, Eggert Pétursson, Ragna Róbertsdóttir, Karin Sander, Egill Sæbjörnsson, Hrafnkell Sigurdsson, Ignacio Uriarte, Thór Vigfússon, Lawrence Weiner

Ibid

London
Los Angeles

Galleries

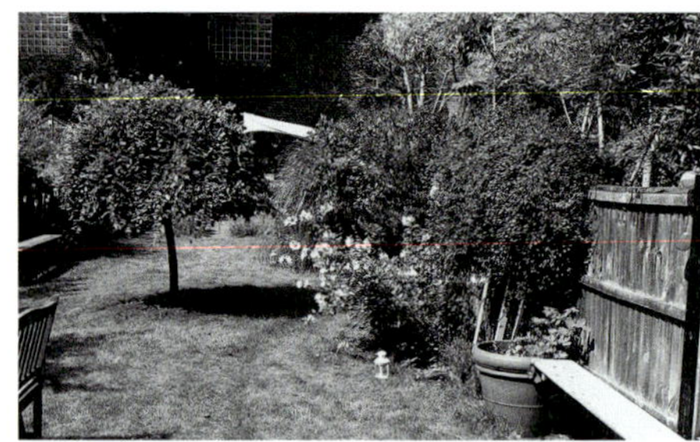

What is your favorite aspect of running a gallery?
Researching and curating shows.

How do you choose the artists you work with?
Firstly the work; but the relationship and the conversation with the artist is of equal importance.

If you weren't running a gallery what else would you do?
Botanist and writer, or a writer on botany.

- **Contact** — Ibid, Magnus Edensvard, magnus@ibidprojects.com
- **Established** — 2003
- **Owner(s) / Partner(s)** — Magnus Edensvard
- **Team** — 6
- **Space(s)** — 800 m²
- **Artists at Art Basel** — Rodrigo Matheus, Carsten Nicolai, Christopher Orr, Despina Stokou, Christoph Weber
- **Further artists represented** — David Adamo, Jānis Avotiņš, Ross Chisholm, Flora Hauser, William Hunt, Jack McConville, Amir Mogharabi, Rallou Panagiotou, Michael Portnoy, Olivier Richon, Christian Rosa, Alex Ruthner, Colin Snapp, Maria Taniguchi

IHN

Seoul

Insights

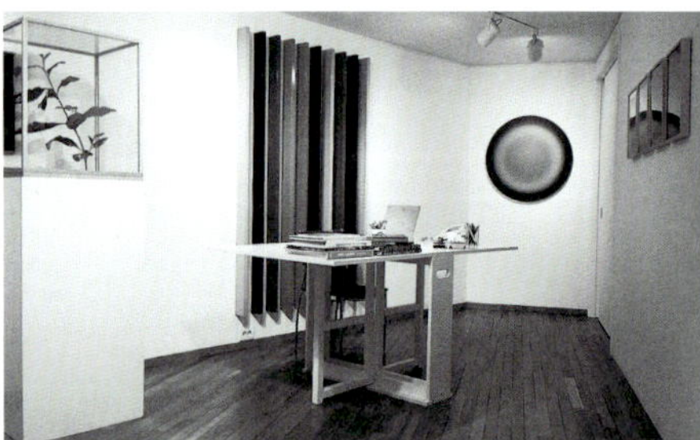

What is your favorite aspect of running a gallery?
I get to see the global art market, meet innovative artists and collectors from all over the world, and of course, I get better opportunities to develop my collection.

How do you choose the artists you work with?
I look for artists with unique and clear concepts, but also artists who share the same vision as the gallery.

If you weren't running a gallery what else would you do?
I would still be involved in the art scene one way or the other. Perhaps I would be part of an art and culture foundation: supporting and bridging artists and institutions, creating a cultural environment, and promoting Korean culture around the world.

- **Contact** Gallery IHN
  Hyein Kim
  galleryihn@gmail.com
- **Established** 1989
- **Owner(s) / Partner(s)** Ihn Yang
- **Team** 5
- **Space(s)** 430 m²
- **Artists at Art Basel** Bae Joonsung
  Bahk Seon Ghi
  Eddie Kang
  Han Unsung
  Hong Sung-Chul
  Hong Sung-Do
  Myeongbeom Kim
  Whang Inkie
- **Further artists represented** Ahn Jinkyun
  Camill Leberer
  James Casebere
  Cheon Kwang-Yup
  Liam Gillick
  Teo González
  Ha Sang-Rim
  Jeong Bo-Young
  Jeong Dae-Hyun
  Joo Myung-Duck
  Kim Young Hun
  Kong Sung Hoon
  Manfred Menz
  William Steiger
  Yoo Hyun-Mi
  Yoon JeongMee

Ingleby

Edinburgh

 Galleries
Galleries

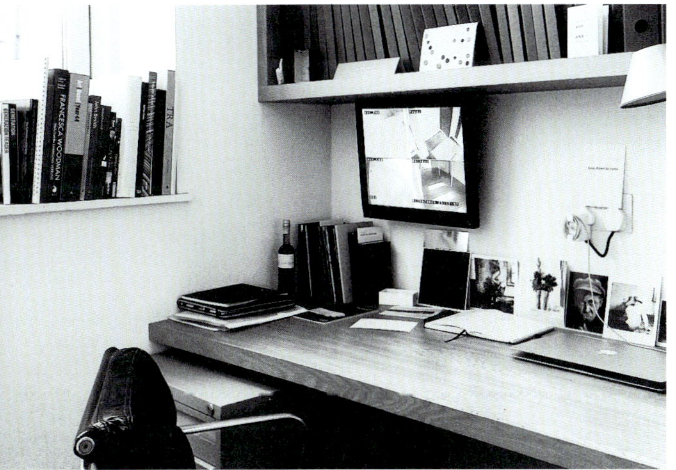

What is your favorite aspect of running a gallery?
Working with interesting people and amazing objects.

How do you choose the artists you work with?
Carefully.

If you weren't running a gallery what else would you do?
Live on a remote Hebridean island.

- **Contact** Ingleby Gallery
  Richard Ingleby
  richard@inglebygallery.com
- **Established** 1998
- **Owner(s) / Partner(s)** Florence Ingleby
  Richard Ingleby
- **Team** 8
- **Space(s)** 557.5 m²
- **Artists at Art Basel** David Austen
  David Batchelor
  Thomas Joshua Cooper
  Richard Forster
  James Hugonin
  Callum Innes
  Peter Liversidge
  Harland Miller
  Andrew Miller
  Jonathan Owen
  Katie Paterson
  Winston Roeth
  Iran do Espírito Santo
  Frank Walter
- **Further artists represented** Roger Ackling
  Ian Davenport
  Susan Derges
  Ian Hamilton Finlay
  Tommy Grace
  Howard Hodgkin
  Jermey Millar
  Garry Fabian Miller
  Kay Rosen
  Sean Scully
  Alison Watt

Instituto de visión

Bogotá

 Nova

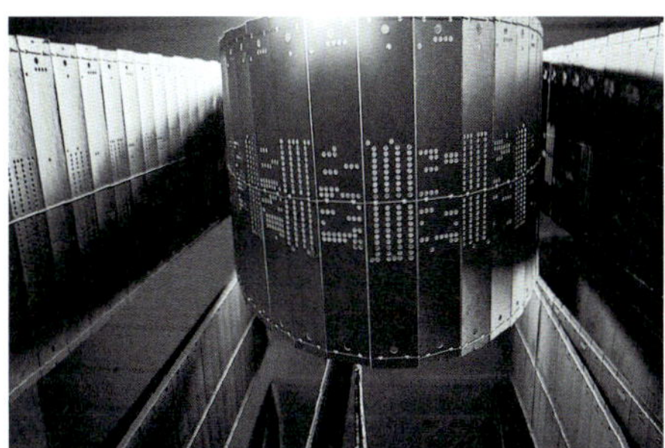

What is your favorite aspect of running a gallery?
Running a gallery is a very exciting experience. We have direct contact with many interesting people, from the artists to producers, collectors, institutions, and the general public. Working with art allows us to contribute to society, create our own micro-political system, and provide our own poetic means to relate with reality.

How do you choose the artists you work with?
The group of Colombian artists we represent belongs to a specific generation born in the 1970s and 1980s. This is what we call the new generation of Colombian art because these artists approach the Colombian context with more poetic leanings and work with more contemporary tools as well as with an international language.

If you weren't running a gallery what else would you do?
We are a very committed group of women. Omayra studied visual art, Karen and Maria studied art history, and Beatriz is a curator. We have no other option than to follow our passions, and being gallerists allows us to collaborate and exchange with our community and society.

- **Contact** Instituto de visión
  Omayra Alvarado
  omayra@institutodevision.com
- **Established** 2013
- **Owner(s) / Partner(s)** Karen Abreu
  Omayra Alvarado
  Beatriz Lopez
  Maria Wills
- **Team** 6
- **Space(s)** 150 m²
- **Artists at Art Basel** Tania Candiani
- **Further artists represented** Luis Ernesto Arocha
  Felipe Arturo
  Marlon de Azambuja
  Alicia Barney
  Otto Berchem
  Pía Camil
  Miguel Angel Cardenas
  Carolina Caycedo
  Nicolás Consuegra
  Wilson Díaz
  Sebastián Fierro
  Fornoll Franco
  Ana María Millán
  Carlos Motta
  Santiago Reyes Villaveces
  Ana Roldán
  Daniel Santiago Salguero
  Manuela Viera-Gallo

Invernizzi

Milan ● Galleries

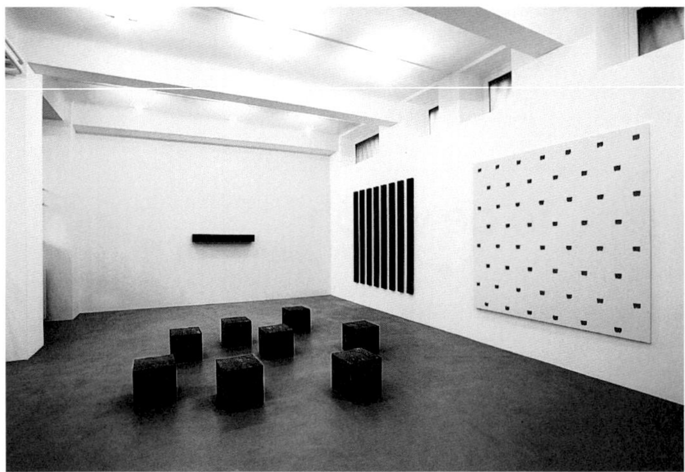

What is your favorite aspect of running a gallery?
My favorite aspect is the creation of projects in close collaboration with the artists. The gallery works with museums and public institutions both in Italy and internationally; yet another fascinating aspect is carrying out projects in Renaissance villas or in historical contexts, as well as participating in national and international fairs, where it is possible to have discussions with people.

How do you choose the artists you work with?
I choose the artists based on my own personal perception of the work, which I have developed since I was a boy by frequenting artists' studios. By choosing artists and through exhibitions, I would like to transmit my point of view, and what I feel when faced by the magic and mystery of a work. A "meeting" that is not only visual but that also sets off a dialogue in the mind.

If you weren't running a gallery what else would you do?
If I had not opened a gallery I would probably have become a chef and opened a restaurant. In fact, art and cooking stimulate the mind by way of sensorial perception, always allowing you to discover new things. Alternatively I would have become a publisher, which is also a way of communicating with people, offering new stimuli and possibilities.

- **Contact** A arte Invernizzi, Epicarmo Invernizzi, info@aarteinvernizzi.it
- **Established** 1994
- **Owner(s) / Partner(s)** Epicarmo Invernizzi
- **Team** 7
- **Space(s)** 400 m²
- **Artists at Art Basel** Rodolfo Aricò, Francesco Candeloro, Enrico Castellani, Alan Charlton, Carlo Ciussi, Gianni Colombo, Dadamaino, Riccardo De Marchi, Lesley Foxcroft, John McCracken, François Morellet, Mario Nigro, Pino Pinelli, Bruno Querci, Ulrich Rückriem, Nelio Sonego, Mauro Staccioli, Niele Toroni, David Tremlett, Günter Umberg, Michel Verjux
- **Further artists represented** Gianni Asdrubali, Nicola Carrino, Bernard Frize, Willi Kopf, Igino Legnaghi, Rudi Wach

iPreciation

Singapore ● Insights, Encounters

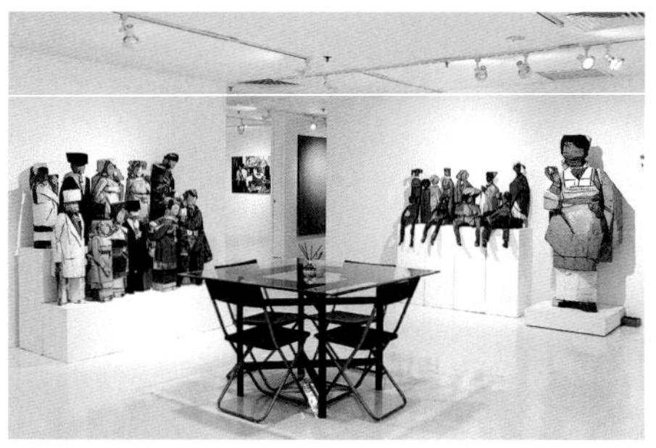

What is your favorite aspect of running a gallery?
Looking at art and simply enjoying it! We love working with the artists in developing art that we believe will be significant pieces of work in time to come. Our favorite challenge is helping an artist from being under-appreciated to being recognized and having his or her works collected and talked about.

How do you choose the artists you work with?
We must love the work of the artists we work with. Their work must be original and distinctive. They should be artists we believe in, and have both the brilliance and tenacity to arrive at their next milestone. Our artists do not stop creating art, they don't get lazy and live on their past ideas and glories, but continuously think about the ideas they want to convey in their work.

If you weren't running a gallery what else would you do?
Retire in the French or British countryside. Preferably near Paris or London, as I need three days of city life and four days of complete quiet.

- **Contact** iPreciation, June Ong, june.ong@ipreciation.com
- **Established** 1999
- **Owner(s) / Partner(s)** Helina Chan
- **Team** 7
- **Space(s)** 464.5 m²
- **Artists at Art Basel** Lee Wen
- **Further artists represented** Au Ka Wai, Jumadi Alfi, Riki Antoni, Samsul Arifin, Boo Sze Yang, Cheung Yee, Irene Chou, Gao Xingjian, Filip Gudovic, Jin Jie, Hilmi Johandi, Ju Ming, Kheng-Li Wee, Michael Lee, Luke Heng, Milenko Prvacki, Sai Hua Kuan, Jeremy Sharma, Tay Bak Chiang, Tang Da Wu, Tse Yim On, Budi Ubrux, Wang Ruobing, Doris Wong, Ye Jian Qing, Zhang Jian

Ishii

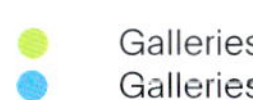

Tokyo ● Galleries
Paris ● Galleries

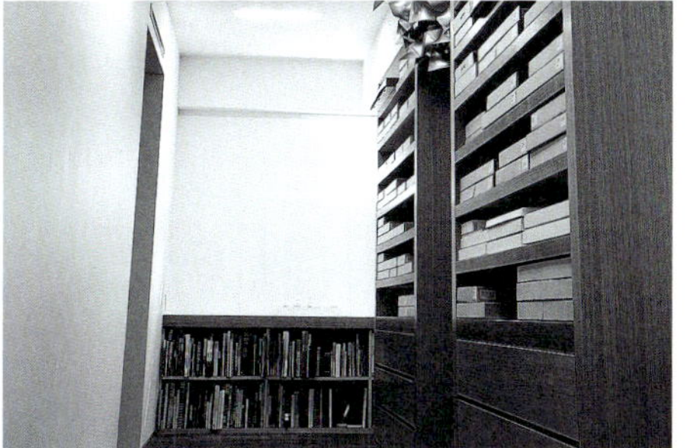

What is your favorite aspect of running a gallery?
Working with artists that are already part of art history, and supporting younger ones who may be engraved in future art history.

How do you choose the artists you work with?
Meeting the artists, talking to them, and seeing if we can establish a long-term working relationship.

If you weren't running a gallery what else would you do?
Artist.

- **Contact** Taka Ishii Gallery
  Takayuki Ishii
  tig@takaishiigallery.com
- **Established** 1994
- **Owner(s) / Partner(s)** Takayuki Ishii
- **Team** 11
- **Space(s)** 231 m²
- **Artists at Art Basel** Ei Arakawa
  Nobuyoshi Araki
  Michael Elmgreen & Ingar Dragset
  Mario García Torres
  Tomoo Gokita
  Naoya Hatakeyama
  Nobuya Hoki
  Takashi Ishida
  Zon Ito
  Naoto Kawahara
  Annette Kelm
  Yuki Kimura
  Yukinori Maeda
  Daido Moriyama
  Kyoko Murase
  William J. O'Brien
  Silke Otto-Knap
  Sterling Ruby
  Hiroe Saeki
  Kunié Sugiura
  Yosuke Takeda
  Kei Takemura
  Marijke van Warmerdam
  Cerith Wyn Evans
- **Further artists represented** Amy Adler
  Thomas Demand
  Luke Fowler
  Dan Graham
  Sean Landers
  Helen Mirra
  Taro Shinoda
  Hirofumi Toyama
  Christopher Wool

Taka Ishii Gallery
Interview with Takayuki Ishii

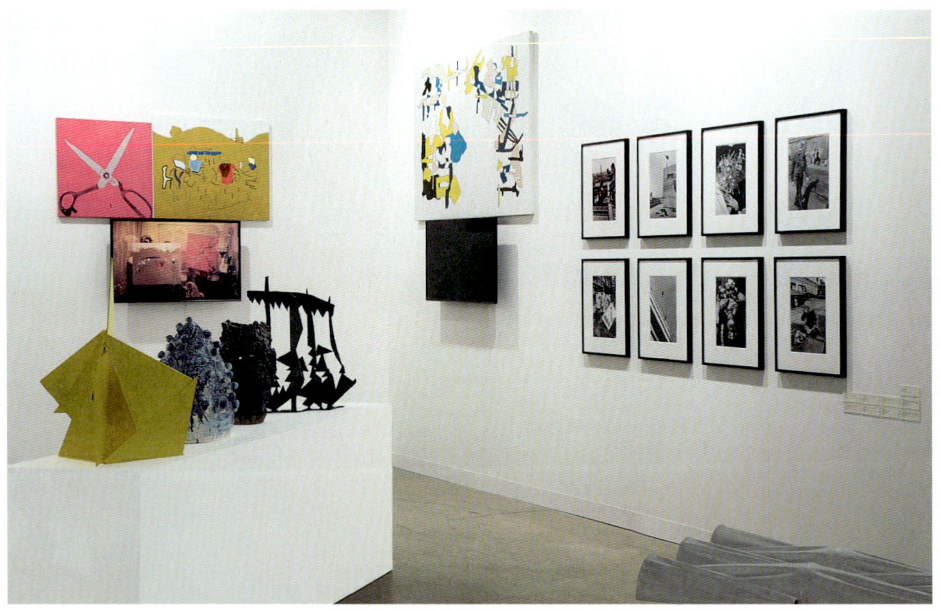

Art Basel in Basel, 2014

Your first exhibition was a show by Larry Clark in 1994. Why did you decide to start your gallery in Tokyo with *Tulsa*?

I saw Larry Clark's portfolio in the mid-1980s at the Los Angeles' Temporary Contemporary (MOCA) in Little Tokyo, when I was still an art student. It made a huge impression on me. When I decided to start the gallery I really wanted to show him in the first show. In the mid-1990s, photography and contemporary art were still part of different fields and thus not shown together. So it was like a double challenge!

You opened the gallery 20 years ago and you now have three spaces in Tokyo: one dedicated to photography, one to modern art, and the third to contemporary art. How did you come up with this triple activity and why this separation between media and fields?

Because of photography: we had a lot of photographers in the program, so we separated this activity in a specific gallery program, in order to show more photographers, mostly Japanese, but also foreign.

You are also very interested in books. You published the Japanese edition of *Tulsa* by Larry Clark, for example.

Yes. I really like photography books, and for almost every show we make a catalogue. We did *Tulsa* in 1996 and we also published the first Japanese edition of *Teenage Lust*. Our catalogue now comprises more than a hundred books.

When did you start participating in Art Basel?

We came to the main sector five years ago and we did Art Nova twice before that: the first one with Kiyoji Otsuji, a historical Japanese artist, and the second with Yuki Kimura, a younger female artist.

What do you think about the current revival of interest in modern and avant-garde Japanese art?

The 2013 Guggenheim Gutai show was a trigger for more international interest in the Japanese avant-garde, but it came too late actually: it should have been happening 20 years ago! I think the interest is becoming apparent: five or six years ago, there were a lot of curators coming to Tokyo and Osaka to research. They came to the gallery too. And for a few years now, collectors have been buying.

How would you describe the Tokyo art scene today, in the middle of the 2010s?

It's a slow scene, but thee are many young galleries, showing internationally and with a good program, like Take Ninagawa and Aoyama|Meguro, who are doing Liste this year. They are in their 20s and 30s, they show contemporary Japanese artists as well as international ones. So it is developing slowly but surely.

You also participate in Art Basel in Hong Kong. What is the main difference for you? Is it easier in Hong Kong?

For the shipping, yes! [*Laughs*] The audience is completely different. I did the Hong Kong art fair once before it became Art Basel. It was hard, very hard. Nobody came into the booth really, they just passed by ... We had Thomas Demand, Sterling Ruby, and Naoya Hatakeyama, but even with these artists ... For the 2014 edition, we were very busy!

Art Basel in Hong Kong, 2014

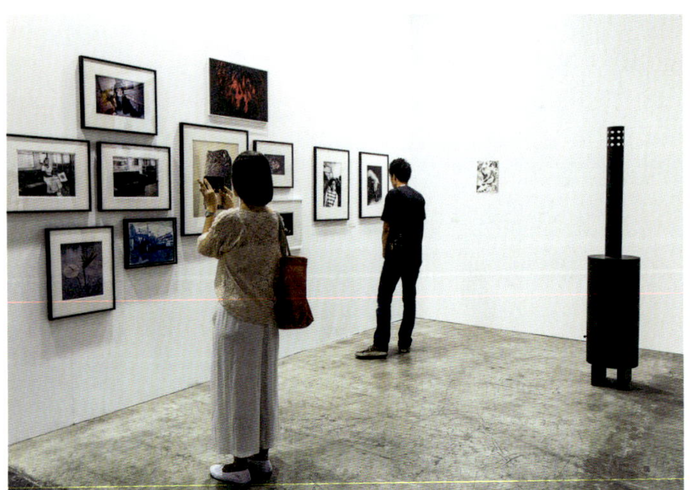

JOOJ
ANNA
JOOJ
NN
ASSA

Joan Jonas
Mirror Check, 1970/1972

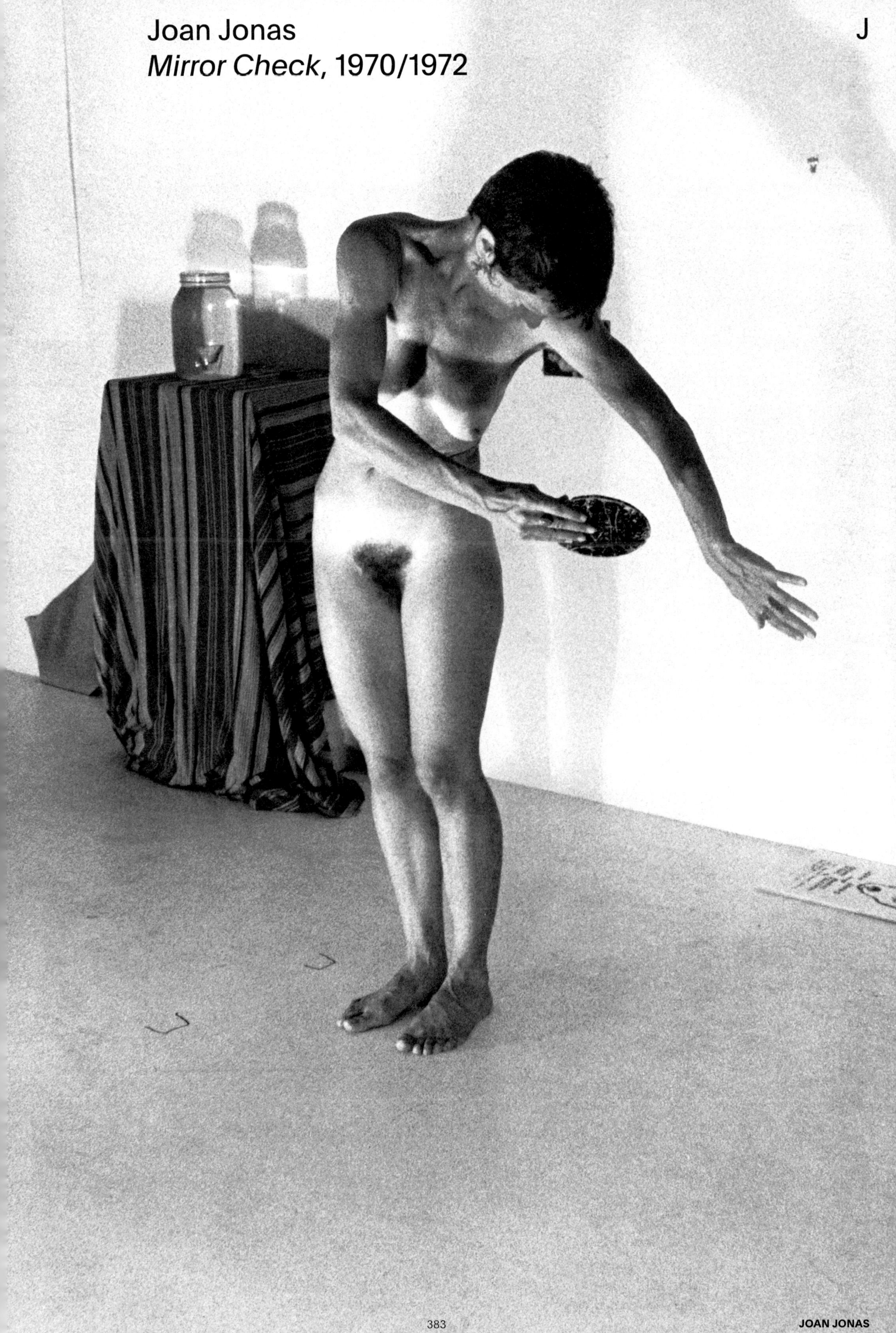

J

Joan Jonas
Mirror Check, 1970/2014

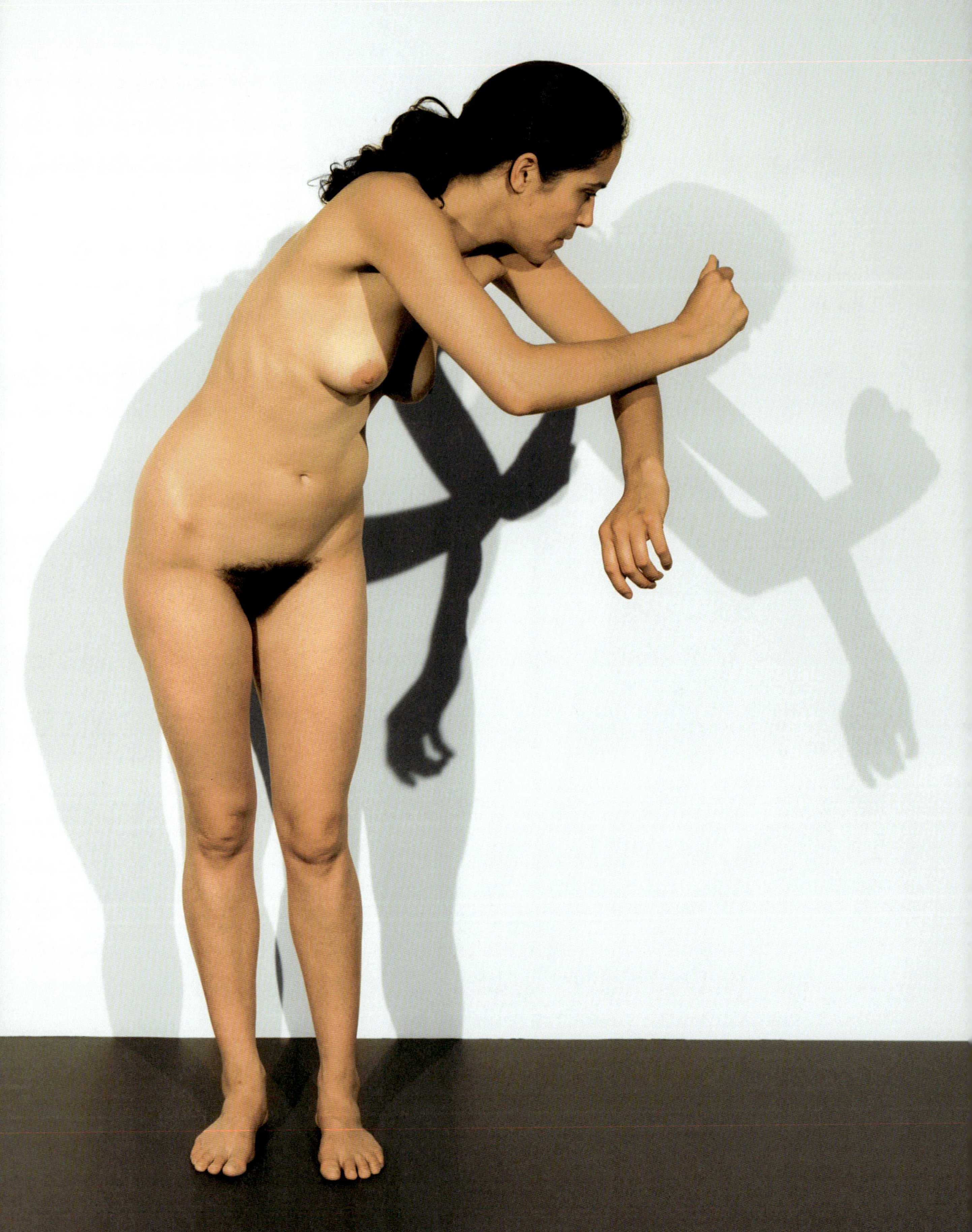

Conversation with Joan Jonas on her *Mirror Check* performance restaged in *14 Rooms*, Basel, June 2014

LIONEL BOVIER Your performance piece *Mirror Check* was created in 1970, i.e. 44 years ago. How do you approach the recreation of this piece given the art context today, the special context of *14 Rooms* during Art Basel art week, the flourishing of performance art and its museification over the last decade, and the evolution of feminism in contemporary Western society? Do you think the meaning and reception of the piece have changed a lot since its first performance?

JOAN JONAS In relation to the movement, it is presented as closely as possible to the way it was originally performed. One big difference is that it was performed in a large gymnasium at a distance from a seated audience and right before one of my *Mirror Piece* performances in which performers carry mirrors that, facing the audience, bring their reflections into the piece. Later, I also did this as an opener for the *Organic Honey* video performances in which the monitor was an ongoing mirror. The idea of *Mirror Check* is that the viewer is prevented from seeing what the performer sees in the mirror as she examines her body. The relation of the mirror to the body was a reference to self-examination and exposure referring to issues of feminism.

In *14 Rooms* the performance takes place in a small room. The piece is repeated over and over again as if it were looped. The audience is allowed to randomly walk in and out of the room, staying as long as they wish. Their perception is quite different from the original performances due the intimacy of the situation. When re-performed, it is more abstract and it can be experienced as a 10-minute dance.

LB Could you tell us more about the origins of your *Mirror Piece* series and the context of the first performance of *Mirror Check* in 1970?

JJ When I began performing in the late 1960s, the mirror was my first major prop. I was originally inspired by the writings of Jorge Luis Borges, in particular the collection of short stories *Labyrinths* (1962). I copied out all of the references to mirrors, memorized them, and then recited them while dressed in a costume covered with mirrors that made a particular sound as I slowly moved from side to side during a performance.

This lead to the choreography of the *Mirror Pieces 1 & 2* in which about 17 performers moved slowly in patterned sequences holding large 18" × 5' mirrors. *Mirror Check* directly came out of thinking about mirrors in relation to the body and the gaze of the viewer.

LB How do you see the fact that you are no longer performing the piece yourself, but delegating its performance? How did you work with the 2014 performers to "teach" them the piece (showing them footage of the original performance, elements of script, etc.)?

JJ It is really a great pleasure to teach this piece to a variety of younger performers. I show them each a video of myself performing the work in 1970 and ask them to copy my movements exactly. Then I meet with them and ask them to perform the piece for me while I give them suggestions and instructions about the speed and variety in their movements. Of course it's impossible to do exactly what I did, but that is a positive aspect, because I like to see how each performer does the performance slightly differently.

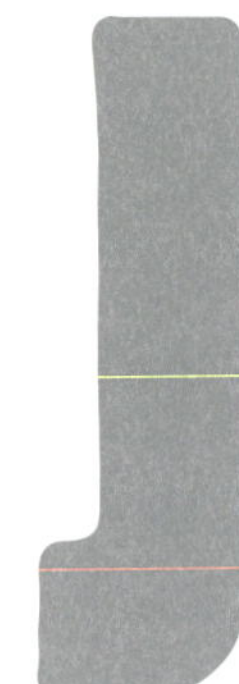

Jablonka

Cologne
Hürth Kalscheuren

Galleries
Unlimited

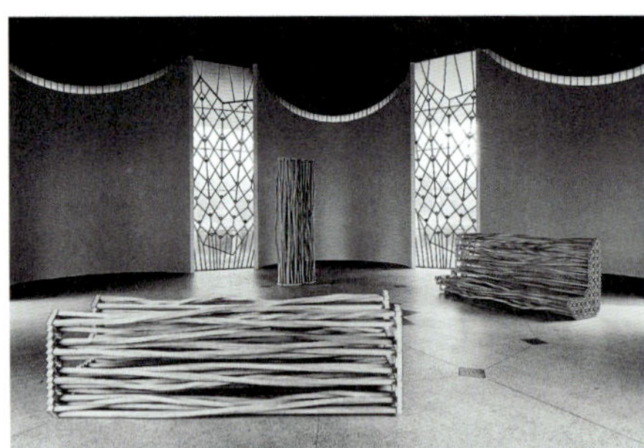

- **Contact** Jablonka Galerie
  Rafael Jablonka
  info@jablonkagalerie.com
- **Established** 1988
- **Owner(s) / Partner(s)** Rafael Jablonka
- **Team** 4
- **Artists at Art Basel** Nobuyoshi Araki
  Ross Bleckner
  Eric Fischl
  Mike Kelley
  Sherrie Levine
  Philip Taaffe
  Andreas Slominski
  Andy Warhol
- **Further artists represented** Platon
  Terry Winters

Jacobson

London
New York

Galleries
Galleries

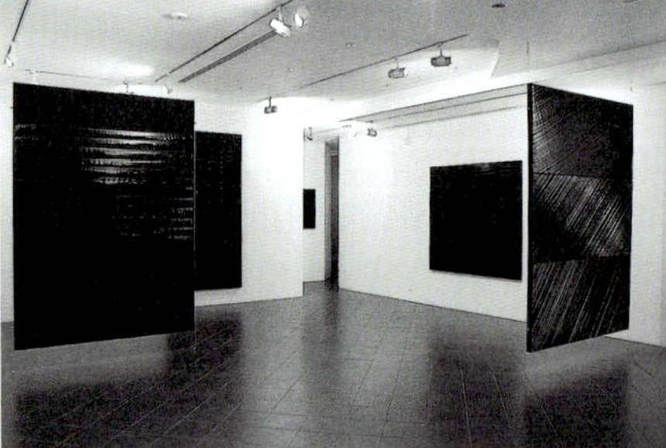

What is your favorite aspect of running a gallery?

Visiting artists' studios.

How do you choose the artists you work with?

They are all artists I have always wanted to work with: Pierre Soulages, Frank Stella, Sam Francis, etc. etc.

If you weren't running a gallery what else would you do?

Writing novels and poetry.

- **Contact** Bernard Jacobson Gallery
  Robert Delaney
  robert@jacobsongallery.com
- **Established** 1969
- **Owner(s) / Partner(s)** Bernard Jacobson
- **Team** 10
- **Space(s)** 464.5 m²
- **Artists at Art Basel** Helen Frankenthaler
  Sam Francis
  Karl Hyde
  Kwang Young Chun
  Bruce Mclean
  Robert Motherwell
  Ben Nicholson
  Pierre Soulages
  Frank Stella
  William Tillyer
  Marc Vaux
  Tom Wesselmann
- **Further artists represented** Pia Fries
  Shirley Kaneda
  Nicholas Pope
  Graham Sutherland

Jacques

London

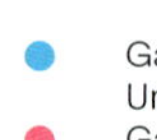

Galleries
Unlimited
Galleries

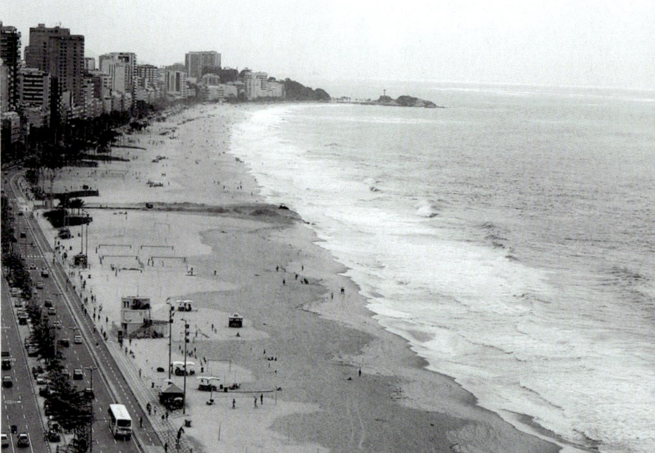

What is your favorite aspect of running a gallery?

Having the freedom to work with artists without the bureaucracy of a large organization. To be able to make things happen and have a voice that makes a difference from a small platform.

How do you choose the artists you work with?

It is always from gut instinct to begin with, that's how I'm drawn to the work in the first place. Sometimes I follow artists for many years—in the case of Lygia Clark and Hannah Wilke, I followed their work for ten years before reaching out to the estates and working with them. I don't like being in a hurry, which is a difficult position to maintain as the art world has got faster and more competitive.

If you weren't running a gallery what else would you do?

I would retain my independence and do something creative like opening a florist … then six months later, I would close it and reopen a gallery and start all over again …

- **Contact** Alison Jacques Gallery
  Alison Jacques
  info@alisonjacquesgallery.com
- **Established** 2004
- **Owner(s) / Partner(s)** Alison Jacques
- **Team** 10
- **Space(s)** 325 m²
- **Artists at Art Basel** Michael Bauer
  Irma Blank
  Lygia Clark
  Tomory Dodge
  Saul Fletcher
  Fernanda Gomes
  Sheila Hicks
  Birgit Jürgenssen
  Ian Kiaer
  Klara Kristalova
  Graham Little
  Robert Mapplethorpe

Ana Mendieta
Ryan Mosley
Hélio Oiticica
Alessandro Raho
Iran do Espirito Santo
Dorothea Tanning
Hannah Wilke
Catherine Yass
Thomas Zipp

Janda

Vienna — Galleries

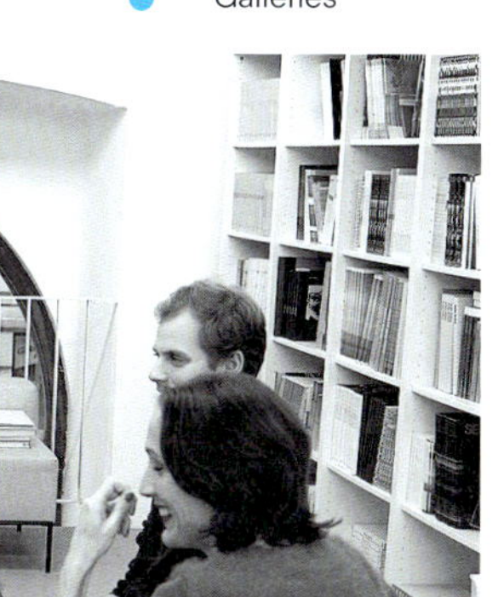

What is your favorite aspect of running a gallery?
I enjoy working with artists—it's a very particular kind of collaboration, accompanying a career, and, in some cases, also developing together. I like selling as a very specific form of art communication, and the fact that a gallery can (and has to) react very quickly to changes, questions, and new ideas.

How do you choose the artists you work with?
By looking at exhibitions, at art works, by reading books, by talking, traveling, and visiting studios. A studio visit can change the whole perception. I think it is important to be very attentive.

If you weren't running a gallery what else would you do?
I have no idea.

- **Contact**: Galerie Martin Janda
  Elisabeth Konrath
  elisabeth.konrath@martinjanda.at
- **Established**: 1992
- **Owner(s) / Partner(s)**: Martin Janda
- **Team**: 9
- **Space(s)**: 500 m²
- **Artists at Art Basel**: Alessandro Balteo Yazbeck
  Svenja Deininger
  Nilbar Güreş
  Július Koller
  Roman Ondák
  Gabriel Sierra
  Roman Signer
  Mladen Stilinović
  Adrien Tirtiaux
  Maja Vukoje
  Sharon Ya'ari
- **Further artists represented**: Martin Arnold
  Benjamin Butler
  Adriana Czernin
  Milena Dragicevic
  Werner Feiersinger
  Giuseppe Gabellone
  Christine & Irene Hohenbüchler
  Raoul De Keyser
  Jakob Kolding
  Jan Merta
  Allen Ruppersberg
  Joe Scanlan
  Corinne Wasmuht
  Donelle Woolford
  Jun Yang

Michael Janssen

Berlin
Singapore

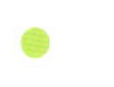

Insights

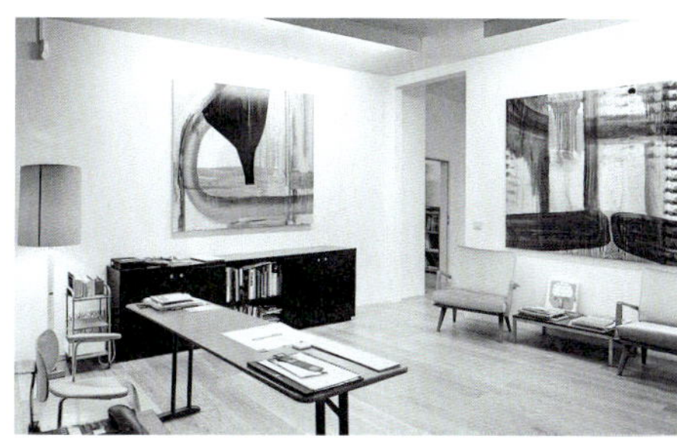

What is your favorite aspect of running a gallery?
Working with artists directly, visiting their studios, exchanging ideas, and creating amazing projects together.

How do you choose the artists you work with?
Instinct.

If you weren't running a gallery what else would you do?
Have a nice restaurant in the countryside, either in Italy or in France.

- **Contact**: Michael Janssen
  Nina Borgmann
  berlin@galeriemichaeljanssen.de
- **Established**: 1995
- **Owner(s) / Partner(s)**: Michael Janssen
- **Team**: 6
- **Space(s)**: 1,000 m²
- **Artists at Art Basel**: Aiko Tezuka
- **Further artists represented**: Stijn Ank
  Meg Cranston
  Lili Dujourie
  Monique van Genderen
  Assaf Gruber
  Thomas Grünfeld
  Ho Tzu Nyen
  Emil Holmer
  Anders Kjellesvik
  Christof Mascher
  Jin Meyerson
  Joris Van De Moortel
  Julika Rudelius
  Jeremy Sharma
  Christoph Steinmeyer
  Eddy Susanto
  Shaan Syed
  Titarubi
  Rose Wylie
  Mario Ybarra Jr.
  Peter Zimmermann

Rodolphe Janssen

Brussels

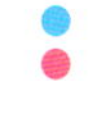

Feature
Galleries
Public

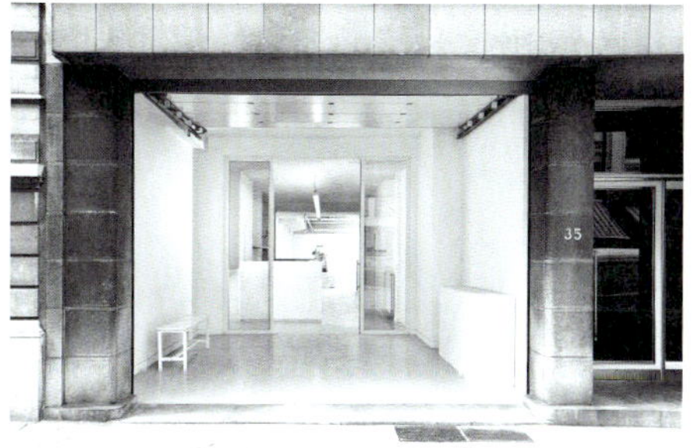

What is your favorite aspect of running a gallery?
Dinner and drinks with my artists.

How do you choose the artists you work with?
I show artists I would collect if I were a collector.

If you weren't running a gallery what else would you do?
Architect.

- **Contact** Galerie Rodolphe Janssen
  Julie Senden
  julie@galerierodolphejanssen.com
- **Established** 1991
- **Owner(s) / Partner(s)** Rodolphe Janssen
- **Team** 7
- **Space(s)** 255 m²
- **Artists at Art Basel** Betty Tompkins
- **Further artists represented** David Adamo, Davide Balula, Walead Beshty, Elaine Cameron-Weir, Wim Delvoye, Jürgen Drescher, Kendell Geers, Sean Landers, Thomas Lerooy, Justin Lieberman, Esko Männikkö, Chris Martin, Adam Mcewen, Farhad Moshiri, Sam Moyer, Marlo Pascual, David Ratcliff, Torbjørn Rødland, Sam Samore, Stephen Shore, Gert & Uwe Tobias, Banks Violette

Jeffries

Vancouver — Galleries Unlimited

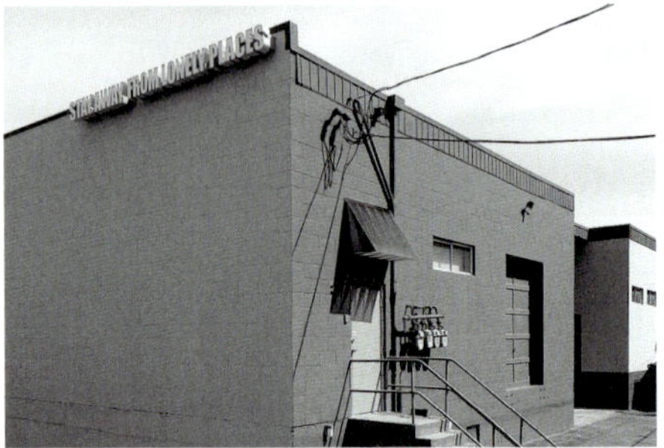

What is your favorite aspect of running a gallery?
Artists … and their stories.

How do you choose the artists you work with?
In the end … intuition.

If you weren't running a gallery what else would you do?
Be a gardener near the sea with a farm up the mountain.

- **Contact** Catriona Jeffries
  Catriona Jeffries
  catriona@catrionajeffries.com
- **Established** 1994
- **Owner(s) / Partner(s)** Catriona Jeffries
- **Team** 7
- **Space(s)** 585 m²
- **Artists at Art Basel** Raymond Boisjoly, Rebecca Brewer, Geoffrey Farmer, Julia Feyrer, Brian Jungen, Janice Kerbel, Christina Mackie, Liz Magor, Gareth Moore, Damian Moppett, Jerry Pethick, Judy Radul, Ron Terada, Ian Wallace
- **Further artists represented** Arabella Campbell, Duane Linklater, Myfanwy Macleod, Isabelle Pauwels, Kevin Schmidt, Jin-Me Yoon

Jensen

Sydney
Auckland — Galleries

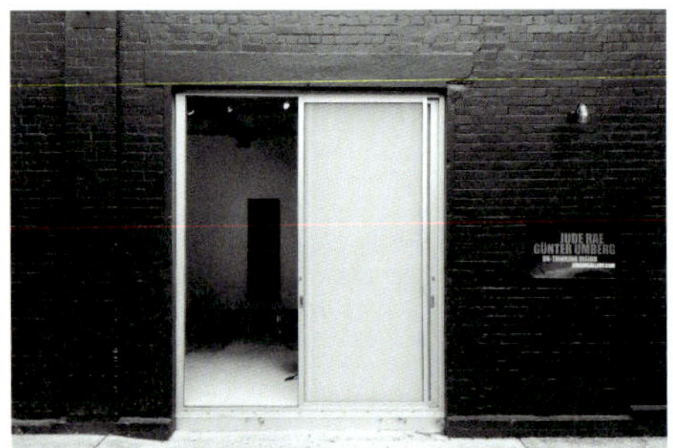

What is your favorite aspect of running a gallery?
Working alongside artists and being an advocate for their work.

How do you choose the artists you work with?
We want to represent artists whose practice we really enjoy and respect.

If you weren't running a gallery what else would you do?
Architecture.

- **Contact** Jensen Gallery
  Andrew Jensen
  gallery@jensengallery.com.au
- **Established** 1988
- **Owner(s) / Partner(s)** Emma Fox
- **Team** 4
- **Space(s)** 650.5 m²
- **Artists at Art Basel** Helmut Federle, Callum Innes, Imi Knoebel, Leigh Martin, Tomislav Nikolic, Tony Oursler, Jude Rae, Fred Sandback, Günter Umberg, Elisabeth Vary
- **Further artists represented** James Casebere, Melissa Coote, Sam Harrison, Jacqueline Humphries, Isabel Nolan, Winston Roeth, Judith Wright

Johnen

Berlin

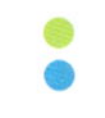

Galleries
Galleries Unlimited

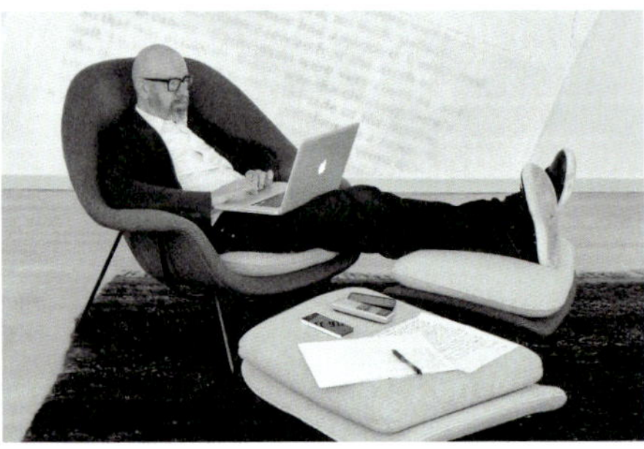

What is your favorite aspect of running a gallery?
Having the possibility to support and promote artists whose work and vision helps to see the world in a different and more complex way.

How do you choose the artists you work with?
By intuition. Sometimes in discussion with friends and other artists. The gallery is interested in artists who are in opposition to the most fashionable trends.

If you weren't running a gallery what else would you do?
I wrote my thesis on Richard Tuttle and I would love to write more books.

- **Contact** Johnen Galerie
  Cornelia Tischmacher
  mail@johnengalerie.de
- **Established** 1984
- **Owner(s) / Partner(s)** Jörg Johnen
- **Team** 8
- **Space(s)** 400 m²
- **Artists at Art Basel** Stephan Balkenhol
  Martin Boyce
  Martin Creed
  Hans-Peter Feldmann
  Rodney Graham
  Andrew Grassie
  Candida Höfer
  Raimer Jochims
  Liu Ye
  Roman Ondák
  Prabhavathi Meppayil
  Thomas Ruff
  Wilhelm Sasnal
  Tino Sehgal
  Wiebke Siem
  Michael van Ofen
  Yoshitomo Nara
- **Further artists represented** Jānis Avotiņš
  Stefan Bertalan
  David Claerbout
  James Coleman
  Slawomir Elsner
  Ryan Gander
  Francesco Gennari
  Dan Graham
  David Hahlbrock
  Olaf Holzapfel
  Martin Honert
  Robert Kusmirowski
  Tim Lee
  Jan Merta
  The Estate of Florin Mitroi
  Anri Sala
  Helmut Stallaerts
  Jeff Wall

Jongma

Amsterdam ● Positions

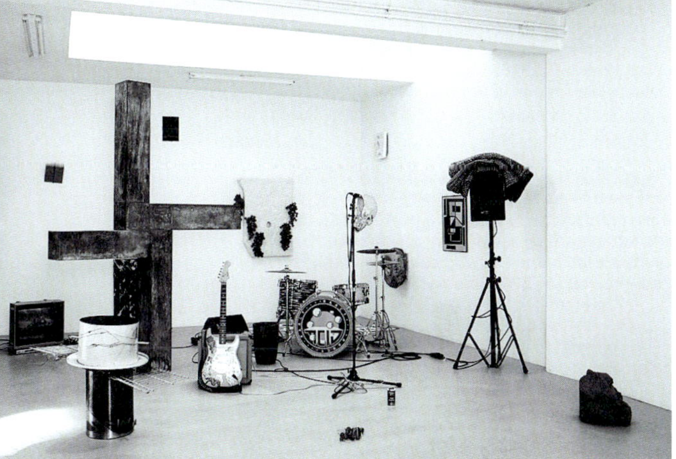

- **Contact** Galerie Juliètte Jongma
  Alie Sonneveldt
  info@juliettejongma.com
- **Established** 2004
- **Owner(s) / Partner(s)** Juliètte Jongma
- **Team** 2
- **Space(s)** 120 m²
- **Artists at Art Basel** Florian & Michael Quistrebert
- **Further artists represented** Chris Evans
  Melissa Gordon
  Donna Huddleston
  Ursula Mayer
  Lisa Oppenheim
  Pablo Pijnappel
  Misha de Ridder
  Karen Sargsyan
  Guido van der Werve
  Arjan van Helmond
  Nina Yuen

Juda

London

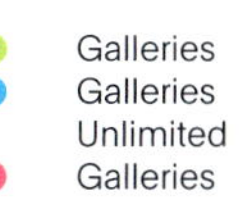

● Galleries
● Galleries Unlimited
● Galleries

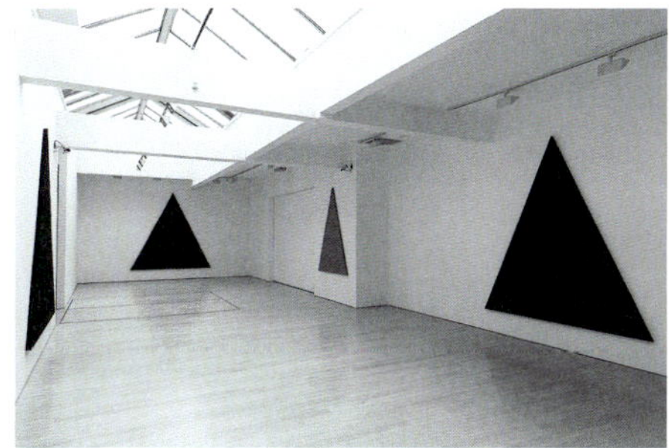

What is your favorite aspect of running a gallery?

Installing exhibitions and having a successful exhibition both in acclaim and sales.

How do you choose the artists you work with?

Many of our artists have been with the gallery for a long time. The newer artists have been chosen through visits to art schools or on personal recommendation from other artists.

If you weren't running a gallery what else would you do?

The only training I have apart from being an art dealer is a First Class waiter on a luxury liner and I would return to that if I had the energy.

- **Contact** Annely Juda Fine Art
  David Juda
  ajfa@annelyjudafineart.co.uk
- **Established** 1960
- **Owner(s) / Partner(s)** David Juda
- **Team** 9
- **Space(s)** 480 m²
- **Artists at Art Basel** Roger Ackling
  Anthony Caro
  Alan Charlton
  Christo
  Katsura Funakoshi
  Naum Gabo
  Nigel Hall
  David Hockney
  Sigrid Holmwood
  Tadashi Kawamata
  Leon Kossoff
  Darren Lago
  Kasimir Malevich
  François Morellet
  David Nash
  Kazuo Shiraga
  Yuko Shiraishi
  Friedrich Vordemberge-Gildewart
- **Further artists represented** Prunella Clough
  Duan Jianyu
  Gloria Friedmann
  Philipp Goldbach
  Werner Haypeter
  Edwina Leapman
  Catherine Lee
  Kenneth Martin
  Mary Martin
  László Moholy-Nagy
  Sarah Oppenheimer
  Alan Reynolds
  Yoshishige Saito Suzanne Treister
  Georges Vantongerloo
  Graham Williams
  Katsuhiro Yamaguchi

Jablonka Galerie
Interview with Rafael Jablonka

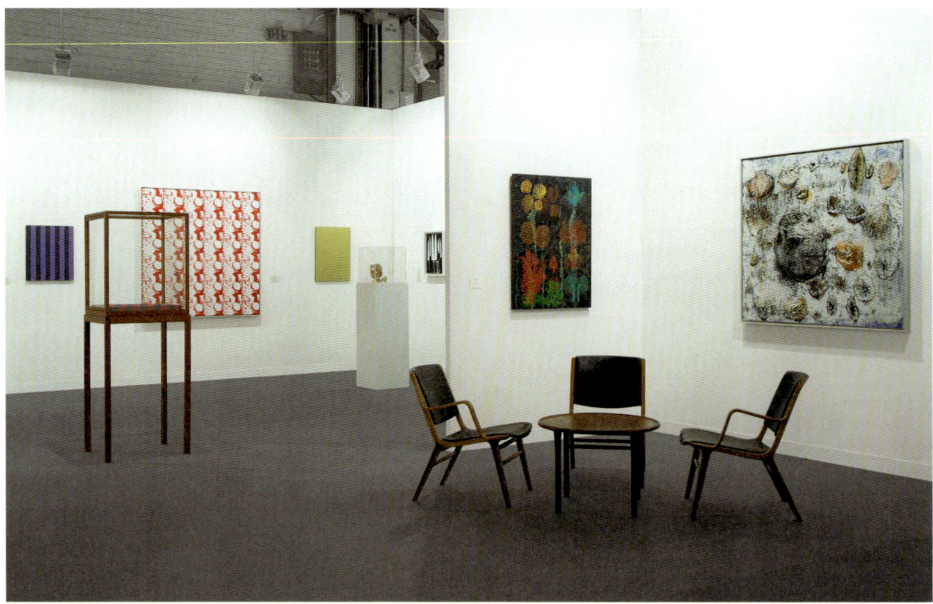

Art Basel in Basel, 2014

You opened your gallery in 1988 in Cologne. What was the inaugural exhibition?
It was a group show and, funnily enough, it included a Carroll Dunham painting that we are showing now in our Zurich space. I started with American artists like Peter Halley, Carroll Dunham, Richard Prince, and soon after, Mike Kelley and Sherrie Levine.

Did you open in Cologne because of the art scene at the time?
Yes. I'm from Poland, and I first worked as a curator—with Kasper König on the exhibition *Von hier aus* (1984), and on the inaugural show of the Ludwig Museum's new building, *Europa/Amerika* (1986). It informed me about the American scene of the 1980s, but also made me realize that museum jobs were not really for me: I knew by then that I wanted to open a gallery.

At the time Cologne was a real center of the art world, with a very strong connection to New York …
Yes, but Cologne was a tiny thing compared to New York … It was only a center for Europe until 1992. It's only an episode in history, mostly due to the fact that people like Rudolf Zwirner and Michael Werner opened their galleries there. We were all going to Cologne for visiting exhibitions. Except for Konrad Fischer in Düsseldorf, all the galleries were in Cologne. Not in Berlin, which was still divided. Cologne was the place where galleries where moving to, from Sweden, Munich, and other cities.

How was the art fair in Cologne at that time?
The Cologne art fair was very strong. It was the first contemporary art fair, but the management drove it against a wall in the 1990s. They have been trying for years to recuperate.

When did you open in Zurich?
Two years ago. My gallery there is a "pièce unique" type of space, more like a shop. We also have a third space since 2011, the Böhm Chapel, in the suburbs of Cologne where we organize long-lasting exhibitions.

What about your first participation in Art Basel?
It was probably in 1989. At that time there weren't many restrictions. I didn't participate in 1990, because of the crisis; the director of the fair came to me and asked me to come back … That was the time when they asked you to come! Now you have a waiting list of a 1,000 galleries.

Do you remember one booth in particular you did at Art Basel, like a solo presentation, or do you always represent all the artists of the gallery?
This year is special: normally I try to put some "classics" within the selection. Right now I have Warhol—I've worked with the Warhol Estate for many years—but it looks like a curated show about Levine and Warhol.

The Art Basel booth is an important presentation, so you take a lot of time devising it. It's not just taking three walls and hanging works: I try to think how I can organize contrasts, tensions, etc., between a work and another one. It's not something that I do in one day: we build a model, a plan, etc.

For me, any show is always like the first one, I never learn from previous mistakes, I guess. So if you ask me if I remember a particular booth I did here, I probably remember them all, but I couldn't say that one was better than another. One would be better than another one just in terms of turnover!

Do you also participate in Miami Beach?
I did Miami Beach for several years, but the jetlag was killing me, so I stopped. I also didn't like the fact that there were so many distractions: so many events and social things going on. For me art is a serious expression of artists' ideas and visions, like poetry. I don't think it is part of a party environment. But I guess we live in a world resembling a global party more and more …

Art Basel in Basel remains focused on the artworks, and the city is clearly less party-oriented. But even here you can witness an evolution: in the 1990s the fair experience was basically focused around the fair's halls and a few good shows in the city. Then maybe you'd go to a bar, but that was it!
I hope that in the future there won't be more distraction. Already now I think there are too many things going on: you can hardly talk to people because they have so much on their menu. This year [2014], they have to see Unlimited, *14 Rooms*, Fondation Beyeler, Schaulager, etc. And by the end of the day they have 5 minutes left to come to your stand. We—meaning the Art Basel community—may also kill ourselves with these expanding programs.

The gallery began 26 years ago. How do you see the evolution of a gallery like yours, with very strong positions and representing famous artists? How do you include new positions within this list, for instance? Who were the last artists you included in your program?
The photographer Platon. He is a star photographer, working for the *New Yorker*, making photographs like Avedon or Irving Penn. It's not a Sherrie Levine type of photography. I don't think there is such a big distance between photography and painting. It is a very different technique, but in terms of expression, I get as much satisfaction from Platon as from a painting by Philip Taaffe.

Have you worked with Philip Taaffe for a long time?
Since 1999 I think. I have known his work since the mid-1980s and really liked it, but he was working with other galleries. I thought I didn't need to show him, but could buy his works for myself, until he asked to come to me. One day he will be considered one of the most important American abstract painters.

K

For the Kabinett sector in Miami Beach, Galleries sector participants are chosen to present curated exhibitions in a separately delineated space within their booths. The concepts within Kabinett are diverse, including thematic group shows, art historical showcases, and solo shows for rising stars. We invited New York-based Pablo León de la Barra, UBS MAP Curator, Latin America, Solomon R. Guggenheim Museum, to choose his four favorite booths

KABI NETT

2014 participants

Galerie 1900-2000
Ivan Serpa

Benzacar
Liliana Porter

Carberry
Judith Rothschild

Casas Riegner
José Antonio Suárez Londoño

Faria
Jaime Davidovich

Gupta
Mickalene Thomas

Hirschl & Adler
Fairfield Porter

Hoffman
Michael Rakowitz

kaufmann repetto
Dianna Molzan

Kicken
Germany's Coming of Age

Krinzinger
Günter Brus

Lehmann Maupin
Teresita Fernández

Lelong
Etel Adnan

Mara-La Ruche
Amalia Nieto

Meile
Yan Xing

Naumann
Leon Kelly

Nolan
Ciprian Mureşan and Şerban Savu

OMR
James Turrell

Roesler
Paulo Bruscky

Rumma
Ettore Spalletti

Schulte
Robert Wilson

Sicardi
Antonio Asis

Sperone Westwater
Guillermo Kuitca

Taylor
Antoni Tàpies

Two Palms
Terry Winters

Van Doren Waxter
Joseph Cornell

Wolff
Miriam Cahn

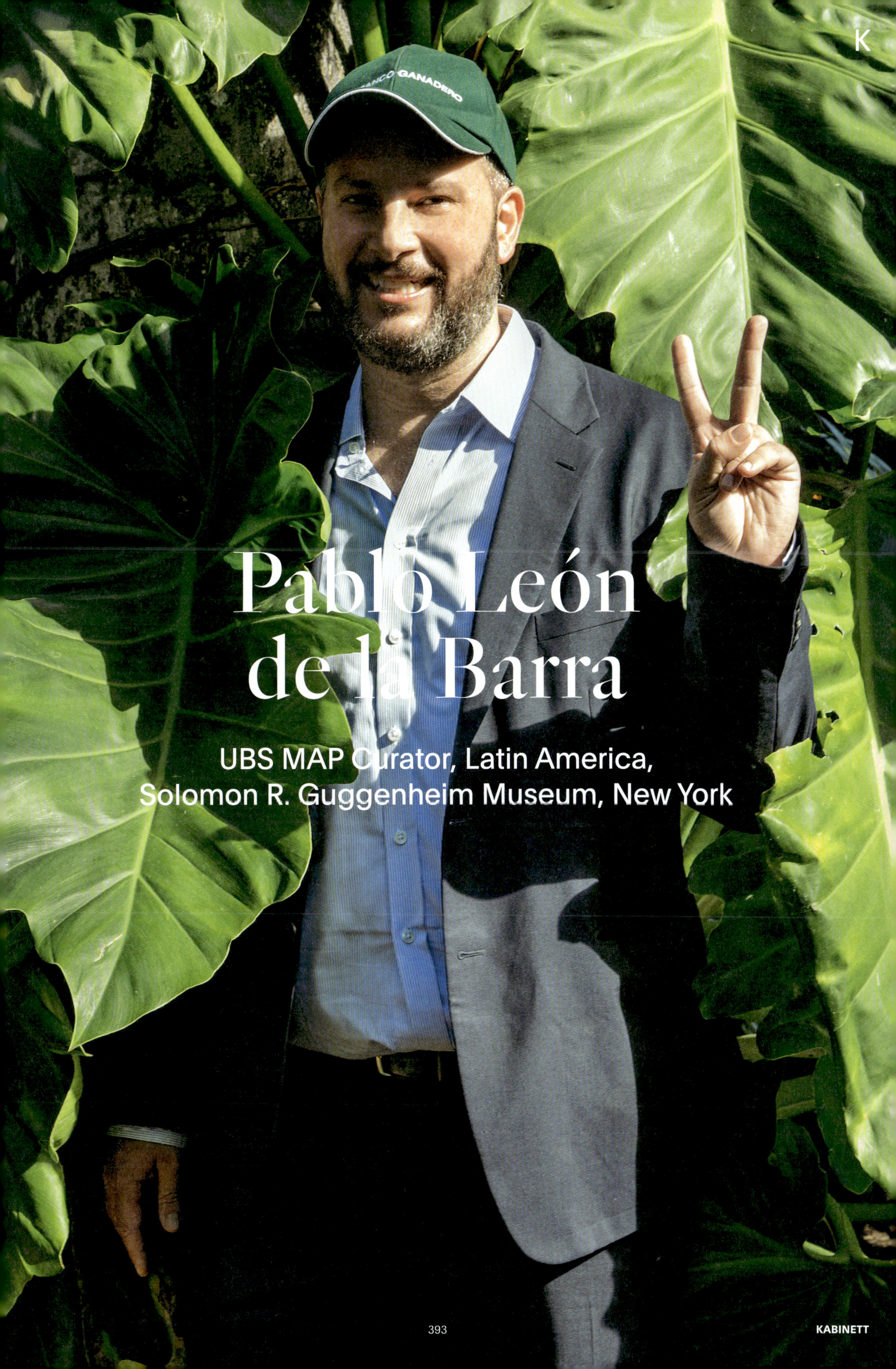

Pablo León de la Barra

UBS MAP Curator, Latin America, Solomon R. Guggenheim Museum, New York

K

Galerie Lelong
Etel Adnan

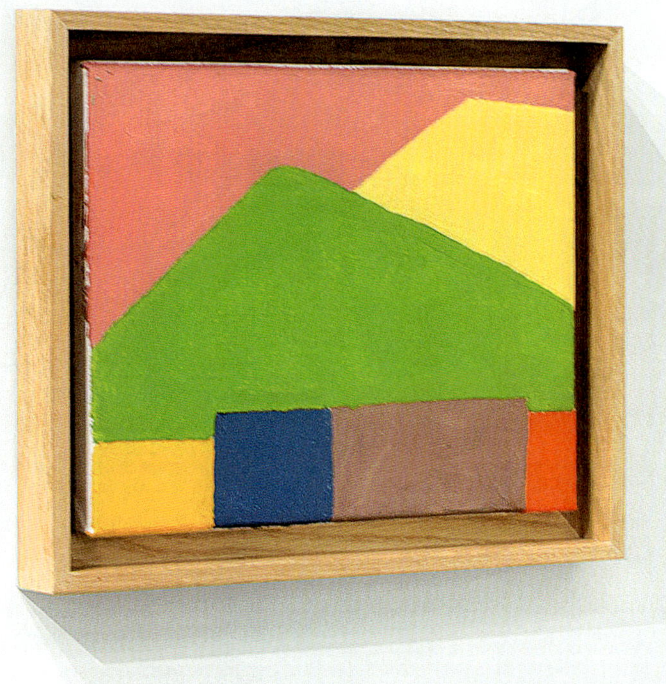

Etel Adnan's paintings were one of the highlights of documenta 13 (2012). I had became aware of her work a year before thanks to a publication and a great interview she did with Hans Ulrich Obrist. A Lebanese poet and painter born in 1925, Adnan has lived in California since 1955. In her beautiful paintings she depicts colorful landscape abstractions of Mount Tamalpais, located north of San Francisco. It wasn't until I visited Lebanon in 2012 that I really understood the power behind her paintings. What she is really painting is the memory of exile and the longing for the place one has left. Her landscapes are also her memory of Mount Lebanon, the mountain range that extends the entire length of the country and which is always present on the horizon. Nevertheless, for Adnan, "Ultimately our real home is our life" (quoted from Hans Ulrich Obrist Instagram post-it project).

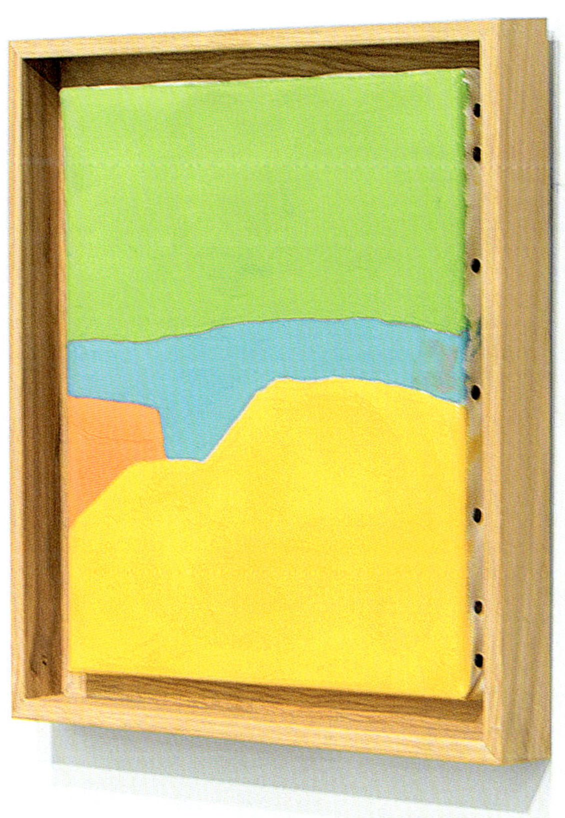

K

Galerie 1900–2000
Ivan Serpa

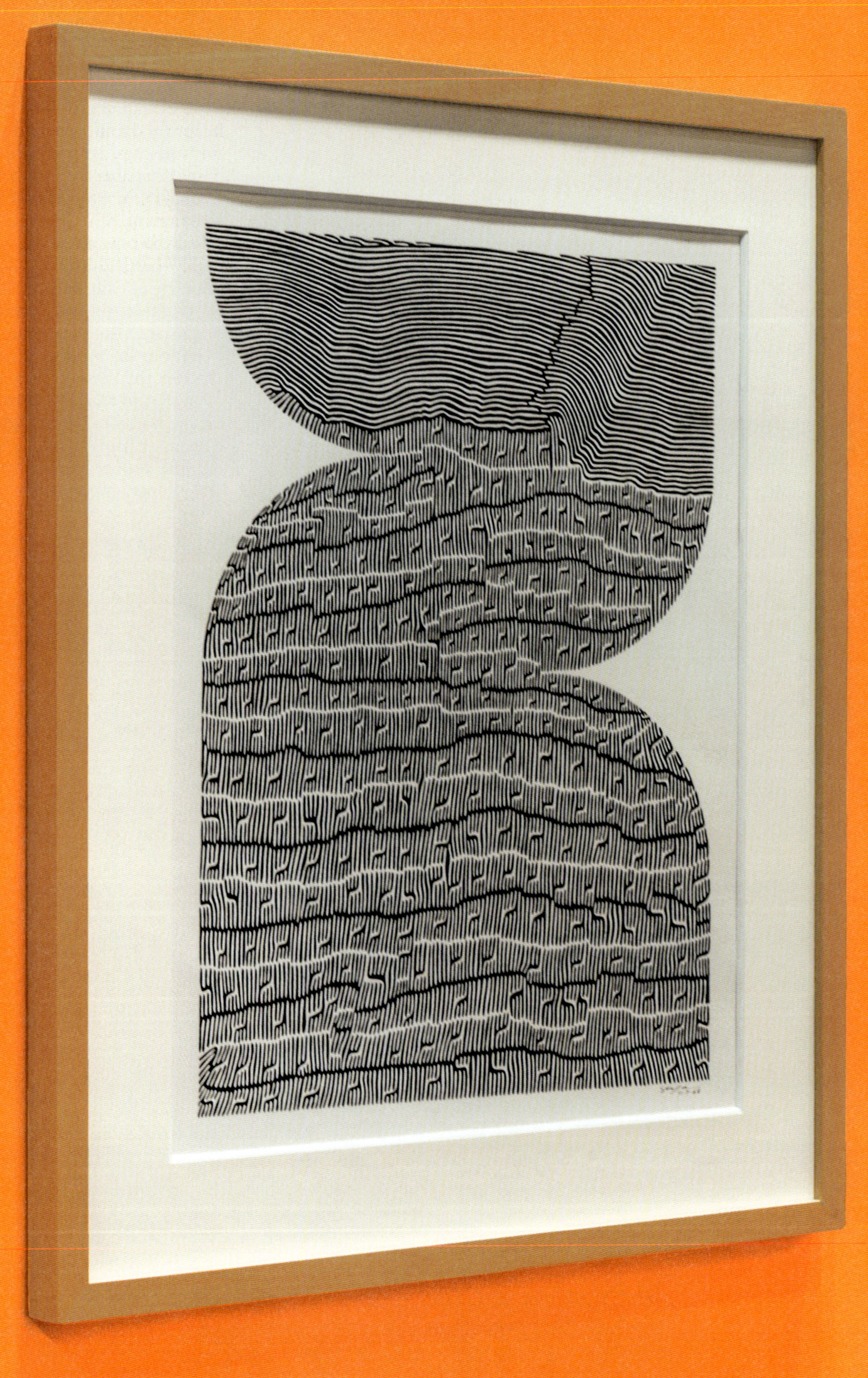

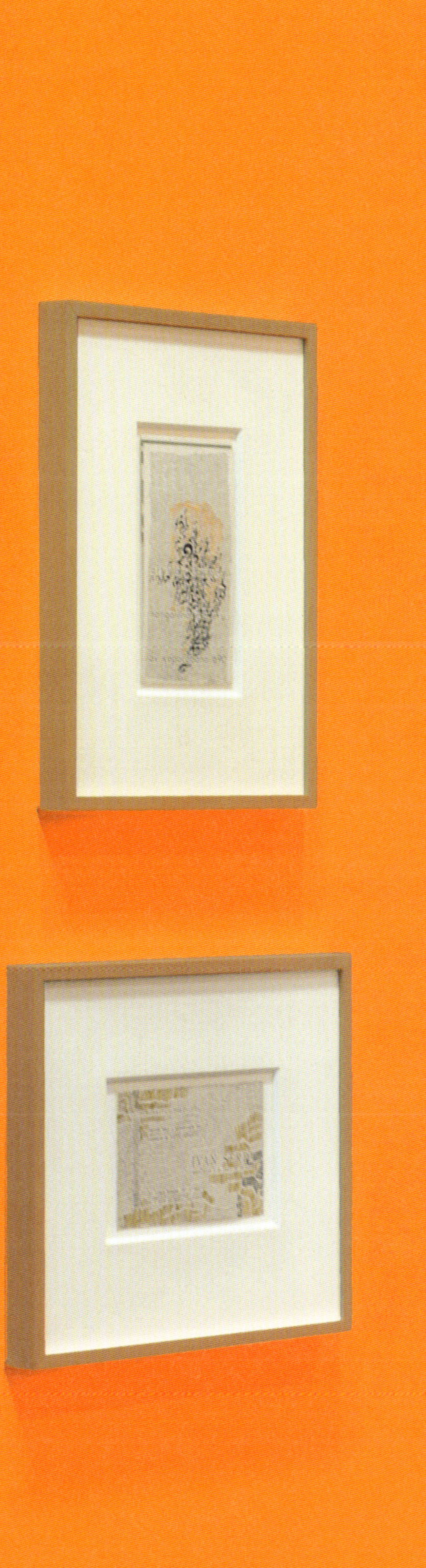

Ivan Serpa is better known today as Hélio Oiticica's teacher. His prolific work ranges from geometrical abstraction to figurative expressionism. The body of work presented here was made at the end of the 1960s and consists of ink drawings on paper. What at first sight looks like beautiful doodles are really obliterations of names and information on postcards, letters, and invitations: a reminder of the disappearance of identity and of the censorship of information happening at the time under the Brazilian dictatorship.

Henrique Faria Fine Art
Jaime Davidovich

I met Jaime for the first time last summer in New York. When I visited his studio I was amazed that he kept a body of work from almost 50 years there, which was virtually unnoticed by museums, institutions, collectors, and the market. The work presented here is part of his 1970s "Tape Projects," in which he covered entire wall surfaces using tape not only as an artistic material, but as a way of intervening and interfering in space. This led later to his interest in video, and the creation of *The Live Show*, a TV program which was transmitted by cable TV, and which was another way of interfering with programmed reality.

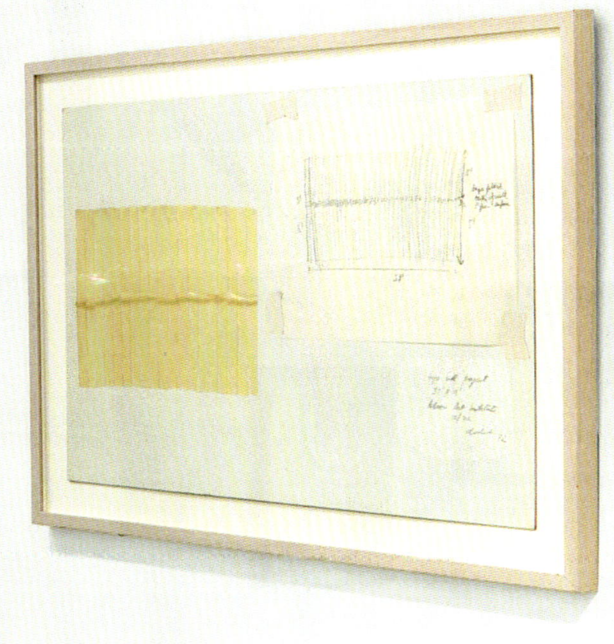

Galeria Nara Roesler
Paulo Bruscky

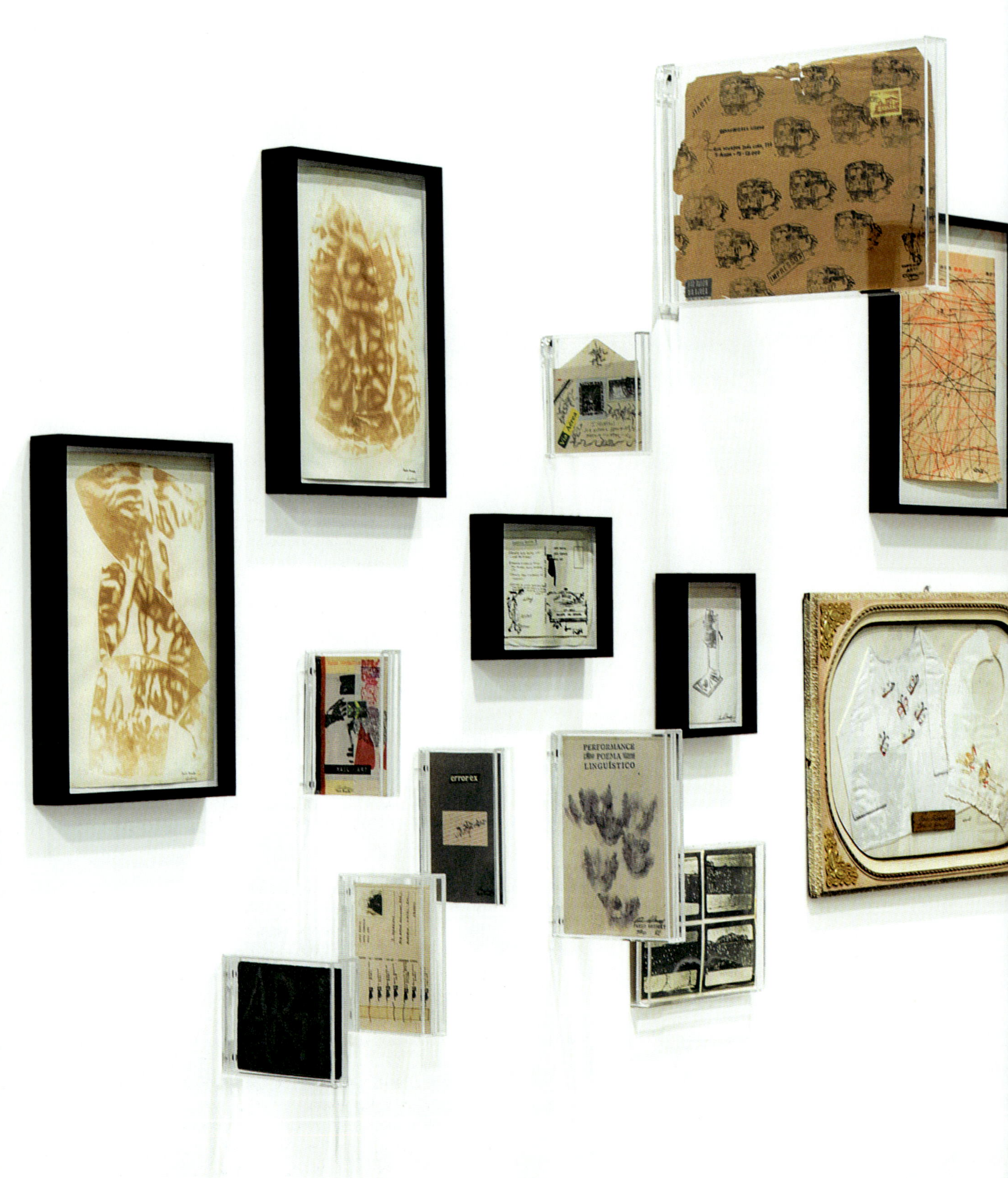

I first came into contact with Paulo Bruscky's work at the Havana Biennial of 2009. There I entered his personal universe of Mail art, ink stamps, and publications. Based in Recife, in the northeast of Brazil, he has been a pioneer of postal art since the 1960s, and has established a network of communication and exchange through this medium that challenged not only the censorship of the dictatorship in Brazil at the time, but also the notion of centers and peripheries. Through his work Bruscky affirms that the center is always the place where one is located, and that it's possible to make an aesthetic revolution from there.

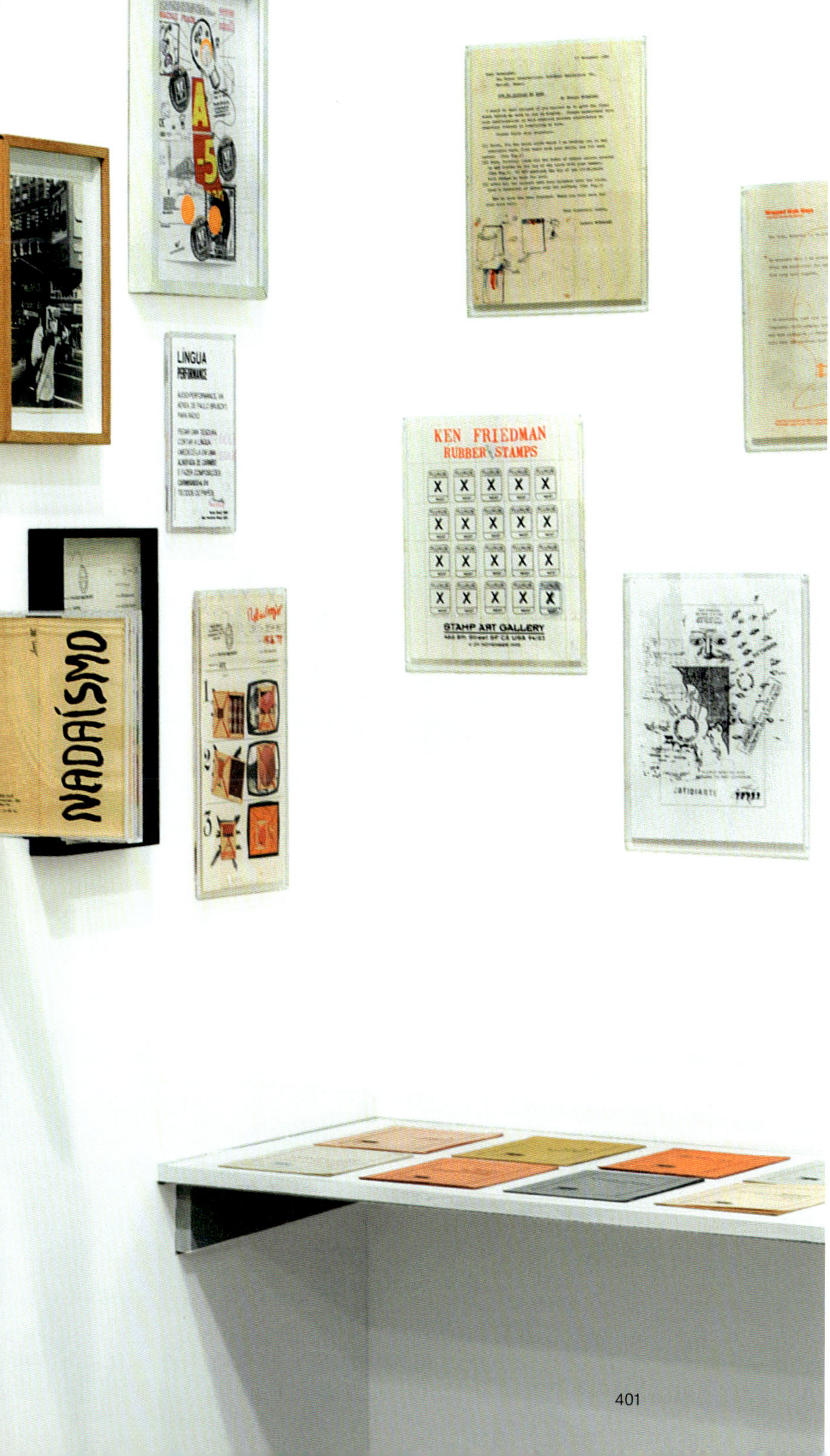

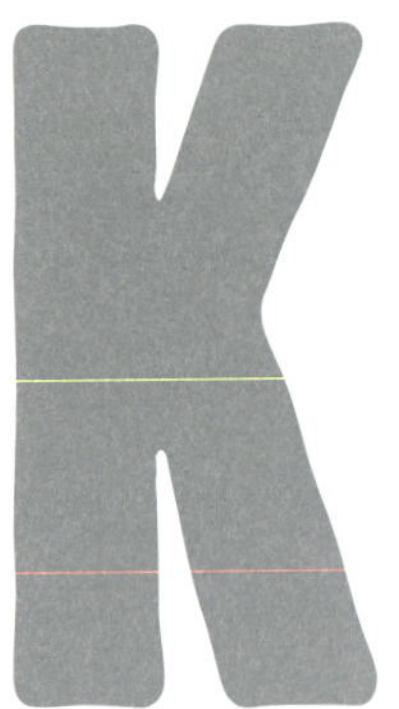

Kadel Willborn

Düsseldorf
Karlsruhe

Feature
Parcours

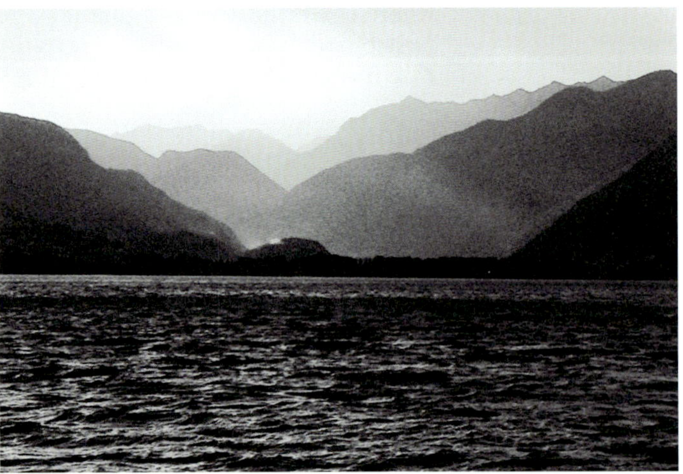

What is your favorite aspect of running a gallery?

Getting a new perspective on the world every day through the artists' works.

How do you choose the artists you work with?

An artist has to push the limits of what we thought we knew and surprise us with his/her work. We also have to connect with the artist as a person.

If you weren't running a gallery what else would you do?

Start running a gallery.

- **Contact** Kadel Willborn
  Iris Kadel
  iris@kadel-willborn.de
- **Established** 2003
- **Owner(s) / Partner(s)** Iris Kadel
  Moritz Willborn
- **Team** 5
- **Space(s)** 200 m²
- **Artists at Art Basel** Art & Language
- **Further artists represented** Matthias Bitzer
  Shannon Bool
  Vlassis Caniaris
  Natalie Czech
  Helmut Dorner
  Helen Feifel
  Dani Gal
  Benedikt Hipp
  Barbara Kasten
  Ane Mette Hol
  Ketty La Rocca
  Mathilde Rosier
  Adrian Williams

Kaikai Kiki

Tokyo — Galleries

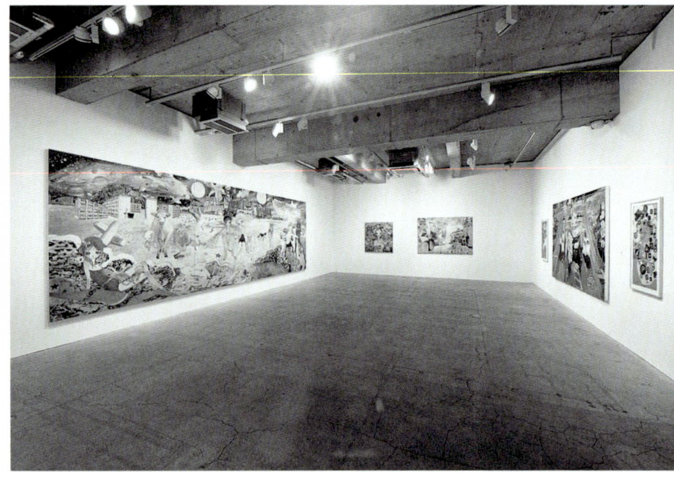

- **Contact** Kaikai Kiki Gallery
  Chiaki Kasahara
  gallery_taiwan@kaikaikiki.co.jp
- **Established** Kaikai Kiki Gallery
- **Owner(s) / Partner(s)** Takashi Murakami
- **Artists at Art Basel** Chiho Aoshima
  Aya Takano
  Mr.
- **Further artists represented** Nick D
  KAWS
  Friedrich Kunath
  Matthew Monahan
  Takashi Murakami
  Kazumi Nakamura
  Anselm Reyle
  Anri Sala
  Hugh Scott-Douglas

Kalfayan

Athens
Thessaloniki

Galleries
Positions

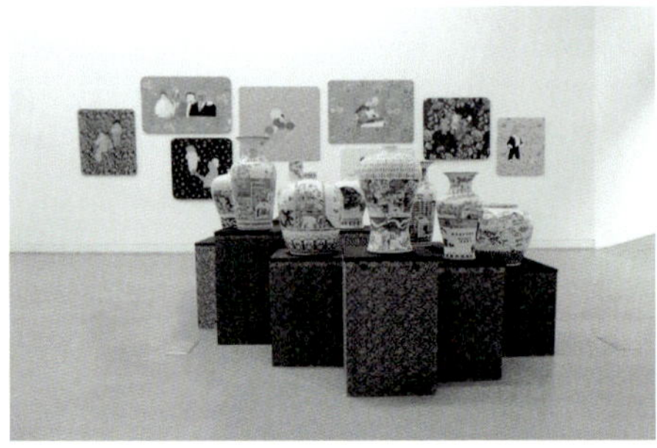

What is your favorite aspect of running a gallery?

Running a gallery feels like an exploration: traveling far afield like a New-Age Marco Polo and Tavernier, discovering new people, artists, ideas! One can only be thankful for all the adventures in the art world and the endless challenges that make our business a source of progress and inspiration.

How do you choose the artists you work with?

See, listen, observe, study, feel … follow your instinct!

If you weren't running a gallery what else would you do?

Arsen Kalfayan: astronaut.

Roupen Kalfayan: gardener at Halkidiki.

- **Contact** Kalfayan Galleries
  Yuli Karatsiki
  yuli@kalfayangalleries.com
- **Established** 1995
- **Owner(s) / Partner(s)** Arsen Kalfayan
  Roupen Kalfayan
- **Team** 8
- **Space(s)** 400 m²
- **Artists at Art Basel** Vartan Avakian
  Maria Loizidou

Nina Papaconstantinou
Hrair Sarkissian
Dimitris Tataris
Stefanos Tsivopoulos
Raed Yassin

- **Further artists represented** Bill Balaskas
Breda Beban
Rania Bellou
Emmanouil Bitsakis
Vlassis Caniaris
Ala Dehghan
Diohandi
Aikaterini Gegisian
Adrian Paci
Sister Corita
Panos Tsagaris
Constantin Xenakis

Kaplan

New York

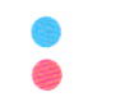

Galleries
Galleries

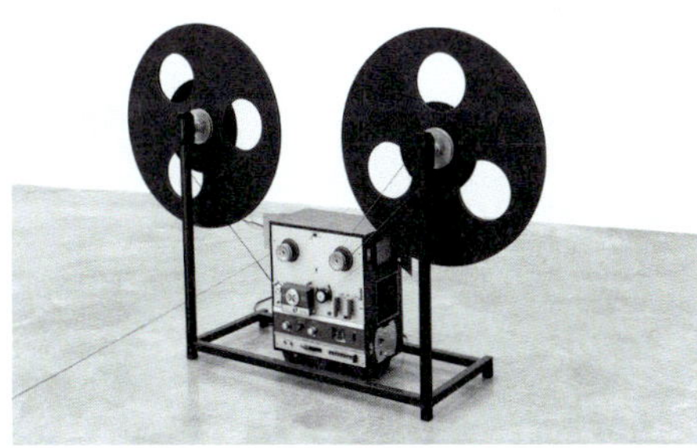

What is your favorite aspect of running a gallery?
Working with artists.

How do you choose the artists you work with?
No divas.

If you weren't running a gallery what else would you do?
General Manager of the New York Yankees.

- **Contact** Casey Kaplan
Casey Kaplan
casey@caseykaplangallery.com
- **Established** 1995
- **Owner(s) / Partner(s)** Casey Kaplan
- **Team** 6
- **Space(s)** 464.5 m²
- **Artists at Art Basel** Kevin Beasley
Matthew Brannon
Nathan Carter
Jason Dodge
Geoffrey Farmer
Liam Gillick
Giorgio Griffa
Brian Jungen
Sanya Kantarovsky
Mateo López
Jonathan Monk
Marlo Pascual
Diego Perrone
Julia Schmidt
David Thorpe
Garth Weiser
Johannes Wohnseifer
- **Further artists represented** Henning Bohl
Jeff Burton
Trisha Donnelly
Annika von Hausswolff
Gabriel Vormstein

Kargl

Vienna

Galleries

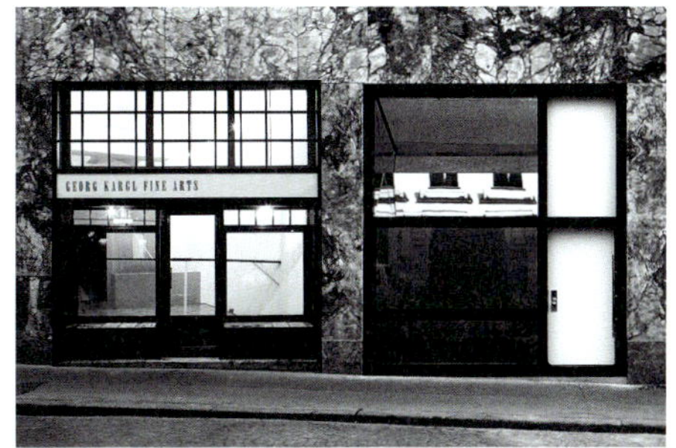

What is your favorite aspect of running a gallery?
To make the artistic avant-garde visible to the public of the city of Vienna and guests.

How do you choose the artists you work with?
By intuition. With a long-term survey of art from tomorrow, and going back to medieval times.

If you weren't running a gallery what else would you do?
Nothing else. This profession involves many professions such as architect, logistics, transportation, technician, superintendent, psychologist, handcraft worker, economist, art historian, archival worker, marketing strategist, cleaning woman, ambassador, librarian, and buddy.

- **Contact** Georg Kargl Fine Arts
Fiona Liewehr
georg.kargl@georgkargl.com
- **Established** 1990 (Galerie Metropol)
1998 (Georg Kargl Fine Arts)
2005 (Georg Kargl BOX)
2006 (Georg Kargl Permanent)
- **Owner(s) / Partner(s)** Georg Kargl
- **Team** 8
- **Space(s)** 350 m² (Fine Arts)
30 m² (BOX)
30 m² (Permanent)
- **Artists at Art Basel** Carter
Clegg & Guttmann
Koenraad Dedobbeleer
Mark Dion
Andreas Fogarasi
Jitka Hanzlová
Herbert Hinteregger
Bernhard Leitner
Thomas Locher
Inés Lombardi
David Maljkovic
Matt Mullican
Muntean/Rosenblum
Gerwald Rockenschaub
Nedko Solakov
Erwin Thorn
Marcel van Eeden
Nadim Vardag
- **Further artists represented** Richard Artschwager
Martin Dammann
Michael Gumhold
Chris Johanson
Björn Kämmerer
Sanna Kannisto
Herwig Kempinger
Harald Klingelhöller
Yves Mettler
Christian Philipp Müller
Max Peintner
Raymond Pettibon
Wolfgang Plöger
Liddy Scheffkencht
Rosemarie Trockel
Marijke van Warmerdam
Costa Vece
Ina Weber
Nicole Wermers
Cerith Wyn Evans
Richard Zeiss

Karma International

Zurich  Discoveries

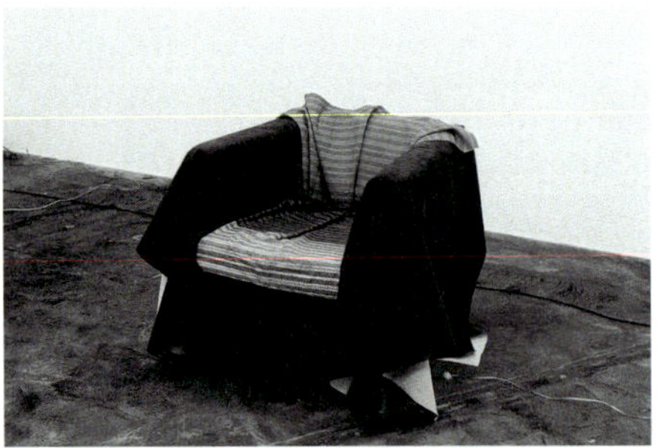

What is your favorite aspect of running a gallery?
A gallery feels like one big family.

How do you choose the artists you work with?
Because we admire them. We are very privileged to work with artists who constantly challenge us! Learning is more compelling than knowing.

If you weren't running a gallery what else would you do?
Journalist or psychiatrist.

- **Contact** Karma International
  Marina Olsen
  marina@karmainternational.org
- **Established** 2008
- **Owner(s) / Partner(s)** Karolina Dankow
  Marina Olsen
- **Team** 5
- **Space(s)** 200 m²
- **Artists at Art Basel** David Hominal
  Pamela Rosenkranz
- **Further artists represented** Kim Seob Boninsegni
  Agnieszka Brzezanska
  Ida Ekblad
  José Rojas
  K8 Hardy
  Carissa Rodriguez
  Emanuel Rossetti
  Thomas Sauter
  Martin Soto Climent
  Keiichi Tanaami
  Sergei Tcherepnin
  Vivian Suter

Kasmin

New York  Galleries
Galleries

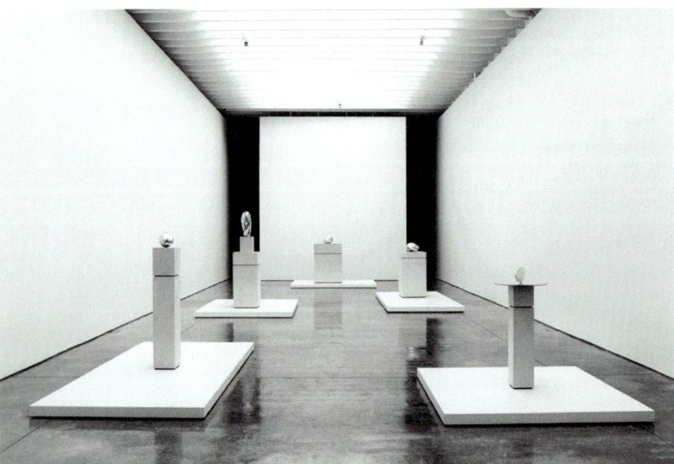

- **Contact** Paul Kasmin Gallery
  Paul Kasmin
  info@paulkasmingallery.com
- **Established** 1989
- **Owner(s) / Partner(s)** Paul Kasmin
- **Team** 25
- **Space(s)** 557.5 m²
- **Artists at Art Basel** Arman
  Mattia Bonetti

Constantin Brancusi
Saint Clair Cemin
Taner Ceylan
William N. Copley
Ian Davenport
Dzine
Barry Flanagan
Caio Fonseca
Walton Ford
Simon Hantaï
Nir Hod
Robert Indiana
Deborah Kass
David LaChapelle
Les Lalanne
Morris Louis
Nyoman Masriadi
Santi Moix
James Nares
Iván Navarro
Jules Olitski
Erik Parker
Elliott Puckette
Nancy Rubins
Mark Ryden
Will Ryman
Makoto Saito
Tseng Kwong Chi
Andy Warhol

kaufmann repetto

Milan 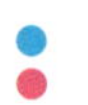 Galleries
New York Galleries
Kabinett

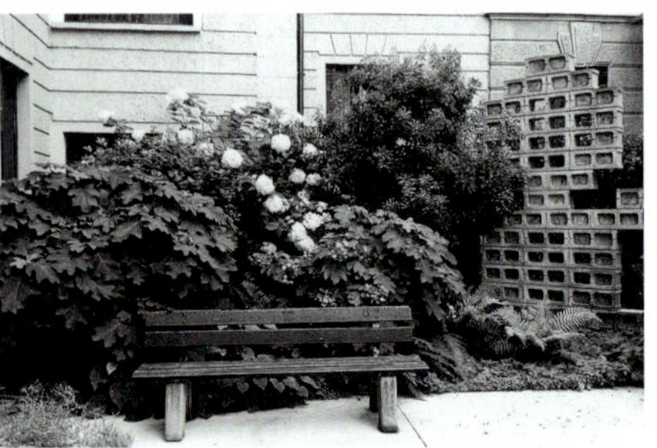

What is your favorite aspect of running a gallery?
The artists.

How do you choose the artists you work with?
With guts.

If you weren't running a gallery what else would you do?
There is nothing else I can do.

- **Contact** kaufmann repetto
  Francesca Kaufmann
  info@kaufmannrepetto.com
- **Established** 2000
- **Owner(s) / Partner(s)** Francesca Kaufmann
  Chiara Repetto
- **Team** 5
- **Space(s)** 370 m²
- **Artists at Art Basel** Thea Djordjadze
  Latifa Echakhch
  Judith Hopf
  Lily van der Stokker
- **Further artists represented** Andrea Bowers
  Candice Breitz
  Pierpaolo Campanini
  Gianni Caravaggio
  Maggie Cardelús
  Talia Chetrit
  Shannon Ebner
  Edi Hila
  Nicola Martini
  Carlo Mollino
  Dianna Molzan
  Yoshua Okon
  Adrian Paci
  Dan Perjovschi
  Eva Rothschild
  Aida Ruilova
  Matt Sheridan Smith
  Billy Sullivan
  Pae White
  Thomas Zipp

Kelly

New York

Galleries
Galleries
Galleries

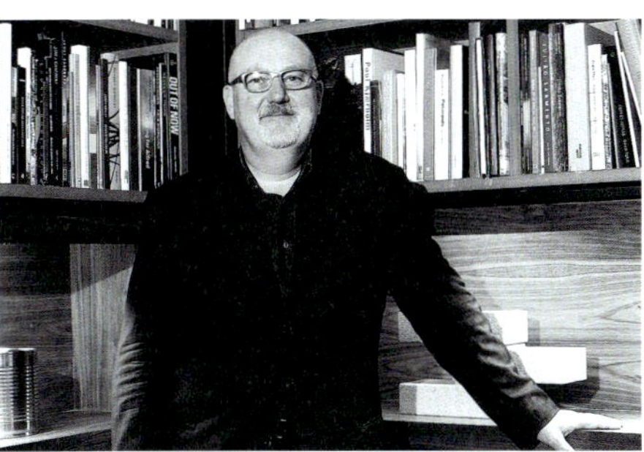

What is your favorite aspect of running a gallery?

The most fulfilling aspect of running a gallery is working with individual artists to support their creative vision and to provide a robust platform and context for their work.

How do you choose the artists you work with?

We are constantly traveling and always on the lookout for new, extraordinary work. We visit studios, exhibitions, museums, art fairs, speak with colleagues, etc., and keep our eyes open. We seek out artists who have the same interests as us, who are intelligent, devoted to their work, interested in developing their careers in a significant manner, and have a profound work relationship with us.

If you weren't running a gallery what else would you do?

In a previous career I loved teaching at art school and miss that interaction with dynamic, open, young people, who are constantly questioning and forming opinions, but at heart I am a frustrated architect. That would be my chosen alternate profession.

- **Contact** Sean Kelly, Thomas Kelly, thomas@skny.com
- **Established** 1991
- **Owner(s) / Partner(s)** Sean Kelly
- **Team** 16
- **Space(s)** 743.5 m²
- **Artists at Art Basel** Marina Abramović, Los Carpinteros, James Casebere, Leandro Erlich, Iran do Espírito Santo, Antony Gormley, Laurent Grasso, Rebecca Horn, Callum Innes, Idris Khan, Joseph Kosuth, Peter Liversidge, Robert Mapplethorpe, Mariko Mori, Julião Sarmento, Alec Soth, Frank Thiel, James White, Kehinde Wiley
- **Further artists represented** David Claerbout, Johan Grimonprez, Tehching Hsieh, Terence Koh, Nathan Mabry, Anthony McCall

Keng

Taipei
Beijing

Galleries

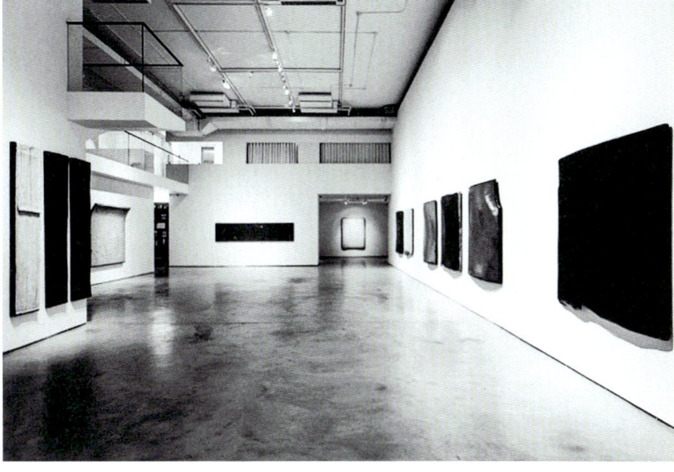

What is your favorite aspect of running a gallery?

Seeking, presenting, and promoting artists who have not received a fair share of attention is the most attractive part for me.

How do you choose the artists you work with?

Artists who have their own unique and distinctive style of creation and a complete set of artworks.

If you weren't running a gallery what else would you do?

A collector would be another option for me since the art world has always fascinated me.

- **Contact** Tina Keng Gallery, Tina Keng, info@tinakenggallery.com
- **Established** 1992
- **Owner(s) / Partner(s)** Tina Keng
- **Team** 17
- **Space(s)** 1,600 m²
- **Artists at Art Basel** Sanyu, Su Xiaobai, Wang Huaiqing, Wu Da-Yu, Xu Jiang, Yun Gee
- **Further artists represented** Chiang Yomei, Chen Chun-Hao, Chu Shu-Hsien, George Chann, Guan Liang, Hou I-Ting, Hung Ying, Kao Chung-Li, Li-lan, Lin Fengmian, Lin Ju, Su Meng-Hung, Tony Wong, Tu Wei-Cheng, Peng Wei, Wu Tien-Chang, Yang Mao-Lin, Yao Jui-Chung, Zao Wou-ki, Zhang Hongtu

Kerlin

Dublin

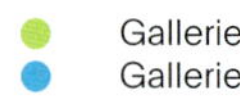

Galleries
Galleries

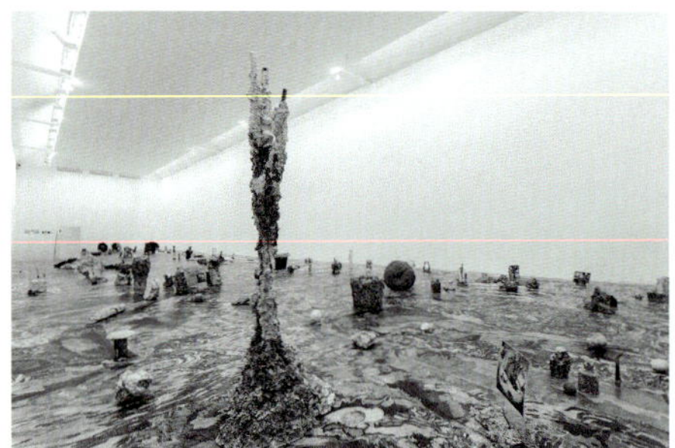

What is your favorite aspect of running a gallery?
The conversation.

How do you choose the artists you work with?
Personality goes a long way.

If you weren't running a gallery what else would you do?
Probably drive an ice-cream truck.

- **Contact** Kerlin Gallery
Darragh Hogan
gallery@kerlin.ie
- **Established** 1988
- **Owner(s) / Partner(s)** John Kennedy
David Fitzgerald
Darragh Hogan
- **Team** 8
- **Space(s)** 334.5 m²
- **Artists at Art Basel** Aleana Egan
Callum Innes
Merlin James
Eoin Mc Hugh
Sean Scully
- **Further artists represented** Phillip Allen
Phil Collins
Dorothy Cross
Willie Doherty
Mark Francis
Maureen Gallace
Mark Garry
Liam Gillick
David Godbold
Siobhán Hapaska
Jaki Irvine
Sam Keogh
Samuel Laurence Cunnane
Elizabeth Magill
Brian Maguire
Stephen McKenna
Isabel Nolan
Kathy Prendergast
Paul Seawright
Paul Winstanley

Kern

New York

Galleries
Unlimited
Galleries

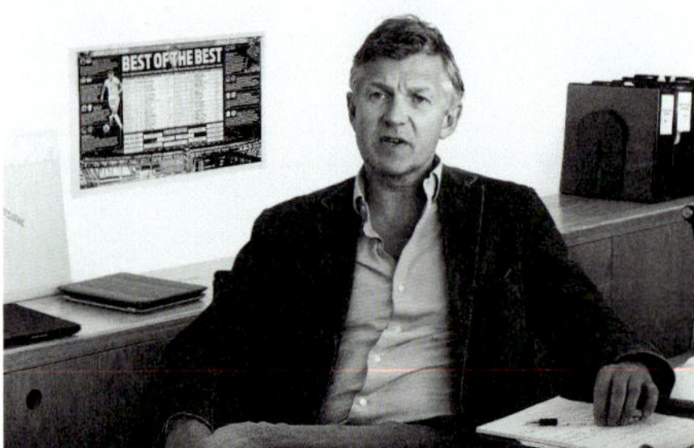

What is your favorite aspect of running a gallery?
Working in a field I consider significant, and doing my part.

How do you choose the artists you work with?
Thinking about the longevity of it.

If you weren't running a gallery what else would you do?
Movie director.

- **Contact** Anton Kern Gallery
Christoph Gerozissis
christoph@antonkerngallery.com
- **Established** 1996
- **Owner(s) / Partner(s)** Anton Kern
- **Team** 9
- **Space(s)** 350 m²
- **Artists at Art Basel** Nobuyoshi Araki
Ellen Berkenblit
John Bock
Brian Calvin
Anne Collier
Saul Fletcher
Mark Grotjahn
Bendix Harms
Eberhard Havekost
Lothar Hempel
Richard Hughes
Sarah Jones
Shio Kusaka
Jim Lambie
Marepe
Chris Martin
Dan McCarthy
Matthew Monahan
Marcel Odenbach
Manfred Pernice
Alessandro Pessoli
Wilhelm Sasnal
Lara Schnitger
David Shrigley
Francis Upritchard
Andy Warhol
Jonas Wood

Kewenig

Berlin
Palma de Mallorca

Galleries
Unlimited
Galleries

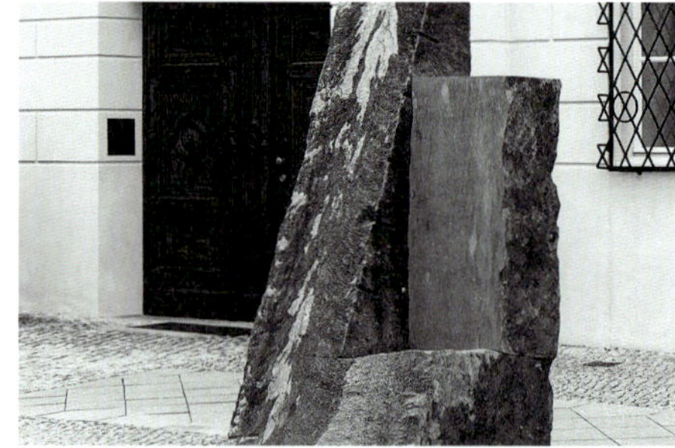

What is your favorite aspect of running a gallery?
The collaboration and friendship with the artists.

How do you choose the artists you work with?
Artists recommended warmly by artists.

If you weren't running a gallery what else would you do?
Lawyer.

- **Contact** Kewenig
Michael Kewenig
gallery@kewenig.com
- **Established** 1986
- **Owner(s) / Partner(s)** Michael & Jule Kewenig
- **Team** 9
- **Space(s)** 1,000 m²
- **Artists at Art Basel** Christian Boltanski
Marcel Broodthaers
James Lee Byars
Hanne Darboven
Wim Delvoye
Elger Esser
Leiko Ikemura
Ilya & Emilia Kabakov
Kimsooja
Imi Knoebel
Jannis Kounellis

Bertrand Lavier
Mario Merz
Pavel Pepperstein
Pedro Cabrita Reis
Sean Scully
Sandra Vásquez de la Horra
Marcelo Viquez
Ralf Ziervogel

- **Further artists represented**
  Giovanni Anselmo
  Ivan Bazak
  Bert de Beul
  Frédéric Bruly Bouabré
  Ian Hamilton Finlay
  Seydou Keïta
  Bernd Koberling
  Hendrik Krawen
  Giuseppe Penone
  A.R. Penck
  Viktor Pivovarov
  Berdardí Roig
  Miroslav Tichý
  Niele Toroni
  James Turrell
  Peter Wüthrich

Kicken

Berlin

- Galleries
- Galleries Kabinett

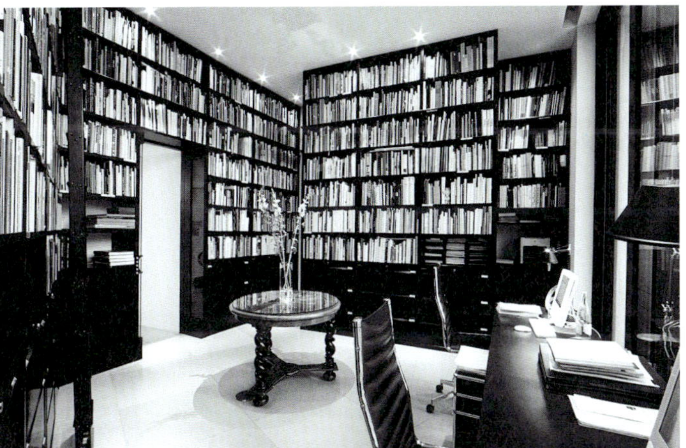

What is your favorite aspect of running a gallery?

To make accessible the incredibly rich universe of photography: show it in its diverse aspects and allow people to benefit from its aesthetic synergy, especially when combined with other media.

How do you choose the artists you work with?

On one hand, the history of photography provides us with essential names such as László Moholy-Nagy, Man Ray, or Rodchenko, whom we think need to be connected to a wider public. Then there are artists of equal standard, but unknown, such as Umbo (Otto Umbehr), or the Czech avant-garde, like Jaromír Funke, Josef Sudek, and František Drtikol who need promotion even more urgently. In the contemporary field, the strong quality of fresh eyes like Jitka Hanzlová's or Charles Fréger's are most convincing.

If you weren't running a gallery what else would you do?

I would, as my late husband Rudolf and I have been doing for the last 15 years, continue to create and transmit aesthetics in contemporary daily life by tracing and placing outstanding works of art, design, or architecture.

- **Contact**
  Kicken Berlin
  Petra Helck
  kicken@kicken-gallery.com
- **Established**
  1974 (Aachen, as Galerie Lichttropfen)
- **Owner(s) / Partner(s)**
  Annette Kicken
- **Team**
  8
- **Space(s)**
  150 m²
- **Artists at Art Basel**
  Bauhaus
  Bernd & Hilla Becher
  Sibylle Bergemann
  Erwin Blumenfeld
  Joachim Brohm
  Lucien Clergue
  Götz Diergarten
  František Drtikol
  Charles Fréger
  Jaromír Funke
  Jitka Hanzlová
  Peter Keetman
  Rudolf Koppitz
  Heinrich Kühn
  Ute & Werner Mahler
  Werner Mantz
  László Moholy-Nagy
  Helmut Newton
  Kiyoshi Niiyama
  Helga Paris
  Man Ray
  Albert Renger-Patzsch
  Heinrich Riebesehl
  Hans-Christian Schink
  Wilhelm Schürmann
  Alfred Seiland
  Otto Steinert
  Christer Strömholm
  Umbo
  Ludwig Windstosser
- **Further artists represented**
  Karl Blossfeldt
  Anna & Bernhard Blume
  Rudolf Bonvie
  Constantin Brancusi
  Harry Callahan
  Hugo Erfurth
  Alfred Ehrhardt
  Arno Fischer
  Fotoform
  Lee Friedlander
  Ernst Fuhrmann
  F. C. Gundlach
  Heinz Hajek-Halke
  Fritz Henle
  André Kertész
  Klaus Kinold
  Helmar Lerski
  Sameer Makarius
  Arnold Newman
  Kaoru Ohto
  Richard Pare
  Walter Peterhans
  Alexander Rodchenko
  Jaroslav Rössler
  August Sander
  Aaron Siskind
  Josef Sudek
  Anton Josef Trcka
  Ed van der Elsken
  Dr. Paul Wolff

Kilchmann

Zurich

- Galleries
- Galleries
- Galleries

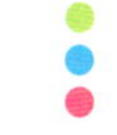

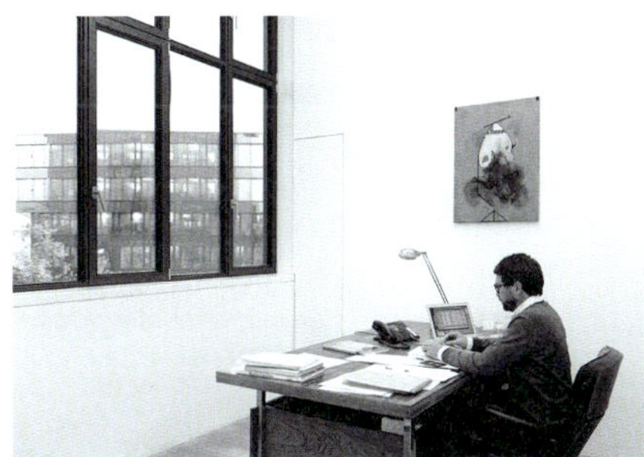

What is your favorite aspect of running a gallery?

The fascinating part of running a gallery is to be in contact with so many different players in the art world, such as artists, collectors, curators, and critics, and meeting interesting people again and again.

How do you choose the artists you work with?

To take on a new artist requires that s/he fits aesthetically and conceptually into the gallery's program, that s/he has a market or the possibility to build one up, and finally that s/he has enough works to sell.

If you weren't running a gallery what else would you do?

That's a good question!

- **Contact** Galerie Peter Kilchmann
  Peter Kilchmann
  info@peterkilchmann.com
- **Established** 1992
- **Owner(s) / Partner(s)** Peter Kilchmann
- **Team** 8
- **Space(s)** 550 m²
- **Artists at Art Basel** Francis Alÿs
  Maja Bajevic
  Hernan Bas
  Michael Bauer
  Armin Boehm
  Monica Bonvicini
  Los Carpinteros
  Willie Doherty
  Valérie Favre
  Marc-Antoine Fehr
  Fernanda Gomes
  Bruno Jakob
  Raffi Kalenderian
  Tobias Kaspar
  Zilla Leutenegger
  Jorge Macchi
  Teresa Margolles
  Fabian Marti
  Claudia & Julia Müller
  Adrian Paci
  David Renggli
  Bernd Ribbeck
  Melanie Smith
  Javier Téllez
  Tercerunquinto
  Erika Verzutti
  Artur Zmijewski

Klosterfelde Edition

Hamburg
Berlin

 Edition

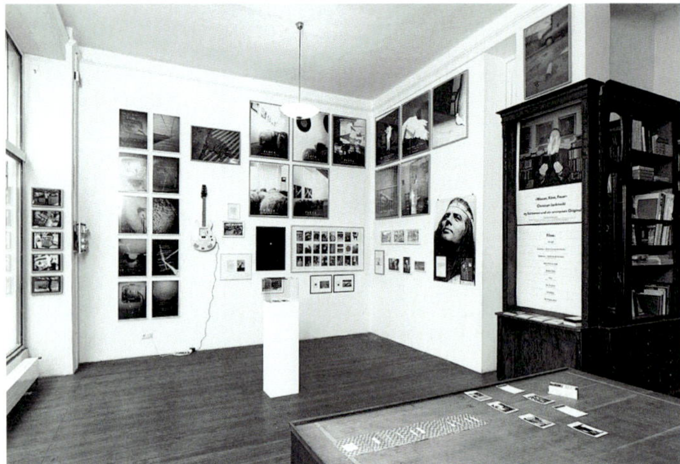

What is your favorite aspect of running a gallery?
Being part of the artistic process.

How do you choose the artists you work with?
A mixture of feeling and respect for the gallery's program.

If you weren't running a gallery what else would you do?
Be a teacher or a nurse.

- **Contact** Helga Maria Klosterfelde Edition
  Alfons Klosterfelde
  office@helgamariaklosterfelde.de
- **Established** 1990
- **Owner(s) / Partner(s)** Helga Maria Klosterfelde
- **Team** 3
- **Space(s)** 110 m²
- **Artists at Art Basel** Matthew Antezzo
  John Bock
  Werner Büttner
  Ulrike Heise
  General Idea
  Christian Jankowski
  Michael Kleine
  Henrik Olesen
  Lisa Oppenheim
  Dan Peterman
  Haim Steinbach
  Rosemarie Trockel
  Jorinde Voigt
  Lawrence Weiner
- **Further artists represented** Donald Baechler
  Tobias Buche
  Hanne Darboven
  Carsten Höller
  Joseph Kosuth
  Jonas Lipps
  Matt Mullican
  Steven Pippin
  Kay Rosen
  Lily dan der Stokker
  Rirkrit Tiravanija

Klüser

Munich

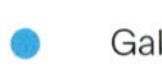 Galleries

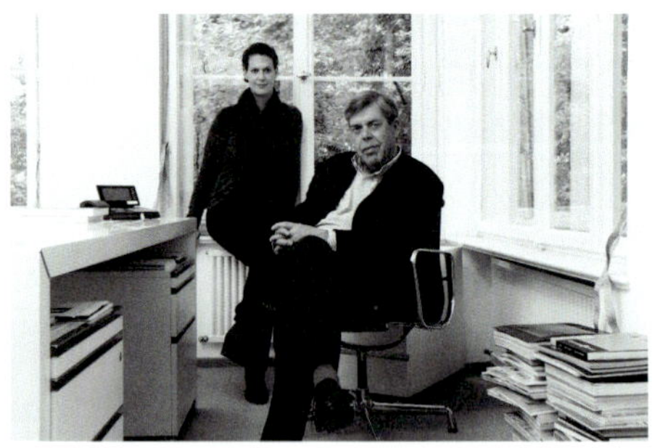

What is your favorite aspect of running a gallery?
The direct work with artists and their pieces. They have enriching personalities and offer new perspectives on a wide range of subjects.

How do you choose the artists you work with?
Quality.

If you weren't running a gallery what else would you do?
I am running a gallery because it is my passion and because I want to. So why should I do something else?

- **Contact** Galerie Klüser
  Julia Klüser
  info@galerieklueser.com
- **Established** 1978
- **Owner(s) / Partner(s)** Bernd Klüser
  Julia Klüser
- **Team** 8
- **Space(s)** 450 m²
- **Artists at Art Basel** Joseph Beuys
  Tony Cragg
  Jack Goldstein
  Gilbert & George
  Alex Katz
  Olaf Metzel
  Lori Nix
  Sigmar Polke
  Jorinde Voigt
  Andy Warhol
- **Further artists represented** Donald Baechler
  Christian Boltanski
  Jeff Cowen
  Enzio Cucchi
  Jan Fabre
  David Godbold
  Isca Greenfield-Sanders
  Mimi Paladino
  Blinky Palermo
  Bernardi Roig
  Glen Rubsamen
  Julião Sarmento
  Sean Scully
  Conrad Shawcross

Knust

Munich

Edition
Edition

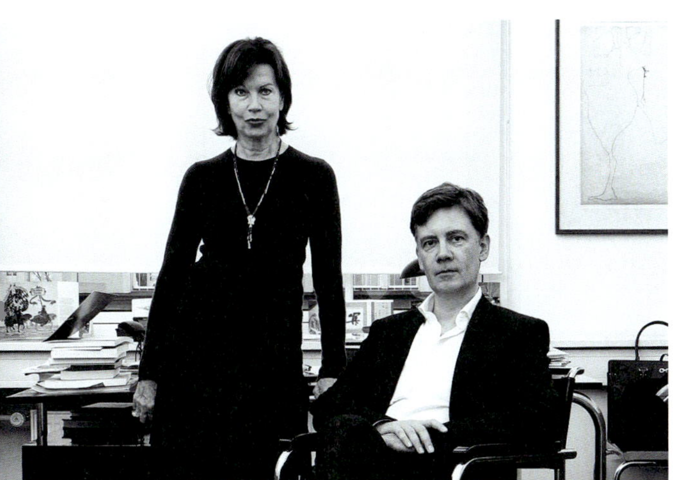

What is your favorite aspect of running a gallery?
Working with artists.

How do you choose the artists you work with?
Representing a range of established artists for 30 years, we seek out new relationships by mutual agreement between us, i.e. Sabine Knust and Matthias Kunz. The new artists we work with meet the standards of the older artists, but also develop new standards adapted to the art of our time.

If you weren't running a gallery what else would you do?
I would collect art.

- **Contact** Sabine Knust
Matthias Kunz
mail@sabineknust.com
- **Established** 1982
- **Owner(s) / Partner(s)** Sabine Knust
Matthias Kunz
- **Team** 5
- **Space(s)** 160 m²
- **Artists at Art Basel** John Baldessari
Georg Baselitz
Marc Brandenburg
Matias Faldbakken
Günther Förg
Liam Gillick
Mark Grotjahn
Eberhard Havekost
Andy Hope 1930
Olaf Holzapfel
Jörg Immendorff
Per Kirkeby
Imi Knoebel
Michael Landy
Jonathan Lasker
Markus Lüpertz
Jonathan Meese
Paul Morrison
Olaf Nicolai
Jorge Pardo
A.R. Penck
Jack Pierson
Richard Prince
Tal R
Arnulf Rainer
Daniel Richter
Thomas Schütte
Katharina Sieverding
Gert & Uwe Tobias
Franz West
Christopher Wool
Thomas Zipp

Kogure

Tokyo

Insights

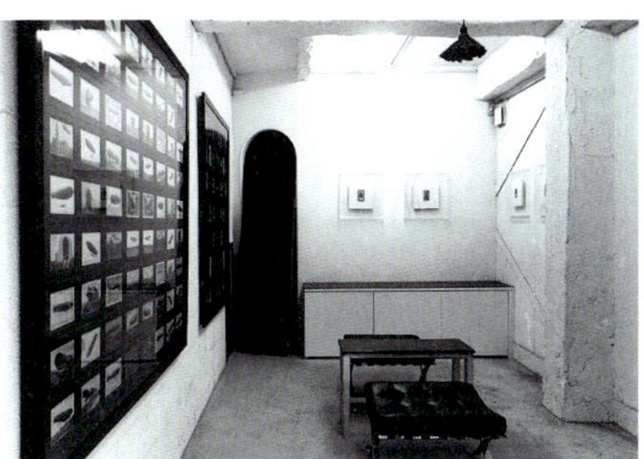

What is your favorite aspect of running a gallery?
A gallery finds its value in a piece of art which enables people to get together on an equal footing and respect each other beyond their occupations, nationalities, and cultures.

How do you choose the artists you work with?
If the gallery possesses a strong power of attraction due to a superior personality, superior artists that match the wavelength of the gallery will naturally be drawn in. Those that gather around me at the gallery who are my greatest supporters and excellent artists will bring other excellent artists. When I see an exhibition I focus on my four principles: technique, design, creativity, and sense of color. And above all, the "power of the object" needs to be strong.

If you weren't running a gallery what else would you do?
Life comes down to art and gastronomy. I would like to manage several restaurants, serving creative dishes that capture a sense of the seasons, using carefully selected safe and delicious ingredients. Tranquil, not very noticeable, and not too big. Guests would be entertained by antique dinnerware and art on the walls. Of course, neither artificial seasoning nor synthetic detergent will be used. I especially want to note that there would be no comprise with genetically modified foods.

- **Contact** Gallery Kogure
Tomoko Kogure
info@gallerykogure.com
- **Established** 2006
- **Owner(s) / Partner(s)** Hiroshi Kogure
- **Team** 4
- **Space(s)** 39.6 m² (Gallery Kogure)
82.5 m² (Lower Akihabara)
- **Artists at Art Basel** Takahiro Yamamoto
- **Further artists represented** Masaharu Fujishiro
Atsuko Goto
Ai Haibara
Shigeki Hayashi
Takahiro Hirabayashi
Tomohide Ikeya
Kenichiro Ishiguro
Yuwa Kato
Hiroyuki Matsuura
Mai Miyake
Takahiro Sanda
Ryo Shiotani
Yuko Soi
Atsushi Suwa
Kazuyuki Takishita
Keita Tatsuguchi
Fuco Ueda
Hidenori Yamaguchi
Takato Yamamoto
Taichiro Yoshida

Kohn

Los Angeles

Galleries

What is your favorite aspect of running a gallery?
I love the idea of presenting a group of artworks to the public. That is my small creative contribution to what artists are able to do.

How do you choose the artists you work with?
Because I work for myself I can choose whomever I want to work with—as long as they want to work with me! The criteria ranges from personal taste to pushing the limits of my personal taste. It is important to go out of my comfort zone in order to keep both me and the public engaged.

If you weren't running a gallery what else would you do?
I would like to construct buildings. Working with the architect and project manager on my new gallery in Hollywood, I learned so much during the long and arduous process that I would be excited to put my knowledge to productive use once again. I will probably do it simultaneously with the gallery!

- **Contact** Kohn Gallery
  Samantha Glaser
  samantha@kohngallery.com
- **Established** 1985
- **Owner(s) / Partner(s)** Michael Kohn
- **Team** 8
- **Space(s)** 1,115 m²
- **Artists at Art Basel** Lita Albuquerque
  John Bauer
  Larry Bell
  Wallace Berman
  Bruce Conner
  Camille Rose Garcia
  Joe Goode
  Dennis Hollingsworth
  Tom LaDuke
  Eddie Martinez
  Ryan McGinness
  William Monk
  Simmons & Burke
  Troika

König

Berlin

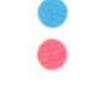

Galleries
Galleries Public

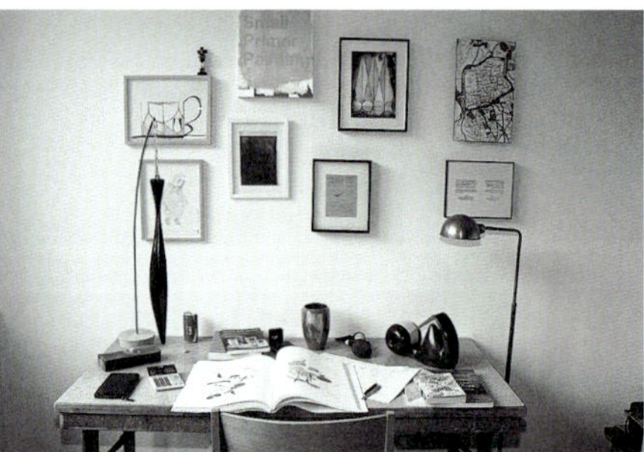

- **Contact** Johann König
  Johanna Chromik
  johanna@johannkoenig.de
- **Established** 2002
- **Owner(s) / Partner(s)** Johann König
- **Team** 10
- **Artists at Art Basel** Monica Bonvicini
  Paul Czerlitzki
  Tue Greenfort
  Katharina Grosse
  Jeppe Hein
  Camille Henrot
  Jessica Jackson Hutchins
  Nathan Hylden
  Annette Kelm
  Alicja Kwade
  Michaela Meise
  Amalia Pica
  Michael Sailstorfer
  Tatiana Trouvé
  Jorinde Voigt
  Johannes Wohnseifer
  David Zink Yi
- **Further artists represented** Micol Assaël
  Henning Bohl
  Andreas Fischer
  Kiki Kogelnik
  Manfred Kuttner
  Lisa Lapinski
  Helen Marten
  Justin Matherly
  Natascha Sadr Haghighian
  Jeremy Shaw
  Corinne Wasmuht

Kordansky

Los Angeles

Galleries Unlimited
Galleries

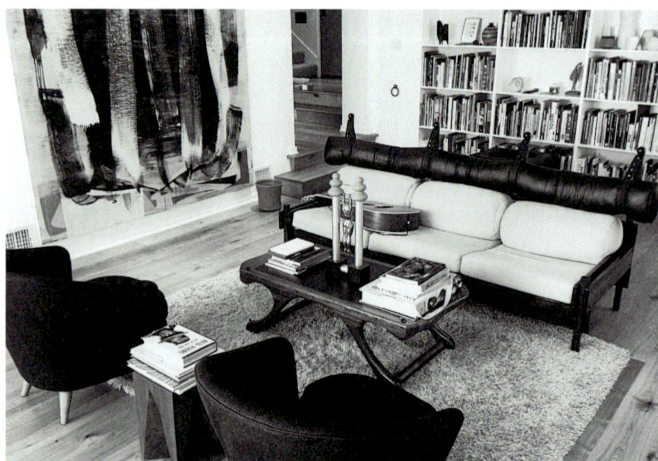

What is your favorite aspect of running a gallery?
Our greatest pleasure comes from working closely with our artists; understanding each artist's unique vision and helping each artist realize her or his ambitions.

How do you choose the artists you work with?
Our gallery has a founding interest in the art and culture of Los Angeles. I started the gallery showing the work of friends and classmates from CalArts. We have since sought to broaden this dialogue by working with artists, of varying generations and locales, who share the sensibility of our program and a spirit sympathetic with the unique perspective of this city.

If you weren't running a gallery what else would you do?
I would be a stay-at-home dad.

- **Contact** David Kordansky Gallery
  Maisey Cox
  maisey@davidkordanskygallery.com
- **Established** 2003
- **Owner(s) / Partner(s)** David Kordansky
- **Team** 13
- **Space(s)** 1,200 m²
- **Artists at Art Basel** Kathryn Andrews
  Matthew Brannon
  Andrea Büttner
  Valentin Carron
  Aaron Curry
  Andrew Dadson
  Tom of Finland
  Sam Gilliam
  Evan Holloway
  Rashid Johnson
  William E. Jones
  Elad Lassry
  Anthony Pearson
  Mai-Thu Perret
  Jon Pestoni
  Ricky Swallow
  Lesley Vance
  Mary Weatherford
  John Wesley
  Jonas Wood

- **Further artists represented**: Markus Amm, Steven Claydon, Heather Cook, Will Fowler, Patrick Hill, Larry Johnson, Thomas Lawson, Chris Martin, John Mason, Alan Michael, Ruby Neri, David Noonan, Pietro Roccasalva

Koru

Hong Kong • Insights

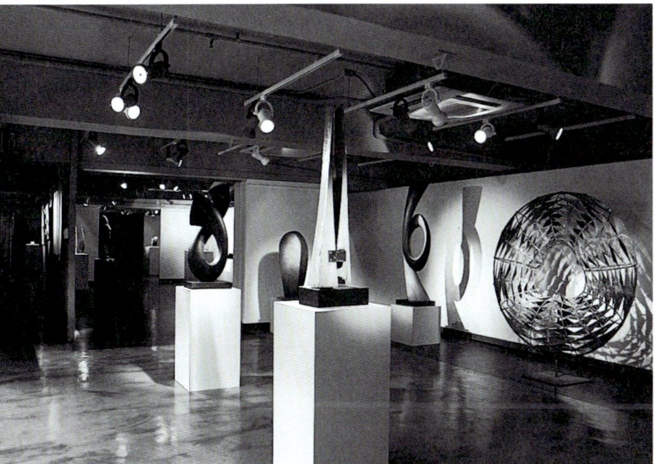

What is your favorite aspect of running a gallery?

We see ourselves and our gallery as a conduit for creativity: we are an intermediary presenting artworks we like, admire, respect, to clients with an interest in art. We find immense satisfaction in fulfilling that role. That pleasure is further compounded thanks to our gallery having become an intertwined network of clients, consultants, and art lovers who are curious and able to appreciate and be inspired by visual art.

How do you choose the artists you work with?

Our gallery focuses on contemporary sculptural works. When we opened in 2001, we initially chose artists we already knew, as well as others recommended to us. Over time that changed: artists, for the most part, now approach us. But what we value has not changed. We continue to choose artists whose sculptural production has a narrative quality, is artistically challenging, and visually arresting. That's primarily based on our gut instinct, without being unduly influenced by trends or fads.

If you weren't running a gallery what else would you do?

We have run a successful gallery in Hong Kong for the past 14 years. We love what we do. We admit we find it difficult to imagine an alternative scenario. However, if such a calamity befell us, we hope we would seek out another area of artistic creativity. One where we might be able to employ our talents and skills in the nurture of such creativity, while whetting and subsequently satisfying the appetites of those who appreciate, enjoy, and wish to possess such works.

- **Contact**: Koru Contemporary Art, ChinChye Lee, info@koru-hk.com
- **Established**: 2001
- **Owner(s) / Partner(s)**: Mark Brian Joyce, ChinChye Lee
- **Team**: 4
- **Space(s)**: 372 m²
- **Artists at Art Basel**: Brian Brake
- **Further artists represented**: Armen Agop, Gretchen Albrecht, Galia Amsel, Tanya Ashken, Alfredo Barbini, Graham Bennett, Claudia Borella, Christine Cathie, Emma Camden, Simone Cenedese, Chris Charteris, Neil Dawson, John Edgar, Egypt, Agneta Ekholm, Bohumil Elias, Chen Feng, Ben Foster, Oriano Galloni, Guan Donghai, Dorothy Helyer, Kazumi Ikemoto, Kira Kim, Osef Marek, David Murray, Etsuko Nishi, David Reekie, Livio Seguso, Terry Stringer, Sun Yi, Rick Swain, Elizabeth Thomson, Csunny Wang, Hiroshi Yamano, Zheng Xuewu

KOW

Berlin • Feature

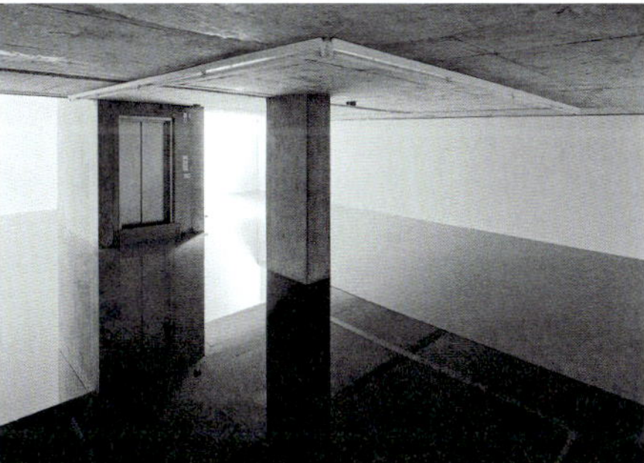

What is your favorite aspect of running a gallery?

Doing what we want to do, showing what we want to show, saying what we want to say, and selling what we want to sell.

How do you choose the artists you work with?

If their work can touch and move the social imaginary, then they're in.

If you weren't running a gallery what else would you do?

Run a museum and a music label.

- **Contact**: KOW, Nikolaus Oberhuber, gallery@kow-berlin.com
- **Established**: 2009
- **Owner(s) / Partner(s)**: Alexander Koch, Nikolaus Oberhuber
- **Team**: 8
- **Space(s)**: 350 m²
- **Artists at Art Basel**: Santiago Sierra
- **Further artists**: Arno Brandlhuber, Chto Delat, Alice Creischer, Eugenio Dittborn, Barbara Hammer, Chris Martin, Frédéric Moser & Philippe Schwinger, Mario Pfeifer, Tina Schulz, Santiago Sierra, Michael E. Smith, Clemens von Wedemeyer, Franz Erhard Walther, Tobias Zielony

K

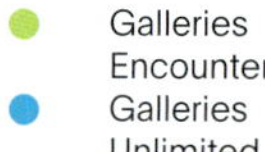

Koyama

Tokyo
Singapore

- Galleries Encounters
- Galleries Unlimited

What is your favorite aspect of running a gallery?
I like that I can see the various artists' production so closely and be there when the artists are acknowledged by collectors and museums.

How do you choose the artists you work with?
I am interested in artists who always work in close relation with their own lives and societies.

If you weren't running a gallery what else would you do?
I think I would work in the film industry.

- **Contact** Tomio Koyama Gallery
  Tetsuya Kamimura
  kamimura@tomiokoyamagallery.com
- **Established** 1996
- **Owner(s) / Partner(s)** Tomio Koyama
- **Team** 14
- **Space(s)** 278 m²
- **Artists at Art Basel** Katsuyo Aoki
  Varda Caivano
  Nana Funo
  Satoshi Hirose
  Hideaki Kawashima
  Makiko Kudo
  Masahiko Kuwahara
  Toru Kuwakubo
  Takuro Kuwata
  Shintaro Miyake
  Yoshitomo Nara
  Rieko Otake
  Makoto Saito
  Kishio Suga
  Hiroshi Sugito
  Shooshie Sulaiman
  Ian Woo
- **Further artists represented** Masako Ando
  Stephan Balkenhol
  Benjamin Butler
  Atsushi Fukui
  Daisuke Fukunaga
  Rieko Hidaka
  Ryan McGinley
  Mika Ninagawa
  Tam Ochiai
  Satoshi Ohno
  Khvay Samnang
  Richard Tuttle

Koyanagi

Tokyo

- Galleries
- Galleries

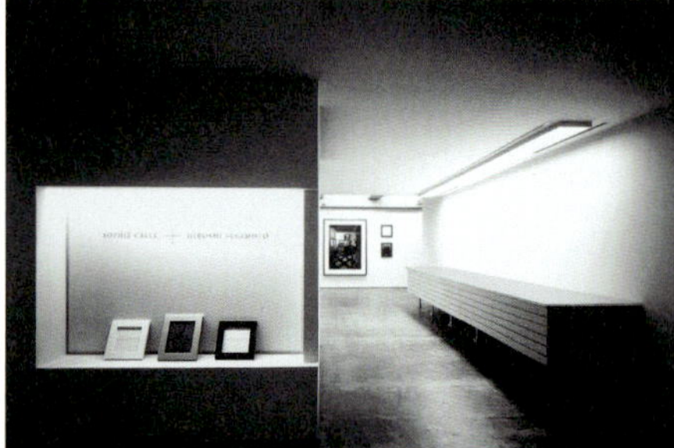

- **Contact** Gallery Koyanagi
  Sho Kuwajima
  mail@gallerykoyanagi.com
- **Established** 1995
- **Owner(s) / Partner(s)** Atsuko Koyanagi
- **Team** 6
- **Space(s)** 210 m²
- **Artists at Art Basel** Michaël Borremans
  Janet Cardiff & George Bures Miller
  Dominique Gonzalez-Foerster
  Federico Herrero
  Ryoji Ikeda
  Kae Masuda
  Rei Naito
  Makoto Ofune
  Thomas Ruff
  Ataru Sato
  Yoshihiro Suda
  Hiroshi Sugimoto
  Risaku Suzuki
  Tabaimo
  Kouichi Tabata
  Yuriko Terazaki
  Yoon Heechang
- **Further artists represented** Sophie Calle
  Marlene Dumas
  Olafur Eliasson
  Junya Ishigami
  Luisa Lambri
  Christian Marclay
  Hellen van Meene
  Tetsuya Nakamura
  Robert Platt
  Noguchi Rika
  Bill Viola
  Tomoko Yamaguchi

Kraupa-Tuskany Zeidler

Berlin

- Statements

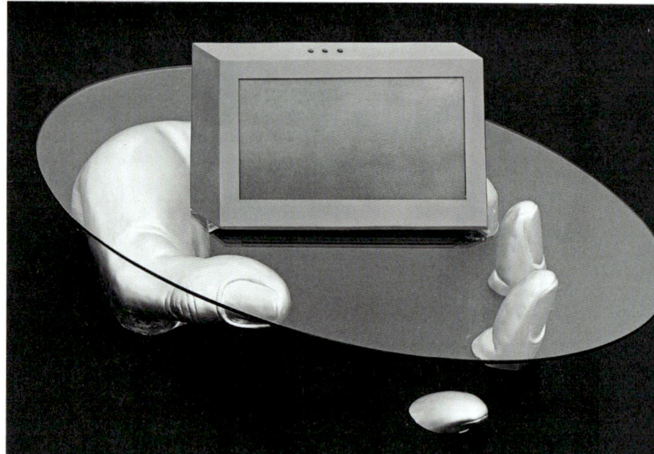

What is your favorite aspect of running a gallery?
Working closely with artists and the diversity of exciting challenges that comes with it.

How do you choose the artists you work with?
Most importantly we have to feel emotionally and intellectually challenged by an artist's practice. At the same time we always keep the overall gallery program in mind before we ask an artist if s/he wants to work with us.

If you weren't running a gallery what else would you do?
I guess we would be thinking about opening one.

- **Contact** Kraupa-Tuskany Zeidler
  Amadeo Kraupa-Tuskany
  office@aktnz.com
- **Established** 2011
- **Owner(s) / Partner(s)** Nadine Zeidler
  Amadeo Kraupa-Tuskany
- **Team** 5
- **Space(s)** 200 m²
- **Artists at Art Basel** Katja Novitskova
- **Further artists represented** Aids-3D
  Florian Auer
  GCC
  Sture Johannesson
  K-HOLE
  Daniel Keller
  Avery Singer
  Slavs and Tatars

Kreps

New York

- Galleries
- Galleries

What is your favorite aspect of running a gallery?
Spending time with artists and thinking about ideas.

How do you choose the artists you work with?
It's an organic process.

If you weren't running a gallery what else would you do?
I can't even begin to think about what else I would do.

- **Contact** Andrew Kreps Gallery
Andrew Kreps
contact@andrewkreps.com
- **Established** 1996
- **Owner(s) / Partner(s)** Andrew Kreps
Liz Mulholland
- **Team** 8
- **Space(s)** 650.5 m²
- **Artists at Art Basel** Ricci Albenda
Darren Bader
Martin Barré
Frank Benson
Andrea Bowers
Daniel Bozhkov
Marc Camille Chaimowicz
Roe Ethridge
Uwe Henneken
Christian Holstad
Jamie Isenstein
Annette Kelm
Maria Loboda
Goshka Macuga
Ján Mančuška
Robert Melee
Robert Overby
Peter Piller
Ruth Root
Cheyney Thompson
Pádraig Timoney
Hayley Tompkins
Fredrik Værslev
Klaus Weber
Honza Zamojski

Krinzinger

Vienna

- Galleries
Encounters
- Galleries
Unlimited
Parcours
- Galleries
Kabinett

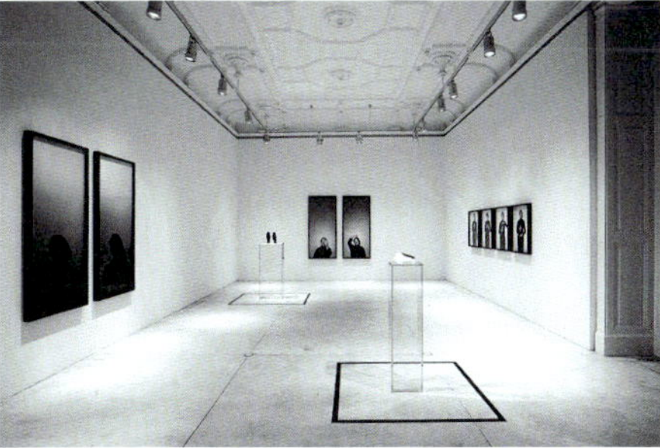

- **Contact** Galerie Krinzinger
Ursula Krinzinger
galeriekrinzinger@chello.at
- **Established** 1971
- **Owner(s) / Partner(s)** Ursula Krinzinger
Thomas Krinzinger
- **Team** 15
- **Space(s)** 600 m²
- **Artists at Art Basel** Marina Abramović
Nader Ahriman
Atelier Van Lieshout
Kader Attia
Gottfried Bechtold
Günter Brus
Chris Burden
Johanna Calle
Andy Coolquitt
Adriano Costa
Angela de la Cruz
István Csákány
Vladimir Dubossarsky & Alexander Vinogradov
Christian Eisenberger
Franz Graf
Sakshi Gupta
Jonathan Hernández
Secundino Hernández
Martha Jungwirth
Waqas Khan
Zenita Komad
Valery Koshlyakov
Angelika Krinzinger
Oleg Kulik
Ulrike Lienbacher
Jonathan Meese
Bjarne Melgaard
Shintaro Miyake
Otto Muehl
Hermann Nitsch
Hans Op de Beeck
Meret Oppenheim
Bernd Oppl
Goran Petercol
Werner Reiterer
Eva Schlegel
Erik Schmidt
Rudolf Schwarzkogler
Christian Schwarzwald
Mithu Sen
Sudarshan Shetty
Daniel Spoerri
Alfred Tarazi
Frank Thiel
Gavin Turk
Erik van Lieshout
Jannis Varelas
Martin Walde
Mark Wallinger
Zhang Ding
Thomas Zipp

Krupp

Basel

- Galleries
Unlimited

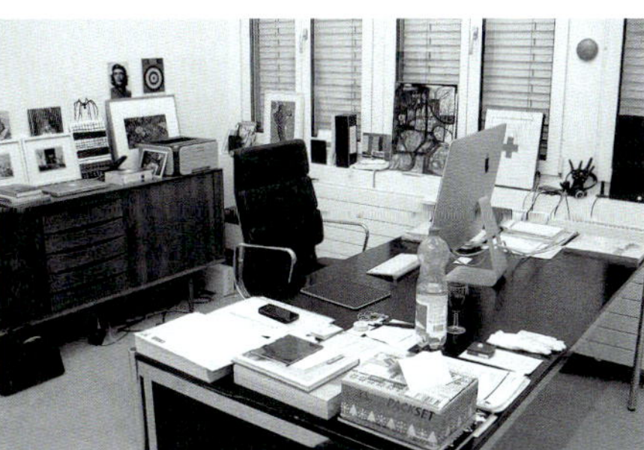

What is your favorite aspect of running a gallery?
Painting, smoking, eating.

How do you choose the artists you work with?
Best is (s)he who s(m)ells most.

If you weren't running a gallery what else would you do?
There is no other profession I could practice with the same enthusiasm.

- **Contact** Nicolas Krupp
Nicolas Krupp
gallery@nicolaskrupp.com
- **Established** 2000
- **Owner** Nicolas Krupp
- **Team** 2
- **Space(s)** 200 m²
- **Artists at Art Basel** Thomas Baumann
Angela de la Cruz
Peter Friedl
Joanne Greenbaum
Lone Haugaard Madsen
Diango Hernández
Dani Jakob
Piotr Janas
Michael Kunze
Atta Kwami

Claudio Moser
Yoan Mudry
Markus Müller
Markéta Othová
Marjetica Potrč
Werner Reiterer
Rico Scagliola / Michael Meier
Dominik Sittig
Studer / van den Berg
Walter Swennen
Heimo Zobernig

Kukje/Kim

Seoul
New York

Galleries
Encounters
Galleries
Unlimited
Galleries

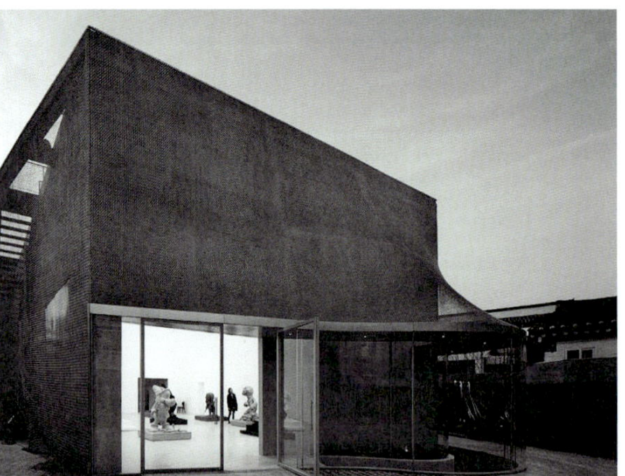

What is your favorite aspect of running a gallery?
One of the most engaging aspects of running a gallery is supporting an artist's creative evolution and playing a part in their careers internationally. It is especially rewarding to see a client's interest grow along with an artist's own development, and to see a young artist's work first acquired by a museum. I still really enjoy traveling, as well as the challenge of working closely with others in the field, such as museum curators, collectors, and other dealers.

How do you choose the artists you work with?
My primary concern is always the quality and creativity of an artist's practice. We watch the artists' work over a long period of time, keeping track of their exhibitions and doing extensive research at the gallery. One of the most important and challenging aspects of running Kukje has been our commitment to introducing important international artists to a Korean audience, as well as showcasing contemporary Korean art on a global stage.

If you weren't running a gallery what else would you do?
I think I would still be in the art world but in a different capacity, for example as a collector. I can't think of a more dynamic and rewarding field to be in than the visual arts.

- **Contact** Kukje Gallery/Tina Kim Gallery
Eliza Ravelle-Chapuis
eliza@tinakimgallery.com
- **Established** 1982
- **Owner(s) / Partner(s)** Hyun-Sook Lee
- **Team** 25
- **Space(s)** 950 m²
- **Artists at Art Basel** Ghada Amer
Louise Bourgeois
Cecily Brown
Alexander Calder
Chung Sang-Hwa
Chung Chang-Sup
Gimhongsok
Ha Chong-Hyun
Kyungah Ham
Candida Höfer
Jenny Holzer
Michael Joo
Donald Judd
Yeondoo Jung
Anish Kapoor
Bharti Kher
Kimsooja
Willem de Kooning
Roy Lichtenstein
Joan Mitchell
Julian Opie
Jean-Michel Othoniel
Seo-Bo Park
Anselm Reyle
Kibong Rhee
Gerhard Richter
Sterling Ruby
Lee Ufan
Bill Viola
Haegue Yang
Yeesookyung
Aaron Young
- **Further artists represented** Anthony Caro
Jae-Eun Choi
Eva Hesse
Hong Seung-Hye
Roni Horn
Eemyun Kang
Anselm Kiefer
Kim Hong-Joo
Kira Kim
Sora Kim
Koo Bohnchang
Joris Laarman
Lee Kwang-Ho
Richard Long
Paul McCarthy
Sungsic Moon
David Nash
Hein-Kuhn Oh
MeeNa Park
Sasa[44]
U Sunok

kurimanzutto

Mexico City

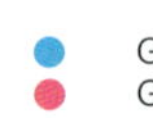

Galleries
Galleries

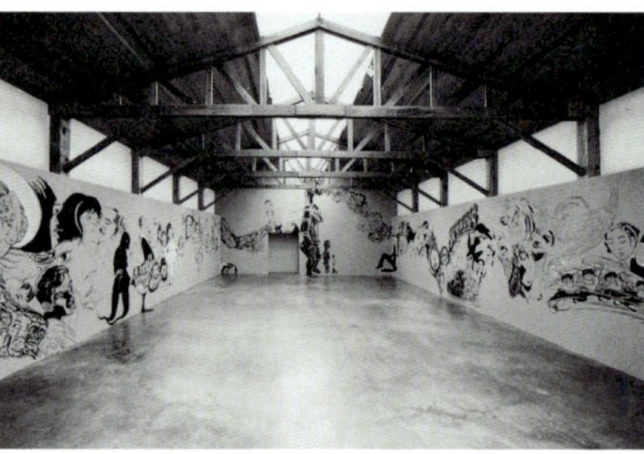

- **Contact** kurimanzutto
info@kurimanzutto.com
- **Established** 1999
- **Owner(s) / Partner(s)** Monica Manzutto
Jose Kuri
- **Team** 16
- **Artists at Art Basel** Eduardo Abaroa
Carlos Amorales
Miguel Calderón
Allora & Calzadilla
Mariana Castillo Deball
Abraham Cruzvillegas
Minerva Cuevas
Jimmie Durham
Daniel Guzmán
Jonathan Hernández
Gabriel Kuri
Dr. Lakra
Sarah Lucas
Roman Ondák
Gabriel Orozco
Damián Ortega
Fernando Ortega
Wilfredo Prieto
Anri Sala
Gabriel Sierra
Monika Sosnowska
Sofía Táboas
Rirkrit Tiravanija
Adrián Villar Rojas
Danh Vo
Apichatpong Weerasethakul
Akram Zaatari

David Kordansky Gallery
Interview with David Kordansky

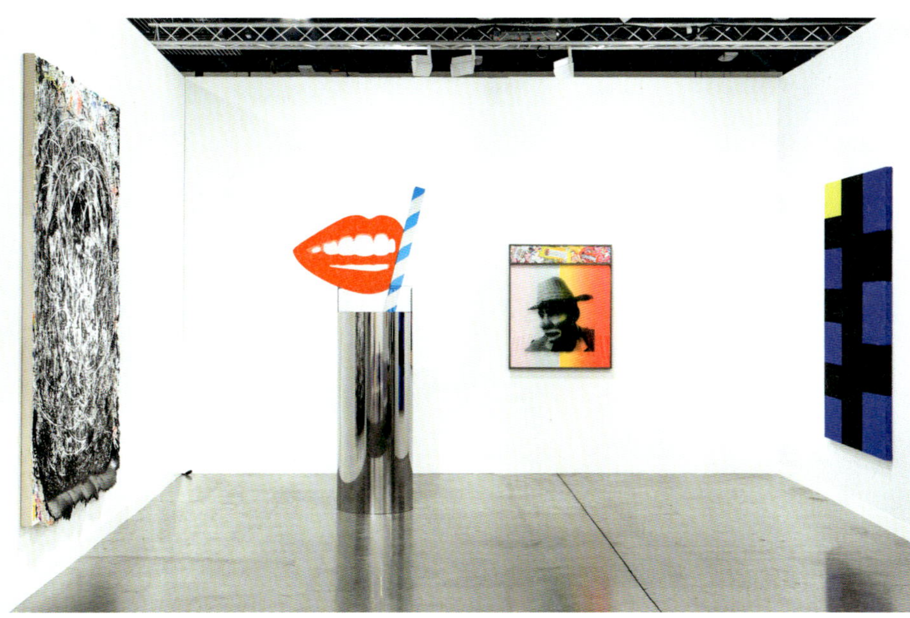

Art Basel in Miami Beach, 2014

When and how did you start the gallery?

I was a graduate student at CalArts in 1999–2000. There was a sort of sea change at that time: a shift away from CalArts being the most important institution, to UCLA and Art Center College of Design. UCLA was able to curate a program of professors that was unbeatable: Paul McCarthy, Barbara Kruger, John Baldessari, Charles Ray, Chris Burden, Mike Kelley, Richard Hawkins, Stephen Prina … The irony is that all of these artists were CalArts graduates! You also had Dennis Cooper and Bruce Hainley going back and forth between Art Center and UCLA. All of a sudden CalArts became the old guard, after having been the most radical position on the West coast. If you wanted to be a professional artist, you went to UCLA or Art Center, not to learn per se, but to be tailored for the real world. At CalArts, on the contrary, you had Michael Asher and his "post-studio critique" class that made some artists never want to make art again.

I was asking myself how I could possibly find success in this landscape. There were great artists and students at CalArts at that time, very interesting people. So I made a conscious decision to open a gallery, a 500 square-foot space in Chinatown. We're talking cockroaches, Domino's pizza and Chinese food every day for the first five years …

Who were the artists that you started with? Your first exhibition was a group show with all your fellow classmates.

I showed my professors, Thomas Lawson, the Dean of CalArts, and William E. Jones, together with classmates such as Lesley Vance, who I still show today. The first exhibition was a mess; I didn't know how to hang a show … even if I had already curated shows of these CalArts artists before. But I was enjoying the process of articulating the intentionality of these artists. I found more happiness in talking about my friends and their practices than in the act of making art myself.

What were you doing as an artist?

I was doing performances, very endurance-based performances, and sculpture, kind of conceptual sculptures that were sort of playing with certain modalities of Modernism.

How was the art scene in Los Angeles when you started? Today it seems everyone wants to go to Los Angeles, open a gallery …

It was … different. You have to remember most artists after graduation still moved right to New York. Now young artists graduating from New York and all over the world are moving to Los Angeles! I am personally very interested in the artistic production that came out of Los Angeles from the 1940s on. Some of the best galleries existed here, like the Eugenia Butler Gallery, but also William Copley's gallery—bringing Magritte, Duchamp, and all of those Surrealists to the West. And of course you have the whole generation of "Light and Space," you have Craig Kaufmann, Billy Al Bengston, Larry Bell, as well as John Mason and the ceramicists working with Peter Voulkos, the first to bring ceramics to the contemporary art world.

If you look at the growth of the gallery, it's a sort of barometer for the growth of the city as an art epicenter. We started in Chinatown, which is where everyone was (though now it's like a ghost town). Then we moved to Culver City in 2008, then the new epicenter, where we opened a second space in 2011. Now as things are even more dispersed, we have found our own place in downtown Hollywood, very much our own corner of the city.

The new gallery is a great building with its exhibition space, its storage, and office spaces. A lot of places are just a gallery with a tiny office: we develop a culture around the gallery that goes beyond just showing the work. Artists and collectors want to come and hang out. It's a home in a way. We have two main spaces for exhibitions and we opened with two very ambitious artists: Rashid Johnson and Jonas Wood. Then in early 2015 Tom of Finland and Betty Woodman. The gallery has always been about tempering the dialogue between generations, geographies, cultures, and juxtapositions.

You started mainly with artists from Los Angeles, but you soon opened your program to European artists, and notably to two Swiss artists: Valentin Carron and Mai-Thu Perret.

For some odd reason I have always had a fascination with this generation of Swiss artists. Mai-Thu Perret's ceramics have this kind of West coast sort of spirit, and her questioning of the Modern canon is really what Los Angeles is about. In a way, Switzerland is like Los Angeles!

Valentin and I have talked a lot about this: it's funny because his production makes so much sense when you put it up in relation with Los Angeles. It's coming from a different place of course, but the kind of material import within the work could be similar to a Paul McCarthy or Charles Ray or even a Mike Kelley! There's a kind of internal logic of Mike Kelley remaking the Chinatown wishing well and Valentin Carron's notion of reverberating and remaking these provincial artworks that exist in small villages and parks, and giving them a second life. It's very much a part of what Mike Kelley was thinking about, especially regionalism, and how you play with the politics of regionalism on large-scale international platforms.

LIFE
LIKE

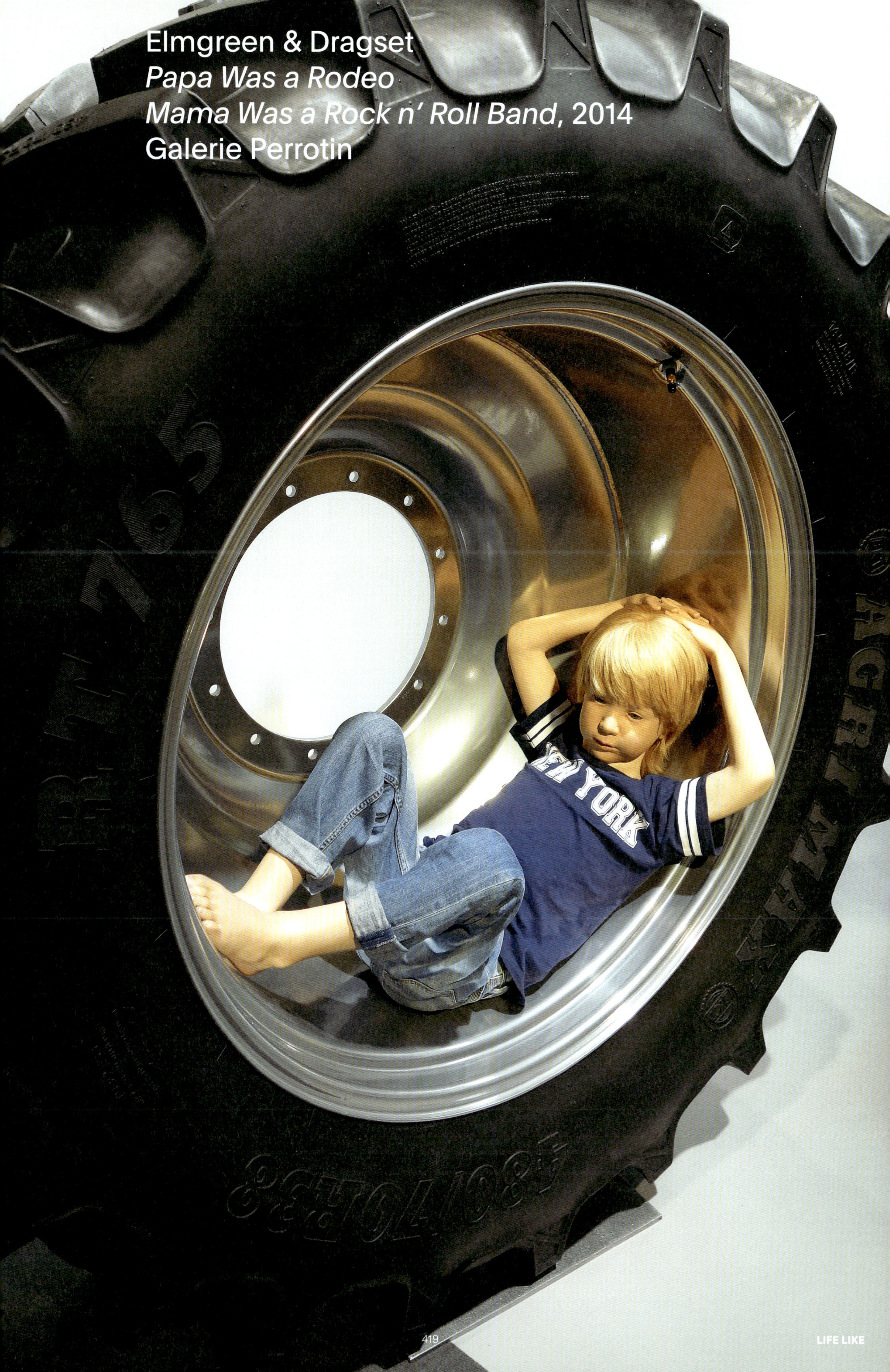

Elmgreen & Dragset
Papa Was a Rodeo
Mama Was a Rock n' Roll Band, 2014
Galerie Perrotin

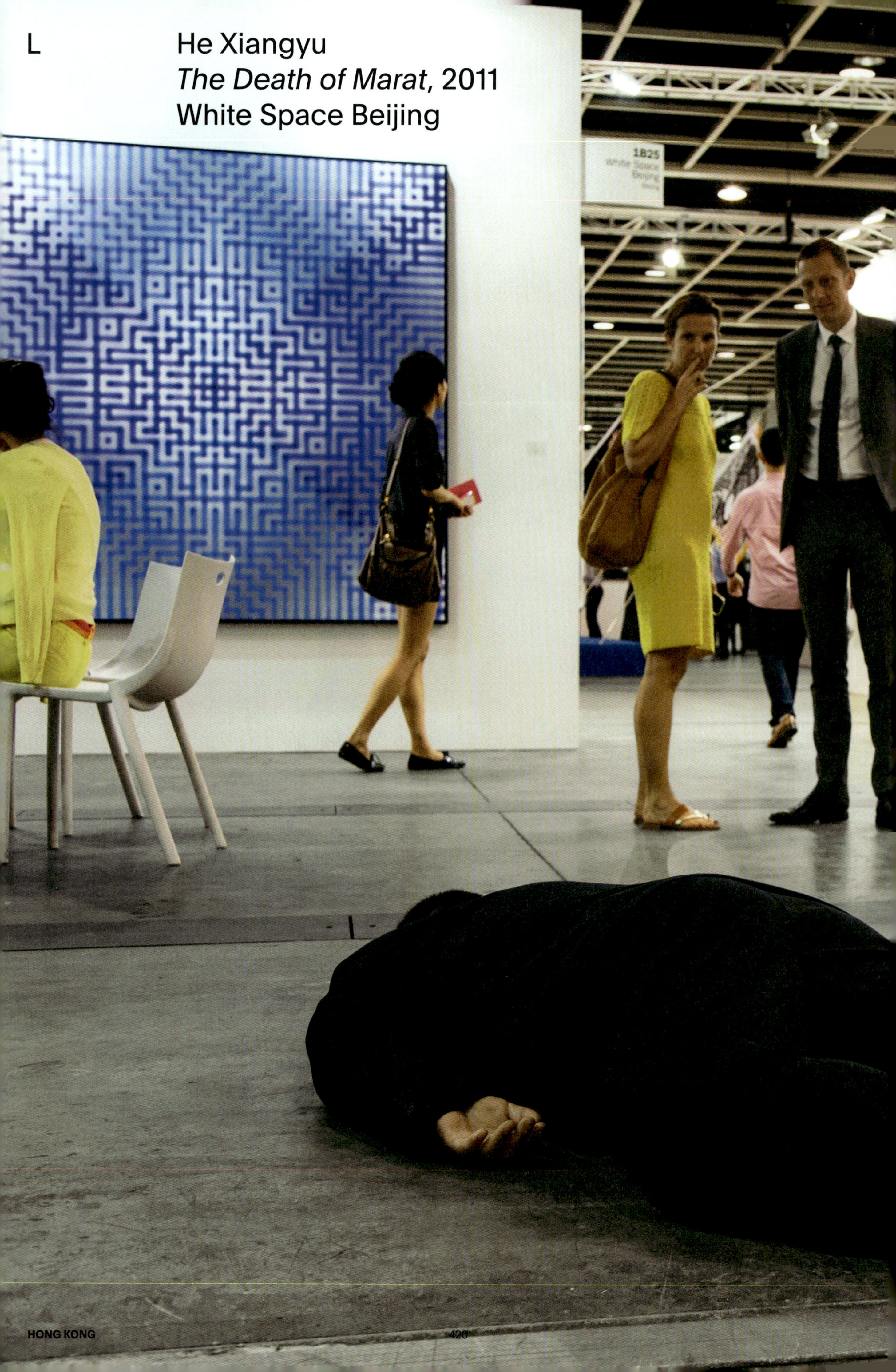

L

He Xiangyu
The Death of Marat, 2011
White Space Beijing

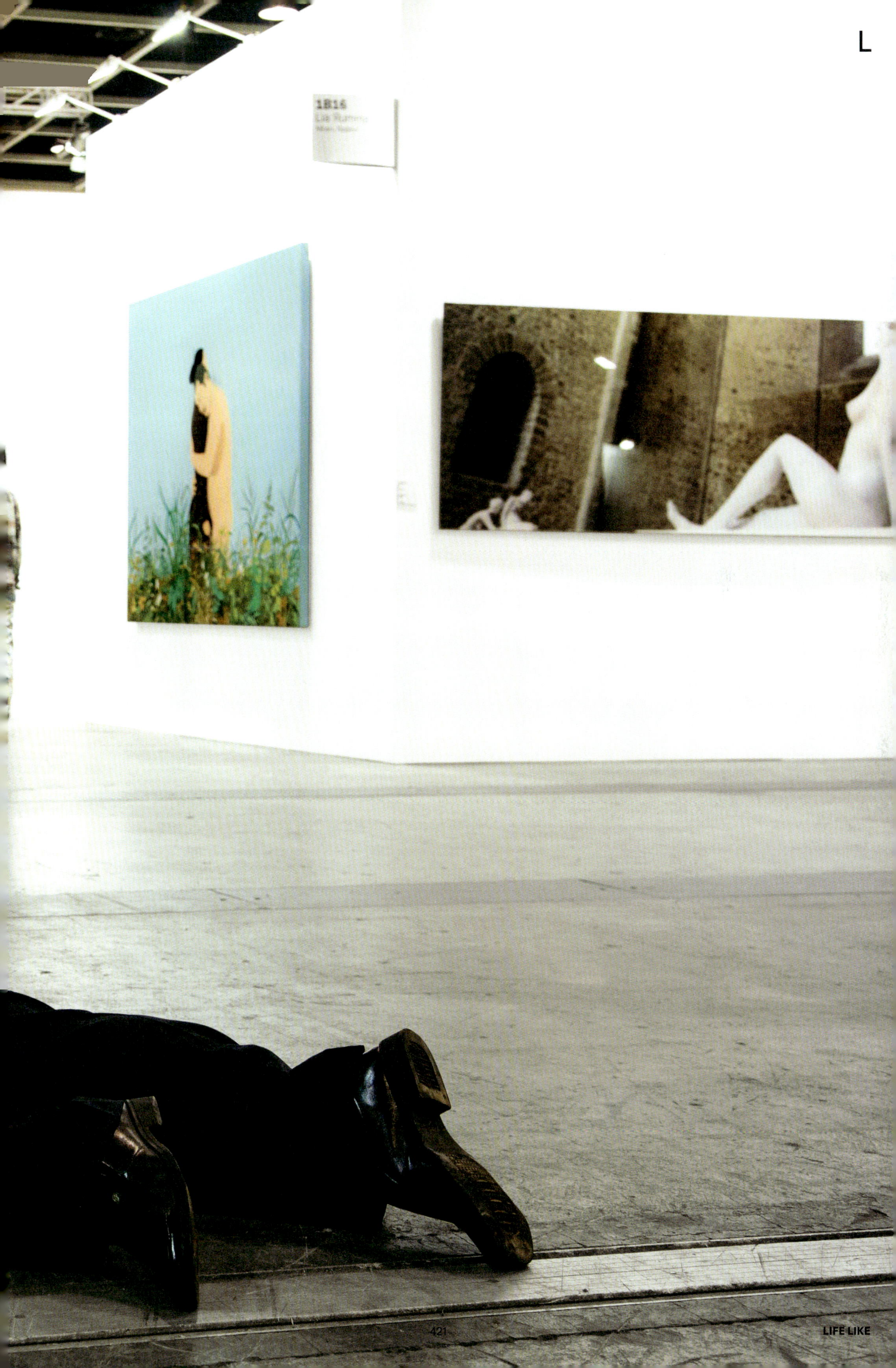

L

Patricia Piccinini
The Comforter, 2010
Tolarno Galleries

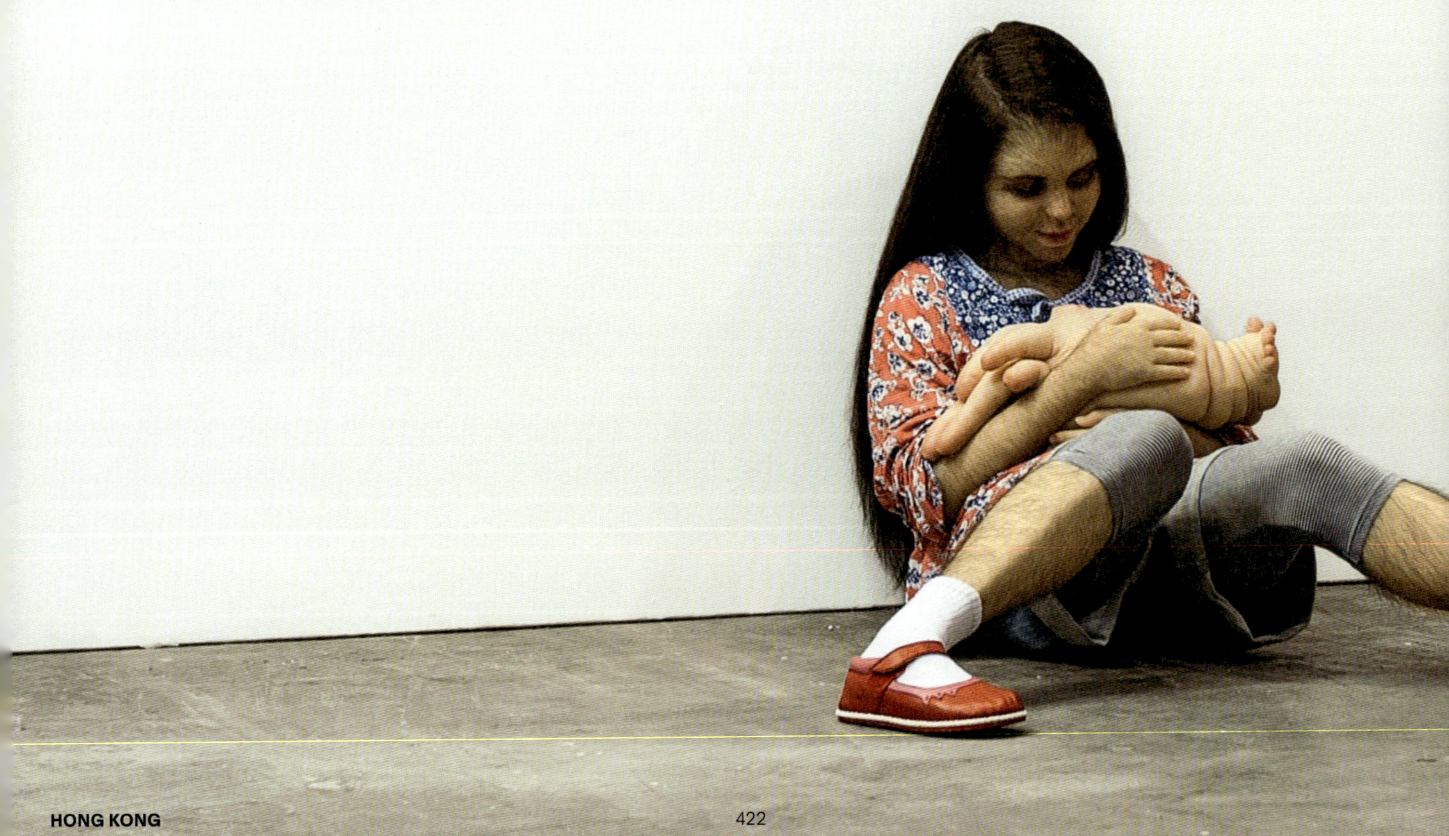

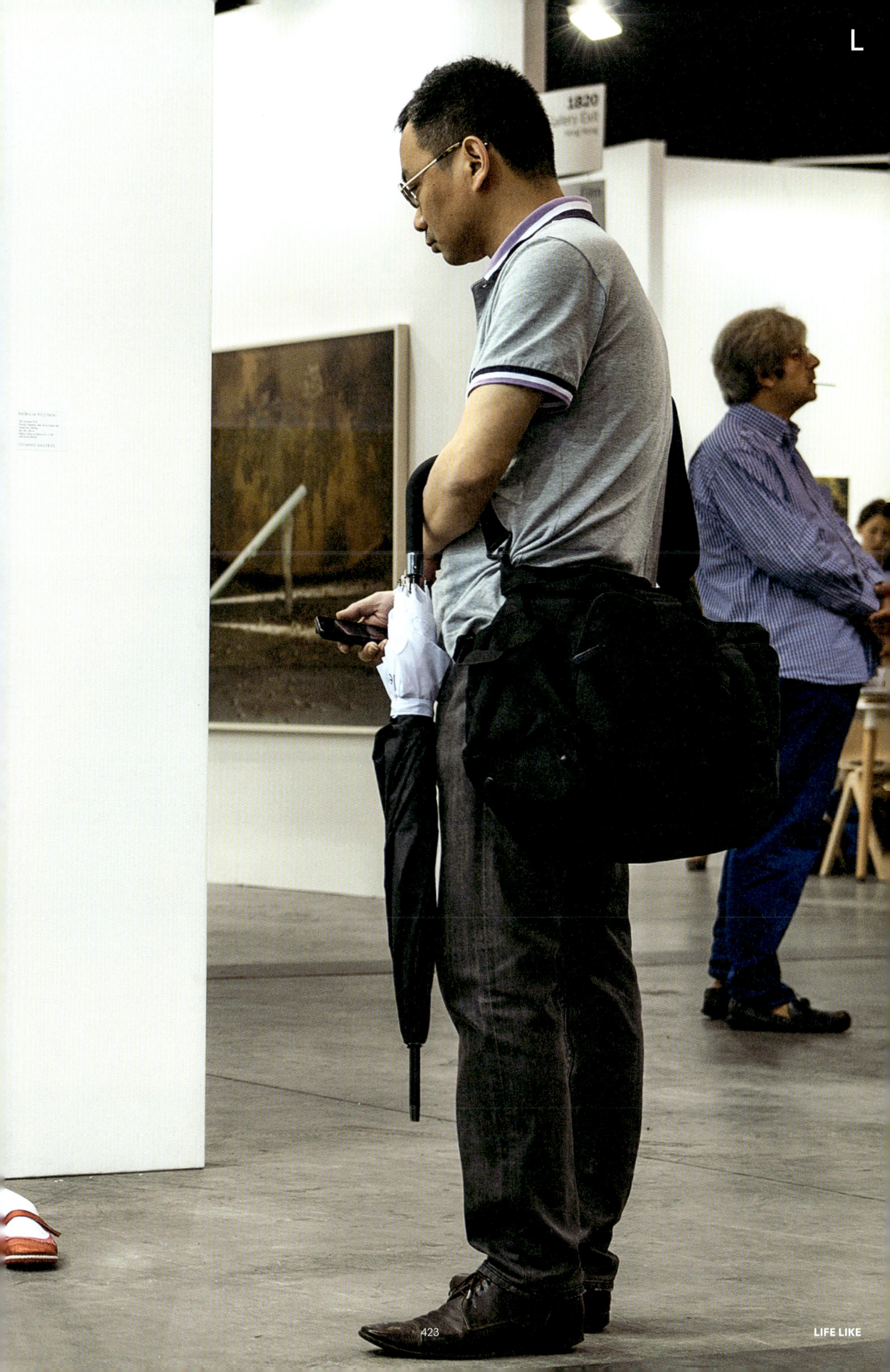
1820

L

Duane Hanson
Chinese Student, 1989
Van de Weghe Fine Art

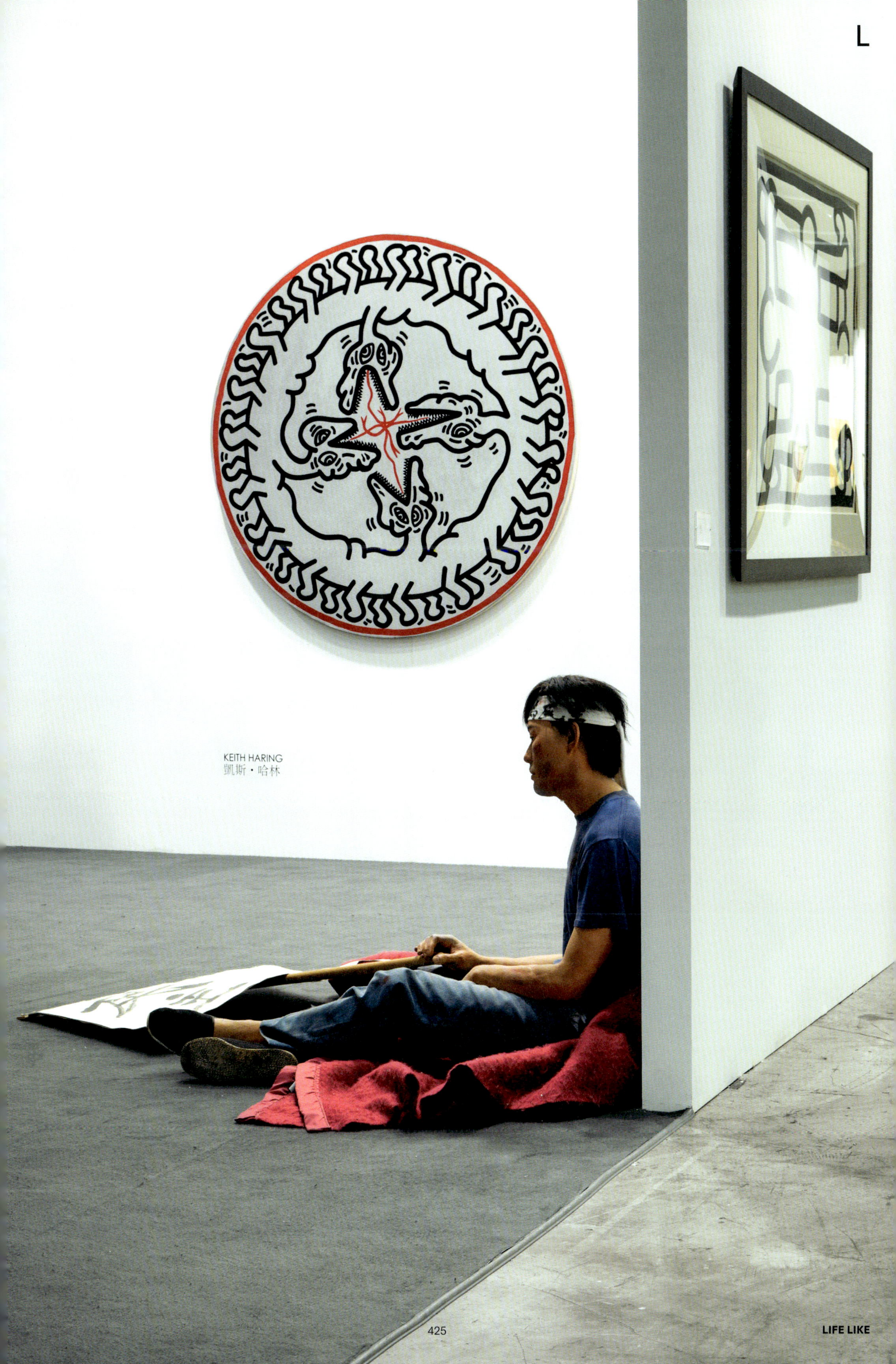
KEITH HARING
凱斯・哈林

L

John Ahearn
Cynthia, 1981; *Sam*, 1981; *Kate*, 1982
Alexander and Bonin

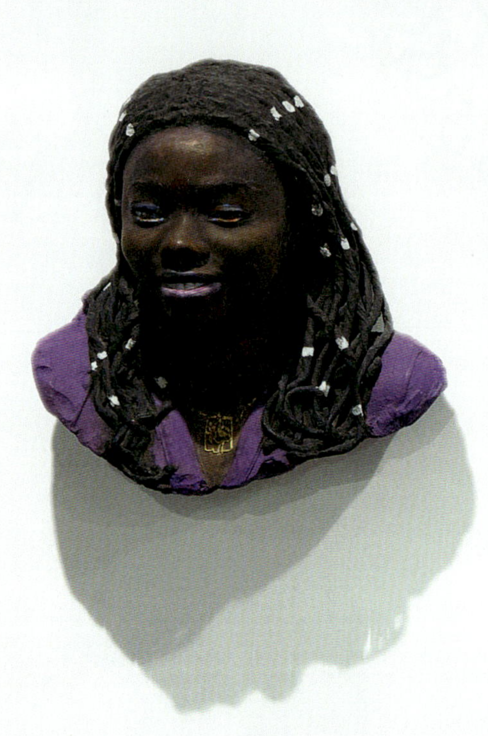

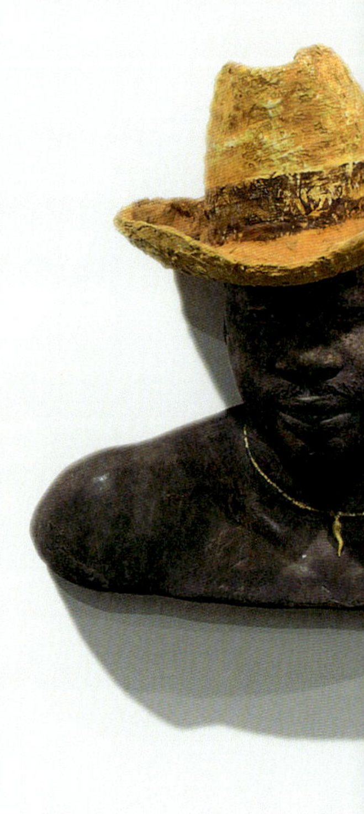

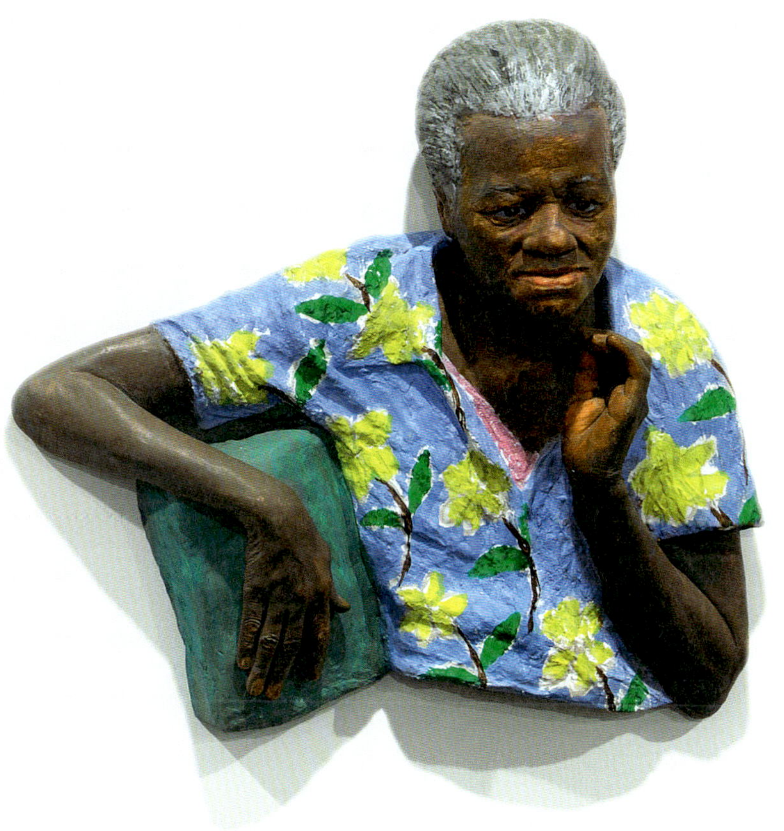

L

Daniel Firman
Fanny, 2013
Galerie Perrotin

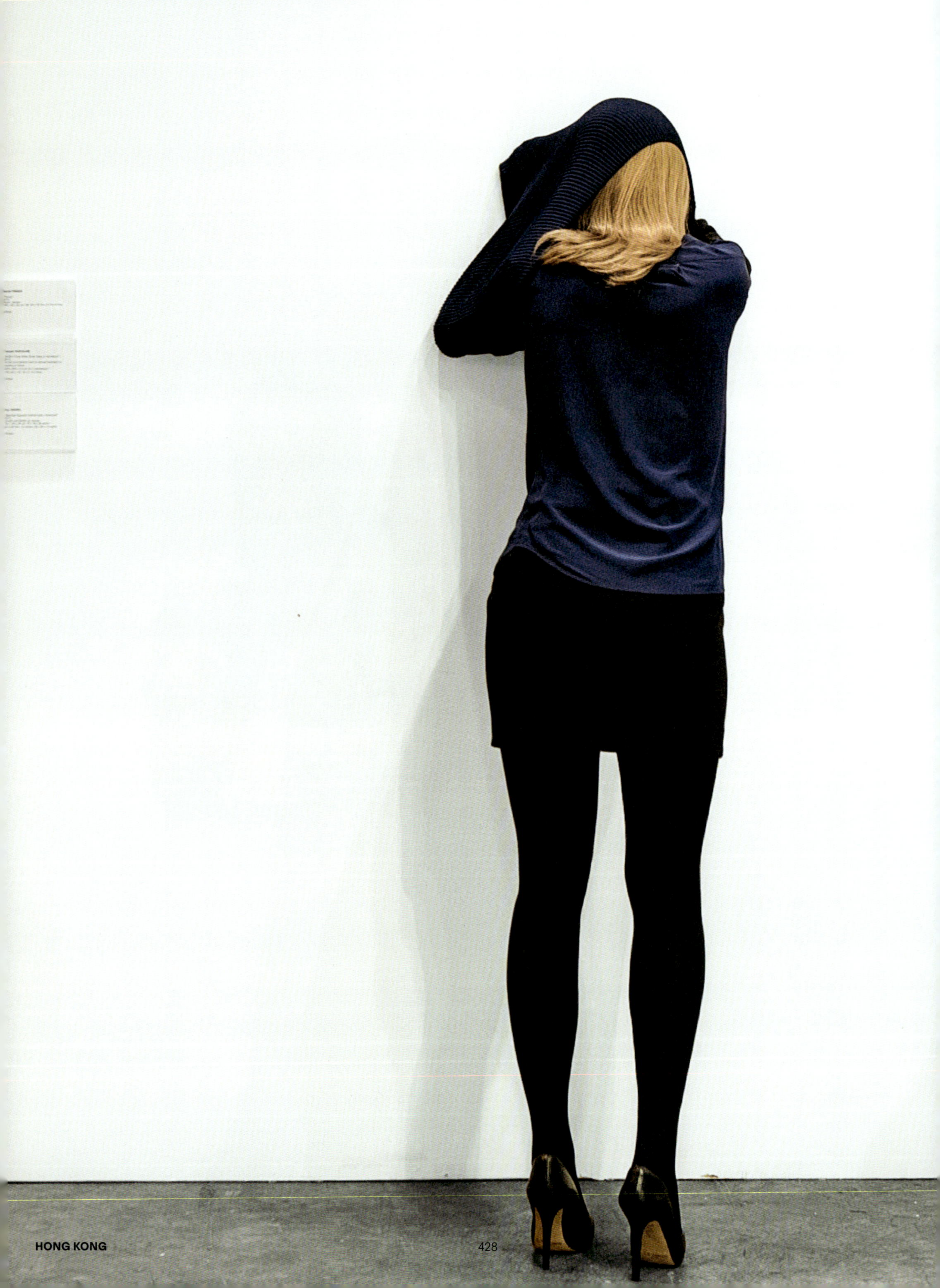

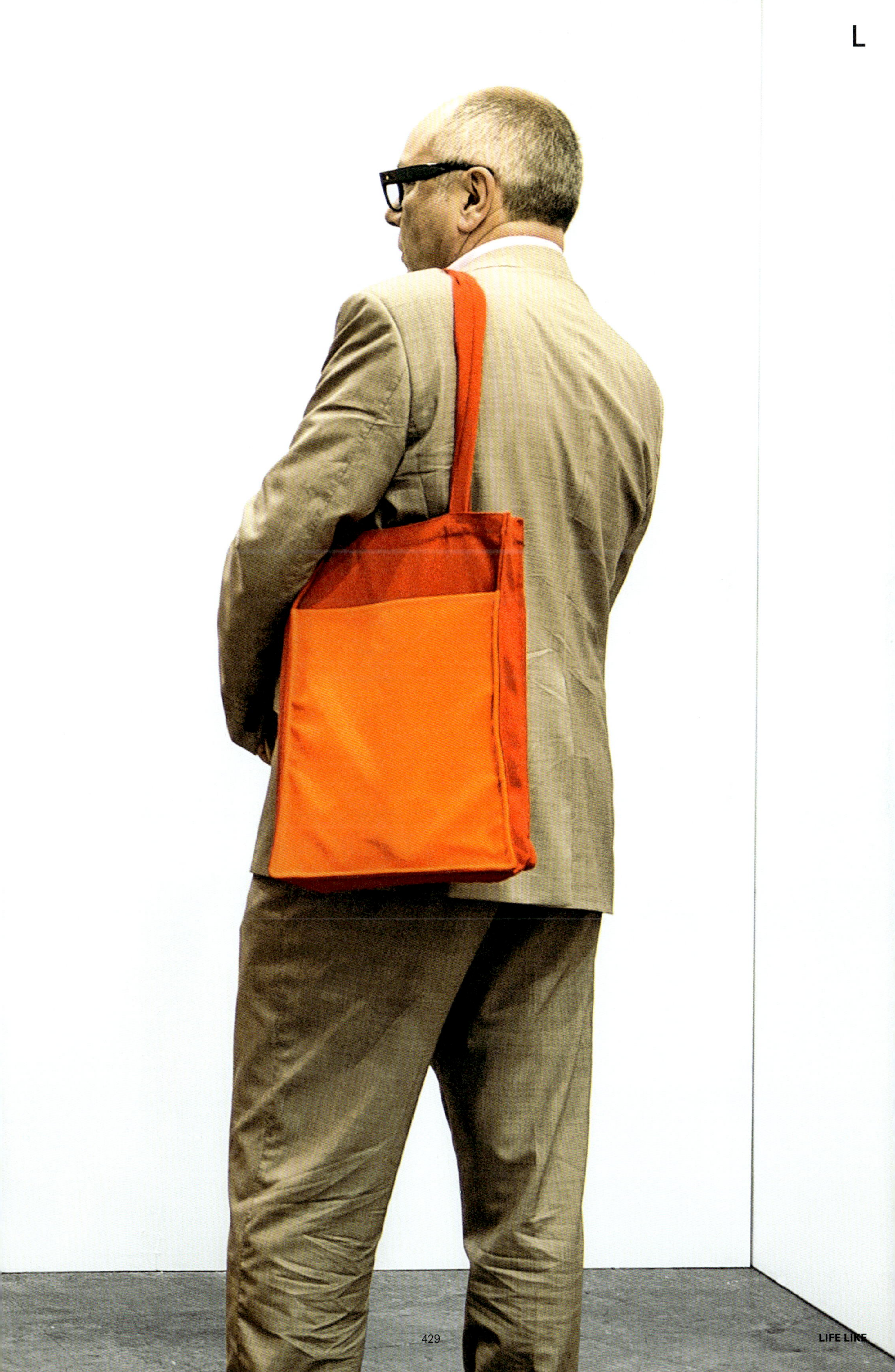

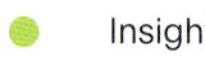

L-Art

Chengdu

Insights

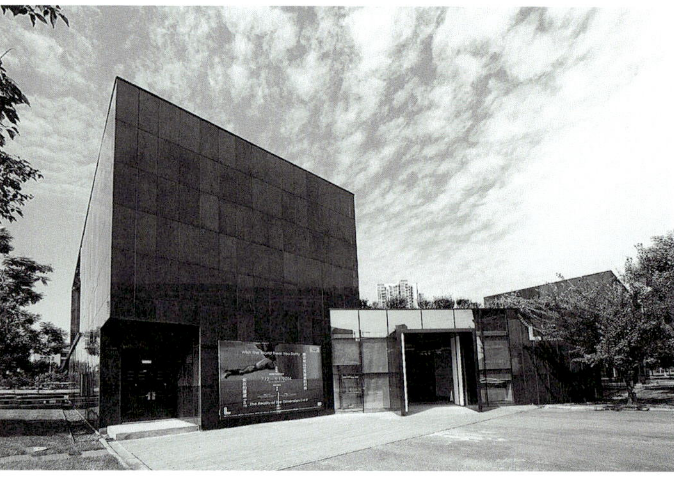

What is your favorite aspect of running a gallery?
Helping and promoting emerging artists, sharing new ideas and opinions with art lovers and collectors, discovering new things everyday.

How do you choose the artists you work with?
Look at their works, their path of creation, their personality, and their attitude toward art.

If you weren't running a gallery what else would you do?
Be a person bridging contemporary art with other fields (such as fashion, music, food, etc.), promoting art and artists in a crossover approach.

- **Contact** L-Art Gallery
  Jing Lu
  rain@l-artgallery.com
- **Established** 2011
- **Owner(s) / Partner(s)** Lu Jing
- **Team** 4
- **Space(s)** 450 m²
- **Artists at Art Basel** Xu Bacheng
- **Further artists represented** Li Rui
  Liu Yujie
  Meng Yangyang
  Xu Bacheng
  Zhang Tianjun
  Zhang Ya

Labor

Mexico City

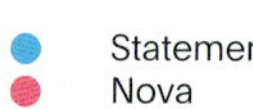

Statements
Nova

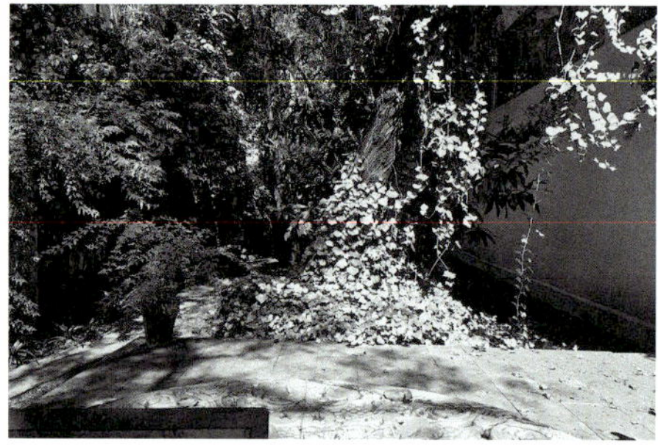

What is your favorite aspect of running a gallery?
Growing through long-term interactions, and the relationships with the artists.

How do you choose the artists you work with?
Taken as a whole, the work of the artists in the gallery implies a certain political statement. Thus, when I choose a new artist, it is important to consider that their practice is aligned with Labor's larger vision of exhibiting art that is research-based and has some social or political dimension.

If you weren't running a gallery what else would you do?
I would dare to study for a PhD in Economics.

- **Contact** LABOR
  Pamela Echeverría
  pamelaes@labor.org.mx
- **Established** 2009
- **Owner(s) / Partner(s)** Pamela Echeverría
- **Team** 5
- **Artists at Art Basel** Jorge Satorre
  Pedro Reyes
  Pablo Vargas Lugo
- **Further artists represented** Erick Beltrán
  Etienne Chambaud
  Terence Gower
  Irene Kopelman
  Jill Magid
  Nicholas Mangan
  Teresa Margolles
  Raphael Montañez Ortíz
  Santiago Sierra
  Antonio Vega Macotela
  Héctor Zamora

Lahumière

Paris

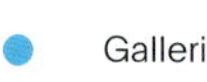

Galleries

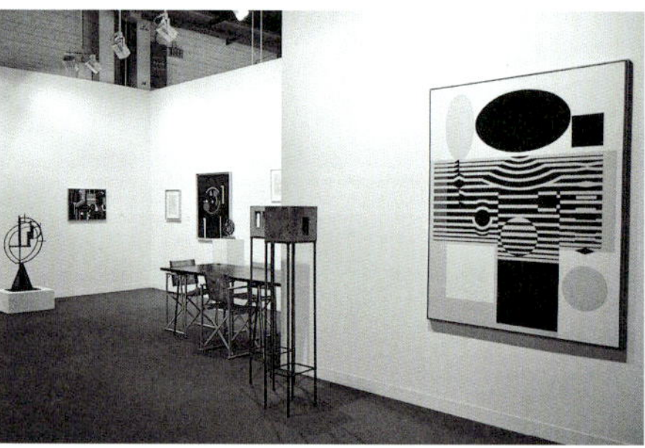

What is your favorite aspect of running a gallery?
The excitement of introducing new artists, helping the public to rediscover forgotten or lesser known classic artists, the pleasure of being at the beginning of this process, and accompanying a number of great public and private collections.

How do you choose the artists you work with?
The gallery today has a name in the field of constructive abstract art; some artists come to see us, others we choose to contact. We expect them to have a certain personal dynamic and a good general knowledge of art history and an interest in their contemporaries.

If you weren't running a gallery what else would you do?
I wanted to be a doctor or a captain on a ship.

- **Contact** Galerie Lahumière
  Anne Lahumière
  anne@lahumiere.com
- **Established** 1963
- **Owner(s) / Partner(s)** Anne & Jean-Claude Lahumière
- **Team** 3
- **Space(s)** 200 m²
- **Artists at Art Basel** Olle Baertling
  Charles Bézie
  Félix Del Marle
  Jean Dewasne
  César Domela
  Adolf Fleischmann
  Emile Gilioli
  Hans Jörg Glattfelder
  Auguste Herbin
  Gottfried Honegger
  Robert Jacobsen
  Jean Legros
  Alberto Magnelli
  Edgard Pillet
  Denis Pondruel
  Victor Vasarely
- **Further artists represented** Bauduin
  Nicholas Bodde
  Andreas Brandt
  Marcelle Cahn
  Jean-Gabriel Coignet
  Nathalie Delasalle
  Jean-François Dubreuil
  Günter Fruhtrunk
  Jean-Michel Gasquet
  Jean Gorin
  Renaud Jacquier Stajnowicz
  Jean Leppien
  Antoine Perrot
  Yves Popet
  Henri Prosi
  Moon-Pil Shim
  André Stempfel

Lam

Shanghai
Hong Kong
Singapore

 Galleries
Encounters

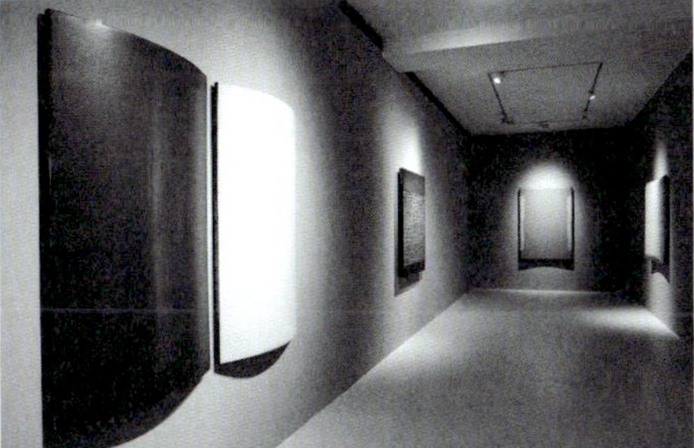

What is your favorite aspect of running a gallery?
I love engaging with curators and academics and learning from their different perspectives on art in order to create cultural dialogue. I also enjoy discovering artists and putting them in touch with curators to contextualize and learn about their works. My goal is to place artists in collections and museums and put them on the international radar or make international artists known in Asia. I also help young collectors start building their collections.

How do you choose the artists you work with?
Many of my artists are recommended by curators and influential academics who know I am passionate about abstract art, particularly abstract art that comes from different routes and pushes boundaries. I work with established, mid-career, and emerging artists from a variety of backgrounds who work in different mediums. I like to work with artists who can surprise me and make me think differently about art and life in general.

If you weren't running a gallery what else would you do?
I would be focusing on my foundation, the China Art Foundation, which helps to ensure that the global interest in contemporary Chinese art has a sustainable future. I would still be working in the arts and, hopefully, bridging the cultural divide between East and West.

- **Contact** Pearl Lam Galleries
  Harriet Onslow
  harriet@pearllamgalleries.com
- **Established** 2002
- **Owner(s) / Partner(s)** Pearl Lam
- **Team** 72
- **Space(s)** 2,600 m²
- **Artists at Art Basel** Jenny Holzer
  Juju Sun
  Li Huasheng
  Michael Chow aka Zhou Yinghua ~O-O~
  Qin Yufen
  Qiu Deshu
  Su Xiaobai
  Morgan Wong
  Yan Binghui
  Zhang Jianjun
  Zhu Jinshi
- **Further artists represented** Choi Jeong Hwa
  Golnaz Fathi
  Syaiful Aulia Garibaldi
  Gonkar Gyatso
  Sayaka Ishizuka
  André Kneib
  Jim Lambie
  Lan Zhenghui
  Lei Hong
  Li Tianbing
  Li Xiaojing
  Jason Martin
  Peter Peri
  Qiu Zhenzhong
  Carlos Rolón
  Yinka Shonibare MBE
  Tsang Kin-Wah
  Mehmet Ali Uysal
  Wang Dongling
  Wang Tiande
  Entang Wiharso
  Zhang Wei
  Zheng Chongbin

Lambert

Paris

 Galleries
Unlimited

- **Contact** Yvon Lambert
  Mathieu Cénac
  mathieu@yvon-lambert.com
- **Established** 1966

Landau

Montreal
Meggen

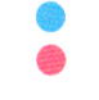 Galleries
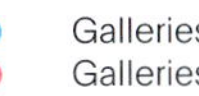 Galleries

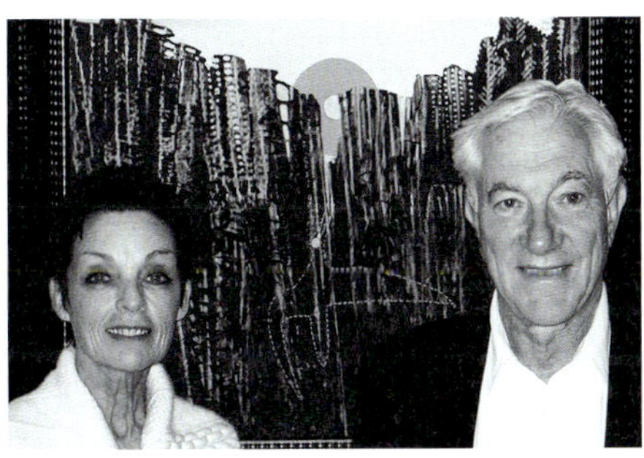

What is your favorite aspect of running a gallery?
A) I love hanging an exhibition to the point that I tend to try to do almost everything myself. This starts with designing the space, planning the exhibit, placing the artworks, lighting the entire booth and even

nailing up the descriptive tags exactly as I want them. Here I am reliant on the advice and input of my wife, Alice. Together, we often buy outstanding masterpieces just so that they can hang under the Landau Fine Art umbrella and enable our exhibit to be a standout amid hundreds of others. B) I cherish meeting people who are enthusiastic about the arts and with whom I share mutual respect. I have often stated that in our business and in the world in which we are intimately involved, people are more important than the actual artworks that we present and sell. The world of art has afforded me the privilege of meeting individuals from all walks of life (not just billionaires) for which I am supremely grateful.

How do you choose the artists you work with?

My wife Alice and I only buy and subsequently present artists and artworks that we love and want to live with. We do not purchase, nor do we sell art as an investment. This might seem confusing in today's world of mega prices, but we hold true to our principles of showing, buying, and selling only those artists that we have chosen to live with long term, regardless of whether they might remain in the gallery collection for five minutes or for five decades. We urge our customers to adhere to this same principle and to shun high-pressure sales techniques sometimes shown by some "hot shot" gallery sales staff.

- **Contact** Landau Fine Art
Nissa Khan
nkhan@landaufineart.ca
- **Established** 1987
- **Owner(s) / Partner(s)** Robert & Alice Landau
- **Team** 10
- **Space(s)** 1,860 m²
- **Artists at Art Basel** Josef Albers
Jean Arp
Fernando Botero
Alexander Calder
Heinrich Campendonk
Massimo Campigli
Lynn Chadwick
Marc Chagall
Chun Kwang Young
Giorgio de Chirico
Edgar Degas
André Derain
Jean Dubuffet
Max Ernst
Lyonel Feininger
Alberto Giacometti
Adolph Gottlieb
Juan Gris
Alexej von Jawlensky
Wassily Kandinsky
Christoph Kiefhaber
Paul Klee
- **Further artists represented** Sara Landau
Henri Laurens
Le Corbusier
Fernand Léger
Jacques Lipchitz
René Magritte
Marino Marini
Henri Matisse
Joan Miró
Amedeo Modigliani
Henry Moore
Giorgio Morandi
Emil Nolde
Pablo Picasso
Georges Rouault
Yves Tanguy
Georges Valmier
Kees van Dongen

Layr

Vienna — Nova

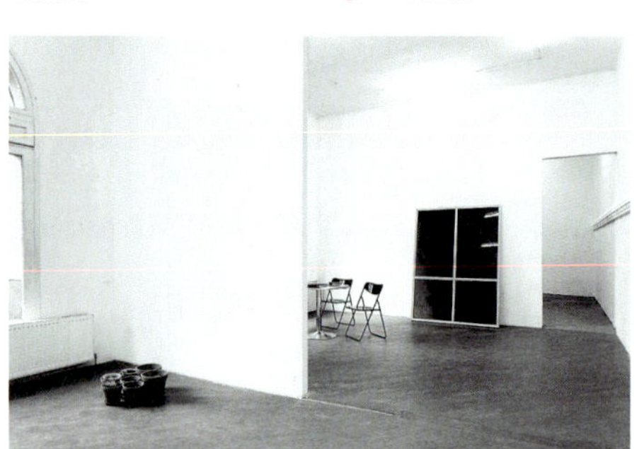

What is your favorite aspect of running a gallery?

As a gallerist I want to offer opportunities to artists, give them space and exhibitions, allow them to develop fully, actively supporting them and maintaining a dialogue.

How do you choose the artists you work with?

I look for and support positions that offer a certain timeliness and simulteanously have a very individual character or personality. It is not about a monoculture or formulating a single thought. It is also about bringing together a group of artists who can be read as a statement. The whole thing should have a good tone or chord—which also means that the artists should feel comfortable within such constellations.

- **Contact** Galerie Emanuel Layr
Emanuel Layr
gallery@emanuellayr.com
- **Established** 2011
- **Owner(s) / Partner(s)** Emanuel Layr
- **Team** 2
- **Space(s)** 200 m²
- **Artists at Art Basel** Marius Engh
Nick Oberthaler
- **Further artists represented** Franz Amann
Julien Bismuth
Andy Boot
Plamen Dejanoff
Stano Filko
Benjamin Hirte
Lisa Holzer
Tillman Kaiser
Mahony
Lili Reynaud-Dewar
Fabian Seiz
Philipp Timischl

Lee

London
Hong Kong
New York

Galleries
Galleries
Unlimited
Parcours
Galleries

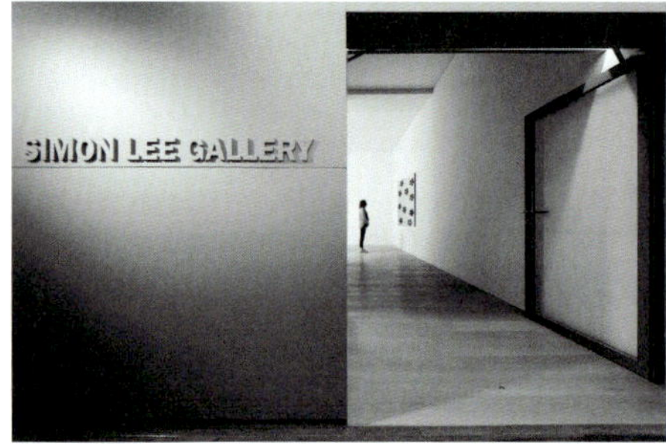

- **Contact** Simon Lee Gallery
Martha Gardikas
martha@simonleegallery.com
info@simonleegallery.com
- **Established** 2002
- **Owner(s) / Partner(s)** Simon Lee
- **Team** 21
- **Artists at Art Basel** Mel Bochner
Angela Bulloch

Merlin Carpenter
Larry Clark
George Condo
Dexter Dalwood
Jeff Elrod
Matias Faldbakken
Hans-Peter Feldmann
Bernard Frize
Ran Huang
Alex Hubbard
Sherrie Levine
Daido Moriyama
Paulina Olowska
David Ostrowski
Claudio Parmiggiani
João Penalva
Michelangelo Pistoletto
Josephine Pryde
Hugh Scott-Douglas
Jim Shaw
Gary Simmons
Valerie Snobeck
Marnie Weber
Christopher Wool
Toby Ziegler
Heimo Zobernig
Nam June Paik
Nam Tchun-Mo
O-Bong Kwon
Patricia Piccinini
David Salle
Jennifer Steinkamp
Eve Sussman
Bernar Venet

Leeahn

Seoul
Daegu

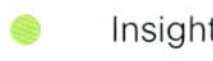

Insights

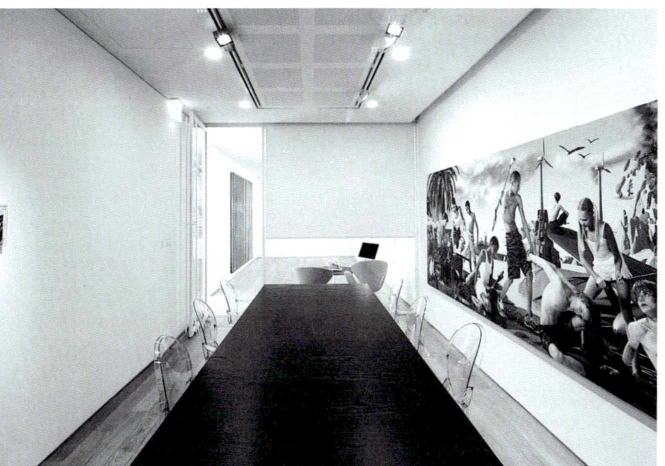

What is your favorite aspect of running a gallery?
I can introduce new positions in contemporary art along with works of leading artists in extensive exhibitions.

How do you choose the artists you work with?
I choose major contemporary artists of our time who actively work both at home and on the international scene, as well as young emerging artists.

If you weren't running a gallery what else would you do?
Collector.

- **Contact** Leeahn Gallery
Haekyung Kim
hkkim@leeahngallery.com
- **Established** 2007
- **Owner(s) / Partner(s)** Haeryung Ahn
- **Team** 9
- **Space(s)** 1,031 m²
- **Artists at Art Basel** Seungjoo Kim
- **Further artists represented** Boomoon
Jim Dine
Dzine
Hyun Wook Ryu
Hyun Soo Kim
Jeong Hwa Choi
Ki-soo Kim
Kim Ho-deuk
Kyo-Jun Lee
Un Kyung Hur
Katinka Lampe
Leenam Lee
Lisa Ruyter
Nak Beom Kho

Lehmann Maupin

New York
Hong Kong

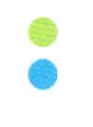

Galleries
Galleries Unlimited
Galleries Kabinett

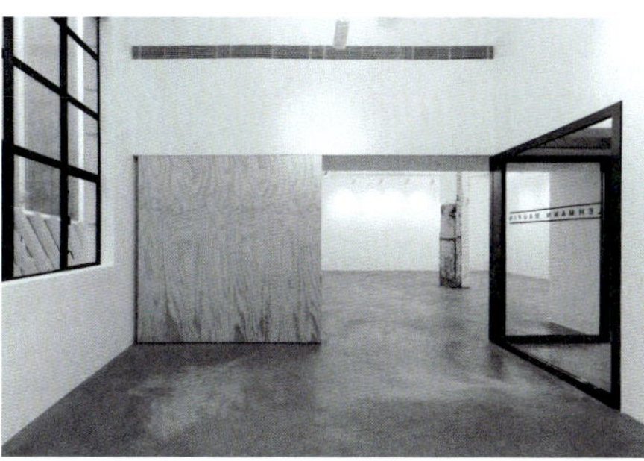

What is your favorite aspect of running a gallery?
Interacting and collaborating with the artists is the most rewarding aspect of running a gallery. Being able to help a development in their careers, offer advice, and provide them with a platform to create their best work are the most vital elements of running a contemporary arts organization. Also, it's invigorating being surrounded by energetic, immensely creative artists, and that is a constant source of meaning and inspiration.

How do you choose the artists you work with?
We look for artists who address contemporary culture at large, rather than solely within the narrow realm of contemporary art. We seek out artists whose work engages with a global perspective, which is reflective of Lehmann Maupin's long-standing commitment to expanding the boundaries of the gallery's international program. We also look for artists who engage with concepts of identity and create their own visual languages.

If you weren't running a gallery what else would you do?
I have always admired the work of talent agents in the film industry and would appreciate the challenges of such a position. Also, my love for architecture and modern design is very important to me, so I have always dreamt of a life as an architect.

- **Contact** Lehmann Maupin
Drew Moody
drew@lehmannmaupin.com
- **Established** 1996
- **Owner(s) / Partner(s)** Rachel Lehmann
David Maupin
- **Team** 30
- **Space(s)** 790 m²
- **Further artists represented** Kader Attia
Hernan Bas
Ashley Bickerton
Billy Childish
Mary Corse
Tracey Emin
Teresita Fernández
Anya Gallaccio
Gilbert & George
Sonia Gomes
Shirazeh Houshiary
Klara Kristalova
Lee Bul
Liu Wei
Mr.
OSGEMEOS
Angel Otero
Tony Oursler
Alex Prager
Robin Rhode
Tim Rollins and K.O.S.
Jennifer Steinkamp

Do Ho Suh
Juergen Teller
Mickalene Thomas
Adriana Varejão
Suling Wang
Nari Ward
Erwin Wurm

Gebrüder Lehmann

Dresden
Berlin

 Galleries

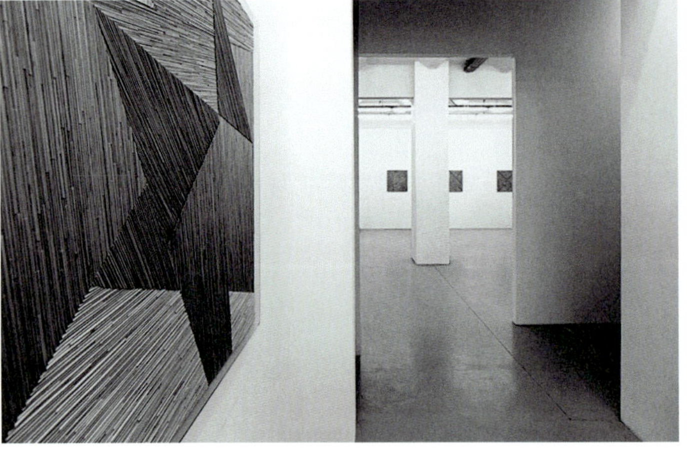

What is your favorite aspect of running a gallery?
Every day I can deal with art. There is nothing more exciting.

How do you choose the artists you work with?
Individualists, those I believe are unique in their generation, pulling me like a magnet and whose paintings touch me.

If you weren't running a gallery what else would you do?
I would collect art. Many works of art that I have sold to collections would have remained with me. But maybe it's more exciting to see them travel …

- **Contact** Galerie Gebr. Lehmann
  Jörg Goedecke
  joerg@galerie-gebr-lehmann.de
- **Established** 1992
- **Owner(s) / Partner(s)** Ralf Lehmann
  Frank Lehmann
- **Team** 6
- **Space(s)** 200 m²
- **Artists at Art Basel** Tatjana Doll
  Slawomir Elsner
  Eberhard Havekost
  Olaf Holzapfel
  Martin Mannig
  Daniel Schubert
  Keiichi Tanaami
  Joep van Liefland
- **Further artists represented** Ellen Harvey
  Hirschvogel
  Herbert Hoffmann
  Martin Honert
  Tilman Hornig
  Thoralf Knobloch
  Dan McCarthy
  Frank Nitsche
  Lara Schnitger
  Kohei Yoshiyuki

Leighton

Berlin

Galleries
Nova

- **Contact** Tanya Leighton
  info@tanyaleighton.com
- **Established** 2008
- **Owner(s) / Partner(s)** Tanya Leighton
- **Artists at Art Basel** David Diao
  Aleksandra Domanović
  Van Hanos
  Sharon Hayes
  Jamian Juliano-Villani
  Sanya Kantarovsky
  Oliver Laric
  Dan Rees
- **Further artists represented** Ayreen Anastas
  Pavel Büchler
  Alejandro Cesarco
  Sean Edwards
  Rene Gabri
  Aurélien Gamboni
  Enzo Mari
  Bruce McLean
  Lucas Ospina
  John Smith

Lelong

Paris
New York

 Galleries
Galleries Unlimited
Galleries Kabinett
Public

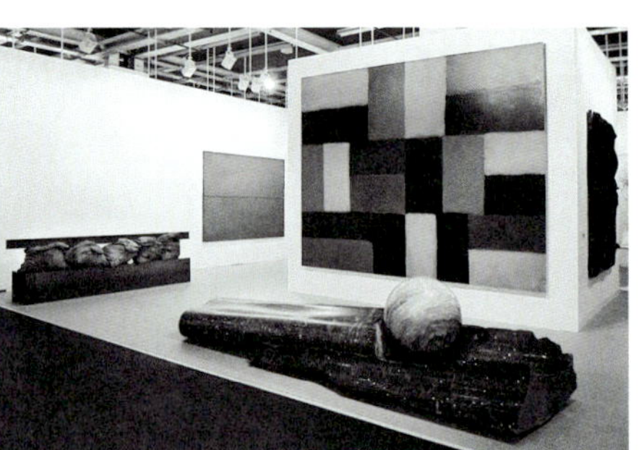

What is your favorite aspect of running a gallery?
Working with artists.

- **Contact** Galerie Lelong
  Jean Frémon
  fremon@galerie-lelong.com
- **Established** 1981
- **Owner(s) / Partner(s)** Jean Frémon
  Daniel Lelong
  Mary Sabbatino
- **Team** 28
- **Space(s)** 600 m²
- **Artists at Art Basel** Etel Adnan
  Pierre Alechinsky
  Ramazan Bayrakoğlu
  Sarah Cain
  Petah Coyne
  Nicola De Maria
  Angelo Filomeno
  Barry Flanagan
  Günther Förg
  Andy Goldsworthy
  Jane Hammond
  David Hockney
  Rebecca Horn
  Alfredo Jaar
  Konrad Klapheck
  Jiří Kolář
  Leon Kossoff
  Jannis Kounellis
  Wolfgang Laib
  Rosemary Laing
  Catherine Lee
  Lin Tianmiao
  Nalini Malani
  Cildo Meireles
  Ana Mendieta
  Joan Miró
  Robert Motherwell
  David Nash
  Hélio Oiticica
  Yoko Ono
  Emilio Perez
  Ernest Pignon-Ernest
  Jaume Plensa
  Arnulf Rainer
  Ursula von Rydingsvard
  Zilia Sánchez
  Sean Scully
  Kate Shepherd

Kiki Smith
Ettore Spalletti
Nancy Spero
Antoni Tàpies
Barthélémy Toguo
Juan Uslé
Jan Voss
Krzysztof Wodiczko
Catherine Yass

Lelong Editions

Paris 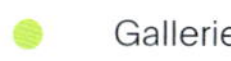 Galleries

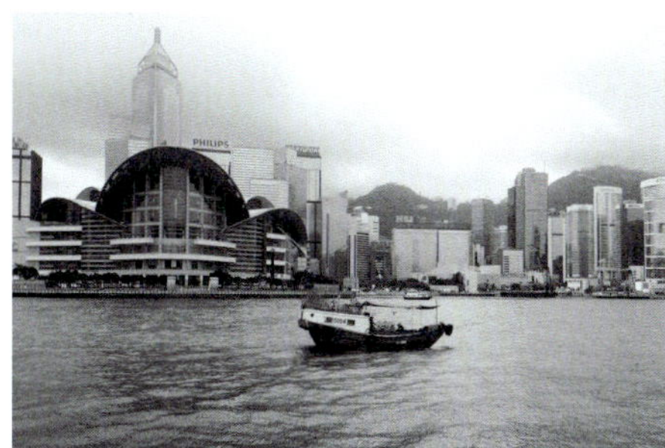

What is your favorite aspect of running a gallery?
Meeting new, young collectors around the world.

- **Contact** Lelong Editions
  Patrice Cotensin
  cotensin@galerie-lelong.com
- **Established** 1981
- **Owner(s) / Partner(s)** Jean Frémon
  Daniel Lelong
- **Team** 5
- **Space(s)** 50 m²
- **Artists at Art Basel** Etel Adnan
  Pierre Alechinsky
  Francis Bacon
  Louise Bourgeois
  Nicola De Maria
  Barry Flanagan
  Günther Förg
  Alberto Giacometti
  Andy Goldsworthy
  David Hockney
  Rebecca Horn
  Konrad Klapheck
  Jiri Kolàr
  Jannis Kounellis
  Lin Tianmiao
  Nalini Malani
  Joan Miró
  Robert Motherwell
  David Nash
  Ernest Pignon-Ernest
  Jaume Plensa
  Arnulf Rainer
  Sean Scully
  Kate Shepherd
  Kiki Smith
  Nancy Spero
  Antoni Tàpies
  Barthélémy Toguo
  Juan Uslé
  Jan Voss

Leme

São Paulo 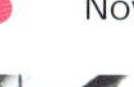 Nova

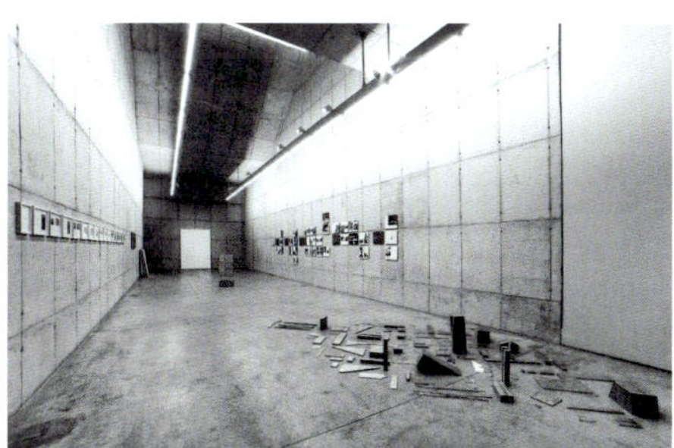

What is your favorite aspect of running a gallery?
Designing and discussing a show with an artist, and seeing the audience's response is one of my favorite aspects of running a gallery. I like the day before an opening a lot.

How do you choose the artists you work with?
We must have a connection with the artist, not just an aesthetic one, but also in terms of a relationship.

If you weren't running a gallery what else would you do?
I would be collecting more for sure!

- **Contact** Galeria Leme
  Camila Siqueira
  camila@galerialeme.com
- **Established** 2004
- **Owner(s) / Partner(s)** Eduardo Leme
- **Team** 8
- **Space(s)** 600 m²
- **Artists at Art Basel** Alexandre Brandão
  Zilvinas Kempinas
- **Further artists represented** Gabriel Acevedo Velarde
  Paulo Almeida
  AVPD
  David Batchelor
  Luiz Braga
  Sebastiaan Bremer
  Felipe Cama
  Paulo Climachauska
  Ana Elisa Egreja
  Luciano Figueiredo
  Richard Galpin
  Sandra Gamarra
  Gustavo von Ha
  Neil Hamon
  Candida Höfer
  Henry Krokatsis
  Jaime Lauriano
  Milton Marques
  José Carlos Martinat
  Mariana Mauricio
  Jessica Mein
  Marcia de Moraes
  Nina Pandolfo
  Mauro Piva
  Frank Thiel
  João Pedro Vale
  Christian Vinck

Lett

Auckland Galleries

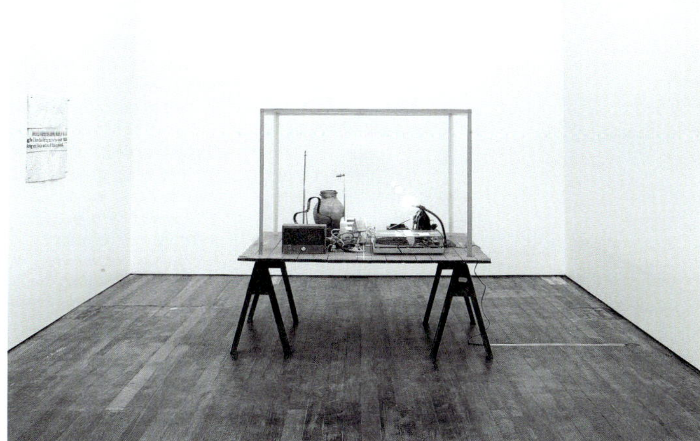

What is your favorite aspect of running a gallery?
Working with artists and facilitating the creation of great work.

How do you choose the artists you work with?
I like working with smart and ambitious people. When I feel pushed by an artist's practice it is usually a good sign too.

If you weren't running a gallery what else would you do?
Something that involved planting trees and tending a beehive.

- **Contact** Michael Lett
  Michael Lett
  michael@michaellett.com
- **Established** 1993
- **Owner(s) / Partner(s)** Michael Lett
  Andrew Thomas
- **Team** 4
- **Space(s)** 464.5 m²
- **Artists at Art Basel** Hany Armanious
  Dan Arps
  Martin Creed
  Julian Dashper
  Simon Denny
  Sriwhana Spong
  Michael Stevenson
  Cerith Wyn Evans
- **Further artists represented** Jim Allen
  Eve Armstrong
  The Estate of L. Budd
  Steve Carr
  Shane Cotton
  et al.
  Jacqueline Fraser
  Zac Langdon-Pole
  Michael Parekowhai
  Campbell Patterson
  Séraphine Pick
  Peter Stichbury
  Imogen Taylor

Lévy

New York
London
Geneva

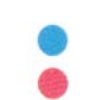

Galleries
Galleries

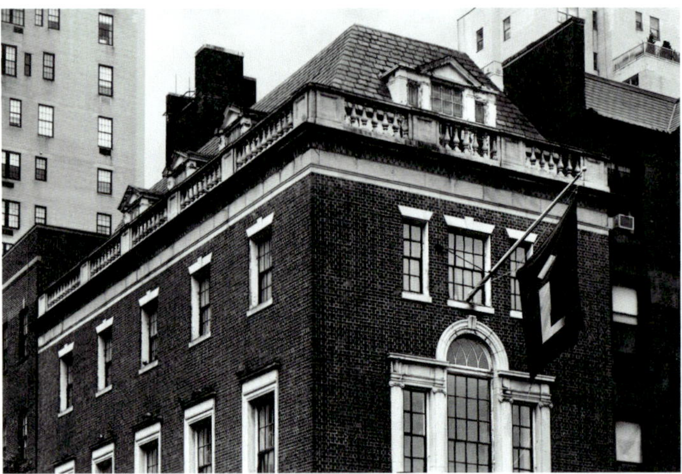

What is your favorite aspect of running a gallery?

It's impossible to single out a "favorite" part, the joy of running a gallery is the sum of all parts, and being fully immersed in art on a daily basis.

How do you choose the artists you work with?

I work with artists and estates that I believe in, and that I am passionate about. The most important aspect is what you can bring to the artist and how you can contribute to their career and legacy.

If you weren't running a gallery what else would you do?

I would love to open a library and tearoom. Perhaps there will be a library and tearoom as part of the Dominique Lévy Gallery in the future!

- **Contact** Dominique Lévy Gallery
  info@dominique-levy.com
- **Established** 2013
- **Owner(s) / Partner(s)** Dominique Lévy
- **Team** 18
- **Artists at Art Basel** Alberto Burri
  Enrico Castellani
  Gilbert & George
  David Hammons
  Keith Haring
  Jeff Koons
  Barbara Kruger
  Sigmar Polke
  Richard Prince
  Thomas Schütte
  Richard Serra
  Frank Stella
  Günther Uecker
  Andy Warhol
  Christopher Wool
- **Further artists** The Estate of Yves Klein
  Boris Mikhailov
  The Estate of Roman Opalka
  The Estate of Germaine Richier
  Pierre Soulages

Lin & Lin

Taipei
Beijing

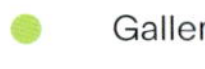

Galleries

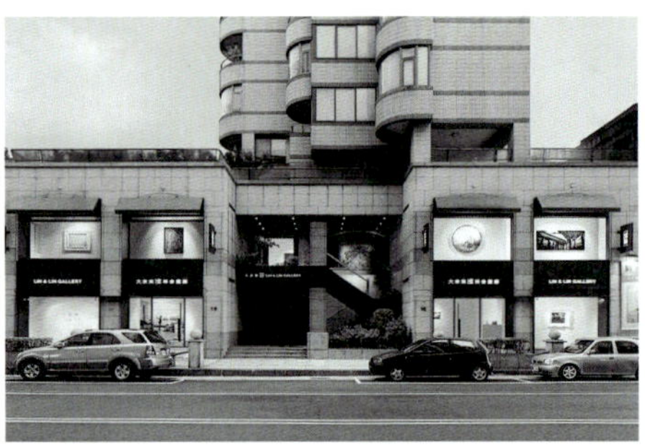

What is your favorite aspect of running a gallery?

As a gallery director now, I am always excited about discovering emerging artists and still amazed by having the opportunity to work with established or internationally recognized artists. The idea of introducing or promoting them and their art to the world is beyond fascinating. You could always feel the energy and possibility anytime, anywhere.

How do you choose the artists you work with?

By focusing on the dissemination of culture, Lin & Lin Gallery is more than just a regular gallery with the basic functions of presenting, collecting, or circulating artifacts; it also serves as a vanguard by interpreting and establishing the local cultural aesthetics within the context of contemporary art. To fulfill Lin & Lin's mission, we keep looking for artists who are living for their own cultural aesthetics and who recognize the unique spirit and value of the different cultures with us.

If you weren't running a gallery what else would you do?

It is tough to imagine not running a gallery like this. Maybe I would keep supporting art and be a part of it by being a serious collector. The passion for art would always be there.

- **Contact** Lin & Lin Gallery
  David Lin
  info@linlingallery.com
- **Established** 1984
- **Owner(s) / Partner(s)** Tien-Min Lin
  David Lin
- **Team** 10
- **Space(s)** 2,000 m²
- **Artists at Art Basel** Chen Chieh-Jen
  Liu Wei
  Mao Yan
  Zhou Chunya
- **Further artists represented** George Chann
  Chen Chieh-Jen
  Chiu Chien-Jen
  Guan Liang
  Hsiao Chin
  Huang Chia-Ning
  Hung Tung-Lu
  Kuo Wei-Kuo
  Lai Chiu-Chen
  Leng Bingchuan
  Liu Shih-Tung
  Liu Wei
  Lu Hsien-Ming
  Mao Yan
  Sanyu
  Wang Huai Qing
  Wu Da-Yu
  Xia Yang
  Xu Jiang
  Ye Nan
  Yin Zhaoyang
  Yun Gee
  Zao Wou-Ki
  Zhao Gang
  Zhou Chunya

Linder

Basel 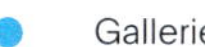 Galleries

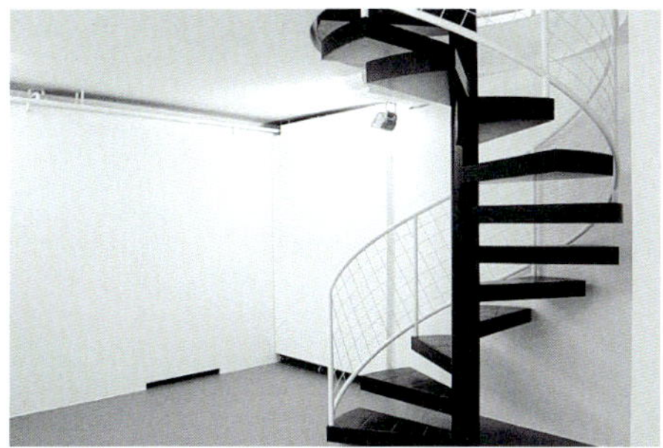

What is your favorite aspect of running a gallery?
I like to organize shows and select works with the artists.

How do you choose the artists you work with?
I visit exhibitions and studios, and I listen to tips from artists I appreciate.

If you weren't running a gallery what else would you do?
Curator of a private collection.

- **Contact** Galerie Gisèle Linder, Gisèle Linder, galerie@galerielinder.ch
- **Established** 1984
- **Owner(s) / Partner(s)** Gisèle Linder
- **Team** 4
- **Space(s)** 120 m²
- **Artists at Art Basel** Roger Ackling, John Beech, Manon Bellet, Renate Buser, Alan Ebnother, Philipp Goldbach, Serge Hasenböhler, Luzia Hürzeler, Clare Kenny, Kathrin Kunz, Ingeborg Lüscher, Luo Mingjun, François Morellet, Ursula Mumenthaler, Carmen Perrin, Michael Rouillard, Anne Sauser-Hall, Werner von Mutzenbecher, Andrea Wolfensberger, Peter Wüthrich
- **Further artists represented** Alfonso Fratteggiani Bianchi, Christoph Eisenring, Takaya Fujii, Maria Elena González, Julije Knifer, Marta Kolendo, Jordan Tinker, Peter Willen

Liprandi

Buenos Aires 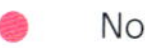 Nova

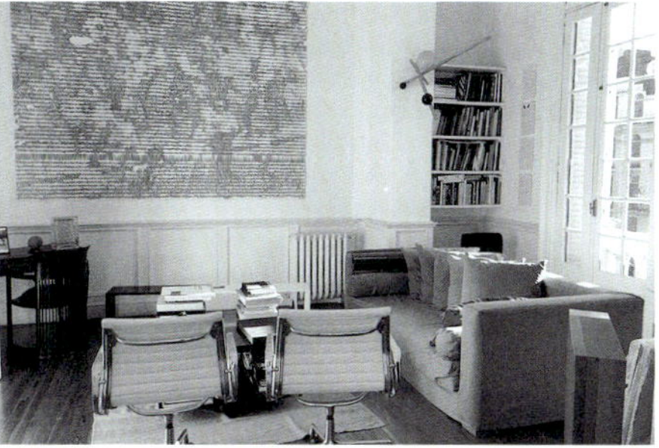

What is your favorite aspect of running a gallery?
I like the constant challenge of discovering and interpreting the artists' minds, and the new horizons and readings of reality that they propose.

How do you choose the artists you work with?
I choose our artists according to a simple rule: I don't sell anything that I wouldn't buy for myself.

If you weren't running a gallery what else would you do?
If I weren't running a gallery I would be playing music all day long!

- **Contact** Ignacio Liprandi Arte Contemporáneo, Ignacio Liprandi, maia@ignacioliprandi.com
- **Established** 2009
- **Owner(s) / Partner(s)** Ignacio Liprandi
- **Team** 3
- **Space(s)** 70 m²
- **Artists at Art Basel** Adriana Bustos, Magdalena Jitrik
- **Further artists represented** Pablo Accinelli, Nicolás Bacal, Fabián Bercic, Tomás Espina, Claudia Fontes, Ana Gallardo, David Lamelas, Mauricio Lupini, Mathieu Mercier, Eduardo Navarro, Jorge Pedro Núñez, Vijai Patchineelam, Cristina Piffer, Rita Ponce de León, José Alejandro Restrepo, Leandro Tartaglia

Lisson

London, Milan, New York, Singapore

- Galleries
- Galleries Unlimited Parcours
- Galleries Public

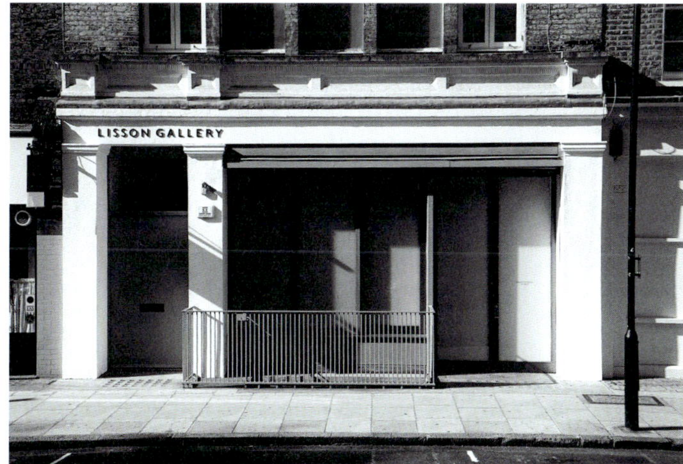

- **Contact** Lisson Gallery, Ossian Ward, contact@lissongallery.com
- **Established** 1967
- **Owner(s) / Partner(s)** Nicholas Logsdail
- **Team** 60
- **Space(s)** 1,500 m²
- **Artists at Art Basel** Ai Weiwei, Allora & Calzadilla, Cory Arcangel, Art & Language, Daniel Buren, James Casebere, Tony Cragg, Angela de la Cruz, Ryan Gander, Rodney Graham

Carmen Herrera
Shirazeh Houshiary
Christian Jankowski
Peter Joseph
Anish Kapoor
John Latham
Lee Ufan
Liu Xiaodong
Richard Long
Jason Martin
Haroon Mirza
Julian Opie
Tony Oursler
Giulio Paolini
Joyce Pensato
Pedro Reyes
Lawrence Weiner

- **Further artists represented** Marina Abramović
Gerard Byrne
Richard Deacon
Nathalie Djurberg & Hans Berg
Spencer Finch
Ceal Floyer
Dan Graham
Tim Lee
Sol LeWitt
Robert Mangold
Tatsuo Miyajima
Jonathan Monk
Florian Pumhösl
Rashid Rana
Santiago Sierra
Sean Snyder
Richard Wentworth

Löhrl

Mönchengladbach 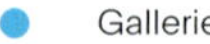 Galleries

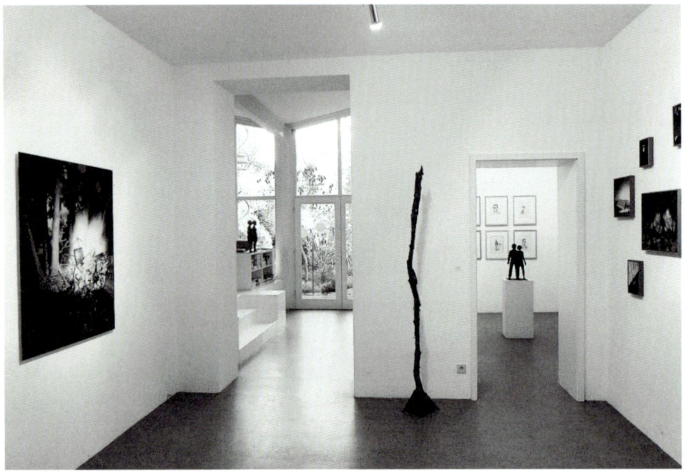

What is your favorite aspect of running a gallery?
Presenting contemporary art to the public, expecting that many visitors will start collecting. Giving young artists the chance to present their work.

How do you choose the artists you work with?
We work with well-known artists for a long time and continue showing their work. We look for young artists at academies who convince us with their concepts and the high quality of their work. Partly through recommendations by our artists.

If you weren't running a gallery what else would you do?
Dietmar Löhrl: Continued my profession as a management consultant, specializing in problem-solving methods and finding new ideas.
Christian Löhrl: I would have continued my career as a professional soccer player, and afterward worked in marketing and sports management.

- **Contact** Galerie Löhrl
Christian Löhrl
info@galerieloehrl.de
- **Established** 1975
- **Owner(s) / Partner(s)** Christa Löhrl
Dietmar Löhrl
Christian Löhrl
- **Team** 7
- **Space(s)** 600 m²

- **Artists at Art Basel** Stephan Balkenhol
Terry Fox
Katsura Funakoshi
Blinky Palermo
Otto Piene
Sigmar Polke
Gerhard Richter
Gregor Schneider
Günther Uecker
- **Further artists represented** Fabian Chiquet
Ulrich Erben
Jochen Gerz
Christof Klute
Roman Kochanski
Julia Rothmund
Ulrich Rückriem
Gil Shachar
Anett Stuth
Keiji Uematsu
Thomas Virnich

Lombard Freid

New York  Galleries

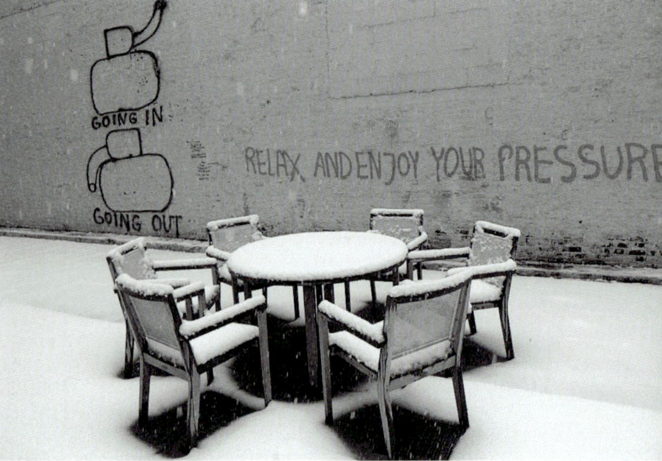

What is your favorite aspect of running a gallery?
The expression on the face of the FedEx man when we have a provocative show.

How do you choose the artists you work with?
Creatively and carefully.

If you weren't running a gallery what else would you do?
Jane: Sleep.
Lea: Read.

- **Contact** Lombard Freid Gallery
Lisa Carlson & Alia Fattouh
info@lombardfreid.com
- **Established** 1995
- **Owner(s) / Partner(s)** Jane Lombard
Lea Freid
- **Team** 7
- **Space(s)** 136 m²
- **Artists at Art Basel** Cao Fei
Teppei Kaneuji
Ulrich Lamsfuss
Lee Kit
Lee Mingwei
Tameka Norris
Eko Nugroho
The Propeller Group
Nina Yuen
- **Further artists represented** Huguette Caland
Sarah Dwyer
Mounir Fatmi
Motoyuki Daifu
Dan Perjovschi
Michael Rakowitz
Lucien Samaha
Mona Vatamanu & Florin Tudor
Kemang Wa Lehulere

Long March

Beijing

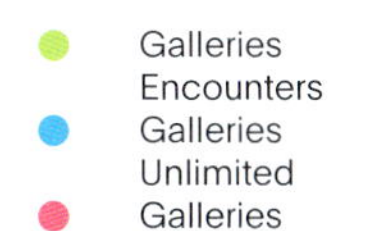

Galleries Encounters
Galleries Unlimited
Galleries

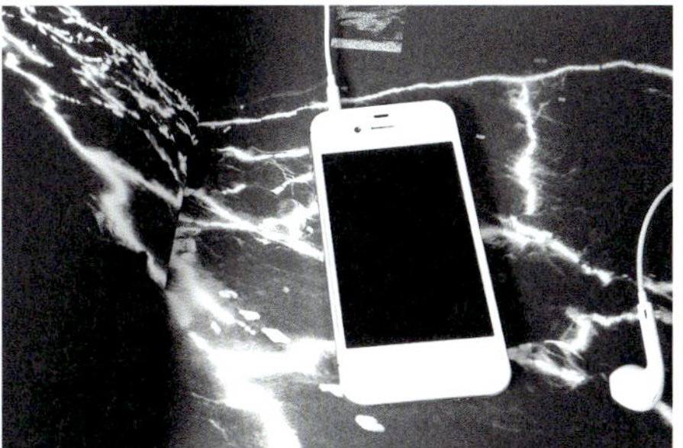

What is your favorite aspect of running a gallery?
The fact that one is required to (metaphorically) speak many languages, walk many circles, the artist's circle, the curator's circle, the collector's circle, and more. I meet so many fascinating characters who are not defined by their professions or the roles they play in the art world.

How do you choose the artists you work with?
We choose each other.

If you weren't running a gallery what else would you do?
Artist.

- **Contact** Long March Space
lm@longmarchspace.com
- **Established** 2002
- **Owner(s) / Partner(s)** Lu Jie
- **Team** 15
- **Space(s)** 2,500 m²
- **Artists at Art Basel** Chen Chieh-Jen
Guo Fengyi
Hu Xiangqian
Ran Huang
Li Tianbing
Liu Wei
Xu Zhen / Madein Company
Wang Jianwei
Wang Sishun
Wu Shanzhuan
Wu Shanzhuan & Inga Svala Thórsdóttir
Yang Shaobin
Yu Hong
Zhan Wang
Zhang Hui
Zhou Xiaohu
Zhu Yu

Luhring Augustine

New York

Galleries Unlimited
Parcours
Galleries

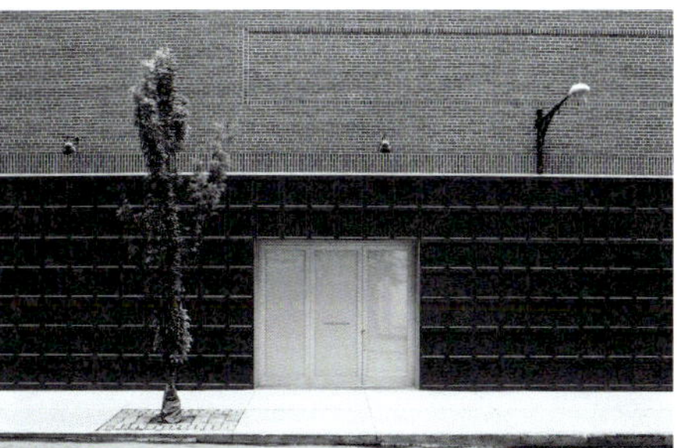

- **Contact** Luhring Augustine
Luhring Augustine
info@luhringaugustine.com
- **Established** 1985
- **Owner(s) / Partner(s)** Lawrence Luhring
Roland Augustine
- **Team** 25
- **Space(s)** 1,022 m²
- **Artists at Art Basel** Janine Antoni
Charles Atlas
Janet Cardiff and George Bures Miller
Larry Clark
William Daniels
Jeff Elrod
Tom Friedman
Roger Hiorns
Johannes Kahrs
Ragnar Kjartansson
Luisa Lambri
Glenn Ligon
Jason Moran
Yasumasa Morimura
Daido Moriyama
Reinhard Mucha
David Musgrave
Michelangelo Pistoletto
Pipilotti Rist
Josh Smith
Joel Sternfeld
Philip Taaffe
Tunga
Guido van der Werve
Rachel Whiteread
Steve Wolfe
Christopher Wool
Zarina

Luxembourg & Dayan

New York
London

Feature

- **Contact** Luxembourg & Dayan
Stephanie Adamowicz
stephanie@luxembourgdayan.com
- **Established** 2009
- **Owner(s) / Partner(s)** Daniella Luxembourg
Amalia Dayan
Alma Luxembourg
- **Artists at Art Basel** Domenico Gnoli
- **Further artists represented** Jean Arp
Alberto Burri
César
Marcel Duchamp
Mark Flood
Lucio Fontana
Lucian Freud
Jeff Koons
Jannis Kounellis
Bjarne Melgaard
Pino Pascali
Michelangelo Pistoletto
Rob Pruitt
Martial Raysse
Mario Schifano
Jerzy 'Jurry' Zieliński

Yvon Lambert

Interview with Yvon Lambert

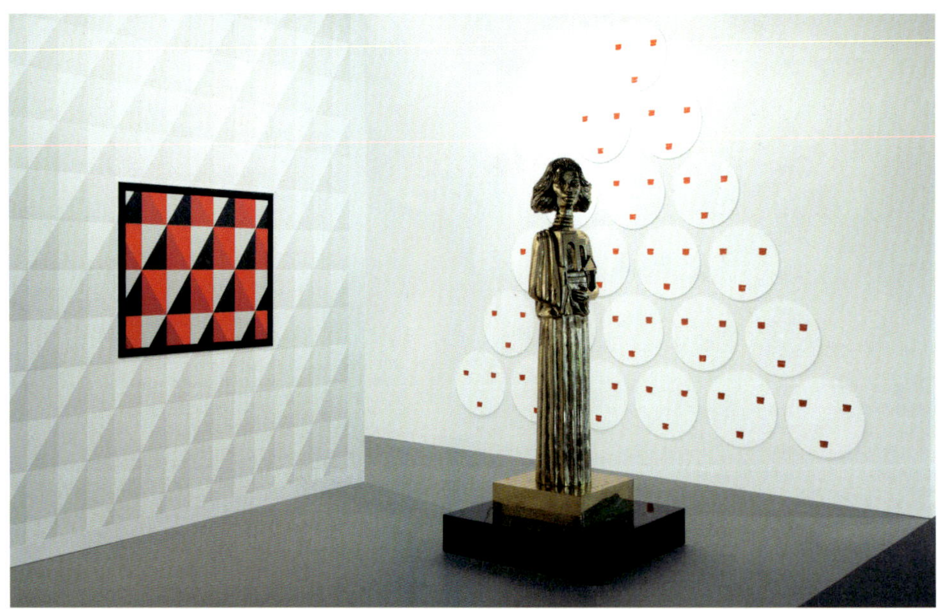

Art Basel in Basel, 2014

You opened your gallery in 1966, four years before Art Basel was launched, and you've participated in the fair from the start. Do you remember those early years?

It wasn't a big art fair, it was still a modest affair in a different venue from today. Things were really very simple. I remember that the flooring was very crude. Funny I should remember that—I can't recall what I showed that first year, but I remember the flooring!

Is that maybe because it wasn't so important to "do" Basel at the time?

Yes it was, but it was still pretty new. The only art fairs were the ones in Basel, Cologne (1969), and then Paris (1974). I remember the Cologne fair very well because one year I showed a different artist every day—it was the first time a gallery dared to do that.

Where was your gallery located at the time? And what spurred you to open it?

I was working out of Rue de l'Échaudé in the 6th arrondissement in Paris. First I'd had a little gallery on Rue de Seine, where I showed a lot of geometric art, but then I was offered a gallery on Rue de l'Échaudé that had been previously run by an American, David Anderson, who was Martha Jackson's son. I was on friendly terms with him and one day he said to me, "I've decided to return to the US. You can have the gallery, if you want it." Next I moved to Rue du Grenier-Saint-Lazare, before setting up here [Le Marais] in 1986. I particularly recall a show I held in 1972, covering the history of the gallery's first five years, ranging from Carl Andre to On Kawara via Dennis Oppenheim, Daniel Buren, Niele Toroni, etc. I also showed Arakawa, Hamish Fulton, Richard Long, and others. Shows stayed up for much less time than today, and a lot less people came. It was much more of a cottage industry. I remember when Richard Long turned up for his show with just a small folder under his arm. "Where's the show?" I asked. "Right here," he said. Then he made a rainbow in glitter—the kind you used to see on greeting cards—straight onto the floor, on the carpet. It was terrific. We took a photo, and that's all that remains.

How did you meet the artists you worked with in the late 1960s and early '70s, notably the Americans?

I went to the US at an early date, because I wasn't really interested in what I saw in Paris. That was the heyday of the Paris School. People were beginning to show Pop art, but I moved pretty quickly and, in fact, fairly naturally from historic geometric art to Sol LeWitt and Carl Andre. They were artists of my own generation, as were Daniel Buren and Niele Toroni. At the time, having a show in Paris was a big deal. It really meant a lot to American artists. So ever since there's been real loyalty between the gallery and those artists, as well as with Lawrence Weiner and Robert Barry. I also ran a gallery in New York for a few years. But, as you know, it's all coming to an end: we're closing on December 31, 2014.

Why are you closing after 40 years in business?

The real reason is that I now find the art-market scene too difficult. I was once part of it and used it, without regret, but it's no longer what I want—it's no longer the world I knew. Today the job isn't the job I once loved. I'm 78. But rather than hanging up everything, I'll be hanging onto something else, that is to say the real world of art, culture, literature, art history and, of course, books. That's what I'm most interested in now. The bookstore in the front of the gallery, which I opened in 2001, is what I really enjoy. So don't worry, I'm not heading for a quiet retirement. "Retirement" is a word I've never used, and it's not about to happen! I'm just going to do something else. You can't get rid of me so easily! (*Laughs*)

When do you think this change occurred? I suppose it's partly related to the increasingly dominant role the auction houses play on the contemporary art scene.

I'd say that by the late 1990s the nature of the game had changed. At auctions, in fact, all the power is in the hands of a few American and Swiss players. These days there are still extremely important galleries doing good work, but as far as I'm concerned I never wanted that kind of power, I never worked that way.

Now your collection has become an important part of your life. You began collecting very early, which was not true of all gallery owners. Some of them buy a work from their artists from time to time, but in order to support an artist, rather than to collect. In contrast, collecting has long been important to you.

I built up my collection over many years, and I've now donated it to the state. It's currently housed in Avignon—the Collection Lambert in Avignon opened in 2000 and has hosted some magnificent shows, such as *Les Papesses* in 2013. To tell the truth, I always used to organize shows with the desire to keep some works, but I never thought it would take on such proportions. I found myself with a great quantity of works and wondered what I could do with them. First I did a show at Villeneuve d'Ascq and Tourcoing in 1992. The collection truly reflects my dealer's eye, because it's composed of artists who interested me, the ones I liked and promoted. It's basically a collection of works by the artists I showed.

Are you planning to do a show that traces the gallery's history?

No. I don't want any celebrations. We will close with the first exhibition of Adel Abdessemed at the gallery; I like the idea of ending with a beginning. Our stand at Basel this year was a big hit, thanks to the efforts of my team. It was magnificent: a Toroni, a Jenny Holzer, Douglas Gordon's wall, Bertrand Lavier's wallpaper, Lawrence Weiner's piece—the stand was a fine tribute to the gallery's history.

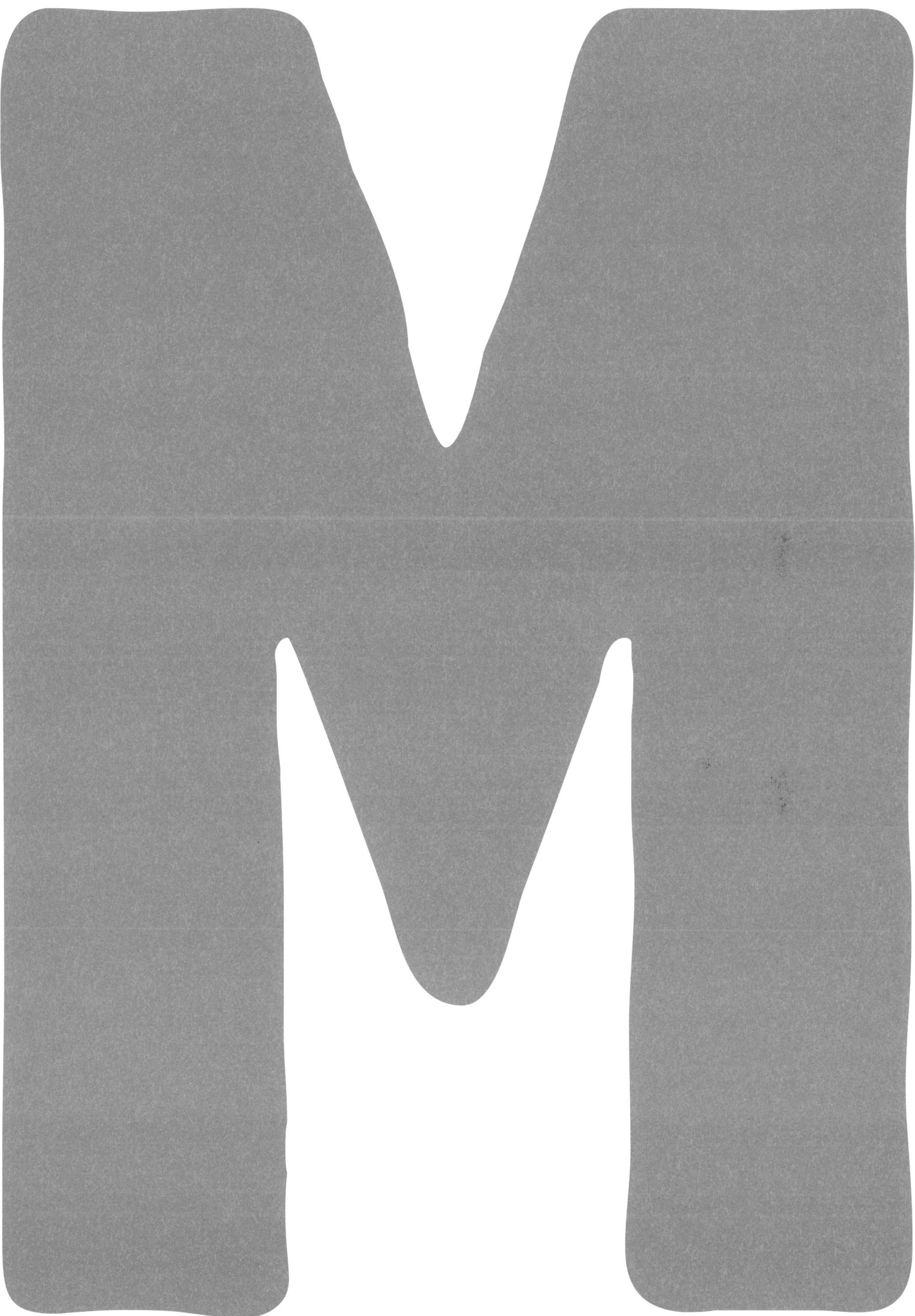

Yishu
$pik€
Art under
Capitalism
Art Basel
16–22
2014
MOUSSE 44
SUMMER
2014
IT'S
BEEN
A
LONG, COLD,
LONELY
WINTER

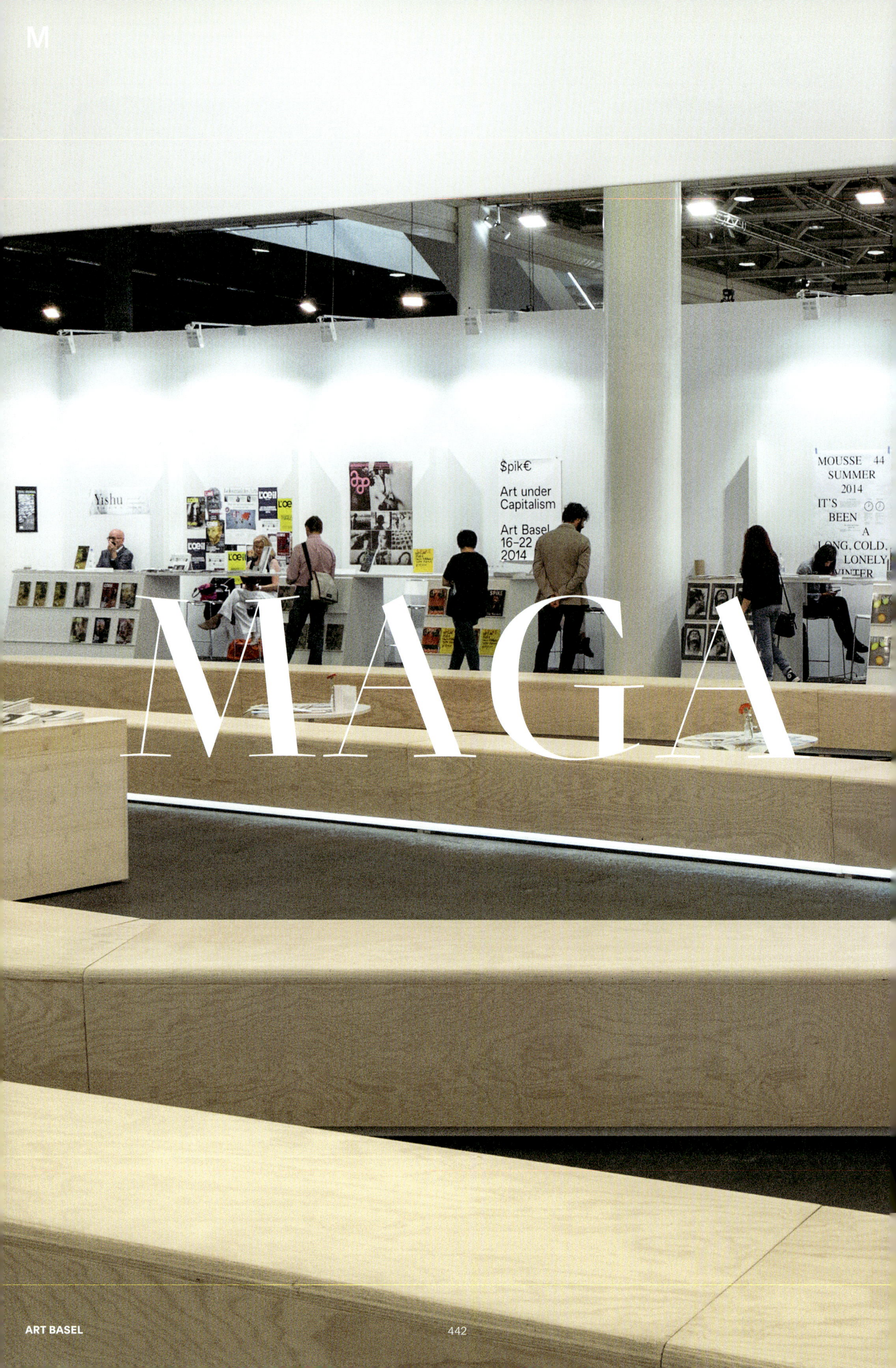

MAGA

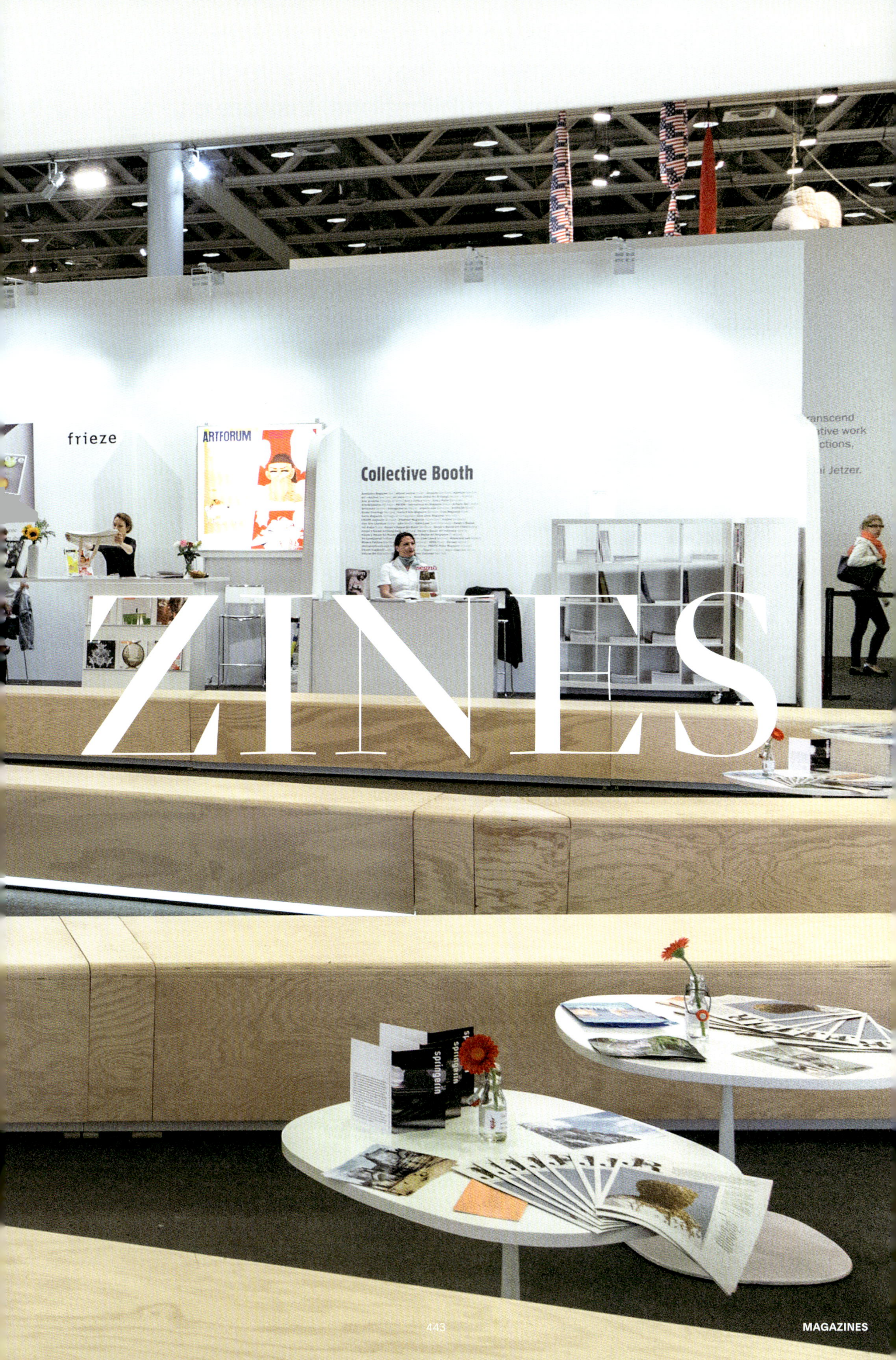
frieze
ARTFORUM
Collective Booth
ZINES.

The Magazines sector, present at all three Art Basel exhibitions, features a selective range of premier publications. Visitors can explore both the art world's major internationally active publications as well as those that cover regional art scenes in greater detail and depth. Each year several publishers also offer limited edition artworks created in direct collaboration with artists.

A

99ArtWeb
Beijing
99ys.com

Aesthetica Magazine
York
aestheticamagazine.com

Afterall Journal
London
afterall.org

Amarello
Rio de Janeiro
amarello.com.br

Aperture
New York
aperture.org

Art & Antiques
Wilmington (NC)
artandantiquesmag.com

Art + Auction
New York
artinfo.com

Artblend Inc
Fort Lauderdale
artblend.com

Artillery
Los Angeles
artillerymag.com

Art in America
New York
artinamericamagazine.com

art ltd. magazine
Woodland Hills
artltdmag.com

Art Metropole
Toronto
artmetropole.com

Art OnCuba
Havana
oncubamagazine.com

Art Papers
Atlanta
artpapers.org

art press
Paris
artpress.fr

art.es
Madrid
art-es.es

Artam Global Art & Design
Macka - Istanbul
artam.com

ArtAsiaPacific
Hong Kong
artasiapacific.com

Arte
Milan
cairoeditore.it

ARTE AL DIA International
Miami
artealdia.com

Arte al Limite
Santiago de Chile
arteallimite.com

Arte e Critica
Rome
arteecritica.it

Arte y Parte
Santander
arteyparte.com

Arte!Brasileiros
São Paulo
artebrasileiros.com.br

ARTEiN International Art Magazine
Venezia Mestre
artein.it

Artfacts.Net Ltd.
London
artfacts.net

ARTFORUM International Magazine
New York
artforum.com

ARTINVESTO
Munich
artinvestor.de

artmagazine.cc
Vienna
artmagazine.cc

ArtNexus
Miami
artnexus.com

artports.com
Karlsruhe
artports.com

ArtPULSE
Miami
artpulsemagazine.com

ArtReview
London
artreview.com

Art World Magazine
Shanghai
yishushijie.com

Baku
London
baku-magazine.com

Beaux Arts magazine
Issy-les-Moulineaux
beauxartsmagazine.com

Bijutsu Techo - BT
Tokyo
bijutsu.co.jp/bt

Blouinartinfo.com Asia
New York
artinfo.com

Border Crossings
Winnipeg
bordercrossingsmag.com

Brownbook Magazine
Dubai
brownbook.me

Camera Austria International
Graz
camera-austria.at

Canvas
Dubai
canvasonline.com

Carrier Pigeon
New York
carrierpigeonmag.com

Carte d'Arte Magazine
Messina
cartedartemagazine.it

Chinese Contemporary Art News
Beijing
canart.com.tw

Contemporary Art Philippines
Pasig City
contemporaryartphilippines.com

Contemporary Artists
Chong Qing
artistchina.org

Cura Magazine
Rome
curamagazine.com

Dardo Magazine
Santiago de Compostela
dardomagazine.com

DASartes
Rio de Janeiro
dasartes.com

Dear Dave Magazine
New York
deardavemagazine.com

DROME magazine
Brussels
dromemagazine.com

E

Elephant Magazine
Amsterdam
frameweb.com/
elephant

esse arts + opinions
Montreal
esse.ca

ETC
Prevost
etcmontreal.com

Eyeline
Brisbane
eyelinepublishing.com

F

Fine Arts Literature
Wuhan
meishuwenxian.com

Fisheye magazine
Poggibonsi (Siena)
carlocambieditore.it

Flash Art
Milan
flashartonline.com

frieze
London
frieze.com

frieze d/e
Berlin
frieze-magazin.de

FUTURO contemporaryart
Meisterschwanden
futuro-magazin.ch

G

g&e
Madrid
grabadoyedicion.com

Gallery.spb
Saint Petersburg
spb-gallery.info

H

Harper's Bazaar Art Arabia
Dubai
itp.com

Harper's Bazaar Art Singapore
harpersbazaar.mx

Harper's Bazaar Art En Espanol
harpersbazaar.mx

Harper's Bazaar Art Brasil
São Paulo
harpersbazaar.com.br

Harper's Bazaar Art China
Beijing
bazaarart.com.cn

Harper's Bazaar Art Hong Kong
Hong Kong
scmpgroup.com

Harper's Bazaar Art Indonesia
Jakarta
harpersbazaar.co.id

Harper's Bazaar Art Russia
Moscow
bazaar.ru

Hi Art
Beijing
hiart.cn

I

Iberoamericana Internacional Magazine
Lima
iberointernacional.com

K

Kaleidoscope
Milan
kaleidoscope-press.com

KQ kunstquartal
Ostfildern
kq-daily.de

Kunst-Bulletin
Zurich
kunstbulletin.ch

L

L'Aperitivo Illustrato
Pesaro
aperitivoillustrato.it

Le Journal des Arts
Paris
lejournaldesarts.fr

Leap Magazine
Beijing
leapleapleap.com

LLEI D'ART
Alpicat - Lleida
lleidart.com

L'Œil
Paris
loeil.fr

L'OFFICIEL Art
Paris
editiionsjalou.com

Look Lateral
Mantova
looklateral.com

M

Masdearte.com
Madrid
masdearte.com

Mirus
Zurich
mirusmag.com

Modern Painters
New York
artinfo.com

Monopol
Berlin
monopol-magazin.de

Mousse Magazine
Milan
moussemagazine.it

Mutualart.com
Brooklyn, NY
mutualart.com

N

NERO
Rome
neromagazine.it

O

Ocula
Hong Kong
ocula.com

P

Parkett
Zurich
parkettart.com

Parnass
Vienna
parnass.at

photography-now.com
Berlin
photography-now.com

Pipeline Magazine
Sheung Wan, Hong Kong
pipelinemag.com

Prefix Photo Magazine
Toronto
prefix.ca

Printed Matter, Inc
New York
printedmatter.org

R

Rooms Magazine
London
roomsmagazine.com

S

Sculpture
Hamilton
sculpture.org

Segno
Pescara
rivistasegno.eu

Select
São Paulo
select.art.br

SFAQ
Los Angeles
sfaqonline.com

sleek magazine
Berlin
sleekmag.com

Spike Art Quarterly
Vienna
spikeart.at

springerin
Vienna
springerin.at

T

Tagboat/ TOKYO ART GUIDE
Tokyo
tagboat.com/artguide

Take on Art
New Delhi
takeonart.wordpress.com

Tar Mag
Florence
tar-mag.com

tasj
New York
tasjmagazine.com

Texte zur Kunst
Berlin
textezurkunst.de

The Art Newspaper
London
theartnewspaper.com

The Pocket Arts Guide
Hong Kong
thepocketartsguide.com

V

Vellum
Brooklyn, NY
vellumartzine.com

W

Weltkunst
Hamburg
zeitkunstverlag.de

White Zinfandel
New York
whitezinf.org

Y

Yishu - Journal of Contemporary Chinese Art
Vancouver
yishu-online.com

Z

Zoom Magazine
zoom-net.com

M

City population
420,000
(Miami Metropolitan Area: 5,817,000)

Population density
4,700 inhabitants per square kilometer

Fair founded in
2001 but postponed to 2002 due to 9/11 attacks

Visitors in 2014
73,000

Number of exhibitors in 2014
267

Number of artists exhibited in 2014
over 4,000

Exhibition Partners: Museums & Cultural Institutions

Art and Culture Center of Hollywood
Dave Muller: *Rock 'n' Old*; Bhakti Baxter: *Returning What Was Borrowed*; Michael Dean: *Yardbird Records*; Annie Buckley: *The People's Tarot*

Art Center/South Florida
30 Years on the Road

Bass Museum
Peter Marino: *One Way*

Boca Raton Museum of Art
Theresa Ferber Bernstein: *A Century in Art*; *Elliot Erwit Photography*; Bryan Drury: *Terrestrial Visions*; Shizuka Yokomizo: *Forever and Again*

CasaLin
Hotbed 2014

Fairchild Tropical Botanic Garden
Chihuly at Fairchild: A Glass Garden; Design at Fairchild by Pakhale

The Patricia & Phillip Frost Art Museum
Wang Qingsong: *Adinfinitum; A Global Exchange: Geometric Abstraction since 1950; Hands of Korea; A Wolfsonian Teaching Exhibition: Koizumi Kishio—Remembering Tokyo*; Gaby Grobo: *Horizonte infinito*

HistoryMiami
Mario Algaze: *A Respect for Light*

Institute of Contemporary Art, Miami
Andra Ursata; Pedro Reyes

Jewish Museum of Florida
The Chosen: Selected Works from Florida Jewish Art Collectors

Locust Projects
Daniel Arsham; Simón Vega: *Project Room*; Ron Terada: *Art on the Move*

Lowe Art Museum
Art in Real Life: Traditional African Art from the Lowe; Transformative Visions: Works by Haitian Artists from the Permanent Collection

MDC Museum & Galleries of Art + Design
Shen Wei: *In Black, White and Gray*

Pérez Art Museum
Beatriz Milhazes: *Jardim Botânico*; Geoffrey Farmer: *Let's Make the Water Turn Black*; Mario García Torres and Nicole Cherubini

Miami Children's Museum
Let's Explore! Dora and Diego

Museum of Art, Fort Lauderdale
Café Dolly: Picabia, Schnabel, Willumsen; *American Scene Photography: Martin Z. Margulies Collection*

Museum of Contemporary Art
George Edozie: *Shifting Paradigms*

Norton Museum of Art
4th annual 'Recognition of Art by Women'; Klara Kristalova: *Turning into Stone*; Terry Haggerty

University Galleries, Florida Atlantic University
Altarations: Built, Blended, Processed (part one)

Vizcaya Museum & Gardens
Vizcaya-fy or Bust!

Wolfsonian – FIU
Myth and Machine: The First World War in Visual Culture

Young At Art Museum
Sebastian Masuda's *Colorful Rebellion—Seventh Nightmare*

Cisneros Fontanals Art Foundation
Impulse, Reason, Sense, Conflict. Abstract Art from the Ella Fontanals-Cisneros Collection

de la Cruz Collection Contemporary Art Space
Beneath The Surface

Girls' Club Collection
The Moment. The Backdrop. The Persona

The Margulies Collection at the Warehouse
Fifteen Year Anniversar Exhibition

Rubell Family Collection
To Have and to Hold; Aaron Curry, Neïl Beloufa, Will Boone, Lucy Dodd, Mark Flood David Ostrowski, and Kaari Upson

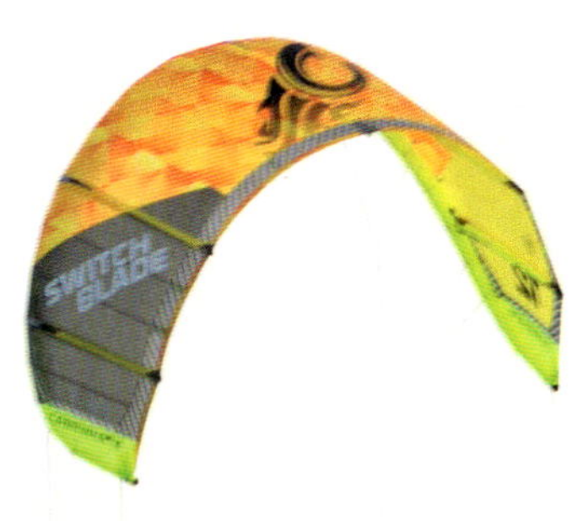

MIAMI BEACH

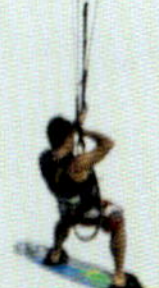

Miami Dodge Island Port

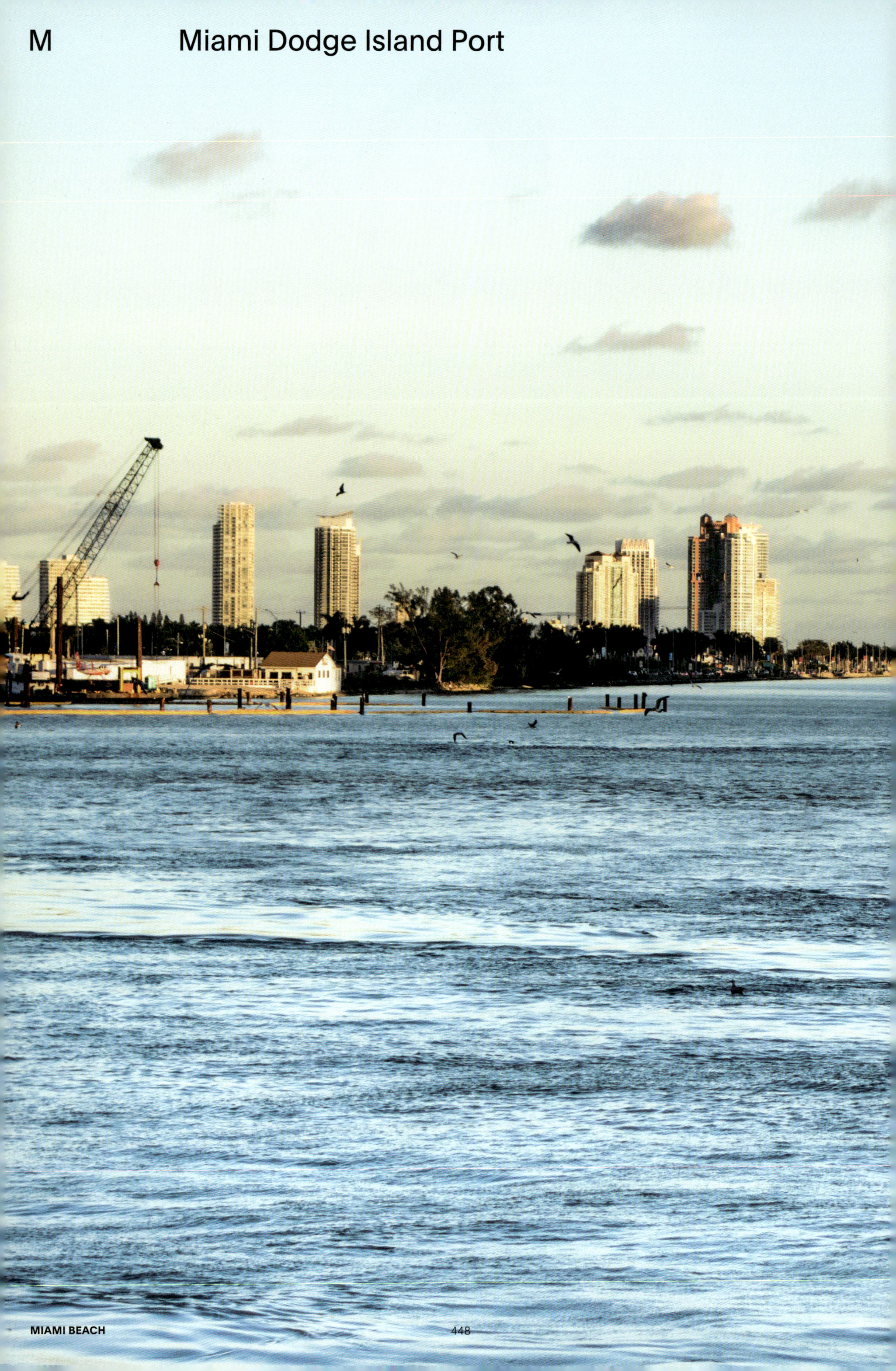

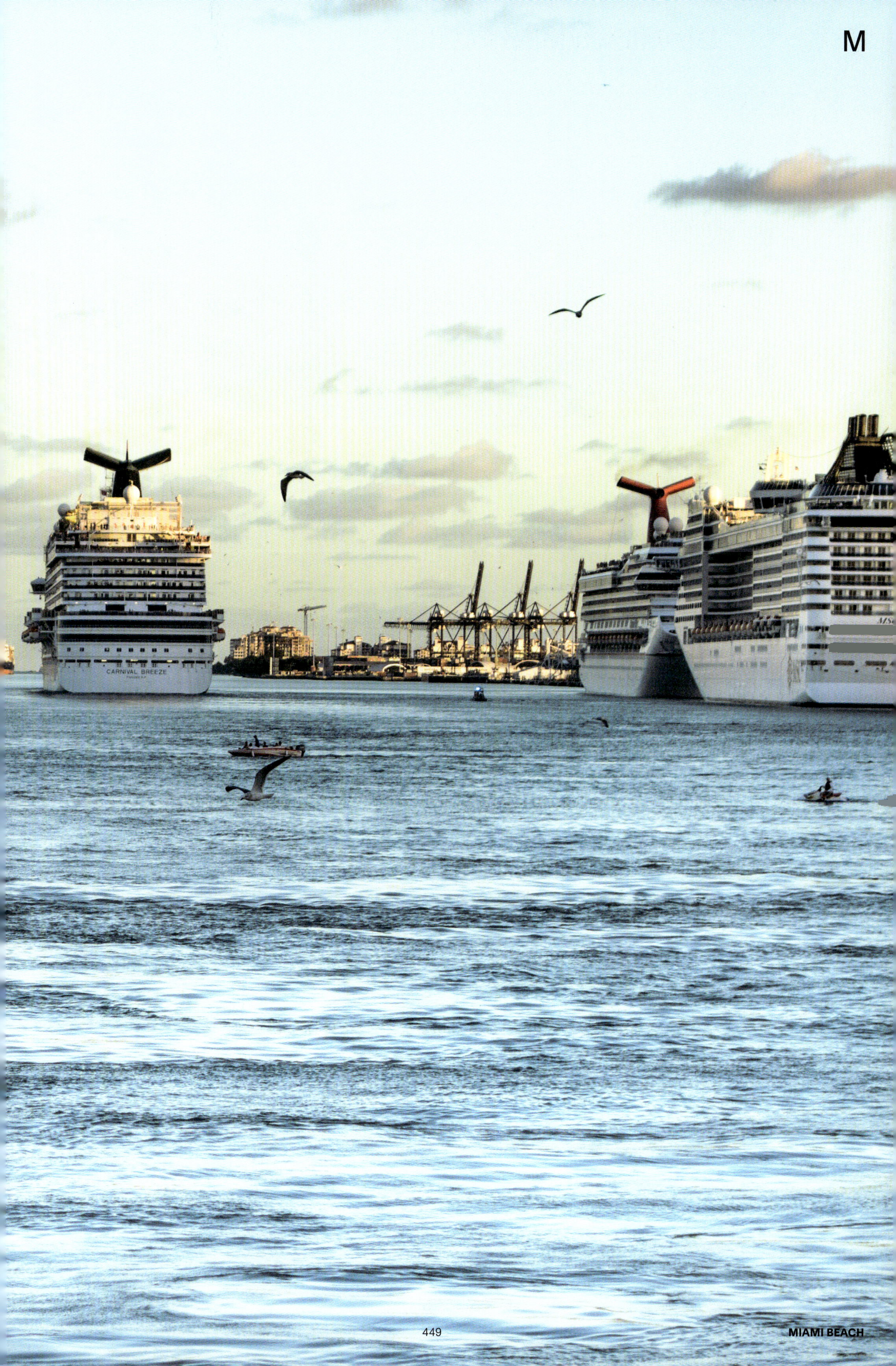
CARNIVAL BREEZE

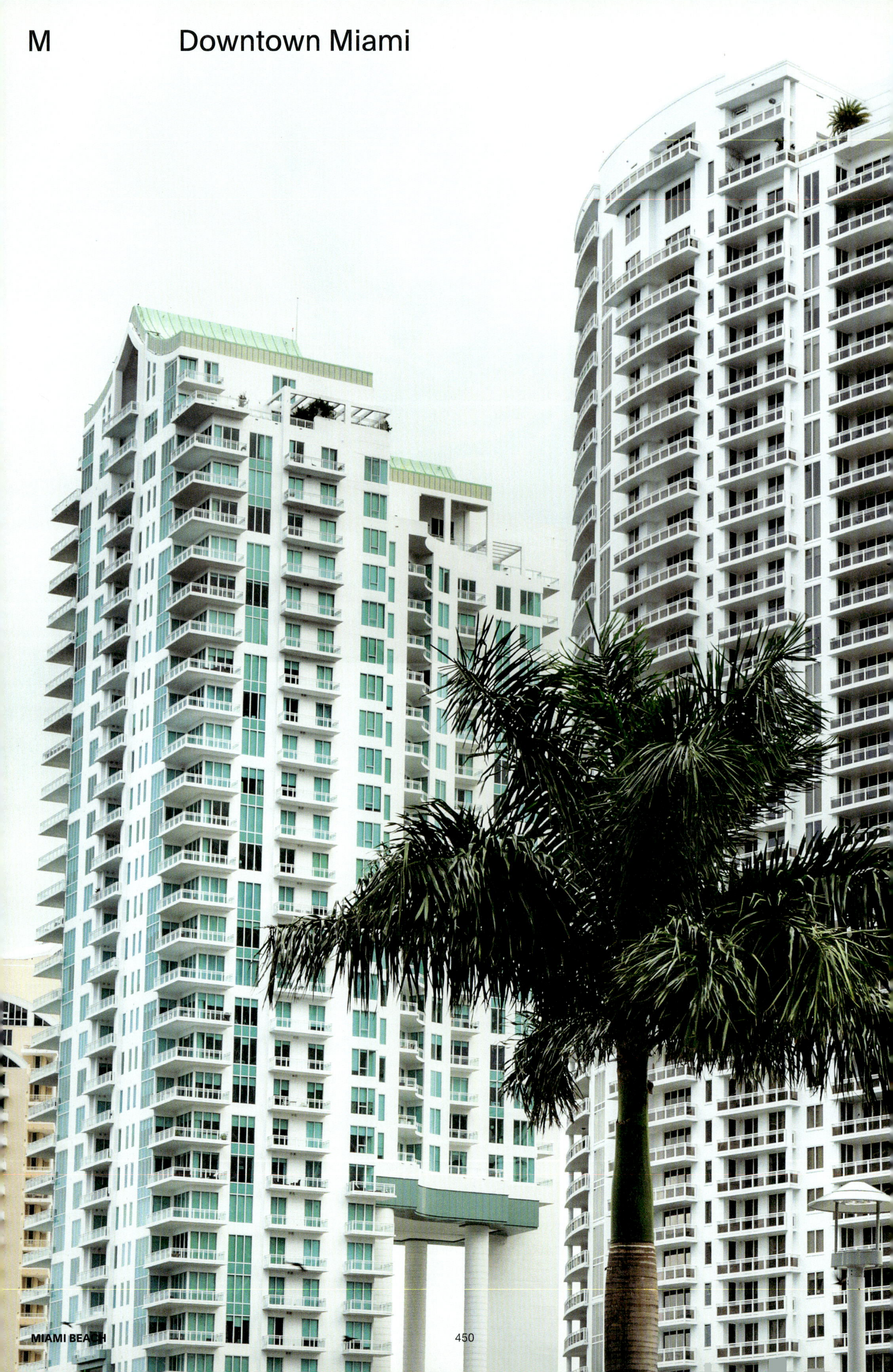

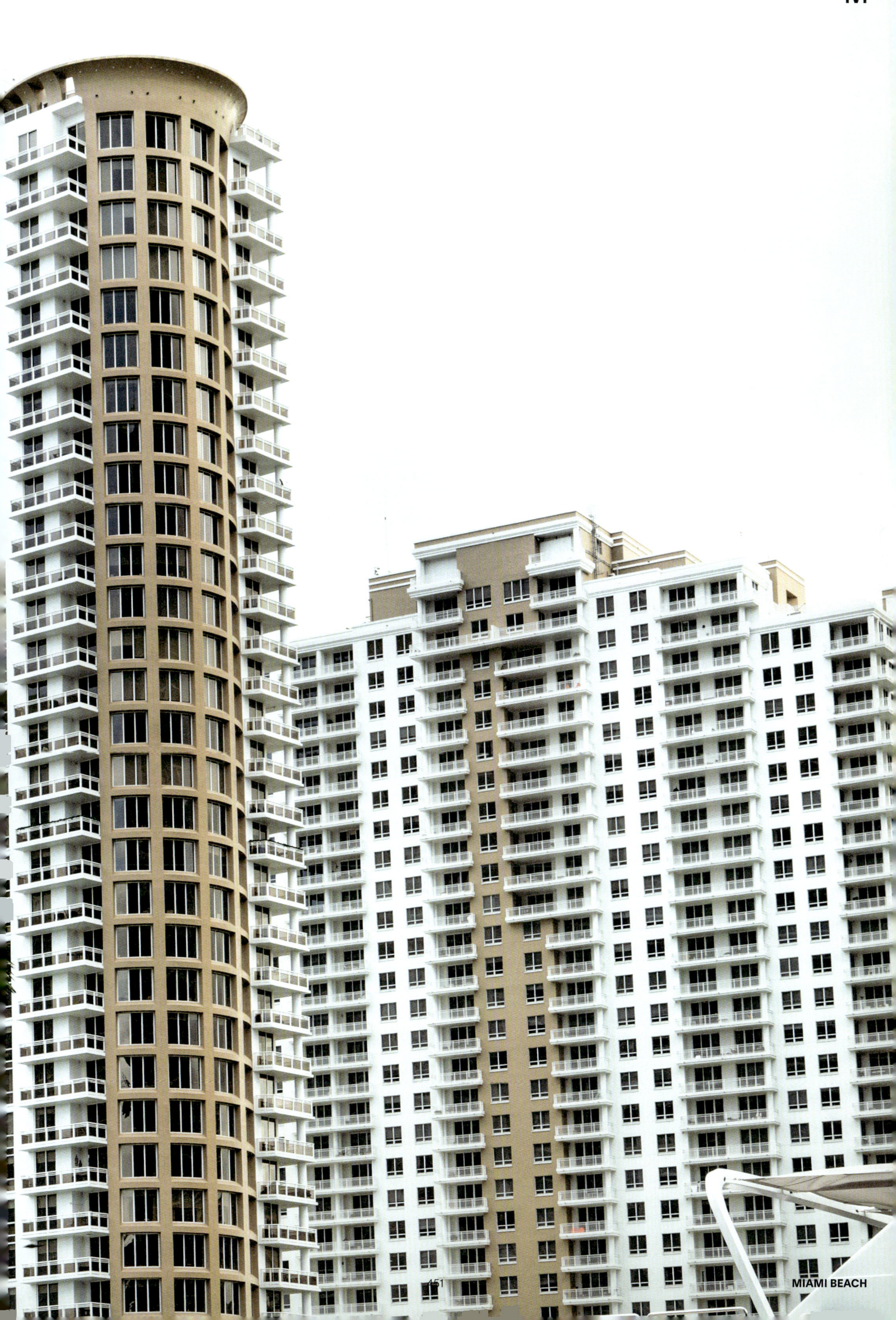

Vizcaya Museum & Gardens

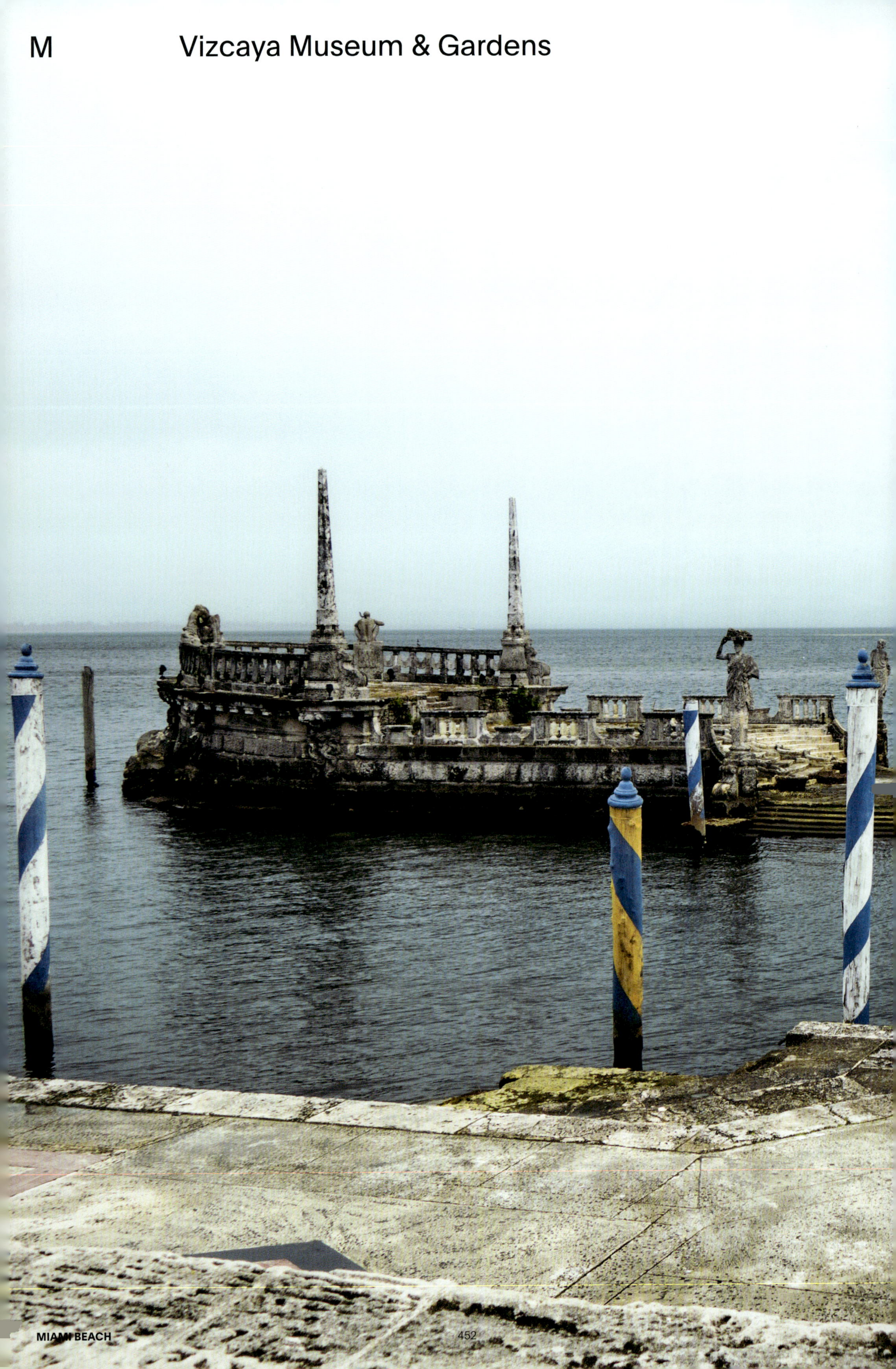

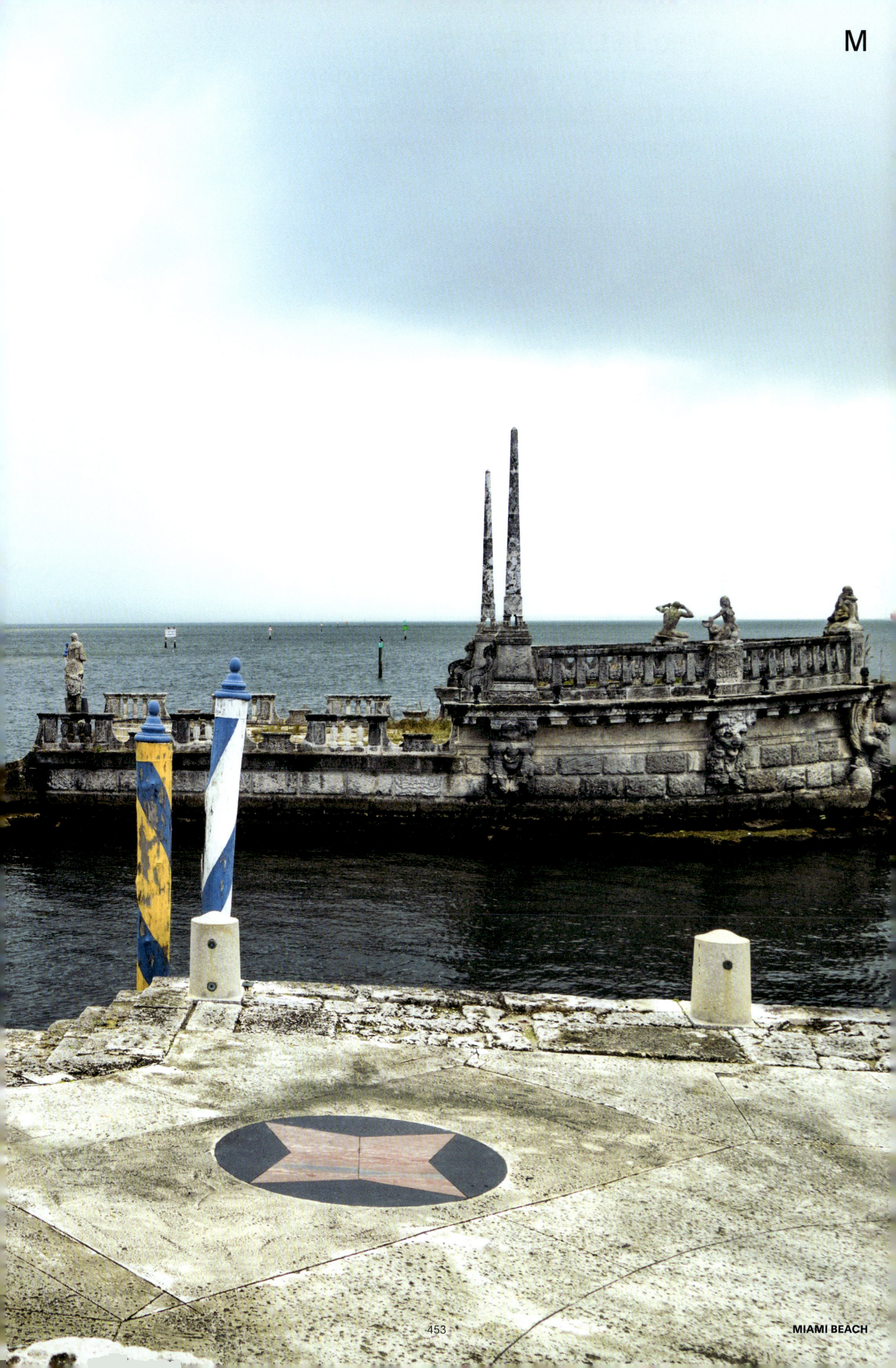

M

Theo Jansen's *Strandbeest* presented by Audemars Piguet and the Peabody Essex Museum Oceanfront, Miami Beach

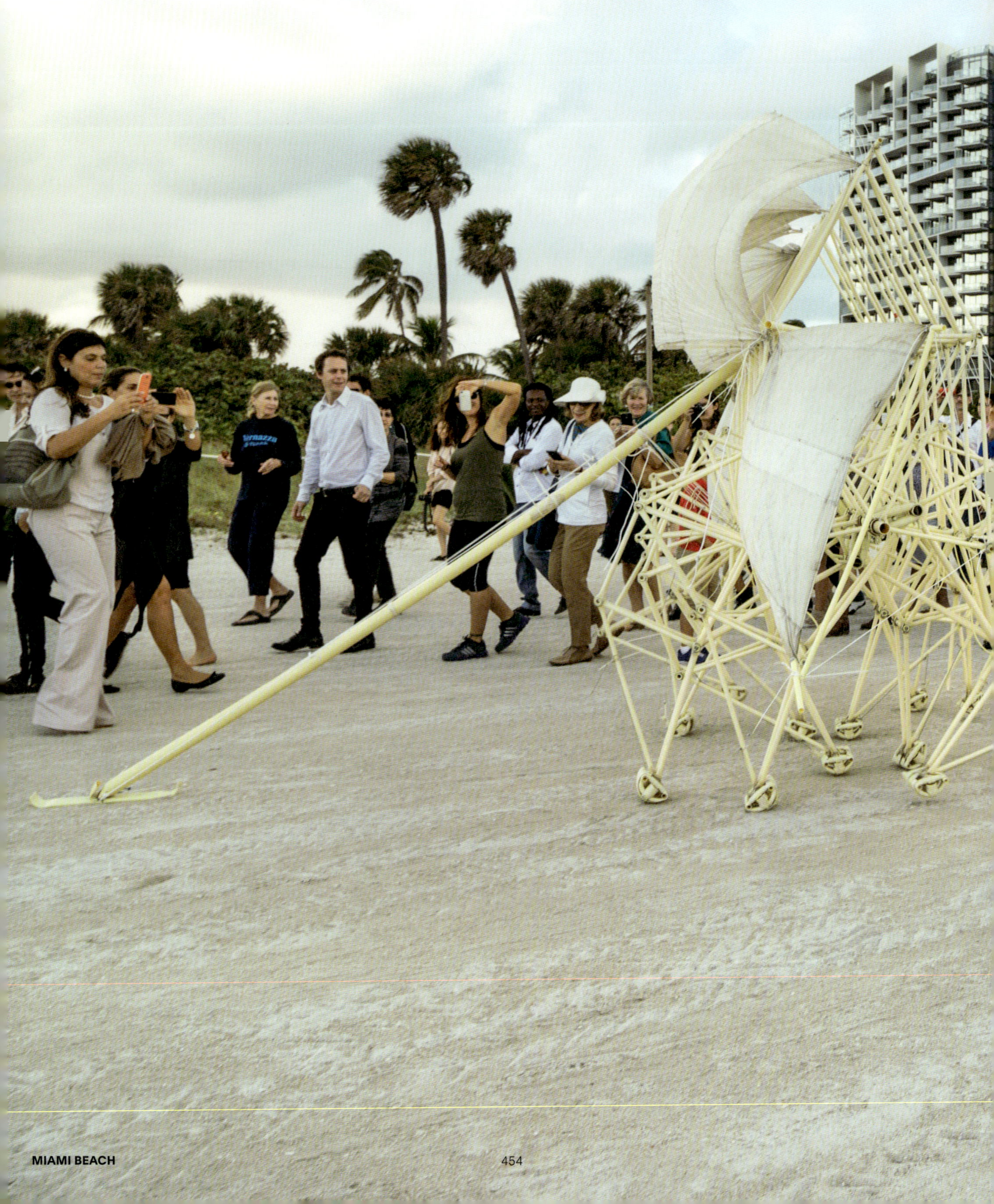

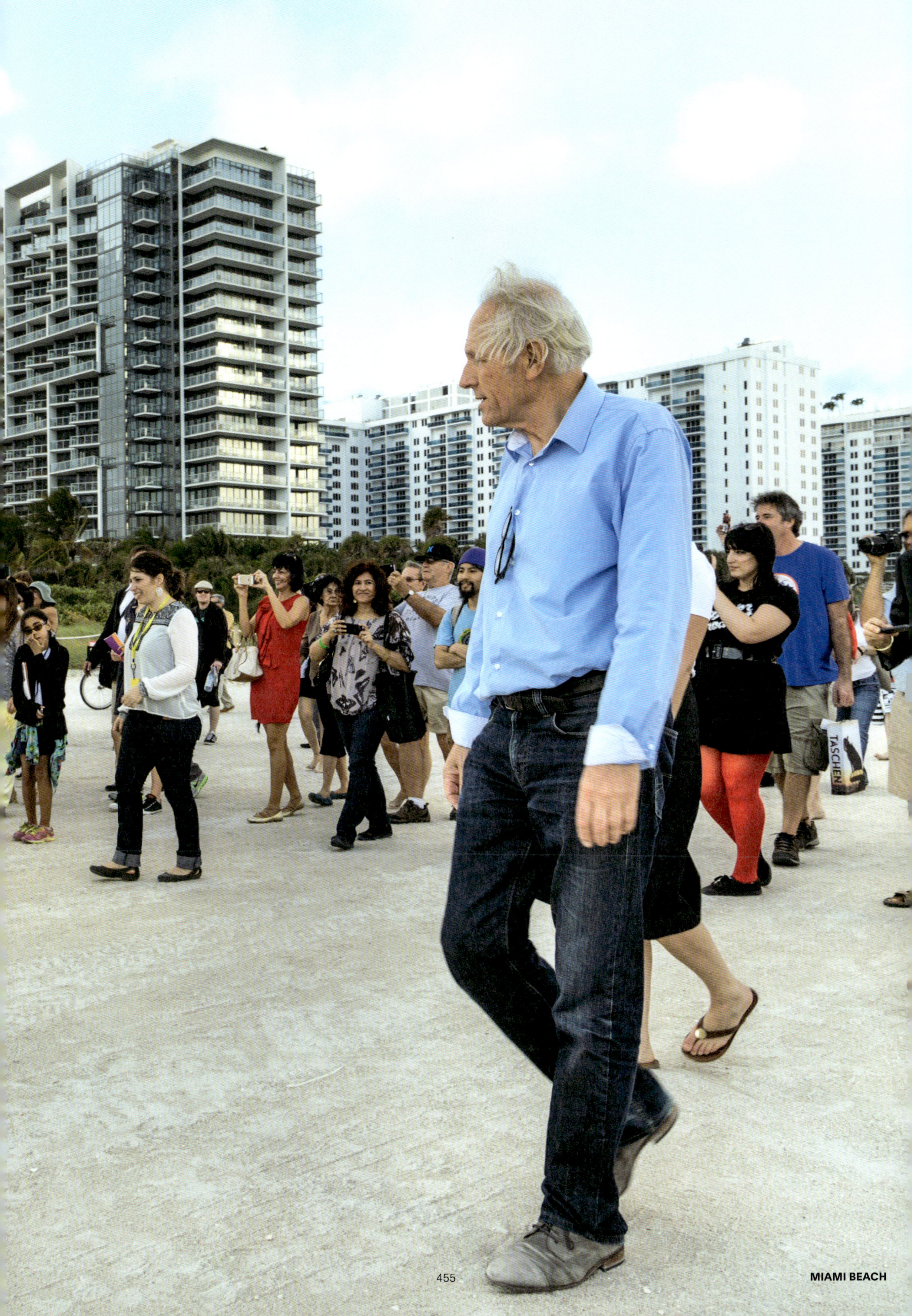
TASCHEN

Edward Tyler Nahem Fine Art

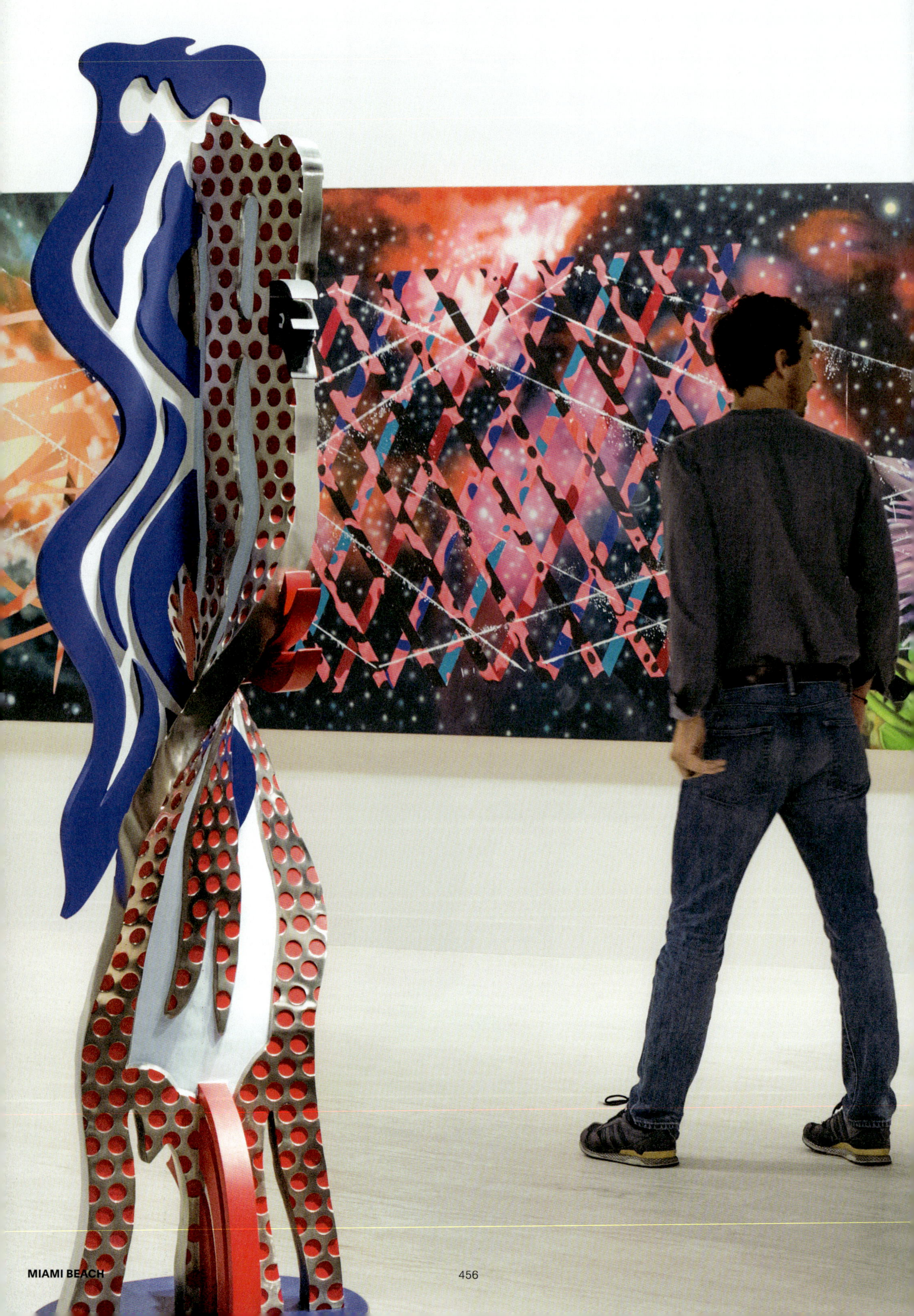

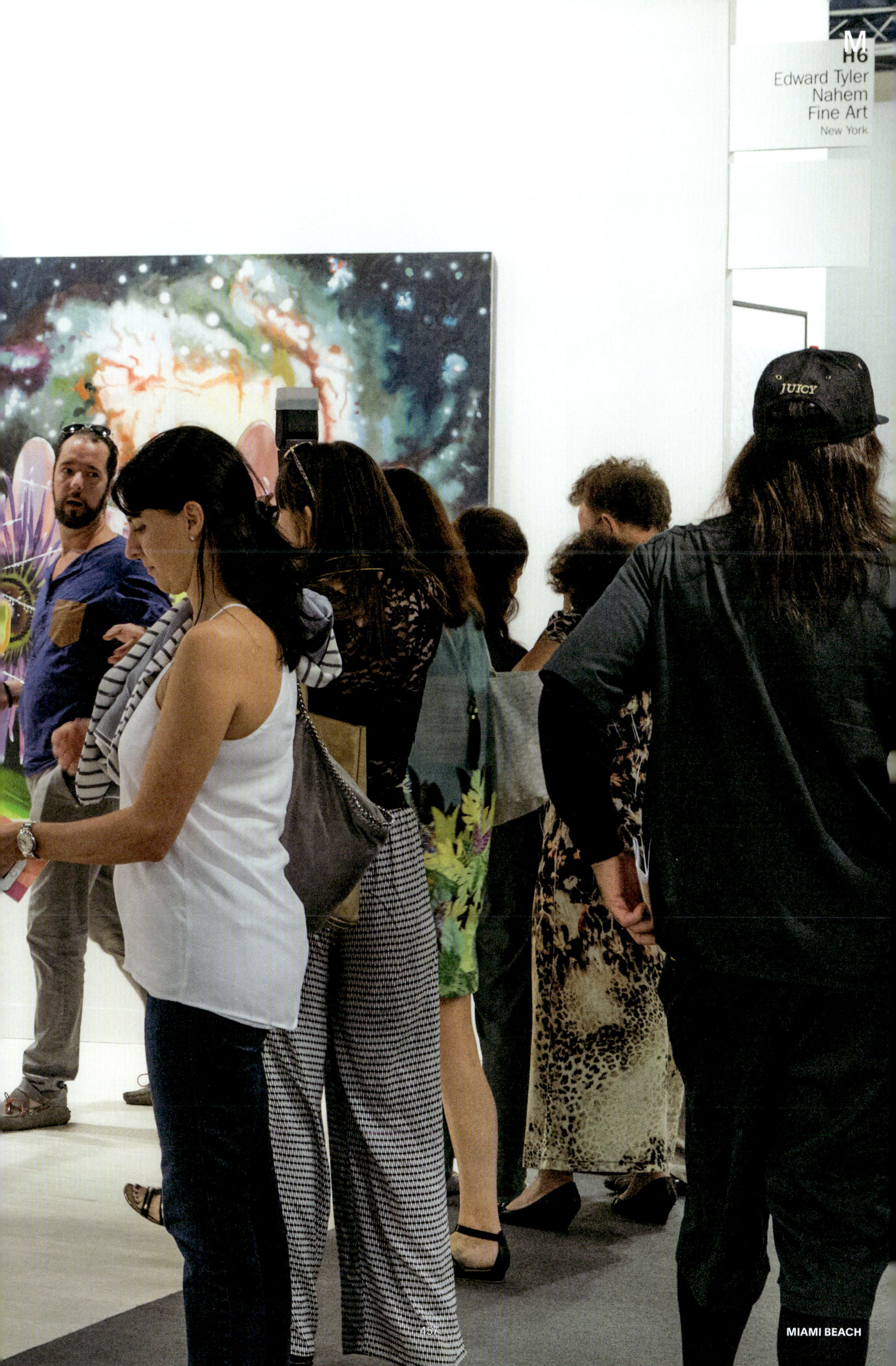
M
H6
Edward Tyler
Nahem
Fine Art
New York
JUICY

Paul Kasmin Gallery

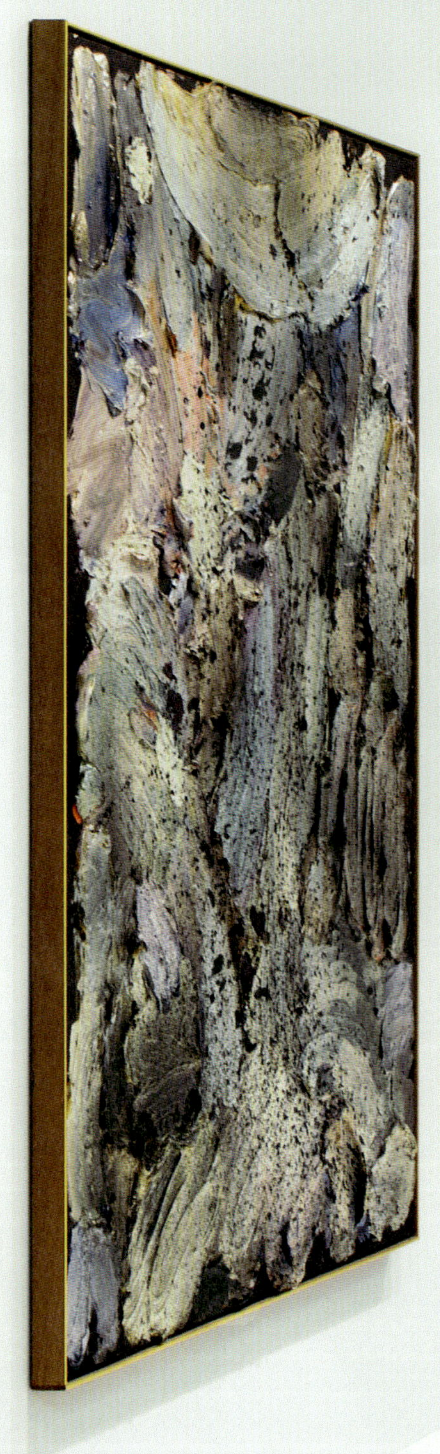

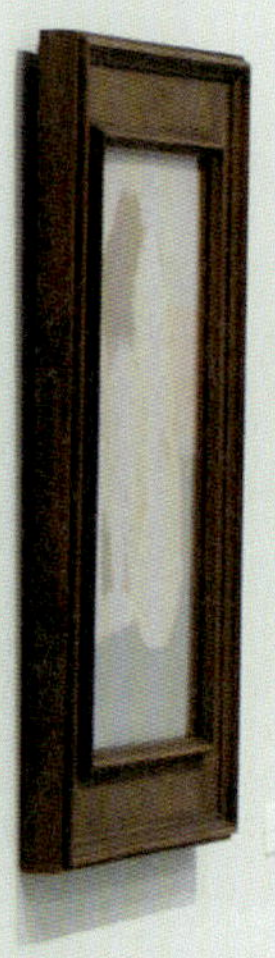

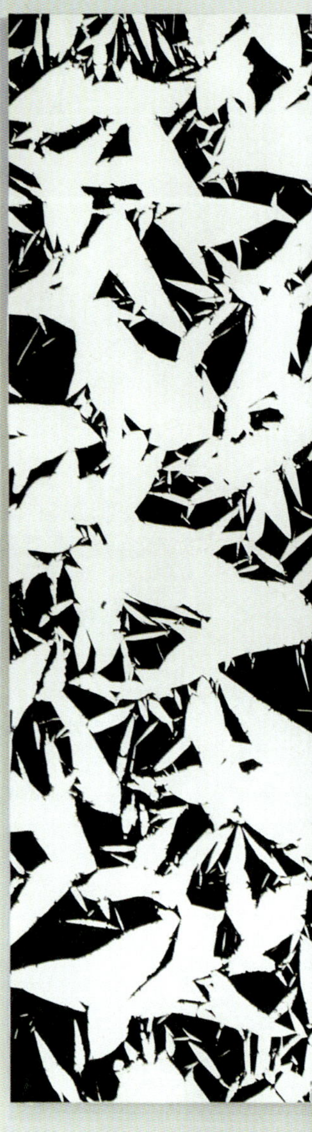

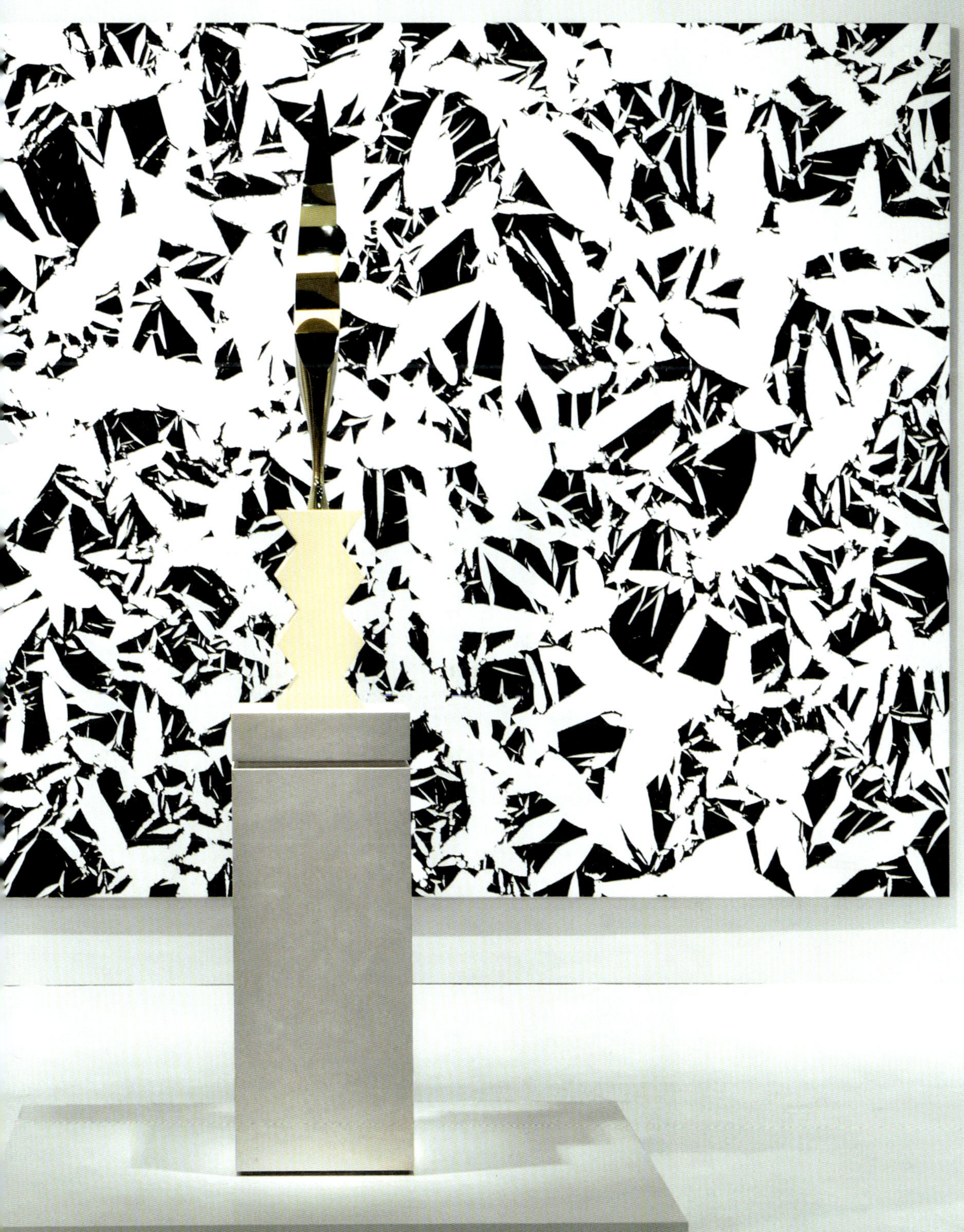

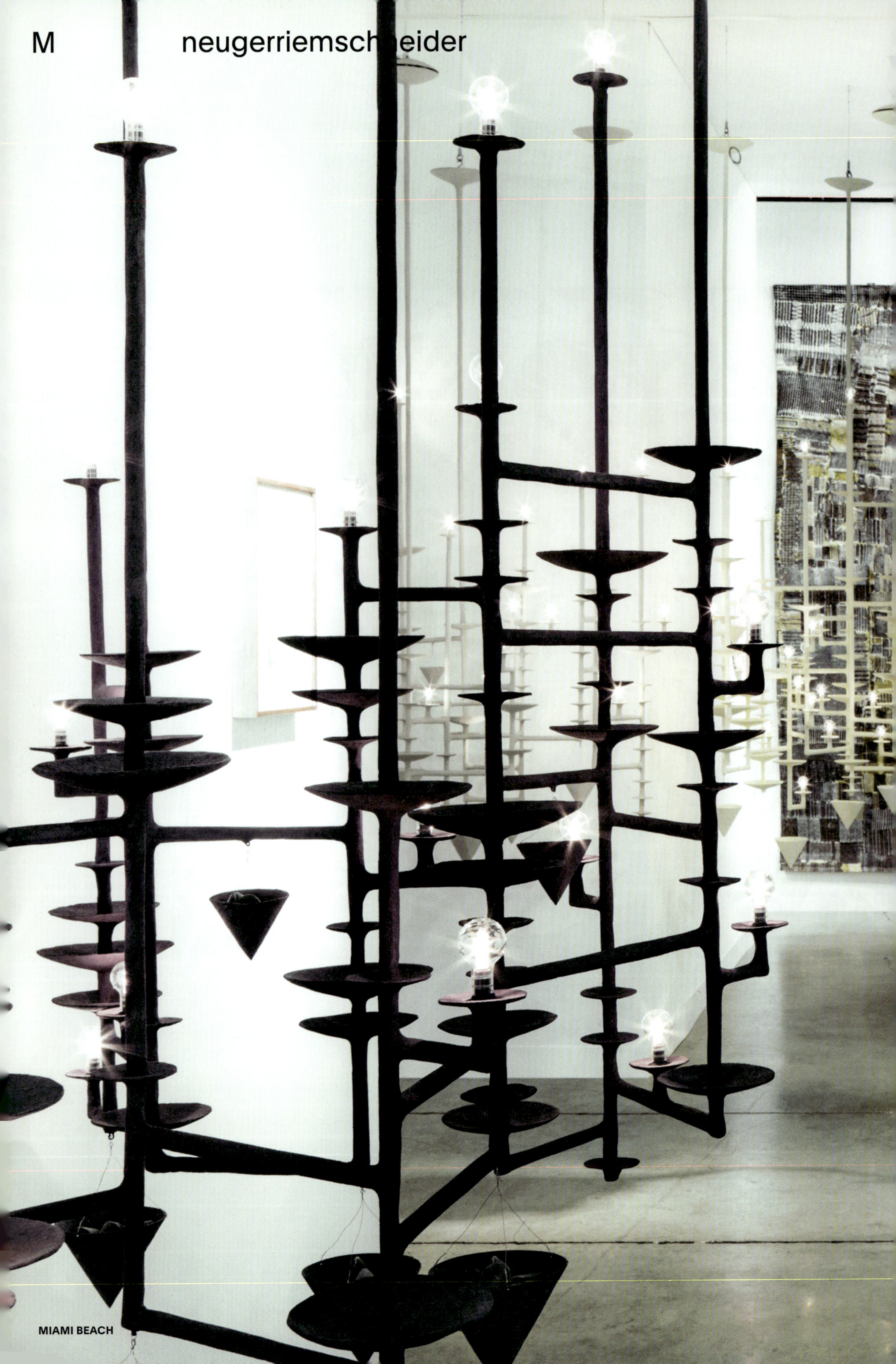
M
neugerriemschneider
MIAMI BEACH

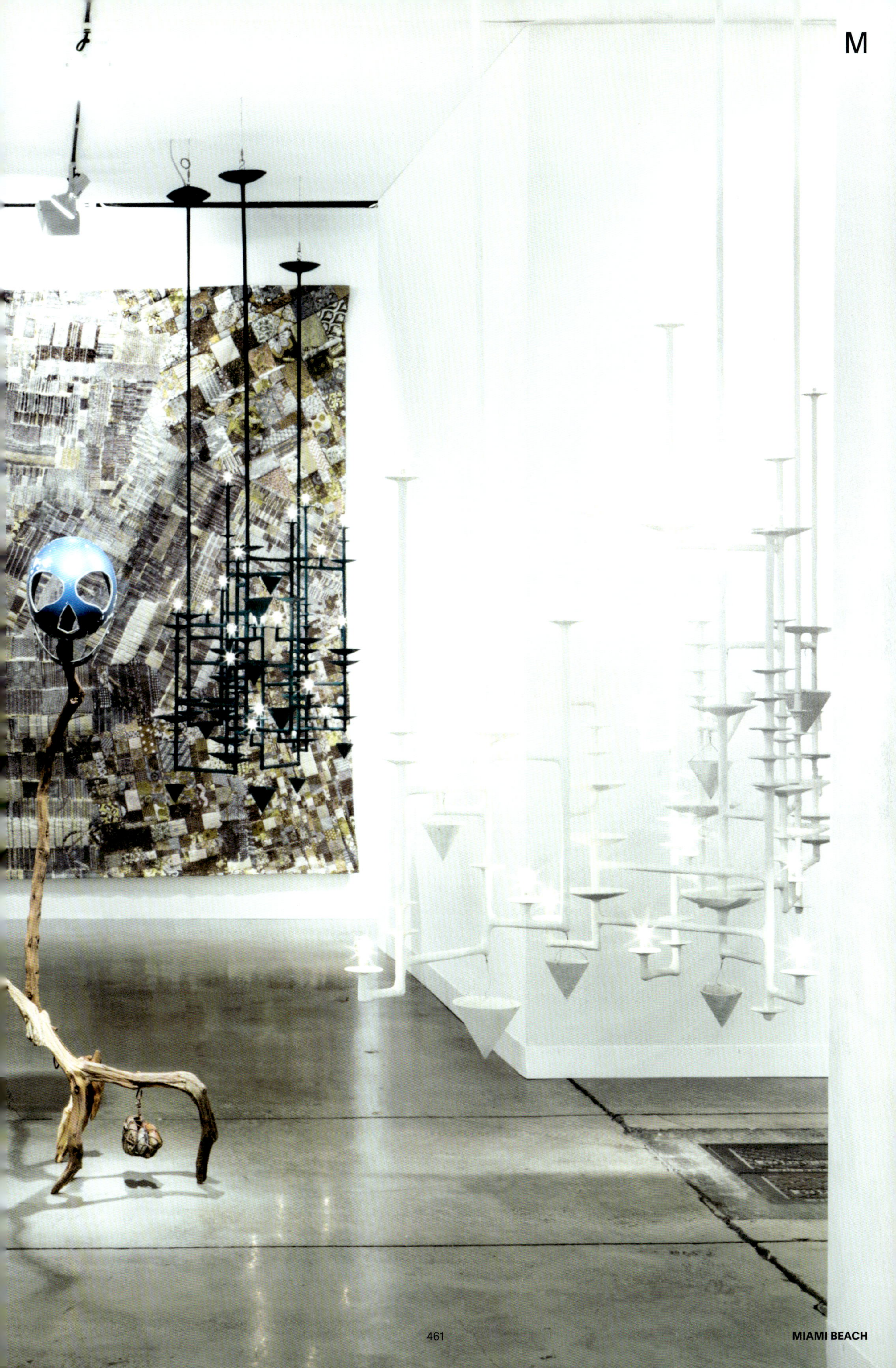

M

Paul Stolper Gallery
Damien Hirst

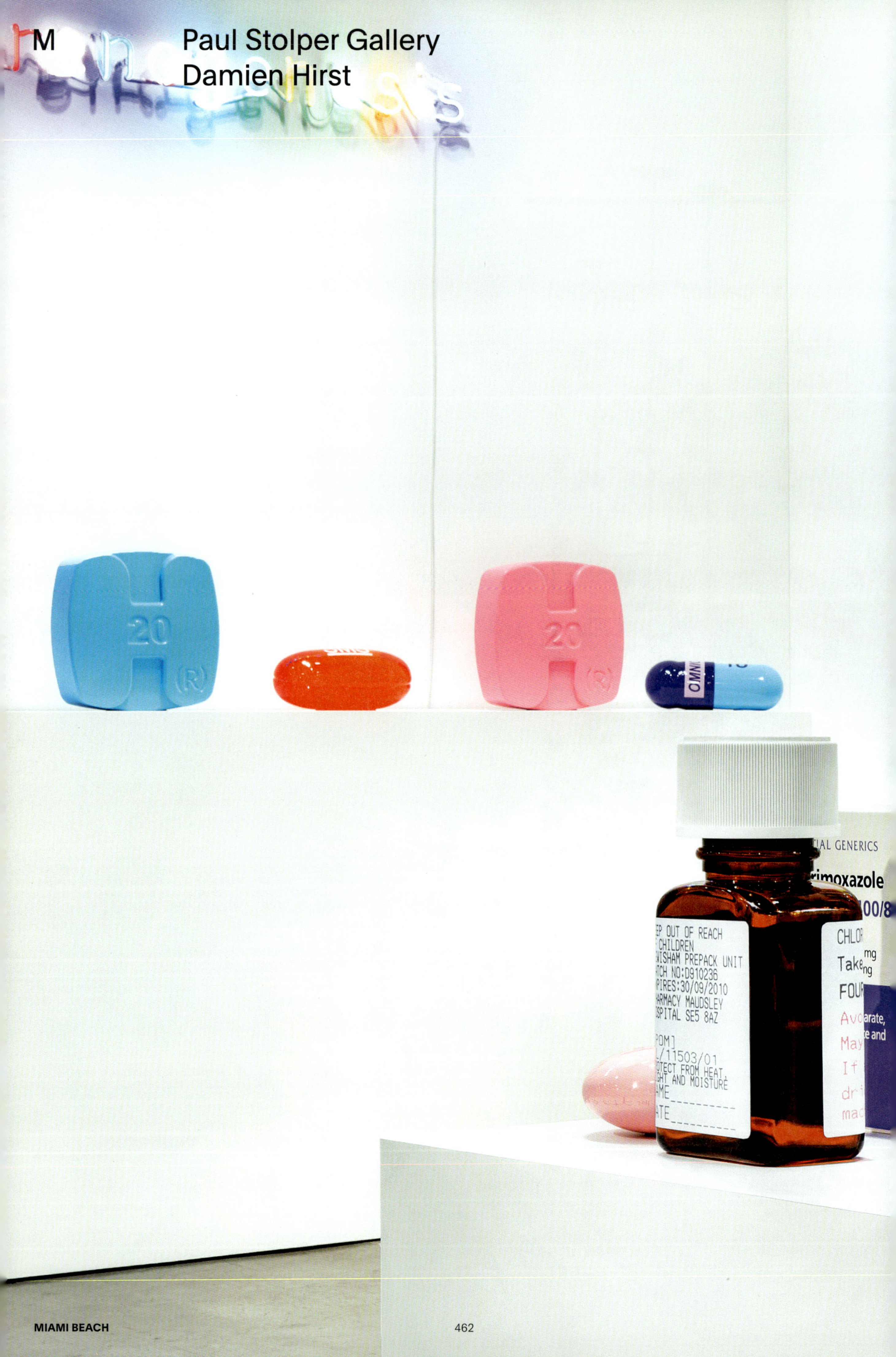

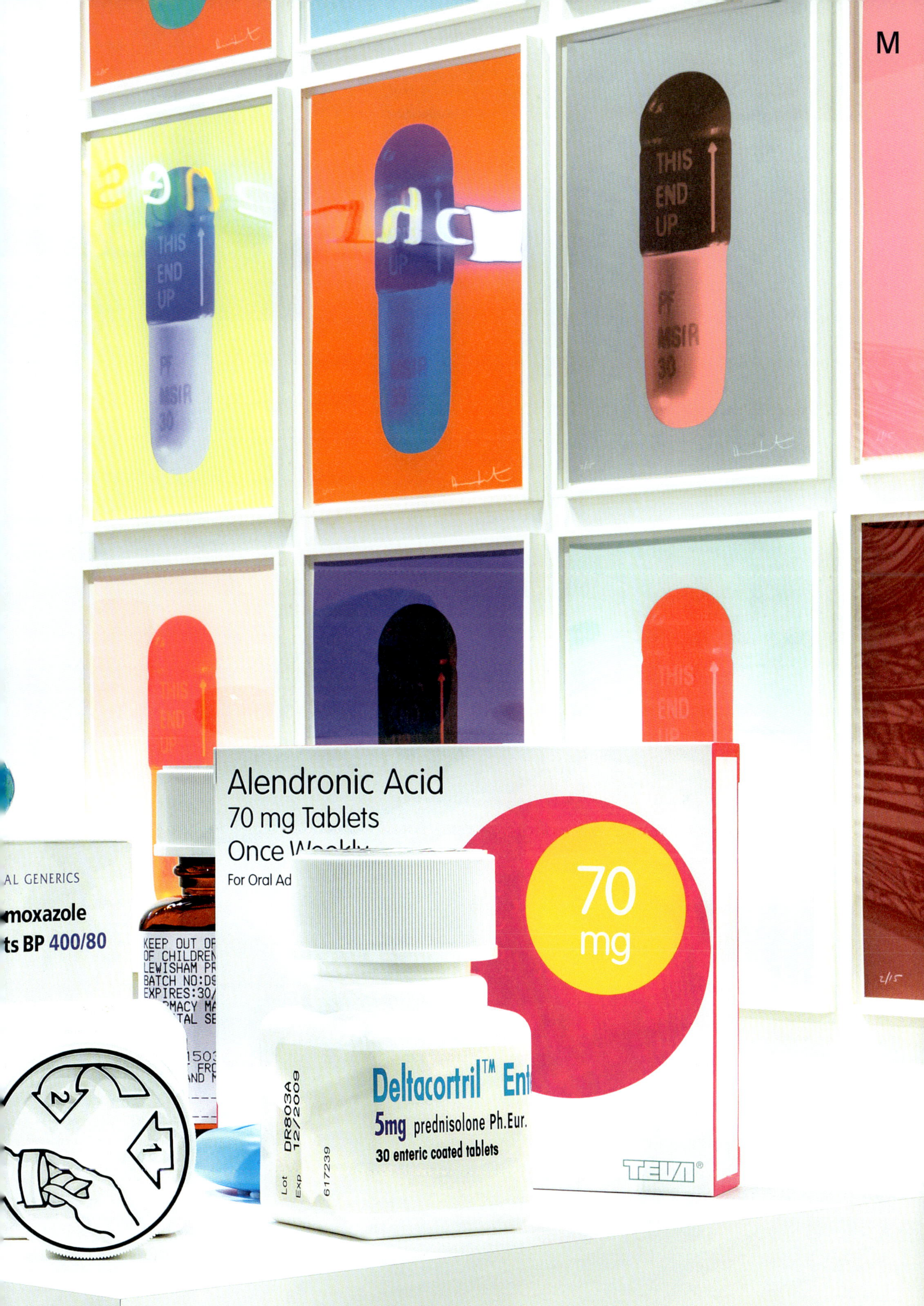
THIS END UP
Alendronic Acid
70 mg Tablets
For Oral Ad
70 mg
AL GENERICS
moxazole
ts BP 400/80
KEEP OUT OF
OF CHILDREN
LEWISHAM PR
BATCH NO:D9
Deltacortril™ Ent
5mg prednisolone Ph.Eur.
30 enteric coated tablets
Lot DR803A
Exp 12/2009
617239
TEVA

M

Galerie Hans Mayer
Sol LeWitt

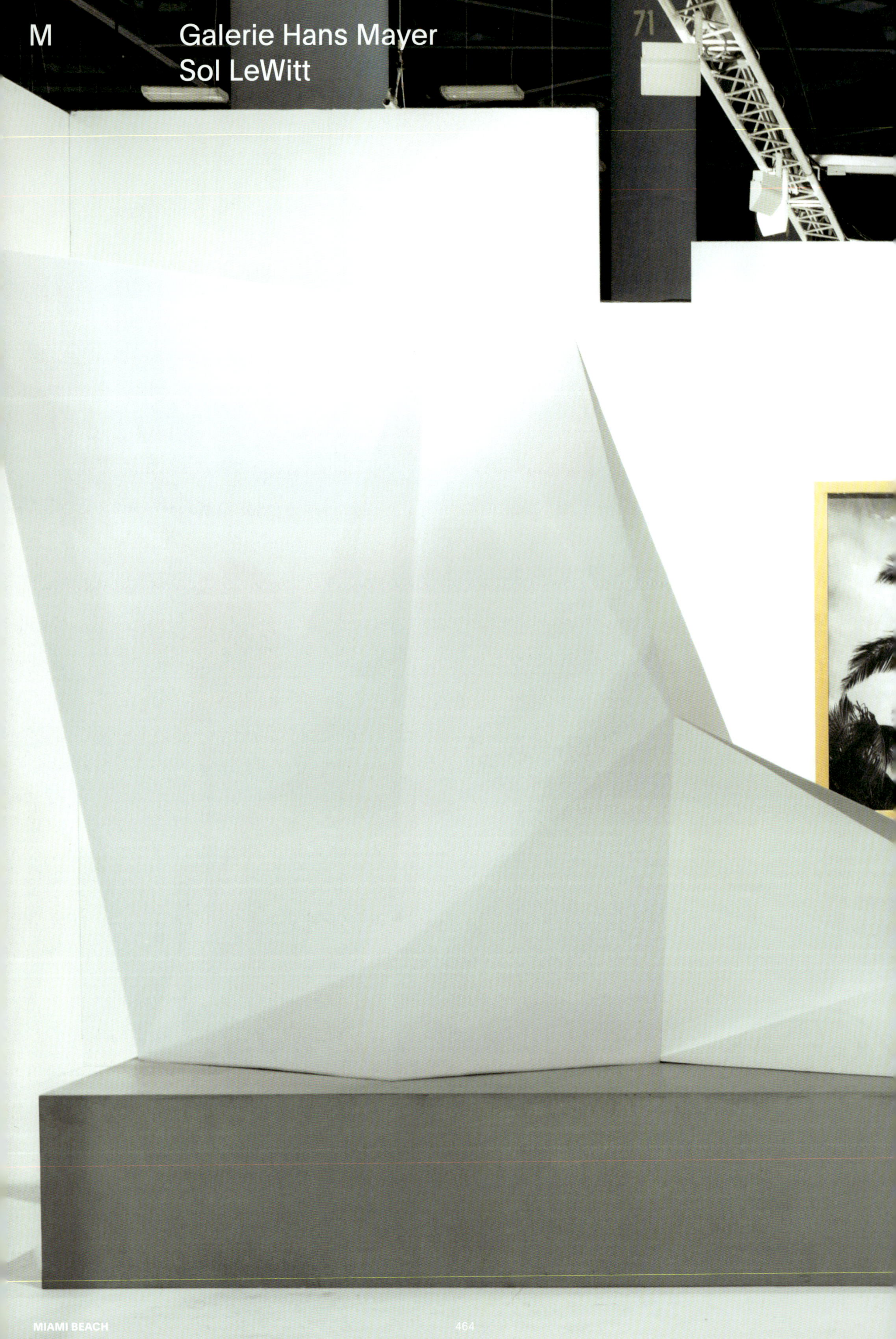

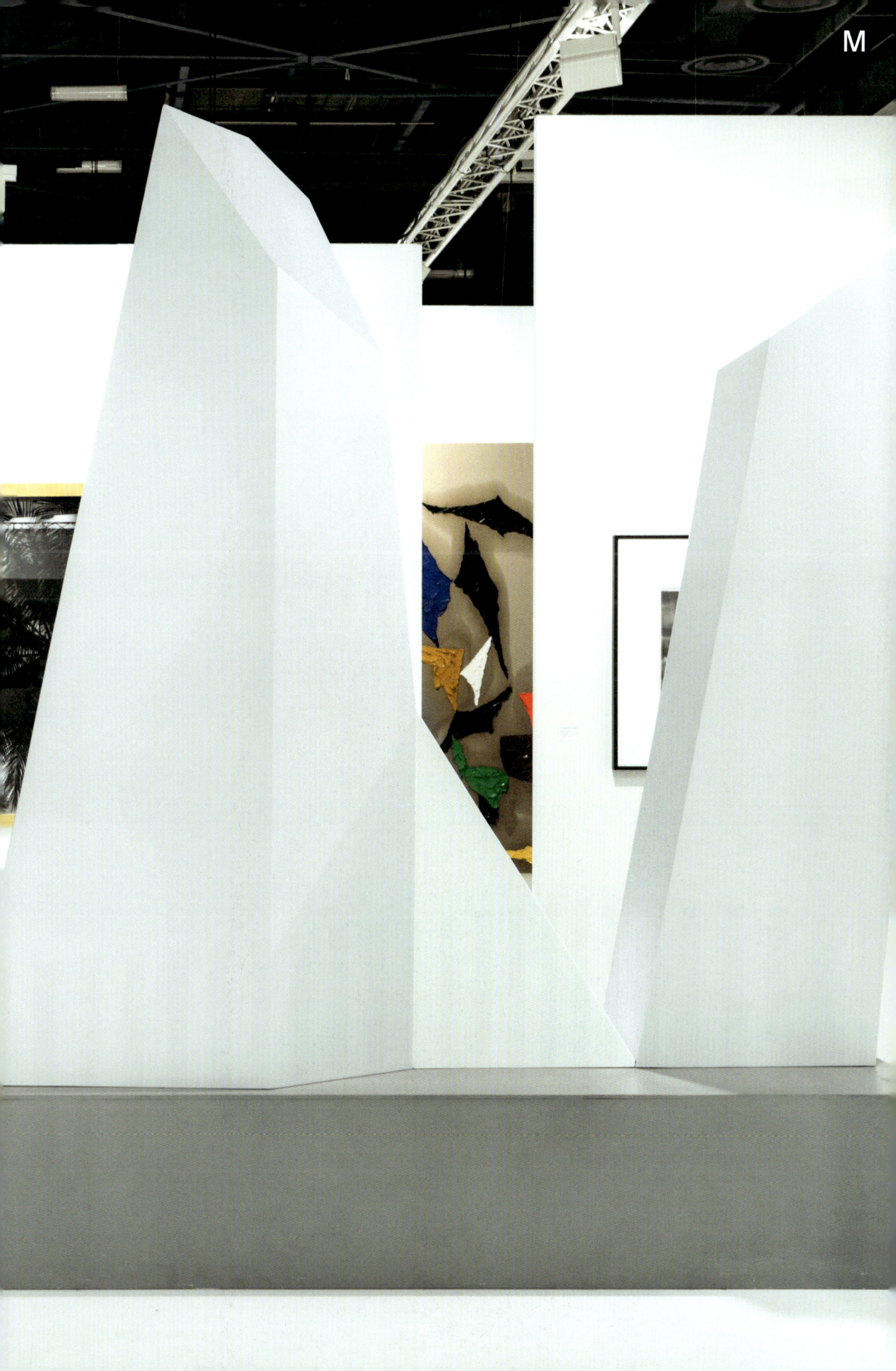

M

Bortolami
Daniel Buren
Jutta Koether

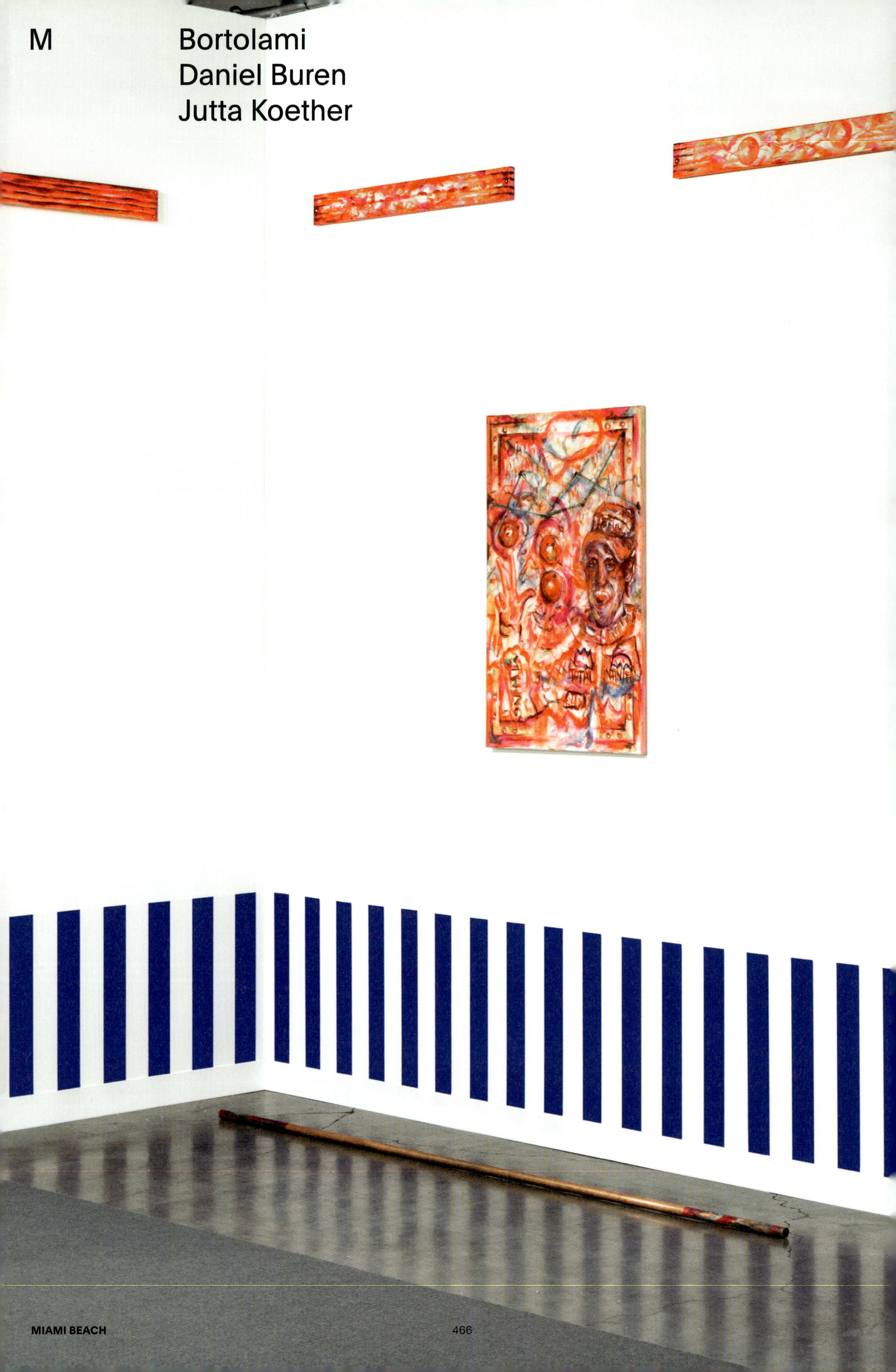

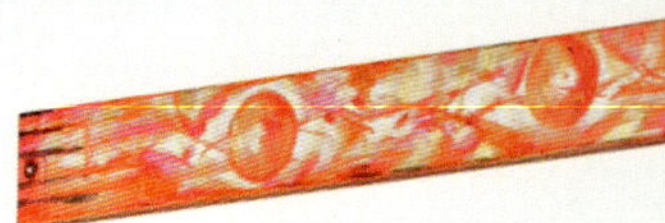

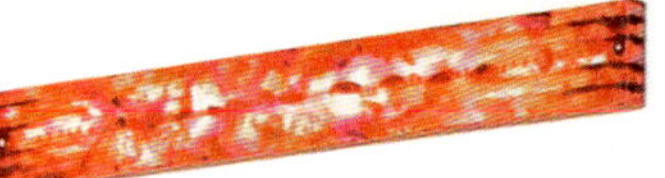

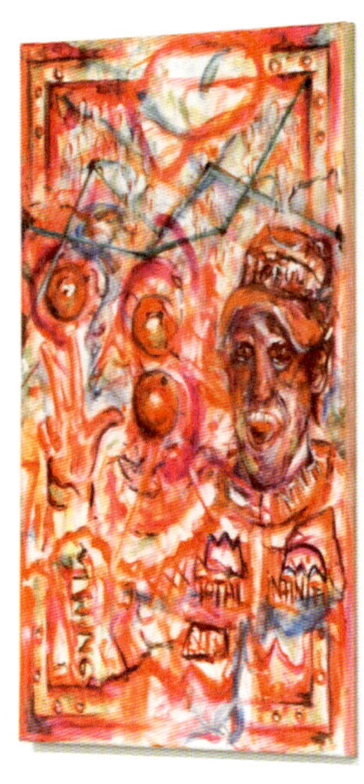

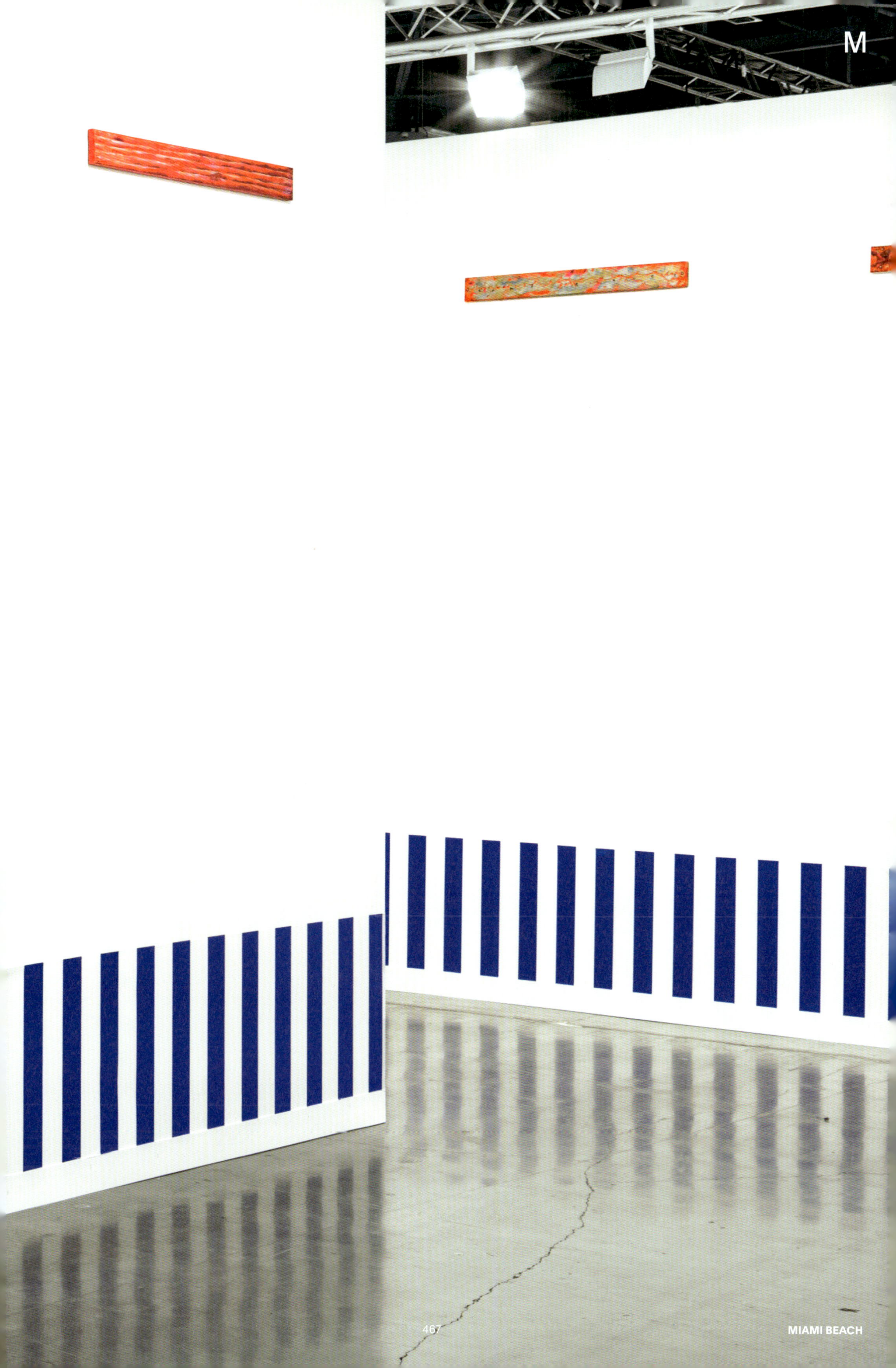

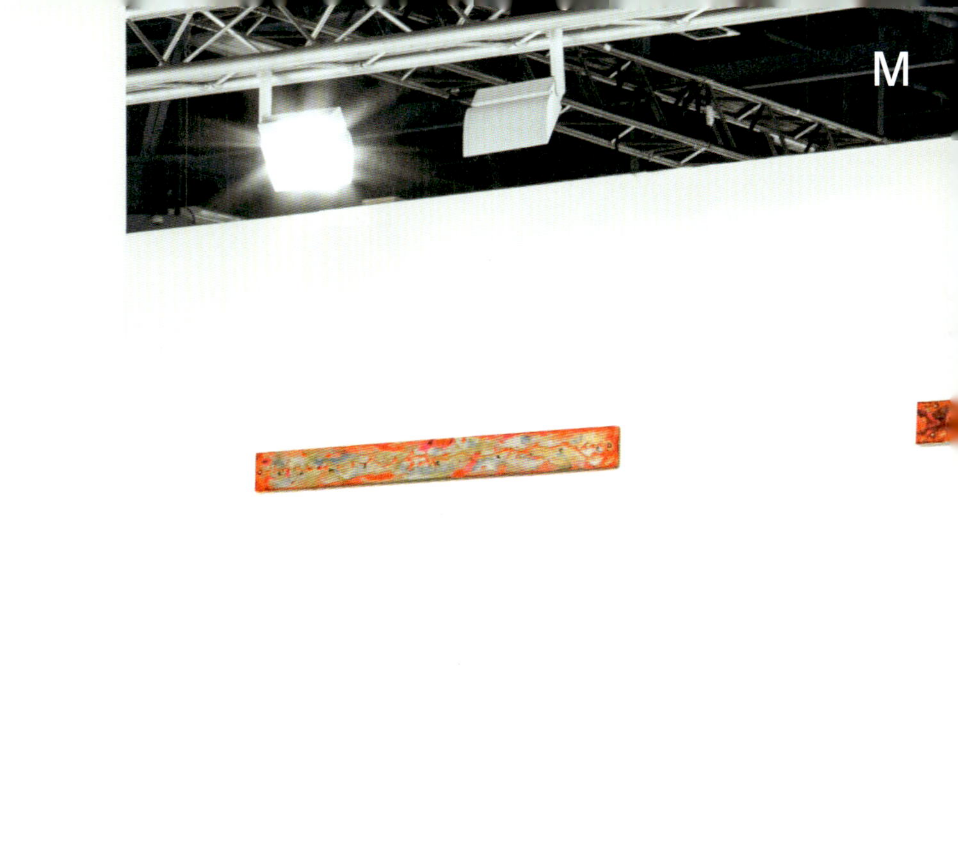

Sies + Höke
Claudia Wieser

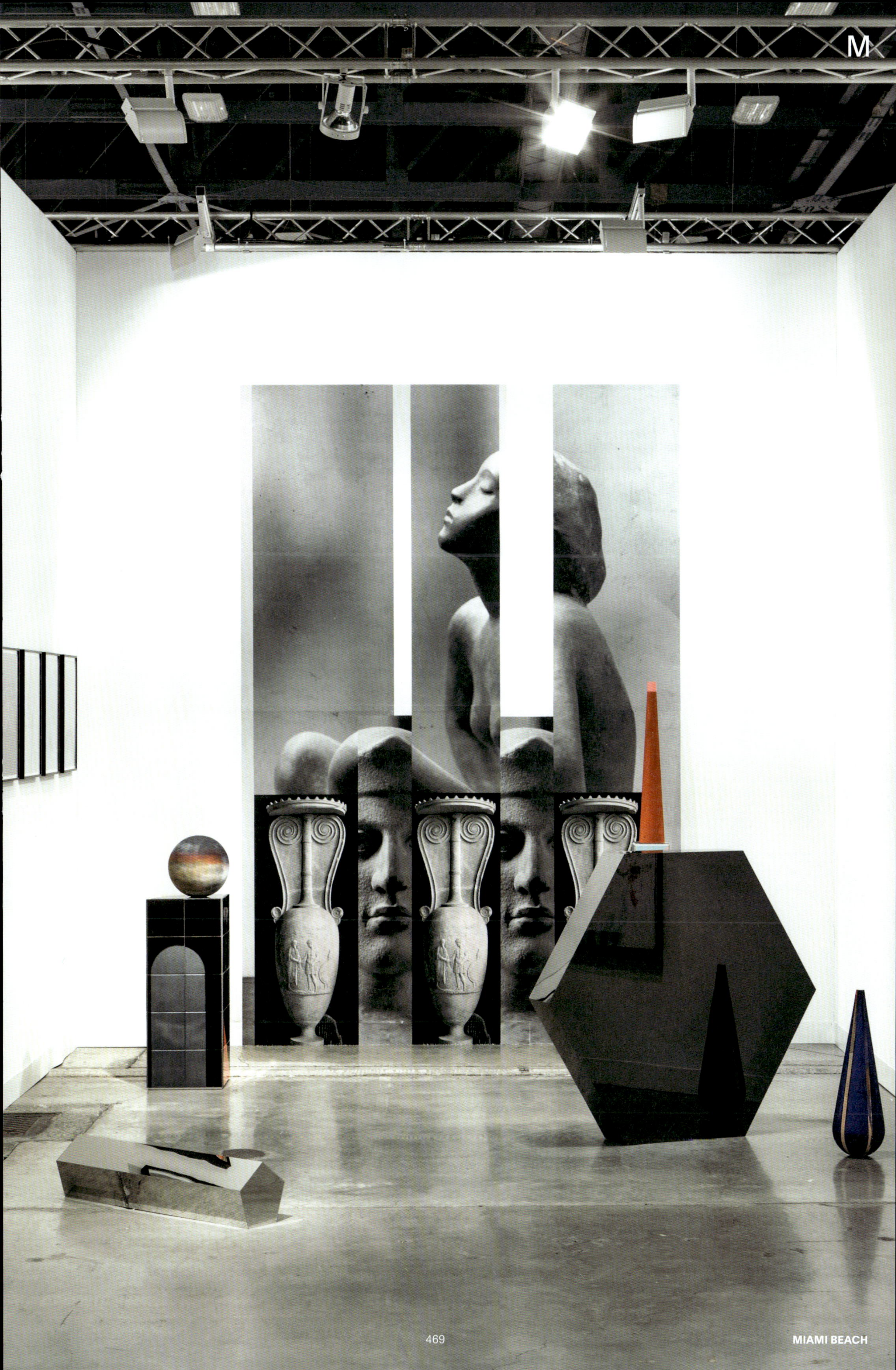

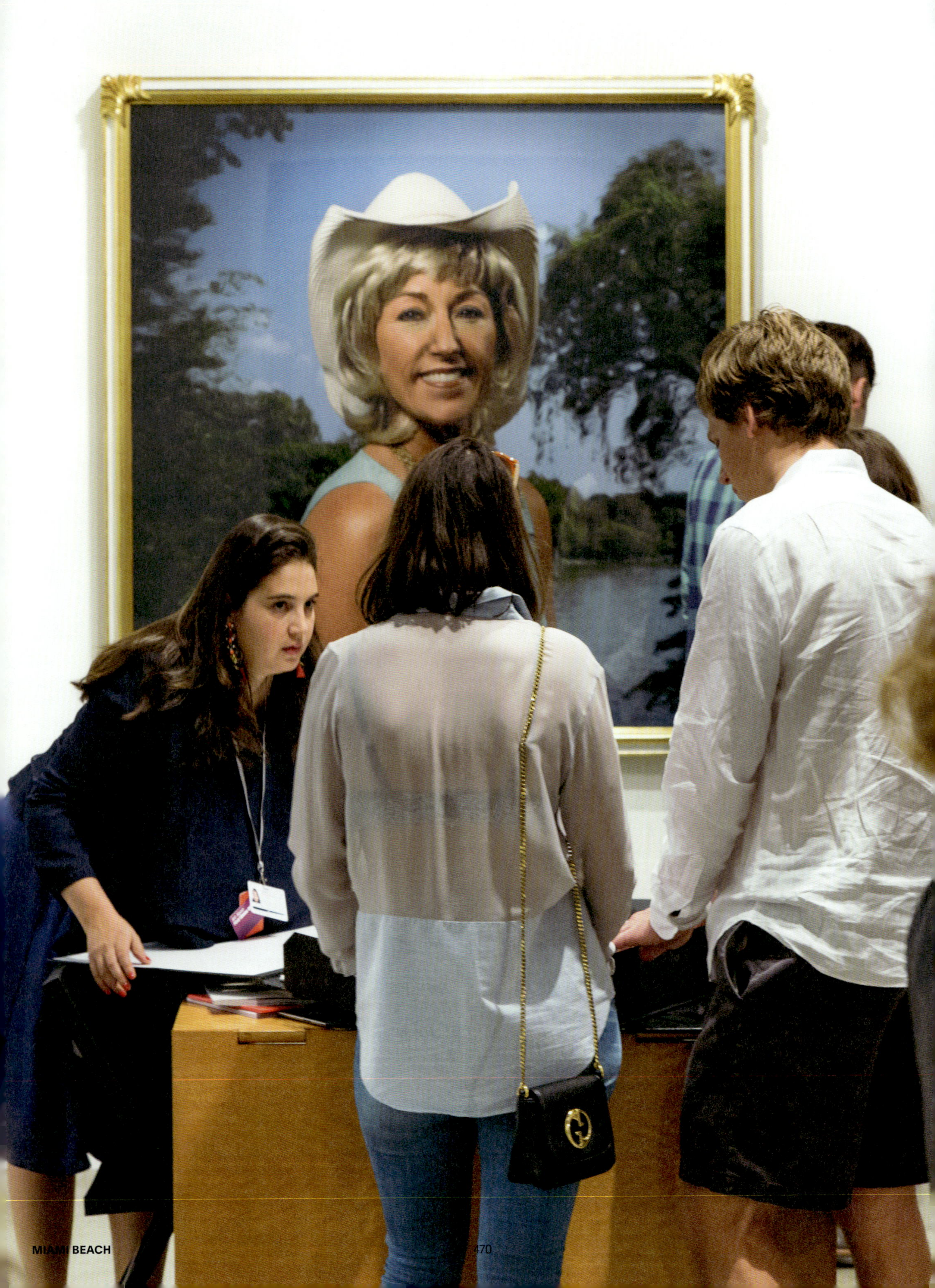

Metro Pictures
Cindy Sherman

Sadie Coles HQ

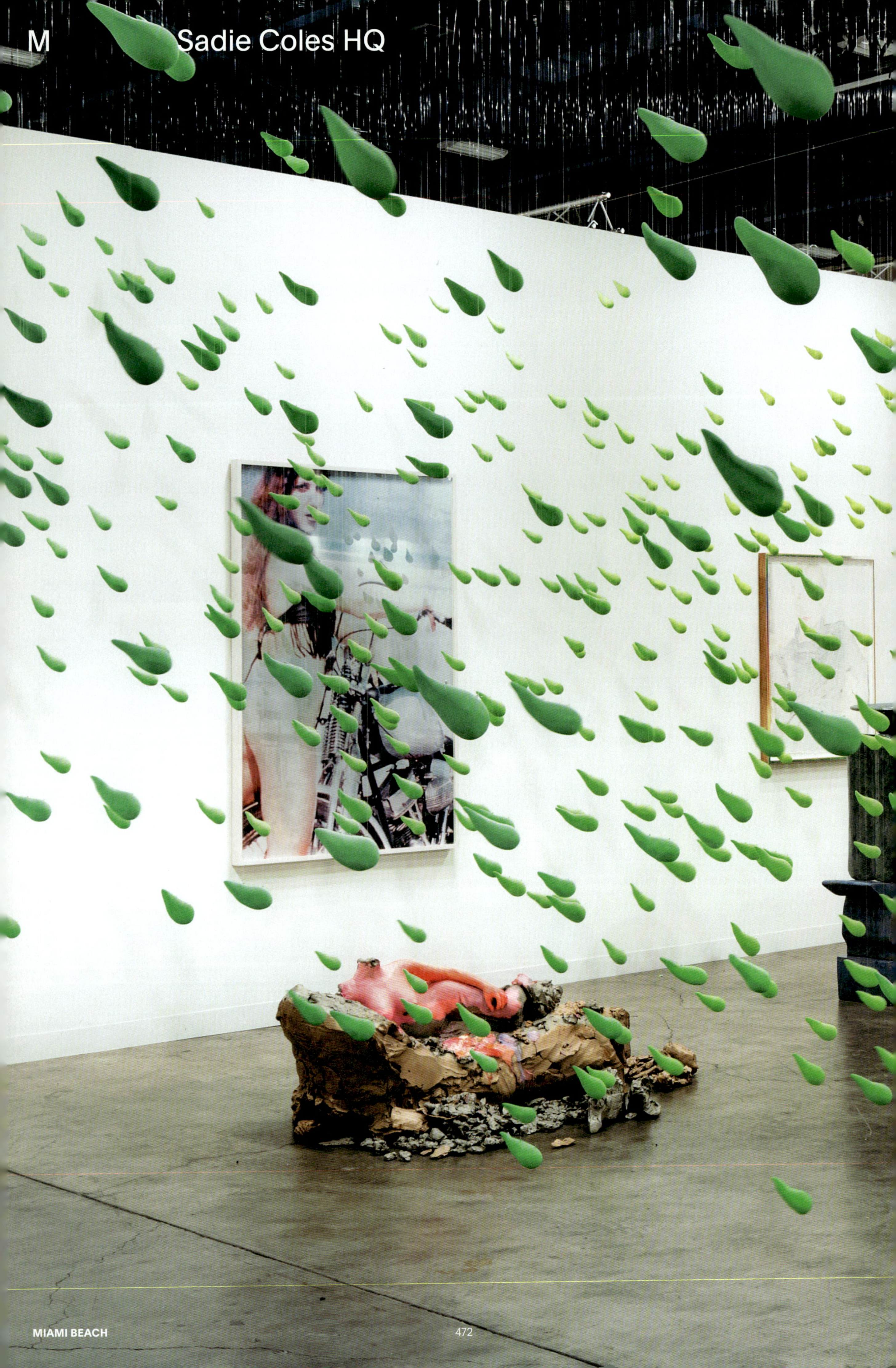

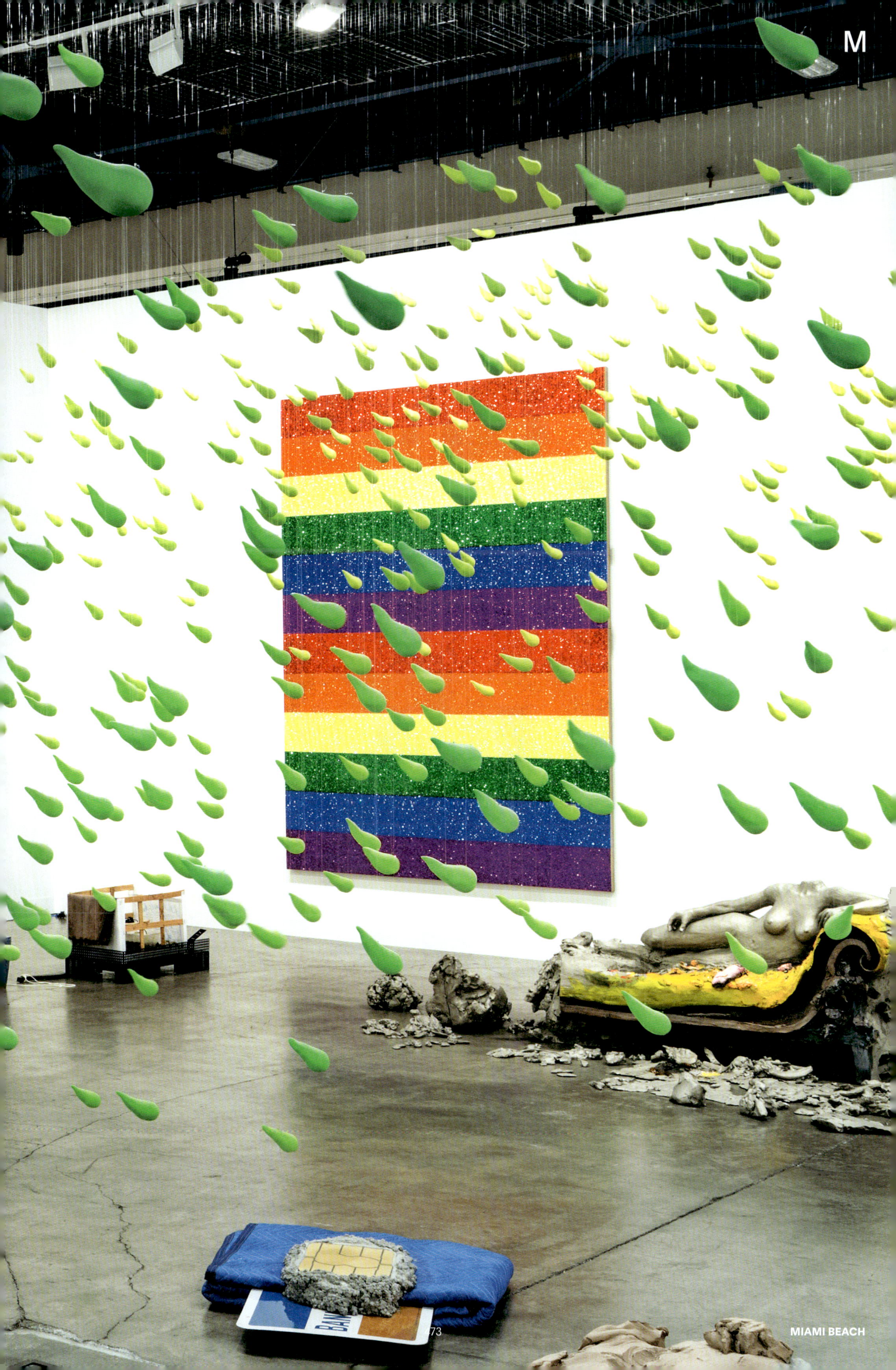

MEEM
4
MIAM
I

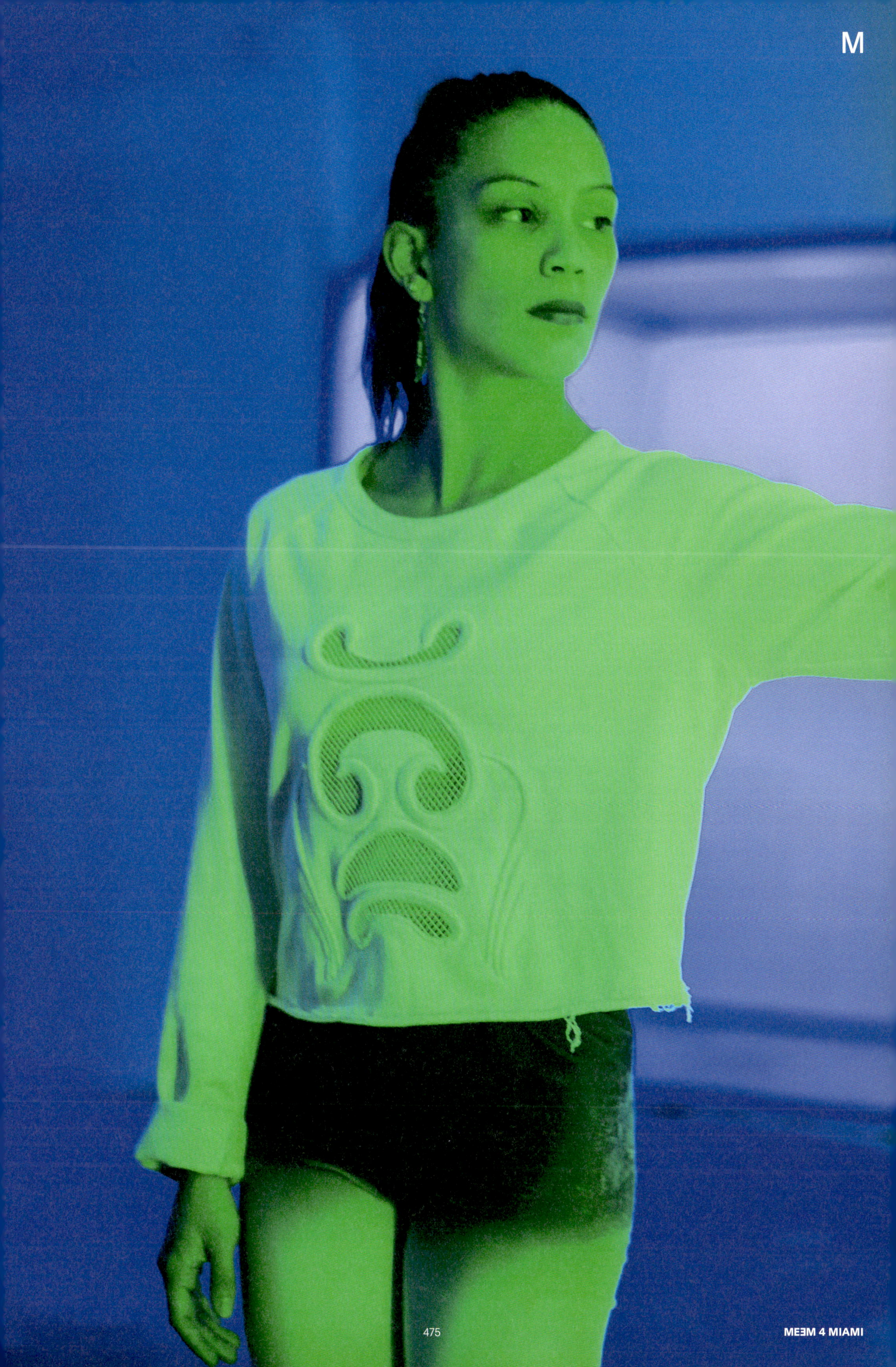

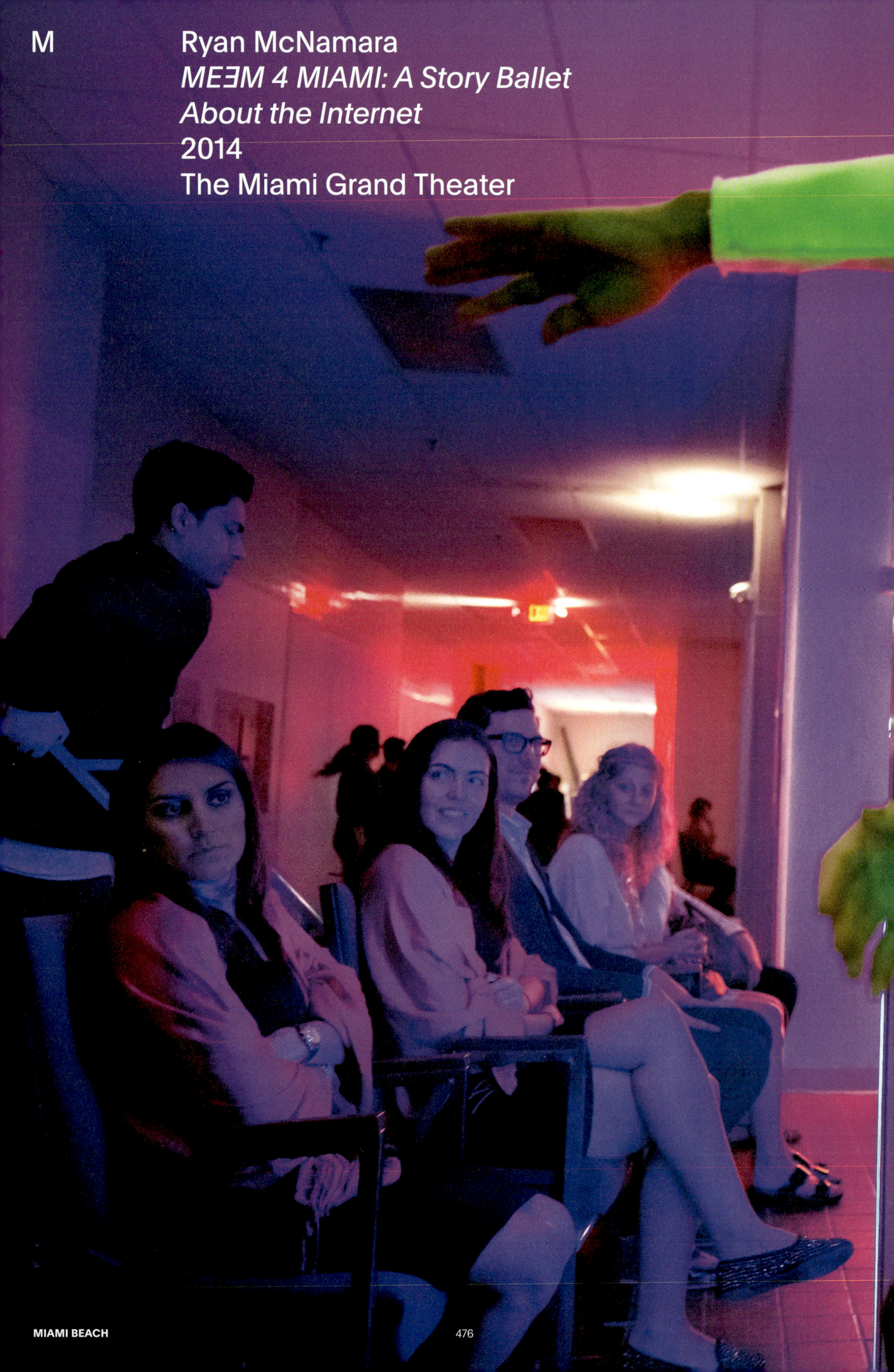

Ryan McNamara
MEƎM 4 MIAMI: A Story Ballet About the Internet
2014
The Miami Grand Theater

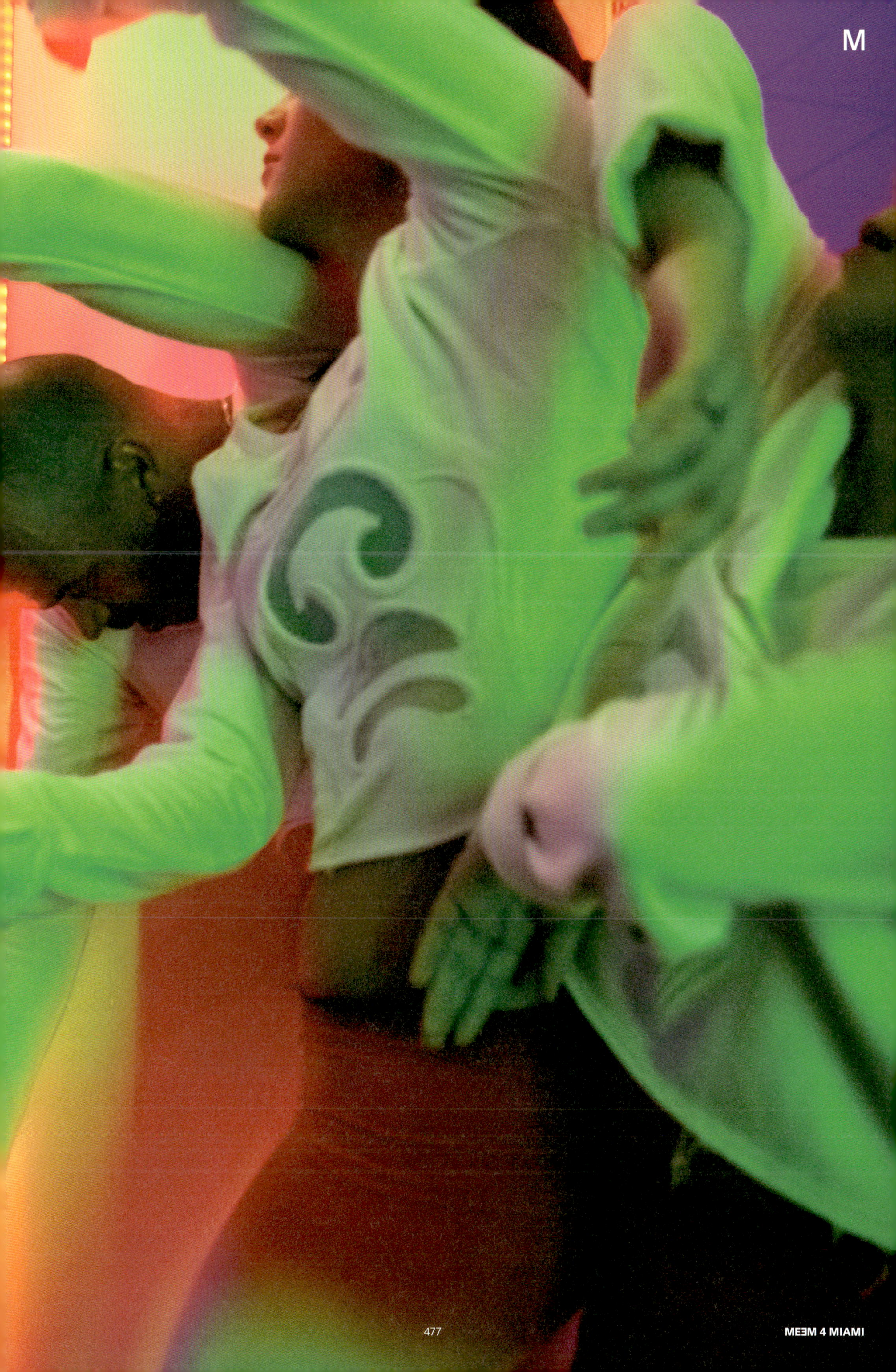

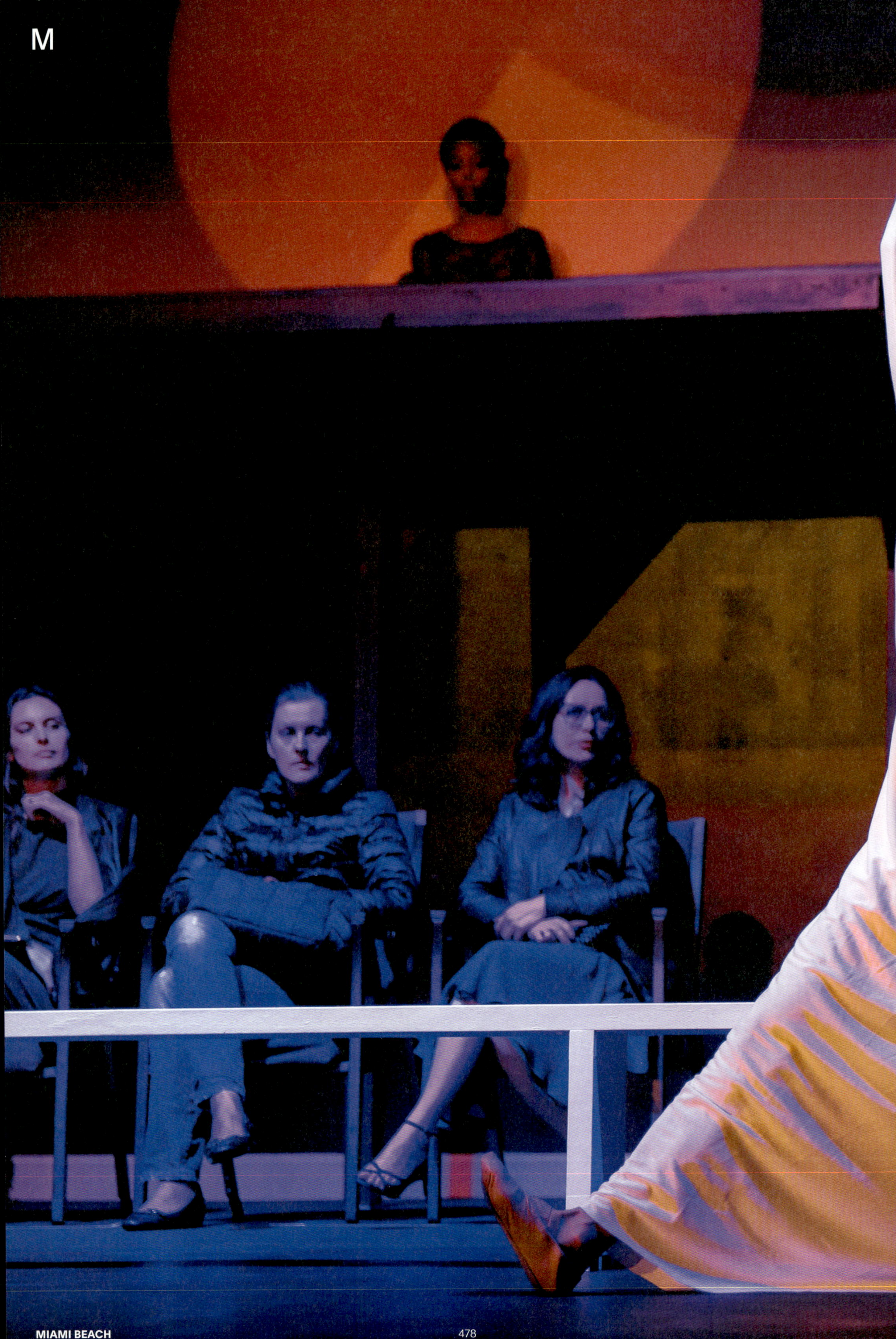

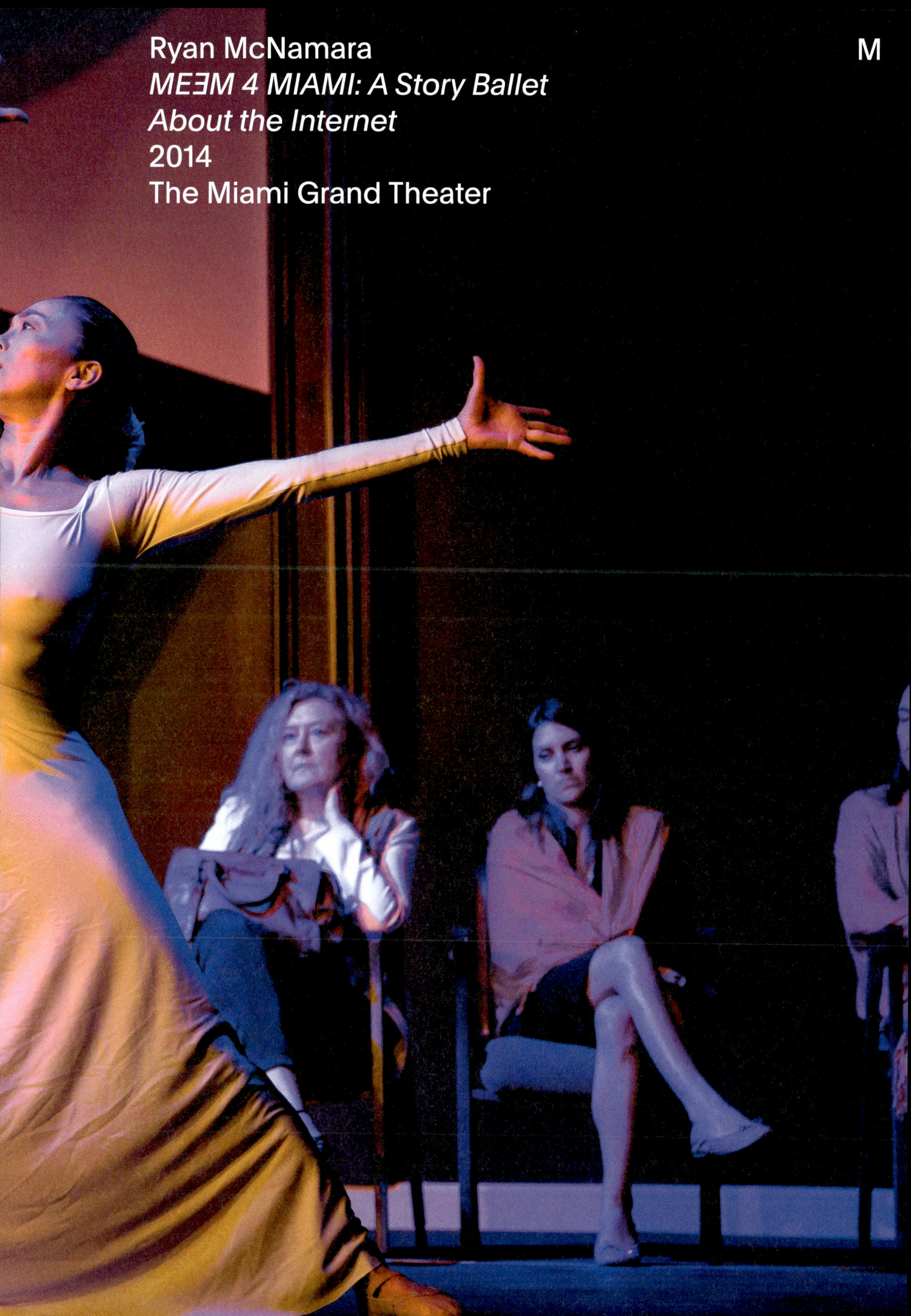
Ryan McNamara
MEƎM 4 MIAMI: A Story Ballet About the Internet
2014
The Miami Grand Theater
M

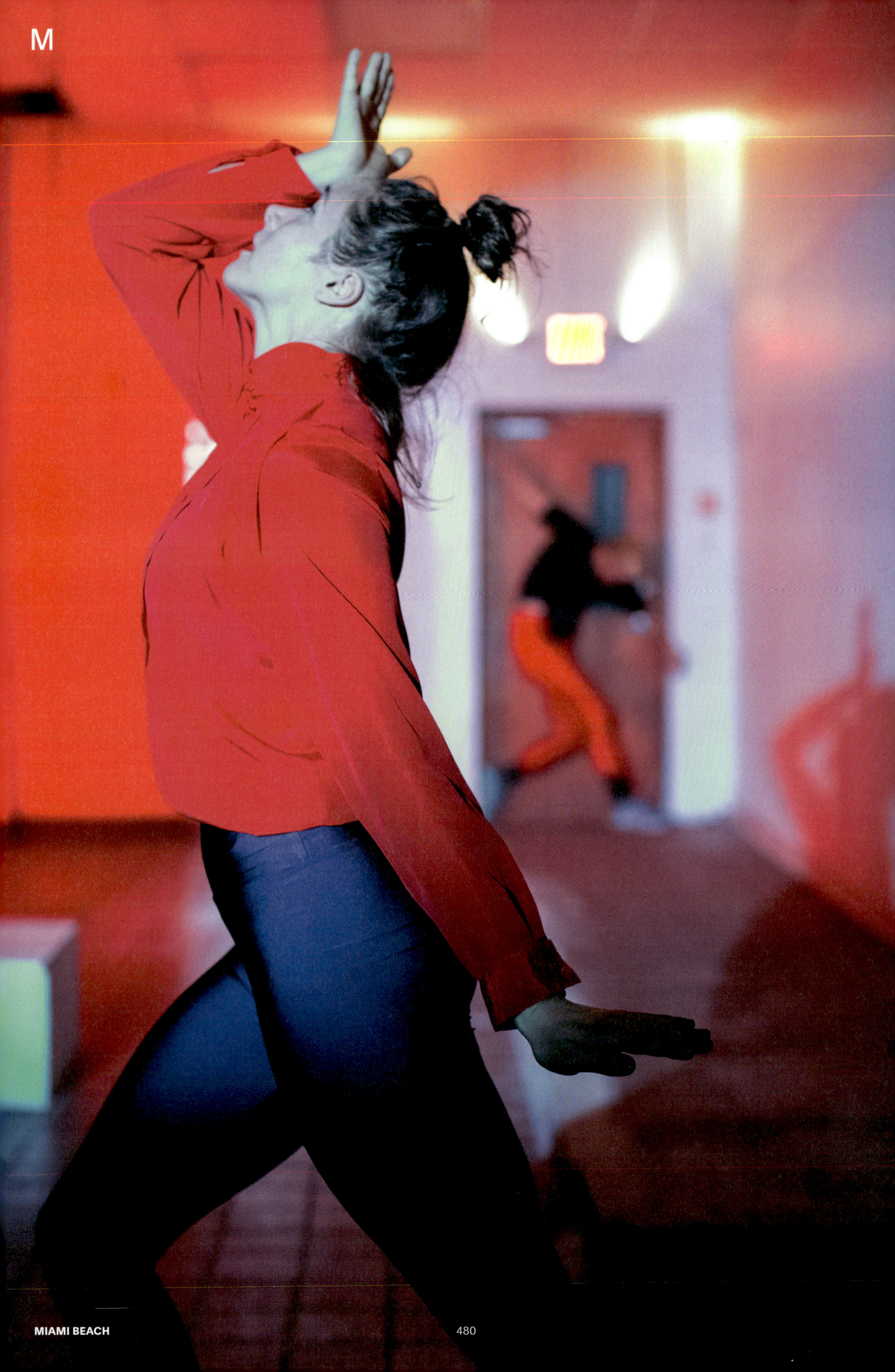

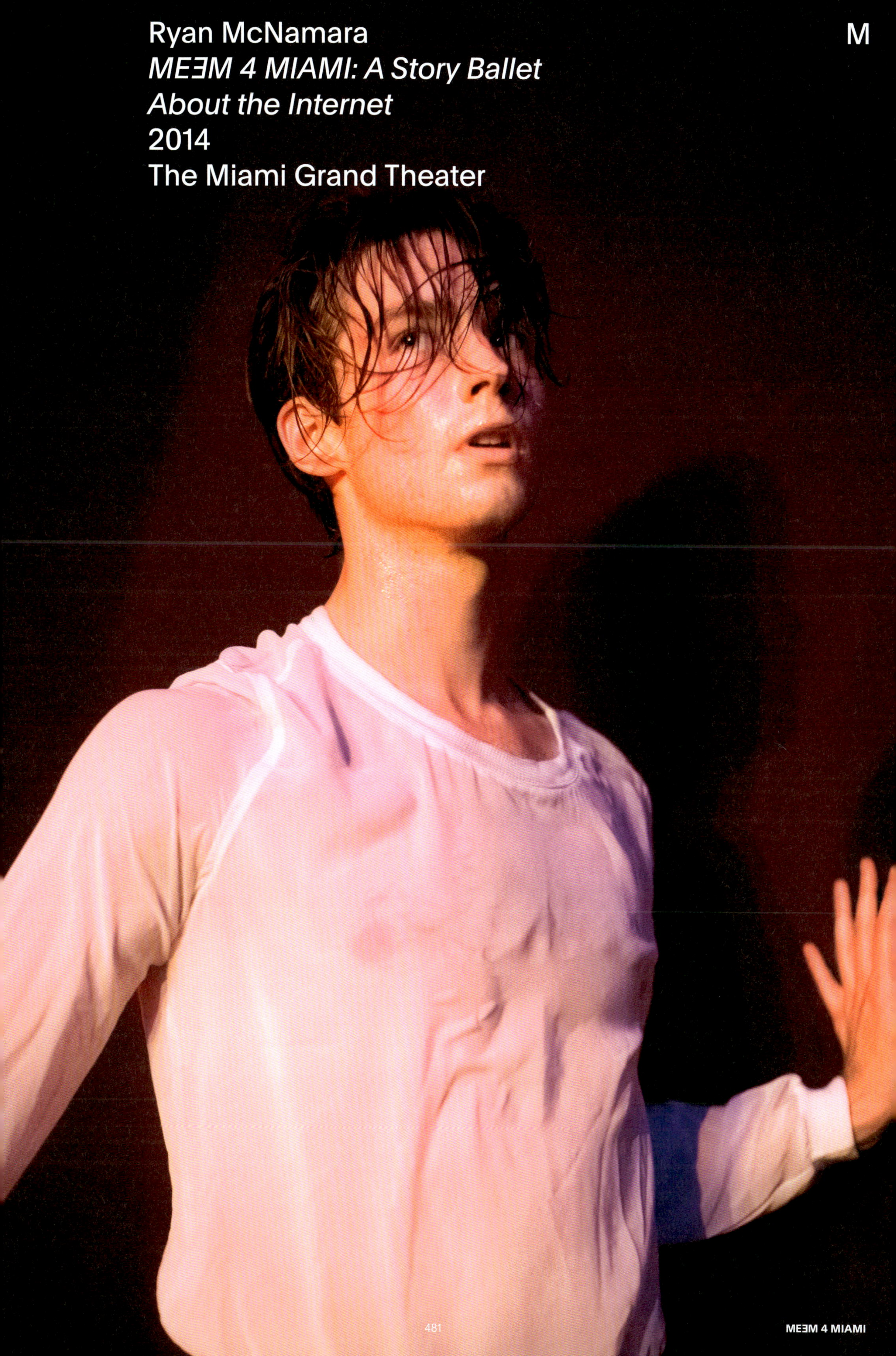

Ryan McNamara
MEƎM 4 MIAMI: A Story Ballet About the Internet
2014
The Miami Grand Theater

M

Claire Bishop speaks with Ryan McNamara about the ambitious and complex event *MEƎM 4 MIAMI* staged at the Miami Grand Theater during Art Basel's show in Miami Beach. A choreographic exploration of the online world, the work was a Performa Commission, presented by Art Basel, and produced by Performa and Art Basel

Salon|Artist Talk
Art Basel in
Miami Beach

December 4, 2014

Ryan McNamara, Artist, Brooklyn, in conversation with Claire Bishop, Art Historian and Critic, New York

CLAIRE BISHOP *MEƎM 4 Miami: A Story Ballet About the Internet* is a hugely ambitious piece with 28 dancers, an incredibly complicated structure that has taken weeks and months to sort out. You are dealing with the supposedly obsolete medium of the story ballet to deal with our experience of the Internet, in particular the way cultural information is circulated and distributed—and, in the process, perhaps also leveled. Why a story ballet, why use this antiquated form to talk about the latest digital technology?

It's a rhizomatic experience, like "clicking" and happening all over the place rather than just plowing through. That was the starting point of making this piece and creating that structure. —Ryan McNamara

RYAN MCNAMARA What is so interesting about *Story Ballet* is that it actually doesn't tell a story: you already know the story and you lay it on top of the movements that you are seeing in front of you. If you don't know *Swan Lake*, you can't actually follow the story by watching the ballet. It is abstract. It is a very difficult thing to translate a narrative into movement. It made sense for me to start working with what I saw at first as an abstract form, and then look at how to deal with narratives.

CB You are also importing familiar stories into that structure, excerpts from pop videos, or other forms of historical dance, as well as more contemporary forms of choreography.

RM Yes, I keep these "known" forms in the work. It was interesting to keep a linear narrative, which is a traditional way of telling a story, and sort of import the architecture of the Internet into it. It's a rhizomatic experience, like "clicking" and happening all over the place rather than just plowing through. That was the starting point of making this piece and creating that structure.

CB How did you develop the choreography in each of the different sequences that one sees as s/he moves around the space?

RM I've been working with dancers in New York for about five years now and I had never really done a piece of which I would consider myself being the choreographer, so when I was given this opportunity I thought it was time to dive in and spend time in the studio with dancers. It was going to be a large cast, but I wanted to work with these dancers in small groups. I also wanted the pieces within the piece to look very diverse, so I asked the dancers to bring in three video clips of a movement that they responded to somewhere online. It ranged from Janet Jackson videos to American bandstands from the 1960s and story ballets. I found interesting that everyone really loves, no matter what their training is, music videos and pop dancing. That ended up being a big part of it; no matter what his or her background was is, everybody wants to be Madonna.

CB In your work it's more or less difficult to identify the references. Could you talk about some of the videos that you used a starting point?

RM My interest is not so much in a kind of pastiche. It's more about using a source material that is expanded, contracted, slowed down, made bigger or smaller. When the three dancers come on stage at first, very slowly, that whole phrase takes about five minutes; it's a three-second excerpt from a Tina Turner clip from 1972 that we expanded into five minutes and added new features to. There are moments where there is something somewhat recognizable about it, but there's essentially Janet Jackson, Balanchine, Jerome Robbins, Trisha Brown … Some moments are more obvious than others, which are then contrasted with a direct quote, for example with the Martha Graham segment.

CB So it's a sort of collage, taking pre-existing elements and inserting them into a new ensemble.

RM Exactly. I'm almost asking for a Martha Graham intervention into my piece, saying "here's your time, put your piece in there," and then we pick up again.

CB You changed the ending a lot since last year's performance in New York: the finale last year culminated in Martha Graham's company piece with 11 dancers on stage doing a group section of salutations to the sun, and now it ends with just one dancer, Miki Ohikara, performing *Deep Song* from 1937. Why did you choose that piece? After a little bit of research, I realized this is the song in response to the Spanish Civil War, which seems miles away from the rest of the things we have been looking at, all very contemporary.

RM The finale of New York's version comes from *Ritual to the Sun*, a late Graham work from 1981 that many say is pastoral, but that I find just over-the-top glorious. It puts a smile on your face. Developing the new (and expanded) work, I started to realize that there was a kind of darkness in this new version: it made me think about how, when the Internet first took off, it was a utopia, the information super highway, the "World Wide Web"— this term we don't use anymore. *Deep Song* is a very political moment for Martha Graham, but it's not the only piece; she made a lot of anti-war pieces in that time.

CB Tell me about your role in the piece. You appear intermittently through it and your style of movement is quite different to the rest of the dancers. I wonder whether this is because you see yourself as a kind of

Ryan McNamara, *MEƎM 4 MIAMI: A Story Ballet About The Internet*, 2014, The Miami Grand Theater

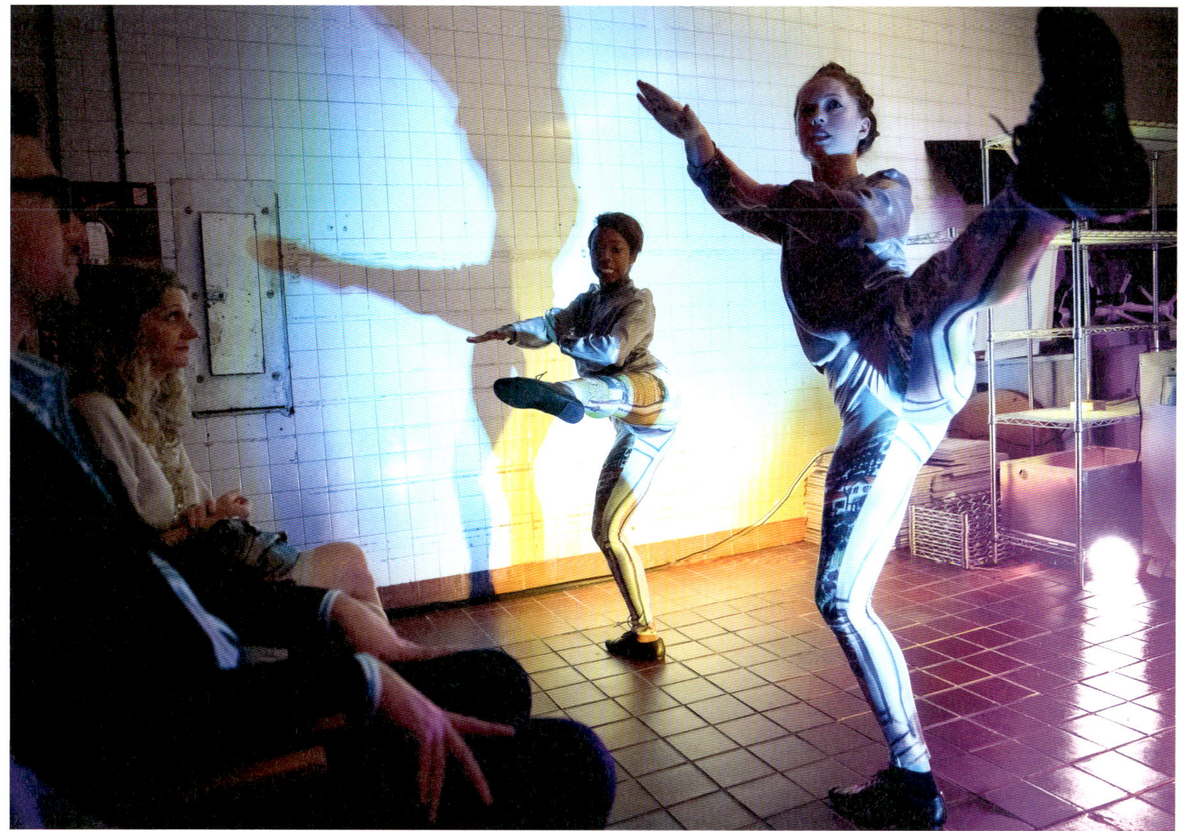

viewer who is moving through the scenes or whether you are submitted to another kind of choreography that I can't define?

RM I describe my role as the "glitch." I am actually the only person in the world that knows the entire piece: no one has seen it in its entirety except me, including the people in it! It's these little moments of different parts of choreography, but done with a body that is barely living, it's a glitchy version of all of the pieces. It's kind of the best-of/worst-of.
I did another piece called *Make Ryan A Dancer* (2010) in which I trained in PS1 for five months, learning how to dance in front of the public everyday. I really like this idea of two bodies doing the same movement that in the end is not the same movement. The press image for *Make Ryan A Dancer* is a ballet dancer and me doing the same leg lift and it doesn't look the same because of our different capacities. My point is that with all this virtuosity—they are all amazing dancers—you forget how amazing all they are doing is, and then when this body flops out there, you realize how good they are.

No matter what his or her background is, everybody wants to be Madonna.
—Ryan McNamara

CB I guess it also contrasts with the viewers' bodies, which are extremely passive. Something very specific happens in the audience that you move around by chairs-movers into different positions around the theater and up to the kitchen areas. Across most 20th-century rhetoric, and especially recently in the notion of "viewer's activation," there is the idea of empowerment about participating in and making decisions within a work of art; here it feels like being in a wheelchair! We are in regular chairs, but we are moved around on wheels, we depend on the chairs-movers and this feels particularly frustrating in the first 20 minutes when you are dispersing the audience to different stations: we are systematically relocated and parked in front of a performance for a period that actually feels slightly too long (sometimes you even see several cycles of it) and it creates this phenomenon of restlessness, where you are constantly looking around and checking what else there is to see. Basically, it creates a fear of missing out: you think that there will be something else going on which actually would be more fun to look at. Are you surprised by how compliant people are by resting in the chairs? Does everyone stay put?

RM Pretty much. Basically I'm hiding the entire time because I am under the stage or under the ramp, so I can't see what is going on and I have no idea if the piece has turned into chaos. I'm waiting for that night where it happens! We have done a lot for that not to happen, but I am always thinking about coming out and maybe everybody is wandering around, giving up on sitting on his or her chair. Maybe that is another reading of my role in the piece.

But actually it's not so different from a traditional spectacle: you are in a chair, you don't do anything, the performer does a lot; and so actually we are not breaking that much of this traditional relationship between spectator and performer. That is part of it. It was very important to have a very active passivity, rather that telling them ok now it's time to go there. This is why we had people pushed around.

CB At what point in your creative process did this became key to the work? Was it a starting point, did you want to do a piece where the audience was moved around, or did the dancing component come first?

RM It might have been somewhere around when you wrote your article in *Artforum* a couple of years ago about why so few artists were dealing with the Internet, "Digital Divide. Contemporary Art and New Media." I found it interesting that there wasn't a lot of work about that as a concept, so I really did start thinking about how to translate that into what seems like a completely opposite experience, during a live dance work. I was trying to figure out what that kind of narrative structure it would be. I knew that there had to be something about a changing of perspectives. The network that I could picture in my head of these bodies moving around really appealed to me: the idea that there would be a kind of structure, that there would be another choreography laid on top of another choreography that is as complicated, and actually as testing for the performers.

CB What is notable also is that it's so low tech and so physical. For something that is discussing the virtual it's a resolutely physical and material experience.

RM Definitely. The most high-tech things are the speakers. I even avoided projected images and similar things to play up this clumsiness of the analog. The digital can be clean, fast. You click and you are there. In this, someone has to get under you, push you over …

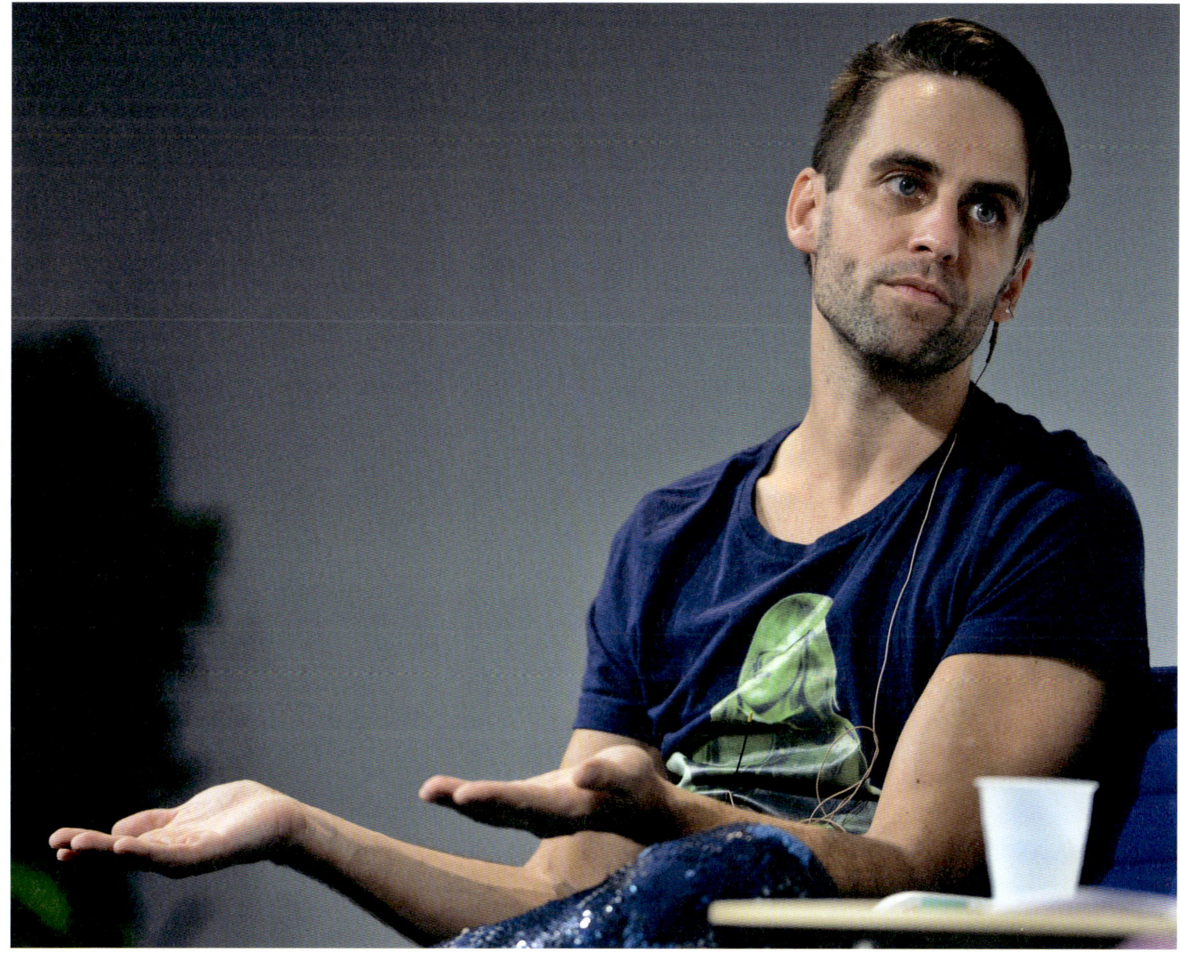

Ryan McNamara, Artist Talk, Art Basel in Miami Beach, December 4, 2014

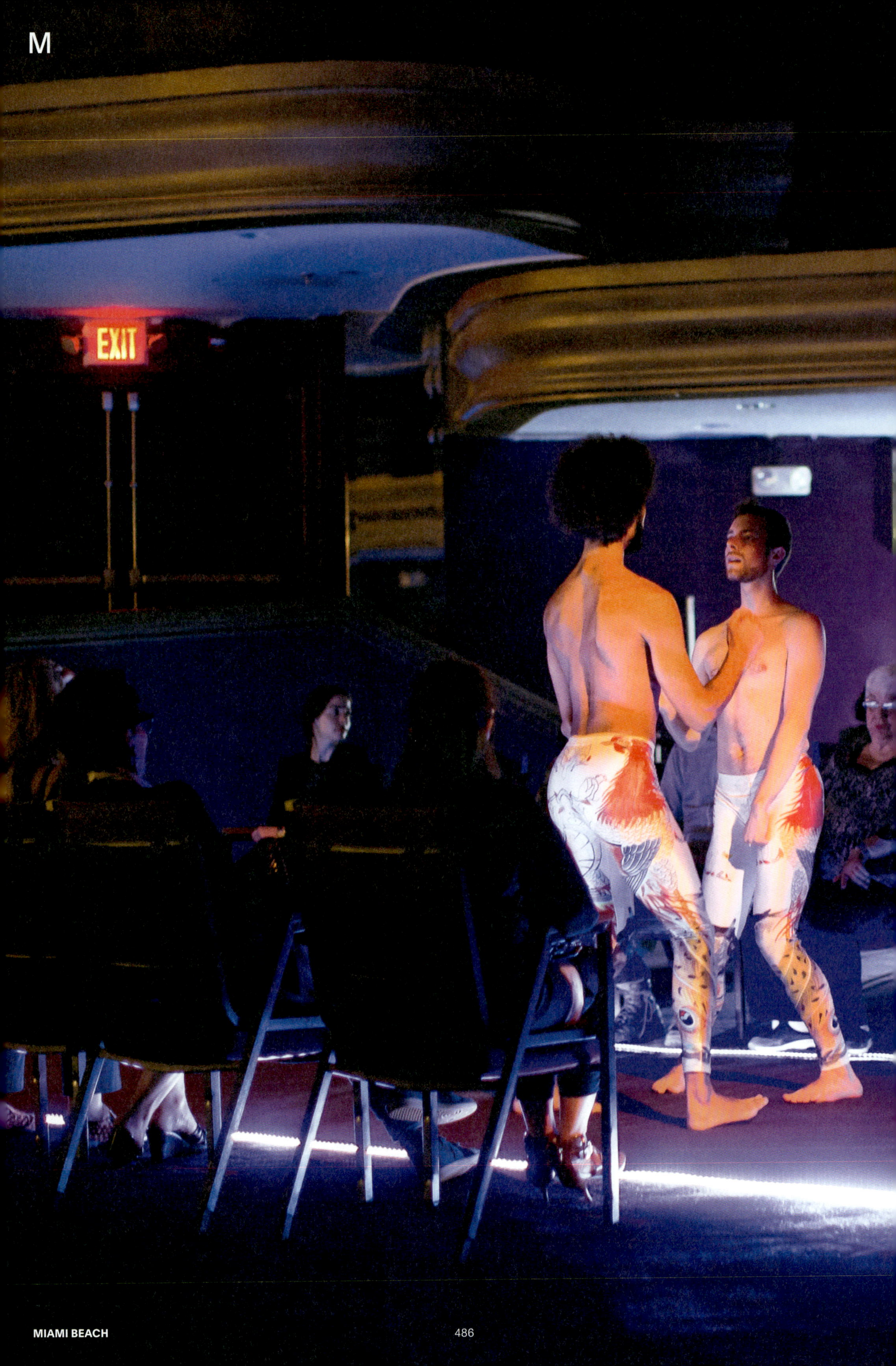
EXIT

Ryan McNamara
MEƎM 4 MIAMI: A Story Ballet About the Internet
2014
The Miami Grand Theater

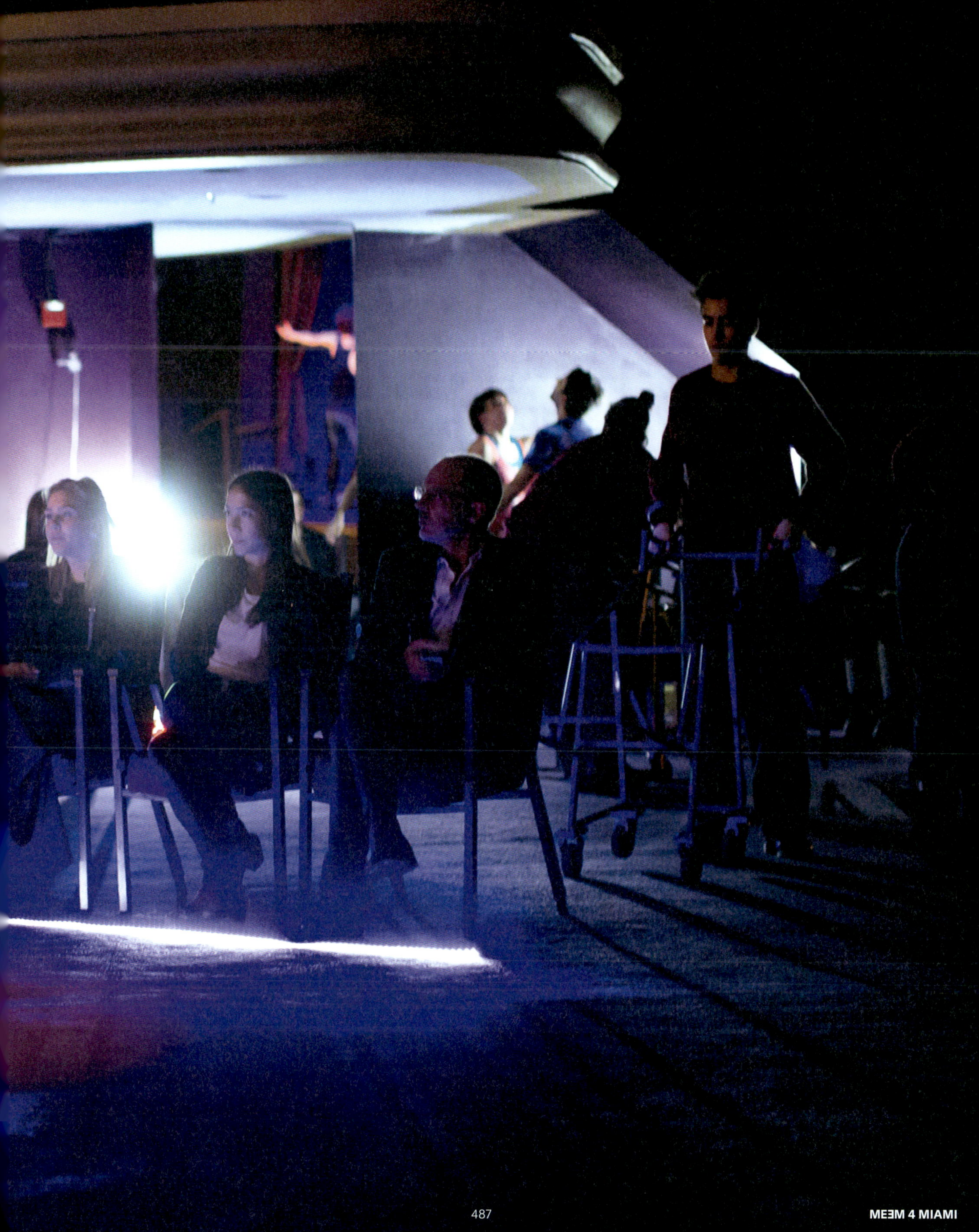

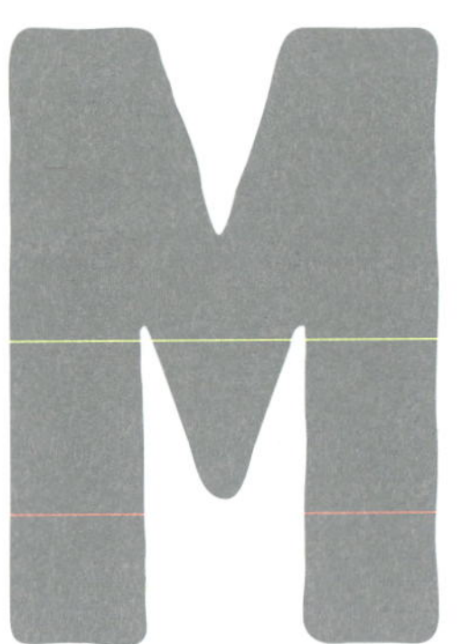

m Bochum

Bochum • Galleries

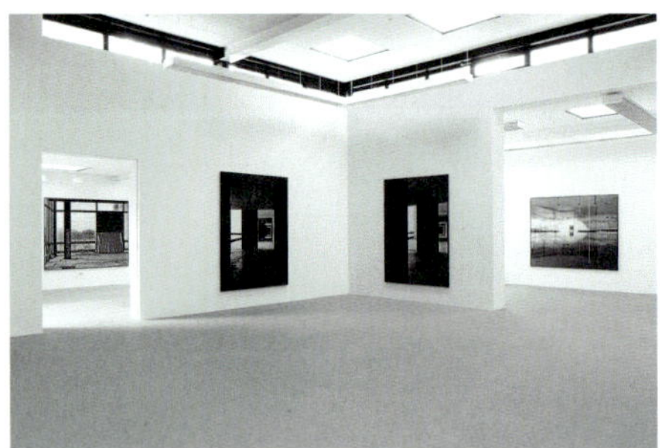

What is your favorite aspect of running a gallery?
ART.

How do you choose the artists you work with?
ART.

If you weren't running a gallery what else would you do?
ART.

- **Contact** Galerie m Bochum
  Susanne Breidenbach
  galerie@m-bochum.com
- **Established** 1969
- **Owner(s) / Partner(s)** Susanne Breidenbach
- **Team** 4
- **Space(s)** 250 m²
- **Artists at Art Basel** Evelina Cajacob
  Lucinda Devlin
  Antje Dorn
  Thomas Florschuetz
  Gotthard Graubner
  Caroline von Grone
  Carla Guagliardi
  Evelyn Hofer
  Aino Kannisto
  Lee Ufan
  François Morellet
  Simone Nieweg
  François Perrodin
  Alfredo Álvarez Plágaro
  Arnulf Rainer
  Richard Serra
  Elisabeth Vary
  Jan Wawrzyniak
  Peter Wegner
- **Further artists represented** Sybille Berger
  Ger van Elk
  Paco Fernández
  Claus Goedicke
  Marta Guisande
  Barbara Köhler
  Norbert Kricke
  Laura Letinsky
  Melanie Manchot
  Kenneth Martin
  Tanya Poole
  David Rabinowitch
  Dirk Reinartz
  Boris Savelev
  Guiseppe Spagnulo
  Apolonija Šušteršič

Maass

Berlin • Galleries

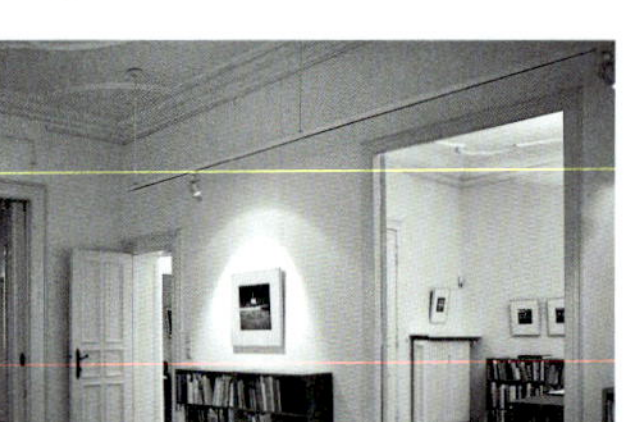

What is your favorite aspect of running a gallery?
Spending all day with great works of art around me.

How do you choose the artists you work with?
On quality and personal relevance; we only handle what we like—I know, it's luxury.

If you weren't running a gallery what else would you do?
An artist; preferably a painter.

- **Contact** Jörg Maass - Kunsthandel
  Jörg Maass
  joerg@kunsthandel-maass.de
- **Established** 1987
- **Owner(s) / Partner(s)** Jörg Maaß
- **Team** 5
- **Space(s)** 300 m²
- **Artists at Art Basel** Max Beckmann
  Otto Dix
  George Grosz
  Erich Heckel
  Ernst Ludwig Kirchner
  Paul Klee
  Otto Mueller
  Emil Nolde
  Max Pechstein
  Karl Schmidt-Rottluff
- **Further artists represented** Georg Baselitz
  Pablo Picasso
  Sigmar Polke
  Gerhard Richter

Maccarone

New York
Los Angeles

• Galleries
Unlimited
• Galleries

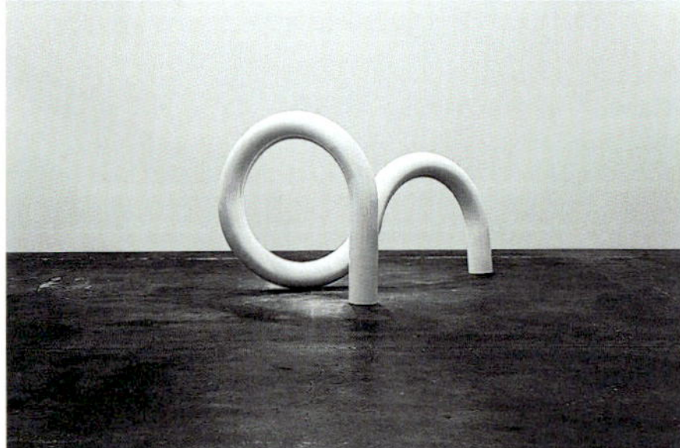

What is your favorite aspect of running a gallery?
I love to create chaos in the space, go broke, and collaborate with artists whose work is poetic or immaterial. I am very drawn to that type of work.

How do you choose the artists you work with?
I look at a lot of work before I take on an artist, but I decide if I like a piece of art very quickly. It is completely a gut reaction.

If you weren't running a gallery what else would you do?
Play tennis.

- **Contact** Maccarone
kitchen@maccarone.net
- **Established** 2001
- **Owner(s) / Partner(s)** Michele Maccarone
Ellen Langan
- **Team** 10
- **Space(s)** 4,367 m²
- **Artists at Art Basel** Scott Benzel
Carol Bove
Ann Craven
Alex Hubbard
Rosy Keyser
David Lamelas
Nate Lowman
Ryan Sullivan
Oscar Tuazon
- **Further artists represented** Sarah Charlesworth
Chivas Clem
Eli Hansen
Phanos Kyriacou
Paul Lee
Hanna Liden
Corey McCorkle
Rodney Mcmillian
Otto Muehl
Claudia & Julia Müller
Daniel Roth
Jeannette Montgomery Barron
Jorge Peris
Alessandro Piangiamore
Daniele Puppi
Serge Spitzer
Vedovamazzei
Ouattara Watts

Magazzino

Rome

Galleries
Galleries

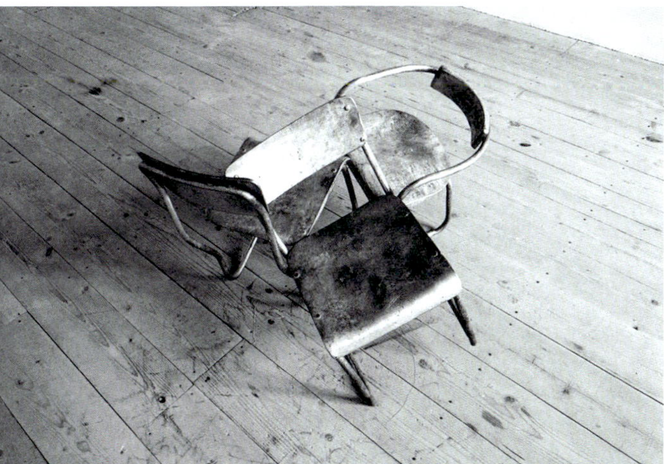

What is your favorite aspect of running a gallery?

Being elsewhere, in any sense. Dealing with different worlds, diverse and new ways of thinking, and hoping to encounter "the beauty that saves the world," which is often hidden and mysterious or evident and illuminating.

How do you choose the artists you work with?

They are fellow travelers who have a special talent in understanding what is happening, and the ability to find images that simultaneously reveal, interrogate, and alleviate our condition.

If you weren't running a gallery what else would you do?

If not arts, something similar that always deals with the "elsewhere": cinema.

- **Contact** Magazzino
Gabriele Gaspari
gabriele@magazzinoartemoderna.com
- **Established** 1997
- **Owner(s) / Partner(s)** Mauro Nicoletti
- **Team** 4
- **Space(s)** 160 m²
- **Artists at Art Basel** Massimo Bartolini
Elisabetta Benassi
Antonio Biasiucci
Pedro Cabrita Reis
Mircea Cantor
Jonas Dahlberg
Jan Fabre
Alberto Garutti
Gianluca Malgeri
Domenico Mangano

Maggiore

Bologna
Paris
New York

 Galleries

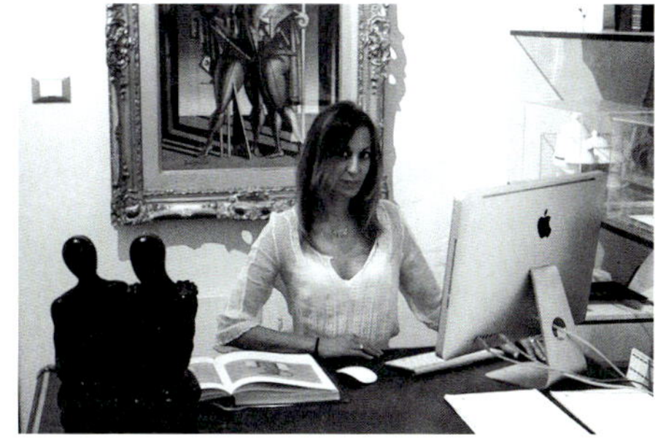

What is your favorite aspect of running a gallery?

I love running an art gallery! There is no other place in the world where you have the freedom to choose what you prefer: learning something, having fun, meeting interesting people (artists, curators, collectors, art lovers, museum directors), or wondering about life. And, most of all, if you are lucky enough in an art gallery you can find an answer: your personal answer! An art gallery is a place where taste is created and oriented.

How do you choose the artists you work with?

Every artist and every single artwork have been selected for their important and innovative contribution not only to the history of art but also to human knowledge. We believe in the quality of an idea realized with a strong aesthetic that can provoke deep emotion. These aspects belong to the artists who become a vehicle between what it was and what it will be.

If you weren't running a gallery what else would you do?

All my life has been art related! Even before I was born, since my parents, Franco and Roberta Calarota, founded our gallery some time before. I grew up in Italy where art and aesthetics are in every corner of the streets, in landscapes, in painting! I was fed with art history. Art was my third word and I cannot remember any moment of my life where art has not been present. I was predestined to art but soon it became a choice. And since I spend hours writing about art, I guess I could be a writer!

- **Contact** Galleria d'Arte Maggiore G.A.M.
Alessia Calarota
info@maggioregam.com
- **Established** 1978
- **Owner(s) / Partner(s)** Roberta Calarota
Franco Calarota
Alessia Calarota
- **Team** 8
- **Space(s)** 400 m²
- **Artists at Art Basel** Giorgio De Chirico
Giorgio Morandi
- **Further artists represented** Arman
Giacomo Balla
Enrico Baj
Per Barclay
Davide Benati
Bertozzi & Casoni
Alighiero Boetti
Georges Braque
Alberto Burri
Alexander Calder
Giuseppe Capogroossi
Marc Chagall
Sandro Chia
Hsiao Chin
Antoni Clavé
Paul Delvaux
Fortunato Depero
Pablo Echaurren
Max Ernst
Lucio Fontana

Sam Francis
Robert Indiana
Allen Jones
Wassily Kandinsky
Paul Klee
Franz Kline
Joseph Kosuth
Wilfred Lam
Fernand Léger
Leoncillo
Nino Longobardi
René Magritte
Marino Marini
Georges Mathieu
Roberto Matta
Fausto Melotti
Joan Miró
Mattia Moreni
Louise Nevelson
Luigi Ontani
Mimmo Paladino
Peter Phillips
Pablo Picasso
Michelangelo Pistoletto
Serge Poliakoff
Arnaldo Pomodoro
Mel Ramos
Gino Severini
Ettore Spalletti
Graham Sutherland
Antoni Tàpies
Andy Warhol
Tom Wesselmann
Zao Wou-Ki

Magician Space

Beijing 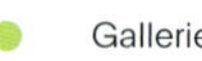 Galleries

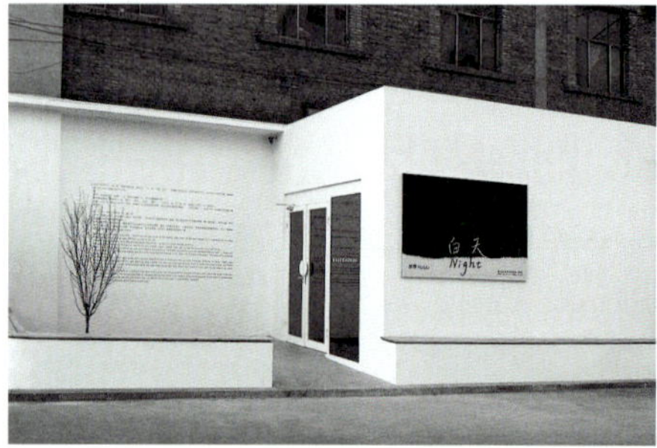

What is your favorite aspect of running a gallery?
As a mediator between artists and society, running a gallery attracts me in two different ways. On the one hand, I can always be in communication with the most creative people in the world—that is the way I can broaden my horizons and become more imaginative. On the other hand, through a gallery, people learn about the artists and get the chance to collect their work. It is really meaningful to help popularize an outstanding work as it contributes and aesthetically enhances a society.

How do you choose the artists you work with?
I choose an artist by judging them on whether they can think and imagine beyond a general level of emotions. I also look at their ability to find something essential among the myriad of issues arising from society—artists who have striven the hardest toward realizing change through a certain path. And I admire those who are brave enough to transcend themselves and push themselves even harder to improve.

If you weren't running a gallery what else would you do?
I would definitely choose to be a full time collector.

- **Contact** Magician Space
  Billy Tang
  billytang@magician-space.com
- **Established** 2008
- **Owner(s) / Partner(s)** Qu Kejie
- **Team** 5
- **Space(s)** 100 m²
- **Artists at Art Basel** Guan Xiao
  Guan Yong
  Jiang Zhi
  Liang Yuanwei
  Tang Yongxiang
  Wang Zhongjie
  Yu Honglei
  Zhuang Hui & Dan'er
- **Further artists represented** Bai Yiluo
  Chen Zhou
  He An
  Hu Yun
  Li Ran
  Yu Bogong
  Wang Wei

Mai 36

Zurich
- Galleries
- Galleries

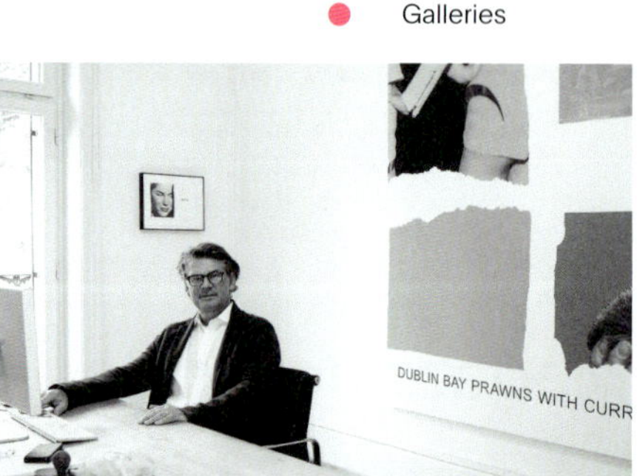

What is your favorite aspect of running a gallery?
I enjoy the close relationship with the artists and their visions, meeting passionate and great personalities, and through showing, talking about, and selling artworks, contributing to the history of the art of today.

How do you choose the artists you work with?
Their work has to get my personal attention and should change my way of looking at things. I am interested in the mind of the artist and in his/her work's potential to enrich our perception and experience of the world.

If you weren't running a gallery what else would you do?
I would most likely show, tell, and sell other ideas and objects such as vintage furniture, glass objects, ceramics, etc.

- **Contact** Mai 36 Galerie
  Victor Gisler
  victor@mai36.com
- **Established** 1988
- **Owner(s) / Partner(s)** Victor Gisler
- **Team** 7
- **Space(s)** 171 m²
- **Artists at Art Basel** Franz Ackermann
  John Baldessari
  Stephan Balkenhol
  Troy Brauntuch
  Pedro Cabrita Reis
  Ernst Caramelle
  Raúl Cordero
  Koenraad Dedobbeleer
  Jürgen Drescher
  Roe Ethridge
  Pia Fries
  Flavio Garciandía
  General Idea
  Luigi Ghirri
  Robert Mapplethorpe
  Rita McBride
  Matt Mullican
  Michel Pérez Pollo
  Manfred Pernice
  Magnus Plessen
  Glen Rubsamen
  Thomas Ruff
  Paul Thek
  Lawrence Weiner
  Rémy Zaugg
- **Further artists represented** Ian Anüll
  Matthew Benedict
  Daan van Golden
  Jitka Hanzlová
  Peter Hujar
  Harald F. Müller
  Christoph Rütimann
  Stefan Thiel
  Matthias Zinn

Maisterravalbuena

Madrid  Nova

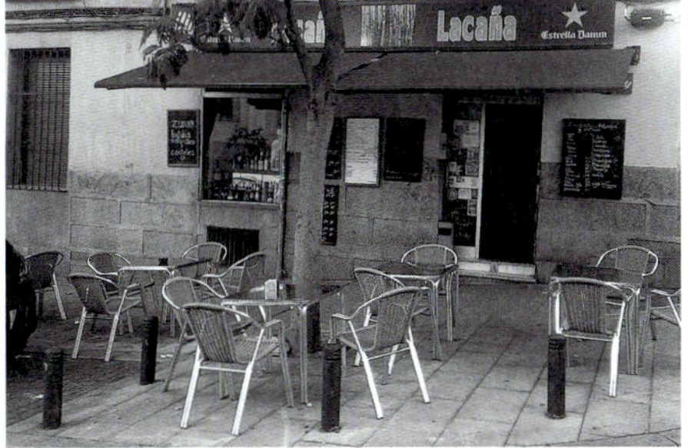

What is your favorite aspect of running a gallery?
The moment we receive a new work and you feel it fits with the artist, with you, with the gallery, with the show. And the moment when a collector falls in love with a work you have shown and explained to them.

How do you choose the artists you work with?
We always start with the idea that there is to be a special feeling and understanding between ourselves and the artists.

If you weren't running a gallery what else would you do?
Pedro Maisterra: I would to open a little restaurant in Navarra.
Belén Valbuena: I would love to run a bookshop and have time to read as much as possible.

- **Contact**: Maisterravalbuena
  Belén Valbuena
  galeria@maisterravalbuena.com
- **Established**: 2007
- **Owner(s) / Partner(s)**: Pedro Maisterra
  Belén Valbuena
- **Team**: 3
- **Space(s)**: 170 m²
- **Artists at Art Basel**: Regina de Miguel
  Hiraki Sawa
  Dan Shaw-Town
- **Further artists represented**: A Kassen
  Antonio Ballester Moreno
  Daniel Jacoby
  Maria Loboda
  Erlea Maneros Zabala
  Néstor Sanmiguel Diest
  Cristián Silva
  B. Wurtz

Malingue

Hong Kong 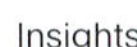 Insights

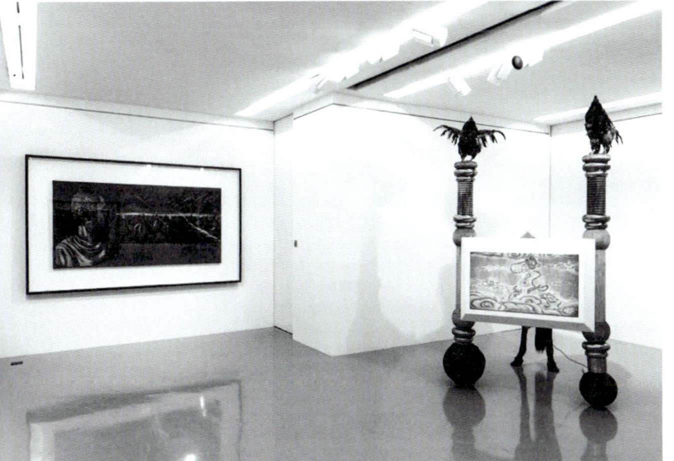

What is your favorite aspect of running a gallery?
Curating shows with the artists.

How do you choose the artists you work with?
It always starts by falling in love with the work.

If you weren't running a gallery what else would you do?
Lorraine would run a lifestyle store and I would write.

- **Contact**: Edouard Malingue Gallery
  Lorraine Malingue
  lorraine@edouardmalingue.com
- **Established**: 2010
- **Owner(s) / Partner(s)**: Edouard Malingue
  Lorraine Malingue
- **Team**: 6
- **Space(s)**: 149 m²
- **Artists at Art Basel**: Yuan Yuan
- **Further artists represented**: Charwei Tsai
  Cui Xinming
  Jeremy Everett
  Laurent Grasso
  Callum Innes
  Nuri Kuzucan
  Los Carpinteros
  Fabien Mérelle
  Song Hyun-Sook
  Sun Xun
  Janaina Tschäpe
  João Vasco Paiva
  Wang Zhibo
  Wu Chi-Tsung

Mara-La Ruche

Buenos Aires 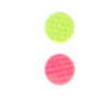 Galleries
Galleries Kabinett

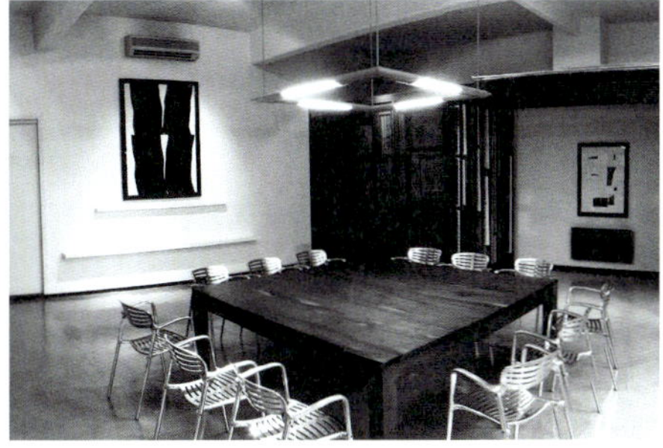

What is your favorite aspect of running a gallery?
Promoting the artist.
Publishing a good "museum-like" catalogue with each exhibition.
Organizing exhibitions.

How do you choose the artists you work with?
The quality of their work.

If you weren't running a gallery what else would you do?
I would write about art.

- **Contact**: Jorge Mara-La Ruche
  Jorge Mara
  info@jorgemaralaruche.com.ar
- **Established**: 2001
- **Owner(s) / Partner(s)**: Jorge Mara & Nelly Corral
- **Team**: 6
- **Space(s)**: 300 m²
- **Artists at Art Basel**: Roberto Aizenberg
  Carlos Arnaiz
  Horacio Coppola
  Sarah Grilo
  Alfredo Hlito
  Macaparana
  Amalia Nieto
  Květa Pacovská
  Ana Sacerdote
  Grete Stern
  Eduardo Stupía
- **Further artists represented**: Natalia Abot Glenz
  Carmelo Arden Quin
  Marcolina Dipierro
  Adolfo Estrada
  José Antonio Fernández-Muro
  León Ferrari
  Kirin
  Juan Lecuona
  Fabio Miniotti
  Fidel Sclavo

M

Marconi

Milan

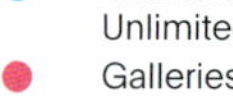

Galleries Unlimited

Galleries

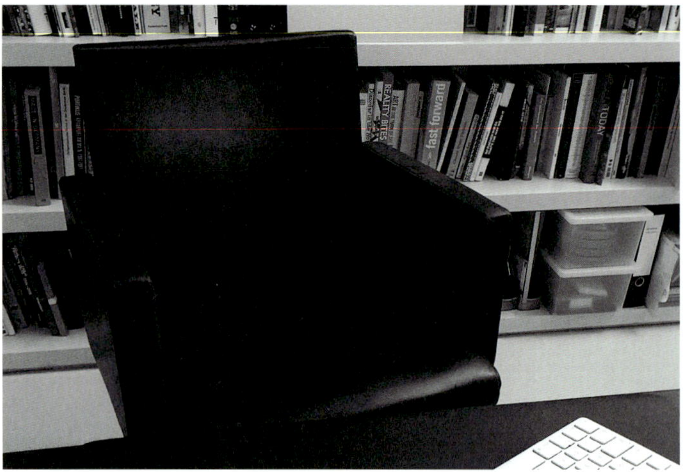

What is your favorite aspect of running a gallery?

One of my favorite aspects of running a gallery is working closely with the artists: having a dialogue, exchanging ideas, and working on gallery shows with my artists. To go and see my artists' studios and be involved in the whole creation process right from the beginning—from the very first idea to the final result.

How do you choose the artists you work with?

It is a long process to choose new artists. It starts with being intrigued by works you see. And then it goes on to visiting the artists' studios and getting to know them and their work better. After that there is usually a wait and see period in which you process all the info, and in which you rethink your possible choice. A show at the gallery or the inclusion in a group show would be the next step.

If you weren't running a gallery what else would you do?

I couldn't imagine what else to do. Art kind of runs in my family: my grandfather was a framer who made frames for the likes of de Chirico, Morandi, and Carrà, and then my father opened his gallery in the 1960s and showed many Italian and international artists. He still runs the Foundation Marconi in Milan. I grew up being surrounded by art and the artists of my father's gallery and it just seemed to be a natural step for me to continue this road …

- **Contact** Gió Marconi
  gio@giomarconi.com
- **Established** 1990
- **Owner(s) / Partner(s)** Gió Marconi
- **Team** 7
- **Space(s)** 400 m²
- **Artists at Art Basel** Franz Ackermann
  Rosa Barba
  Will Benedict
  John Bock
  Kerstin Brätsch
  Matthew Brannon
  André Butzer
  Nathalie Djurberg & Hans Berg
  Günther Förg
  Simon Fujiwara
  Nikolas Gambaroff
  Wade Guyton
  Lothar Hempel
  Annette Kelm
  Sharon Lockhart
  Jorge Pardo
  Tobias Rehberger
  Markus Schinwald
  Dasha Shishkin
  Lucie Stahl
  Catherine Sullivan
  Grazia Toderi
  Fredrik Værslev
  Atelier Van Lieshout
  Francesco Vezzoli
  Amelie von Wulffen

Marks

New York
Los Angeles

Galleries
Galleries

- **Contact** Matthew Marks Gallery
  Jacqueline Tran
  jacqueline@matthewmarks.com
- **Established** 1991
- **Owner** Matthew Marks
- **Artists at Art Basel** Robert Adams
  Darren Almond
  Nayland Blake
  Peter Cain
  Thomas Demand
  Vincent Fecteau
  Peter Fischli/David Weiss
  Lucian Freud
  Katharina Fritsch
  Luigi Ghirri
  Robert Gober
  Nan Goldin
  Martin Honert
  Gary Hume
  Jasper Johns
  Ellsworth Kelly
  Michel Majerus
  Brice Marden
  Ken Price
  Martin Puryear
  Charles Ray
  Paul Sietsema
  Tony Smith
  Anne Truitt
  Rebecca Warren
  Terry Winters

Marlborough London

London
New York
Barcelona
Madrid
Monaco
Santiago

Galleries
Galleries

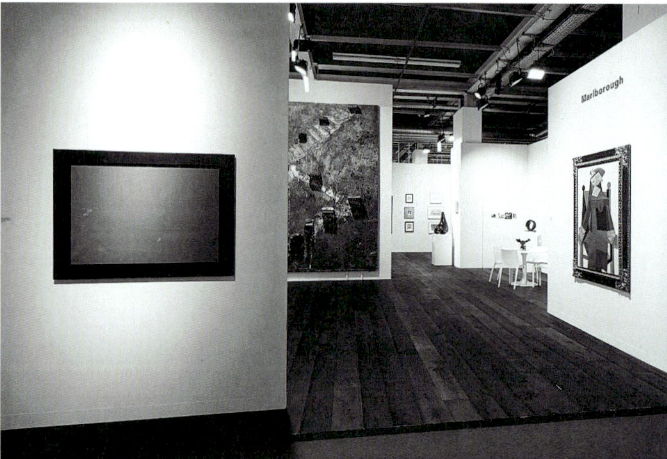

What is your favorite aspect of running a gallery?

There is magic in following the life of an artwork from its conception in the artist's mind to its creation and handling. Bringing works to the gallery, setting up an exhibition, and witnessing collectors or museum directors fall in love with the works is a very special experience.

How do you choose the artists you work with?

The gallery has an international reputation for representing artists. The gallery directors actively visit museum and commercial exhibitions, as well as art schools to keep informed about established and emerging artists. One of our former directors, the late Miss Valerie Beston, set up a fund to sponsor an art student graduating from the Royal College of Art in London. Each of these artists is given an exhibition at the gallery in early autumn.

If you weren't running a gallery what else would you do?
I would certainly be working in a related field to the arts. Possibly a creative film producer, with all the artistic choices they have from selecting a script, to casting actors, and working on the costumes, lighting, and set designs. I guess there is common ground between this and what I actually do. Still, I would miss the thrill of art dealing enormously.

- **Contact** Marlborough Fine Art (London) Ltd.
  Alexander Platon
  aplaton@marlboroughfineart.com
- **Established** 1946
- **Owner(s) / Partner(s)** The heirs of Frank Lloyd
- **Team** 20
- **Space(s)** 279 m²
- **Artists at Art Basel** Frank Auerbach
  Francis Bacon
  Chen Yifei
  Chu Teh-Chun
  Lyonel Feininger
  Paul Klee
  Jacques Lipchitz
  Pablo Picasso
  Paula Rego
  Gerhard Richter
  George Rickey
  Kurt Schwitters
  Manolo Valdés
  Zao Wou-Ki
  Zeng Fanzhi
- **Further artists represented** Avigdor Arikha
  Robert Devriendt
  Clive Head
  Bill Jacklin
  R.B. Kitaj
  Oskar Kokoschka
  Nina Murdoch
  Hughie O'Donoghue
  Victor Pasmore
  Joe Tilson
  John Virtue

Marlborough New York

New York  Galleries
Chelsea Galleries

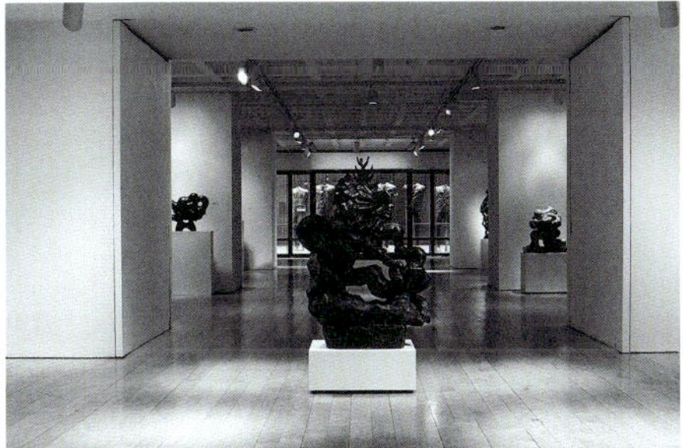

What is your favorite aspect of running a gallery?
Pierre Levai:
To promote artists.

How do you choose the artists you work with?
They choose me.

If you weren't running a gallery what else would you do?
I would be a bullfighter!

- **Contact** Marlborough Gallery Inc.
  Pierre Levai
  treddi@marlboroughgallery.com
- **Established** 1946
- **Owner(s) / Partner(s)** Pierre Levai
  Gilbert Lloyd
- **Team** 5
- **Space(s)** 1,347 m²
- **Artists at Art Basel** Frank Auerbach
  Marc Chagall
  Chu Teh-Chun
  Richard Estes
  Fernand Léger
  Jacques Lipchitz
  Piet Mondrian
  Robert Motherwell
  Pablo Picasso
  Ad Reinhardt
  George Rickey
  Auguste Rodin
  Manolo Valdés
  Zao Wou-Ki

Martin

New York 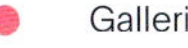 Galleries

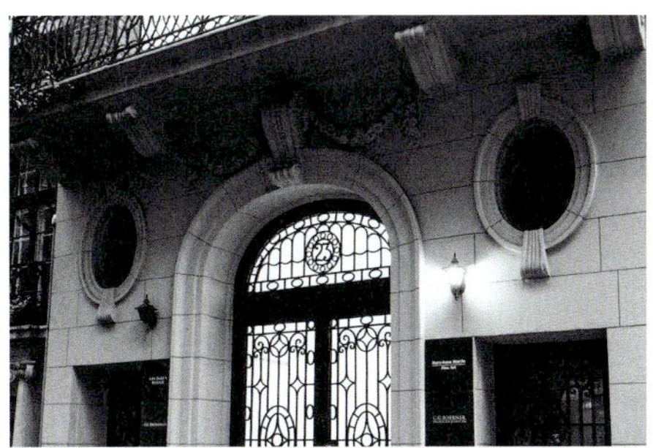

What is your favorite aspect of running a gallery?
I am often consulted on matters of expertise in my field of Mexican and Latin American Art. I see many, many forgeries, some that are horrible and some that are quite amusing. Every so often I discover a long lost treasure, and this gladdens my heart. For this reason every day is different; I am never bored.

How do you choose the artists you work with?
I have to love the work and love the artist, too.

If you weren't running a gallery what else would you do?
I would be working in my library, researching painting and drawings. There is still so much to learn. I would love to form a major collection, based only on aesthetic value, not on "investment" potential.

- **Contact** Mary-Anne Martin / Fine Art
  Mary-Anne Martin
  mamartin@mamfa.com
- **Established** 1982
- **Owner(s) / Partner(s)** Mary-Anne Martin
- **Team** 6
- **Space(s)** 200 m²
- **Artists at Art Basel** Antonio Bandeira
  Leonora Carrington
  Miguel Covarrubias
  Isabel de Obaldía
  Gunther Gerzso
  Mathias Goeritz
  Frida Kahlo
  Wifredo Lam
  Roberto Matta
  Alice Rahon
  Diego Rivera
  Rufino Tamayo
  Joaquin Torres-Garcia
  Francisco Toledo
  Alejandro Xul Solar
  Francisco Zúñiga
- **Further artists represented** Alfredo Castañeda
  Elena Climent
  Carlos Mérida
  José Clemente Orozco
  Carlos Orozco Romero
  Wolfgang Paalen
  David Alfaro Siqueiros
  Remedios Varo

Mathes

New York

Galleries
Galleries

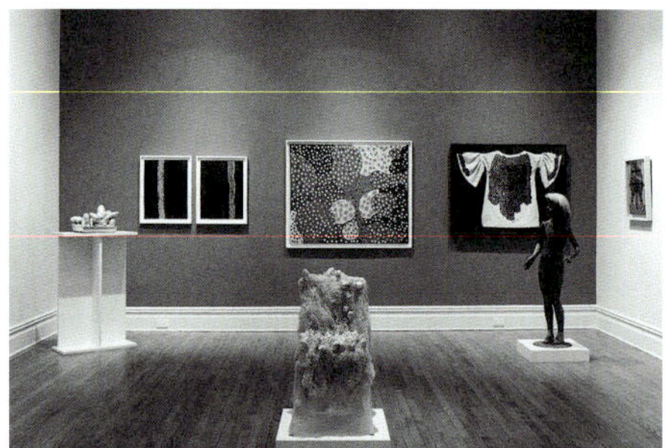

What is your favorite aspect of running a gallery?

I enjoy the challenge of discovering great pictures and sharing my knowledge and enthusiasm for these works with collectors.

The gallery has an ongoing history of organizing solo exhibitions of artists long due for reappraisal. I also look to create a dialogue between American and European art and this frequently guides my choices.

How do you choose the artists you work with?

I often search for artists who have been overlooked, or areas of the market that have been under-appreciated.

If you weren't running a gallery what else would you do?

If I were not running a gallery I would be a docent at the Met or MoMA.

- **Contact** Barbara Mathes Gallery
  Jill Bishins
  jill@barbaramathesgallery.com
- **Established** 1978
- **Owner(s) / Partner(s)** Barbara Mathes
- **Team** 4
- **Space(s)** 372 m²
- **Artists at Art Basel** Carla Accardi
  Giacomo Balla
  Agostino Bonalumi
  Alexander Calder
  Pier Paolo Calzolari
  Enrico Castellani
  John Chamberlain
  Allan D'Arcangelo
  Jean Dubuffet
  Neil Jenney
  Yayoi Kusama
  Fausto Melotti
  Pablo Picasso
  Michelangelo Pistoletto
  Robert Rauschenberg
  Gerhard Richter
  Ed Ruscha
  Sophie Taeuber-Arp
  Richard Tuttle
  Günther Uecker

Mayer

Düsseldorf

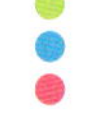

Galleries
Galleries
Galleries

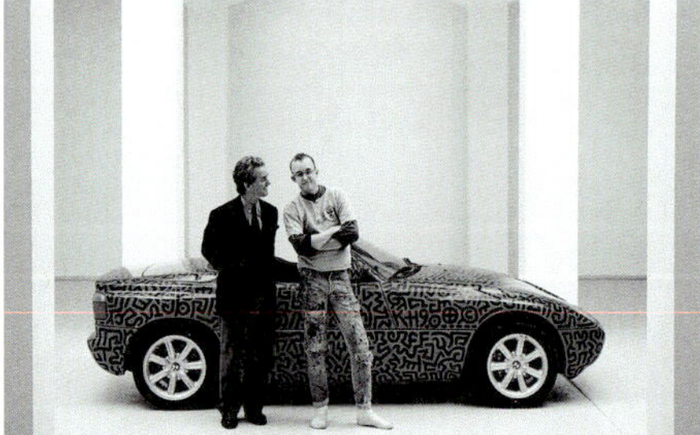

What is your favorite aspect of running a gallery?

Having been a gallerist now for 50 years, I can say that, despite all the problems one has, being inside the myth of creative forces and getting enormous energy out of it still is the most important aspect!

How do you choose the artists you work with?

By immediately seeing and feeling that the artist's work thrills me immensely—like a "coup de foudre"!

If you weren't running a gallery what else would you do?

I would be in the music business or I would be an architect. Generally, every aspect of culture interests me very much, I have always worked as a "cross-cultural-agent."

- **Contact** Galerie Hans Mayer
  Marie Mayer
  marie.mayer@galeriehansmayer.de
- **Established** 1965
- **Owner** Hans Mayer
- **Team** 7
- **Space(s)** 1,800 m²
- **Artists at Art Basel** Bill Beckley
  Zander Blom
  Keith Haring
  Dennis Hopper
  Jürgen Klauke
  Robert Longo
  Heinz Mack
  Takashi Naraha
  Markus Oehlen
  Tony Oursler
  C.O. Paeffgen
  Nam June Paik
  Julio Le Parc
  Robert Rauschenberg
  Kenny Scharf
  Jesus Rafael Soto
  Günther Uecker
  Andy Warhol
  Tom Wesselmann
- **Further artists represented** Mark Adrian
  David Bill
  Menashe Kadishman
  Bertrand Lavier
  Peter Lindbergh
  Hans Peter Reuter
  Ena Swansea
  Bernar Venet
  Ben Willikens

Mayor

London

Galleries

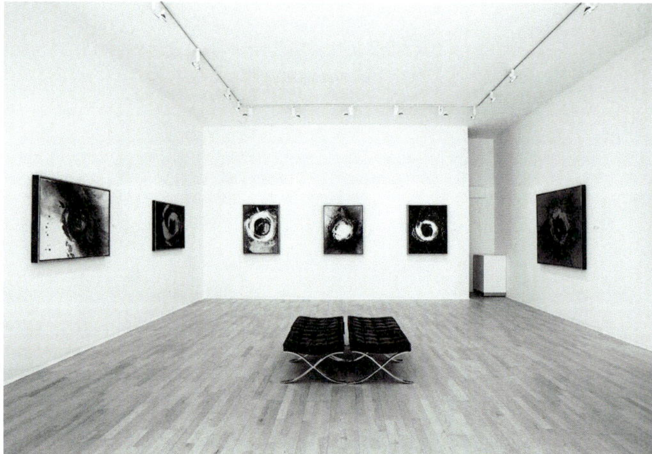

What is your favorite aspect of running a gallery?

Planning an exhibition program, and then starting to buy the works by the various artists in order to be able to do the exhibitions.

How do you choose the artists you work with?

By carefully looking back at earlier movements of the 1950s, 1960s, and 1970s, and choosing temporarily forgotten artists who deserve to be an important part of art history.

If you weren't running a gallery what else would you do?

An artist (and probably a very bad one!).

- **Contact** The Mayor Gallery
Christine Hourde
christine@mayorgallery.com
- **Established** 1925
- **Owner(s) / Partner(s)** James Mayor
- **Team** 5
- **Space(s)** 109.5 m²
- **Artists at Art Basel** Armando
Alberto Biasi
Enrico Castellani
Carlos Cruz-Diez
Dadamaino
Jan Henderikse
Walter Leblanc
Heinz Mack
Almir da Silva Mavignier
François Morellet
Otto Piene
Henk Peeters
Mira Schendel
Jan Schoonhoven
Turi Simeti
Luis Tomasello
Günther Uecker
Nanda Vigo
Gerhard von Graevenitz
- **Further artists represented** Ivor Abrahams
Billy Apple®
Anne Appleby
Antony Donaldson
Sylvia Heider

Mazzoleni

Turin
London

Galleries

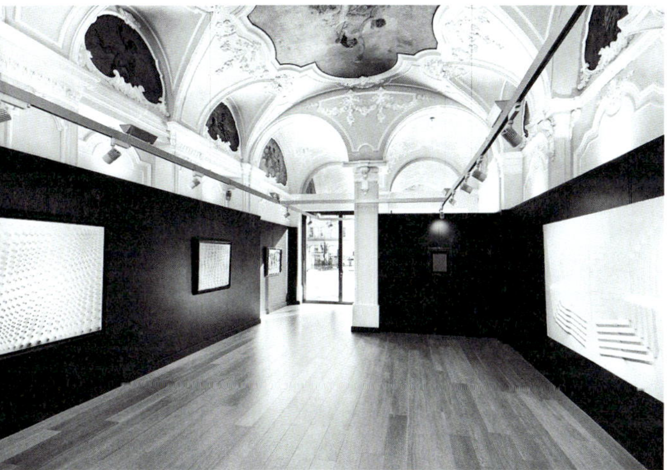

What is your favorite aspect of running a gallery?

The best aspect of working in the art world is dealing with real and entusiastic art lovers. The growing number of collectors—including young collectors—that are emerging is what drives me to continue my business with more vivacity and reliability. I love to advise my collectors on artworks that have historical and artistic aesthetic relevance, and whose value will endure overtime.

How do you choose the artists you work with?

Great artists have always succeeded in challenging the collective imagination, transcending the boundaries of their predecessors. The criteria are: ability, originality, initiative, and perseverance.

If you weren't running a gallery what else would you do?

I inherited the passion for the artworld from my parents. My dream has always been to do the job of my father Giovanni. Otherwise, I would have liked to work in the clothing industry, with a leading Italian fashion house.

- **Contact** Mazzoleni Galleria d'Arte
Davide Mazzoleni
davidemazzoleni@mazzoleniarte.it
- **Established** 1986
- **Owner(s) / Partner(s)** Giovanni Mazzoleni
- **Team** 6
- **Space(s)** 350 m²
- **Artists at Art Basel** Alighiero Boetti
Agostino Bonalumi
Alberto Burri
Enrico Castellani
Lucio Fontana
Piero Manzoni
Mario Merz
Giulio Paolini
Michelangelo Pistoletto
Paolo Scheggi
- **Further artists represented** Afro
Karel Appel
Enrico Baj
Afro Basaldella
Pier Paolo Calzolari
Giuseppe Capogrossi
Marc Chagall
Gianni Colombo
Dadamaino
Giorgio De Chirico
Piero Dorazio
Hans Hartung
Asger Jorn
Wassily Kandinsky
Wifredo Lam
Alberto Magnelli
René Magritte
Georges Mathieu
Fausto Melotti
Nunzio
Tancredi Parmeggiani
Giuseppe Penone
Gianni Piacentino
Pablo Picasso
Serge Poliakoff
Arnaldo Pomodoro
Jean-Paul Riopelle
Gino Severini
Cy Twombly
Victor Vasarely
Emilio Vedova
Gilberto Zorio

McCaffrey

New York
Saint Barthelemy

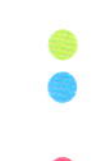

Galleries
Galleries Unlimited
Galleries

- **Contact** Fergus McCaffrey
Lisa Panzera
info@fergusmccaffrey.com
- **Established** 2006
- **Owner(s) / Partner(s)** Fergus McCaffrey
- **Team** 7
- **Space(s)** 548 m²
- **Artists at Art Basel** Jack Early
Koji Enokura
Noriyuki Haraguchi
Tatsuo Ikeda
Birgit Jürgenssen
Nobuaki Kojima
Sadamasa Motonaga
Saburo Murakami
Tomoharu Murakami
Natsuyuki Nakanishi
Hitoshi Nomura
Richard Nonas
Kiyoji Otsuji
Sigmar Polke
Gary Rough
William Scott
Nobuo Sekine
Kazuo Shiraga
Jiro Takamatsu
Atsuko Tanaka
Andy Warhol

McKee

New York

Galleries

- **Contact** McKee Gallery
Anders Bergstrom
anders@mckeegallery.com
- **Owner(s) / Partner(s)** David McKee

Meert

Brussels

Galleries Unlimited

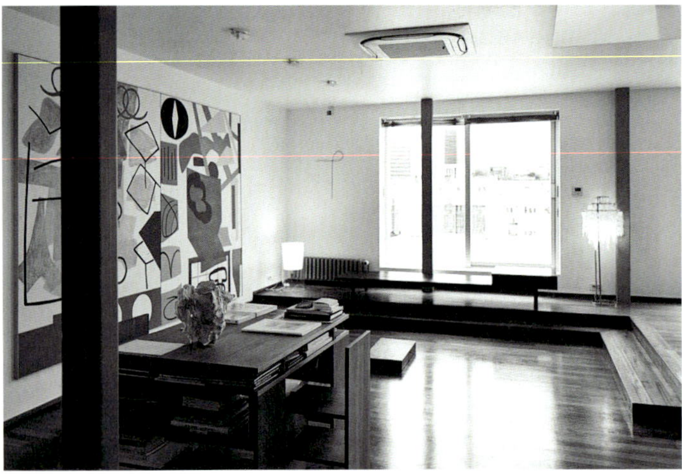

What is your favorite aspect of running a gallery?
My favorite aspect of running a gallery is to have a more personal contact with the artists that I respect and select for the program. Solely buying and selling art on the secondary market, without knowing the artist, wouldn't give me any pleasure. Running a gallery also has a strong curatorial side to it, which forces one to continuously study and analyze, in order to present relevant, interesting exhibitions.

How do you choose the artists you work with?
The program of the gallery was framed 27 years ago. From the beginning, an important, though not exclusive, focus was put on Minimal and Conceptual art. This within different time frames, from the 1960s to a younger generation, whose practice connects to the historical program. For the selection of the artists it is most important that they demonstrate an autonomous, personal reflection on art and its practice.

If you weren't running a gallery what else would you do?
I was (and am) a collector before running a gallery. Collecting art is and was a necessity, so I would continue to collect, even more.

- **Contact** Galerie Greta Meert, Frédéric Mariën, info@galeriegretameert.com
- **Established** 1988
- **Owner(s) / Partner(s)** Greta Meert, Frédéric Mariën
- **Team** 5
- **Space(s)** 500 m²
- **Artists at Art Basel** Carla Accardi, Carl Andre, John Baldessari, Johannes Döring, Peter Joseph, Louise Lawler, Robert Mangold, Anne Neukamp, Thomas Struth, Catharina van Eetvelde, Pieter Vermeersch, Didier Vermeiren, Johannes Wald
- **Further artists represented** Robert Adams, Robert Barry, Gianfranco Baruchello, Eric Baudelaire, Iñaki Bonillas, Enrico Castellani, Hanne Darboven, Edith Dekyndt, Sylvie Eyberg, Suzan Frecon, Shirley Jaffe, Mimmo Jodice, Brandt Junceau, Donald Judd, Valerie Krause, Melissa Kretschmer, Sol LeWitt, Liliana Moro, Jean-Luc Moulene, Anne Neukamp, Sophie Nys, Tobias Putrih, Fred Sandback, Niele Toroni, Richard Tuttle, Koen van den Broek, Michael Venezia, Ian Wallace

Meessen De Clercq

Brussels

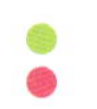
Galleries
Nova

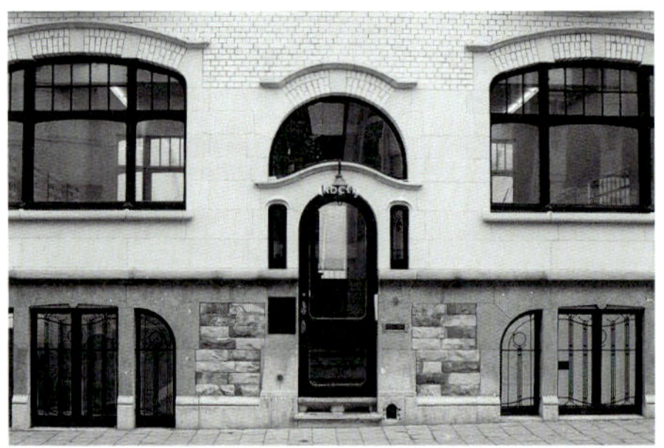

What is your favorite aspect of running a gallery?
Collaborating with the artists.

How do you choose the artists you work with?
Quality of the work, conviction, poetic strength.

If you weren't running a gallery what else would you do?
Read more.

- **Contact** Meessen De Clercq, Isa Deslypere, isa@meessendeclercq.be
- **Established** 2008
- **Owner(s) / Partner(s)** Olivier Meessen, Jan De Clercq
- **Team** 6
- **Space(s)** 400 m²
- **Artists at Art Basel** Lieven De Boeck, Hreinn Friðfinnsson, Adam Henry, Nicolás Lamas, Claudio Parmiggiani, Fabrice Samyn, José María Sicilia
- **Further artists represented** Ignasi Aballí, Sarah Bostwick, Susan Collis, Jordi Colomer, Ellen Harvey, Jorge Méndez Blake, Bruno Perramant, Evariste Richer, Kelly Schacht, Katrín Sigurðardóttir, Thu Van Tran, Maarten Vanden Eynde, Leon Vranken

Meier

San Francisco

Galleries Unlimited
Galleries

NINETEEN NINETEEN

The Story of the deYoung House at 1919 California Street San Francisco

By Helen deYoung Cameron

What is your favorite aspect of running a gallery?
Finding young talent and nurturing those artists' careers.

If you weren't running a gallery what else would you do?
Professional trapshooting.

- **Contact**
  Anthony Meier Fine Arts
  Megan McConnell
  gallery@anthonymeierfinearts.com
- **Established** 1984
- **Owner(s) / Partner(s)** Anthony Meier
- **Team** 6
- **Space(s)** 102 m²
- **Artists at Art Basel**
  Hurvin Anderson
  Janine Antoni
  Nicholas Byrne
  Sarah Cain
  Rosana Castrillo Diaz
  Michael DeLucia
  Jeremy Dickinson
  Leonardo Drew
  Cecilia Edefalk
  Tony Feher
  Teresita Fernández
  Barnaby Furnas
  David Gilbert
  Gonkar Gyatso
  Joseph Havel
  Richard Hoblock
  Jim Hodges
  Roy McMakin
  Donald Moffett
  Kristen Morgin
  Dave Muller
  Jockum Nordström
  Rob Reynolds
  Kate Shepherd
  Jasmin Sian
  Gary Simmons
  Caragh Thuring
  Tam Van Tran
  Michael Wetzel
  Yuh-Shioh Wong
- **Further artists represented**
  John Chamberlain
  Donald Judd
  Agnes Martin
  Sigmar Polke
  Gerhard Richter
  Robert Ryman

Meile

Beijing
Lucerne

Galleries
Encounters
Galleries
Galleries
Kabinett

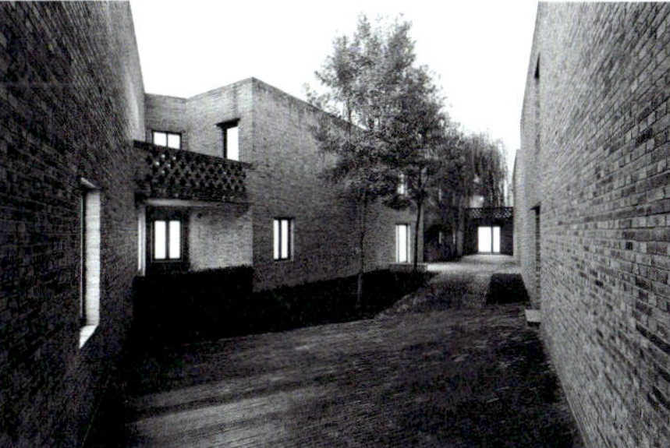

What is your favorite aspect of running a gallery?
The exchange with artists and collectors, and being around people who are enthusiastic about contemporary art.

How do you choose the artists you work with?
Their quality and potential according to my own taste. It is also important for me to discover artists at an early stage and to lead them to be world class.

If you weren't running a gallery what else would you do?
I would write.

- **Contact**
  Galerie Urs Meile
  Elena Kaiser
  elenakaiser@galerieursmeile.com
- **Established** 1992
- **Owner(s) / Partner(s)** Urs Meile
- **Team** 21
- **Space(s)**
  170 m² (Lucerne)
  450 m² (Beijing)
- **Artists at Art Basel**
  Ai Weiwei
  Hu Qingyan
  Li Gang
  Qiu Shihua
  Tobias Rehberger
  Shan Fan
  Shao Fan
  Julia Steiner
  Not Vital
  Wang Xingwei
  Xie Nanxing
  Yan Xing
- **Further artists represented**
  Andreas Golder
  Chen Hui
  Lang/Baumann
  Li Zhanyang
  Liu Ding
  Meng Huang
  Anatoly Shuravlev
  Xia Xiaowan

Menconi + Schoelkopf

New York

 Survey

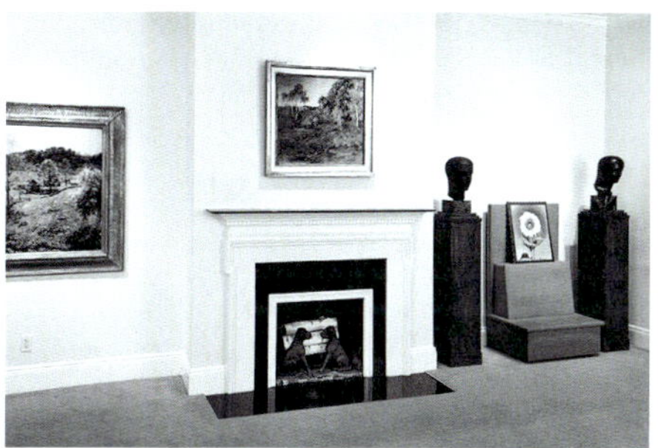

What is your favorite aspect of running a gallery?
Our favorite part of the job is augmenting the connoisseurship of our most passionate and educated clients—when the right piece finds the right home, it is tremendously gratifying.

How do you choose the artists you work with?
Presenting American art from the 19th and early 20th centuries, we are always looking for work that we believe in, regardless of whether scholarship and the market have yet admitted the artist to the canon. This sometimes means working with household names, and sometimes means making a case for renewed consideration of lesser-known lights.

If you weren't running a gallery what else would you do?
Susan Menconi would be an artist herself—a sculptor—and Andrew Schoelkopf remarks, "I really love the partnership between advisor and client and if not in the art business, I would probably find a similar business in which to maintain those same types of relationships. Helping a client to make a better informed decision is very gratifying."

- **Contact**
  Menconi + Schoelkopf
  Jonathan Spies
  jspies@msfineart.com
- **Established** 2001
- **Owner(s) / Partner(s)**
  Susan Menconi
  Andrew Schoelkopf
- **Team** 5
- **Space(s)** 186 m²
- **Artists at Art Basel** Ralston Crawford
- **Further artists represented**
  The Estate of Charles Biederman
  Elie Nadelman
  Joseph Stella

Mendes Wood

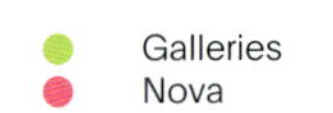

São Paulo

- Galleries
- Nova

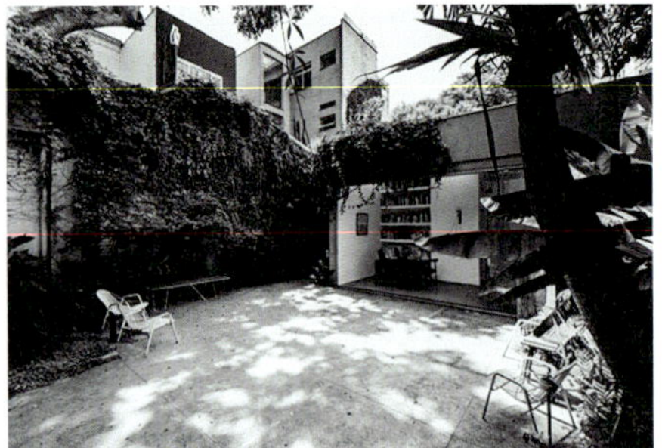

What is your favorite aspect of running a gallery?

Being in touch with ideas, with individuals who are pushing the boundary of expression and narrative structure. Art has never been so comprehensively plural. This plurality allows us to connect, relate, change, and update the world around us. Whether art calls itself "engaged" or otherwise, we strongly feel that in some evolutionary sense, access to art increases human agency, making us freer, more critical and empathetic individuals, awake to the lives of others. And our own.

How do you choose the artists you work with?

Mostly, we listen to the artists we already work with and to artists we admire. Of course, curators also do a wonderful job of bringing ideas to the fore, so we visit many, many exhibitions around the world.

If you weren't running a gallery what else would you do?

Matthew Wood: Good question. In all honesty,I would probably be a gardener.

- **Contact** Mendes Wood DM
Cecilia Tanure
cecilia@mendeswooddm.com
- **Established** 2010
- **Owner(s) / Partner(s)** Pedro Mendes
Matthew Wood
Felipe Dmab
- **Team** 20
- **Space(s)** 1,158 m²
- **Artists at Art Basel** Lucas Arruda
Cibelle Cavalli Bastos
Neïl Beloufa
Paloma Bosquê
Anna Bella Geiger
Sonia Gomes
Patricia Leite
Paulo Nazareth
Daniel Steegmann Mangrané
Tunga
- **Further artists represented** Adriano Costa
Michael Dean
Mariana Castillo Deball
Thiago Martins De Melo
f.marquespenteado
Deyson Gilbert
Runo Lagomarsino
Paulo Monteiro
Paulo Nimer Pjota
Marina Perez Simão
Leticia Ramos
Roberto Winter
Francesca Woodman

mennour

Paris

- Galleries
- Unlimited
- Galleries

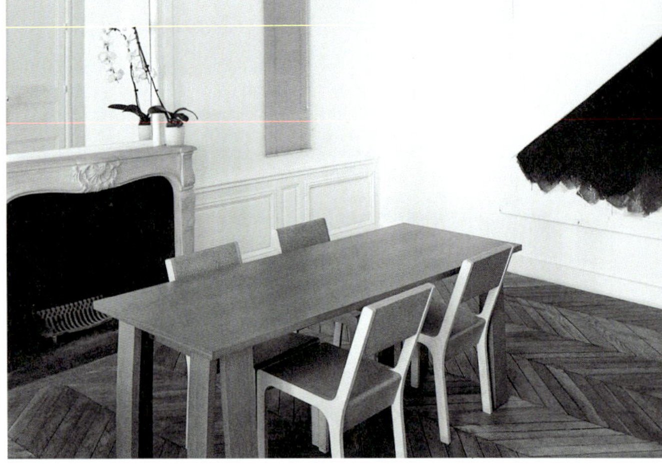

What is your favorite aspect of running a gallery?

Working with the artists and accompanying their projects.

How do you choose the artists you work with?

Visiting artists' studios and exhibitions as much as I can.

If you weren't running a gallery what else would you do?

Ballet dancer or soccer player.

- **Contact** kamel mennour
Kamel Mennour
galerie@kamelmennour.com
- **Established** 1999
- **Owner(s) / Partner(s)** Kamel Mennour
- **Team** 25
- **Space(s)** 800 m²
- **Artists at Art Basel** Hicham Berrada
Mohamed Bourouissa
Marie Bovo
Daniel Buren
Pier Paolo Calzolari
Valentin Carron
Latifa Echakhch
Dario Escobar
Michel François
Alberto Garcia-Alix
Petrit Halilaj
Camille Henrot
David Hominal
Huang Yong Ping
Alfredo Jaar
Ann Veronica Janssens
Anish Kapoor
Tadashi Kawamata
Alicja Kwade
Lee Ufan
Claude Lévêque
François Morellet
Gina Pane
Martin Parr
Martial Raysse
Lili Reynaud-Dewar
Zineb Sedira
Miri Segal
Shen Yuan

Metro Pictures

New York

- Galleries Unlimited
- Galleries

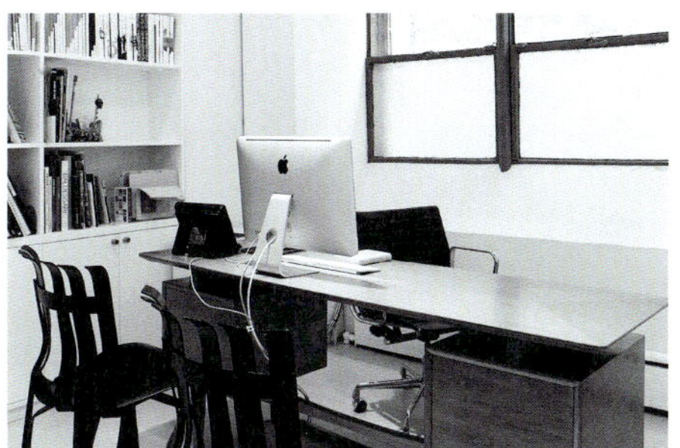

What is your favorite aspect of running a gallery?
The regular interaction with the artists and their art.

How do you choose the artists you work with?
We pay attention. We look for artists who have an uncommon vision, are making a significant contribution, and who we believe we can effectively represent and support.

If you weren't running a gallery what else would you do?
Not much.

- **Contact** Metro Pictures
  Helene Winer
  helene@metropictures.com
- **Established** 1980
- **Owner(s) / Partner(s)** Helene Winer
  Janelle Reiring
- **Team** 12
- **Space(s)** 650 m²
- **Artists at Art Basel** Nina Beier
  Olaf Breuning
  René Daniëls
  Claire Fontaine
  Camille Henrot
  Isaac Julien
  Louise Lawler
  Robert Longo
  David Maljkovic
  Paulina Olowska
  Tony Oursler
  Trevor Paglen
  Jim Shaw
  Cindy Sherman
  Gary Simmons
  Sara VanDerBeek
  Iris Vonna-Michell
  B. Wurtz
- **Further artists represented** André Butzer
  Andy Hope 1930
  John Miller
  Alexandre Singh
  Andreas Slominski
  Catherine Sullivan

Meyer Riegger

Berlin
Karlsruhe

- Galleries
- Galleries Unlimited
- Galleries

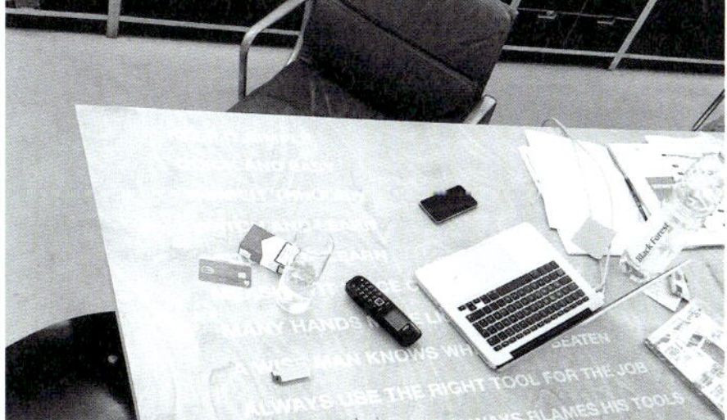

What is your favorite aspect of running a gallery?
The creative part of it, which means working closely with the artist and dealing with certain artistic concepts.

How do you choose the artists you work with?
It needs a certain moment, which can't be described.

If you weren't running a gallery what else would you do?
Maybe driving a racing car, flying an airplane, or sailing an America's Cup sailboat.

- **Contact** Meyer Riegger
  Eva Scherr
  eva@meyer-riegger.de
- **Established** 1997
- **Owner(s) / Partner(s)** Jochen Meyer
  Thomas Riegger
- **Team** 7
- **Space(s)** 560 m²
- **Artists at Art Basel** Franz Ackermann
  Rosa Barba
  Katinka Bock
  Armin Boehm
  Björn Braun
  Miriam Cahn
  Henrik Håkansson
  Eva Kotátková
  Ján Mančuška
  Meuser
  John Miller
  Helen Mirra
  Jonathan Monk
  Melvin Moti
  Scott Myles
  Paulo Nazareth
  Daniel Roth
  Julia Schmidt
  David Thorpe
  Gabriel Vormstein
  Waldemar Zimbelmann
- **Further artists represented** Heike Aumüller
  Jeanne Faust
  Uwe Henneken
  Anna Lea Hucht
  Jamie Isenstein
  Korpys/Löffler
  Kalin Lindena
  Silke Schatz

Mezzanin

Vienna
Geneva

- Galleries
- Galleries

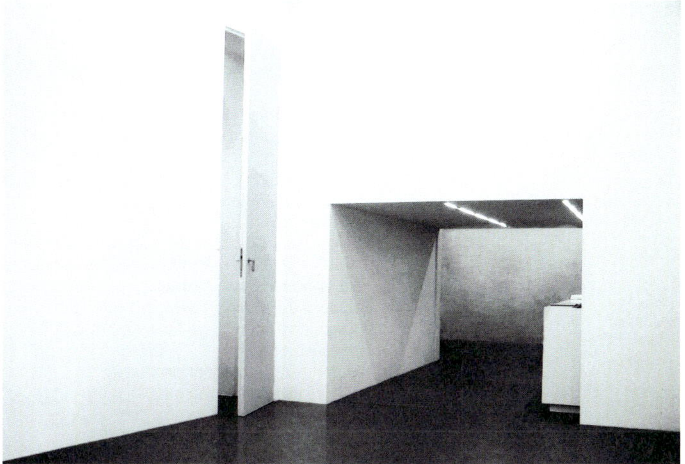

What is your favorite aspect of running a gallery?
Working closely with our artists.

How do you choose the artists you work with?
Galerie Mezzanin's program and curatorial concept is to consistently show and represent younger artists in context with established and historical artists. When choosing artists to work with I follow what interests me personally while bearing in mind the aforementioned orientation.

If you weren't running a gallery what else would you do?
I would be working for UNICEF or a similar organization.

- **Contact**: Galerie Mezzanin
  Karin Handlbauer
  office@galeriemezzanin.com
- **Established**: 2002
- **Owner(s) / Partner(s)**: Karin Handlbauer
- **Team**: 6
- **Space(s)**: 250 m²
- **Artists at Art Basel**: Etti Abergel
  Thomas Bayrle
  Bernhard Frue
  Peter Kogler
  Christian Mayer
  Katrin Plavcak
  Stephen Prina
  Mandla Reuter
  Alexander Wolff
  Christina Zurfluh
- **Further artists represented**: Sunah Choi
  Gerald Domenig
  Marino Formenti
  Michael Hakimi
  Lisa Lapinski
  Marzena Nowak
  Michelangelo Pistoletto
  Sturtevant
  Santos R. Vasquez

Michael Jon

Miami
Detroit  Nova

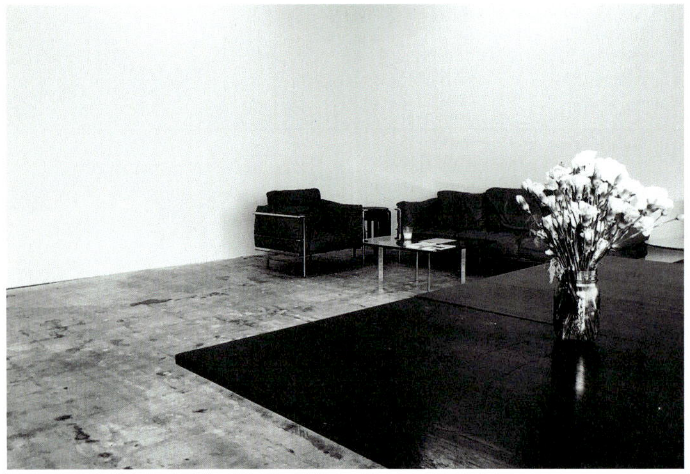

What is your favorite aspect of running a gallery?
Engaging in critical discourses and presenting new aesthetic and philosophical executions.

How do you choose the artists you work with?
Developing a personal relationship with artists that are committed to their practice—a unique vision, a confident approach to materials, and a willingness to question themselves, and thus evolve.

If you weren't running a gallery what else would you do?
Michael: A used belt salesman.
Alan: Pursue a pro tennis career.

- **Contact**: Michael Jon Gallery
  Alan Gutierrez
  info@michaeljongallery.com
- **Established**: 2012
- **Owner(s) / Partner(s)**: Michael Radziewicz
  Alan Gutierrez
- **Team**: 2
- **Space(s)**: 316 m²
- **Artists at Art Basel**: Sayre Gomez
  JPW3
- **Further artists represented**: Kelly Akashi
  Math Bass
  Egan Frantz

Millan

São Paulo ● Galleries

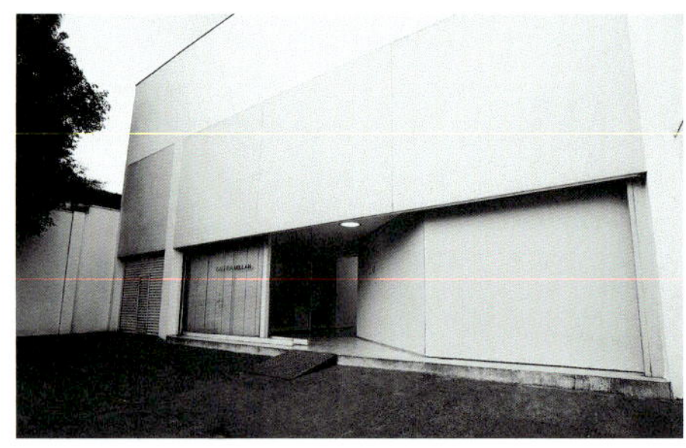

How do you choose the artists you work with?
We have a commitment to a historical and critical view of art, introducing relationships between contemporary artists, and modern artists who influenced their education. The belief in this dialogue between generations allows us to represent a team of consistent artists, ranging from well-knowns to young artists.

- **Contact**: Galeria Millan
  Caroline Carrion
  caroline@galeriamillan.com.br
- **Established**: 1986
- **Owner(s) / Partner(s)**: André Millan
  Socorro De Andrade Lima
- **Team**: 16
- **Space(s)**: 450 m²
- **Artists at Art Basel**: Rodrigo Andrade
  Artur Barrio
  Lenora de Barros
  Tatiana Blass
  Sofia Borges
  Felipe Cohen
  Nelson Felix
  Anna Maria Maiolino
  Rubens Mano
  Emmanuel Nassar
  Henrique Oliveira
  Paulo Pasta
  Ana Prata
  Berna Reale
  José Resende
  Miguel Rio Branco
  Thiago Rocha Pitta
  Mira Schendel
  Tunga
- **Further artists represented**: Rodrigo Bivar
  Dudi Maia Rosa
  Otavio Schipper
  Bob Wolfenson

Ming

Taipei ● Insights

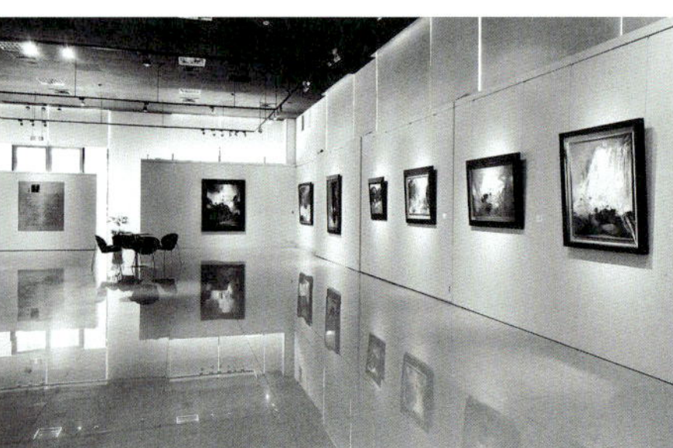

What is your favorite aspect of running a gallery?
Meeting new artists and admiring their beautiful works. It is also very exciting to attend art fairs around the world.

How do you choose the artists you work with?
The reason we choose an artist is not based on his/her academic background: we try to read their minds, see if they can express their thoughts in their artwork, and have enough passion. We assume that's where their potential is.

If you weren't running a gallery what else would you do?
Be a consultant, or a museum guide who can always admire the art.

- **Contact** Ming Art Gallery
  Chu Yin Cheng
  mingart8@gmail.com
- **Established** 2005
- **Owner(s) / Partner(s)** Chu Yin Cheng
- **Team** 6
- **Space(s)** 80 m²
- **Artists at Art Basel** Chiu Ya-Tsai
- **Further artists represented** Tang Hay Wen

Francesca Minini

Milan

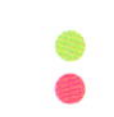

Discoveries
Nova

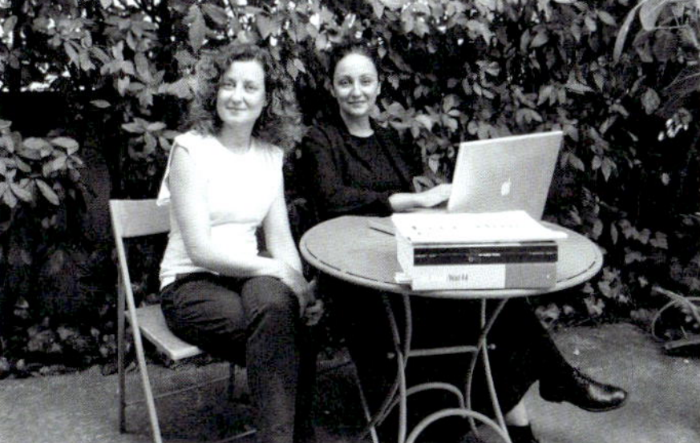

What is your favorite aspect of running a gallery?

Every aspect of the gallery interests me. First of all the relationship with the artists and the great ideas they have for all their projects. The important contacts with collectors and the constant exchange with curators. The experience of seeing shows, museums, the numerous biennials, and the large number of fairs we participate in allow mutual debate to constantly enrich the curatorial aspect of our research.

How do you choose the artists you work with?

It comes from passion and interest in their artistic research. Following this, the commercial aspect starts. Maybe it is too naive but I still believe in the artwork-comes-first idea.

If you weren't running a gallery what else would you do?

It is very difficult to say. I come from a family of art dealers, and artists and art have always surrounded me. When I opened my gallery in 2006 it was kind of natural for me to continue this history and I still think it was my best choice. Recently Alessandra, my sister, joined my gallery, and now every member of the family is deeply involved in art. It is a family madness for sure!

- **Contact** Francesca Minini
  Anna Abbà
  anna@francescaminini.it
- **Established** 2006
- **Owner(s) / Partner(s)** Francesca Minini
- **Team** 5
- **Space(s)** 210 m²
- **Artists at Art Basel** Paolo Chiasera
  Simon Dybbroe Møller
  Giulio Frigo
  Mandla Reuter
  Alice Ronchi
- **Further artists represented** Ghada Amer
  Becky Beasley
  Matthias Bitzer
  Armin Boehm
  Daniel Buren
  Jan De Cock
  Flavio Favelli
  Dan Graham
  Ali Kazma
  Deborah Ligorio
  Gabriele Picco
  Riccardo Previdi
  Francesco Simeti

Massimo Minini

Brescia

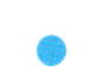

Galleries

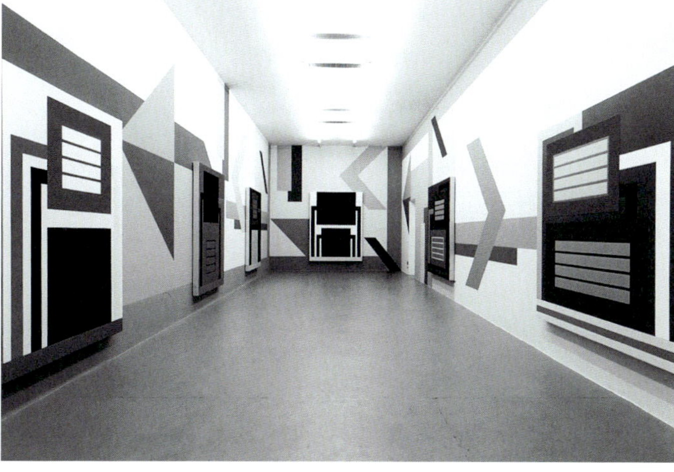

What is your favorite aspect of running a gallery?

"Running a gallery" can be a funny job. It's not a job, really, it's a passion and a trap. You always start wanting to do all kinds of things, show how good you are, how much you know about art, artists, artworks, stories, and art history. Then, bit by bit, routine takes over. Running a gallery means fighting with shippers, builders, printers, customs offices, collectors who want to pay less, artists who want to raise prices.

How do you choose the artists you work with?

There are people who believe in the originality of their ideas. They think their decisions are based just on their own judgment and that they are impervious to the world's opinions. I think our thoughts and convictions are molded and modified by all kinds of input that comes to us from the press, from exhibitions, from critics, from debates, and so my choices of artists are also shaped by this array of "advice" that the art world offers us on a daily basis.

If you weren't running a gallery what else would you do?

In a previous life I was a sales rep, selling goods throughout Europe. By driving around and visiting various countries, I learned there was an art world out there, working and showing and selling things. So at a certain point I chucked it all in and opened the gallery. It was 1973 and I was 29 years old. If I hadn't run a gallery, I would have liked to write. And so gradually I've turned from a dealer into a writer. Some people actually say to me me, "Why don't you close the gallery? You're better at writing."

- **Contact** Galleria Massimo Minini
  Massimo Minini
  info@galleriaminini.it
- **Established** 1973
- **Owner(s) / Partner(s)** Massimo Minini
  Daniella Betta
- **Team** 8
- **Space(s)** 700 m²
- **Artists at Art Basel** Carla Accardi
  Roger Ballen
  Robert Barry
  Monica Bonvicini
  Stanley Brouwn
  Daniel Buren
  Haris Epaminonda
  Hans-Peter Feldmann
  Alberto Garutti
  Luigi Ghirri
  Paolo Gioli
  Dan Graham
  Anish Kapoor
  Sol LeWitt
  David Maljkovic
  Ryan Mendoza
  Sabrina Mezzaqui
  Paul P.
  Giulio Paolini
  Nedko Solakov
  Ettore Spalletti
  Ian Wilson
  Francesca Woodman

- **Further artists represented** Ghada Amer
Stefano Arienti
Olivo Barbieri
Gabriele Basilico
Vanessa Beecroft
Letizia Cariello
Jota Castro
Paolo Chiasera
Jan De Cock
Maurizio Donzelli
Ian Hamilton Finlay
Yona Friedman
Peter Halley
Bertrand Lavier
Eva Marisaldi
Ryan Mendoza
Mathieu Mercier
Paolo Novelli
Gerwald Rockenschaub
Haim Steinbach
Paul Thorel
Betty Woodman

Miro

London

- Galleries
- Galleries Unlimited
- Galleries Public

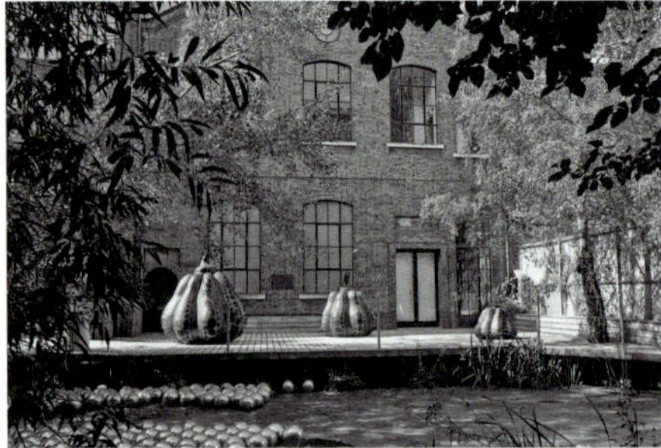

What is your favorite aspect of running a gallery?
Visiting artists in their studios.

How do you choose the artists you work with?
Intuitively.

If you weren't running a gallery what else would you do?
I would be an artist.

- **Contact** Victoria Miro
info@victoria-miro.com
- **Established** 1985
- **Owner(s) / Partner(s)** Victoria Miro
Glenn Scott Wright
W.P. Miro
- **Team** 30
- **Space(s)** 1,067 m²
- **Artists at Art Basel** Doug Aitken
Jules de Balincourt
Hernan Bas
Varda Caivano
Verne Dawson
Peter Doig
Stan Douglas
William Eggleston
Michael Elmgreen & Ingar Dragset
Inka Essenhigh
Ian Hamilton Finlay
Barnaby Furnas
David Harrison
NS Harsha
Alex Hartley
Secundino Hernández
Christian Holstad
Chantal Joffe
Isaac Julien
Idris Khan
John Kørner
Udomsak Krisanamis
Yayoi Kusama
Wangechi Mutu
Alice Neel
Maria Nepomuceno
Chris Ofili
Jacco Olivier
Celia Paul
Grayson Perry
Tal R
Conrad Shawcross
Sarah Sze
Adriana Varejão
Kara Walker
Suling Wang
Stephen Willats
Francesca Woodman

Mitchell-Innes & Nash

New York

- Galleries
- Galleries Unlimited
- Galleries Public

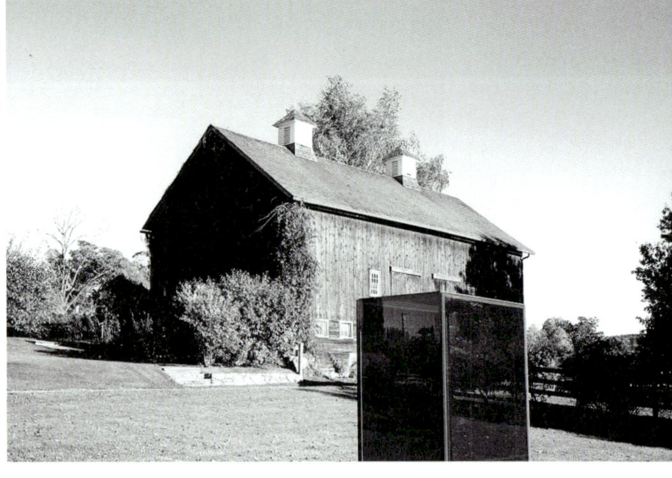

What is your favorite aspect of running a gallery?
I love working with our contemporary artists, seeing the exhibitions they create for our space, and working with artists' Estates to put on shows such as our recent Jay DeFeo exhibition.

How do you choose the artists you work with?
It's a slightly different process every time, but ultimately it comes down to having that instinctive "green light" feeling about the work.

- **Contact** Mitchell-Innes & Nash
Josie Nash
josie@miandn.com
- **Established** 1996
- **Owner(s) / Partner(s)** David Nash
Lucy Mitchell-Innes
- **Team** 14
- **Space(s)** 464.5 m²
- **Artists at Art Basel** Jean Arp
Sarah Braman
Anthony Caro
Jay DeFeo
Keltie Ferris
Gonzalo Fonseca
Nancy Graves
Karl Haendel
Chris Johanson
Martin Kersels
Julije Knifer
Leon Kossoff
Justine Kurland
Leigh Ledare
Daniel Lefcourt
Alexander Liberman
Virginia Overton
William Pope.L
Martha Rosler
Amanda Ross-Ho
Julian Stanczak
Jessica Stockholder
Brent Wadden
Paul Winstanley
- **Further artists represented** Alberto Burri
Allan D'Arcangelo
Christopher Miner
Norbert Schwontkowski

Mizuma

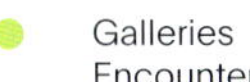

Tokyo
Singapore

Galleries
Encounters

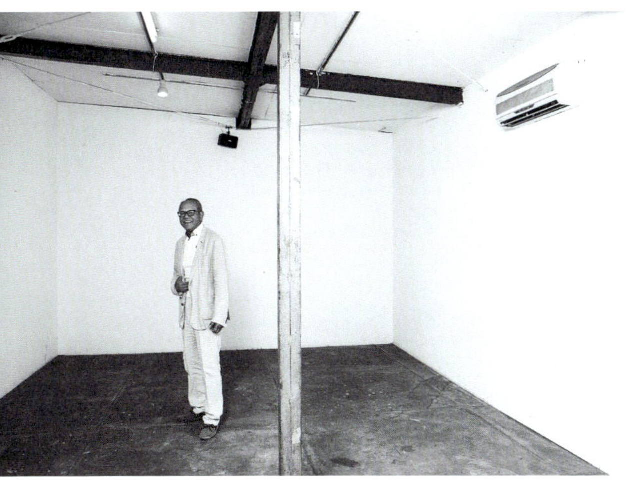

What is your favorite aspect of running a gallery?
Sharing their successes and growing with the artists.

How do you choose the artists you work with?
I believe that using hands to create works is connected to using the brain. So I have chosen artists who perform manual tasks, with unseen and profound concepts.

If you weren't running a gallery what else would you do?
I would be a collector of contemporary art.

- **Contact** Mizuma Art Gallery
Sueo Mizuma
gallery@mizuma-art.co.jp
- **Established** 1994
- **Owner(s) / Partner(s)** Sueo Mizuma
- **Team** 10
- **Space(s)** 285 m²
- **Artists at Art Basel** Miyanaga Aiko
Yamaguchi Akira
Darbotz
DU Kun
Tanada Koji
Yoga Mahendra
Kumazawa Mikiko
Jun Nguyen-Hatsushiba
O Jun
Albert Yonathan Setyawan
Kaneko Tomiyuki
Amano Yoshitaka
- **Further artists represented** Yamaguchi Ai
Kondoh Akino
Okamoto Eli
Okada Hiroko
Matsukage Hiroyuki
Tenmyouya Hisashi
Indieguerillas
Kurashige Jin
Mori Junichi
Motomiya Kaoru
Jane Lee
Aida Makoto
Ikeda Manabu
Yamamoto Masao
Nasirun
Susan Philipsz
Angki Purbandono
Rongrong & Inri
Yamamoto Ryuki
Aoyama Satoru
Tsutsui Shinsuke
Karasumaru Yumi

Mnuchin

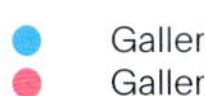

New York

Galleries
Galleries

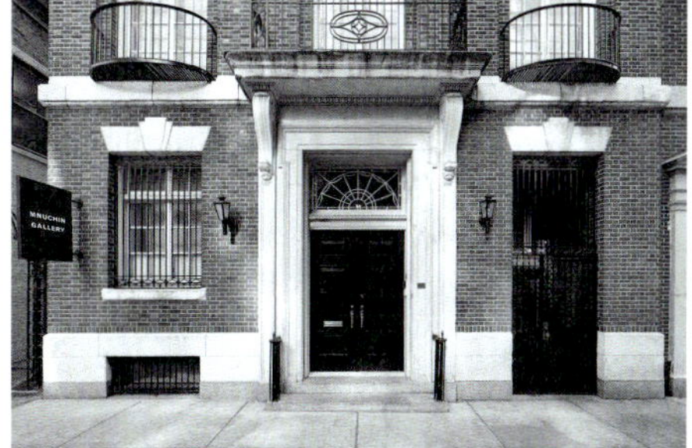

What is your favorite aspect of running a gallery?
I became a dealer because I had a craving to make exhibitions.

How do you choose the artists you work with?
There are many artists with whom we would be proud to work. Our choice comes down to what opportunities we have to present what we consider to be outstanding material.

If you weren't running a gallery what else would you do?
I would follow my second great interest, which is landscaping and trees.

- **Contact** Mnuchin Gallery
Liana Gorman
liana@mnuchingallery.com
- **Established** 1993
- **Owner(s) / Partner(s)** Robert Mnuchin
Sukanya Rajaratnam
- **Team** 8
- **Space(s)** 895.5 m²
- **Artists at Art Basel** Mark Bradford
Alexander Calder
John Chamberlain
Joseph Cornell
Richard Diebenkorn
Dan Flavin
Simon Hantaï
Donald Judd
Jacob Kassay
Ellsworth Kelly
Franz Kline
Willem de Kooning
Henri Laurens
Morris Louis
Conrad Marca-Relli
Brice Marden
Agnes Martin
Robert Motherwell
Mark Rothko
Robert Ryman
Cy Twombly
Andy Warhol
Christopher Wool

Modern Art

London

Galleries
Galleries
Parcours
Galleries

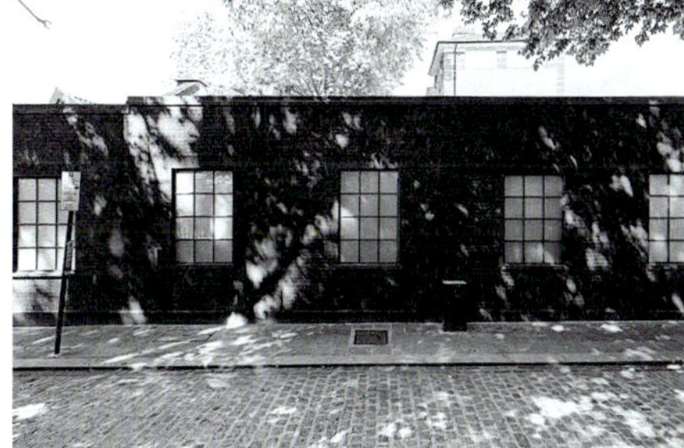

What is your favorite aspect of running a gallery?
Artists.

How do you choose the artists you work with?
Intuition, recommendation from other artists, and research.

If you weren't running a gallery what else would you do?
Psychoanalyst.

- **Contact** Stuart Shave / Modern Art
  Ryan Moore
  ryan@modernart.net
- **Established** 1998
- **Owner(s) / Partner(s)** Stuart Shave
  Jimi Lee
- **Team** 9
- **Space(s)** 464.5 m²
- **Artists at Art Basel** David Altmejd
  Karla Black
  Tom Burr
  Mark Flood
  Tim Gardner
  Lothar Hempel
  Yngve Holen
  Jacqueline Humphries
  Ansel Krut
  Phillip Lai
  Paul Lee
  Linder
  Barry McGee
  Jonathan Meese
  Matthew Monahan
  Katy Moran
  David Noonan
  Anna-Bella Papp
  Eva Rothschild
  Bojan Šarčević
  Lara Schnitger
  Collier Schorr
  Steven Shearer
  Ricky Swallow
  Richard Tuttle

Modern Institute

Glasgow

Galleries
Unlimited
Parcours
Galleries

- **Contact** The Modern Institute
  Margot Samel
  margot@themoderninstitute.com
- **Established** 1998
- **Owner(s) / Partner(s)** Toby Webster
  Andrew Hamilton
- **Team** 16
- **Space(s)** 1,342 m²
- **Artists at Art Basel** Dirk Bell
  Martin Boyce
  Anne Collier
  Jeremy Deller
  Alex Dordoy
  Urs Fischer
  Kim Fisher
  Luke Fowler
  Martino Gamper
  Henrik Håkansson
  Mark Handforth
  Thomas Houseago
  Richard Hughes
  Chris Johanson
  William E. Jones
  Andrew Kerr
  Shio Kusaka
  Jim Lambie
  Liz Larner
  Tobias Madison
  Adam McEwen
  Victoria Morton
  Scott Myles
  Nicolas Party
  Toby Paterson
  Simon Periton
  Manfred Pernice
  Mary Redmond
  Eva Rothschild
  Monika Sosnowska
  Simon Starling
  Katja Strunz
  Tony Swain
  Spencer Sweeney
  Joanne Tatham & Tom O'Sullivan
  Pádraig Timoney
  Hayley Tompkins
  Sue Tompkins
  Cathy Wilkes
  Michael Wilkinson
  Gregor Wright

Moeller

New York
Berlin

Galleries

What is your favorite aspect of running a gallery?
Selling to collectors who appreciate great art.

If you weren't running a gallery what else would you do?
Play the violin.

- **Contact** Moeller Fine Art
  Achim Moeller
  mail@moellerfineart.com
- **Established** 1972
- **Owner** Achim Moeller
- **Team** 8
- **Space(s)** 279 m²

Monitor

Rome
New York

Discoveries

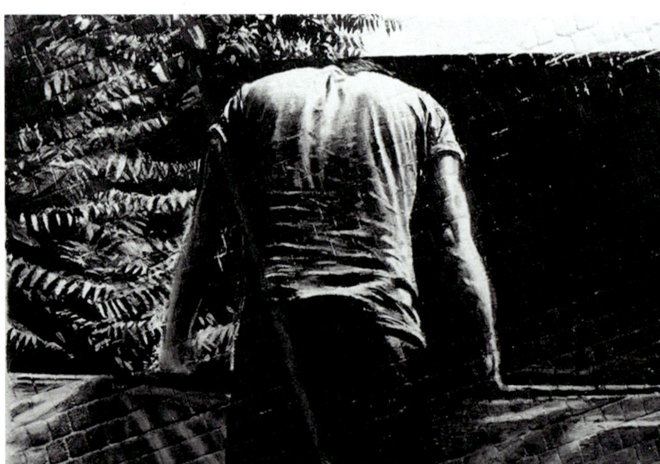

What is your favorite aspect of running a gallery?
Working with the artists, developing projects, seeing them grow.

How do you choose the artists you work with?
I see the potentiality of the works and the person behind this.

If you weren't running a gallery what else would you do?
Running a gallery still looks like a good option.

- **Contact** Monitor
  Paola Capata Manuela Contino
  monitor@monitoronline.org
- **Established** 2003
- **Owner(s) / Partner(s)** Paola Capata
- **Team** 3
- **Space(s)** 120 m²
- **Artists at Art Basel** Ian Tweedy
- **Further artists represented** Francesco Arena
  Jesse Ash
  Adam Avikainen
  Tomaso De Luca
  Graham Hudson
  Rä di Martino
  Ursula Mayer
  Nathaniel Mellors
  Antonio Rovaldi
  Alexandre Singh
  Ian Tweedy
  Nico Vascellari
  Kostis Velonis
  Guido van der Werve
  Zimmerfrei

mor charpentier

Paris 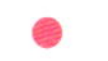 Nova

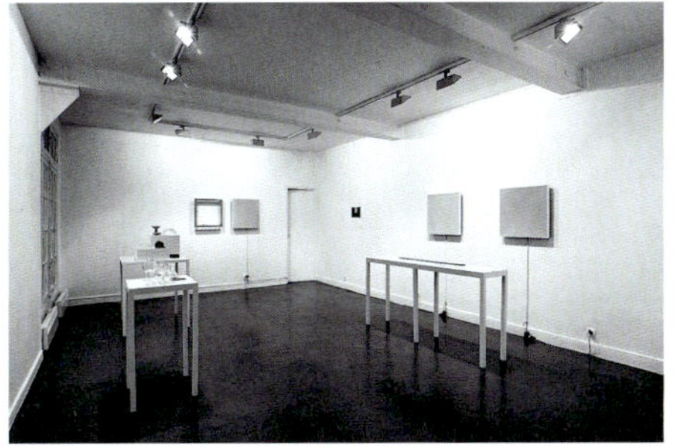

What is your favorite aspect of running a gallery?
The most exciting part is working closely with artists in all the steps of their creative process. We also love the great variety of interesting people we meet everyday.

How do you choose the artists you work with?
We are interested in socially or politically engaged artists, even though "instinct" plays a major role in our choices.

If you weren't running a gallery what else would you do?
Before being gallerist, I (Alex) was a marketing manager and Philippe was a financial consultant, but fortunately we were saved by the art world!

- **Contact** mor charpentier, Alex Mor, alex@mor-charpentier.com
- **Established** 2010
- **Owner(s) / Partner(s)** Alex Mor, Philippe Charpentier
- **Team** 6
- **Space(s)** 130 m²
- **Artists at Art Basel** Voluspa Jarpa, Teresa Margolles, Oscar Muñoz
- **Further artists represented** Lara Almarcegui, Alexander Apóstol, Julieta Aranda, Marwa Arsanios, Milena Bonilla, María José Arjona, Cevdet Erek, Maria Elvira Escallon, Voluspa Jarpa, Enzo Mianes, Teresa Margolles, Mohamed Namou, Yoshua Okón, Uriel Orlow, Liliana Porter, Charwei Tsai

Mot

Brussels, Mexico City 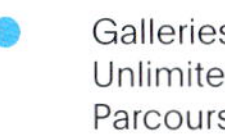 Galleries, Unlimited, Parcours

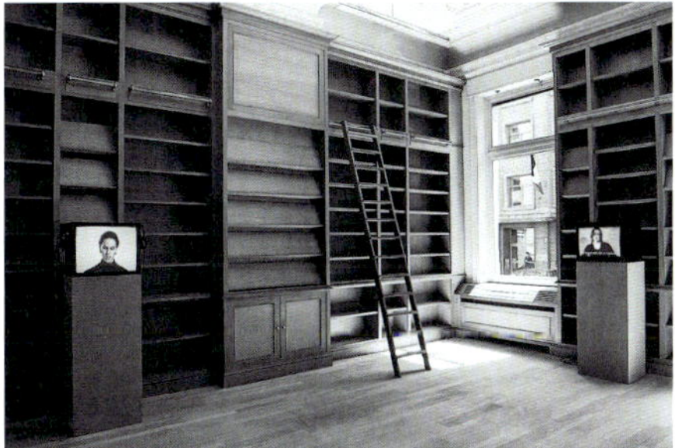

- **Contact** Jan Mot, Jan Mot, office@janmot.com
- **Established** 1996
- **Owner(s) / Partner(s)** Jan Mot
- **Team** 3
- **Artists at Art Basel** Robert Barry, Pierre Bismuth, Rineke Dijkstra, Mario García Torres, Joachim Koester, David Lamelas, Philippe Thomas, Ian Wilson
- **Further artists represented** Sven Augustijnen, Manon de Boer, Dominique Gonzalez-Foerster, Douglas Gordon, Sharon Lockhart, Tino Sehgal, Tris Vonna-Michell

MOT International

London, Brussels — Feature, Unlimited, Nova

What is your favorite aspect of running a gallery?
Art.

How do you choose the artists you work with?
Research.

- **Contact** MOT International, Nicola Wright, nicola@motinternational.com
- **Established** 2006
- **Owner(s) / Partner(s)** Chris Hammond, Aly Afshar
- **Artists at Art Basel** Dennis Oppenheim, Elizabeth Price, Laure Prouvost

mother's tankstation

Dublin  Discoveries, Nova

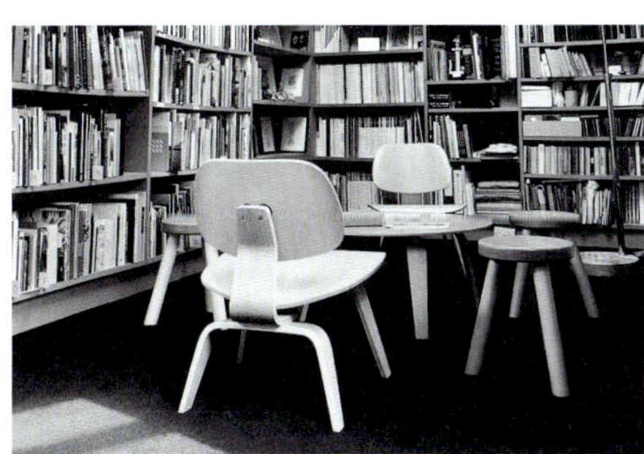

What is your favorite aspect of running a gallery?
mother's tankstation is honoured with a reputation for finding emerging talent, creating early opportunities, and growing together with the artists. This is not only my favorite aspect of running a gallery, but the one closest to my heart. It takes rigor, restless research, and endless travel; an essential, yet hotly debated cornerstone of contemporary gallery existence. Personally I don't mind, given that everything we do is actually a real privilege.

How do you choose the artists you work with?
Finding artists is key to any gallery's success, and certainly essential to its identity, yet it is arguably one of the hardest things to achieve and balance. Sometimes the simplest, most tangential things attract my attention, but in the end it always comes down to an artist's focus and passion. I adore when personality and individualism shine through a practice like a beacon, even in a raw state—this will make me travel across the planet to visit a studio.

If you weren't running a gallery what else would you do?
I've thought about astrophysics or animal dentistry as possible alternatives to running a gallery, but given that before mother's tankstation I practiced as an artist alongside curatorial work and running a Master's program, I think I'm best

suited to the visual arts. I loved making work, but the gallery essentially employs and heightens all those creative, curatorial, and organizational skills to a focused and highly rewarding end. Watching the gallery grow is even better than gardening.

- **Contact** mother's tankstation
  Finola Jones
  gallery@motherstankstation.com
- **Established** 2006
- **Owner(s) / Partner(s)** Finola Jones
- **Team** 5
- **Space(s)** 250 m²
- **Artists at Art Basel** Uri Aran
  Ara Dymond
  Noel McKenna
  Mairead O'hEocha
- **Further artists represented** Sam Anderson
  Ian Burns
  Nina Canell
  Kevin Cosgrove
  Brendan Earley
  Fergus Feehily
  Atsushi Kaga
  Shane McCarthy
  Noel McKenna
  Alasdair McLuckie
  Matt Sheridan Smith
  David Sherry

Mujin-to

Tokyo Discoveries

What is your favorite aspect of running a gallery?
Being able to connect with people and access society through artists. Collaborating with artists to promote their ideas is the most exciting part of running a gallery.

How do you choose the artists you work with?
How they observe society (and history) and how they represent society.

If you weren't running a gallery what else would you do?
There is neither time to look back, nor in other directions: I just deal with now and look forward to the future.

- **Contact** Mujin-to Production
  Mayumi Wakaguri
  info@mujin-to.com
- **Established** May 2006
- **Owner(s) / Partner(s)** Rika Fujiki
- **Team** 4
- **Space(s)** 70 m²
- **Artists at Art Basel** Tsubasa Kato
- **Further artists represented** Kazuhiko Hachiya
  Lyota Yagi
  Chim↑Pom
  Sachiko Kazama
  Ryohei Usui
  Yoko Asakai
  Yukihiro Taguchi
  Osamu Matsuda
  Kenta Nishimura

Müller

Zurich 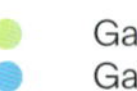 Galleries
Galleries

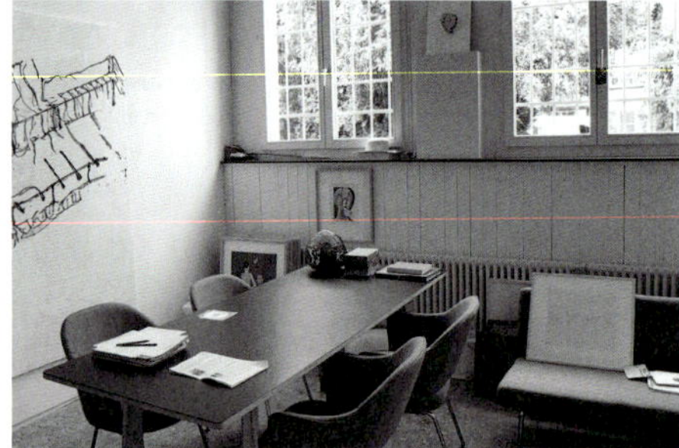

What is your favorite aspect of running a gallery?
Showing strong exhibitions as well as the close relationships with the artists, and being able to see their growth and development.

How do you choose the artists you work with?
I need to be impressed by the quality and consistency of their work over time.

If you weren't running a gallery what else would you do?
Be a collector.

- **Contact** Galerie Mark Müller
  Mark Müller
  mail@markmueller.ch
- **Established** 1990
- **Owner(s) / Partner(s)** Mark Müller
- **Team** 2
- **Space(s)** 220 m²
- **Artists at Art Basel** Joachim Bandau
  Reto Boller
  Urs Frei
  Stefan Gritsch
  Katharina Grosse
  Marcia Hafif
  Joseph Marioni
  Martín Mele
  Judy Millar
  François Morellet
  Patrick Rohner
  Giacomo Santiago Rogado
  Christine Streuli
  Markus Weggenmann
- **Further artists represented** Heike Kati Barath
  Francis Baudevin
  Sabian Baumann
  Monika Brandmeier
  Dennis Hollingsworth
  Axel Lieber
  John Nixon
  François Perrodin
  Hans Stalder
  Jürg Stäuble
  Michel Verjux
  Duane Zaloudek

Munro

Hamburg  Galleries

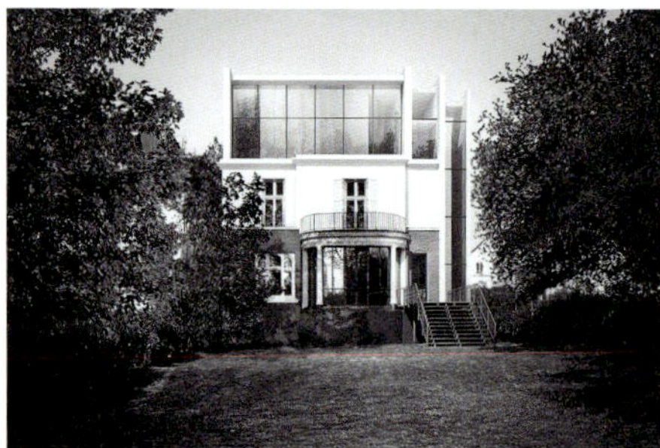

What is your favorite aspect of running a gallery?
Through my friendship with Alfred Schmela I felt the challenge to show strong art in my hometown of Hamburg, something which almost didn't exist at that time.

How do you choose the artists you work with?
Interest in their work.

If you weren't running a gallery what else would you do?
Collect/buy/sell art.

- **Contact** Galerie Vera Munro
Vera Munro
gallery@veramunro.de
- **Established** 1977
- **Owner(s) / Partner(s)** Vera Munro
- **Team** 6
- **Space(s)** 600 m²
- **Artists at Art Basel** Eriks Apalais
John M Armleder
Janis Avotins
Silvia Bächli
Jean-Marc Bustamante
Helmut Dorner
Günther Förg
Teresa Hubbard/
Alexander Birchler
Imi Knoebel
Linda McCue
Kohei Nawa
Miwa Ogasawara
Gerwald Rockenschaub
Wawrzyniec Tokarski
Franz-Erhard Walther
Paul Winstanley
- **Further artists represented** Mary Heilmann
Donald Judd
Richard Long
Blinky Palermo
Sigmar Polke
Gerhard Richter

Murphy

Fortitude Valley 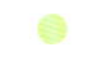 Insights

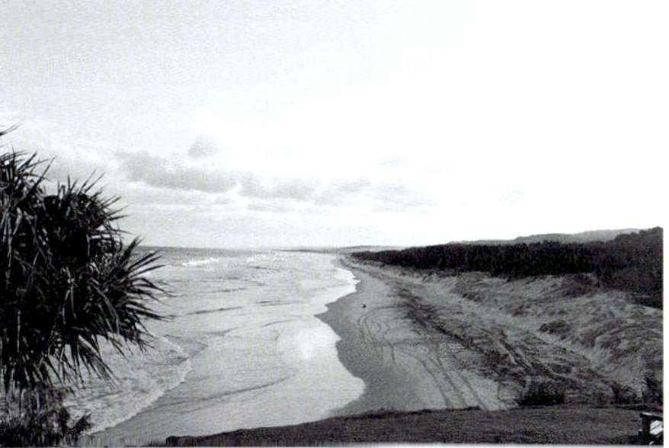

What is your favorite aspect of running a gallery?
Working with an incredibly diverse group of artistic talent and the collectors who are willing to support them is both challenging and professionally rewarding. The relationships formed over time, with both artists and clients is quite unique. With up to 12 exhibitions a year, there is never the opportunity for boredom, and one never tires of installing a new body of work.

How do you choose the artists you work with?
I spend a lot of time researching and visiting exhibitions both locally and nationally. I look at artists with a strong and consistent commitment to their practice—even if they are emerging. My nose is always in a catalogue, book, or art magazine. Other artists are the greatest barometers; they tend to be in tune with who to watch, so I will always consider their recommendations.

If you weren't running a gallery what else would you do?
This is a very difficult question—for as long as I can remember I have always wanted to be the director of a commercial gallery. A life without artists, clients, and a beautiful working environment is difficult to imagine. I have no doubt I would be working in another area of the visual arts, perhaps a curatorial position in a private museum. It sounds clichéd, but I understand and appreciate just how fortunate I am to have a career that is so much more than a "job."

- **Contact** Jan Murphy Gallery
Jan Murphy
jan@janmurphygallery.com.au
- **Established** 1995
- **Owner(s) / Partner(s)** Jan Murphy
- **Team** 3
- **Space(s)** 150 m²
- **Artists at Art Basel** Danie Mellor
- **Further artists represented** Jason Benjamin
Natasha Bieniek
Kim Buck
Julia deVille
Richard Dunlop
Jason Fitzgerald
James Guppy
Linde Ivimey
Kirra Jamison
Rhys Lee
Adam Lester
Robert Malherbe
Lara Merrett
Michael Muir
Ben Quilty
Victoria Reichelt
Leslie Rice
Monica Rohan
Alex Seton
Marina Strocchi
A.J. Taylor
Huang Xu
Heidi Yardley
Liu Zhuoquan

Murray White

Melbourne 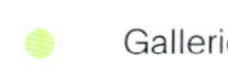 Galleries

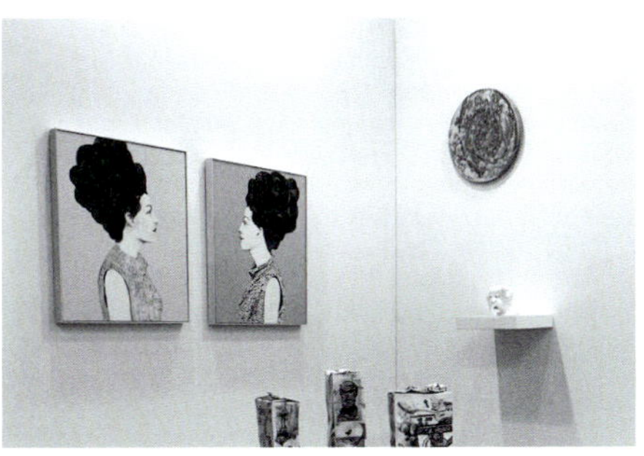

What is your favorite aspect of running a gallery?
The continuity and ongoing relationship with artists as opposed to the singular project context of the public museum sector.

How do you choose the artists you work with?
"Choosing" an artist to represent and work with is an ongoing, long-term relationship that is developed through a mutual appreciation and understanding of their particular practice.

If you weren't running a gallery what else would you do?
Nothing.

- **Contact** Murray White Room
Murray White
email@murraywhiteroom.com
- **Established** 2006
- **Owner(s) / Partner(s)** Murray White
- **Team** 5
- **Space(s)** 110 m2
- **Artists at Art Basel** Bastien Aubry
/Dimitri Broquard
Polly Borland
Tony Clark
Richard Giblett
Anne-Marie May
Alasdair McLuckie
Alex Pittendrigh
Sally Ross
Sangeeta Sandrasegar
Constanze Zikos
- **Further artists represented** Judith Van Heeren
Eliza Hutchison
Alexander Knox

Mendes Wood DM
Interview with Matthew Wood

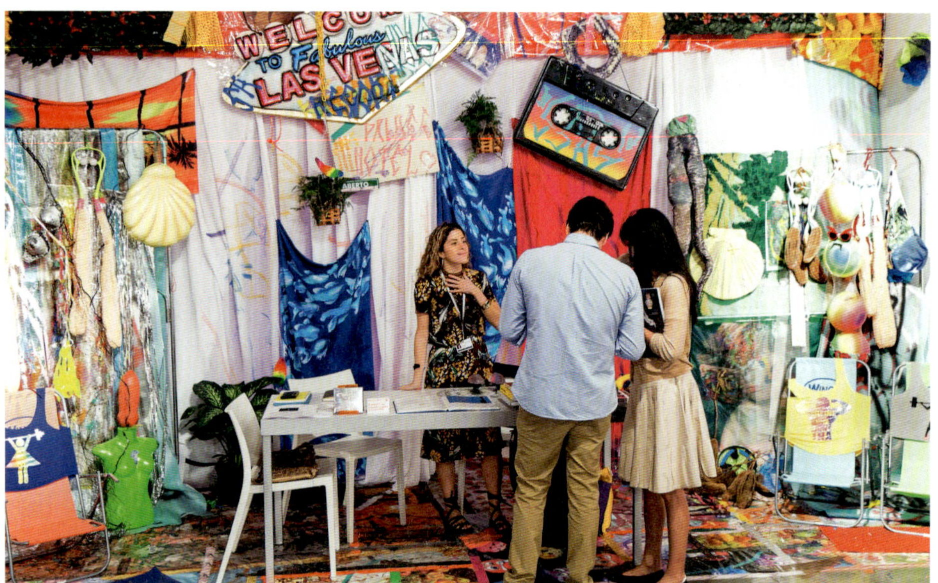

Art Basel in Miami Beach (Nova), 2014

Let's start with the history of the Mendes Wood gallery. When was it created? Why did you open in São Paulo?

There is a sort of complex hidden story to our three-partner gallery. I met Pedro [Mendes] 11 years ago while we were studying philosophy in Paris. We met on a course on the philosophy of aesthetics: I was more about Baudelaire and *l'art pour l'art*; he was studying Schopenhauer and the question of the representation of art in the world. We completely disagreed about everything! Over time I realized how rich our differences were: we ended up finding a common ground in contemporary art practice. Pedro eventually convinced me to move to Brazil where he is from. I'm from the US, having grown up in Tanzania, France, and Belgium. Brazil was just a stunning, new horizon where in 2008 we started JACA, an artists' residency located in Belo Horizonte—Pedro's hometown. I met Paulo Nazareth there, one of the first artists we represented.

After that, it became quite obvious that São Paulo is really the cultural center of South America. Unlike North America, where New York has this centralizing power, South America has always had a disparate cultural life. So it was hard to get the critical mass, the energy, which is something that has finally happened. Obviously Mexico City is an incredible capital, but it's really too close to the United States. Like New York, São Paulo is a city that was built by immigrants, having rich conversations with Black history and Native Indians, as well as a massive Italian population, the largest Japanese population outside Japan, a lot of Eastern European and Jewish immigrants. In São Paulo we met Felipe [Dmab]—the third partner—who has a background in history and philosophy. He was running an art space and we started frequenting each other's spaces. Thinking in the same way, we joined forces and opened in 2010.

How did you build the program?

In my spare time I'm a gardener, and in the middle of the gallery there's a large garden. When I first moved to Brazil I tried to make a kind of Northern hemisphere garden, which died within three weeks. So I learned about tropical plants. I see the garden growing alongside the gallery—it may sound silly and romantic—but the gallery came together as organic encounters of energy. If your artists tell you to listen to this music, you should check it out; if they tell you that there's this artist that no one's ever heard of living in a garage in the Amazon, just get a flight. So our first artists kind of happened naturally. We work with believers for the large part. If they weren't artists they would explode or move to the moon or bury themselves under the Antarctic continent. They are people that desperately have to be artists.

We started representing mainly younger Brazilians, people of our generation. We were advancing this vision of Brazil that had not yet made its space in the world. Unfortunately in Brazil there are very few Afro-Brazilian artists that are represented, and Paulo Nazareth and Sonia Gomes are the only ones to be represented in the country. Paulo is speaking for a whole set of social questions that really interest us—given that Brazil has a massive number of social problems and questions. There's no reason to have a gallery if you can't change the world.

That was our basis; but then we realized that to make this generation blossom, we needed them to be in contact with a context of international artists. So every month we do at least two international shows—we do 20 to 24 shows a year. The whole art world knows that Brazil massively taxes foreign goods, as we are the last great protectionist economy. It really is an adventure to get things in, and in the past there's unfortunately been too little contact with international art. It has been hard for galleries to bring it to Brazil. So we've been coming up with ways to bring artists to Brazil and to produce the works in situ. The artists stay for two months and get to know the local artists and the curators. There's a sort of social responsibility of having a space in a country that has some of the most fascinating collectors in the world, wonderfully sophisticated collectors who have been collecting conceptual art since the 1970s.

To do so many show you need different spaces.

Right. Our first three spaces are just next door to each other, and then we have a warehouse space that is like a dream space, an active laboratory for about half the year for a series of six exhibitions. In the other spaces we run programming on a sort of six-week basis. Some of our shows are even in the street, like this huge urban occupation we did with Lawrence Weiner in 2014.

Do you feel more and more people are coming to Brazil to visit the spaces and the galleries?

It's amazing. I have been in São Paulo for four years and I see it: you wake up and there is a new group of Swedish people in the garden, with the map upside down, lost. It used to happen on a weekly basis and now it happens every day.

Do you think São Paulo could be the new city in South America, with Miami Beach becoming less frequented?

São Paulo is a capital. Miami is a capital of a sort ... for ten days! I like Miami but it just doesn't compare to São Paulo. People don't always realize to what extent Brazil is just about the same size as the US. It's huge and it has really preserved its cultural complexity. São Paulo is a tough city, but a very refreshing place. To me it represents a model for Southern leadership.

Part of the reason why we've been going to Hong Kong for four years now is because we are interested in an exchange with Asia, which isn't mediated necessarily by London or New York. I see us as agents of change. I am always fascinated by context, by how different ideas have different meanings in different cultural contexts. It's really interesting to bring a Brazilian artist from Minas Gerais to Hong Kong and see what happens. It's increasingly time for North–North, South–South, North–South conversations to unfold and take place.

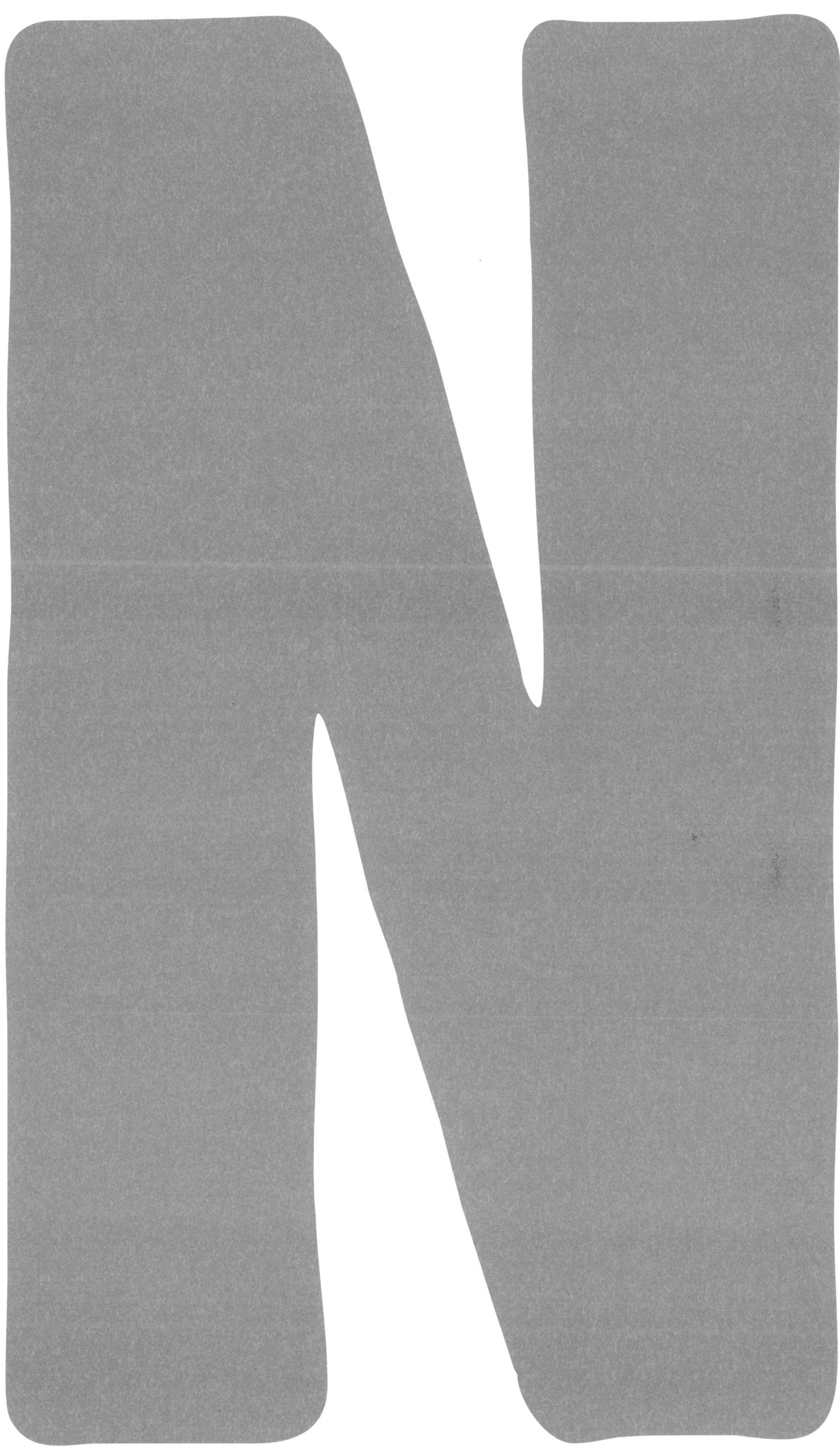

N

Michelle Grabner
Lynne Cooke
Glenn Ligon
NEXT
Andrea Bellini
Agustín Pérez Rubio

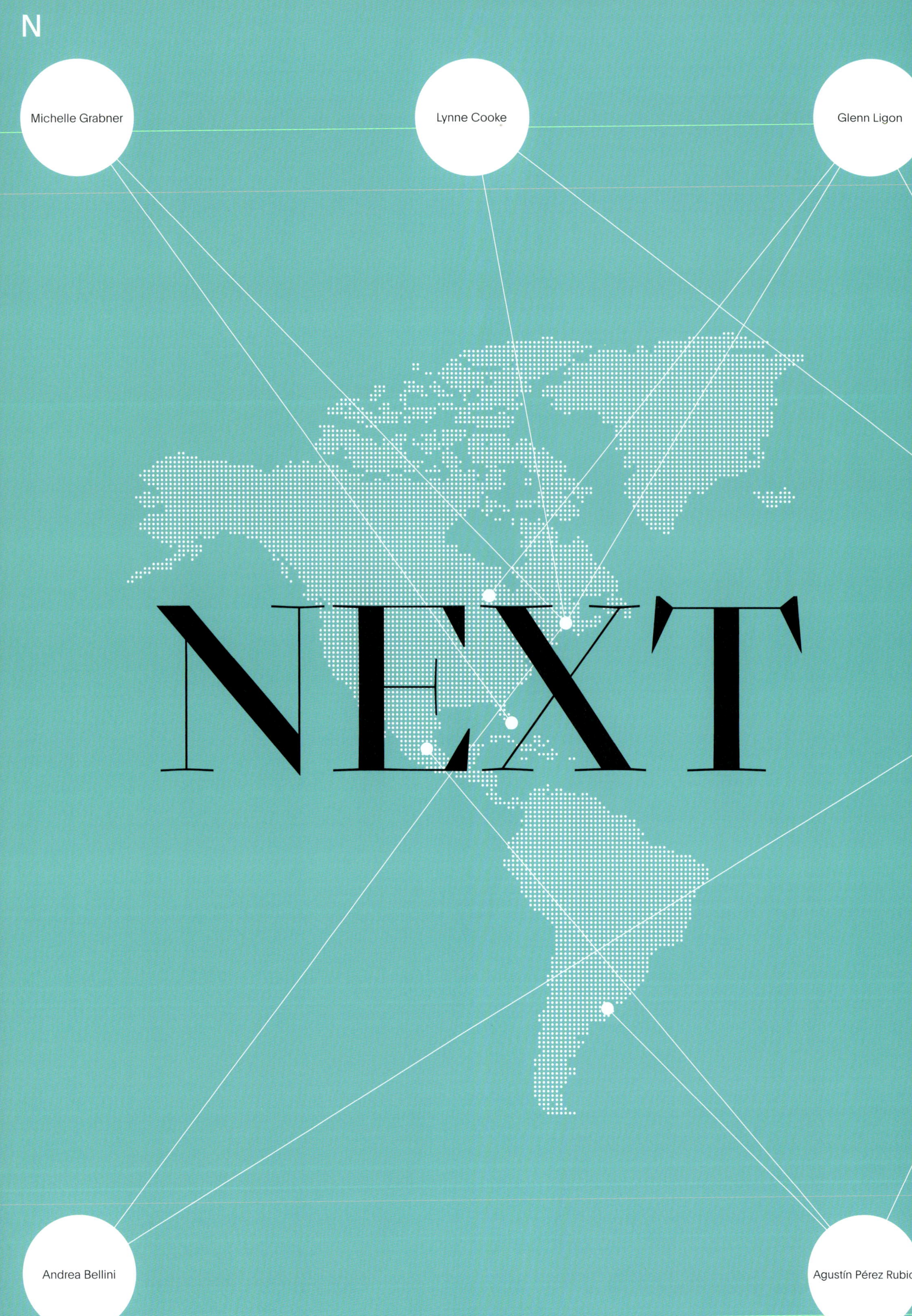

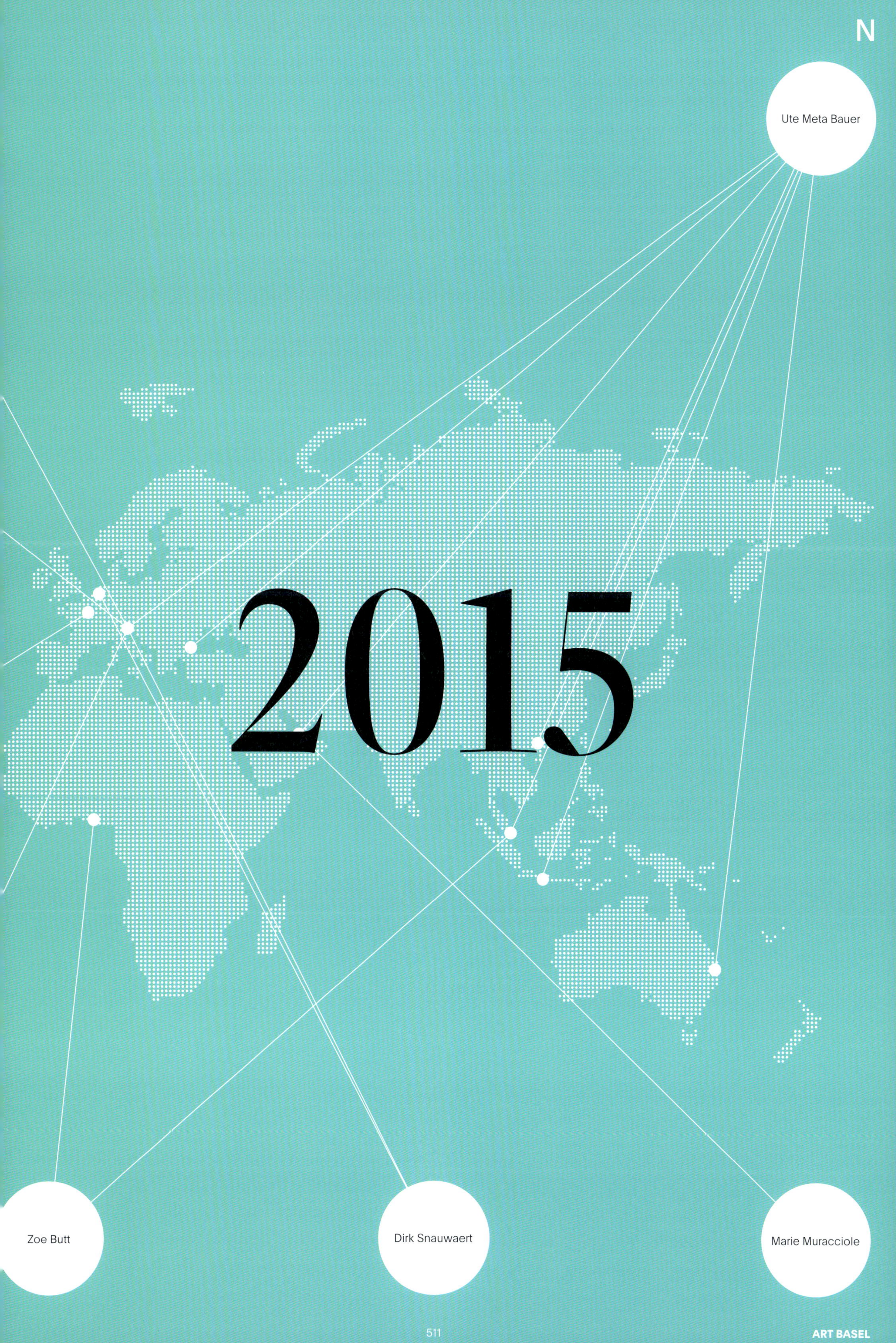
N
Ute Meta Bauer
2015
Zoe Butt
Dirk Snauwaert
Marie Muracciole

Andrea Bellini

Director, Centre d'art contemporain; Director, Biennale de l'image en mouvement, Geneva

01 *2015 Triennial: Surround Audience*, curated by Lauren Cornell and Ryan Trecartin, New Museum, New York, until June 24

2015 will offer no better opportunity than to see how digital technology and late capitalism are altering our vision of the world, or—put less ambitiously—to at least ascertain their effects on visual artists. This for sure is a must see next year.

02 2015 United Nations Climate Change Conference, Paris, November 30–December 11

The last opportunity to save the planet from deadly gases post-Tokyo comes on the back of the recent gentleman's agreement between China and the USA. Something more is needed, which makes this an absolutely crucial step for all of us, big, and—above all—small. According to the organizing committee, the objective of the 2015 conference is to achieve, for the first time in over 20 years of UN negotiations, a binding and universal agreement on climate from all of the world's nations.

03 *The Tale of Tales*, a film by Matteo Garrone

Italian director of *The Embalmer* (2002), *First Love* (2003), and *Gomorrah* (2008), Matteo Garrone is about to present maybe his most ambitious work, *The Tale of Tales*, inspired by *Lo cunto de li cunti*, the 17th-century collection of classic fairy tales in Napolitan dialect (among them *Rapunzel*, *Cinderella*, *Snow White*, and *Beauty and the Beast*), by Giambattista Basile, which is universally recognized as the precursor to all later fairy tales. I'm sure Garrone is at the top of his game.

Zoe Butt

Executive Director and Curator, Sàn Art, Ho Chi Minh City

01 ASEAN Economic Community

A supposed single market competitive economy with equitable development between South East Asian nations by the end of 2015: Will we see visa restrictions ease? A passion for regional expression in art collecting? An improved educational exchange program within the region?

02 Opening of the National Gallery of Art, Singapore, October 2015

Slated to be the hub of South East Asian exchange for regional and international artistic production, this institution is rumored to have a robust budget, with its exhibition program being hotly debated!

03 Asian Studies in Africa: Challenges and Prospects of a New Axis of Intellectual Interactions, Accra, Ghana, September 24–26, 2015

One of the first gatherings of minds showcasing art historical, cultural, and social developments, side by side, with a dynamic set of international speakers tracing new trajectories of knowledge within and for the Global South.

Lynne Cooke

Senior Curator, Special Projects in Modern Art, National Gallery of Art, Washington

01 Douglas Crimp's forthcoming memoir, *Before Pictures*

This much-anticipated book is a fascinating exploration of a richly interwoven medley of visual arts, dance, performance, fashion, and gay scenes in New York City, in the decade leading up to Crimp's landmark *Pictures* show in 1977.

02 Whitney Museum of American Art, New York, May 2015

The (revisionist?) histories of American art that will be charted when the Whitney Museum installs its collection in its new premises. Whose perspectives, and whose investments, will shape those histories of the national narratives?

03 Joan Jonas, United States Pavilion, the 56th International Art Exhibition, Venice Biennale, May 9–November 22

A seminal figure in the founding of Performance art in the 1960s, Joan Jonas has never lost her edge.

Michelle Grabner

Artist, Chicago, and Co-curator, 2014 Whitney Biennial, New York

01 Whitney Museum of American Art, New York, May 2015

The opening of the Whitney Museum on Gansevoort Street in downtown Manhattan—and of course the Metropolitan Museum of Art squatting in the Whitney's Marcel Breuer building on Madison Avenue for the next eight years.

02 Shana Lutker's research into the history of Surrealist fistfights continues

Chapter 3 debuts at the Pérez Art Museum Miami in May 2015 (until September) and in the fall at the Hirshhorn Museum (Washington DC).

03 Benjamin Buchloh, *Formalism and Historicity: Models and Methods in 20th-Century Art*

Published by October Books, a volume of essays including the influential "Conceptual Art 1962–1969: From the Aesthetics of Administration to the Critique of Institutions" (1989) and "Allegorical Procedures: Appropriations and Montage in Contemporary Art" (1982).

Glenn Ligon

Artist, New York

01 The 56th International Art Exhibition, Venice Biennale, May 9–November 22

All the World's Futures, Okwui Enwezor's curatorial vision for the Venice Biennale, signals a paradigm shift from previous exhibitions. Rather than focusing on a central theme, he has chosen several "filters" through which the work in the exhibition will be considered. Under the headings *Liveness: On Epic Duration*, *Garden of Disorder*, and *Capital: A Live Reading*, he will present readings, film, video, photography, theater, painting, and installations with the rigor and sense of inquiry that he brings to all his curatorial endeavors.

02 *Stephen Andrews: A Survey*, Art Gallery of Ontario, April–September

Masterfully curated by Kitty Scott, curator of modern and contemporary art, Andrews' much anticipated show will focus on his investigation of memory, identity, and technology, and their representations in the media of drawing, painting, and animation. Andrews will also being exhibiting his recent work in ceramics, signaling a move into the three-dimensional work that has echoes in his ongoing interest in process and chance.

03 Whitney Museum of American Art, New York, May 2015

They had a good run at the magnificent Marcel Breuer-designed building on Madison Avenue but their new Renzo Piano designed home on the shores of the Hudson River will dramatically increase their exhibition space and serve as a sparkling showcase for the more than 20,000 objects in their permanent collection as well as exhibitions devoted to the work of Archibald Motley, Frank Stella, Laura Poitras, and David Wojnarowicz.

Ute Meta Bauer

Founding Director, NTU Center for Contemporary Art, Singapore

Asia on the move, 2015

Biennales still play a crucial role throughout Asia and serve as point of entry. Several new art institutions will provide more insight into and scholarship about the rich and varied, but less known art histories across this vast continent. Get a suitcase packed and visas in place for an extensive trip through Asia and the Pacific to get to know the variety of artistic scenes and practices, there's so much to see and so much to learn.

01 Winter/Spring

The Past, The Present, The Possible, 12th Sharjah Biennial curated by Eungie Joo (March 5–June 5).

02 Summer

Although Venice is not Asia, exploring the various Asian contributions to *All the World's Futures* revealed by Okwui Enwezor curating the 56th International Art Exhibition, Venice Biennale (May 9–November 22); and *ArtJog* in Jogjakarta in June, which serves as springboard for young artists from Indonesia.

03 Fall/Winter

The fifth edition of the Guangzhou Triennial, the 1st-Asia-Biennial, curated by Henk Slager and Zhang Qing (December 11, 2015–April 10, 2016) will wrap up the year after the 14th Istanbul Biennial "drafted" by Carolyn Christov-Bakargiev (September 5–November 1); the 8th SCAPE Public Art engaging with Christchurch after the earthquake in New Zealand, curated by Rob Garrett (October 3–November 15); the 8th Asia Pacific Triennial in Brisbane (November 12, 2015–April 10, 2016); and the long awaited National Gallery of Art of Singapore opening under Eugene Tan's direction.

Marie Muracciole

Director, Beirut Art Center, Beirut

01 Changes in Africa and solidarity between Arab countries

First and foremost.

02 Sharjah Biennial & March Meeting

With *The Past, The Present, The Possible*, 12th Sharjah Biennial curated by Eungie Joo (March 5–June 5) and the March Meeting 2015 organized by the Sharjah Art Foundation (May 11–15).

03 Joseph Massad, *Islam in Liberalism*

Published by The University of Chicago Press and presented as a book which "explores what Islam has become in today's world, with full attention to the multiplication of its meanings and interpretations. It is an unflinching critique of Western assumptions and of the liberalism that Europe and Euro-America blindly present as a type of salvation to an assumingly unenlightened Islam."

Agustín Pérez Rubio

Artistic Director, Malba–Museo de Arte Latinoamericano, Buenos Aires

01 The 56th International Art Exhibition, Venice Biennale, May 9–November 22

All the World's Futures curated by Okwui Enwezor.

02 Francis Alÿs, Museo Tamayo, Mexico City, March 19–August

A solo sow of Mexico City-based Belgian artist Francis Alÿs curated by Cuauhtémoc Medina.

03 Presidential and Legislative Elections, Argentina, October 25

Dirk Snauwaert

Director, Wiels, Brussels

01 Vincent Messen, Belgian Pavilion, the 56th International Art Exhibition, Venice Biennale, May 9–November 22

As well as Okwui Enwezor's central exhibition.

02 Our challenging exhibition program at Wiels, Brussels

With Pierre Leguillon's *Le Musée des erreurs* in January–February, the *Body Talk* exhibition featuring six female African artists starting in February, a nine-week live dance exhibition by choreographer Anne Teresa De Keersmaeker (Spring), and the premiere of Stan Douglas' new film *The Secret Agent* (Fall).

03 *Atopolis*, Mons, June 13–October 18

Mons in 2015 is European Capital of Culture and Wiels is co-organizing the *Atopolis* exhibition, whose title alludes to Edouard Glissant's ideas, dedicated to artists interested in the phenomena of circulation, diaspora, and cultural dislocation, and opposed to the homogenization of globalization.

N

Designed for galleries to present one, two or three artists showing new works that have been created within the last three years, the Nova sector in Miami Beach is a site for discoveries, featuring features never-before-seen pieces direct from the artist's studio and strong juxtapositions. We invited Alex Gartenfeld, Deputy Director and Chief Curator of the Institute of Contemporary Art, Miami, to choose his four favorite booths.

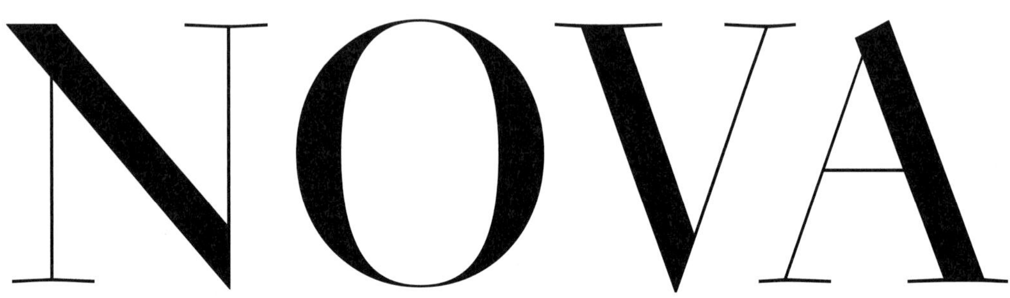

2014 participants

47 Canal
Michele Abeles
Ajay Kurian

80m2
David Zink Yi
Rita Ponce de León

Altman Siegel
Liam Everett

Beijing Commune
Hu Xiaoyuan
Wang Guangle

Bureau
Erica Baum
Jaya Howey

Cervera
David Diao

Cherry and Martin
Brian Bress

Cintra + Box 4
Cristina Canale
Pedro Motta
Maria Klabin

Instituto de visión
Tania Candiani

Labor
Pablo Vargas Lugo
Pedro Reyes

Layr
Marius Engh
Nick Oberthaler

Leighton
Van Hanos
Jamian Juliano-Villani

Leme
Alexandre Brandão
Zilvinas Kempinas

Liprandi
Adriana Bustos
Magdalena Jitrik

Maisterravalbuena
Dan Shaw-Town
Regina de Miguel
Hiraki Sawa

Meessen De Clercq
Nicolás Lamas
José María Sicilia
Lieven de Boeck

Mendes Wood
Cibelle Cavalli Bastos
Patricia Leite

Michael Jon
Sayre Gomez
JPW3

Francesca Minini
Paolo Chiasera

mor charpentier
Oscar Muñoz
Voluspa Jarpa
Teresa Margolles

MOT International
Laure Prouvost

mother's tankstation
Uri Aran
Ara Dymond
Mairead O'hEocha

Parra & Romero
Lara Almarcegui
Luis Camnitzer
Oriol Vilanova

Peres Projects
Dorothy Iannone
Mike Bouchet

Real Fine Arts
Jon Pestoni
Sam Pulitzer

Anita Schwartz
Waltercio Caldas
Angelo Venosa
Otavio Schipper

Silverman
Ruairiadh O'Connell
Hugh Scott-Douglas
Dashiell Manley

SKE
Astha Butail
Srinivasa Prasad
Sudarshan Shetty

Société
Sean Raspet
Timur Si-Qin and Ned Vena

Supportico Lopez
Michael Dean
Christina Mackie
Zin Taylor

T293
May Hands
Erica Mahinay

Take Ninagawa
Shinro Ohtake
Tsuruko Yamazaki
Ryoko Aoki

Travesía Cuatro
Sarah Crowner
Milena Muzquiz

Wallspace
David Korty
Nancy Lupo

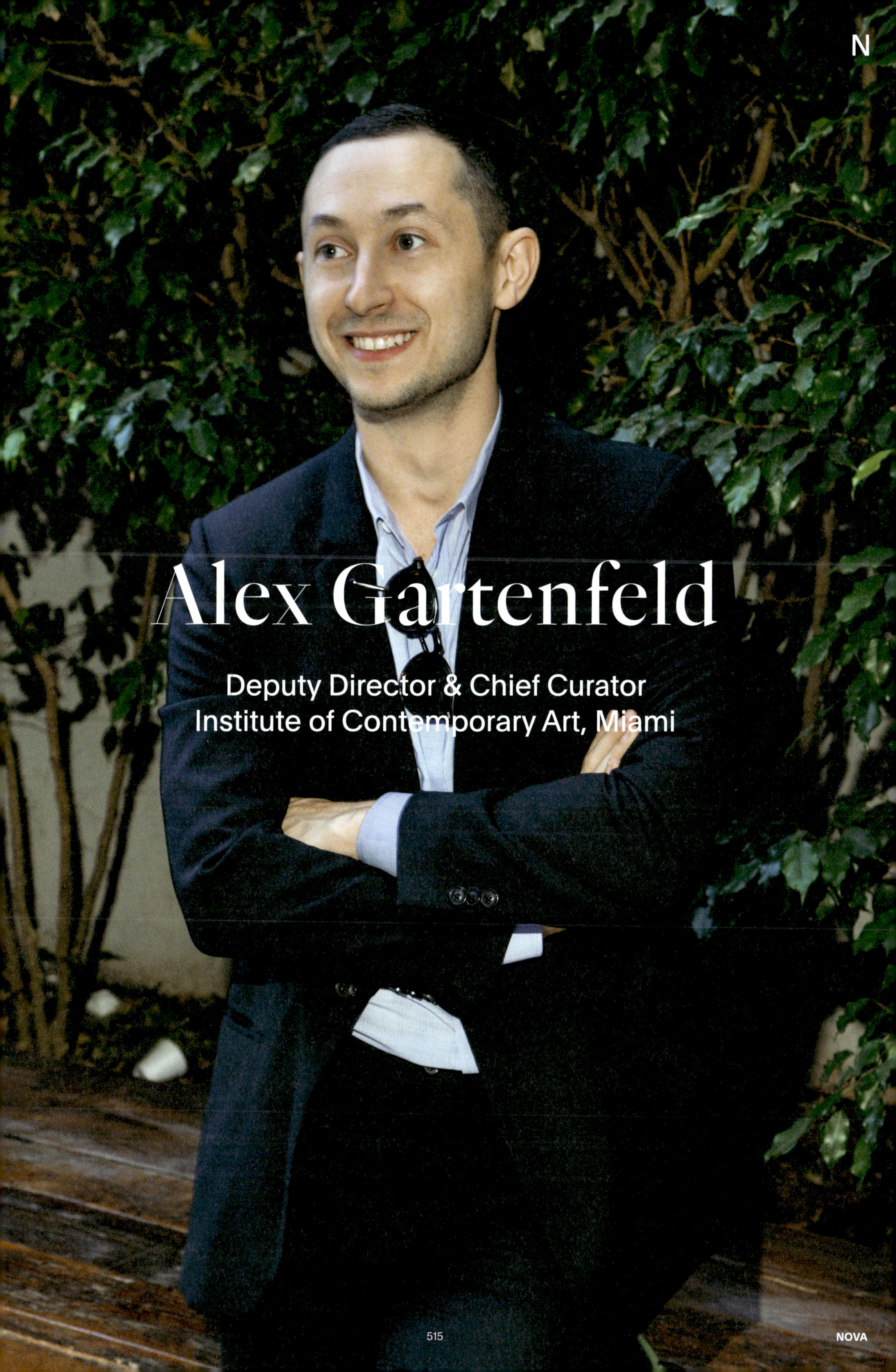

Alex Gartenfeld

Deputy Director & Chief Curator
Institute of Contemporary Art, Miami

47 Canal
Michele Abeles

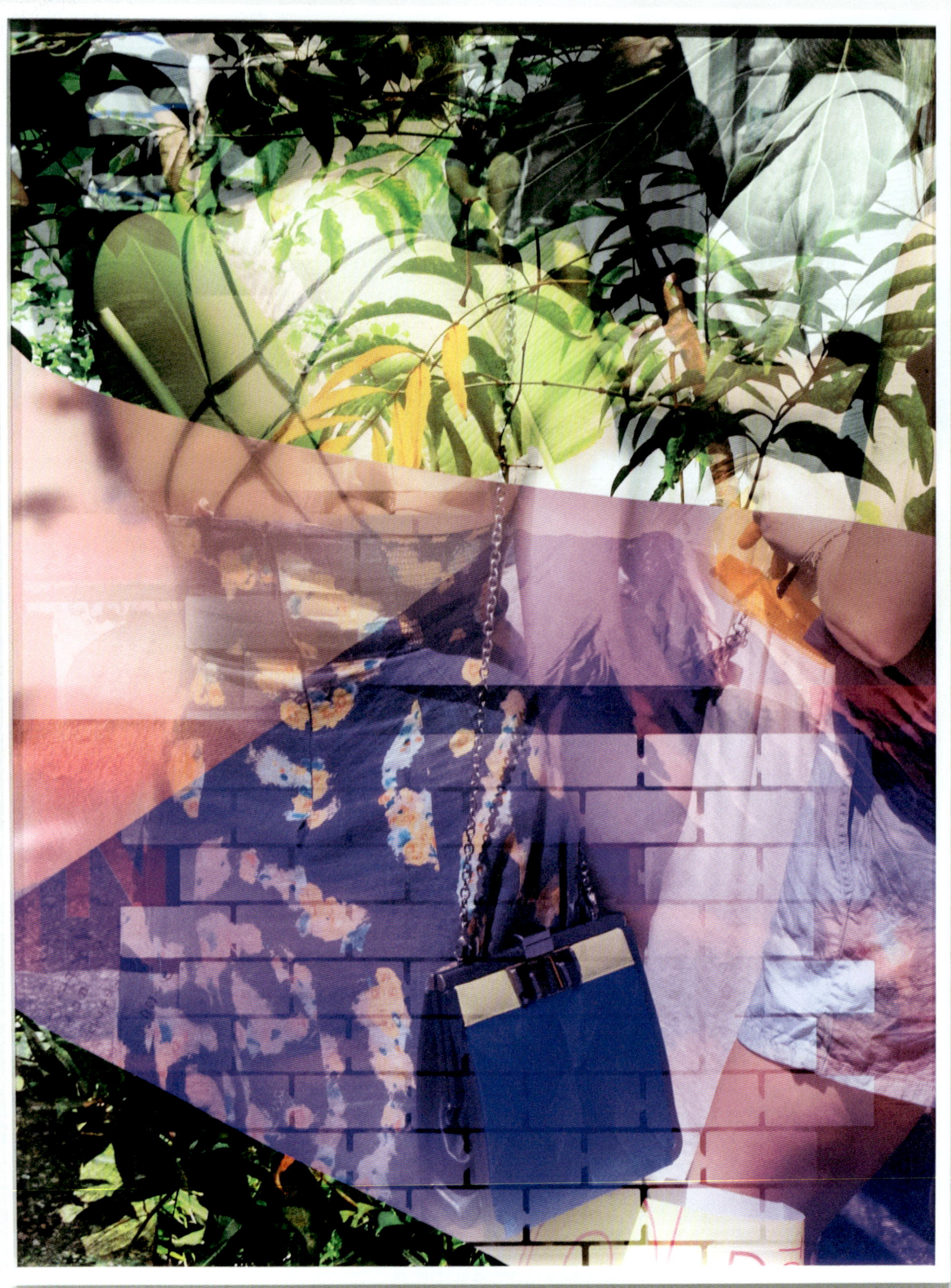

Over the last few years, Michele Abeles has been creating increasingly complex images that involve (digitally and physically) compressed space. In this homage to the relationship between New York and Miami, the artist shows how pointedly critical her image production really is. There is real, awkward intimacy between viewer and image, layer and layer, subject and monogrammed handbag.

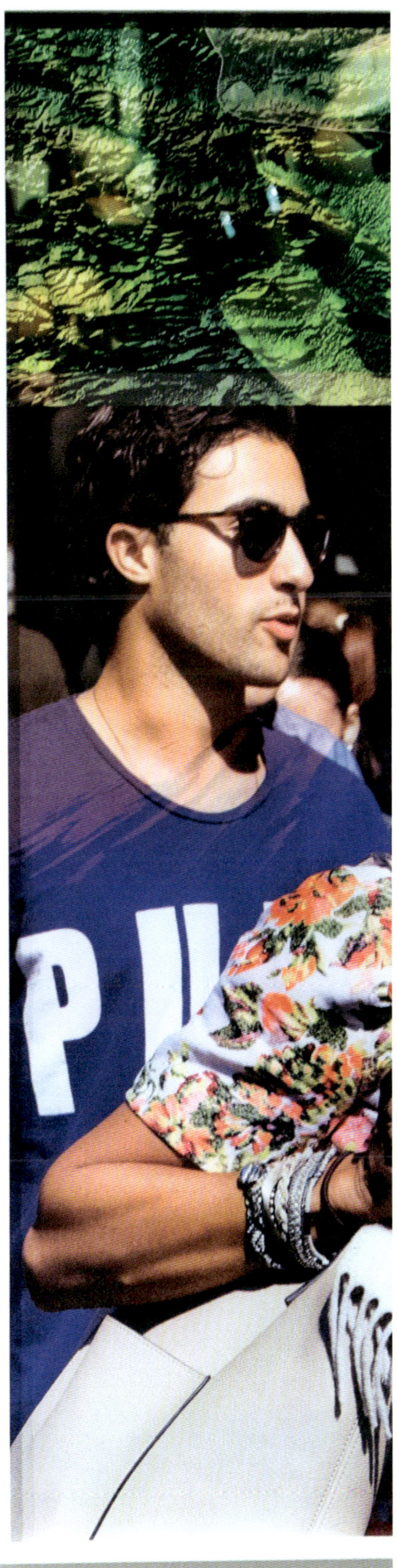

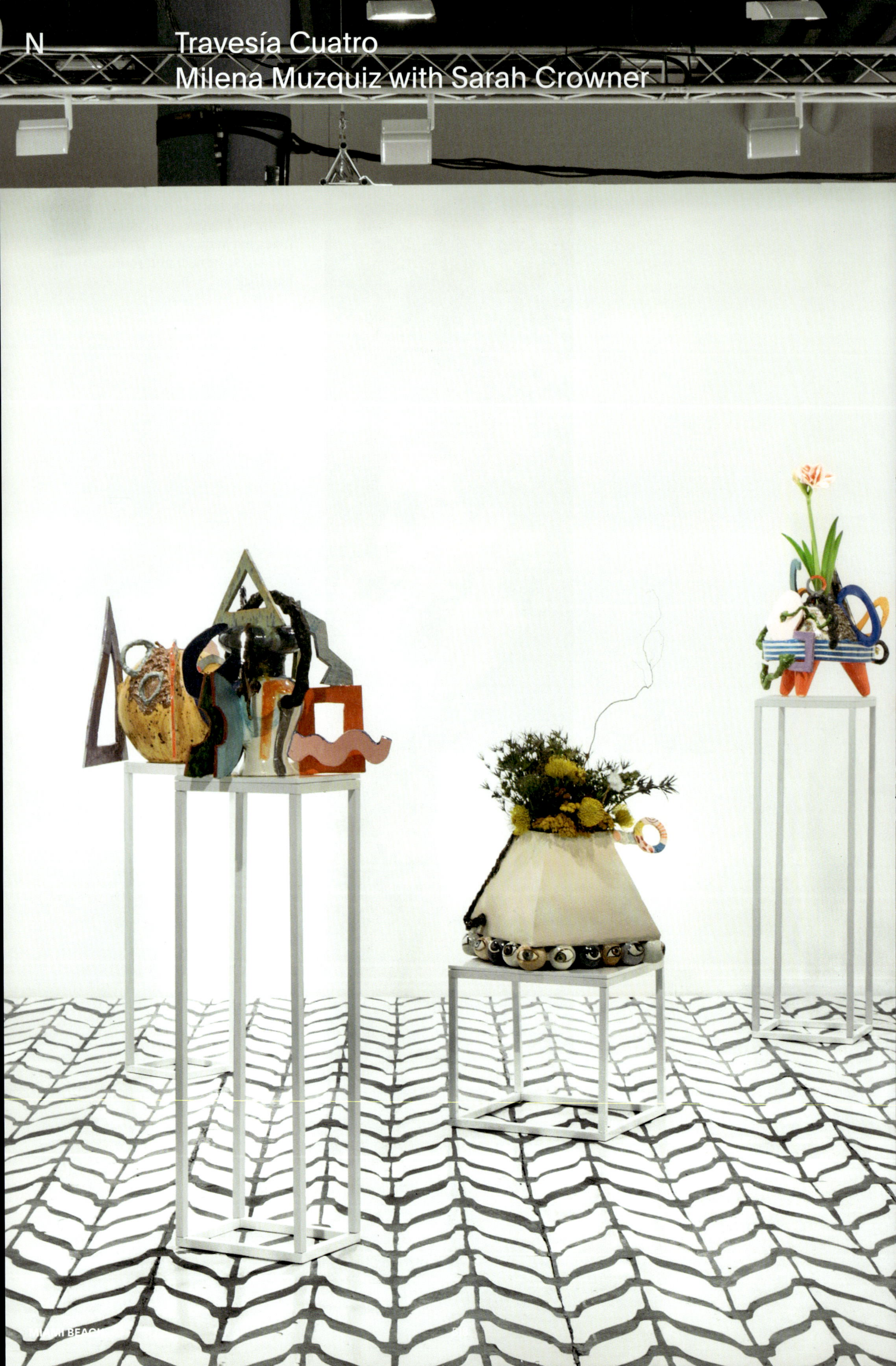

N

Travesía Cuatro
Milena Muzquiz with Sarah Crowner

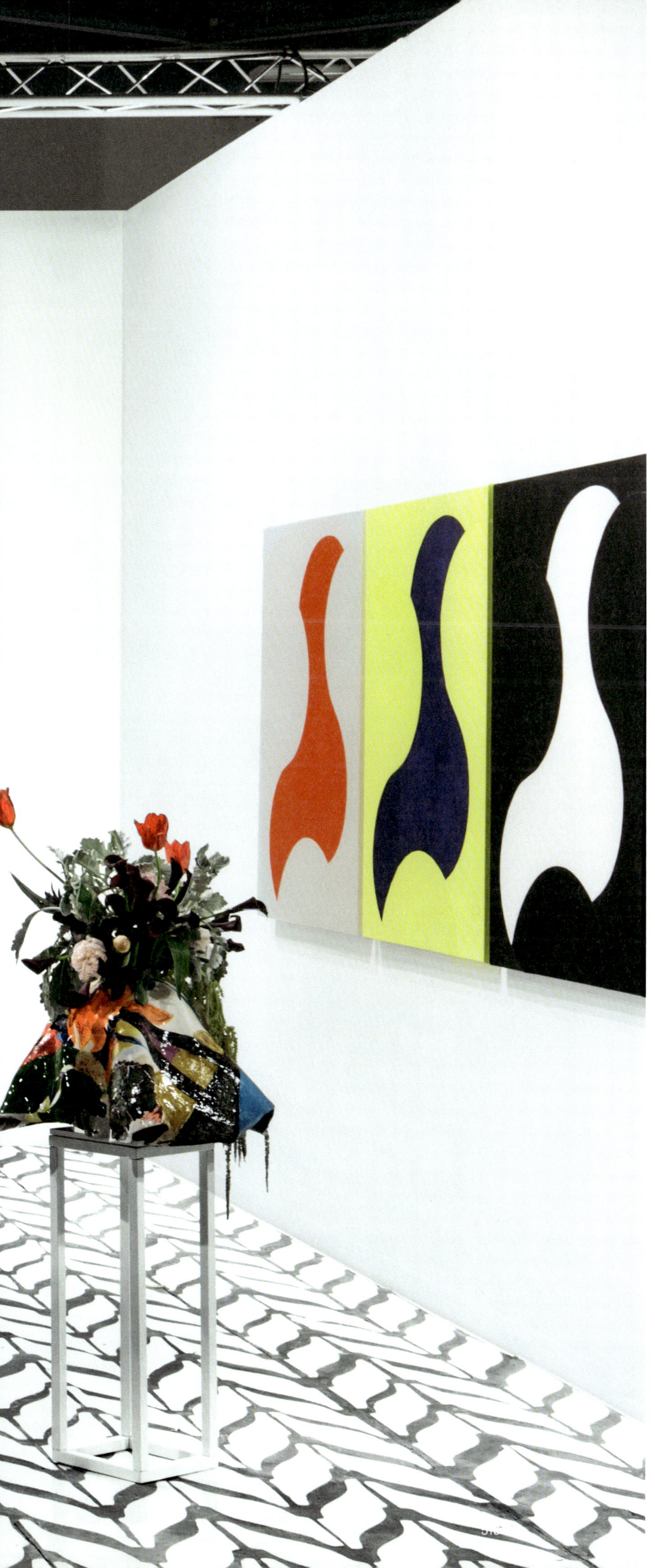

I liked that the gallery kept the best ceramics, those with ruffled lips, on the floor under the desk. The indelicacy amplified the work's perversity; and the asymmetry of Sarah Crowner's paintings, which appeared wonkier and more poetic than I had previously realized.

N

An artist whose insistent brushwork is proof that painting is critical to generating new images. The recently increased scale gives the artist, who moves between abstraction and figuration, greater psychological and allegorical space.

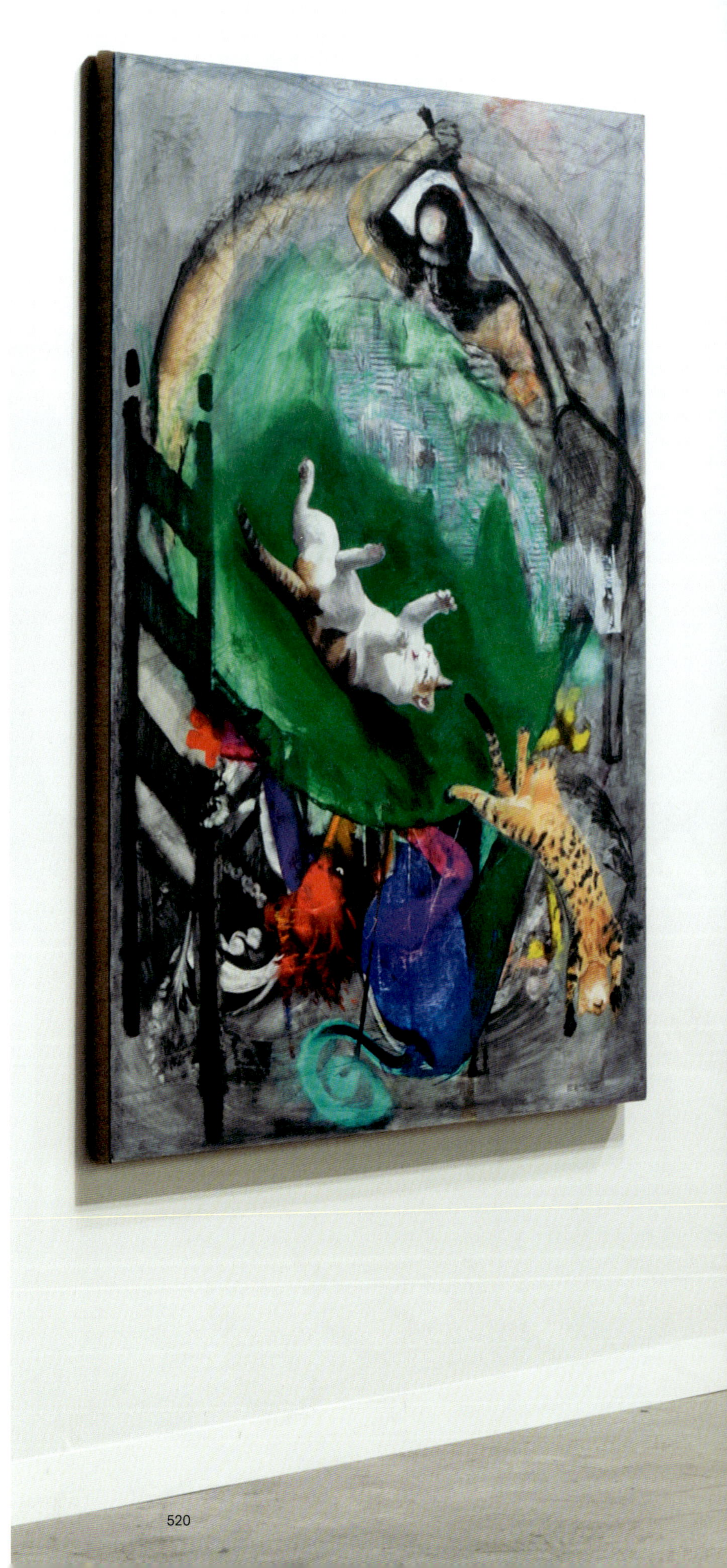

Tanya Leighton
Van Hanos

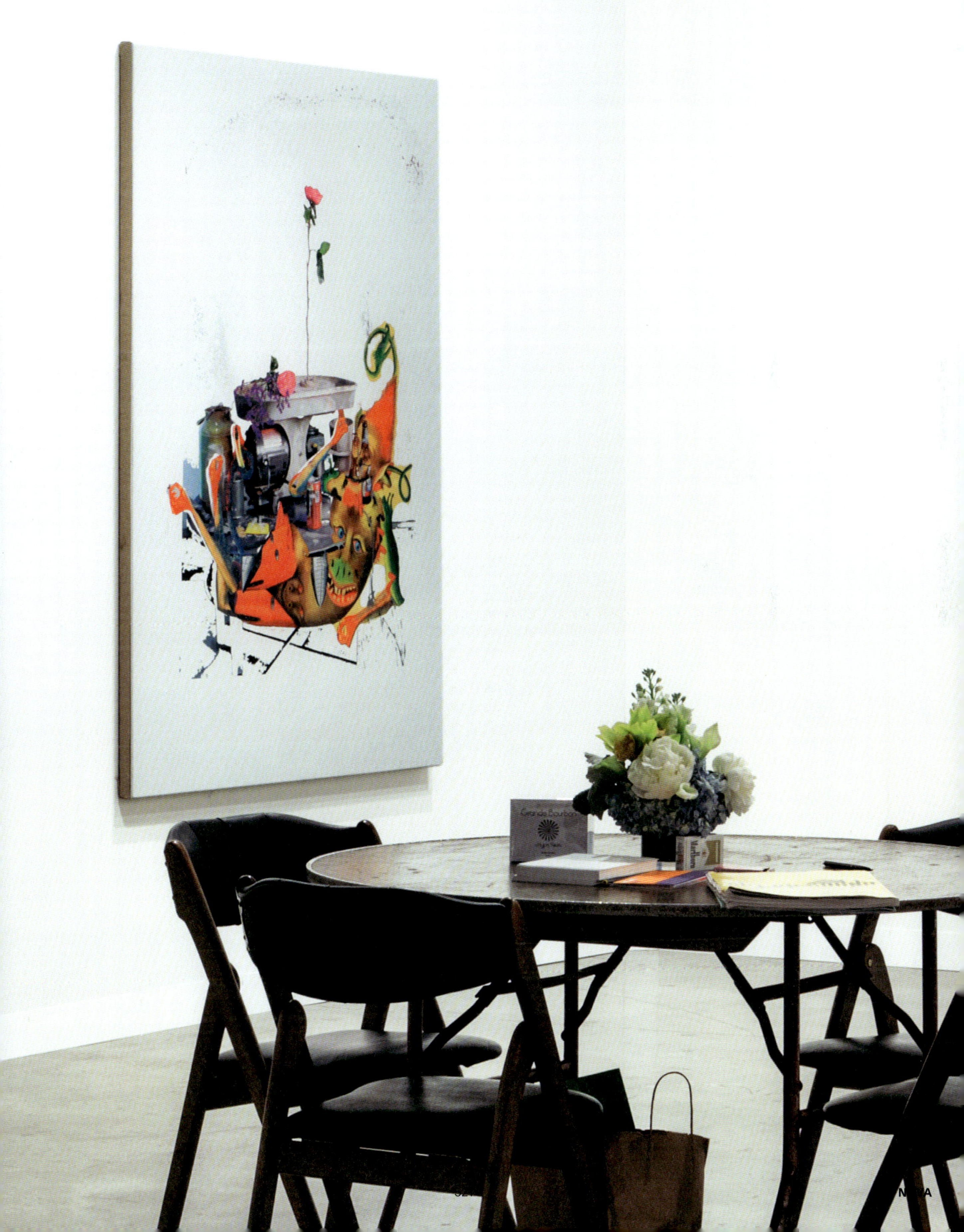

Take Ninagawa
Shinro Ohtake

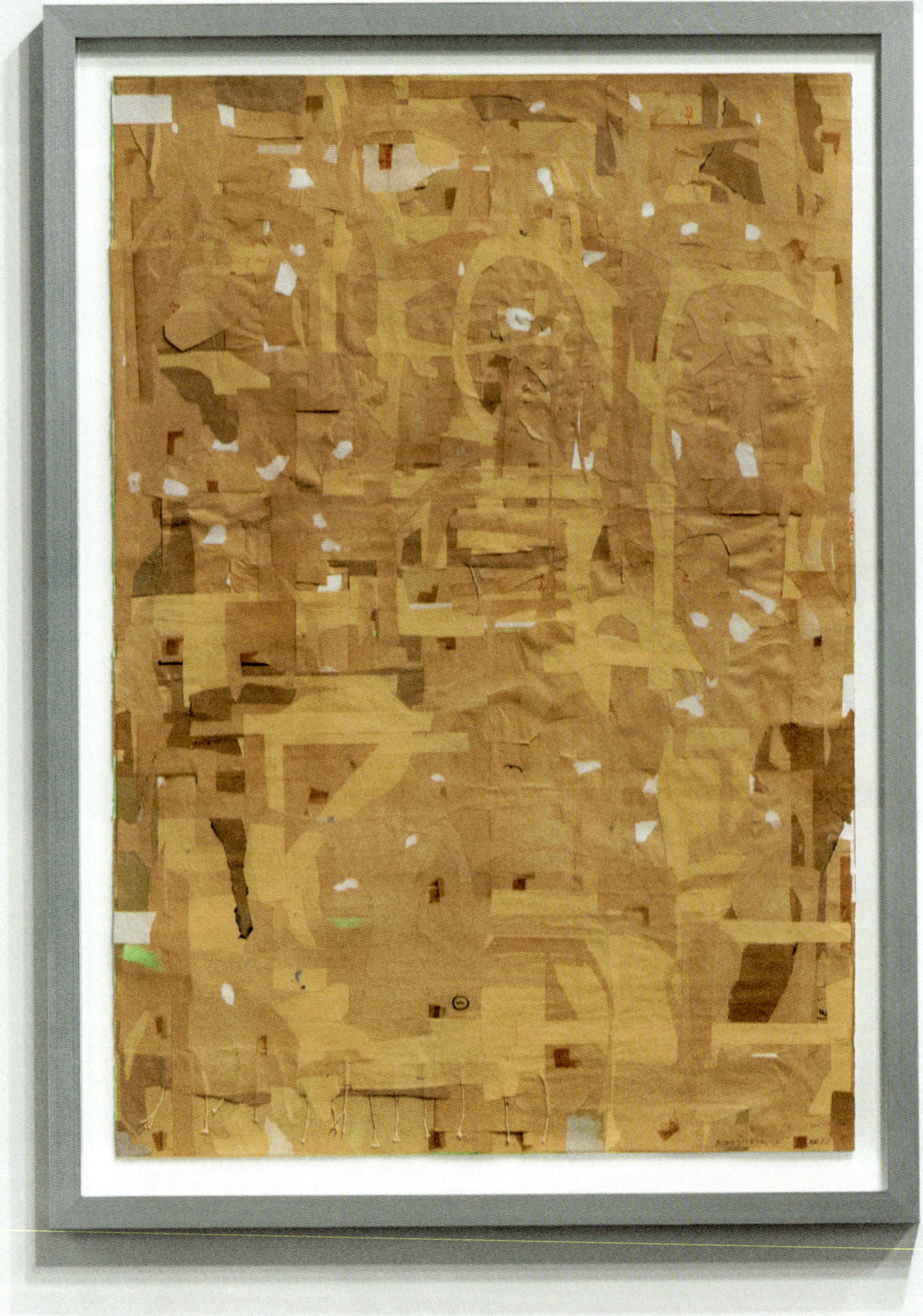

Japan's Höch. The artist's collages from the past three decades are masterful additions to the history of collage: endlessly engrossing, and possessed of the abjection of a turned-over book.

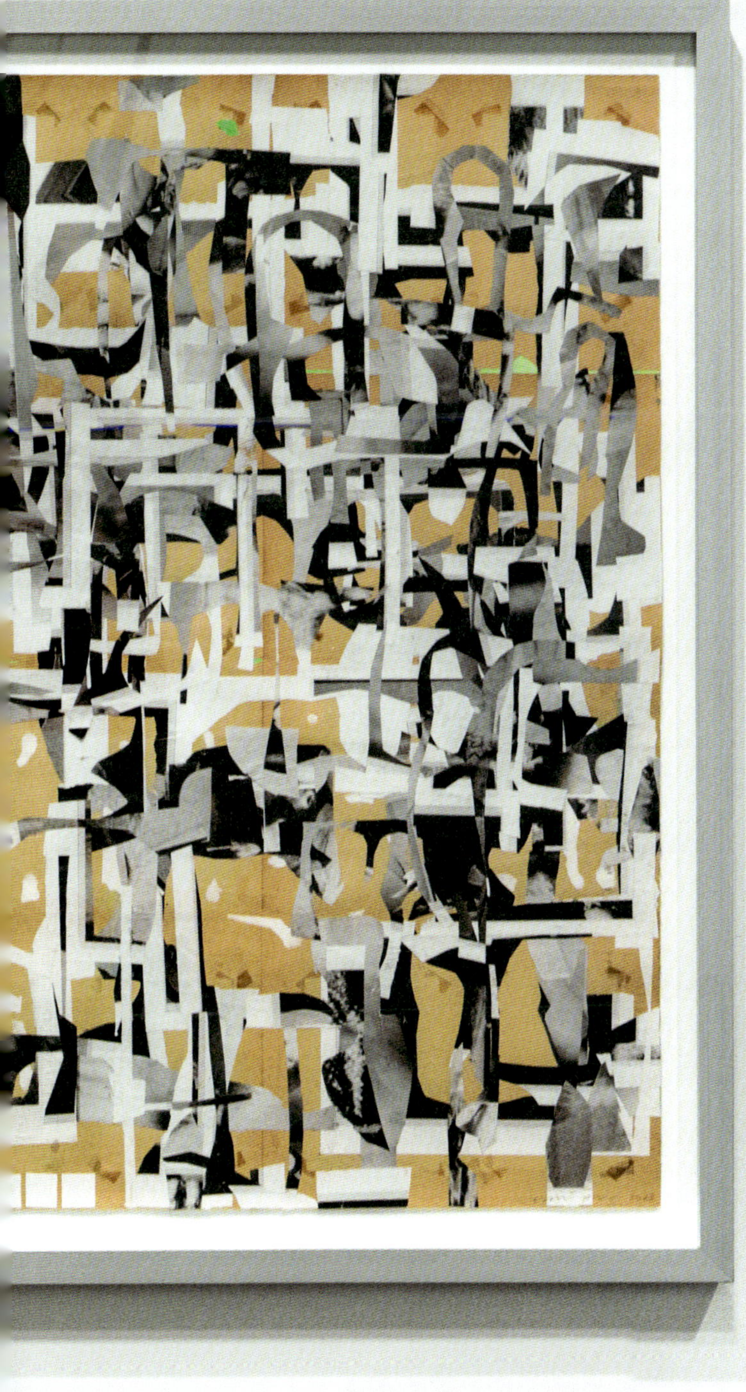

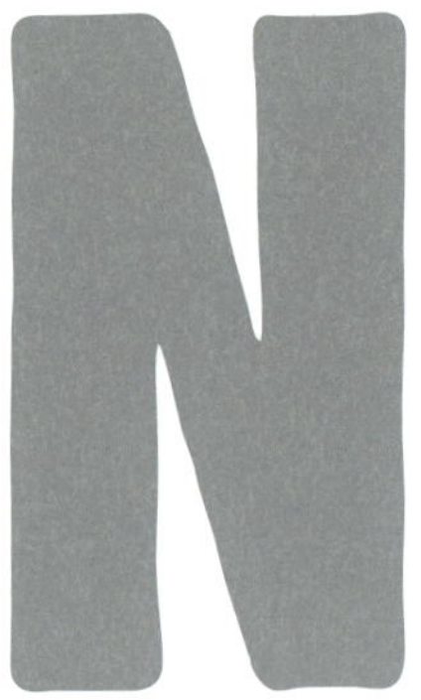

nächst St. Stephan

Vienna

Galleries
Galleries

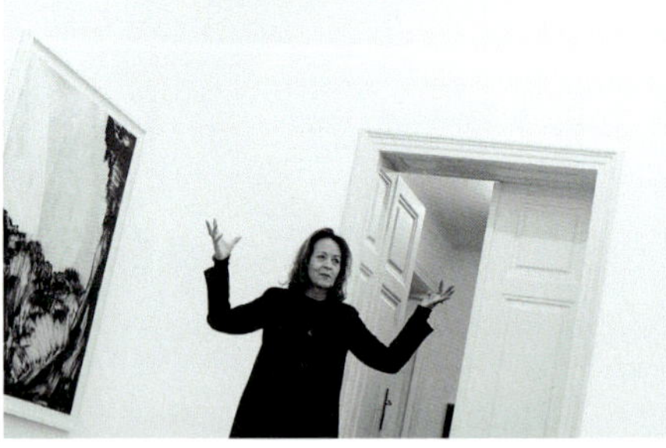

What is your favorite aspect of running a gallery?
It's a profession that requires many different talents. You need a holistic approach to art, business, and life. You never get bored.

How do you choose the artists you work with?
In terms of what is and what is not (yet) part of my program, I like to think of it as a necklace or as a chain with different pendants. I have been working with a reliable group of artists for many, many years. It takes a long time to choose new artists. You have to look at their work closely—you have to examine and consider it first. And yet you still have to count on your instinct! There's still that love at first sight. I don't want to get too comfortable with what I show at the gallery. If I stopped questioning things, that would mean missing out what's happening today.

If you weren't running a gallery what else would you do?
No idea. I can't imagine doing anything else. This is my calling.

- **Contact**
  Galerie nächst St. Stephan
  Rosemarie Schwarzwälder
  Deniz Pekerman
  galerie@schwarzwaelder.at
- **Established**
  1954 (by Msgr. Otto Mauer)
  1978 (with Director Rosemarie Schwarzwälder)
  1987 (privatized)
- **Owner(s) / Partner(s)**
  Rosemarie Schwarzwälder
- **Team**
  10
- **Space(s)**
  200 m²
- **Artists at Art Basel**
  Adam Adach
  Polly Apfelbaum
  Herbert Brandl
  Michał Budny
  Ernst Caramelle
  Heinrich Dunst
  Helmut Federle
  Bernard Frize
  Katharina Grosse
  Luisa Kasalicky
  Imi Knoebel
  Daniel Knorr
  Lee Ufan
  Sonia Leimer
  Isa Melsheimer
  Manfred Pernice
  Karin Sander
  Jörg Sasse
  Adrian Schiess
  Jessica Stockholder
  Walter Swennen
  Joëlle Tuerlinckx
  Günter Umberg
  Christoph Weber
  James Welling
- **Further artists represented**
  Sabine Boehl
  Rainer Ganahl
  Aneta Grzeszykowska
  Agnieszka Kalinowska

Nadi

Jakarta

Galleries

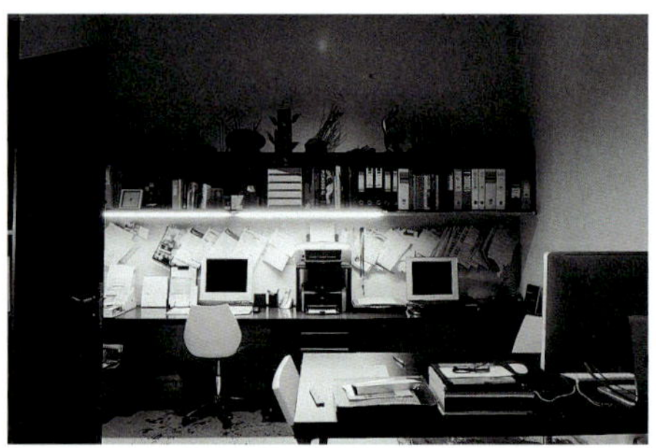

What is your favorite aspect of running a gallery?
My favorite aspect of running a gallery is its similarity with my hobby. I love art and I love the art world.

How do you choose the artists you work with?
First, I observe young artists over several years. If their works show quality improvements, I will then ask them to work with me.

If you weren't running a gallery what else would you do?
I am an architect, so I would practice architecture.

- **Contact**
  Nadi Gallery
  Meli Angkapradipta
  nadigallery@gmail.com
- **Established**
  2000
- **Owner(s) / Partner(s)**
  Biantoro Santoso
- **Team**
  5
- **Space(s)**
  250 m²
- **Artists at Art Basel**
  Jumaldi Alfi
  Eddie Hara
  Yuli Prayitno
  Yusra Martunus
  Handiwirman Saputra
  Arin Dwihartanto Sunaryo
  Agus Suwage
- **Further artists represented**
  Heri Dono
  S. Teddy D.
  Laksmi Shitaresmi

Nagel Draxler

Berlin
Cologne

Galleries

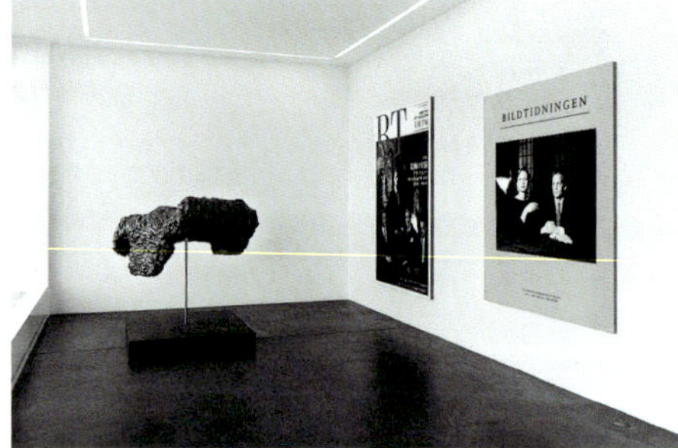

What is your favorite aspect of running a gallery?
Being a driving force in art production and the art market.

How do you choose the artists you work with?
This is a lifetime challenge that requires a high level of experience and knowledge and a good eye.

If you weren't running a gallery what else would you do?

Museum director or writer.

- **Contact** Galerie Nagel Draxler
  Denise Moser
  berlin@galerie-nagel.de
- **Established** 1990
- **Owner(s) / Partner(s)** Christian Nagel
  Saskia Draxler
- **Team** 10
- **Space(s)** 300 m²
- **Artists at Art Basel** Kader Attia
  Michael Beutler
  Guillaume Bijl
  Mark Dion
  Andrea Fraser
  Hans-Jörg Mayer
  Christian Philipp Müller
  Martha Rosler
  Dominik Sittig
  Joëlle Tuerlinckx
  Gang Zhao
  Heimo Zobernig
- **Further artists represented** Lutz Braun
  Clegg & Guttmann
  Keren Cytter
  Stephan Dillemuth
  Renée Green
  Julia Haller
  Sven Johne
  Kiron Khosla
  Thomas Kilpper
  Till Krause
  Kalin Lindena
  Ken Lum
  Lone Haugaard Madsen
  Christian Mayer
  John Miller
  Akiyoshi Mishima
  Stefan Müller
  Josephine Pryde
  Cornelius Quabeck
  Stephanie Taylor
  Mirjam Thomann
  Jan Timme
  Luca Vitone
  Joseph Zehrer

Nagy

London — Galleries

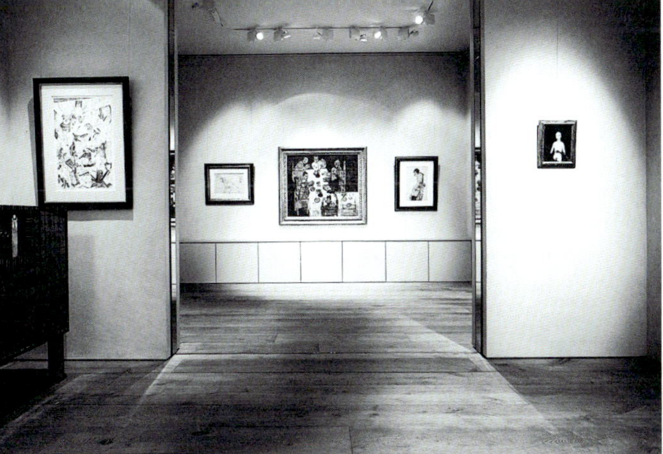

- **Contact** Richard Nagy Ltd.
  Nina Hartl
  info@richardnagy.com
- **Established** 1989
- **Owner(s) / Partner(s)** Richard Nagy
- **Team** 4
- **Artists at Art Basel** Francis Bacon
  Max Beckmann
  Heinrich Campendonk
  Otto Dix
  James Ensor
  Lyonel Feininger
  Lucian Freud
  Alberto Giacometti
  George Grosz
  Erich Heckel
  Karl Hubbuch
  Ernst Ludwig Kirchner
  Gustav Klimt
  Oskar Kokoschka
  Alfred Kubin
  Wilhelm Lehmbruck
  Henri Matisse
  George Minne
  Emil Nolde
  Hermann Max Pechstein
  Anton Peschka
  Pablo Picasso
  Odilon Redon
  Auguste Rodin
  Christian Schad
  Egon Schiele
  Rudolf Schlichter
  Karl Schmidt-Rottluff
  Stanley Spencer

Nahem

New York — Galleries  Galleries

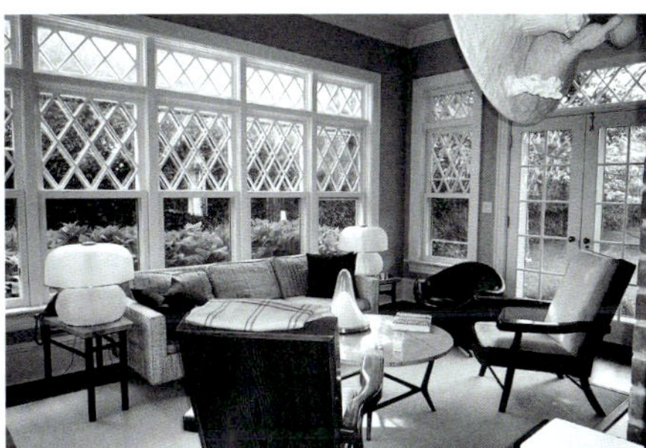

What is your favorite aspect of running a gallery?

Placing a great work of art in the collection of impassioned collectors is one of the more gratifying parts of running a gallery. A superlative work by an artist has the potential to excite on many levels—intellectually, aesthetically, and spiritually. Be it the recent sale of extraordinary paintings by Rothko, Mitchell, and Basquiat—any one could be such an example. The collector connected deeply with the painting immediately and it was very satisfying to be the conduit for this experience.

How do you choose the artists you work with?

Above all, I look for the highest quality and coherence of vision in an artist and in the individual works of art that I choose to represent. I won't take on anything that I don't believe in or for which I do not have a certain degree of enthusiasm. Whether the work is a rare portrait by Francis Bacon, an important mobile by Alexander Calder, or a richly abstract painting by Gerhard Richter, the criteria remain the same. And the same holds true for any of the gallery artists we represent.

If you weren't running a gallery what else would you do?

If I weren't running a gallery I would spend more time doing what I already do as my "night job": producing theater and films that offer both a clear, humanitarian message, and the visual style and soundtrack to go with them. As one of the chief producers of *Fela!* on Broadway, I had the enormous pleasure to bring the music and message of the pioneering Nigerian musician and political activist, Fela Kuti, to amazed audiences on three continents.

- **Contact** Edward Tyler Nahem Fine Art
  Janis Cecil
  janis@etnahem.com
- **Established** 1985
- **Owner(s) / Partner(s)** Edward Nahem
- **Team** 9
- **Space(s)** 325 m²
- **Artists at Art Basel** Francis Bacon
  Jean-Michel Basquiat
  Alighiero Boetti
  Alexander Calder
  John Chamberlain
  Richard Diebenkorn
  Jean Dubuffet

Sam Francis
Alberto Giacometti
Philip Guston
Keith Haring
Donald Judd
Ellsworth Kelly
Franz Kline
Willem de Kooning
Roy Lichtenstein
Henri Matisse
Joan Miró
Joan Mitchell
Claes Oldenburg
Pablo Picasso
Richard Prince
Robert Rauschenberg
Gerhard Richter
Mark Rothko
Ed Ruscha
Frank Stella
Antoni Tàpies
Wayne Thiebaud
Andy Warhol
Tom Wesselmann

- **Further artists represented** Erik Benson
Alejandra Icaza
iROZEALb (iona rozeal brown)
Miron Schmückle
Andres Serrano
José María Sicilia

Nahmad

New York — Galleries
London — Galleries

- **Contact** Helly Nahmad Gallery
Marzina Marzetti
info@hellynahmadgallery.com
- **Established** 2001
- **Owner(s) / Partner(s)** Helly Nahmad
- **Team** 5
- **Artists at Art Basel** Alexander Calder
Jean Dubuffet
Lucio Fontana
Fernand Léger
René Magritte
Joan Miró
Pablo Picasso
- **Further artists represented** Jean Arp
Salvador Dalí
Max Ernst
Alberto Giacometti
Henri Matisse
Pierre-Auguste Renoir

Nanzuka

Tokyo  Galleries

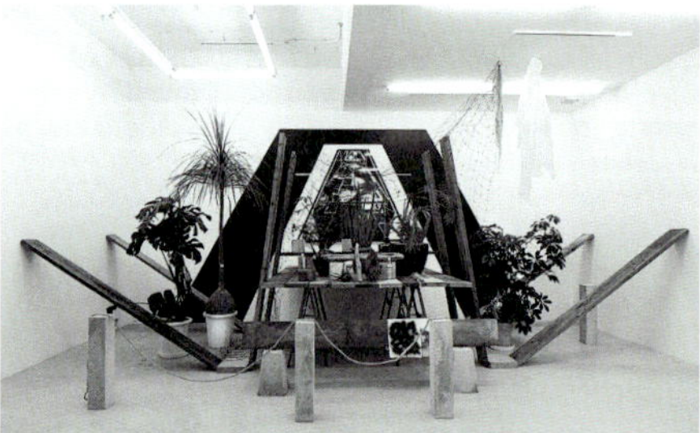

What is your favorite aspect of running a gallery?
Supporting artists, taking part in the art scene and in history is worth more than the businesses.

How do you choose the artists you work with?
In Japan there are many great artists overlooked for geographical reasons and because of a conservative art market. I have been excavating artists who deserve to be re-evaluated, such as Keiichi Tanaami, Hajime Sorayama, and Masayuki Nagare. I also support young artists.

If you weren't running a gallery what else would you do?
Curator, art writer, collector, in a business related to art and culture.

- **Contact** Nanzuka
Yuki Itaya
itaya@nug.jp
- **Established** 2005
- **Owner(s) / Partner(s)** Shinji Nanzuka
Aisho Miura
- **Team** 4
- **Space(s)** 70 m²
- **Artists at Art Basel** Julia Chiang
Yuji Honbori
Todd James
Toru Kamei
Hajime Sorayama
Keiichi Tanaami
Makoto Taniguchi
Hiroki Tsukuda
- **Further artists represented** Agnieszka Brzezanska
Tatjana Doll
Sumiyo Ito
Tomoki Kurokawa
Jompet Kuswidananto
Martin Mannig
Akiyoshi Mishima
Mustone
Frank Nitsche
Oliver Payne
Dirk Skreber
Hiroko Yamaji
Yuichi Yokoyama

Naumann

New York  Galleries
Kabinett

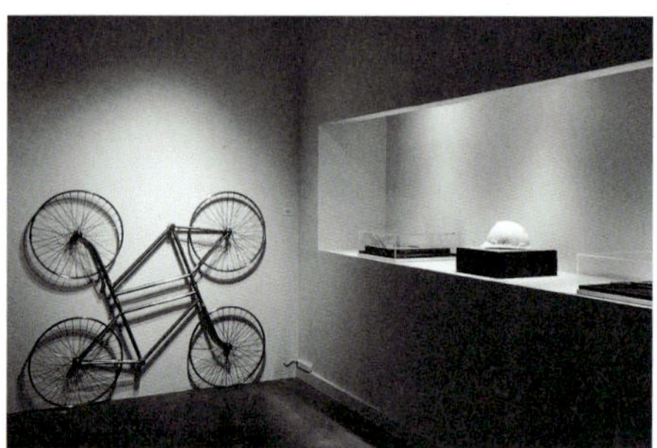

What is your favorite aspect of running a gallery?
Opening up a new work of art and seeing it for the first time (after that: installation).

How do you choose the artists you work with?
Entirely on my own personal taste, but with all artists, it must be apparent that their work is derived from sources of history of art.

If you weren't running a gallery what else would you do?
I would do research and writing, and return full-time to my earlier life as a scholar.

- **Contact** Francis M. Naumann Fine Art LLC
Francis Naumann
francis@francisnaumann.com
- **Established** 2001
- **Owner(s) / Partner(s)** Francis M. Naumann
- **Team** 2
- **Space(s)** 167.5 m²
- **Artists at Art Basel** John Atherton
Eugene Berman
Joseph Cornell
Marcel Duchamp
Suzanne Duchamp
James Guy
Marcel Jean
Leon Kelly
Michael Lenson
Dora Maar
Stanton MacDonald-Wright
George J. Marinko
Francis Picabia
Walter Quirt
Robert Rauschenberg
Man Ray
Kay Sage
Jacques Villon
Beatrice Wood

- **Further artists represented**
  Ai Weiwei
  Nancy Becker
  Rafael Leonardo Black
  Katherine S. Dreier
  Baroness Elsa von Freytag-Loringhoven
  Kathleen Gilje
  Philip Haas
  Stanley William Hayter
  Don Joint
  Pamela Joseph
  Carlo Maria Mariani
  Walter Pach
  Naomi Savage
  Douglas Vogel
  Tetsuya Yamada

Navarro

Madrid 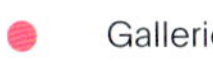 Galleries

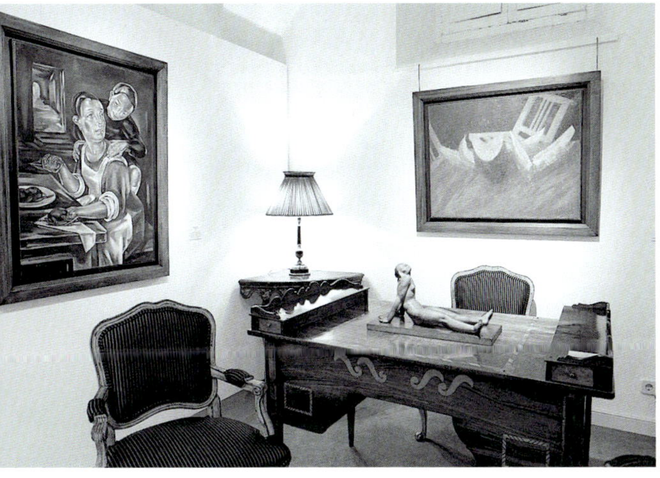

What is your favorite aspect of running a gallery?
Being able to establish contact with artists, collectors, curators, and with the artistic and cultural world.

How do you choose the artists you work with?
I choose the artists because of the quality of their work and their influence on the following generations. We deal with avant-garde and modern artists.

If you weren't running a gallery what else would you do?
I have a degree in Law and if it was not for my family connection to the gallery I would most probably have worked as a lawyer.

- **Contact** Galeria Leandro Navarro
  Iñigo Navarro
  galeria@leandro-navarro.com
- **Established** 1978
- **Owner(s) / Partner(s)** Galeria Leandro Navarro S.L.
- **Team** 5
- **Space(s)** 450 m²
- **Artists at Art Basel**
  Josef Albers
  Francisco Bores
  Lucian Freud
  Pablo Gargallo
  Juan Gris
  Wassily Kandinsky
  Baltasar Lobo
  Manolo Millares
  Pablo Picasso
  Manuel Rivera
  Oskar Schlemmer
  Joaquín Torres García
- **Further artists represented**
  Juan Barjola
  Giorgio Morandi
  Joan Miró
  Pablo Palazuelo
  Benjamin Palencia
  Gerardo Rueda
  Kurt Schwitters
  Maria Helena Vieira da Silva

Neu

Berlin Galleries

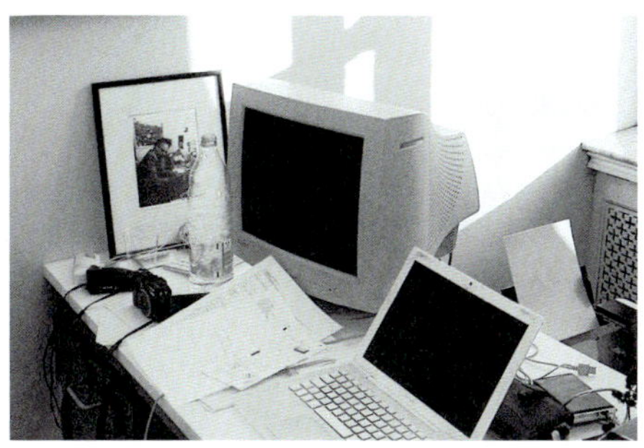

What is your favorite aspect of running a gallery?
Just as we have been partners, complementing each other for the past 20 years, the variety of the tasks and being confronted with new challenges every day are very stimulating and a source of inspiration.

How do you choose the artists you work with?
More than a rational decision or the product of a selective screening, the choice of an artist results from an instinct, a feeling that this particular artist is going to fit into our program. Often, in fact, it is our artists that introduce us to the new artists, so we would say that a common state of mind is key for us.

If you weren't running a gallery what else would you do?
Considering the wonderful array of people we have met, and the places and situations experienced, it is difficult to imagine that we could do something else in another life.

- **Contact** Galerie Neu
  Marta Fontolan
  mail@galerieneu.com
- **Established** 1994
- **Owner(s) / Partner(s)** Alexander Schroeder & Thilo Wermke
- **Team** 11
- **Space(s)** 380 m²
- **Artists at Art Basel**
  Kai Althoff
  Tom Burr
  Marc Camille Chaimowicz
  Bernadette Corporation
  Jana Euler
  Matias Faldbakken
  Keith Farquhar
  Christian Flamm
  Saul Fletcher
  Claire Fontaine
  Florian Hecker
  Ull Hohn
  Yngve Holen
  Karl Holmqvist
  Alex Hubbard
  Sergej Jensen
  Kitty Kraus
  Klara Lidén
  Hilary Lloyd
  Victor Man
  Birgit Megerle
  Manfred Pernice
  Daniel Pflumm
  Josephine Pryde
  Gedi Sibony
  Andreas Slominski
  Sean Snyder
  Francesco Vezzoli
  Cosima von Bonin
  Katharina Wulff
  Cerith Wyn Evans

neugerriemschneider

Berlin

Galleries
Encounters
Galleries
Galleries

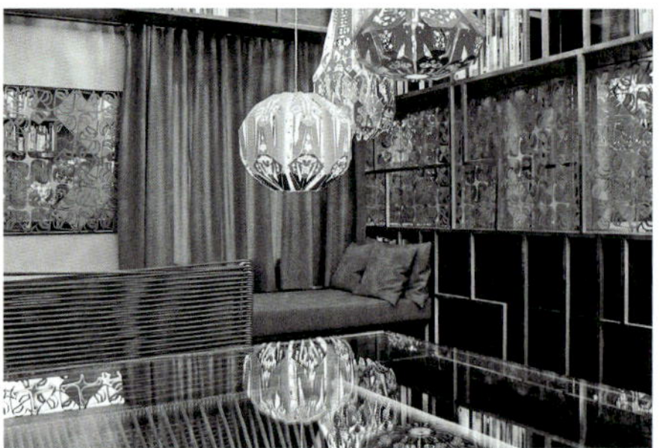

- **Contact** neugerriemschneider
mail@neugerriemschneider.com
- **Established** 1994
- **Owner(s) / Partner(s)** Tim Neuger
Burkhard Riemschneider
- **Artists at Art Basel** Franz Ackermann
Ai Weiwei
Paweł Althamer
James Benning
Billy Childish
Keith Edmier
Olafur Eliasson
Noa Eshkol
Mario García Torres
Isa Genzken
Sharon Lockhart
Renata Lucas
Michel Majerus
Antje Majewski
Mike Nelson
Jorge Pardo
Elizabeth Peyton
Tobias Rehberger
Simon Starling
Thaddeus Strode
Rirkrit Tiravanija
Pae White

Ning

Hong Kong

Galleries

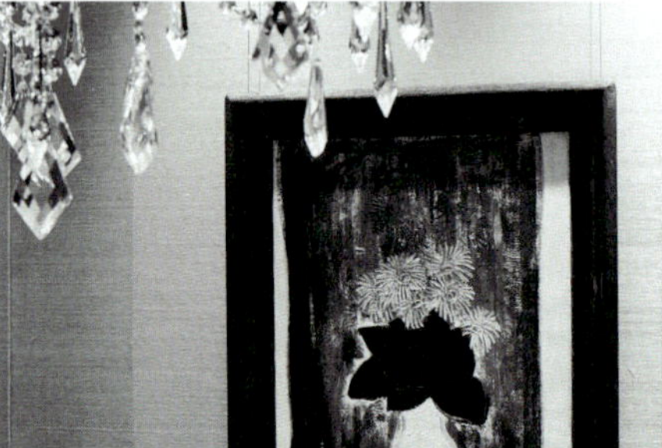

What is your favorite aspect of running a gallery?

I enjoy exhibiting Chinese art and promoting it to a wider international audience. My work brings me into contact with clients in both the East and the West, which I find fascinating. I enjoy traveling to see clients and finding artworks.

How do you choose the artists you work with?

My main interest lies in 20th-century Chinese art and contemporary Chinese art. I am lucky to have established good relationships with the contemporary artists I represent. This is very important, so we can discuss their work and future direction.

If you weren't running a gallery what else would you do?

Actually I find it hard to imagine another life other than running a gallery!

- **Contact** Anna Ning Fine Art
Anna Ning
info@annaningfineart.com
- **Established** 2005
- **Owner(s) / Partner(s)** Anna Ning
- **Team** 3
- **Space(s)** 93 m²
- **Artists at Art Basel** Sanyu
Teh-Chun Chu
Wu Guanzhong
Yun Chee
Zao Wouki

Nitsch

New York

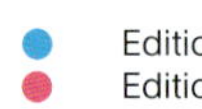

Edition
Edition

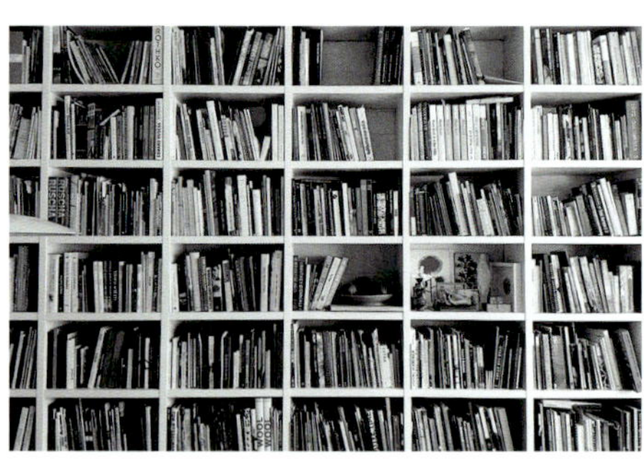

- **Contact** Carolina Nitsch
Carolina Nitsch
info@carolinanitsch.com
- **Established** 2000
- **Team** 3
- **Space(s)** 186 m²
- **Artists at Art Basel** Ai Weiwei
Louise Bourgeois
E.V. Day
Richard Dupont
Tracey Emin
Robert Gober
Paula Hayes
Donald Judd
Jenny Holzer
Anish Kapoor
Martin Kippenberger
Jeff Koons
Vera Lutter
Bruce Nauman
Olaf Nicolai
Carolee Schneemann
Thomas Schütte
Alyson Shotz
Laurie Simmons
Matthew Weinstein
Carrie Mae Weems

Noero

Turin

Galleries
Galleries
Unlimited
Parcours
Galleries

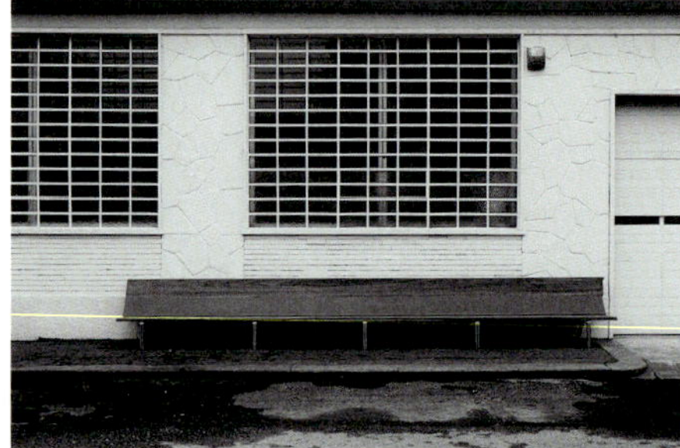

What is your favorite aspect of running a gallery?

The privilege of working with a rising idea, believing in it, and fighting for its statement alongside the artist who has conceived it. This is the most beautiful challenge. It is not comparable to the launch of a product: we are talking about Art and Poetry—and trying to build an economy with poetry is unbelievably sexy.

How do you choose the artists you work with?
It is not a daily quest per se, but rather something that one finds on one's path. It is exceptional and extraordinary when one discovers the work of an artist and decides to support it, and then see it develop and grow.

If you weren't running a gallery what else would you do?
Franco Noero:
I always dreamt of having a hotel. Maybe a little chain …
Pierpaolo Falone:
I always dreamt of being a tennis champion.

- **Contact** Galleria Franco Noero
Elisa Facchin
elisa@franconoero.cm
- **Established** 1999
- **Owner(s) / Partner(s)** Franco Noero
Pierpaolo Falone
- **Team** 8
- **Space(s)** 600 m²
- **Artists at Art Basel** Darren Bader
Pablo Bronstein
Tom Burr
Jeff Burton
Neil Campbell
Andrew Dadson
Jason Dodge
Lara Favaretto
Martino Gamper
Henrik Håkansson
Mark Handforth
Arturo Herrera
Gabriel Kuri
Phillip Lai
Jim Lambie
Robert Mapplethorpe
Paulo Nazareth
Mike Nelson
Henrik Olesen
Kirsten Pieroth
Steven Shearer
Simon Starling
Tunga
Costa Vece
Francesco Vezzoli

Nolan

New York

Galleries
Galleries
Kabinett

What is your favorite aspect of running a gallery?
Producing catalogues and the ability to interact with both contemporary and historical art, as well as sharing my ideas with people interested in collecting art.

How do you choose the artists you work with?
Visiting shows and studios.

If you weren't running a gallery what else would you do?
My invitation-only private island with a swim up bar and library.

- **Contact** David Nolan Gallery
David Nolan Maureen Bray
info@davidnolangallery.com
- **Established** 1987
- **Owner(s) / Partner(s)** David Nolan
- **Team** 6
- **Space(s)** 279 m²
- **Artists at Art Basel** Richard Artschwager
Steve DiBenedetto
Carroll Dunham
Ian Hamilton Finlay
Julia Fish
Neil Gall
George Grosz
David Hartt
Mel Kendrick
Barry Le Va
Alice Maher
Wardell Milan
Ciprian Muresan
Jim Nutt
Christina Ramberg
Alexander Ross
Serban Savu
Eugen Schönebeck
Gavin Turk
Sandra Vásquez de la Horra
Jorinde Voigt

Nordenhake

Berlin
Stockholm

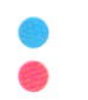
Galleries
Galleries
Public

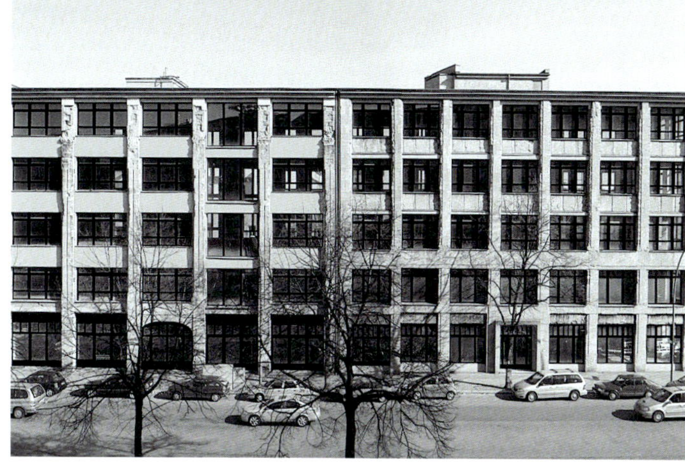

- **Contact** Galerie Nordenhake
Isabelle Köhncke
isabelle@nordenhake.com
- **Established** 1976
- **Owner(s) / Partner(s)** Claes Nordenhake
- **Team** 10
- **Space(s)** 348 m²
- **Artists at Art Basel** Meriç Algün Ringborg
Christian Andersson
Olle Baertling
Mirosław Bałka
John Coplans
Sarah Crowner
Ann Edholm
Paul Fägerskiöld
Spencer Finch
Hreinn Friðfinnsson
Franka Hörnschemeyer
Gunilla Klingberg
Eva Löfdahl
Esko Männikkö
Meuser
Helen Mirra
Sirous Namazi
Walter Niedermayr
Scott Olson
Marjetica Potrč
Håkan Rehnberg
Michael Schmidt
Florian Slotawa
Leon Tarasewicz
Johan Thurfjell
Alan Uglow
Günter Umberg
Not Vital
Magnus Wallin
Stanley Whitney
Rémy Zaugg
John Zurier
- **Further artists represented** Anna Barham
Ann Böttcher
Jonas Dahlberg
Felix Gmelin
Mikael Olsson
Ulrich Rückriem

Nothelfer

Berlin  Galleries

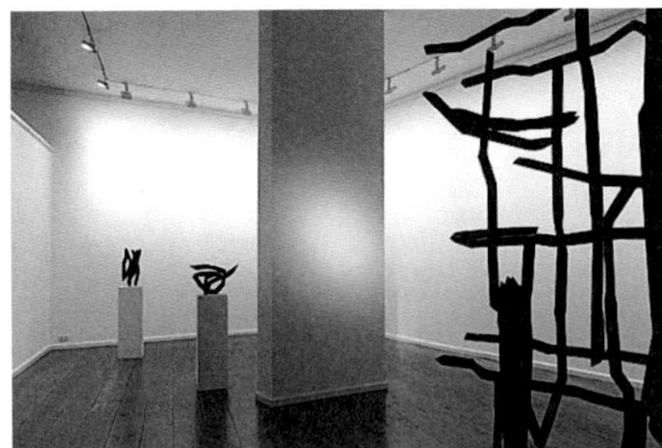

What is your favorite aspect of running a gallery?
I am a collector at heart. The gallery gives me the choice to be in very close contact with the art world and share art with other collectors and art enthusiasts.

How do you choose the artists you work with?
With a special understanding of the art; I use this understanding to discover artists who are important to my gallery and me, and finally to my collectors.

If you weren't running a gallery what else would you do?
I would continue collecting! On top of that I would publish more catalogues and books, which deal with all the different aspects of the artworld.

- **Contact**: Galerie Georg Nothelfer
Vera Ehe
nothelfer@galerie-nothelfer.de
- **Established**: 1971
- **Owner(s) / Partner(s)**: Georg Nothelfer
- **Team**: 5
- **Space(s)**: 270 m² (Tiergarten)
60 m² (Charlottenburg)
- **Artists at Art Basel**: Christo & Jeanne-Claude
Madeleine Dietz
Christoph M. Gais
Thomas Hartmann
Gerhard Hoehme
Henri Michaux
Herta Müller
Georges Noël
Robert Schad
Emil Schumacher
Kazuo Shiraga
K.R.H. Sonderborg
Walter Stöhrer
Fred Thieler
Jan Voss
- **Further artists represented**: Adochi
Pierre Alechinsky
Shusaku Arakawa
Armando
Peter Brüning
Michael Buthe
Ouhi Cha
Eduardo Chillida
K.F. Dahmen
Lothar Fischer
K.O. Götz
Manfred Hamm
Anton Heyboer
Edgar Hofschen
Rolf Iseli
Asger Jorn
László Lakner
Michel Macréau
Walter Menne
Jürgen Messensee
Robert Motherwell
Max Neumann
Markus Prachensky
Arnulf Rainer
Dieter Roth
Arno C. Schmetjen
Bernard Schultze
Richard Serra
Daniel Spoerri
Helmut Sturm
Antoni Tàpies
Wolfgang Troschke
Cy Twombly

Nuoart

Beijing Insights

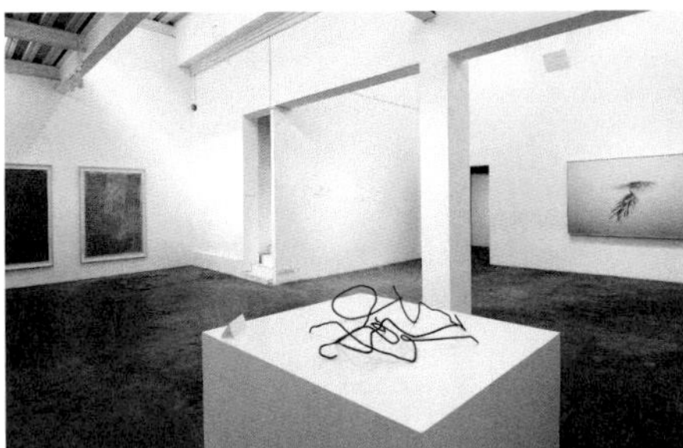

What is your favorite aspect of running a gallery?
We position ourselves as a "super" artist, and we regard every exhibition as a work of art. Our ideal is top business, and our fun lies in constant exploration and discovery.

How do you choose the artists you work with?
Capability and energy are the two aspects that we value most. To be specific, an artist has to be extraordinary in his ability to express. This includes sensibility, techniques, and the charisma from his inner heart. We think the combination makes a very charming artist.

If you weren't running a gallery what else would you do?
A collector. It is my favorite hobby. If the gallery is out of the question, then I will devote more time to the cultural industry, which has a wider dissemination, like an art hotel, or book planning, which actually is what we are currently doing.

- **Contact**: Nuoart
Lisa Sun
lisasun@nuoart.com
- **Established**: 2010
- **Owner(s) / Partner(s)**: Zheng Nuo
- **Team**: 8
- **Space(s)**: 600 m²
- **Artists at Art Basel**: Guo Gong
Wang Yabin
- **Further artists represented**: Chen Nong
Liang Quan
Shi Jinsong

Richard Nagy Ltd.
Interview with Richard Nagy

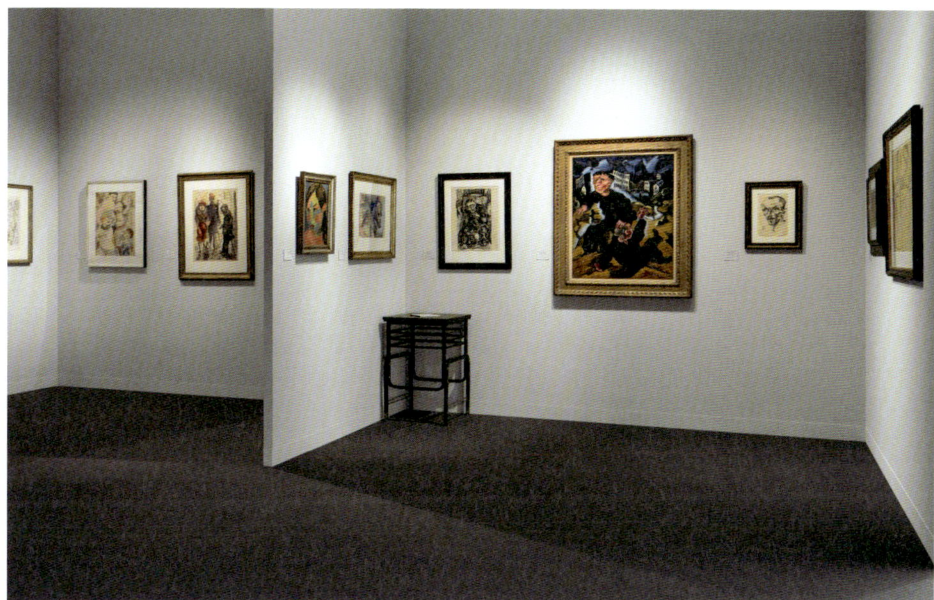

Art Basel in Basel, 2014

You opened your gallery in 1980 and your speciality is German Expressionism and Austrian artists such as Egon Schiele and Gustav Klimt. Why this particular period?

I began my career with Old Master paintings. Looking at auction catalogues from previous years—from 1970 to 1980—the quality of Old Master works coming to the market was diminishing quickly and I thought: "OK, this is an area that is drying up, so I'll go into something that I personally like," and there seemed to be a lot of material around. Thirty-five years later, what I was finding with Old Masters is now happening with Classic Modernism, and hence the rise of the contemporary market because there's simply not enough material from Classic Modernism, Post-Impressionism, and Impressionism to fulfill the demands of collectors.

Do you think this will change the occupation and focus of your gallery?

No. I'll do more of the same. I'm not interested in dealing in the emperor's new clothes.

How did you build the gallery's program—you have organized solo and "group" exhibitions about Klimt's and Schiele's circles?

I like art that is perhaps a bit confrontational, that addresses the human condition in extremis. I also like art that is intellectually provocative, and the artists I work with fulfill all those demands. I'm not interested in art that turns into wallpaper after you've looked at it and walked past it 20 times and that doesn't engage you anymore, which is probably why I will stay clear of the contemporary market—not because there aren't great artists working today, of course there are, but unfortunately 90% of what is produced lacks those qualities for me.

How do you build your exhibitions?

Well, I have been selling this material for 30 years, so I know where a lot of it is. Most of the exhibitions are works borrowed back, that the gallery has handled in previous years.

A lot of this historical material has to be traced to establish provenance: that's one of the complex tasks that is very particular to your type of dealership.

That's certainly the case. I think in today's market, the majority of collectors have no understanding of art before Andy Warhol and I don't even think they are curious about it. So one needs to know history, if one is talking about George Grosz and the Dada Movement, these artists require a political understanding.

Also all the artists you're working with are not equal. Schiele is the darling of the audience and Otto Dix and George Grosz are not ...

Less so. They are much more difficult and confrontational, they address politics from the left of the political spectrum. In Grosz's case he was a member of the Communist Party briefly; a trip to Moscow cured him of that. Then for a lot of people they find the work ugly because it's very tough, dealing with the realities of life in Berlin after the First World War, where there were mutilated soldiers returning home whose only means of support was begging. Something like one in four women had to prostitute themselves at some point in their lives. These are tough subjects that polite society is not very interested in.

You also participate in TEFAF in Maastricht. Is your approach to it the same?

Yes, the same sort of material, the same artists. The only difference is that what is being lost in Art Basel now, which I feel is a great mistake, is that there is not enough critical mass around Classic Modernism to tempt collectors to come here anymore. What this fair used to be was the greatest fair of 20th-century art, Classic Modernism through to Avant-Garde; this is being lost, I think, in the pursuit of something that could easily backfire. This fair was set up by Ernst Beyeler, Jan Krugier, and a few other great dealers of the second half of the 20th century. One should be careful not to forget that.

In Maastricht it's completely different, there's really no Avant-Garde so the audience there is not coming for the circus. It sounds like I'm quite negative and bitter about it, but it is a realistic view. You only have to look at the terrace of the Hotel Trois Rois, on Tuesday and Wednesday nights, where they have to have bouncers allowing people in or not, and you have the feel of the new Basel. And of course by tonight, the circus has moved on already. It's not about art anymore unfortunately; people are buying the lifestyle.

Hasn't there always been that? A bit of lifestyle is always included, notably in the second half of the 20th century, and it's not a new phenomenon in itself.

I disagree, I don't think Basel was like that at all, the collectors tended to be knowledgeable, knowing what art they wanted and understanding what it was, and its historical context ... In relation to dealers today you could argue that the contemporary art market's exactly the same, but I would suggest that the knowledge-base is skin deep.

Carla Accardi
1924–2014

Terry Adkins
1953–2014

Markus Brüderlin
1958–2014

Frédéric Bruly Bouabré
1923–2014

René Burri
1933–2014

Lynne Cohen
1944–2014

Pierre Daix
1922–2014

Harun Farocki
1944–2014

Jan Hoet
1936–2014

Nancy Holt
1938–2014

On Kawara
1933–2014

Walter Keller
1953–2014

Rudolf Kicken
1947–2014

Jean-Claude Lahumière
1929–2014

Maria Lassnig
1919–2014

Otto Piene
1928–2014

Francisco Sobrino
1932–2014

Sturtevant
1924–2014

Ger van Elk
1941–2014

Ultra Violet
1935–2014

OVA TIONS

O

Something No One Talks About Better than Artists

Harry Bellet

Death is something no one talks about better than artists. "I want to make death lively and playful, I want death to be like the famous *danse macabre* from Basel," said Jean Tinguely in 1989, two years before death asked him to dance. More recently, Maurizio Cattelan envisaged a headstone for collector François Pinault engraved with the question, "Why me?" Fortunately, the two latter individuals are still with us. Others, alas, have been so rude as to leave us this year—for as Tinguely also said, "It is always impolite to die, with regard to everyone else."

Carla Accardi in her studio, Rome, 1999

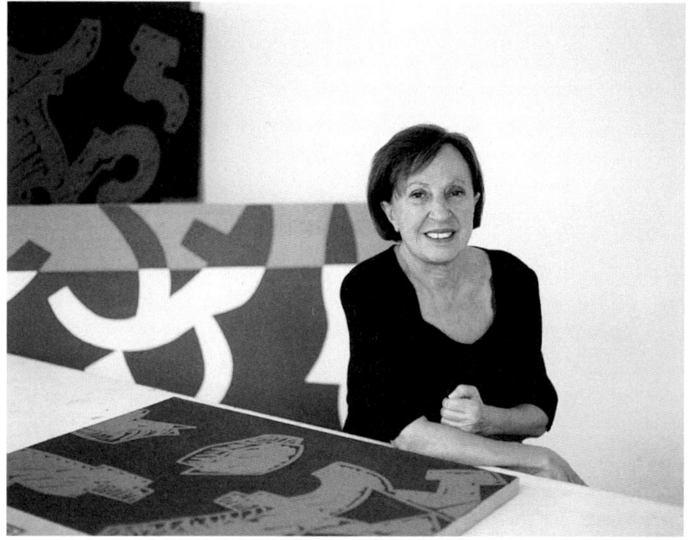

I trust I'll be forgiven for beginning this sad roll call with a fellow Frenchman, Pierre Daix. If I had to describe Pierre in one word, it would be "courage." As the French Communist daily newspaper, *L'Humanité,* put it the day following his death, "his heart never missed a drumbeat." Indeed, it took a valiant heart to join the outlawed French Communist Party in 1939, when Daix was only 17. And the very next year he joined the Resistance. Arrested and imprisoned, he was deported to the Mathausen concentration camp. After the Liberation, he briefly served as chief of staff to government minister Charles Tillon, then became editor-in-chief of *Lettres Françaises,* published by Louis Aragon. At about that time he met Picasso, who became a close friend. Indeed, Daix's last public outing, just a few days before he died, was a visit to the Picasso Museum in Paris. He wrote some 15 books on Picasso, including part of the catalogue raisonné. Courage was also required when Daix came to the defense of Alexander Solzhenitsyn, and when he broke with the Communist Party after having been a vital cog in that organization. He recounted it all in a book with the explicit title of *J'ai cru au matin* (I Believed in Dawn, 1976). He also published books on Delacroix, Manet, Gauguin, and Pierre Soulages, as well as, more surprisingly, a biography of François Pinault. The two men met at the home of artist Antoni Clavé, where the former Communist and the wealthy businessman discovered they shared a passion for cycling. For a long time afterward they would cycle together on the roads around Saint-Tropez.

I lost another friend in Markus Brüderlin. It was in Basel, where he was born in 1958, that I first met Markus. He was a curator who inaugurated the foundation that Ernst Beyeler opened in Riehen, Switzerland, in 1997. There Brüderlin organized several memorable exhibitions including one called *ArchiSculpture* (2004), and another devoted to the relationship between abstraction and ornamentation (2001), based on his doctoral dissertation for the University of Vienna. He also faithfully attended the lectures then being given by Joseph Beuys, and he founded and headed the Kunstraum Wien as well as the art magazine *Springer.* He later became a Commissioner of Education and Arts for the Austrian federal government, charged with allocating funds to innovatory projects. "I, a Swiss citizen, was distributing Austrian taxpayers' money," he admitted with amusement in 2008 on the SwissInfo website. Ernst Beyeler summoned him back to Basel during the construction of the foundation, on which Brüderlin wrote a monograph, *Renzo Piano: Fondation Beyeler, A Home for Art* (Birkhauser). In 2006 Brüderlin left to run the Kunstmuseum in Wolfsburg, Germany, where he organized highly original exhibitions, such as one in 2010 devoted to the influence on contemporary art of Rudolf Steiner (1861–1925), the theosophist and founder of the Anthroposophical Society.

Jan Hoet, from Belgium, was another outstanding curator. Born in Leuven in 1936, he became interested in artists from his own country in 1979 when he organized a contemporary art show titled *Aktuele Kunst in België: Inzicht/Overzicht–Overzicht/Inzicht.* Contemporary art was one thing, getting the general public to like it was another—better—thing. That was the idea—often plagiarized since—that prompted Hoet to organize a now-legendary event in Ghent, titled *Chambres d'amis*, in 1986. Artists' works were not displayed in the museum, but rather in the "guest rooms" of private residents in Ghent who opened their homes to visitors. The dynamic Fleming soon drew the attention of his foreign counterparts, and in 1992 he was charged with running documenta 9 in Kassel, where he deliberately challenged the certainties of the art scene by mingling stars with lesser known artists, and by overturning chronological frameworks, for example by hanging David, Gauguin, and Ensor in the same room (each represented by just one painting), followed by Beuys, Giacometti, and James Lee Byars. In 1999 he made one of his dreams come true by opening the Stedelijk Museum voor Actuele Kunst (SMAK) in a former casino next to the Musée des Beaux-Arts in Ghent. The collection he had assembled over 20 years—Artschwager, Buren, Beuys, Cragg, Flanagan, Judd, Merz, Nauman, etc.—had finally found a home. But Hoet left Ghent in 2003 for the modest city of Herford, Germany (population 65,000), which asked him to set up a museum. The architect he chose was Frank Gehry. When a reporter from *Le Monde* asked him why, he replied, "Because this area is know for its narrow-mindedness. A museum has to be viewed as a critical apparatus rather than a decorative symbol of society."

Equally active was Walter Keller, born near Zurich in 1953. By turns journalist, publisher, photographer, and gallery owner, in 1984 he cofounded *Parkett* magazine with Bice Curiger (who penned a fine obituary of Keller for *Artforum*) and Jacqueline Burckhardt. It served as a model for many others—few art magazines have been the subject of exhibitions at the Pompidou Center in Paris and The Museum of Modern Art in New York. Keller left *Parkett* in 1993 to found a publishing house (Scalo Verlag) that specialized in photography, putting out books on the likes of Nan Goldin, Larry Clark, Robert Frank, Gilles Peress, and Richard Prince. The same year, alongside George Reinhart and Urs Stahel, he co-founded the Fotomuseum Winterthur, which soon became a leading institution of its kind. From January to June 2008 he served briefly as the editor-in-chief of *DU* magazine, then opened a Zurich gallery linked to his publishing outfit. In 2012 he surprised everyone by organizing a show at the Swiss National Museum titled *CAPITAL—Merchants in Venice and Amsterdam,* which traced the economic history of those two cities back to the 13th century, highlighting the development of financing, credit, and trade that generated prosperity and even opulence, creating two centers of high life, art, and culture. The topic is still relevant today.

Terry Adkins

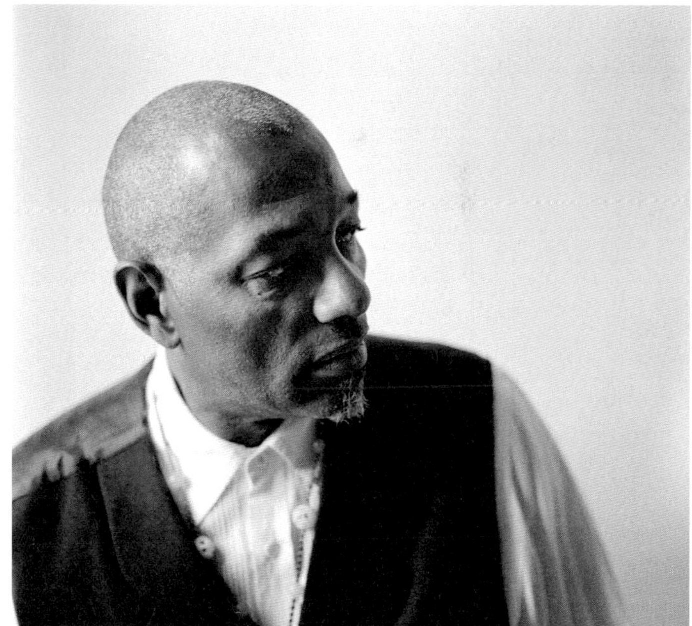

If Keller was partly a dealer in photography, Rudolf Kicken was entirely so. Born in 1947, he opened his first gallery in his home town of Aachen in 1974, moving it to Cologne in 1979 and then Berlin in 2000. He specialized in the Czech and German avant-gardes of the 1920s and 1930s—showing the work of Josef Sudek as early as 1976—but was also interested in historic individuals such as the Viennese Secessionist Heinrich

Kühn, Man Ray, and László Moholy-Nagy, as well as younger photographers like Dieter Appelt. Such was his expertise that he was chosen for the selection committee, along with Eleanor Barefoot and Harry Lunn from New York, Andrew Cowan from London, and Alain Paviot from Paris, for the first Paris Photo Salon in 1997. The exhibitions he organized in his gallery and on fair stands were always of museum quality.

René Burri

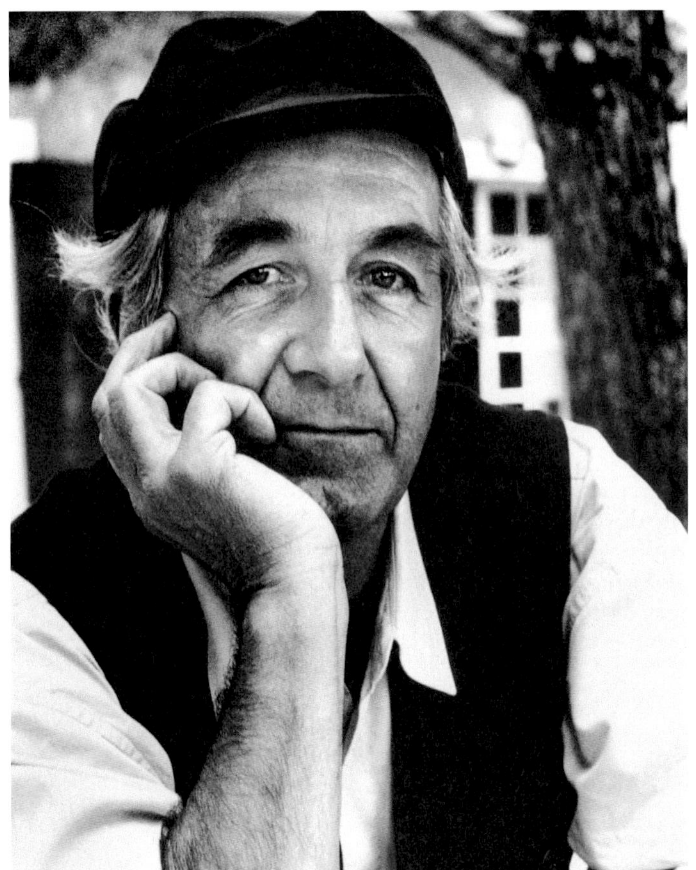

Another regular to the Art Basel fair has also left us: we will miss the tall, lanky figure, full beard, and humor of Jean-Claude Lahumière, even if his wife Anne and daughter Diane will continue to run the gallery that has been present at the Basel fair from the start. Born in 1929, Lahumière was also an artist and designer who went by the name Jean d'Imbleval, having studied in André Lhote's studio and worked with Jean Dewasne. But above all he was a man of strong commitments: we recall with fondness his delight at showing photos taken in 1972 outside the Grand Palais in Paris, where the young and already bearded man participated in the "unhanging" of work by artists who refused to participate in an exhibition sponsored by French president Georges Pompidou, titled *60–72: Douze ans d'art contemporain en France.* Much later, aged 82, Lahumière would still take to task French politicians who he felt were falling down on the job, just as he enjoyed telling off journalists if necessary.

The Galerie Lahumière specializes in geometric abstraction, a movement that lost an eminent member this year in the person of Francisco Sobrino. Born in 1932 in Guadalajara, Spain, Sobrino studied fine art in Madrid and Buenos Aires, where he met Demarco, Garcia Rossi, and Le Parc. In Paris, along with the two latter artists, and Morellet, Stein, and Yvaral, he founded the Groupe de Recherche d'Art Visuel (GRAV), a group that explored new techniques in a move from geometric abstraction toward kinetic art. Sobrino first used Plexiglas, stacking clear or colored sheets of it in juxtapositions that created new shapes, bending light and space as the beholder moved around them. One of GRAV's mottoes was "Please Touch." Subsequently, from 1964 onward, Sobrino used mirror-polished steel to make what he called "permutational structures" in which reflections created an interaction between artwork and environment. Later, the introduction of movement added a further dimension to his art, which Sobrino hoped would take to the streets (as did the other members of GRAV). A museum of his work is being planned for Guadalajara.

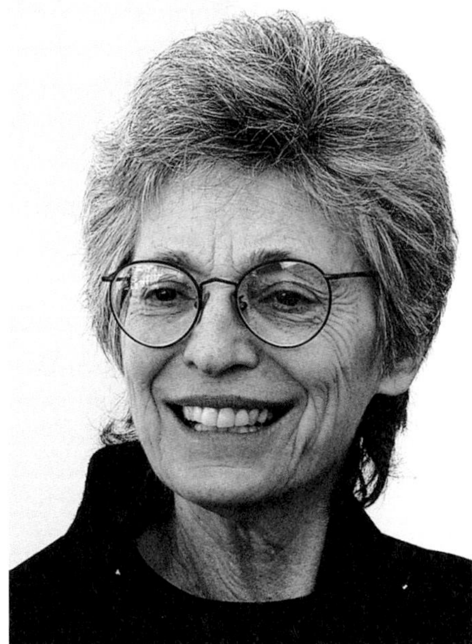

Lynne Cohen

Similar concerns interested Otto Piene, who also worked on light and movement, although his art took a very different path. Born in 1928 in Bad Laasphe, Germany, he studied art in Munich and Düsseldorf, and philosophy in Cologne. In 1957 he co-founded ZERO with Heinz Mack and Günther Uecker, a group whose ambitions were somewhat similar to GRAV's. He devised paintings based on a grid—his "grid pictures"—that made his monochrome canvases vibrate. In 1962, Piene and his two companions designed a "Salon of Light" for the Stedelijk Museum in Amsterdam, and he experimented with new techniques occasionally related to performance art, employing light, fire, and smoke as well as helium balloons. He later left for the Massachusetts Institute of Technology (MIT), where Gyorgy Kepes had founded the Center for Advanced Visual Studies in 1967. Piene was the first guest artist there, and in 1974 he succeeded Kepes as the Center's director, a job he held for 20 years, exploring potential links between art, nature, and technology.

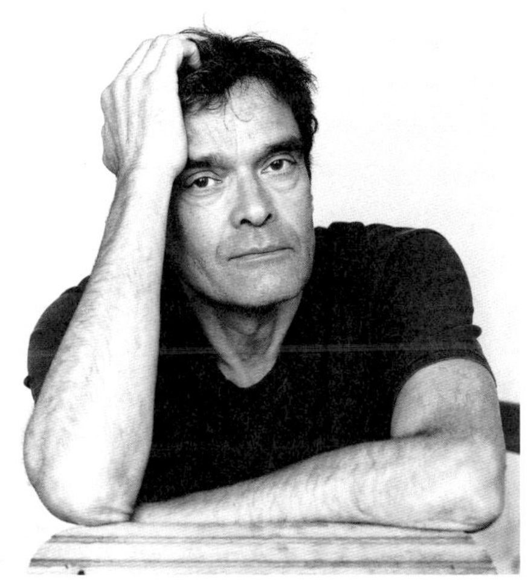

Harun Farocki

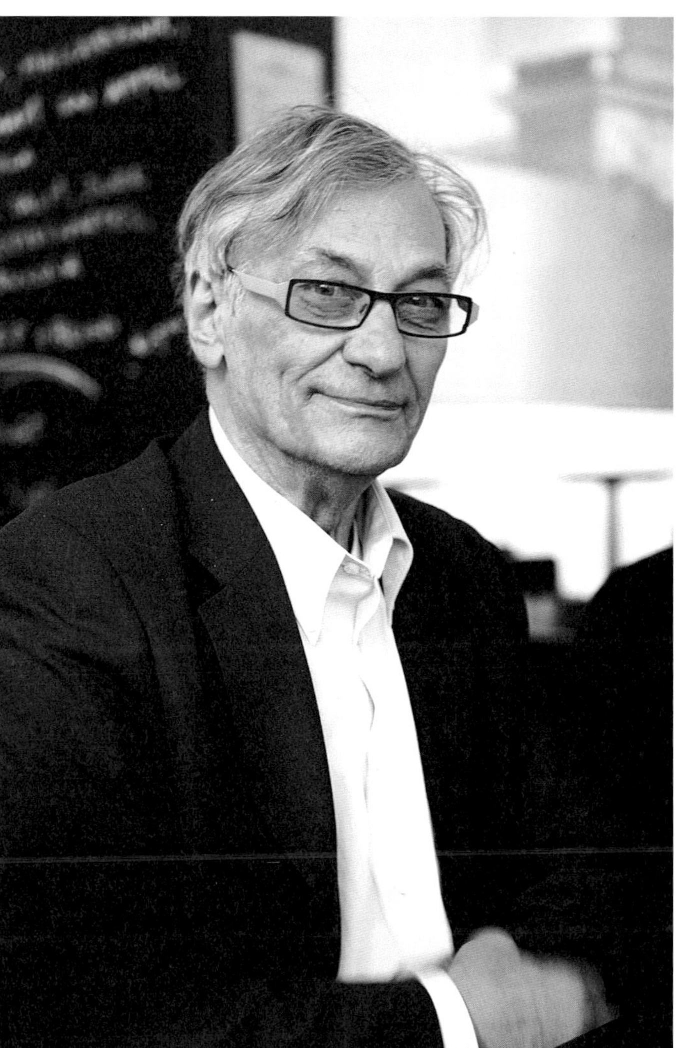

Jan Hoet

Maria Lassnig was born in Kappel am Krappfeld, Austria, in 1919. Although she was an abstract painter for a while, she was known above all for her decades-long exploration of a highly singular method that focused on her own body, often with a delightful sense of self-mockery. She liked to call her paintings *Körperbilder*, "body images" or "body awareness." The principle was very simple: she depicted only those parts of her body of which she was aware at the moment she painted. If she wasn't aware of her nose or an ear, they would not appear in the painting—shades of the work of Edvard Munch, as well as of her friendship with André Breton and Benjamin Péret, whom she met during a stay in Paris in 1951. In 1968 she moved to New York, where she made several films. Recognition came late, but was authentic. It began with a show at the Pompidou Center in Paris in 1996, and peaked with a Golden Lion for career achievement at the Venice Biennale in 2013. Lassnig was also interested in the *danse macabre,* and a large painting some six feet by four, done in 1999 and titled *Death and the Girl*, showed her dancing with the Grim Reaper.

Humor was something that Elaine Sturtevant also had in abundance. Born in Lakewood, Ohio, in 1924 (or possibly 1926 or 1930), she studied at the Art Institute of Chicago and the Art Students League in New York. It was the heyday of Abstract Expressionism and Pop art, and she headed down the latter path, exhibiting her own versions of works by Johns, Rauschenberg, Stella, and Rosenquist—not forgetting a Segal-style plaster cast—at New York's Bianchini Gallery in 1965. The show also included a silkscreen from Warhol's *Flowers* series. She might have been charged with plagiarism, and yet some artists apparently appreciated the homage, because Warhol himself provided the silkscreen he used for his *Flowers.* These appropriations, which Sturtevant signed with her own name, radically raised the issues of originality in art and the status of the artist. Although some artists were sympathetic to her approach, others remained hostile, as did the critics. Her perfect replica, in 1967, of Claes Oldenburg's 1961 installation of *The Store* earned her some ire, as did her replicas of Joseph Beuys' works in the early 1970s. She subsequently spent a good ten years

O

in the wilderness, when no one would give her a show. Then in 1986, other artists such as Sherrie Levine, Mike Bidlo, and Richard Prince began to practice the art of "appropriation." Sturtevant suddenly went from pariah to precursor. She carried on, adding new generations to her collection: Haring, Kiefer, Gonzalez-Torres, and McCarthy joined her list, as did the artist who might have been her mentor, so fond was he of remake his own works, namely Marcel Duchamp—to whom she paid a tribute at the Whitney Biennial of 2006. Formerly reviled, her work received a Golden Lion at the 2011 Venice Biennale, demonstrating that much of the art community no longer considered originality to be a key artistic criterion.

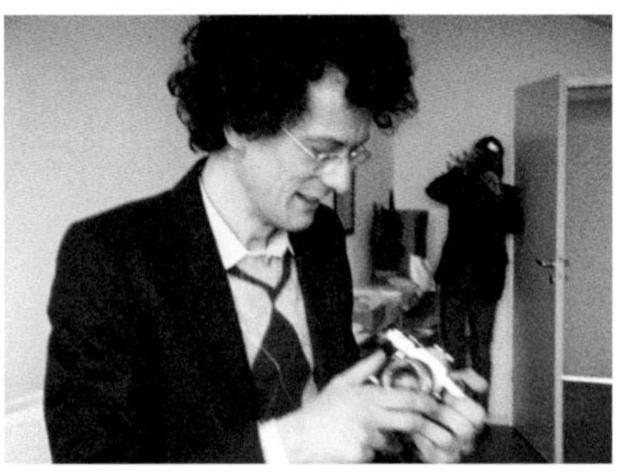

Walter Keller in a still from a film by Sigmar Polke in 1984

Nor is even *making* a work a criterion, unless one's own life is considered an artwork. That is what the career of Ultra Violet seems to demonstrate. Born Isabelle Collin Dufresne in Grenoble in 1935 to a grand bourgeois family (including a cabinet minister in De Gaulle's administration), to whom she caused great concern, she ran away and found refuge in New York. She first became a model and muse for Salvador Dalí, who liked to stroke her with a lobster. "Our sexual relationship was Dalí-esque, that is to say theatrical and preposterous, but never penetrating in the clinical sense of the term," she told *Le Monde* in 2009. In 1963 she met Andy Warhol at the St. Regis hotel, where Dalí was living. Warhol asked her to be in one of his films. Upon joining the gang at the Factory, Isabelle changed her name: Warhol suggested Poly Ester or Notre Dame, but she preferred Ultra Violet, dying her hair, eyelashes, nails, and clothes that color. The new woman who emerged became famous. According to Warhol, "She'd tell journalists, 'I collect art and love.' But what she really collected were press clippings … She was popular with the press because she had a freak name, purple hair, an incredibly long tongue, and a mini-rap about the intellectual meaning of underground movies." But there were too many deaths, suicides, and overdoses, so in 1973 Ultra Violet broke with that scene. She went on to write for the theater and opera and even took up painting, but that's not what made her famous.

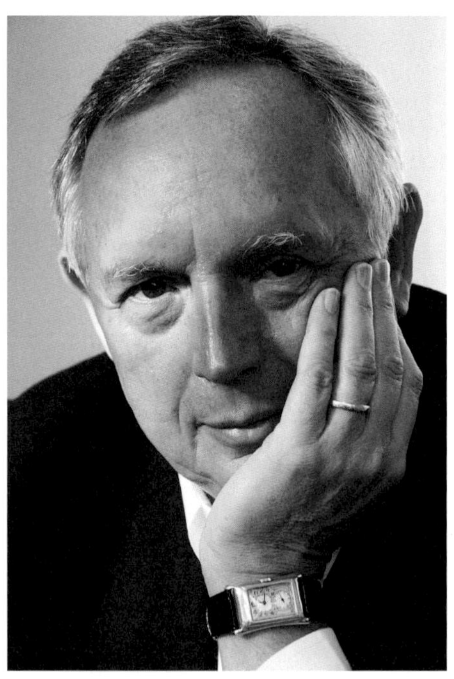

Rudolf Kicken

Conceptual art, in its various forms, lost three major figures in 2014: Dutchman Ger van Elk, American Terry Adkins, and an artist of Japanese origin, On Kawara.

Born in Amsterdam in 1941, van Elk long explored the way that pictures lie to us. In his 1974 series *The Adieu,* he used a set of photographs showing him waving farewell, but the photos were repainted in an illusionistic manner. Distorted frames created strange effects of perspective, so that the beholder was no longer certain of the viewing angle. Evoking the tradition of 17th- and 19th-century Dutch genre painting, van Elk would also call upon the repertoire of Arte Povera, Pop art, Fluxus, and Minimal art in order to interrogate both subject and material. Although little known on the art market, van Elk was fully recognized by the great exhibition curators, beginning with Harald Szeemann, who included van Elk in the legendary 1969 show at the Kunsthalle in Bern, *When Attitudes Become Form.* Ger van Elk also represented his country at the Venice Biennale in 1980, and was selected for no fewer than three documentas.

Born in 1953 in Washington, DC, Terry Adkins was a teacher, performer, musician, sculptor, and certainly other things I've overlooked. "My quest," he said, "has been to find a way to make music as physical as sculpture might be, and sculpture as ethereal as music is." But that was not his only drive. He was also keen to pay tribute to Afro-American heroes, some of whom are well known—the abolitionist John Brown, Martin Luther King, musicians Bessie Smith, John Coltrane, and Jimi Hendrix (whom Adkins liked to point out had been a paratrooper with the 101st Airborne Division before becoming an inspired guitarist)—while others have been forgotten, like Matthew Henson, an Afro-American who accompanied Robert Peary on his polar exploration of 1909. In homage to Henson, Adkins himself traveled to the Arctic. Similarly, when existing musical instruments did not suit him, he would invent new ones, such as the "arkaphone," an 18-foot-long horn which, being very sculptural, suggests that he fulfilled his original quest, as did his growing recognition—the *New York Times* described him as "a newly minted breakaway star on the international art scene."

ean-Claude Lahumière

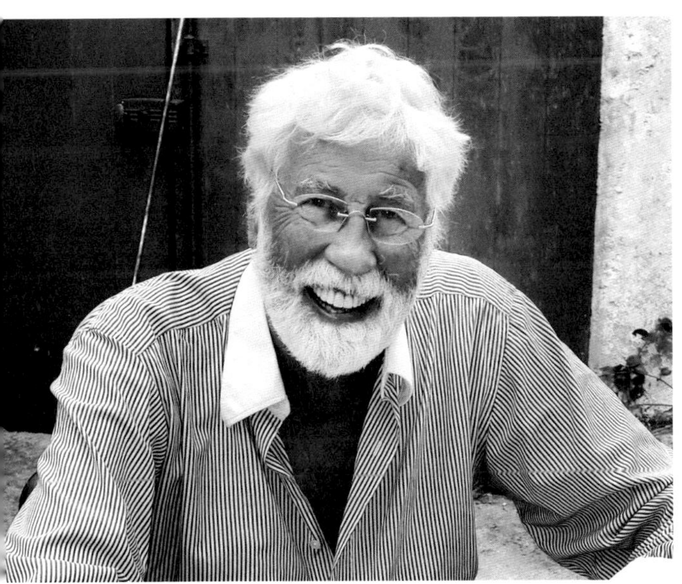

Death seems to have been on Kawara's mind all the time. Or rather, it was time—which brought the end ever nearer—that he had on his mind. We might view each of his *Date Paintings* as a victory over the Reaper, as were his telegrams, sent to a growing circle of correspondents around the world, with the message, "I'm still alive." Then there were the daily postcards that stated the time he awoke ("I got up at … "). Born in 1933 in Kariya, Japan, like many Japanese people On Kawara had been traumatized by the bombings of Hiroshima and Nagasaki. They inspired his first drawings, a series called "Thanatophanies," featuring feverish, disfigured, distraught faces. Having moved to New York in 1965, he abandoned representational art and began his *Date Paintings* early the following year (January 4). Every canvas bears, in the same white lettering, the date it was made. If it couldn't be completed in a day, it was left unfinished. All that varied were size and background color, going from red to blue and, most often, black. To this he would add a newspaper of that day—and place—framed in a little cardboard box. In 1970 On Kawara went further in time with a series titled *One Million Years (Past)*, making a systematic list of the million years between 998,031 BCE and 1969 CE, filling ten volumes of 200 pages each. Ten years later he traveled into the future with *One Million Years (Future)*, listing the million years to come. Death may always catch up with us, but artists know how to toy with it.

Some artists even cheat death by leaving their mark in history. That was the case with Carla Accardi, inseparably linked with the history of postwar Italian art. Born in Trapani, Sicily, in 1924, she studied at the school of fine arts in Florence before moving to Rome. Early on she demonstrated her keen political awareness by co-founding the Forma Uno group with Consagra, Dorazio, Perilli, Sanfilippo, and Turcato. At a time when Europe's Communist parties were following the socialist-realist line laid down by their Soviet big brother, the group sought to reconcile Marxism and abstract art. Nor was that Accardi's only commitment: in 1970 she drew up the *Manifesto di Rivolta Femminile* with Carla Lonzi and Elvira Banotti, making her one of the earliest feminist activists in Italy. Marxism and abstraction were not the only apparently incompatible terms Accardi attempted to unite, because her early work displayed a determined synthesis of geometry and physical gesture. She later forsook canvas in favor of clear plastic sheeting known as Sicofoil. This approach prompted her to abandon

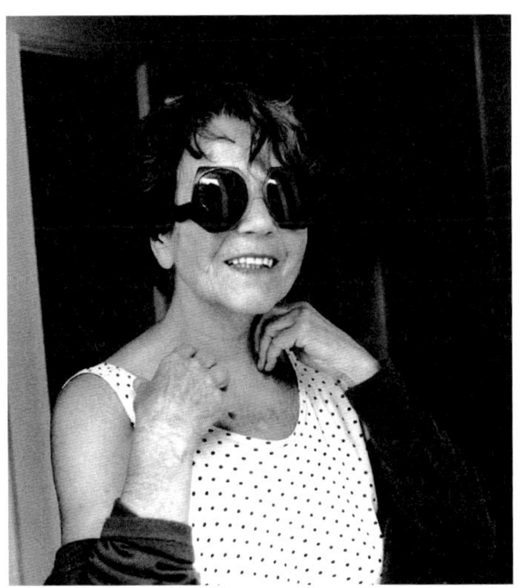

Maria Lassnig

the traditional stretcher, and she began to organize compositions in the form of huts and tents that created veritable environments, which she called by the Italian term *ambiente*. Her work influenced the Arte Povera artists of the following generation, but they were not the only ones to study her oeuvre—a retrospective held at the musée d'Art moderne de la Ville de Paris in 2002 drew admiring comments from the likes of Fabrice Hyber, Bertrand Lavier, Franz West, and Paola Pivi.

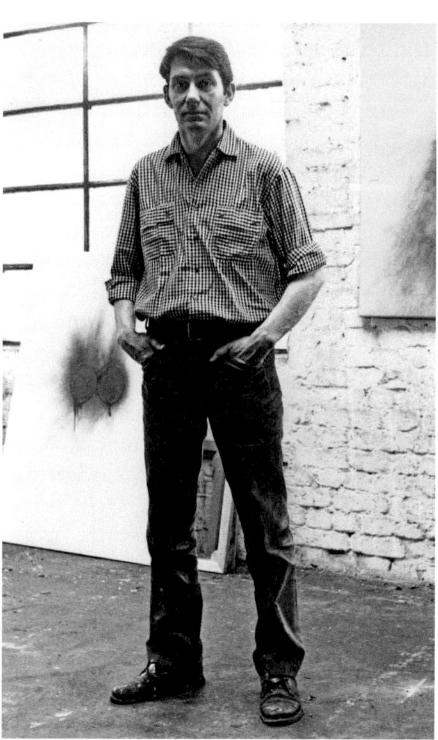

Otto Piene in his studio, 1966, Dusseldorf

No less surprising was poet and artist Frédéric Bruly Bouabré from the Ivory Coast. He quite simply invented a writing system, called the Bété syllabary, in the presence of no less a figure than God himself, who appeared on March 11, 1948, to Bouabré, then working as a clerk for the railroad linking Dakar to Niger. "The heavens opened before my eyes and seven colored stars drew a beauteous circle around their Mother-Sun, and I became Cheik Nadro, 'he who does not forget.'" The revelation inspired Bouabré to invent an African writing system based on geometric shapes, signs, and symbols, some of them inspired by the ancient carvings he saw on rock faces near the village of Békora, not far from Zéprégühé, where he was born around 1923. Bouabré employed this visual idiom both to recount mythological sagas and to depict current or everyday events, using colored pencils on small cards. Fortunately for people unfamiliar with the subtleties of Bété, Bouabré labeled the cards in French. He was discovered as early as 1958 not by an art critic but by the French naturalist and anthropologist Théodore Monod, who published an article on the new language. It was not until 1989, however, that Bouabré attained international recognition thanks to the *Magiciens de la Terre* exhibition curated by Jean-Hubert Martin in Paris. Subsequently, Bouabré's artistic reputation continued to grow, from his selection for documenta in Kassel in 2002 to his participation in the Venice Biennale in 2013.

Lady Death took a heavy toll on photographers in 2014. They included René Burri, born in Zurich, Switzerland, in 1933. His first news photograph was a shot of Winston Churchill, homburg on head, standing proudly in the back of an open car during a visit to Switzerland. The year was 1946, and Burri was just 13. Keen on the visual arts, he studied at the highly respected school of applied arts in Zurich, a "little Swiss Bauhaus" where Johannes Itten notably taught. There Burri acquired notions of formal rigor and compositional geometry. He joined the Magnum photography agency in 1954, covering major international events including wars and revolutions. He didn't like to show blood and death. "I'm convinced that showing the bullet that killed a soldier, or a mass grave, doesn't mean I've explained anything or really shown anything," he told *Le Monde* in 1984. The most famous portrait of Che Guevara, cigar between his lips, was by Burri. But he also liked artists (having snapped Picasso, Kokoschka, Klein, Giacometti, and his friend Tinguely) and architects such as Le Corbusier (whom he frequented from 1955 to 1965) and the Mexican Luis Barragán. Indeed, he published photographic monographs on both of the latter.

Lynne Cohen worked on a completely different register. Born in Racine, Wyoming, in 1944, she, too, went to art school—intending to be a sculptor—and thereby became familiar with 20th-century art, which she sometimes mentioned when discussing her work. "I want so show how society merges with modern art," she told *Le Monde* in 1992. "I'm amazed how readymade the world is." She could thus compare a stainless-steel bathtub to a Brancusi, sandbags to a Beuys, or black stains on a wall to abstract expressionism. These are the features that populate her photographs, which eschew human presence. The type of places she chose to photograph—hospitals, reception rooms, factories, office buildings, gyms, lobbies, laboratories, pools—had three

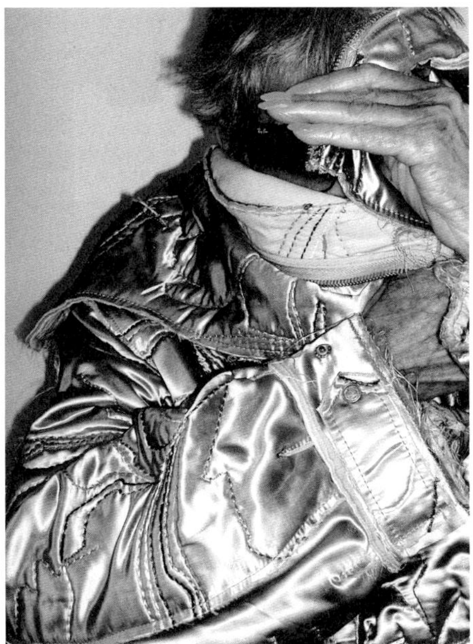
Sturtevant

things in common: they were functional, collective, and totally void of their usual occupants. "You can talk more easily about someone when he's not there," she said. A first set of photographs was published by Aperture in New York in 1988, with the unsettling title of *Occupied Territory*, and exhibited that same year in Europe at the Samia Saouma gallery in Europe. Cohen was honored with one retrospective at the National Gallery of Canada in 2002, and another the following year at the Musée de l'Élysée in Lausanne, Switzerland.

Nancy Holt, born in Worcester, Massachusetts, in 1938, was the widow of Robert Smithson, sculptor of the legendary *Spiral Jetty*. But more than that, her own oeuvre is now acquiring symbolic status. I'm thinking notably of *Sun Tunnels* (1976), four huge concrete cylinders set in the Utah desert so as to align with the sun's rays at the winter and summer solstices. It is not only a major contribution to Land art, but also a monumental reflection on the nature of the photographic lens—Holt was also a photographer and filmmaker. The cylinders are sufficiently large to allow a person to stand up inside and observe the way the landscape is thus framed. In 2012, at the Université d'Avignon in France, one of her last installations resuscitated a sculpture conceived 40 years earlier in Montana: eight steel tubes set on five-foot-high poles are arranged in a compass rose. Twice a year, in March and September, the sun sets in alignment with the western tube. The rest of the time, the tubes point to an isolated fragment of the campus. "More than a sculpture to look at," she said, "it is a sculpture to look through."

Within this list of obituaries, Harun Farocki represents something of an exception. First of all because he was primarily a filmmaker, a key figure on the experimental documentary scene who was dubbed "the German Godard" by *Der Spiegel*. Born in 1944 in Novy Jicin, Czechoslovakia, Farocki spent his childhood in Indonesia before moving to Berlin, studying at the academy of film and television there from 1966 to 1968. He later taught at the academy in the 1980s, and later still became a professor at Berkeley. As far as I know, the first time anyone considered the fine-art aspect of his work was in 1994 when Chris Dercon, co-curator of an exhibition on the way the avant-garde reacted to historical events—then being organized for the Pompidou Center in Paris, where it opened in 1996 under the title *Face à l'Histoire*—decided to include Farocki in the show. It was a shrewd choice, because Farocki's films constitute a meticulous critique of the media, scrupulously deciphering the strategies that ideology adopts in order to infiltrate imagery. He was one of the first to analyze the advent of a total-surveillance society, and also one of the first to denounce the military's use of video simulations, notably in Iraq—*Serious Games* (2009–2010) showed just how disembodied modern warfare has become. Farocki also participated in documenta 12 in Kassel, was given a retrospective at the Jeu de Paume in Paris, and exhibitions at MoMA in New York and Tate Modern in London. The art world is beginning to take a closer look at his work, and it is about time—for therein lies our salvation.

Ger van Elk

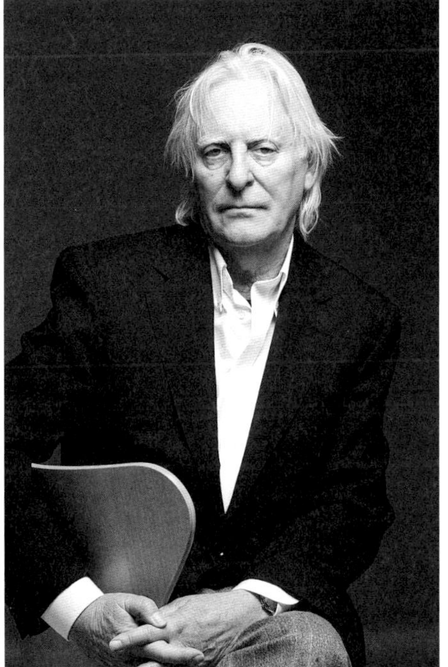

O'Neill

Rome

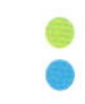

Galleries
Feature

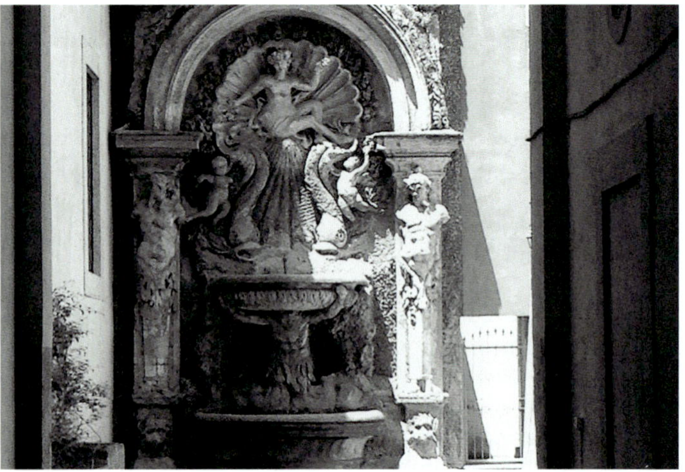

What is your favorite aspect of running a gallery?
Collaborating with artists to make new work. Enabling new work to exist.

How do you choose the artists you work with?
Artists often suggest other artists to work with, and the combination of a sense of the work with a liking of the person guides decisions. A gallerist kind of marries an artist, so there has to be a good personal feeling.

If you weren't running a gallery what else would you do?
Make furniture or buildings.

- **Contact** Galleria Lorcan O'Neill Roma
Serena Basso
serena@lorcanoneill.com
- **Established** 2003
- **Owner(s) / Partner(s)** Lorcan O'Neill
Laura Chiari
- **Team** 10
- **Space(s)** 600 m²
- **Artists at Art Basel** Martin Creed
Tracey Emin
Richard Long
Luigi Ontani
Eddie Peake
Rachel Whiteread
- **Further artists represented** Manfredi Beninati
Don Brown
Enrico Castellani
Juliana Cerqueira Leite
Francesco Clemente
Giorgio Griffa
Gary Hume
Anselm Kiefer
Matvey Levenstein
Hanna Liden
Masbedo
Carsten Nicolai
Emilio Prini
Max Renkel
Pietro Ruffo
Prem Sahib
Kiki Smith
Sam Taylor-Johnson
Jeff Wall
Cerith Wyn Evans

Obadia

Paris
Brussels

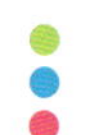

Galleries
Galleries
Galleries

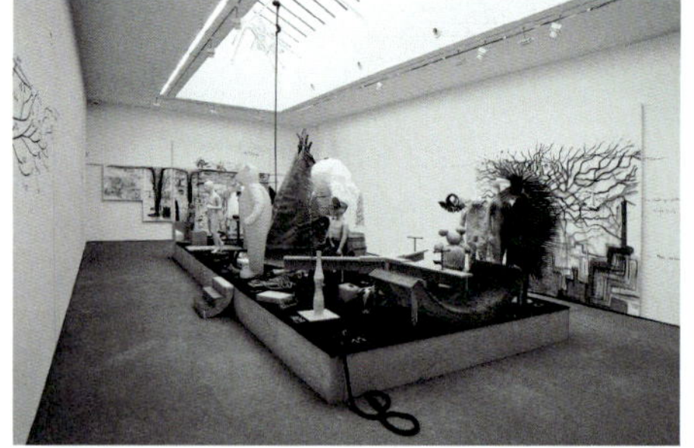

What is your favorite aspect of running a gallery?
I like to promote artists that I believe in and support their career within an international context, alongside getting institutions and influential collectors to know their work.

How do you choose the artists you work with?
First there has to be a personal sensibility for a work, which brings something new and different from art history, and the will to work harmoniously and together with a similar ambition to reach the best international level.

If you weren't running a gallery what else would you do?
I would be working for political and economic international strategy institutions or private companies.

- **Contact** Galerie Nathalie Obadia
Bianca Duclert
bianca.duclert
@galerie-obadia.com
- **Established** 1993
- **Owner(s) / Partner(s)** Nathalie Obadia (Owner)
Rachel Rechner (Paris)
Anne-Laure Buffard (Paris)
Constance Dumas (Brussels)
- **Team** 12
- **Space(s)** 1,200 m²
- **Artists at Art Basel** Brook Andrew
Rina Banerjee
Martin Barré
Valérie Belin
Fabrice Hyber
Manuel Ocampo
Fiona Rae
Sarkis
Lorna Simpson
Mickalene Thomas
Joris Van de Moortel
Joana Vasconcelos
Xu Zhen
- **Further artists represented** Mequitta Ahuja
Barry X Ball
Carole Benzaken
Huma Bhabha
Guillaume Bresson
Rosson Crow
Luc Delahaye
Michael DeLucia
Jean Dewasne
Patrick Faigenbaum
Roland Flexner
Ramin Haerizadeh
Rokni Haerizadeh
Shirley Jaffe
Sophie Kuijken
Thomas Lerooy
Eugène Leroy
Meuser
Youssef Nabil
Frank Nitsche
Enoc Perez
Chloe Piene
Pascal Pinaud
Laure Prouvost
Jorge Queiroz
Pieter Schoolwerth
Mithu Sen
Andres Serrano
Jessica Stockholder
Nicola Tyson
Agnès Varda
Brenna Youngblood

OMR

Mexico City

- Galleries
- Galleries Unlimited
- Galleries Kabinett

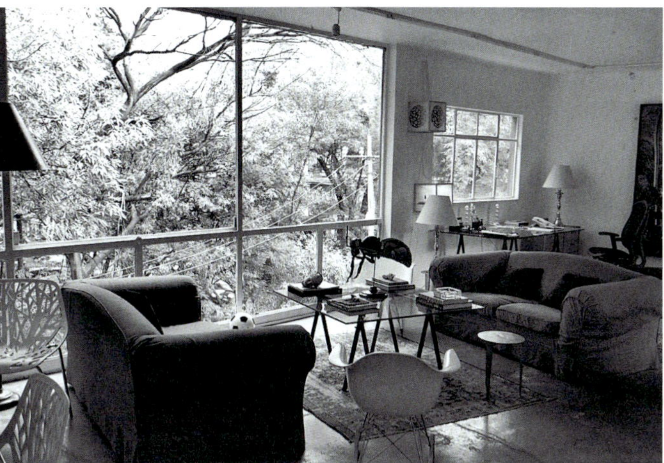

What is your favorite aspect of running a gallery?

For more than 30 years the gallery has allowed us to open our minds and our world to an incredibly diverse and interesting array of people and ideas. Our relationships with the artists and the challenges we confront to realize groundbreaking projects are the most rewarding aspects of running the gallery. Walking into a studio and experiencing great work for the first time is a thrill that ignites fresh dialogues and new ideas, processes, and projects. For us, there is nothing else like it.

How do you choose the artists you work with?

Over the years we have learned to keep our eyes open to fresh languages that shift paradigms. Our evolving red thread lies in artistic practices that methodically explore the threshold between art, science, and culture. For us the individual and collective experience of this higher field of knowledge is and will continue to be one of art's most relevant contributions to the evolution of culture. We seek artists who display honesty, individuality, quality, consistency, discipline, and a sense of humor.

If you weren't running a gallery what else would you do?

I would be a traveler, an archeologist, a gardener. My husband Jaime says that if I see a bus pass by, I jump in, and then ask where it is going. I believe there is always something interesting at the end of the road, and at the middle and the start, one just has to be aware. History and plants are another passion of mine. I would love to spend a lot of time exploring and studying the ecological reservation and archeological site of Calakmul, on the Yucatan peninsula.

- **Contact** OMR
Kerstin Erdmann
kerstin@galeriaomr.com
- **Established** 1983
- **Owner(s) / Partner(s)** Jaime Riestra
Patricia Ortiz Monasterio
- **Team** 15
- **Space(s)** 800 m²
- **Artists at Art Basel** Julieta Aranda
Ryan Brown
Pia Camil
Aldo Chaparro
Jose Dávila
Gabriel De La Mora
Candida Höfer
Artur Lescher
Rafael Lozano-Hemmer
Jorge Méndez Blake
Theo Michael
David Moreno
Rubén Ortiz-Torres
Bonnie Seeman
Daniel Silver
Troika
James Turrell
Atelier Van Lieshout
- **Further artists represented** José Arnaud-Bello
Sofia Borges
Raúl Cárdenas (Torolab)
Félix Curto
Alberto García-Alix
Yishai Jusidman
Adolfo Riestra
Maruch Santiz Gómez

One and J.

Seoul

- Galleries

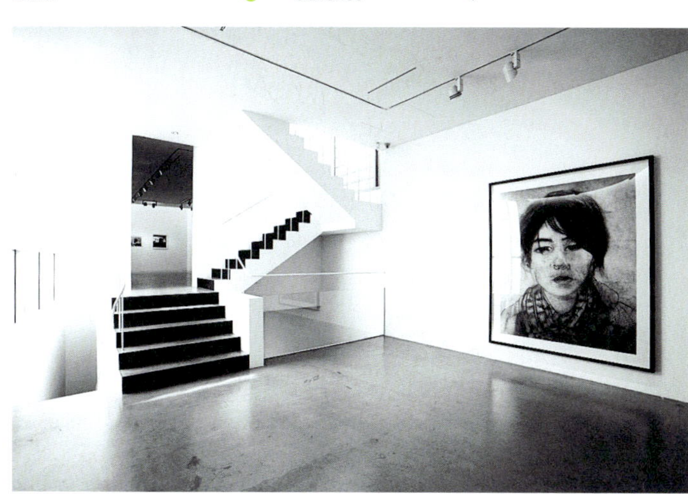

What is your favorite aspect of running a gallery?

The interaction with all the interesting people that play some role in the art world.

How do you choose the artists you work with?

It is a two-way street, the artists also choose us. We both search for some intelligence, passion, commitment, a little integrity, and trust.

If you weren't running a gallery what else would you do?

Live to support the uniquely human endeavors in art and culture in some way.

- **Contact** One and J. Gallery
Pat Lee
pat@oneandj.com
- **Established** 2005
- **Owner(s) / Partner(s)** Pat Lee
Won Jae Park
- **Team** 5
- **Space(s)** 140 m²
- **Artists at Art Basel** Eimei Kaneyama
Suyoung Kim
Taeyoon Kim
Jung Lee
Seung Yul Oh
Jina Park
- **Further artists represented** Minseung Jang
Honggoo Kang
Chosil Kil
Yunho Kim
Kyunghwan Kwon
Nikki S. Lee
Dongwook Suh
Joongho Yum

Ora-Ora

Hong Kong ● Insights

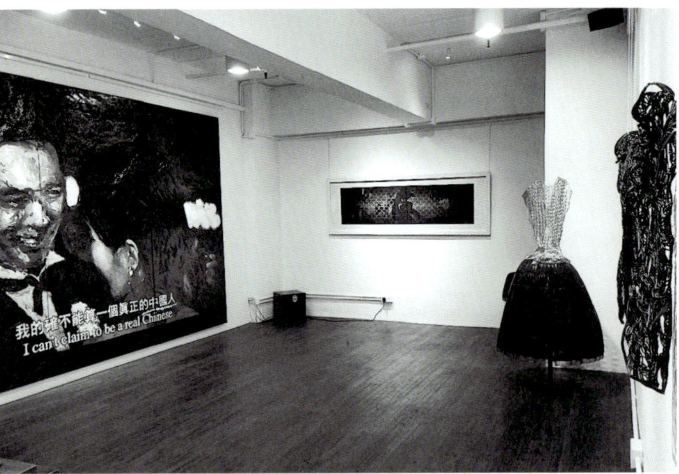

What is your favorite aspect of running a gallery?
Sharing ideas with artists and understanding them and their works. The best part of my work is the frequent visits to artists' studios and being the first person to see their new works.
How do you choose the artists you work with?
The quality and impact of their artworks is key. As importantly, I choose to work with artists who are mature and diligent, and are eager to have an artistic career. I like curious artists.

If you weren't running a gallery what else would you do?
My dream job is to be an artist and to create artworks in my studio. I would also set up organizations to provide better art curriculums for schools in Hong Kong.

- **Contact** Galerie Ora-Ora
Henrietta Tsui-Leung
info@ora-ora.com
- **Established** 2006
- **Owner(s) / Partner(s)** Henrietta Tsui-Leung
Alfred Leung
- **Team** 8
- **Space(s)** 400 m²
- **Artists at Art Basel** Peng Wei
- **Further artists represented** Halley Cheng
Will Clift
Gao Qian
Hang Chunhui
Hao Liang
Huang Dan
Huang Haifei
Huang Yongyu
Kum Chi Keung
Lai Jing
Liu Dewei
Liu Qi
Ma Jun
Man Fung-Yi
Mok Yat-San
Cindy Sio-Ieng Ng
Pan Wenxun
Peng Jian
Nina Pryde
Qin Xiuping
Joseph Maria Subirachs
Stephen Chun Hei Wong
Wu Qiang
Xiao Xu
Xu Hualing
Xu Hongfei
Yayoi Kusama
Zeng Guoqing
Zhang Yanzi

Osage

Hong Kong
Shanghai
Beijing ● Galleries
Encounters

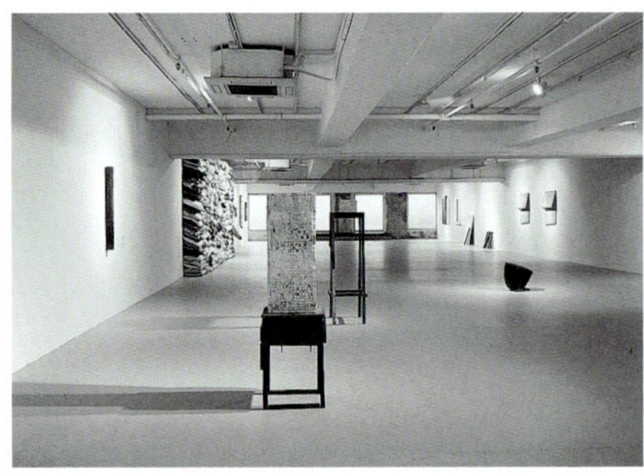

What is your favorite aspect of running a gallery?
Osage Gallery was initiated to extend the work of the Osage Art Foundation, fulfilling the need for a commercial platform that promotes thought-provoking and often overlooked artists. This is what continues to drive us.

How do you choose the artists you work with?
Osage has a focus on contemporary Asian art; the artists we work with critically address and challenge wide-ranging issues, examine questions that shape us as individuals and cultures, and activate such discussions in diverse ways with different audiences.

If you weren't running a gallery what else would you do?
We would be exploring public arts projects, such as an arts festival.

- **Contact** Osage Gallery
Chloe Chu
chloechu@osagegallery.com
- **Established** 2004
- **Owner(s) / Partner(s)** Agnes Lin
- **Team** 8
- **Space(s)** 2,462 m²
- **Artists at Art Basel** Au Hoi Lam
Louie Cordero
Leung Mee-Ping
Li Xinping
Ma Shuqing
Miao Xiaochun
Ng Joon Kiat
Wilson Shieh
Ian Woo
Tintin Wulia
- **Further artists represented** Kingsley Ng
Liang Quan
Sara Tse

Ota

Tokyo
Singapore ● Galleries

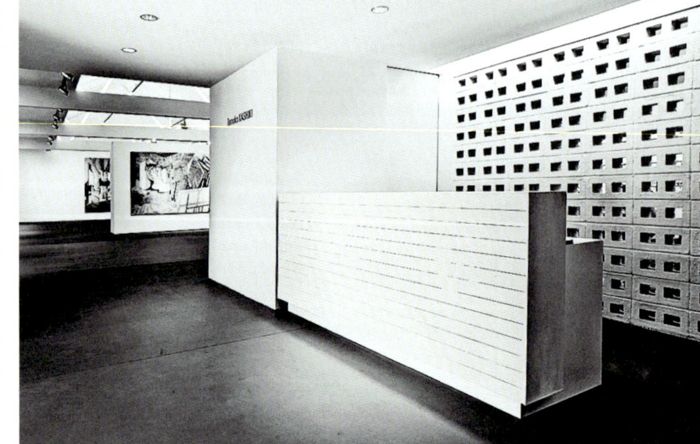

- **Contact** Ota Fine Arts
  sg@otafinearts.com
- **Established** 1994
- **Owner(s) / Partner(s)** Ota Hidenori
- **Team** 9
- **Space(s)** 500 m²
- **Artists at Art Basel** Ay Tjoe Christine
  Rina Banerjee
  Tomoko Kashiki
  Zai Kuning
  Yayoi Kusama
  Nobuaki Takekawa
  Yeesookyung
- **Further artists represented** Monir Farmanfarmaian
  Akira The Hustler
  Masanori Handa
  Tsuyoshi Hisakado
  Manami Koike
  Bubu de La Madeleine
  Firoz Mahmud
  Takao Minami
  Masayasu Mitsuke
  Hiraki Sawa
  Yoshiko Shimada
  Shinchika
  Tang Dixin
  Yuken Teruya
  Umeda Tetsuya

Oxley9

Sydney — Galleries

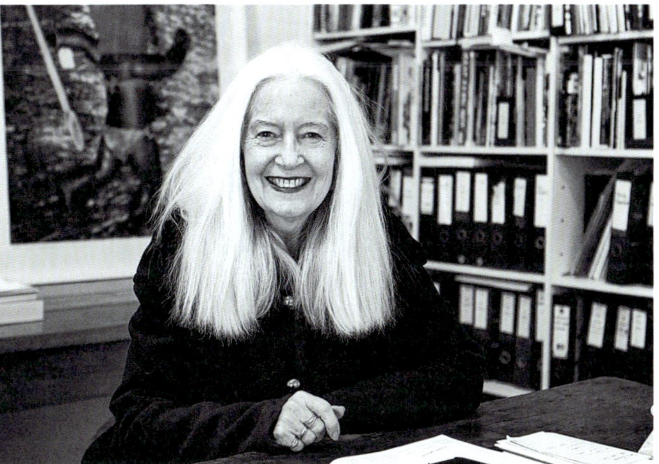

What is your favorite aspect of running a gallery?

The shows. They are my driving force. The more familiar an artist becomes, the more intense and vital the experience is of seeing the development and progression of their work. Every show is like a challenge the artist undertakes, which can surprise, delight, and on occasion disappoint! But it is experiencing an artist's journey through their shows that I love.

How do you choose the artists you work with?

It is very intuitive. You instinctively know where the artist is headed and believe they will go the distance. There is a connection with the integrity of their art, and an understanding of the intentions within their practice. Sometimes you have to wait for that special body of work to come, but you know it is there.

If you weren't running a gallery what else would you do?

I can't imagine not running a gallery.

- **Contact** Roslyn Oxley9 Gallery
  Roslyn Oxley
  roslyn@roslynoxley9.com.au
- **Established** 1982
- **Owner(s) / Partner(s)** Roslyn & Tony Oxley
- **Team** 10
- **Space(s)** 700 m²
- **Artists at Art Basel** Daniel Boyd
  Fiona Hall
  Bill Henson
  Isaac Julien
  Teppei Kaneuji
  David Noonan
- **Further artists represented** James Angus
  Hany Armanious
  Del Kathryn Barton
  Tony Clark
  Sarah Contos
  Sean Cordeiro & Claire Healy
  Marley Dawson
  Destiny Deacon
  Wim Delvoye
  Mikala Dwyer
  Dale Frank
  Jacqueline Fraser
  Rosalie Gascoigne
  Newell Harry
  Louise Hearman
  Lindy Lee
  Linda Marrinon
  Tracey Moffatt
  TV Moore
  Callum Morton
  Nell
  Nyapanyapa Yunupingu
  Bronwyn Oliver
  Michael Parekowhai
  Patricia Piccinini
  Gareth Sansom
  Glenn Sorensen
  Kathy Temin
  Imants Tillers
  Jenny Watson
  Rohan Wealleans
  John Wolseley

One and J. Gallery

Interview with Patrick Lee

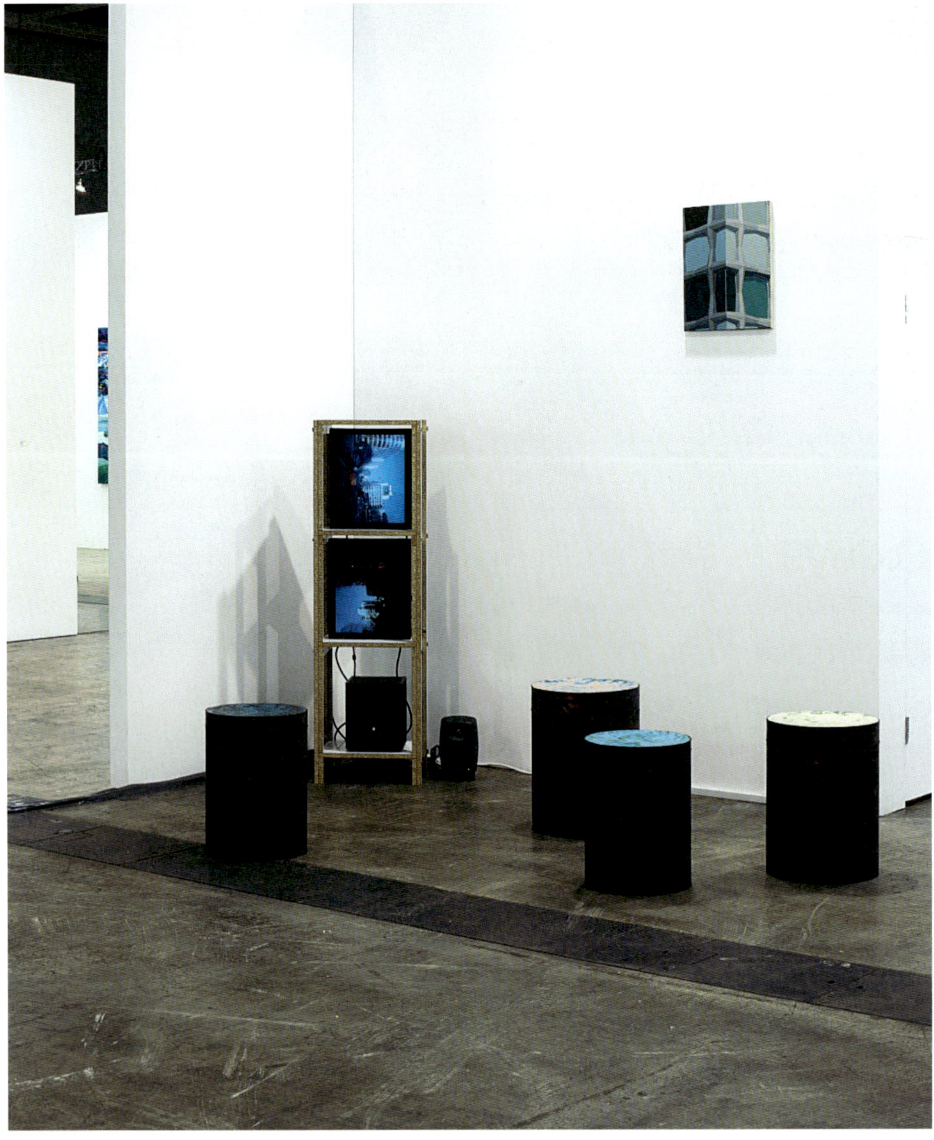

Art Basel in Hong Kong, 2014

One and J. Gallery opened in 2005 in Seoul. Could you tell us about its beginnings?

I joined the gallery six months after its foundation by Won Jae Park and another partner who left soon afterward. There were no Korean galleries at that time that really focused on young artists. There were some alternative spaces and residencies, but One and J. is one of the first galleries that really showed emerging Korean contemporary artists. I used to go to the gallery just to see the shows at the beginning, but I soon realized it was a chance for me: I come from a law and finance background, but running a gallery had always been a dream job. I first joined them to help on the business side and then I basically bought the other partner's share in 2006.

When did you start participating in Art Basel?

We have done Art Basel in Hong Kong since its first edition, and before that ART HK. 2013 was the first year we showed in Basel, with a Statement with Chosil Kil, a fantastic conceptual Korean artist based in London. We did Art Basel in Miami Beach as well, with Seung Yul Oh, a very talented young artist with whom we did Encounters last year in Hong Kong. It was a really great year! We didn't go to Basel in 2014. We applied but it didn't work out. It's very tough, but I actually think it is a good thing: it forces the galleries make amazing proposals! As the space is limited and everyone wants to go there, it really motivates us to think about what we will be proposing for the next year.

How would you define your program? Is there an aesthetic that unites the list of artists you work with?

People say we have a certain "color": I don't know if I can articulate it, because all our artists work very differently and with different media. They are painters, sound artists, video artists, photographers ... We work with artists for a very long time before "signing" them on, because it's almost like a marriage, you really have to trust each other. We are a relatively small gallery and staff, and we currently represent 12 artists, all Korean. We have started to show non-Korean artists, about two a year, and we invite curators to show young artists that aren't necessarily in our program.

Do you feel that the Gwangju Biennial is now an important destination for art, collectors, and curators? Is it the main event in Korea?

Every two years the whole art crowd comes to Gwangju, but Seoul is the real art scene "home." The level of this biennial is very good: Massimiliano Gioni did one, and Jessica Morgan curated it in 2014. It's a serious event and a lot of galleries do their best shows in September, us included. The biennial really helped the market and the whole scene in Korea, because many curators and collectors came here for the first time and they get to see the quality of Korean art and galleries.

You also organize a film and video program at the gallery.

We like to think of the gallery as a sort of platform for the advancement of contemporary culture. Rachel Lehman (from Lehman Maupin) was in Seoul last week and we hosted a talk for her. She said something to me: "I don't really consider the 'art world' as just fine arts. The people involved in music, design, writing, film, are all artists." We believe this as well. We try to foster links in those communities, organizing musicians and DJ sets, screening films, launching books. It's fun, I get excited about those projects as much as about our shows!

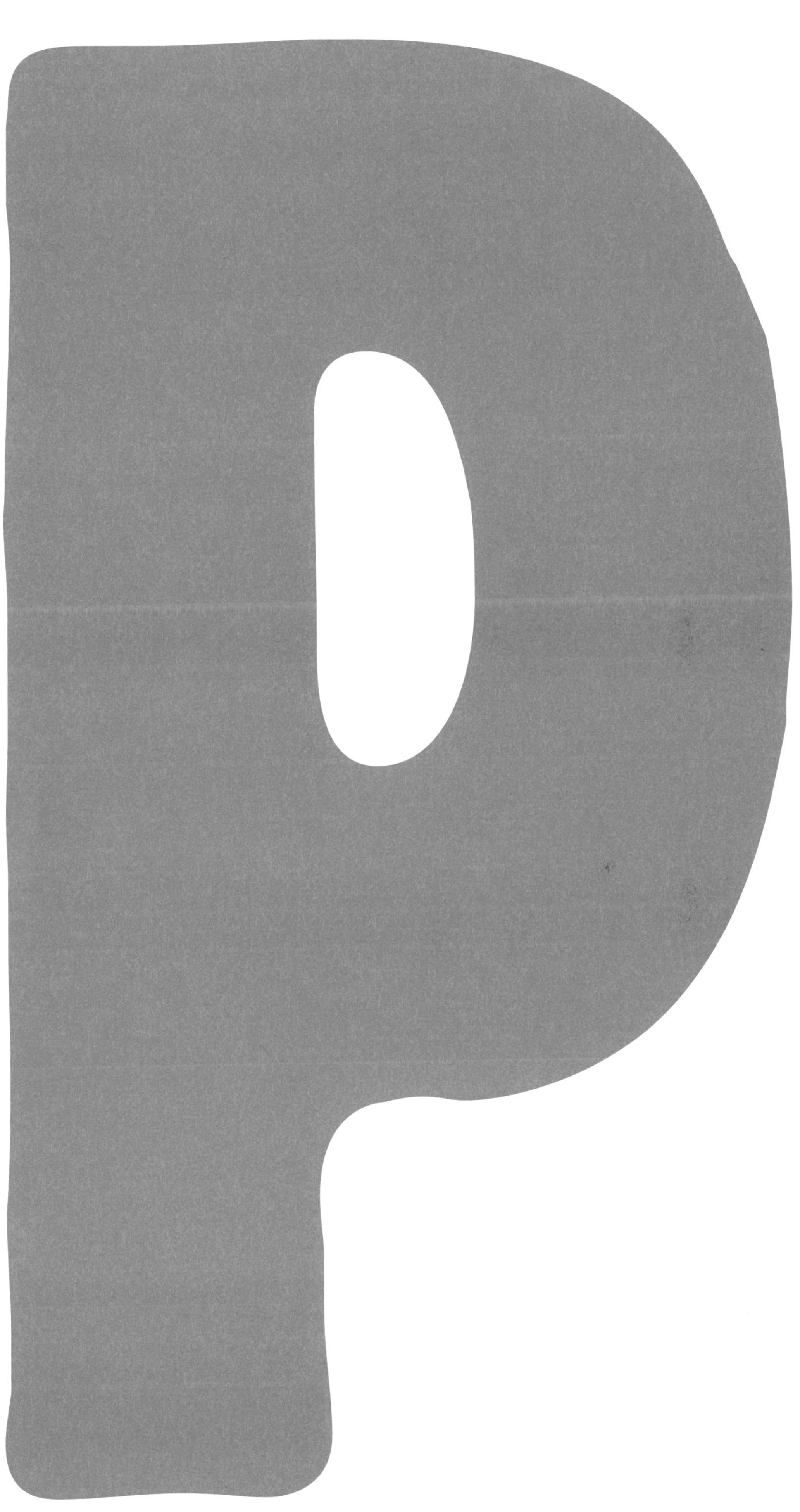

P

Parcours engages Basel's historical neighborhoods with site-specific sculptures, interventions, and performances by renowned international artists and emerging talents. In 2014 the sector curated by Florence Derieux, Director of the FRAC Champagne-Ardenne was sited on and around Rheingasse in Kleinbasel.

PAR COURS

2014 participants

Francesco Arena
Willborn

Darren Bader
Coles

Gottfried Bechtold
Krinzinger

Pierre Bismuth
Bugada & Cargnel

Jean-Luc Blanc
Art : Concept

Chris Burden
Gagosian

Ryan Gander
gb agency
Lisson

Mark Handforth
Gavin Brown
Modern Institute
Noero
Presenhuber

Iman Issa
Rodeo

João Penalva
Lee

Seth Price
Capitain
Petzel

Eva Rothschild
Presenhuber
Modern Art

Mario García Torres
Proyectos Monclova
Mot

Guido van der Werve
Foxx
Luhring Augustine

Zeng Fanzhi
Gagosian

Ryan Gander
Make Everything Like It's Your Last, 2013
Kartausgasse

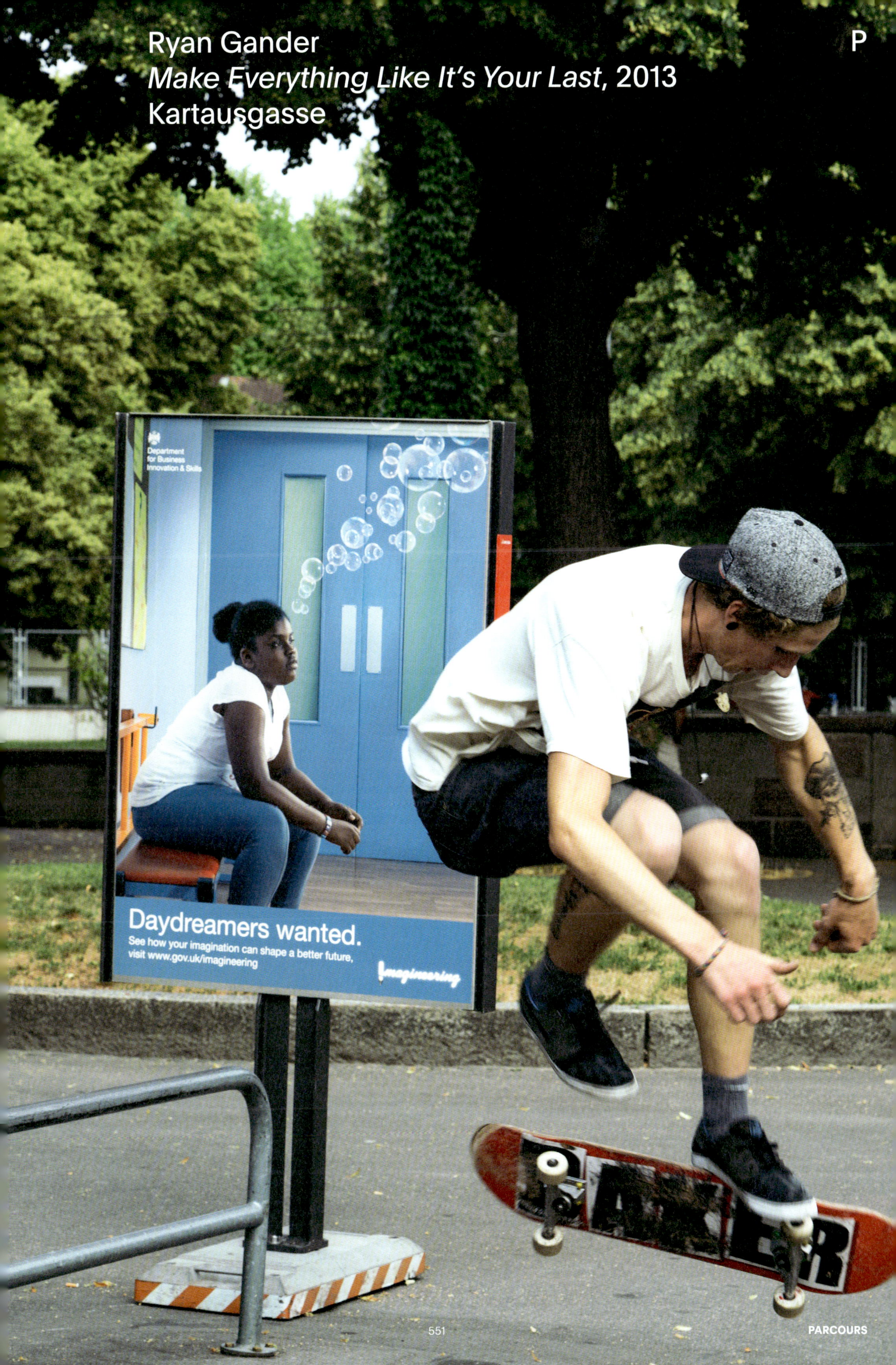

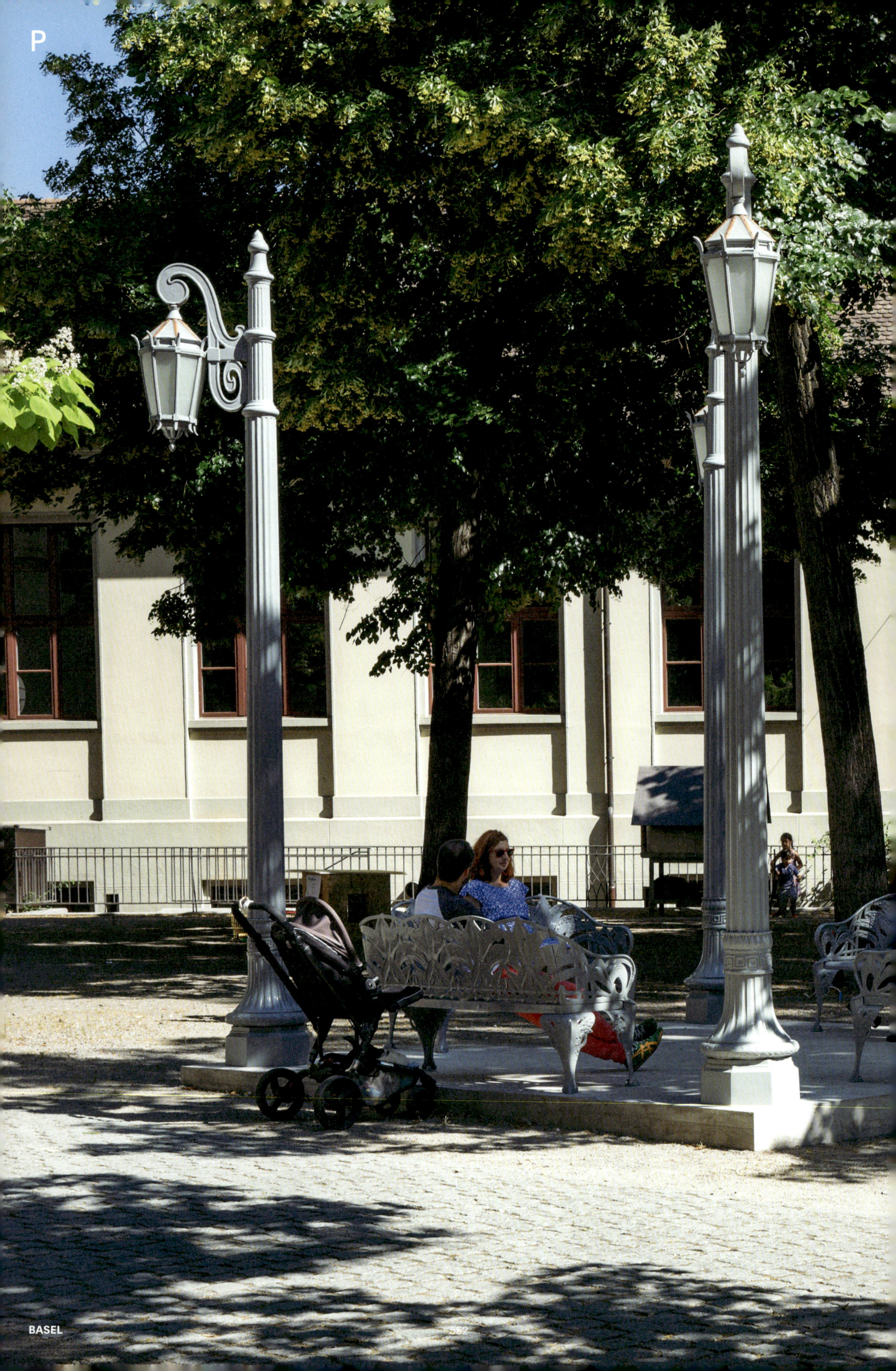

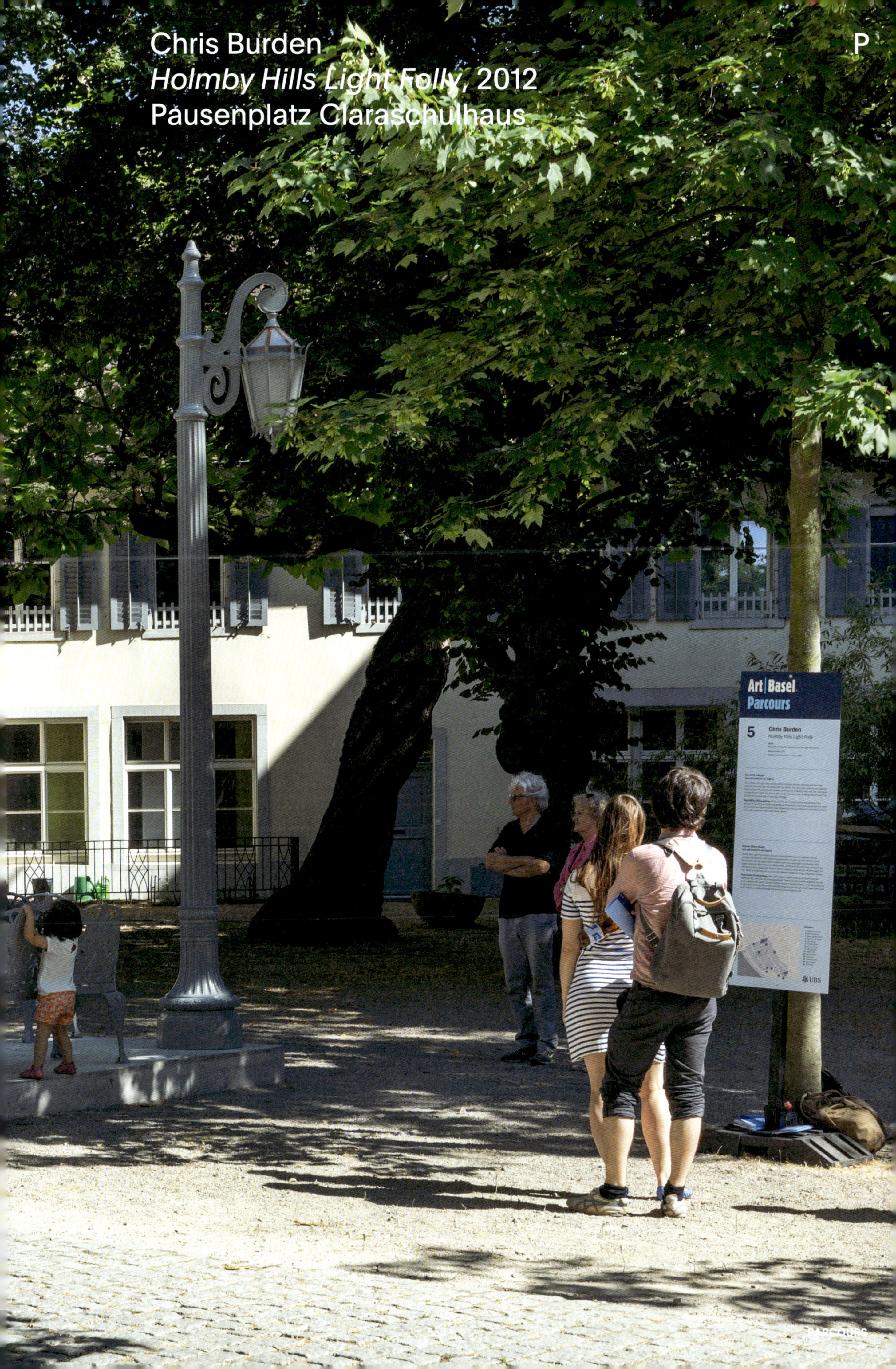

Chris Burden
Holmby Hills Light Folly, 2012
Pausenplatz Claraschulhaus

P

P

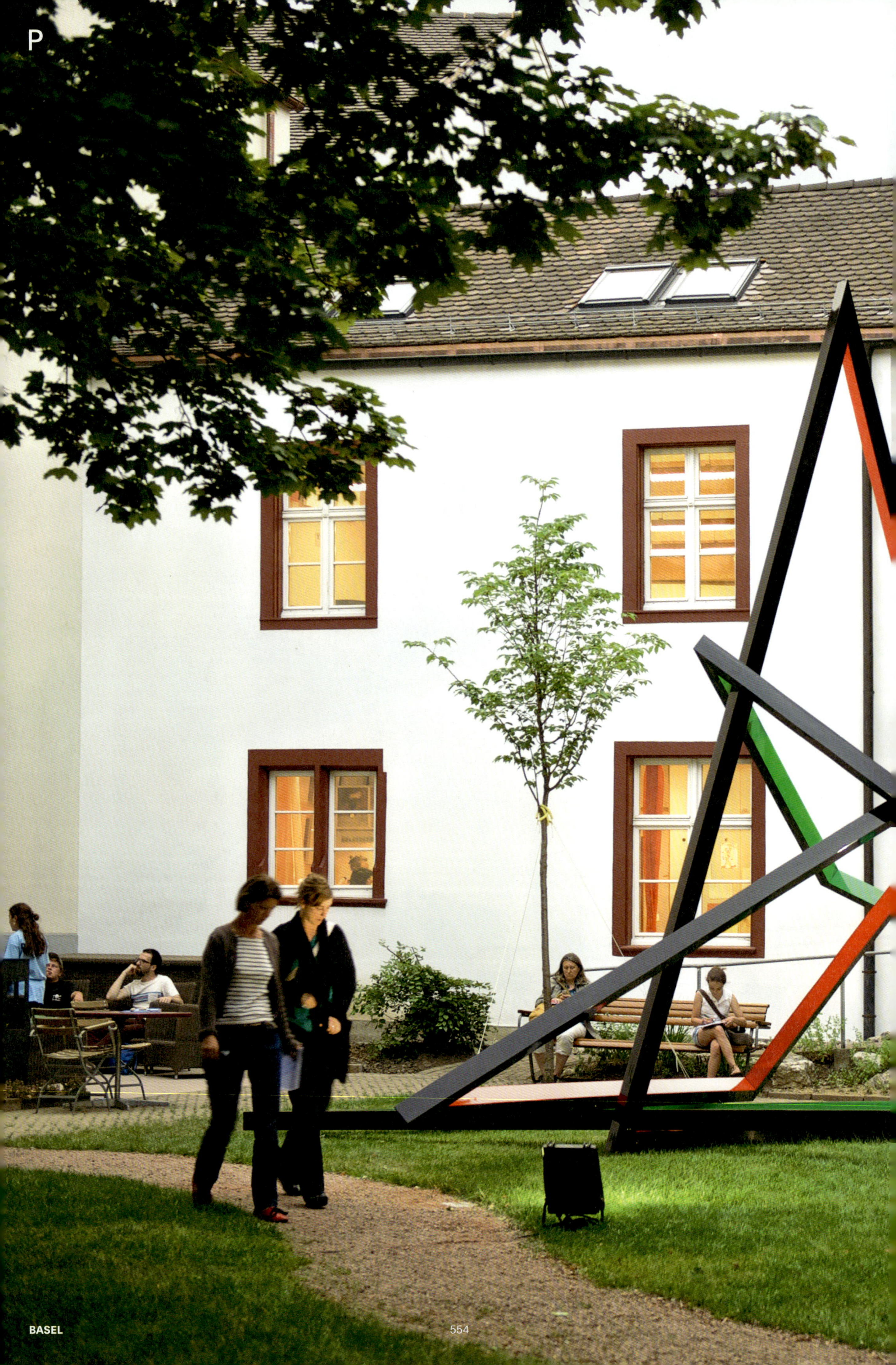

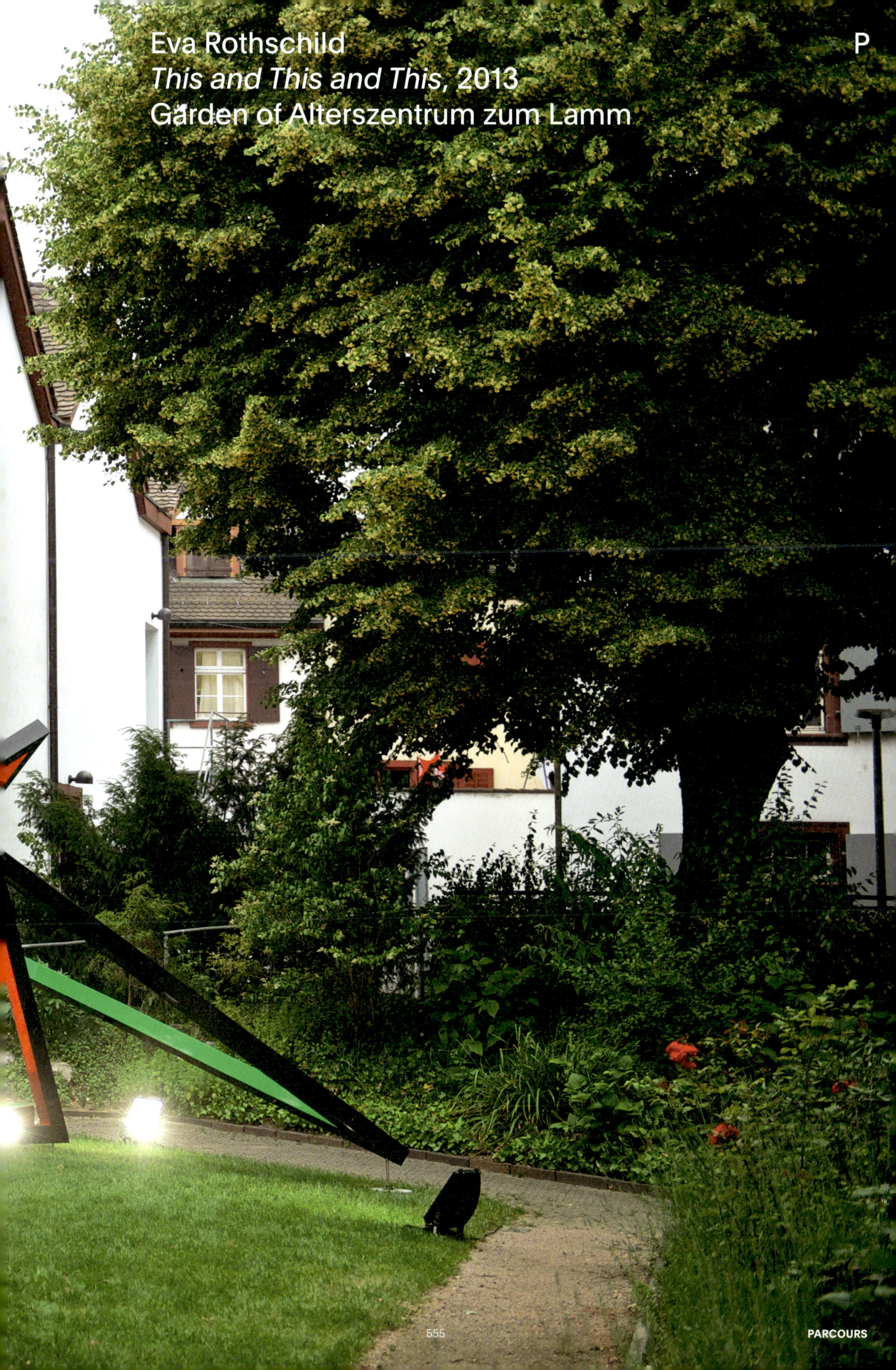

Eva Rothschild
This and This and This, 2013
Garden of Alterszentrum zum Lamm

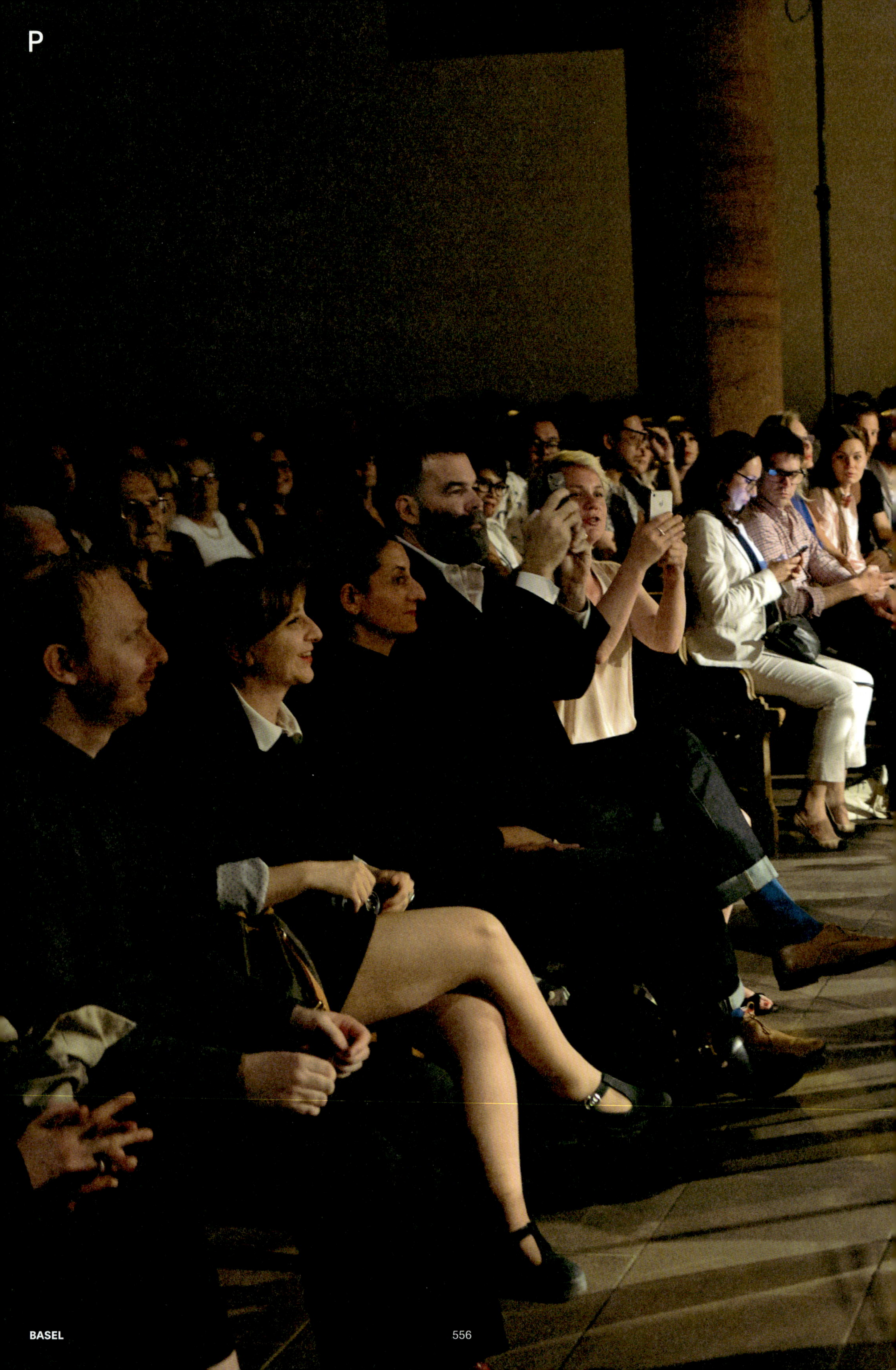

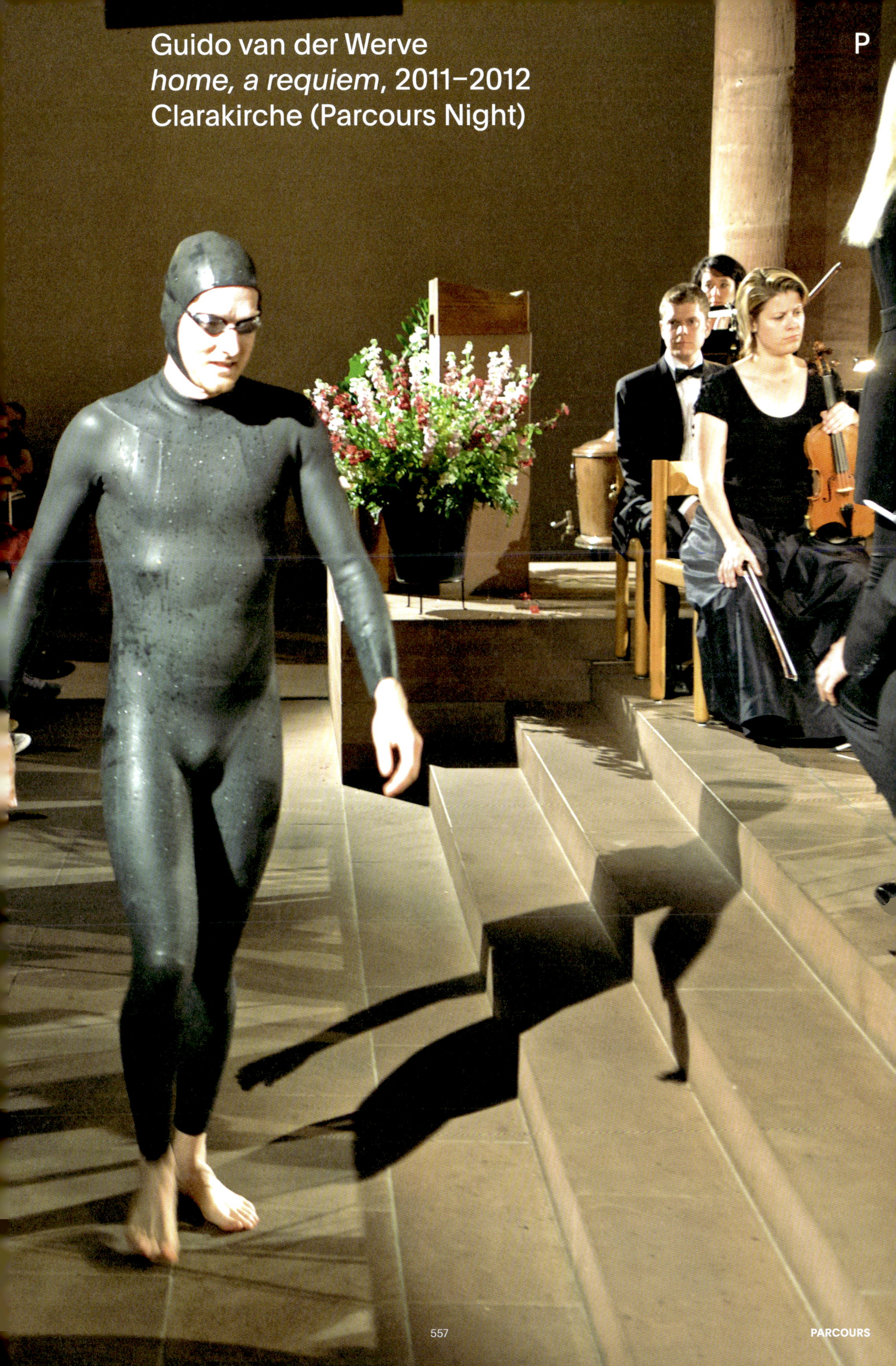

Guido van der Werve
home, a requiem, 2011–2012
Clarakirche (Parcours Night)

Mark Handforth
Magenta Torque Moment & Tilted Shadow,
2014/2013
Entrance to Clarakirche

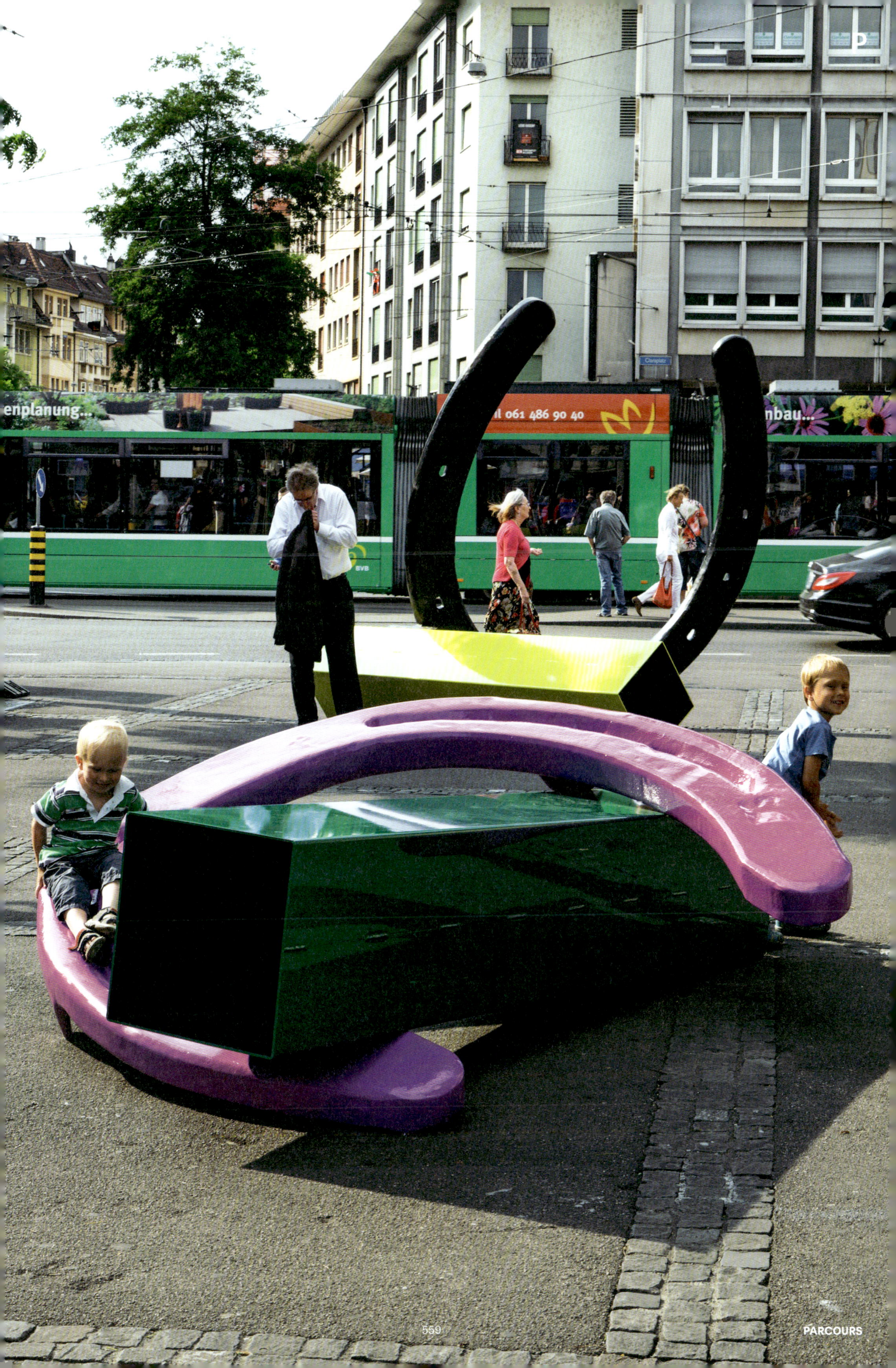
enplanung...
061 486 90 40
nbau...

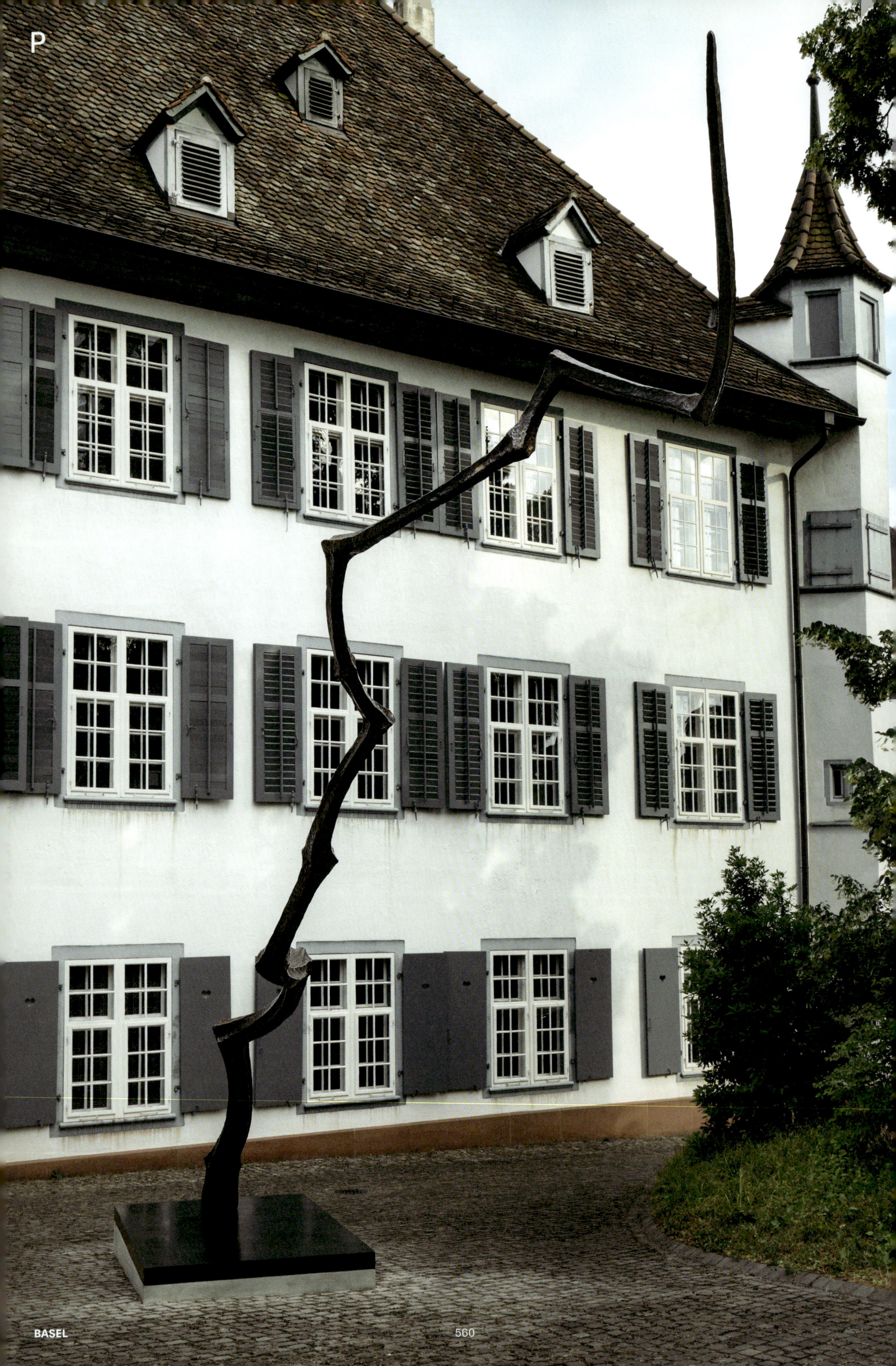
P

Zeng Fanzhi
Untitled, 2014
Hatstätterhof

P

Giving curators, critics, and collectors the opportunity to discove[r] ambitious new talents from all over the globe, the Positions sector in Miami Beach offers a platform for a single artist to present one major project. We invited New York's SculptureCente[r] Curator Ruba Katrib to choose her three favorite booths.

POSIT ION S

2014 participants

Carroll / Fletcher
Constant Dullaart

Central
Nino Cais

Clifton Benevento
Zak Kitnick

Crèvecoeur
Julien Carreyn

Fraser
Meleko Mokgosi

Freedman Fitzpatrick
Lucie Stahl

Gunn
Tracey Rose

Jongma
Florian & Michael Quistrebert

Kalfayan
Hrair Sarkissian

RaebervonStenglin
Thomas Julier

Ramiken Crucible
Borden Capalino

Razuk
Maria Laet

Revolver
Ishmael Randall Weeks

SlyZmud
Faivovich & Goldberg

SpazioA
Esther Kläs

Subal
Sam Ekwurtzel

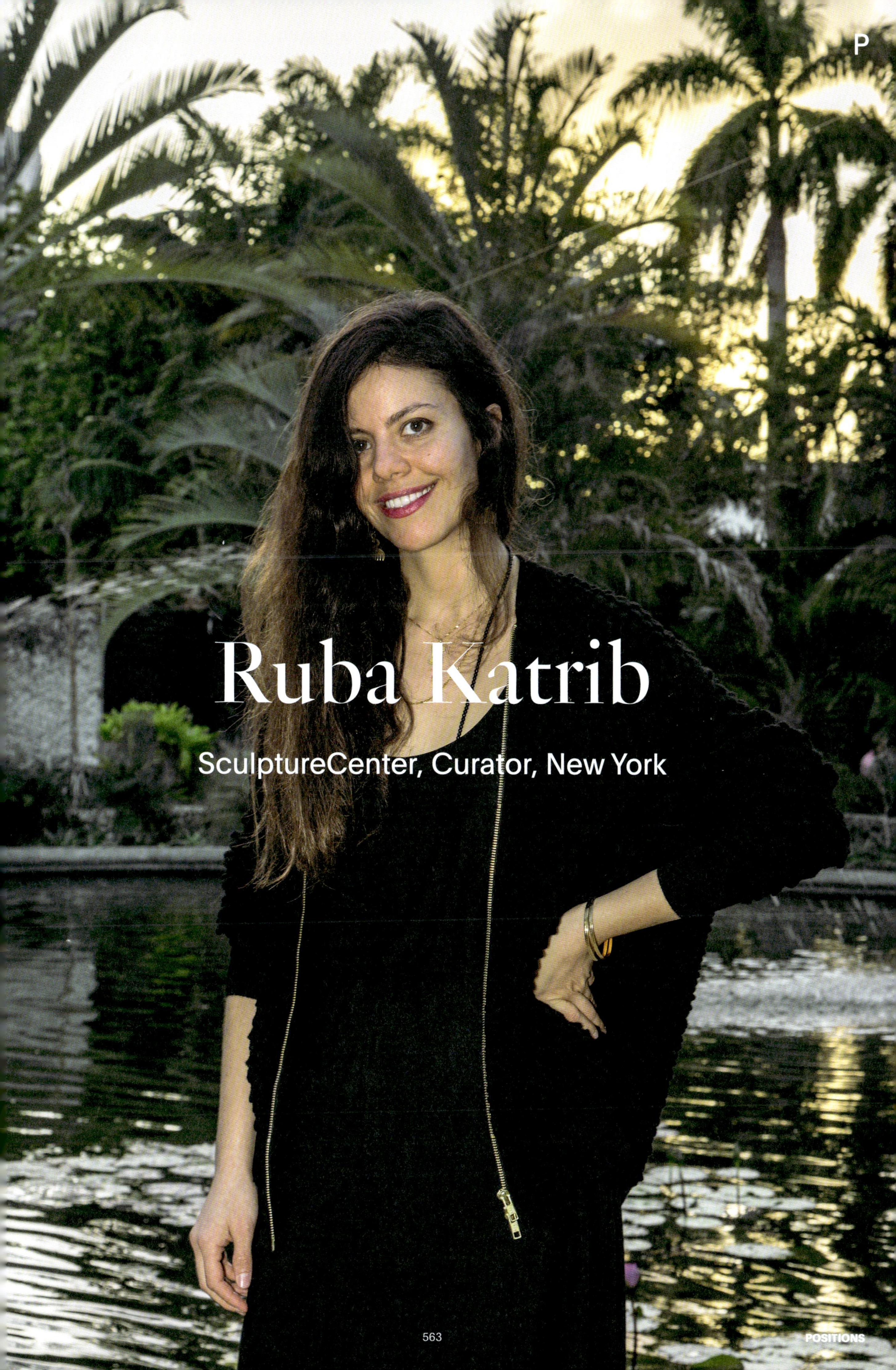

Ruba Katrib

SculptureCenter, Curator, New York

P

SpazioA
Esther Kläs

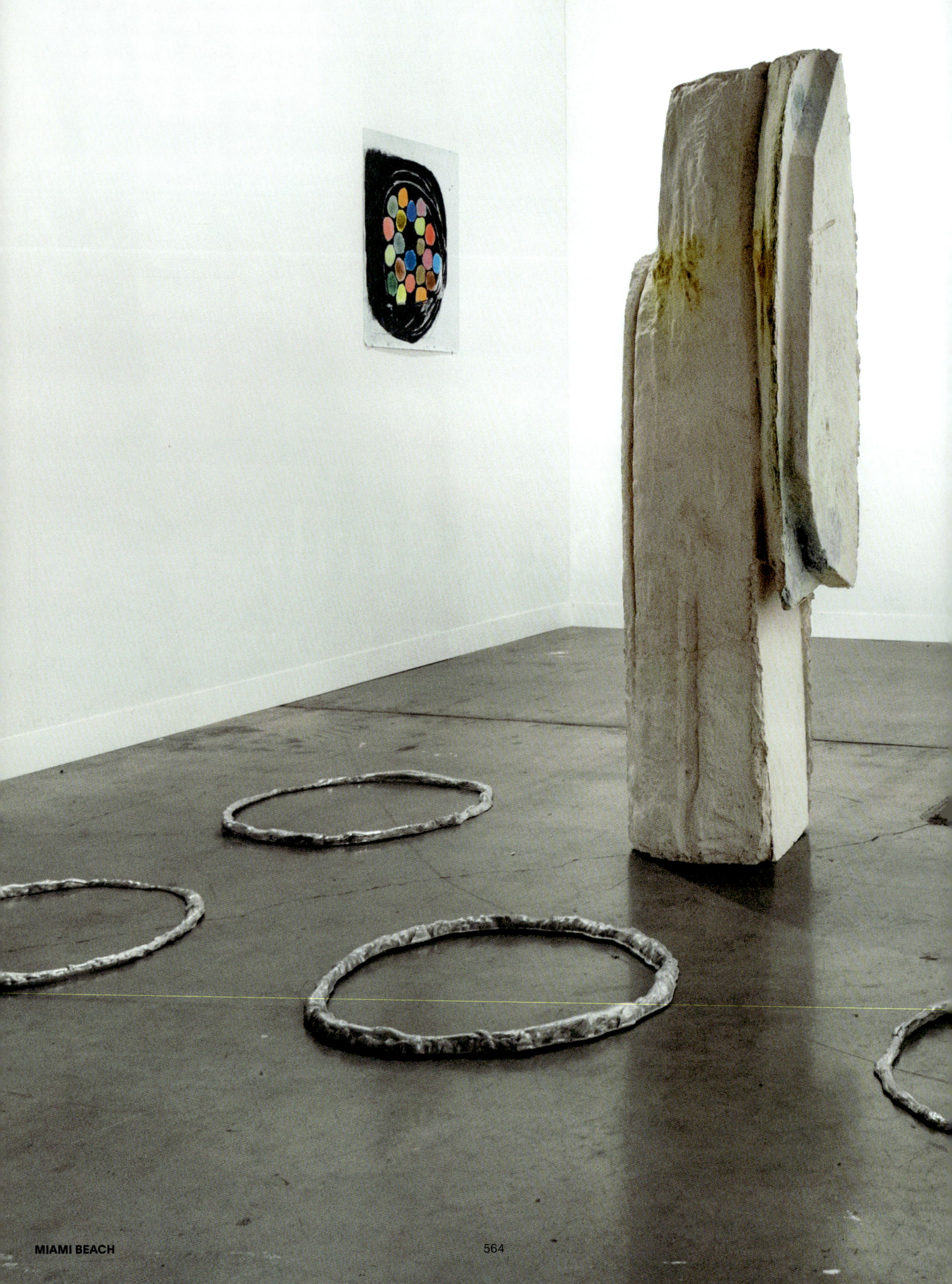

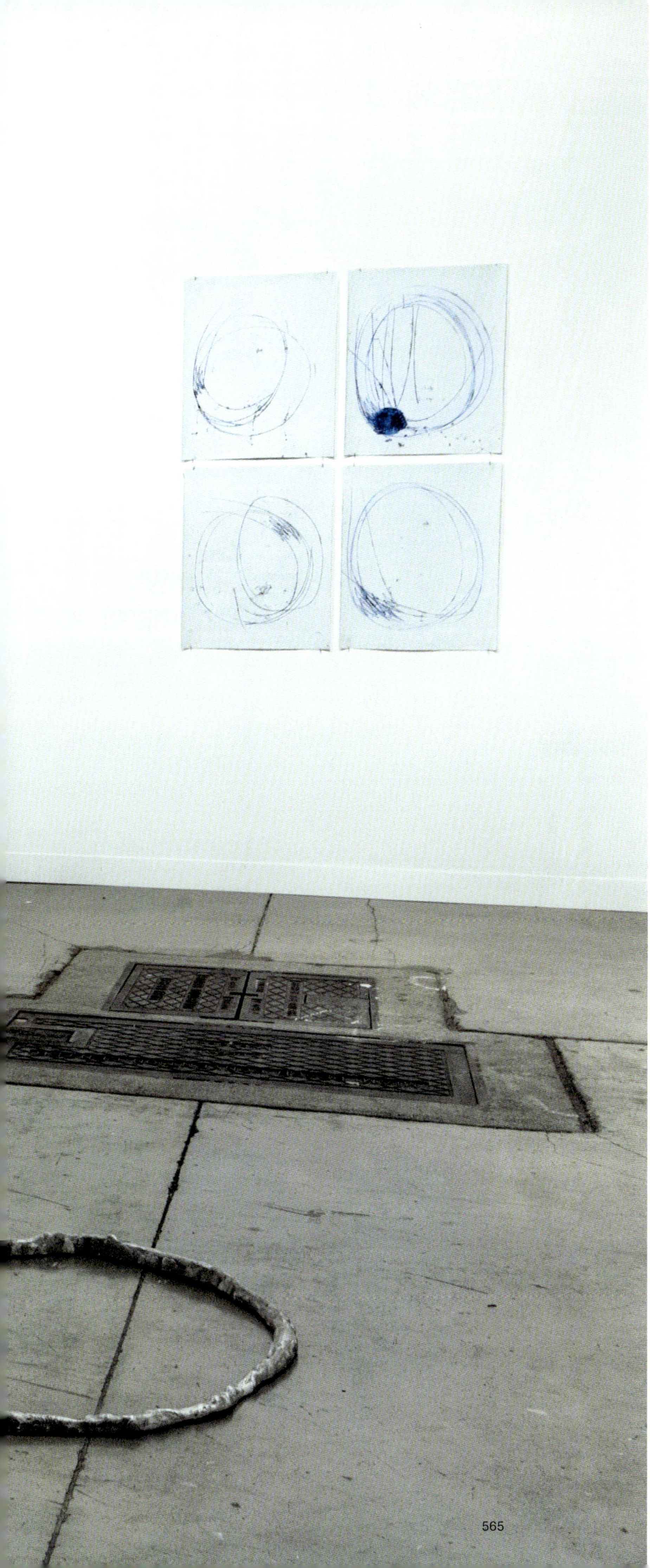

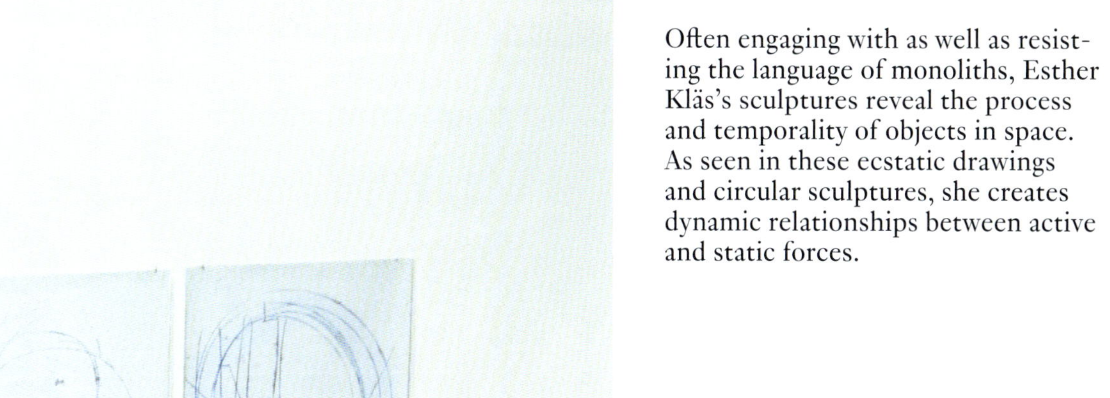

Often engaging with as well as resisting the language of monoliths, Esther Kläs's sculptures reveal the process and temporality of objects in space. As seen in these ecstatic drawings and circular sculptures, she creates dynamic relationships between active and static forces.

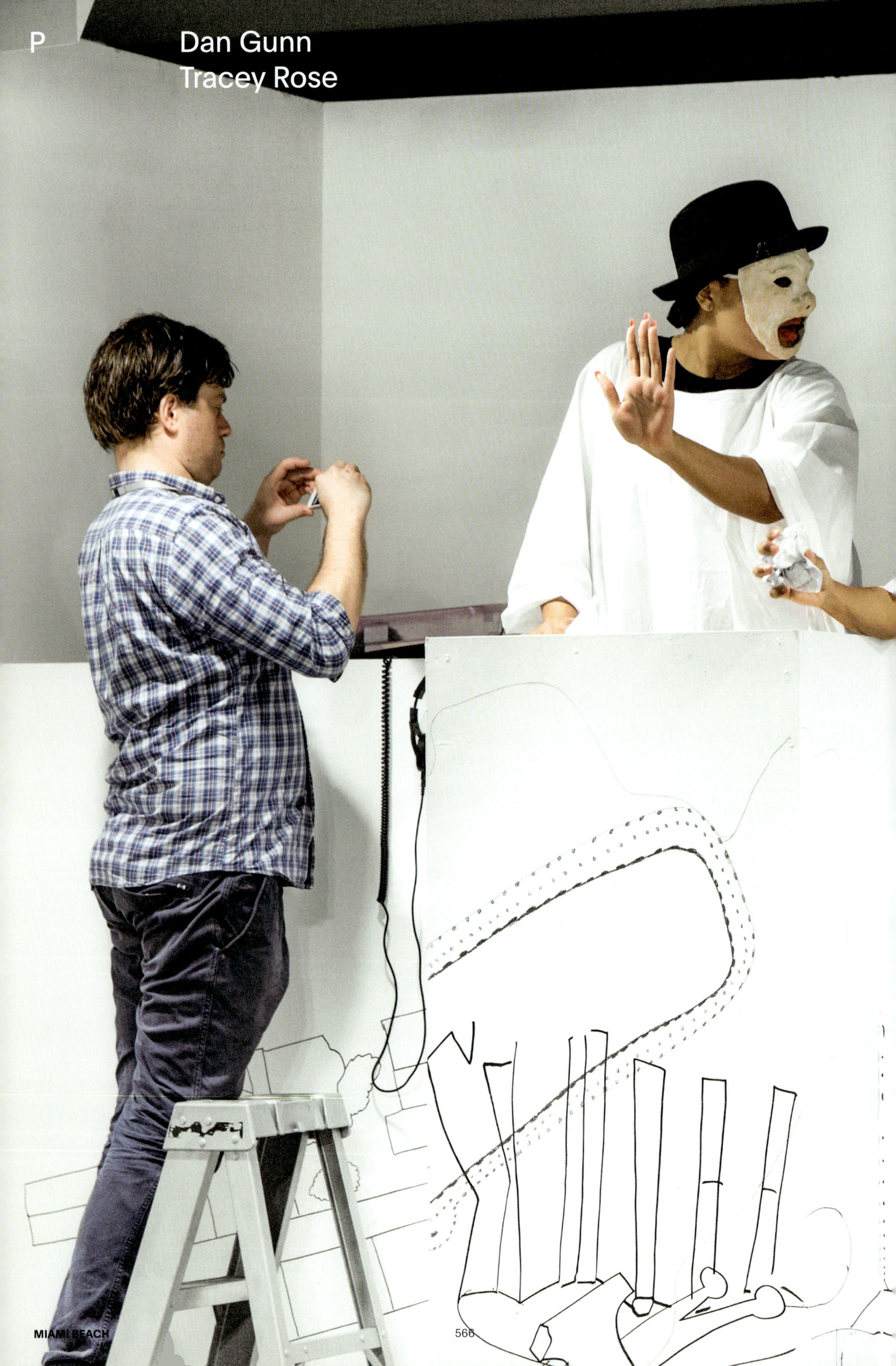

P

Dan Gunn
Tracey Rose

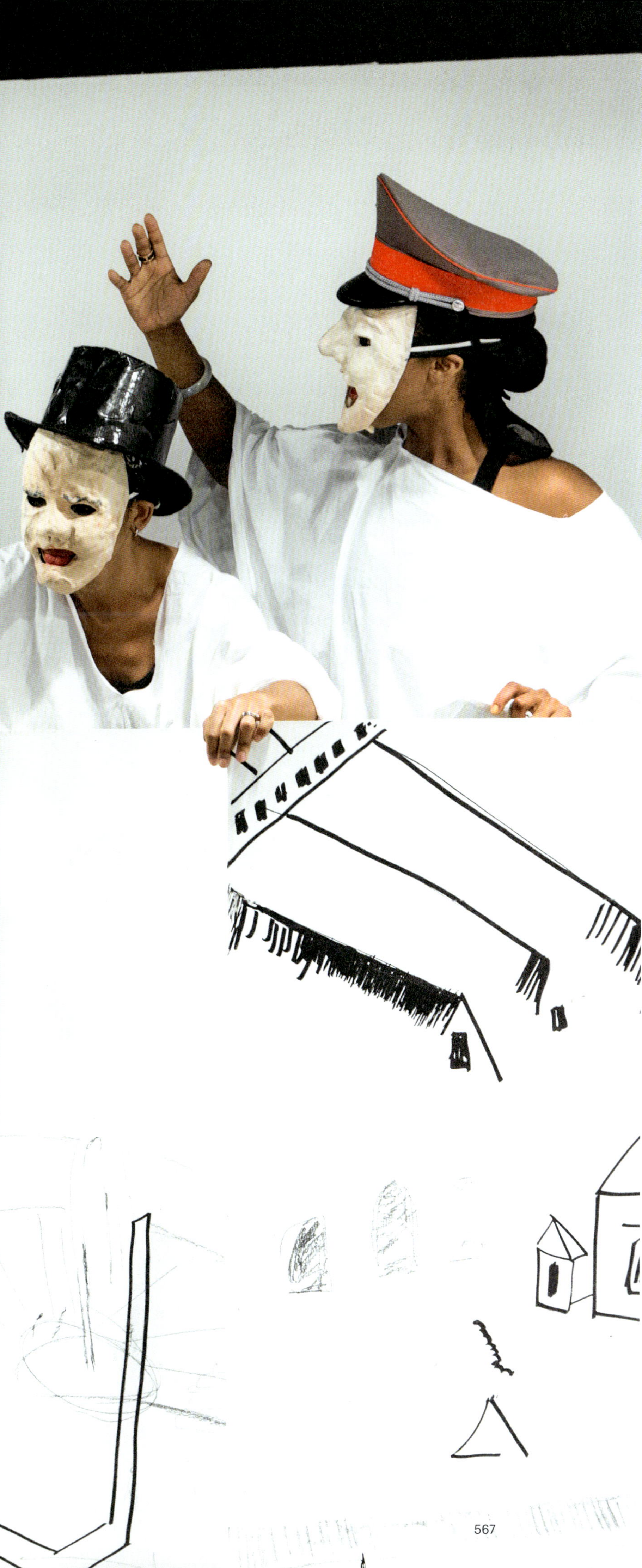

P

Staging a sort of play—while slurring and punning on the context of the work in the title—*Art Thou Not Fair: KniggerKhaffirKhoon, aka "KKK"* features three black women in white face, performing above a screen and lip-syncing to a prerecorded script. Abstract and poetic, Tracey Rose's narrative speaks of the politics around power and race.

Freedman Fitzpatrick
Lucie Stahl

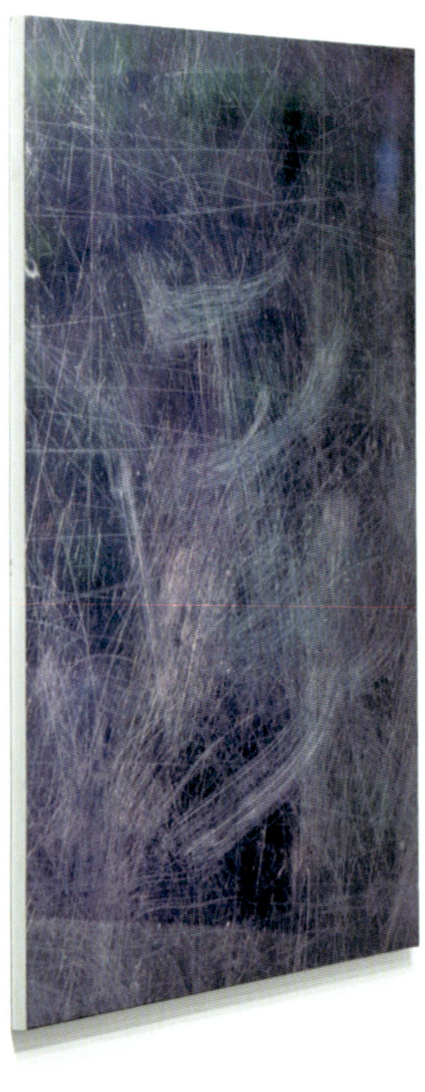

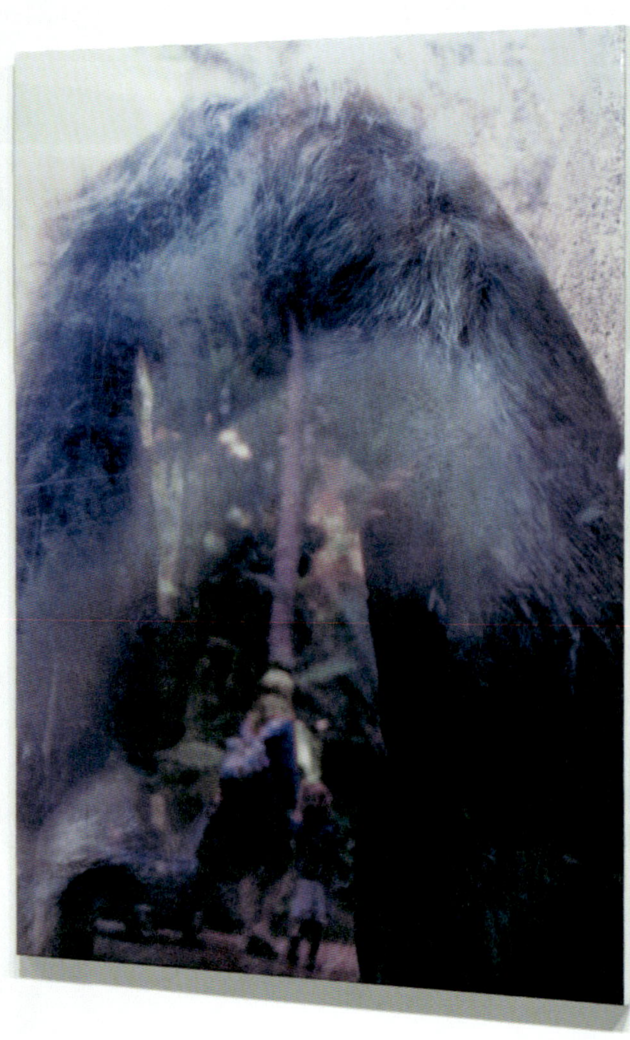

Lucie Stahl makes images that echo back to their origin, creating deeply layered works that encourage us to question what we are looking at. Surface takes on a new meaning through her manipulation of image-based technologies and processes.

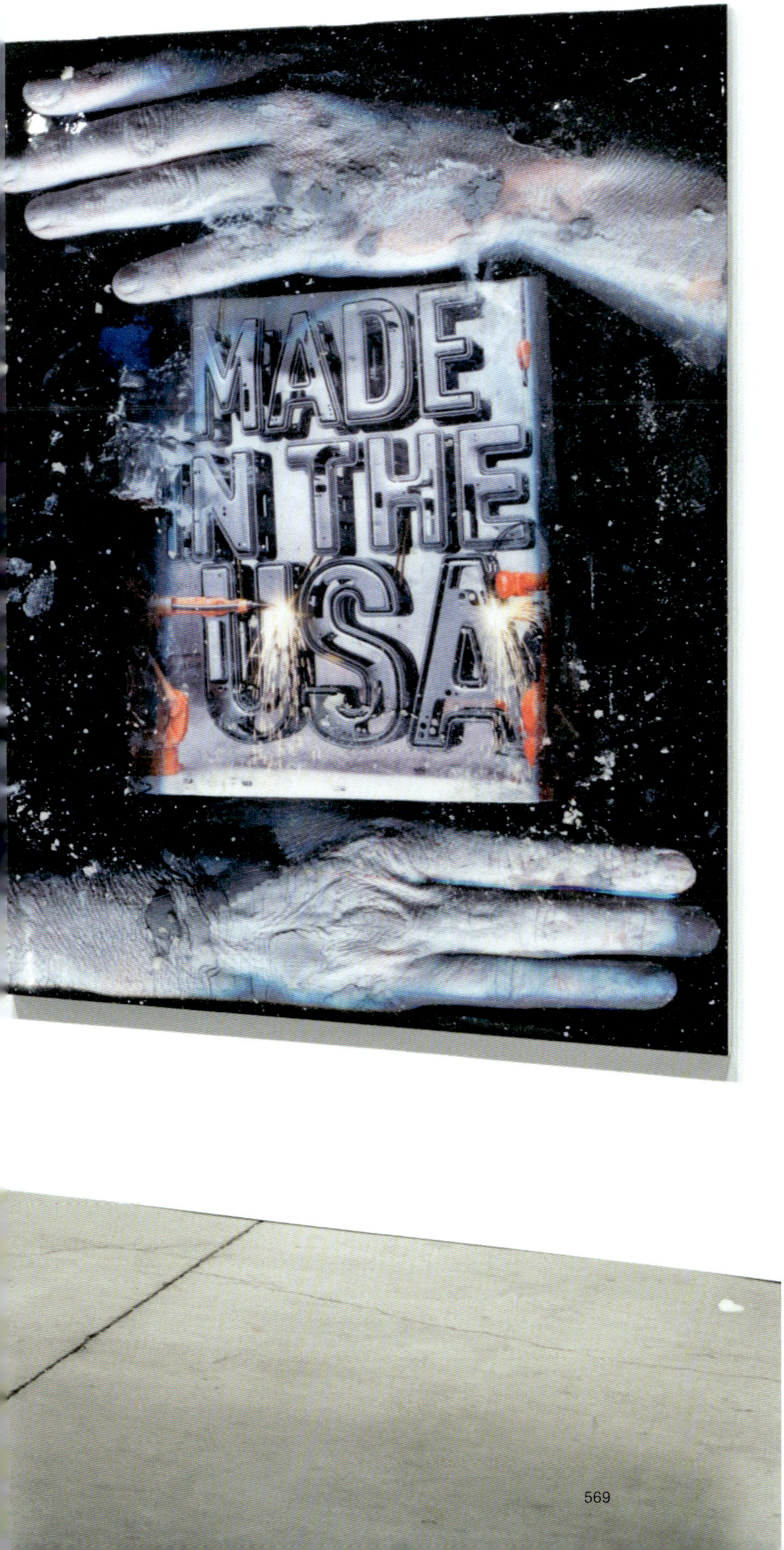

P

The Public sector offers its visitors a chance to see outdoor sculptures, interventions, and performances sited within an open and public exhibition format at Collins Park. The sector has been produced in collaboration with the Bass Museum of Art since 2011, and is curated by New York-based Nicholas Baume, Director and Chief Curator of the Public Art Fund.

PUBLIC

2014 participants

Georg Baselitz
Ropac

Lynda Benglis
Cheim & Read

Matthias Bitzer
Boesky
Rech

Sarah Braman
Mitchell-Innes & Nash

Ana Luiza Dias Batista
Razuk

Sam Ekwurtzel
Subal

Elmgreen & Dragset
Miro

Faivovich & Goldberg
SlyZmud

Nuria Fuster
Cervera

Ryan Gander
Lisson

Jeppe Hein
König

Jessica Jackson Hutchins
König

Alfredo Jaar
Lelong
Goodman Gallery
Schulte

Gunilla Klingberg
Nordenhake

José Carlos Martinat
Revolver

Justin Matherly
Cooper

Olaf Metzel
Wentrup

Sam Moyer
Rodolphe Janssen

Ernesto Neto
Bonakdar

Ugo Rondinone
Gladstone
Presenhuber

Nancy Rubins
Gagosian

Yinka Shonibare MBE
Cohan

Jessica Stockholder
Gupta

Barthélémy Toguo
Lelong

Tatiana Trouvé
Gagosian

Hank Willis Thomas, Ryan Alexiev, and Jim Ricks
Shainman
Goodman Gallery

Performances during Public Opening Night by:
Alix Pearlstein
Liz Glynn & Dawn Kasper
Ryan Gander
Christian Falsnaes

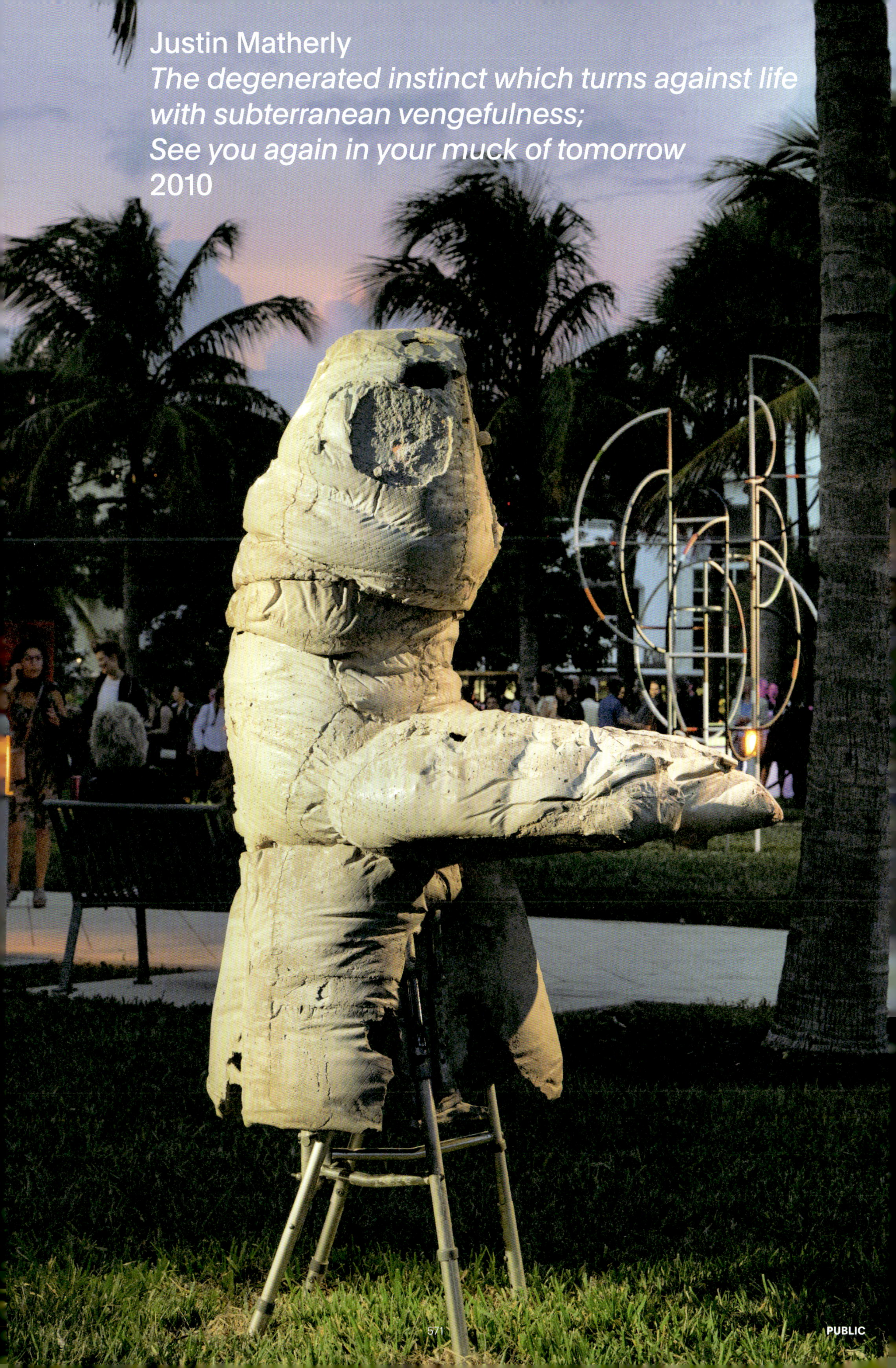

Justin Matherly
The degenerated instinct which turns against life with subterranean vengefulness; See you again in your muck of tomorrow
2010

Alix Pearlstein
The Shining
2014

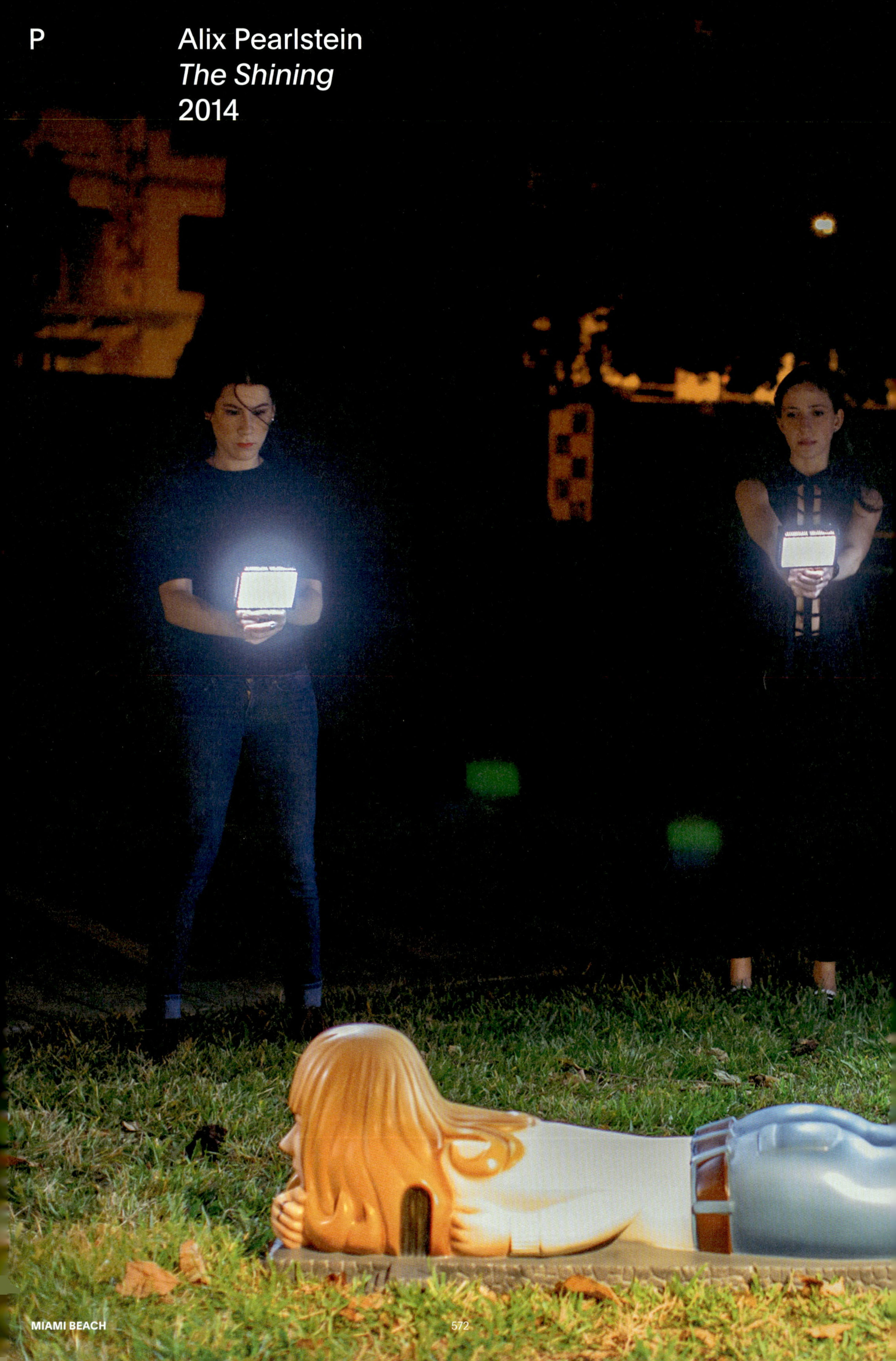

Ana Luiza Dias Batista
Eva (Eve)
2014

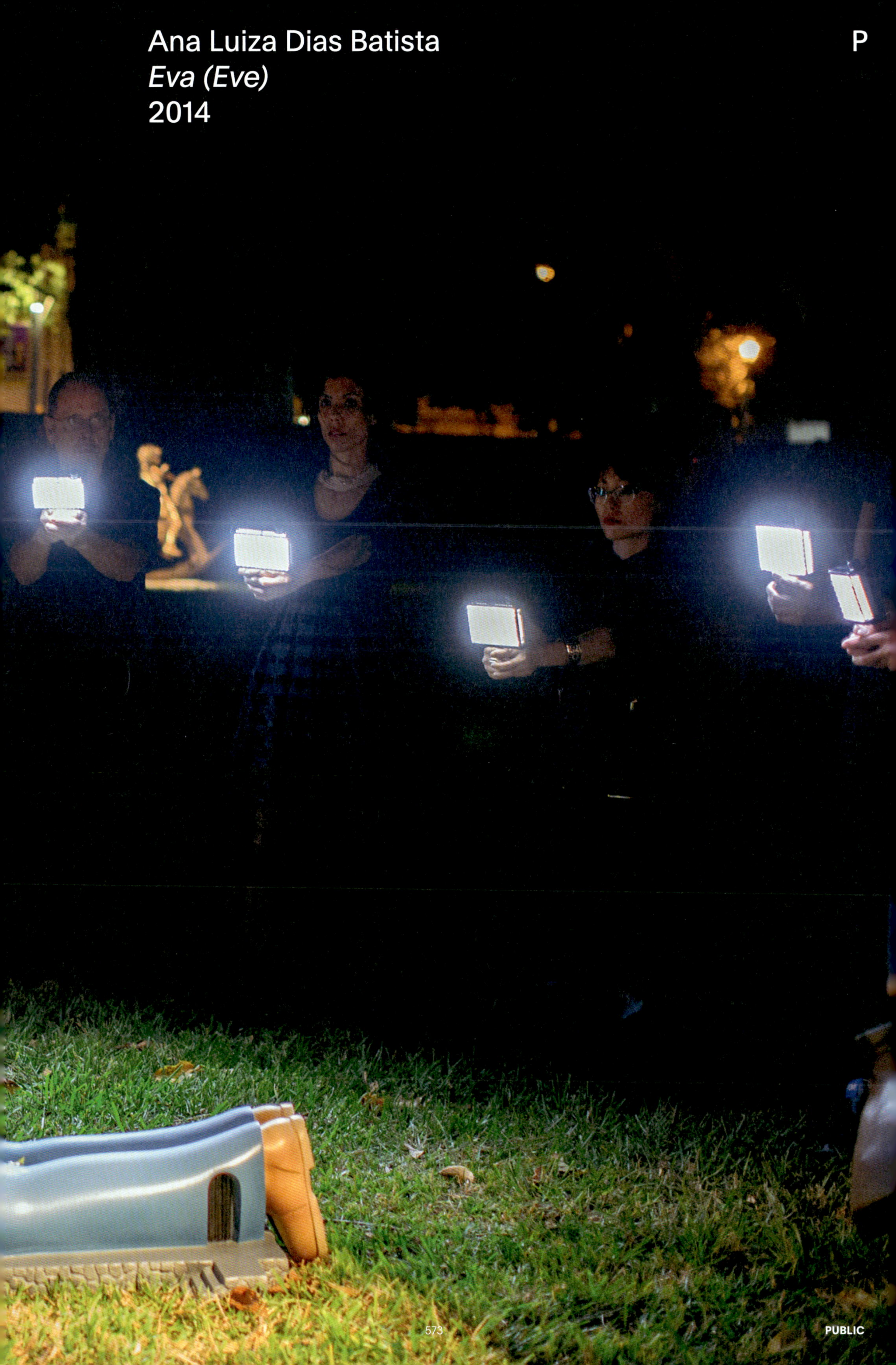

Nancy Rubins
Our Friend Fluid Metal, Chunkus Majoris
2013

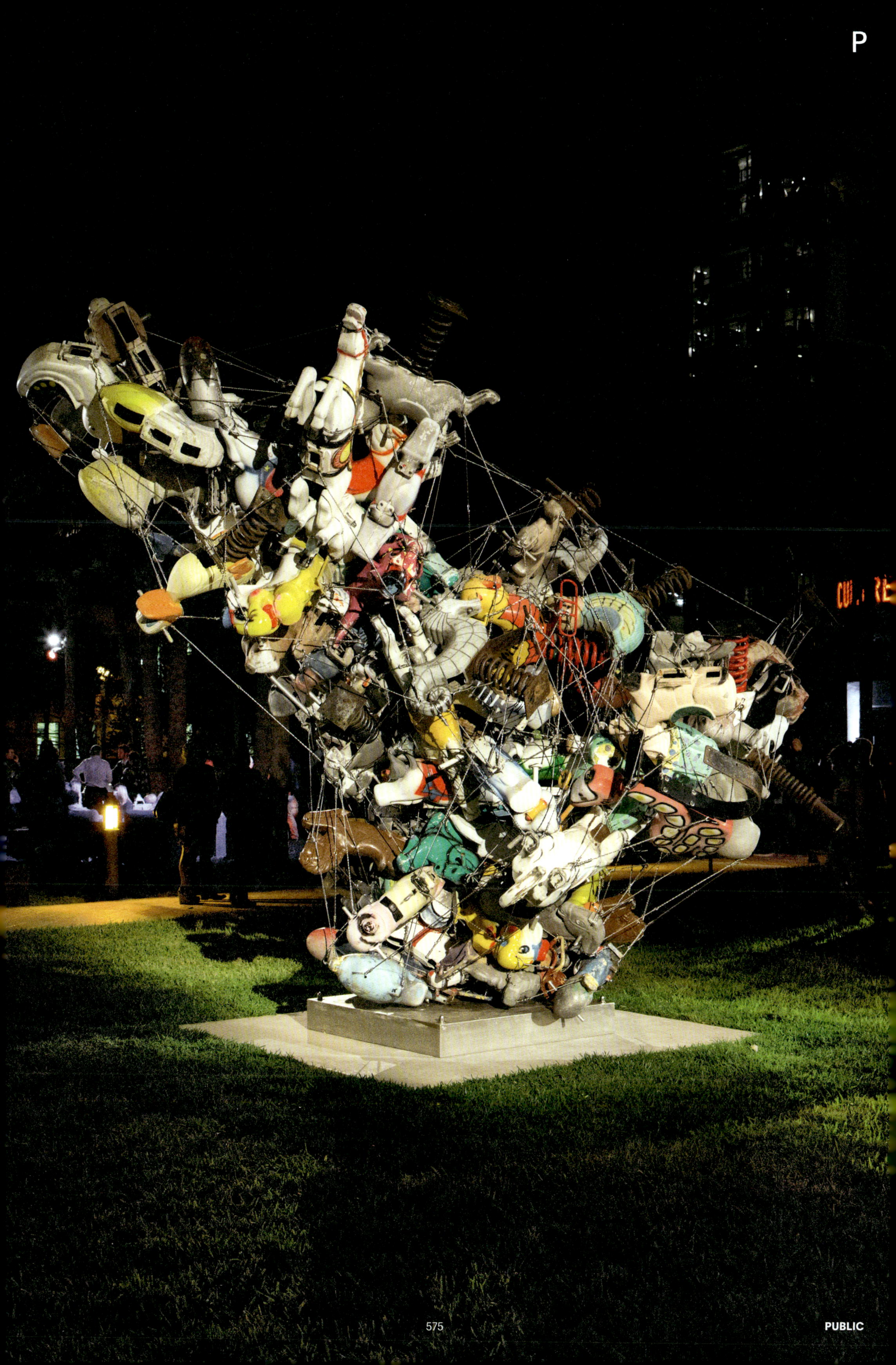

Lynda Benglis
Pink Lady
2013

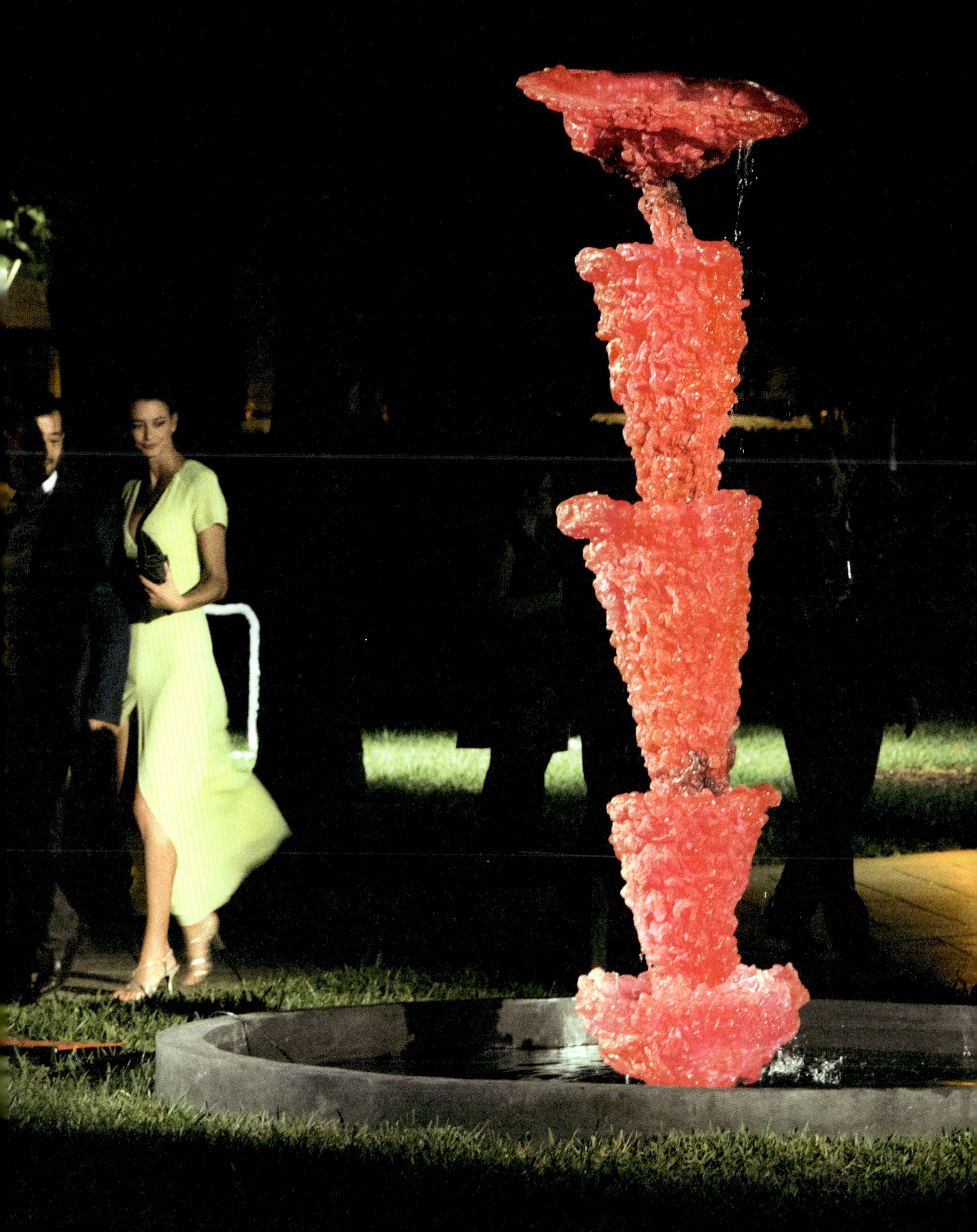

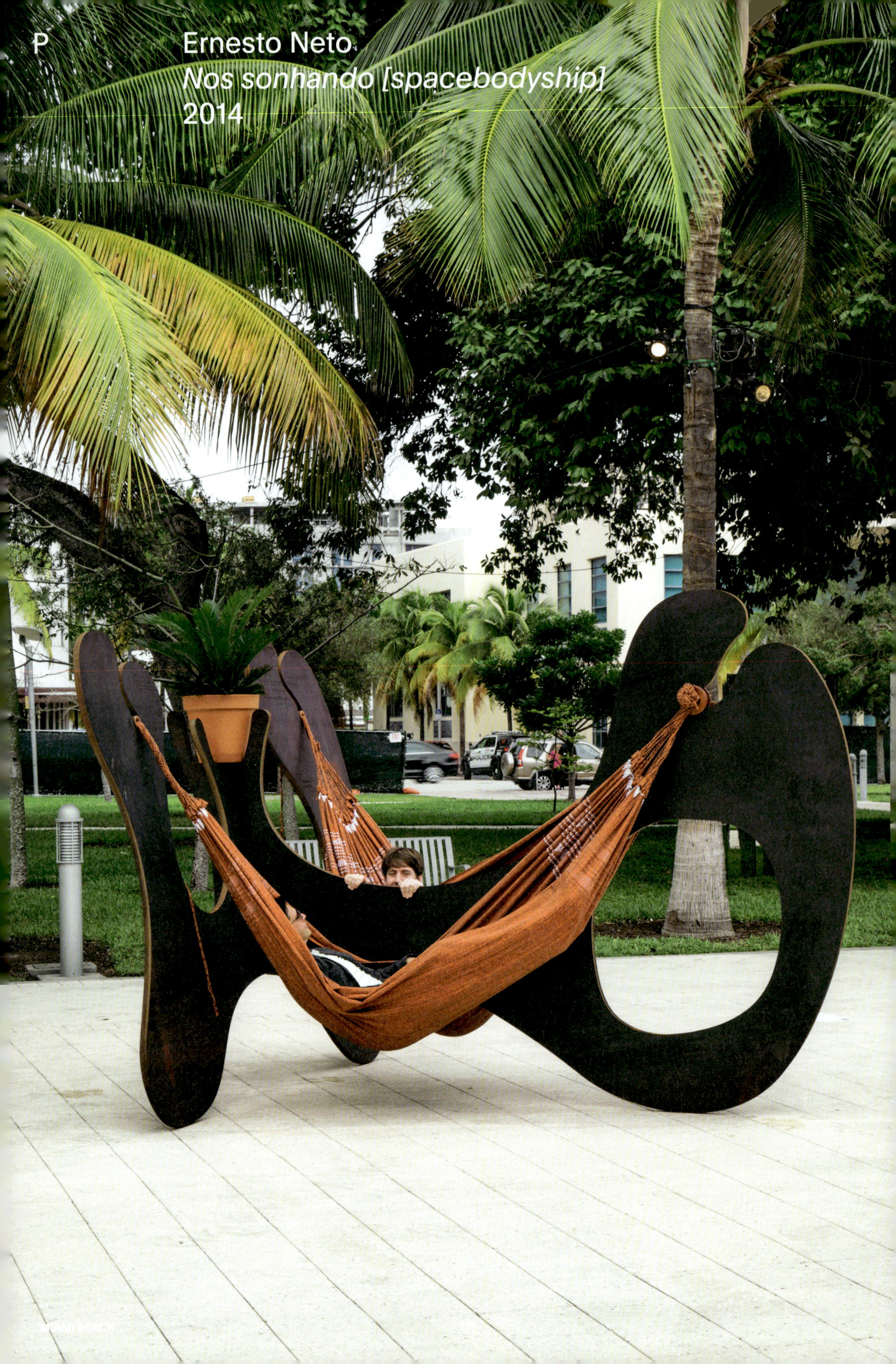

P

Ernesto Neto
Nos sonhando [spacebodyship]
2014

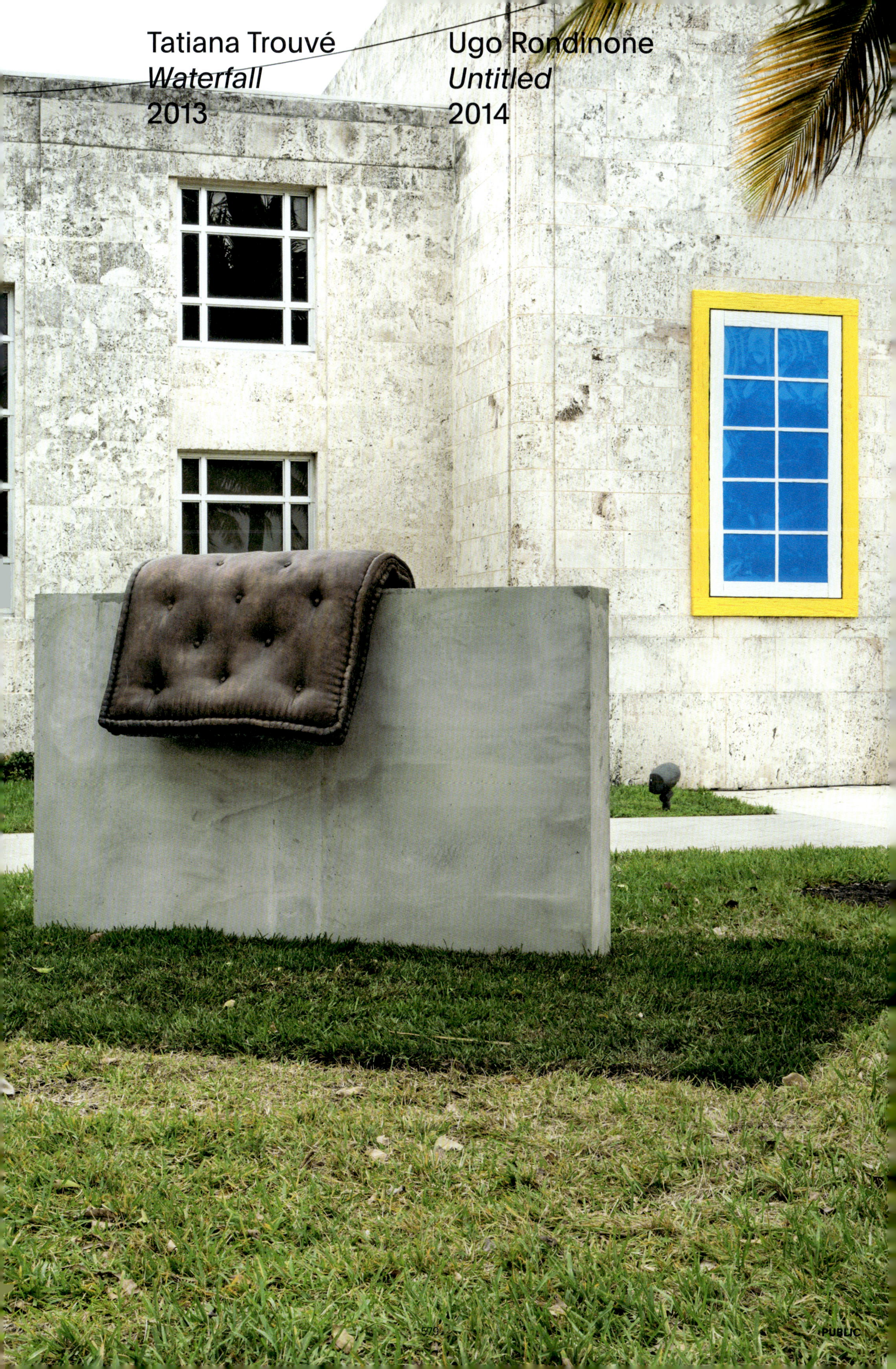

Tatiana Trouvé
Waterfall
2013

Ugo Rondinone
Untitled
2014

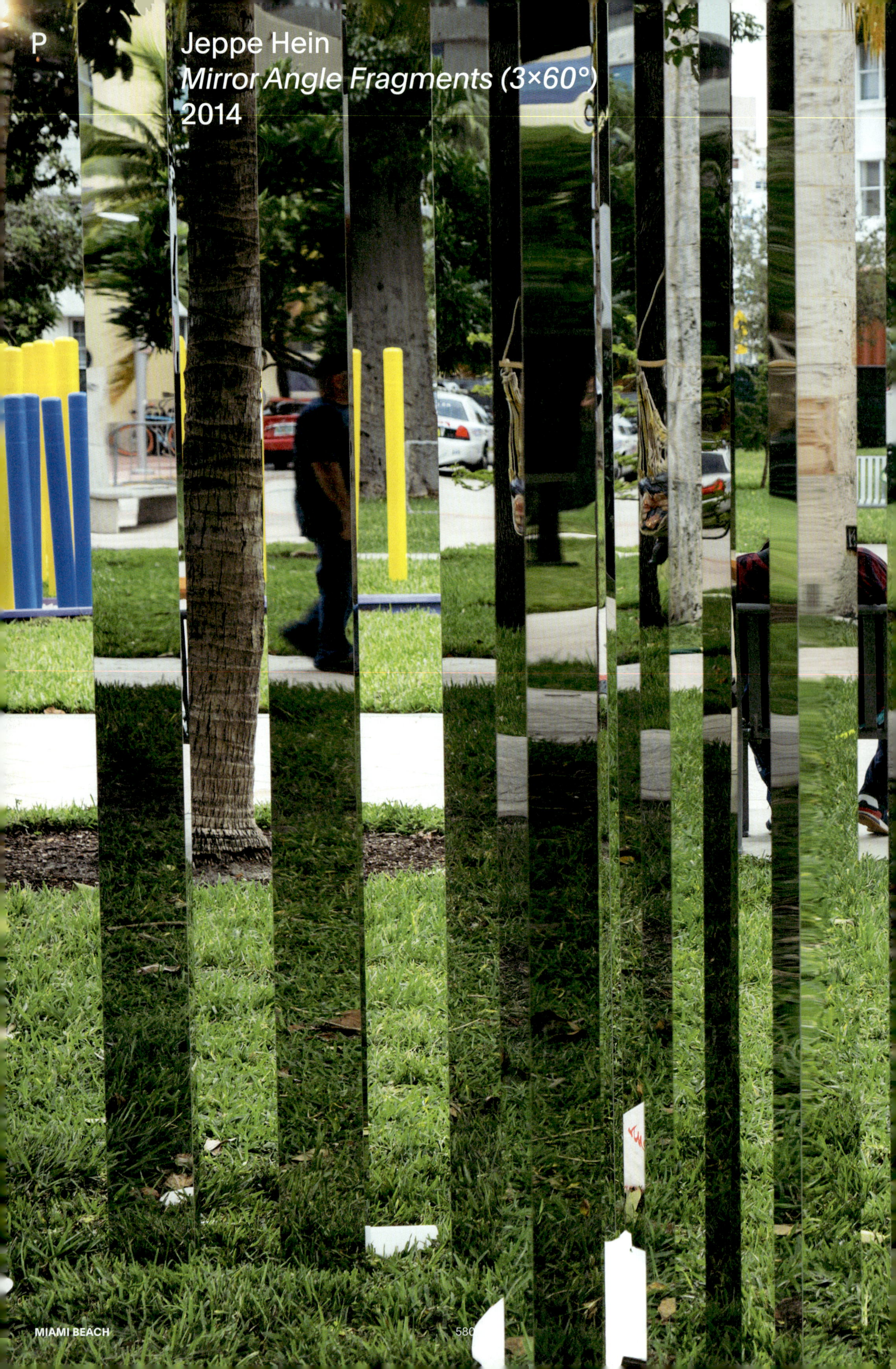
P
Jeppe Hein
Mirror Angle Fragments (3×60°)
2014

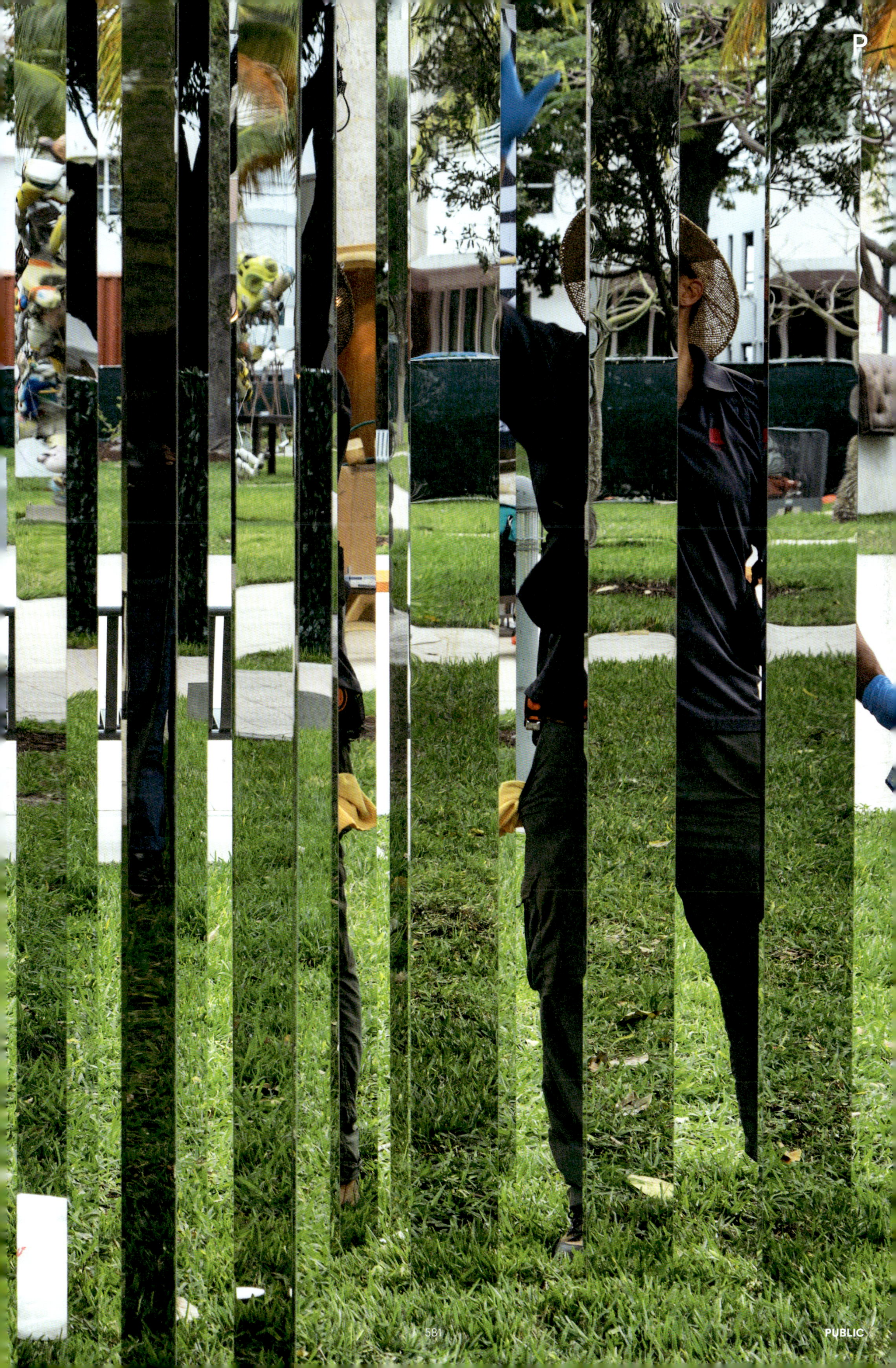

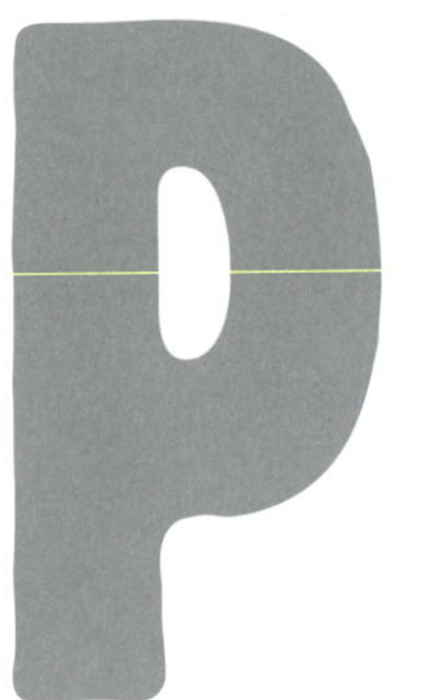

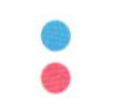

P.P.O.W

New York — Feature, Galleries

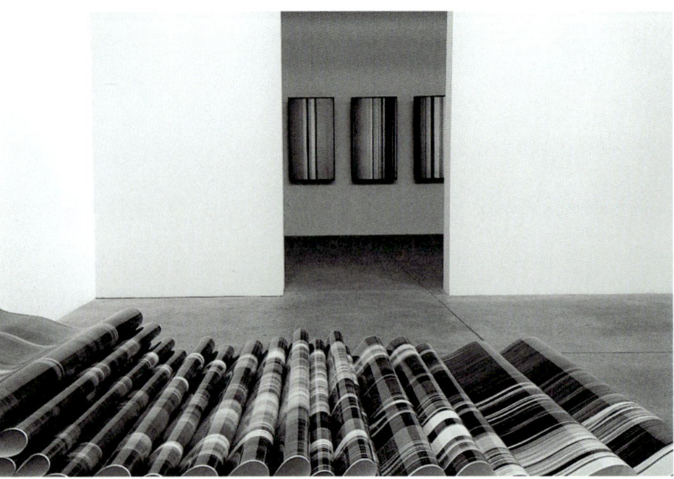

What is your favorite aspect of running a gallery?

I love my work! No two days are alike and we are constantly learning. We meet amazing artists and people from all walks of life. Most importantly we contribute to history and society in the most positive ways.

How do you choose the artists you work with?

We work with artists that contribute, deepen, and build on our history. We also look for artists that will grow and benefit from our support, who can contribute and add to our program formally and intellectually.

If you weren't running a gallery what else would you do?

Wendy would be a gardener and Penny would be an architectural historian.

- **Contact** P.P.O.W
  Anneliis Beadnell
  anneliis@ppowgallery.com
- **Established** 1983
- **Owner(s) / Partner(s)** Wendy Olsoff
  Penny Pilkington
- **Team** 6
- **Space(s)** 372 m²
- **Artists at Art Basel** Carolee Schneemann
  David Wojnarowicz
  Martin Wong
- **Further artists represented** Ann Agee
  Dotty Attie
  Sandow Birk
  Judy Fox
  Ben Gocker
  Julie Heffernan
  Timothy Horn
  Dinh Q. Lê
  Walter Martin & Paloma Muñoz
  Adam Putnam
  Hunter Reynolds
  Jessica Stoller
  Suzanne Treister
  Anton van Dalen
  Timothy Wehrle
  Thomas Woodruff

Pace

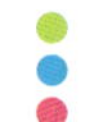

New York — Galleries
London — Galleries
Beijing — Galleries
Hong Kong
Menlo Park

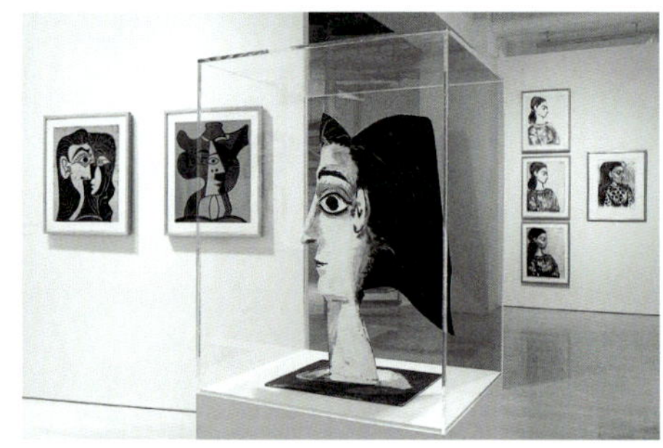

- **Contact** Pace
  Madeline Lieberberg
  mlieberberg@pacegallery.com
- **Established** 1960
- **Owner(s) / Partner(s)** Arne Glimcher
  Marc Glimcher
- **Space(s)** 3,640 m²
- **Artists at Art Basel** Josef Albers
  Yto Barrada
  Alexander Calder
  Brian Clarke
  Chuck Close
  Nigel Cooke
  Keith Coventry
  Willem de Kooning
  Jim Dine
  Tara Donovan
  Rosalyn Drexler
  Jean Dubuffet
  Tim Eitel
  Lee Friedlander
  Adrian Ghenie
  Adolph Gottlieb
  Paul Graham
  Kevin Francis Gray
  Loris Gréaud
  Hai Bo
  Tim Hawkinson
  Barbara Hepworth
  David Hockney
  Hong Hao
  Robert Irwin
  Alfred Jensen
  Donald Judd
  Ilya & Emilia Kabakov
  Lee Tzu-hsun
  Lee Ufan
  Sol LeWitt
  Li Songsong
  Maya Lin
  Liu Jianhua
  Robert Mangold
  Mao Yan
  Agnes Martin
  Roberto Matta
  Prabhavathi Meppayil
  Mario Merz
  Vik Muniz
  Elizabeth Murray
  Yoshitomo Nara
  Louise Nevelson
  Carsten Nicolai
  Isamu Noguchi
  Kenneth Noland
  Thomas Nozkowski
  Claes Oldenburg
  & Coosje van Bruggen
  Adam Pendleton
  Pablo Picasso
  Richard Pousette-Dart
  Qiu Xiaofei
  Robert Rauschenberg
  Mark Rothko
  Michal Rovner
  Robert Ryman
  Lucas Samaras
  Joel Shapiro
  Raqib Shaw
  James Siena
  Kiki Smith
  Bosco Sodi
  Song Dong
  Keith Sonnier

Saul Steinberg
Hiroshi Sugimoto
Sui Jianguo
Antoni Tàpies
Team Lab
Paul Thek
James Turrell
Richard Tuttle
Keith Tyson
Corban Walker
Robert Whitman
Fred Wilson
Xiao Yu
Yin Xiuzhen
Yue Minjun
Zhang Huan
Zhang Xiaogang

Pace Prints

New York

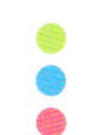

Galleries
Edition
Edition

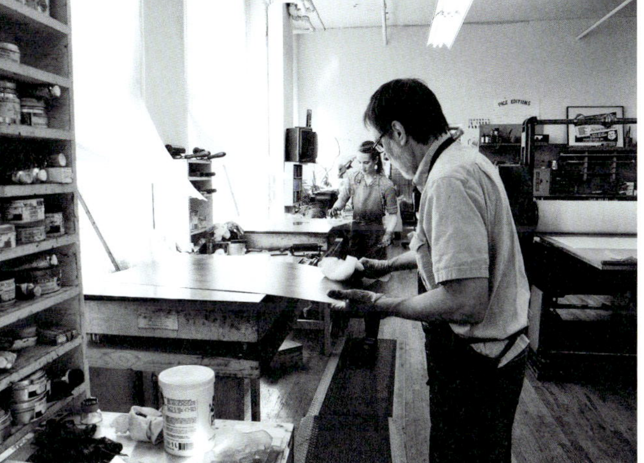

What is your favorite aspect of running a gallery?

One of the most interesting aspects of managing Pace Prints is interacting with the people with whom I associate—artists, collectors, colleagues including our staff, competitors, trade associations and numerous other art organizations, etc. As a publisher, orchestrating the creation of works of art that are appreciated and valued is extremely gratifying.

How do you choose the artists you work with?

As a print publisher and operating two print galleries, it is important to maintain a broad point of view in selecting artists both to publish and from whom to acquire works for sale. Our main objective is to publish, represent, and offer editions by a wide spectrum of artists in terms of age, gender, nationality and, most importantly, imagery. Of greatest importance is the artists' potential to successfully translate their imagery into editions and monoprints using various graphic mediums.

If you weren't running a gallery what else would you do?

If I were to retire, I would spend my time at the Metropolitan Museum of Art and at other national and international museums in an effort to acquire a greater knowledge of Asian, African, Oceanic, and Ancient art.

- **Contact** Pace Prints
  Richard (Dick) Solomon
  dick@paceprints.com
- **Established** 1968
- **Owner(s) / Partner(s)** Richard Solomon
- **Team** 32
- **Space(s)** 1,393.5 m²
- **Artists at Art Basel** Ghada Amer & Reza Farkhondeh
  Donald Baechler
  Rina Banerjee
  John Chamberlain
  Francesco Clemente
  Chuck Close
  Will Cotton
  Tara Donovan
  Leonardo Drew
  Jean Dubuffet
  Inka Essenhigh
  Lee Ufan
  Sol LeWitt
  Ling Jian
  Nicola López
  Robert Mangold
  Ryan McGinness
  Paul Morrison
  Wangechi Mutu
  Yoshitomo Nara
  Louise Nevelson
  Kenneth Noland
  Claes Oldenburg
  Kenny Scharf
  Sea-Hyun Lee
  Kiki Smith
  Pat Steir
  James Turrell
  Dan Walsh
  Yue Minjun
  Zhang Huan
  Zhang Xiaogang

Pace/MacGill

New York

Galleries

- **Contact** Pace/MacGill Gallery
  Margaret Kelly
  info@pacemacgill.com
- **Established** 1983
- **Owner(s) / Partner(s)** Peter Macgill
- **Team** 13
- **Artists at Art Basel** David Byrne
  Harry Callahan
  William Christenberry
  Robert Frank
  Lee Friedlander
  Jim Goldberg
  Emmet Gowin
  Paul Graham
  Peter Hujar
  Mark Klett
  Josef Koudelka
  Annie Leibovitz
  Richard Misrach
  Vik Muniz
  Susan Paulsen
  Irving Penn
  Paolo Roversi
  Michal Rovner
  Kiki Smith
  Alfred Stieglitz
  Paul Strand
  Hiroshi Sugimoto
  Joann Verburg
  William Wegman
- **Further artists represented** Adou
  Diane Arbus
  Richard Benson
  Chuck Close
  Walker Evans
  Hai Bo
  Hiro
  Jocelyn Lee
  Boris Mikhailov
  Nicholas Nixon
  Tod Papageorge
  Robert Rauschenberg
  Lucas Samaras
  Fazal Sheikh
  Frederick Sommer
  John Szarkowski
  Andy Warhol
  Henry Wessel
  Garry Winogrand

Paley

London

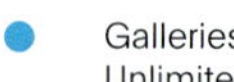

Galleries Unlimited

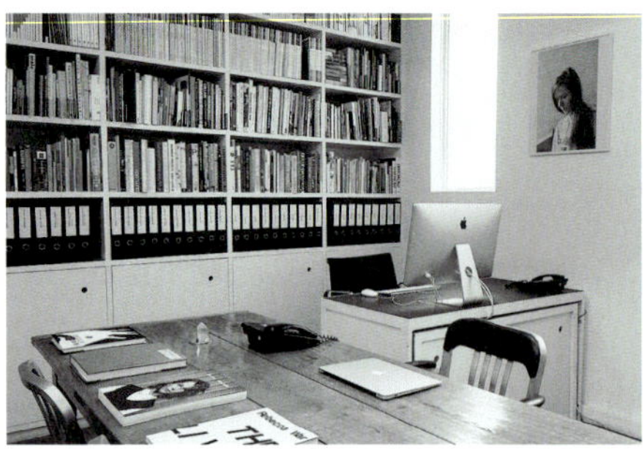

What is your favorite aspect of running a gallery?

Working closely with the artists in creative response to their creativity.

How do you choose the artists you work with?

Their clarity of vision—always looking to improve my ability to choose. With guidance from "gathering together" from the I-Ching.

If you weren't running a gallery what else would you do?

Work as a curator in a museum.

- **Contact** Maureen Paley, Oliver Evans, oliver@maureenpaley.com
- **Established** 1984
- **Owner(s) / Partner(s)** Maureen Paley
- **Team** 10
- **Space(s)** 464.5 m²
- **Artists at Art Basel** AA Bronson, Kaye Donachie, Morgan Fisher, Hamish Fulton, General Idea, Liam Gillick, Anne Hardy, Peter Hujar, Michael Krebber, Stephen Prina, Tim Rollins & K.O.S., David Salle, Wolfgang Tillmans, Rebecca Warren, Gillian Wearing, James Welling
- **Further artists represented** Thomas Eggerer, Gardar Eide Einarsson, Maureen Gallace, Andrew Grassie, Sarah Jones, Lars Laumann, Erik van Lieshout, Daria Martin, Maaike Schoorel, Hannah Starkey, Dirk Stewen, David Thorpe, Gert & Uwe Tobias, Donald Urquhart, Banks Violette

Paragon

London

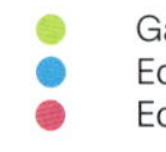

Galleries
Edition
Edition

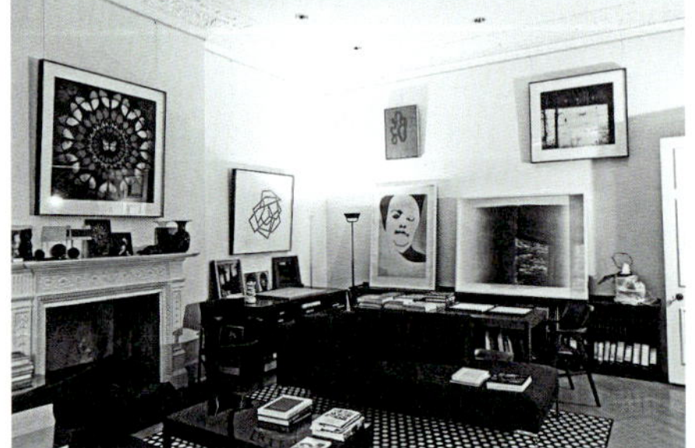

What is your favorite aspect of running a gallery?

The most fulfilling aspect of being a publisher is the collaboration between artists, fabricators, and ourselves.

How do you choose the artists you work with?

We work with artists who we believe we can help in the creation of a significant work of art in print.

If you weren't running a gallery what else would you do?

A gamekeeper.

- **Contact** Paragon, Florian Simm, florian@paragonpress.co.uk
- **Established** 1986
- **Owner(s) / Partner(s)** Charles Booth-Clibborn
- **Team** 4
- **Space(s)** 150 m²
- **Artists at Art Basel** Gillian Carnegie, Leda Catunda, Jake & Dinos Chapman, Damien Hirst, Gary Hume, Anish Kapoor, Sarah Morris, Marc Quinn, Grayson Perry
- **Further artists represented** Kai Althoff, Hurvin Anderson, Richard Deacon, Peter Doig, Eberhard Havekost, Michael Landy, Christopher Le Brun, Elizabeth Magill, Paul Morrison, Ged Quinn, George Shaw, Corinne Wasmuht, Richard Wathen, Rachel Whiteread, Thomas Zipp

Galerie Paris-Beijing

Beijing
Paris
Brussels

Insights

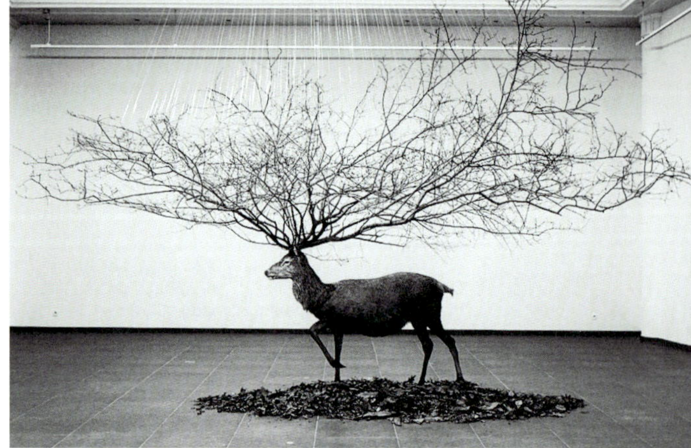

What is your favorite aspect of running a gallery?

Running a gallery means to be able to complete ten different jobs in one. There are so many steps from the first meeting with an artist until their first sale … from hanging an artwork to selling it. It is very exciting to do a job that is never the same and is linked to the ideas of creativity, exchange, movement …

How do you choose the artists you work with?

We need to be moved by his/her works and his/her personnality: our artists usually become our friends.

If you weren't running a gallery what else would you do?

We would probably be running a hotel or a restaurant with a strong connection to the art world.

- **Contact** Galerie Paris-Beijing
  Romain Degoul
  paris@galerieparisbeijing.com
- **Established** 2006
- **Owner(s) / Partner(s)** Flore & Romain Degoul
- **Team** 9
- **Space(s)** 1,000 m²
- **Artists at Art Basel** Fu Site
  Ren Hang
  Wang Haiyang
  Yang Yongliang
  Zhu Xinyu
- **Further artists represented** Li Wie
  Liu Bolin
  Myeongbeom Kim
  Martin Parr
  Rero
  Alex Seton
  Yi Hwan-Kwon
  Wang Ningde
  Wang Qingsong

Park Ryu Sook

Seoul — Insights

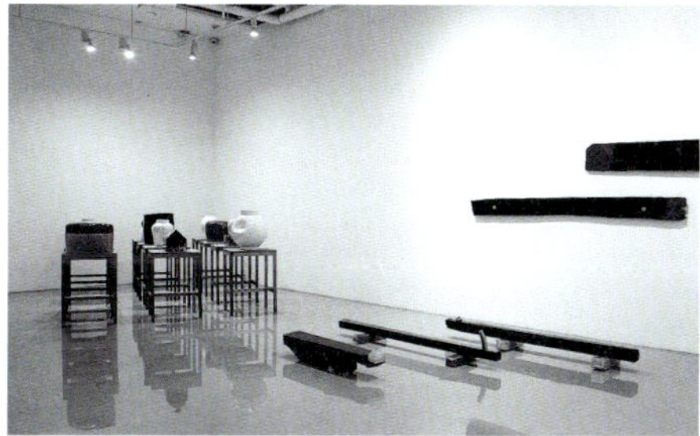

What is your favorite aspect of running a gallery?
The art fairs.

How do you choose the artists you work with?
By following what my gut tells me.

If you weren't running a gallery what else would you do?
I can't imagine myself doing anything else.

- **Contact** Park Ryu Sook Gallery
  Soo Choi
  info@parkryusookgallery.com
- **Established** 1983
- **Owner(s) / Partner(s)** Park Ryu Sook
- **Team** 5
- **Space(s)** 300 m²
- **Artists at Art Basel** Kim Tschang-Yeul
- **Further artists represented** Choi Jeong Hwa
  Kim Kang Yong
  Kim Sung Ho
  Koo Sung Soo
  Kwon Ki-Soo
  Lee Hun Chung
  Lee Lee Nam
  Park Jong-Pil
  Park Seo-Bo

Parra & Romero

Madrid
Santa Gertrudis/Ibiza 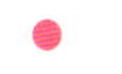 Nova

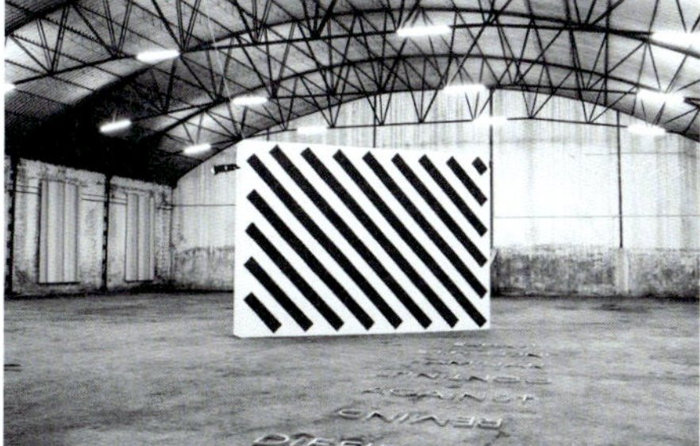

What is your favorite aspect of running a gallery?
It is an extraordinary way of life.

How do you choose the artists you work with?
They need to have a coherent conceptual dialogue with their peers, no matter their gender, media, or age.

If you weren't running a gallery what else would you do?
I cannot imagine doing something else.

- **Contact** Parra & Romero
  Guillermo Romero Parra
  guillermo@parra-romero.com
- **Established** 2005
- **Owner(s) / Partner(s)** Guillermo Romero Parra
- **Team** 6
- **Space(s)** 1,450 m²
- **Artists at Art Basel** Lara Almarcegui
  Luis Camnitzer
  Philippe Decrauzat
  Oriol Vilanova
- **Further artists represented** Stefan Brüggemann
  Alejandro Cesarco
  Kajsa Dahlberg
  Martina Klein
  Germaine Kruip
  David Lamelas
  Paloma Polo
  Thomas Scheibitz
  Conrad Shawcross

Parrasch

New York  Galleries

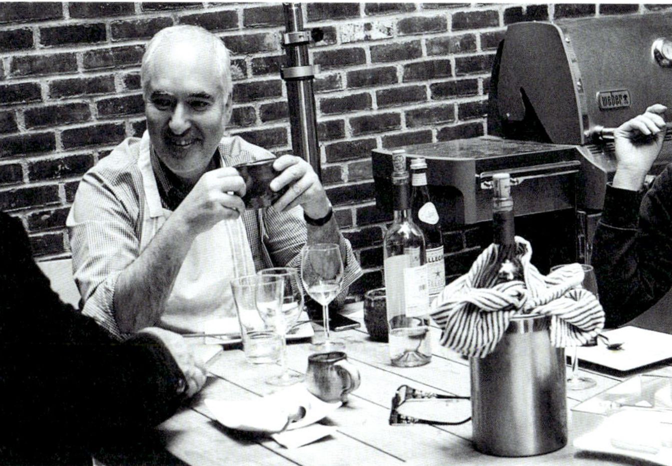

What is your favorite aspect of running a gallery?
Cooking lunch for my staff and gallery guests every day.

How do you choose the artists you work with?
Their work chooses me.

If you weren't running a gallery what else would you do?
Cook.

- **Contact** Franklin Parrasch Gallery
  Katharine Overgaard
  info@franklinparrasch.com
- **Established** 1986
- **Owner(s) / Partner(s)** Franklin Parrasch
- **Team** 6
- **Space(s)** 288 m²
- **Artists at Art Basel** Billy Al Bengston
  Ron Cooper
  Mary Corse
  Joe Goode
  Marcia Hafif
  Craig Kauffman
  John McCracken
  John McLaughlin
  Bruce Nauman
  Ken Price
  Joan Snyder
- **Further artists represented** Mark Gonzales
  Daniel Turner

Pauli

Lausanne — Galleries

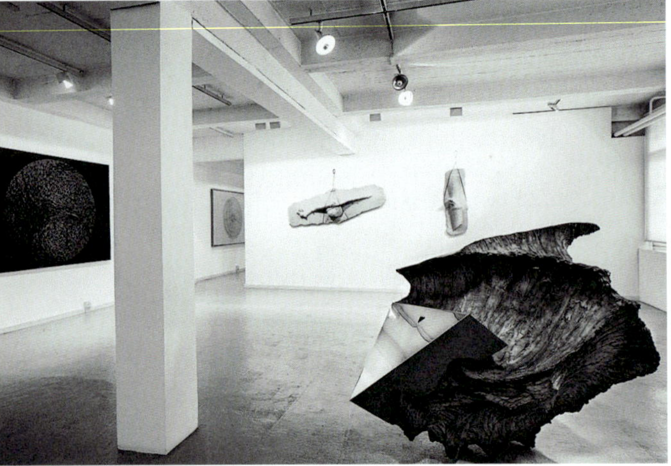

What is your favorite aspect of running a gallery?
Discovering new artists, new works by the gallery's artists, visiting their studios, organizing their exhibitions, and keeping close contact with collectors.

How do you choose the artists you work with?
Reading about artists in art magazines, watching films about them, visiting museums and foundations, art fairs, biennales, etc.

If you weren't running a gallery what else would you do?
I can't imagine doing something different—art is so important to me!

- **Contact** Galerie Alice Pauli
Alice Pauli
info@galeriealicepauli.ch
- **Established** 1962
- **Owner(s) / Partner(s)** Alice Pauli
- **Team** 3
- **Space(s)** 400 m²
- **Artists at Art Basel** Julius Bissier
Philippe Cognée
Stéphane Guiran
Rebecca Horn
Christian Lapie
Flavio Paolucci
Jaume Plensa
Giuseppe Penone
Nunzio
Pierre Soulages
Mark Tobey
Peter Wüthrich
- **Further artists represented** Geneviève Asse
Jim Dine
Monique Frydman
Loïc Le Groumellec
Mimmo Paladino
Alicia Penalba
Anne & Patrick Poirier
Fabienne Verdier

Pékin

Beijing
Hong Kong

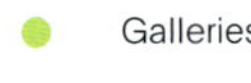

Galleries

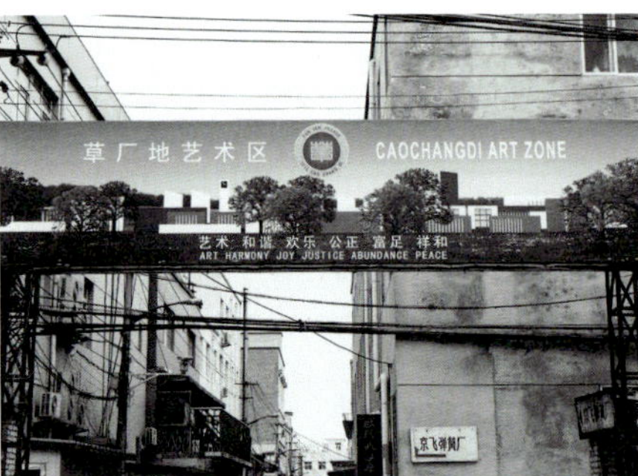

What is your favorite aspect of running a gallery?
Easy: the daily interaction with artists.

How do you choose the artists you work with?
Not easy: there are many talented artists who would not fit comfortably alongside the artists we represent and choose to exhibit. It takes time to build the relationship and a mutual trust. It's very much like choosing a marriage partner!

If you weren't running a gallery what else would you do?
Be an art collector.

- **Contact** Pékin Fine Arts
Meg Maggio
meg@pekinfinearts.com
- **Established** 2005
- **Owner(s) / Partner(s)** Meg Maggio
- **Team** 8
- **Space(s)** 600 m² (Beijing)
150 m² (Hong Kong)
- **Artists at Art Basel** Chen Shaoxiong
Huang Zhiyang
Kata Legrady
Arik Levy
Luo Mingjun
Liu Zheng
Liu Ding
Nashunbatu
Wang Luyan
Suling Wang
Zhang Dali
- **Further artists represented** Liu Di
Yang Dongxue
Fang Lu
Zhang Xiao
Xie Qi
Yu Likwai
Zhao Liang

Peres Projects

Berlin

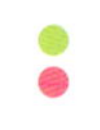

Galleries
Nova

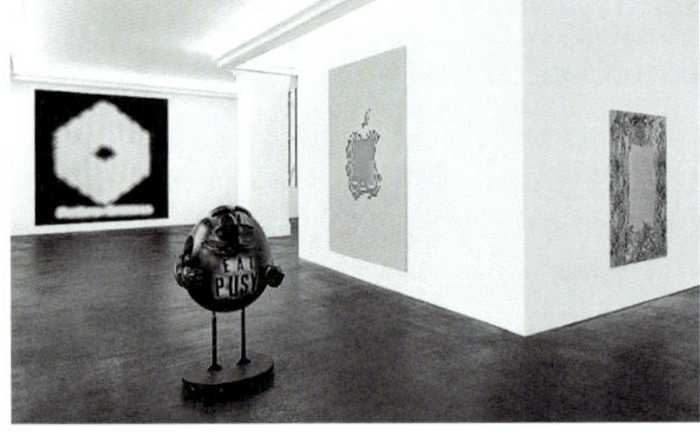

What is your favorite aspect of running a gallery?
The creative aspect of working with artists.

How do you choose the artists you work with?
Organically, through personal interests and relationships.

If you weren't running a gallery what else would you do?
A lawyer, like I was before.

- **Contact** Peres Projects
Nick Koenigsknecht
berlin@peresprojects.com
- **Established** 2002
- **Owner(s) / Partner(s)** Javier Peres
- **Team** 12
- **Space(s)** 500 m²
- **Artists at Art Basel** Dan Attoe
Mike Bouchet
Mark Flood
Alex Israel
David Ostrowski
- **Further artists represented** Assume Vivid Astro Focus
Antonio Ballester Moreno
Leo Gabin
Dorothy Iannone
Bruce LaBruce
Eddie Peake
Dean Sameshima
Marinella Senatore
Brent Wadden

Perrotin

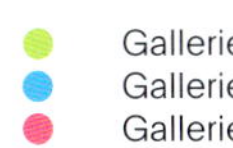

Paris — Galleries
Hong Kong — Galleries
New York — Galleries

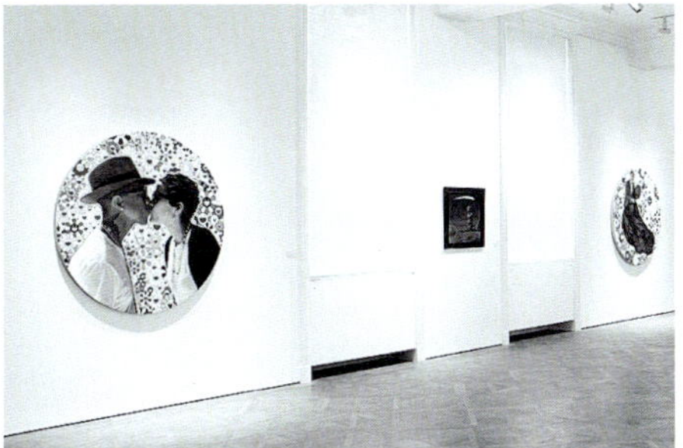

What is your favorite aspect of running a gallery?

The artists' studios are particularly stimulating, talking about art and life. My aim is to make the artists' dreams come true, from the production to the exhibition.

How do you choose the artists you work with?

The exhibition celebrating the 25 years of the gallery at the Tri Postal, a 6,000 m² space in Lille, showed that my choices were both eclectic and thoughtful. It is also often the magic of an encounter with an artist and his work that is necessary and that becomes obvious.

If you weren't running a gallery what else would you do?

When I was young, I wrote scripts. Maybe I could have been a scriptwriter or a film director.

- **Contact**: Galerie Perrotin
Raphaël Gatel
raphael@perrotin.com
- **Established**: 1989
- **Owner(s) / Partner(s)**: Emmanuel Perrotin
- **Team**: 50
- **Space(s)**: 1,300 m² (Paris Turenne)
700 m² (Paris Salle de Bal)
400 m² (New York)
650 m² (Hong Kong)
- **Artists at Art Basel**: Ivan Argote
Daniel Arsham
Hernan Bas
Sophie Calle
Maurizio Cattelan
Wim Delvoye
Elmgreen & Dragset
Ericson & Ziegler
Lionel Esteve
Daniel Firman
Bernard Frize
Gelitin
Laurent Grasso
Thilo Heinzmann
John Henderson
Gregor Hildebrandt
JR
Jesper Just
Izumi Kato
Kaws
Bharti Kher
Kolkoz
Klara Kristalova
Guy Limone
Ryan McGinley
Farhad Moshiri
Mr.
Takashi Murakami
Kaz Oshiro
Jean-Michel Othoniel
Paola Pivi
Germaine Richier
Claude Rutault
Michael Sailstorfer
Jesús Rafael Soto
Pierre Soulages
Aya Takano
Tatiana Trouvé
Xavier Veilhan
Pieter Vermeersch
Peter Zimmermann

Petzel

New York — Galleries
Parcours — Galleries

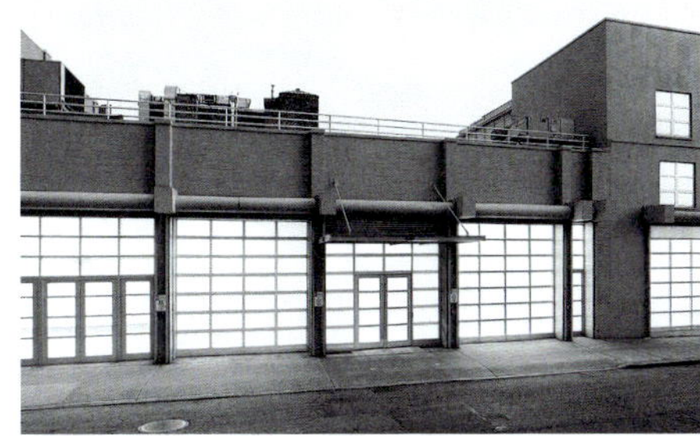

What is your favorite aspect of running a gallery?

Successful exhibitions. An exhibition is successful when the artist receives critical acclaim, institutional support, and seduces enough collectors to actually purchase the works on the walls. My teams are adept at advance press, visiting studios with curators, and, of course, sales. I love it when five or six weeks later another artist surprises us again with his or her vision. I can't think of a better job that offers a framework for my pursuit of intellectual satisfaction and economic independence.

How do you choose the artists you work with?

I have known and admired Charline von Heyl since the 1980s; we practically moved to New York together as I wanted to show her in my new gallery. I rarely experience the sensation I had visiting the Seth Price and Wade Guyton exhibition at PS1. I had no clue what they were up to. I wanted to get involved! Yael Bartana's *And Europe Will Be Stunned* blew me away. I hope for each artist to have an individual voice in my gallery, whether it is ambitious, critical, or even disrespectful; but always historically informed.

If you weren't running a gallery what else would you do?

Learn from Arsene Wenger at Arsenal London to coach a soccer team in the USA.

- **Contact**: Petzel Gallery
Laura Higgins
laura@petzel.com
- **Established**: 1994 (New York)/2008 (Berlin)
- **Owner(s) / Partner(s)**: Friedrich Petzel
Andrea Teschke
Samantha Tsao (New York)
Gisela Capitain
Friedrich Petzel (Berlin)
- **Team**: 20
- **Space(s)**: 1,115 m² (New York)
1,393.5 m² (Berlin)
- **Artists at Art Basel**: Yael Bartana
Walead Beshty
Troy Brauntuch
Simon Denny
Thomas Eggerer
Wade Guyton
Robert Heinecken
Charline von Heyl
Sean Landers
Maria Lassnig
Robert Longo
Adam McEwen
Sarah Morris
Jorge Pardo
Joyce Pensato
Seth Price
Dana Schutz
Dirk Skreber
Nicola Tyson
Heimo Zobernig
- **Further artists represented**: Cosima Von Bonin
Keith Edmier
Georg Herold
Christian Jankowski
Rezi van Lankveld
Allan McCollum
Stephen Prina
Jon Pylypchuk
Willem de Rooij
Corinne Wasmuht

Pi

Istanbul
London

Insights

What is your favorite aspect of running a gallery?
Being in-between creation and placement.

How do you choose the artists you work with?
Some works have a way of talking to me.

If you weren't running a gallery what else would you do?
Honestly I cannot think of anything else that would make me feel this connected to life.

- **Contact** Pi Artworks
  Yesim Turanli
  yt@piartworks.com
- **Established** 1998
- **Owner** Yesim Turanli
- **Team** 9
- **Space(s)** 500 m²
- **Artists at Art Basel** Nezaket Ekici
- **Further artists represented** Yeşim Akdeniz
  Mehmet Ali Uysal
  Volkan Aslan
  Nancy Atakan
  Tayeba Begum Lipi
  Osman Dinc
  Maria Friberg
  Susan Hefuna
  Horasan
  Nejat Sati
  Paul Schwer
  Gulay Semercioglu
  Ayten Turanli
  Farniyaz Zaker

Pia

Zurich

Galleries

What is your favorite aspect of running a gallery?
The combination of being in conversation with artists and organizing shows with them, as well as working in a team.

How do you choose the artists you work with?
Often through contact with other artists or curators, or being struck by a show of an artist you haven't seen before.

If you weren't running a gallery what else would you do?
There is not much else I could do.

- **Contact** Galerie Francesca Pia
  Patricia Hartmann
  p.hartmann@francescapia.com
- **Established** 1990
- **Owner** Francesca Pia
- **Team** 7
- **Space(s)** 600 m²
- **Artists at Art Basel** Thomas Bayrle
  Isabelle Cornaro
  Stéphane Dafflon
  Philippe Decrauzat
  Hans-Peter Feldmann
  Vidya Gastaldon
  Aloïs Godinat
  Joseph Grigely
  Juan José Gurrola
  Wade Guyton
  Fabrice Gygi
  Emil M. Klein
  Jutta Koether
  Elad Lassry
  Tobias Madison
  Kaspar Müller
  Marta Riniker-Radich
  Mai-Thu Perret
  Bruno Serralongue
  David Shrigley
  Josef Strau
  Joanne Tatham & Tom O'Sullivan
  John Tremblay
  Betty Woodman

PKM

Seoul

Galleries
Galleries

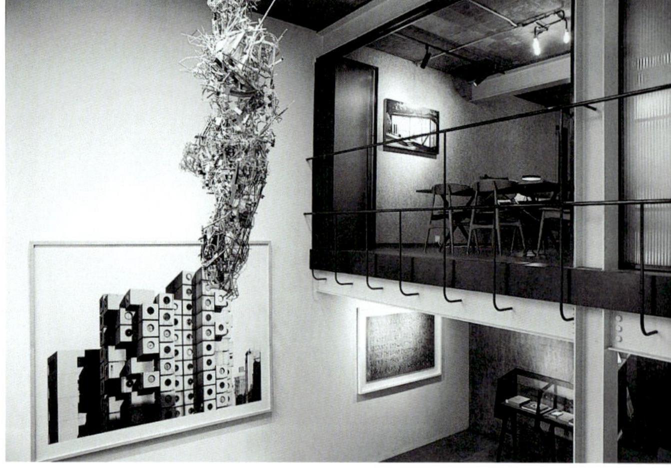

What is your favorite aspect of running a gallery?
From its foundation, PKM Gallery has actively supported and successfully promoted emerging Korean artists on the international stage through its creative exhibition programs. At the same time, the gallery has introduced internationally acclaimed artists to a Korean audience. By running the gallery, I've had great opportunities that allowed me to play a leading role in the advancement of Korean contemporary art.

How do you choose the artists you work with?
I encourage artists at various stages of their development and recognition—from young and emerging to mid-career and established—to have a dialogue around a set of ideas and questions that recur in the works of artists through exhibitions. Therefore I have kept close ties with established artists for over ten years and I have endeavored to discover talented young artists.

- **Contact** PKM Gallery
  Kyoungeun Hwang
  hke@pkmgallery.com
- **Established** 2001
- **Owner(s) / Partner(s)** Kyung-Mee Park
- **Team** 6
- **Space(s)** 245 m²
- **Artists at Art Basel** Cho Duck-Hyun
  Choi Jeong Hwa
  Heeseung Chung
  Kim Tschang-Yeul
  Koo Hyunmo
  Sangbin Im
  Wonwoo Lee
  Young Do Jeong
  Yun Hyong-Keun
- **Further artists represented** Darren Almond
  Bae Young-Whan
  Hernan Bas
  Cody Choi
  Michael Craig-Martin
  Jonas Dahlberg
  Thomas Demand
  Olafur Eliasson
  Steven Gontarski
  Ham Jin
  Byron Kim
  Jiwon Kim
  Sanggil Kim
  Koo Hyunmo
  Lee Bul
  Lee Kangso
  Noori Lee
  Sang Nam Lee
  Wonwoo Lee
  Bruce Nauman
  Claes Oldenburg
  & Coosje Van Bruggen
  Gabriel Orozco
  Jorge Pardo
  Katie Paterson
  Yun Hyong-Keun

Plan B

Cluj
Berlin

Discoveries

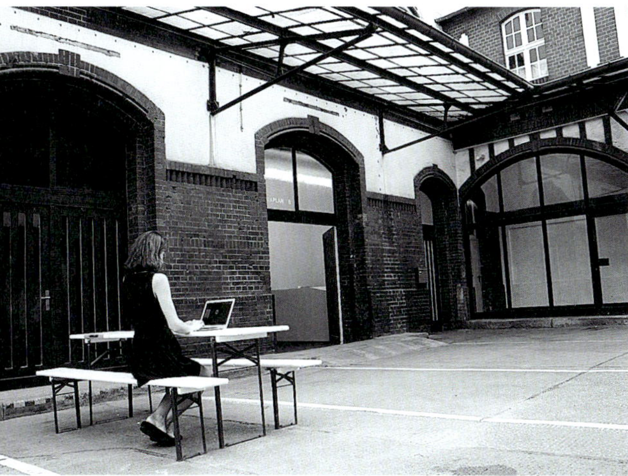

What is your favorite aspect of running a gallery?

Production tasks, sometimes bordering on the impossible; it is a challenge that is amplified also by the different geographical locations we operate in. "The production crisis" converts itself into the energy one needs to put on a good show, the moment of maximum tension which involves everybody altogether. Beyond that, the most challenging moment is the moment when the show starts to take shape in the gallery space, bringing the initial plan to a good conclusion.

How do you choose the artists you work with?

Our gallery works mainly with a generation of artists from Cluj whose international debut coincides with our intensified presence on the international scene in the mid-2000s. The belief that their works have a bigger meaning than the stakes of the local context helped the initial group of artists of the gallery to grow stronger over time. Apart from the geographical aspect, the capacity to access and reveal the sublime meaning of reality functions as an important criteria as well.

If you weren't running a gallery what else would you do?

Mihai Pop: At this point I do not see myself doing something else and the decision to give up a potential career as an artist to the possibility of being a gallerist was very thoroughly thought about. This doesn't mean that I dedicate all my time to the gallery; such a commitment would burn out the creative, investigative side of my work and would turn me slowly but surely into a bureaucrat. To do nothing is acceptable in Eastern Europe and I am trying not to lose the bad habits of my original location.

- **Contact** Galeria Plan B
  Mihaela Lutea
  contact@plan-b.ro
- **Established** 2005
- **Owner(s) / Partner(s)** Mihai Pop
  Mihaela Lutea
- **Team** 7
- **Space(s)** 400 m²
- **Artists at Art Basel** Ciprian Muresan
  Serban Savu
- **Further artists represented** Ioana Batranu
  Rudolf Bone
  Alexandra Croitoru
  Belu-Simion Fainaru
  Adrian Ghenie
  Istvan Laszlo
  Victor Man
  Navid Nuur
  Miklos Onucsan
  Cristi Pogacean
  Cristian Rusu
  Achraf Touloub
  Gabriela Vanga

Platform China

Beijing
Hong Kong

Galleries

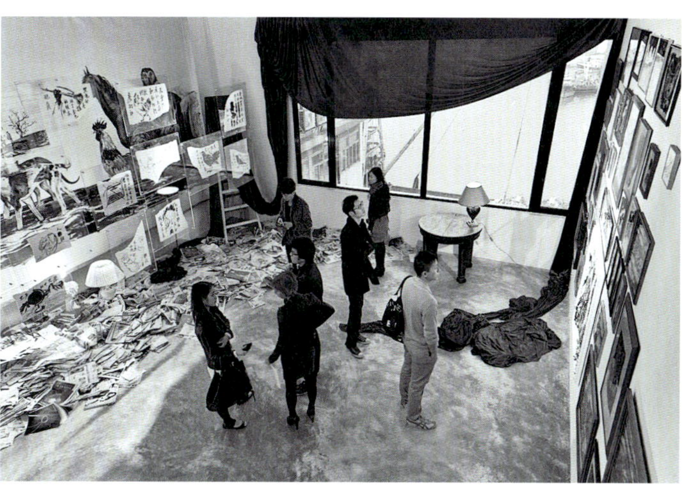

What is your favorite aspect of running a gallery?

Running a gallery can often be like riding a horse with no reins: the thrill, the passion, the unexpected, and the wilderness of it all are what keep me excited about it day after day.

How do you choose the artists you work with?

Platform China's activity evolves around continuous research into the freshest, most experimental, and alternative art forms. We choose the artists we work with for the energy, the language, and the innovation they transmit. There is no rule that can be explained: we work with artists we fall in love with and the love is reciprocal, as it is in a relationship … with its ups and downs.

If you weren't running a gallery what else would you do?

If I weren't running a gallery I would be sailing a boat across the globe while writing books and poems.

- **Contact** Platform China
  Claudia Albertini
  hk@platformchina.org
- **Established** 2005
- **Owner(s) / Partner(s)** Sun Ning
  Chen Haitao
  Claudia Albertini
- **Team** 10
- **Space(s)** 1,600 m²
- **Artists at Art Basel** Jia Aili
  Ma Ke
  Qin Qi
  Qiu Ruixiang
  Song Yuanyuan
  Tang Dayao
  Wang Ningde
  Wang Yin
  Yang Maoyuan
  Zhao Gang
  Zhang Yexing
  Zhou Yilun
- **Further artists represented** Bi Jianye
  Huang Liang
  Jin Shan
  Li Ming
  Lou Shen Yi
  Shi Jinsong
  Sun Xun
  Wang Gongxin
  Zhao Zhao

Podnar

Berlin
Ljubljana

● Galleries

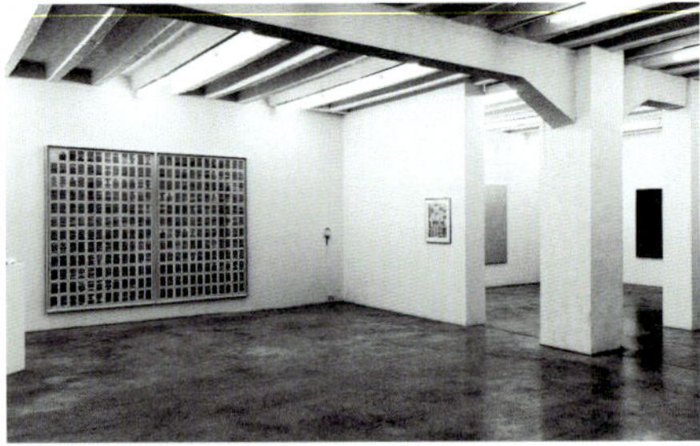

What is your favorite aspect of running a gallery?

Since its establishment in 2003 Galerija Gregor Podnar has been one of the most internationally active Slovene/German commercial galleries, and has brought not only Slovene artists to greater international recognition, but artists from the greater Central and Eastern European region as well. Given our international collaborations with many museums and galleries, the gallery is highly respected and regularly participates in the most prominent international art fairs.

How do you choose the artists you work with?

The gallery presents internationally well-known and established artists mostly from Eastern European centers, as well as young emerging artists from a wider context, in whose case only the quality of the work is what counts.

If you weren't running a gallery what else would you do?

I started out as a curator in the early 1990s and had been running an international program as artistic director of Galerija Škuc in Ljubljana, where I also established the gallery's commercial activity and its presence on the international art market. I have continued with solo exhibitions of the most recent production by the artists represented by the gallery, where my curatorial strategy stays recognizable and significant. I have been publishing monographs and book projects by individual artists.

- **Contact** Galerija Gregor Podnar
  Kati Simon
  berlin@gregorpodnar.com
- **Established** 2003 (Kranj, Slovenia)
- **Owner(s) / Partner(s)** Gregor Podnar
- **Team** 7
- **Space(s)** 136 m²
- **Artists at Art Basel** Irma Blank
  Attila Csörgö
  Ion Grigorescu
  Alexander Gutke
  Anne Neukamp
  Tobias Putrih
  Ariel Schlesinger
- **Further artists represented** Primož Bizjak
  Vadim Fishkin
  Irwin
  Yuri Leiderman
  Marzena Nowak
  Dan Perjovschi
  Goran Petercol
  Goran Trbuljak
  Francisco Tropa
  B. Wurtz

Polígrafa

Barcelona

● Galleries
● Edition
● Edition

What is your favorite aspect of running a gallery?

The relationship with the artists and bringing them to Barcelona to do special projects in our studio.

How do you choose the artists you work with?

Searching all around the world and taking into account not only their quality, but also the possibilities of translating their art into editions.

If you weren't running a gallery what else would you do?

Collecting.

- **Contact** Polígrafa Obra Gráfica S.L.
  José Aloy
  aloy@poligrafa.net
- **Established** 1964
- **Owner(s) / Partner(s)** Joan De Muga
  José Aloy
  Alvaro Puigdengolas
- **Team** 11
- **Space(s)** 500 m²
- **Artists at Art Basel** Antonio Asis
  Massimo Bartolini
  Luis Camnitzer
  Nathan Carter
  Michael Craig-Martin
  Carlos Cruz-Diez
  Claire Fontaine
  Gao Xingjian
  Leiko Ikemura
  Atsushi Kaga
  Jacob Kassay
  Marco Maggi
  Joan Miró
  Paul P
  Laure Prouvost
  Su Xiaobai
  Derek Sullivan
  Antoni Tàpies
  Luis Tomasello
  Scott Treleaven
  Bernar Venet
  Wang Huai-Qing
  Zao Wou-Ki

Presenhuber

Zurich

● Galleries
● Galleries Unlimited Parcours
● Galleries Public

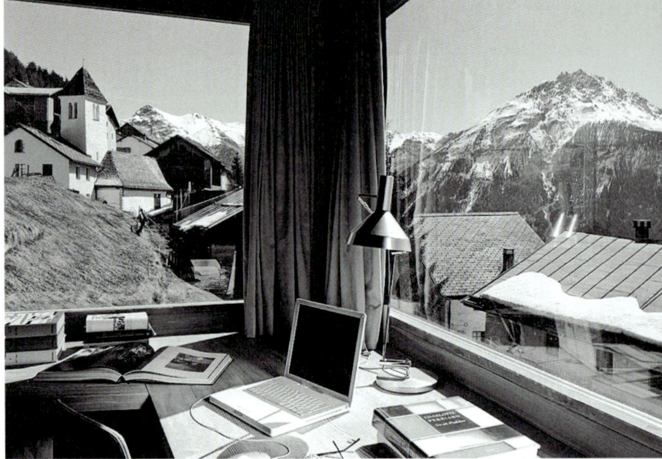

What is your favorite aspect of running a gallery?

I wanted to become an artist and studied art in Vienna; I soon realized that I would not be able to make great art. A very close friend of mine Ugo Rondinone attended the same art school; he advised me to become a gallerist. I thought that was a great idea and started an exhibition program at Walcheturm Gallery in Zurich in October 1989.

How do you choose the artists you work with?

It is always good to talk to artists you already work with. They can be great advisers.

If you weren't running a gallery what else would you do?

I love architecture and design, so it might be a field I could work in instead.

- **Contact** Galerie Eva Presenhuber
Anna Helwing
a.helwing@presenhuber.com
- **Established** 2002
- **Owner(s) / Partner(s)** Eva Presenhuber
- **Team** 18
- **Space(s)** 1,100 m²
- **Artists at Art Basel** Doug Aitken
Martin Boyce
Joe Bradley
Angela Bulloch
Valentin Carron
Verne Dawson
Jay Defeo
Trisha Donnelly
Carroll Dunham
Latifa Echakhch
Matias Faldbakken
Sam Falls
Peter Fischli / David Weiss
Liam Gillick
Douglas Gordon
Mark Handforth
Candida Höfer
Alex Hubbard
Wyatt Kahn
Karen Kilimnik
Andrew Lord
Gerwald Rockenschaub
Tim Rollins & K.O.S.
Ugo Rondinone
Dieter Roth
Eva Rothschild
Jean-Frédéric Schnyder
Steven Shearer
Josh Smith
Oscar Tuazon
Franz West
Sue Williams
Michael Williams

Project Fulfill

Taipei

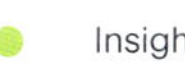

Insights

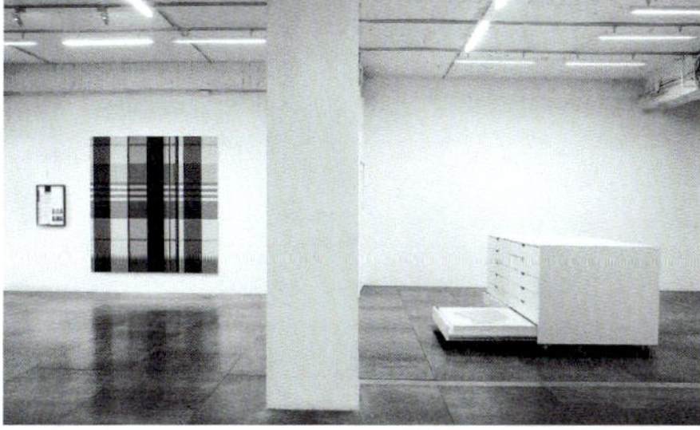

What is your favorite aspect of running a gallery?

Working with our favorite artists and getting to know them better, not only their work but also their personality.

Growing with artists either in a positive way or a painful one is a blessed journey.

How do you choose the artists you work with?

I am looking for artists who show focus, consistency, passion, not trend followers, and who can bare the loneliness before getting somewhere. Their work should show intriguing concepts, and be visually pleasant so that I cannot stop thinking about them overnight.

If you weren't running a gallery what else would you do?

I would be in the fashion business, be an event coordinator, and a collector.

- **Contact** Project Fulfill Art Space
Pei Yu Lin
infopfarts@gmail.com
- **Established** 2008
- **Owner** Pei Yu Lin
- **Team** 2
- **Space(s)** 198 m²
- **Artists at Art Basel** Chou Yu-Cheng
LuxuryLogico
Wang Chung-Kun
Wang Fuijui
- **Further artists represented** Chen Sung-Chih
Hsu Chiao-Yen
Teng Chao Ming
Tu Pei-Shih
Wang Sean
Wu Chang-Jung

ProjecteSD

Barcelona

Galleries

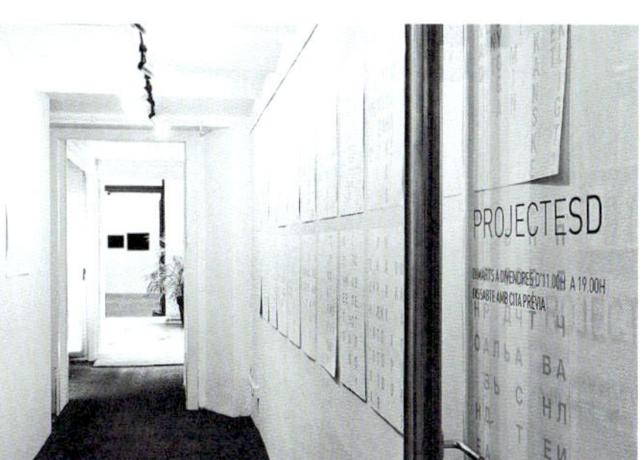

What is your favorite aspect of running a gallery?

The interaction with the artists and the mediation between them, their art, and the audience (collectors, museums, curators, but also visitors and students).

How do you choose the artists you work with?

The quality of the work is the key thing. I also have to be able to develop a good relationship with the artist. I am more a gallerist than a dealer and in my view to represent an artist is a long-term issue.

If you weren't running a gallery what else would you do?

I would simply work. Sometimes you cannot choose, but I would fit best in a working environment that involves research and that can give me intellectual gratification. I also very much like the interaction with people.

- **Contact** ProjecteSD
Silvia Dauder
sd@projectesd.com
- **Established** 2003
- **Owner(s) / Partner(s)** Silvia Dauder
- **Team** 3
- **Space(s)** 250 m²
- **Artists at Art Basel** Iñaki Bonillas
Raimond Chaves
Patricia Dauder
Koenraad Dedobbeleer
Dora García
Guillaume Leblon
Jochen Lempert
Asier Mendizabal
Matt Mullican
Marc Nagtzaam
Peter Piller
Christoph Weber
- **Further artists represented** Hans-Peter Feldmann
Xavier Ribas
Pieter Vermeersch

P

Proyectos Monclova

Mexico City

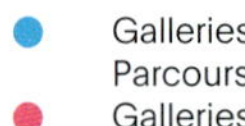

Galleries
Parcours
Galleries

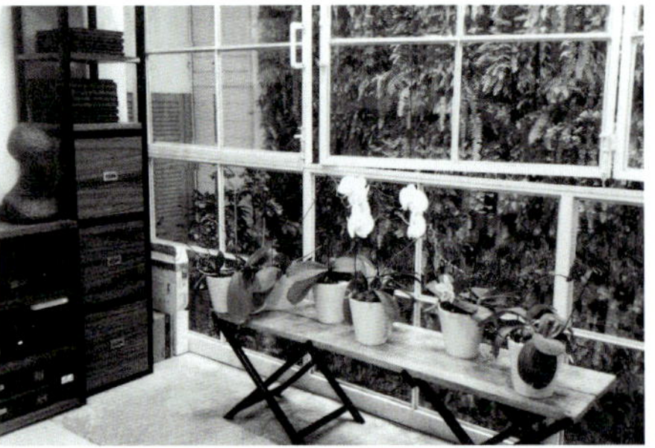

What is your favorite aspect of running a gallery?

Of course working with the artists and making connections in order to provide the meanings for great things to happen, and then looking at the results, being able to enjoy and share them.

How do you choose the artists you work with?

It's been very organic and different each time. I have never literally gone out searching for artists. The artists that we have been working with are artists with whom we have a strong connection in terms of the work as well as on a personal level.

If you weren't running a gallery what else would you do?

While working at the gallery I realized that I love temporary constructions and building with drywall panels. If I were not directing the gallery I would perhaps be doing that.

- **Contact** — Proyectos Monclova
  Polina Stroganova
  polina@proyectosmonclova.com
- **Established** — 2005
- **Owner(s) / Partner(s)** — José García Torres
  Teofilo Cohen
  David Trabulsi
- **Team** — 7
- **Space(s)** — 430 m²
- **Artists at Art Basel** — Nina Beier
  Mario García Torres
  Federico Herrero
  Christian Jankowski
  Tercerunquinto
  Eduardo Terrazas
- **Further artists represented** — Edgardo Aragón
  François Bucher
  José León Cerrillo
  Simon Fujiwara
  Marie Lund
  Tania Pérez Córdova
  Julia Rometti & Victor Costales
  Eduardo Sarabia

PSM

Berlin

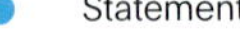

Statements

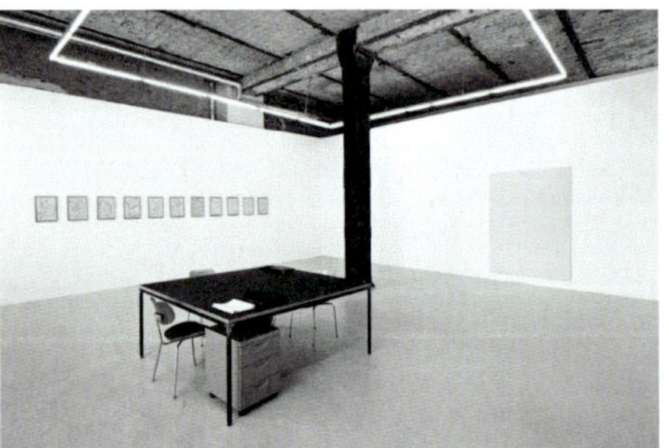

What is your favorite aspect of running a gallery?

Running a gallery means managing young and emerging artists and growing together with them toward an international career. My favorite aspect is the close and ongoing relationship with the artists and their work.

How do you choose the artists you work with?

The artists I work with catch my attention by creating works with new twists of either theoretical or physical practices with an emphasis on authentic, deep, personal connections.

If you weren't running a gallery what else would you do?

After working in a museum and galleries and running a project space together with a co-curator, my choice was to start gallery. It is what I want to do.

- **Contact** — PSM
  Sabine Schmidt
  sabine@psm-gallery.com
- **Established** — 2008
- **Owner(s) / Partner(s)** — Sabine Schmidt
- **Team** — 5
- **Space(s)** — 200 m²
- **Artists at Art Basel** — Christian Falsnaes
  Nadira Husain
  Daniel Jackson
  Nathan Peter
- **Further artists represented** — Øystein Aasan
  Awst & Walther
  Eduardo Basualdo
  Thomas Chapman
  Paolo Chiasera
  Pauline Curnier Jardin
  Sophie Erlund
  Ujino Muneteru
  Anca Munteanu Rimnic
  Ariel Reichman

P.P.O.W

Interview with Wendy Olsoff

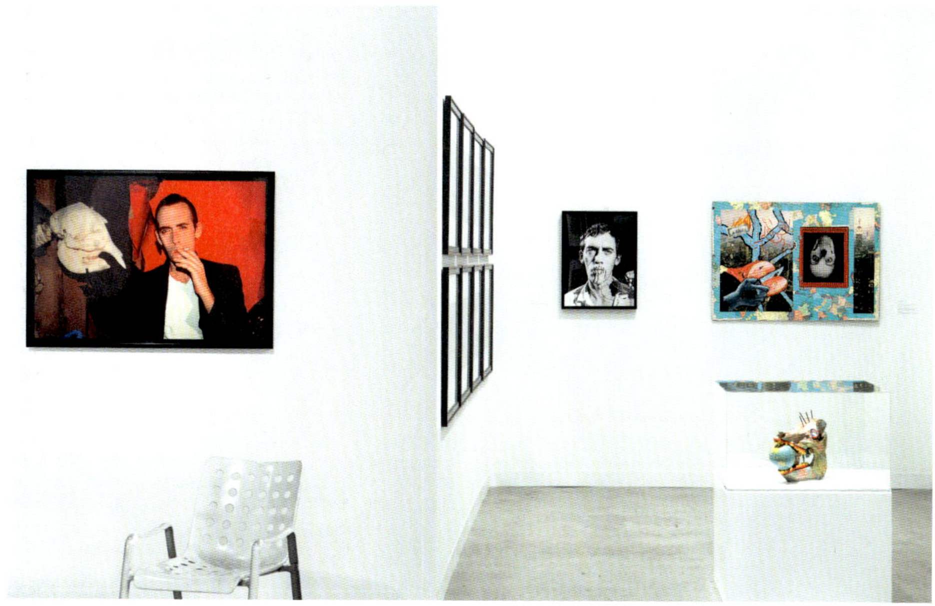

Art Basel in Miami Beach, 2014

What does P.P.O.W mean?

When we opened in the East Village in 1983, galleries had names like Civilian Warfare or Gracie Mansion, and we didn't want either a traditional name or a "creative one": it's a combination of my initials and those of my business partner, Penny Pilkington. At the time it also referred to "prisoner of war" and reflected a feeling in the East Village, a neighborhood where there was a lot of drug dealing, poverty. It fit into that time and has lasted for 32 years!

What did you do before opening the gallery?

I worked at other galleries, including a South American gallery in New York. Penny's parents owned a gallery called Piccadilly Gallery that showed at Art Basel at the very beginning of the fair—she's English. We met at Leslie Waddington's gallery.

What was opening a gallery in the East Village in the early 1980s like?

We were 25 years old, living Uptown, and often going to the East Village. We asked Gracie Mansion how her gallery was doing, she said fine. We decided within two weeks to open ours. We found a little storefront on 10th Street and an apartment, a 6th-floor walk up in a tenement. We did everything ourselves, painted it, renovated it, and we started to frantically visit artists' studios. It was an amazing moment because we had just opened and all of a sudden limousines, collectors, and museum curators pulled up—and we had no idea of what we were really doing! I think if we had known we wouldn't have done it, or we would have taken more time to think about it. So we very much developed in the public eye. Penny and I were not that interested in contemporary art before: Penny's parents showed George Grosz, I studied Renaissance and Rococo-Baroque art; but we wanted to show artists that we chose.

Our first show was very important to us: Sue Coe is a very important illustrator and political artist. The show sold out and was reviewed in *Artforum*. We really thought it was going to be that easy all the time! Because of Sue, we instantly became a gallery that political and feminist artists, people who had a connection with politics, immediately appreciated. And we've stayed true to that.

When did you start showing David Wojnarowicz?

We started showing him in 1988. It was after his East Village fame, when he was diagnosed with AIDS. He was having a resurgence of popularity because he started making such strong work about the AIDS crisis and speaking out about it, fusing photography and language, painting and performance. He had also been censored by the American Family Foundation and taken to court. We were supporting him through all of that. It was a spectacular time. We also represented Carrie Mae Weems at that time. We showed her for 15 years. These artists kind of defined us in the 1990s; we learned so much from them.

Later we added Martha Wilson. We also show Carolee Schneemann now—she fits into our history. But we keep looking for younger voices that can add to that dialogue. The times have changed, but they are out there.

You are also showing Martin Wong and now represent his estate.

We showed and promoted his work for years, though no one was interested. We worked with two estates [Wong and Wojnarowicz], kind of shepherding them, and waiting, for a long time. All of a sudden young curators get interested in them because they studied them in graduate school, because their professors were intellectuals, and they want to bring these works to the public. It's a wonderful process to live through as a dealer, but it takes time, sometimes decades.

You mentioned the specific political identity of your gallery: one can easily understand how it relates to museum curators and academics, but how does it work with a younger generation of artists?

I think artists can serve as role models for what a gallery can be: we can be a commercial gallery, we can be at an art fair, we can also have a connection to politics and social change, because I believe that the art that we showed preceded gay marriage, President Obama, etc. The artists know first what's going to happen and the gallery supports them. You can witness and participate in real social change.

I don't know what the artists think, but I feel I understand our role as being in turn role models for younger dealers: to maintain integrity, even in this commercial atmosphere, to say that art dealers are not bad, are not villains, are not greedy: we are art workers, and we work very hard.

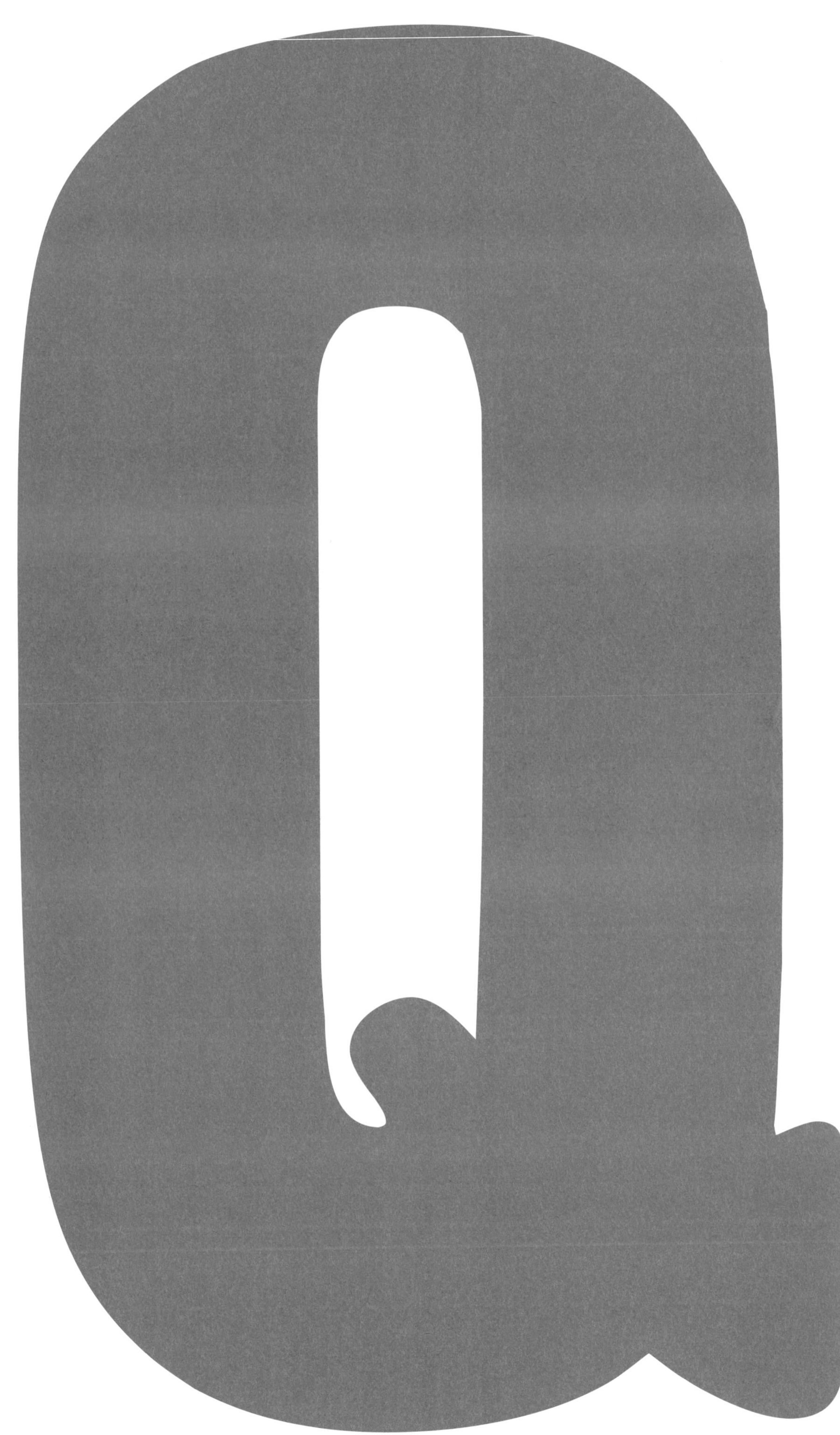

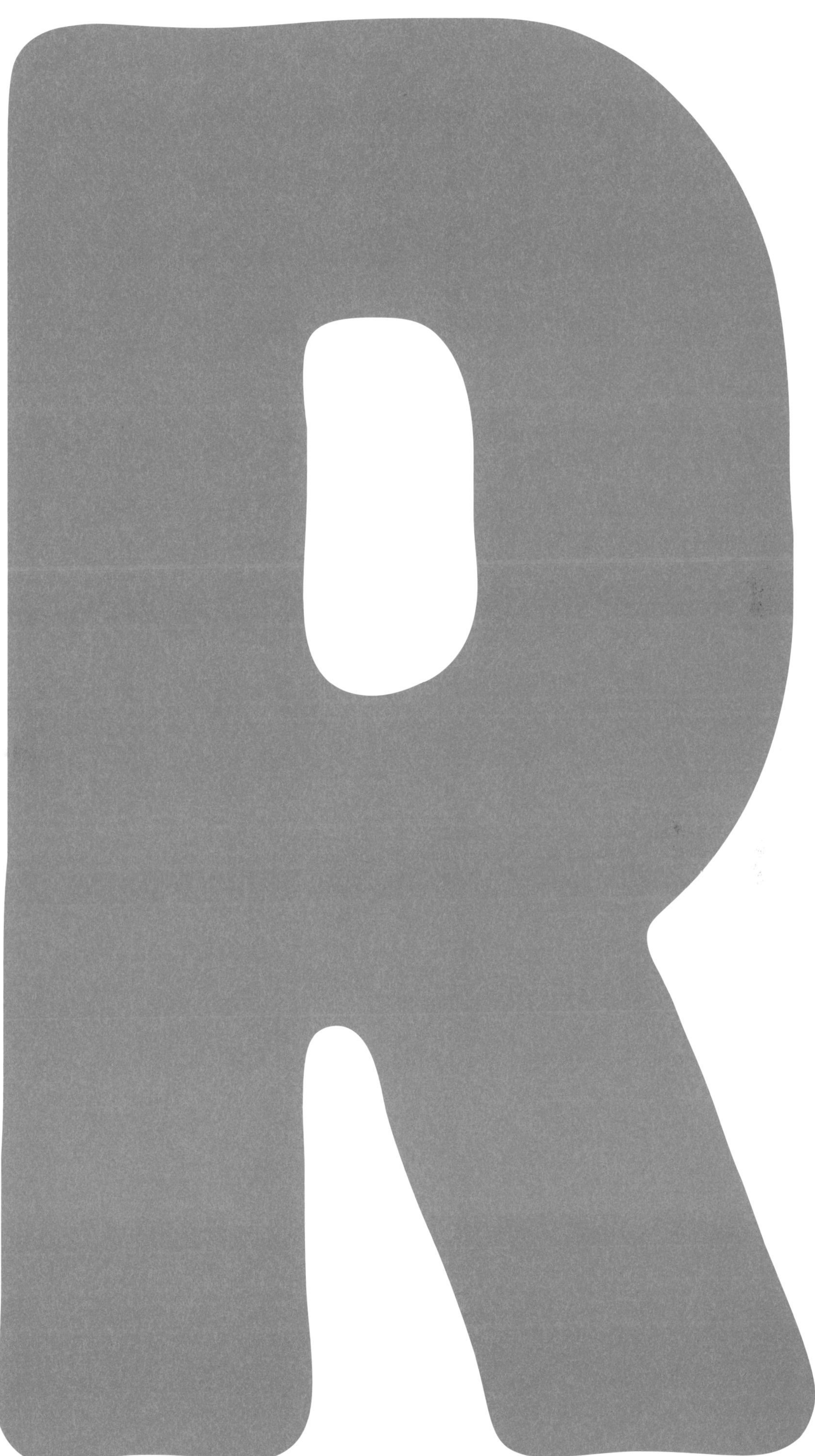

Rudolf Stingel
Untitled (Paula), 2012
Unlimited, Art Basel, 2012

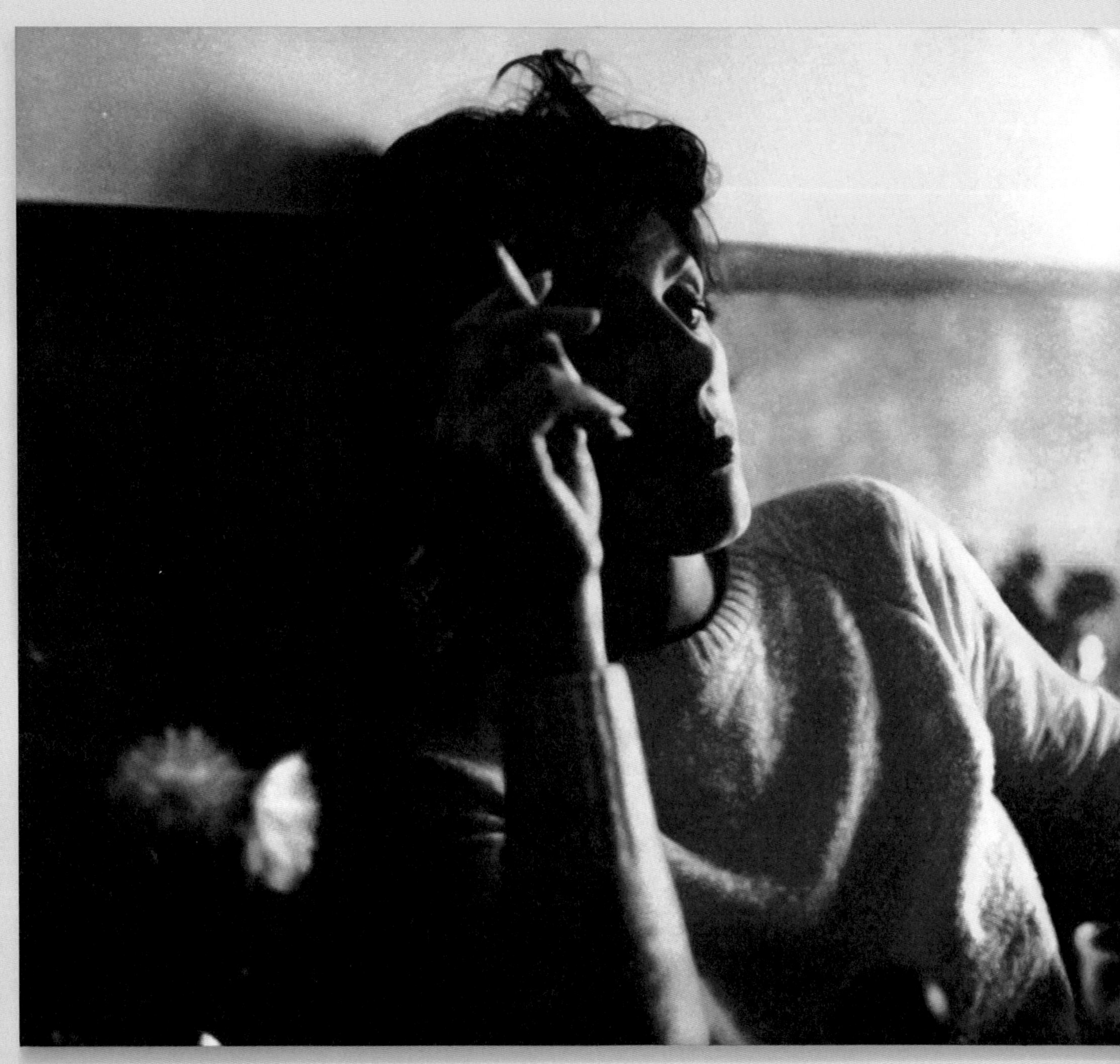

RETRO SPECT IVE: PAULA COO PER

"To Work Magic of a Sort"
A Retrospective Conversation with Paula Cooper

CLÉMENT DIRIÉ When talking to Matthew Higgs you once said that you had wanted to start a gallery and to work with artists since you were 17 or 18 years old—at the time you were living in Paris—and that you couldn't have done anything but art …

PAULA COOPER Most of my time in Paris was spent looking at art and visiting galleries. I knew the exact location of every Degas and Manet in the Louvre. I had no idea what I was going to do or how to do it. I wasn't even finished with school … But art was always on my mind, and I knew that I wanted to help artists. I purposely refused to learn how to type; I'd be damned if I would be anyone's secretary. Never! When I moved to New York, not knowing how to do anything really, I worked for Chanel perfumes, then for the Japan Trade Center, which was rather hilarious and very interesting. The Japanese are so hip. It was the first year of Kabuki in New York and through a friend I met and spent the whole of their visit with the star Kanzaburō Nakamura and his wife. We saw *Psycho*, spent a lot of time with fans in transvestite clubs in the Village and sight saw. They became dear friends. I did many things until I finally began work at the World House Gallery, which was designed by Frederick Kiesler, with whom I became friendly. It was my apprenticeship and it was incredible—the gallery showed Alberto Giacometti, Jean Fautrier, Max Ernst, Jean Dubuffet, many European artists. The first show I ever installed was a Giorgio Morandi exhibition. Cordier & Ekstrom across the street (in Gagosian's first space) became my hangout and Arne Ekstrom a good friend. Henry Geldzahler, who had just started his post at the Met, would stop by the gallery and bring me news about the contemporary art world. It was because of him that I first started attending "Happenings." In 1962 or 1963 I met Steve Pepper, a graduate student of art history who had a space uptown on Broadway. He showed contemporary artists like Red Grooms, held performances and introduced me to artist Bob Thompson. He later became a professor of art history at Johns Hopkins University and disappeared from the New York art scene. He was an important influence on me. He made me aware that a gallery could be free, something else, a space for all kinds of artistic endeavors.

I opened my gallery with an exhibition against the war in Vietnam. There was a great divide: people who were strongly pro and con. I had friends who wouldn't speak to me because of my beliefs. –Paula Cooper

CD You opened your gallery in 1968, but before that you briefly ran a first gallery [Paula Johnson Gallery in 1964].

PC Yes. I showed Bob Thompson … He, his wife Carol, and I became friends and frequently would hang out at the Five Spot. Walter De Maria had his first New York one-person show at the gallery, and through him I met a lot of other younger artists. I remember Walter's opening: there were about 15–20 people—La Monte Young and Marian Zazeela were there, Simone Forti and Robert Whitman too—and at one point the room became silent, people sat down around the perimeter of the room and remained silent for about 5 minutes. It was the kind of mystical "event" that Walter would inspire. All of this was very exciting to me …

I had met artists at World House but not so many young ones. However I really didn't know how to make the business side of it work. I married very young and got divorced around that time, too. I then went to work for Park Place [1965–1967], a cooperative of ten artists—five painters and five sculptors. I still work with two of them: Mark di Suvero and Robert Grosvenor, and I'm close to David Novros.

LIONEL BOVIER They called themselves the "Park Place group"?

PC That was the name of the street where they were originally located. I was there for two and a half years during which time I met Carl Andre and Sol LeWitt, who were my idols. I knew their work quite well, but I had never met them. It was a very small art world and artists of different disciplines supported each other—dancers, musicians, composers, visual artists. We did a concert with Steve Reich, for two nights. It was packed! I remember Philip Glass and Terry Riley played with the other musicians. I convinced Hohner, a piano company, to loan us equipment, telling them: "You'll get tremendous publicity from this concert," and you know, they actually did! It was that kind of environment. Everyone was supportive of everyone else. Everyone was poor, everyone was young, and had time …

CD You organized readings of Gertrude Stein's *The Making of Americans* and James Joyce's *Ulysses* for 25 years at the gallery, you did symposia, and organized concerts with Pandit Prân Nath, S.E.M. Ensemble, the Chamber Music Society, and others. Where did this diversity come from?

PC We had a continuous and varied series of concerts and dance at the gallery. Artists needed spaces to perform in. It's good for the space too. I believe in Karma … [*laughs*]

CD How did this idea of Gertrude Stein and James Joyce readings every January come about?

PC Jean Rigg, Alison Knowles, and John Cage came to me with the idea, and I said: "That's great! Let's do it!" And we did for years.

CD The first exhibition you did in 1968 was a benefit exhibition. So there was also this idea of supporting political issues.

PC Yes, I opened my gallery with an exhibition against the war in Vietnam. There was a great divide: people who were strongly pro and con. I had friends who wouldn't speak to me because of my beliefs.

CD In this exhibition Sol LeWitt made his first wall drawing. It was really a seminal exhibition for this generation of Minimal and Conceptual artists.

Paula Cooper,
New York, 1970

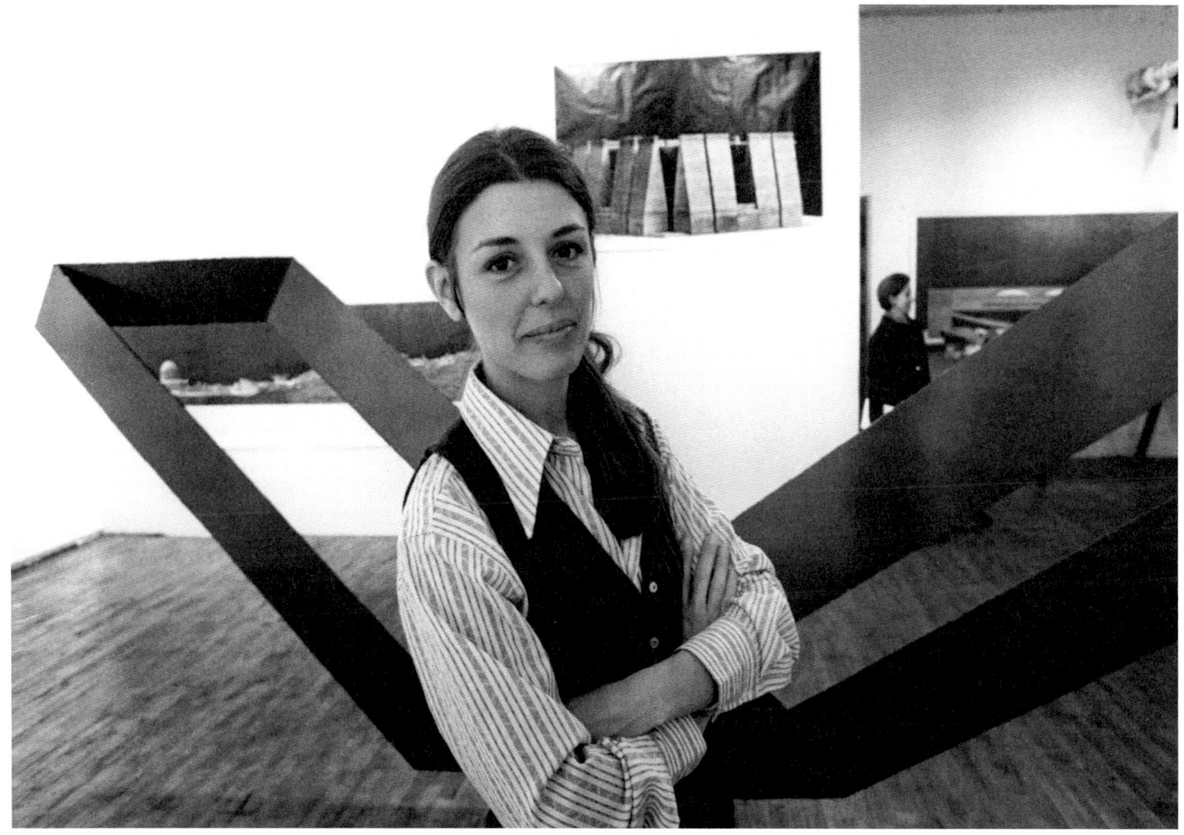

PC To me, these artists were already well known. Donald Judd, Dan Flavin, Robert Ryman, Carl Andre, etc. were already recognized as important artists by their peers. The show was put together by Lucy Lippard, Ron Wolin—who was Head of the Veterans Against the War—and the painter Robert Huot. The show was a benefit for the Student Mobilization Committee to End the War in Vietnam. It was a fabulous exhibition.

CD Was it a message to open the gallery with such a show? Was it intended as a statement about the relationship between art and society?

PC No. The way I approach things is more organic, not programmatic. It was about what I believed in, what many people believed in, and about true art. It was a way to act. Just act.

LB You were called an "activist" gallery several times ...

PC We had many events at the gallery. We have manifested our support for many political, moral, and social issues as well as various disciplines in the arts.

Art Basel in Basel, 2014

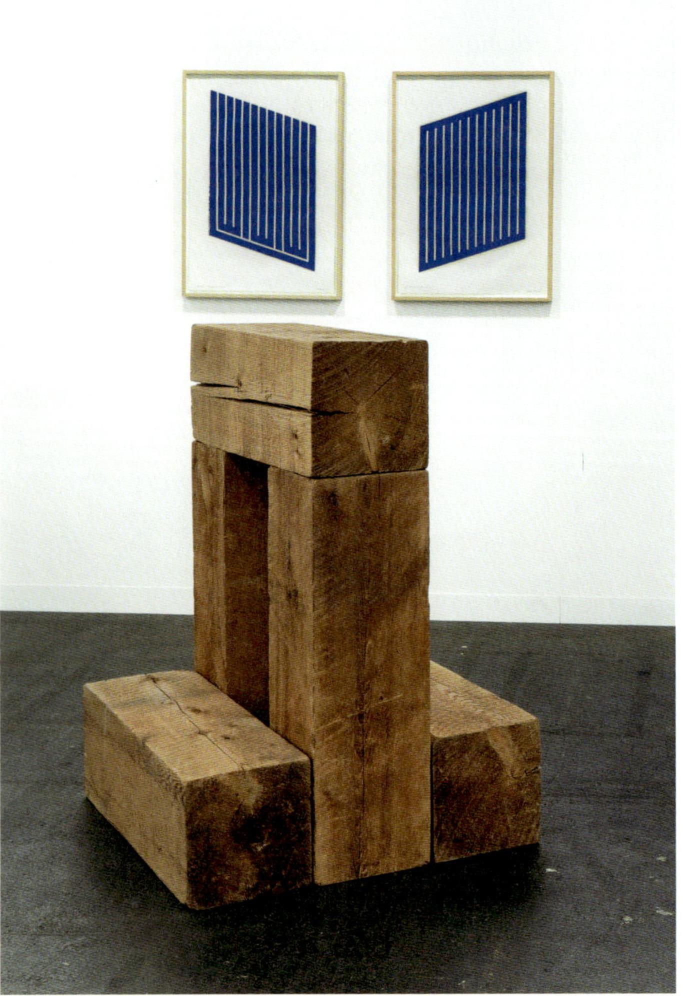

LB Speaking of activism, what was the atmosphere in New York like when you opened your gallery? Weren't the majority of dealers male at that time?

PC There have always been women dealers in New York. Edith Halpert was important. She dealt with work in the 1920s through the 1950s and she was very effective. There was also Martha Jackson, Eleanor Ward, Marian Willard, etc. But they never had the power or cachet that men had. They were often considered "second tier." The two biggest dealers, when I started, were Sidney Janis and Leo Castelli—Sidney was a great dealer. He bequeathed one of the most generous gifts ever to MoMA, with no restrictions.

LB What is it like to be at the beginning of a historical moment and to see now, with the distance of time, what history has made of it? There's a lot of interest, mostly genuine, for this period: a lot of documentation has been retrieved, a lot of publications have been done, some people even reenact shows of the past, and of course a commercial interest has been mixed with this research.[1] How do you look at this?

PC That's a complicated question with many facets. It's rewarding in many ways but it's hard to look at, too. There are too many distortions and manipulations at play. The art world is so different, even from ten years ago, that any connection with the past seems dislocated. It has absolutely nothing to do with what we were doing, nothing at all.

LB If everything changed that means even the artists did?

PC Of course, some artists are affected by this world. Thank God, some aren't.

LB What about the ways of collecting?

PC The whole economic and global situation is constantly changing. It's changed even since we began this interview!

LB You say that major changes are happening now, but wasn't this true already in the 1980s?

PC The change was slower then. The number of changes has increased in such a way that there is no precedent. The first auction of contemporary

1 The archives of the Paula Cooper Gallery from 1968 to 1973 were given by the gallery to the Archives of American Art (Washington).

works, the Scull sale, took place in 1973. There had never been a single evening sale devoted exclusively to contemporary art before. Thereafter, it never stopped. This November, Christie's contemporary sale brought in the highest-ever total for an auction, outdoing all other categories.

The art world is so different, even from ten years ago, that any connection with the past seems dislocated. It has absolutely nothing to do with what we were doing, nothing at all. —Paula Cooper

LB You've been working with artists such as Carl Andre over a very long period of time, so you've lived through changes.

PC Yes, over a period of several decades, an artist's financial success frequently ebbs and flows. It's happened to almost everyone: Warhol, Stella, Rauschenberg, etc. Donald Judd is the example I know best: he was well known but there was no market for his work in the early 1980s. We so believed in him, concentrated on the work, persistently exhibited it. We resurrected his career and made a huge market for him—then Pace stole him away! When you are working with artists, you have to be prepared for highs and lows. It's normal.

LB And you think that's part of the gallery's work to maintain that relationship with the artist even when it goes down?

PC Absolutely.

LB How many artists are, let's say, at the core of your gallery?

PC Something like 18 artists. We work with well-established, mid-career, very young artists, and, unlike 20 years ago, we also work with estates.

LB Do you continue to bring in young artists?

PC Yes! Most recently Justin Matherly, Tauba Auerbach, Matias Faldbakken, and Liz Glynn. And we've also started working with Charles Gaines, who is not a young artist but is new to the gallery.

CD Do you collect the artists you show?

PC Early on, if I wanted to keep a work and a collector came along and wanted that very work, I would give it up. I thought it more important that it get out into the world. So I missed a lot of great opportunities. I've never been a big collector. I do have works that I love and are meaningful to me and of course quite a few by artists we don't exhibit too—and I frequently drive people who work with me crazy because I say "no, no that's not for sale." But I have a modest collection.

CD I was surprised to discover that your first participation in Art Basel was in 1999, quite late compared to the creation of the gallery, which opened in 1968. Why is this?

PC For a long time I thought that it wasn't my job to "advertise," in the broadest sense of the term. I thus wouldn't publish books, nor advertise in magazines, nor have a booth at art fairs. As for the fair, I thought "I'd better do it once before I die, just to see what it's like, to experience it." The first time I visited Art Basel was right after documenta in 1972, and I was horrified! [*Laughs*] It was like an automobile show. I went straight to the Kunstmuseum after ... I must say you see some wonderful works from time to time. One year, there was an exhibition of Max Beckmann's portraits from the 1920s. That was very special. And then a lot of galleries started doing one-person exhibitions. When did that start?

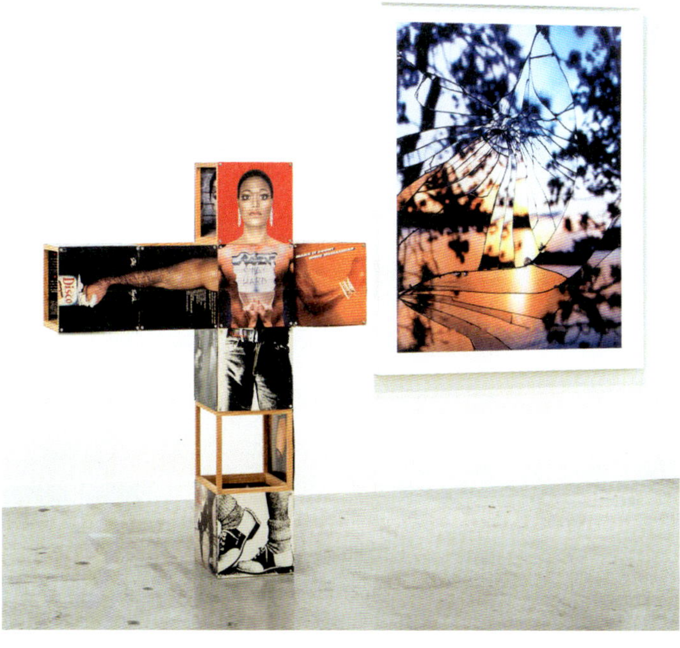

Art Basel in Miami Beach, 2014

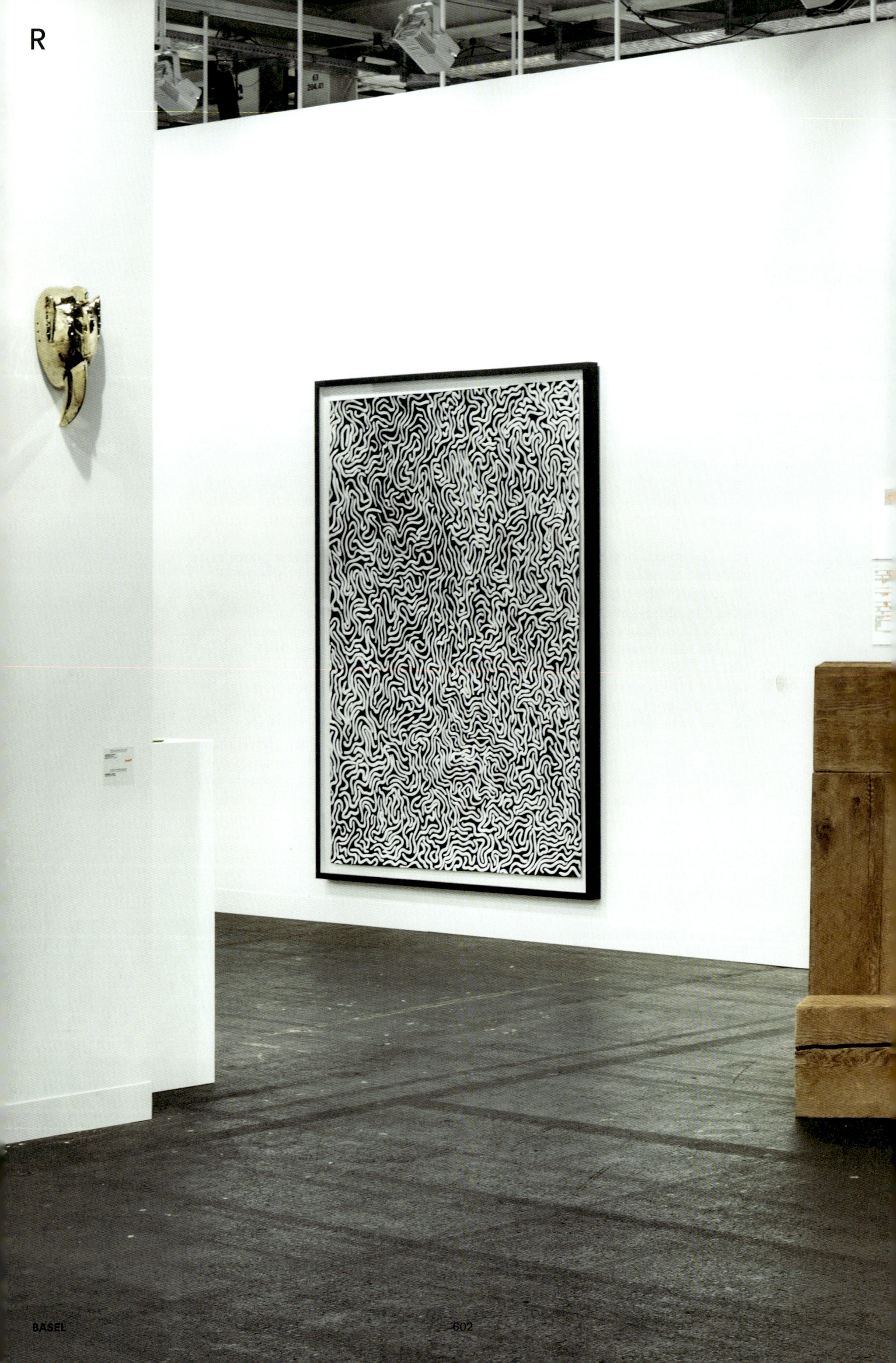

Paula Cooper Gallery
Art Basel in Basel
2014

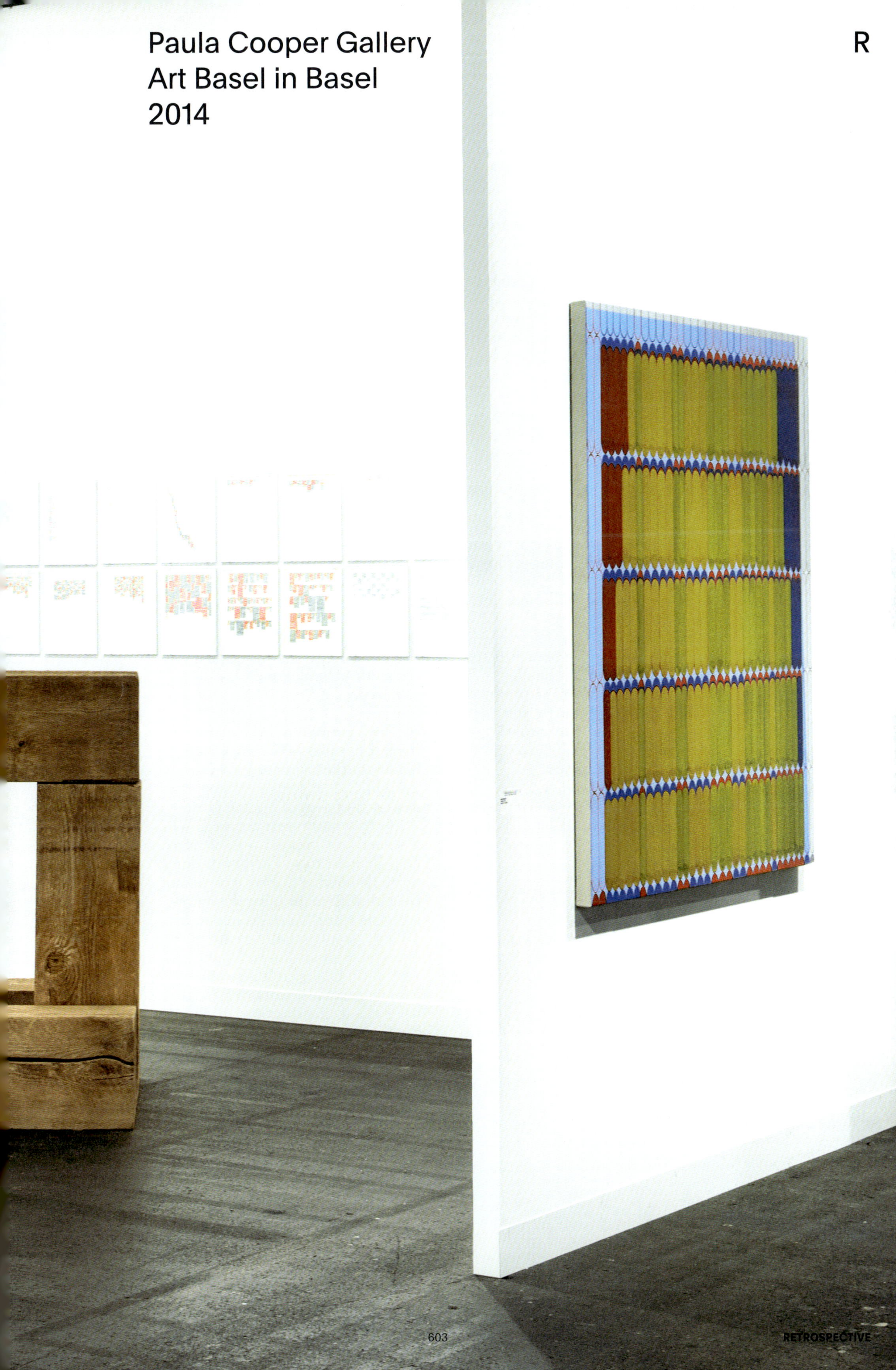

LB The "Perspective" platform was created in 1979 to showcase young artists through solo shows. It modified itself over the years and reappeared in 1996 with "Statements," again for showing young artists. The "Unlimited" platform and its large-scale installations started in 2000. They brought video in once as a separate sector, in the mid-1990s, through a sort of special gallery. Unlimited was, I think, a major factor of change for the fair as whole, because suddenly it really looked like an exhibition. Probably that had an impact on the way people conceived their own gallery booth: you also want to represent fully the capacity of the gallery to work on complex projects, not just on being transportable. But the project you mention could basically have been done any year by one of the modern art galleries ...

CD Why did you decide to continue to attend the fair after 1999?

PC After the first impulse of "I want to do it once," it worked somehow ...

LB So, it's been good for meeting new collectors?

PC Now it's very nice because I see people I've known for years in Europe and that I don't see often. A lot of them don't come to New York, or do so rarely. I also love to install works and we've always been very conscious of that aspect.

LB I think your space is installed as if it were the gallery. It's not about using all the space, it's more about doing a nice show.

PC Yes.

LB Have you ever done special projects for the fair, like inviting an artist to do something specific for the booth?

PC No and some artists actually won't participate in a fair, like Hans Haacke.

LB I'm surprised to hear you didn't want to publish books, as I've always seen you having a great affinity with books. There are also connections with some of the artists you work with: one can see for instance a lot of Carl Andre poems in this fair; Sol LeWitt was a great amateur and a great maker of artists' books, and co-founded Printed Matter. Dan Walsh and Tauba Auerbach make books. There's a thread of people who like books in your gallery. And some years ago you even opened a bookshop!

PC I was always a voracious reader. My husband is a publisher and I love bookstores. But to me, at the time, publishing a book equaled self-promotion. If an outside entity like a museum published a book, it was different, it was a bona fide validation of the artist. Now, from time to time, we do venture into some publishing projects. We also have a little record label, Dog w/a Bone.

CD You gave an interview in which you said that the history of your gallery reflects the history of the art world over the last few decades in New York. How would you consider the legacy of the gallery, not only regarding artists and works, but also the spirit behind it and what you achieved.

PC My history is not the history of the last decades—Gagosian is the history of the last decades. Leo Castelli, Sidney Janis were important dealers, in terms of placing great works by mostly great artists ... What has been very important to me is to help an artist to succeed in the long term. Of course, I've been fortunate to work with many outstanding artists. The word "spirit" is important. To help people see things differently, open their minds, infuse their lives with a wholeness, at least while looking at a particular work of art—to work magic of a sort.

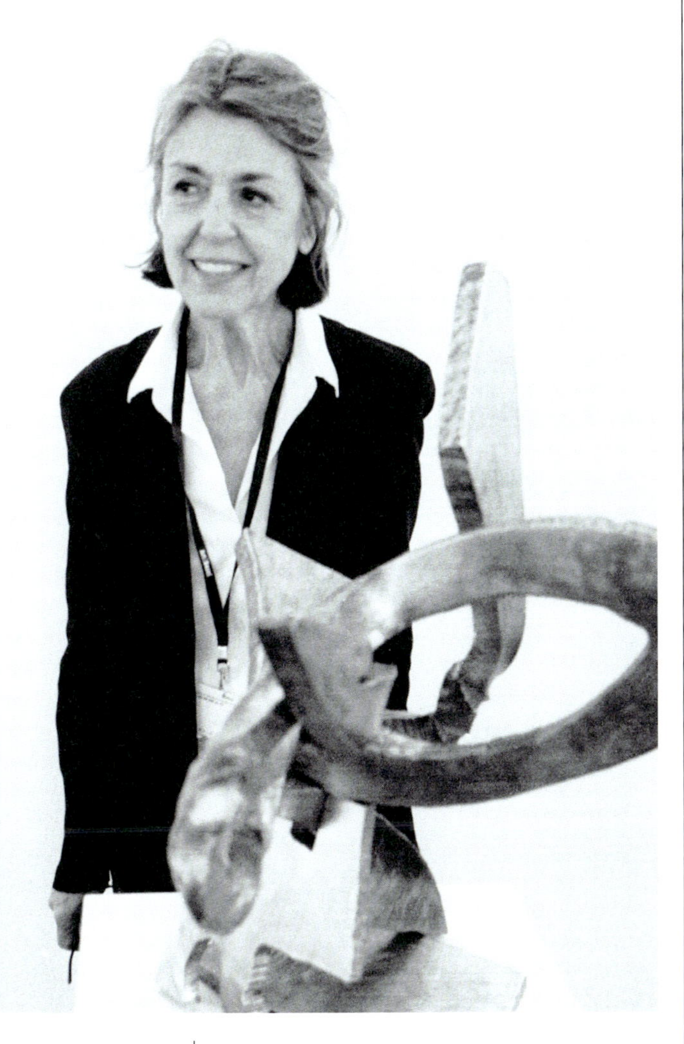

To help people see things differently, open their minds, infuse their lives with a wholeness, at least while looking at a particular work of art—to work magic of a sort.
—Paula Cooper

Justin Matherly, *Sunrise*, 2013, Art Basel in Basel, Unlimited, 2013

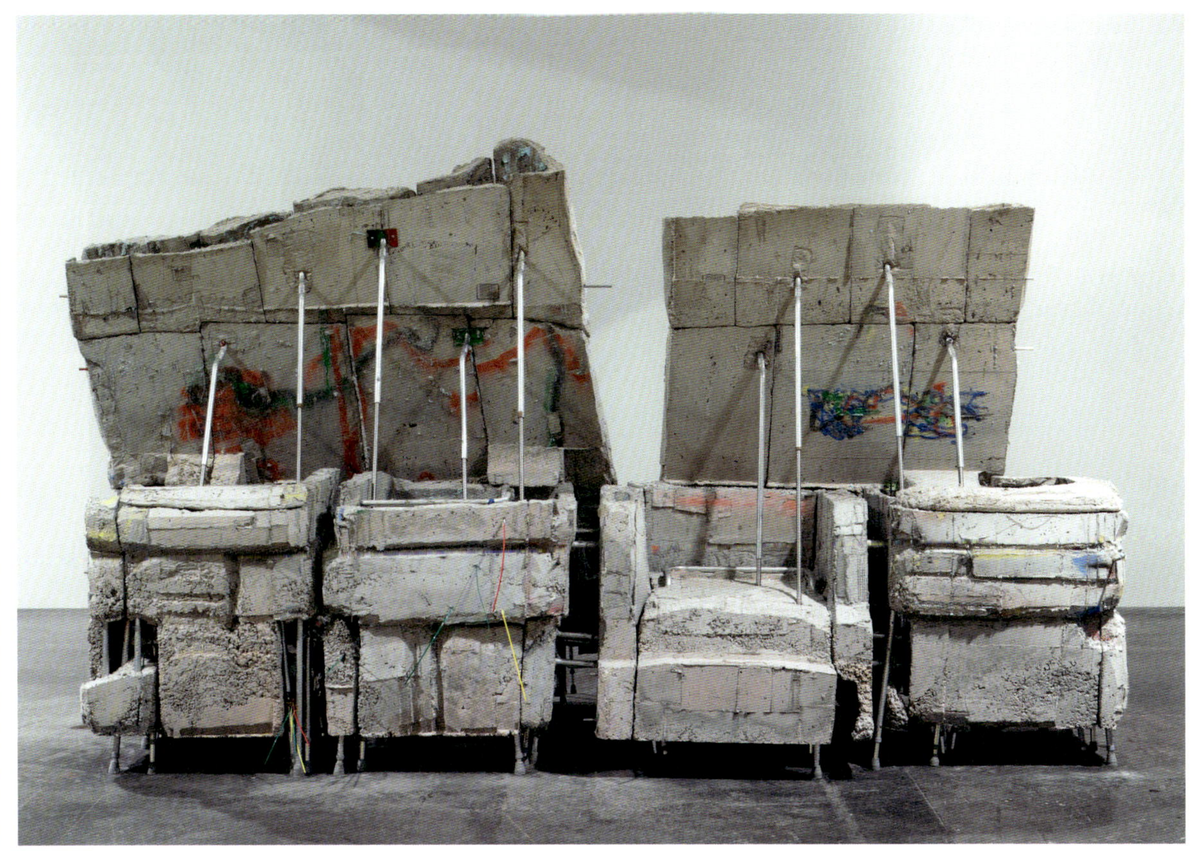

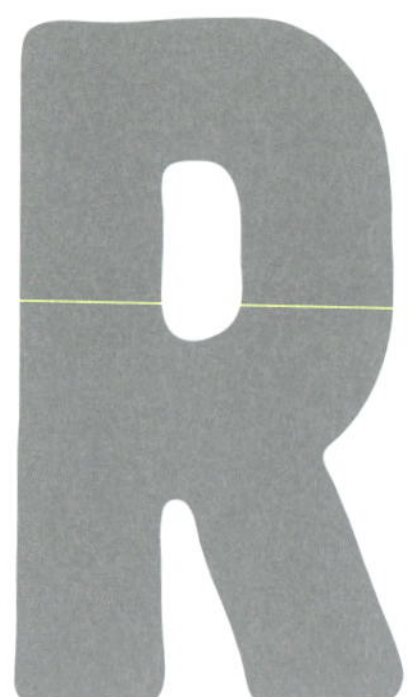

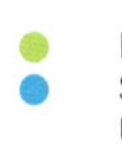

RaebervonStenglin

Zurich

- Discoveries
- Statements
- Unlimited
- Positions

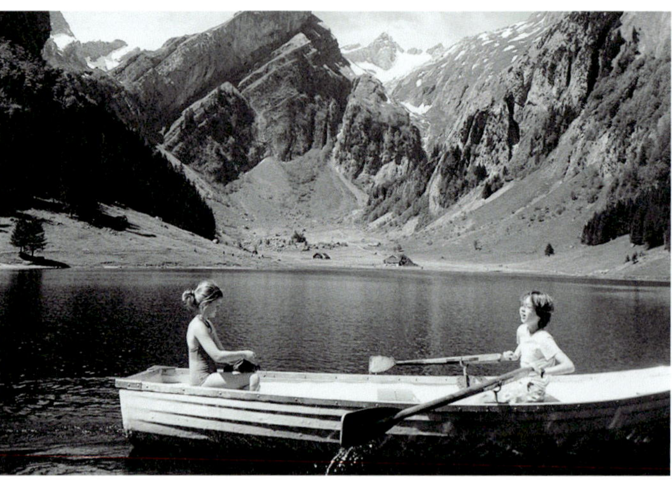

What is your favorite aspect of running a gallery?
Inviting all of our artists and friends at the openings for beer and sausages.

How do you choose the artists you work with?
We turn the wheel of fortune.

If you weren't running a gallery what else would you do?
Run a bar in Barbados.

- **Contact** RaebervonStenglin
Matthias von Stenglin
info@raebervonstenglin.com
- **Established** 2010
- **Owner(s) / Partner(s)** Beat Raeber
Matthias von Stenglin
- **Team** 3
- **Space(s)** 100 m²
- **Artists at Art Basel** Thomas Julier
Dane Mitchell
Taiyo Onorato & Nico Krebs
- **Further artists represented** Saâdane Afif
Andrew Dadson
Karsten Födinger
Raphael Hefti
Sofia Hultén
David Keating
Robert Kinmont
Susanne Kriemann
Manuela Leinhoß
Jill Magid
Kilian Rüthemann
Ivan Seal
Alexander Wagner

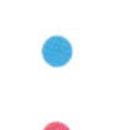

Ramiken Crucible

New York

- Statements
- Unlimited
- Positions

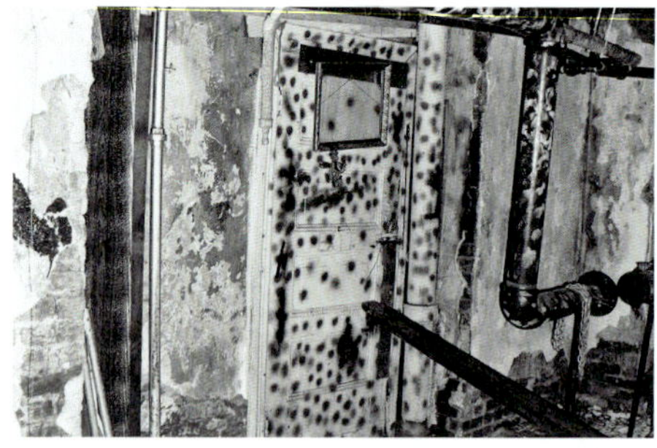

What is your favorite aspect of running a gallery?
Time.

How do you choose the artists you work with?
We consult the Buzz-o-tron 5,000 index.

If you weren't running a gallery what else would you do?
Even more drugs.

- **Contact** Ramiken Crucible
Blaize Lehane
blaize@ramiken.biz
- **Established** 2009
- **Owner(s) / Partner(s)** Blaize Lehane
Mike Ursuta
- **Artists at Art Basel** Lucas Blalock
Borden Capalino
Gavin Kenyon
Andra Ursuta

Razuk

São Paulo

- Positions
Public

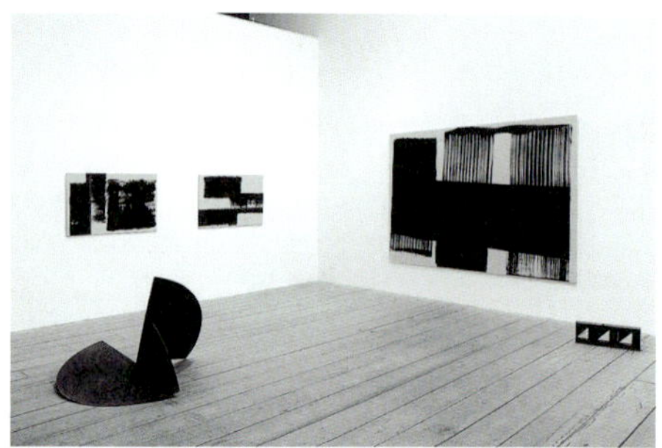

What is your favorite aspect of running a gallery?
Being in contact with art and artists, and having the opportunity to introduce them to the public.

How do you choose the artists you work with?
Visiting studios, exhibitions, talking to curators, reading, researching, and also using my feeling.

If you weren't running a gallery what else would you do?
I would work for a museum.

- **Contact** Galeria Marilia Razuk
Marcela Razuk
marcela@galeriamariliarazuk.com.br
- **Established** 1992
- **Owner** Marilia Razuk
- **Team** 10
- **Space(s)** 200 m²
- **Artists at Art Basel** Ana Luiza Dias Batista
Maria Laet
Wagner Malta Tavares
- **Further artists represented** Marlon de Azambuja
José Bechara
Cabelo
Johanna Calle
Alexandre Canonico

Amilcar de Castro
Rodrigo de Castro
Raquel Garbelotti
Vanderlei Lopes
Fabricio Lopez
Lucia Mindlin Loeb
Julio Plaza
Gustavo Rezende
Sergio Romagnolo
Hilal Sami Hilal
Mariana Serri
Marina Weffort
Paulo Whitaker

Real Fine Arts

New York — Nova

- **Contact** Real Fine Arts
  Tyler Dobson
  realfinearts@gmail.com
- **Established** 2008
- **Owner(s) / Partner(s)** Tyler Dobson & Ben Morgan-Cleveland
- **Team** 4
- **Space(s)** 65 m²
- **Artists at Art Basel** Jon Pestoni
  Sam Pulitzer
- **Further artists represented** Yuji Agematsu
  Nicolas Ceccaldi
  Whitney Claflin
  Jana Euler
  Flame
  Manuel Gnam
  Bill Hayden
  Lena Henke
  Anne Imhof
  Morag Keil
  Andrei Koschmieder
  Caitlin MacBride
  Mathieu Malouf
  Alissa McKendrick
  Dave Miko
  Heji Shin
  Stefan Tcherepnin
  Ned Vena
  Amelie von Wulffen
  Antek Walczak

Rech

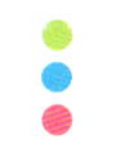

Paris — Galleries
Brussels — Galleries
London — Galleries
Public

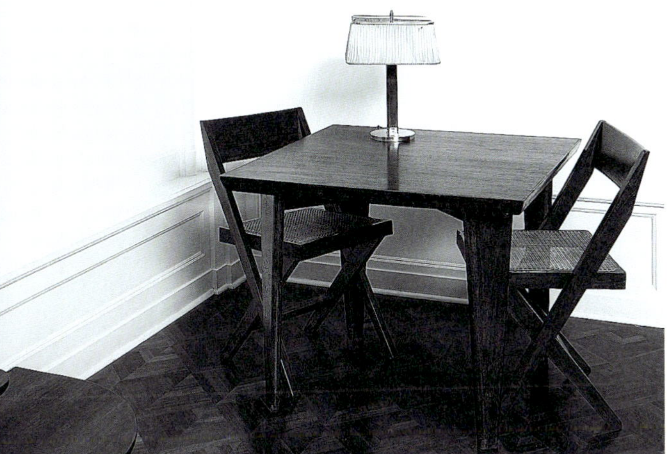

What is your favorite aspect of running a gallery?

My favorite aspect is when I can visit an artist's studio, an established artist or an emerging one.

How do you choose the artists you work with?

I travel around the world a lot and visit diverse places seeing shows, and if there is an artwork that strongly catches my eye I try to contact the artist. And then when I see more works in the studio and still like it, the human relation comes into play, as obviously it's important to get along with an artist to collaborate well. I have no aesthetic criteria in my choices, they are my personal choices.

If you weren't running a gallery what else would you do?

I did film studies, so that could have been the field I work in.

- **Contact** Almine Rech Gallery
  Marie Jasseron
  marie@alminerech.com
- **Established** 1997
- **Owner(s) / Partner(s)** Almine Rech
- **Team** 18
- **Space(s)** 905 m²
- **Artists at Art Basel** Jo Baer
  Matthias Bitzer
  Don Brown
  Alexander Calder
  Mary Corse
  Aaron Curry
  Ayan Farah
  Mark Hagen
  Gregor Hildebrandt
  Jeff Koons
  Jannis Kounellis
  Erik Lindman
  Joel Morrison
  David Ostrowski
  Helen Pashgian
  Peter Peri
  Pablo Picasso
  Richard Prince
  Ugo Rondinone
  Joel Shapiro
  Turi Simeti
  Taryn Simon
  Ida Tursic & Wilfried Mille
  Dewain Valentine
  Francesco Vezzoli
  Brent Wadden
  Su Xiaobai
  Aaron Young
- **Further artists represented** Ziad Antar
  Joe Bradley
  Tom Burr
  Beatrice Caracciolo
  Johan Creten
  Philip-Lorca Di Corcia
  Sylvie Fleury
  John Giorno
  Adam Helms
  Patrick Hill
  Alex Israel
  Thomas Kiesewetter
  Joseph Kosuth
  Ange Leccia
  Daniel Lergon
  John McCracken
  Sarah Parke & Mark Barrow
  Anselm Reyle
  Matthieu Ronsse
  Katja Strunz
  Eduardo Terrazas
  Gavin Turk
  James Turrell
  Not Vital
  Liu Wei
  Franz West
  Tsuruko Yamazaki
  Yeesookyung

Reena Spaulings

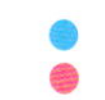

New York — Galleries
Galleries

- **Contact** Reena Spaulings Fine Art
  Jake Palmert
  jake@reenaspaulings.com
- **Established** 2003
- **Owner(s) / Partner(s)** John Kelsey
  Emily Sundblad
- **Team** 6
- **Space(s)** 279 m²
- **Artists at Art Basel** Merlin Carpenter
  Michaela Eichwald
  Matias Faldbakken
  K8 Hardy
  Klara Liden
  Valentina Liernur

Georgie Nettell
Ken Okiishi
Henrik Olesen
Seth Price
Josephine Pryde
Peter Wächtler
Stephen Willats

- **Further artists represented** Shadi Habib Allah
Ei Arakawa
Stephan Dillemuth
Kim Gordon
Jutta Koether
Nora Schultz

Regen Projects

Los Angeles

Galleries Unlimited
Galleries

- **Contact** Regen Projects
Shaun Caley Regen
office@regenprojects.com
- **Established** 1989
- **Owner** Shaun Caley Regen
- **Artists at Art Basel** Doug Aitken
Matthew Barney
Walead Beshty
John Bock
Abraham Cruzvillegas
Lizzie Fitch/Ryan Trecartin
Dan Graham
Rachel Harrison
Elliott Hundley
Christian Jankowski
Sergej Jensen
Anish Kapoor
Toba Khedoori
Gabriel Kuri
Liz Larner
Glenn Ligon
Scott McFarland
Marilyn Minter
Catherine Opie
Jennifer Pastor
Manfred Pernice
Raymond Pettibon
Elizabeth Peyton
Jack Pierson
Lari Pittman
Richard Prince
Daniel Richter
Willem de Rooij
Gary Simmons
Wolfgang Tillmans
Ryan Trecartin
Gillian Wearing
Lawrence Weiner
James Welling
Sue Williams
Andrea Zittel

René

Paris

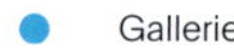

Galleries

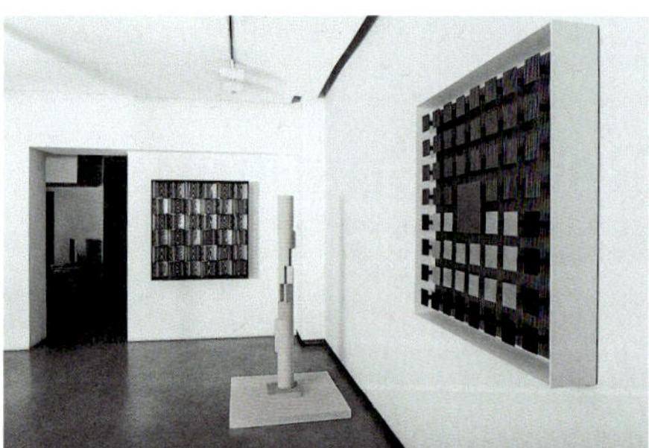

What is your favorite aspect of running a gallery?
The main focus of the work in the gallery is contact with the artists, workshop visits, and discussions about their art. These exchanges allow us to understand their approach better and always remain up-to-date with the new generation of creators and new techniques of conception and realization, so that I can carefully select works that will be shown in exhibitions. The conception and realization of an exhibition is a delicate moment: you have to highlight each artist in a set that can be heterogeneous.

How do you choose the artists you work with?
When Denise René created the gallery, she defined a strong artistic line: geometric abstraction and kinetic art. The artists she defended are still exhibited by the gallery. The younger ones are chosen in the same spirit. We are lucky enough to have a new generation of creators; I am attentive to their works and I try to select those that I think will become the masters of tomorrow. Beyond technique and technology, I make my selection on the quality and the poetry of their proposals.

If you weren't running a gallery what else would you do?
Apart from being a gallery, I have also had a career in architecture and publishing. These professions are quite similar to the conception and realization of a finished object. If I had to change, I would like to participate in the integration of art in architecture and in the city. For me, with the artists of our gallery we must continue to work for the diffusion of art for the greatest number.

- **Contact** Galerie Denise René
Denis Kilian
info@deniserene.com
- **Established** 1944
- **Owner(s) / Partner(s)** Denis Kilian
- **Team** 4
- **Space(s)** 200 m²
- **Artists at Art Basel** Yaacov Agam
Jean Arp
David Bill
Jakob Bill
Max Bill
Anne Blanchet
Geneviève Claisse
Elias Crespin
Carlos Cruz-Diez
Karl Gerstner
Gun Gordillo
Auguste Herbin
Youri Jeltov
Matti Kujasalo
LAb[au]
Pe Lang
Julio Le Parc
Vincent Leroy
Aurélie Nemours
Jesus Rafael Soto
Haruhiko Sunagawa
Sophie Taeuber-Arp
Santiago Torres
Wolfram Ullrich
Victor Vasarely
Zimoun
- **Further artists represented** Josef Albers
Olle Baertling
Martha Boto
Pol Bury
Marcelle Cahn
Waltercio Caldas
Chryssa
Cicero Dias
Sonia Delaunay
Hugo Demarco
Ángel Duarte
Equipo 57
Günter Fruhtrunk
Horacio Garcia-Rossi
Jean Gorin
André Heurtaux
Robert Indiana
Robert Jacobsen
Lajos Kassák
Michalis Katzourakis
František Kupka
Le Corbusier
Walter Leblanc
Richard Paul Lohse
Angel Luque
José Macaparana
Heinz Mack
François Morellet
Richard Mortensen
Mehdi Moutashar
Takashi Naraha
César Paternosto
Dario Perez-Flores
Ivan Picelj
Nicolas Schöffer
Francisco Sobrino

Henryk Stazewski
Joël Stein
Jean Tinguely
Luis Tomasello
Gregorio Vardanega
Wen-Ying Tsai
Jean-Pierre Yvaral

Revolver

Lima

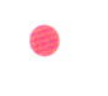

Positions
Public

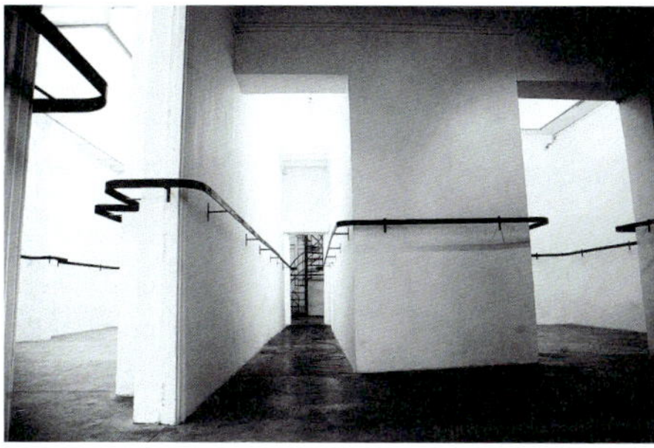

What is your favorite aspect of running a gallery?
We like the fact that we promote art, not only within our community but also worldwide, and continue to expand our culture.

How do you choose the artists you work with?
The first group of artists that formed the gallery was a group of friends from the same generation. Then we started to include artists from older generations who trusted us and our project.

If you weren't running a gallery what else would you do?
I am an artist. As this is an artists' gallery, I think that if I were not a gallerist I would still be an artist.

- **Contact**: Revolver Galería
  Giancarlo Scaglia
  gscaglia@revolvergaleria.com
- **Established**: 2008
- **Owner(s) / Partner(s)**: Giancarlo Scaglia Barrios
- **Team**: 4
- **Space(s)**: 100 m²
- **Artists at Art Basel**: José Carlos Martinat
  Ishmael Randall-Weeks
- **Further artists represented**: Daniel Barclay
  Elena Damiani
  Matías Duville
  Philippe Gruenberg
  Gilda Mantilla
  Andrés Marroquín Winkelmann
  Jerry B. Martin
  Juan Salas
  Giancarlo Scaglia

Reynolds

London

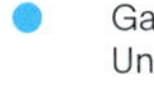

Galleries
Unlimited

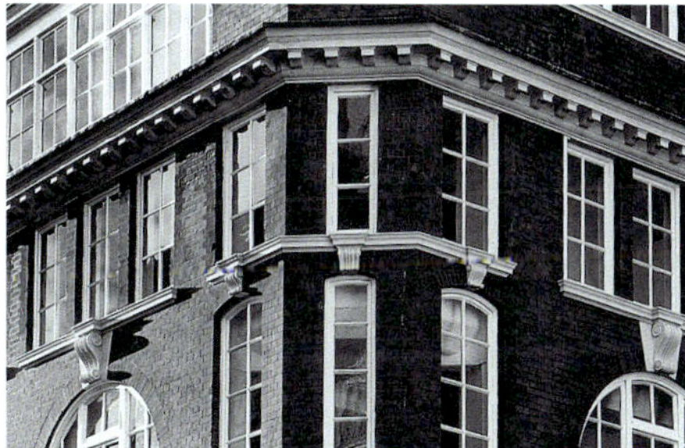

What is your favorite aspect of running a gallery?
Putting on the shows.

How do you choose the artists you work with?
Each one is different.

If you weren't running a gallery what else would you do?
Write.

- **Contact**: Anthony Reynolds Gallery
  Anthony Reynolds
  ar@anthonyreynolds.com
- **Established**: 1985
- **Owner(s) / Partner(s)**: Anthony Reynolds
- **Team**: 5
- **Space(s)**: 111.5 m²
- **Artists at Art Basel**: Richard Billingham
  Ian Breakwell
  Erik Dietman
  Peter Gallo
  Paul Graham
  Lewis Klahr
  Lucia Nogueira
  Walid Raad
  Georgia Sagri
  Nancy Spero
  Jon Thompson
  Amikam Toren
  Apichatpong Weerasethakul
- **Further artists represented**: Lucy Harvey
  Emily Jacir
  Kai Kaljo
  Nobuko Tsuchiya

Riis

Oslo
Stockholm

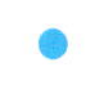

Galleries
Unlimited

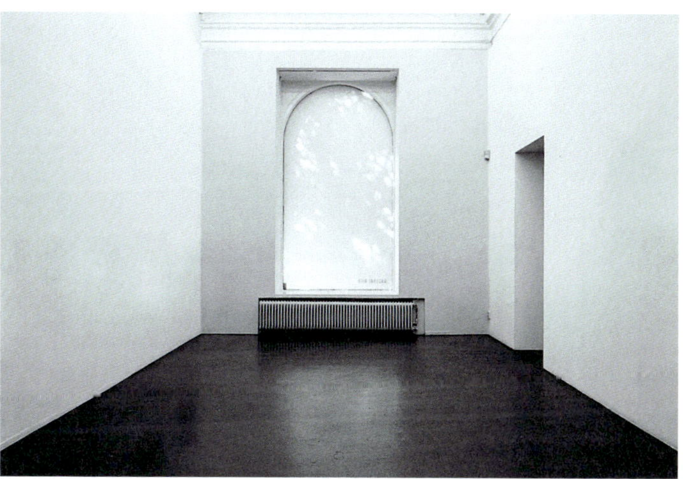

What is your favorite aspect of running a gallery?
The firsthand experience of the creative process in the creation and presentation of artworks.

How do you choose the artists you work with?
That decision often requires an assessment of many factors, but the power and the sincerity of the art and the artist always come first.

If you weren't running a gallery what else would you do?
I honestly don't know, but I believe the skills and experience from running a gallery would be useful also in other professions and areas of work.

- **Contact**: Galleri Riis
  Espen Ryvarden
  espen@galleririis.com
- **Established**: 1972
- **Owner(s) / Partner(s)**: Espen Ryvarden
  Kristin Elisabeth Bråten
- **Team**: 5
- **Space(s)**: 500 m²
- **Artists at Art Basel**: Morten Andenæs
  Andreas Eriksson
  Hamish Fulton
  Jan Groth
  Håvard Homstvedt
  Olav Christopher Jenssen
  Daido Moriyama
  Eline Mugaas
  Christine Ödlund
  Rallou Panagiotou

Stein Rønning
Fredrik Söderberg
Tone Vigeland
Marijke van Warmerdam
Sverre Wyller

- **Further artists represented** Martin Erik Andersen
Signe Marie Andersen
Per Berntsen
Per Inge Bjørlo
Bård Breivik
Sofia Ekström
Katrine Giæver
Kristján Gudmundsson
Marte Johnslien
Arne Malmedal
Kristina Matousch
Paul Osipow
Günter Umberg
Dan Wolgers
Troels Wörsel

Roberts & Tilton

Culver City  Galleries

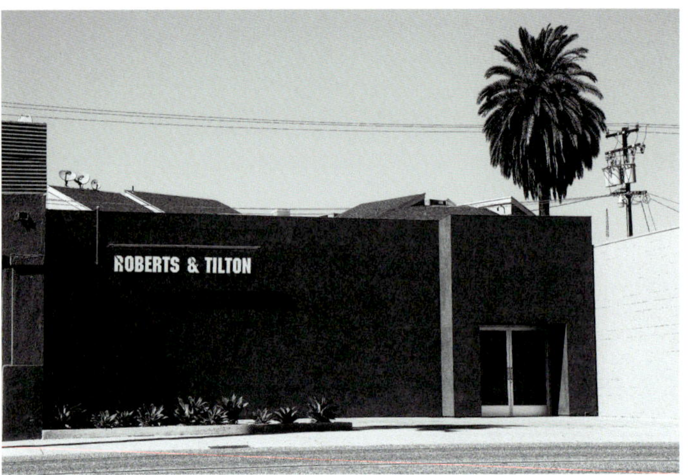

What is your favorite aspect of running a gallery?
Constantly being challenged by the art we exhibit.

How do you choose the artists you work with?
It is all about intuition and a gut feeling, plus an innate ability to know where to look.

If you weren't running a gallery what else would you do?
We would start a non-profit institution to support the arts.

- **Contact** Roberts & Tilton
Mary Skarbek
mary@robertsandtilton.com
- **Established** 1999
- **Owner(s) / Partner(s)** Bennett Roberts
Julie Roberts
Jack Tilton
- **Team** 8
- **Space(s)** 279 m²
- **Artists at Art Basel** Michael Dopp
Egan Frantz
Dean Levin
Evan Nesbit
Thomas Wachholz
- **Further artists represented** Eberhard Havekost
Thomas Kiesewetter
Israel Lund
Daniel Joseph Martinez
Barry McGee
Betye Saar
Ed Templeton
Kehinde Wiley
Zhao Zhao

Rodeo

Istanbul
London
 Feature
Parcours

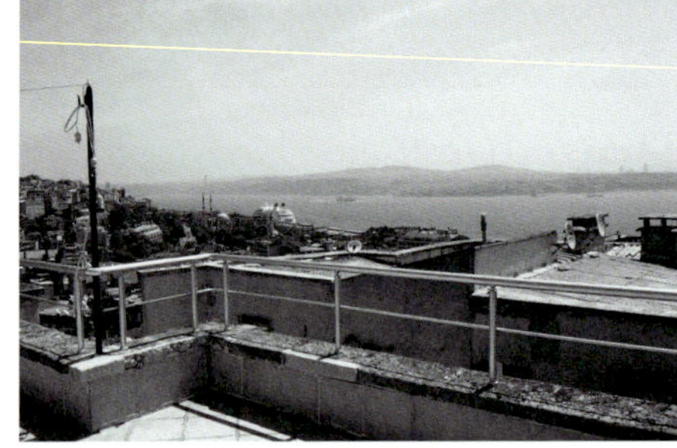

Contact Rodeo
Katy Green
katy@rodeo-gallery.com
- **Established** 2007
- **Owner** Sylvia Kouvali
- **Team** 4
- **Artists at Art Basel** Haris Epaminonda
Iman Issa
- **Further artists represented** Duncan Campbell
Banu Cennetoğlu
Lukas Duwenhögger
Apostolos Georgiou
Tamara Henderson
Emre Hüner
Ian Law
Shahryar Nashat
Christodoulos Panayiotou
Eftihis Patsourakis
James Richards
Mark Aerial Waller

Roesler

São Paulo
Rio de Janeiro
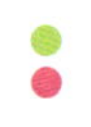 Galleries
Galleries Kabinett

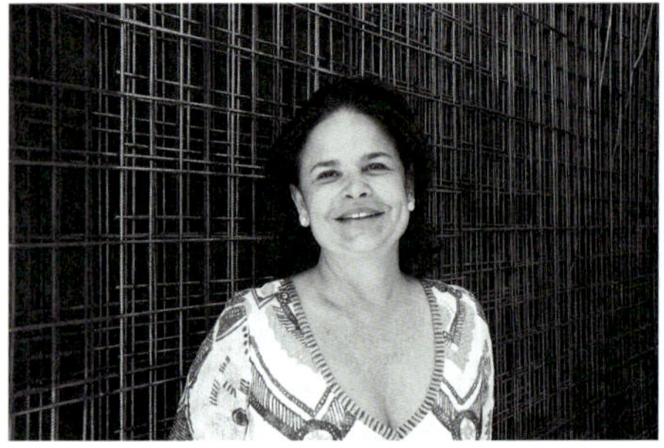

What is your favorite aspect of running a gallery?
No doubt that it is the privilege of working closely with such group of gifted artists, with their very special ways of experiencing and engaging with the sensible world, and being able to translate their views to our public.

How do you choose the artists you work with?
I trust my intuition, first and foremost. But I receive a lot of information from my artists, the gallery directors, and a few trusted curators.

If you weren't running a gallery what else would you do?
I would be showing the world to my grandchildren!

- **Contact** Galeria Nara Roesler
Nara Roesler
nara@nararoesler.com.br
- **Established** 1989
- **Owner(s) / Partner(s)** Nara Roesler
Daniel Roesler
Alexandre Roesler
- **Team** 27
- **Space(s)** 720 m²
- **Artists at Art Basel** Carlito Carvalhosa
Marcos Chaves
Eduardo Coimbra
Antonio Dias
Isaac Julien

Lucia Koch
Artur Lescher
Milton Machado
Marco Maggi
Vik Muniz
Sérgio Sister

- **Further artists represented** Brígida Baltar
Alberto Baraya
Paulo Bruscky
Cristina Canale
Bruno Dunley
O Grivo
Cao Guimarães
Karin Lambrecht
Julio Le Parc
Virginia de Medeiros
Alice Miceli
Fábio Miguez
Raul Mourão
Tomie Ohtake
Hélio Oiticica
Oscar Oiwa
Abraham Palatnik
Rodolpho Parigi
José Patrício
Paul Ramirez Jonas
Marcelo Silveira
Luzia Simons
Melanie Smith
Angelo Venosa
Laura Vinci

ROH

Jakarta

Insights

What is your favorite aspect of running a gallery?
Building the careers of emerging artists.

How do you choose the artists you work with?
Personal relationship.

If you weren't running a gallery what else would you do?
Travel the world.

- **Contact** ROH Projects
Laksamana Tirtadji
jun@rohprojects.net
- **Established** 2012
- **Owner(s) / Partner(s)** Laksamana Tirtadji
Rachel Ibrahim
- **Team** 5
- **Space(s)** 750 m²
- **Artists at Art Basel** Bagus Pandega
- **Further artists represented** Windi Apriani
Syaiful Garibaldi
Triyadi Guntur Wiratmo
Gede Mahendra Yasa

Rokeby

London

Discoveries

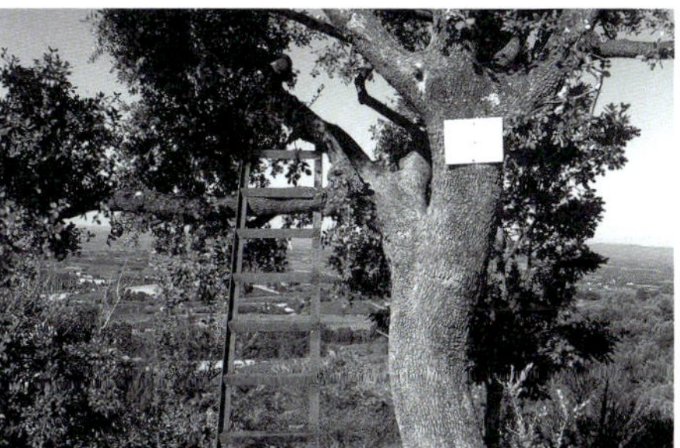

What is your favorite aspect of running a gallery?
Working together (as a couple).

How do you choose the artists you work with?
Shared interests and an admiration of their commitment, ability, and ambition.

If you weren't running a gallery what else would you do?
Sex, drugs, and rock 'n' roll.

- **Contact** Rokeby
Edward Greenacre
edward@rokebygallery.com
- **Established** 2005
- **Owner(s) / Partner(s)** Beth Greenacre
Edward Greenacre
- **Team** 2
- **Space(s)** 40 m²
- **Artists at Art Basel** Bettina Buck
- **Further artists represented** Eli Cortiñas
Sam Dargan
Doug Fishbone
Leung Chi Wo
Kate Newby
Ian Pedigo
Gideon Rubin
Michael Samuels
Conrad Ventur

Ropac

Paris
Salzburg

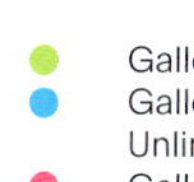

Galleries
Galleries Unlimited
Galleries Public

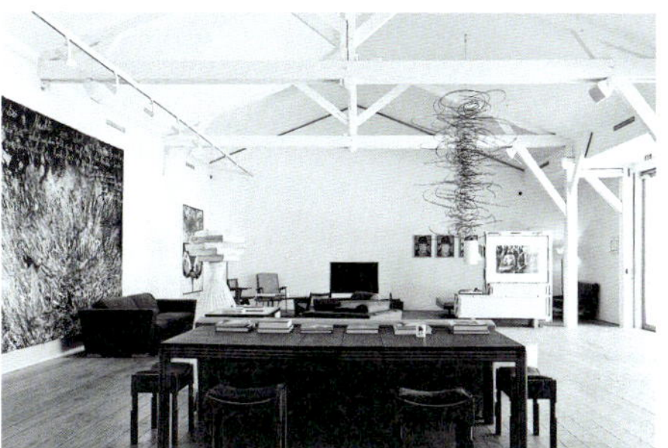

What is your favorite aspect of running a gallery?
The relationships we build with the artists to participate in their universe and to help them realize their projects and their vision.

How do you choose the artists you work with?
We are constantly looking at artists of each period: very young artists, mid-career ones, and very established ones. We can see works in magazines, at biennales, and at exhibitions in remote places. There are many ways to discover new artists if you are constantly aware and curious. We try to learn as much as possible about the artist's content and practice before a first relationship is established. Sometimes it finalizes in a new working collaboration, but it is always challenging.

If you weren't running a gallery what else would you do?
As I am fascinated by classical music, opera, and theater, I could have imagined finding my way in this very inspiring world.

- **Contact** Galerie Thaddaeus Ropac
Katja Schoppe
katja@ropac.net
- **Established** 1983
- **Owner(s) / Partner(s)** Thaddaeus Ropac
- **Team** 60
- **Space(s)** 4,800 m²
- **Artists at Art Basel** Cory Arcangel
Jules de Balincourt
Georg Baselitz
Oliver Beer
Joseph Beuys
Tony Cragg
Richard Deacon
Antony Gormley
Ilya & Emilia Kabakov
Alex Katz
Anselm Kiefer
Imi Knoebel
Robert Longo
Robert Mapplethorpe
Tom Sachs
Sturtevant
Andy Warhol
Erwin Wurm
Yan Pei-Ming

- **Further artists represented** Claire Adelfang
Art & Language
Mahmoud Bakhshi
Stephan Balkenhol
Ali Banisadr
The Estate of Philippe Bradshaw
Marc Brandenburg
Lee Bul
Jean-Marc Bustamante
Matali Crasset
Elger Esser
Harun Farocki
Sylvie Fleury
Gilbert & George
Amos Gitaï
Wolfgang Laib
Jonathan Lasker
Liza Lou
Marcin Maciejowski
Jason Martin
Farhad Moshiri
Nick Oberthaler
Jack Pierson
Arnulf Rainer
Daniel Richter
Gerwald Rockenschaub
David Salle
Raqib Shaw
Andreas Slominski
Not Vital

Rosen

New York — Galleries, Galleries

- **Contact** Andrea Rosen Gallery
Rebekah Bowling
r.bowling@rosengallery.com
- **Established** 1990
- **Owner(s) / Partner(s)** Andrea Rosen
- **Team** 26
- **Artists at Art Basel** David Altmejd
Walker Evans
Lizzie Fitch/Ryan Trecartin
Felix Gonzalez-Torres
Al Hansen
Elliott Hundley
Tetsumi Kudo
Friedrich Kunath
Jose Lerma
Josiah McElheny
Josephine Meckseper
László Moholy-Nagy
Katy Moran
Dan Peterman
Michael Raedecker
Matthew Ritchie
Matthew Ronay
Mika Rottenberg
Ryan Trecartin
Andrea Zittel

Rosenfeld

New York — Galleries

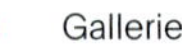

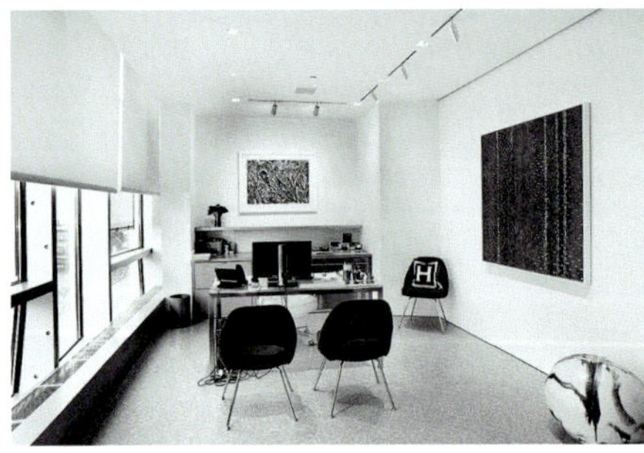

What is your favorite aspect of running a gallery?
The serendipity of the every day and meeting extraordinary art enthusiasts/scholars/professionals. No two days are the same and because the gallery specializes in 20th- and 21st-century American art—promoting many of the aesthetic movements of those decades—the gallery audience is diverse and global. One minute we might be sharing a selection of Romare Bearden collages with a curator, and the next we might be giving a gallery talk on Nancy Grossman's assemblages.

How do you choose the artists you work with?
We choose artists that we admire and respect; artists that have passionately pursued their craft with integrity and purpose.

If you weren't running a gallery what else would you do?
Art is a sixth sense for Michael Rosenfeld; he needs it near and he needs to share it with others, so most likely he would be in a museum curatorial role; Halley K. Harrisburg would be designing/editing art books or working in a PR firm, promoting the arts.

- **Contact** Michael Rosenfeld Gallery
Halley Harrisburg
hkh@michaelrosenfeldartart.com
- **Established** 1989
- **Owner(s) / Partner(s)** Michael Rosenfeld
Halley K. Harrisburg
- **Team** 12
- **Space(s)** 604 m²
- **Artists at Art Basel** Ruth Asawa
Harry Bertoia
Barbara Chase-Riboud
Jay DeFeo
Beauford Delaney
Claire Falkenstein
Michael Goldberg
Morris Graves
Nancy Grossman
Hughie Lee-Smith
Norman Lewis
Boris Margo
Fairfield Porter
Richard Pousette-Dart
Theodore Roszak
Betye Saar
Alma Thomas
Toshiko Takaezu
Mark Tobey
- **Further artists represented** Benny Andrews
John Biggers
Federico Castellon
Seymour Lipton
Alfonso Ossorio
Louis Stone
Bob Thompson
Charmion von Wiegand

Rossi & Rossi

London
Hong Kong — Galleries

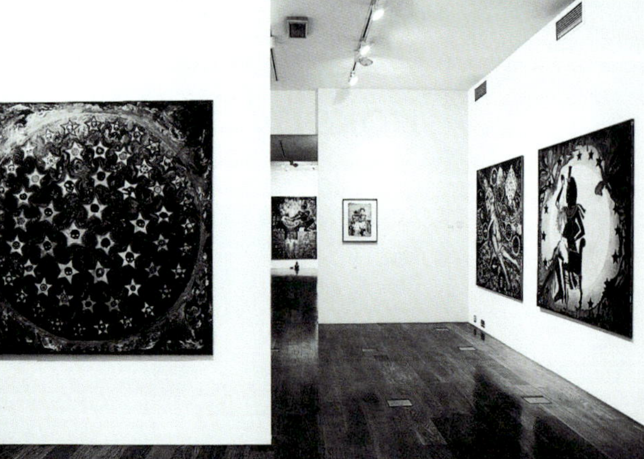

What is your favorite aspect of running a gallery?
The constant surprise and wonder inspired by the work of the artist. The realization that at times we can make a difference to the career of an artist by nurturing them and giving them the space to grow. Building up relationships with collectors and curators, traveling a common path on a journey of discovery.

How do you choose the artists you work with?
Quality of the work, integrity, humility, commitment to spending time in the studio and not chasing the market, depth

of content, wanting to be part of a "family" which is what the gallery is.

If you weren't running a gallery what else would you do?
I love what I do and I can't think of doing anything else except spending time with my family. I guess if I were not a gallerist I would find other ways to be involved with artists: curating, publishing, collecting.

- **Contact** Rossi & Rossi
  Fabio Rossi
  fabio@rossirossi.com
- **Established** 1985
- **Owner(s) / Partner(s)** Anna Maria Rossi & Fabio Rossi
- **Team** 7
- **Space(s)** 300 m²
- **Artists at Art Basel** Leang Seckon
- **Further artists represented** Fereydoun Ave
  Benchung
  Konstantin Bessmertny
  Bhutanese Textile Project
  Faiza Butt
  Heman Chong
  Lois Conner
  Shane Cotton
  Dedron
  Heri Dono
  Christopher Doyle
  Gade
  Naiza H. Khan
  Abbas Kiarostami
  Kesang Lamdark
  Desheng Ma
  Erbossyn Meldibekov
  Nortse
  Tsering Nyandak
  Tenzing Rigdol
  Tsherin Sherpa
  Tsewang Tashi
  Palden Weinreb
  Nicole Wong

Rumma

Milan — Galleries
Naples — Galleries Kabinett

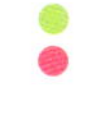

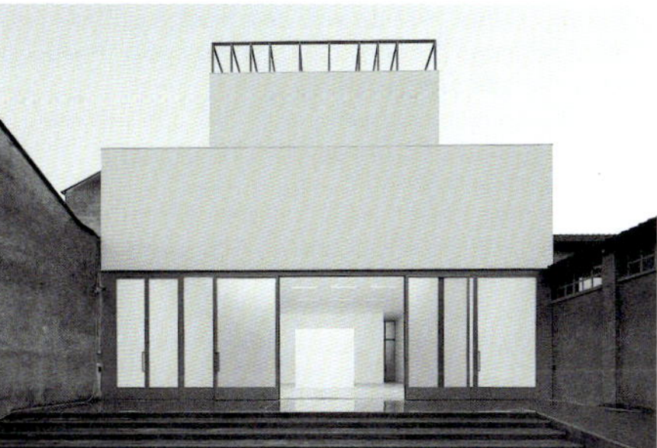

What is your favorite aspect of running a gallery?
To always be free to choose the artists and to be able to have a productive dialogue with my team.

How do you choose the artists you work with?
Usually I am impressed by an artwork and it is the work that leads me to be willing to meet the artist, since I believe that the artwork, in some ways, is the portrait of the artist.

If you weren't running a gallery what else would you do?
I would pilot a spacecraft.

- **Contact** Lia Rumma
  Lia Rumma
  info@liarumma.it
- **Established** 1971
- **Owner(s) / Partner(s)** Lia Rumma
  Paola Potena
- **Team** 15
- **Space(s)** 1,200 m²
- **Artists at Art Basel** Marina Abramović
  Vanessa Beecroft
  Enrico Castellani
  Clegg & Guttmann
  Gino De Dominicis
  Andreas Gursky
  Alfredo Jaar
  Ilya & Emilia Kabakov
  William Kentridge
  Joseph Kosuth
  Hendrik Krawen
  David Lamelas
  Marzia Migliora
  Ugo Mulas
  Michelangelo Pistoletto
  Thomas Ruff
  Ettore Spalletti
  Haim Steinbach
  Tobias Zielony
  Gilberto Zorio
- **Further artists represented** Victor Burgin
  Alberto Burri
  Gary Hill
  Anselm Kiefer
  Reinhard Mucha
  Dré Wapenaar

Ruzicska

Salzburg — Galleries

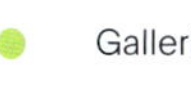

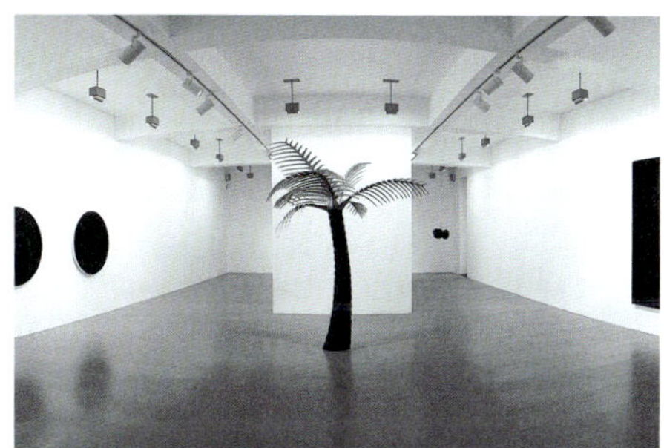

What is your favorite aspect of running a gallery?
Having to do with art.

If you weren't running a gallery what else would you do?
Garden architecture.

How do you choose the artists you work with?
Gut feeling.

- **Contact** Galerie Nikolaus Ruzicska
  Nikolaus Ruzicska
  ruzicska@ruzicska.com
- **Established** 2001
- **Owner(s) / Partner(s)** Nikolaus Ruzicska
- **Team** 8
- **Space(s)** 350 m²
- **Artists at Art Basel** Henrik Eiben
  Imi Knoebel
  Brigitte Kowanz
  Niko Luoma
  Gerold Miller
  François Morellet
- **Further artists represented** AES+F
  Olaf Otto Becker
  Ross Bleckner
  Herbert Brandl
  Manfred Erjautz
  Josef Hoflehner
  Axel Hütte
  Peter Kogler
  Cameron Martin
  Olivier Mosset
  Maurizio Nannucci
  Kenton Nelson
  Andy Ouchi
  Alessandro Raho
  Ruth Root
  Katja Strunz
  Vincent Szarek
  Clemens Wolf

R

Anthony Reynolds Gallery

Interview with Anthony Reynolds

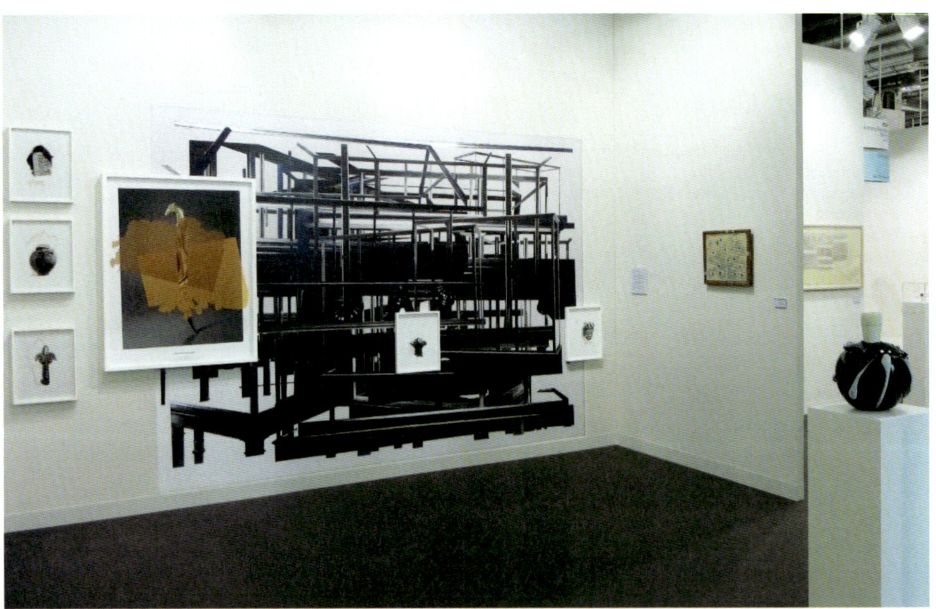

Art Basel in Basel, 2014

Since you founded Anthony Reynolds Gallery in 1985 in London, your program has been quite unique, and has included British artists (Richard Billingham, Mark Wallinger) and foreign ones (Walid Raad, Emily Jacir), older generations (Leon Golub, Erik Dietman, Sturtevant), contemporary art, and photography (Paul Graham)—even showing a filmmaker (Apichatpong Weerasethakul). How would you describe your program and your list of artists?

You have described it yourself! With a crucial difference—that it is the artists who demonstrate singularity rather than the program itself. Art never ceases to surprise me. I have never followed one path, because some stranger always pops up with an interesting alternative. To those you rightly mention, I must add several other extraordinary encounters: the late, great Ian Breakwell, master of word and image, polymath, and visual raconteur; Lucy Harvey, whose *Guide To Life* is an ever-expanding work of pure genius; the apparently unlimited ability of Amikam Toren to cajole any material object into improving itself; Jon Thompson's stunning interrogation and re-awakening of the modernist project in painting; the total originality of Nobuko Tsuchiya's sculpture; the disarming ability of Peter Gallo to invest a formal and painterly mastery with a political and personal psychology; the unrelenting, uncompromising rigor of Nancy Spero; Giorgia Sagri, Asier Mendizabal, Lucia Nogueira …

You are celebrating your 30th anniversary in 2015. Looking back, which are the exhibitions, artists, gallery events, etc. that make you proud?

I don't spend much time looking back except for the constant need to remind oneself of the contemporary presence of all worthwhile art of the past. It's a little invidious to single out particular collaborations, though one show that is hard to top was Sturtevant's *Vertical Monad*; Spinoza on God spoken from a cyber-world in the original Latin, staged in a total environment of Payne's grey. Absolutely riveting: repetition and difference incarnate. I am also happy to have been the first gallery to show Richard Billingham, Mark Wallinger, Walid Raad, Lewis Klahr, Keith Farquhar, Mark Alexander, Keith Tyson, Steve McQueen, Andrew Mansfield, and Nobuko Tsuchiya. I am proud of our stubborn championing of great artists like Leon Golub through antipathetic times. Long relationships are worth celebrating too. Toren, Mansfield, and Breakwell for 31 years, Wallinger for 30 years, Graham for 25 years, Billingham for 19 years. I guess it is too much to hope to repeat this with Weerasethakul and Klahr, both of whom we showed for the first time this year, but we'll give it a go!

Your first participation in Art Basel in Basel was in 1992. Do you remember that edition? How do you approach each year's participation in terms of presentation?

I will never forget that first time. What an experience—to be welcomed into the company of all of one's most admired peers. And it's still the fair where I feel most honored, excited, and proud to participate.

Planning the booth is always an interesting challenge. You are presented with roughly the same space and you try to maintain your identity while ringing the changes. We plan the space to allow a focus on one or two artists while representing several more; there are usually threads and connections that are not necessarily apparent; we tend to favor curiosity over spectacle—that we have reserved for Unlimited in which we have participated all but once—and have usually sold the work(s).

In parallel, what role do you see for the gallery space today, as it seems to be a very important "locus" for your activity?

Things were very different in the early 1990s: there were only a few contemporary art worlds, nearly all of a Western orientation, and one knew to which one belonged; now there are almost as many art worlds as there are artists and as many other worlds feeding off them, many with precious little interest in the art but a great deal of interest in the market. And as long as a work of art fulfills the profit motive it becomes less important to see it beyond, at best, an online check. Meanwhile exhibition programs have become more and more event-based and celebrity conscious. So where does the traditional gallery model fit in, with its investment in the unproven, its still substantial overheads, and its dependence on loyal relationships? It is true the gallery space is an important locus of activity, but while it can still function, it is not the only way. While fairs like Art Basel remain the best and biggest source of new clients, we might also need to examine the process whereby auctions and art fairs are becoming the prime sources of income; art fairs for which the gallery "program" is an increasingly costly ancillary expense. The trend for solo presentations or thematic exhibitions at fairs is perhaps one sign of the difficulty facing galleries to maintain a live audience and to project a singular identity—if the viewer/buyer won't come to the exhibition, then the exhibition shall be taken to the viewer. Maybe it's just a problem of saturation—it's a global industry and there are so many galleries. How to choose which galleries, in which countries, to visit? Why not go to a few fairs and see all (those pre-selected) at once?

The power of art as a force for regeneration is well-proven; now we need to regenerate ourselves. The traditional role and identity of the progressive gallery will change. As I began by saying, art will always surprise. By remaining open and responsive to surprise, while never losing sight of our history, we can still offer a valuable contribution.

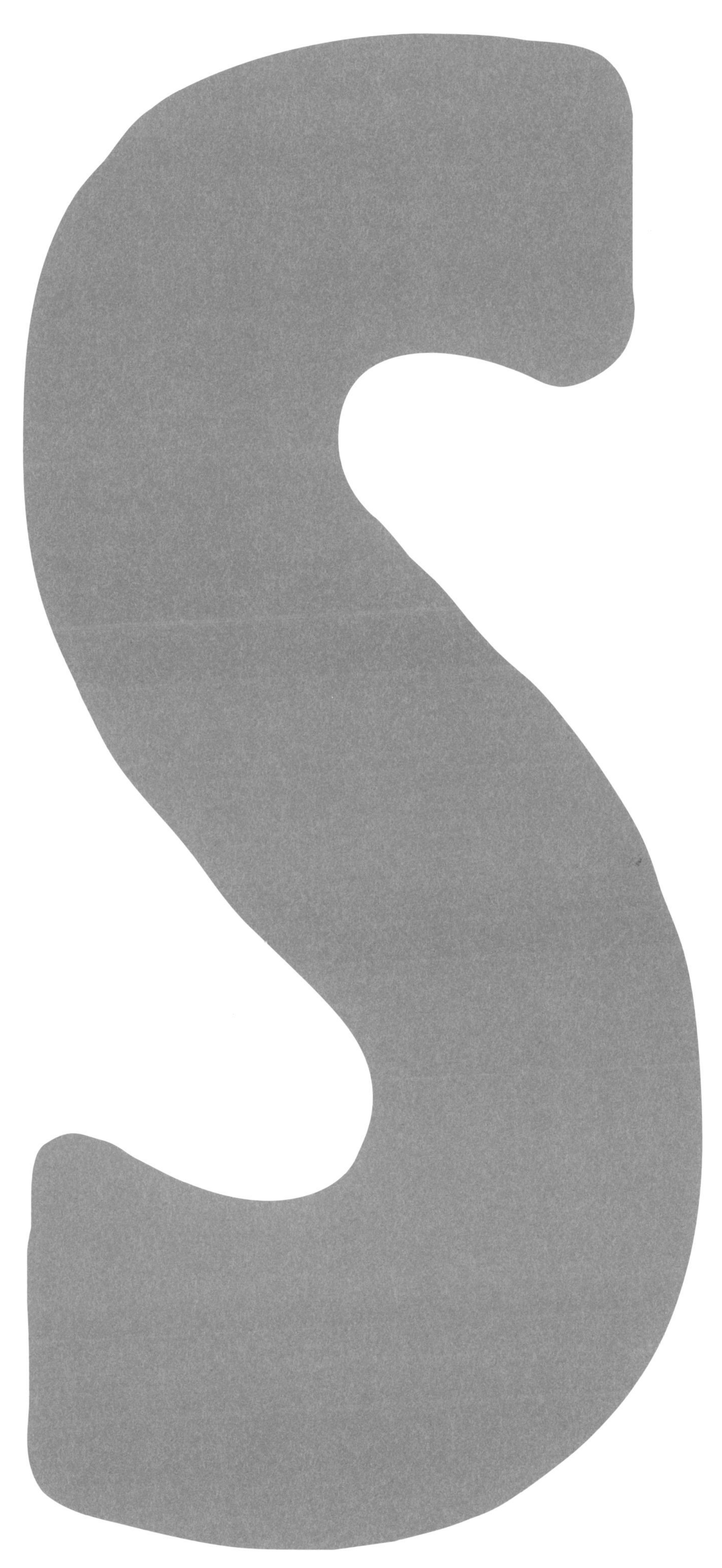

Statements at Art Basel presents exciting new solo projects by young, emerging artists. The Baloise Group has been giving awards to one or two artists in this sector since 1999. It also acquires works by the award-winning artist(s), which it donates to important European art institutions. In 2014, the prize winner was John Skoog, with his 2014 project *Reduit (Redoubt)*, presented by Pilar Corrias. We invited Chus Martinez, Head of the Art Institute/Institut Kunst, Basel, to choose her four favorite booths.

STATE MENTS

2014 participants

American Contemporary
David Brooks

Aninat
Paula de Solminihac

Arratia Beer
Pablo Rasgado

Bartlett
Marie Lund

Bureau
Ellie Ga

Corrias
John Skoog

Kraupa-Tuskany Zeidler
Katja Novitskova

Labor
Jorge Satorre

PSM
Christian Falsnaes

RaebervonStenglin
Taiyo Onorato & Nico Krebs

Ramiken Crucible
Lucas Blalock

Side 2
Fumito Urabe

Société
Trisha Baga

Werble
Anna Betbeze

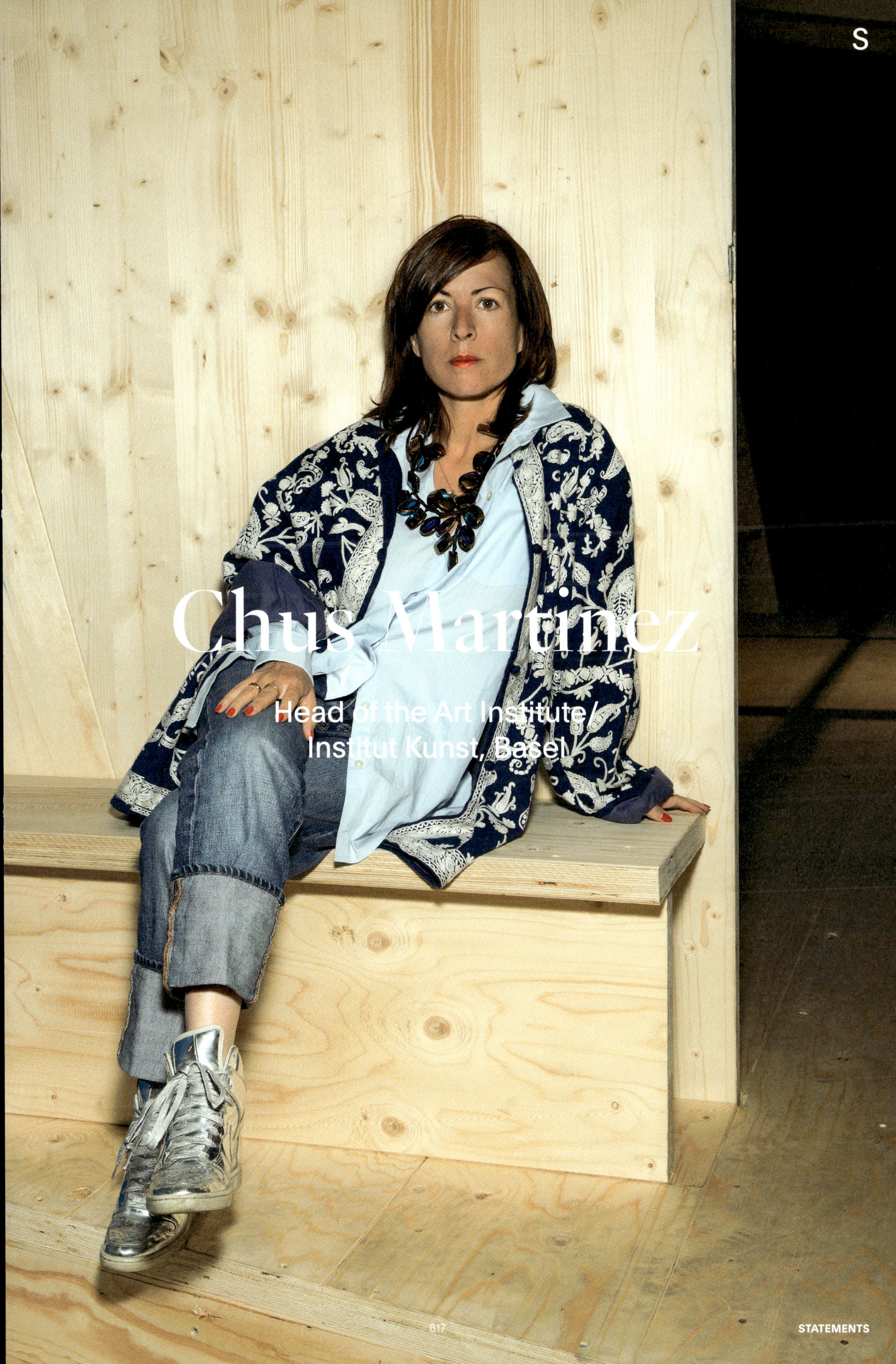

Chus Martinez

Head of the Art Institute/
Institut Kunst, Basel

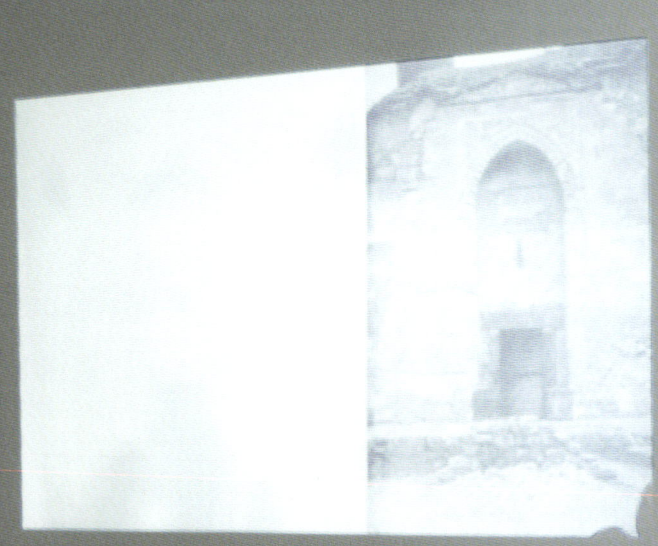

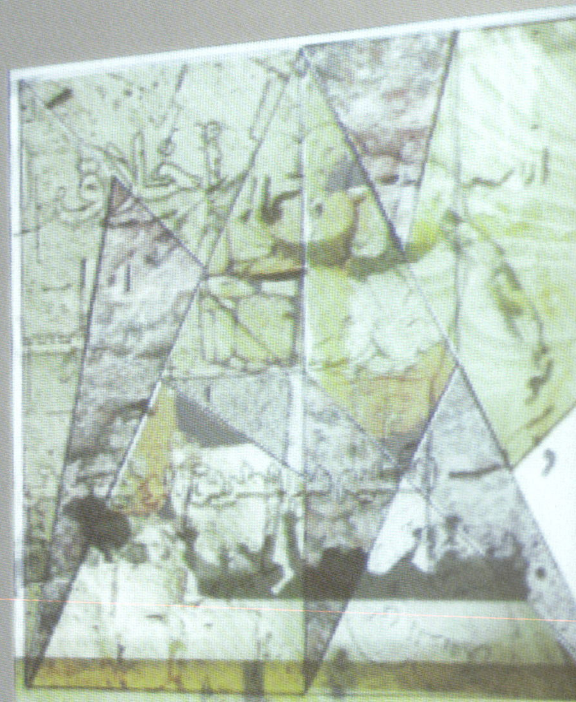
built with the pink granite stones from the Lighthouse,

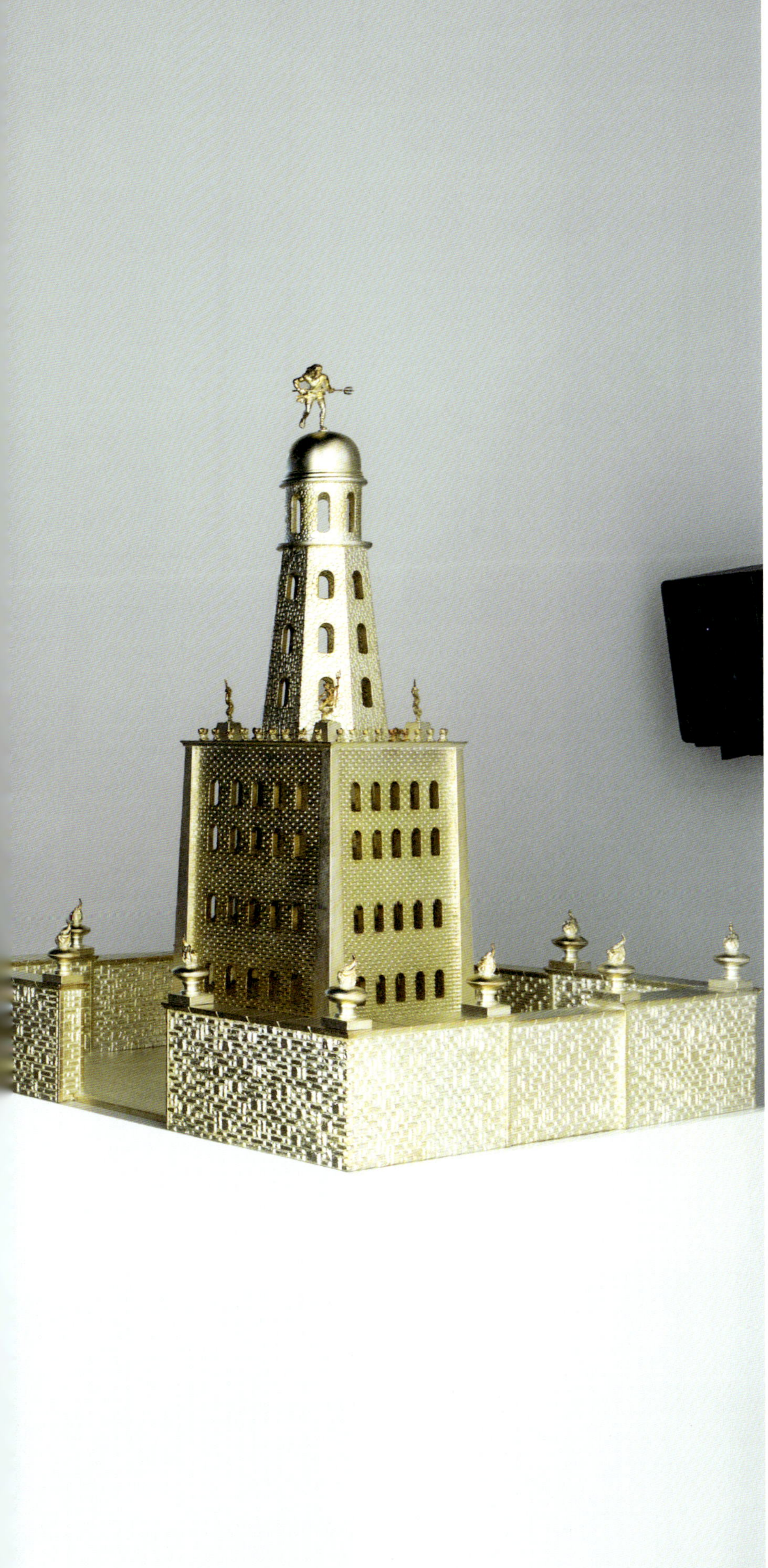

In her film and drawings Ellie Ga shows a polyvalent landscape, an attempt to embody an understanding of place, form, and how both merge into one another. Architecturally enveloping the viewer, the drawings and the movie grow steadily in front of our eyes, producing a very beautiful notion of structure. Method and gesture are one, drawing and telling are one. To see and to remember is the same thing and therefore, to be here is to be there, in her story, in the past, inside a form, part of a fiction, part of a narrative.

S

A location comes into existence only by virtue of a manmade object being built, or an action. Jorge Satorre's stones create a location, the "past." It is a landscape in which he situates materials, but also the very possibility of the future. Archeology is his way of redoubling the present with a past dimension that is primarily facing the future.

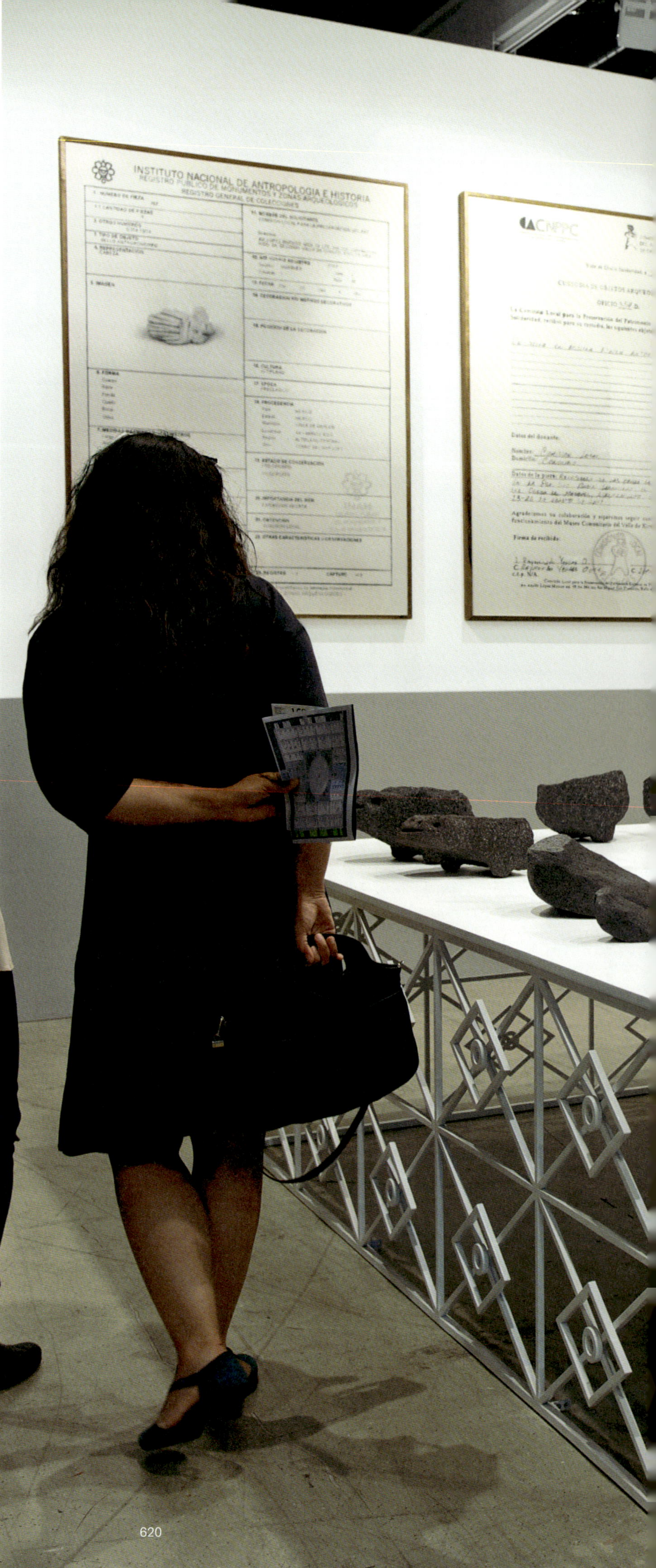

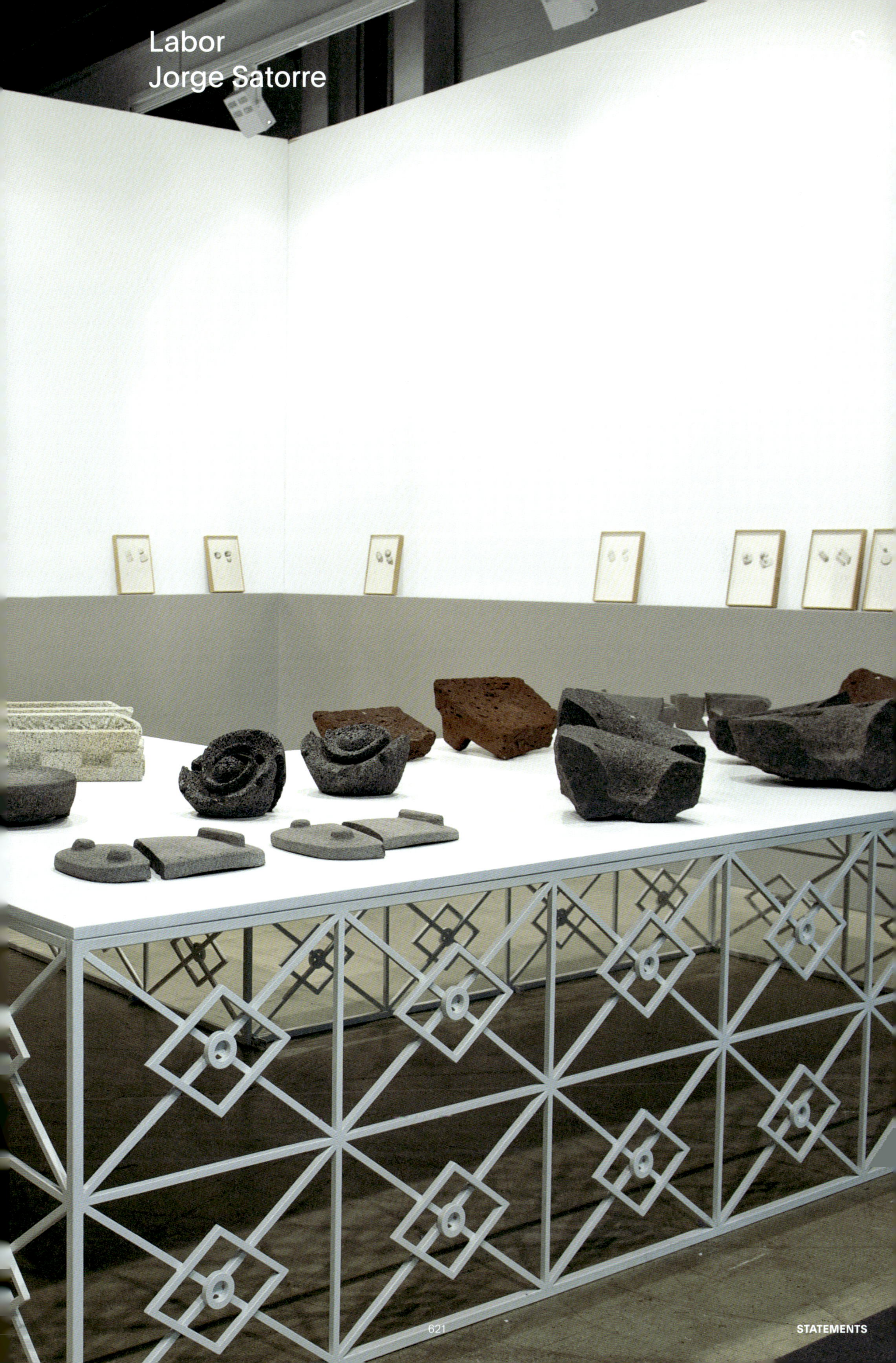

Labor
Jorge Satorre

S

Image is emotion. Nature is tenacious, man too. Observing nature one inserts oneself like a tree among the other trees. So does architecture, or any other element that conforms to what we call "a landscape." Everything is rooted in the ground ... its resistance to movement is absolute. John Skoog's films capture a perceptual resoluteness that transforms nature into pure emotion.

Pilar Corrias
John Skoog

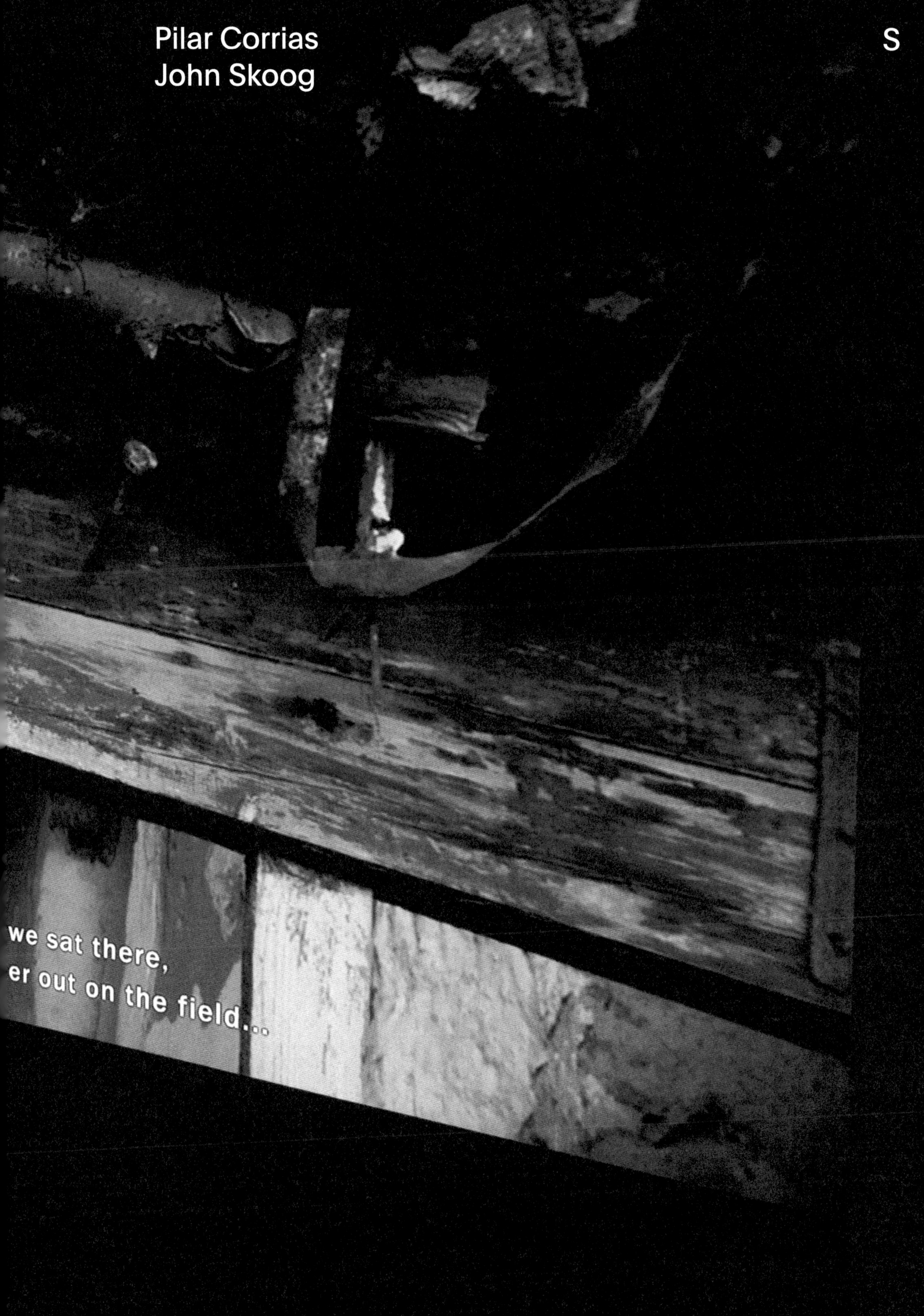

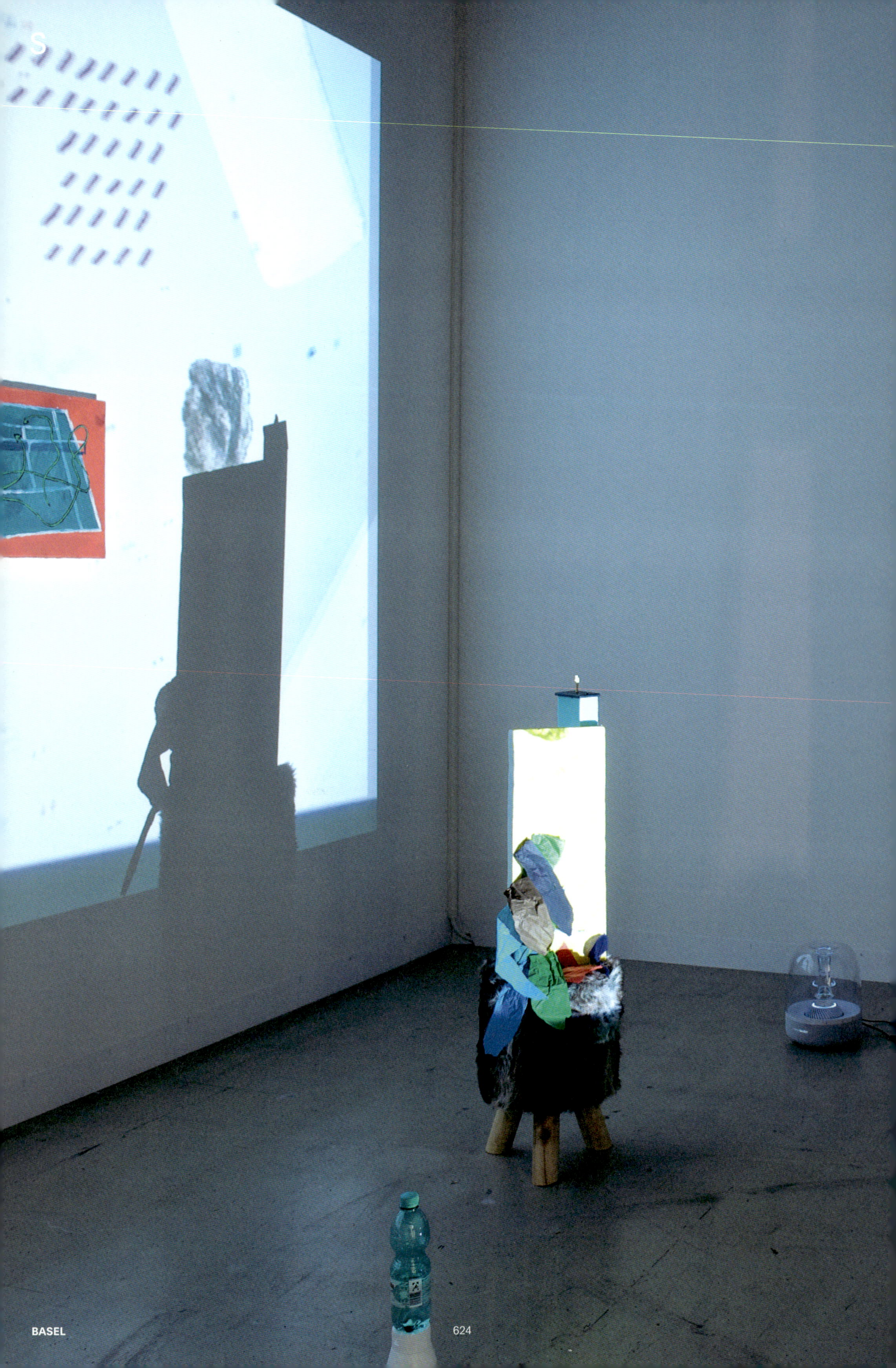

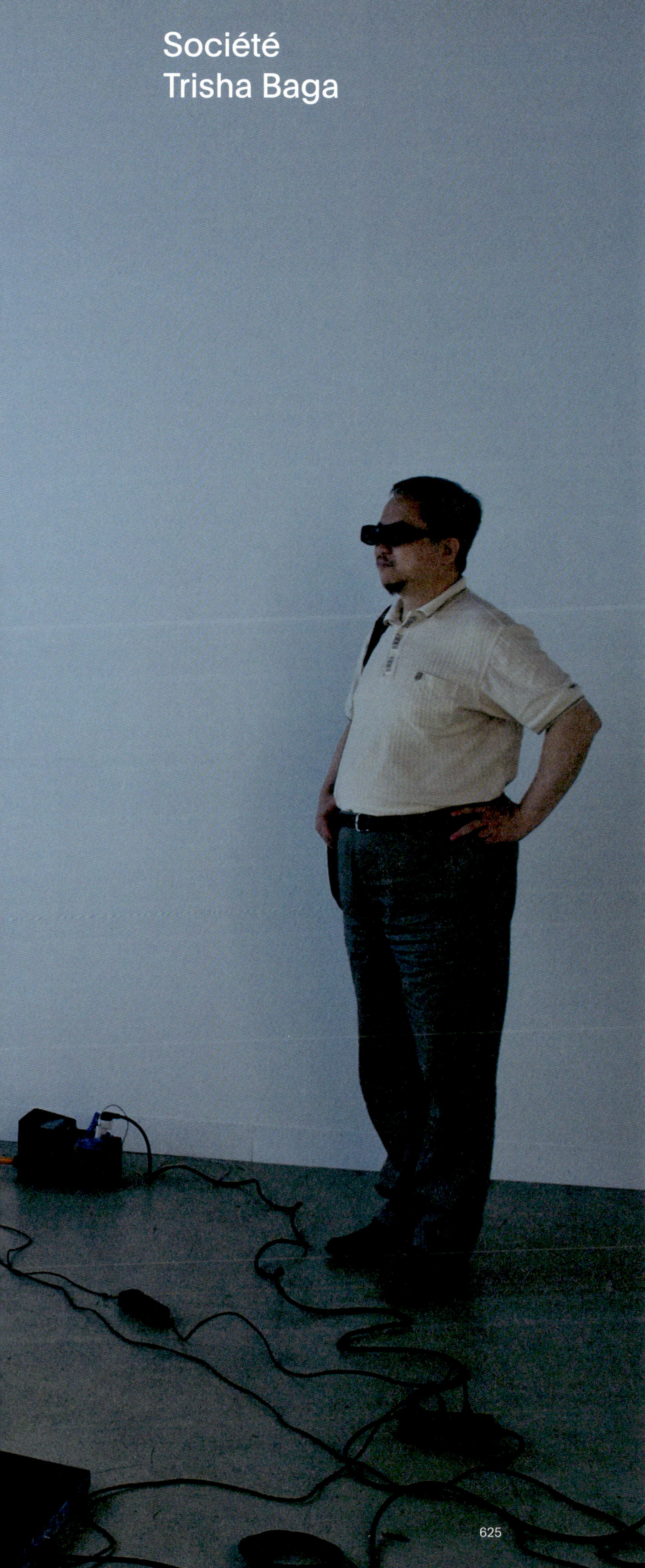

Société
Trisha Baga

Trisha Baga's film is a pure surprise of elements in dance. The 3-D effect combined with the objects present in the room creates a scenography where we see, think, and sense the movie all in one. Playful, performative, and intelligent in the way she makes technology think about us instead of forcing us into technology's logic.

S

A new sector in Art Basel in Miami Beach, Survey presents precise art historical projects—including solo presentations or juxtapositions and thematic exhibitions—from artists representing a range of cultures, generations, and artistic approaches.

SURVEY

2014 participants

Bergamin
Alfredo Volpi

Bjerggaard
Poul Gernes

Broadway 1602
Gina Pane
Rosemarie Castoro
Lenora de Barros
Lydia Okumura

Charim
Andrei Monastyrski
Valie Export
Alfons Schilling

de Torres
Taller Torres-García

Edlin
Henry Darger
Marcel Storr

espaivisor
Lotty Rosenfeld

Fuentes
Alison Knowles

Greenan
Paul Feeley

Menconi + Schoelkopf
Ralston Crawford

Tonkonow
Michelle Stuart

Vallois
Niki de Saint Phalle

Y++ Wada
Tetsuya Ishida

James Fuentes
Alison Knowles

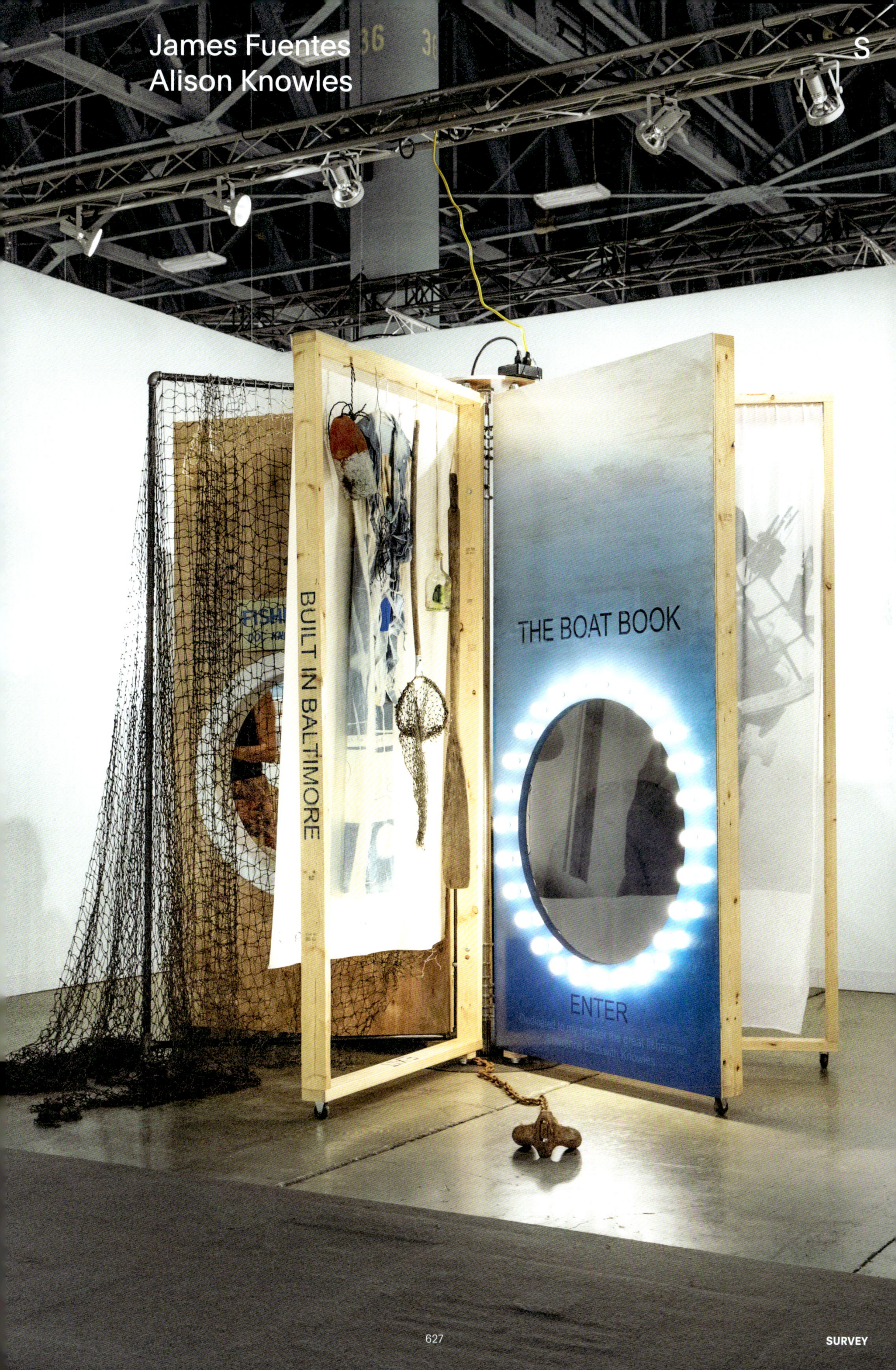

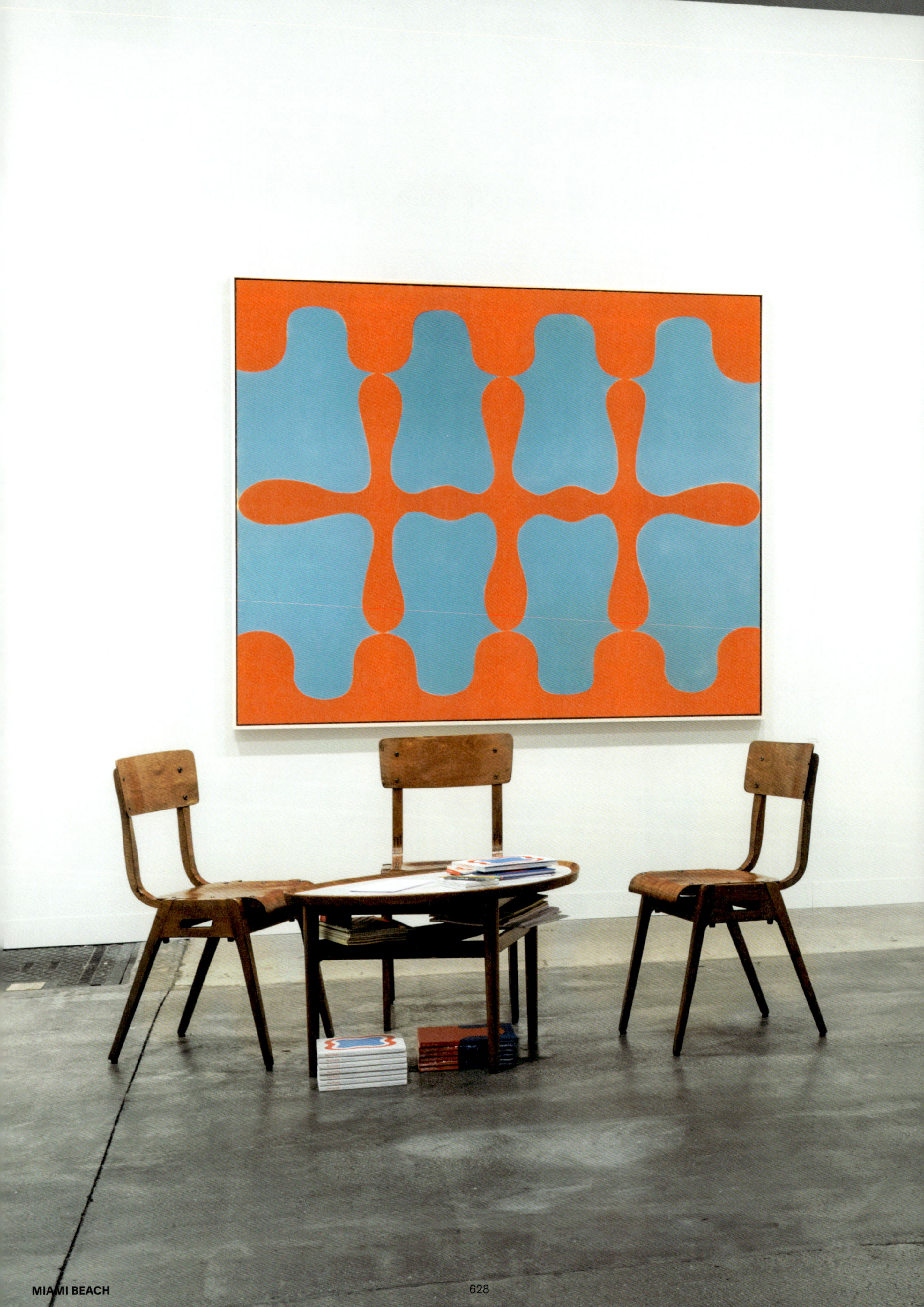

Garth Greenan Gallery
Paul Feeley

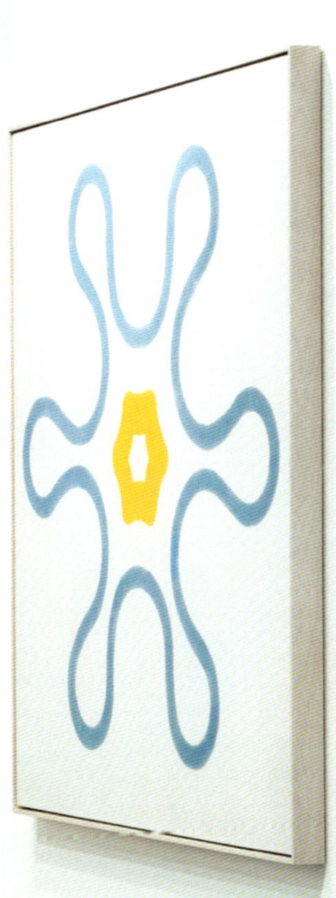

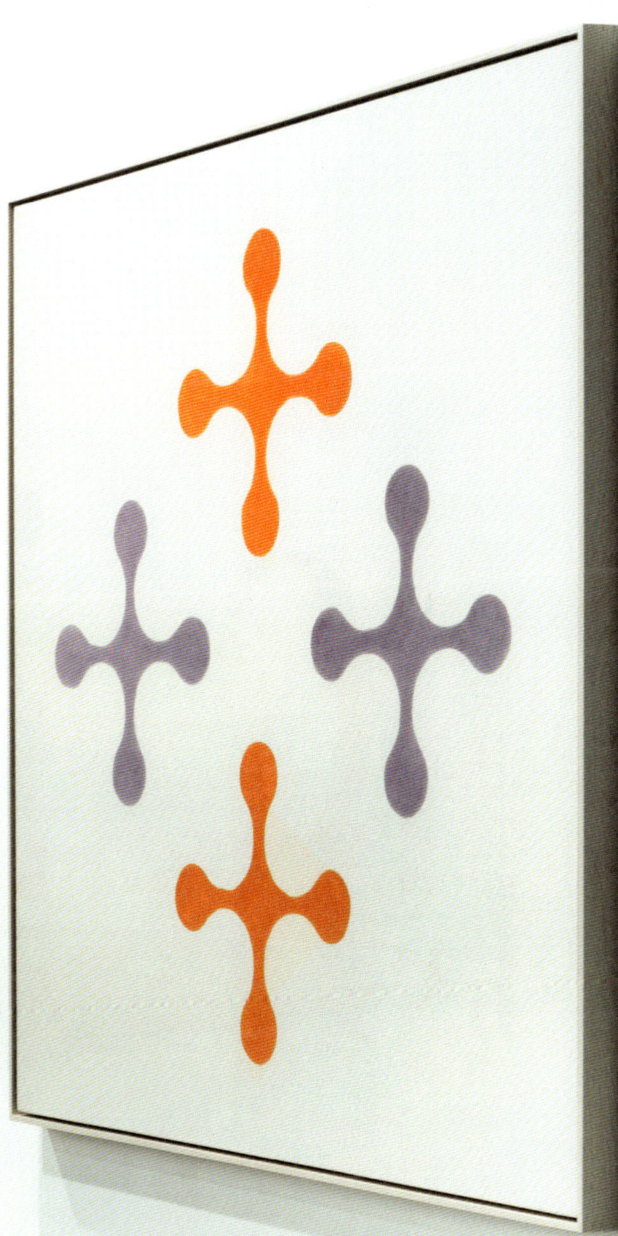

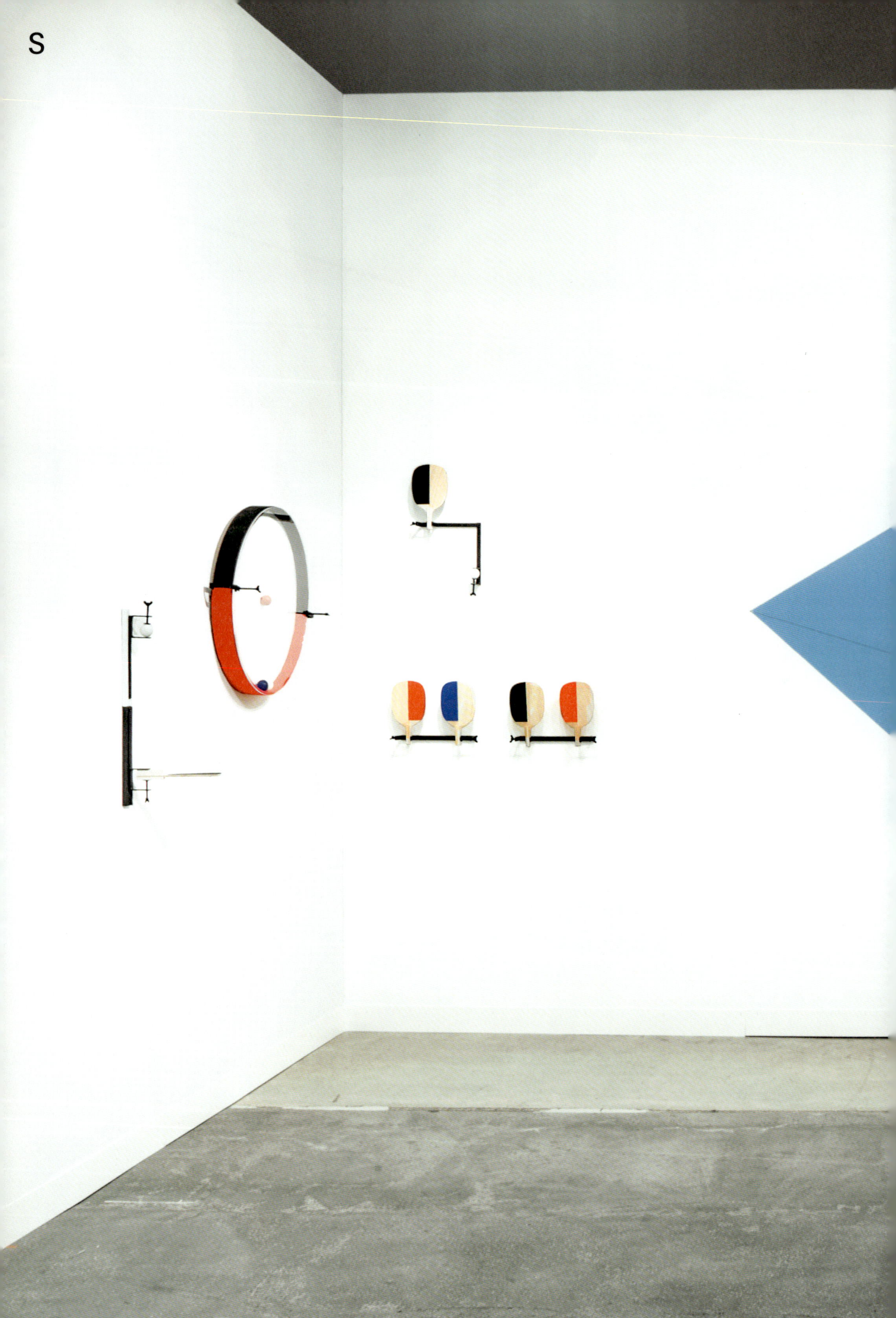

Broadway 1602
Lenora de Barros
Lydia Okumura

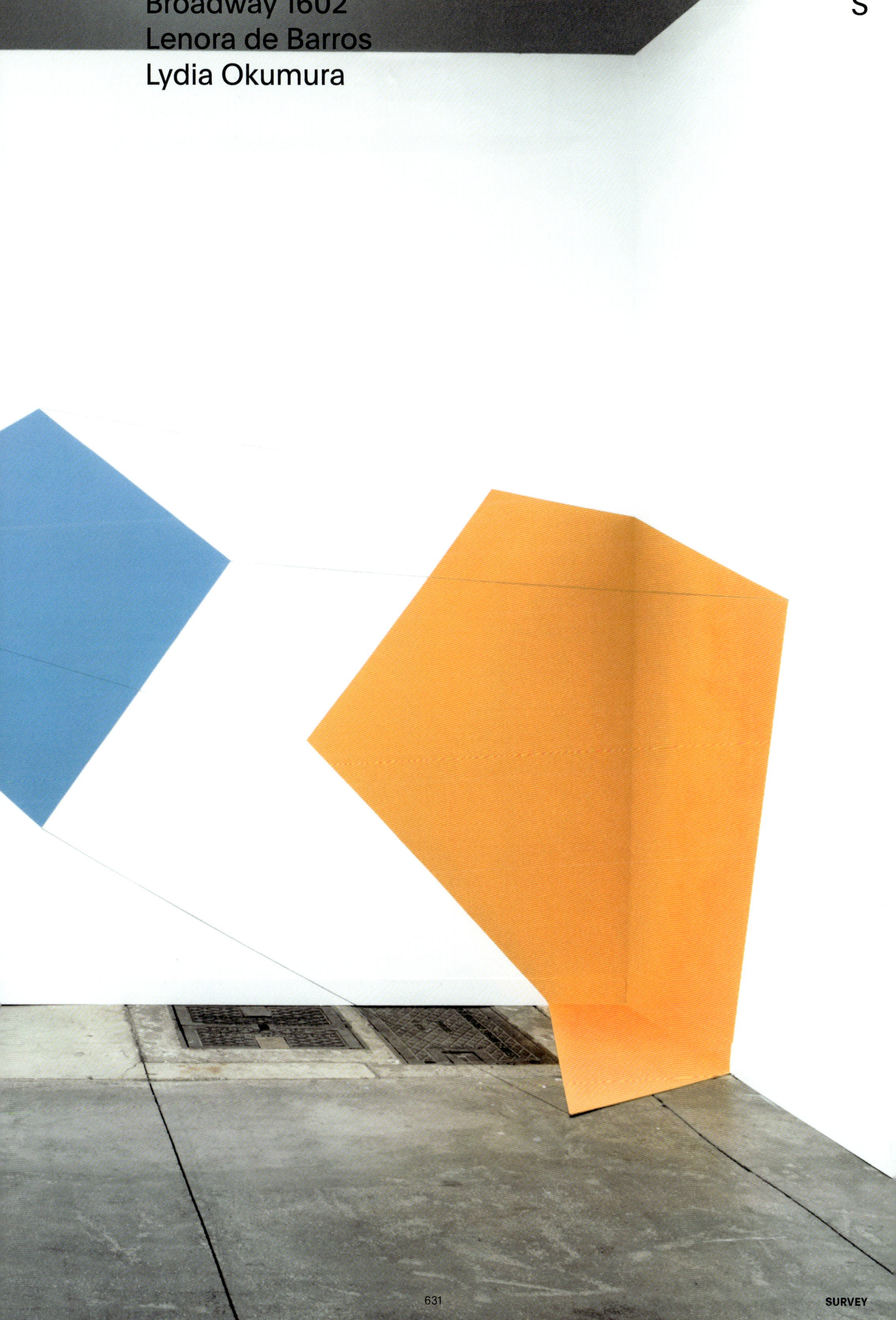

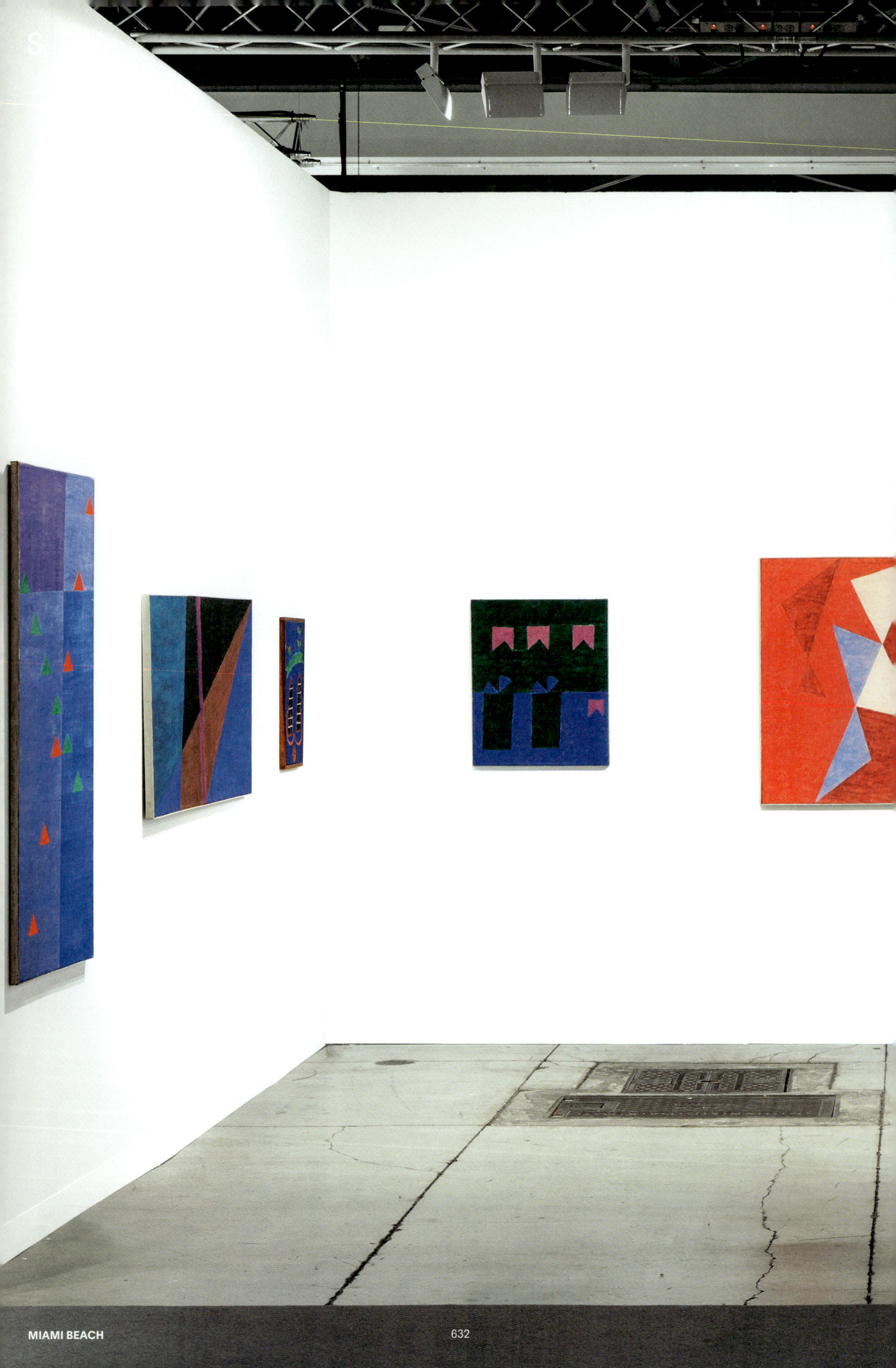

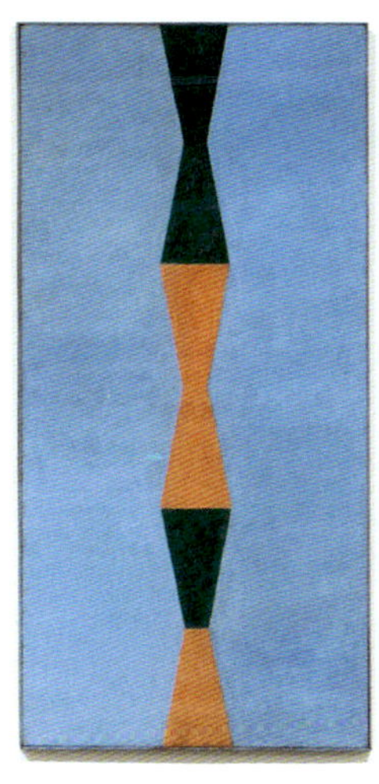
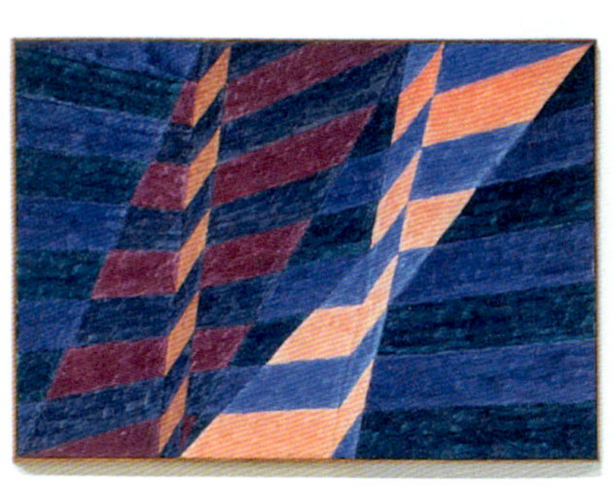
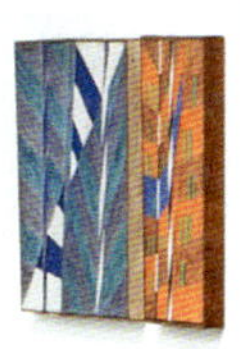
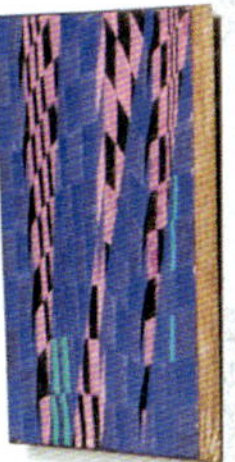
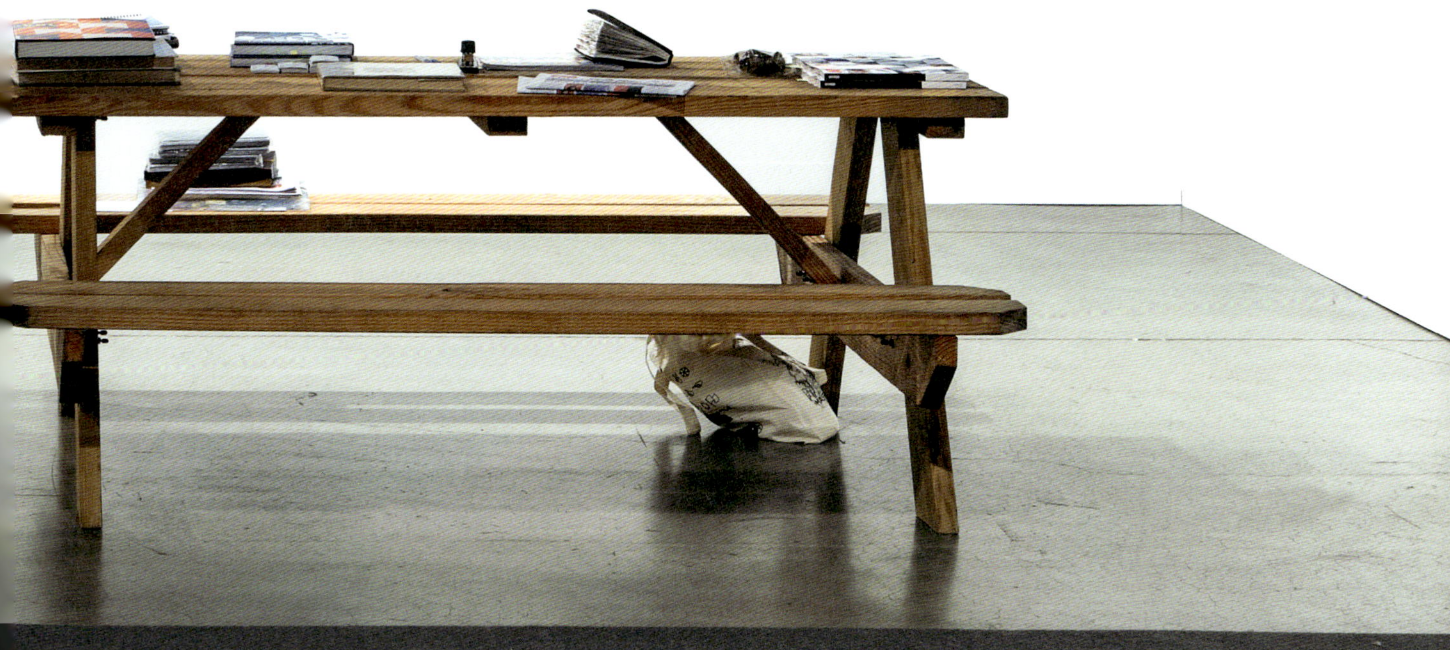

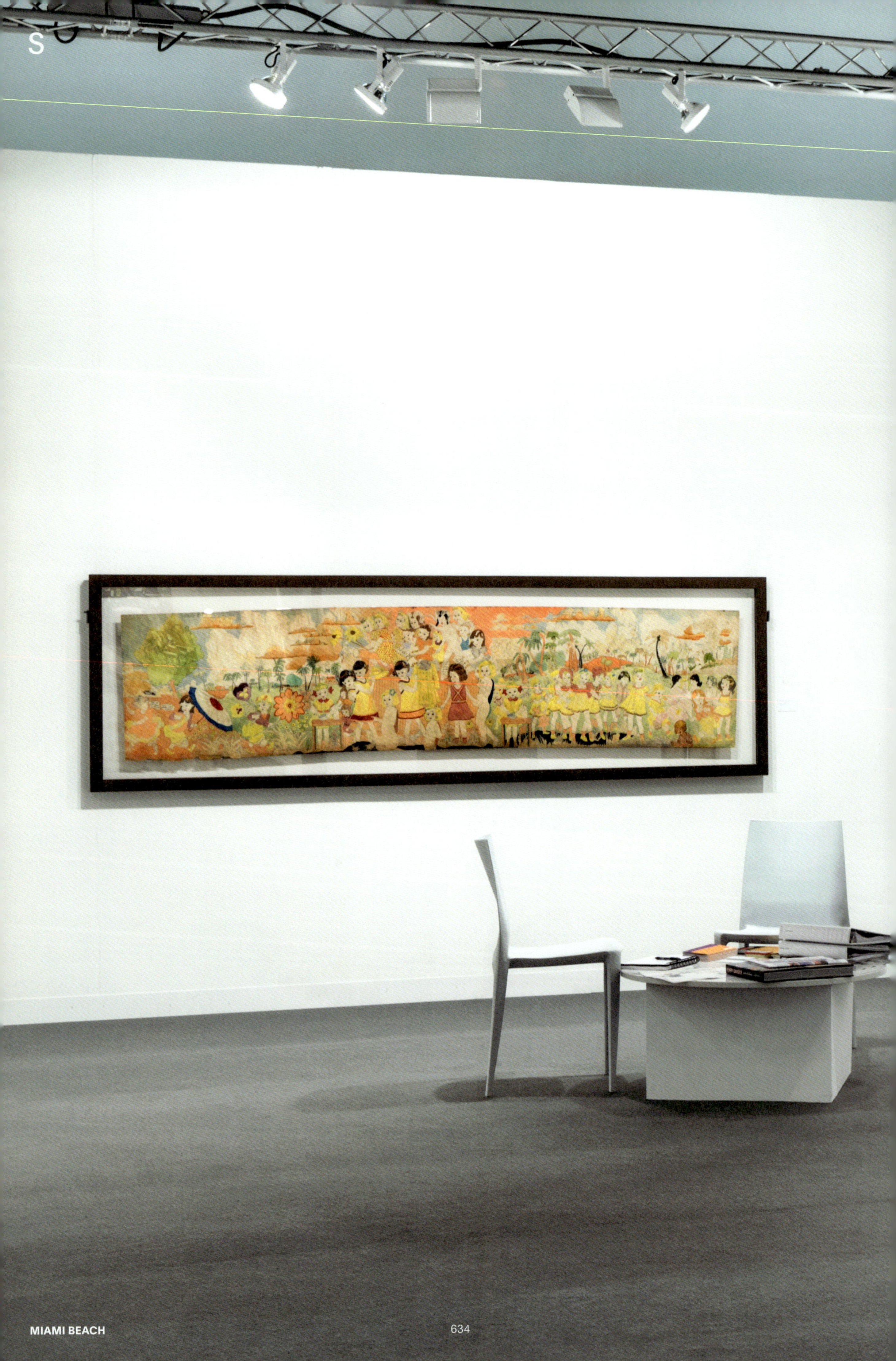

Andrew Edlin Gallery
Henry Darger
Marcel Storr

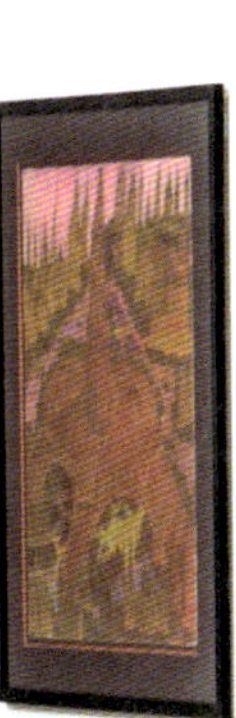

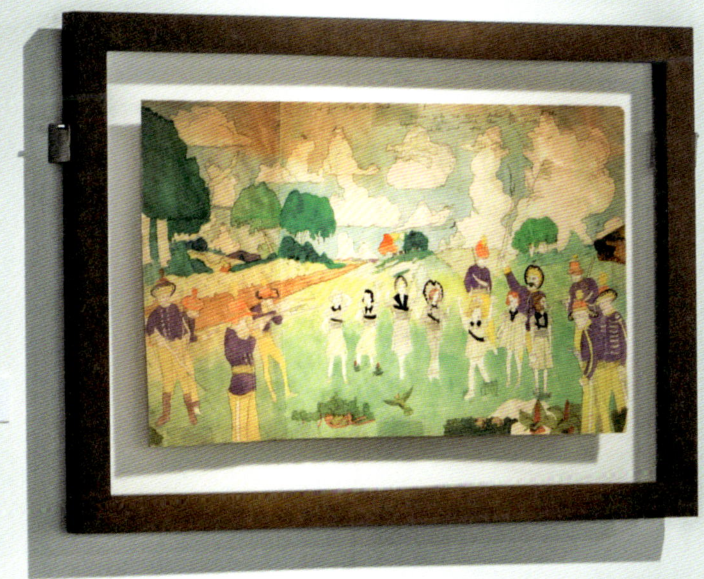

S

Galerie Georges-Philippe & Nathalie Vallois
Niki de Saint Phalle

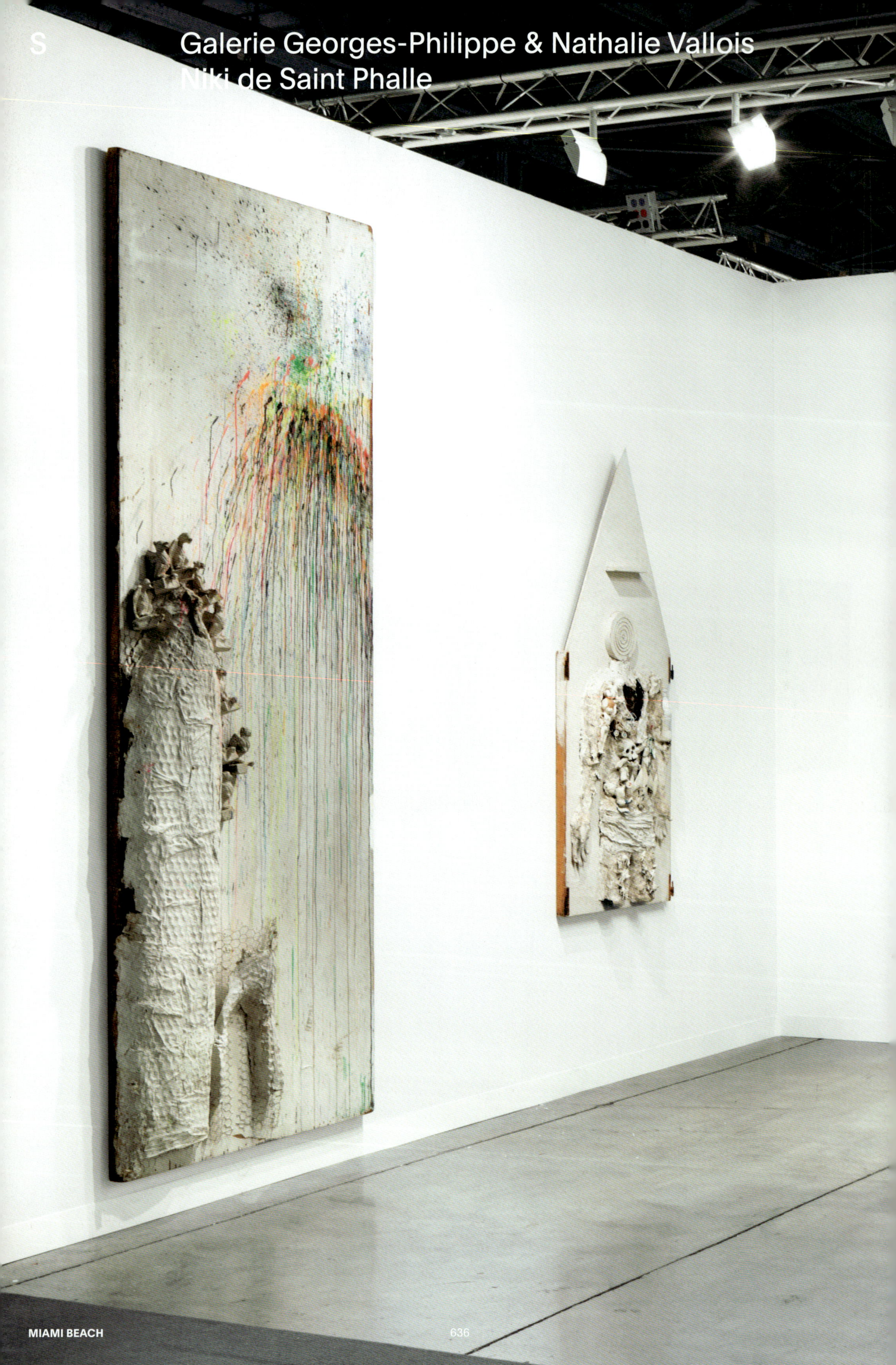

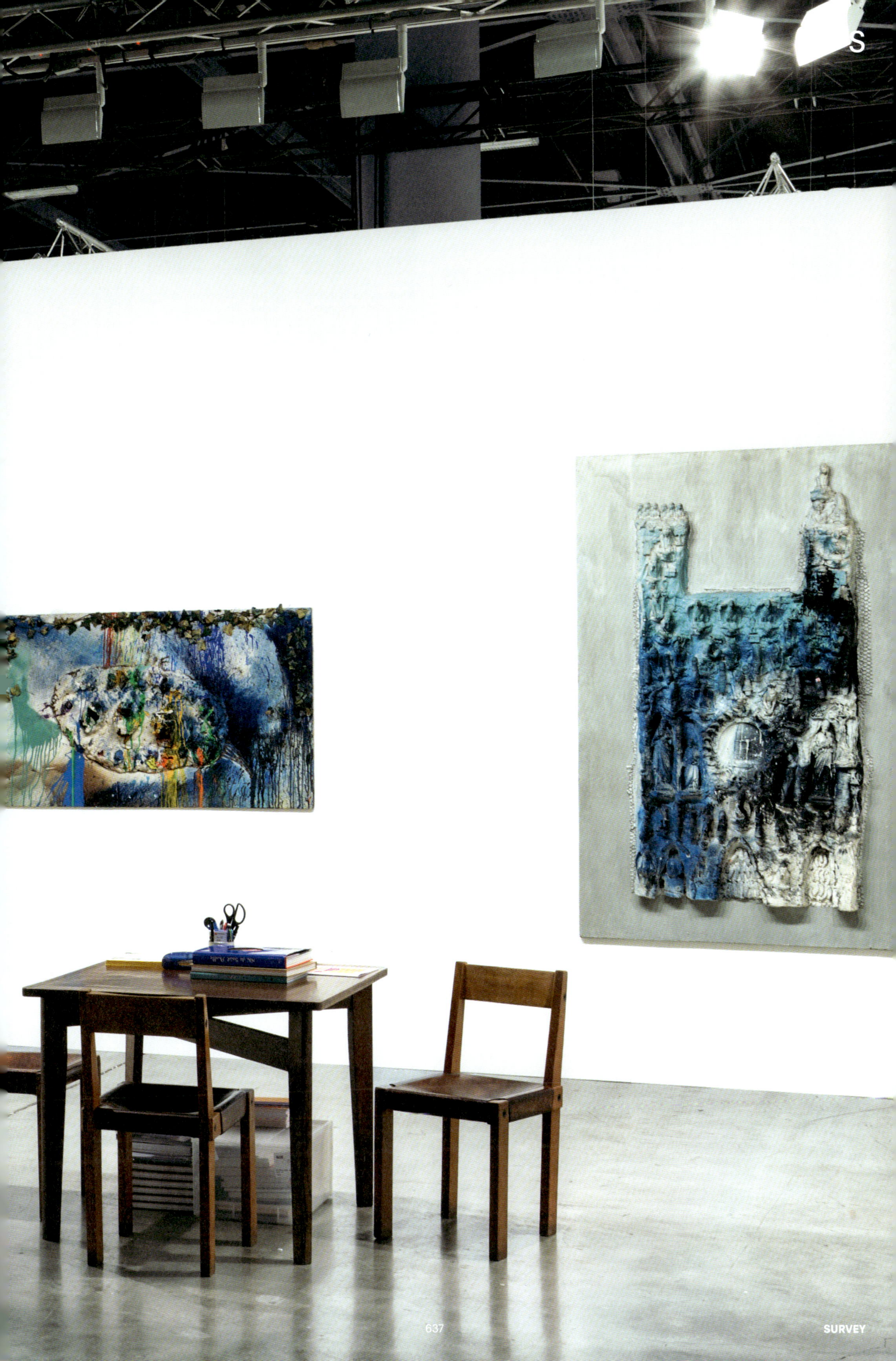

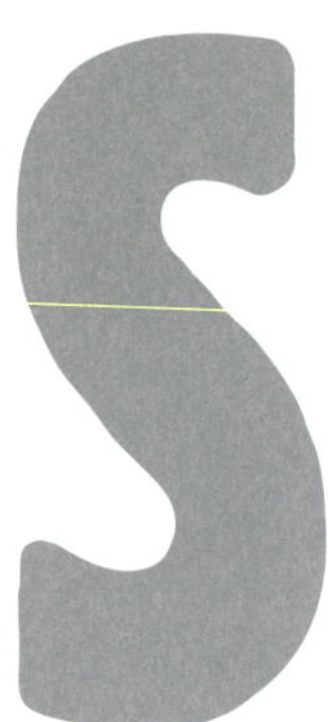
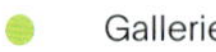

Sakshi

Mumbai ● Galleries

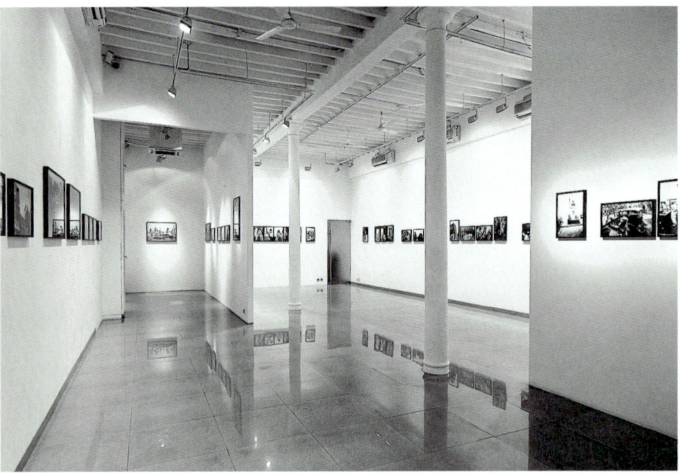

What is your favorite aspect of running a gallery?
I enjoy programming and interacting with creative minds.

How do you choose the artists you work with?
More by intuition honed over the years.

If you weren't running a gallery what else would you do?
Designer.

- **Contact** Sakshi Gallery
Geetha Mehra
art@sakshigallery.com
- **Established** 1984
- **Owner(s) / Partner(s)** Geetha Mehra
V Sanjay Kumar
- **Team** 15
- **Space(s)** 148.5 m²
- **Artists at Art Basel** Safaa Erruas
Sunil Gawde
Manjunath Kamath
Dhruva Mistry
Rekha Rodwittiya
Valay Shende
Vivek Vilasini
- **Further artists represented** El Anatsui
Anirban Mitra
Surendran Nair
Julian Opie
Ravinder Reddy
K. G. Subramanyan
Waswo X. Waswo

Salon 94

New York ● Galleries

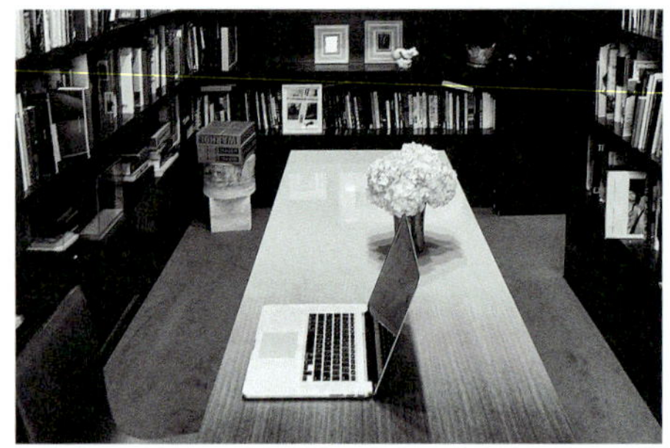

What is your favorite aspect of running a gallery?
My favorite aspect of running a gallery is helping artists realize their vision.

How do you choose the artists you work with?
I look at a lot of art, visit a lot of studios, and I like to listen to recommendations by artists who I admire.

If you weren't running a gallery what else would you do?
A movie producer perhaps?

- **Contact** Salon 94
Fabienne Stephan
fabienne@salon94.com
- **Established** 2002
- **Owner(s) / Partner(s)** Jeanne Greenberg Rohatyn
Alissa Friedman
Fabienne Stephan
- **Team** 13
- **Space(s)** 325 m²
- **Artists at Art Basel** The Estate of Terry Adkins
Huma Bhabha
Francesca DiMattio
Katy Grannan
Takuro Kuwata
Marilyn Minter
Warlimpirrnga Tjapaltjarri
- **Further artists represented** Amy Bessone
Liz Cohen
Jules de Balincourt
The Estate of Jimmy DeSana
Sylvie Fleury
Paula Hayes
Jon Kessler
The Estate of Carlo Mollino
Takeshi Murata
Jayson Musson
Carlos Rolon
David Benjamin Sherry
Laurie Simmons
Lorna Simpson
Betty Woodman

SCAI

Tokyo

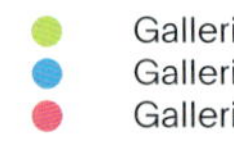

Galleries
Galleries
Galleries

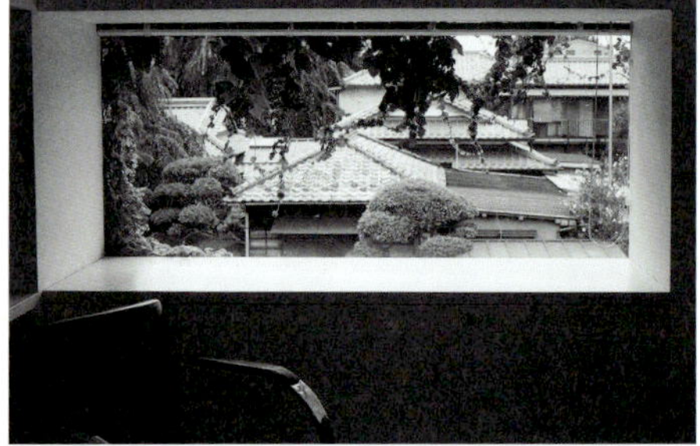

What is your favorite aspect of running a gallery?
I like the thrill of working with artists and collectors who are always onto something new. I push forward the realization of ideas through open and frank dialogues. It is stimulating and also fulfilling. For me, the gallery is a platform through which new ideas are formed,

developed, and put into action. My role is to grow and manage its entirety, taking the right decisions at the right moments. It is often intense and I enjoy the whole process.

How do you choose the artists you work with?

I think about how the artist and the gallery could benefit from each other from multiple perspectives, and what each presentation could mean in the broader context of the gallery's programs and activities. I also seek to promote young talented artists from Japan abroad, and vice versa.

If you weren't running a gallery what else would you do?

I would be a hotel concierge who could respond to your curiosity by giving tips and advice. I would find delight in this job.

- **Contact** SCAI the Bathhouse
Koichiro Osaka
info@scaithebathhouse.com
- **Established** 1993
- **Owner(s) / Partner(s)** Masami Shiraishi
- **Team** 10
- **Space(s)** 90 m²
- **Artists at Art Basel** Genpei Akasegawa
Darren Almond
Noriko Ambe
Toshikatsu Endo
He Xiangyu
Jeppe Hein
Anish Kapoor
Yusuke Komuta
Lee Ufan
Tatsuo Miyajima
Mariko Mori
Natsuyuki Nakanishi
Kohei Nawa
Miwa Ogasawara
Daisuke Ohba
Julian Opie
Tomoko Shioyasu
Apichatpong Weerasethakul
- **Further artists represented** Brian Alfred
Choe U-Ram
Dzine
Kaoru Hirano
Jeon Joonho
Naoki Ishikawa
Toru Kamiya
Haruka Kojin
Yurie Nagashima
Katsuhiro Saiki
Tomoaki Suzuki
Nobuko Tsuchiya
Tadanori Yokoo

Schipper

Berlin

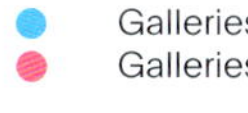
Galleries
Galleries

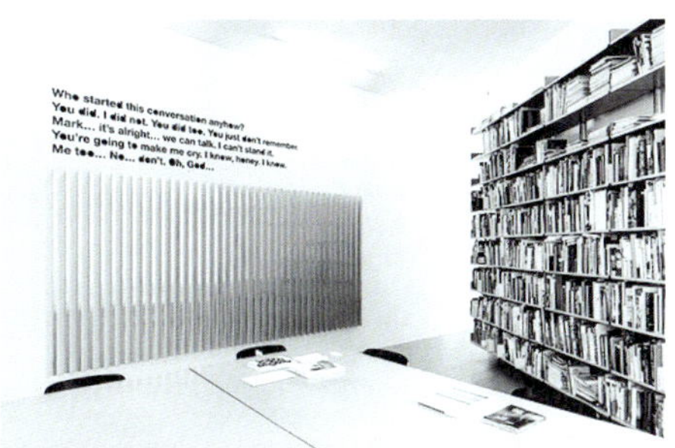

What is your favorite aspect of running a gallery?

The artists are what drive my work. When I started my gallery in 1989 I was working very closely with artists to develop new practices of exhibiting art and also of commodifying these works. Artists such as Liam Gillick, Dominique Gonzalez-Foerster, Pierre Huyghe, and Philippe Parreno have made important contributions to the way we think about exhibitions. Working to define what constitutes a work of art and how to find a market for it continues to be a very interesting and challenging process.

How do you choose the artists you work with?

I take a long time before deciding to take an artist on board because once we work with someone we want to do a very thorough job. I am extremely aware of committing to a long-term, perhaps even a lifelong relationship. That being said, I think that education, culture, and history shape our understanding of art and influence the choices we make. My first consideration always concerns the conceptual aspects of an artist's practice.

If you weren't running a gallery what else would you do?

I don't want to do anything else.

- **Contact** Esther Schipper
office@estherschipper.com
- **Established** 1989
- **Owner(s) / Partner(s)** Esther Schipper
Florian Wojnar
- **Team** 20
- **Space(s)** 450 m²
- **Artists at Art Basel** Matti Braun
AA Bronson
Angela Bulloch
Nathan Carter
Thomas Demand
Jean-Pascal Flavien
Ceal Floyer
The Estate of General Idea
Liam Gillick
Dominique Gonzalez-Foerster
Grönlund-Nisunen
Pierre Huyghe
Ann Veronica Janssens
Christoph Keller
Gabriel Kuri
Isa Melsheimer
Ari Benjamin Meyers
Philippe Parreno
Ugo Rondinone
Christopher Roth
Karin Sander
Tomás Saraceno
Julia Scher
Daniel Steegmann Mangrané

Schöttle

Munich

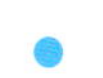
Galleries

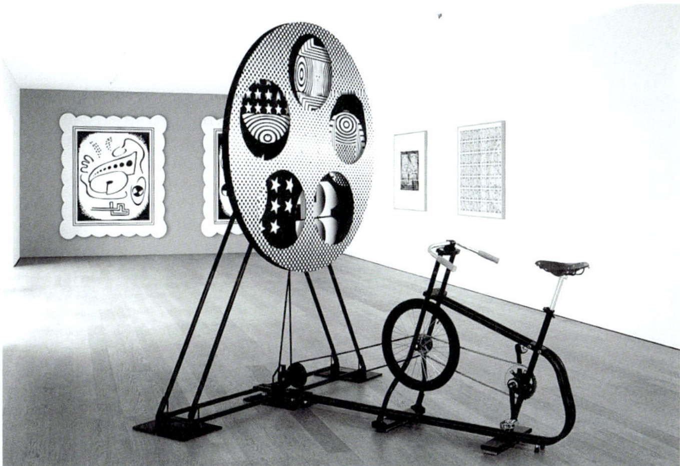

What is your favorite aspect of running a gallery?

An important motivation for bringing a gallery into being and maintaining it is, in my opinion, to capture and present the essential moments of the fluidity of movement in art.

How do you choose the artists you work with?

We choose the artists according to the above criterion.

If you weren't running a gallery what else would you do?

I would like to be an ornithologist.

- **Contact** Galerie Rüdiger Schöttle
Rüdiger Schöttle
info@galerie-schoettle.de
- **Established** 1968
- **Team** 4
- **Space(s)** 450 m²
- **Artists at Art Basel** Janis Avotins
Stephan Balkenhol

Maria Bartuszova
Steven Claydon
Heinz Frank
Lorena Herrera Rashid
Candida Höfer
Goshka Macuga
Alex Mirutziu
Andrew Palmer
Thomas Ruff
Thomas Struth
Florian Süssmayr
Chen Wei

- **Further artists represented** Armin Boehm
Martin Boyce
Geta Brătescu
David Claerbout
Anders Clausen
James Coleman
Martin Creed
Slawomir Elsner
Elger Esser
Liam Gillick
Dan Graham
Rodney Graham
Thomas Helbig
On Kawara
John Knight
Bela Kolarova
Tim Lee
Jan Merta
Anri Sala
Thomas Schütte
Jeff Wall
Thomas Zipp

Schulte

Berlin

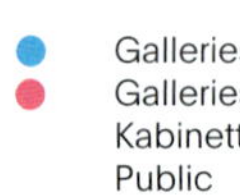

Galleries
Galleries
Kabinett
Public

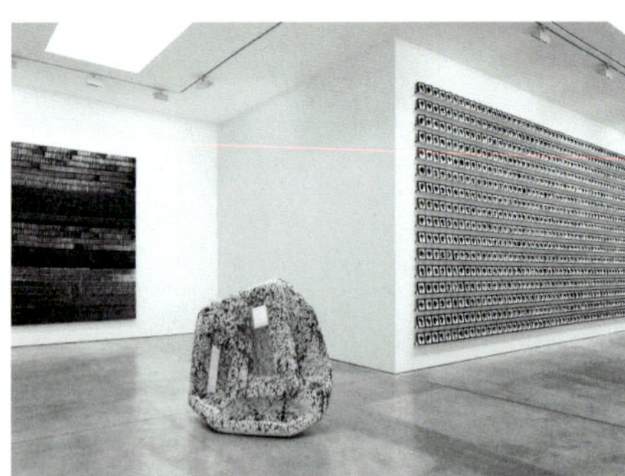

What is your favorite aspect of running a gallery?
The multitude of aspects to be mastered and the freedom to determine my own path.

How do you choose the artists you work with?
Substance, vision, awareness, stamina.

If you weren't running a gallery what else would you do?
Teach.
Work in a museum.
Practice Bach's cello suites.

- **Contact** Galerie Thomas Schulte
Gonzalo Alarcón
gonzalo@galeriethomasschulte.de
- **Established** 1991
- **Owner(s) / Partner(s)** Thomas Schulte
Stefan Roepke
- **Team** 9
- **Space(s)** 340 m²
- **Artists at Art Basel** Richard Deacon
Mark Francis
Paco Knöller
Gordon Matta-Clark
Allan McCollum
Jacco Olivier
João Penalva
Hermann Pitz
Peter Rogiers
Leunora Salihu
Iris Schomaker
Katharina Sieverding
Stephen Willats
Robert Wilson

- **Further artists represented** Alice Aycock
Danilo Dueñas
Alfredo Jaar
Idris Khan
Jonathan Lasker
Iñigo Manglano-Ovalle
Robert Mapplethorpe
Fabian Marcaccio
Bernhard Martin
Michael Müller
David Reed
Albrecht Schnider
Juan Uslé

Anita Schwartz

Rio de Janeiro

Nova

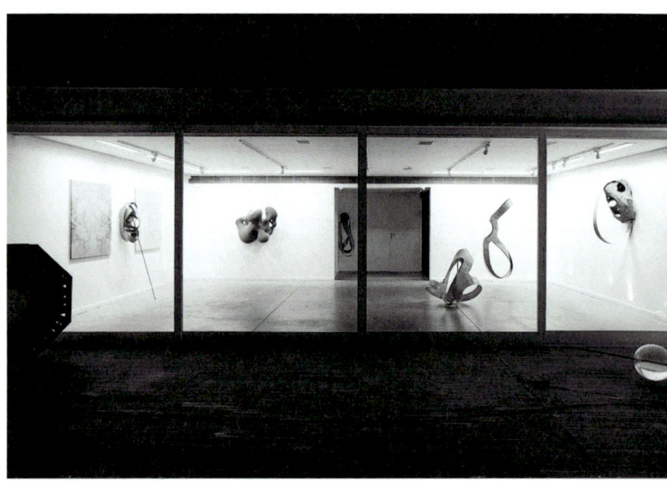

What is your favorite aspect of running a gallery?
The thing that I enjoy the most is the permanent contact with the artists.

How do you choose the artists you work with?
I am always researching artists through worldwide exhibitions and attending art fairs. I usually pay attention to the new generations.

If you weren't running a gallery what else would you do?
Maybe I would have been a great chef …

- **Contact** Anita Schwartz Galeria de Arte
Anita Schwartz
anita@anitaschwartz.com.br
- **Established** 1998
- **Owner(s) / Partner(s)** Anita Schwartz
- **Team** 6
- **Space(s)** 700 m²
- **Artists at Art Basel** Waltercio Caldas
Otavio Schipper
Angelo Venosa
- **Further artists represented** Claudia Bakker
Niura Bellavinha
Rochelle Costi
Célia Euvaldo
Thomas Florschuetz
Carla Guagliardi
Ana Holck
Artur Lescher
Maria Lynch
Antonio Manuel
Everardo Miranda
Wagner Morales
Abraham Palatnik
José Paulo
Paulo Pereira
Wanda Pimentel
Fernanda Quinderé
Nuno Ramos
Estela Sokol
Gustavo Speridião
Ana Vidigal
Bruno Vilela
Daisy Xavier
Carlos Zilio

Anna Schwartz

Melbourne
Sydney

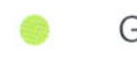 Galleries

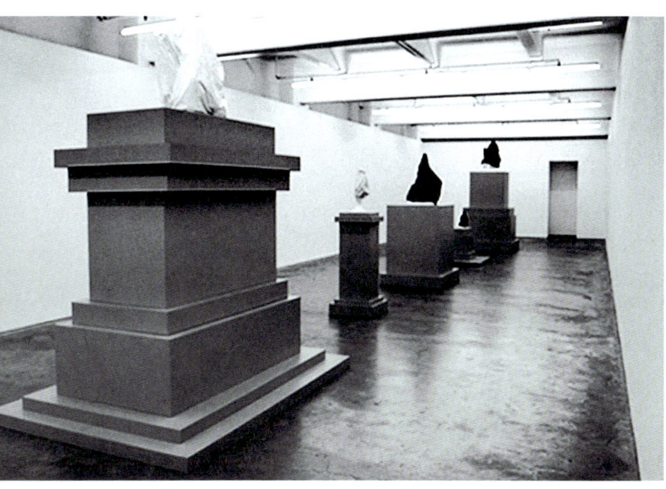

What is your favorite aspect of running a gallery?
Representing the salient ideas of our time rendered by inventive artists. Creating new audiences and challenging those that already exist.

How do you choose the artists you work with?
They are the originators of ideas and forms. They reflect and catalyze the world and its psycho-social conditions. They are various. Each is unique.

If you weren't running a gallery what else would you do?
This has been my choice in life. I would not consider doing anything else.

- **Contact** Anna Schwartz Gallery
  Anna Schwartz
  anna@annaschwartzgallery.com
- **Established** 1982
- **Owner(s) / Partner(s)** Anna Schwartz
- **Team** 10
- **Space(s)** 253 m² (Melbourne)
  337 m² (Sydney)
- **Artists at Art Basel** Heman Chong
  Angela de la Cruz
  Marco Fusinato
  Shaun Gladwell
  Callum Morton
  Mike Parr
  Yinka Shonibare MBE
  Jane and Louise Wilson
- **Further artists represented** AES+F
  Lida Abdul
  Christine Borland
  Stephen Bram
  Lauren Brincat
  Louisa Bufardeci
  Ian Burns
  Mutlu Çerkez (Estate)
  Susan Cohn
  Daniel Crooks
  Mikala Dwyer
  Emily Floyd
  Joseph Kosuth
  Gabriella Mangano
  & Silvana Mangano
  Clement Meadmore
  Angelica Mesiti
  Jan Nelson
  John Nixon
  Clement Meadmore (Estate)
  Stieg Persson
  Kerrie Poliness
  Vivienne Shark LeWitt
  Kathy Temin
  Peter Tyndall
  Daniel von Sturmer
  Jenny Watson
  Warwick Thornton

Semarang

Semarang

Galleries

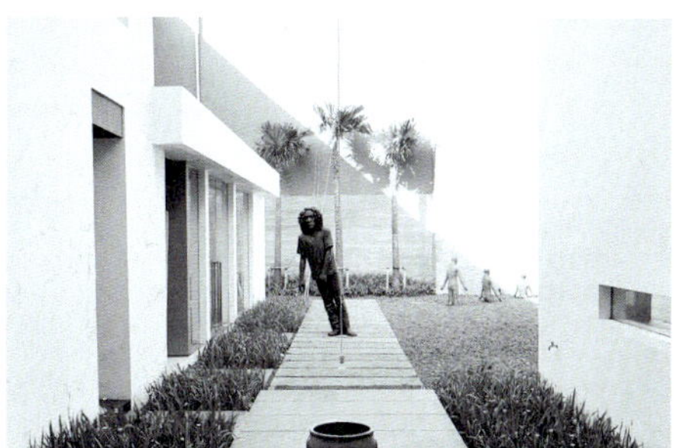

What is your favorite aspect of running a gallery?
As an art lover, running a gallery is a way to express this love.

How do you choose the artists you work with?
By discovering the special talents of each artist.

If you weren't running a gallery what else would you do?
Run a property (developer) business.

- **Contact** Semarang Gallery
  Devi Ariany
  galeri_semarang@yahoo.com
- **Established** 2001
- **Owner(s) / Partner(s)** Chris Dharmawan
- **Team** 6
- **Space(s)** 1,179 m²
- **Artists at Art Basel** Rudi Mantofani
- **Further artists represented** Samsul Arifin
  Bestrizal Besta
  Andy Dewantoro
  Sugiyo Dwiarso
  Eddie Hara
  I Gusti Ngurah Udiantara (Tantin)
  I Made Widya Diputra (Lampung)
  Mella Jars
  Agapetus Kristiandana
  Krisna Murti
  Eko Nugroho
  Erik Pauhrizi
  Agus Suwage

Seroussi

Paris

 Galleries

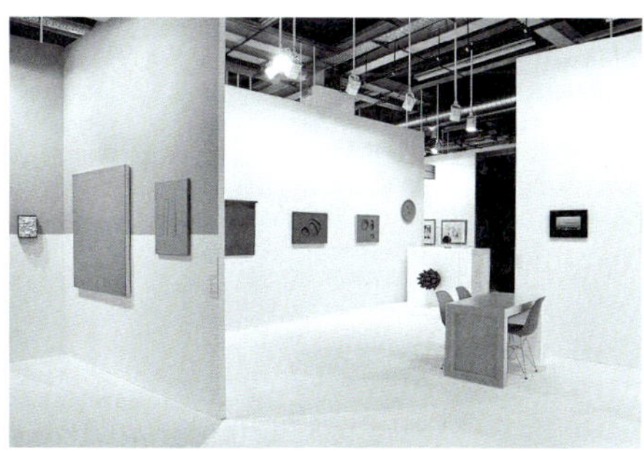

What is your favorite aspect of running a gallery?
Creating links between historical and contemporary art.

If you weren't running a gallery what else would you do?
I would have been a shrink.

- **Contact** Galerie Natalie Seroussi
  Natalie Seroussi
  galerie@natalieseroussi.com
- **Established** 1983
- **Owner(s) / Partner(s)** Natalie Seroussi
- **Team** 5
- **Space(s)** 70 m²
- **Artists at Art Basel** Hans Arp
  Alexander Calder

- **Further artists represented**
  Sergio Camargo
  Enrico Castellani
  Dadamaino
  Lucio Fontana
  Anish Kapoor
  Yves Klein
  Le Corbusier
  Man Ray
  Piero Manzoni
  Salvatore Scarpitta
  Paolo Scheggi
  Salvador Dalí
  Jean Dubuffet
  Max Ernst
  Jean Hélion
  Francis Picabia
  Martial Raysse
  Kurt Schwitters
  Gil Joseph Wolman

Sfeir-Semler

Beirut
Hamburg

 Galleries

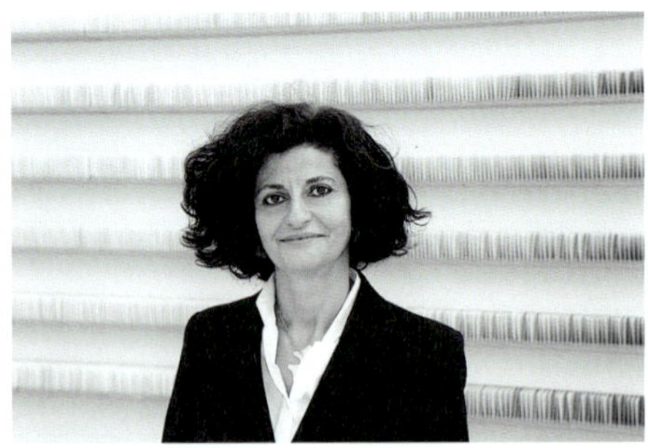

What is your favorite aspect of running a gallery?
I love working closely with artists and seeing the work from early conception to its final realization. There is something truly fascinating about seeing the evolution of the creative process.

How do you choose the artists you work with?
I look everywhere to find qualities in an artist and, of course, I compare and study all the details carefully before deciding.

If you weren't running a gallery what else would you do?
I won't stray too far, I would have liked to be a museum director.

- **Contact** Sfeir-Semler Gallery
  Andrée Sfeir-Semler
  galerie@sfeir-semler.com
- **Established** 1985
- **Owner(s) / Partner(s)** Andrée Sfeir-Semler
- **Team** 5
- **Space(s)** 850 m²
- **Artists at Art Basel**
  Etel Adnan
  The Atlas Group
  Yto Barrada
  Anna Boghiguian
  Balthasar Burkhard
  Marwan
  Timo Nasseri
  Walid Raad
  Marwan Rechmaoui
  Wael Shawky
  Rayyane Tabet
  Akram Zaatari
- **Further artists represented**
  Haig Aivazian
  Mounira Al Solh
  Robert Barry
  Taysir Batniji
  Ian Hamilton Finlay
  Günter Haese
  Hiroyuki Masuyama
  Rabih Mroué
  Khalil Rabah
  Christine Streuli
  Hoda Tawakol

Shainman

New York
Kinderhook

 Galleries
Public

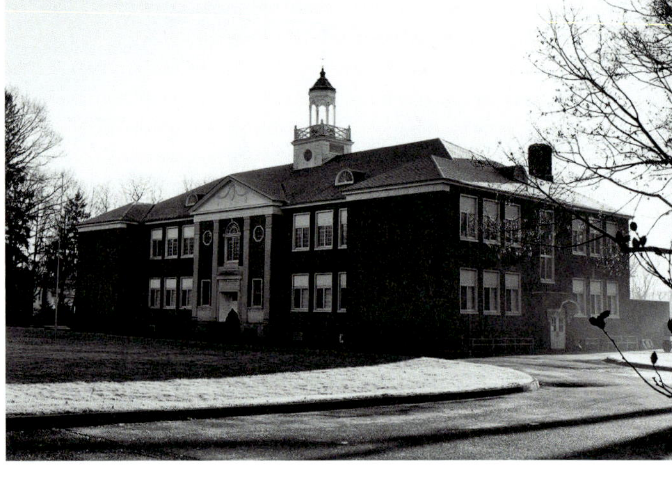

What is your favorite aspect of running a gallery?
Watching an artist develop, and being a part of his/her story. I am truly privileged to champion the artists that I am most passionate about.

How do you choose the artists you work with?
With heart, mind, and soul.

If you weren't running a gallery what else would you do?
I would be riding horses full-time and competing with my jumper.

- **Contact** Jack Shainman Gallery
  Joeonna Bellorado-Samuels
  joeonna@jackshainman.com
- **Established** 1984
- **Owner(s) / Partner(s)** Jack Shainman
- **Team** 14
- **Space(s)** 3,224 m²
- **Artists at Art Basel**
  El Anatsui
  Shimon Attie
  Radcliffe Bailey
  Yoan Capote
  Nick Cave
  Gehard Demetz
  Vibha Galhotra
  Kay Hassan
  Brad Kahlhamer
  Hayv Kahraman
  Titus Kaphar
  Tallur L.N.
  Kerry James Marshall
  Enrique Martínez Celaya
  Richard Mosse
  Adi Nes
  Jackie Nickerson
  Odili Donald Odita
  Toyin Odutola
  Claudette Schreuders
  Michael Snow
  Hank Willis Thomas
  Carlos Vega
  Leslie Wayne
  Carrie Mae Weems
  Lynette Yiadom-Boakye
- **Further artists represented**
  Tim Bavington
  Pierre Dorion
  Barkley L. Hendricks
  Deborah Luster
  Zwelethu Mthethwa
  Malick Sidibé
  Susana Solano

Shanghai Gallery

Shanghai 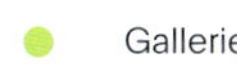 Galleries

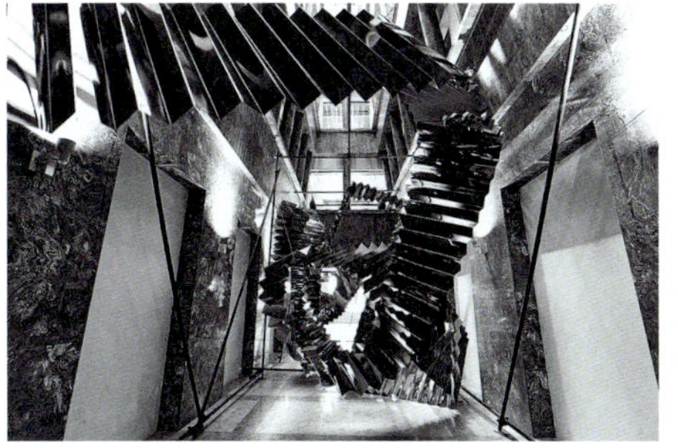

- **Contact** Shanghai Gallery of Art
Josef Ng
gr@on-the-bund.com
- **Established** 2004
- **Space(s)** 1,200 m²
- **Artists at Art Basel** Cui Xiuwen
Gao Weigang
Yang Yongliang
Zheng Lu
- **Further artists represented** Feng Mengbo
Jin Jiangbo
Map Office
Qiu Jie
Shao Yinong & Mu Chen
Tang Yuhan
Wu Di
Xu Bing
Zheng Chongbin

ShanghART

Shanghai
Beijing
Singapore

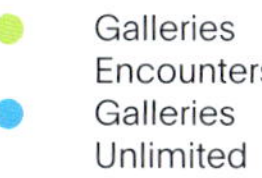

Galleries
Encounters
Galleries
Unlimited
Galleries

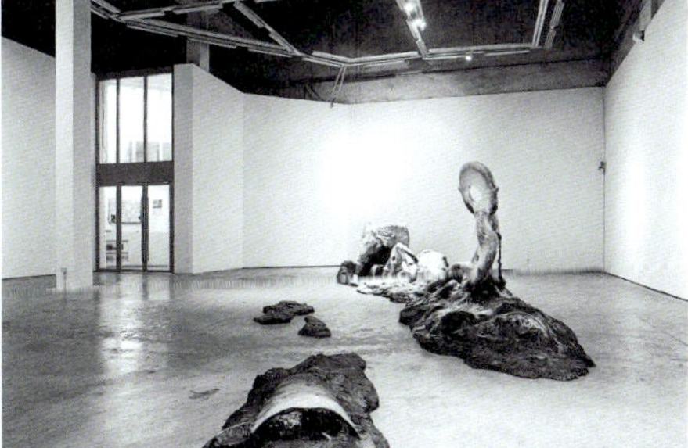

What is your favorite aspect of running a gallery?

The aspect of creating space, physical as well as mental space.

How do you choose the artists you work with?

We are looking for artists who add something to the world and are in dialogue with the other artists we are working with.

If you weren't running a gallery what else would you do?

I would probably lead a rather quiet life, trying to be a farmer or a librarian perhaps.

- **Contact** ShanghART Gallery
Betty Yang Jun
betty@shanghartgallery.com
- **Established** 1996
- **Owner(s) / Partner(s)** Lorenz Helbling
Chen Yan
Helen Zhu
- **Team** 30
- **Space(s)** 3,000 m²
- **Artists at Art Basel** Birdhead
Chen Xiaoyun
Ding Yi
Geng Jianyi
Han Feng
Hu Jieming
Huang Kui
Ji Wenyu & Zhu Weibing
Jiang Pengyi
Liang Shaoji
Liang Yue
Liu Weijian
Lu Lei
Pu Jie
Shao Yi
Shen Fan
Shi Qing
Shi Yong
Sun Xun
Tang Guo
Tang Maohong
Wang Youshen
Wu Yiming
Xu Zhen / Madein Company
Xue Song
Yang Fudong
Yang Zhenzhong
Yu Youhan
Zhang Ding
Zhang Enli
Zhang Qing
Zhou Tiehai
Zhou Zixi
Zhu Jia
- **Further artists represented** Chen Yanyin
Li Shan
Xiang Liqing
Wei Guangqing
Wang Guangyi
Yuan Yuan
Zeng Fanzhi
Zhao Bandi
Li Pinghu

Shin

Tokyo 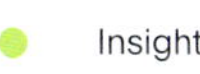 Insights

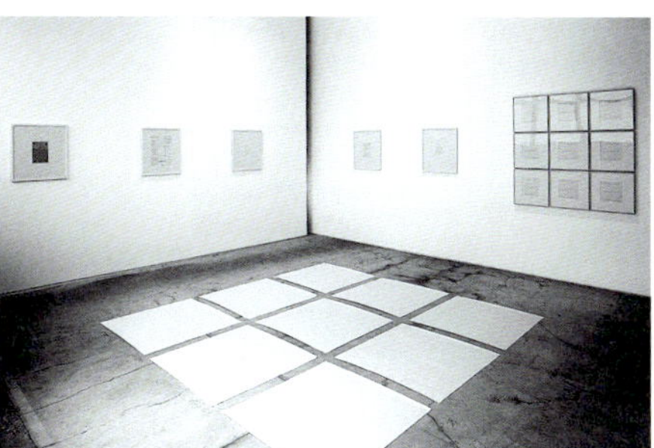

What is your favorite aspect of running a gallery?

To create new values in the history of art.

How do you choose the artists you work with?

I like to work with artists who represent the zeitgeist.

If you weren't running a gallery what else would you do?

I cannot think of any other professions. If I had been born in the 19th century, I would have liked to become an opera singer in Italy.

- **Contact** Misa Shin Gallery
info@misashin.com
- **Established** 2010
- **Owner(s) / Partner(s)** Misa Shin
- **Team** 5
- **Space(s)** 70 m²
- **Artists at Art Basel** Tsuyoshi Ozawa
- **Further artists represented** Ai Weiwei
Seung Woo Back
Shingo Francis
Yasuko Iba
Arata Isozaki
Tadashi Kawamata
Ken Lum
Yutaka Matsuzawa
Jio Shimizu
Shomei Tomatsu
Momoyo Torimitsu

ShugoArts

Tokyo

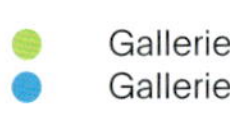

Galleries
Galleries

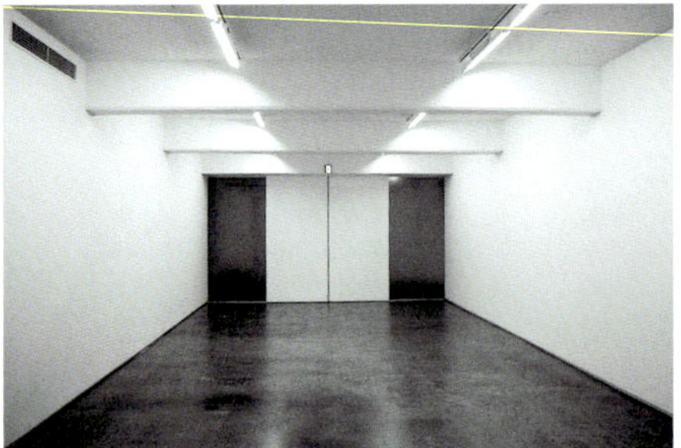

What is your favorite aspect of running a gallery?
I am proud of running the gallery as "art dojo" for our artists, clients, and team members of ShugoArts. (The dojo is a traditional-style training hall for judo or kendo.)

How do you choose the artists you work with?
Intuition.

If you weren't running a gallery what else would you do?
Astronaut or monk.

- **Contact** ShugoArts
  Mika Mizuno
  mika.shugoarts@gmail.com
- **Established** 2000
- **Owner(s) / Partner(s)** Shugo Satani
  Satoko Oe
- **Team** 5
- **Space(s)** 123 m²
- **Artists at Art Basel** Masaya Chiba
  Yukio Fujimoto
  Carsten Höller
  Leiko Ikemura
  Teppei Kaneuji
  Shinichiro Kano
  Masato Kobayashi
  Aki Kondo
  Lee Kit
  Naofumi Maruyama
  Ritsue Mishima
  Morimura Yasumasa
  Kazuna Taguchi
  Tomoko Yoneda
- **Further artists represented** Candice Breitz
  Mitsuhiro Ikeda
  Takuya Ikezaki
  Tadasuke Iwanaga
  Ilya Kabakov
  Runa Islam
  Boris Mikhailov
  Takuma Nakahira
  Ylva Ogland
  Shigeo Toya
  Jun Yang

Sicardi

Houston

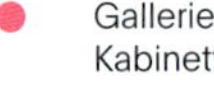

Galleries
Kabinett

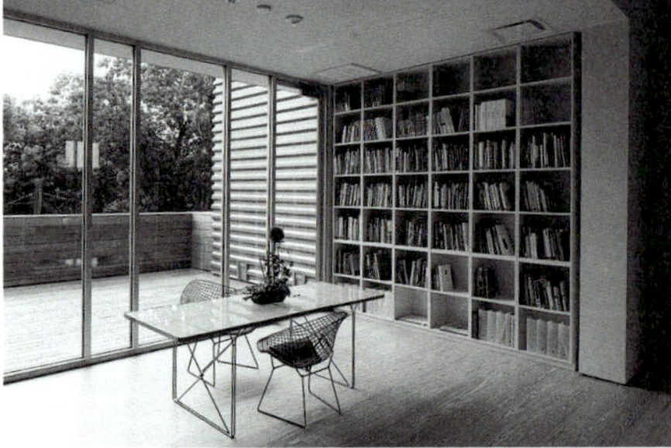

- **Contact** Sicardi Gallery
  Laura Wellen
  laura@sicardi.com
- **Established** 1994
- **Owner(s) / Partner(s)** María Inés Sicardi
  Allison Ayers
  Carlos Bacino
- **Team** 10
- **Space(s)** 550 m²
- **Artists at Art Basel** Antonio Asis
  Carlos Cruz-Diez
  León Ferrari
  Gego
  Francisco Sobrino
  Jesús Rafael Soto
  Luis Tomasello
- **Further artists represented** Maria Fernanda Cardoso
  Dias & Riedweg
  Sérvulo Esmeraldo
  Manuel Espinosa
  Thomas Glassford
  Graciela Hasper
  Marco Maggi
  Gabriel de la Mora
  Oscar Muñoz
  Liliana Porter
  Miguel Angel Ríos
  Miguel Ángel Rojas
  Pablo Siquier
  Melanie Smith
  Ana Maria Tavares
  Clarissa Tossin

Side 2

Tokyo

Insights
Statements

What is your favorite aspect of running a gallery?
Learning about artists' ideas and works, encountering people who are also excited about them.

How do you choose the artists you work with?
By instinct and through discussions.

If you weren't running a gallery what else would you do?
That is hard to imagine.

- **Contact** Gallery Side 2
  Yuko Fukamizu
  info@galleryside2.net
- **Established** 1997
- **Owner(s) / Partner(s)** Junko Shimada
- **Team** 5
- **Space(s)** 80 m²
- **Artists at Art Basel** Takeo Hanazawa
  Masaru Tatsuki
  Fumito Urabe
- **Further artists represented** Michelangelo Consani
  Jun Fujita
  Maureen Gallace
  Takahiro Inamori
  Udomsak Krisanamis
  Peter McDonald
  Yuko Murata
  Steven Pippin
  Yusuke Saito
  Shinako Sato
  Rirkrit Tiravanija
  Yasuko Watanabe

Sies + Höke

Düsseldorf

Galleries
Galleries Unlimited
Galleries

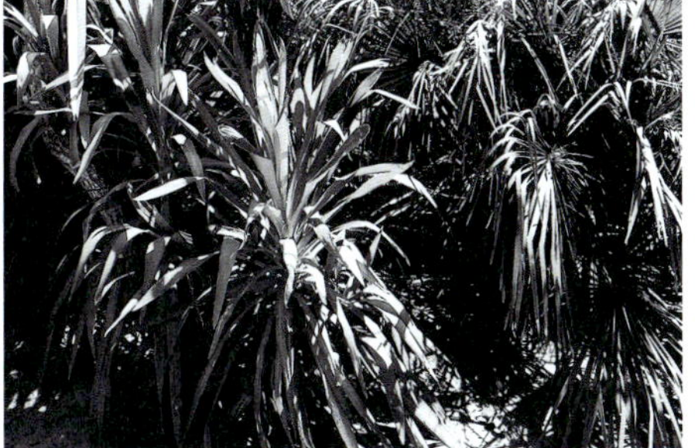

What is your favorite aspect of running a gallery?
There is not just one. There are: following ideas, working together with artists, detailed research, and dealing with their works. Long-term relationships and growing together are the main aspects.

How do you choose the artists you work with?
Follow what you don't understand.

If you weren't running a gallery what else would you do?
Be a collector.

- **Contact** Sies + Höke, Tine Lurati, tine@sieshoeke.com
- **Established** 1999
- **Owner(s) / Partner(s)** Nina Höke, Alexander Sies
- **Team** 10
- **Space(s)** 850 m²
- **Artists at Art Basel** Abel Auer, Etienne Chambaud, Talia Chetrit, Daniel Gustav Cramer, Björn Dahlem, Marcel Dzama, João Maria Gusmão + Pedro Paiva, Federico Herrero, Dorota Jurczak, Thomas Kiesewetter, Kris Martin, Jonathan Meese, Michael van Ofen, Taiyo Onorato + Nico Krebs, Fabrice Samyn, Florian Slotawa, Claudia Wieser

Sikkema Jenkins

New York

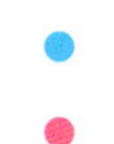

Galleries Unlimited
Galleries

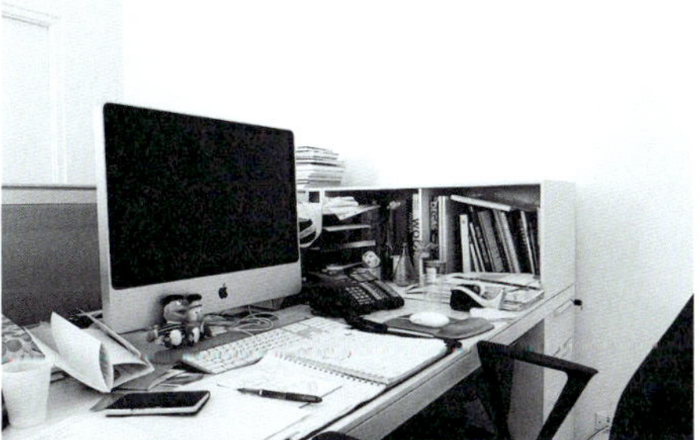

What is your favorite aspect of running a gallery?
Seeing an artist's work evolve in the studio and being able to present it in the gallery.

How do you choose the artists you work with?
Visiting artists' studios and exhibitions, and conversing with our artists and colleagues. We tend to follow an artist's work for a few years before making a commitment to it.

If you weren't running a gallery what else would you do?
After all these years it is hard to imagine anything else. However, seeing art and exhibitions and building a collection full time would be great.

- **Contact** Sikkema Jenkins & Co., Katie Rashid, katie@sikkemajenkinsco.com
- **Established** 1991
- **Owner(s) / Partner(s)** Brent Sikkema, Michael Jenkins, Meg Malloy
- **Team** 10
- **Space(s)** 929 m²
- **Artists at Art Basel** William Cordova, Leonardo Drew, Mitch Epstein, Tony Feher, Terry Haggerty, Josephine Halvorson, Arturo Herrera, Sheila Hicks, Jennie C. Jones, Vik Muniz, Elizabeth Neel, Kay Rosen, Erin Shirreff, Amy Sillman, Kara Walker
- **Further artists represented** Antony, Burt Barr, Trisha Brown, Marc Handelman, Jan Henle, Leslie Hewitt, Merlin James, Nikki S. Lee, Marlene McCarty, Jorge Queiroz, Shahzia Sikander

Silverlens

Makati City
Singapore

Galleries

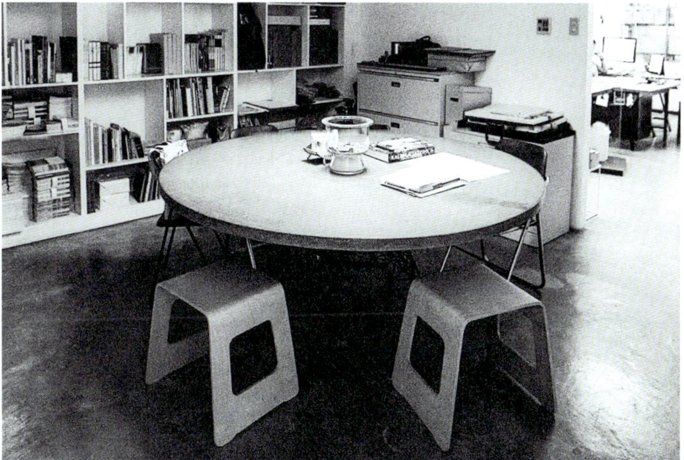

What is your favorite aspect of running a gallery?
Installing the shows is definitely a highlight, the moment when the work is coming together in the exhibition space. Studio visits are another favorite.

How do you choose the artists you work with?
We must like the work. It is so special to stand in front of the artist's work and have that feeling. We must respect the process of the artist and believe in what s/he is doing. Focus and discipline are very important to be a good artist, so we like artists who have both.

If you weren't running a gallery what else would you do?
Isa Lorenzo: Be a psychiatrist.
Rachel Rillo: Be an artist.

- **Contact** Silverlens, Isa Lorenzo, isa@silverlensgalleries.com
- **Established** 2004
- **Owner(s) /** Isa Lorenzo

- **Partner(s)** Rachel Rillo
- **Team** 13
- **Space(s)** 700 m²
- **Artists at Art Basel** Pio Abad, Luis Lorenzana, Patricia Perez Eustaquio, Hanna Pettyjohn, Maria Taniguchi, Yee I-Lann
- **Further artists represented** Frank Callaghan, Mariano Ching, Chati Coronel, Christina Dy, Dina Gadia, Gregory Halili, Isa Lorenzo, Wawi Navarroza, Gina Osterloh, Bernardo Pacquing, Gary-Ross Pastrana, Rachel Rillo, Corinne de San Jose, Ryan Villamael, Costantino Zicarelli

Silverman

San Francisco 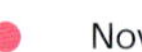 Nova

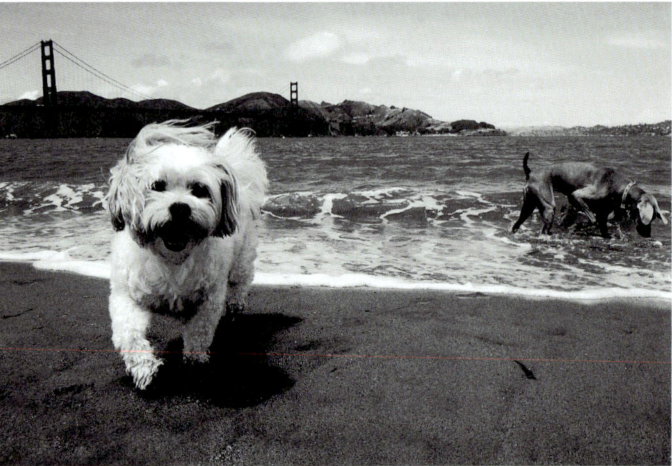

What is your favorite aspect of running a gallery?

I enjoy discovering artists and building a dialogue around their practice in order to promote their work and contribute to an enduring career. I also relish the editorial process when curating exhibitions. It is gratifying when artists feel confident and comfortable with my input. Although many dealers complain about art fairs, I love them. They are hard work, but when your gallery is located in an outlier city like San Francisco, their heavy footfall is exciting.

How do you choose the artists you work with?

I have a slow, deliberate process when working with artists, one that is based on seeing something special in their work, assessing the seriousness of their practice, and developing mutual trust. While I may be interested in their current work, I'm also looking toward the next series, as well as at their personal ambitions as artists. I look for artists who do what they do, who are keen to push the boundaries of contemporary art, and who are not easily swayed by passing ephemeral trends.

If you weren't running a gallery what else would you do?

The truth is I can't imagine not doing what I do. However, there are a few other activities that I enjoy that are welcomed extensions to the gallery. I recently joined the board of the Tenderloin Museum, which will act as a dynamic cultural space. I'm also on the San Francisco Arts Commission where I can suggest exciting public projects in the Bay Area. Lastly, I am lucky to curate exhibitions at Fused Space, a 2,500 sq. foot exhibition space offered to me by renowned designer Yves Béhar.

- **Contact** Jessica Silverman Gallery, Rina Kim, rina@jessicasilvermangallery.com
- **Established** 2008
- **Owner(s) / Partner(s)** Jessica Silverman
- **Team** 4
- **Space(s)** 223 m²
- **Artists at Art Basel** Dashiell Manley, Ruairiadh O'Connell, Hugh Scott-Douglas
- **Further artists represented** Christopher Badger, Luke Butler, Tammy Rae Carland, Shannon Finley, Barbara Kasten, Matt Lipps, Hayal Pozanti, Sean Raspet, Conrad Ruiz, Amikam Toren, Susanne M. Winterling

Silverstein

New York Galleries

What is your favorite aspect of running a gallery?

Running a gallery is immensely challenging and, for the most part, extraordinarily satisfying. I enjoy collaborating with talented and passionate individuals. I greatly appreciate the human element of running a gallery; connecting with artists, curators, staff, and collectors—many of whom have become close friends. Yet, in the end, facilitating a connection to art is the ultimate challenge and reward, and continues to bring me great pleasure.

How do you choose the artists you work with?

Foremost, I look for artists who create because they have no other choice but to do so. For mature artists, I look for the development of a unique language, one that has evolved over a period of time. And for emerging artists, I look at their works in search of a foundation, which that unique language can build upon. Beyond their ideas, I also try to gain insight into their state of being—motivations, goals, etc.—to ultimately determine if they will be a solid partner.

If you weren't running a gallery what else would you do?

I would enjoy having more time to curate, as well as spending more time with some of the incredible people I have met along the way. I would certainly dedicate more time to supporting the Center for Arts Education, here in New York, as I believe that it is imperative to our future that every child in public or private school be exposed to the arts.

- **Contact** Bruce Silverstein, Bruce Silverstein, bruce@brucesilverstein.com
- **Established** 2001
- **Owner(s) / Partner(s)** Bruce Silverstein
- **Team** 10
- **Space(s)** 650 m²
- **Artists at Art Basel** Diane Arbus, Bernd and Hilla Becher, Ilse Bing, Constantin Brancusi, Harry Callahan, John Coplans, Elger Esser, Walker Evans, Robert Frank, Jaromir Funke, E.O. Hoppé, André Kertész, Dorothea Lange, Dora Maar, Man Ray, Robert Mapplethorpe, Shinichi Maruyama, László Moholy-Nagy, Henry Moore, Barbara Morgan, Daido Moriyama, Max Neumann, Paul Outerbridge, Alexander Rodchenko, Charles Sheeler, Cindy Sherman, Aaron Siskind

Keith Smith
Frederick Sommer
Trine Søndergaard
Edward Steichen
Alfred Stieglitz
Paul Strand
Josef Sudek
Hiroshi Sugimoto
Michael Wolf
Silvio Wolf
John Wood
Francesca Woodman

- **Further artists represented** Erwin Blumenfeld
Marie Cosindas
Todd Hido
Nicolai Howalt
Nathan Lyons
Maria Mameli
Lisette Model
Eileen Neff
Larry Silver
Rosalind Solomon
Brea Souders
Zoe Strauss
Randy West
Joel-Peter Witkin

Skape

Seoul 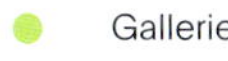 Galleries

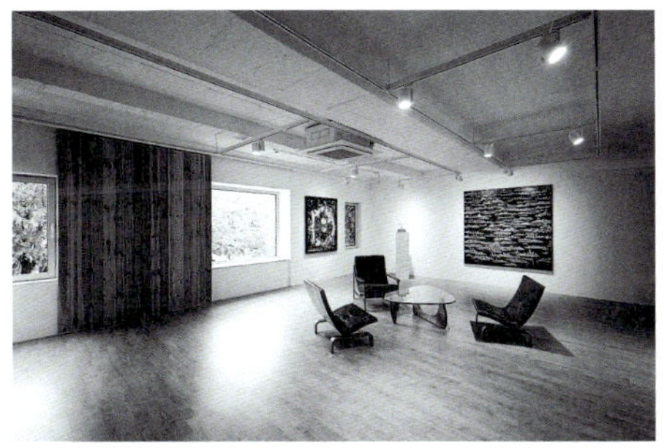

What is your favorite aspect of running a gallery?
I am fond of preparing a creative and innovative exhibition by communicating with various artists who view the world from different perspectives. The sense of achievement that I feel from the successful result of continuous promotion of artists also excites me.

How do you choose the artists you work with?
I tend to work with artists who have their own world, built through research and continuous communication.

If you weren't running a gallery what else would you do?
If I hadn't opened my own gallery, probably I would have worked for someone else's gallery.

- **Contact** Gallery Skape
Kyung Ae Sohn
ska@skape.co.kr
- **Established** 2004
- **Owner(s) / Partner(s)** Kyung Ae Sohn
- **Team** 6
- **Space(s)** 440 m²
- **Artists at Art Basel** Soojung Choi
Suejin Chung
Jungwook Kim
Sungsoo Kim
Hyeseung Lee
Hyungkoo Lee
Sodam Lim
Jeongwon Yoon
- **Further artists represented** Kyuchul Ahn
Yujung Chang
Sungmyung Chun
Jihyun Jung
Jungyeob Jung
Hyuenjun Kim
Myeongbeom Kim
Taeheon Kim
Myungkeun Koh
Sun K. Kwak
B.G. Muhn
Reinoud Oudshoorn
Zhang Yingnan
Youngjin Yoo

Skarstedt

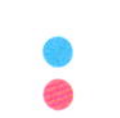

New York — Galleries
London — Galleries

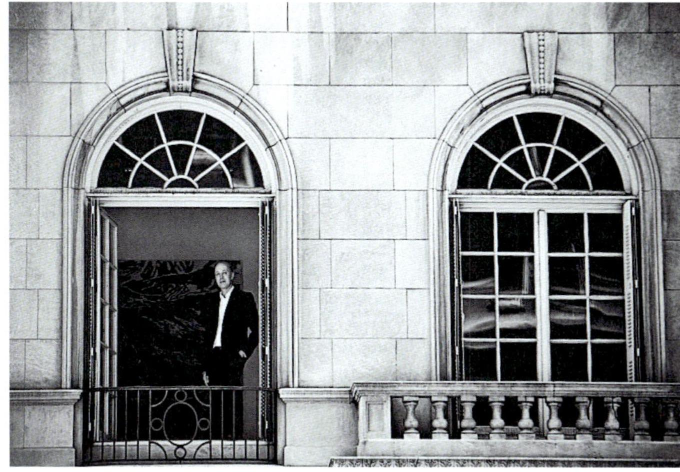

What is your favorite aspect of running a gallery?
I love every aspect of it. It is a big privilege to run a gallery and get to hang out with eccentric collectors and some of the great artists of our time.

How do you choose the artists you work with?
Most of the artists I work with I have been collaborating with for a very long time. Once I decide I like an artist—which can sometimes take a long time—I remain committed.

If you weren't running a gallery what else would you do?
I would definitely be a full time collector.

- **Contact** Skarstedt
Brady Doty
info@skarstedt.com
- **Established** 1994
- **Owner(s) / Partner(s)** Per Skarstedt
Bona Colonna Montagu
- **Team** 19
- **Space(s)** 604 m²
- **Artists at Art Basel** Francis Bacon
Georg Baselitz
George Condo
Carroll Dunham
Eric Fischl
Peter Fischli / David Weiss
Günther Förg
Keith Haring
Jenny Holzer
Mike Kelley
Martin Kippenberger
Yves Klein
Barbara Kruger
Louise Lawler
Sherrie Levine
Robert Mapplethorpe
Juan Münoz
Cady Noland
Albert Oehlen
Sigmar Pölke
Richard Prince
David Salle
Thomas Schütte
Cindy Sherman
Lucien Smith
Rosemarie Trockel
Andy Warhol
Franz West
Christopher Wool

SKE

Bangalore
New Delhi

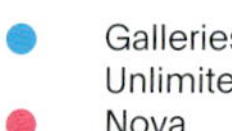

Galleries
Unlimited
Nova

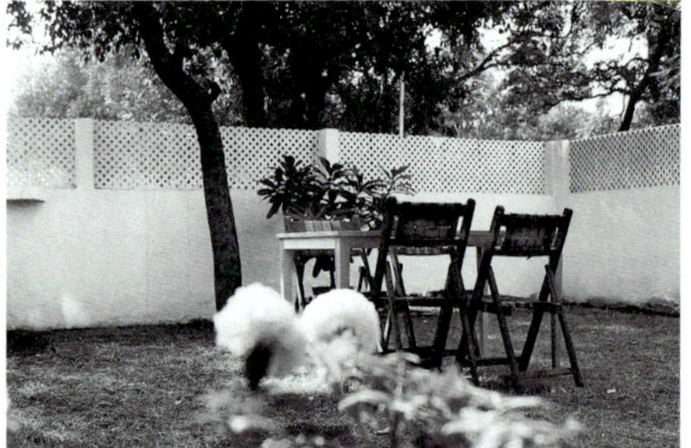

What is your favorite aspect of running a gallery?
Visiting artists' studios to get an insight into the artist and their practice, and working on the gallery program.

How do you choose the artists you work with?
I go with my instinct and discuss new additions with gallery artists; it makes a more democratic process.

If you weren't running a gallery what else would you do?
I would run a public space in a wider cultural context that would include literature, film, architecture, design, performance, and visual art.

- **Contact** GALLERYSKE
  Aruna Keshav
  aruna@galleryske.com
- **Established** 2003
- **Owner(s) / Partner(s)** Sunitha Kumar Emmart
- **Team** 14
- **Space(s)** 557.5 m²
- **Artists at Art Basel** Sheela Gowda
  Bharti Kher
  Prabhavathi Meppayil
  Pors & Rao
  Srinivasa Prasad
  Sudarshan Shetty
  Navin Thomas
- **Further artists represented** Krishnaraj Chonat
  Sakshi Gupta
  Abhishek Hazra
  Sreshta Rit Premnath
  Mariam Suhail
  Anup Mathew Thomas

Skopia

Geneva

Galleries
Unlimited

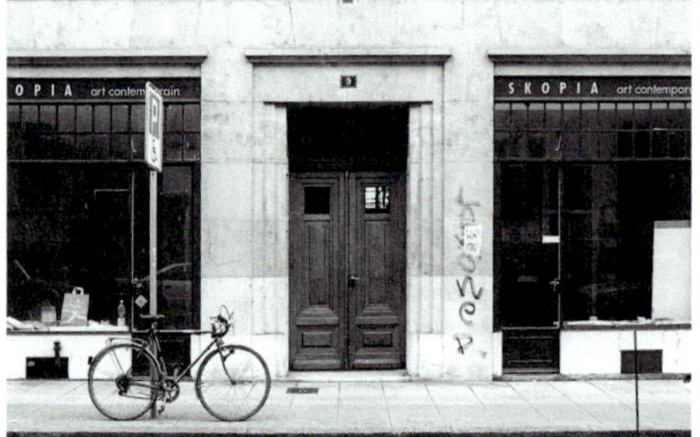

What is your favorite aspect of running a gallery?
Almost everything (except numbers). But what I really enjoy is visiting the studio, the discovery of a work. Then putting on the show.

How do you choose the artists you work with?
In an intuitive manner and with curiosity: I think a lot about it, and then try to forget. In the end, I think I am looking for something that is related to space. Artists I am interested in deal with this question.

If you weren't running a gallery what else would you do?
Probably nothing!

- **Contact** Skopia P.-H. Jaccaud
  Pierre-Henri Jaccaud
  info@skopia.ch
- **Established** 1989
- **Owner(s) / Partner(s)** Pierre-Henri Jaccaud
- **Team** 4
- **Space(s)** 160 m²
- **Artists at Art Basel** Silvia Bächli & Eric Hattan
  Francis Baudevin
  Erik Bulatov
  Jean Crotti
  Thomas Huber
  Alain Huck
  Claudio Moser
  Franz Erhard Walther
- **Further artists represented** Pierre-Olivier Arnaud
  Alexandre Bianchini
  Jérémy Chevalier
  Pierre André Ferrand
  Franz Gertsch
  Alex Hanimann
  Robert Ireland
  Stanislaw Koba
  Jean-Luc Manz
  Olivier Mosset
  Vanessa van Obberghen
  Christoph Rütimann
  Hinrich Sachs
  Simone Schardt
  Pierre Schwerzmann
  Marion Tampon-Lajarriette

SlyZmud

Buenos Aires

Positions
Public

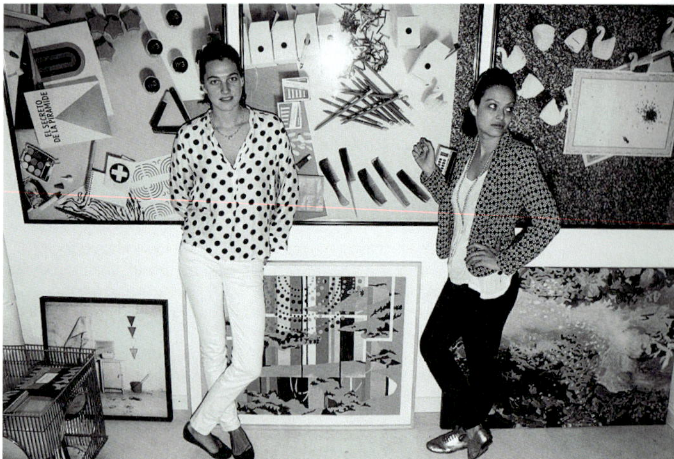

What is your favorite aspect of running a gallery?
Our favorite aspect of running a gallery is the possibility of having a platform to exhibit the production and ideas of contemporary artists that are the most interesting to us from our time and country. To expand their point of view into the world is what we consider the best thing about our job.

How do you choose the artists you work with?
The selection of our artists relies on two important factors: the conceptual value of their work that enables us to question ideas of the times we are living in (political, poetic aspects) and an aesthetic impact. It is important for us to visually feel attracted to what we are showing and how we present it in our space.

If you weren't running a gallery what else would you do?
Larisa Zmud: I would have an organic food restaurant and be a theater actress.
Natalia Sly: If I wasn't running a gallery I would run a farm somewhere far away from the buzz of the city.

- **Contact** SlyZmud
  Natalia Sly
  natalia@slyzmud.com
- **Established** 2011
- **Owner(s) / Partner(s)** Natalia Sly
  Larisa Zmud
- **Team** 2
- **Space(s)** 55 m²

- **Artists at Art Basel** Guillermo Faivovich & Nicolás Goldberg
- **Further artists represented** Gabriel Baggio
Daniel Basso
Nicolás Bedel
Azul Caverna
Jimena Croceri
Sebastián Garbrecht
Diego Gravinese
Vicente Grondona
Valeria Maculán
Miguel Mitlag
Jill Mulleady
Hernán Paganini
Deborah Pruden
Martina Quesada
Hernán Salamanco
Juan Stoppani
Lorena Ventimiglia
Juan Andrés Videla
Pablo Ziccarello

Snitzer

Miami 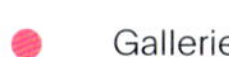 Galleries

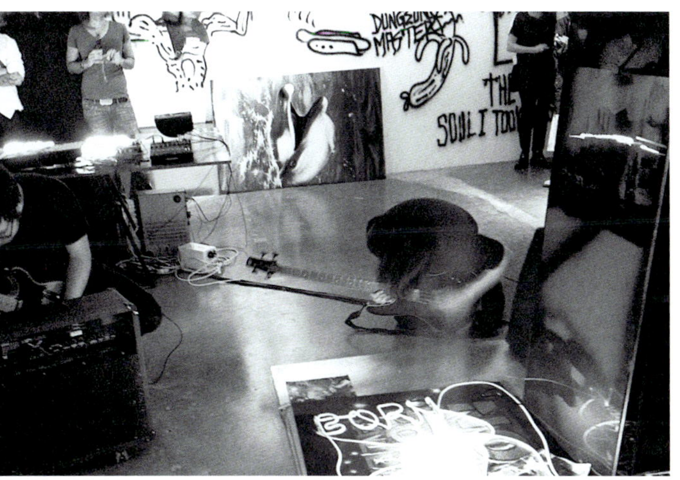

What is your favorite aspect of running a gallery?
Exposing new talent.

If you weren't running a gallery what else would you do?
Make art.

How do you choose the artists you work with?
It's like getting married … a complex process.

- **Contact** Fredric Snitzer Gallery
Fredric Snitzer
info@snitzer.com
- **Established** 1977
- **Owner(s) / Partner(s)** Fredric Snitzer
- **Team** 6
- **Space(s)** 279 m²
- **Artists at Art Basel** Alice Aycock
Hernan Bas
Maria Martinez Canas
Enrique Martinez Celaya
Alexander Kroll
Jon Pylypchuk
Diego Singh
- **Further artists represented** Zhivago Duncan
Naomi Fisher

Société

Berlin 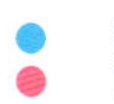 Statements
Nova

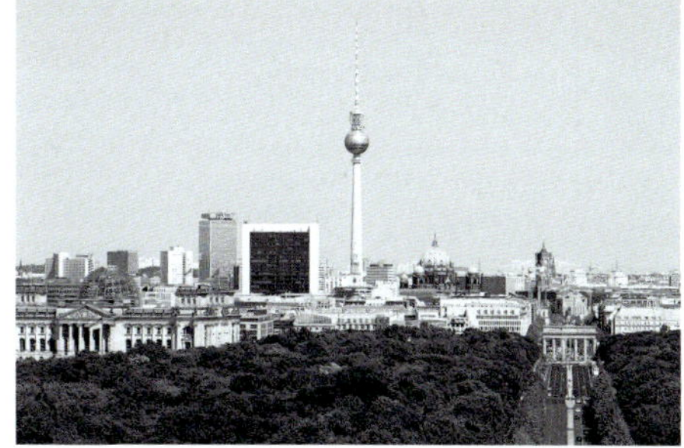

What is your favorite aspect of running a gallery?
Artists.

If you weren't running a gallery what else would you do?
Farm.

How do you choose the artists you work with?
Intuition.

- **Contact** Société
Daniel Wichelhaus
daniel@societeberlin.com
- **Established** 2009
- **Owner(s) / Partner(s)** Daniel Wichelhaus
Hans Bülow
- **Team** 4
- **Space(s)** 450 m²
- **Artists at Art Basel** Trisha Baga
Sean Raspet
Timur Si-Qin
Ned Vena
- **Further artists represented** Josh Kolbo
Kaspar Müller
Davis Rhodes
Bunny Rogers
Matthew Schlanger

Soka

Taipei
Beijing
Tainan

Galleries

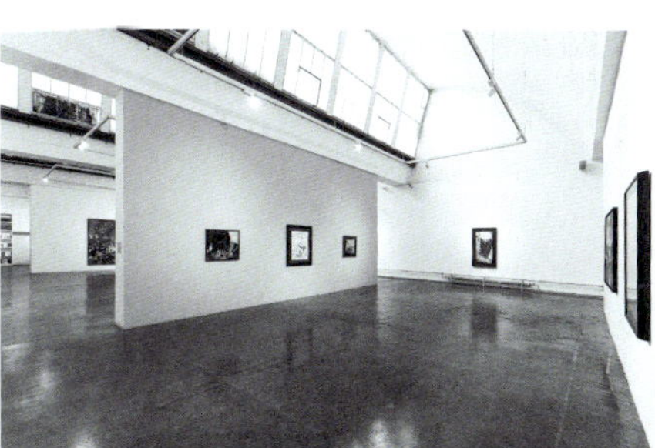

What is your favorite aspect of running a gallery?
The best part is getting to know artists, collectors, and art lovers. We have private clients and museum clients from all around the world and we have the chance to visit them, introduce them to our culture, and, at the same time, learn from them, which makes the gallery's task more interesting and fun.

How do you choose the artists you work with?
Usually we choose artists who have their own aesthetic values and persist in their own line of creation in the long-term. We work closely with our artists in order to present them well.

If you weren't running a gallery what else would you do?
Running the gallery is the only thing I want to do as a lifelong job.

- **Contact** Soka Art
Crystal Cheng
crystal.chengs@gmail.com
- **Established** 1992
- **Owner(s) / Partner(s)** Hsiao Fuyuan

- **Team** 20
- **Space(s)** 1,500 m²
- **Artists at Art Basel** Hong Ling, Hsi Shih-Ping, Iida Kiriko, Liang Quan, Mao Xuhui, Zeng Jianyong, Zeng Yongning

SpazioA

Pistoia — Positions

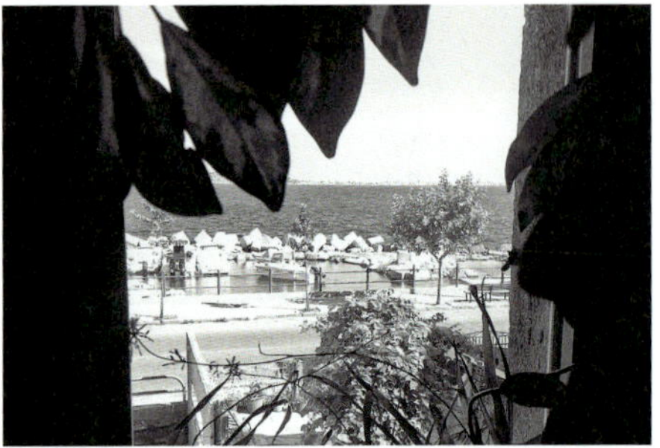

What is your favorite aspect of running a gallery?
I like to support artists and their projects, getting involved in the various phases of the their work.

How do you choose the artists you work with?
I'm working with a group of young artists. Right from the start, I've always made highly personal choices, a role I still think I play today, at least partially.

If you weren't running a gallery what else would you do?
I would travel the world, teaching yoga and meditation wherever I found a need.

- **Contact** SpazioA
  Giuseppe Alleruzzo
  info@spazioa.it
- **Established** 2008
- **Owner(s) / Partner(s)** Giuseppe Alleruzzo
- **Team** 2
- **Space(s)** 200 m²
- **Artists at Art Basel** Esther Kläs
- **Further artists represented** Luca Bertolo, Chiara Camoni, Francesco Carone, Giulia Cenci, Dina Danish, Maxim Liulca, Alessandro Mencarelli, Katarina Zdjelar

Sperone Westwater

New York — Galleries, Galleries Kabinett

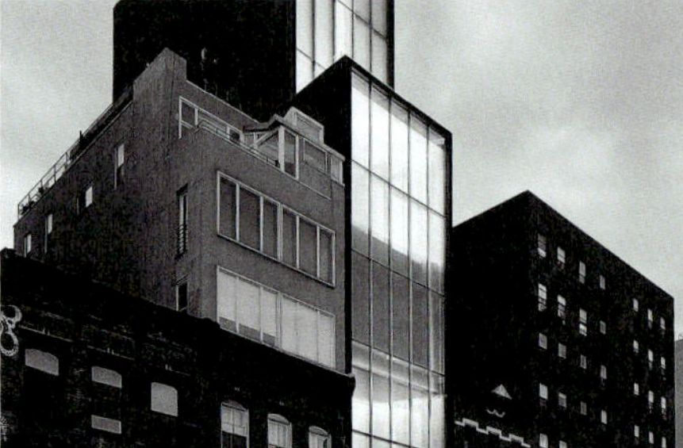

- **Contact** Sperone Westwater
  Juliette Premmereur
  juliette@speronewestwater.com
- **Established** 1975
- **Owner(s) / Partner(s)** Gian Enzo Sperone, Angela Westwater
- **Team** 12
- **Space(s)** 1,579.5 m²
- **Artists at Art Basel** Carla Accardi, Barry X Ball, Ali Banisadr, Bertozzi & Casoni, Alighiero Boetti, Wim Delvoye, Braco Dimitrijevic, Kim Dingle, Lucio Fontana, Mark Greenwold, Guillermo Kuitca, Wolfgang Laib, Charles Ledray, Liu Ye, Richard Long, Emil Lukas, Heinz Mack, Piero Manzoni, Mario Merz, Frank Moore, Malcolm Morley, Nabil Nahas, Bruce Nauman, Evan Penny, Otto Piene, Alexis Rockman, Susan Rothenberg, Tom Sachs, Julian Schnabel, Andrew Sendor, Fabio Viale, Not Vital, William Wegman, Martin Wilner, Jan Worst

Sprüth Magers

Berlin, London — Galleries, Unlimited, Galleries

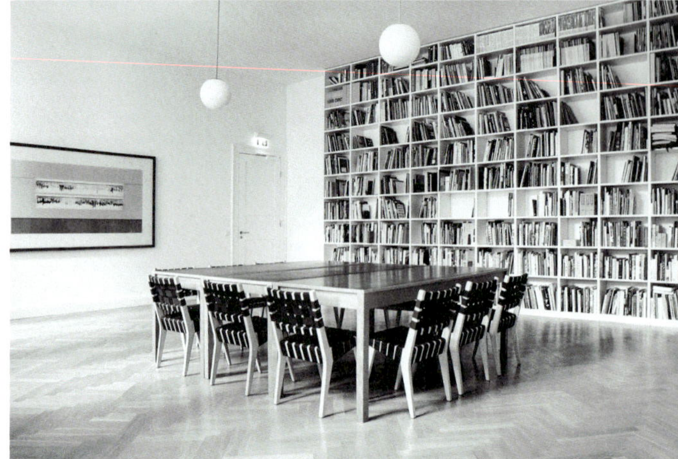

- **Contact** Sprüth Magers Berlin London
  Craig Burnett
  info@spruethmagers.com
- **Established** 1983
- **Owner(s) / Partner(s)** Monika Sprüth, Philomene Magers
- **Team** 45
- **Space(s)** 700 m²
- **Artists at Art Basel** Keith Arnatt, John Baldessari, Bernd & Hilla Becher, John Bock, George Condo, Walter Dahn, Hanne Darboven, Thomas Demand, Thea Djordjadze, Peter Fischli & David Weiss, Cyprien Gaillard, Andreas Gursky, Jenny Holzer, Gary Hume, Karen Kilimnik, Astrid Klein, Barbara Kruger, David Lamelas, Louise Lawler

Reinhard Mucha
Michail Pirgelis
Sterling Ruby
Ed Ruscha
Analia Saban
Thomas Scheibitz
Andreas Schulze
Cindy Sherman
Stephen Shore
Rosemarie Trockel

- **Further artists represented** Kenneth Anger
Siegfried Anzinger
Richard Artschwager
Alighiero Boetti
Philip-Lorca Dicorcia
Marcel van Eeden
Robert Elfgen
Sylvie Fleury
Donald Judd
Axel Kasseboehmer
Joseph Kosuth
Kraftwerk
David Maljkovic
Anthony McCall
Robert Morris
Jean-Luc Mylayne
Nina Pohl
Richard Prince
Gerda Scheepers
Frances Scholz
Alexandre Singh
Robert Therrien
Ryan Trecartin
John Waters
Andro Wekua
Andrea Zittel

St. Etienne

New York ● Galleries

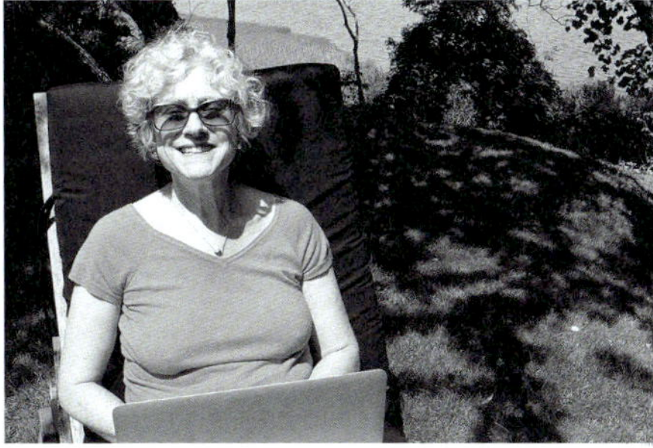

What is your favorite aspect of running a gallery?
Working with art that engages me passionately, and the endless variety of ways in which that passion can be shared with others.

How do you choose the artists you work with?
All our artists share a humanist sensibility: they speak to some aspect of the human condition.

If you weren't running a gallery what else would you do?
I would expand in one or more of the areas in which I am already invovled, such as writing or museum curating.

- **Contact** Galerie St. Etienne
Jane Kallir
jkallir@gseart.com
- **Established** 1939
- **Owner(s) / Partner(s)** Jane Kallir & Hildegard Bachert
- **Team** 7
- **Space(s)** 1,500 m²
- **Artists at Art Basel** Max Beckmann
Otto Dix
Lyonel Feininger
George Grosz
Erich Heckel
Ernst Ludwig Kirchner
Gustav Klimt
Oskar Kokoschka
Käthe Kollwitz
Paula Modersohn-Becker
Emil Nolde
Hermann Max Pechstein
Egon Schiele
Karl Schmidt-Rottluff

- **Further artists represented** Ernst Barlach
Leonard Baskin
Sue Coe
Lovis Corinth
Paul Klee
Alfred Kubin
Grandma Moses
Marie-Louise Motesiczky
Otto Mueller

Staerk

Copenhagen  Galleries
● Galleries

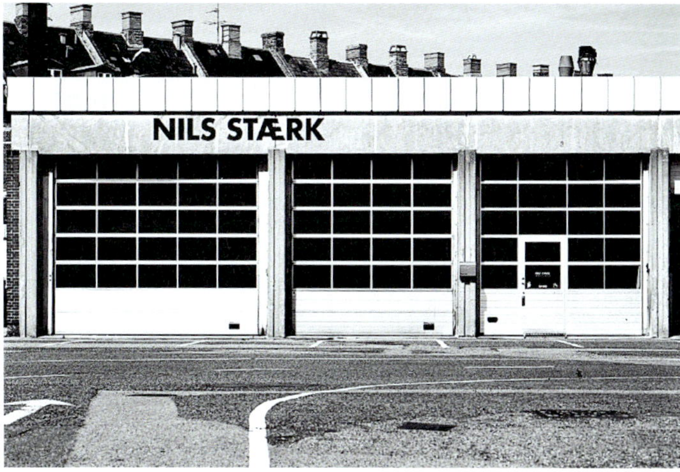

What is your favorite aspect of running a gallery?
Freedom to do what I want.

How do you choose the artists you work with?
Gut reaction.

If you weren't running a gallery what else would you do?
No idea.

- **Contact** Nils Stærk
Nils Stærk
nils@nilsstaerk.dk
- **Established** 1997
- **Owner(s) / Partner(s)** Nils Stærk
- **Team** 6
- **Space(s)** 900 m²
- **Artists at Art Basel** Miriam Bäckström
Olaf Breuning
Gardar Eide Einarsson
Mads Gamdrup
Nils Erik Gjerdevik
Jone Kvie
Michael Kvium
Runo Lagomarsino
Torbjørn Rødland
Matthew Ronay
Tom Sandberg
Tove Storch
Superflex
Ed Templeton
Eduardo Terrazas
- **Further artists represented** Ingvar Cronhammar
Richard Hughes
Thaddeus Strode

STAMPA

Basel 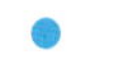 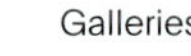 Galleries

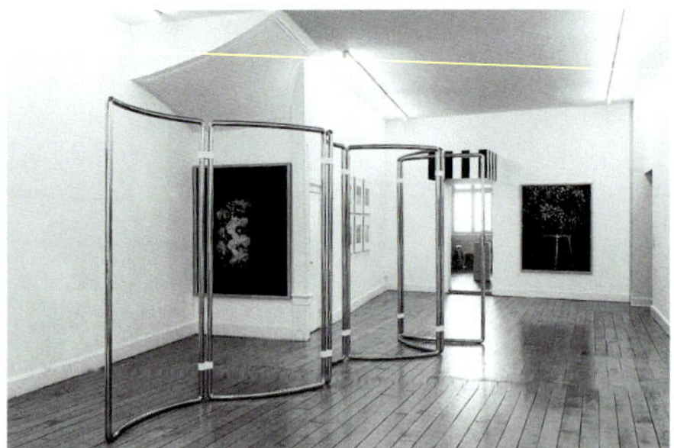

What is your favorite aspect of running a gallery?

Our main interest has always been the discovery of artists and their support on a long-term basis, with exhibitions that are conceived and realized in close collaboration with them. The mediation of contemporary art is a central part of our activities. Following the original idea of an open space, our program is completed by interdisciplinary events (contemporary music, architecture, academic research), our integrated art bookshop, and cooperation with Plattfon music shop.

How do you choose the artists you work with?

Generally we are open-minded regarding all artistic forms of expression. On the one hand, our selection is a mixture of curiosity, interest, and instinct. A key aspect is the originality of the work. On the other hand, it is based on a vivid exchange with other galleries and cultural institutions. We are passionate visitors of art exhibitions and keep ourselves updated with the latest publications on art.

If you weren't running a gallery what else would you do?

Most likely we would still be engaged in cultural management or in a field of scientific research, namely in chemistry, physics, medicine, or microbiology.

- **Contact** — STAMPA
Gilli and Diego Stampa
info@stampa-galerie.ch
- **Established** — 1969
- **Owner(s) / Partner(s)** — Gilli & Diego Stampa
- **Team** — 5
- **Space(s)** — 350 m²
- **Artists at Art Basel** — Silvia Bächli
Miriam Cahn
Marlene Dumas
General Idea
Martina Gmür
Sabine Hertig
Hanspeter Hofmann
Daniela Keiser
Eva-Fiore Kovacovsky
Zilla Leutenegger
Guido Nussbaum
A.R. Penck
Pipilotti Rist
Cindy Sherman
Roman Signer
Erik Steinbrecher
Gerda Steiner & Jörg Lenzlinger
Valentina Stieger
Vivian Suter
Rosemarie Trockel
- **Further artists represented** — Vito Acconci
Jonas Burkhalter
Monika Dillier
Ian Hamilton Finlay
Herzog & de Meuron
Christine & Irene Hohenbüchler
Udo Koch
Dorit Margreiter
Josef Felix Müller
Marcel Odenbach
Dennis Oppenheim

Standard (Oslo)

Oslo ● Galleries Unlimited ● Galleries

- **Contact** — Standard (Oslo)
Eivind Furnesvik
info@standardoslo.no
- **Established** — 2005
- **Owner(s) / Partner(s)** — Eivind Furnesvik
- **Team** — 6
- **Space(s)** — 700 m²
- **Artists at Art Basel** — Tauba Auerbach
Nina Beier
Ian Cheng
Gardar Eide Einarsson
Marius Engh
Matias Faldbakken
Aaron Garber-Maikovska
Goutam Ghosh
Kim Hiorthøy
Alex Hubbard
Ann Cathrin November Høibo
Michaela Meise
Anders Nordby
Chadwick Rantanen
Nick Relph
Torbjørn Rødland
Josh Smith
Oscar Tuazon
Fredrik Værslev
Emily Wardill

Standing Pine

Nagoya 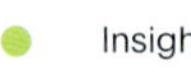 Insights

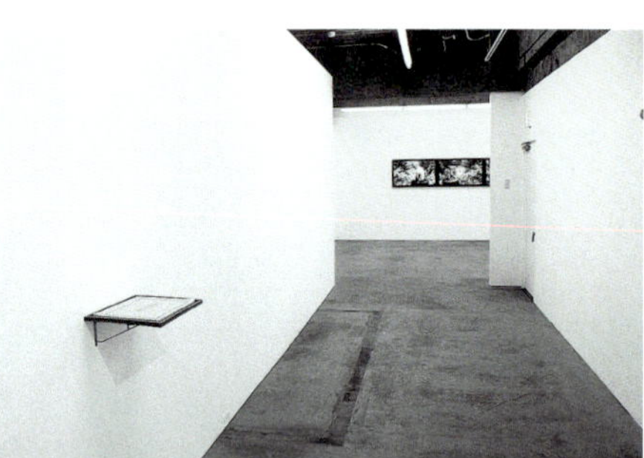

What is your favorite aspect of running a gallery?

I like to have exhibitions at the gallery and be surrounded by my favorite artworks. I can see and touch artists' work before anyone else. Also, it is my pleasure to share new values with art collectors who purchase the works.

How do you choose the artists you work with?

First of all, an important criterion is whether I like the artist's work or not. Second, it is also important wether I can get along with the artist in terms of working together for a long time because I believe that relationship between an art dealer and an artist is like husband and wife.

If you weren't running a gallery what else would you do?

I think I would work in the music field because I like music very much. However, running a gallery is my life, so I cannot think of any other job.

- **Contact** — Standing Pine
Takeshi Tatematsu
info@standingpine.jp
- **Established** — 2009
- **Owner(s) / Partner(s)** — Takeshi Tatematsu
- **Team** — 3
- **Space(s)** — 99 m²
- **Artists at Art Basel** — Youki Hirakawa
Shinji Ogawa
- **Further artists represented** — Masayuki Arai
Mayumi Inukai
Pe Lang
Tomoaki Shitara
Kenji Sugiyama

Star

Beijing — Insights

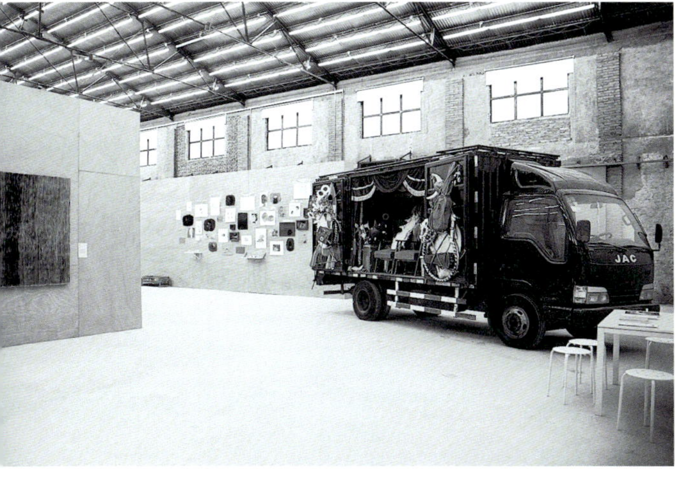

What is your favorite aspect of running a gallery?
What I love most is that I can have a close relationship with artists and works of art in a very special way, and I prove my vision in art.

How do you choose the artists you work with?
I choose artists on the basis of my feelings. Of course these "feelings" are continuously modified and revised.

If you weren't running a gallery what else would you do?
I might do something related to art documentation or engage in research in art history.

- **Contact** Star Gallery
  Jie Cui
  cuij@stargallery.cn
- **Established** April 1, 2005
- **Owner(s) / Partner(s)** Fang, Fang
- **Team** 8
- **Space(s)** 1,000 m²
- **Artists at Art Basel** Wen Ling
  Yan Cong
- **Further artists represented** Chen Fei
  Chen Ke
  Chen Tianzhuo
  Chen Xi
  Gao Yu
  Jin Nü
  Jü Ting
  Kensuke Karasawa
  Qiu Jiongjiong
  Sun Yanchu
  Wang Yifan
  Wei Jia
  Xu Maomao

Starkwhite

Auckland

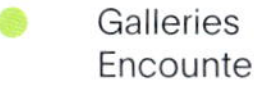

Galleries
Encounters

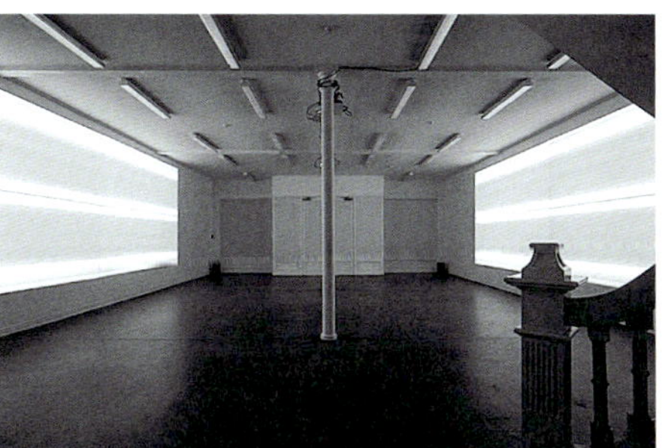

What is your favorite aspect of running a gallery?
Developing art fair presentations with the attributes of the fair and its location in mind—fairs like Art Basel in Hong Kong, with the brand power and multi-faceted edges required to perform their market-driven role, and also a space between the art museum and the art market where we can present exhibitions that deliver a variety of outcomes, opening up new possibilities for Starkwhite and the artists we work with.

How do you choose the artists you work with?
We look for artists whose work is concept-based, rich in content, and with a distinctive aesthetic. We work across time: looking back to the great artistic legacies of the recent past created by artists like abstract pioneer Gordon Walters, and looking forward by working with artists who are shaping and defining the current and future direction of contemporary art practice in the Asia-Pacific region.

If you weren't running a gallery what else would you do?
I would be working full time for a new art foundation established in Auckland this year to support cross-cultural projects in the visual arts, with an initial focus on exchanges between New Zealand and China.

- **Contact** Starkwhite
  John McCormack
  john@starkwhite.co.nz
- **Established** 2003
- **Owner(s) / Partner(s)** Dominic Feuchs & John McCormack
- **Team** 3
- **Space(s)** 929 m²
- **Artists at Art Basel** Rebecca Baumann
  Gordon Walters
- **Further artists represented** Billy Apple®
  Martin Basher
  Whitney Bedford
  Alicia Frankovich
  Trenton Garratt
  Gavin Hipkins
  Jin Jiangbo
  Richard Maloy
  Ross Manning
  Seung Yul Oh
  John Reynolds
  Layla Rudneva-Mackay
  Jim Speers
  Grant Stevens
  Clinton Watkins
  Michael Zavros

Starmach

Krakow

Galleries

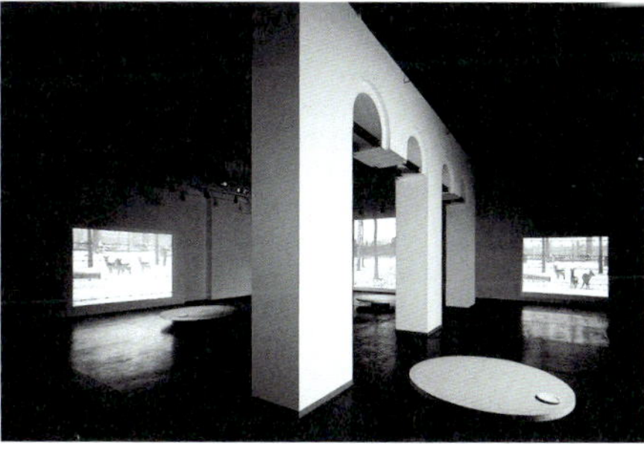

What is your favorite aspect of running a gallery?
The exhibitions.

How do you choose the artists you work with?
Through interest in their art.

If you weren't running a gallery what else would you do?
Collect.

- **Contact** Starmach Gallery
  Andrzej Szczepaniak
  andrzej@starmach.eu
- **Established** 1989
- **Owner(s) / Partner(s)** Andrzej Starmach
- **Team** 4
- **Space(s)** 589 m²
- **Artists at Art Basel** Magdalena Abakanowicz
  Tadeusz Kantor
  Edward Krasiński
  Roman Opałka
  Henryk Stażewski
  Alina Szapocznikow

- **Further artists represented** Mirosław Bałka
Jerzy Bereś
Tadeusz Brzozowski
Marek Chlanda
Władysław Hasior
Maria Jarema
Katarzyna Kobro
Piotr Lutyński
Jerzy Nowosielski
Teresa Rudowicz
Mikołaj Smoczyński
Jonasz Stern
Władysław Strzemiński
Jan Tarasin
Marian Warzecha
Ryszard Winiarski
Krzysztof Zieliński

Stein

Milan

● Galleries Unlimited
● Galleries

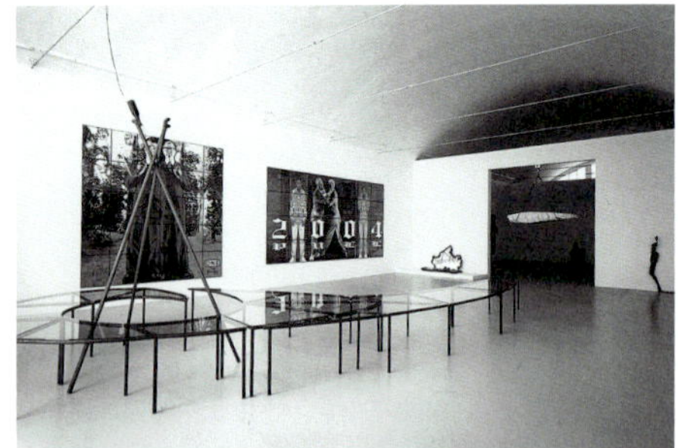

- **Contact** Christian Stein
Silvia Bagnara
christianstein@iol.it
- **Established** 1966
- **Owner(s) / Partner(s)** Gianfranco Benedetti
- **Team** 10
- **Space(s)** 1,800 m²
- **Artists at Art Basel** Marco Bagnoli
Domenico Bianchi
Alighiero Boetti
Pier Paolo Calzolari
Paolo Canevari
Luciano Fabro
Lucio Fontana
Jannis Kounellis
Piero Manzoni
Fausto Melotti
Mario Merz
Marisa Merz
Mimmo Paladino
Giulio Paolini
Giuseppe Penone
Jack Pierson
Michelangelo Pistoletto
Remo Salvadori
Christopher Wool
Peter Wüthrich

Stevenson

Cape Town
Johannesburg

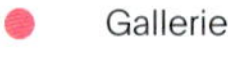
● Galleries

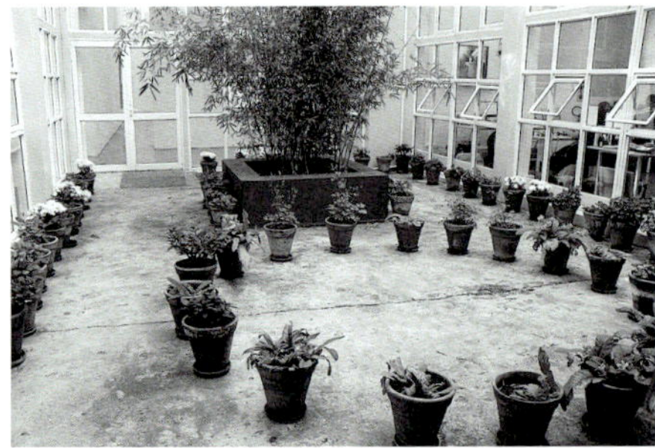

What is your favorite aspect of running a gallery?
Paying our artists.

How do you choose the artists you work with?
It feels like the artists choose us—our paths cross and they grant us the privilege of representing them …

If you weren't running a gallery what else would you do?
Doing anything else is unimaginable.

- **Contact** Stevenson
Joost Bosland
joost@stevenson.info
- **Established** 2003
- **Owner(s) / Partner(s)** Federica Angelucci
Joost Bosland
David Brodie
Andrew Da Conceicao
Darren Levy
Sophie Perryer
Michael Stevenson
- **Team** 27
- **Space(s)** 560 m²
- **Artists at Art Basel** Wim Botha
Serge Alain Nitegeka
Barthélémy Toguo
- **Further artists represented** Zander Blom
Dineo Seshee Bopape
Edson Chagas
Steven Cohen
Ângela Ferreira
Meschac Gaba
Ian Grose
Simon Gush
Nicholas Hlobo
Pieter Hugo
Samson Kambalu
Anton Kannemeyer
Mawande Ka Zenzile
Estate Of Ernest Mancoba
Sabelo Mlangeni
Nandipha Mntambo
Zanele Muholi
Daniel Naudé
Mame-Diarra Niang
Odili Donald Odita
Deborah Poynton
Jo Ractliffe
Robin Rhode
Viviane Sassen
Claudette Schreuders
Penny Siopis
Guy Tillim
Kemang Wa Lehulere
Portia Zvavahera

Stolper

London

● Edition

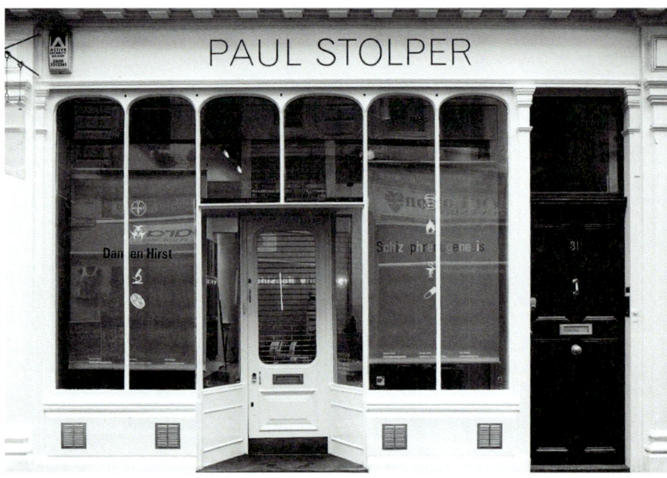

What is your favorite aspect of running a gallery?
Working closely with artists and seeing projects come to fruition.

How do you choose the artists you work with?
I have always trusted my own instinct and followed that through.

If you weren't running a gallery what else would you do?
I'd like to work in radio.

- **Contact** Paul Stolper Gallery
  Alexandra Sterling
  alexandra@paulstolper.com
- **Established** 1998
- **Owner(s) / Partner(s)** Paul Stolper
- **Team** 5
- **Space(s)** 130 m²
- **Artists at Art Basel** Jeremy Deller
  Don Brown
  Keith Coventry
  Shepard Fairey
  Damien Hirst
  Julian Simmons
  Mark Wallinger

STPI

Singapore

Galleries
Encounters
Edition
Edition

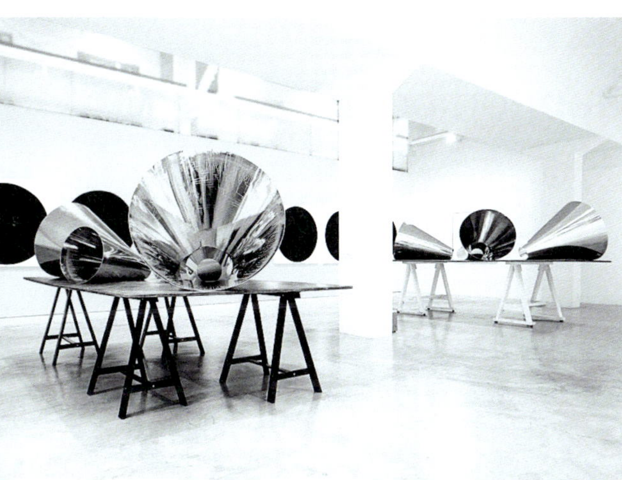

What is your favorite aspect of running a gallery?
Working with an amazing team.

How do you choose the artists you work with?
From my dream list.

If you weren't running a gallery what else would you do?
Go back to school.

- **Contact** STPI
  Yen Hui Teng
  tengyenhui@stpi.com.sg
- **Established** 2002
- **Owner(s) / Partner(s)** Emi Eu
- **Space(s)** 400 m²
- **Artists at Art Basel** Heman Chong
  Richard Deacon
  Do Ho Suh
  Haegue Yang
  Sun Xun
  Teppei Kaneuji
  Rirkrit Tiravanija
  Ronald Ventura
  Wu Shanzhuan
  & Inga Svala Thórsdóttir
- **Further artists represented** Ashley Bickerton
  Eko Nugroho
  Teresita Fernández
  Ryan Gander
  Qiu Zhijie
  Tabaimo
  Zhan Wang

Strina

São Paulo

Galleries
Galleries

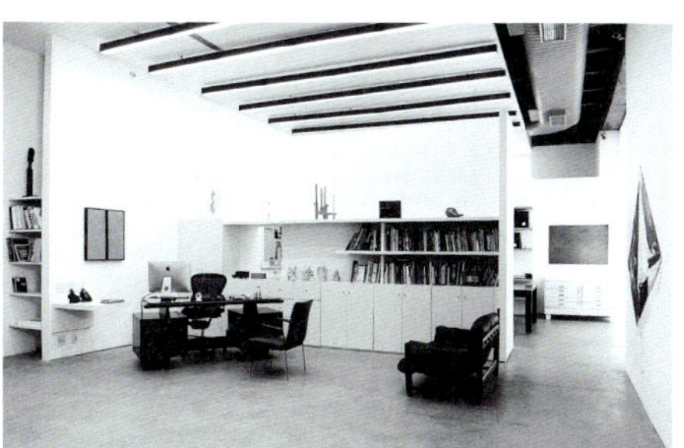

What is your favorite aspect of running a gallery?
The possibility of being in contact with new art, new thinking, has always fascinated me. That's the best part of my job, to accommodate new ideas within the means of a gallery space.

How do you choose the artists you work with?
I believe my choices are always guided by personal taste and a great, great deal of intuition.

If you weren't running a gallery what else would you do?
I would probably be an artist-photographer.

- **Contact** Galeria Luisa Strina
  Patricia Dominguez
  patricia@galerialuisastrina.com.br
- **Established** 1974
- **Owner(s) / Partner(s)** Luisa Malzoni Strina
- **Team** 16
- **Space(s)** 544 m²
- **Artists at Art Basel** Caetano de Almeida
  Leonor Antunes
  Juan Araujo
  Alexandre da Cunha
  León Ferrari
  Marcius Galan
  Carlos Garaicoa
  Fernanda Gomes
  Marcellvs L.
  Laura Lima
  Mateo López
  Renata Lucas
  Jorge Macchi
  Anna Maria Maiolino
  Antonio Manuel
  Marepe
  Cildo Meireles
  Pedro Reyes
  Adrián Villar Rojas
  Gabriel Sierra
- **Further artists represented** Pablo Accinelli
  Tonico Lemos Auad
  Eduardo T. Basualdo
  Laura Belém
  Erick Beltrán
  Matías Duville
  Olafur Eliasson
  Brian Griffiths
  Federico Herrero
  Magdalena Jitrik
  Luisa Lambri
  Armin Linke
  Jarbas Lopes
  Gilberto Mariotti
  Pedro Motta
  Muntadas
  Bernardo Ortiz
  Nicolás Paris
  Marina Saleme
  Beto Shwafaty
  Edgard de Souza
  Alessandro Balteo Yazbeck

Subal

New York

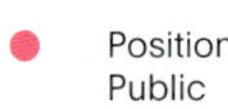

Positions
Public

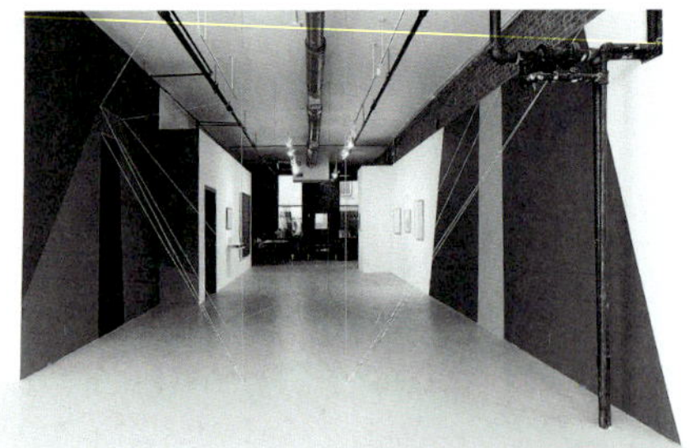

What is your favorite aspect of running a gallery?
Perhaps it sounds cliché̀d, but the most pleasurable aspect of running the gallery is working with the artists. I love developing ideas, helping each artist realize their goals. Nothing is better than starting with something abstract—a concept for a show, for instance, that initially seems logistically and conceptually impossible—and seeing the idea materialize into an exhibition.

How do you choose the artists you work with?
I tend to think of my program and my space curatorially. I often seek out the suggestions of curators, writers, and artists, and make as many studio visits as possible. I am drawn to what one might call "artist's artists." I like work that is difficult to figure out, that needs time to understand both the formal and the theoretical complexities. I want to know that I can have a long-term engagement with someone's practice.

If you weren't running a gallery what else would you do?
I would have a restaurant in the mountains of Austria.

- **Contact** Simone Subal Gallery
  Simone Subal
  simone@simonesubal.com
- **Established** 2011
- **Owner(s) / Partner(s)** Simone Subal
- **Team** 2
- **Space(s)** 111.5 m²
- **Artists at Art Basel** Sam Ekwurtzel
- **Further artists represented** Sonia Almeida
  Larry Bamburg
  Julien Bismuth
  Frank Heath
  Anna K.E.
  Kiki Kogelnik (Estate)
  Florian Meisenberg
  Brian O'Doherty
  B. Ingrid Olson
  Yorgos Sapountzis
  Erika Vogt

Sullivan+Strumpf

Sydney

Insights

What is your favorite aspect of running a gallery?
Running a gallery means you are contributing to the future world—the artists that we support and nurture today will have work in existence when we are all dead and gone. It is exciting to think we are somehow enabling that communication with future audiences.

How do you choose the artists you work with?
Artists need to be earnest, hardworking, and interested in the idea of excellence. It sounds old-fashioned I know, but if they are not those things, they won't get far.

If you weren't running a gallery what else would you do?
A very sad curator!

- **Contact** Sullivan+Strumpf
  Ursula Sullivan
  ursula@sullivanstrumpf.com
- **Established** 2005
- **Owner(s) / Partner(s)** Ursula Sullivan & Joanna Strumpf
- **Team** 5
- **Space(s)** 440 m²
- **Artists at Art Basel** Tony Albert
  eX de Medici
  Sam Leach
  Alex Seton
- **Further artists represented** Matthew Allen
  Sydney Ball
  Leah Emery
  Juan Ford
  Gregory Hodge
  Sam Jinks
  Joanna Lamb
  Michael Lindeman
  Dane Lovett
  Alasdair Macintyre
  Judy Millar
  Kate Shaw
  Tim Silver
  Darren Sylvester
  Hiromi Tango
  Daniel Templeman
  TextaQueen
  Aida Tomescu

Supportico Lopez

Berlin

Feature
Unlimited
Nova

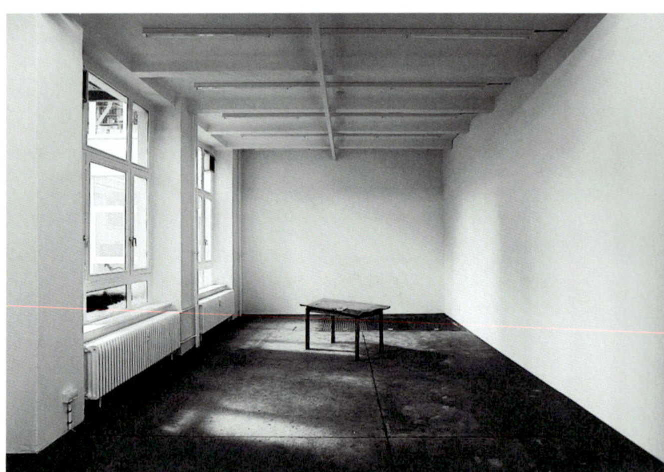

What is your favorite aspect of running a gallery?
The curatorial aspect of running a gallery is the anchor point of our work and this is what drives our motivation day by day. Working very closely with artists, "guiding" and supporting them throughout their careers, as well as bringing together young artists with historical positions are the most important aspects of our job.

How do you choose the artists you work with?
We are constantly on the search for new positions that complete our program on the one hand and boost our curiosity on the other. This may include rediscovering old and neglected positions that accentuate a significant interest, as well as young and emerging artists that are not "hot" and fulfill the needs of the current art market situation, but that embody a potential to develop solid careers in the long run.

If you weren't running a gallery what else would you do?
I would probably run a restaurant in some sunny place together with my husband.

- **Contact** Supportico Lopez
  Stefania Palumbo
  info@supporticolopez.com
- **Established** 2008
- **Owner(s) / Partner(s)** Gigiotto Del Vecchio
  Stefania Palumbo
- **Team** 3
- **Space(s)** 250 m²
- **Artists at Art Basel** Henri Chopin
  Michael Dean
  Christina Mackie
  Zin Taylor

- **Further artists represented**

Armando Andrade Tudela
Julian Beck
Steve Bishop
Danilo Correale
Maria Adele Del Vecchio
Giulio Delvè
Marius Engh
Jan Peter Hammer
Natalie Häusler
Franziska Lantz
J. Parker Valentine
Niels Trannois

Sur

Punta del Este
Montevideo

 Galleries

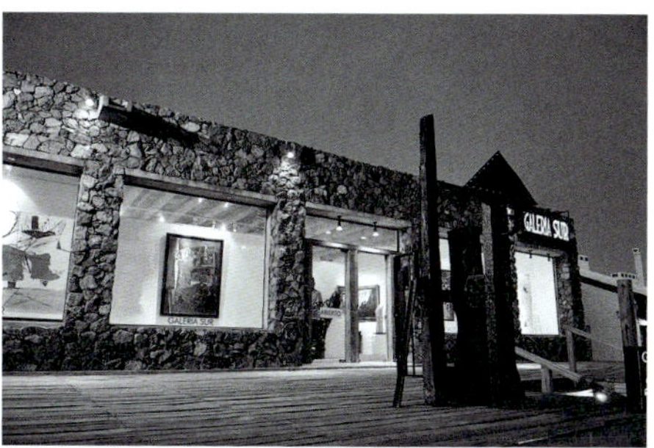

What is your favorite aspect of running a gallery?

The passion for art and creativity that comes into play in each historical or contemporary exhibition. The research and preparation for a show, whether about an artist or an art movement, which afterward will be embodied in the gallery space and, of course, in its respective catalogue.

How do you choose the artists you work with?

Our work focuses on Latin American historical avant-gardes, which were related to the European and American movements of the 1920s, 1930s, and 1940s and their later influences. This election is a direct consequence of a deep analysis of the historical and artistic value of the artist. To deal with this, I carefully try to understand what my sensitivity and taste have to say; I strongly believe in them.

If you weren't running a gallery what else would you do?

I would spend a considerable amount of my time traveling and collecting works and other art objects. Inevitably I would attempt to mount exhibitions in alternative spaces. I would be working hard to recover the memory of some key artists who have been forgotten by history.

- **Contact**: Galería Sur
Martin Castillo
sur@montevideo.com.uy
- **Established**: 1984
- **Owner(s) / Partner(s)**: Jorge Castillo
Martin Castillo
- **Team**: 7
- **Space(s)**: 380 m²
- **Artists at Art Basel**:

Pablo Atchugarry
Rafael Barradas
Antonio Berni
Fernando Botero
Eduardo Cardozo
Emiliano di Cavalcanti
José Pedro Costigliolo
Wifredo Díaz Velez
Pedro Figari
Gonzalo Fonseca
Maria Freire
Oswaldo Guayasamin
José Gurvich
Wifredo Lam
Marcelo Legrand
Francisco Matto
Roberto Matta
Joan Miró
Miguel Angel Pareja
Pablo Picasso
Cândido Portinari
Diego Rivera
Lasar Segall
David Alfaro Siqueiros
Nicolás de Staël
Fernando de Szyszlo
Rufino Tamayo
Joaquín Torres García
Alfredo Volpi

Szwajcer

Brussels

 Galleries Unlimited

- **Contact**: Galerie Micheline Szwajcer
Dimitri Riemis
dimitri@gms.be
- **Established**: 1980
- **Owner(s) / Partner(s)**: Micheline Szwajcer
- **Team**: 5
- **Artists at Art Basel**:

Giovanni Anselmo
Stanley Brouwn
Angela Bulloch
David Claerbout
James Coleman
François Curlet
Koenraad Dedobbeleer
Daniel Dewar & Grégory Gicquel
Luciano Fabro
Hans-Peter Feldmann
Bernard Frize
Liam Gillick
Dan Graham
Jos de Gruyter & Harald Thys
Carsten Höller
Ann Veronica Janssens
On Kawara
Peter Lemmens
Zoe Leonard
Mark Luyten
Lucy McKenzie
Guy Mees
Matt Mullican
Manfred Pernice
Tobias Rehberger
Allen Ruppersberg
Daan van Golden
Lawrence Weiner
Marthe Wéry
Christopher Wool

Sfeir-Semler Gallery
Interview with Andrée Sfeir-Semler

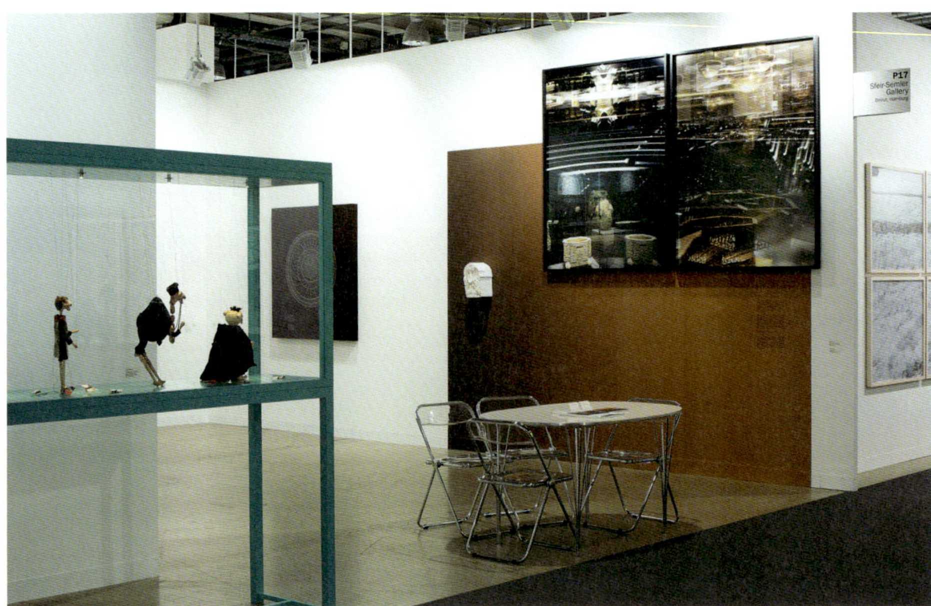

Art Basel in Basel, 2014

You opened your gallery in 1985, in Kiel (Germany). Why did you decide to open a gallery and why there?

I studied History and Art History and I was writing my PhD in northern Germany because of my husband. I was wondering what I was going to do with this PhD when a local gallery moved out of the city and offered me the space. I was so naive that I immediately agreed, even if I had no experience whatsoever. I had no exhibitions planned, no commitments to anyone. I took the gallery from an art dealer who was mainly focused on German Expressionism, but I was sure I didn't want to do that: I wanted to work with living artists. One of the very first exhibitions was with Arnulf Rainer. Shortly after it was Ian Hamilton Finlay, Ulrich Rückriem … And for some reason, it worked. As a scholar, I wanted to understand contemporary art by myself, so I did also a few thematic exhibitions such as *Lapis Lazuli & Gold* (in 1995)—the two most precious materials in the Middle Ages—in which I included artists such as Marcel Broodthaers and Yves Klein; one on Kinetic art; and one called *Allegory*, which was about the sublimity of things, with people like Giulio Paolini …

How did you work with other galleries, artists, and what was your network?

Times were different. I had no money, but I managed to do a show with Lyonel Feininger. I had to commit to buy one work. I didn't have a penny. I couldn't sleep. But I got lucky: a museum bought a piece … Today this would be completely impossible. The big difference back then was that you were really able to call people like Michelangelo Pistoletto or Giulio Paolini and they would give you some work. At that time, I was young and good-looking, it was easier than it would be today! [*Laughs*]

You have participated in Art Basel since very early on, since 1989, but not on the first floor: on the ground floor.

It's funny that the young women are downstairs now and the older women upstairs, right? [*Laughs*] I brought works by Georg Baselitz, a whole series of beautiful drawings, pretty much in the very first year. I remember bringing a huge asphalt piece by Enzo Cucchi and a white Paolini, also at the beginning. Soon after I met Lucebert and started to show Cobra artists. The artists were much older than I was, like my fathers or grandparents, and now it's the contrary, all my artists are much younger than I am!

When did you start to work more with artists of your generation or younger? Was this shift also a question of region, because you moved from Germany to the Middle East …

That's true! I encountered the work of Walid Raad through Catherine David, in an exhibition she organized in the late 1990s at Kunst-Werke in Berlin. It was a work of the Atlas Group. This name didn't ring a bell to me, but it was Beirut. I was extremely interested to see art from Beirut.

So you closed the first gallery?

No, I met Walid and started working with him in 2002: he integrated very beautifully with other conceptual artists I had shown for a long time, such as Robert Barry and Sol LeWitt. In 2003 Art Basel threw me out. So I was left without a booth. It really was a surprise. I had been there for 14 years! I started thinking about why they picked me out? They explained that there were too many German galleries and that they wanted to open up to new countries, etc. So, I asked myself "What should I do?" I started thinking very much about how to become a "solitaire," how to become someone you cannot avoid, you cannot work without. That might have been one reason in the back of my head, but the real reason for opening in Beirut was that the war had finished: we had spent all our holidays in the country, even during the very bad war years, we baptized our daughter in Beirut under the bombs, we never stopped going, and there were just no galleries whatsoever in the country!

In 2002, I started supporting Ashkal Alwan, a non-profit initiative. They had invited Walid, so I co-financed the show. Everything felt like a new start in the country. Rafic Hariri, Prime Minister of Lebanon, was doing great things: he built a new airport, the city was beautiful! I went to dinner with an architect friend, Bernard Khoury, and he told he had just rented a new office. It was in the middle of nowhere, in the Quarantaine Area, a non-place, a "non-lieu" as you would say in French. I fell in love with the building. It was 1,400 square meters but I thought if I come back to this country, it should not be through a side door! I rented the space, and we started modeling it. When I was at ARCO, in Madrid, they killed Hariri; there were car bombs exploding everywhere … I considered postponing the opening, but then I thought that everything in our life has always been postponed because of the war. By that time, through Walid I had met several Lebanese and Arab artists who were in his peer group—Akram Zaatari, Marwan Rechmaoui—and we decided to open, no matter what! We had the most amazing opening ever, with thousands of visitors! It had a beautiful energy because it was like the hope of a new start.

And since then you operate in Hamburg and in Beirut.

It was clear that it was going to be difficult to establish a gallery in Beirut, so I wanted to keep a position in Germany. But the Beirut gallery became a hub, almost like an institution, and we started writing a new page in contemporary art of that part of the world with the artists we exhibited there. I think that contemporary art cannot exist outside of a socio-geographical context. I am a disciple of Bourdieu, so I always saw art as a vehicle for a cultural and socio-historical context. I am really thankful and proud to say that we now have a group of artists who are not only important for our part of the world, but who are also collected by all major museums around the world, MoMA, the Centre Pompidou, Tate Modern, the Kunsthaus Zürich …

We asked nine art world players for their ten favorite elements present anywhere in the city during the Art Basel week.

TOP TEN TEN TEN TEN TEN TEN TEN TEN TEN TEN

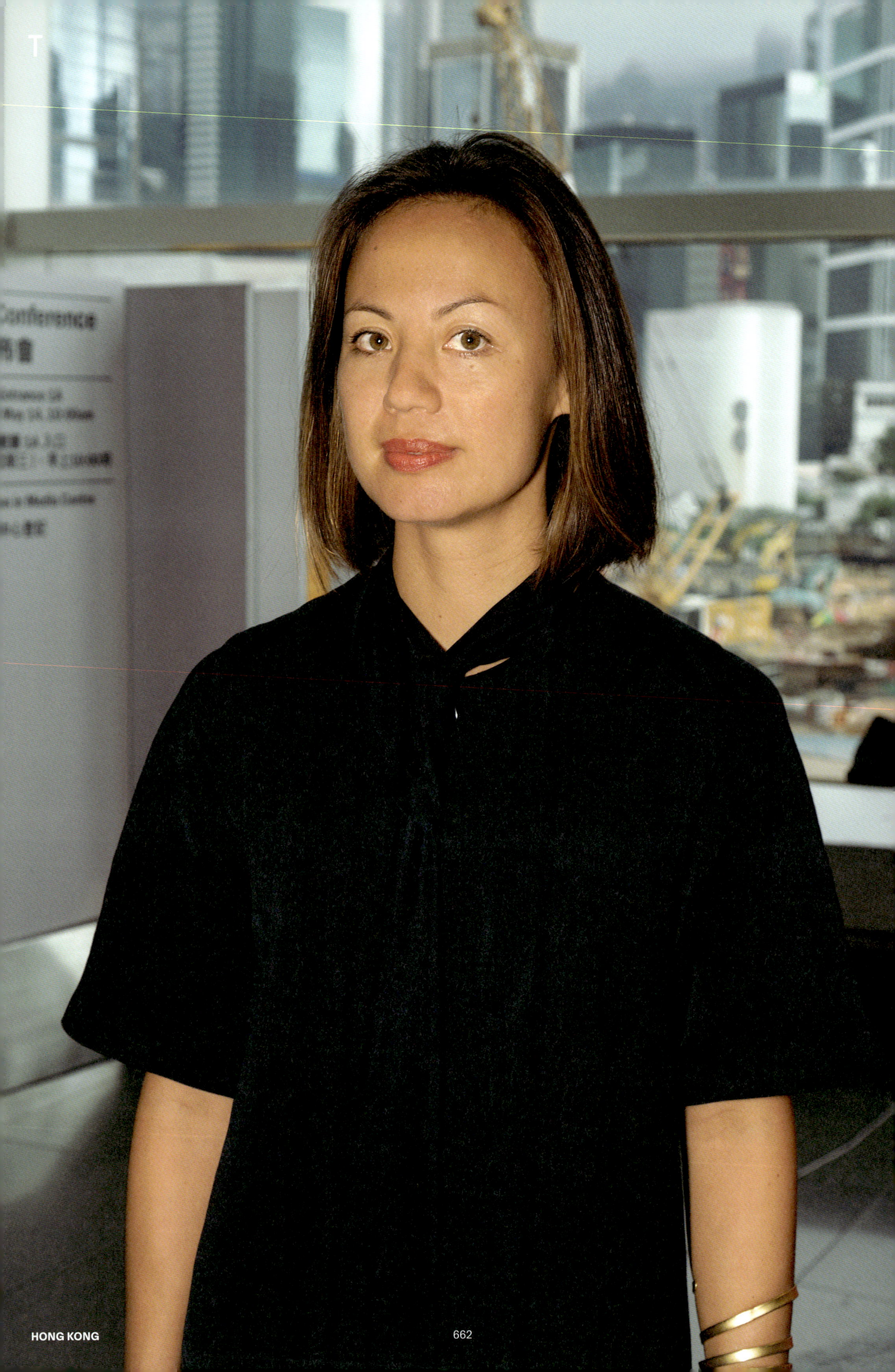

Claire Hsu

Co-Founder and Director, Asia Art Archive,
Hong Kong

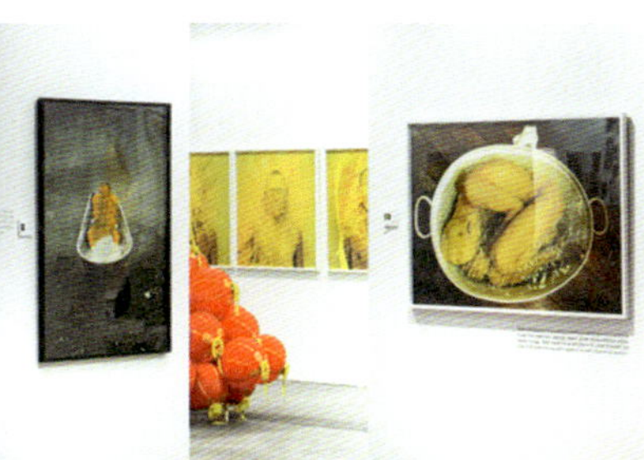

01 **Lee Wen**
Yellow Man series, 1992–2012
iPreciation (Insights)

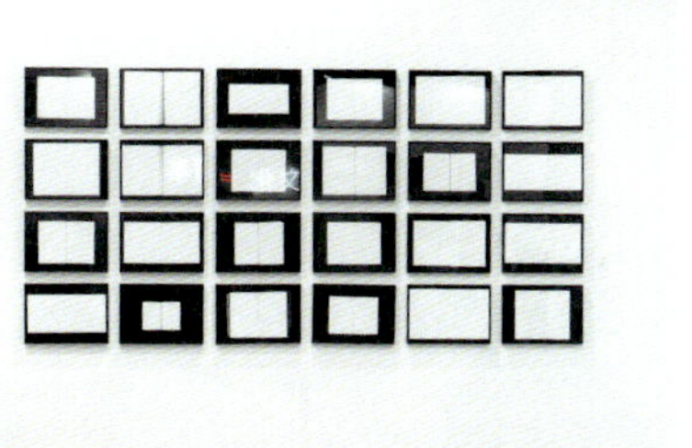

02 **Pak Sheung Chuen**
White Library/A Mind Reaching for Emptiness, 2009
Vitamin Creative Space

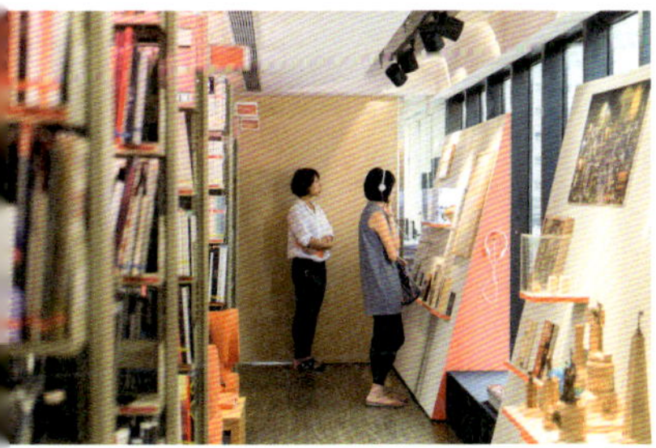

03 ***Mapping Asia***
Exhibition, Asia Art Archive, Hong Kong

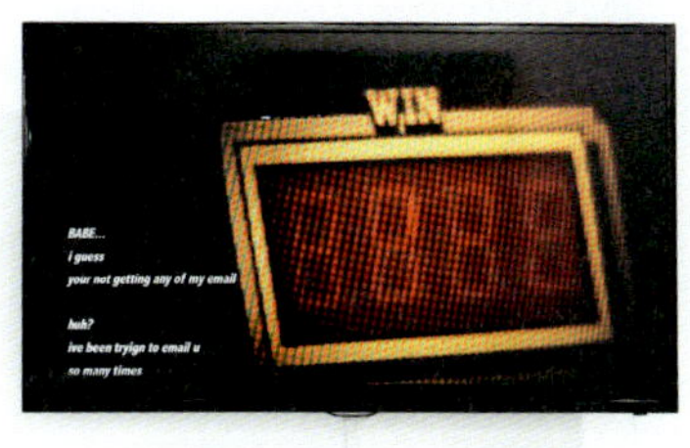

04 **Cheng Ran's video**
Leo Xu Projects (Discoveries)

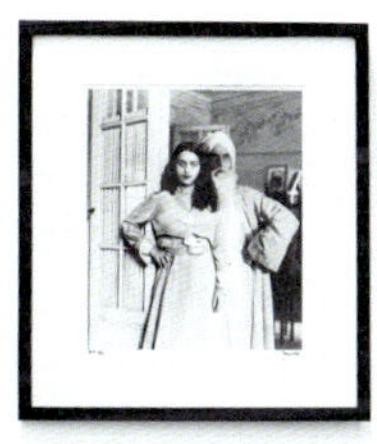

05 **Vivan Sundaram**
Re-Take of Amrita series, 2001–2002
Chemould Prescott Road

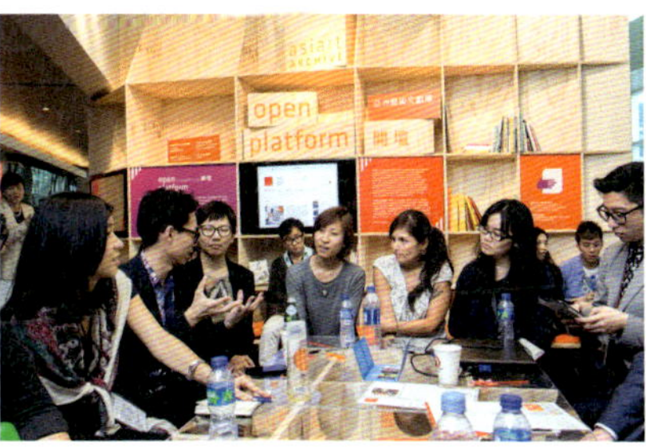

06 **Open Platform 2014**
Asia Art Archive Booth

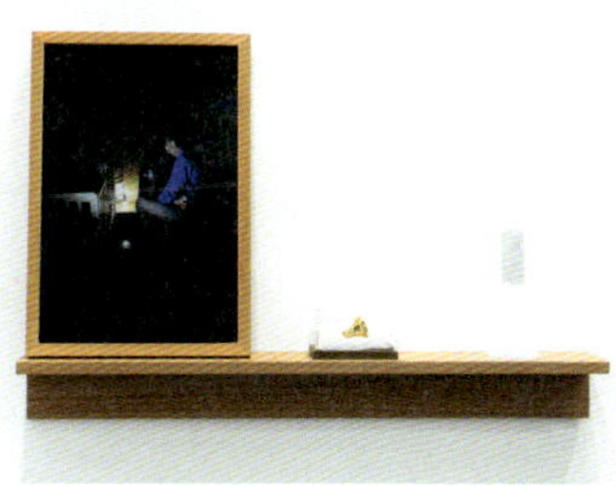

07 **Kwan Sheung Chi & Wong Wai Yin**
Man's Future Fund–Gold Nipple, 2014
Gallery EXIT

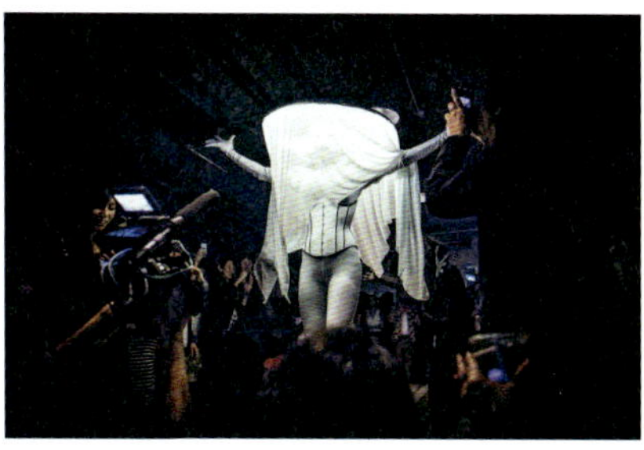

08 **Nadim Abbas and Ming Wong**
Apocalypse Postponed, Absolut Art Bar, Causeway Bay, Hong Kong

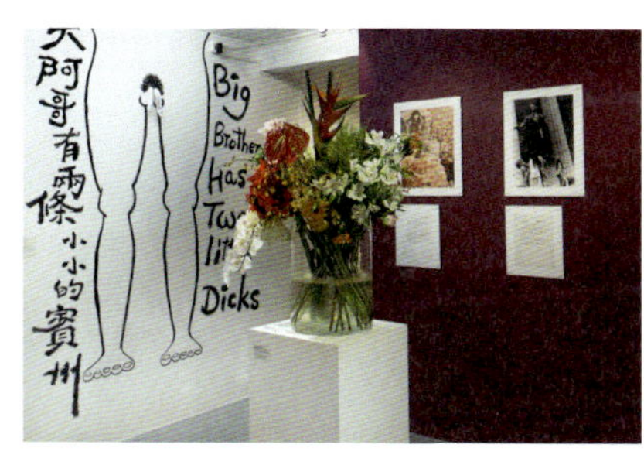

09 ***Ten Million Rooms of Yearning. Sex in Hong Kong***
Exhibition, Para Site, five different locations in Hong Kong

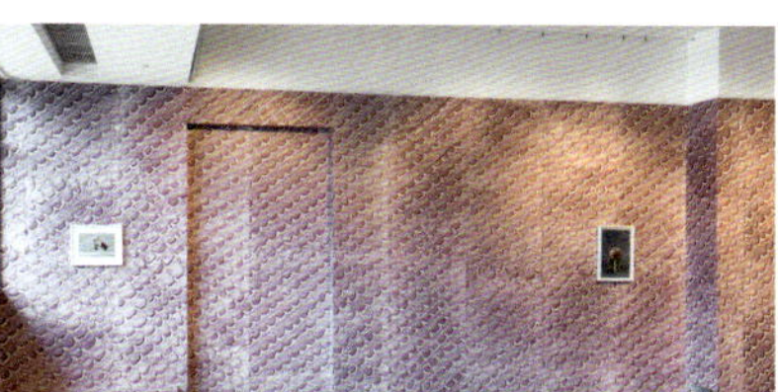

10 **Christodoulos Panayiotou & Philip Wiegard**
The Permeability of Certain Matters
Spring Workshop, Aberdeen, Hong Kong

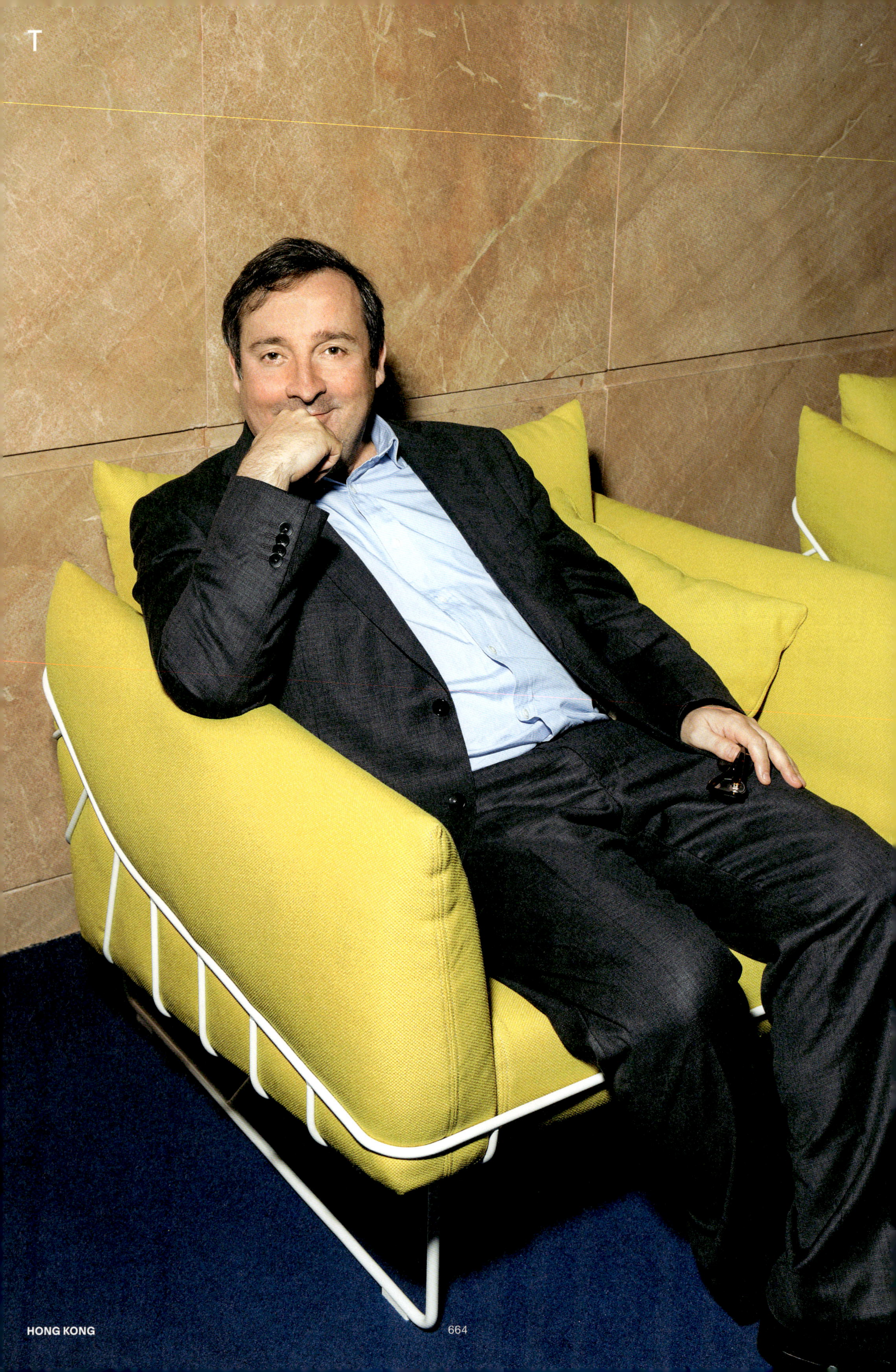
T

Gregor Muir

Executive Director
Institute of Contemporary Arts, London

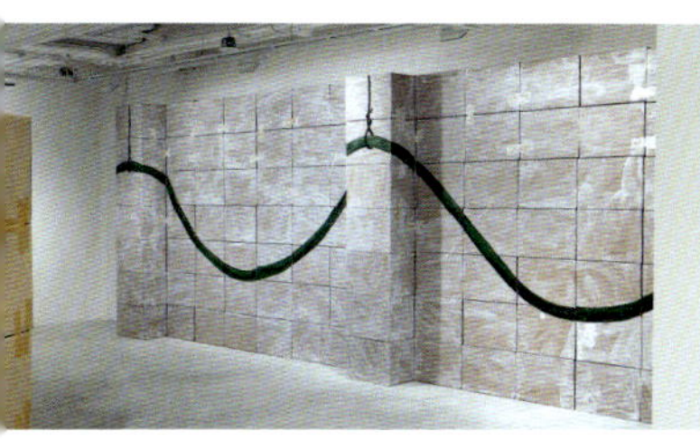

1 Zhang Enli
K11 Art Foundation, Cosco Tower, Hong Kong

hang Enli continues to delight us with his latest *pace Painting* project, which saw broad swirling rushstrokes applied to a temporary structure nade from cardboard boxes.

2 Eloise Hawser
Balice Hertling

ou travel halfway across the globe to discover an tist you like, who just happens to be from your ometown. Eloise Hawser continues to intrigue as ne goes about her transformation of discarded nd appropriated objects.

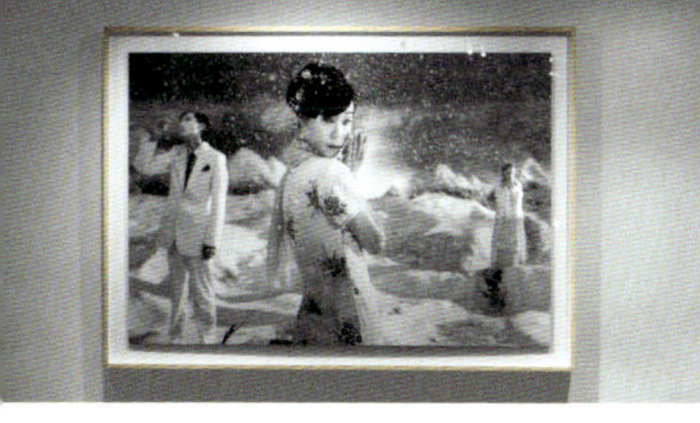

3 *Aftermath: Post-Sense Sensibility, Fifteen Years On*
Duddell's, Shanghai Tang Mansion Hong Kong

nilip Tinari staged a thought-provoking group ow, displaying across the bar artworks referenc- g a period of late-1990s Chinese contemporary t that was, in part, inspired by the 1997 *Sensation* xhibition in London. Artists included Yang dong, Zhao Liang, Xiao Yu, and Jiang Zhi.

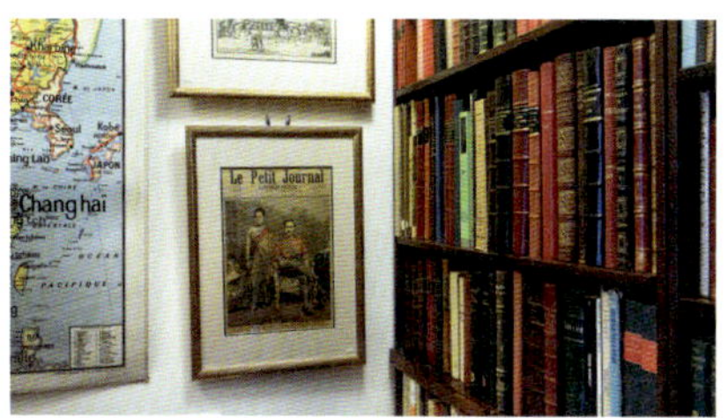

04 Indosiam Rare Books
Hollywood Road, Hong Kong

Try a visit to Indosiam Rare Books. Here you find beautiful books relating to China, Indochina, and other Far Eastern countries.

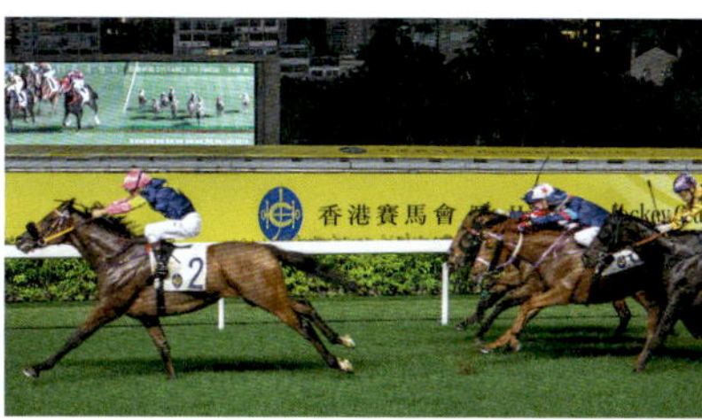

05 Happy Valley Racecourse

There's a palpable energy in the air that makes these races unlike any others anywhere else in the world.

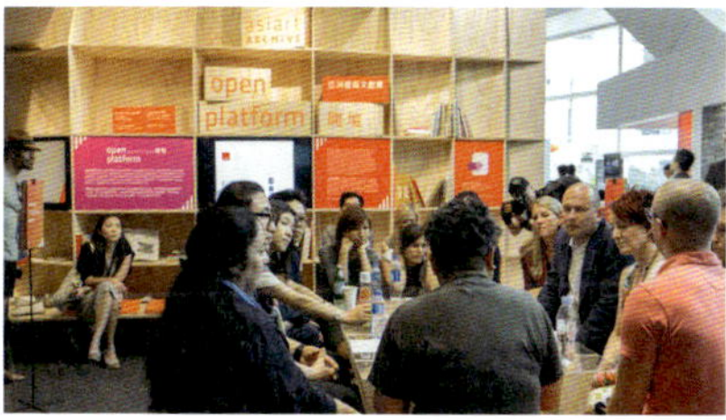

06 Open Platform 2014
Asia Art Archive Booth

An impressive community project that started with a single bookshelf in 2000 and now holds over 50,000 physical and digital items, AAA had the inspired idea to turn their art fair booth into a talks space.

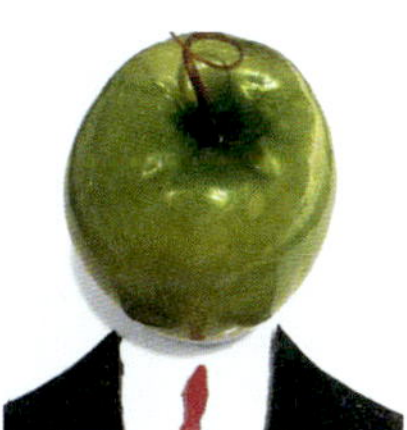

07 Mandarin Oriental Bar & Grill

Richard Chang and Hauser & Wirth joined forces to host a "curated" dinner at the Mandarin Oriental Bar & Grill. The *pièce de résistance* was a dessert resembling a René Magritte painting.

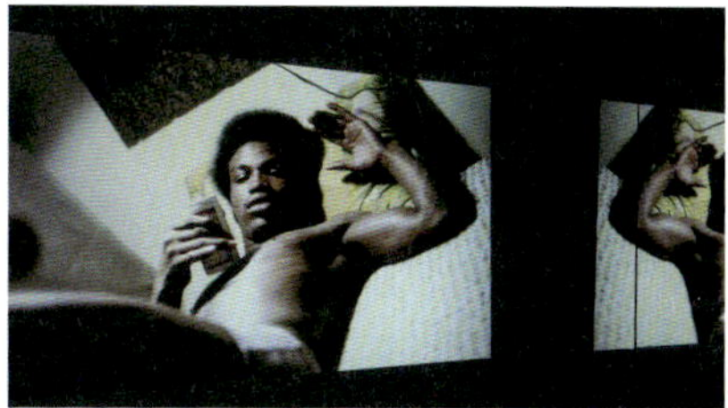

08 *Ten Million Rooms of Yearning. Sex in Hong Kong*
Exhibition, Para Site, five different locations in Hong Kong

One of the works was presented in a private flat in a cramped apartment block. Having climbed five floors on a humid day, what lay in store was a visual treat: Hélio Oiticica's slideshow *Babylonest* (1972–2014). It never ceases to surprise me how modest artworks such as this often prove the most haunting.

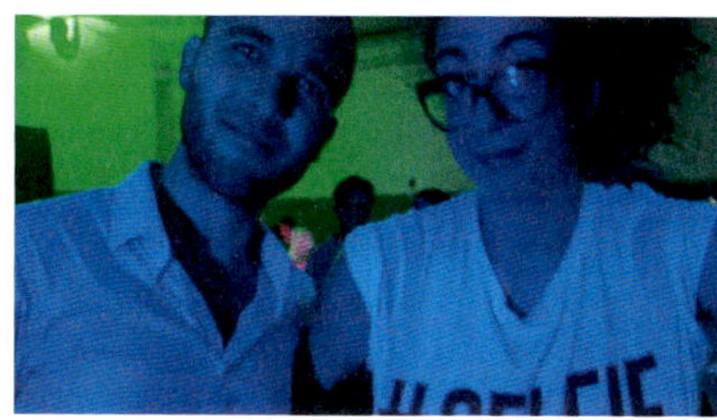

09 Ryan McNamara
Chai Wan Nites, May 16, 2014, Asia One Tower

In this industrial zone I suddenly found myself in a super-heated rave club with flashing lights and pounding techno. I encountered Yana and Stephen Peel, who had sponsored the event, and Aya Mousawi and Simon Sakhai from The Moving Museum (pictured).

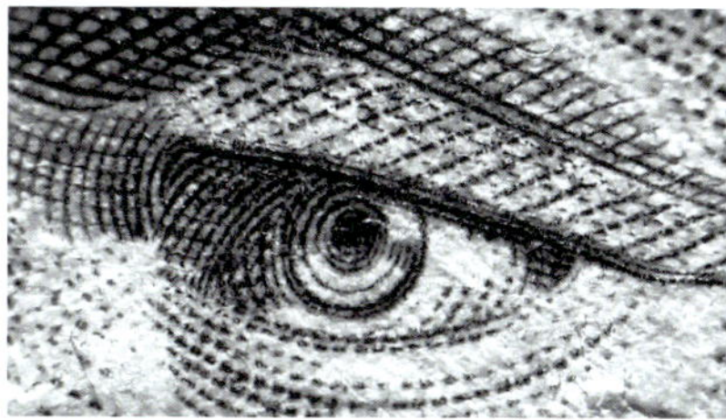

10 James Richards' screening
Asia Society, Hong Kong

James Richards showed several of his films at the Asia Society, followed by a discussion with London-based curator Fatima Hellberg, presented by the Asia Society in collaboration with Institute of Contemporary Arts, London.

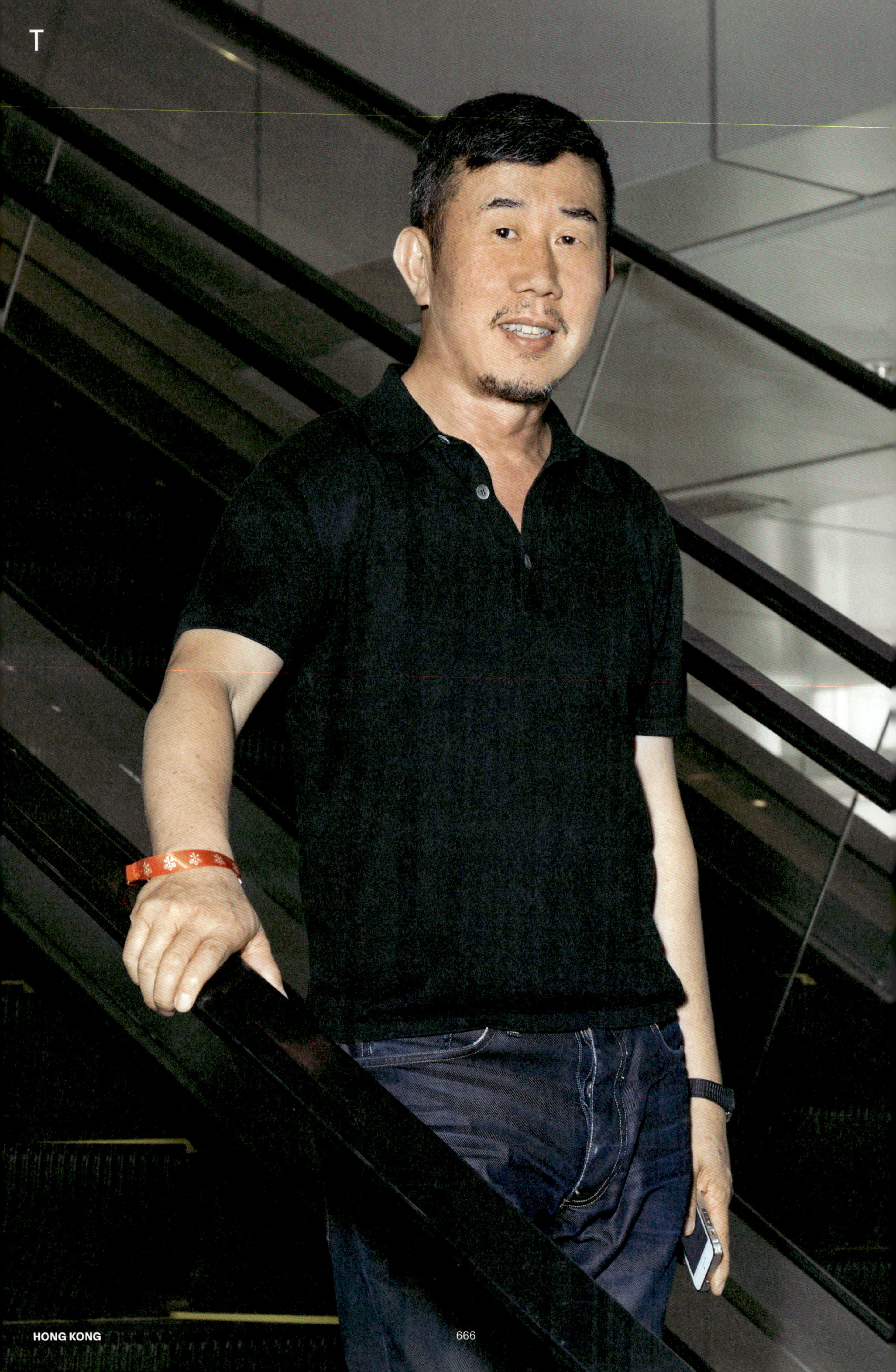

Rudy Tseng

Collector, Taipei

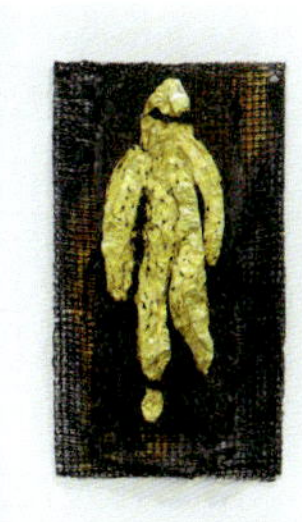

01 **Kesang Lamdark**
Fire-proof Suit Over Palden Choetso, 2013
Rossi & Rossi

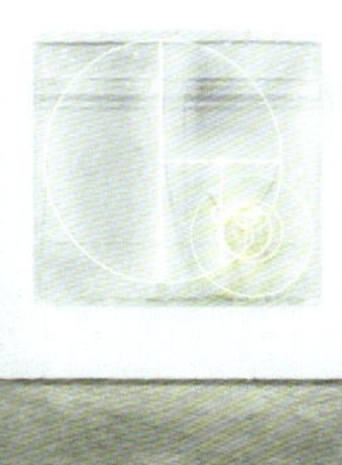

02 **Carsten Höller**
Divisions (White Lines and White Circles), 2014
ShugoArts

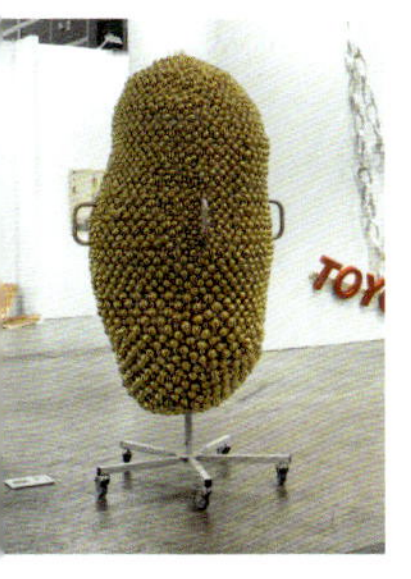

03 **Haegue Yang**
Sonic Dance – Twin Sister, 2014
Galerie Chantal Crousel

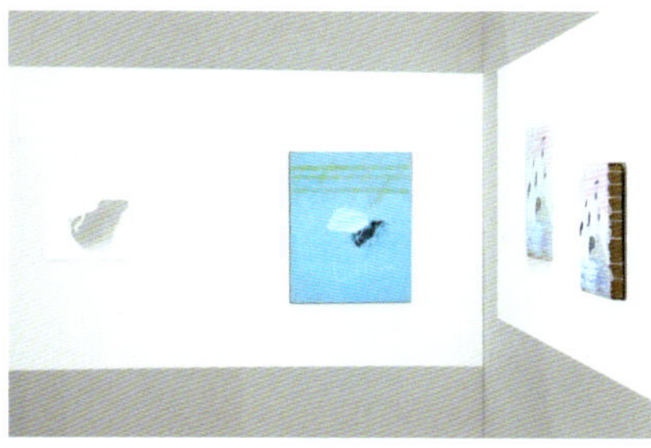

04 **Lee Kit**
Lillian, 2014
Vitamin Creative Space

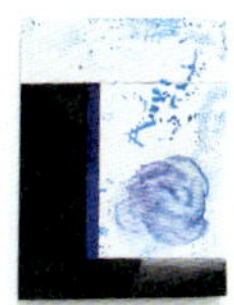

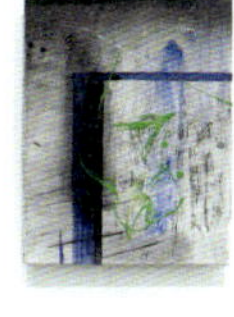

05 **Nick Mauss**
Untitled, 2012, and *lower*, 2013
303 Gallery

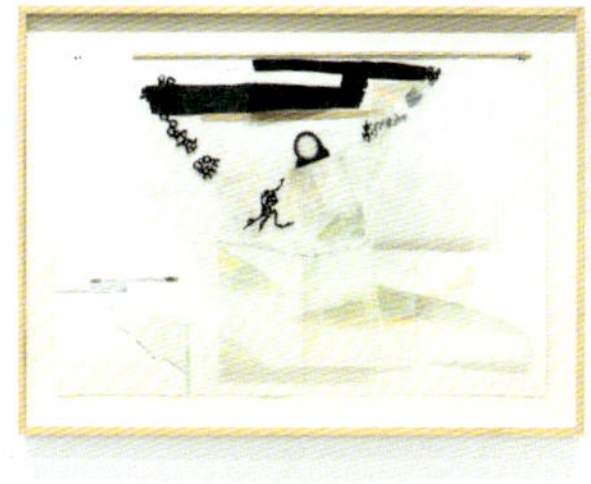

06 **Sung Hwan Kim**
Untitled, 2014
Wilkinson

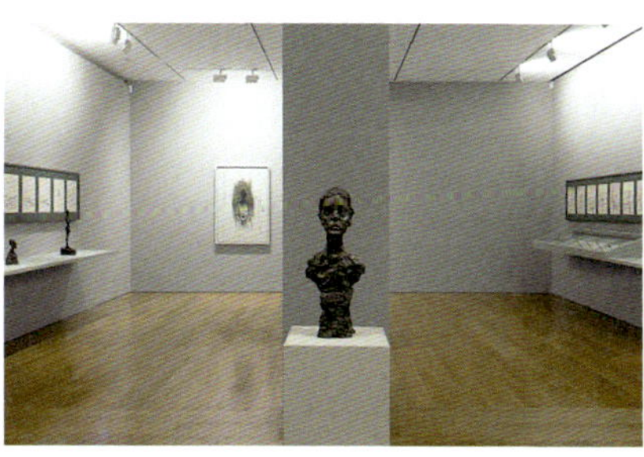

07 ***Giacometti Without End***, exhibition,
Gagosian Gallery, Pedder Building,
Hong Kong

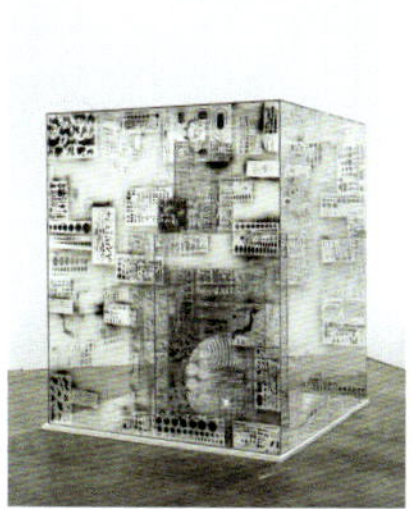

08 **Teppei Kaneuji**
Model of Something #3, 2011
Lombard Freid Gallery

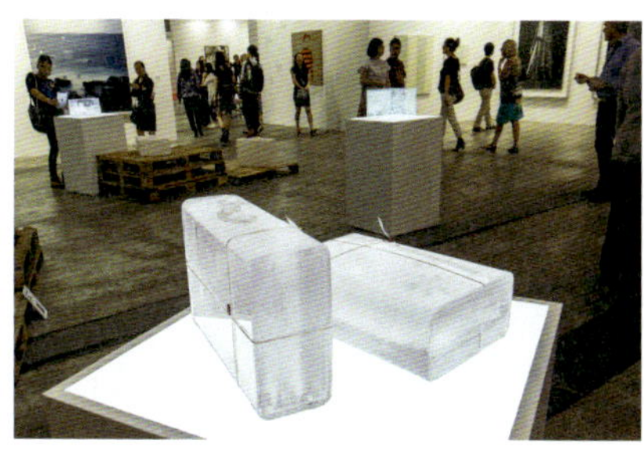

09 **Miyanaga Aiko**
Letter (Hong Kong), 2013
Mizuma Art Gallery (Encounters)

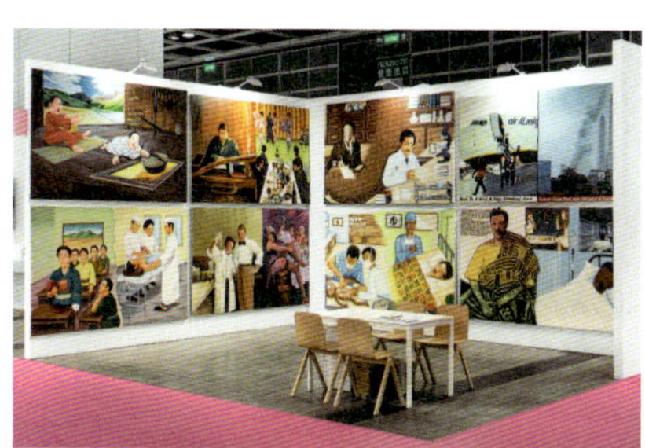

10 **Tsuyoshi Ozawa**
The Return of Dr. N, 2013
Misa Shin Gallery (Insights)

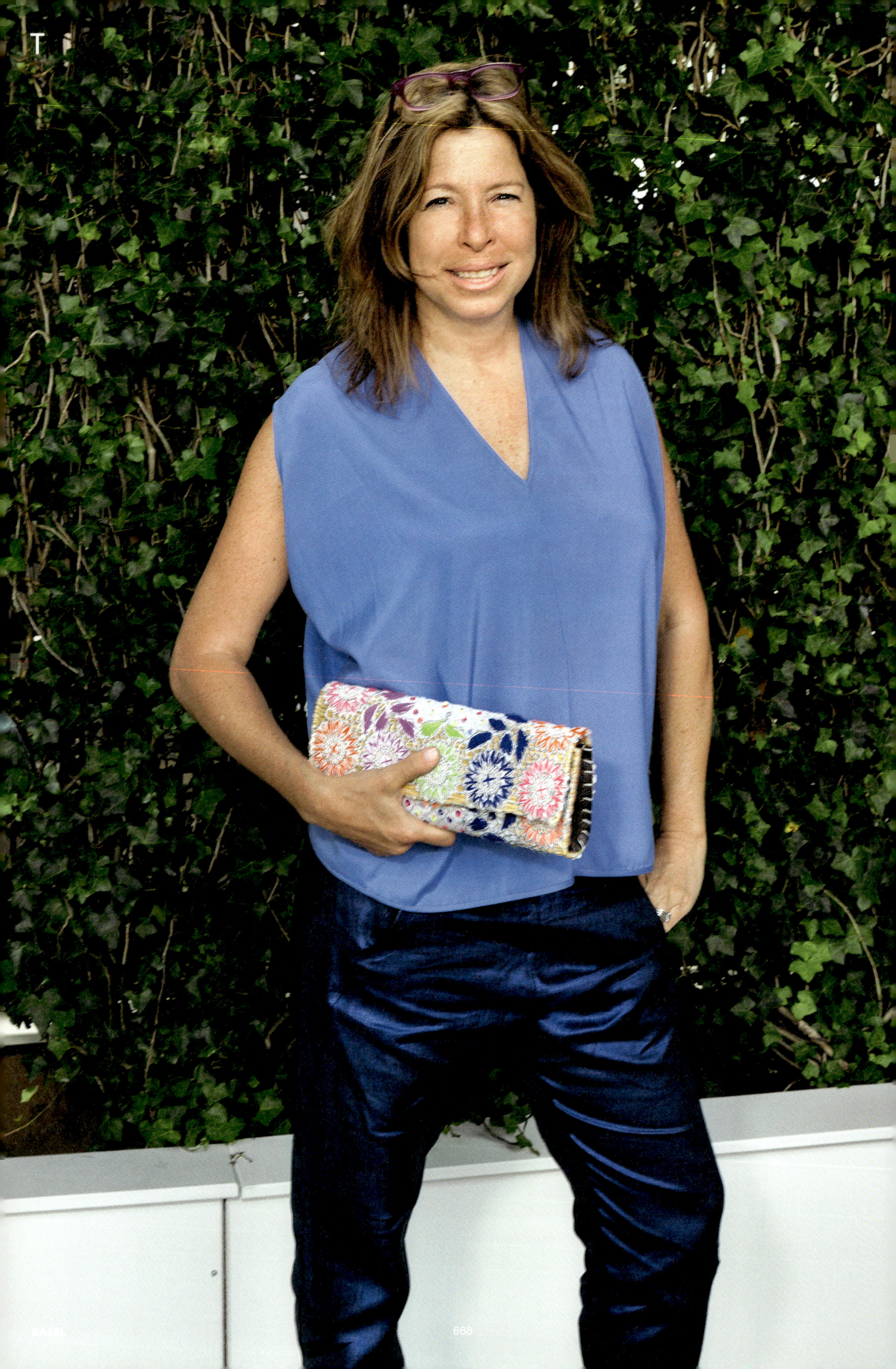

Anne Pasternak

President and Artistic Director,
Creative Time, New York

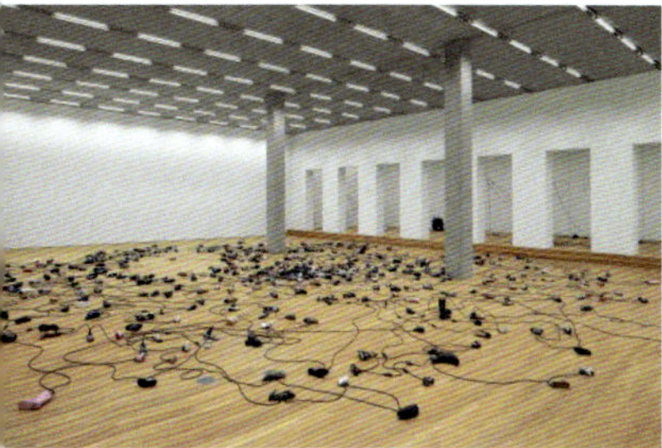

1 **Paul Chan**, *Master Argument*, 2013
Paul Chan - Selected Works, Schaulager, Basel

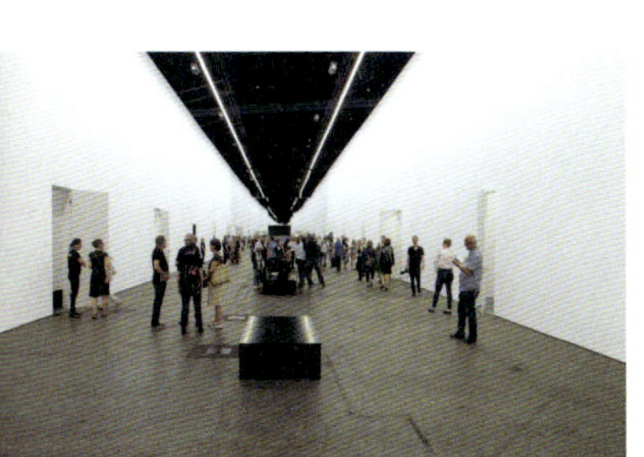

2 ***14 Rooms*** exhibition presented by Fondation Beyeler, Art Basel, and Theater Basel

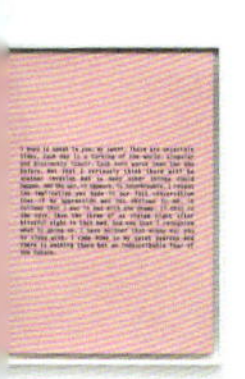
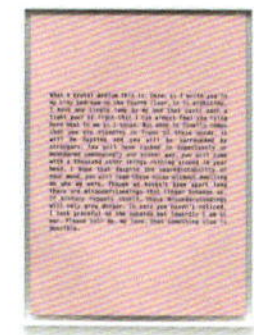

3 **Sharon Hayes**
May 1st, 2012
Tanya Leighton

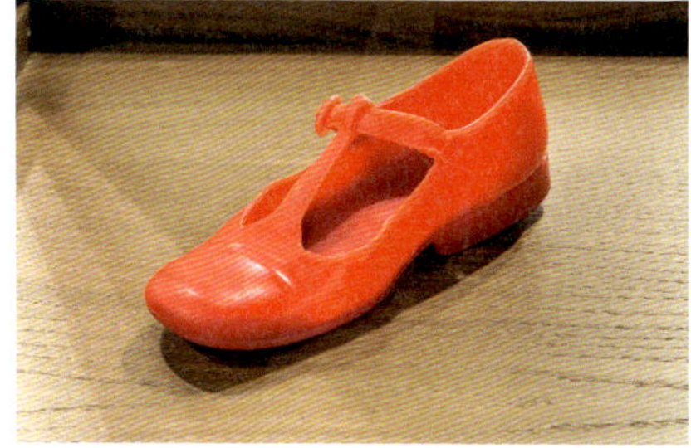

04 **Robert Gober**
Red Shoe, 1990
Anthony Meier Fine Arts

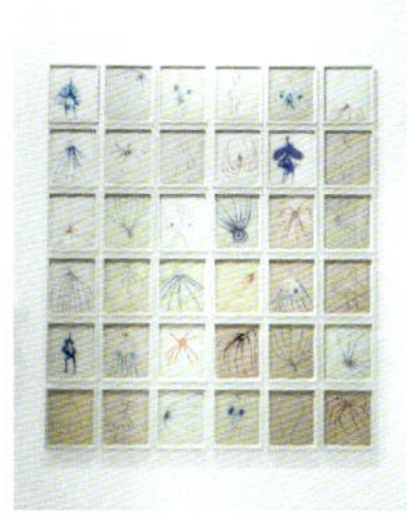

05 **Louise Bourgeois**
The Fragile, 2007
Carolina Nitsch

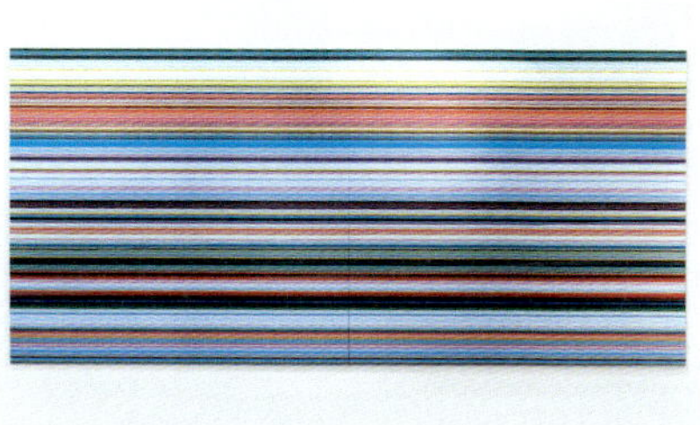

06 **Gerhard Richter**
921-3 STRIP, 2011
Marian Goodman Gallery

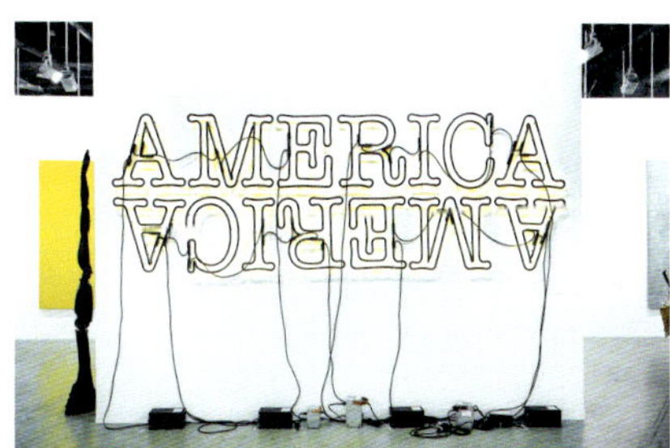

07 **Glenn Ligon**
Double America 2, 2014
Regen Projects

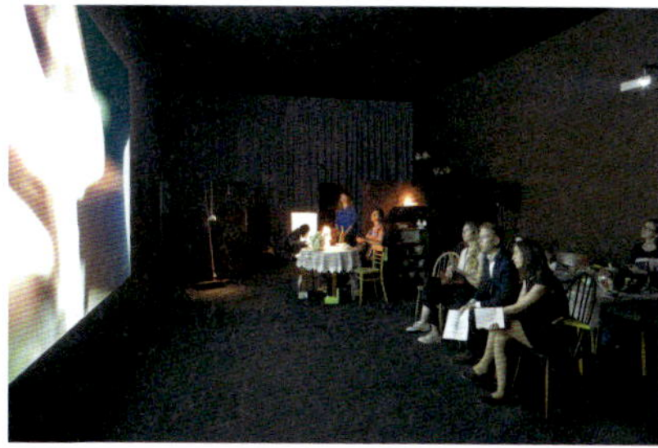

08 **Laure Prouvost**
Wantee, 2013
MOT International (Unlimited)

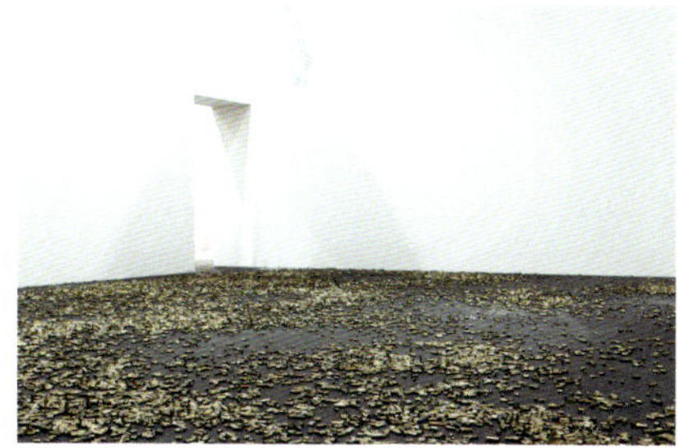

09 **Matias Faldbakken**
20'000 Gun Shells, 2011
Galerie Eva Presenhuber & Standard (Unlimited)

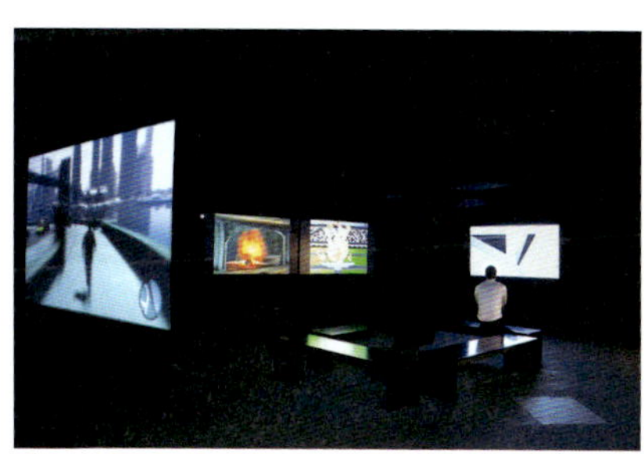

10 **Harun Farocki**
Parallele I-IV, 2012–2014
Galerie Thaddaeus Ropac (Unlimited)

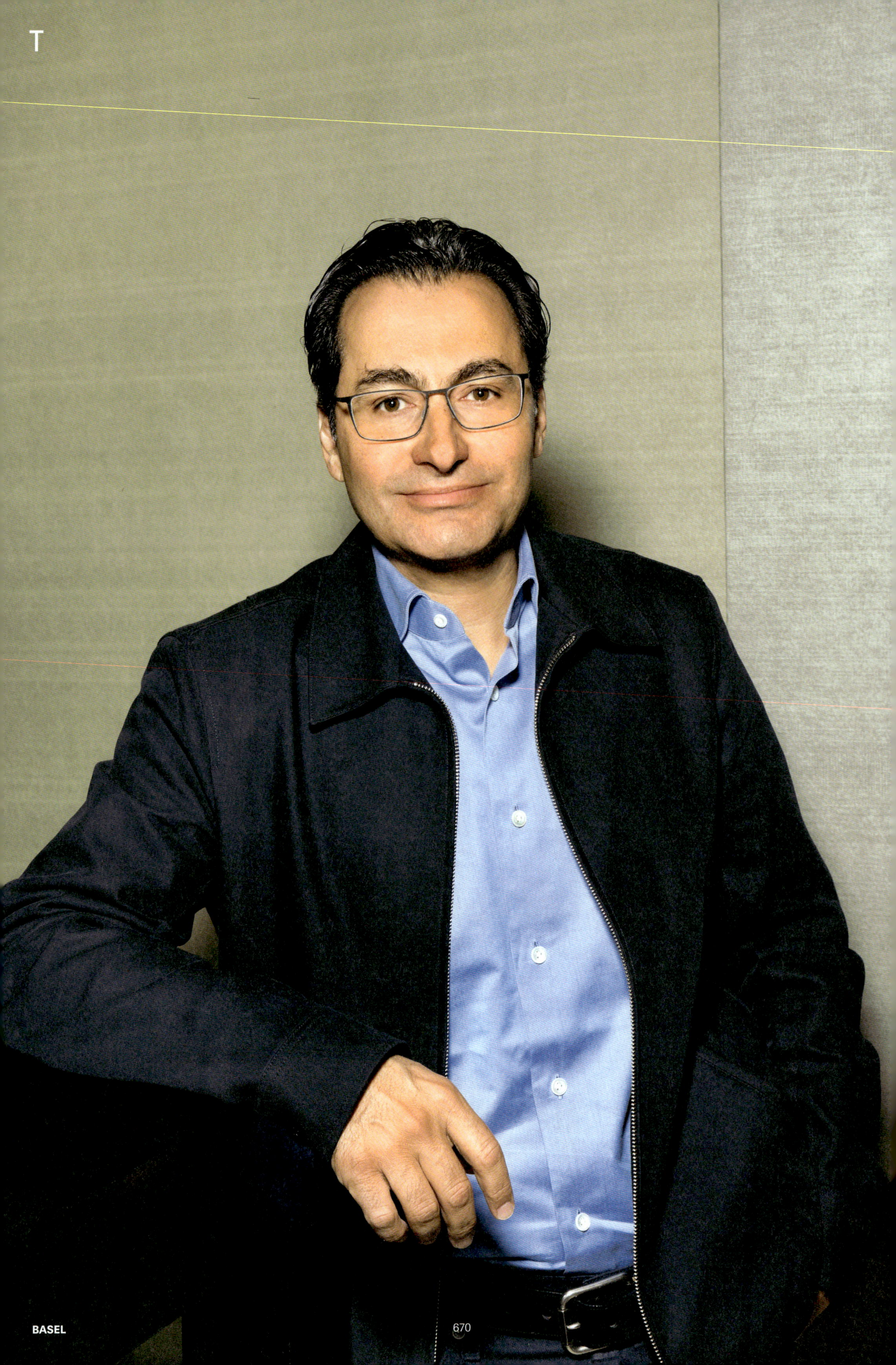

Tony Salamé

Collector, Beirut

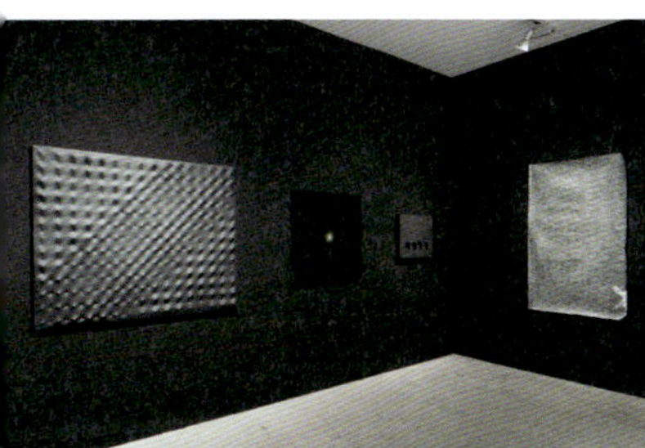

01 **Massimo De Carlo booth** with works by Paola Pivi, Dadamaino, Enrico Castellani, Piotr Uklanski, Paolo Scheggi, and Tony Lewis

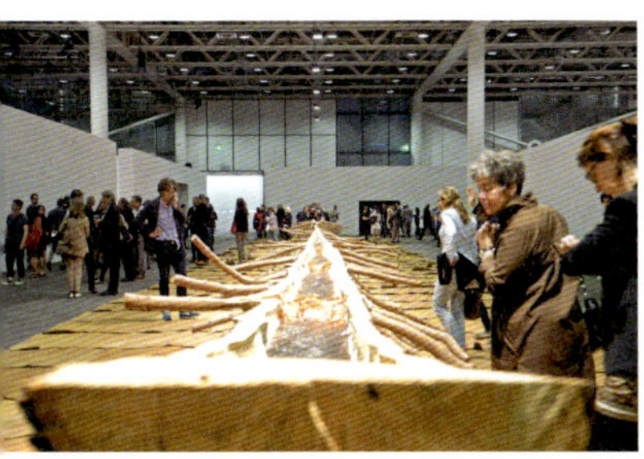

02 **Giuseppe Penone**
Matrice di linfa, 2008
Tucci Russo Studio per l'Arte Contemporanea (Unlimited)

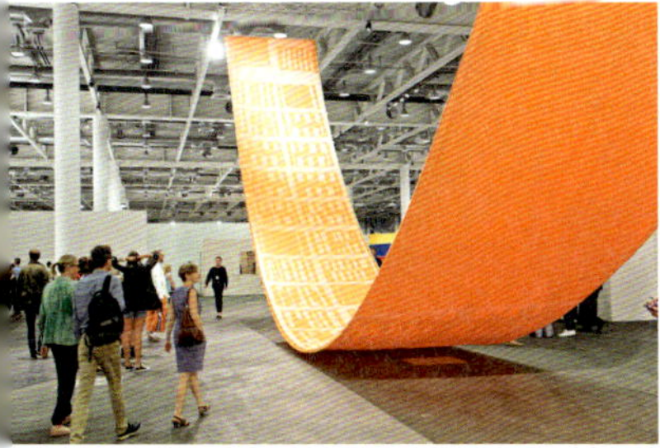

03 **Sam Falls**
Untitled (Pallet 9, Pomona), 2013
Galerie Eva Presenhuber (Unlimited)

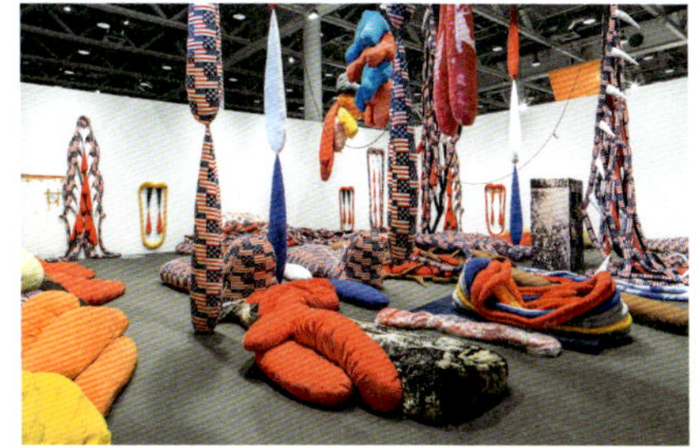

04 **Sterling Ruby**
Soft Work, 2011–2013
Xavier Hufkens and Sprüth Magers Berlin London (Unlimited)

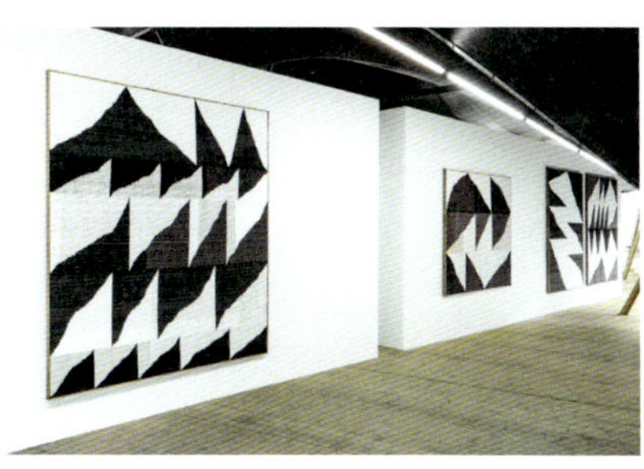

05 **Brent Wadden**
Peres Projects, Liste Art Fair

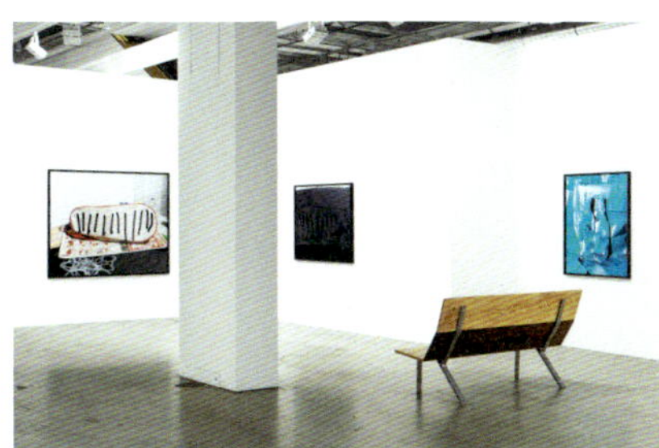

06 **Lucas Blalock**
Ramiken Crucible (Statements)

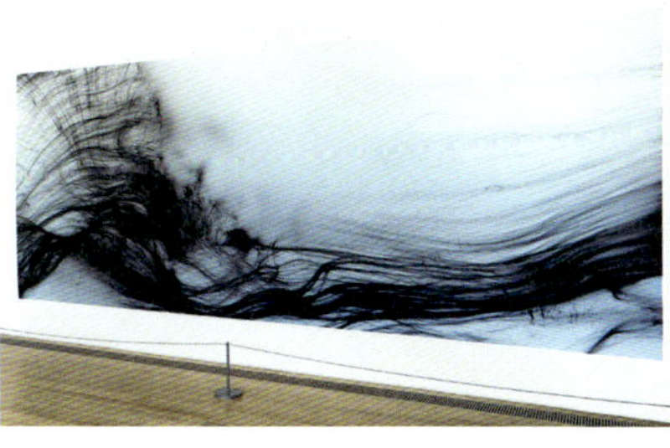

07 **Wolfgang Tillmans**
Solo exhibition, Fondation Beyeler, Riehen

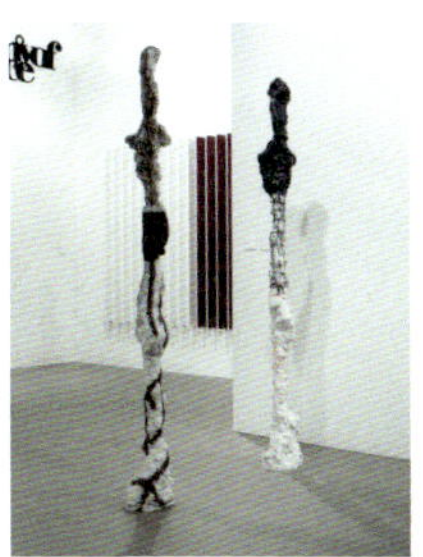

08 **Rebecca Warren**
Sieben and *Zwei*, 2013
Maureen Paley

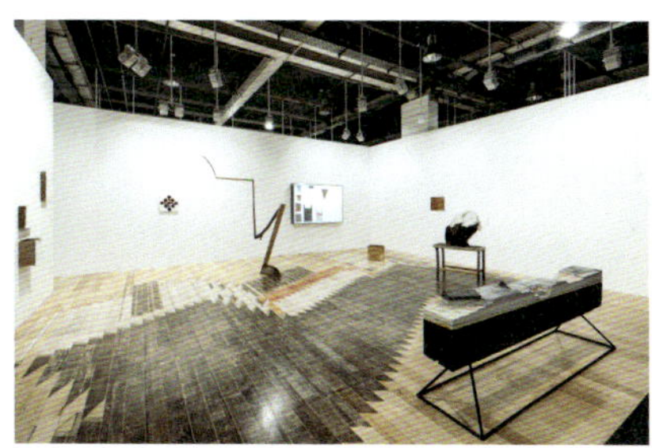

09 **Damián Ortega**
Misunderstanding Alfred, Alfred Arndt I. Bauhaus masters' houses, 1926, 2014
kurimanzutto

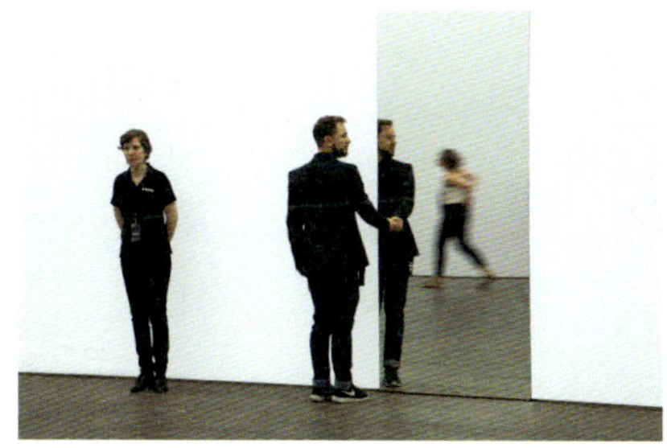

10 ***14 Rooms*** exhibition presented by Fondation Beyeler, Art Basel, and Theater Basel

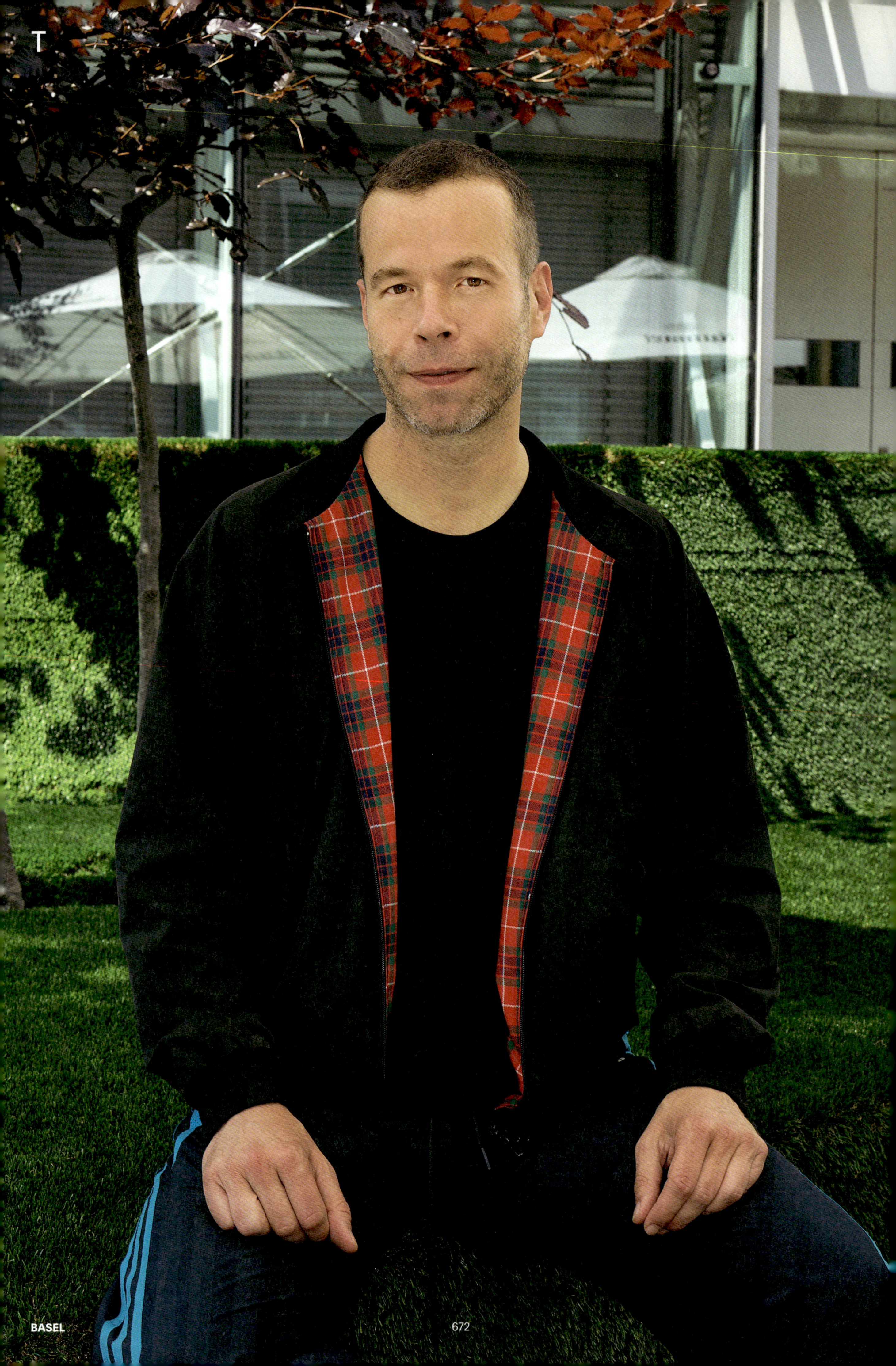

Wolfgang Tillmans

Artist, Berlin & London

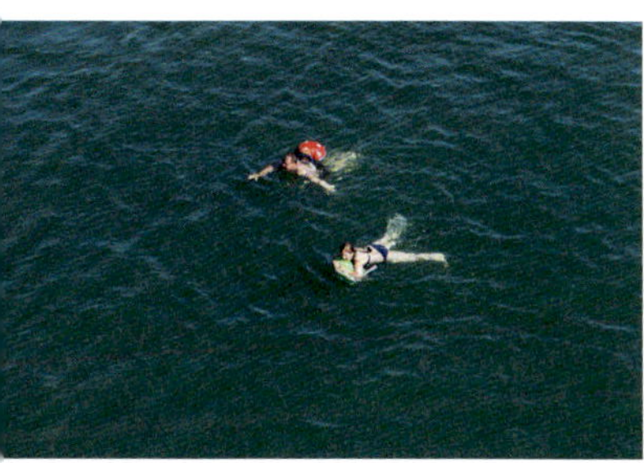

1 **The Rhine**

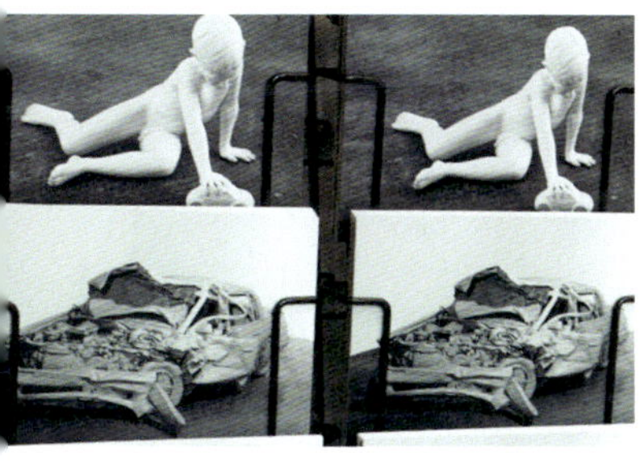

2 **Charles Ray**, *Sculptures 1997–2004*
Kunstmuseum and Museum für Gegenwartskunst, Basel

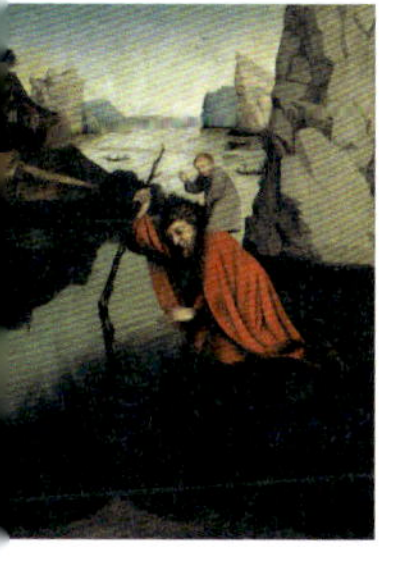

3 **Konrad Witz**
Kunstmuseum, Basel

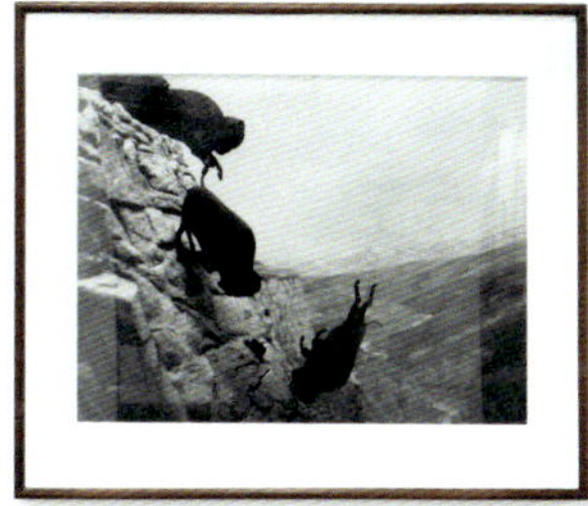

04 **David Wojnarowicz**
Untitled (Buffalos), 1968/69–1992
P.P.O.W (Feature)

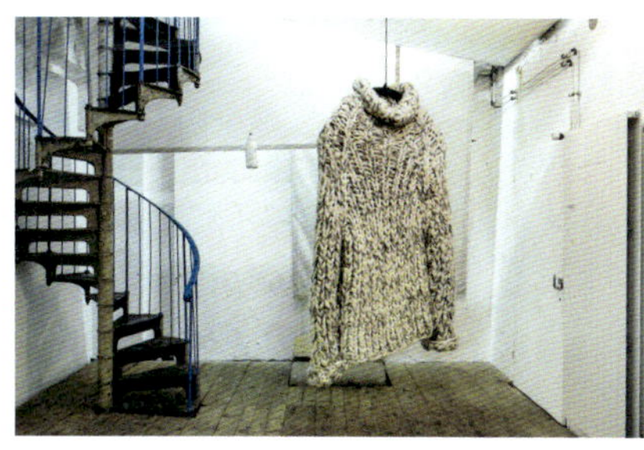

05 **Dewar & Gicquel**
Pull (Jersey), 2014, & *Pull (Torsadé)*, 2014
Truth & Consequences, Liste Art Fair

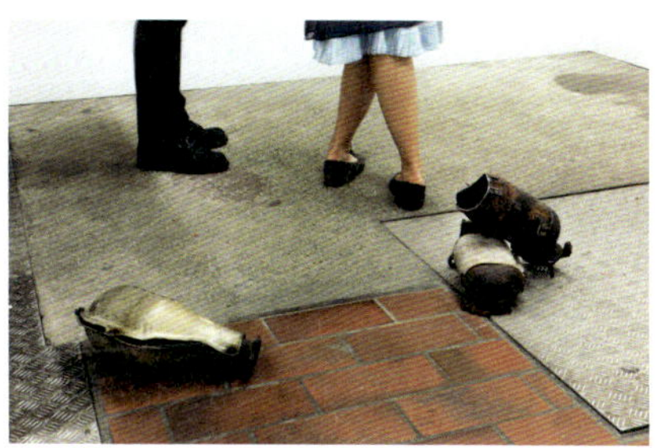

06 **Cameron Rowland**
255, 155–175, 10, 2014
Essex Street, Liste Art Fair

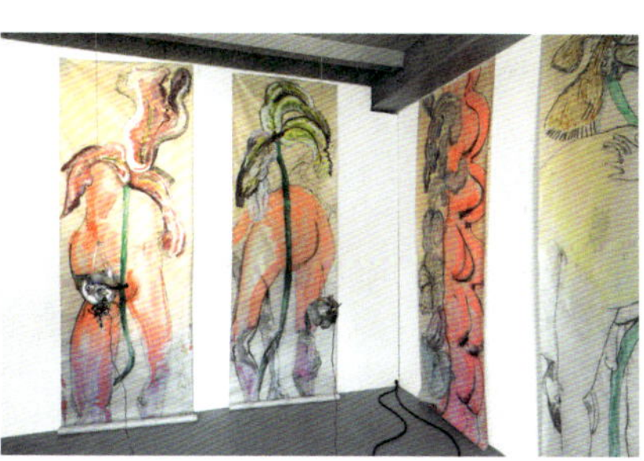

07 **Matthew Lutz-Kinoy**
Loose Bodies, 2013
Freedman Fitzpatrick, Liste Art Fair

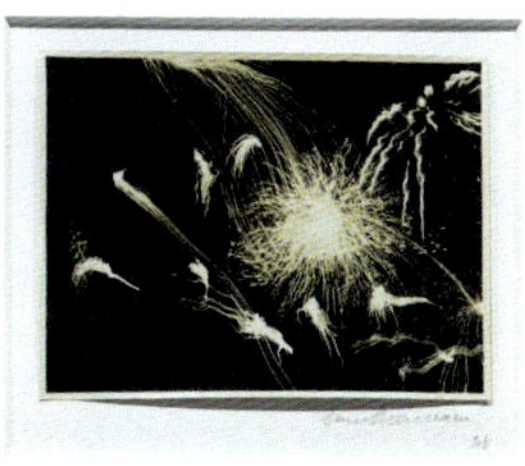

08 **Aenne Biermann**
Fireworks, c. 1930
Galerie Berinson

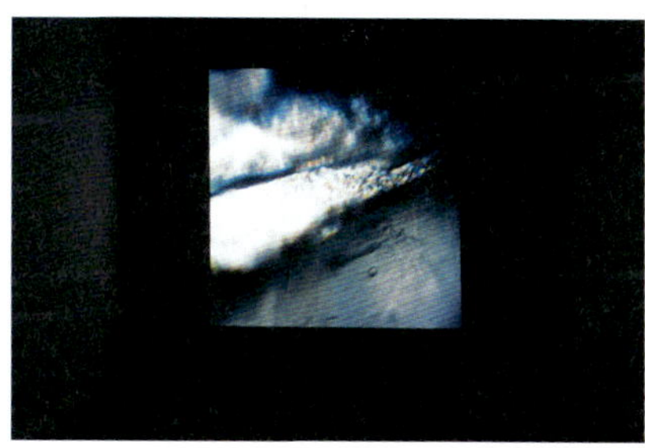

09 **Melvin Moti**
The Eightfold Dot, 2013
Meyer Riegger (Unlimited)

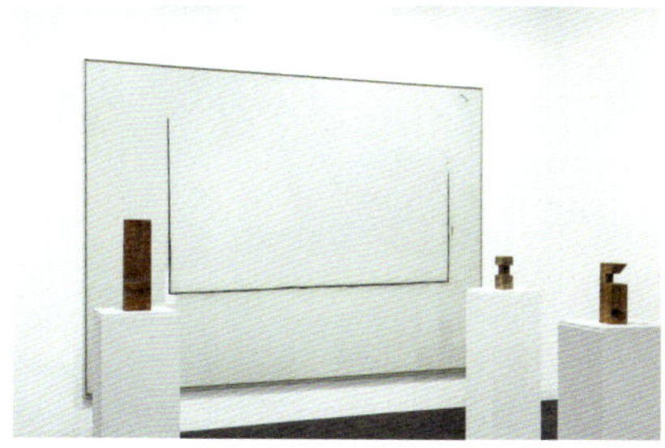

10 **Robert Motherwell**
Open No. 22, 1968

Carl Andre
Untitled, 1957–1959
Andrea Rosen Gallery

T

DAMIEN HIRST
THE NABIS
REGENCY DESIGN
IN-FINITUM
LAND ART
THE SPIRITUAL IN ART
PRINT/OUT
THE BRITANNICA ENCYCLOPEDIA OF AMERICAN ART
ON CLASSIC GROUND
American Master Drawings and Watercolors
I AM A CAMERA
BRASIL

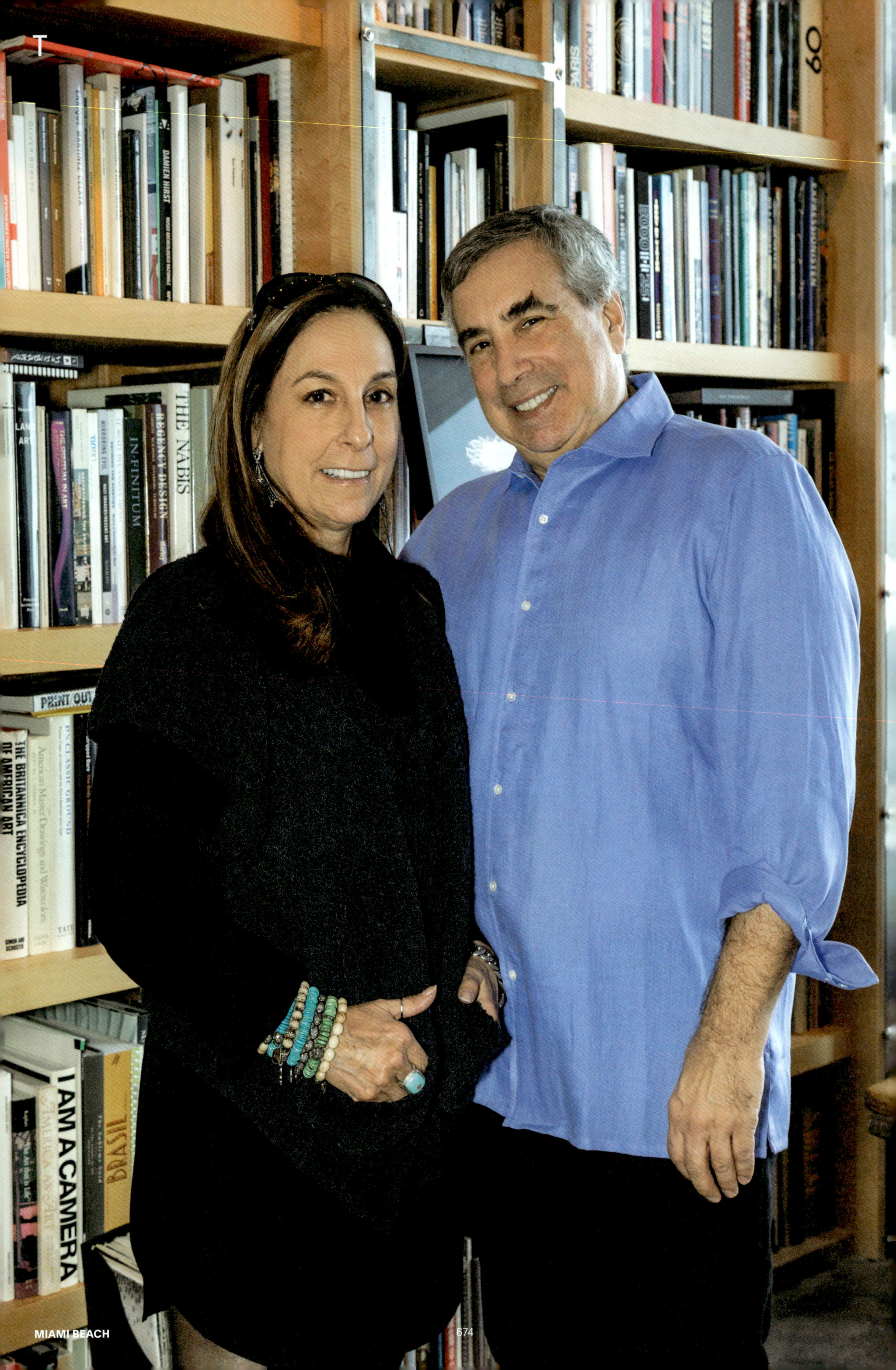

Shelley Fox Aarons & Philip Aarons

Collectors, New York

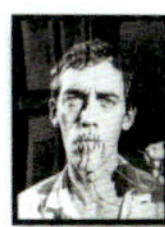
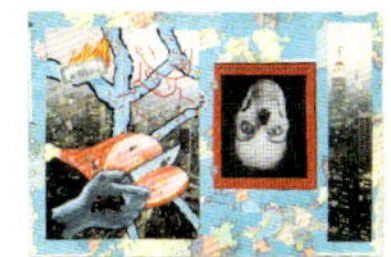

01 **P.P.O.W booth** with works by Martin Wong, David Wojnarowicz, and their circles

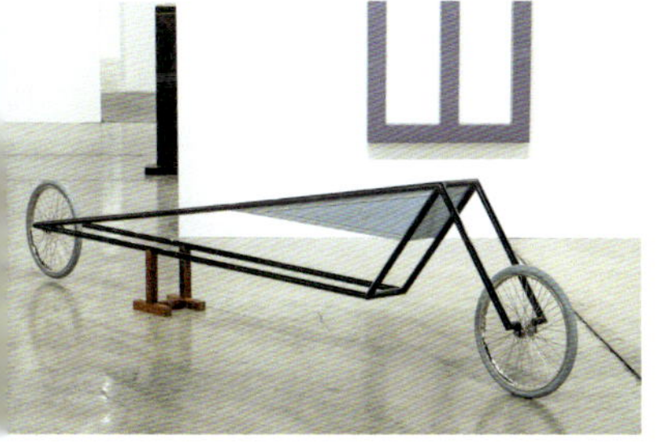

02 **Gianni Piacentino**, *Black Frame Vehicle with Light Blue-gray Triangle Tank*, 1970–1971
Michael Werner

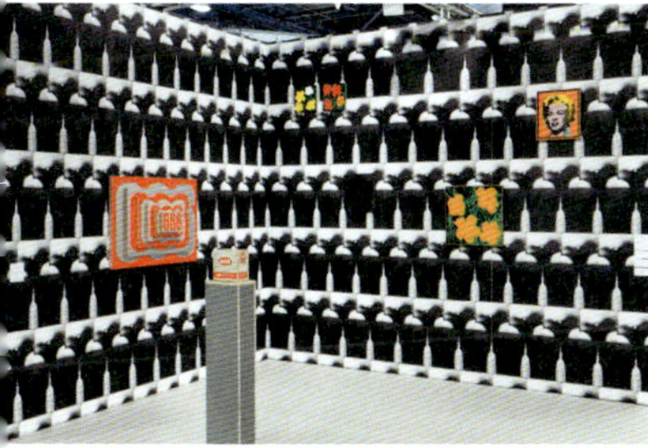

03 **Tom Sachs and Sturtevant** on Sturtevant's *Empire State Building* wallpaper installation, Galerie Thaddaeus Ropac

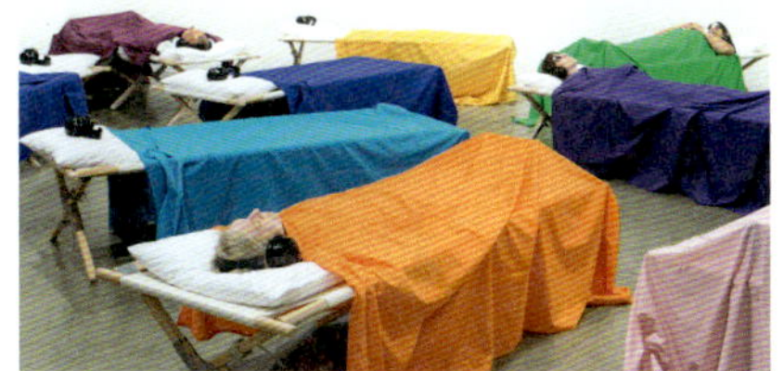

04 **Marina Abramović/MAI**, *Sleeping Exercise*, 2014, presented by Fondation Beyeler

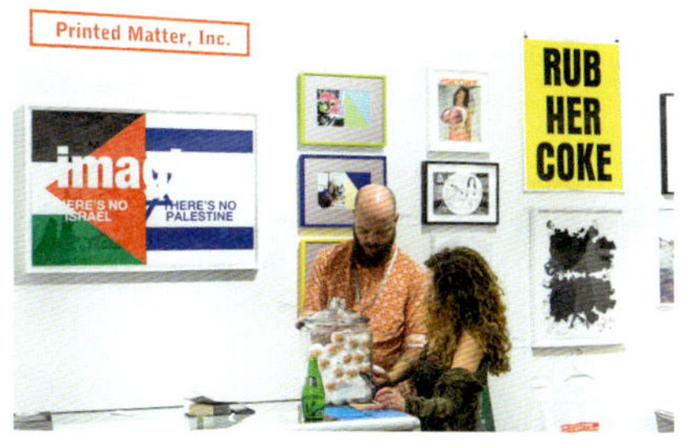

05 **Printed Matter booth**

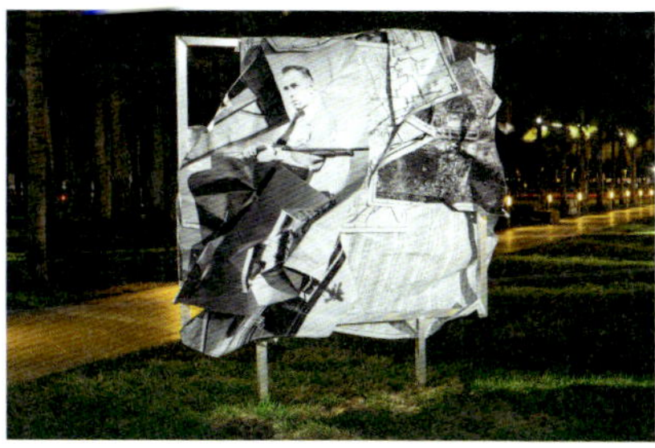

06 **Olaf Metzel**, *Untitled*, 2014
Wentrup (Public)

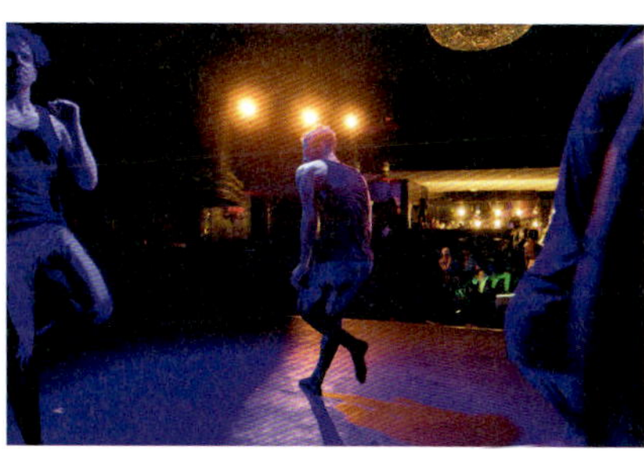

07 **Ryan McNamara**, *MEƎM 4 Miami: A Story Ballet about the Internet*, 2014, a Performa commission presented by Art Basel
Miami Grand Theater (Former Playboy Theater), Castle Beach Resort, Miami Beach

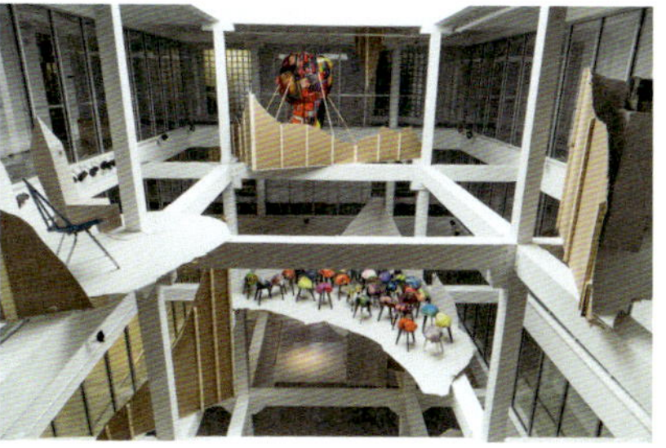

08 **Andra Ursuta**, *As I Lay Drying*, Institute of Contemporary Art, Miami, solo exhibition

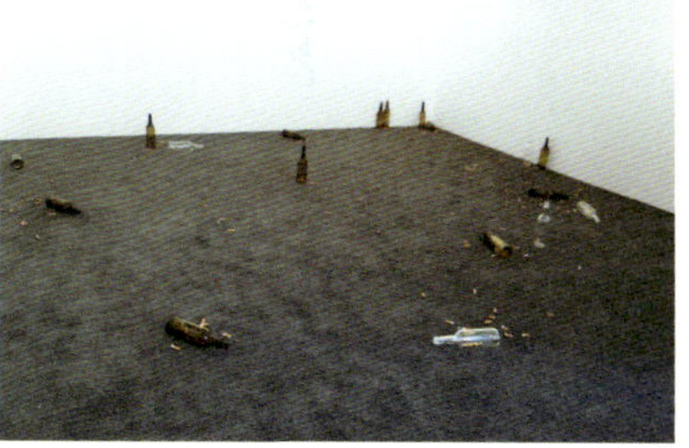

09 **Dan Colen**, one-day installation, 2014
Karma Gallery, Nada Art Fair

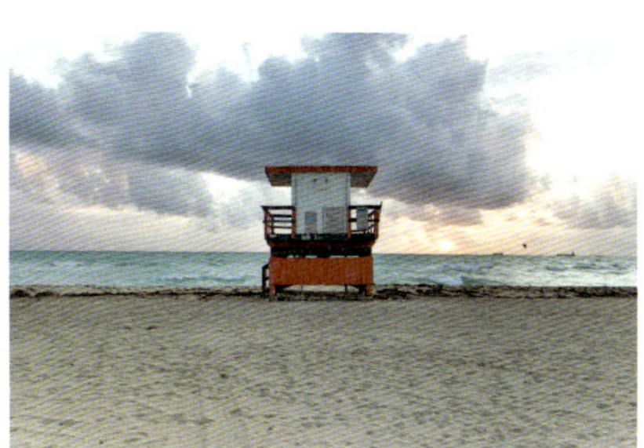

10 **The Atlantic Ocean**

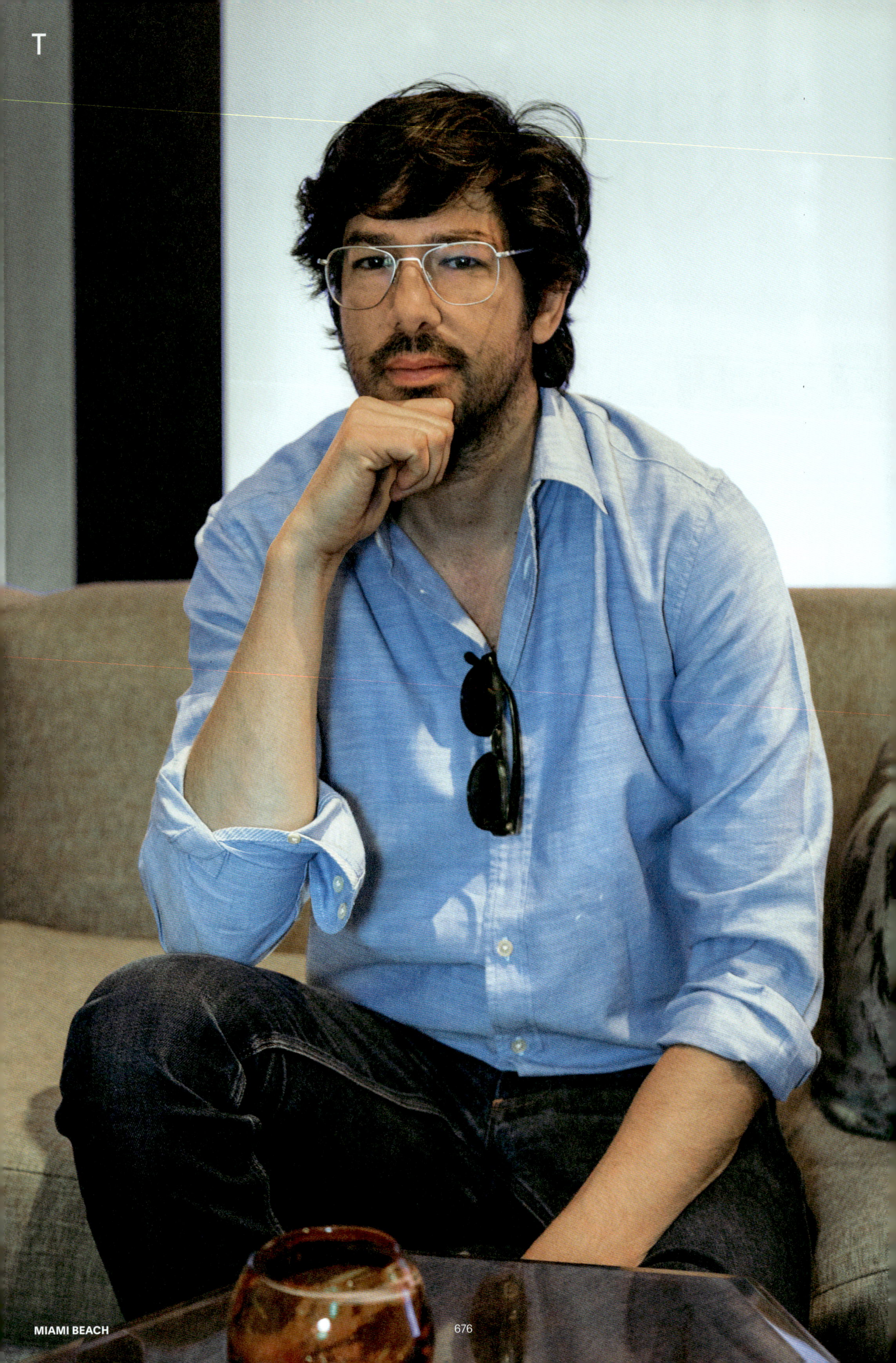

Mario García Torres

Artist, Mexico City

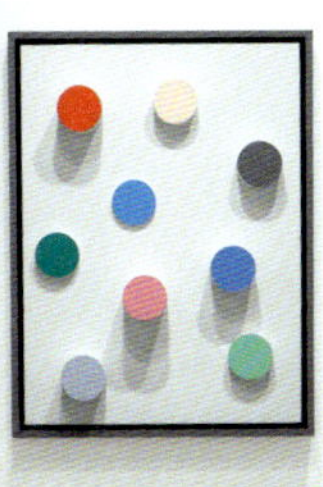

01 **Rodney Graham**
Cylindro-chromatic Abstraction Construction, 2014
303 Gallery

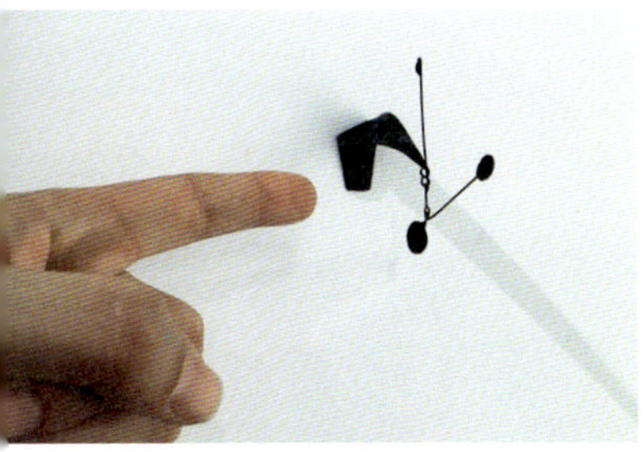

02 **Alexander Calder**
Untitled, 1955
Van de Weghe Fine Art
(Photo by Ryan Gander; scale by Mario García Torres)

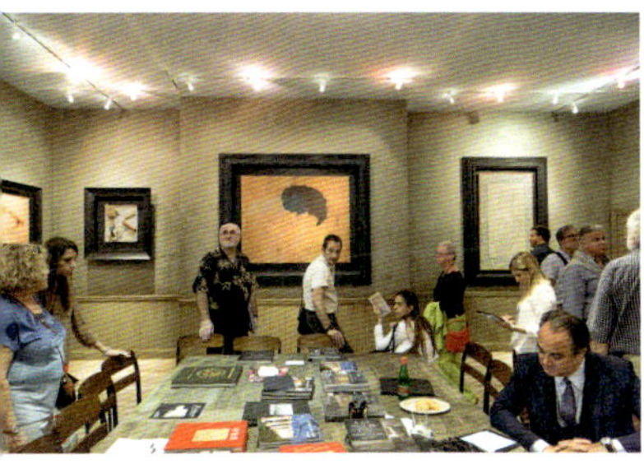

03 **Non-white booths**
(here: Galerie Gmurzynska)

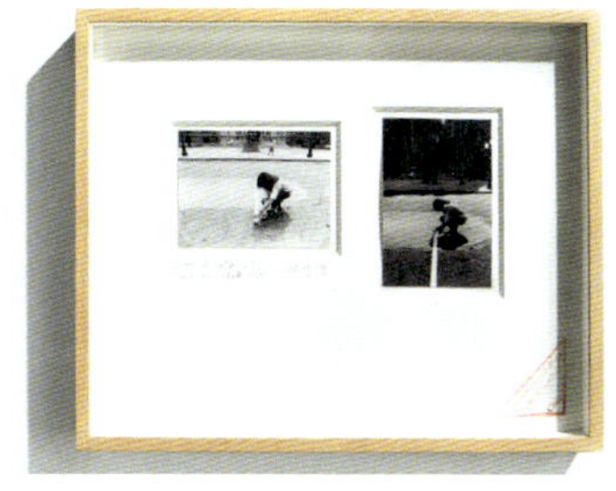

04 **Lotty Rosenfeld**
Acciones de Arte, 1979–1999
espaivisor (Survey)

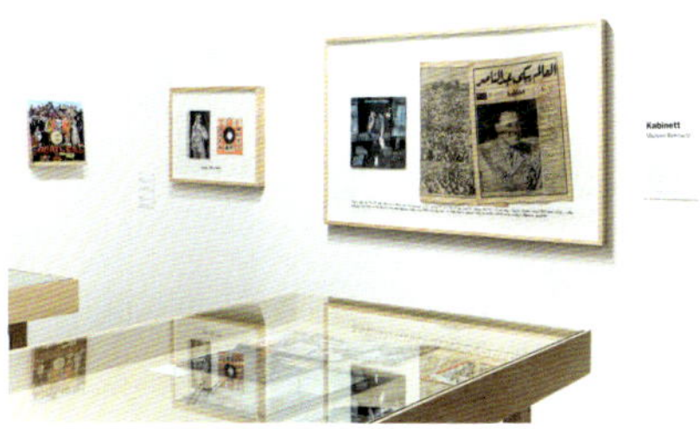

05 **Michael Rakowitz**
The Breakup, 2010–2014
Rhona Hoffman Gallery (Kabinett)

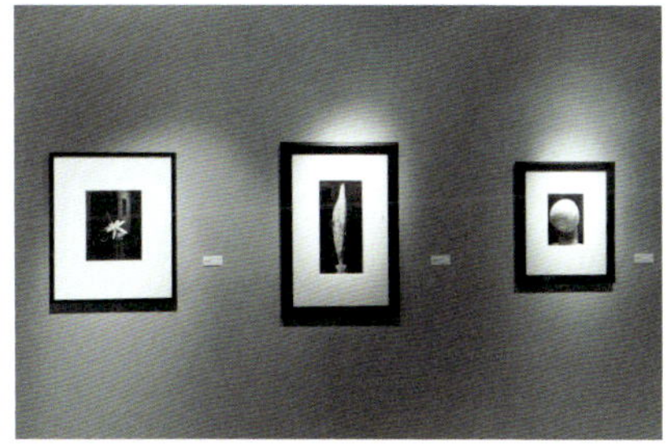

06 **Brancusi: The Photographs**
The Margulies Collection at the Warehouse, Wynwood, Miami

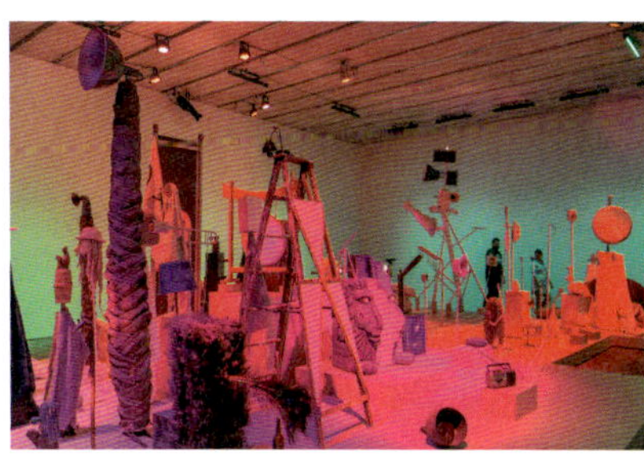

07 **Geoffrey Farmer**
Let's Make the Water Turn Black, Pérez Art Museum Miami, solo exhibition

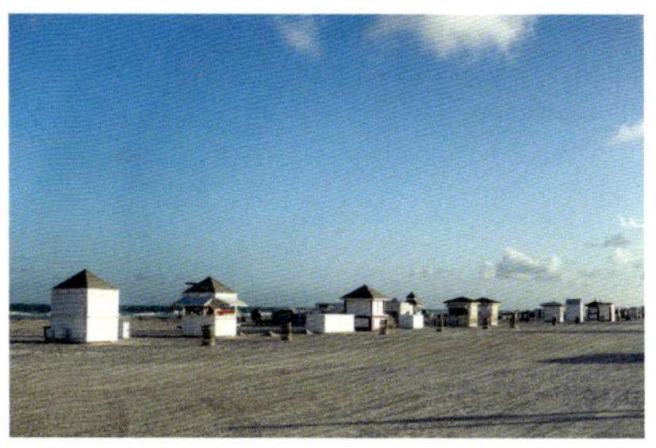

08 **Miami Beach weather**

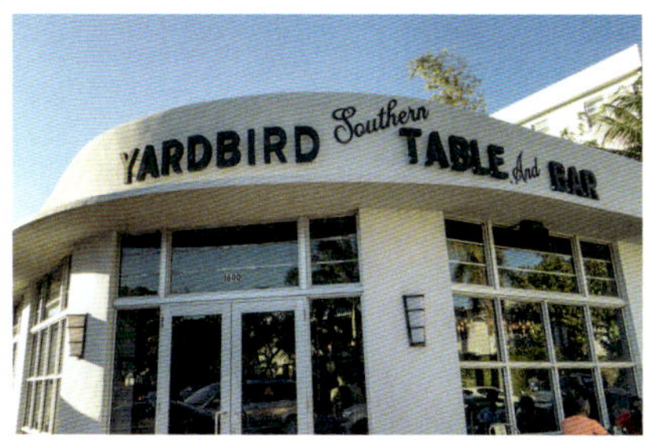

09 **Fried Green Tomato BLT and Blackberry Burbon Lemonade**
Yardbird, 1600 Lennox Avenue, Miami Beach

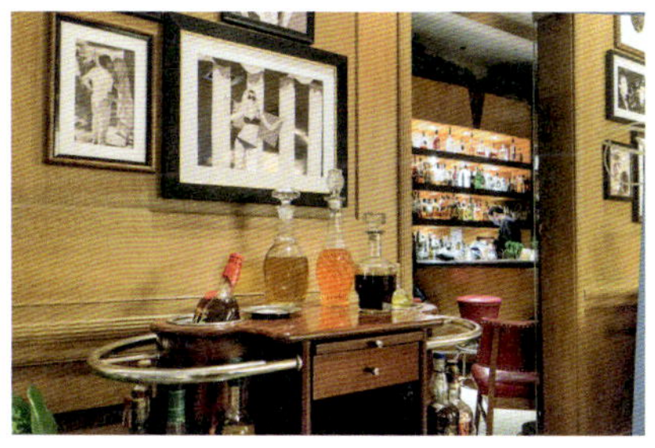

10 **Negronis** at the Raleigh Hotel, Miami Beach

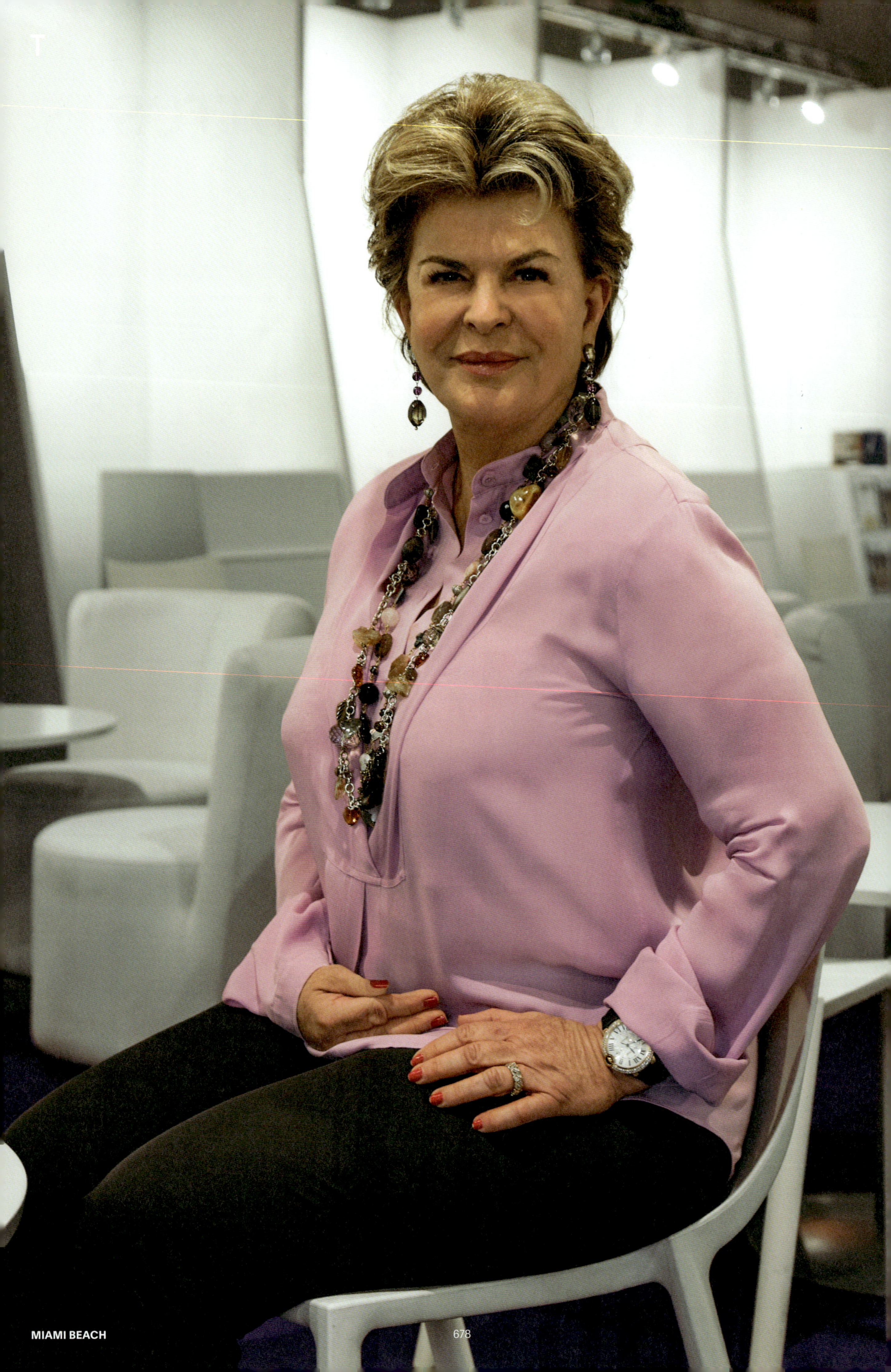
T

Ella Fontanals-Cisneros

Collector and Founder, Cisneros Fontanals Art Foundation, Miami

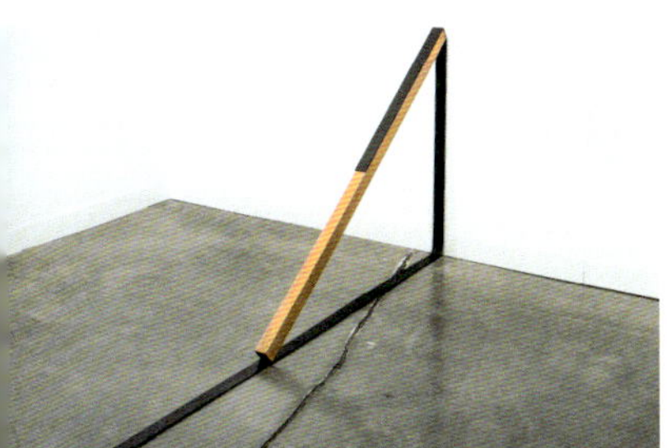

01 **Marcius Galan**
Unstable Piece, 2013
Galeria Luisa Strina

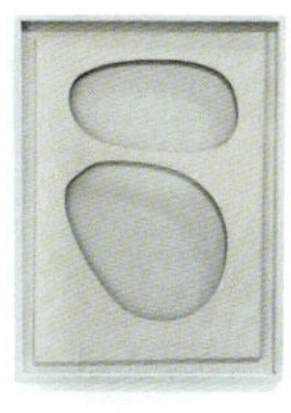

02 **Dadamaino**
Volume, 1958
Galería Guillermo de Osma

03 **Anish Kapoor**
Untitled, 2014
Galleria Continua

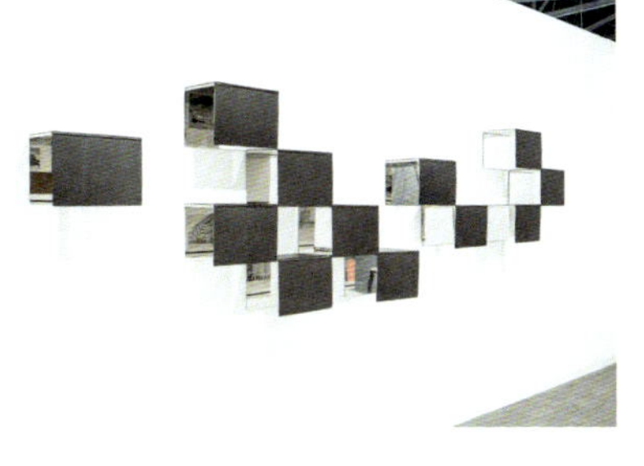

04 **Fernanda Fragateiro**
Common Front/Frente comun, 2013
Galería Elba Benítez

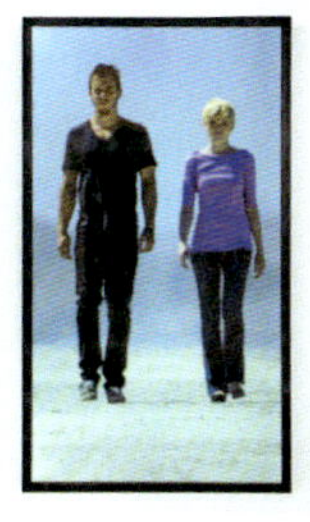

05 **Bill Viola**
Delicate Thread, 2012
Kukje Gallery / Tina Kim Gallery

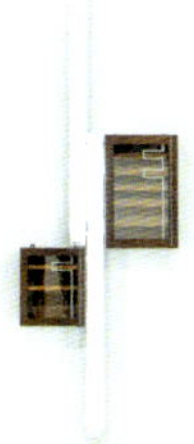

06 **Reinhard Mucha**
Uetzen, 2014
Sprüth Magers Berlin London

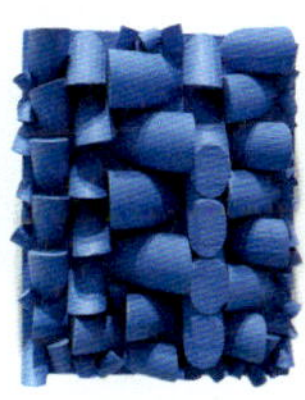

07 **Sergio Camargo**
Construction bleue, 1963
DAN Galería

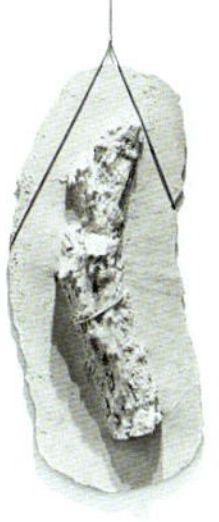

08 **Giuseppe Penone**
Germinazione, 2005
Marian Goodman Gallery

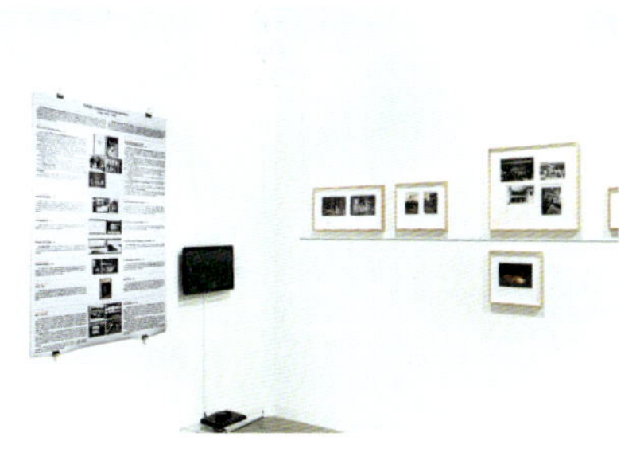

09 **Lotty Rosenfeld**
Acciones de Arte, 1979–1999
espaivisor (Survey)

10 **Shirazeh Houshiary**
Genesis, 2014
Lisson Gallery

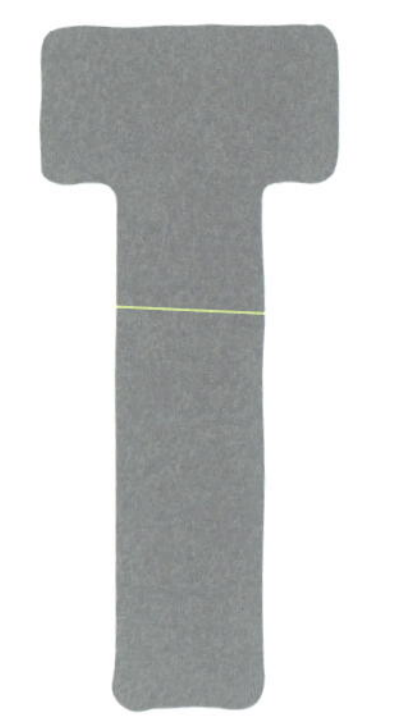

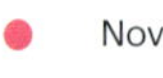

T293

Rome
Naples

● Nova

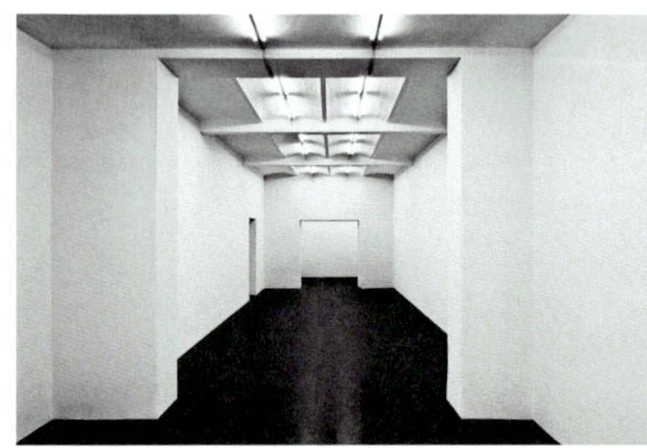

- **Contact** T293
  Vanessa Saraceno
  vaness@t293.it
- **Established** 2002
- **Owner(s) / Partner(s)** Giuseppe Altavilla
- **Team** 5
- **Artists at Art Basel** Sam Falls
  May Hands
  Wyatt Kahn
  Erica Mahinay

Take Ninagawa

Tokyo

● Discoveries
● Feature
● Nova

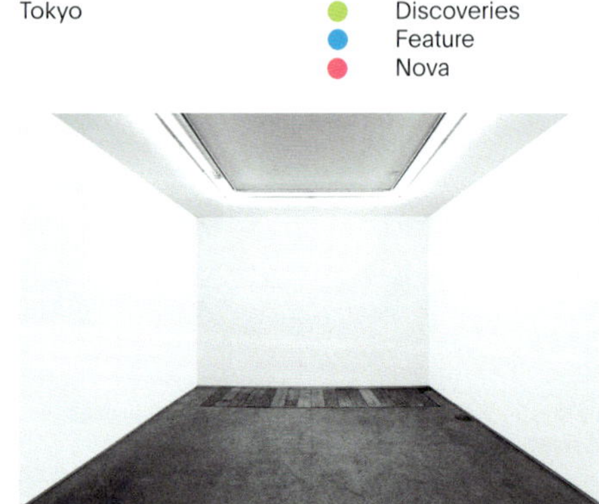

What is your favorite aspect of running a gallery?

My favorite aspect of running a gallery is being able to witness the production of great works, and share the excitement of creation with the artists.

How do you choose the artists you work with?

I am interested in artists who can show us a way of being both inside and outside at the same time.

If you weren't running a gallery what else would you do?

Nothing.

- **Contact** Take Ninagawa
  Atsuko Ninagawa
  info@takeninagawa.com
- **Established** 2008
- **Owner(s) / Partner(s)** Atsuko Ninagawa
- **Team** 4

- **Space(s)** 80 m²
- **Artist at Art Basel** Shinro Ohtake
- **Further artists represented** Ryoko Aoki
  Dale Berning
  Aki Goto
  Taro Izumi
  Shinpei Kageshima
  Misaki Kawai
  Yoriko Kita
  Chikara Matsumoto
  Yuuki Matsumura
  Ken Okiishi
  Aki Sasamoto
  Yukiko Suto
  Soju Tao
  Tsuruko Yamazaki

Tang

Beijing

● Galleries
Encounters

- **Contact** Tang Contemporary Art
  Zhao Ting Ting
  zhaotingting@tangcontemporary.com
- **Established** 2001
- **Owner(s) / Partner(s)** Zheng Lin

tanzer

Melbourne

● Insights

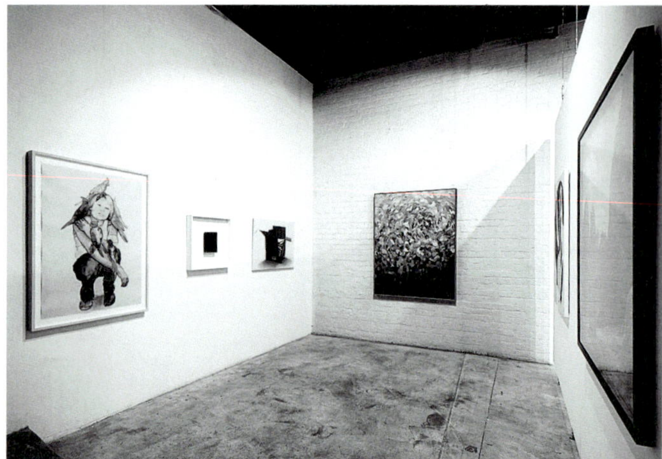

What is your favorite aspect of running a gallery?

My favorite aspect is the relationships I have built with the artists. I love that I get to meet such a diverse range of people and be part of their success and career development.

How do you choose the artists you work with?

My main aim is to create an innovative and creative platform for Australian contemporary art. In order to achieve this, I feel I need to create an environment and context where I can showcase a combination of emerging and mid-career artists that challenge and push boundaries both locally and internationally. I don't really choose artists as such, it is more of an organic process and collaboration.

If you weren't running a gallery what else would you do?

Running a commercial gallery is a very intellectually challenging career, in which there are huge expectations and many disappointments, but, at the end of the day, the rewards outweigh everything. I love the everyday challenges and I truly can't imagine doing anything else, although if I didn't have the gallery I would probably return to my earlier career in medicine.

- **Contact** dianne tanzer gallery + projects
  Lucy Hughes
  dtanzer@ozemail.com.au

- **Established** 1990
- **Owner(s) / Partner(s)** Dianne Tanzer
- **Team** 6
- **Space(s)** 200 m²
- **Artists at Art Basel** Yhonnie Scarce
- **Further artists represented** Abdul Rahman Abdullah, Natasha Bieniek, Kevin Chin, Michael Cook, Marian Drew, Juan Ford, Petrina Hicks, Tony Lloyd, Janelle Low, Donna Marcus, Becc Orszag, Izabela Pluta, Victoria Reichelt, Roh Singh, Owen Leong, Jacqui Stockdale, Amy Joy Watson

Taylor

London

Galleries
Galleries
Galleries Kabinett

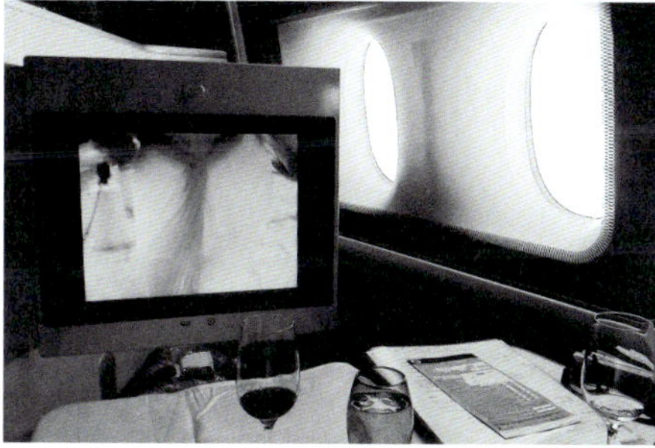

What is your favorite aspect of running a gallery?
There are a number of things I enjoy, but overall I would say spending the majority of my time being immersed in and surrounded by art. It is an enormous privilege.

How do you choose the artists you work with?
Firstly through instinct, and then more practical issues come into play, such as how the artist would fit into our program, and whether I can create opportunities for them internationally. I am always thinking long-term. I want these relationships to endure and mature.

If you weren't running a gallery what else would you do?
I have been in the art world since college, it is where I have always wanted to be. I have never considered doing anything else.

- **Contact** Timothy Taylor Gallery, mail@timothytaylorgallery.com
- **Established** 1996
- **Owner(s) / Partner(s)** Tim Taylor
- **Space(s)** 615 m²
- **Artists at Art Basel** Estate of Craigie Aitchison, Diane Arbus, Robert Bechtle, Jean-Marc Bustamante, Armen Eloyan, Lee Friedlander, Adam Fuss, Ewan Gibbs, Philip Guston, Simon Hantaï, Hans Hartung, Susan Hiller, Volker Hüller, Jessica Jackson Hutchins, Eemyun Kang, Alex Katz, Jonathan Lasker, Agnes Martin, Eddie Martinez, Josephine Meckseper, Richard Patterson, Mai-Thu Perret, Serge Poliakoff, Fiona Rae, Sean Scully, Kiki Smith, Tony Smith, Antoni Tàpies, Eduardo Terrazas, Liliane Tomasko, Lucy Williams

team

New York
Venice

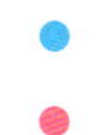
Galleries
Unlimited
Galleries

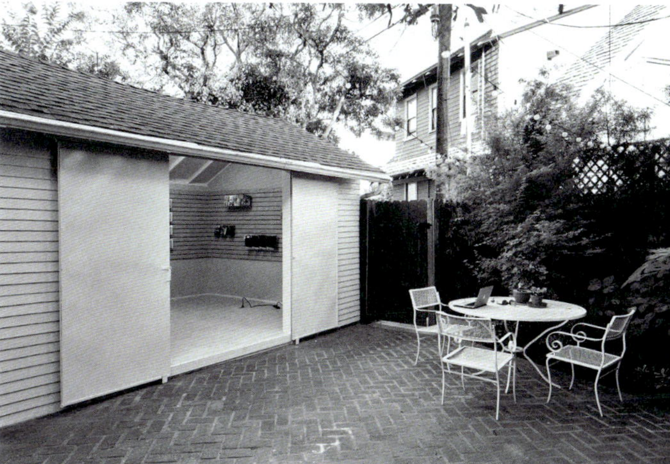

What is your favorite aspect of running a gallery?
Striving to keep the exhibition program strong and evolving.

How do you choose the artists you work with?
Some combination of chemical processes and logical thought brings me to each individual selection.

If you weren't running a gallery what else would you do?
I would sell popcorn at a suburban multiplex.

- **Contact** team (gallery inc.), José Freire, jose@teamgal.com
- **Established** 1996
- **Owner(s) / Partner(s)** José Freire
- **Team** 14
- **Space(s)** 743 m²
- **Artists at Art Basel** Cory Arcangel, Robert Janitz, Suzanne McClelland, Ryan McGinley, David Ratcliff, Tabor Robak, Sam Samore, Andreas Schulze, Stanley Whitney
- **Further artists represented** Alex Bag, Pierre Bismuth, Carina Brandes, Brice Dellsperger, Gardar Eide Einarsson, Massimo Grimaldi, Marc Hundley, Ross Knight, Jakob Kolding, Tam Ochiai, Davis Rhodes, Santiago Sierra, Gert & Uwe Tobias, Pieter Vermeersch, Banks Violette

Tega

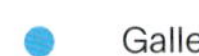

Milan ● Galleries

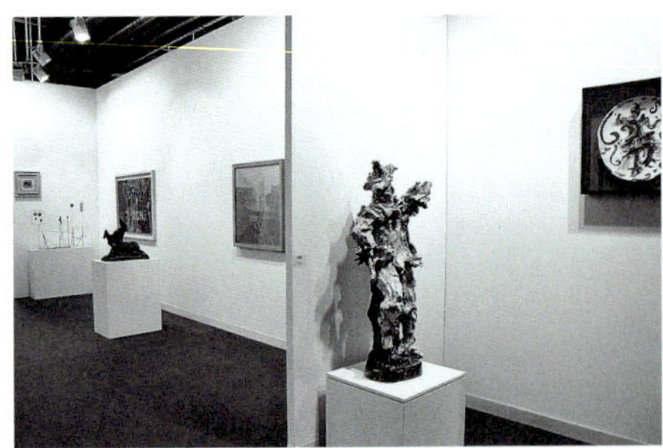

What is your favorite aspect of running a gallery?

The ongoing work: it is always changing and I also continue the tradition started by my grandfather (with Massimo Campigli, Giorgio de Chirico, and Giorgio Morandi, collaborating with their estate and archives) and my father (continuing to work with the archives of Carla Accardi, Piero Consagra, Piero Dorazio, Gastone Novelli, and Mimmo Rotella), promoting artists through collaborations with the major worldwide art insititutions.

How do you choose the artists you work with?

I select artists who do not already have relationships with other galleries in Milan or in Italy in general. We have always focused on maintaining a very high level of quality. Keeping only the leading exponents of each artistic period: Transavanguardia, Arte Povera, Figurative, and Abstract art. We have only ever worked with international artists: Fernando Botero, Christo, Nicola De Maria, Achille Perilli, and Sophia Vari.

If you weren't running a gallery what else would you do?

I would always have worked in the art world, curating exhibitions, more in the organizational, critical, and the communication side of it.

- **Contact** Galleria Tega
Eleonora Tega
info@galleriatega.it
- **Established** 1979
- **Owner(s) / Partner(s)** Eleonora Tega & Francesca Tega
- **Team** 4
- **Space(s)** 160 m²
- **Artists at Art Basel** Carla Accardi
Valerio Adami
Afro
Alighiero Boetti
Fernando Botero
Alberto Burri
Pier Paolo Calzolari
Massimo Campigli
Giuseppe Capogrossi
Enrico Castellani
Christo
Pietro Consagra
Dadamaino
Giorgio de Chirico
Nicola de Maria
Max Ernst
Lucio Fontana
Riccardo Gusmaroli
Damien Hirst
Robert Indiana
Paul Klee
Fernand Léger
Piero Manzoni
Marino Marini
Fausto Melotti
Joan Miró
Amedeo Modigliani
Giorgio Morandi
Giulio Paolini
Achille Perilli
Gianni Piacentino
Pablo Picasso
Michelangelo Pistoletto
Mimmo Rotella
Ed Ruscha
Salvatore Scarpitta
Paolo Scheggi
Antoni Tàpies
Cy Twombly
Sophia Vari
Tom Wesselmann
- **Further artists represented** Enrico Baj
Giacomo Balla
Jean-Michel Basquiat
Agostino Bonalumi
Marc Chagall
Nicolas De Stäel
Piero Dorazio
Jean Dubuffet
Luciano Fabro
Jean Fautrier
Hans Hartung
Wassily Kandinsky
Kcho
Sol LeWitt
Osvaldo Licini
Alberto Magnelli
Mario Merz
Gastone Novelli
Mimmo Paladino
Claudio Parmiggiani
Giuseppe Penone
Serge Poliakoff
Mel Ramos
Alberto Savinio
Mario Schifano
Gino Severini
Mario Sironi
Giuseppe Uncini
Andy Warhol
Gilberto Zorio

Templon

Paris ● Galleries
Brussels ● Galleries Unlimited

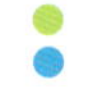

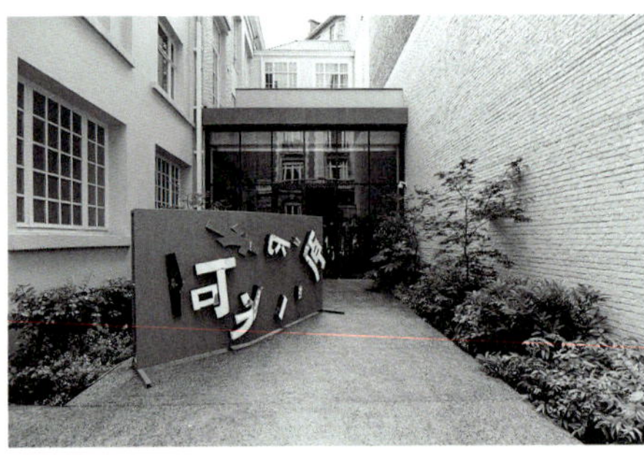

What is your favorite aspect of running a gallery?

I love the challenge of having to always stay in touch with current creation. There is a multiplicity of art scenes and we need to travel all the time. I spend 50% of my time traveling: in the US, China, India, but also in Dubai, Latin America, and Europe of course.

How do you choose the artists you work with?

I am more interested in working with "strong personalities," great artists, rather than finding the new "hot" trend. I wish to find the most significant artists of our times, whatever the medium, style, or origin. I am not only looking for talent, but also for artists who have ambition, the desire to succeed and mark history. My gallery was of one of the first to exhibit important American artists in France: Andre, Judd, Serra, Basquiat, Haring, Lichtenstein, de Kooning, Warhol …

If you weren't running a gallery what else would you do?

In another life, I would have liked to become an architect. Architecture is where all art begins. Architects leave the most significant and visible mark in civilization. Mies van der Rohe, Louis Kahn, Philip Johnson, Richard Meier, Frank Gehry, Renzo Piano, Tadao Ando, among many others, prove that.

- **Contact** Galerie Daniel Templon
Anne-Claudie Coric
accoric@danieltemplon.com
- **Established** 1966
- **Owner(s) / Partner(s)** Daniel Templon
- **Team** 14
- **Space(s)** 660 m²
- **Artists at Art Basel** Valerio Adami
Jean-Michel Alberola
Norbert Bisky
Anthony Caro
Philippe Cognée

Daniel Dezeuze
Jim Dine
Atul Dodiya
Jan Fabre
Eric Fischl
Gérard Garouste
He An
Jitish Kallat
David LaChapelle
Mao Yan
Jonathan Meese
Ivan Navarro
Jules Olitski
Pierre et Gilles
Joel Shapiro
Sudarshan Shetty
Chiharu Shiota
Frank Stella
Tunga
Kehinde Wiley
Yue Minjun

- **Further artists represented**
Arman
Larry Bell
Ben
Saint Clair Cemin
Gregory Crewdson
Anju Dodiya
Raymond Hains
Oda Jaune
Clay Ketter
Ulrich Lamsfuss
Loïc Le Groumellec
Philip Pearlstein
Julião Sarmento
Victor Vasarely
Claude Viallat
Asim Waqif

Thomas

Munich

 Galleries
Galleries

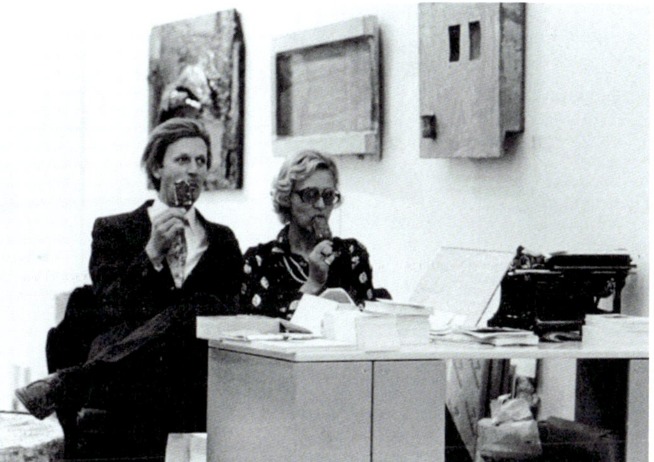

What is your favorite aspect of running a gallery?
Living with art!

How do you choose the artists you work with?
By switching off my brain and by opening my eyes!

If you weren't running a gallery what else would you do?
Build houses!

- **Contact** Galerie Thomas
Raimund Thomas
info@galerie-thomas.de
- **Established** 1964
- **Owner(s) / Partner(s)** Raimund Thomas
Silke Thomas
- **Team** 25
- **Space(s)** 900 m²
- **Artists at Art Basel**
Josef Albers
Georg Baselitz
Max Beckmann
Joseph Beuys
Fernando Botero
Marc Chagall
Eduardo Chillida
Willem de Kooning
Jim Dine
Max Ernst
Lyonel Feininger
Sam Francis
Robert Indiana
Alexej von Jawlensky
Wassily Kandinsky
Anselm Kiefer
Ernst Ludwig Kirchner
Paul Klee
Fernand Léger
Franz Marc
Joan Miró
Joan Mitchell
Otto Mueller
Edvard Munch
Gabriele Münter
Emil Nolde
Max Pechstein
Pablo Picasso
Sigmar Polke
Oskar Schlemmer
Karl Schmidt-Rottluff
Chaïm Soutine
Andy Warhol
Tom Wesselmann

- **Further artists represented**
Alexander Archipenko
Jean Arp
Alexander Calder
Heinrich Campendonk
Lovis Corinth
Tony Cragg
Robert Delaunay
Otto Dix
Lucio Fontana
Gotthard Graubner
Peter Halley
Erich Heckel
Imi Knoebel
Georg Kolbe
Roy Lichtenstein
August Macke
Henri Matisse
Ernst Wilhelm Nay
Louise Nevelson
Otto Piene
Marc Quinn
Robert Rauschenberg
Gerhard Richter
George Rickey
Simon Schubert
George Segal
Jesús Rafael Soto
Cy Twombly
Günther Uecker
Victor Vasarely

Three Star

Paris

 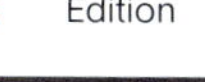
Edition

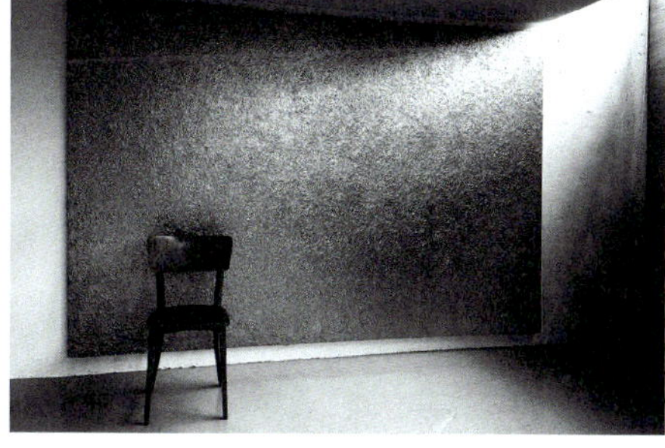

What is your favorite aspect of running a gallery?
We like collaborating with artists we love, encouraging them to use our specific experience and expertise to develop incredible projects, each time redefining the boundaries of artists' book production.

How do you choose the artists you work with?
We choose artists whose sensibilities we find complementary with our desire to create real projects following the tradition of the *livre d'artiste*.

If you weren't running a gallery what else would you do?
We are currently testing the menus for restaurants that we will open, sooner or later!

- **Contact** Three Star Books
  Melanie Scarciglia
  contact@threestarbooks.com
- **Established** 2007
- **Owner(s) / Partner(s)** Christophe Boutin
  Cornelia Lauf
  Melanie Scarciglia
- **Team** 5
- **Space(s)** 118 m²
- **Artists at Art Basel** John Armleder
  Tauba Auerbach
  Matthew Brannon
  Maurizio Cattelan
  Ryan Gander
  Liam Gillick
  Dominique Gonzalez-Foerster
  Thomas Hirschhorn
  Sam Lewitt
  Jonathan Monk
  Olivier Mosset
  Matt Mullican
  Slavs and Tatars
  Simon Starling
  Haim Steinbach
  Lawrence Weiner
  Heimo Zobernig
- **Further artists represented** Alison Knowles & Rirkrit Tiravanija
  Ken Lum & Hubert Damisch
  Blake Rayne
  Tobias Rehberger

Tilton

New York
Los Angeles

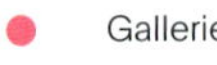 Galleries

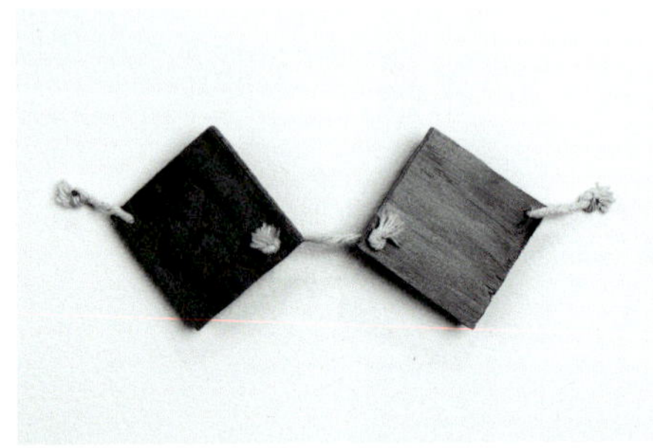

What is your favorite aspect of running a gallery?
Living with the exhibitions and helping young artists.

How do you choose the artists you work with?
The work has to move me.

If you weren't running a gallery what else would you do?
Maybe venture capital and collecting art.

- **Contact** Tilton Gallery
  Lauren Hudgins
  laurenh@jacktiltongallery.com
- **Established** 1983
- **Owner(s) / Partner(s)** Jack Tilton
- **Team** 5
- **Space(s)** 300 m²
- **Artists at Art Basel** Noel Anderson
  Ed Clark
  Luca Dellaverson
  Egan Frantz
  Sakshi Gupta
  Yashua Klos
  Simone Leigh
  Jarbas Lopes
  John Outterbridge
  Henk Peeters
  Rebecca Purdum
  Kianja Strobert
  Ruth Vollmer
  Brenna Youngblood
- **Further artists represented** Derrick Adams
  Noah Davis
  David Lynch
  Sudarshan Shetty
  Leonid Sokov
  Jeff Sonhouse
  Berend Strik
  Zhang Peili

TKG+

Taipei

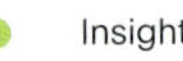 Insights

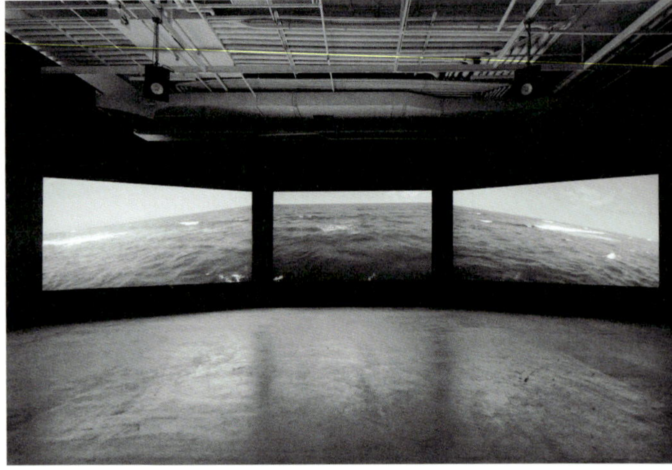

What is your favorite aspect of running a gallery?
Being able to work with artists I really like, promoting them, and seeing them being recognized internationally.

How do you choose the artists you work with?
The work must first strike me with amazement. Then I observe the artist's practice for a period of time, learn about his or her creative process, and decide for myself that the artist is significant in some way. If everything goes well in my communication with the artist, I would then consider signing him or her.

If you weren't running a gallery what else would you do?
I would probably work at a museum or art institution, or become a collector if I had the means. I can't see myself leaving this field.

- **Contact** TKG+
  Lijhen Chen
  info.tkgplus@gmail.com
- **Established** 2009
- **Owner(s) / Partner(s)** Shelly Wu
- **Team** 3
- **Space(s)** 500 m²
- **Artists at Art Basel** Charwei Tsai
  Jao Chia-En
- **Further artists represented** Chen Ching-Yuan
  Su Yu-Hsien
  Yuan Goang-Ming
  Wang Yahui
  Wu Chi-Tsung

Tokyo + BTAP

Tokyo
Beijing

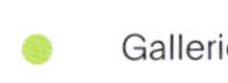 Galleries

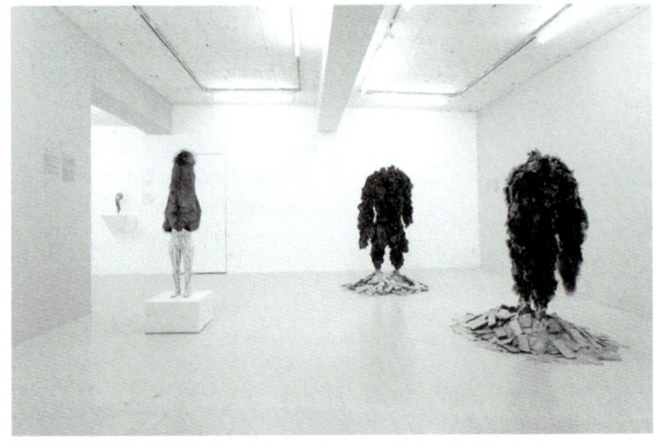

What is your favorite aspect of running a gallery?
Being a gallerist allows me to meet artists from different generations and countries. You can always learn so much about their culture and history through their works.

How do you choose the artists you work with?
It is important to see if the work and the artist's sensibility match the concept that Tokyo Gallery + BTAP has cultivated throughout its history. Also, I am interested in working with artists who challenges my imagination.

If you weren't running a gallery what else would you do?
I enjoy this profession because art always connects me to new people. So I would still be part of the art industry. But being an architect also interests me since I am very passionate about architecture.

- **Contact** Tokyo Gallery + BTAP
  Hiroyuki Sasaki
  hiroyuki.sasaki@tokyo-gallery.com
- **Established** 1950
- **Owner(s) / Partner(s)** Hozu Yamamoto
  Yukihito Tabata
- **Team** 11
- **Space(s)** 400 m²
- **Artists at Art Basel** Koji Enokura
  Susumu Koshimizu
  Katsuhiko Narita
  Yoshishige Saito
  Nobuo Sekine
  SHIMURAbros
  Kishio Suga
  Jiro Takamatsu
  Katsuro Yoshida
- **Further artists represented** Cai Guo-Qiang
  Takeshi Hayashi
  Saya Irie
  Showichi Kaneda
  Hiroto Kitagawa
  Issei Kurihara
  Lu Hao
  Shiro Matsui
  Hiroyuki Matsuura
  Danshaku Miyazawa
  Koh Myung-Keun
  Chiharu Nishizawa
  Oscar Oiwa
  Shinjiro Okamoto
  Yoshio Sekine
  Yuan Shun
  Song Dong
  Isao Sugiyama
  Miki Taira
  Yoshito Takahashi
  Mitsukuni Takimoto
  Lee Ufan
  Wu Qiang
  Xu Bing
  Go Yayanagi
  Ye Jian Qing
  Gyoko Yoshida
  Shigoki Yoshida
  Zeng Jiangyong
  Zhang Xiaotao
  Zhu Jian Zhong

Tolarno

Melbourne 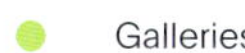 Galleries

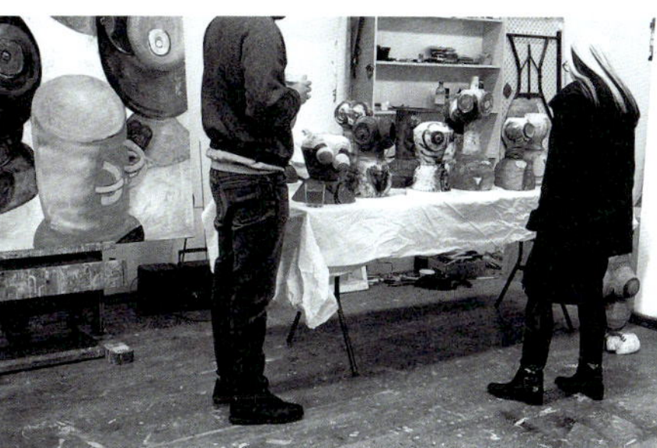

What is your favorite aspect of running a gallery?
Matching a great work with a great collector.

How do you choose the artists you work with?
I try to find out what they think about their own work. I try to understand what they are trying to achieve. The person is more important than the CV.

If you weren't running a gallery what else would you do?
Listen to music.

- **Contact** Tolarno Galleries
  Jan Minchin
  mail@tolarnogalleries.com
- **Established** 1967
- **Owner(s) / Partner(s)** Jan Minchin
- **Team** 3
- **Space(s)** 171 m²
- **Artists at Art Basel** Brent Harris
  Brendan Huntley
  Anastasia Klose
  Patricia Piccinini
  Ben Quilty
  Caroline Rothwell
- **Further artists represented** Brook Andrew
  Benjamin Armstrong
  Peter Atkins
  Martin Bell
  Andrew Browne
  Peter Graham
  Louise Hearman
  Peter Hennessey
  Bill Henson
  Tim Johnson
  Rosemary Laing
  Christopher Langton
  Tim Maguire
  Dan Moynihan
  Robert Rooney
  David Wadelton
  Judy Watson

Tonkonow

New York 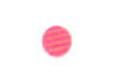 Survey

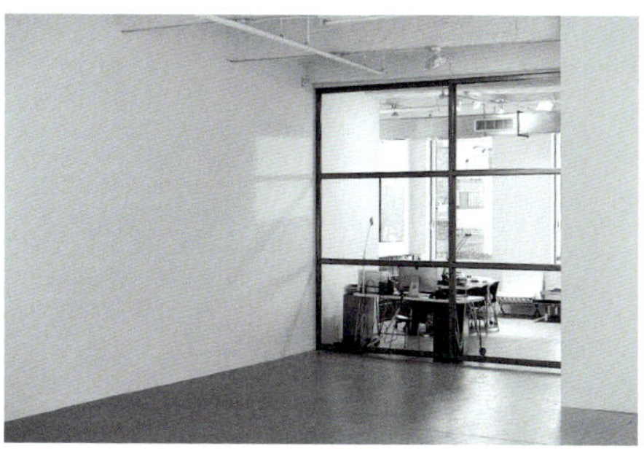

What is your favorite aspect of running a gallery?
Working closely with historically significant artists, identifying exciting younger artists, nurturing the careers of both, and placing their works in great museum and private collections is the best part of having a gallery.

How do you choose the artists you work with?
Mostly by instinct.

If you weren't running a gallery what else would you do?
Curate, write, teach, and cook dinner.

- **Contact** Leslie Tonkonow Artworks + Projects
  Tyler Auwarter
  info@tonkonow.com
- **Established** 1997
- **Owner(s) / Partner(s)** Leslie Tonkonow
- **Team** 4
- **Space(s)** 232 m²
- **Artists at Art Basel** Michelle Stuart
- **Further artists represented** Tracey Baran
  Dean Byington
  Amy Cutler
  Ian Davis
  Agnes Denes
  Danny Jauregui
  Betsy Kaufman
  Malerie Marder
  Laurel Nakadate
  Julia Oschatz
  Tokihiro Sato
  Kunié Sugiura
  Robert Watts
  Saya Woolfalk

Tornabuoni

Paris
Florence
Milan
Portofino
Forte dei Marmi

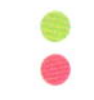 Galleries
● Galleries

- **Contact** Tornabuoni Art
  Francesca Piccolboni
  fpiccolboni@tornabuoniart.fr
- **Established** 1981
- **Owner(s) / Partner(s)** Roberto Casamonti
- **Team** 30
- **Space(s)** 500 m²
- **Artists at Art Basel** Agostino Bonalumi
  Alberto Burri
  Enrico Castellani
  Dadamaino
  Lucio Fontana
  Piero Manzoni
  Francesca Pasquali
  Paolo Scheggi
  Turi Simeti
- **Further artists represented** Carla Accardi
  Giacomo Balla
  Jean-Michel Basquiat
  Umberto Boccioni
  Alighiero Boetti
  Georges Braque
  Mario Ceroli
  Enzo Cucchi
  Giorgio De Chirico
  Piero Dorazio
  Jean Dubuffet
  Hans Hartung
  Jannis Kounellis
  Wifredo Lam
  Sebastián Matta
  Joan Miró
  Giorgio Morandi
  Pino Pascali
  Pablo Picasso
  Michelangelo Pistoletto
  Serge Poliakoff
  Arnaldo Pomodoro
  Mimmo Rotella
  Victor Vasarely
  Emilio Vedova
  Andy Warhol
  Tom Wesselmann

Travesía Cuatro

Madrid
Guadalajara

 Nova

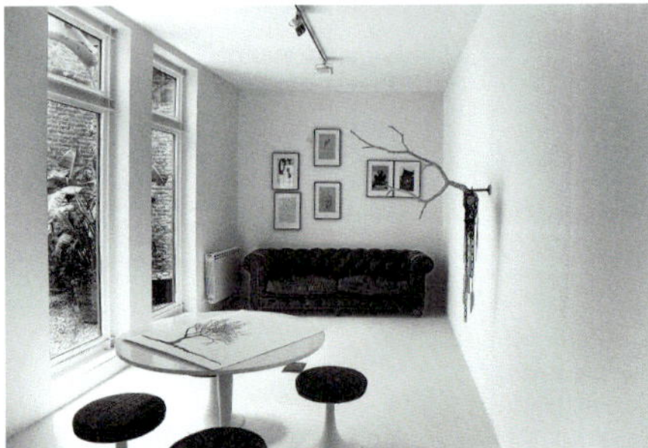

What is your favorite aspect of running a gallery?
The relationship with the artists and with the artworks, and having the possibility to travel around the world.

How do you choose the artists you work with?
We select the artists on different criteria, generated by some kind of shot of love.

If you weren't running a gallery what else would you do?
Ines Lopez-Quesada would be a singer and Silvia Ortiz would be a writer or a poet.

- **Contact** Travesía Cuatro
  Alberto Sanchez
  alberto@travesiacuatro.com
- **Established** 2003
- **Owner(s) / Partner(s)** Ines Lopez-Quesada
  Silvia Ortiz
- **Team** 7
- **Space(s)** 475 m²
- **Artists at Art Basel** Sarah Crowner
  Milena Muzquiz
- **Further artists represented** Jose Dávila
  John Isaacs
  Jis
  Jorge Méndez Blake
  Asunción Molinos Gordo
  Jorge Pardo
  Gonzalo Lebrija
  Mateo López
  Juan de Sande
  Carolina Silva
  Vicky Uslé

Tschudi

Zuoz

● Galleries Unlimited

What is your favorite aspect of running a gallery?
To be part of the creation process of exhi-bitions and artworks.

How do you choose the artists you work with?
The work should challenge and fascinate, be significant beyond the time.

If you weren't running a gallery what else would you do?
Being part of a field of creation.

- **Contact** Galerie Tschudi
  Elsbeth Bisig
  info@galerie-tschudi.ch
- **Established** 1985
- **Owner(s) / Partner(s)** Ruedi Tschudi
  Elsbeth Bisig
- **Team** 3
- **Space(s)** 600 m²
- **Artists at Art Basel** Carl Andre
  Stanley Brouwn
  Balthasar Burkhard
  Alan Charlton
  Hamish Fulton
  Bethan Huws
  Callum Innes
  Kimsooja
  Martina Klein
  Richard Long
  Niele Toroni
  Su-Mei Tse
  Dan Walsh
  Petra Wunderlich
- **Further artists represented** Mario Merz
  Ulrich Rückriem
  Serge Spitzer
  Not Vital

Tucci Russo

Torre Pellice

 Galleries Unlimited

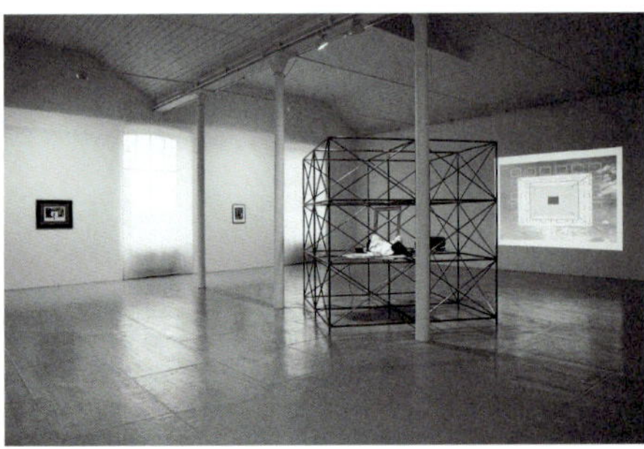

What is your favorite aspect of running a gallery?
Working with the artists and the possibility of contact with their creativ-ity. Step by step you realize that you are involved in a new world presenting things that did not exist before. Art is able to change our understanding of reality and extend our

imagination. It is like becoming part of an endless story, which is available to everyone.

How do you choose the artists you work with?
I was a poet before having a gallery and I had the chance to live in Turin in the mid-1960s. I knew the artists of Arte Povera personally and in 1975, when I opened my own gallery, I tried to establish a dialogue among these artists, the younger generation, and the international panorama. This is what we still try to do. For instance, in May 2014 we opened three solo shows: Giulio Paolini, Tony Cragg, and Robin Rhode.

If you weren't running a gallery what else would you do?
We will celebrate 40 years of activity in 2015. Running a gallery is part of my life. I cannot imagine anything else.

- **Contact** Tucci Russo Studio per l'Arte Contemporanea
  Elisabetta Di Grazia
  gallery@tuccirusso.com
- **Established** 1975
- **Owner(s) / Partner(s)** Antonio Tucci Russo
  Elisabetta Di Grazia
- **Team** 4
- **Space(s)** 1,200 m²
- **Artists at Art Basel** Mario Airò
  Giovanni Anselmo
  Gianni Caravaggio
  Tony Cragg
  Francesco Gennari
  Christiane Löhr
  Giulio Paolini
  Giuseppe Penone
  Robin Rhode
  Conrad Shawcross
- **Further artists represented** Daniel Buren
  Harald Klingelhöller
  Richard Long
  Mario Merz
  Marisa Merz
  Paolo Mussat Sartor
  Alfredo Pirri
  Paolo Piscitelli
  Thomas Schütte
  Jan Vercruysse

Two Palms

New York

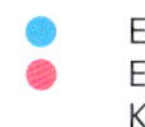

Edition
Edition Kabinett

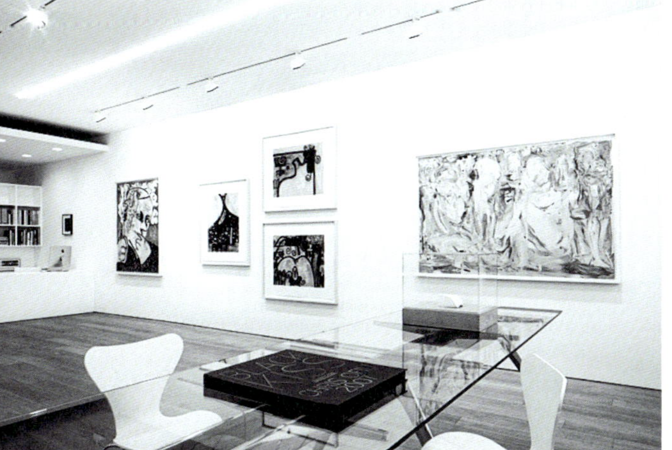

What is your favorite aspect of running a gallery?
Bringing new and challenging work into the public eye.

How do you choose the artists you work with?
We choose our artists based upon work we like with a strong conceptual underpinning.

If you weren't running a gallery what else would you do?
Make art.

- **Contact** Two Palms
  Evelyn Day Lasry
  evelyn@twopalms.us
- **Established** 1994
- **Owner(s) / Partner(s)** Evelyn Day Lasry
  David Lasry
- **Team** 10
- **Space(s)** 697 m²
- **Artists at Art Basel** Mel Bochner
  Cecily Brown
  Richard Prince
  Terry Winters
- **Further artists represented** Chuck Close
  Peter Doig
  Carroll Dunham
  Ellen Gallagher
  Per Kirkeby
  Sol LeWitt
  Chris Ofili
  Elizabeth Peyton
  Matthew Ritchie
  David Row
  Dana Schutz
  Jessica Stockholder

Tornabuoni Art
Interview with Michele Casamonti

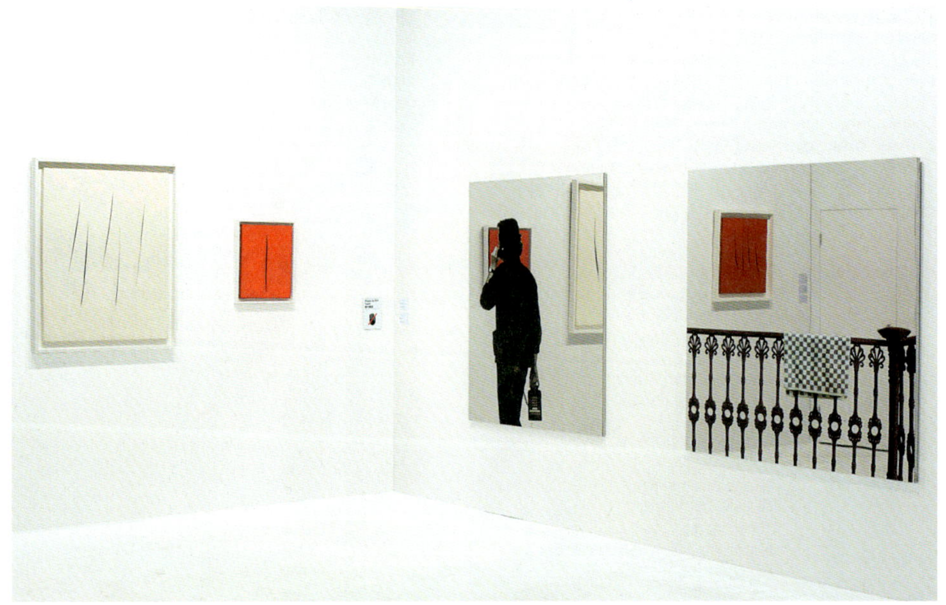

Art Basel in Hong Kong, 2014

What's the history behind Galleria Tornabuoni?

The gallery opened in Florence in 1981 on the Via de' Tornabuoni—it was named after the street rather than Casamonti, the family name of its founder, my father. The gallery went international in the 1990s—we opened a branch in the Swiss resort of Crans-Montana in 1993, followed by Milan in 1995. We later launched two seasonal premises in Portofino and Forte Dei Marni, and in 2009 we opened a branch here in Paris. We are now thinking about opening a London branch.

The gallery's expansion is linked to the "growth" of the artists with whom we have always worked on a consistent basis. Perhaps Tornabuoni Art's greatest strength is our specific, highly focused artistic line: we are interested in all 20th-century art, but specialize in postwar Italian art. Whenever we take part in a fair for the first time—as was the case at Art Basel in Miami Beach in 2014—we organize a Lucio Fontana show. It serves as a good indicator of our policy. Fontana was a seminal artist, one we followed right from the start, when it was a question of pure enthusiasm, since the market for his work wasn't very attractive. As well as Fontana, we also deal in other postwar artists such as Manzoni, Burri, Castellani, Boetti, Scheggi, Rotella, Pomodoro, Ceroli, and Bonalumi. Why those choices? Not because we're Italian—that's pure coincidence—but because I'm convinced that Italy of the 1960s represented a key moment in art history. There was a real paradigm shift, a change that lies at the heart of most of today's experimentation. Milan in the 1960s was where the key protagonists in that shift in artistic vocabulary from what is called modern art to contemporary art lived, met, and worked together. I'm not thinking only of Italians when I say that—Milan was where Yves Klein's first show was held.

What do you think explains the special atmosphere in Milan in the 1960s?

Just after World War II, Milan was where an extraordinary historic event occurred, thanks to Lucio Fontana: the making of the first monochrome—purely monochrome—painting in the history of art. The only precedent was Malevich's *White on White* (1918), but that work was still painted in a way that structurally "divided" figure from ground. It was obviously a revolutionary work, and Malevich is clearly one of the most important artists of the 20th century. But when Fontana did his early monochrome paintings in 1949, they were not designed to be "painted," but to be monochrome, thereby laying down the roots of contemporary art. Monochrome reached France in the 1950s via Klein, and starting in 1959–60 the Milanese generation decided to pursue and radicalize Fontana's discovery. The concept of monochrome implies work on relief, on the sculptural aspect of a canvas—Manzoni, Castellani, and Dadamaino all took this exploration in personal directions. Ever since, I feel, there has been an unbroken line that really runs through the art world. I think Anish Kapoor's work—and I think he would admit it himself—finds the roots of its vocabulary in what happened in Milan and in Fontana's work. That moment was therefore absolutely crucial, and I feel there's still a lot of work to be done on the international level to make everyone realize it. I'd say we're the world leader in this field, we're the authoritative gallery, on an international level, for that entire generation of artists.

So why was the gallery founded in 1980 rather than before?

My grandfather was a collector, and my father was a collector, too. They collected all their lives. When my grandfather died, the two collections were united and my father decided to devote all his free time to art—advising collectors, meeting artists, going to studios, helping other galleries to mount shows, and so on. At some point it became a question of opening our own premises. So my father founded the gallery; my arrival, however, altered its scope and profile. Opening a branch in Paris has strengthened the gallery, and we have begun working closely with a publishing house to produce a series of authoritative books on our artists. Major museum directors have contributed to these publications, which I feel are as important as the shows we've organized. More than a third of the Boetti show held here in 2010 was exhibited at Tate Modern in London and MoMA in New York. In 2010 there was also the magnificent show of work by Giuseppe Capogrossi, organized by the Guggenheim Foundation in Venice before it came here to Paris. I feel strongly that there's a future in this type of collaboration between galleries and major institutions. For instance, we're the largest lender to the Lucio Fontana retrospective hosted in the summer of 2014 by the Musée d'art moderne de la Ville de Paris.

I think a gallery can have a bright future, even when it deals mainly in artists who are no longer alive, if it is able to function on the primary market, which means promoting the work among major institutions, developing a cultural program, publishing catalogues. Although we're also obliged to deal with the complexity of the resale market in our search for works, in order to remain a leader in the market we have to be able to operate like a primary-market gallery. I think that's where our winning formula lies.

At art fairs your stands are highly recognizable because they are often white, with a very meticulous hang. You clearly want to create a space that differs from other galleries. How do you approach this issue of your presence at art fairs?

At one time, art fairs were "market" fairs, but today there's this idea that fairs have become—at least the main international ones—the prime showcase for a gallery's activities. So I think carefully arranging a stand to reflect the gallery's identity represents a gesture of respect toward visitors. In our case, we follow one very simple principle: we try to construct a space that is as coherent as possible with the content of our display. And what happens to suit us best is the "white cube" idea—a pure, luminous space that enhances the monochrome impact of the artists we handle.

U

Art Basel's pioneering exhibition platform, established in 2000, Unlimited in Basel boasts ambitious contemporary and historical works, including massive sculptures and paintings, video projections, large-scale installations, and live performances. In 2014 Unlimited was curated by New York-based Gianni Jetzer.

2014 participants

Rita Ackermann
Hauser & Wirth

Richard Aldrich
Bortolami

Harold Ancart
Hufkens

Carl Andre
Fischer

John Bock
Coles
Kern
Marconi
Regen Projects
Sprüth Magers

Ian Breakwell
Reynolds

Anthony Caro
Juda
Mitchell-Innes & Nash
Templon

Alice Channer
Approach

Andrew Dadson
Kordansky
Noero
RaebervonStenglin

Hanne Darboven
Fischer
Sprüth Magers

Tacita Dean
Borch Jensen

Philippe Decrauzat
Chouakri

Edith Dekyndt
Meert

Matias Faldbakken
Presenhuber
Standard (Oslo)

Sam Falls
Presenhuber

Harun Farocki
Ropac

Tony Feher
Meier
Sikkema Jenkins

Hamish Fulton
Paley
Riis
Tschudi

Ryan Gander
gb agency
Lisson

Ron Gorchov
Cheim & Read

Jos de Gruyter & Harald Thys
Bortolozzi
Szwajcer

João Maria Gusmão + Pedro Paiva
Fortes Vilaça
Sies + Höke
ZERO

Sabine Hornig
Guerra

Thomas Houseago
Hauser & Wirth

Alex Hubbard
Maccarone
Presenhuber

Bethan Huws
Tschudi

Ann Veronica Janssens
Artiaco
mennour
Szwajcer

Gavin Kenyon
Blum & Poe
Ramiken Crucible
ZERO

David Lamelas
Maccarone
Mot
Sprüth Magers

William Leavitt
Greene Naftali

Julio Le Parc
Bugada & Cargnel

Lee Ufan
Kukje/Kim

Richard Long
Lisson

Christina Mackie
Herald St
Jeffries
Supportico Lopez

Christian Marclay
Cooper

Nick Mauss
303 Gallery

Rodney McMillian
Maccarone
Vielmetter

Ana Mendieta
Cortese
Jacques
Lelong

Mario Merz
Kewenig

Yasumasa Morimura
Luhring Augustine

Claudio Moser
Krupp
Skopia

Melvin Moti
Meyer Riegger

David Nash
Juda
Kukje/Kim
Lelong

Bruce Nauman
Hauser & Wirth
Zwirner

Carsten Nicolai
EIGEN + ART

Richard Nonas
McCaffrey

Saskia Olde Wolbers
Paley

Trevor Paglen
Metro Pictures
Zander

Giuseppe Penone
Tucci Russo

Jack Pierson
Stein

Michelangelo Pistoletto
Lee
Luhring Augustine
Stein

Alex Prager
Lehmann Maupin

Laure Prouvost
MOT International

Sterling Ruby
Hufkens
Sprüth Magers

Markus Schinwald
Lambert
Marconi

Jim Shaw
Blum & Poe
Lee
Metro Pictures

Sudarshan Shetty
Krinzinger
SKE
Templon

Wiebke Siem
Johnen

Andreas Slominski
Jablonka

Mikhael Subotzky
Goodman Gallery

Shooshie Sulaiman
Koyama

Pascale Marthine Tayou
Continua

Rirkrit Tiravanija
Gavin Brown

Rosemarie Trockel
Gladstone
Sprüth Magers

Troika
OMR

Daniel Turner
team

Andra Ursuta
De Carlo
Ramiken Crucible

Kara Walker
Miro

Guido van der Werve
Foxx
Luhring Augustine

Doug Wheeler
Zwirner

Cathy Wilkes
Hufkens
Modern Institute

Ming Wong
carlier gebauer
Vitamin

Xu Zhen
Long March

Haegue Yang
Crousel
Kukje/Kim

Yang Fudong
Marian Goodman
ShanghART

Zhan Wang
Long March

Zhang Huan
White Cube

Heimo Zobernig
Aizpuru

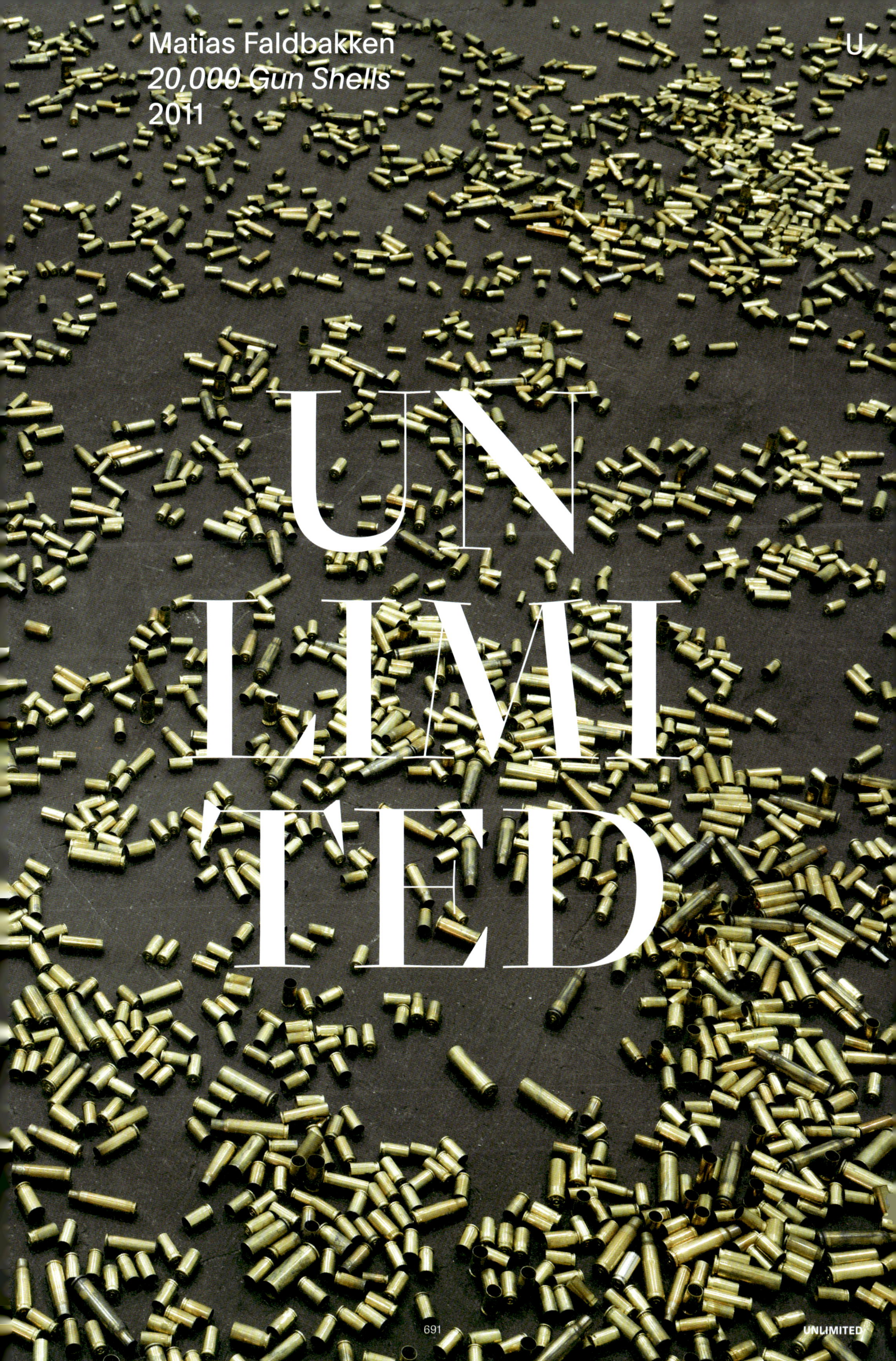
Matias Faldbakken
20,000 Gun Shells
2011
UN
LIMI
TED

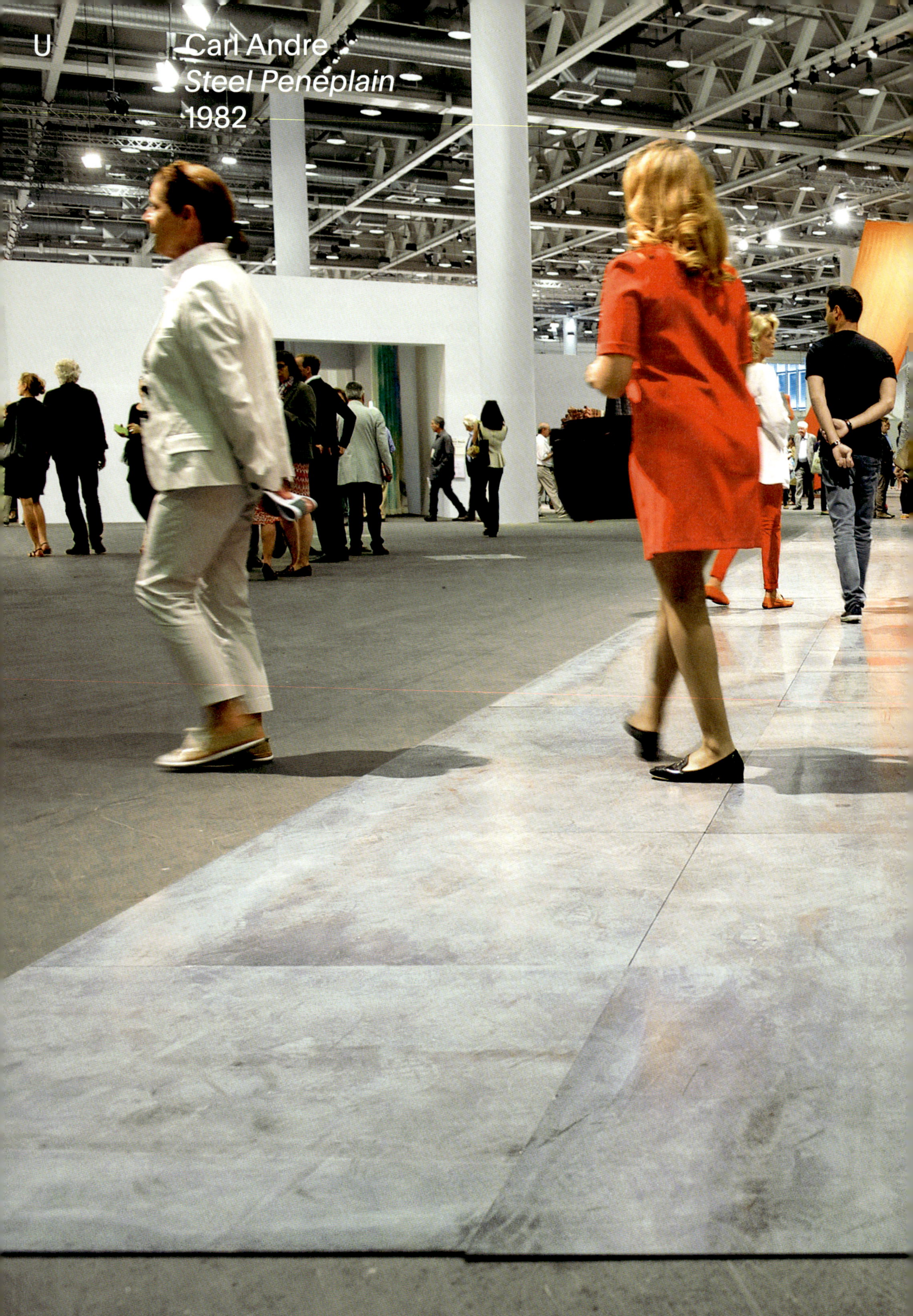
U

Carl Andre
Steel Peneplain
1982

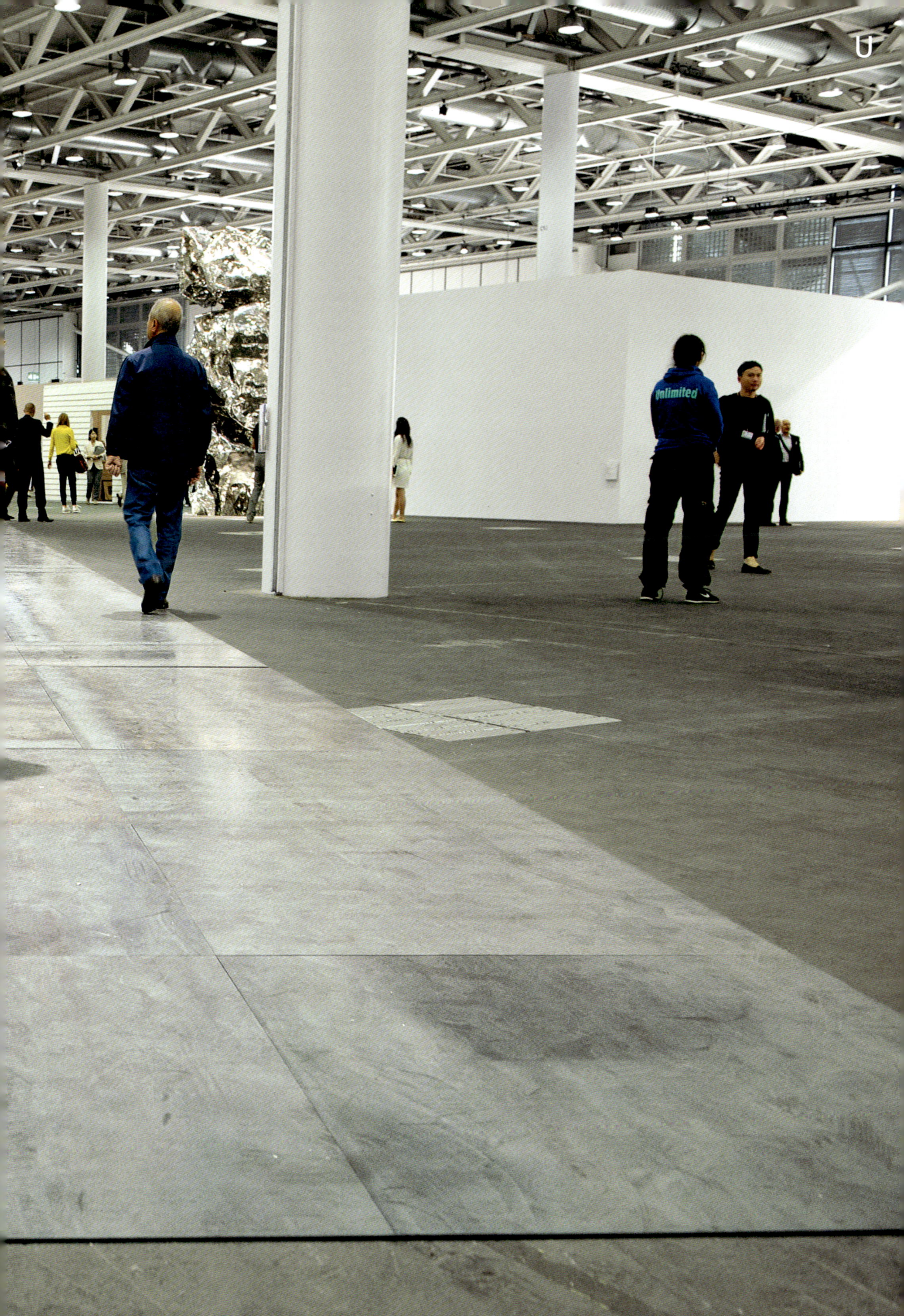
Unlimited

Gavin Kenyon
Farrow
2014 (foreground)

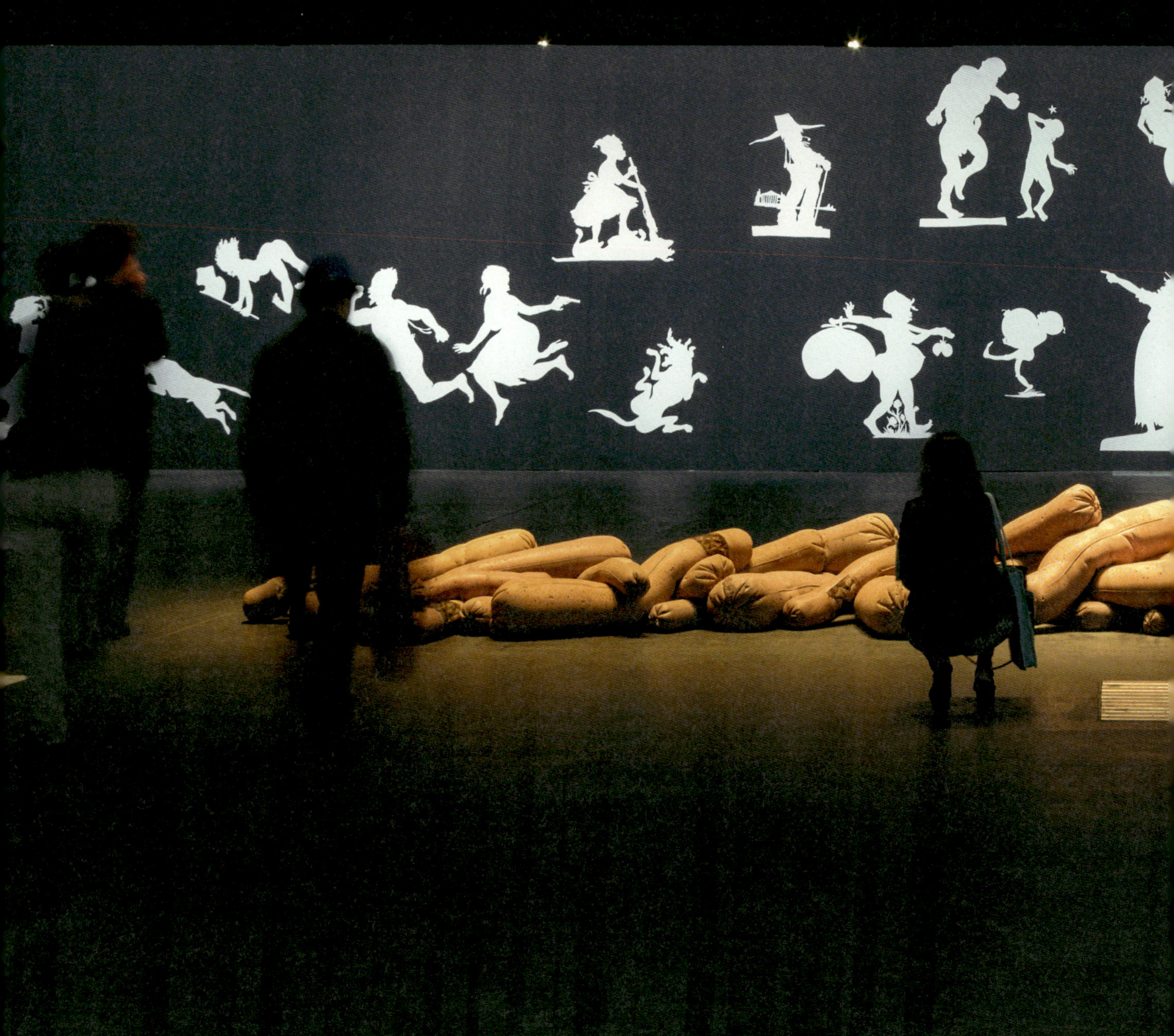

Kara Walker
The Sovereign Citizens Sesquicentennial Civil War Celebration
2013 (background)

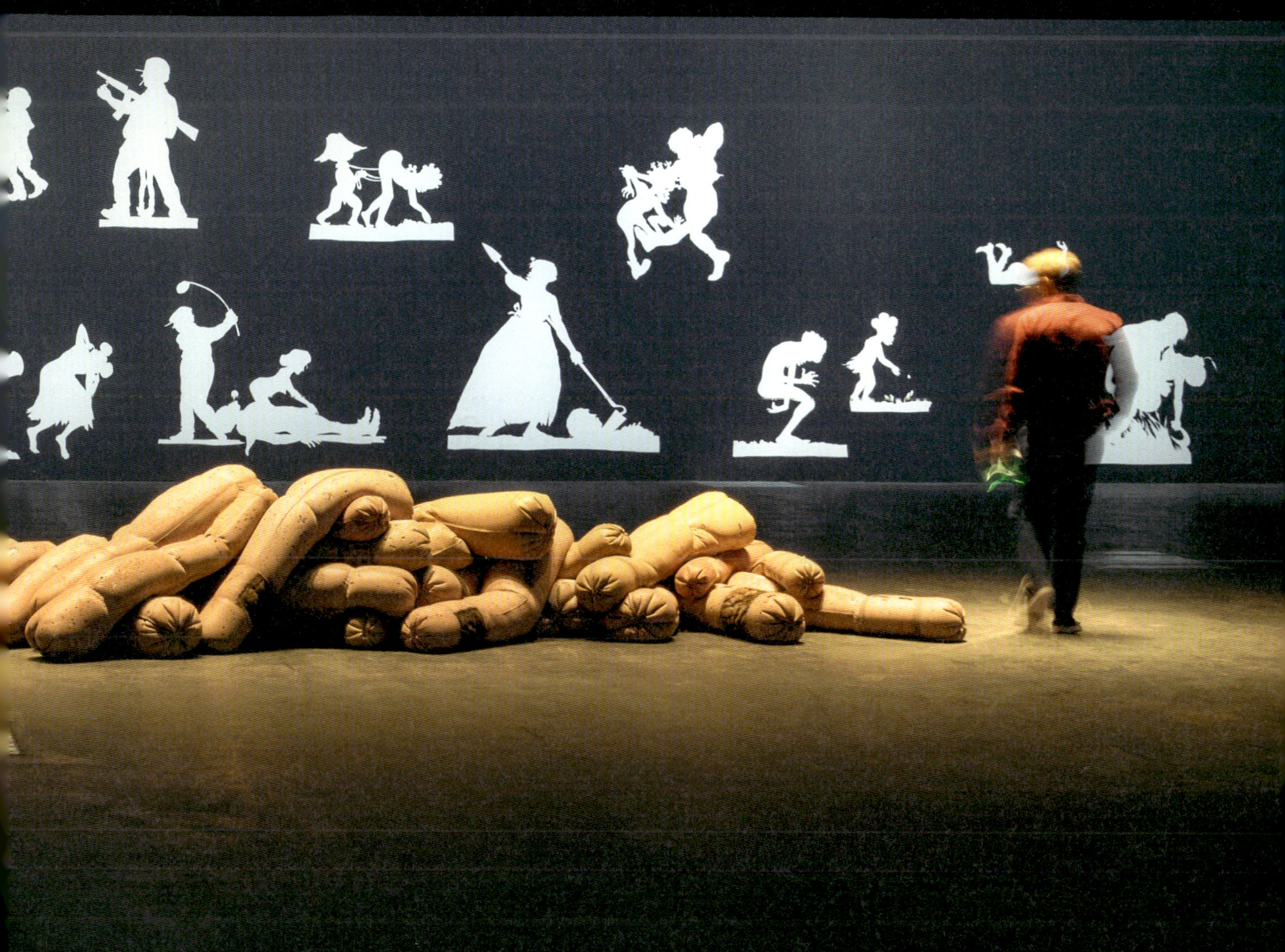

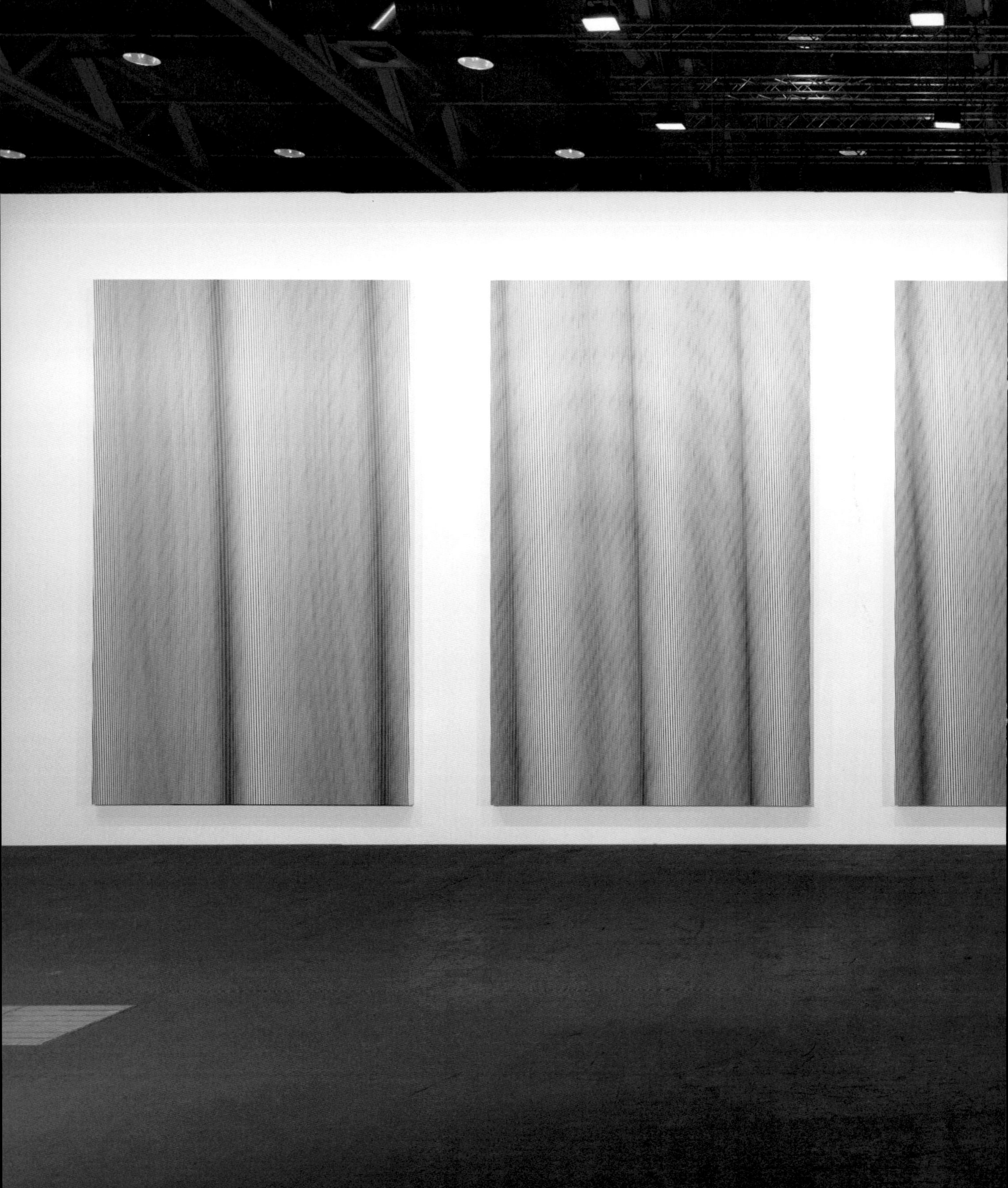

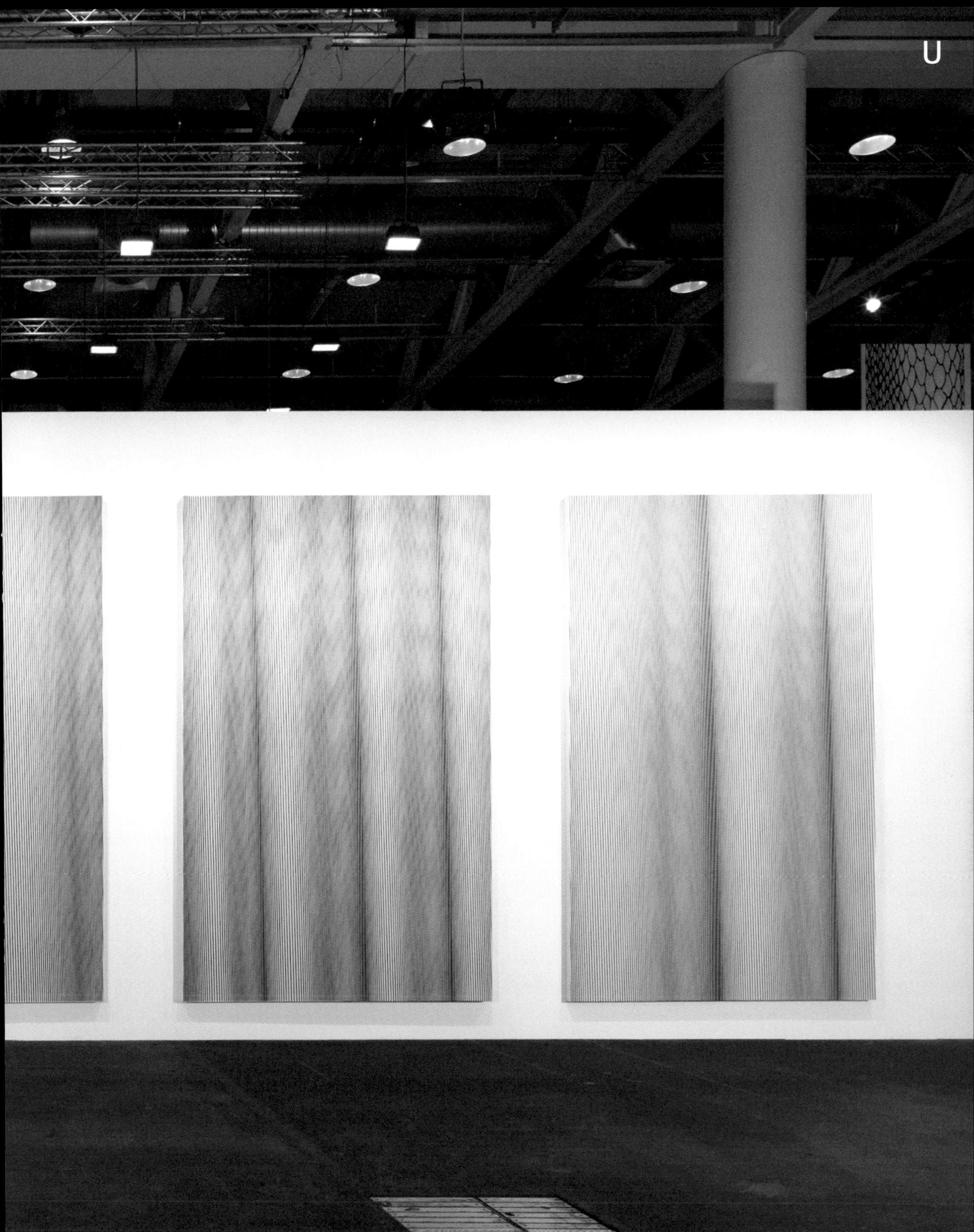

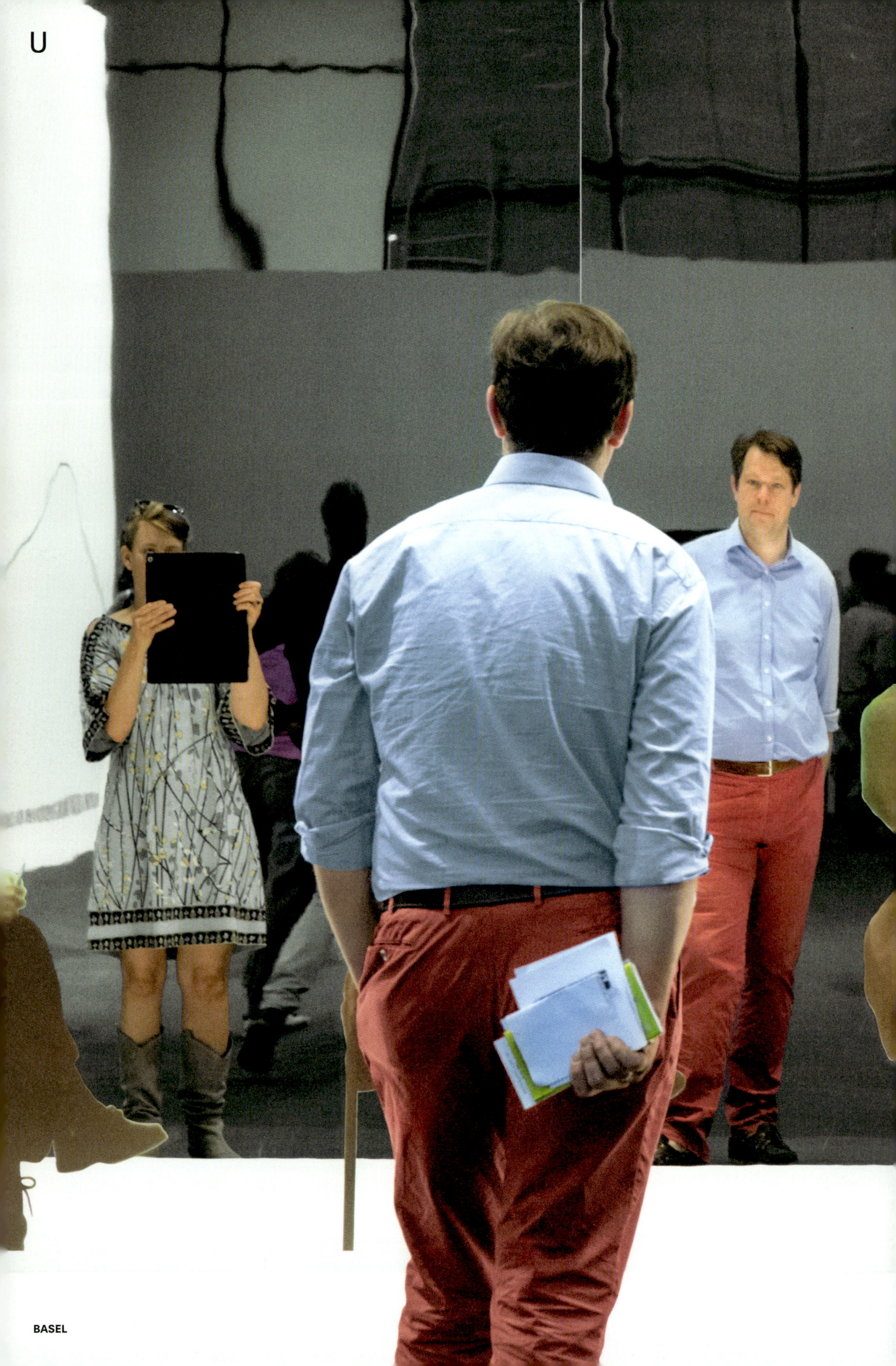

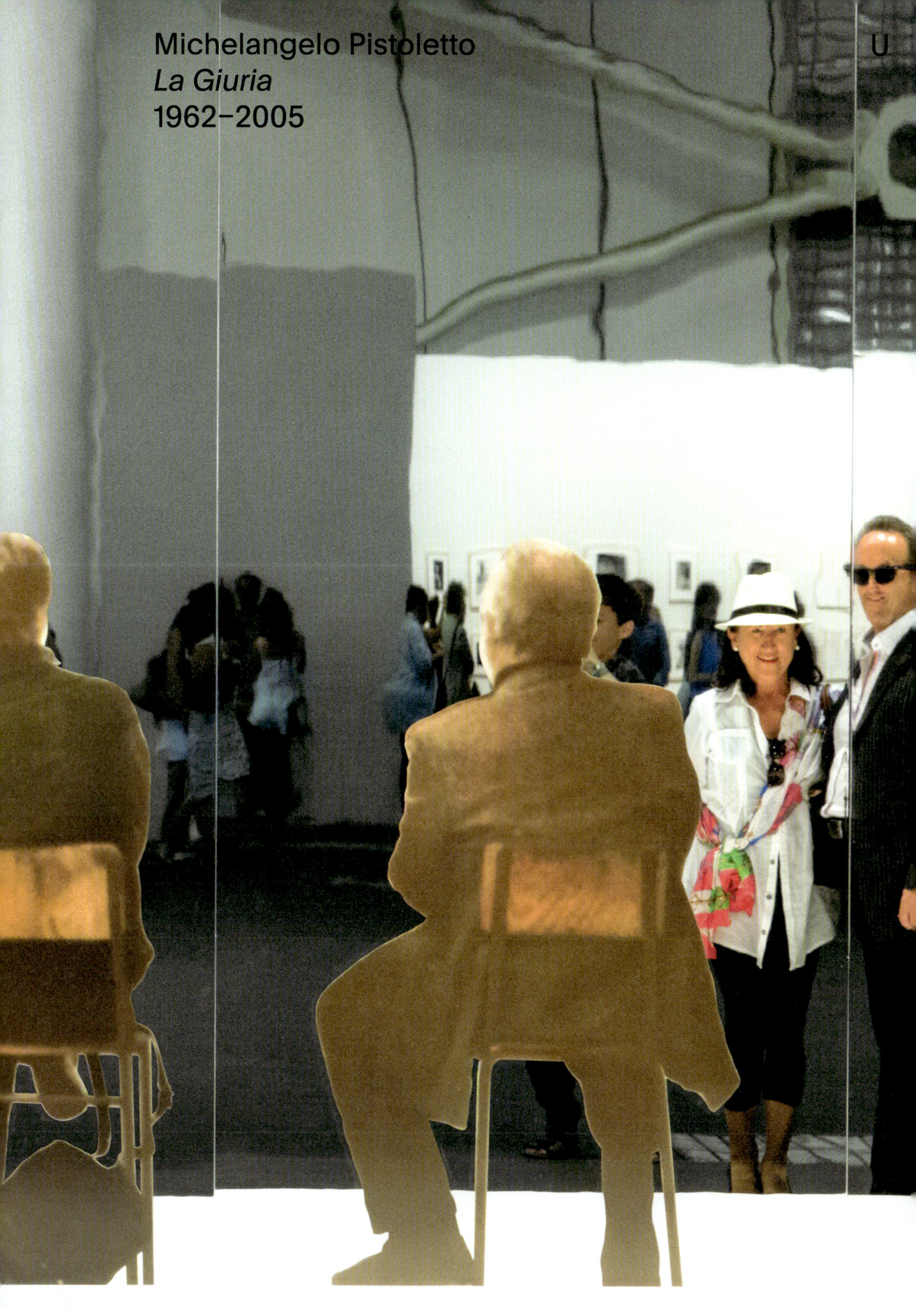

Michelangelo Pistoletto
La Giuria
1962–2005

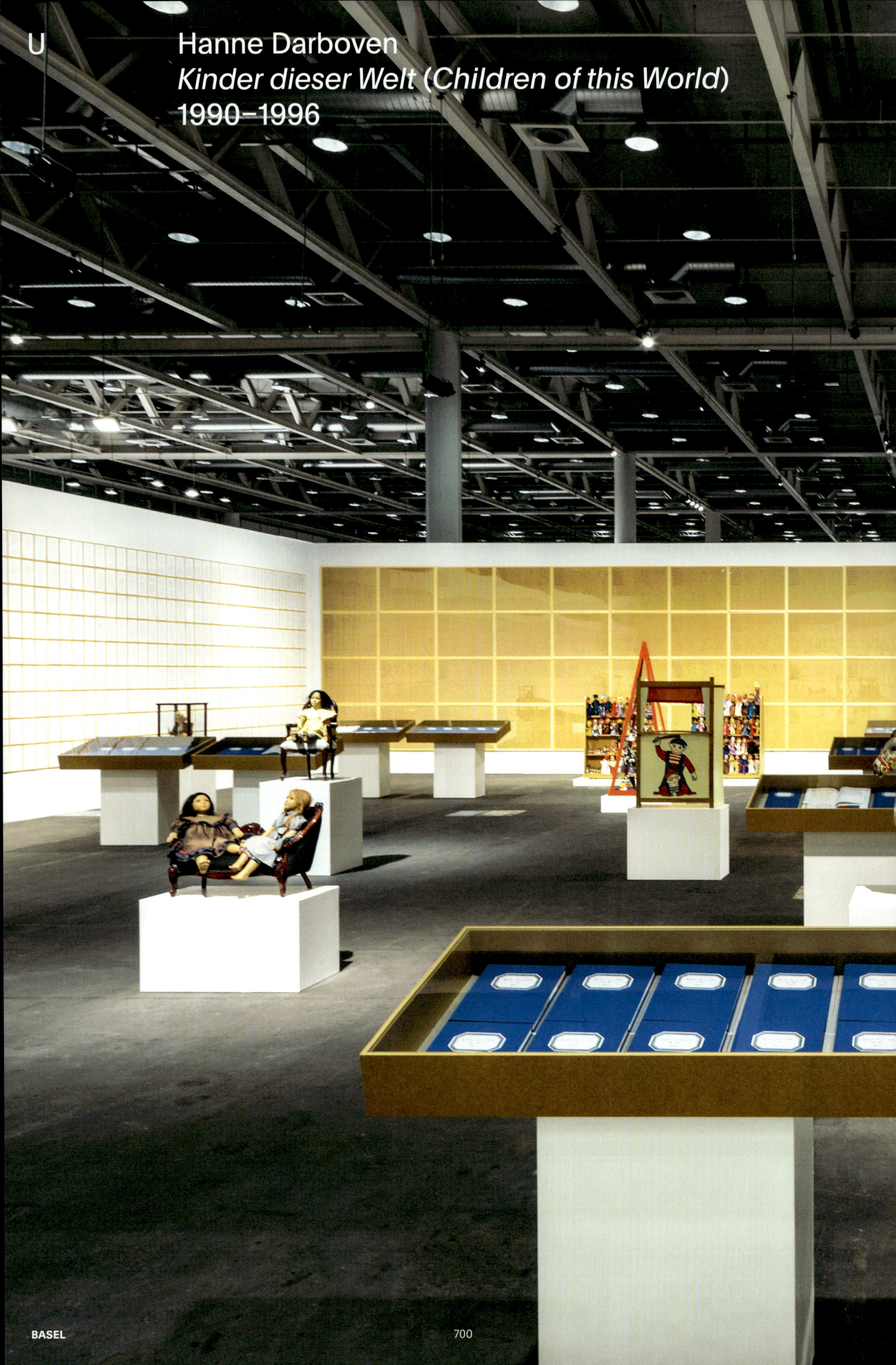

U

Hanne Darboven

Kinder dieser Welt (Children of this World)

1990–1996

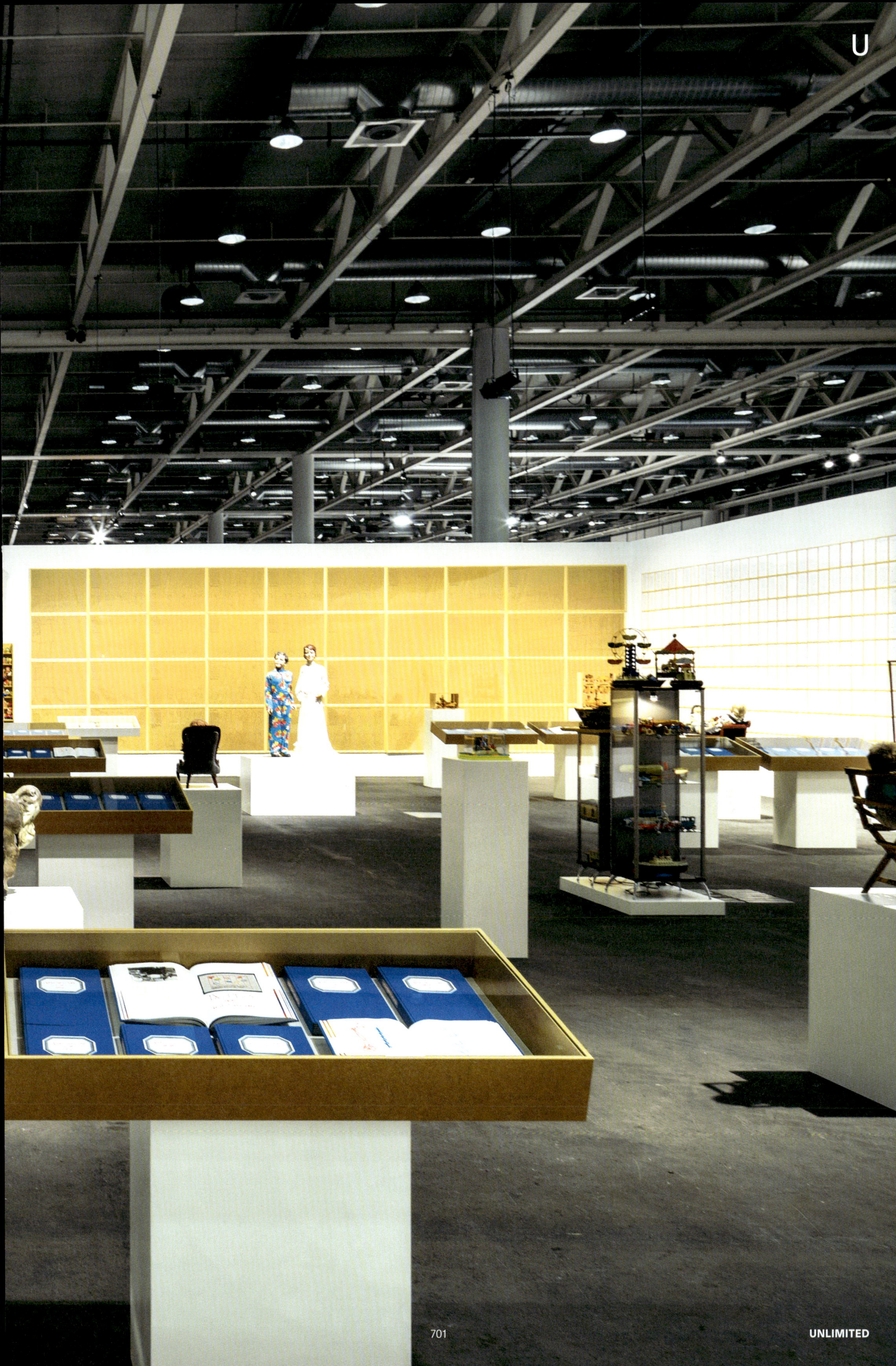

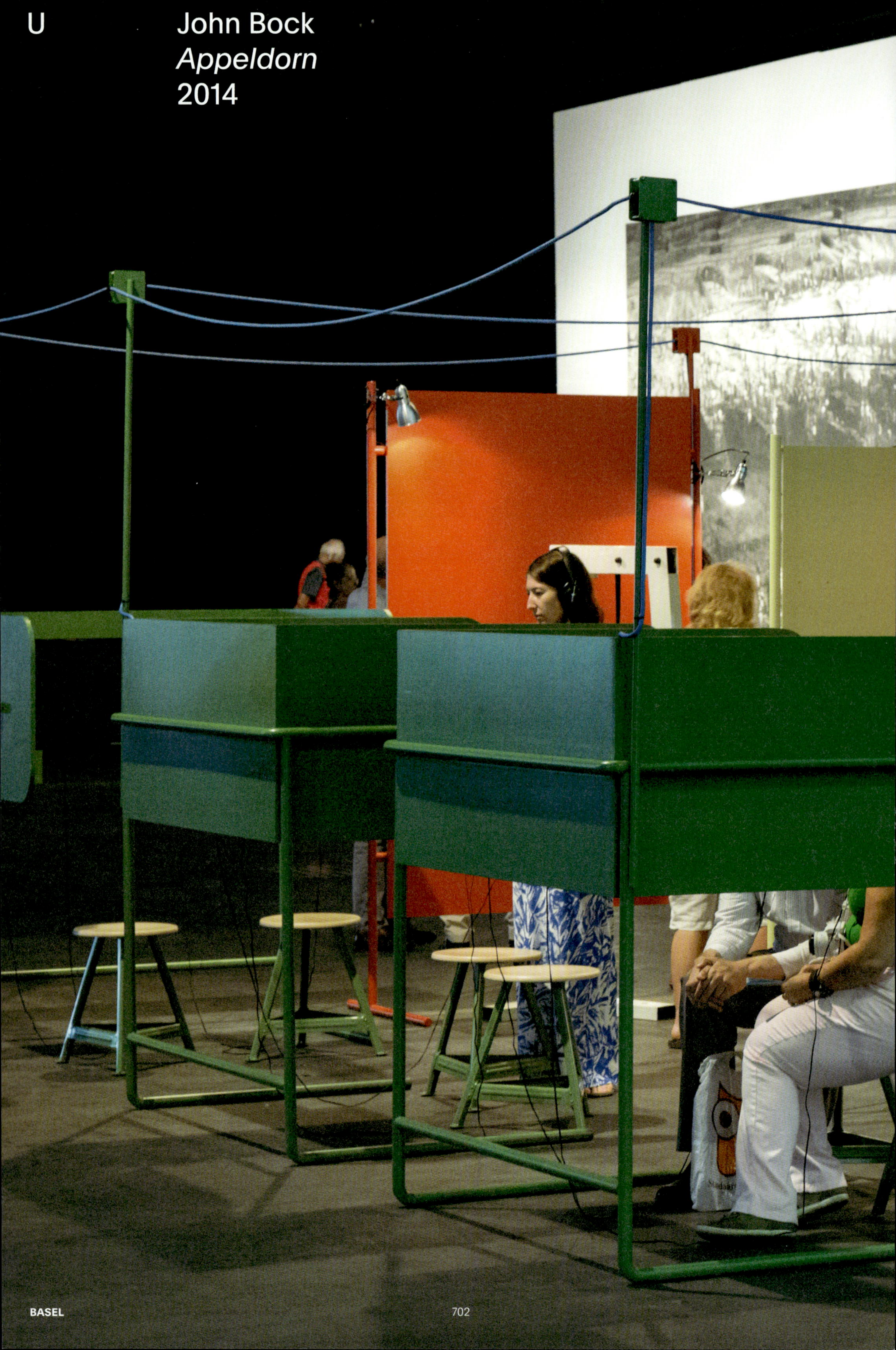

U John Bock
Appeldorn
2014

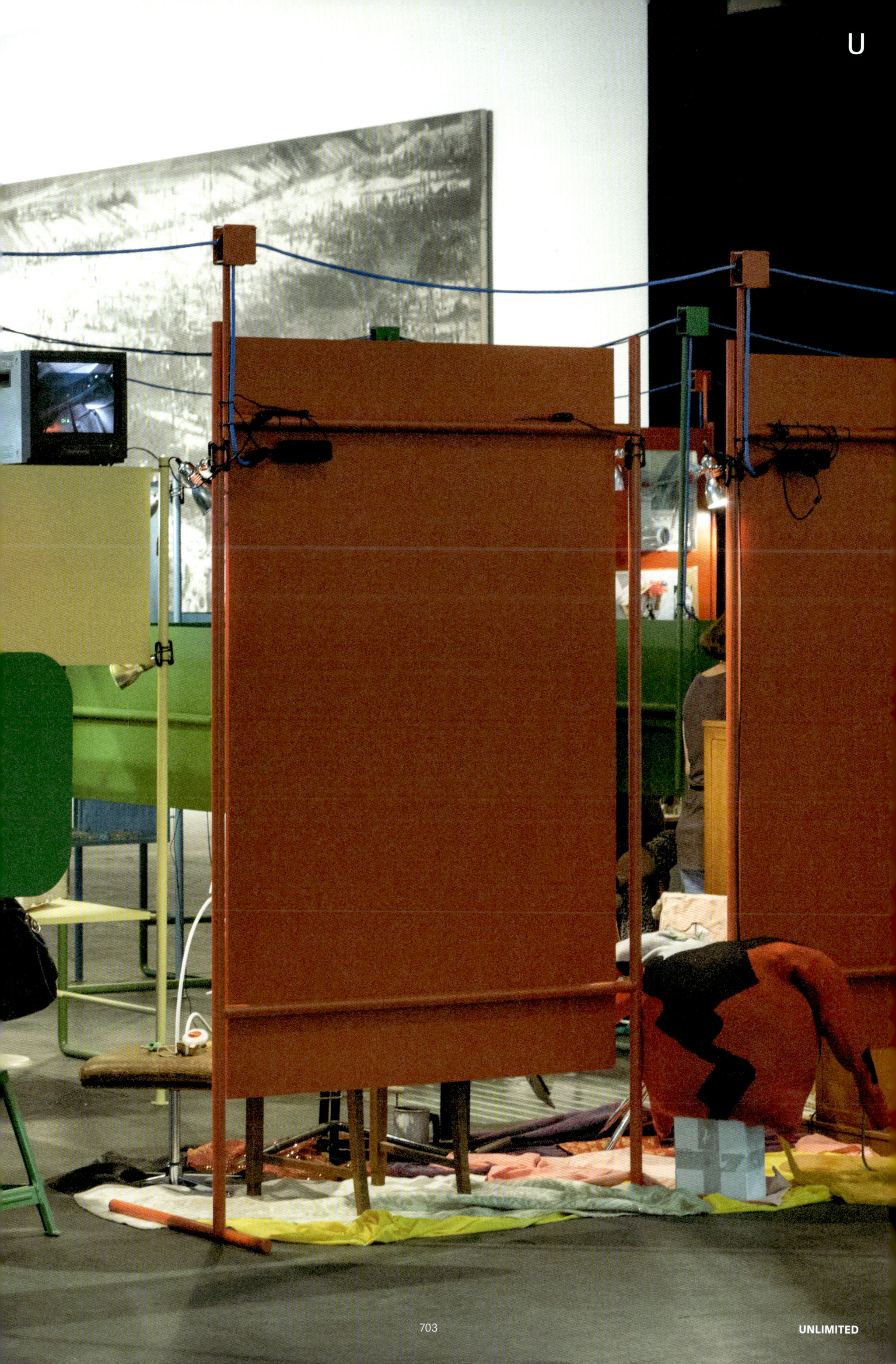

Sterling Ruby
Soft Work
2011–2013

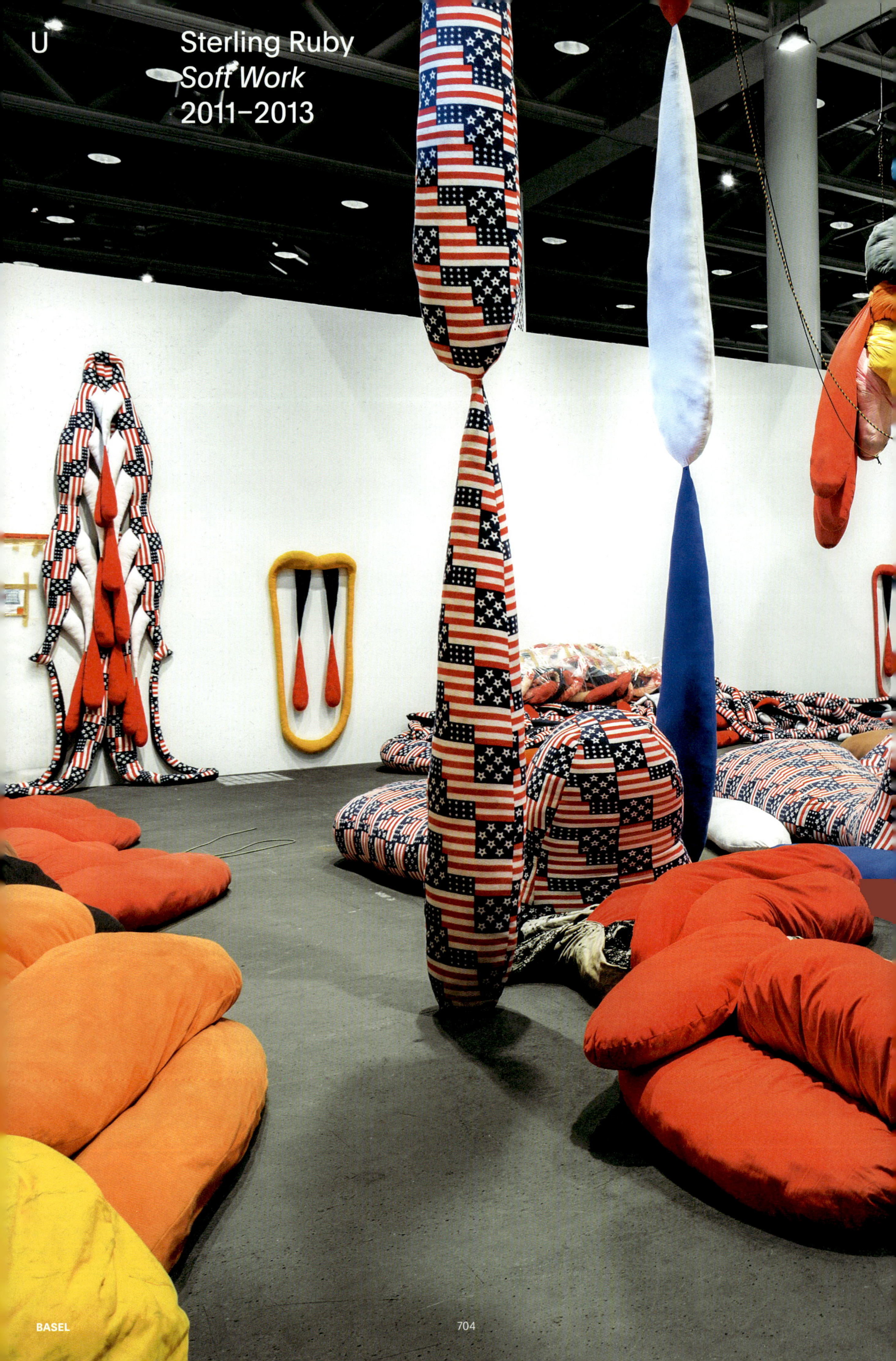

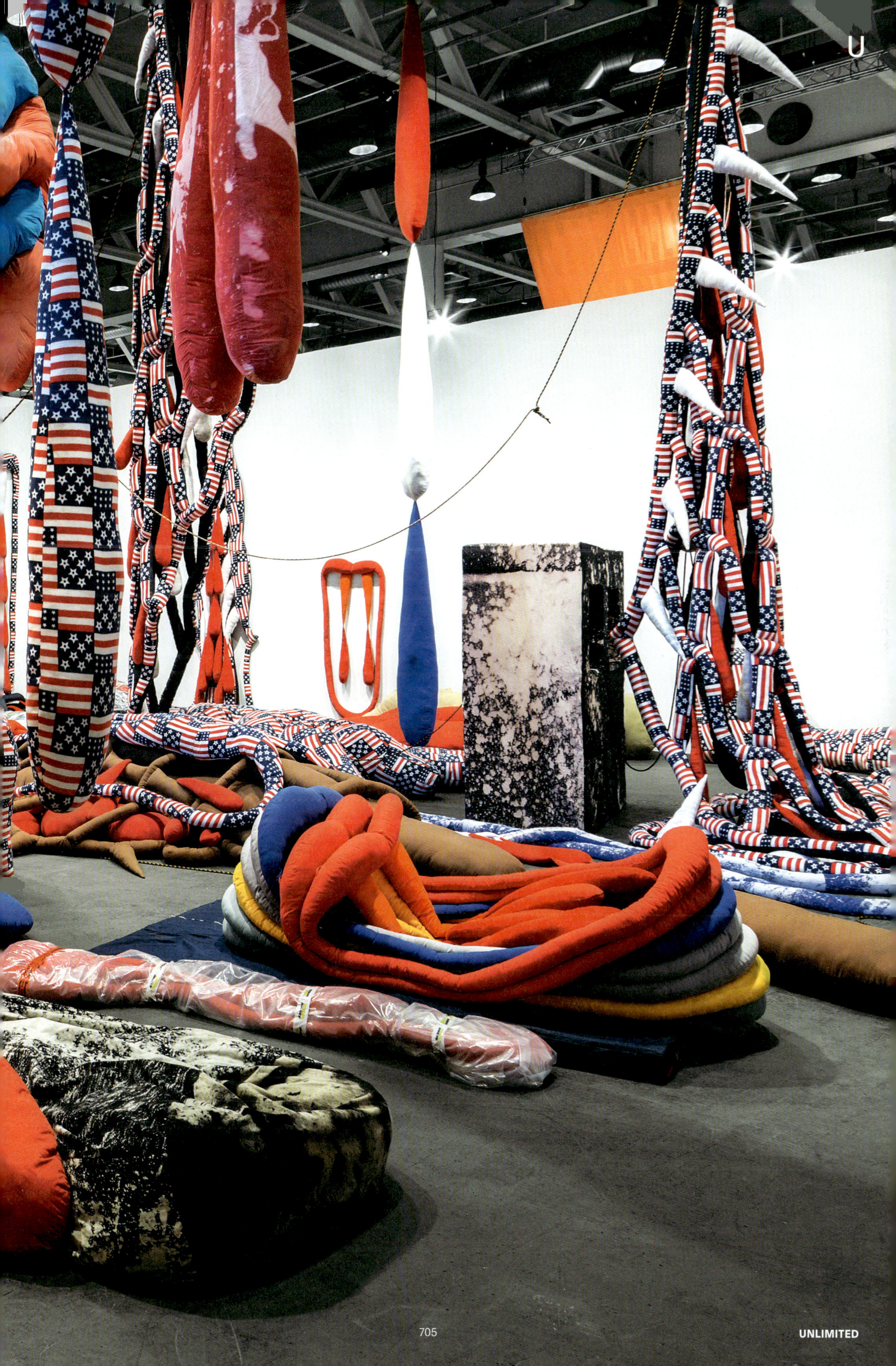

U

Pascale Marthine Tayou
Tayouwood
2014

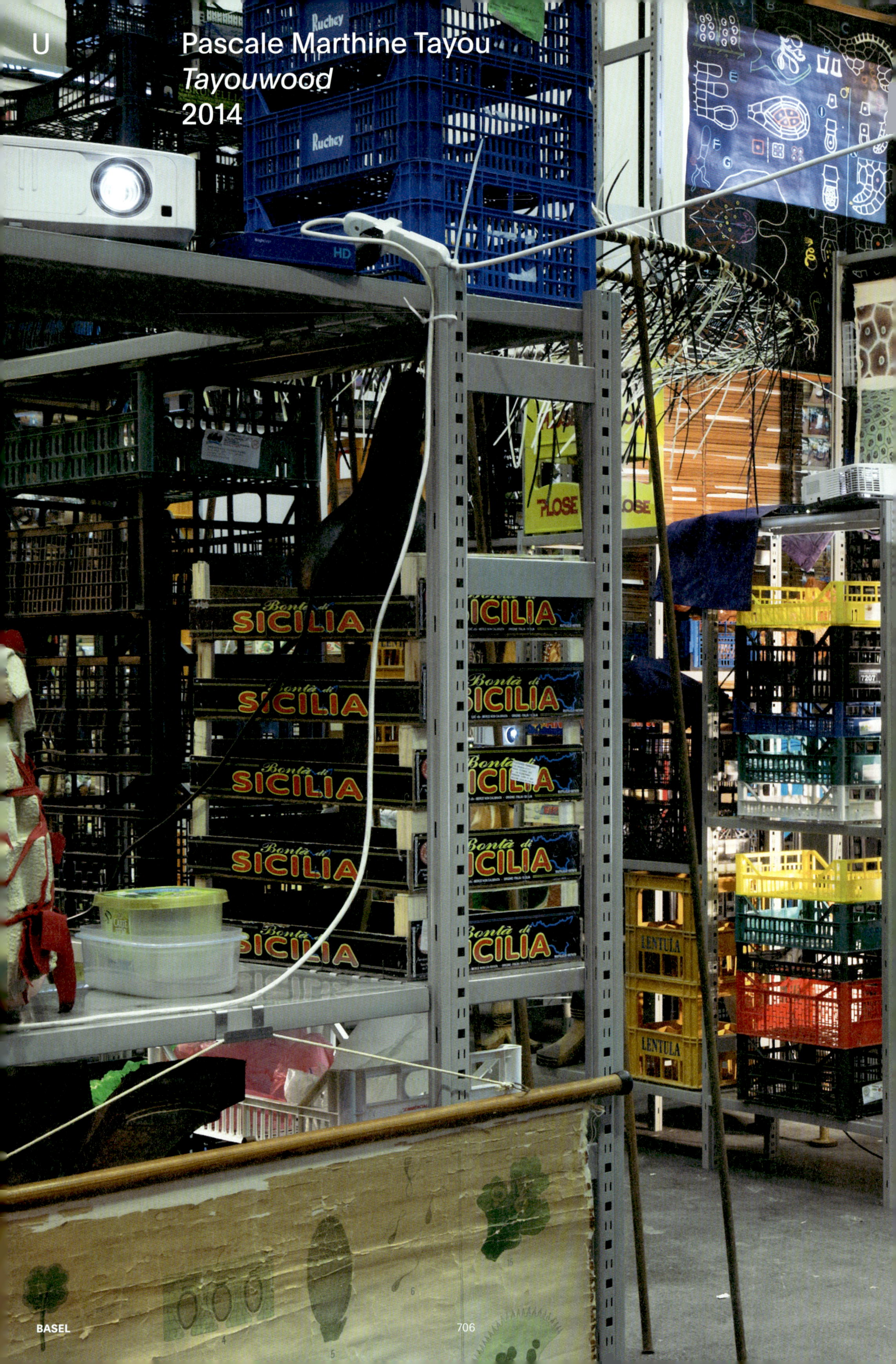

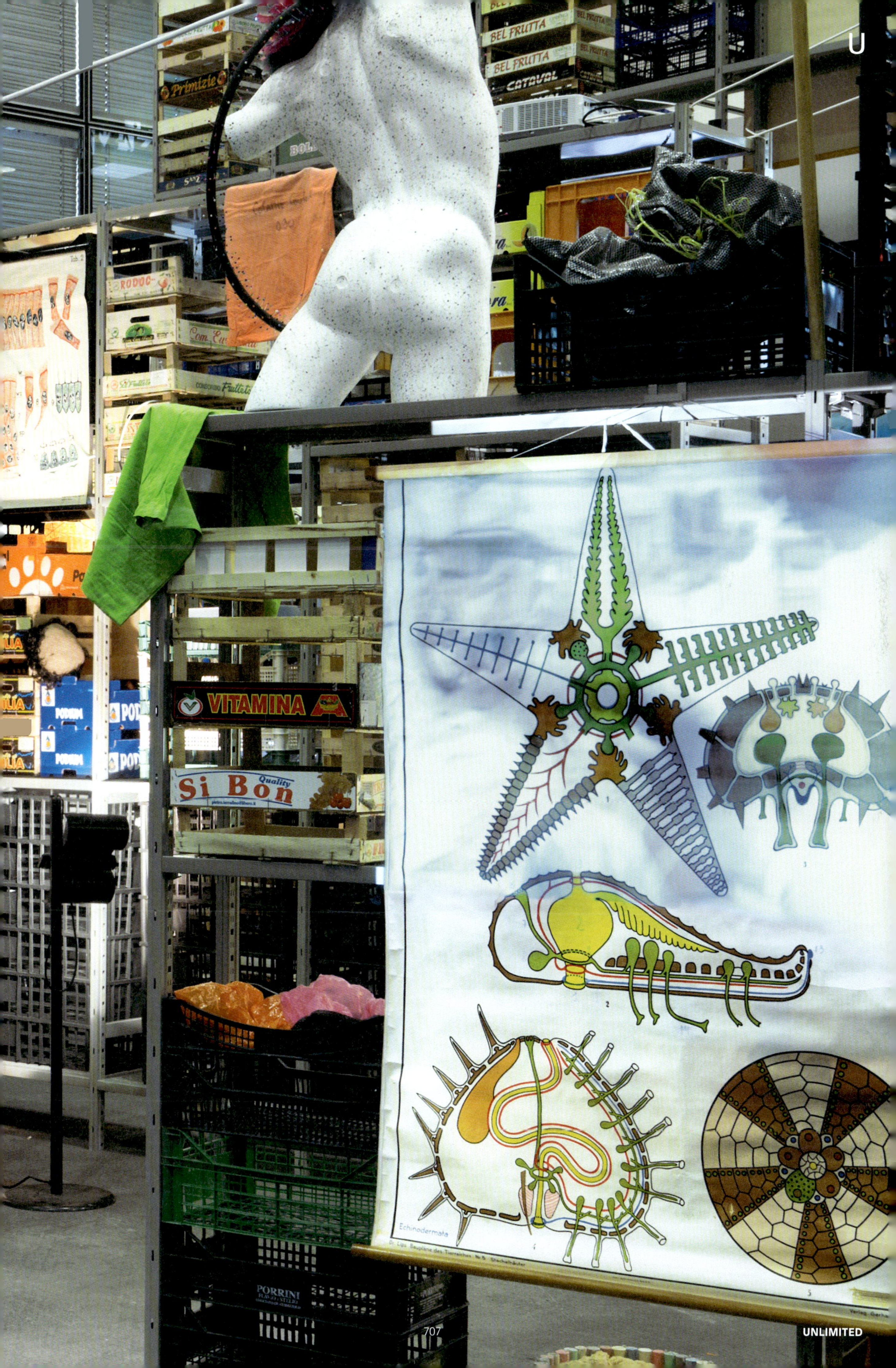
BEL FRUTTA
BEL FRUTTA
CATAVAL
Primizie
VITAMINA
Si Bon
Quality
Echinodermata

U

Jim Shaw
Capital Viscera Applicances Mural
2011

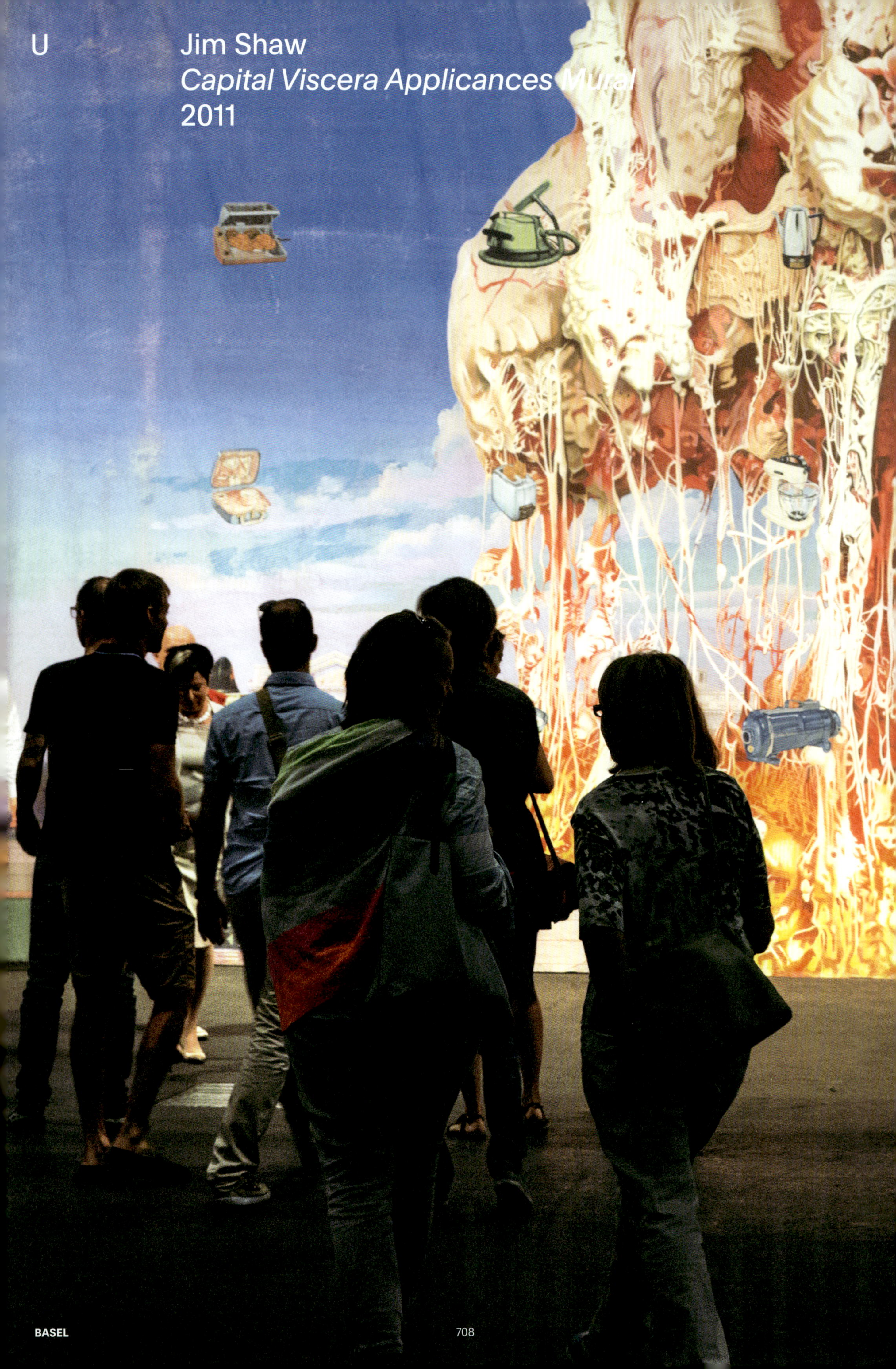

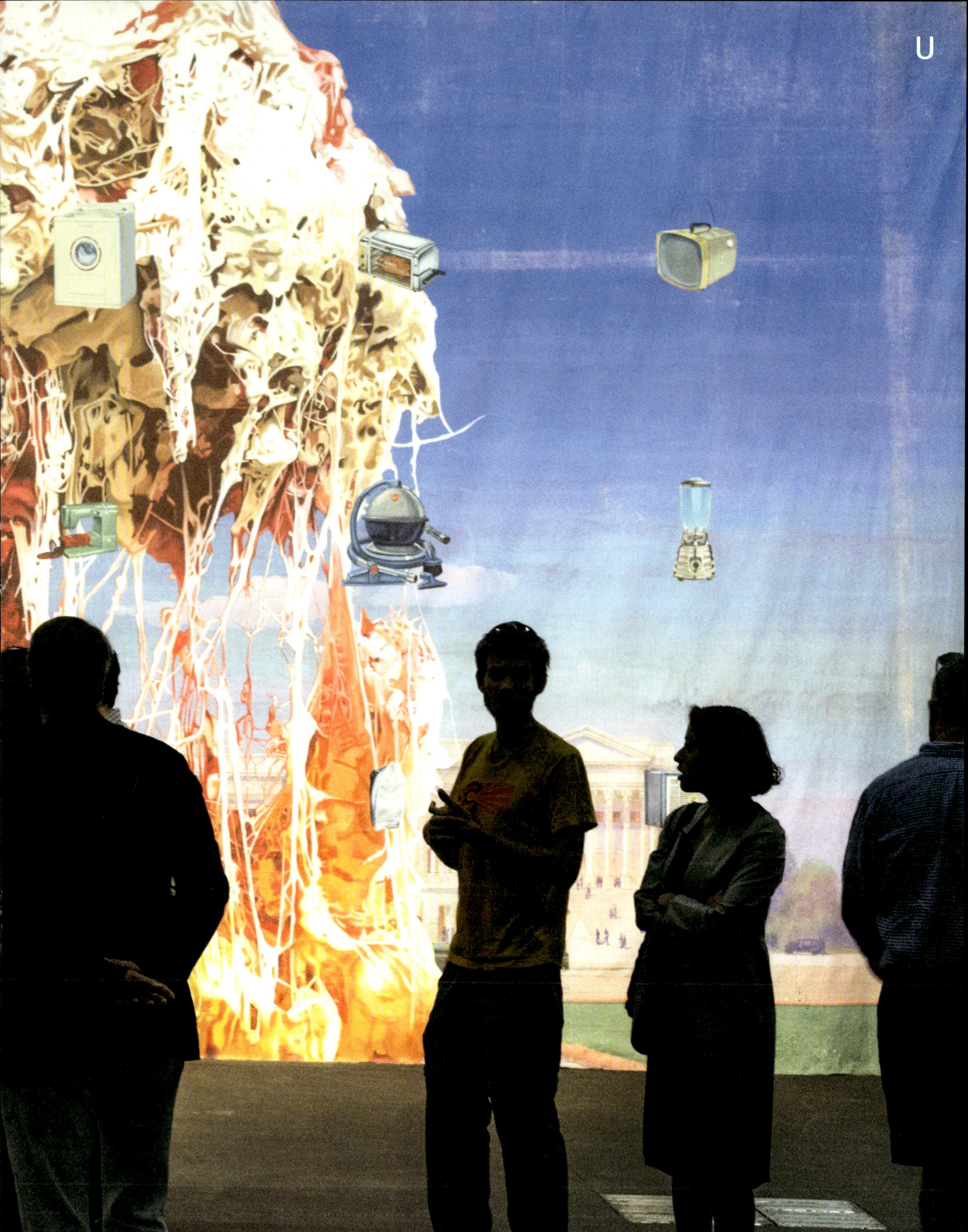

Sam Falls
Untitled (Pallet 9, Pomona)
2013

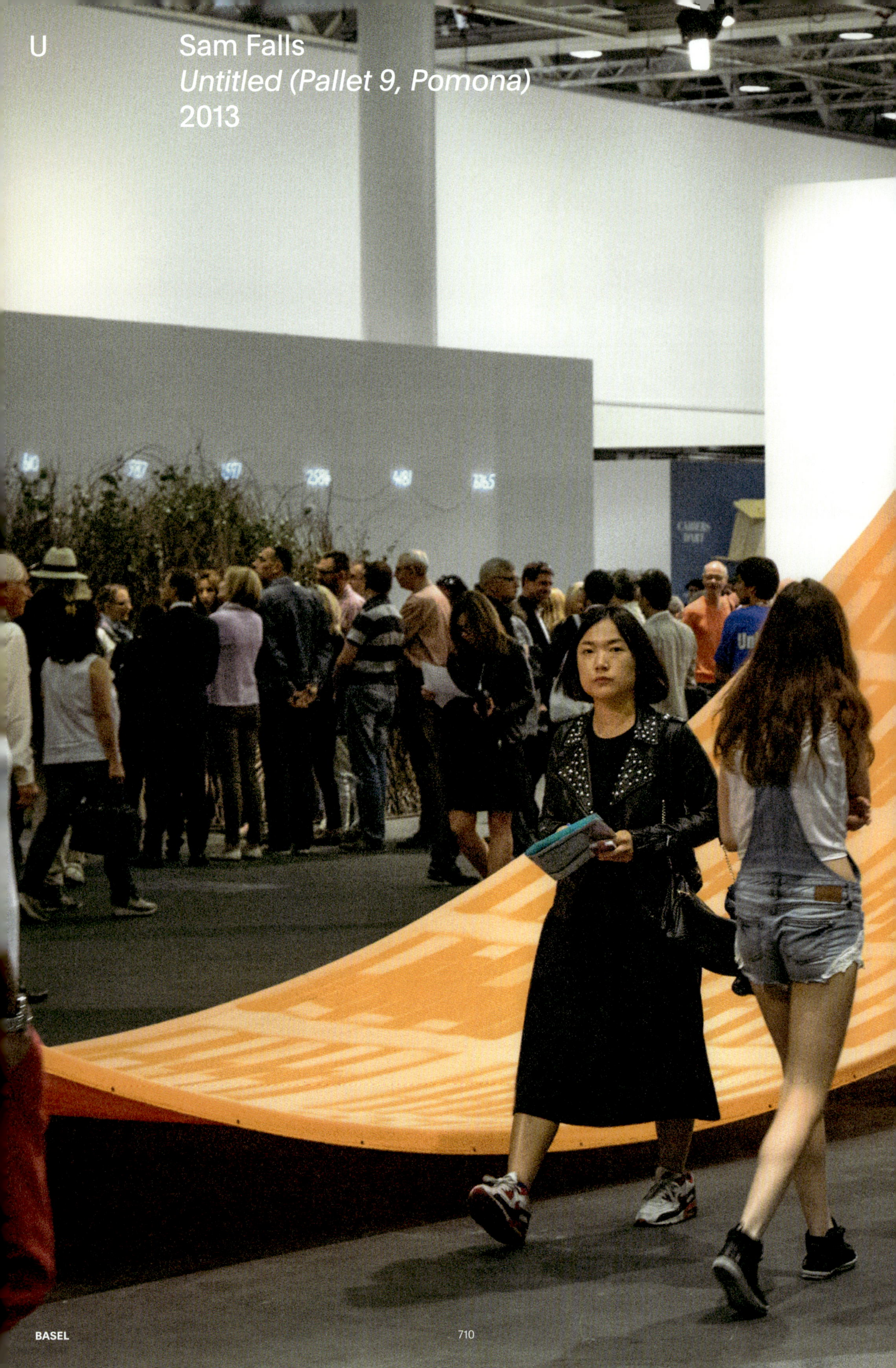

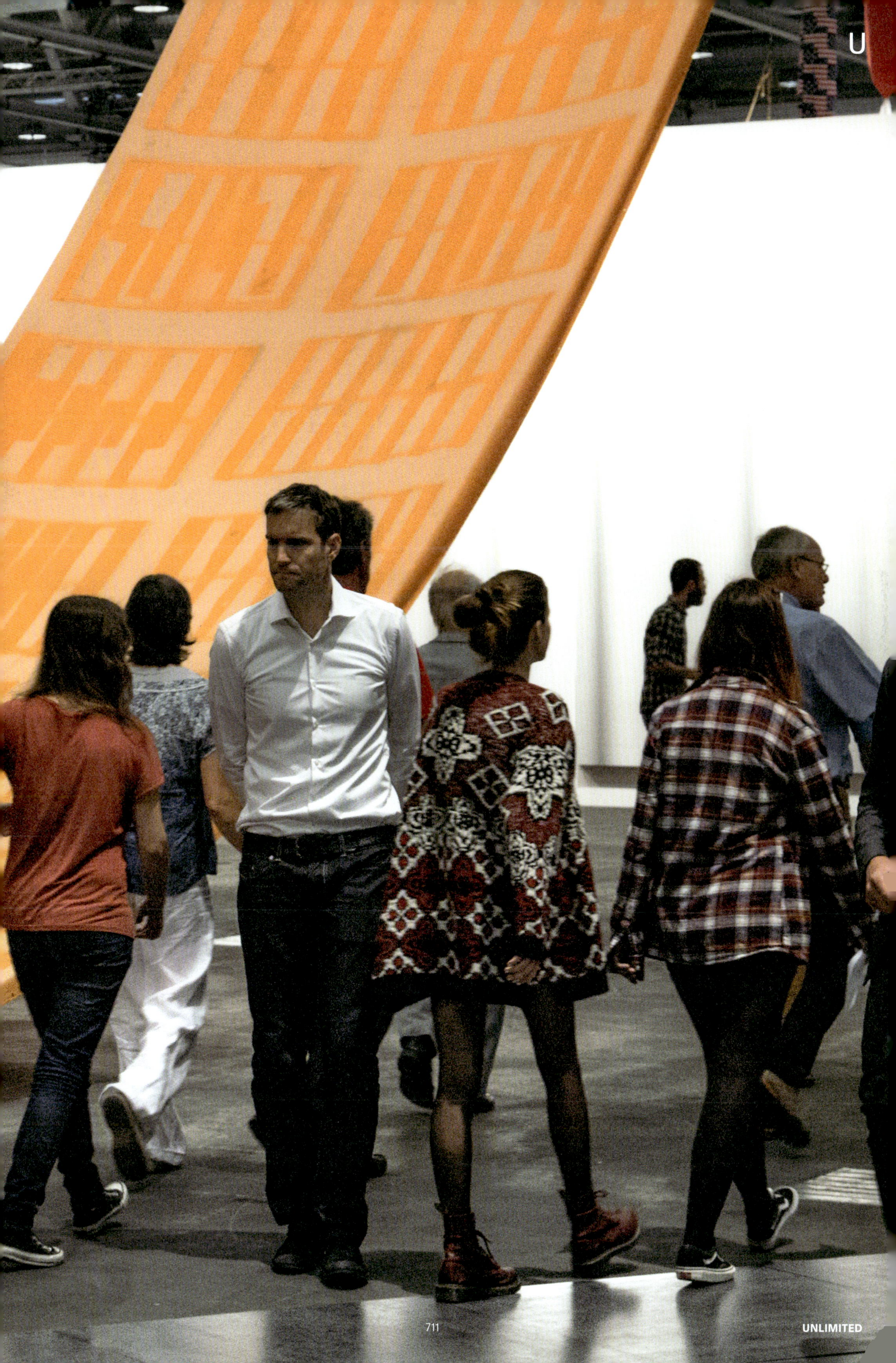

Anthony Caro
River Run
2013

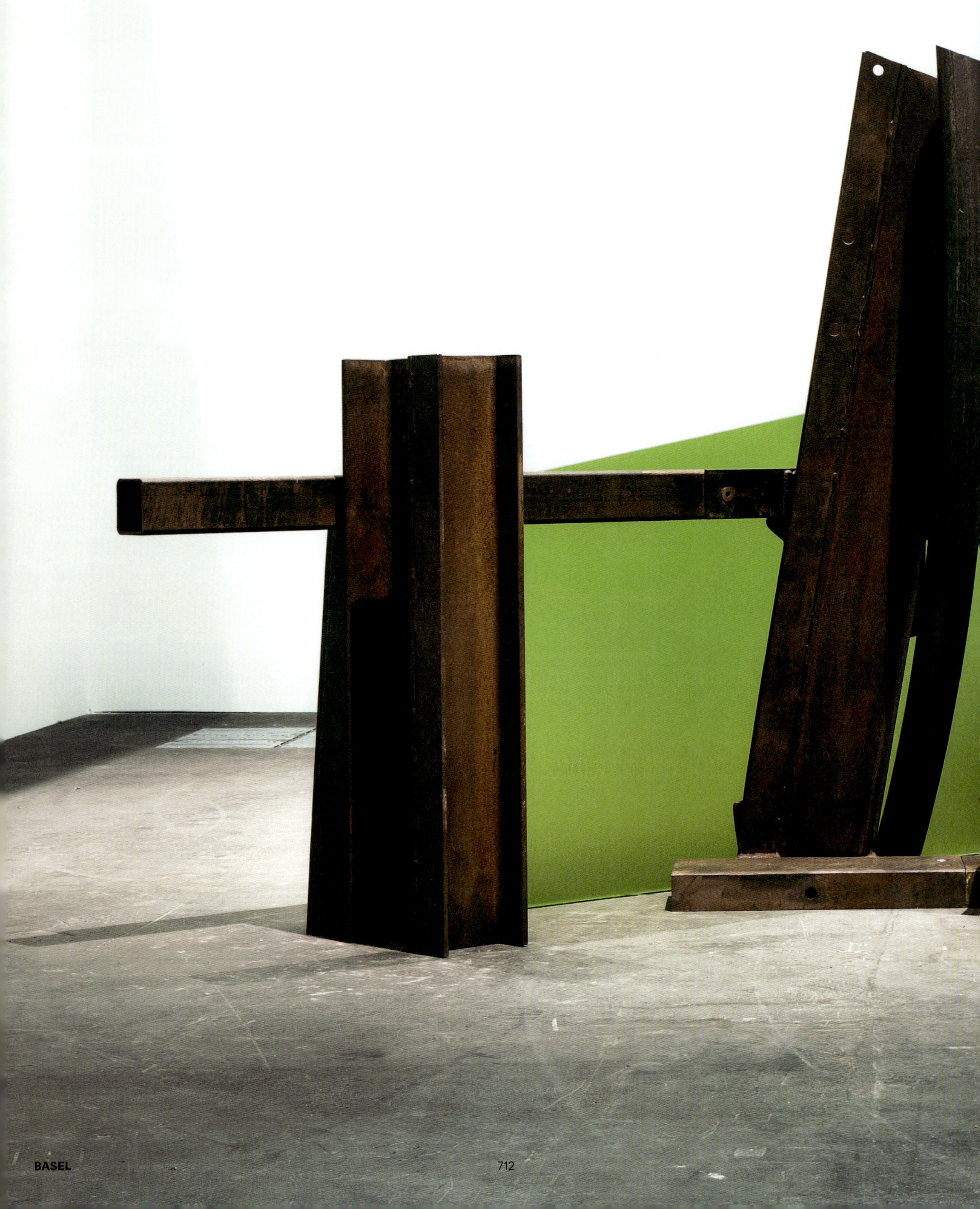

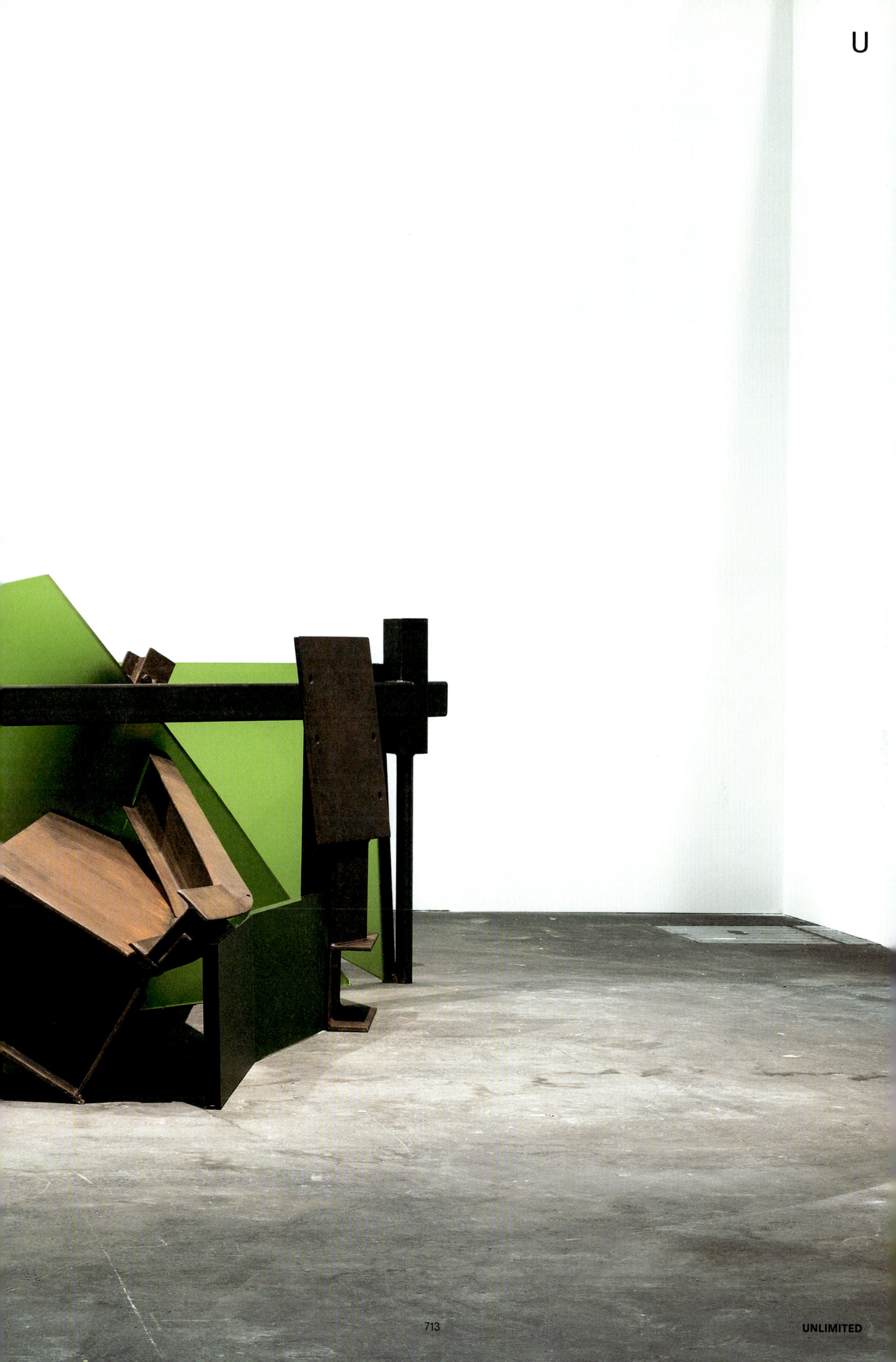

U

Rosemarie Trockel
As Far as Possible
2012

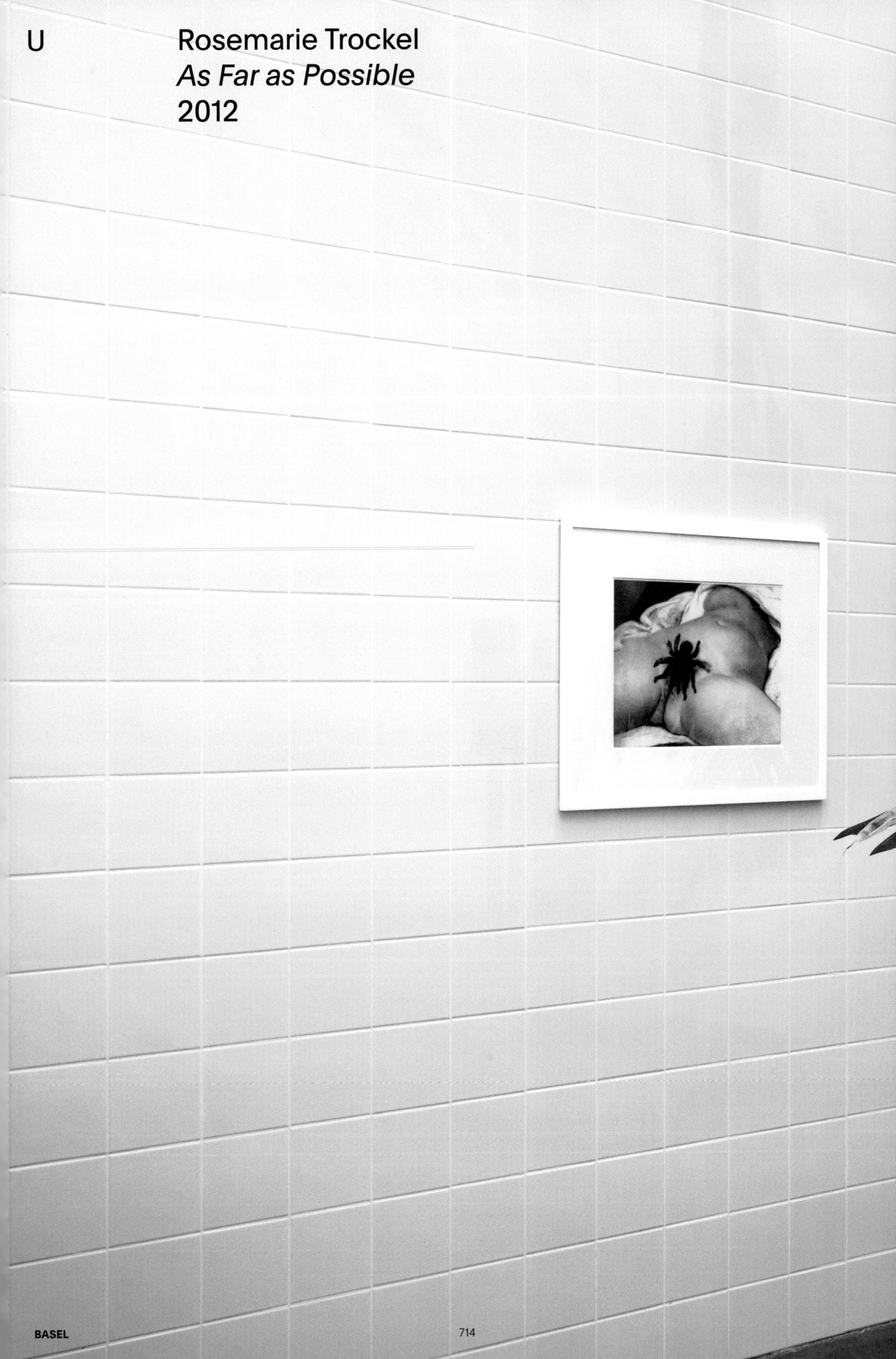

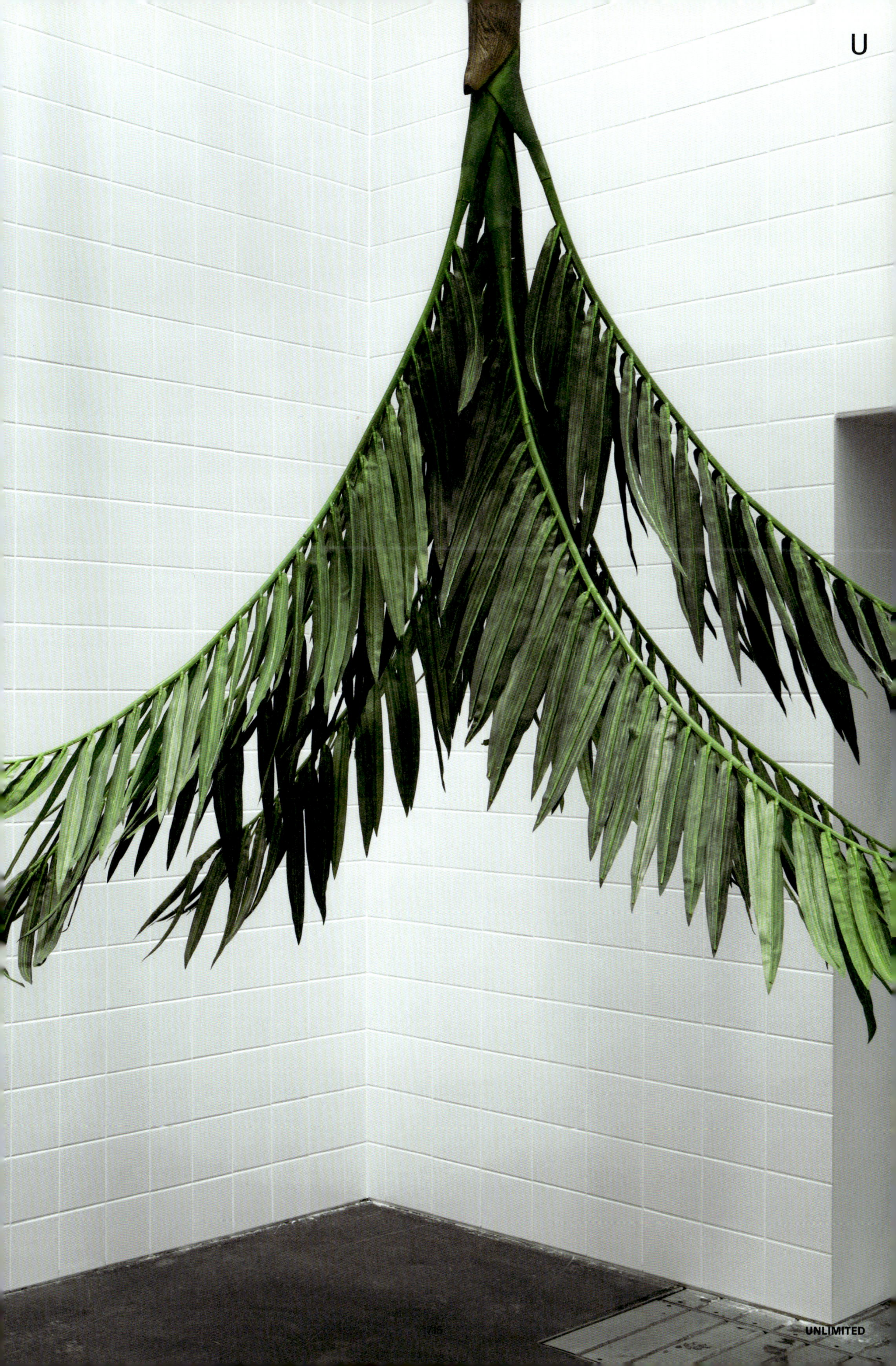

U

Ann Veronica Janssens
RR Lyrae
2014

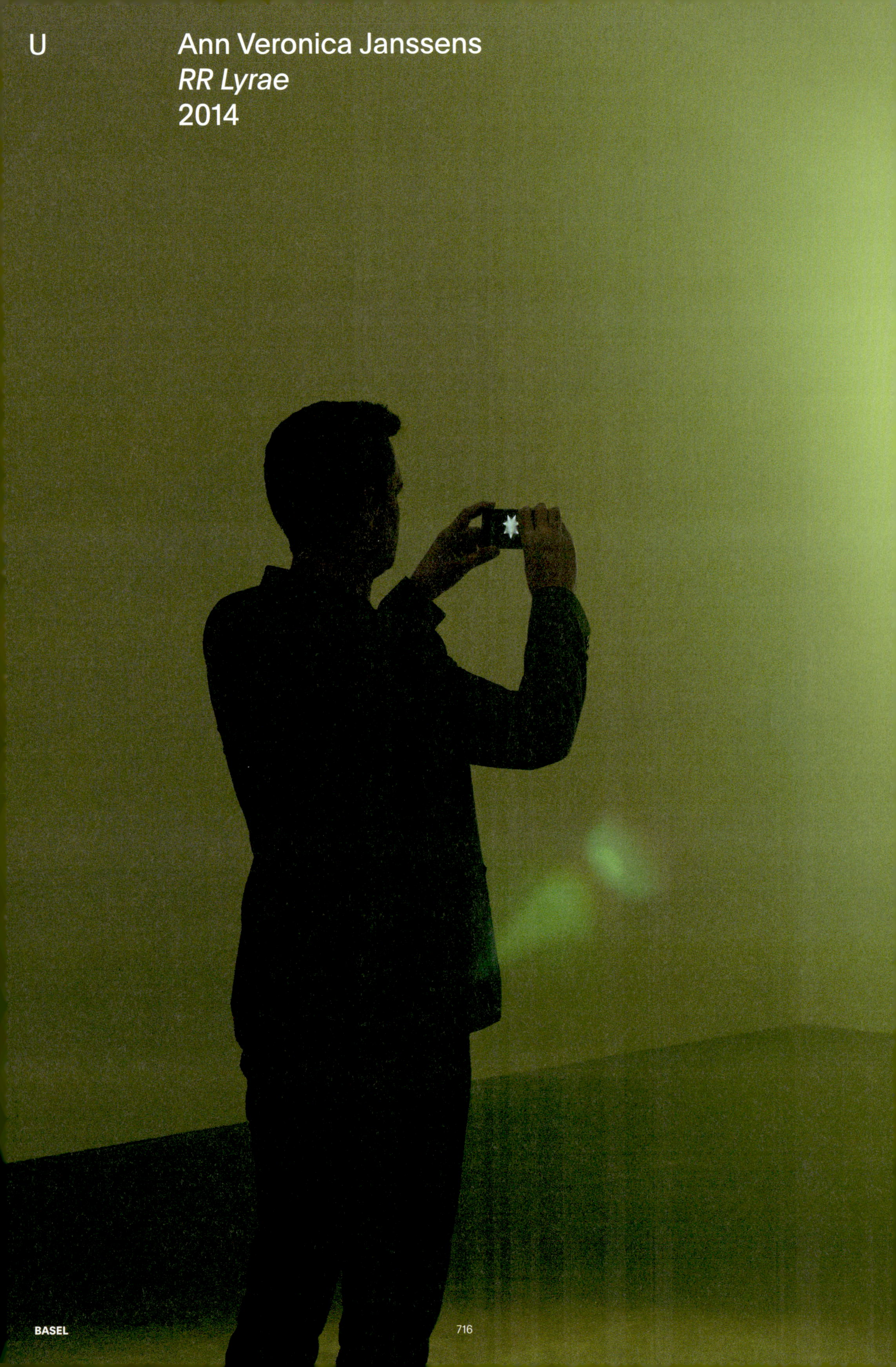

Upstream

Amsterdam ● Discoveries

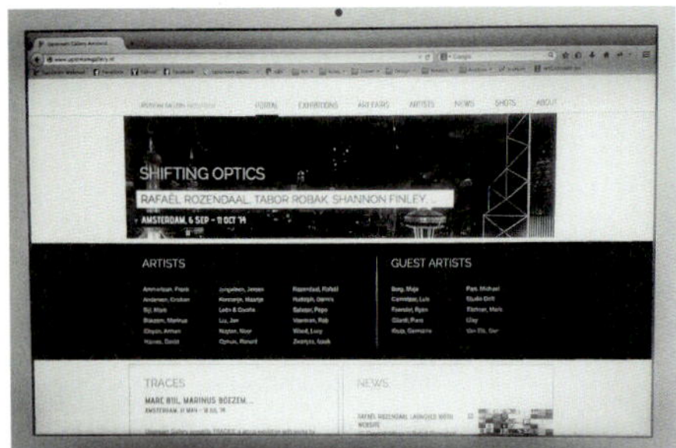

What is your favorite aspect of running a gallery?
The fact that it is a truly international company that brings you to great places and brings you in contact with some of the most inspirational spirits in the world.

How do you choose the artists you work with?
It is a process of spotting a great work, looking into the artist's oeuvre, meeting up, and doing studio visits. When everything feels right we start working together.

If you weren't running a gallery what else would you do?
That is unthinkable.

- **Contact** Upstream Gallery
Nieck de Bruijn
nieck@upstreamgallery.nl
- **Established** 2003
- **Owner(s) / Partner(s)** Nieck de Bruijn
Martijn Dijkstra
- **Team** 4
- **Space(s)** 150 m²
- **Artists at Art Basel** David Haines
- **Further artists represented** Frank Ammerlaan
Cristian Andersen
Marc Bijl
Marinus Boezem
Armen Eloyan
Jeroen Jongeleen
Maartje Korstanje
León & Cociña
Jen Liu
Noor Nuyten
Ronald Ophuis
Rafaël Rozendaal
Dennis Rudolph
Pepo Salazar
Rob Voerman
Lucy Wood
Izaak Zwartjes

Utopian Slumps

Melbourne ● Discoveries

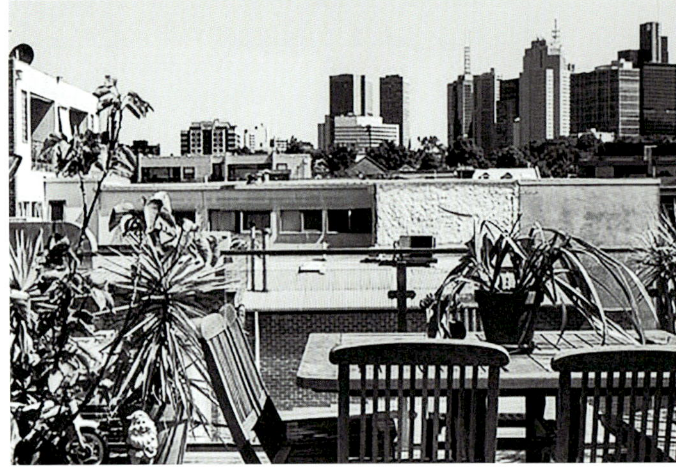

What is your favorite aspect of running a gallery?
Essentially I am a curator who also deals art; therefore the conception, planning, and delivery of exhibitions are the most exciting aspects of running a gallery for me. In particular, I love the research and initial planning stages of curating exhibitions.

How do you choose the artists you work with?
I try to keep up with what is happening in artist-run initiatives, experimental spaces, and curated exhibitions in Australia and abroad, which is often where the most interesting artists can be found. I also rely on the recommendations of my artist and curator friends, and keep a keen eye on *Contemporary Art Daily*.

If you weren't running a gallery what else would you do?
My second passion to art is fashion, so perhaps I'd have my own label, my own boutique, or be working in styling.

- **Contact** Utopian Slumps
Melissa Loughnan
melissa@utopianslumps.com
- **Established** 2010
- **Owner(s) / Partner(s)** Melissa Loughnan
- **Team** 3
- **Space(s)** 140 m²
- **Artists at Art Basel** Sanné Mestrom
- **Further artists represented** Jake Walker
Steven Asquith
Lauren Berkowitz
Fergus Binns
Starlie Geikie
Nathan Gray
Misha Hollenbach
Thomas Jeppe
Rhys Lee
Richard Lewer
William Mackinnon
Dylan Martorell
Mark Rodda
Caleb Shea
Esther Stewart
Amber Wallis

Upstream Gallery
Interview with Nieck de Bruijn

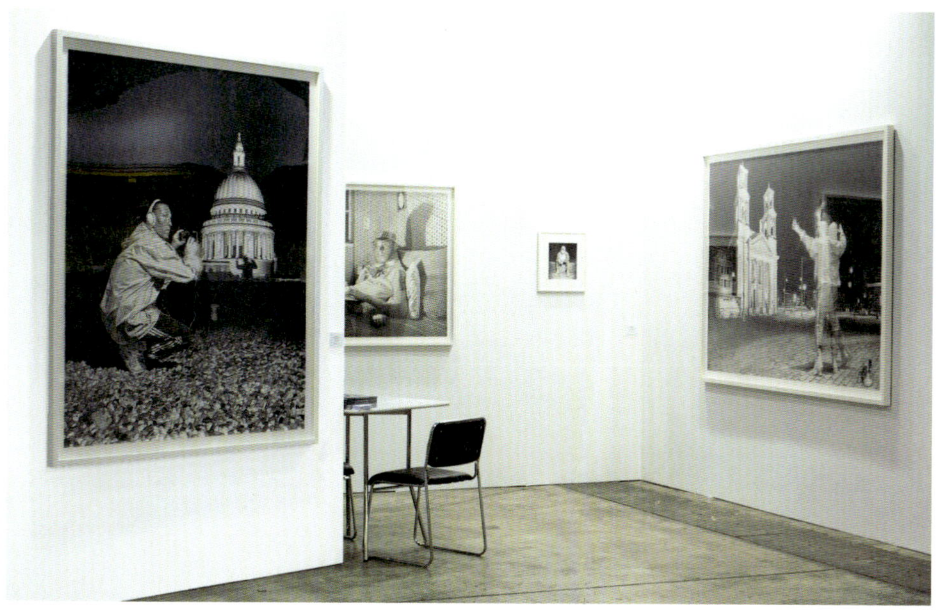

Art Basel in Hong Kong, 2014

How did you start Upstream Gallery?

Ever since I started collecting in the mid-1990s I wanted to create a gallery, although I didn't immediately have the courage to do so. It took me some years, and looking back it was probably a good thing because I made a much better start than I would have otherwise. From the start, I have seen the gallery as an international one, so my focus has always been to promote international artists in Holland alongside our Dutch artists abroad. We were very lucky at the beginning because we were already at Liste in Basel in our first year. It's a fantastic fair for a young gallery to build up an international network of clients and curators. Given that the market was also very good then, I could say I had a really smooth start. We did Liste for many years and started to also do Nada Art Fair in Miami, Art Forum in Berlin, Zoo Art Fair in London. Now we're moving up: we've been at the Armory in New York for some years now and we did Art Basel Statements in 2012 and now Art Basel in Hong Kong. In 2007 Martijn [Dijkstra] joined me as a business partner.

Who is the artist you are showing in Art Basel in Hong Kong and why did you choose him?

David Haines (b. 1969) is a British artist who studied at the Rijksakademie and lives in Amsterdam. He makes pencil drawings on paper and videos. We thought that it might be a good fit here, because it's a sort of hyper-realistic drawings, showing some obvious craftsmanship. We thought it would make it easier to attract people and talk to them about the conceptual aspects of the work. I can say it worked out well, touching local visitors and collectors alike.

How would you describe the gallery scene in Amsterdam, as you've been there for ten years now and have recently changed the location of the gallery?

We started as a typical Amsterdam gallery, in an old canal house, a small space with high ceiling. In 2008, we moved to De Pijp, which is Amsterdam's hippest area at the moment. It's a much bigger gallery and a great area to be in, surrounded by some of the best young galleries in town. The scene developed along with the number of active collectors in Holland: 15 years ago, people were saying that we only had a couple interesting collectors and Belgium was more renowned; now there are a lot of interesting collectors and they are very supportive of the galleries.

One thing in the Netherlands that has always been important is the museum network, the presence of regional museums alongside international institutions such as the Stedelijk. Does this still function as a component of the contemporary art world in the Netherlands?

It does, although recent political changes have decreased the funding. On the other hand, in Amsterdam, most museums were closed for many years. As the Stedelijk and the Rijkmuseum have now reopened, we have had many more international clients and curators coming out to Amsterdam in the last two years.

You work with both younger and older artists (you organized shows with Marinus Boezem and Piero Gilardi), how would you describe your program?

We started with young artists who often showed a sort of rebellious character. The artists developed and I think we are now in line with a more abstract and conceptual approach. Three years ago we started working with an older generation of artists: we now fully represent Marinus Boezem, one of the best representatives of Dutch Conceptual art, together with Ger Van Elk and Jan Dibbets. Because the Netherlands played a leading role in the Conceptual art movement, he is an important historical figure, but a little overlooked. He just turned 80 this year and he is still working and making unbelievable works. I believe both the older and younger generations appreciate being in exhibitions together and benefit from this exchange through the gallery's work.

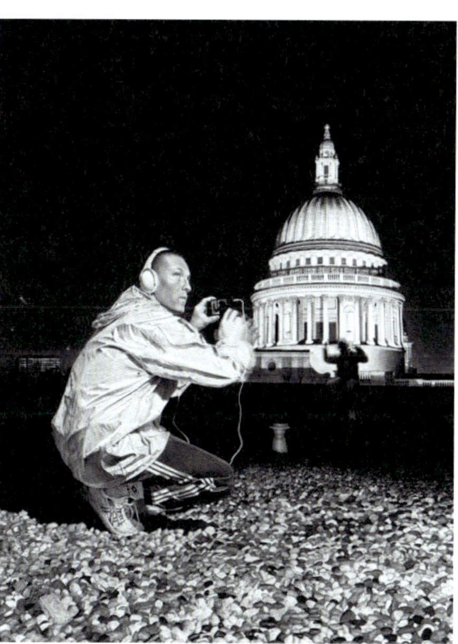

David Haines, *More Than Domes*, 2014

V

Rachel Rose
A Minute Ago, 2014
HD Video, 8'43"

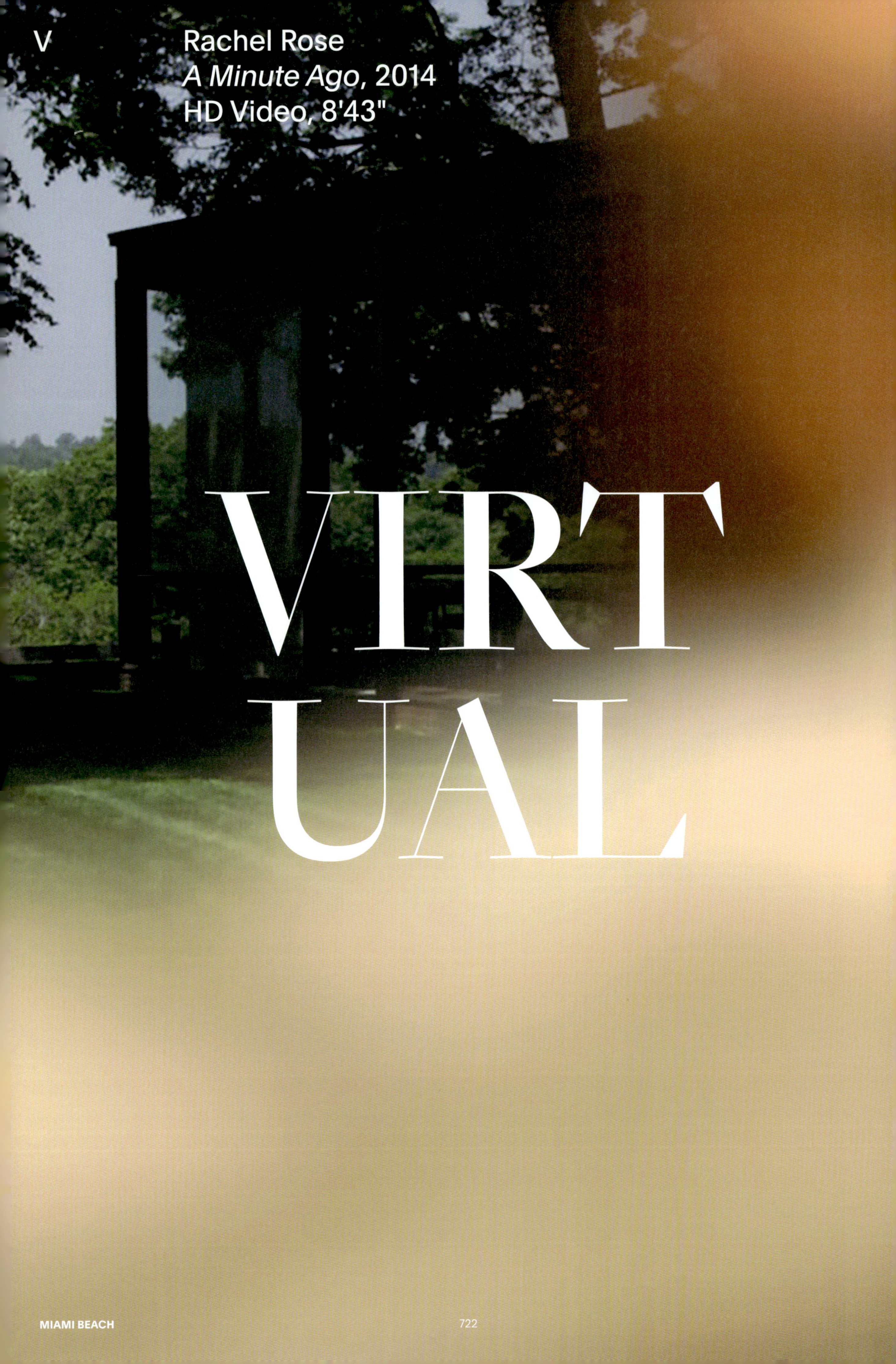

VIRT UAL

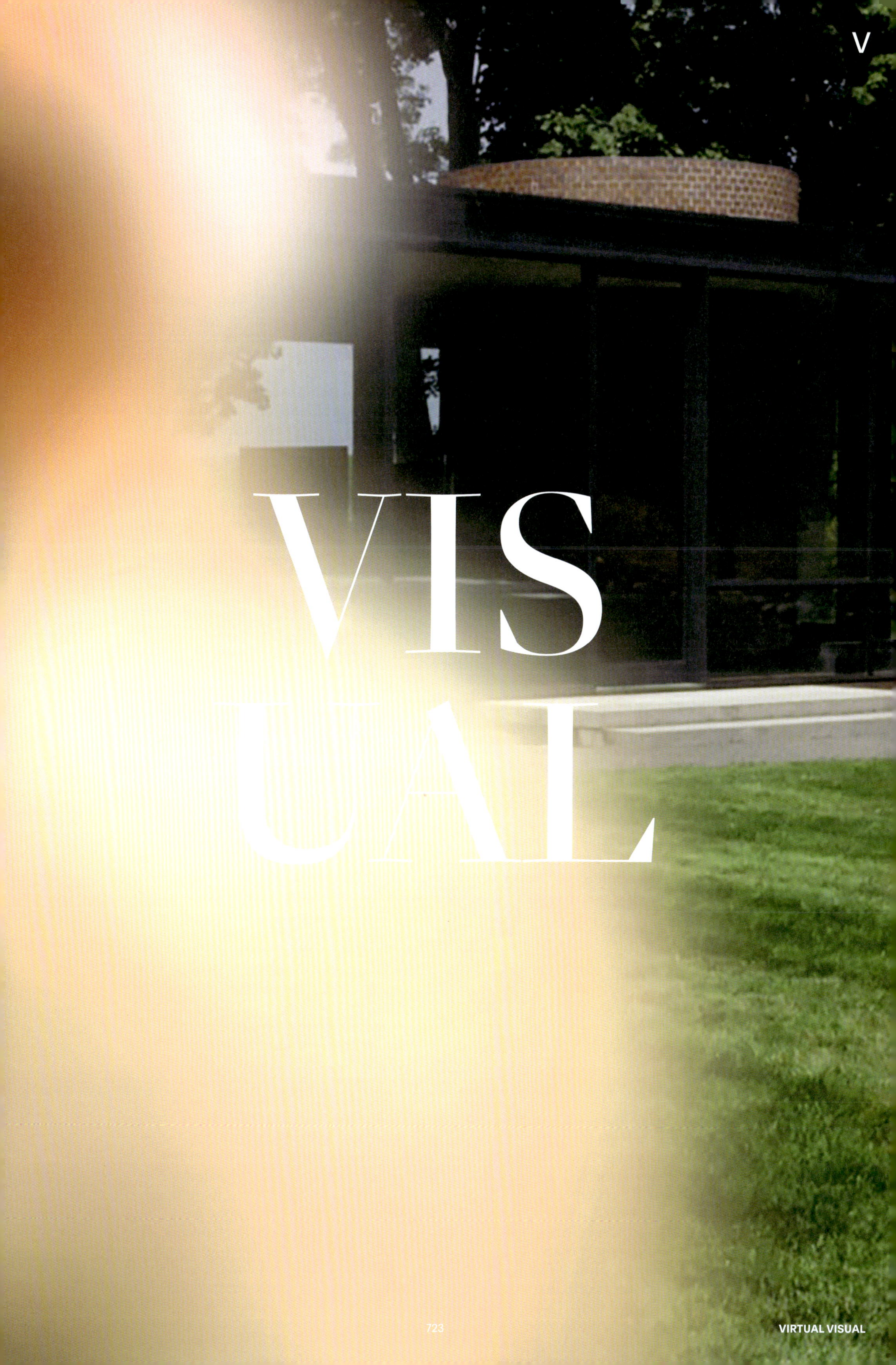

VIS UAL

Chrissie Iles speaks with Rachel Rose and Tabor Robak about *Playfulness: Artists as Online Gamers, Surfers, and Armchair Digital Revolutionaries*

Salon|Artist Talk

Art Basel in Miami Beach

December 5, 2014

With David Gryn, Curator of Art Basel's Film sector and Founder of Artprojx, London; Tabor Robak, Artist, Brooklyn; Rachel Rose, Artist, New York

Moderator: Chrissie Iles, Curator, New York

CHRISSIE ILES It has always been a deep human instinct to explore states of altered perception, and that exploration has always played out through an internalized visual world. In other words, it has always been played out *visually*. A thousand years ago, this experience might have been triggered by psychotropic drugs and, in the last 500 years, the mirror, light, darkness, and optical instruments became primary tools for approaching those states. Until the invention of a camera that was pretty much how it was; still or moving images have since become the primary vehicles, through prosthetic extensions of the body, for exploring these changing relationships with reality.

From the beginning of 20th-century projection to more tactile engagements with surface, be it the surface of the screen or surfaces inside or beyond the screen, the body no longer had to have a physical contact with something. Video games have occupied a really important role in this shift and become the predominant way in which teenagers engage with narrative, fiction, and the moving image. The works of the two artists present here talk about the impact of new technology on that shift.

That's how I think about the absence of the camera or a centralized body: it's almost like a robotic recreation of a body. —Rachel Rose

TABOR ROBAK In my work there is nothing really photographic: I'm not using imagery pulled from real life. It's easier to imagine it like a video game or a 3D-rendered movie. My work really exists in this sort of fantasy, 3D, virtual world. But despite that, despite how it is about this really fantastic surface that doesn't exist in the real world, my work is also about my body, my mind, and my emotions. Emotion is a big part of *A**, a 14-channel piece, about 14 feet by 14 feet, in which I tried to map out the cycle of my emotions in a year, to illustrate the process of being aware of your emotions, and trying to change them for the better.

CI In both of your work it seems that the surface is very important as a kind of permeable membrane through which we can move. The 14 screens are like a body on a certain level, as well as a map of the emotions over a period of time, and in Rachel Rose's case, her use of a particular lens gives a forensic quality to the images. In both of your work there is this sense that we are not really looking from the point of view of a camera. One doesn't feel that there is a camera but something else. Because the camera is an extension of the body, if the camera disappears, where is the body?

RACHEL ROSE In *Palisades in Palisades* (2014) I was very interested in how one space can hold different scales of time: a deep history, like a geological time because the park is on top of a 200-million-year old cliff; an historical time on a more local scale, as it was there during the revolutionary war; and the time of the body now. I was working with a remote control lens to develop these shots that start from 200 feet away and then come right up to the pores of the skin of the protagonist's body. This movement from metaphor to pure sensorial material became like a bone structure for the work.

A Minute Ago (2014) is a work that I shot at the Philip Johnson Glass House, and with this I was really interested in looking at the relationship between collage and natural catastrophe. I was thinking about how to look at natural catastrophe not from a moral or political perspective, but actually from one which is rooted in the history of filmmaking. This is just one axiom, but eventually the house gets disintegrated in a hailstorm and Philip Johnson is being rotoscoped back into the house.

Regarding what you said about the camera and the loss of the body and the way Tabor talked about transferring emotions into a kind of surface, I think I feel similarly: the Philip Johnson work really came out of this daily anxiety about the weather, but not really ever being able to take the time to feel where that unease is and where is it coming from and how that is related to a deeper scale of time, place, and maybe narrative. For me, video and film are like containers for processing out and giving space to these subtle feelings. In that way, the tempo and the methodology for editing become its own body. That's how I think about the absence of the camera or a centralized body: it's almost like a robotic recreation of a body.

TR In a painting you can see the brushstrokes and you can understand how the body has evolved. In digital work, it's less clear because we have pixels and when you get very close the image breaks apart. I'm always looking for a way to bring the brushstrokes or the mark of the hand back into the work. One way I do this is through these very intricate elements that look like they are being hand-moved. Another way is to set up 3D simulations where I've programmed a camera that I control in real time, like in a video game, so the camera-control has actually recorded my body.

CI What you are both describing seems to me to also have a very interesting historical trajectory and I just wonder whether you think about and look at art history or at what Dan Graham calls the "just past" when you make your work? How does the linear trajectory of history collide with the experience of being able to go back and forth across history every time we Google an image?

RR I was thinking a lot about Dan Graham. Looking into the past has much to do with the way I put together my projects rather than a linear historical perspective: the way things position themselves in relationship to ideas that I am working on. Poussin's *The Burial of Phocion* (1648) is the only painting in the Glass House, and in the painting, a body covered by a white sheet is being moved down a pathway to be buried. But it's sort of indefinitely unburied, held there, everything is in a sort of frozen state, where not a leaf is moving, there's not a ripple in the water, it's a perfectly held moment, which is partially how I was looking at Johnson's body. I "activated" this painting because of this relationship.

CI It's interesting because there was a break when the camera was discovered, between the sublime and the picturesque. The sublime became the picturesque through the camera. Poussin is this pivotal figure between the ending of the sublime in painting and the beginning of the picturesque, the beginning of the mechanical image. Taken to its ultimate conclusion, the picturesque is becoming the kitsch sunset, the photographed sunset.

In a funny way Dan Graham is much more about the sublime than you are. His use of the glass surfaces, translucency, and light is very "romantic." In the way you dealt with the surface of the glass house, you have introduced time into the glass: it doesn't look like clear, see-through, glass. But because it also doesn't feel like a camera is involved, you are rearticulating our relationship to light, to translucency, to where the body is. This is something I see is happening very much now in the world in general and in particular in your work, this sense of moving through physical surfaces.

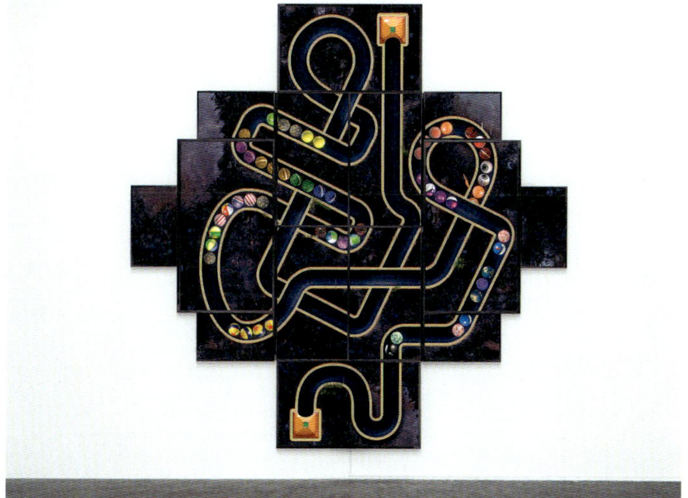

Tabor Robak
*A**
2014
14-channel HD video, real time 3D, 10 min

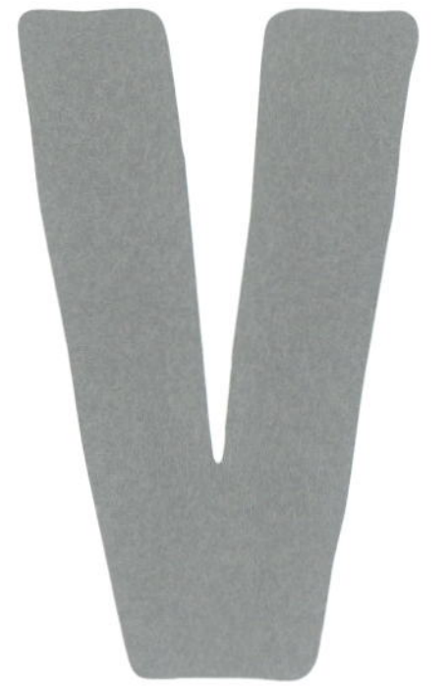

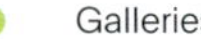

Vadehra

New Delhi ● Galleries

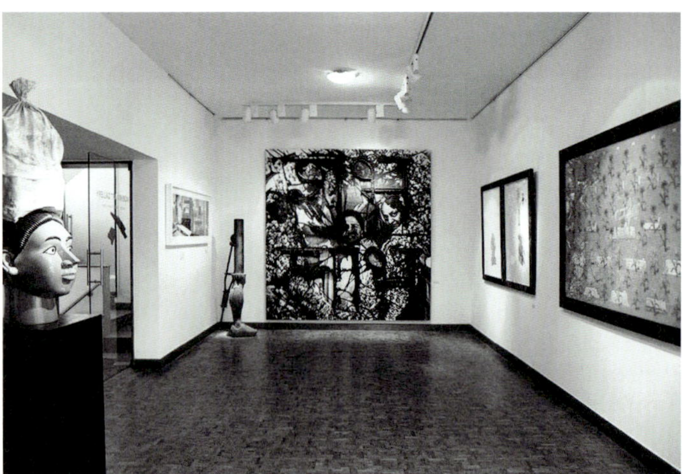

What is your favorite aspect of running a gallery?
Having the opportunity everyday to interact with such interesting people and creative minds—artists, intellectuals, collectors, and art lovers. Building long-lasting relationships with the artists, following their careers and understanding their evolution as creators is very enriching. Also, being able to play an important role in promoting the Indian art scene and help shape the current development of the market is what excites us immensely.

How do you choose the artists you work with?
We have been working with most of our artists for many years, closely following their careers and development. When we approach new artists, it is often after a lengthy process of study and comprehension of the new practitioner carried out by our team of in-house curators and the gallery directors.

If you weren't running a gallery what else would you do?
Run a gallery!

- **Contact** Vadehra Art Gallery
  Parul Vadehra
  parul@vadehraart.com
- **Established** 1987
- **Owner(s) / Partner(s)** Arun Vadehra
  Roshini Vadehra
- **Team** 10
- **Space(s)** 929 m²
- **Artists at Art Basel** Atul Bhalla
  Anju Dodiya
  Atul Dodiya
  Shilpa Gupta
  Zakkir Hussain
  Armando Miguélez
  Paribartana Mohanty
  Shibu Natesan
  Jagannath Panda
  Ashim Purkayastha
  Arpita Singh
  Praneet Soi
  Hema Upadhyay
- **Further artists represented** Binode Behari Mukherjee
  Jayashree Chakravarthy
  Jogen Chowdhury
  M.H. Husain
  George Martin PJ
  Anjolie Ela Menon
  Ganesh Pyne
  A Ramachandran
  Chameli Ramachandran
  Jamini Roy
  Gulammohammed Sheikh
  F.N. Souza
  K.G. Subramanyan

Vallois

Paris ● Survey

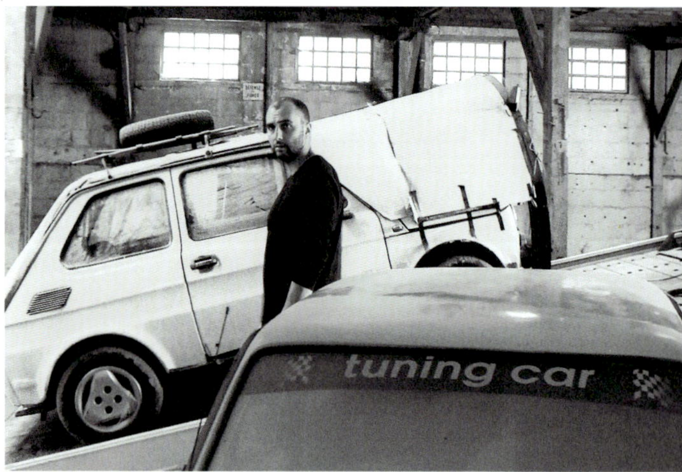

What is your favorite aspect of running a gallery?
Discovering new artists, sharing time, talks (and drinks) with those we work with. Selling a work we love to a passionate collector.

How do you choose the artists you work with?
Acuity, personality, contemporaneity … and humor!

If you weren't running a gallery what else would you do?
What else?

- **Contact** Galerie Georges-Philippe & Nathalie Vallois
  Georges-Philippe Vallois
  info@galerie-vallois.com
- **Established** 1990
- **Owner(s) / Partner(s)** Georges-Philippe Vallois
  Nathalie Vallois
- **Team** 8
- **Space(s)** 320 m²
- **Artists at Art Basel** Pilar Albarracín
  Julien Berthier
  Julien Bismuth
  Raymond Hains
  Taro Izumi
  Niki de Saint Phalle
  Jacques Villeglé
- **Further artists represented** Gilles Barbier
  Alain Bublex
  Massimo Furlan
  Richard Jackson
  Alain Jacquet
  Adam Janes
  Jean-Yves Jouannais
  Martin Kersels
  Paul Kos
  Paul McCarthy
  Jeff Mills
  Arnold Odermatt
  Henrique Oliveira
  Pierre Seinturier
  Jean Tinguely
  Keith Tyson
  Olav Westphalen
  Winshluss
  Virginie Yassef

Van de Weghe

New York

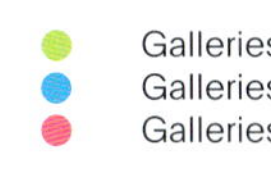

Galleries
Galleries
Galleries

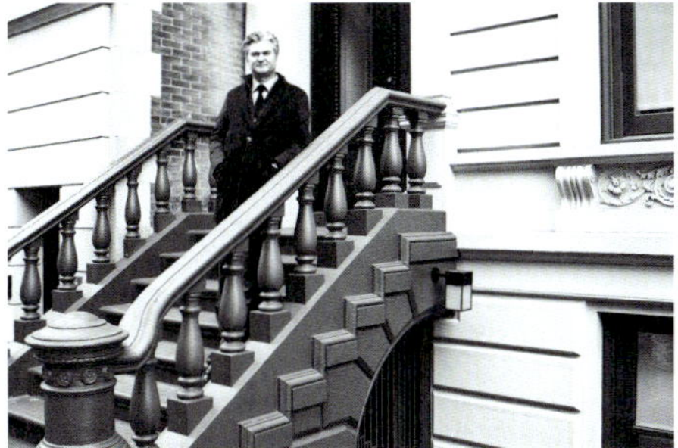

What is your favorite aspect of running a gallery?
Meeting interesting and diverse people.

How do you choose the artists you work with?
I choose them depending on if I would buy their artworks for my personal collection or hang them on my walls.

If you weren't running a gallery what else would you do?
I would work in real estate.

- **Contact** Van de Weghe Fine Art
Pierre Ravelle-Chapuis
pierre@vdwny.com
- **Established** 1999
- **Owner(s) / Partner(s)** Christophe Van de Weghe
- **Team** 4
- **Space(s)** 150 m²
- **Artists at Art Basel** Jean-Michel Basquiat
Alexander Calder
Duane Hanson
Keith Haring
Damien Hirst
Donald Judd
Franz Kline
Roy Lichtenstein
René Magritte
Henry Moore
Pablo Picasso
Richard Prince
Andy Warhol

van den Eynde

Dubai

Insights

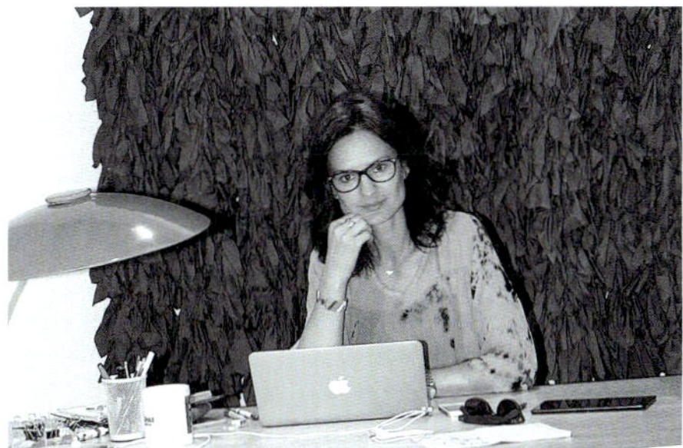

What is your favorite aspect of running a gallery?
We currently think that the word "gallery" doesn't really describe what we do anymore because our artists' projects often take us beyond the standardized practices of the industry. The lack of institutional non-profit platforms in the region and the need to produce projects without any constraints has led us to make some adventurous, challenging decisions and shows. Perhaps it is this "unknown" that creates our most exciting outcomes.

How do you choose the artists you work with?
We mutually chose each other. Today our artists call their practice "collaborative," embracing the members of the gallery team in many aspects of their projects.

If you weren't running a gallery what else would you do?
Whatever I would do would have to be as challenging and hands-on. Tennis player, maybe?

- **Contact** Gallery Isabelle van den Eynde
Isabelle van den Eynde
isabelle@ivde.net
- **Established** 2009
- **Owner(s) / Partner(s)** Isabelle van den Eynde
Jean-Marc Decrop
- **Team** 6
- **Space(s)** 300 m²
- **Artists at Art Basel** Mohammed Kazem
Hassan Sharif
- **Further artists represented** :Mentalklinik
Abdelkader Benchamma
Zoulikha Bouabdellah
Bita Fayyazi
Ramin Haerizadeh
Rokni Haerizadeh
Nargess Hashemi
Aisha Khalid
Idris Khan
Farshid Maleki
Ahmad Amin Nazar
Hesam Rahmanian
Haleh Redjaian

Van Doren Waxter

New York

Galleries
Kabinett

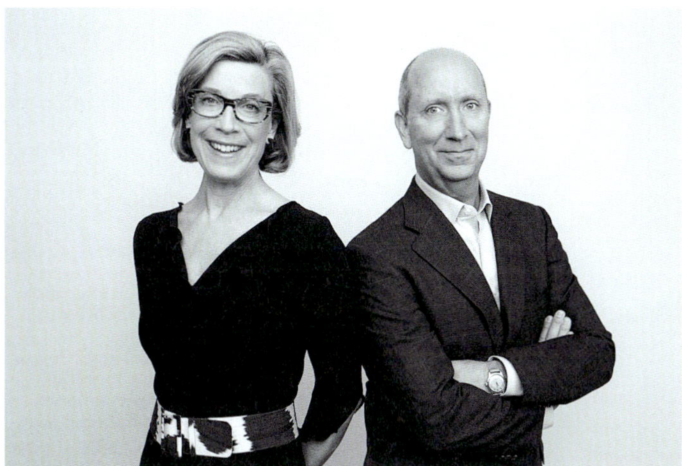

What is your favorite aspect of running a gallery?
Being surrounded by beautiful and challenging objects, and having the opportunity to interact with artists, clients, and the world of people who care about art.

How do you choose the artists you work with?
As in any relationship, both sides have to feel comfortable in their choice. An aspect of that comfort from the gallery side must be an abiding respect for the artist and his or her practice.

If you weren't running a gallery what else would you do?
Find some other way to be surrounded by beautiful, intellectually stimulating objects, and the people who make them.

- **Contact** Van Doren Waxter
Dorsey Waxter
dorsey@vandorenwaxter.com
- **Established** 1999
- **Owner(s) / Partner(s)** John Van Doren
Dorsey Waxter
- **Team** 10
- **Space(s)** 276 m²
- **Artists at Art Basel** Joseph Cornell
Tim Davis
Richard Diebenkorn
Manny Farber
Sam Francis
Helen Frankenthaler
Joe Goode
Al Held
Ellsworth Kelly
John McLaughlin
Dorothea Rockburne
Pat Steir

- **Further artists represented**
  Frank Stella
  James Brooks
  Anthony Caro
  John Chamberlain
  Tim Davis
  Richard Diebenkorn
  Jean Dubuffet
  Manny Farber
  Judy Fiskin
  Sam Francis
  Helen Frankenthaler
  Katsura Funakoshi
  Alexander Gorlizki
  Al Held
  Hans Hofmann
  Ellsworth Kelly
  Eva Lundsager
  Cameron Martin
  John McLaughlin
  Joan Mitchell
  Robert Motherwell
  Georgia O'Keeffe
  Dorothea Rockburne
  Ed Ruscha
  Alan Shields
  Alexis Smith
  David Smith

---

van Orsouw

Zurich  Galleries

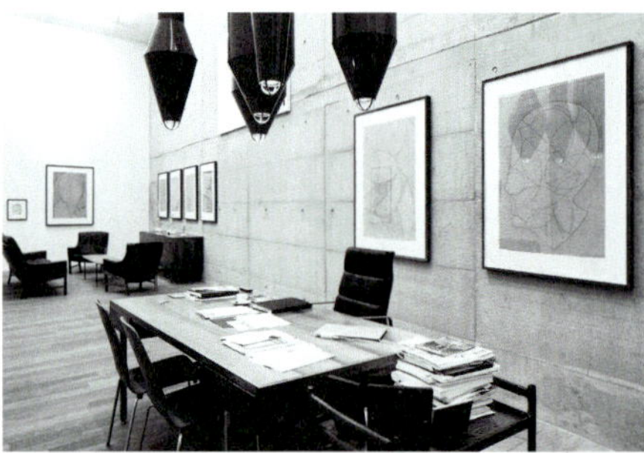

What is your favorite aspect of running a gallery?
Being connected daily with interesting and fascinating people spanning the arts and beyond, including fashion, design, music, publishing, etc. No day looks like another; so, the fact that I know that tomorrow anything could happen is my favorite aspect.

How do you choose the artists you work with?
I trust my instincts; believing in myself and what I read, see, hear, and smell. For me art involves all the senses.

If you weren't running a gallery what else would you do?
Thankfully I have no answer to this question, because I run a gallery and I am more than grateful for this.

- **Contact**
  Galerie Bob van Orsouw
  Bob van Orsouw
  mail@bobvanorsouw.ch
- **Established** 1988
- **Owner(s) / Partner(s)** Bob van Orsouw
- **Team** 6
- **Space(s)** 280 m²
- **Artists at Art Basel**
  Cristian Andersen
  Marcel van Eeden
  Anton Henning
  Klaas Kloosterboer
  Lutz & Guggisberg
  Paul Morrison
  Muntean/Rosenblum
  Julian Opie
  Albrecht Schnider
  Shirana Shahbazi
  Nedko Solakov
  Bernard Voïta
- **Further artists represented**
  Philipp Akkerman
  Nobuyoshi Araki
  Alexander Birchler
  Ger van Elk
  Hannah Greely
  Teresa Hubbard
  Daido Moriyama
  Ernesto Neto
  Walter Pfeiffer

Vermelho

São Paulo 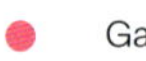 Galleries

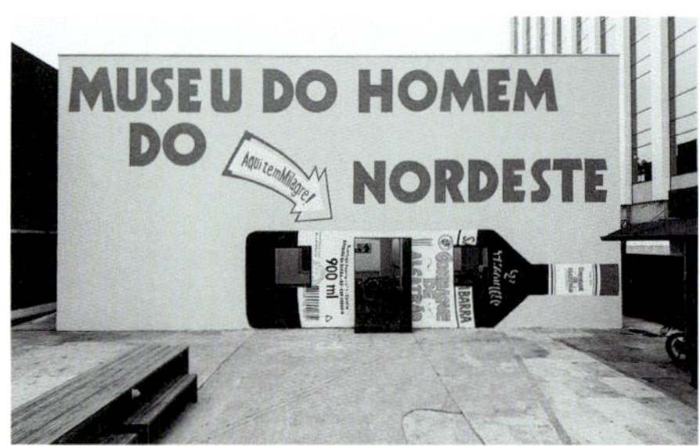

What is your favorite aspect of running a gallery?
Eduardo Brandão: Promoting art where it is not normally shown and making it reach places where it does not easily go.

How do you choose the artists you work with?
To start with, I have to admire the artist as a person.

If you weren't running a gallery what else would you do?
Gardening.

- **Contact**
  Vermelho
  Jan Fjeld
  jan@galeriavermelho.com.br
- **Established** 2002
- **Owner(s) / Partner(s)**
  Eduardo Brandão
  Eliana Finkelstein
- **Team** 17
- **Space(s)** 1,000 m²
- **Artists at Art Basel**
  Gabriela Albergaria
  Jonathas de Andrade
  Claudia Andujar
  Chiara Banfi
  Rodrigo Braga
  Cadu
  Lia Chaia
  Cia. de Foto
  Marcelo Cidade
  Marilá Dardot
  Dias & Riedweg
  Chelpa Ferro
  Carmela Gross
  Maurício Ianês
  Enrique Ježik
  André Komatsu
  Detanico Lain
  Dora Longo Bahia
  Cinthia Marcelle
  Odires Mlászho
  Leya Mira Brander
  Fabio Morais
  Gisela Motta & Leandro Lima
  Rosângela Rennó
  Nicolás Robbio
  Daniel Senise
  Ana Maria Tavares
  Carla Zaccagnini
- **Further artists represented**
  Ivan Argote
  Rafael Assef
  Nicolás Bacal
  Henrique César
  Clara Ianni
  João Loureiro
  Guilherme Peters
  Marco Paulo Rolla

Verna

Zurich  Galleries

What is your favorite aspect of running a gallery?
Art and beauty.

How do you choose the artists you work with?
We don't choose, it is an organic development related to art history.

If you weren't running a gallery what else would you do?
Look at art.

- **Contact**
  Annemarie Verna Galerie
  Gianfranco Verna
  office@annemarie-verna.ch

- **Established** 1969
- **Owner(s) / Partner(s)** Annemarie & Gianfranco Verna
- **Team** 3
- **Space(s)** 100 m²
- **Artists at Art Basel** James Bishop, Antonio Calderara, Andreas Christen, Joseph Egan, Dan Flavin, Richard Francisco, Donald Judd, Sol LeWitt, Robert Mangold, Rita McBride, Giulio Paolini, Sylvia Plimack Mangold, David Rabinowitch, Glen Rubsamen, Fred Sandback, Richard Tuttle, Robert Wilson, Jerry Zeniuk
- **Further artists represented** Agnes Martin, Mario Merz, Ree Morton

Vielmetter

Culver City

- Galleries
- Feature
- Unlimited
- Galleries

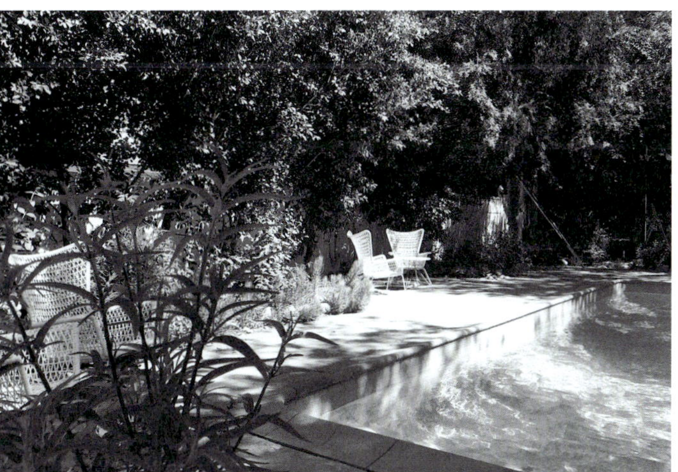

What is your favorite aspect of running a gallery?

I love working with artists. There is no place in the art world where you work more closely and directly with an artist than at a gallery. I enjoy both the daily decisions that I make in collaboration with an artist, as well the as the farther reaching long-term decisions on how to build a lasting career. A gallery is a small, ever-changing universe, and as it has grown it has challenged me on many different levels—there is never a dull moment!

How do you choose the artists you work with?

I listen a lot to artists I respect—they are often more connected to what is going on in terms of new emerging talents. I expect a serious engagement, hard work, and a mature studio practice—and I look for a unique visual language that has enough weight to carry through a lifetime career. It is extremely important to me that my program reflects a rich cultural diversity and I pay attention that we include an equal number of male and female artists.

If you weren't running a gallery what else would you do?

Running a gallery means coaching incredibly talented creative people. If I weren't running a gallery I would be coaching incredibly talented creative people in another context. In my free time, I love gardening and having guests over to my house, so if I had more time, I would start an art hotel in Los Angeles that included an organic café.

- **Contact** Susanne Vielmetter Los Angeles Projects, Kevin Scholl, kevin@vielmetter.com
- **Established** 2000
- **Owner(s) / Partner(s)** Susanne Vielmetter
- **Team** 9
- **Space(s)** 418 m²
- **Artists at Art Basel** Edgar Arceneaux, Andrea Bowers, Jedediah Caesar, Nicole Eisenman, Charles Gaines, Monique van Genderen, Raffi Kalenderian, Rodney McMillian, Wangechi Mutu, Ruben Ochoa, Steve Roden, Amy Sillman, Mickalene Thomas, Nicola Tyson, Tam Van Tran, Patrick Wilson
- **Further artists represented** My Barbarian, Whitney Bedford, Sean Duffy, Karl Haendel, Jutta Koether, Olga Koumoundouros, Shana Lutker, Dave McKenzie, Yunhee Min, Elizabeth Neel, Mary Reid Kelley, Dasha Shishkin

Vitamin

Guangzhou
Beijing

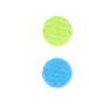

- Galleries
- Galleries Unlimited

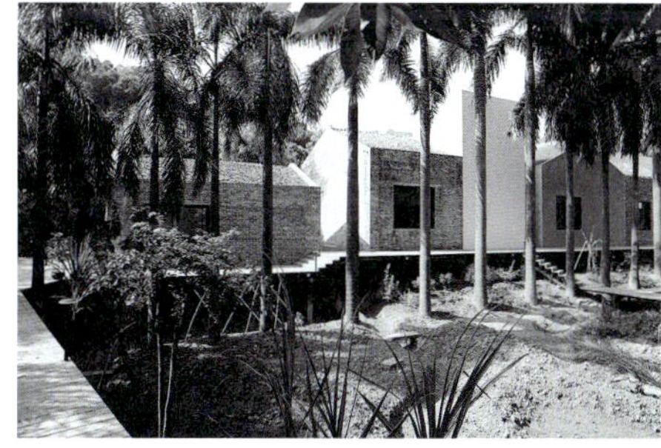

What is your favorite aspect of running a gallery?

The double life.

How do you choose the artists you work with?

Yuanfen (fate, destiny, coincidence ...).

If you weren't running a gallery what else would you do?

Perhaps be a farmer.

- **Contact** Vitamin Creative Space, Chuan Yan, brookeyan@vitamincreativespace.com
- **Established** 2002
- **Owner(s) / Partner(s)** Zhang Wei
- **Artists at Art Basel** Cao Fei, Hao Liang, Sou Fujimoto, Zheng Guogu, Zhou Tao
- **Further artists represented** Tarek Atoui, Heman Chong, Chu Yun, Danh Vo, Duan Jianyu, Olafur Eliasson, Koki Tanaka, Firenze Lai, Lee Kit, Lu Chunsheng, Ming Wong, Pak Sheung Chuen, Xu Tan, Yangjiang Group, Jun Yang

Annemarie Verna Galerie

Interview with Annemarie & Gianfranco Verna

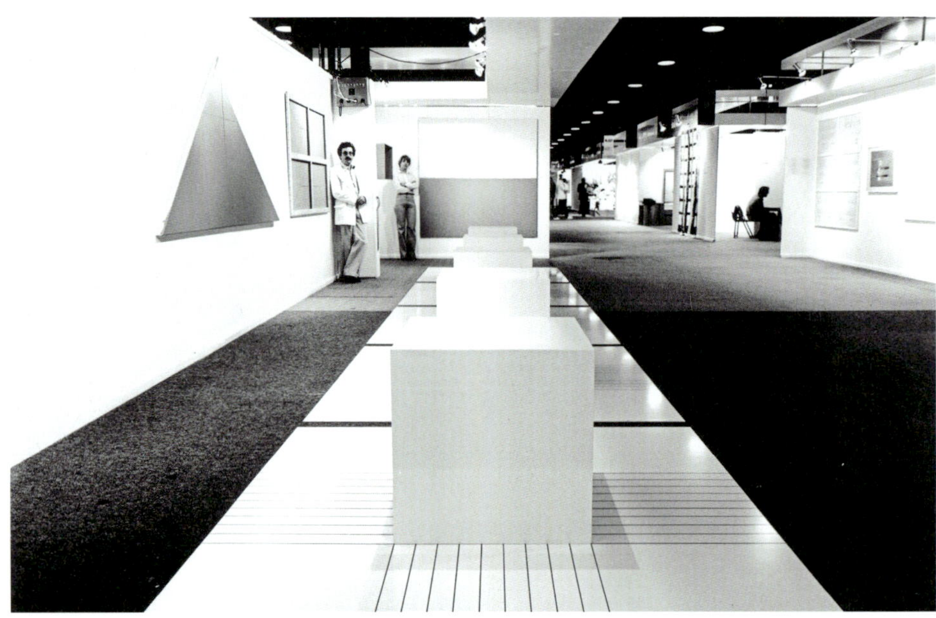

Art Basel, 1977

You founded the gallery in 1969. How did this happen and who were the first artists you invited?

Annemarie Verna: At that time, everything was different: you didn't have a "plan" to open a gallery, you just observed other galleries function and got into the system yourself … We had absolutely no experience, just enthusiasm!

Gianfranco Verna: We were in Paris from 1964 to 1966 and we visited all the galleries; Annemarie started saying she wanted to open her own. I told her it was impossible, that we needed money for the space, the frames, the lamps, etc. But she really insisted. It was the end of Paris as the capital of the art world, but it was still an interesting moment. We tried to find a job in Paris but it didn't work so we came back to Switzerland. After several experiences with a group of partners, we created our own gallery. Our first show was with a group of Bernese artists associated with Harald Szeemann, probably the most advanced group of Swiss artists at that time. We thought that you just needed a price list for people to buy something—but nobody was buying. After a year, the little money we had saved was gone.

AV: But I remained convinced and continued to tell Gianfranco to be patient and that our next show would be successful.

GV: From the beginning, and it was confirmed with time, the idea for the gallery was almost to have a space, and to offer artists the possibility to show their work in it. They could come and work in the space, freely. The first artists we showed were Antonio Calderara in 1969 and Fred Sandback, very early on, in 1971.

Art Basel, 1988

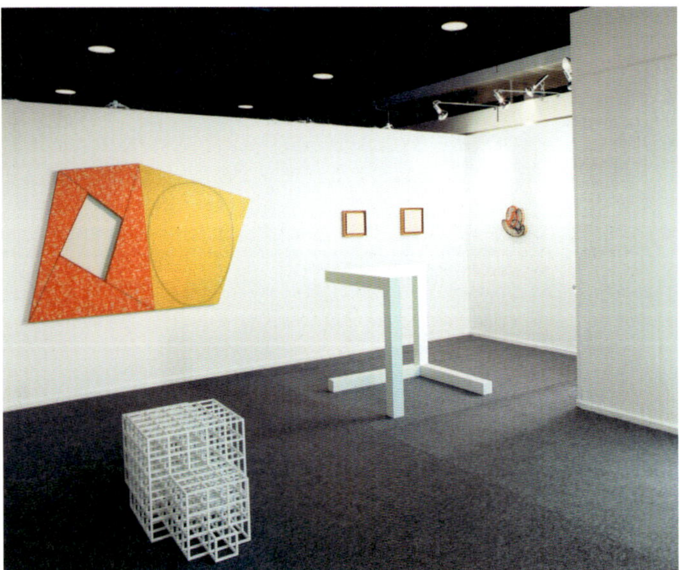

You also exhibited Dan Flavin and Donald Judd. This piece by the latter in your booth is titled *To the Vernas on opening a new …*

AV: This work dates from 1993. It was when done for his show in our then new space on Neptunstrasse, where we still are. Flavin was thrilled at the idea that we would open this new space with this work and he dedicated the show to us. He never decided about the colors, he was very sick at the time and wasn't able to travel anymore: we were waiting for his phone call, we had all the constructions on the walls, waiting for him to tell us whether it should be green or blue. And then at the last minute, before the opening, he told us what combinations he wanted …

Can you tell us about the gallery's initial program? Did you show a lot of Swiss artists?

AV: We had almost no Swiss artists actually, and it was a bit problematic, because people in Zurich didn't like the fact that we were rather showing Americans and Italians. We didn't have a supportive relationship with the audience there. People like Max Bill and artists of his generation came to the openings much more than younger artists, and even though I'm not sure they really understood or liked what we were showing, they were curious and interested. And maybe a little anxious about this new art, a form of competition to Concrete art. When Judd came to Zurich, he went to see Max Bill and I think they admired each other's lifestyle, their curiosity about art, and collecting it. Max Bill was one of the few people who bought two small pieces at the first Judd exhibition in 1973. He also bought Piero Manzoni. But it was a very hard time for us, at least until the mid-1980s.

Do you remember your first participations at Art Basel during the 1970s?

AV: We started to attend the fair in 1971. There were many local galleries, though few of good quality and with ambitious programs. It wasn't so international until the American galleries came. But the most interesting thing is that galleries with similar interests could get to know each other. It was more a community than a power play.

Did you buy at Art Basel?

AV: We had no money. But since there were so few sales, we tried to buy things from the artists we were showing. We started early on to buy one thing in each exhibition. Our collection is now a nice memory of the projects we did. For a long period of time, the prices were very reasonable; you didn't need to be rich to buy artworks. You certainly had to have some money, but you didn't need millions. A lot of European collectors were doctors, lawyers, they had good jobs and a little extra money. This was the Art Basel audience for quite a time.

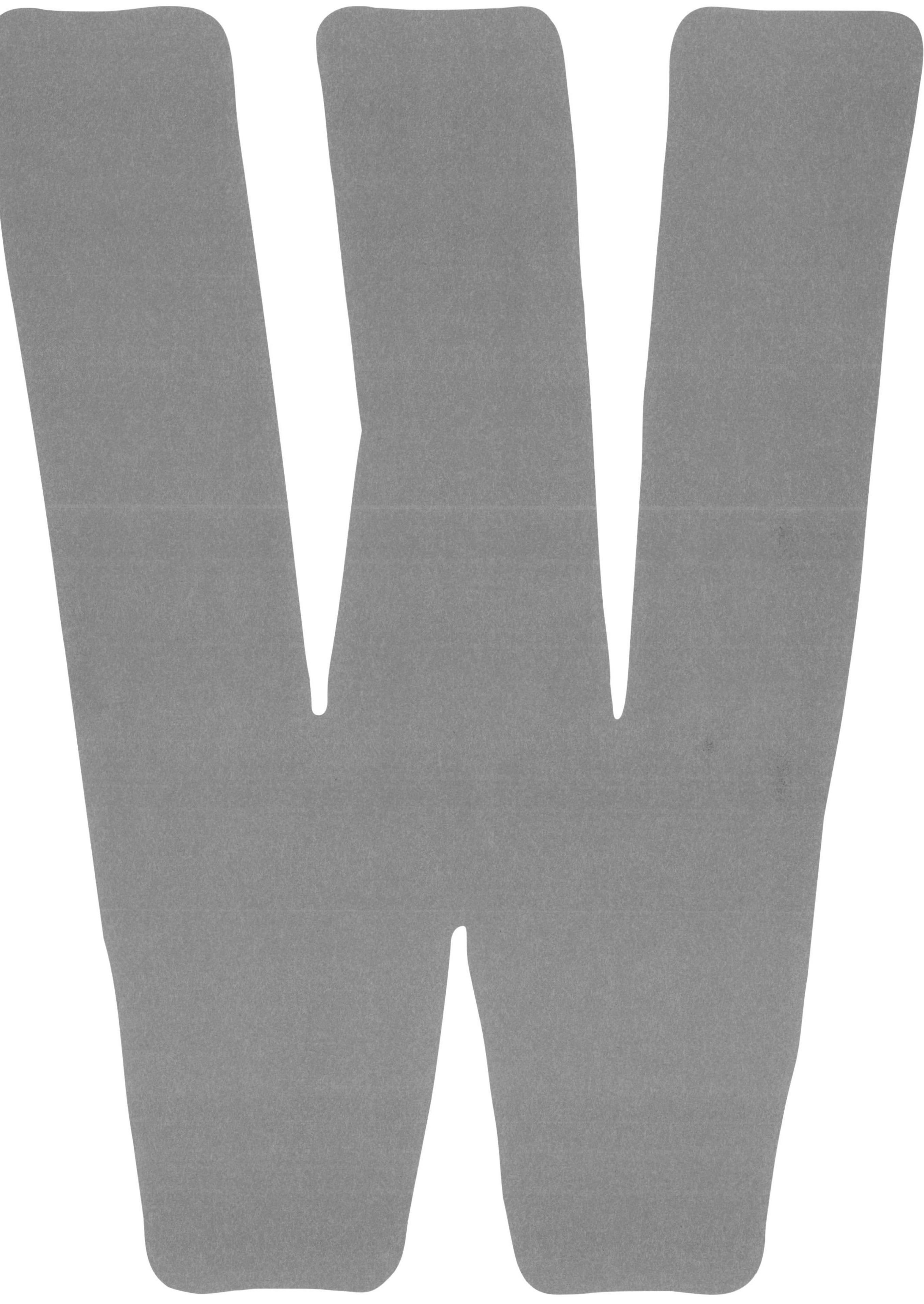

Basel photographer Kurt Wyss has covered the Art Basel fair since its inception. He is known for portraiture as well as his interest in art and his friendship with many artists, and his archive thus documents each edition since 1970. For this portfolio, we have selected photographs from the 1990s: they chronicle the decade during which Art Basel became the center of the art world.

KURT WYSS

Pipilotti Rist
Bankverein Prize Winner
Art 25 Basel
1994

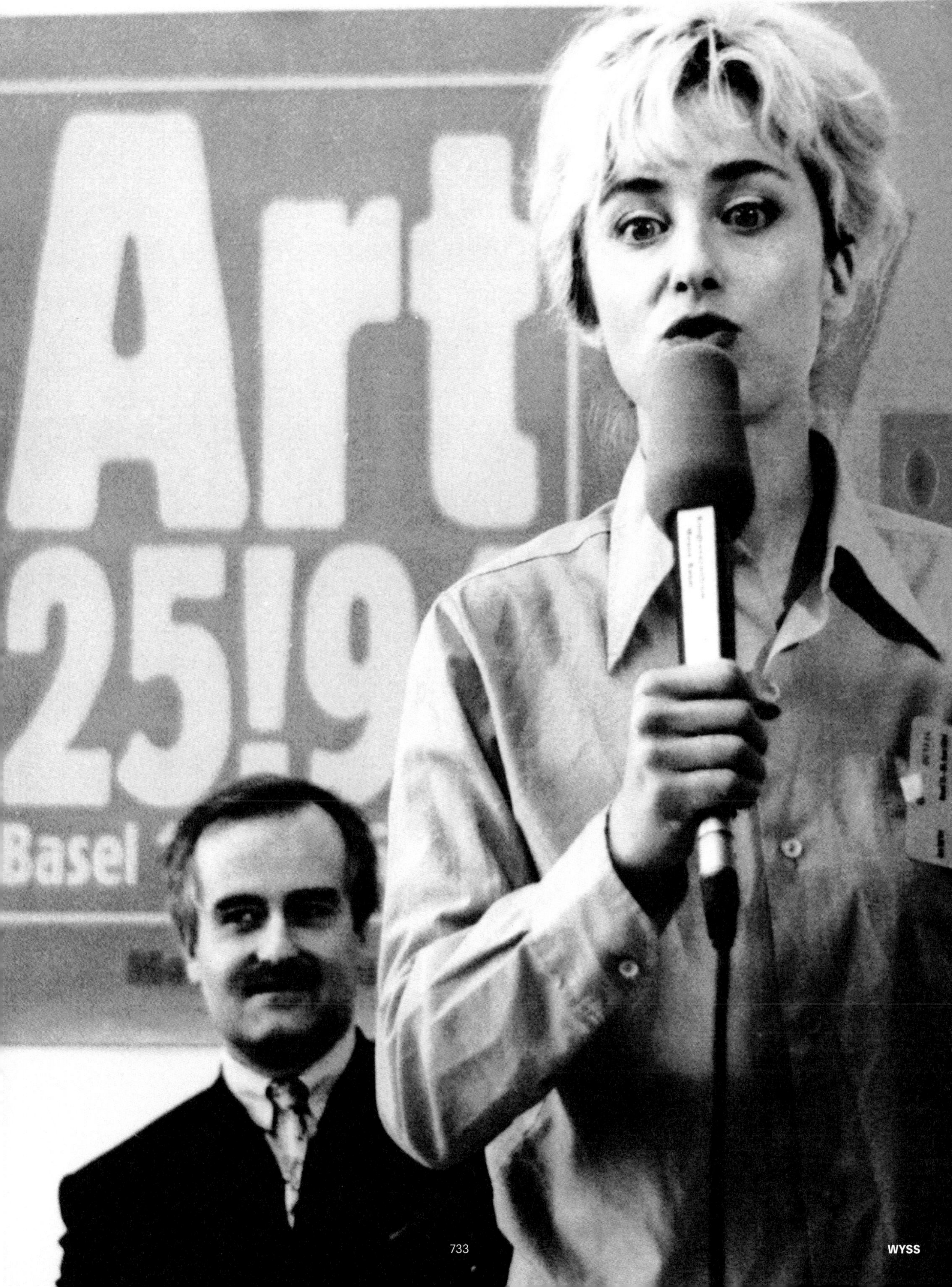

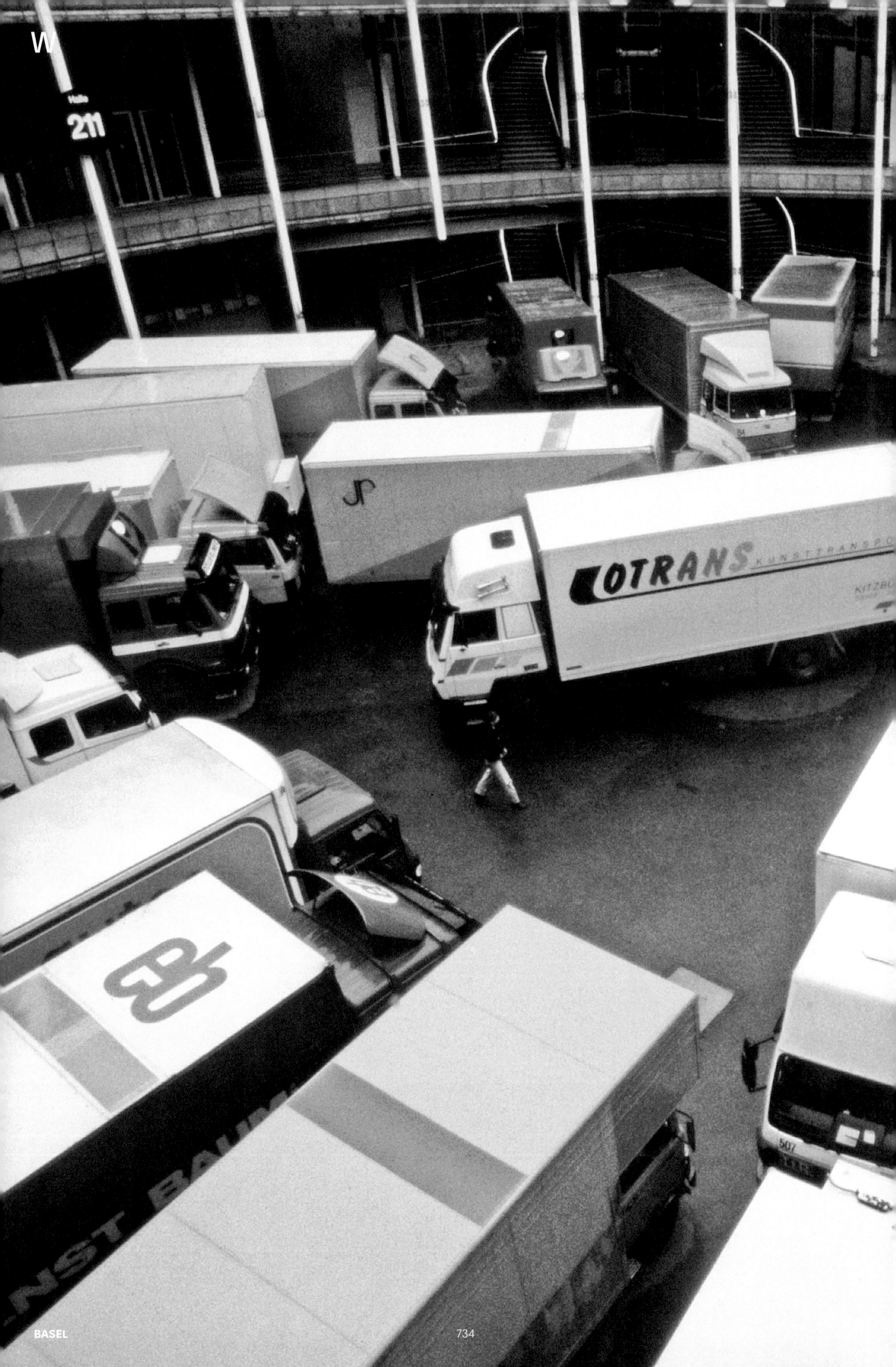
Halle
211
COTRANS KUNSTTRANSPO
KITZBÜ
507

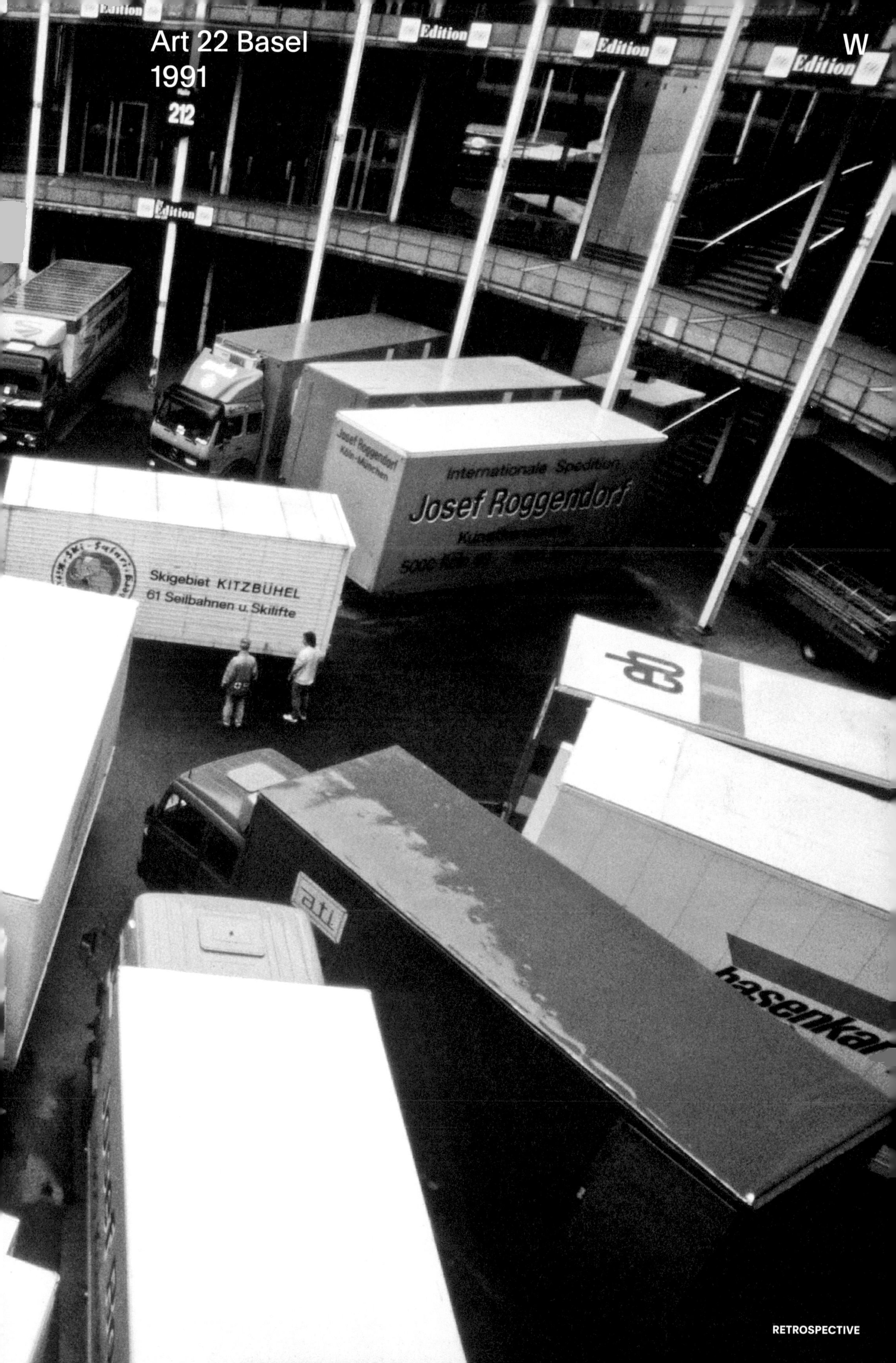

Art 22 Basel
1991

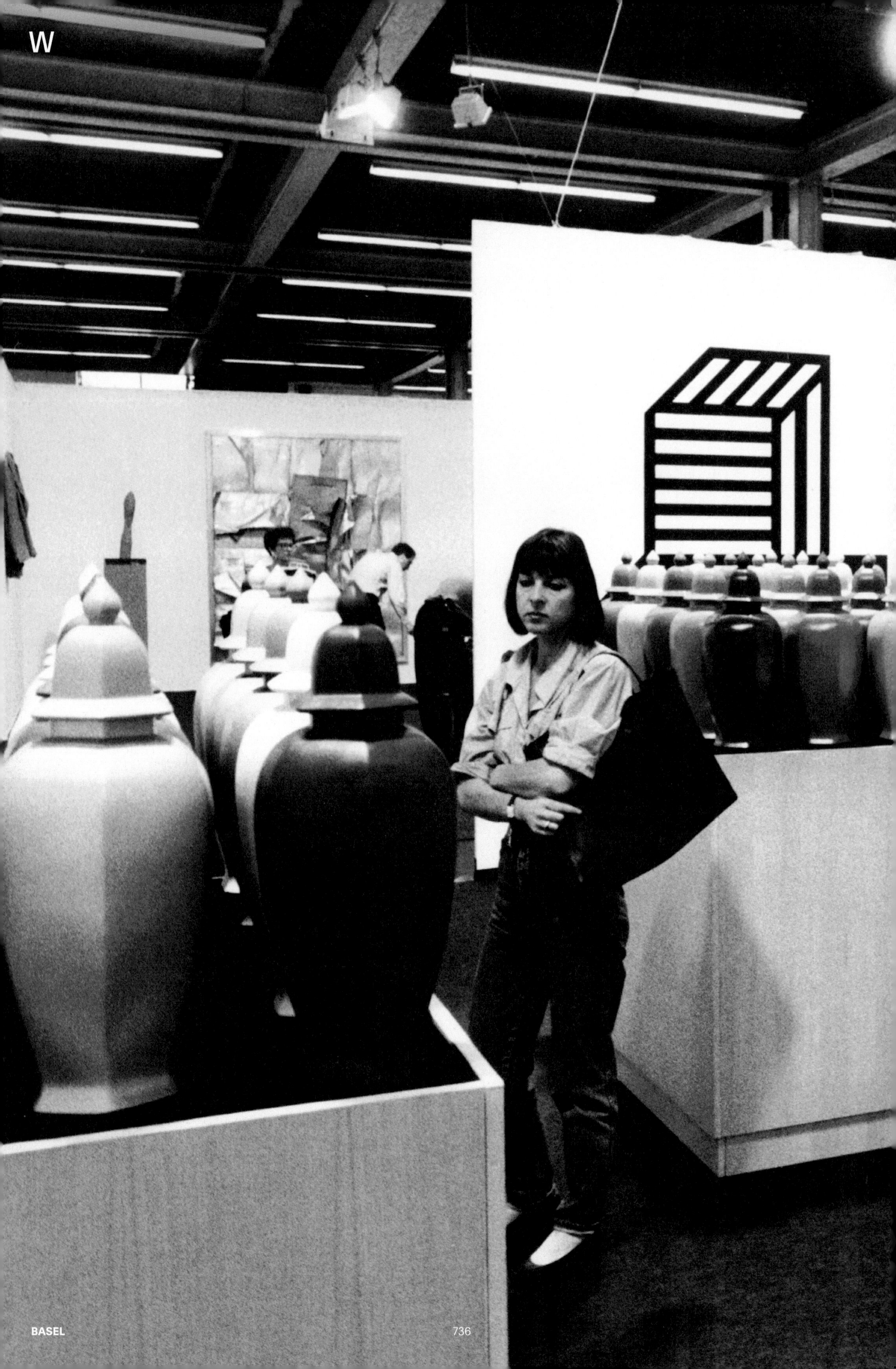

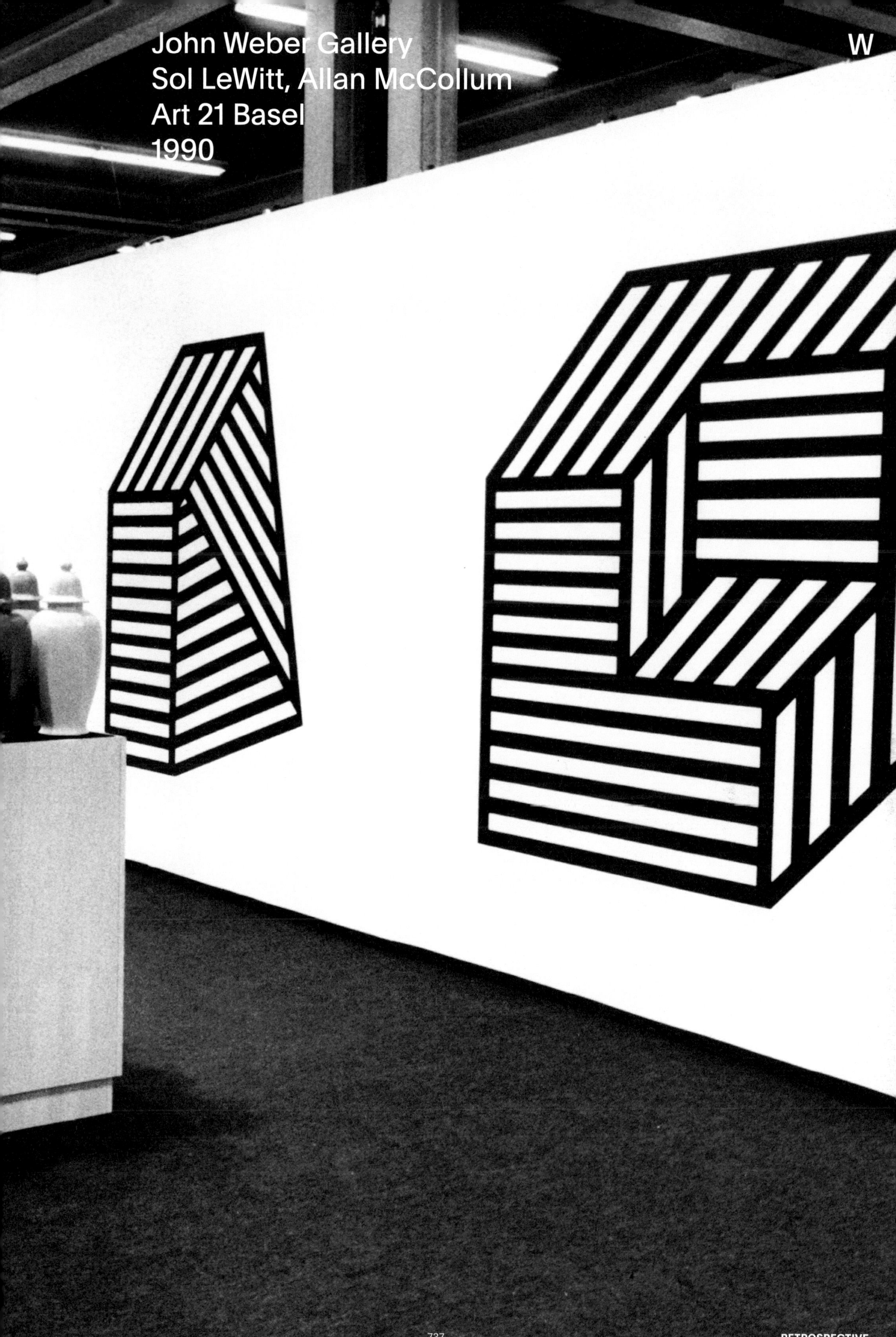

John Weber Gallery
Sol LeWitt, Allan McCollum
Art 21 Basel
1990

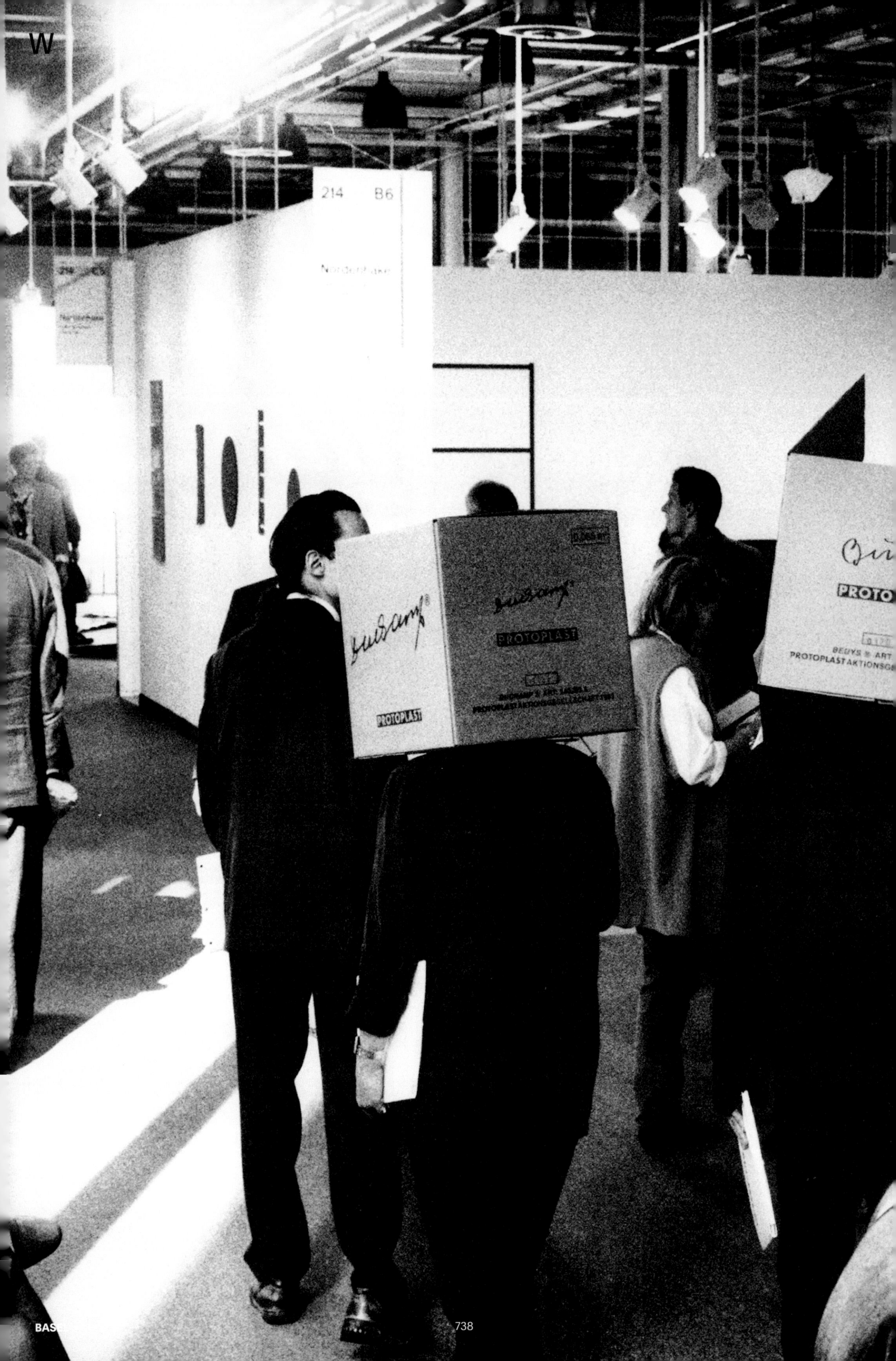
214 B6
PROTOPLAST
PROTOPLAST
PROTOPLAST
BEUYS & ART

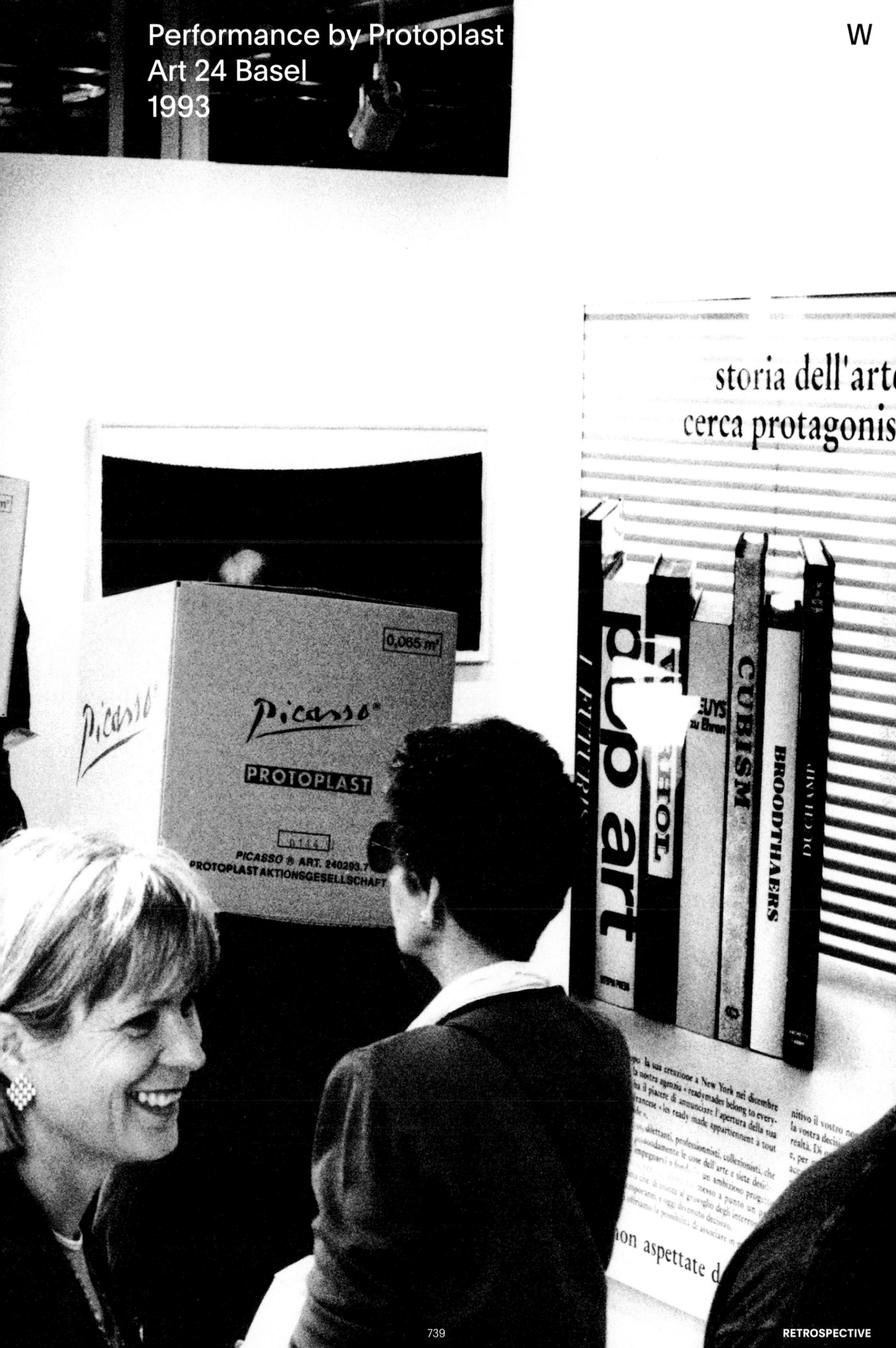

Performance by Protoplast
Art 24 Basel
1993

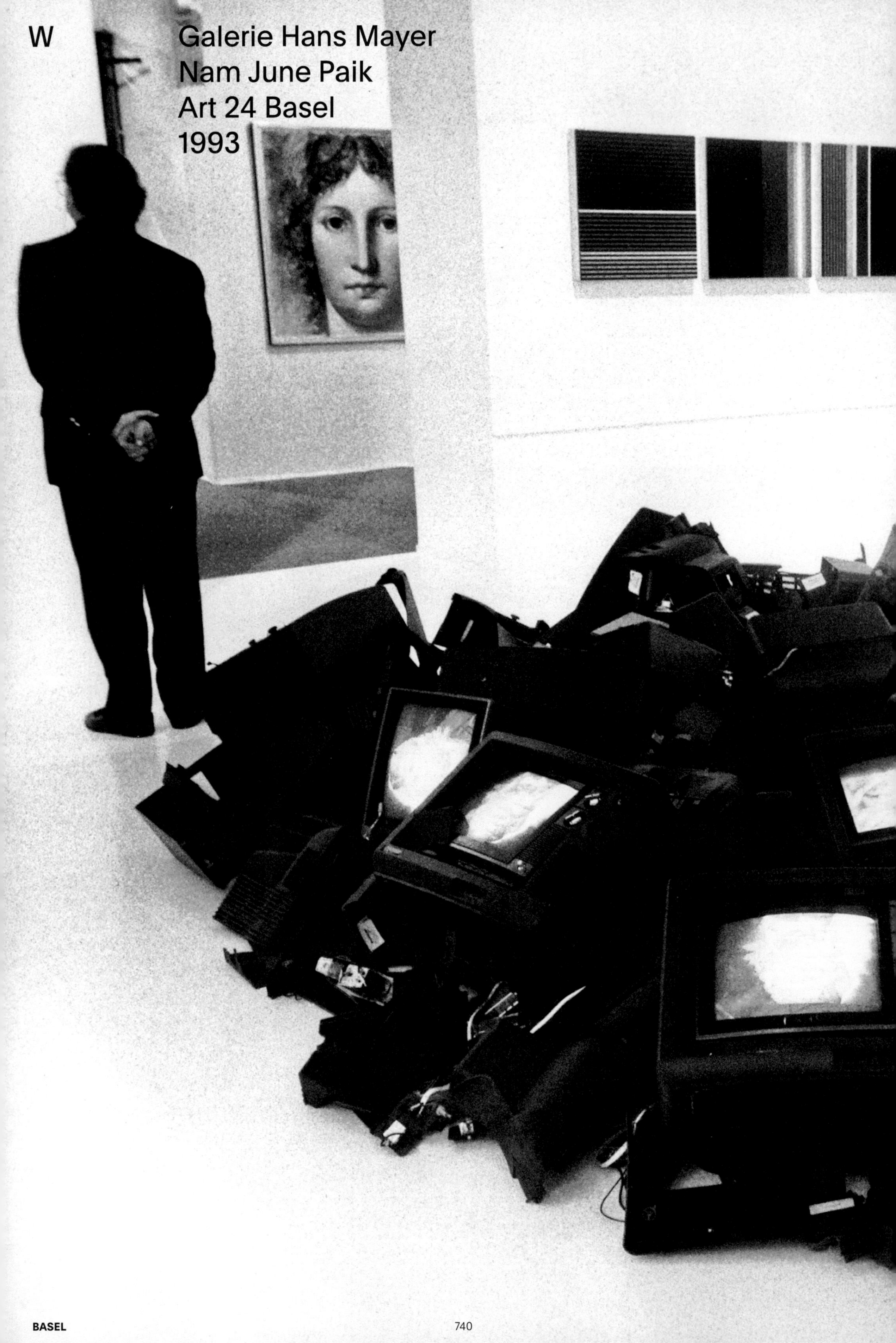

W

Galerie Hans Mayer
Nam June Paik
Art 24 Basel
1993

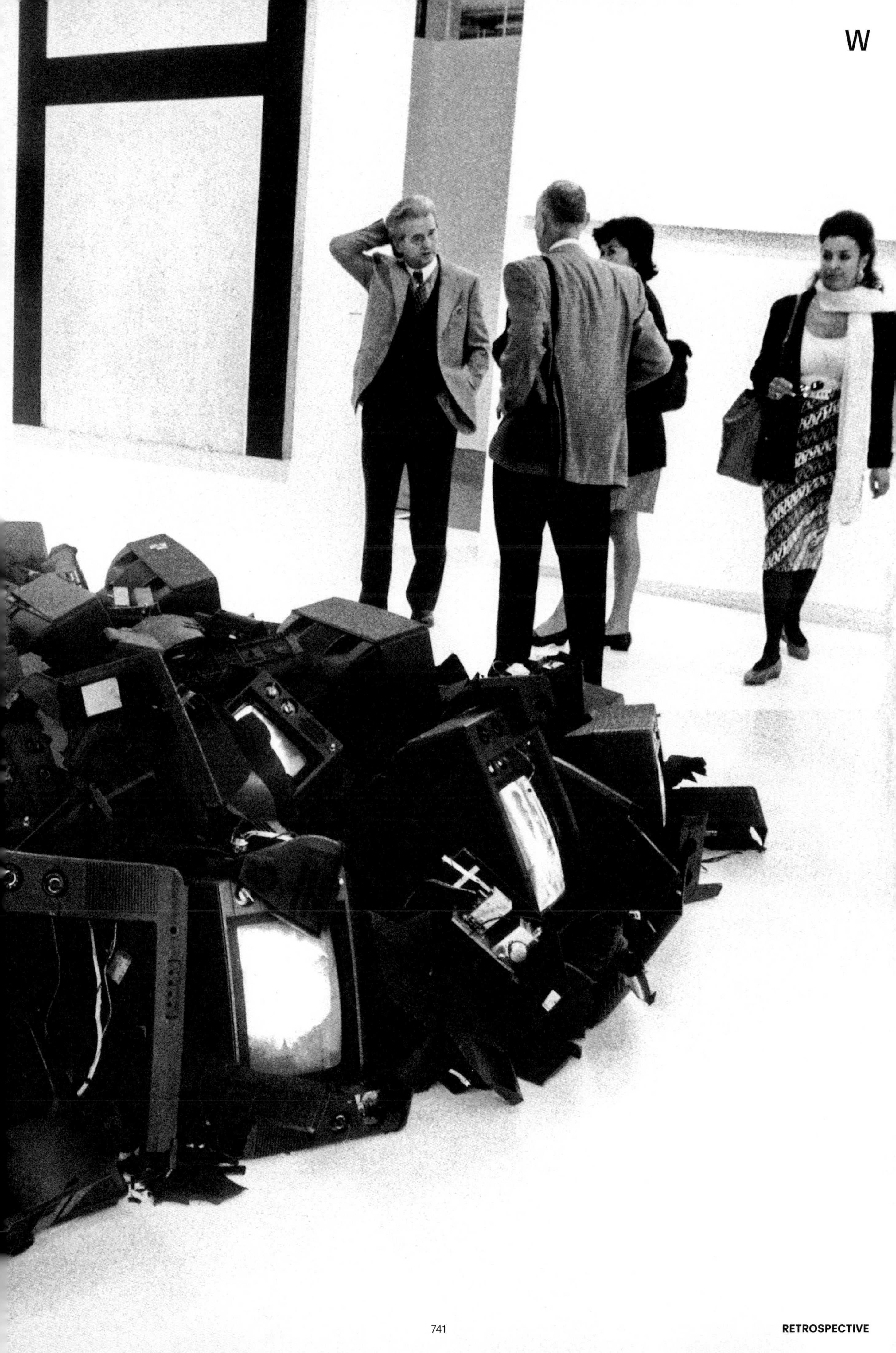

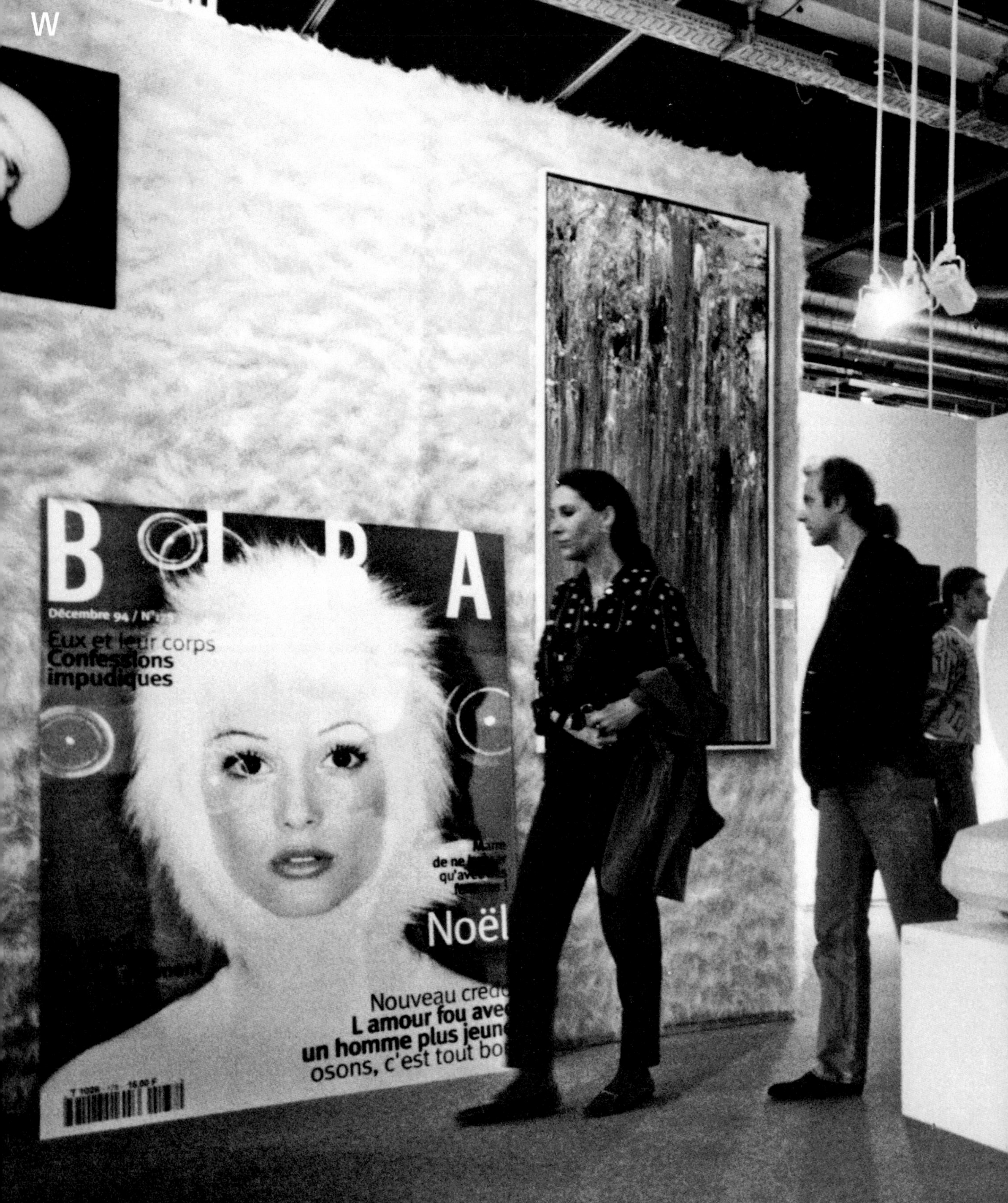
B A
Décembre 94
Eux et leur corps
Confessions
impudiques
Noël
Nouveau credo
L amour fou ave
un homme plus jeune
osons, c'est tout bo

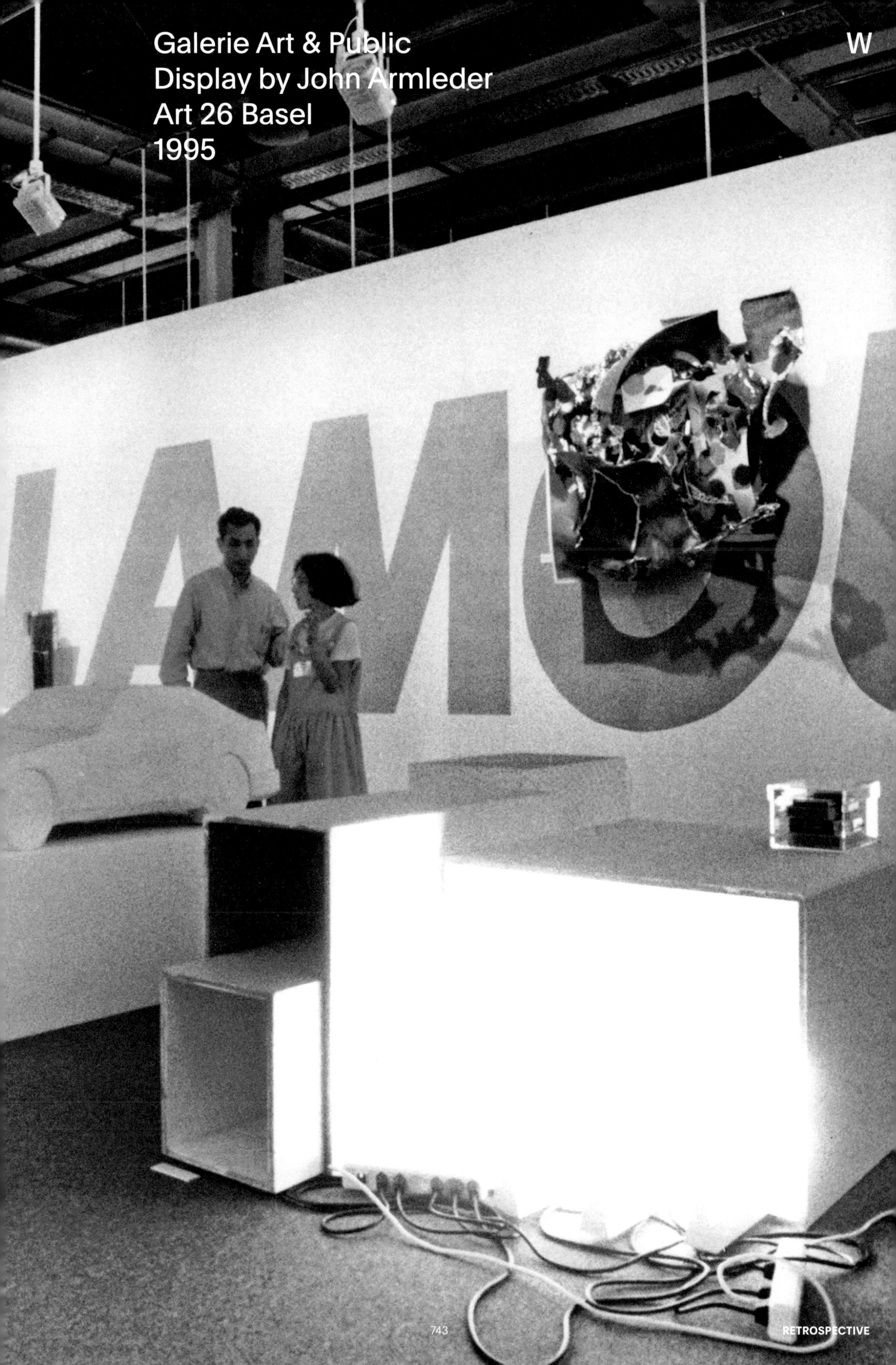

Galerie Art & Public
Display by John Armleder
Art 26 Basel
1995

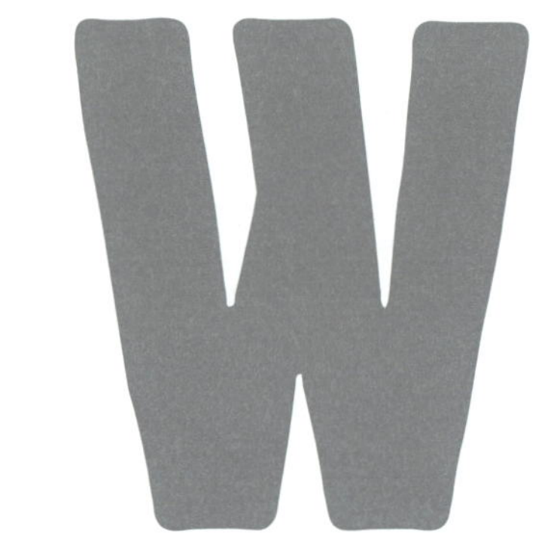

Waddington Custot

London 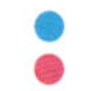 Galleries
Galleries

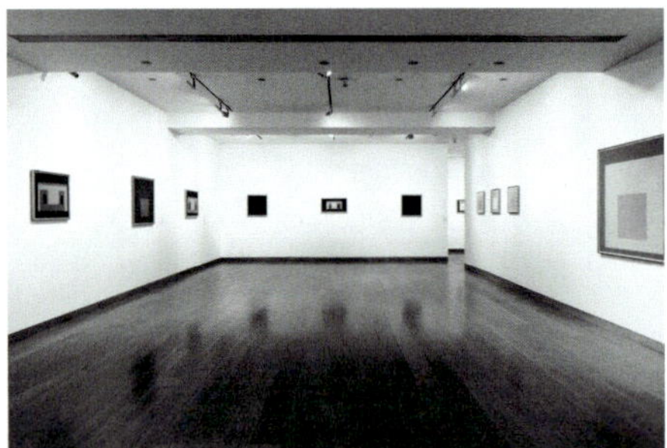

What is your favorite aspect of running a gallery?

Stephane Custot: Above all it's the human interaction. Our business is undeniably a profession of encounters. Encounters with many interesting actors—artists, curators, museums, collectors, fellow gallerists—every day is different, a world in perpetual motion. It's stimulating. Very few industries allow for the combination of business and emotional intelligence; where sensitivity is a strength.

How do you choose the artists you work with?

We have long-term partnerships with artists and estates and are proud to have relationships that have lasted decades. Nothing is short term; we plan and prepare for the future by nurturing our artists now. We've worked with artists who've shaped movements and created change. It has been a privilege to witness this firsthand.

If you weren't running a gallery what else would you do?

I would be a music producer.

- **Contact** Waddington Custot Galleries
Jessica Ramsay
jessica@waddingtoncustot.com
- **Established** 1966
- **Owner(s) / Partner(s)** Leslie Waddington & Stephane Custot
- **Space(s)** 250 m²
- **Artists at Art Basel** Josef Albers
Milton Avery
Peter Blake
Patrick Caulfield
John Chamberlain
Ian Davenport
Jean Dubuffet
Barry Flanagan
Julio González
Peter Halley
Robert Indiana
Henri Matisse
Roberto Matta
Fausto Melotti
Joan Miró
Henry Moore
Ben Nicholson
Pablo Picasso
Robert Rauschenberg
Bridget Riley
Lucas Samaras
Frank Stella
Antoni Tàpies
John Wesley

Wallner

Copenhagen  Galleries
Galleries

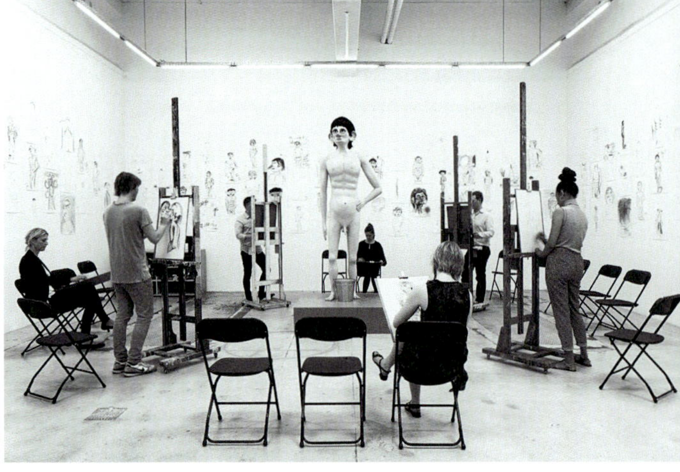

What is your favorite aspect of running a gallery?

Running a gallery has allowed me to combine passion with work. Many of the gallery's artists had their first exhibition with us, and it is a privilege not only to watch them develop, but to work closely with them throughout this ongoing process, allowing for great friendships to develop. The same can be said for artists we have just begun to collaborate with. Besides that, there's nothing like seeing new work when it arrives at the gallery—it is like it is my birthday every day.

How do you choose the artists you work with?

My favorite artists are those that really make me see. I am very interested in artists who have a strong narrative that runs through their work. I am also interested in artists who work with the audience, inviting them to become part of the work. I find both of these aspects very compelling, and am immediately inspired. These are the artists I choose to work with.

If you weren't running a gallery what else would you do?

I can't really think of anything else that would make me as happy as running a gallery would. I suppose if I had to choose it would be something like the President of the United States, or maybe an astronaut. That would be really cool.

- **Contact** Galleri Nicolai Wallner
Marie Gellert Jensen
mgj@nicolaiwallner.com
- **Established** 1993
- **Owner(s) / Partner(s)** Nicolai Wallner
- **Team** 7
- **Space(s)** 1,000 m²
- **Artists at Art Basel** Daniel Buren
Elmgreen & Dragset
Douglas Gordon
Dan Graham
Jeppe Hein
Jakob Kolding
Chris Johanson
Jesper Just
A Kassen
Joachim Koester
Alicja Kwade
Peter Land
Jonathan Monk
Clare Rojas
Christoph Ruckhäberle
Christian Schmidt-Rasmussen
David Shrigley
Glenn Sorensen
Alexander Tovborg
Richard Tuttle
Gitte Villesen

Wallspace

New York 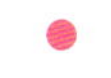 Nova

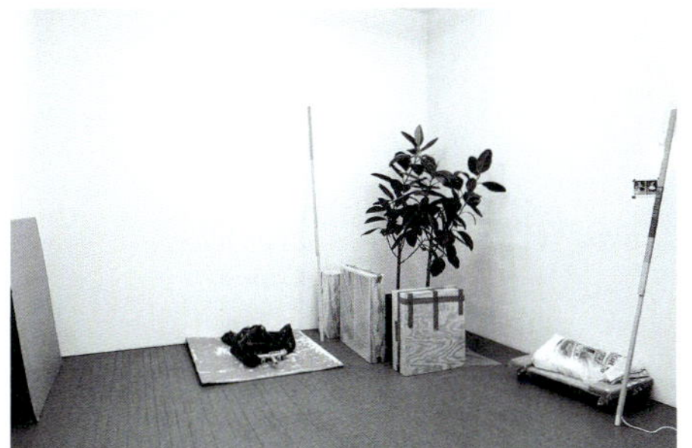

What is your favorite aspect of running a gallery?
Working with artists. Working with our peers and colleagues that make up our community, be they curators, other dealers, writers, or friends.

How do you choose the artists you work with?
A ton of research, and very often the recommendations of our artists.

If you weren't running a gallery what else would you do?
Build a non-collecting institution!

- **Contact** Wallspace
  Nichole Caruso
  nichole@wallspacegallery.com
- **Established** 2003
- **Owner(s) / Partner(s)** Janine Foeller
  Jane Hait
- **Team** 5
- **Space(s)** 186 m²
- **Artists at Art Basel** David Korty
  Nancy Lupo
- **Further artists represented** Ron Amstutz
  Kate Costello
  John Divola
  Harry Dodge
  Shannon Ebner
  Paul Elliman
  Martha Friedman
  Gaylen Gerber
  Daniel Gordon
  Jiří Kovanda
  Scott Olson
  Laura Riboli
  Patricia Treib
  Helen Verhoeven
  Donelle Woolford

Washburn

New York Galleries
Galleries

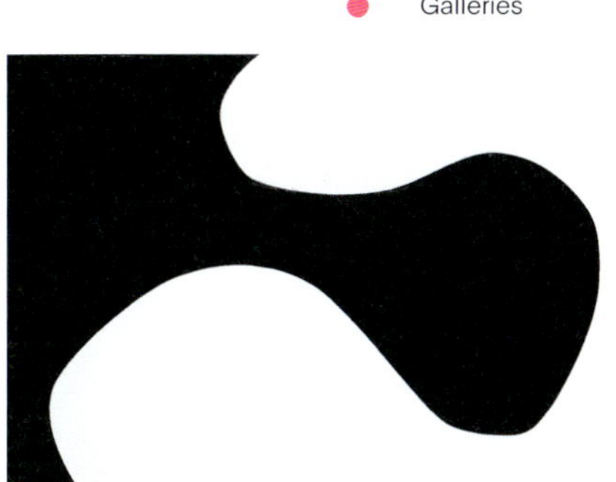

What is your favorite aspect of running a gallery?
Exhibitions. We present the work of artists in frequent chronological exhibitions over years to examine their influences, developments in style, and exploration of media in depth. Each exhibition is accompanied by a brochure with a critical essay and reproductions.

How do you choose the artists you work with?
Quality.

- **Contact** Washburn Gallery
  Brian Washburn
  jwashburn@earthlink.net
- **Established** 1971
- **Owner(s) / Partner(s)** Joan Washburn
- **Team** 4
- **Space(s)** 650 m²
- **Artists at Art Basel** Ilya Bolotowsky
  Nicolas Carone
  Tom Levine
  Alice Trumbull Mason
  Doug Ohlson
  Ray Parker
  Jackson Pollock
  Anne Ryan
  David Smith
  Leon Polk Smith
  Richard Stankiewicz
  Myron Stout
  Jack Youngerman
- **Further artists represented** Norman Bluhm
  Stuart Davis
  Willem de Kooning
  Fritz Glarner
  Gwynn Murrill
  Georgia O'Keeffe
  Richard Pousette-Dart
  Mark Rothko
  Alfred Stieglitz

Wei-Ling

Kuala Lumpur
Penang  Insights

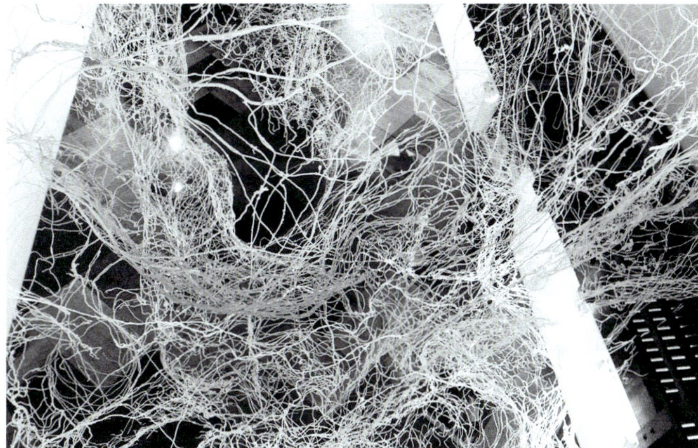

What is your favorite aspect of running a gallery?
I find fulfillment in watching the development and growth of the works and lives of the artists with whom I work. It gives me great joy and moves me no end to see an artwork grow and unfold before my eyes, to understand the reasons behind why a work of art has arrived at where it is, and the inspiration behind it. Artists are my teachers. In my journey, I have learned so much from them and they have generously allowed me a glimpse into their lives and the way they see the world.

How do you choose the artists you work with?
We look to artists who have reached some level of intellectual maturity, have something to "say" in their art, and possess an individual artistic language. To find that language is just the beginning, to constantly push against it, to search and to find, to come to some sort of resolution each time is the relentless journey of an artist.

If you weren't running a gallery what else would you do?
Design jewellery and run an animal sanctuary.

- **Contact** Wei-Ling Gallery
  Shaza Sofi
  weilinggallery@gmail.com
- **Established** 2002
- **Owner(s) / Partner(s)** Lim Wei-Ling
- **Team** 6
- **Space(s)** 1,800 m²
- **Artists at Art Basel** Choy Chun Wei
  Ivan Lam
- **Further artists represented** Claudia Bueno
  Chen Wei Meng
  Cheng Yen Pheng

Chin Kong Yee
Amin Gulgee
Hamidi Hadi
Anurendra Jegadeva
Sean Lean
Hh Lim
Kim Peow Ng
Nor Azizan Rahman Paiman
Rajinder Singh
Wong Chee Meng
Yau Bee Ling
Zulkifli Yusoff

Weingrüll

Karlsruhe ● Discoveries

What is your favorite aspect of running a gallery?
The possibilities.

How do you choose the artists you work with?
If I believe in what they do and they believe in what I do.

If you weren't running a gallery what else would you do?
Probably working for one.

- **Contact** Weingrüll
  Florian Weingrüll
  info@weingruell.com
- **Established** 2010
- **Owner(s) / Partner(s)** Florian Weingrüll
- **Team** 2
- **Space(s)** 160 m²
- **Artists at Art Basel** Sascha Pohle
  Maeghan Reid
- **Further artists represented** Benjamin Appel
  Enrico Bach
  Jakup Ferri
  David Godbold
  Otto D. Handschuh
  Eric Hattan
  Stephanie Kiwitt
  Gabriela Oberkofler
  Sascha Pohle
  Maeghan Reid
  Christian Schmuck

Weiss

Berlin ● Galleries

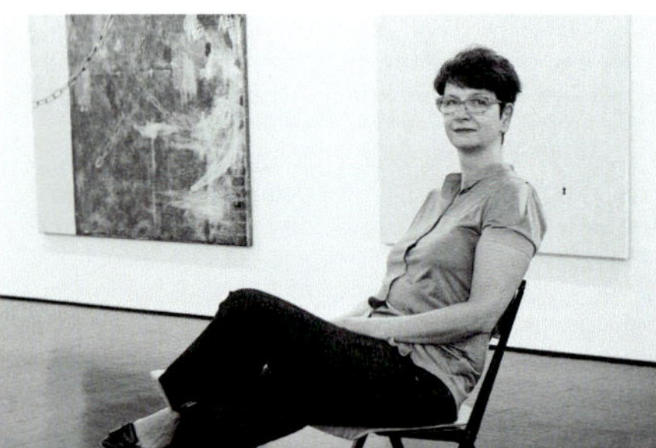

What is your favorite aspect of running a gallery?
The dialogue and collaboration with the artists and their works.

How do you choose the artists you work with?
By their attitude, their work, and their personality.

- **Contact** Galerie Barbara Weiss
  Sophia von Westerholt
  svw@galeriebarbaraweiss.de
- **Established** 1992
- **Owner(s) / Partner(s)** Barbara Weiss
- **Team** 6
- **Space(s)** 600 m²
- **Artists at Art Basel** Monika Baer
  Heike Baranowsky
  Thomas Bayrle
  Geta Brătescu
  Raoul De Keyser
  Maria Eichhorn
  Nicole Eisenman
  Ayşe Erkmen
  Harun Farocki
  Friederike Feldmann
  Berta Fischer
  Mary Heilmann
  Christine & Irene Hohenbüchler
  Laura Horelli
  Jonathan Horowitz
  Boris Mikhailov
  John Miller
  Rebecca Morris
  Deimantas Narkevičius
  Susanne Paesler
  Mai-Thu Perret
  Collier Schorr
  Andreas Siekmann
  Roman Signer
  Niele Toroni
  Suse Weber

Wentrup

Berlin ● Galleries
 Galleries
Public

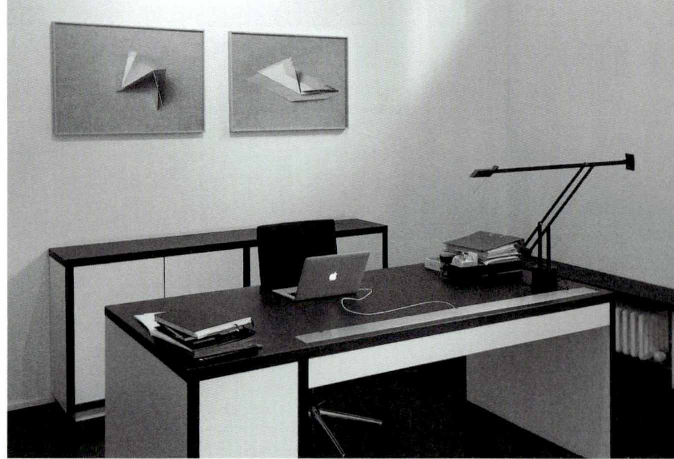

What is your favorite aspect of running a gallery?
Excitement.

How do you choose the artists you work with?
With my eyes, heart, and knowledge.

If you weren't running a gallery what else would you do?
Relax.

- **Contact** Wentrup
  Sascha Welchering
  sascha@wentrupgallery.com
- **Established** 2004
- **Owner(s) / Partner(s)** Tina & Jan Wentrup
- **Team** 6
- **Space(s)** 300 m²
- **Artists at Art Basel** Nevin Aladag
  Miriam Böhm
  Gregor Hildebrandt
  Florian Meisenberg
  Olaf Metzel
  Peles Empire
  Jen Ray
  David Renggli
- **Further artists represented** Cristian Andersen
  Axel Geis
  Mathew Hale
  Wawrzyniec Tokarski
  Timm Ulrichs

Werble

New York

● Statements

What is your favorite aspect of running a gallery?
Working with the artists and realizing the exhibitions.

How do you choose the artists you work with?
Studio visits, recommendations through other artists, open studios.

If you weren't running a gallery what else would you do?
I would be back in school.

- **Contact** Kate Werble Gallery
  Kate Werble
  kate@katewerblegallery.com
- **Established** 2008
- **Owner(s) / Partner(s)** Kate Werble
- **Team** 3
- **Space(s)** 214 m²
- **Artists at Art Basel** Anna Betbeze
- **Further artists represented** Ernesto Burgos
  Christopher Chiappa
  Brock Enright
  Gerard & Kelly
  John Lehr
  Gareth Long
  Rancourt/Yatsuk
  Melanie Schiff
  Molly Smith
  Luke Stettner
  Sarah E. Wood

Werner

New York
London
Märkisch Wilmersdorf

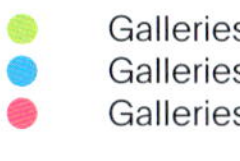

Galleries
Galleries
Galleries

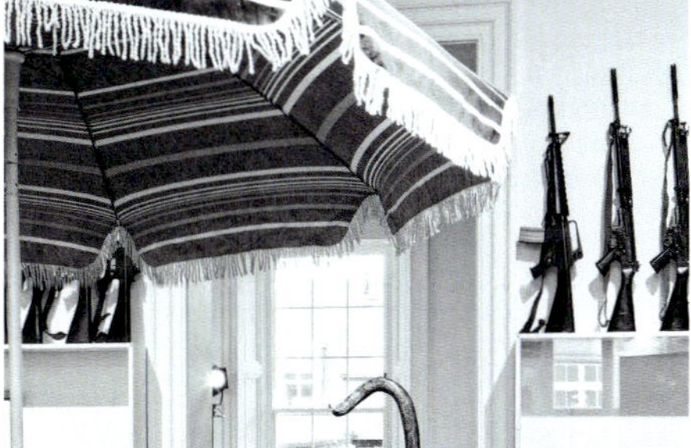

- **Contact** Michael Werner
  Joe Brittain
  joe@michaelwerner.com
- **Established** 1963
- **Owner(s) / Partner(s)** Gordon Veneklasen
  Michael Werner
- **Team** 22
- **Space(s)** 390 m²
- **Artists at Art Basel** Hurvin Anderson
  Georg Baselitz
  Marcel Broodthaers
  Aaron Curry
  Enrico David
  Peter Doig
  Jörg Immendorff
  Per Kirkeby
  James Lee Byars
  Eugène Leroy
  Markus Lüpertz
  Ernst Wilhelm Nay
  A.R. Penck
  Sigmar Polke
  Don Van Vliet
  Michael Williams
- **Further artists represented** Hans Arp
  Joseph Beuys
  Ernst Ludwig Kirchner
  Wilhelm Lehmbruck
  Piero Manzoni
  Francis Picabia
  Kurt Schwitters

White Cube

London
Hong Kong
São Paulo

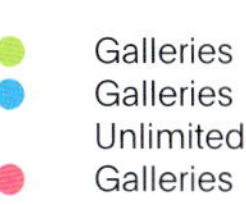

Galleries
Galleries
Unlimited
Galleries

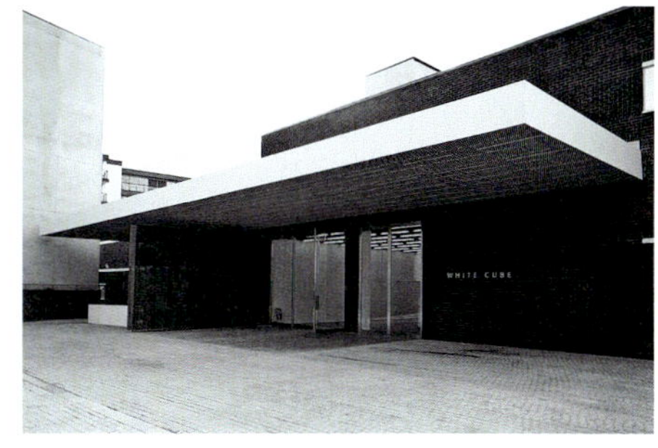

- **Contact** White Cube
  David Chadwick
  davidchadwick@whitecube.com
- **Established** 1993
- **Owner(s) / Partner(s)** Jay Jopling
  Daniela Gareh
  Susan May
  Laura Zhou
  Karla Meneghel
- **Team** 126
- **Space(s)** 5,440 m² (Bermondsey)
  1,110 m² (Mason's Yard)
  550 m² (Hong Kong)
  298 m² (São Paulo)
- **Artists at Art Basel** Franz Ackermann
  Darren Almond
  Ellen Altfest
  Mirosław Bałka
  Georg Baselitz
  Larry Bell
  Ashley Bickerton
  Mark Bradford
  Candice Breitz
  Jake & Dinos Chapman
  Chuck Close
  Gregory Crewdson
  Tracey Emin
  Katharina Fritsch
  Theaster Gates
  Gilbert & George
  Antony Gormley
  Andreas Gursky
  David Hammons
  Mona Hatoum
  Eberhard Havekost
  Damien Hirst
  Gary Hume
  Runa Islam
  Sergej Jensen
  Anselm Kiefer
  Rachel Kneebone
  Friedrich Kunath
  Elad Lassry
  Jac Leirner
  Liu Wei
  Liza Lou
  Christian Marclay
  Kris Martin
  Josiah McElheny
  Julie Mehretu
  Harland Miller
  Sarah Morris
  Gabriel Orozco
  Damián Ortega
  Virginia Overton
  Eddie Peake
  Richard Phillips
  Magnus Plessen
  Marc Quinn
  Jessica Rankin
  Christian Rosa
  Doris Salcedo
  Raqib Shaw
  Haim Steinbach
  Sam Taylor-Johnson
  Fred Tomaselli
  Jeff Wall
  Cerith Wyn Evans
  Zhang Huan

White Space Beijing

Beijing 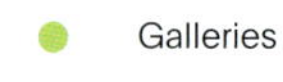 Galleries

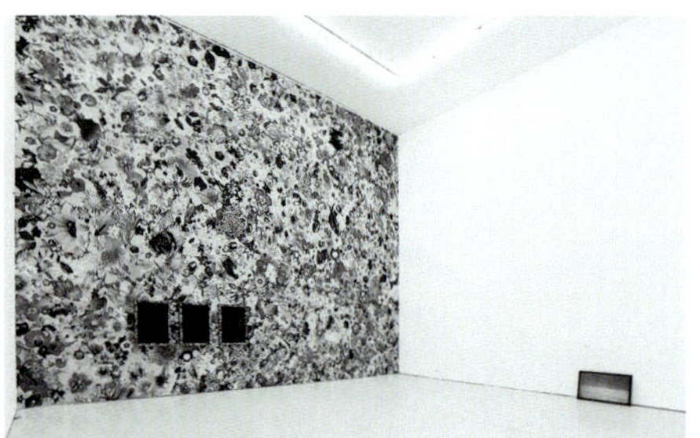

What is your favorite aspect of running a gallery?
Seeing and getting involved in artists' processes.

How do you choose the artists you work with?
I have no standard metrics for choosing artists.

If you weren't running a gallery what else would you do?
I think I would have nothing to do.

- **Contact** White Space Beijing
  Di Zhang
  zhangdi@whitespace-beijing.com
- **Established** 2004
- **Owner(s) / Partner(s)** Tian Yuan
  Zhang Di
- **Team** 6
- **Space(s)** 1,110 m²
- **Artists at Art Basel** Gao Lei
  Gao Ludi
  He Xiangyu
  Jian Ce
  Li Jingxiong
  Li Shurui
  Liu Ren
  Liu Shiyuan
  Liu Wentao
  Liu Xinyi
  Shi Zhiying
  Xie Fan
  Xie Lei
  Wang Haiyang
  Wang Qiang
  Yang Jian
  Zhai Liang
  Zhang Ruyi
- **Further artists represented** Ignacio Uriarte
  Xing Jun Qin

Wigram

London 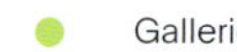 Galleries

- **Contact** Max Wigram Gallery
  Sophie Braine
  sophie@maxwigram.com
- **Established** 2001
- **Owner(s) / Partner(s)** Max Wigram

. Wilkinson

London 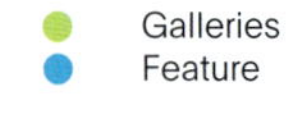 Galleries
Feature

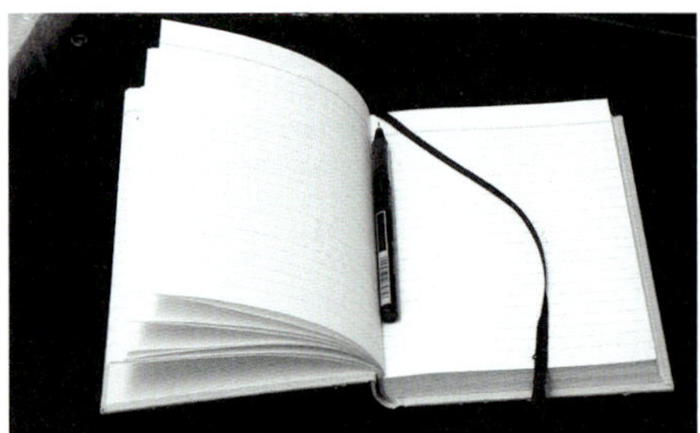

What is your favorite aspect of running a gallery?
The best part of running a gallery is having the opportunity to present exhibitions. It is an honor to work alongside artists and watch their ideas develop and careers grow. The relationship between an artist and a gallery is complex, sometimes stressful, but ultimately rewarding, and the dialogue and exchange is an ongoing learning process. It is through the planning and execution of exhibitions that we become close to the artists, allowing us to fully articulate their work.

How do you choose the artists you work with?
We find artists by having conversations with other artists, writers, and curators, constantly traveling and looking at exhibitions. We look for individuality, artists who have the strength and commitment to have their own voice without following trends either in terms of the market or contemporary art theory. In a world abundant with information, visual and otherwise, it is becoming more challenging for artists to define a position where their work will be seen and heard.

If you weren't running a gallery what else would you do?
Many of our artists write or use text as part of their practice and we have just started working with a writer, Travis Jeppesen (including him in our list as we would a gallery artist), as an experiment to explore the act of writing and use of text in the visual field. If we didn't have a gallery we might become a literary agent or a publisher.

- **Contact** Wilkinson
  Rhian Smith
  rhian@wilkinsongallery.com
- **Established** 2001
- **Owner(s) / Partner(s)** Amanda Wilkinson
  & Anthony Wilkinson
- **Team** 6
- **Space(s)** 550 m²
- **Artists at Art Basel** Dara Birnbaum
  Heman Chong
  Joan Jonas
  Sung Hwan Kim
  Elizabeth Magill
  Jewyo Rhii
  George Shaw
  Laurie Simmons
  Shimabuku
  Phoebe Unwin
- **Further artists represented** Mark Alexander
  Juliette Bonneviot
  Matt Calderwood
  Clegg & Guttmann
  Jimmy De Sana
  AK Dolven
  Harm van den Dorpel
  Matthew Higgs
  Estate of Derek Jarman
  Travis Jeppesen
  Tillman Kaiser
  Ilja Karilampi
  Thoralf Knobloch
  Makiko Kudo
  Marcin Maciejowski
  Renzo Martens
  Ciprian Muresan
  Anna Parkina
  Barbara Probst
  Estate of Ketty La Rocca
  Silke Schatz

Winter

Vienna 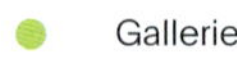 Galleries

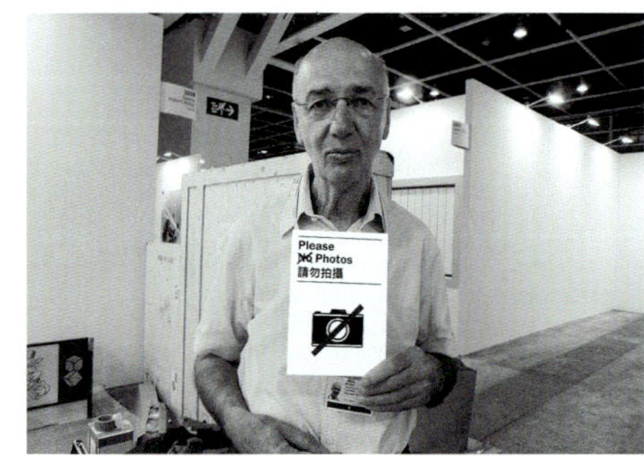

What is your favorite aspect of running a gallery?
Not being a cook.

How do you choose the artists you work with?
Spontaneously.

If you weren't running a gallery what else would you do?
I would be a cook.

- **Contact** Galerie Hubert Winter
  Melanie Wagner
  office@galeriewinter.at
- **Established** 1971
- **Owner(s) / Partner(s)** Hubert Winter
- **Team** 4
- **Space(s)** 350 m²
- **Artists at Art Basel** Judith Fegerl
  Michael Höpfner
  Birgit Jürgenssen
  Fred Sandback
  Lawrence Weiner
  Lei Xue
- **Further artists represented** William Anastasi
  Guillaume Bijl
  Mary Ellen Carroll
  Marcia Hafif
  Ian Hamilton Finlay
  Nancy Haynes
  Michael Kidner Ra
  Tina Lechner
  Paul Etienne Lincoln
  Urs Lüthi
  Ingo Nussbaumer
  Danica Phelps
  Katherine Porter
  Laura Ribero
  Stephen Skidmore
  Haim Steinbach
  Franz Vana
  Francesca Woodman
  Nil Yalter

Wolff

Paris

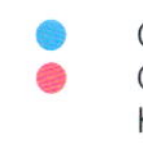

Galleries
Galleries Kabinett

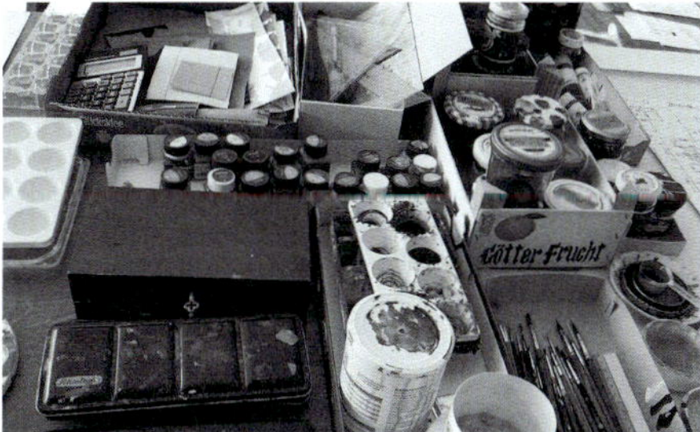

What is your favorite aspect of running a gallery?
I love participating in the movement of the "oeuvre in progess." It's all about trusting that your own time will be able to produce great artists.

How do you choose the artists you work with?
I choose artists who take risks: the risk of not being understood, the risk of not being academic (academism is by definition where it is not expected to be).

If you weren't running a gallery what else would you do?
I love paleontology.

- **Contact** Galerie Jocelyn Wolff
  Jocelyn Wolff
  jocelyn.wolff@galeriewolff.com
- **Established** 2003
- **Owner(s) / Partner(s)** Jocelyn Wolff
- **Team** 6
- **Space(s)** 150 m²
- **Artists at Art Basel** William Anastasi
  Katinka Bock
  Miriam Cahn
  Guillaume Leblon
  Francisco Tropa
  Franz Erhard Walther
- **Further artists represented** Clemens Von Wedemeyer
  Zbyněk Baladrán
  Diego Bianchi
  Isa Melsheimer
  Frédéric Moser & Philippe Schwinger
  Hans Schabus
  Prinz Gholam
  Ulrich Polster
  Elodie Seguin
  Christoph Weber

Workplace

Gateshead
London

Discoveries

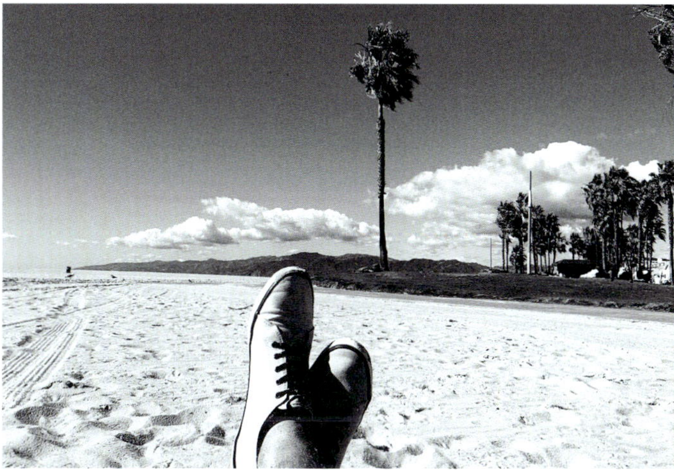

What is your favorite aspect of running a gallery?
First and foremost spending time with artists either in the studio or in the process of selecting, curating, and hanging a new exhibition. We also take great pleasure in meeting and spending time with other gallerists, collectors, and curators who are passionate about supporting artists.

How do you choose the artists you work with?
We are interested in artists who make outstanding work that is (or has the potential to be) exhibited internationally in the art world at the highest level. The list of artists we currently represent has evolved from a close, local peer group into a more diverse and international stable. We try to strike a careful balance between our international reputation and our role, responsibility, and investment into the cultural ecology of the place in which we live and work.

If you weren't running a gallery what else would you do?
Make art.

- **Contact** Workplace Gallery
  Paul Moss
  paul@workplacegallery.co.uk
- **Established** 2005
- **Owner(s) / Partner(s)** Paul Moss
  Miles Thurlow
- **Team** 4
- **Space(s)** 557 m²
- **Artists at Art Basel** Hugo Canoilas
- **Further artists represented** Tanya Axford
  Eric Bainbridge
  Darren Banks
  Sophie Lisa Beresford
  Catherine Bertola
  Cath Campbell
  Joe Clark
  Marcus Coates
  Jo Coupe
  Jacob Dahlgren
  Jennifer Douglas
  Peter J. Evans
  Laura Lancaster
  Rachel Lancaster
  Paul Merrick
  Mike Pratt
  Richard Rigg
  Cecilia Stenbom
  Matt Stokes
  Wolfgang Weileder

Waddington Custot Galleries
A Tribute to Leslie Waddington*

Nicholas Serota

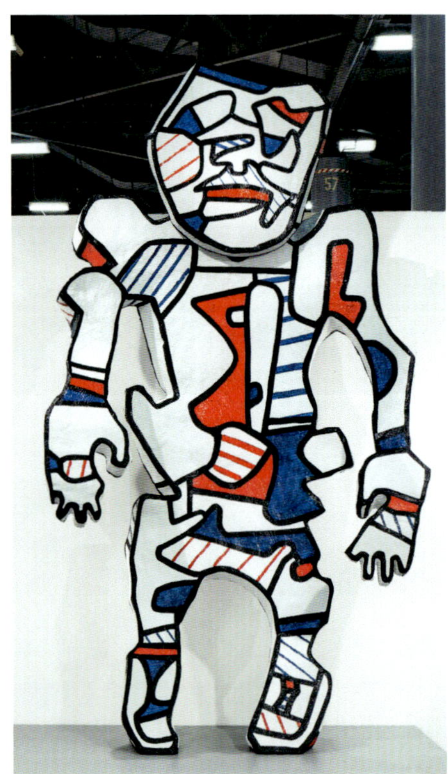

Jean Dubuffet,
Cherche-Aubaine,
1973–2014
Art Basel in
Miami Beach, 2014

There are very few dealers who can claim really long service in the premier battalion of the art world. Many of the most famous survive only one campaign, promoting the artists of their own generation. A few also succeed as agents for the next generation. Almost none are successful for as long as 30 years. Leslie Waddington, who celebrated his 80th birthday in February 2014, has been on the front line for more than 50 years and is a now a campaign veteran without equal in the profession.

The strengths of Leslie's approach to the art of dealing come from his background and formation. The soft lilt of his voice reminds us that he was born into a Jewish family in Ireland and he has always been a slight outsider in the London art establishment. His father, Victor, ran a successful gallery in Dublin for 30 years, dealing in Irish artists such as Jack Yeats, and works from the School of Paris. However, Leslie's spiritual and intellectual roots lie in the literature rather than the art of Ireland, especially in the writings of James Joyce and in the Modernist tradition as it developed in Paris between the wars. It was this interest that took him to Paris and the Sorbonne in the early 1950s, rather than to a British university. There he encountered Existentialism, Sartre, Giacometti, and Camus, and gained a respect for the intellectual that has conditioned the whole way he has lived his life. It made him open to the work of Samuel Beckett in a way that was unusual in Britain in the 1950s and 1960s, but it also gave him an abiding interest in words and literature that has allowed him to keep the daily machinations of the art world at a distance. It is that regard for intellect and for the pleasures of conversation that makes him such a great companion. It has brought him respect from critics including David Sylvester and Clement Greenberg, the friendship of artists such as William Turnbull and Patrick Heron, and a close association with powerful collectors such as Alistair McAlpine and EJ "Ted" Power.

In 1957, Victor Waddington decided to move his gallery from Dublin to London. He was joined in the new business in 1958 by his 24-year-old son Leslie. Initially, the gallery continued on a familiar path, but by 1960 Leslie's influence had brought to it the emerging St Ives painters. In the early 1960s London discovered postwar American art, rapidly embracing Abstract Expressionism, Pop, and the emergent Color Field painting. Leslie, along with James Mayor at Mayor Gallery and John Kasmin at Kasmin Gallery presented enormously influential shows of Louis, Noland, Olitski, Poons, and others. By the mid-1960s, Kasmin and Waddington, along with Alex Gregory Hood's Rowan Gallery, were also showing Anthony Caro's colored welded steel sculptures and what became known as "The New Generation" following Bryan Robertson's exhibitions at the Whitechapel Art Gallery in 1964 and 1965. Waddington became independent of his father in 1966 when he formed Waddington Galleries, with Alex Berstein of Granada television as his silent partner.

Waddington never really embraced Conceptual or American Minimal art, but by the 1980s he was showing new European and American painting and sculpture with his representation of Baselitz, Paladino, Flanagan, and Craig-Martin. Interspersed with these new figures, he remained loyal to British painters such as Patrick Caulfield and Peter Blake, and to lifelong passions such as Dubuffet, Matisse, and Picasso. One of my pleasures during that period would be to visit the viewing room at the gallery on a Saturday morning and have Leslie pull out in quick succession great works by Picasso, Matisse, Baselitz, Morandi, Flanagan, Arp, Laurens, Léger, Miró, Caulfield, Tàpies, and Dubuffet in a random cascade of finely chosen images. You always had the sense that it was the excitement of sharing his passion with others that made Leslie such an effective salesman. At a time when the Tate and other institutions in London were far less ambitious than today, he made his gallery in Cork Street a place where young artists and collectors could receive an education in modern art. He also brought in younger colleagues. Both Alan Cristea and Tim Taylor learned their craft with Leslie, and Hester van Roijen was for some years an influential partner.

In the uncertain commercial years of the early 1990s, Waddington continued to embrace new art, taking on Fiona Rae, Ian Davenport, and Lisa Milroy from the next generation. In recent years the gallery has continued to prosper with secondary market sales working alongside beautifully presented shows by figures such as Heron, Caulfield, Halley, Tapies, and Woodrow, and focused exhibitions by earlier masters such as Picabia, Albers, and Milton Avery, an enduring enthusiasm both of Leslie and his father, Victor. And, of course, Waddington has been a feature of Art Basel and other the other major fairs since the early 1970s, always showing important masterworks alongside new work by the artists he represents.

*This text is excerpted from a tribute given by Nicholas Serota at the FEAGA Award 2013 Ceremony in June 2013. The Federation of European Art Galleries Association (FEAGA) represents the interests of over 2,000 modern and contemporary art galleries in the EU and Switzerland. In addition, FEAGA, whose headquarters are in Brussels is active in European policy. Each year, FEAGA awards two prizes: the Lifetime Award and the Award for Creativity and New Inspiration. Leslie Waddington was the recipient of the Lifetime Award in June 2013.

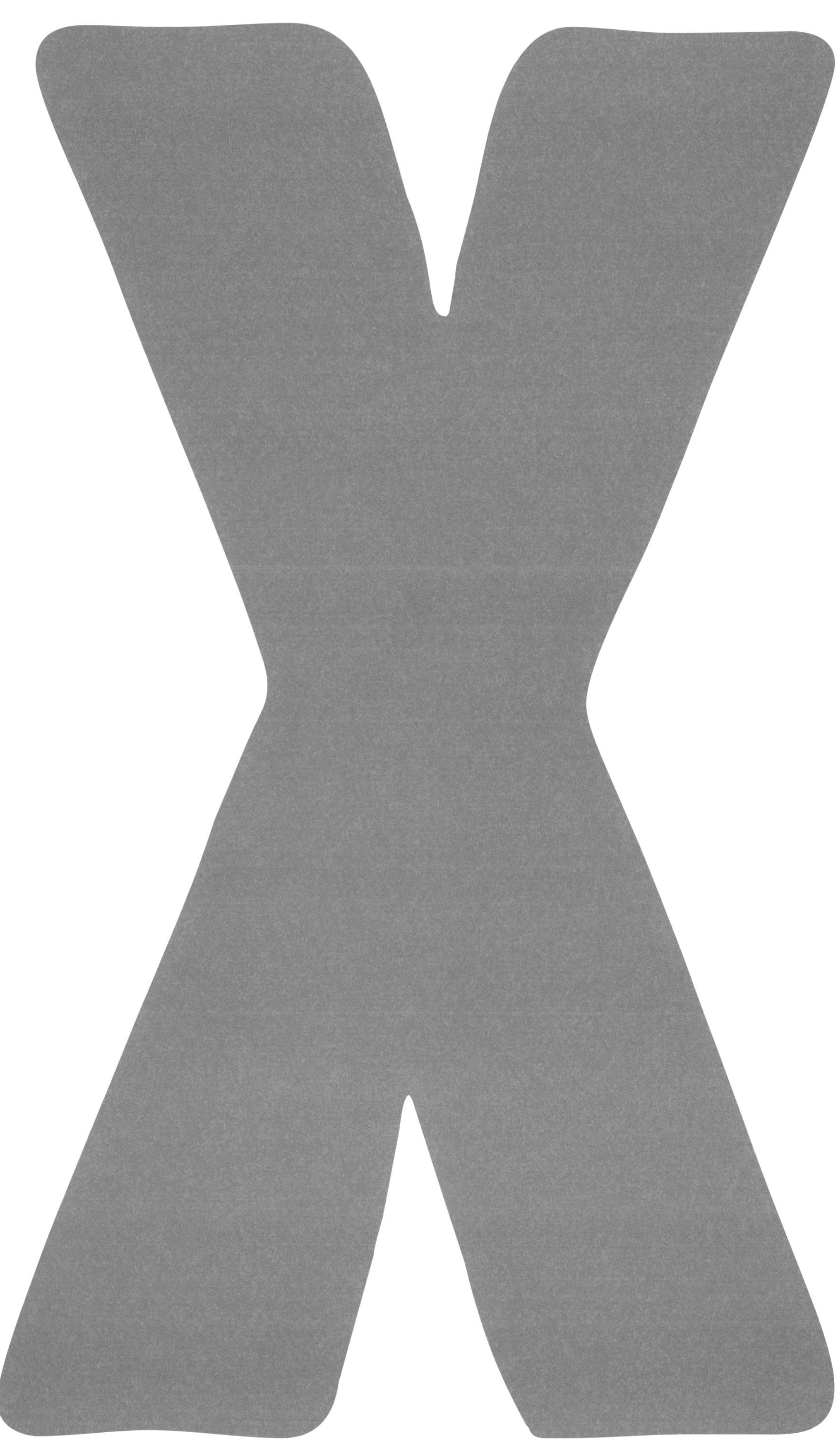

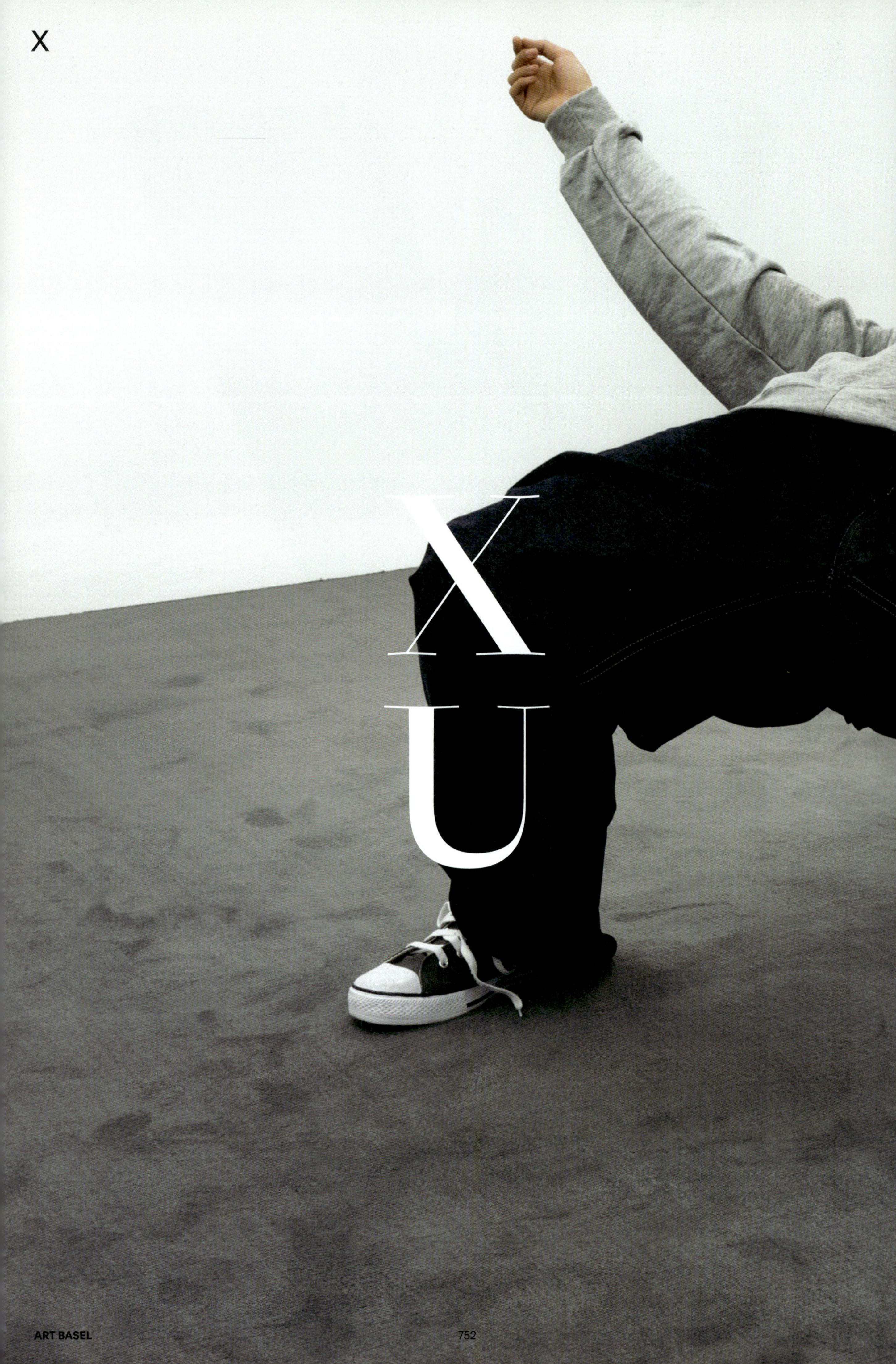
XU

Xu Zhen
In Just a Blink of an Eye, 2005–2014
14 Rooms, Basel, 2014

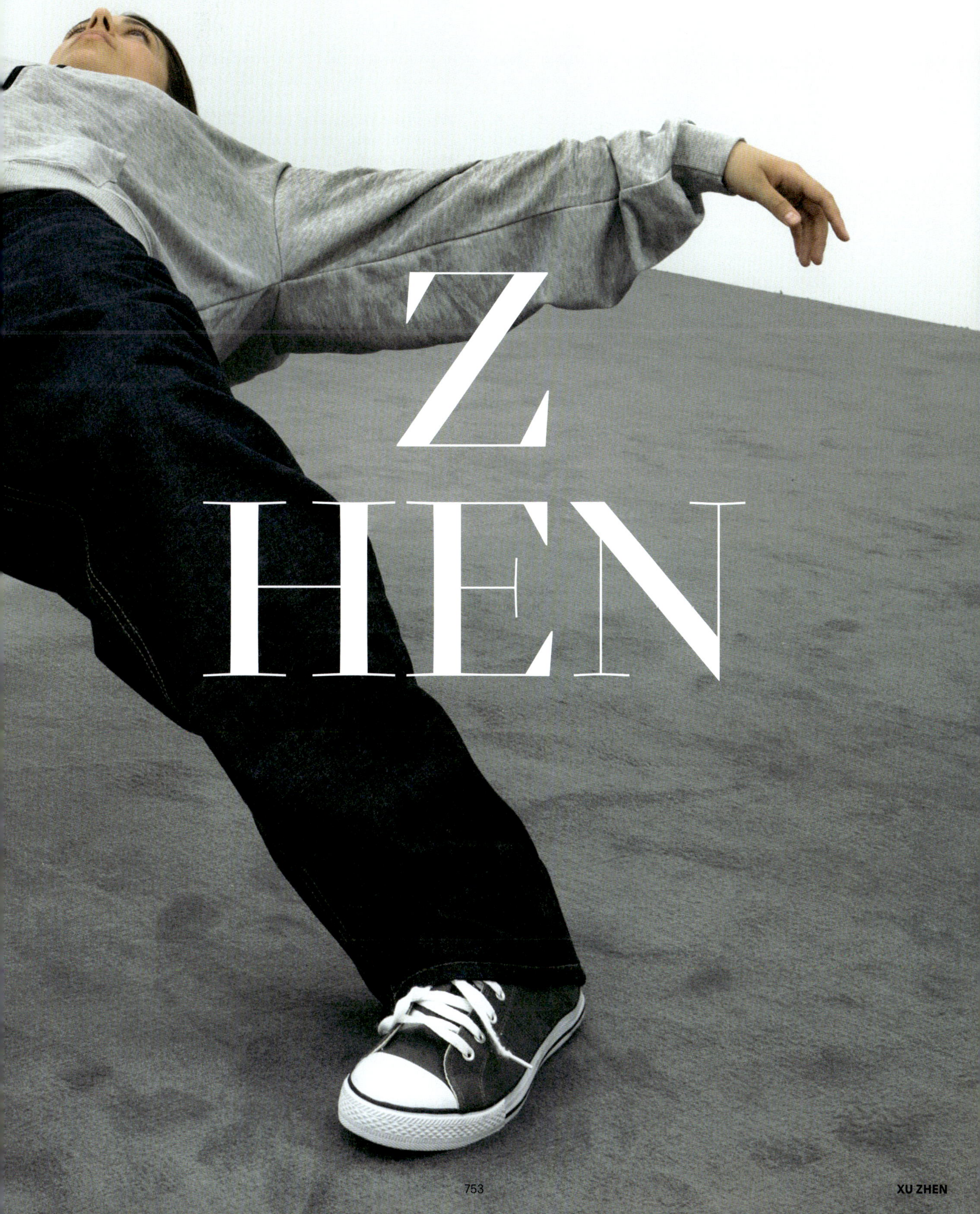

A Year through Art Basel
Interview with Xu Zhen

Born in 1977, Xu Zhen graduated from the Shanghai School of Arts and Crafts in 1996 and currently lives and works in Shanghai. His practice ranges from installation, painting, and sculpture to video, performance, and interventions. In 2006 he participated in the launch of Art-Ba-Ba, an online platform dedicated to contemporary art; he founded BizArt in 2008, one of the first independent art spaces in Shanghai. In 2009 he created the "contemporary art creation company" MadeIn Company, which launched the "Xu Zhen" brand in 2012. Exhibiting since the mid-2000s, he recently had a retrospective exhibition at the Ullens Center for Contemporary Art (Beijing) from January to April 2014.

CLÉMENT DIRIÉ Could you tell us about your life and formation in China in the 1990s? Why did you create MadeIn Company in 2009, and what exactly is it? How does it function?

XU ZHEN I started to curate exhibitions with other artists in the late 1990s. The main difference between then and now is that in the 1990s there were only two to three exhibitions a year in Beijing and Shanghai. Nowadays there are two to three exhibitions a day. However, there still aren't so many exhibitions that are interesting. In 2009 I started to realize that I was becoming an international artist. I thought I had to communicate to everyone how I understood culture, and I think that MadeIn Company is the best window to understand us.

ELÉONOR DE PESTERS Your work has been exhibited at Art Basel in the Galleries and Unlimited sectors. What is your point of view on Art Basel?

XZ I have never been to Art Basel in Switzerland, but if I remember well I started to participate at this fair in 2004. Today most people around me have been to Art Basel in Basel. So the main impressions I have of it are those of people around me who've been there: it's faster, higher, and stronger.

EDP From your point of view, how does Art Basel help artists to be more present on the international art scene? How was it for you?

XZ The viewers at Art Basel are more varied and specialized. It is widely covered by the media, and reviews are very comprehensive. These are all aspects that are very important in the promotion of artists. For example, when I participated in Unlimited in 2014, I saw numerous reviews on our work.

> I believe that like Art Basel, we all have a certain curiosity and openness toward culture. —Xu Zhen

EDP Your recent sculptural compositions are created from Western and Asian statues displayed in museums throughout the world. Among other things these pieces reflect colonial history, violence, cultural conflicts and relations, but the elements that you bring together, even though they come from different civilizations, somehow combine into one new single object. Was your piece *Eternity…* (presented by Beijing's Long March Space in the Unlimited sector) conceived especially for Art Basel? Do you see the choice of this work as a strategic one on the part of Art Basel to symbolize constructive connections between East and West—knowing that the fair was newly expanded in Hong Kong last year?

XZ Created in 2013–2014, *Eternity…* was one of the main works in my mid-career exhibition that I had just had at that time. I think it directly refers to the sensitive issues between Eastern and Western cultures. At the same time, it presents globalization taking place in spite of cultural clashes. I believe that like Art Basel, we all have a certain curiosity and openness toward culture, and I think that choosing this piece was very appropriate for today's Art Basel.

CD In 2014 you were also part of *14 Rooms* at Art Basel in Basel with a captivating performance piece. Could you tell us the story of this work?

XZ According to reviews, and generally speaking, it seems this work has been well received in various countries. It indeed may give a "feeling of loosing control toward the unknown," which is a common anxiety shared by people nowadays.

EDP What major differences do you see between the three fairs? And what would be the assets and weak points of Art Basel in Hong Kong?

XZ The main differences are those between the developing rhythm of each place, and the reality of society.

CD How would you describe the current Asia-Pacific Region art scene and the one in China?

XZ I think that what is important is to develop the future through the past, and to understand the past through the future. Both should be done simultaneously.

Xu Zhen (Made in Company) *Safe House A*, 2012, ShangArt, Art Basel in Miami Beach, 2014

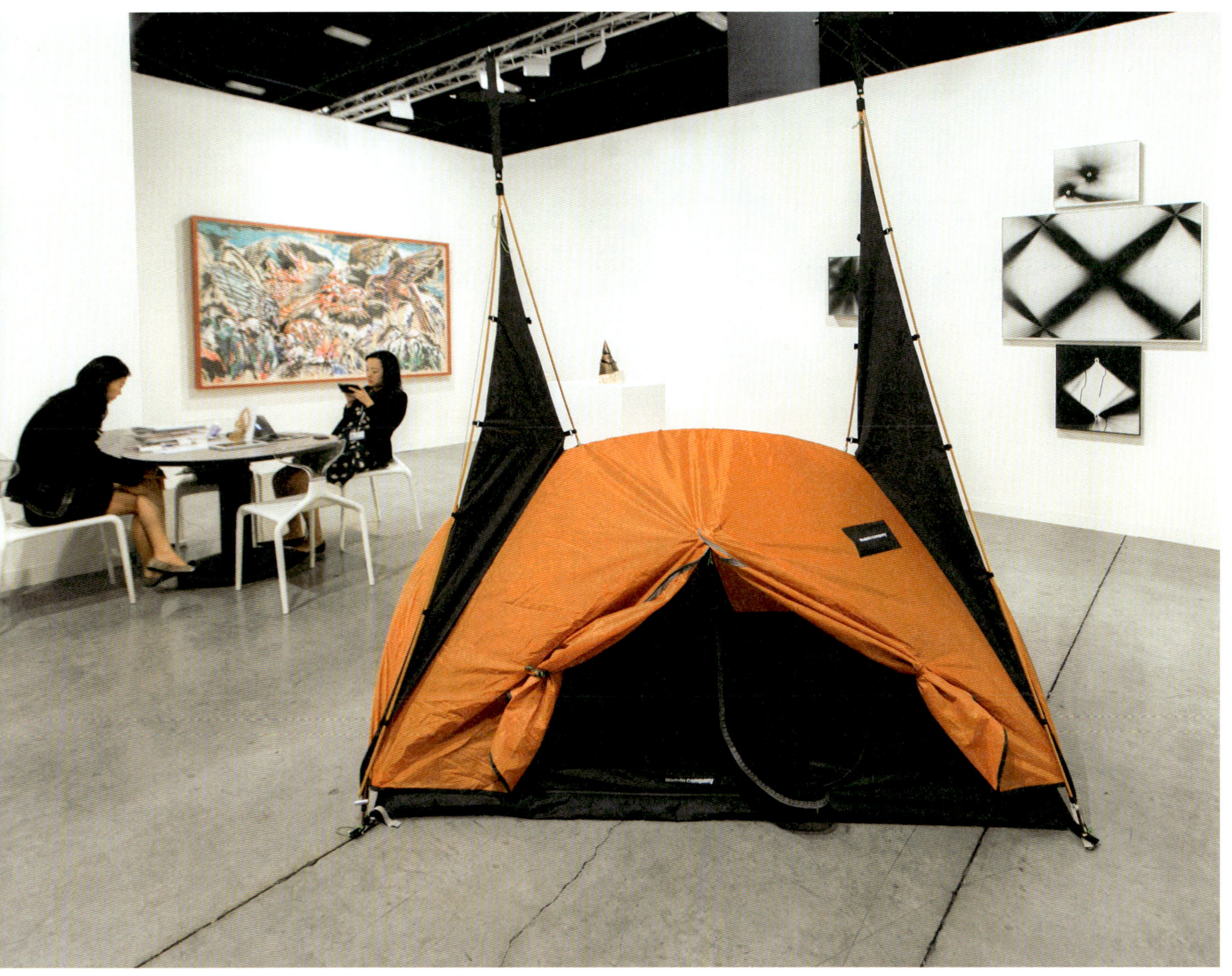

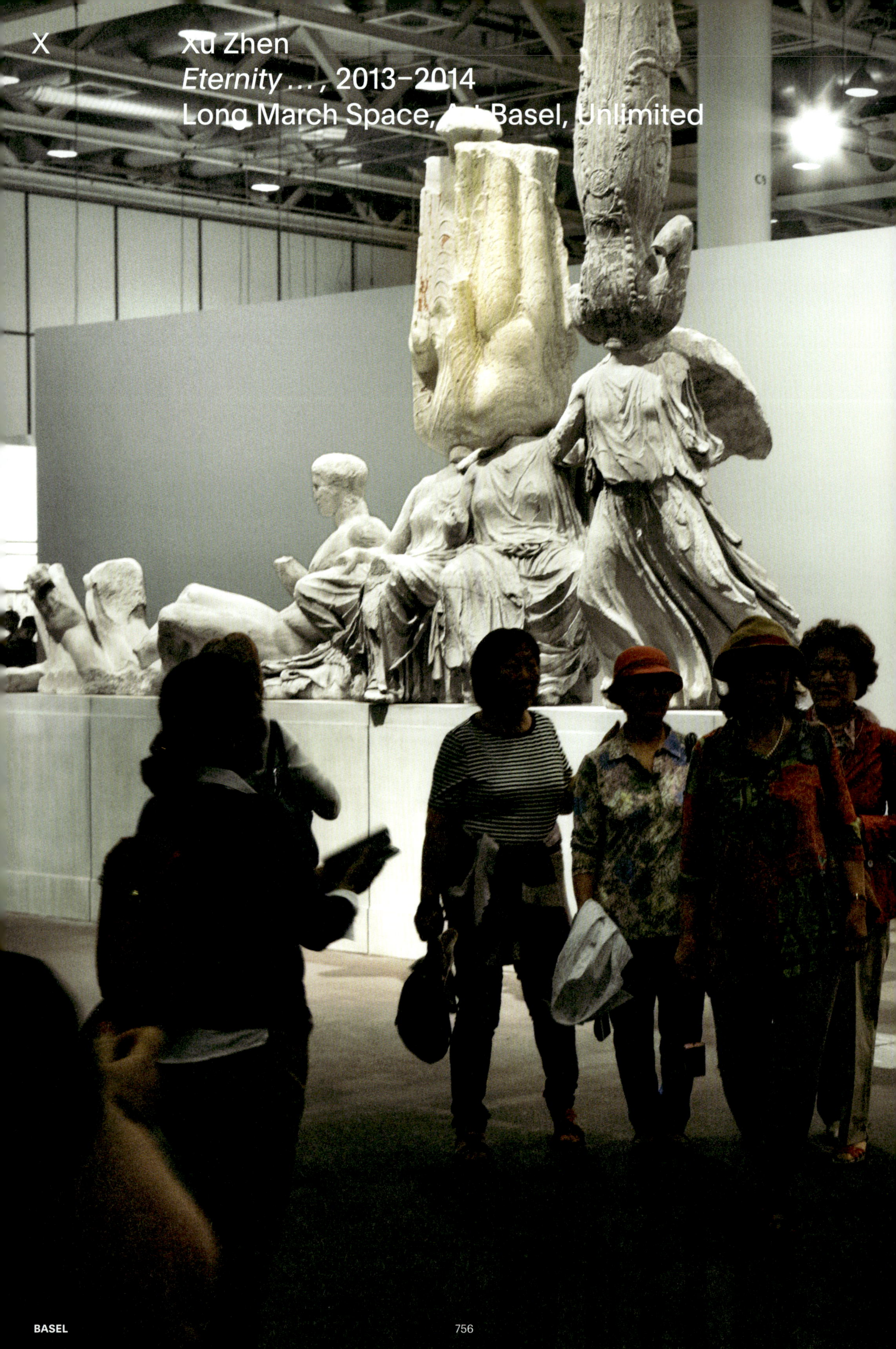

X Xu Zhen
Eternity . . . , 2013–2014
Long March Space, Art Basel, Unlimited

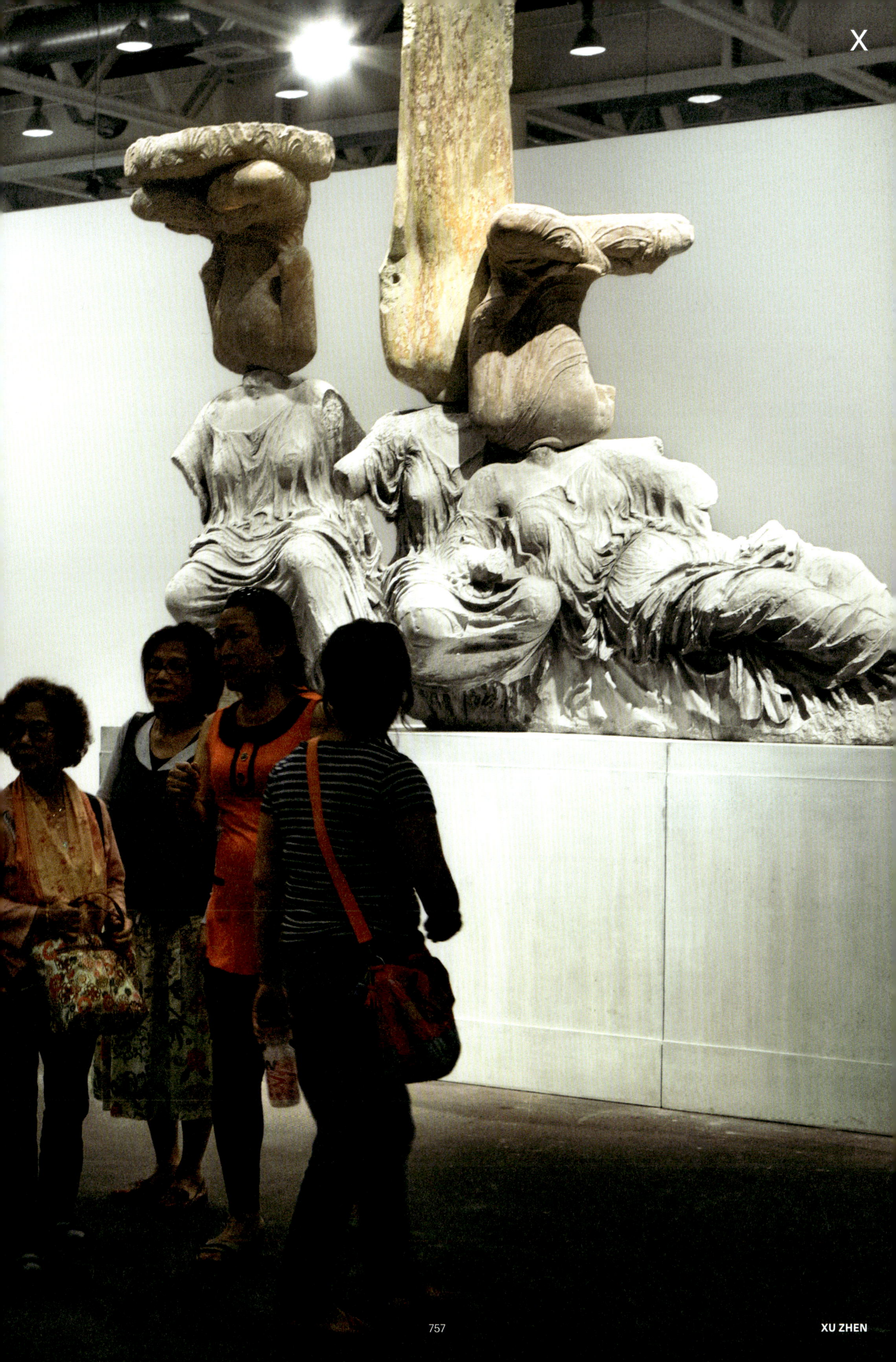

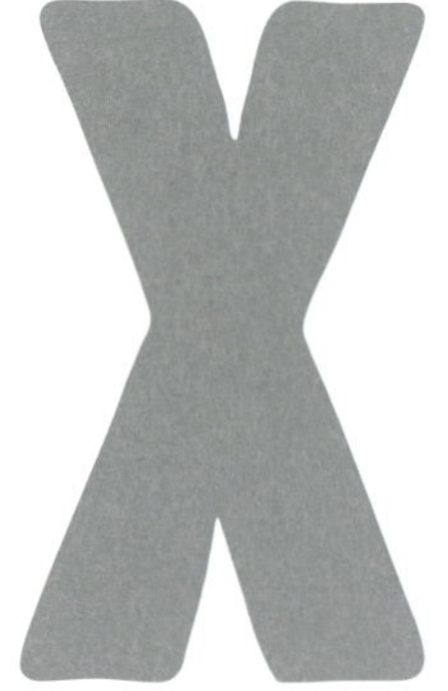

Xu

Shanghai ● Discoveries

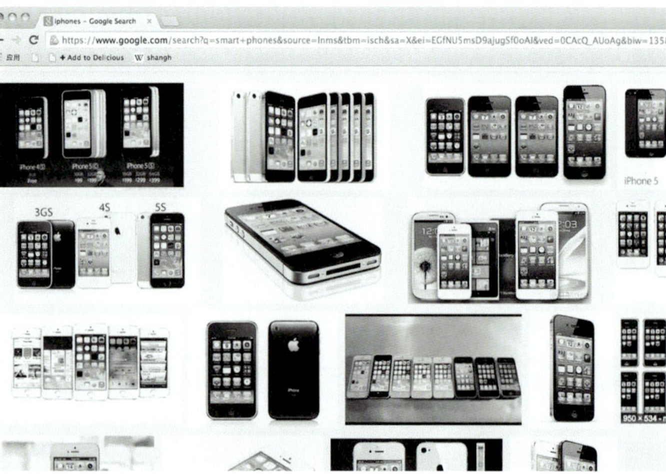

What is your favorite aspect of running a gallery?
Seen through the light of business, the gallery is supposedly a flexible engine exempted from institutional bureaucracy and provides an entrepreneurial adventure into merging the sales side with curating and programming. The aspect I enjoy the most is this possible new gallery model of selling bigger pictures or concepts to various social sectors and individuals so that artistic ideas can be applied and extended in diverse disciplines and businesses, rather than simply placing some art on clients' walls.

How do you choose the artists you work with?
I choose artists who are sensitive to media and who work with/on the time and milieu s/he lives in, rethinking the role of an artist in the 2010s. The choice is finalized only after a long testing between us, through visits, conversations, correspondence, and projects …

If you weren't running a gallery what else would you do?
I would make my own art and curate shows. Alternatively, be a poet who wants to play rock 'n' roll, a critic that reviews volleyball. All would be as good as running a gallery.

- **Contact** Leo Xu Projects
  Leo Xu
  leo@leoxuprojects.com
- **Established** 2011
- **Owner(s) / Partner(s)** Leo Xu & Partners
- **Team** 3
- **Space(s)** 250 m²
- **Artist at Art Basel** Li Qing
- **Further artists represented** Aaajiao
  Chen Wei
  Cheng Ran
  Cui Jie
  Guo Hongwei
  Gabriel Lester
  Michael Lin
  Liu Chuang

XVA

Dubai ● Insights

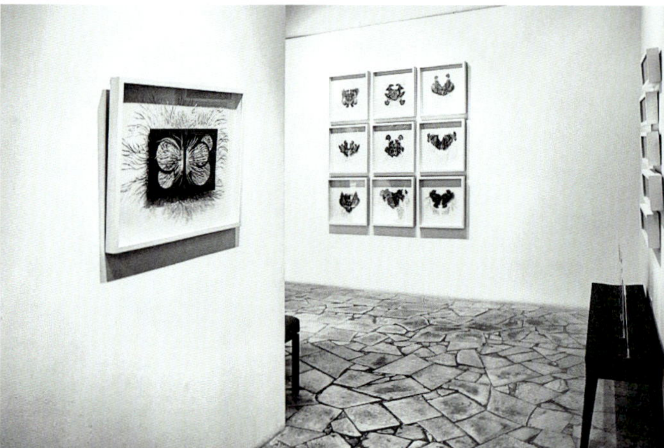

What is your favorite aspect of running a gallery?
Working with art, finding people to buy the art I love. Connecting the two.

How do you choose the artists you work with?
I look for artists who have a purpose to their life in art, who can say something to the community of collectors who constitute XVA's client list.

If you weren't running a gallery what else would you do?
Run an art hotel with a cafe!

- **Contact** XVA Gallery
  Eleanor Smith
  ellie@xvagallery.com
- **Established** 2003
- **Owner(s) / Partner(s)** Mona Hauser
- **Team** 4
- **Space(s)** 55 m²
- **Artists at Art Basel** Faiza Butt
  Imran Channa
  Halim al Karim
- **Further artists represented** Mohsen Ahmadvand
  Arezu
  Al Braithwaite
  Simeen Farhat
  Jonathan Gent
  Mahmoud Hamadani
  Halona Hilbertz
  Sami Al Karim
  Hussein Al-Mohasen
  Colleen Quigley
  Fereydoon Omidi
  Walid Siti
  Morteza Zahedi

XVA Gallery
Interview with Mona Hauser

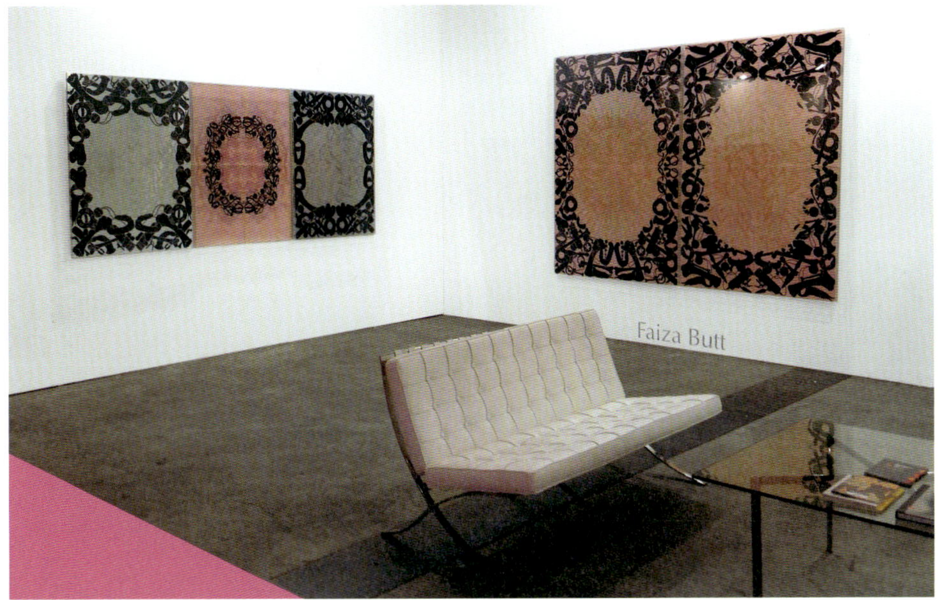

Art Basel in Hong Kong (Insights), 2014

Why did you decide to open in Dubai and to represent mainly Middle Eastern artists?

In 1993 I had planned to open a gallery in Miami, but HRH Sheikh Mohammed summoned us to Dubai. So instead of Miami I thought, why not Dubai? My intent was then to show art from this region, regardless of nationality. To me art has no nationality—often it can add a perspective integral to the work created, but I do not believe it necessary for classification.

How was the art scene there when you opened in 2003?

It was both literally and figuratively a desert, with only two galleries working with artists. It reinforced our desire to show contemporary art. I wanted XVA to become a hub for art created in the region, knowing there had to be an underground of artists in the United Arab Emirates, and that XVA would be a place for them.

As a gallery based in Dubai since 2003, how would you describe the evolution of the art scene and the art market there?

Since 2003 the art scene has reached heights I would have never imagined. There were no art classes in colleges in 2003, now there are degree programs and it is accepted as a career path. Emirati-owned art galleries have blossomed and their artists are in museum shows and collections around the world. Unthinkable ten years ago!

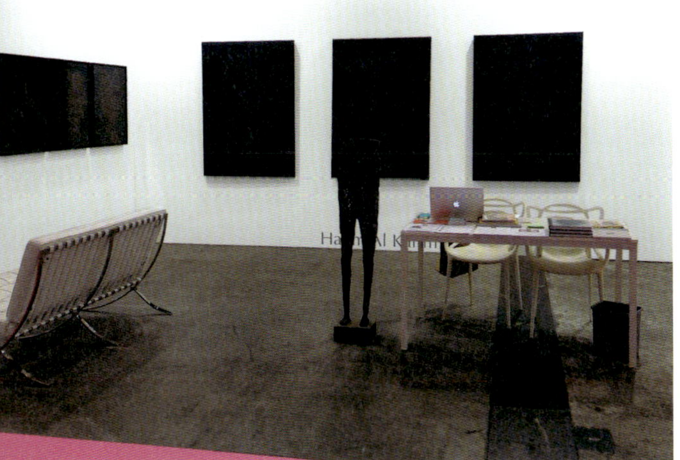

How is this scene dealing both with the Asia-Pacific Region and the West?

XVA has shown in Asian fairs since 2007. We have exhibited at Art Basel in Hong Kong for the past two years, and before that at ART HK, as well as in Shanghai, and at the Asian Contemporary Art Fair in New York. I feel that Middle Eastern art benefits from the Asian context and is well received on its market. We have sold several works by Halim al Karim (Iraqi) and Morteza Zahedi (Iranian) to the MOCA in Yinchuan, for instance. Several of our artists will be showing in the museum's inaugural exhibition in 2015, in a show focusing on Islamic Art.

At Art Basel in Hong Kong in 2013 you showed Imran Channa, and in 2014 Faiza Butt and Halim al Karim. Could you tell us more about these two booths?

Conceptual multimedia Pakistani artist Imran Channa questions the manipulation of memory and history by the media, which is somehow a power construction. The works in this series are entitled *Age of Mythology*, and create a dialogue between art and the illusion of magic, the manipulated story told in history, with its inevitable gaps.

Our booth in 2014 was curated and titled *Objects*: it featured works by Pakistani artist Faiza Butt and Iraqi artist Halim al Karim. Butt's works are large-scale, hand painted, acrylic glazes on paper that show taboo objects displayed in an Orientalist style, reminiscent of manuscript covers. Al Karim's photographs focus on capturing the innocent faces of young girls in an objectified way. Al Karim, who endured extreme trauma under Saddam Hussein's regime in Iraq, expresses suppressed pain in his work. His story is buried in his work, and captures the beauty of the soul in spite of the traces of trauma. His work is beautiful and is haunted by beauty and pain. The booth also featured his new work made with the world's largest wet plate collodion camera. Halim al Karim has done something no other photographer has done by building such a large-scale collodion camera. We sold these works in Art Basel in Hong Kong, making history in the world of photography and the fair.

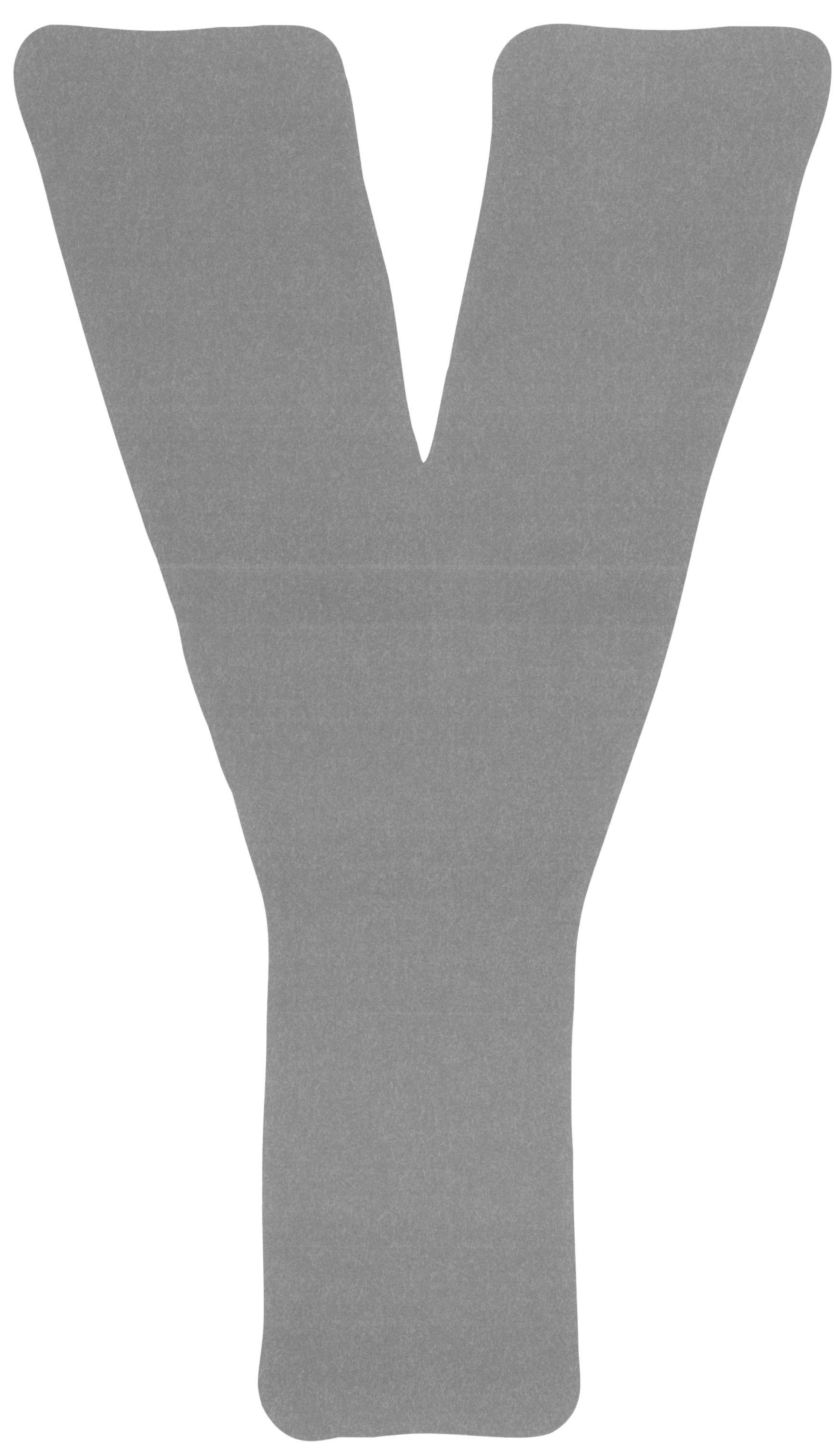

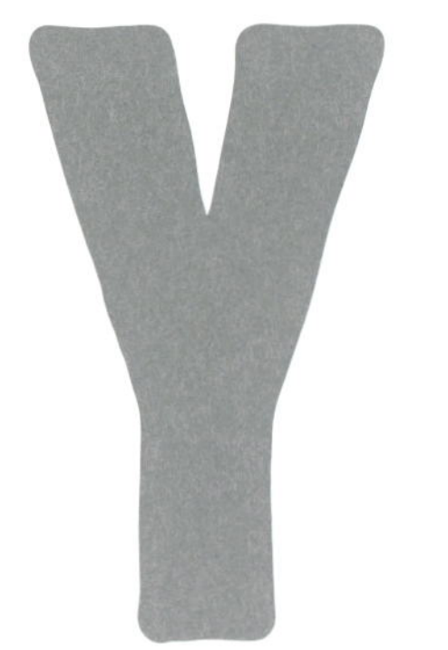

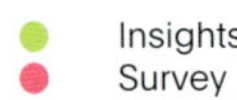

Y++ Wada

Tokyo

Insights
Survey

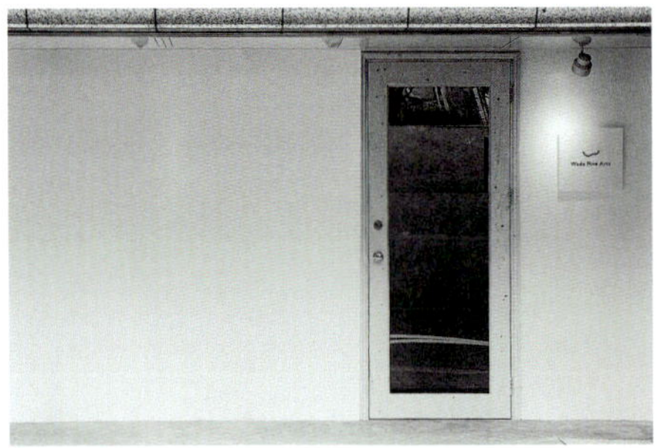

What is your favorite aspect of running a gallery?
I enjoy finding gifted artists at an early stage and "incubating" them. That is why the gallery is proud to be a pure primary market gallery that takes care of young Asian artists, not only from Japan.

How do you choose the artists you work with?
Y++ Wada Fine Arts targets young artists who are at a very early stage of their career, showing the following elements: contemporary expression, outstanding originality, and visual understandability. The gallery also picks up unknown professional artists if they give us a powerful impression with their artworks, their self-confidence, and positive ambitions.

If you weren't running a gallery what else would you do?
Be an artist.

- **Contact** Y++ Wada Fine Arts
  Yumie Wada
  wada@wadafinearts.com
- **Established** 2008 (Y++)
  2007 (Wada Fine Arts)
  1990 (Iseyoshi)
- **Owner(s) / Partner(s)** Yumie Wada
- **Team** 3
- **Space(s)** 80 m²
- **Artists at Art Basel** Tetsuya Ishida
  Hisako Sugiyama
- **Further artists represented** Heri Dono
  Yasushi Ebihara
  Zhao Gang
  Takafumi Hara
  Yan Heng
  Tarui Hideki
  Atsuko Imaizumi
  Miori Inata
  Ryoko Kawashima
  Shinichiro Kitaura
  Takahiro Miura
  Yoichi Miyajima
  Shunsuke François Nanjo
  Hiroshi Ohashi
  Anna Oya
  Marina Qrze
  Keiko Sakamoto
  Takehiko Sugawara
  Takafumi Tsuchiya
  Tomoko Yokoyama
  ZhanFa Zhi

Yamaki

Kobe

Insights

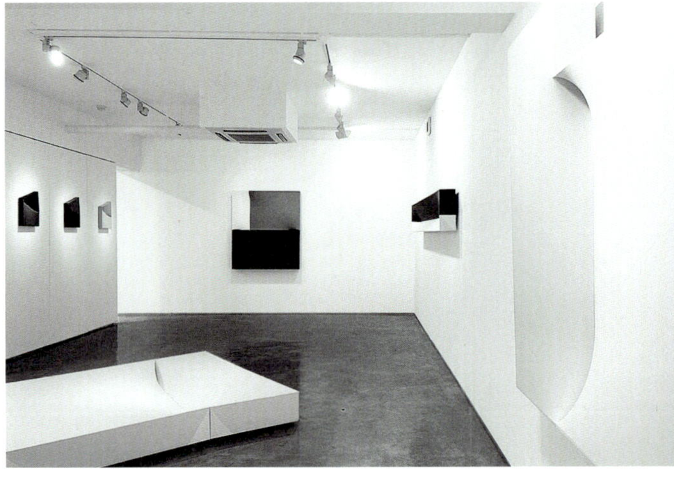

What is your favorite aspect of running a gallery?
Having the chance to share exquisite artworks with collectors, and being able to encounter new works by our artists.

How do you choose the artists you work with?
Whether I can feel empathy with the artists' concepts and statements, as well as their visual expressions, is the basic factor.

If you weren't running a gallery what else would you do?
Having studied fine arts at the university, I would probably still be working in the art field. Among other jobs related to the field, I can see myself in public relations or being an art coordinator.

- **Contact** Gallery Yamaki Fine Art
  Seika Abe
  info@gyfa.co.jp
- **Established** 2006
- **Owner(s) / Partner(s)** Kanako Yamaki
- **Team** 4
- **Space(s)** 120 m²
- **Artists at Art Basel** Tatsuo Kawaguchi
  Takesada Matsutani
- **Further artists represented** Jean-Michel Alberola
  Benoît Broisat
  Louis Cane
  Veronika Dovers
  Michio Fukuoka
  Yuki Hayashi
  Sadaharu Horio
  Kenji Inumaki
  Christian Jaccard
  Louis Jammes
  Susumu Koshimizu
  Jean Le Gac
  Joerg Lehmann
  Frederique Lucien
  Min-Ho Lee
  Kimiyo Mishima
  Sadamasa Motonaga
  Kozo Nishino
  Florian Sussmayr
  Ringo Tang
  Jun Tsukawaki
  Keiji Uematsu
  Takuma Uematsu
  Claude Viallat
  Nobuko Watanabe

Yamamoto Gendai

Tokyo 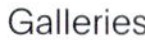 Galleries

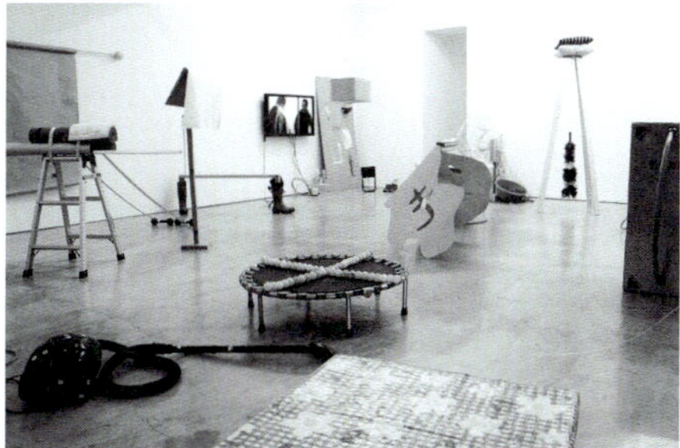

What is your favorite aspect of running a gallery?
Sharing the exhibition build-up process with the artists, and looking at the accomplished show as a first viewer.

How do you choose the artists you work with?
Artists who have their own opinion about art and the world, and who ask us good questions rather than giving us answers.

If you weren't running a gallery what else would you do?
A librarian, reading books as much as possible.

- **Contact** Yamamoto Gendai
  Kazumasa Nonaka
  i@yamamotogendai.org
- **Established** 2004
- **Owner(s) / Partner(s)** Yuko Yamamoto
- **Team** 4
- **Space(s)** 100 m²
- **Artists at Art Basel** Yayoi Deki
  Kei Imazu
  Erina Matsui
  Motohiko Odani
  Richard Serra
  Keisuke Tanaka
  Tiger Tateishi
- **Further artists represented** Etsuko Fukaya
  Shinichi Hara
  Kohei Kobayashi
  Nile Koetting
  Edgar Martins
  Osamu Mori
  Ruriko Murayama
  Hermann Nitsch
  Tsukasa Ohtake
  Masakatsu Takagi
  Naohiro Ukawa
  Kenji Yanobe

Yang

Beijing  Insights

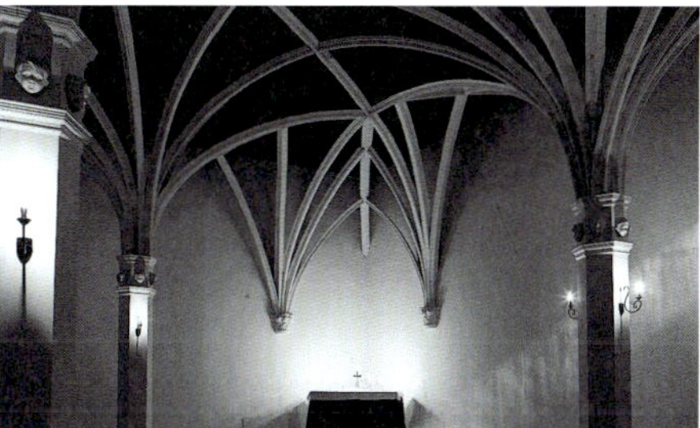

What is your favorite aspect of running a gallery?
Helping young artists to develop their own artistic personality, organizing exhibitions, and triggering discussions with the public.

How do you choose the artists you work with?
We are not looking for artists with similar creative thinking or works. They must be serious in exploring in art. At the end of the day we are not working for one or two artists, but for the values we share.

If you weren't running a gallery what else would you do?
Promote art and educate about it.

- **Contact** Gallery Yang
  Jinpeng Mu
  jinpeng.mu@galleryyang.com
- **Established** 2009
- **Owner(s) / Partner(s)** Yang Yang
- **Team** 5
- **Space(s)** 265 m²
- **Artists at Art Basel** Dong Yuan
- **Further artists represented** Chen Zhuo
  Kong Lingnan
  Li Binyuan
  Liang Shuo
  Lin Ke
  Yan Bing
  Yan Heng
  Ye Linghan
  Zhan Chong
  Zhang Yue

Yavuz

Singapore  Insights

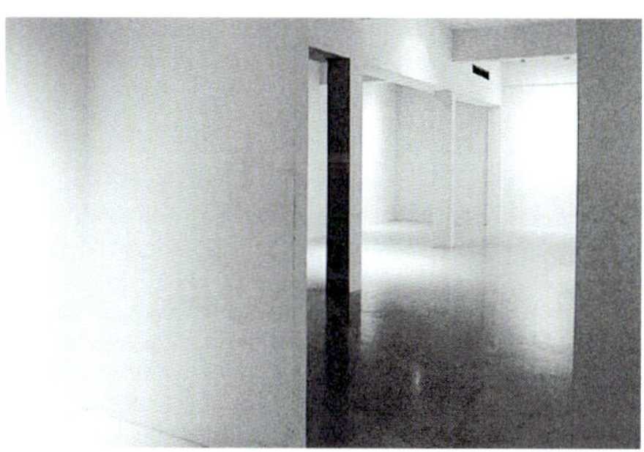

What is your favorite aspect of running a gallery?
Being at the forefront of new art, from visiting artists' studios, collaborating with curators, or working with artists, developing exhibition ideas and concepts, to seeing the finished works on our gallery walls for the very first time. I also enjoy matching a client with a good piece of art.

How do you choose the artists you work with?
There is no stylistic or general thread in the gallery's curatorial program; artists are selected according to the social significance of their artwork and the perception that, within their chosen field of endeavor, they are among those leading their field.

If you weren't running a gallery what else would you do?
I would probably be doing something else related to art.

- **Contact** Yavuz Gallery
  Stella Chang
  info@yavuzfineart.com
- **Established** 2010
- **Owner(s) / Partner(s)** Can Yavuz
- **Team** 4
- **Space(s)** 223 m²
- **Artists at Art Basel** Jakkai Siributr
- **Further artists represented** Iwan Effendi
  Shadi Ghadirian
  Winner Jumalon
  Morvarid K.
  Uttaporn Nimmalaikaew
  Saskia Pintelon
  Navin Rawanchaikul
  Pinaree Sanpitak
  Shin Kwang Ho
  Manit Sriwanichpoom
  Lale Tara

Y++ Wada Gallery
Interview with Yumie Wada

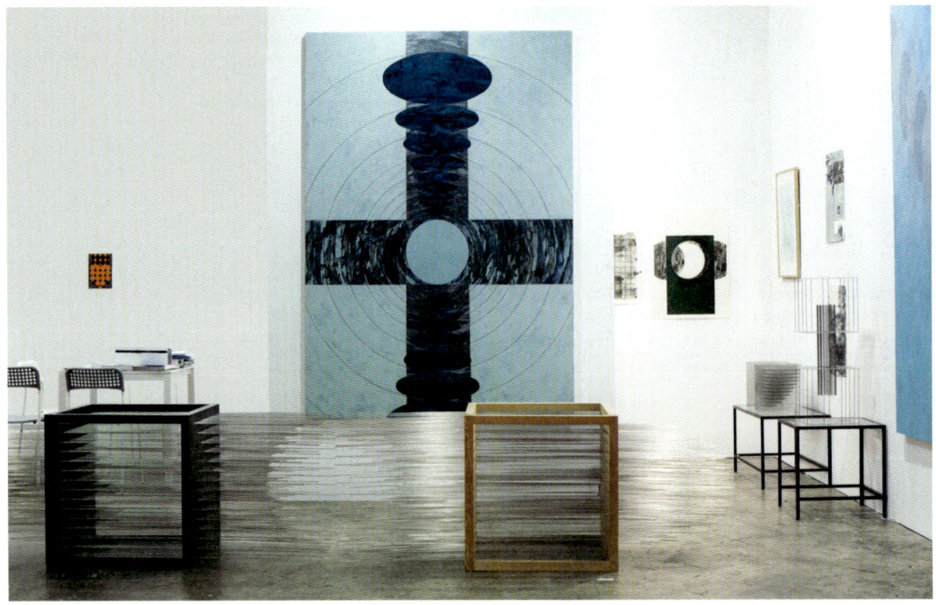

Art Basel in Hong Kong (Insights), 2014

When did the gallery open and what was its initial program?

I established my gallery in 1990 as Gallery Iseyoshi and then, in 2007, I changed its name and established my own company under Wada Fine Arts. Iseyoshi is our family business name for a kimono shop in Ginza (Tokyo). I first set up the gallery in that same building. Furthermore, from 2008 to 2012, I had a gallery in Beijing, called Y++: that's why we are now Y++ Wada. I'm thinking about opening a new gallery in Hong Kong now, or Singapore. I feel it's important to have a gallery in Japan and another one somewhere else in Asia. Even if we represent mainly Japanese artists we also work with artists coming from all over Asia—Indonesia, the Philippines, China, Singapore, Taiwan, etc.

At Art Basel in Honk Kong, your booth is dedicated to only one artist. Could you tell us more about Hisako Sugiyama?

Hisako Sugiyama (b. 1955) is somehow a bridge between Japanese contemporary art and Gutai, between these different generations. There are many other artists from her generation, but her work is of great quality and I love the way she thinks. We have already organized six solo exhibitions with her in my gallery. We've worked together for more than 20 years. And I feel it's important to show people that Japanese art is not only about the artistic trend Takashi Murakami represents …

After graduating in Fine Arts and Music in Japan, she studied at the Academy of Fine Arts in Vienna under the important artist Arnulf Rainer; she also related to Minimalism. She reached this kind of mix between Minimal art and Expressionism. Before her generation, these categories were self-enclosed, but she managed to mix the two, creating a new form of Expressionism. I think this is what makes her a serious and outstanding artist.

Here she proposes a mixture of new large paintings and drawings, as well as her "yellow objects" from 1998 to 2014. Her idea is to convey "a substantial form in nonexistence" to quote the great 20th-century novelist Italo Calvino.

You have been participating in Art Basel in Hong Kong since it began and before that you participated in ART HK. How do you feel the change?

Before Art Basel in Hong Kong, ART HK was a very good art fair. The organizers did a very good job. But with Art Basel our customers changed: many Western people come now and it's a very good way to promote our artists.

In Art Basel in Miami Beach you participated in the first edition of the Survey sector with a solo show of Tetsuya Ishida.

Until his untimely death in 2005, Tetsuya Ishida (b. 1973) sought to create work that captured Japan's tenuous post-bubble economic environment and the urban loneliness of the 1990s and early 2000s. After his death, he became a kind of icon for those fragile decades, his paintings being reproduced on many books and CD covers. When we remember him, we cannot ignore the vulnerability of human beings who cannot resist against social cruelty shown in his work, the despair it expresses, in the lineage of Franz Kafka. Having worked with him when he was alive as a friend and a gallerist, I was very glad to be able to organize this solo show in Miami Beach in order to allow a greater audience to know his incredible work.

Art Basel in Miami Beach (Survey), 2014

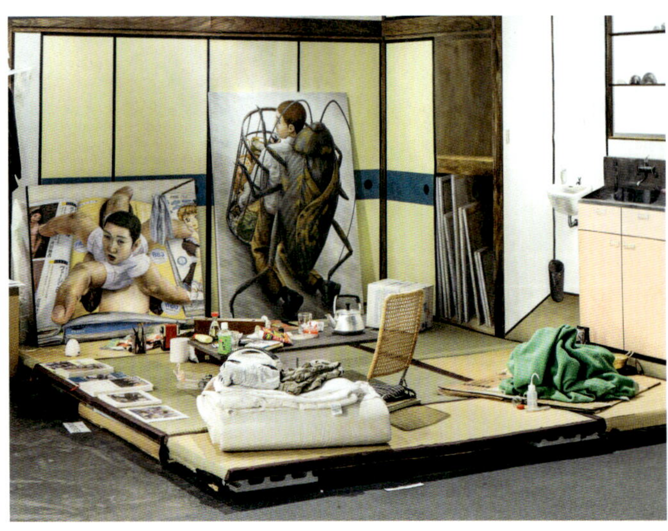

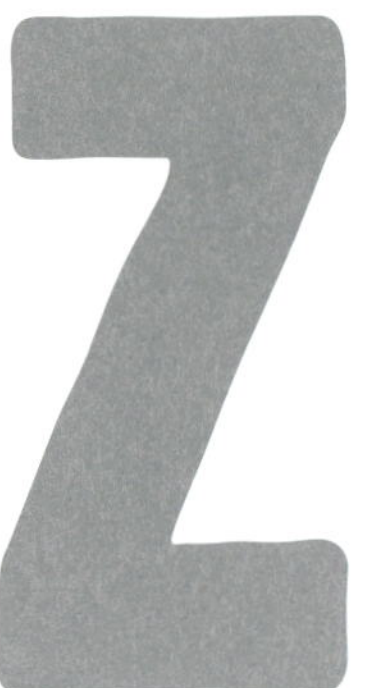

Thomas Zander

Cologne

 Galleries Unlimited

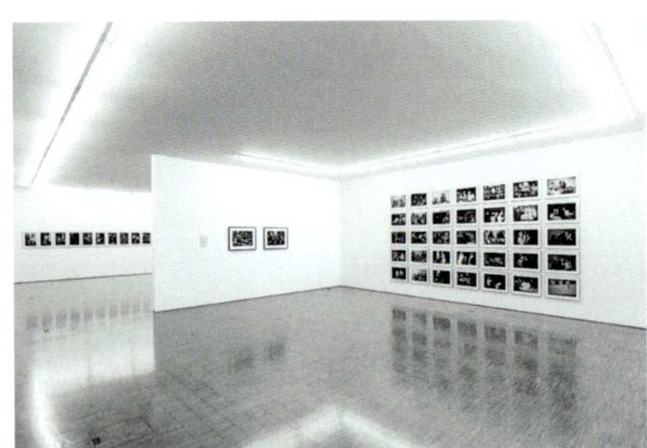

What is your favorite aspect of running a gallery?
Passion.

How do you choose the artists you work with?
Intuition.

If you weren't running a gallery what else would you do?
Music producer.

- **Contact** Galerie Thomas Zander
  Natalie Gaida
  mail@galeriezander.com
- **Established** 1996
- **Owner(s) / Partner(s)** Thomas Zander
- **Team** 10
- **Space(s)** 500 m²
- **Artists at Art Basel** Diane Arbus
  Lewis Baltz
  Lothar Baumgarten
  Victor Burgin
  Peter Downsbrough
  Mitch Epstein
  Walker Evans
  Lee Friedlander
  Andrea Geyer
  Anthony Hernandez
  Candida Höfer
  Mike Mandel
  Gordon Matta-Clark
  Anthony McCall
  Dieter Meier
  Trevor Paglen
  Tod Papageorge
  Albert Renger-Patzsch
  Gerhard Richter
  Ed Ruscha
  Stephen Shore
  Santiago Sierra
  Larry Sultan
  Henry Wessel
  Garry Winogrand
- **Further artists represented** Jean-Paul Deridder
  Don Dudley
  Philippe Gronon
  John McLaughlin
  Gabriele & Helmut Nothhelfer
  Max Regenberg
  Molly Springfield

Zeno X

Antwerp

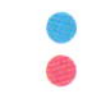 Galleries
Galleries

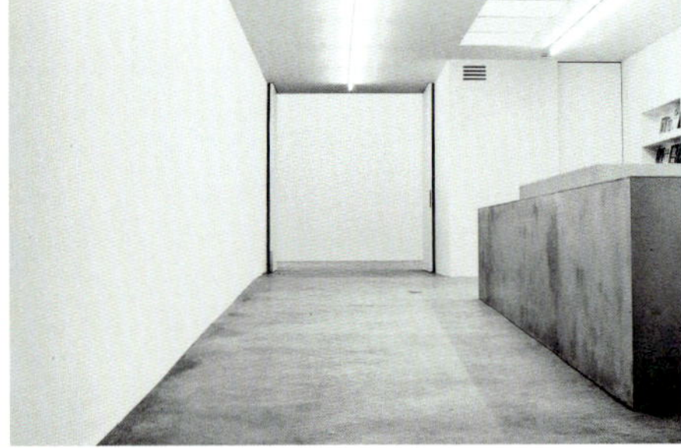

What is your favorite aspect of running a gallery?
Working with the artists.

How do you choose the artists you work with?
I know that I want to work with an artist when I would like to own a work by him/her myself.

If you weren't running a gallery what else would you do?
I would be in another creative field.

- **Contact** Zeno X Gallery
  Frank Demaegd
  info@zeno-x.com
- **Established** 1981
- **Owner(s) / Partner(s)** Frank Demaegd
- **Team** 8
- **Space(s)** 1,200 m²
- **Artists at Art Basel** Michaël Borremans
  Dirk Braeckman
  Anton Corbijn
  Raoul De Keyser
  Jan De Maesschalck
  Marlene Dumas
  Kees Goudzwaard
  Susan Hartnett
  Yun-Fei Ji
  Kim Jones
  Johannes Kahrs
  Naoto Kawahara
  John Körmeling
  Mark Manders
  Jockum Nordström
  Pietro Roccasalva
  Grace Schwindt
  Jenny Scobel
  Bart Stolle
  Mircea Suciu
  Luc Tuymans
  Patrick van Caeckenbergh
  Anne-Mie van Kerckhoven
  Jack Whitten
  Cristof Yvoré

ZERO

Milan

Galleries Unlimited

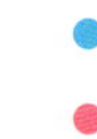 Galleries

What is your favorite aspect of running a gallery?
I enjoy the curatorial and research aspect, which is where I really see myself. I am attracted by the artists' mind, their ideas, and the creative process behind their works.

How do you choose the artists you work with?
There is a magical moment, almost an epiphany when I come into the "right" artwork. My mind is touched and at the same time my rational side starts calculations: from the possibilitiy of production in numeric terms, to the technique, to the physical force invested in the creation of the work, etc. The artist is an exceptional entity and I evaluate the person and the work in their entirety, paying attention to a variety of variables that should coexist at the highest level.

If you weren't running a gallery what else would you do?
I would be a fisherman.

- **Contact** ZERO
  Paolo Zani
  info@galleriazero.it
- **Established** 2000
- **Owner(s) / Partner(s)** Paolo Zani
- **Team** 5
- **Space(s)** 200 m²
- **Artists at Art Basel** Yuri Ancarani
  Giorgio Andreotta Calò
  Micol Assaël
  Mark Barrow
  Neïl Beloufa
  Cezary Bodzianowski
  Hubert Duprat
  Christian Frosi
  Giuseppe Gabellone
  Francesco Gennari
  Massimo Grimaldi
  João Maria Gusmão + Pedro Paiva
  Thomas Houseago
  Gavin Kenyon
  Victor Man
  Jurgen Ots
  Pietro Roccasalva
  Michael Sailstorfer
  Hans Schabus
  Shimabuku
  Gedi Sibony
  Michael E. Smith

Zilberman

Istanbul — Insights

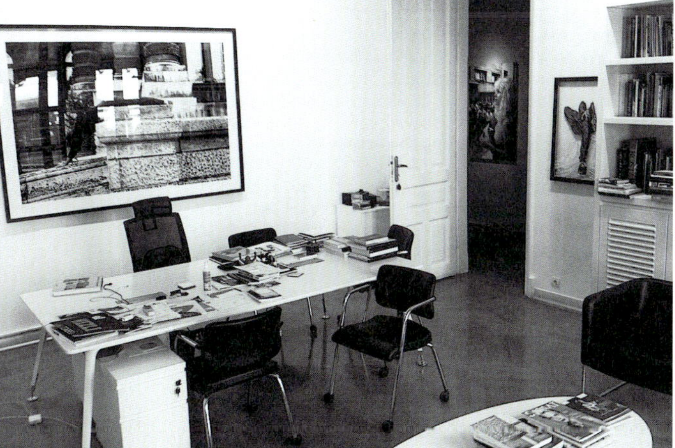

What is your favorite aspect of running a gallery?

Running a gallery provides an environment in which you get to communicate with artists, curators, and art enthusiasts. There is an opportunity to see new and exciting projects in the making, and to express your opinions and suggestions about them. It is a very fulfilling feeling to be supporting artists and contributing to the art scene.

How do you choose the artists you work with?

Most of our young artists are introduced to us through *Young Fresh Different*, our annual group show in which we exhibit works from artists that have applied to our nationwide open call. Some artists we track down after we see their work in exhibitions or fairs, and have an instant attraction to their work. One of the most important things is to see if we have a good dialogue and mutual understanding with the artist. It is wonderful to be friends with our artists.

If you weren't running a gallery what else would you do?

Running a gallery is not my main source of income, it is something I chose to do out of pure interest and enthusiasm. Therefore I think I would be running a gallery in all alternative scenarios of my life.

- **Contact** Galeri Zilberman
  Ayşe Aydoğan
  ayse.aydogan@gmail.com
- **Established** 2008
- **Owner(s) / Partner(s)** Moiz Zilberman
- **Team** 8
- **Space(s)** 225 m²
- **Artists at Art Basel** Selçuk Artut
  Alpin Arda Bağcık
  Janet Bellotto
  Burçak Bingöl
  Guido Casaretto
  Ahmet Elhan
  Zeren Göktan
  Zeynep Kayan
  Azade Köker
  Şükran Moral
  Fırat Neziroğlu
  Walid Siti
  Funda Susamoğlu
  Gülin Hayat Topdemir
  Aslı Torcu
  Eşref Yıldırım

Zwirner

New York
London

Galleries
Galleries Unlimited
Galleries

- **Contact** David Zwirner
  Greg Lulay
  information@davidzwirner.com
- **Established** 1993
- **Owner(s) / Partner(s)** David Zwirner
  Kristine Bell
  Angela Choon
  Christopher D'Amelio
  Bellatrix Hubert
  Julia Joern
  Tracy Nolder
  Hanna Schouwink
- **Team** 120
- **Space(s)** 929 m² (19th Street)
  2,787 m² (20th Street)
  2,787 m² (Grafton Street, London)
- **Artists at Art Basel** Adel Abdessemed
  Tomma Abts
  Francis Alÿs
  Mamma Andersson
  Michaël Borremans
  Carol Bove
  Raoul De Keyser
  Philip-Lorca diCorcia
  Stan Douglas
  Marlene Dumas
  Marcel Dzama
  Dan Flavin
  Suzan Frecon
  Isa Genzken
  Donald Judd
  Jeff Koons
  Yayoi Kusama
  John McCracken
  Oscar Murillo
  Alice Neel
  Jockum Nordström
  Chris Ofili
  Raymond Pettibon
  Neo Rauch
  Jason Rhoades
  Michael Riedel
  Thomas Ruff
  Fred Sandback
  Richard Serra
  Yutaka Sone
  Al Taylor
  Wolfgang Tillmans
  Luc Tuymans
  James Welling
  Christopher Williams
  Jordan Wolfson
  Lisa Yuskavage
- **Further artists represented** Karla Black
  R. Crumb
  On Kawara
  Toba Khedoori
  Kerry James Marshall
  Gordon Matta-Clark
  Ad Reinhardt
  Bridget Riley
  Thomas Ruff
  Fred Sandback
  Katy Schimert
  Diana Thater
  Doug Wheeler

Zeno X Gallery
Interview with Frank Demaegd

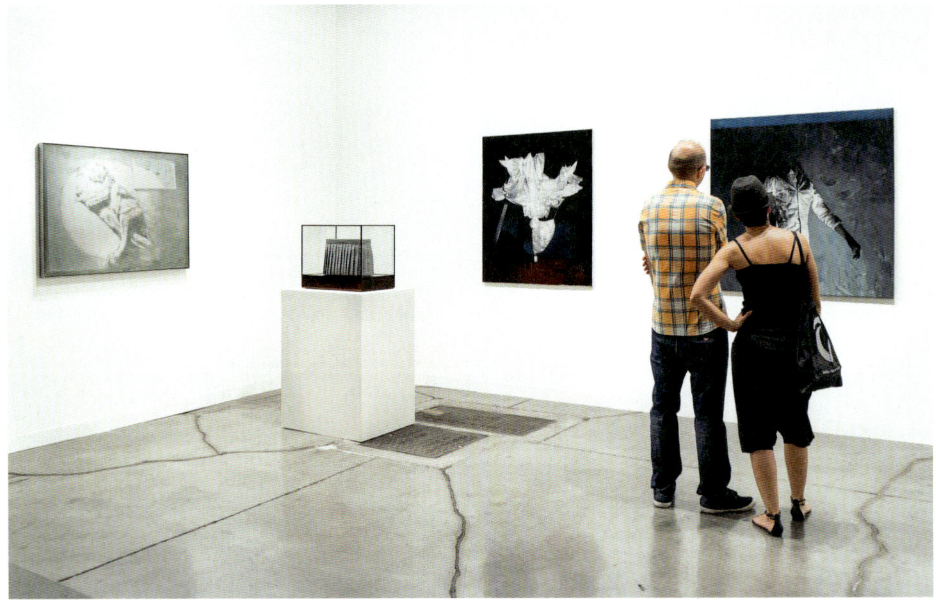

Art Basel in Miami Beach, 2014

Could you tell us how and why you started your gallery, coming from an architecture practice?

I was working as an architect and urban planner in Holland, and I had just bought a house in Antwerp; it was a big house, too big for two people, so we used the ground floor for the exhibitions. I started quite naively: I was not involved in the art market, but I thought that if I organize good exhibitions I'd be able to sell something. The first three or four years, we didn't sell anything…

I started in 1981 with an exhibition by Luc Deleu, a Belgian artist and architect. I also exhibited Rem Koolhaas in 1983. At that time, in the modernist narrative, painting was considered dead, so I showed a lot of installations. Later, I rediscovered painting and felt that I could show it: the result is what you can see now in my program.

Why did you decide to open in Antwerp? How was the art scene in Belgium in the 1980s?

I was working in Holland, my wife was working in Brussels, and Antwerp was in the middle. The art scene was small: there was only one contemporary art museum in Ghent. In Antwerp itself, there were no museums until 1987. Any place between Cologne and New York was on the periphery somehow. When Jan Hoet was nominated for documenta in 1992, Belgium came into the spotlight. It was a very important moment for the Belgian scene.

Was Jan Hoet close to the gallery program?

With Jan you never knew. He professed to dislike galleries, but I admired him, his passion for art. When he did documenta, there was one piece by an artist at the gallery that he wanted to buy, but the museum had no money; I told him to forget about my commission and to just pay the artist's half. He wrote me a very nice letter back and in the same week he had paid the artist. If I had asked him for the money, it would probably have taken four or five years …

You have become almost an institution in Belgium, not only because of your gallery's long history, but also because of the artists you represent: Marlene Dumas, Raoul De Keyser, Guillaume Bijl, etc. You really grew up with your artists.

I think that's very important, yes. Next year, it will be my 25th year working with Luc Tuymans and my 24th year with Marlene Dumas. It's almost like a marriage.

What is the secret to keeping the artists in the gallery?

If you're not in London or New York, you can develop a close relationship with artists without thinking about making money all the time. The pressure is lower than in those capitals, you can build friendships with artists and you are in a position where you can tell them what you like and what you don't. Artists, when successful, need someone who is critical to discuss what they do—not just to talk about how much you've sold or so on. I like that about our relationships.

You first participated in Art Basel in Basel in 1994 with Mark Manders. Could tell us about this first participation?

It was a special project: only cushions and carpets on the floor. I think it is important when you are invited for the first time to a fair that you really make a statement. So that's what we did with Mark Manders who was still unknown at the time. Again, we have a long relationship with him, we've been working with him for 20 years.

How would you define the gallery's program? Do you mainly show Belgian artists?

I don't mainly show Belgian artists, but artists that I like to work in depth with. And not only young artists: I started to work with Jack Whitten, a very important abstract painter who never got the recognition he deserved. We've sold his work to Tate and the SFMOMA, so after all these years, he is finally getting it.

Index

ʾlease note that this ndex includes the ames of all persons, galleries, and institutions cited in *Year 45*, but not of every single artist presented at the Art Basel shows in 2014 or represented by participating galleries. Numbers refer to pages and bold indicates an illustration.

10 Chancery Lane (Gallery) **46**
1900-2000, Galerie **46** 392 **396–397**
1a Space 316
303 Gallery **47** **49** **667** **677** 690
47 Canal 47 514 **516–517**
4A Centre **300**
55 **47** 208
80m2 (Livia Benavides) **48** **188** **514**

A

A Gentil Carioca **68**
Aarons, Philip & Shelley Fox 661 **674–675**
Abbas, Nadim **60–67** **663**
Abdessemed, Adel 440
Abeles, Michele 514 **516–517**
Abramović, Marina 6 36 38 **675**
Abreu, Miguel (Gallery) 68
Absolut **62–67** **663**
Accardi, Carla 534 **536** 541 682
Achiampong, Larry 280
Ackermann, Rita 690
Acquavella 69 314
Adkins, Terry 534 **537** 540–541
Adnan, Etel 125 392 **394–395**
Ahearn, John **426–427**
Ai Weiwei 6
Aike-Dellarco **69** 208
Aiko, Miyanaga 230 **240–241** **667**
Air de Paris **69** **92–93**
Aitken, Doug 49
Aizpuru, Juana de (Galería) **70** **79** 690
Al Bengston, Billy 415
al Karim, Halim 364 759
Albarracín, Pilar 280
Albers, Josef 750
Albert, Tony 364
Aldrich, Richard 690
Alexander and Bonin **70**–71 **426-427**
Alexander, Brooke (Inc.) 70 246
Alexander, Mark 614
Alexiev, Ryan 570
Alfi, Jumaldi 364
Alfred, Brian 280
Alisan Fine Arts **71**
Allora & Calzadilla 36 38 **42**
Almarcegui, Lara 514
Althamer, Paweł 293
Altman Siegel **71** 514
Alva Noto 54 56
Alwan, Ashkal 658
Alÿs, Francis 513
American Contemporary **72** 616
Ameringer/McEnery/Yohe **72**
Ammann, Thomas (Fine Art AG) **72**
Ancart, Harold 690
Andersen's (Contemporary) 73
Anderson, David 440
Andre, Carl 440 599 601 **673** 682 690 **692–693**
Andréhn-Schiptjenko **73**
Angelidakis, Andreas 280
Aninat, Isabel (Galería) **73** 616
Anthology Film Archives 124
Antikenmuseum 82
Anwander, Maria 280
Aoki, Ryoko 514
AoyamaIMeguro 380
Appelt, Dieter 538
Apples, Silver **63**
Applicat-Prazan **74**
Approach (The) **74** 690
Arakawa, Shusaku 440
Aran, Uri 514
Arario (Gallery) **74**–75
ARATANIURANO **75** 208
ARCO 79 658
Arena, Francesco 550
Armleder, John M 256 **742–743**
Armory (New York) 719
Arnaud, Raquel (Galeria) **75** 264
Arndt **76** **330-331**
Arp, Jean 750
Arratia Beer 76 616
Arroyo, Eduardo 79
Arsham, Daniel **297** 300
Art : Concept **76** 550
Art & Language 264 **274–275**
Art and Culture Center 446
Art Center College of Design 415
Art Center/South Florida 446
Art Forum (Berlin) 719
Art Gallery of Ontario 513
Art Institute/Institut Kunst (Basel) 616
Artiaco, Alfonso **77** 690
Artinformal **77** 364 **370–371**
Artschwager, Richard 537
Asia Art Archive (AAA) 298 **663** **665**
Asia Pacific Triennial 513
Asia Society Hong Kong Center 316
Asian Contemporary Art Fair 759
Asis, Antonio 392
Atelier Van Lieshout 230
Athr (Gallery) **77**–78 **158** 364 **368–369**
Atkins, Ed 36 **40**
Atlas (Gallery) 78
Atlas, Charles 280
Atoui, Tarek 362
Attia, Kader 123
Audemars Piguet **28–29** **454–455**
Auerbach, Tauba 601 604
Avakian, Vartan 280
Avery, Milton 309 750
Avia, Amalia 79
AXA ART **32**
Axell, Evelyne 140
Aye (Gallery) **78** 264

B

Bacon, Francis 7 143 525
Bader, Darren 550
Bae Joon Sung 364
Baertling, Olle 143
Baga, Trisha 616 **624–625**
Balaskas, Bill 280
Baldessari, John 5 36 39 415
Balice Hertling **128** **665**
Bałka, Mirosław 293
Baloise **34** 293 616
Barefoot, Eleanor 538
Baronian, Albert **128**
Barragán, Luis 542
Barry, Hannah (Gallery) **129** 208
Barry, Robert 440 658
Bartana, Yael 587
von Bartha **129** **143**
von Bartha, Miklos 143
von Bartha, Stefan 143
Bartlett, Laura (Gallery) **129** 616
Baselitz, Georg 570 658 750
Basquiat, Jean-Michel 143 525
Bass Museum of Art 570
Bastos, Cibelle Cavalli 514
Baudach, Guido W. (Galerie) **130**
Bauer, Ute Meta 511 513
Baum, Erica 514
Baumann, Rebecca 230
Baume, Nicholas 570
Baumeister, Willi 264
Bearden, Romare 612
Beaumont, Clark 38
Bechtold, Gottfried 550
Beck & Eggeling **130**
Beckmann, Max 601
Beijing Art Now (Gallery) 130
Beijing Commune **130** 514
Beirut Art Center 513
Bell, Larry 415
Bellet, Harry 536–543
Bellini, Andrea 510 512
Bellou, Rania 280
Beloufa, Neïl 208 **218–219**
Benglis, Lynda 570 **576–577**
Benítez, Elba (Galería) **131** **679**
Benzacar, Ruth (Galeria de Arte) 131 392
Bergamin (Galeria) **131** 626 **632–633**
Berggruen, John (Gallery) 132
Berinson (Galerie) **132** **673**
Bernier/Eliades **132–133**
Berstein, Alex 750
Betbeze, Anna 616
Beuys, Joseph 79
Beyeler (Fondation) 8–11 **36–43** 82 **133** 390 537 **669** **671** **675**
Beyeler, Ernst 536 537 539 542

Bianchini (Gallery) 539
Bidlo, Mike 540
Bieniek, Natasha 364
Biermann, Aenne **673**
Biesenbach, Klaus 8–11 36–39 **44–45**
Bijl, Guillaume 768
Bill, Max 730
Billingham, Richard 614
BIM (Geneva) 512
Bingöl, Burçak 364
Birnbaum, Dara 264 **268–269**
Bischofberger, Bruno 143
Bishop, Claire 482–485
Bismuth, Pierre 550
bitforms (gallery) **133** 264
Bitzer, Matthias 570
Bjerggaard, Bo (Galleri) 133 626
Black, Karla 206
Blake, Peter 750
Blalock, Lucas 616 **671**
Blanc, Jean-Luc 550
Blau, Daniel **98–99** **134**
Blindspot (Gallery) **134** 364
Blondeau (& Cie) **90–91** **134**
Blum & Poe **135** 690
Blum, Peter (Gallery) **108–109** **135**
BMW **30–31** **147–150**
Boca Raton Museum of Art 446
Bochner, Mel **247**
Bock, John 690 **702–703**
Boers-Li (Gallery) **135**–136
Boesky, Marianne (Gallery) 136 570
Boetti, Alighiero 688
Boezem, Marinus 719
Boltanski, Christian 293
BolteLang **136** 208
Bonakdar, Tanya (Gallery) **136** 570
Bonalumi, Agostino 688
Boone, Mary (Gallery) **137**
Borch Jensen, Niels (Gallery) **137** 246 690
Borland, Polly 280
Borowski, Wiesław 293
Bortolami **138** **466–467** 690
Bortolozzi, Isabella (Galerie) 138 690
Botero, Fernando 682
Bouabré, Frédéric Bruly 534 542
Bouchet, Mike 514
Bourgeois, Louise **669**
Boyce, Nate 280
BQ **112–113** **138**–139
Brake, Brian 364
Braman, Sarah 570
Brame & Lorenceau **139**
Brancusi, Constantin 542 **677**
Brandão, Alexandre 514
Breakwell, Ian 614 690
Breeder (The) **139**
Bress, Brian 280 514
Breton, André 178 539
Breuning, Olaf 280
Brito, Luciana (Galeria) **140**
Broadway 1602 **140** 626 **630–631**
Broodthaers, Marcel 658
Brooks, David 616
Brown, Ben (Fine Arts) **141**
Brown, Gavin (enterprise) **100–101** 141 550 690
Brucker, Trudi 143
Brüderlin, Markus 534 536–537
Brunner, This 280
Brus, Günter 392
Bruscky, Paulo 392 **400–401**
Buchholz (Galerie) **141**–142
Buchloh, Benjamin 512
Buchmann (Galerie) 142
Buchmann, Felix 314
Buck, Bettina 208 280
Bugada & Cargnel **142** 264 550 690
Bundesamt für Kultur 82
Burckhardt, Jacqueline 537
Burden, Chris 415 550 **552–553**
Bureau 142 514 616 **618–619**
Buren, Daniel 440 **466–467** 537
Burgin, Victor 362
Burri, René 534 **538** 542
Bustos, Adriana 514
Butail, Astha 514
Butt, Faiza 364 759
Butt, Zoe 511–512
Büttner, Werner 206
Byars, James Lee 122 537

C

Cabinet **86–87** 192
CAC (Geneva) 512
Cage, John 148 599
Cahn, Miriam 392
Cais, Nino 562
CalArts 49 410 415
Caldas, Waltercio 264 514
Calder, Alexander **677**
Calderara, Antonio **171** 730
Calle, Johanna 264
Camargo, Sergio **679**
Camnitzer, Luis 514
Campoli Presti 192
Canale, Cristina 514
Candiani, Tania **190** 514
Canna (Galeri) 192 364
Canoilas, Hugo 208 **214–215**
Capalino, Borden 562
Capitain, Gisela 206
Capitain, Gisela (Galerie) 192 **206** 550
Capogrossi, Giuseppe 688
Capper, James 208
CAR 280
Carberry, Valerie (Gallery) **192** 392
carlier gebauer **193** 690
Carnegie International 277
Caro, Anthony **712–713** 750
Carrà, Carlo 492
Carreyn, Julien 562
Carroll / Fletcher **193** 208 562
Carron, Valentin 415
Carzaniga (Galerie) **194**
Casa Triângulo **194**
CasaLin 446
Casamonti, Michelle 688
Casas Riegner **194**–195 264 392
Castellani, Enrico **671** 688
Castelli (Gallery) **195**
Castelli, Leo 314 600 604
Castoro, Rosemarie 140 626
Cattelan, Maurizio 536
Caulfield, Patrick 750
CCA (Singapore) 613
Central (Galeria de Arte) **195** 562
Central Police Station 64
Cera, Pedro (Galeria) **196**
Ceroli, Mario 688
Ceruti, Mary 298 301
Cervera, Marta (Galería) **196** 514 570
Chambaud, Étienne 280
Chambers (Fine Art) **196**–197 364
Chan, Paul **669**
Chang, Chien-Chi 280
Chang, Richard **665**
Channa, Imran 759
Channer, Alice 690
Chao, Emily 261
Charim (Galerie) 197 626
Cheim & Read 197 570 690
Chemould Prescott Road **167** **197**–198 **663**
Chen Chieh-Jen 356
Chen Jialing 71
Chen Sai Hua Kuan 280
Chen Zhou 280
Cheng Ran **159** **163** 208 280 **663**
Cherry and Martin **198** 264 514
Chi-Wen (Gallery) **198** 230
Chiasera, Paolo 514
Chilindron, Marta 230
Chillida, Eduardo 79
Chim↑Pom 280
Chinese Contemporary Art 316
Chiu Ya-Tsai 364
Chopin, Henri 264 **266–267**
Chouakri, Mehdi **198**–199 690
Choy Chun Wei 364
Christo 682
Christov-Bakargiev, Carolyn 513
Chu Teh-Chun 364
CIFO (Miami) 446 679
Cintra + Box 4 **199** 614
Clark, Larry 380 537
Clark, Lygia 386
Clavé, Antoni 536
Clifton Benevento **199** 562
Cobra 151 758
Cociña, Joaquín & Cristobal, León 280
Coe, Sue 59
Cohan, James (Gallery) **199** **340–341** 570
Cohen, Lynne 534 **538** 542
Colen, Dan **675**

Sadie Coles (HQ) **106–107** **200** **472–473** 550 690
Comer, Stuart 154 **180**–185
Consagra, Pietro 541 682
Contemporary Fine Arts **200**–201
Continua (Galleria) **201** **334–335** **679** 690
Cooke, Lynne 510 512
Cooper, Dennis 415
Cooper, Paula **596–605**
Cooper, Paula (Gallery) **170** **201** 570 **596–605** 690
Corbett vs. Dempsey **202**
Cordier & Ekstrom 598
Cornell, Joseph 392
Cornell, Lauren 512
Coronel Jr., Vermont 364
Corrias, Pilar **165** **202** **352** 616 **622–623**
Cortese, Raffaella (Galleria) **202**–203 264 690
Costinas, Cosmin **364–375**
Cowan, Andrew 538
Cragg, Tony 537 687
Craig-Martin, Michael 750
Cramer, Daniel Gustav 208
Crawford, Ralston 626
Creative Time 669
Creed, Martin 280
Crèvecoeur **203** 562
CRG (Gallery) 203
Crimp, Douglas 512
Cristea, Alan 750
Cristea, Alan (Gallery) **203**–204 246 **250**
Crousel, Chantal (Galerie) 204 **667** 690
Crowdfunding Initiative **296–301**
Crown Point (Press) **204** 246
Crowner, Sarah 514 **518–519**
Cuc (Gallery) **205** 364 **366–367**
Cucchi, Enzo 658
Curiger, Bice 154 **168–173** 537

D

d'Imbleval, Jean 538
Dadamaino **671** **679** 688
Dadson, Andrew 690
Daix, Pierre 534 536
Dalí, Salvador 79 540
Damani, Abdelkader 123
DAN (Galería) **220** **679**
Dane, Thomas (Gallery) **220**
Darboven, Hanne **175** 690 **700–701**
Darger, Henry 626 **634–635**
Davenport, Ian 750
David, Catherine 658
Davidoff (Oettinger) **27** **151–153**
Davidovich, Jaime 392 **398–399**
Davidson, Maxwell (Gallery) **220**–221
Dávila, Jose 280
Davis, Tim 280
de Aizpuru, Juana 79
de Alvear, Helga (Galería) **221**
de Barros, Lenora 140 626 **630–631**
de Beer, Sue 280
de Boeck, Lieven 514
de Boer, Manon 280
de Bruijn, Nieck 719
De Carlo, Massimo **176** **221** **227** **671** 690
De Chirico, Giorgio 492
De Gruyter, Jos & Thys, Harald 690
De Keersmaeker, Anne Teresa 513
De Keyser, Raoul 768
de Kooning, Willem 682
de la Cruz Collection 446
de Land, Colin 49
De Maria, Nicola 682
De Maria, Walter 599
de Medici, eX 365
de Miguel, Regina 514
de Montferrand, Hadrien (Gallery) **222**
de Osma, Guillermo (Galería) **222** **679**
de Saint Phalle, Niki 626 **636–637**
de Sarthe Gallery **223**
de Solminihac, Paula 616
de Torres, Cecilia (Ltd.) 223 230 626
Dean, Michael 264 **266–267** 514
Dean, Tacita **172** 690
Decrauzat, Philippe 690 **696–697**
Dee, Elizabeth **223**–224
DeFeo, Jay 502
Dekyndt, Edith 690
Dela Cruz, Bembol 364
Deleu, Luc 768
Delfina Foundation 298 **301**
Delhi Art Gallery **224**
Demaegd, Frank 768
Demand, Thomas 380
Demarco, Hugo 538
Dercon, Chris 543
Derieux, Florence 550
Dewar & Gicquel **673**
Dewasne, Jean 538
di Suvero, Mark 599
Dia Art Foundation 162
Diao, David 514
Dias Batista, Ana Luiza 570 **572–573**
Dibbets, Jan 719
didier, michèle (mfc) **224** 246
Dijkstra, Martijn 719
Dine, Jim 309
Dirimart 225
Dix, Otto 531
Dmab, Felipe 508
documenta 172 227 395 537 543 601 768
Dong Yuan 364
Dorazio, Piero 541 682
Doyle, Chris 280
Dr. Sun Yat-sen Museum 316
Drawing Room (The) **225** 364
Drtikol, František 407
du Monde (Galerie) **225** 364
Dubuffet, Jean 598 **750**
Duchamp, Marcel 5 38 122 148 150 415 540
Duclós, Teresa 79
Dullaart, Constant 562
Dumas, Marlene 768
Dunham, Carroll 390
Dvir (Gallery) **226**
Dymond, Ara 514
Dzama, Marcel 280

E

East of Borneo **299**
Ecart **256**
Echakhch, Latifa 169
Edlin, Andrew (Gallery) **256** **634–635** 626
Edwin's (Gallery) 256–257 364
EIGEN + ART (Galerie) **257** 690
Eisenman, Nicole 264 **276–277**
Ekstrom, Arne 598
Ekwurtzel, Sam 562 570
elbaz, frank (galerie) **257**
Eliasson, Olafur 149 **150**
Elmgreen & Dragset **419** 570
EM (Gallery) **257**–258 364
Engh, Marius 514
Enwezor, Okwui **126–127** 513
Epaminonda, Haris 264
Equipo Crónica 79
Equipo Realidad 79
Erben, Thomas (Gallery) **208** 258
Ermotti, Sergio P. 20–23
Ernst, Max 598
Eslite (Gallery) 230 **258** **261**
espaivisor **184** **259** 264 **278–279** 626 **677** **679**
Essex Street **673**
Eu, Emi **251–254**
Eugenia Butler (Gallery) 415
Evangelista, Diogo 280
Everett, Liam 514
Exhibit 320 **259**
Exit (Gallery) 230 **259**–260 **663**
Experimenter **208–213** **260**

F

Fairchild Tropical Botanic Garden 446
Faivovich & Goldberg 562 570
Faldbakken, Matias **102–103** 601 **669** **691**
Falls, Sam **671** 690 **710–711**
Falsnaes, Christian 570 616
Fanal (Atelier-Editions) 246 **286**
Faria, Henrique (Fine Art) **286** 392 **398–399**
Farmer, Geoffrey **677**
Farocki, Harun 280 534 **539** 543 **669** 690
Farquhar, Keith 614
Farquhar, Nicola 208

Fautrier, Jean 598
Feeley, Paul 626 **628–629**
Feher, Tony 690
Feigen, Richard L. (& Co.) 286
Feininger, Lyonel 658
Feldmann, Hans- Peter 49
Fernández, Teresita 392
Ferreras de la Maza, Monica **151**
Feuer, Zach (Gallery) **287**
Finale (Art File) **287** 364
Fine Arts Literature (Art Center) **287**–288
Finlay, Ian Hamilton 658
Firman, Daniel **428–429**
Fischer, Konrad (Galerie) **175** **288** 390 690
Fischer, Nina & Maroan el Sani 280 282
Flagstaff House Museum 316
Flanagan, Barry 537 750
Flavin, Dan 600 730
Fogle, Douglas **264–279**
Foksal (Gallery Foundation) **179** **185** **288** **293**
Fondation Van Gogh 168
Fontana, Lucio 688
Förg, Günther 206 362
Forma Uno 541
Forster, Norman 49
Fortes Vilaça (Galeria) **288**–289 690
Forti, Simone 598
Fost (Gallery) **289** 364
Fotomuseum Winterthur 537
Foxx, Marc (Gallery) 264 **270–271** **289** 550 690
FRAC Champagne-Ardenne 550
Fraenkel (Gallery) **290**
Fragateiro, Fernanda **679**
Francis, Sam 386
Frank, Robert 537
Fraser, Honor **290** 562
Freedman, Carl (Gallery) 208 290
Freedman Fitzpatrick **290**–291 562 **568–569** **673**
Freeman, Peter (Inc.) **291**
Fréger, Charles 407
Friedman, Dara 280
Friedman, Stephen (Gallery) **291**
Friedman, Tom 283
Friese, Klaus Gerrit (Galerie) 264 292
Frigo, Giulio 208
Frith Street (Gallery) **172** **292**
Fudong, Yang **346–347** **665** 690
Fuentes, James **182** 292 **627**
Fujiwara, Simon 38
Fulton, Hamish 440 690
Funke, Jaromír 407
Fuster, Nuria 570
FX Harsono 364

Ga, Ellie 616 **618–619**
Gabin, Leo 280
Gagosian (Gallery) **302** 550 570 604 **667**
Gaines, Charles 601
Gajah (Gallery) **302**
Galan, Marcius **679**
Galhotra, Vibha 364
Galleria dello Scudo **302**
Gander, Ryan **328–329** **551** 570 690
Gandhara (Art) **303**
García Torres, Mario **191** 446 550 661 **676**–677
Garibaldi, Syaiful Aulia 364
Gartenfeld, Alex **514–523**
Gaskell, Anna 280
Gasworks **300**
Gavlak (Gallery) **303**
Gazelli (Art House) 208 **303**–304
gb agency **304** 550 690
GDM 246 **304**–305
Gehry, Frank 280 537 682
Geldzahler, Henry 598
Gelink, Annet (Gallery) **305**
Gemini G.E.L. (LLC) 246 **305**
Gerhardsen Gerner **305**–306
Gernes, Poul 626
Geyer, Andrea 280
Ghebaly, François (Gallery) 208 **218–219** **306**
Giacometti, Alberto 537 542 598 **667**
Gilardi, Piero 719
Gillick, Liam 639
Gioni, Massimiliano 154 **174–179**
Girls' Club Collection 446
Girst, Thomas 148–150
Gladstone (Gallery) 306 314 570 690
Glass, Philip 599
Glissant, Edouard 513
Glöde, Marc 282–285
Glynn, Liz 601
Glynn, Liz & Kasper, Dawn 570
Gmurzynska (Galerie) **306**–307 **677**
Gnoli, Domenico 264
Gober, Robert 206 362 **669**
Goethe-Institut Hongkong 316
Goldberg, RoseLee **124**
Goldin, Nan 537
Gomes, Sonia 508
Gomez, Sayre 208 **218–219** 514
Gonzalez-Foerster, Dominique 36 282 639
Gonzalez-Foerster, Dominique & Bera, Tristan 280
Gonzalez-Torres, Felix 49 362 540
González, Beatriz 264
González, Elvira (Galería) **120** **307**
Goodman Gallery **307** 570 690
Goodman, Marian (Gallery) 308 **346–347** **669** **679** 690
Gorchov, Ron 690
Gordon, Douglas 293 **344–345**
Gordon, Walters 653
Gorky, Arshile 309
Gostomski, Zbigniew 293
Gotovac, Tomislav 280
Grabner, Michelle 280 510 512
Graham, Dan 725
Graham, Martha 483
Graham, Rodney **677**
Grässlin, Bärbel (Galerie) **308**
Gray, Alexander (Associates) **308**–309
Gray, Richard (Gallery) **309**
Green, Brent 280
Greenan, Garth (Gallery) **309** 626 **628–629**
Greenberg, Clement 750
Greenberg, Howard (Gallery) **310**
Greene Naftali (Gallery) 310 690
greengrassi 310
Greve, Karsten 314
Greve, Karsten (Galerie) **310**–311 **314**
Grieder (Contemporary) **311**
Grimm 230 **311**
Grooms, Red 598
Grossman, Nancy 612
Grosvenor, Robert 599
Grosz, George 531 593
Grotto (Fine Art Limited) **312**
G.R.A.V. 538
Gryn, David 280 724
Gu Wenda 230 **236–237** **350–351**
Guan Xiao 280
Guangzhou Triennial 513
Guerra, Cristina **312** 690
Guggenheim Museum 20 21 22 23 392 393
Gunn, Dan **312** 562 **566–567**
Guo Gong 364
Gupta, Kavi (Chicago | Berlin) 313 392 570
Gursky, Andreas 49
Gusmão, João Maria + Pedro Paiva 690
Guyton, Wade 206 587
Gwangju Biennial 548

Haacke, Hans 604
Haas, Michael (Galerie) **178** **354**
Haines, David 208
Hainley, Bruce 415
Hains, Raymond 362
Hakgojae (Gallery) **354**–355
Hales (Gallery) 208 **355**
Halley, Peter 390 750
Halpert, Edith 600
Hamilton, Richard 79
Hammer (Galleries) **355**
Hammer, Jan Peter 280
Han, Ishu 280
Hanart TZ (Gallery) 230 264 **350–351** **356**
Hanazawa, Takeo 364
Handforth, Mark 550 **558–559**
Hands, May 514
Hanos, Van 514 **520–521**
Hanson, Duane **424–425**
Hanzlová, Jitka 407
Hao Shiming 364
Haring, Keith 540 682

Hartt, David 280
Harvey, Lucy 614
Hasegawa, Yuko **230–245**
Hatakeyama, Naoya 380
Hatoum, Mona 362
Haus für elektronische Kunst 82
Hauser & Wirth **114–115** **356** **541** **665** 690
Hauser, Mona 759
Hawkins, Richard 415
Hawser, Eloise **665**
Hayes, Sharon **669**
Hazlitt Holland-Hibbert **357**
He Xiangyu **420–421**
Heath, Frank 280
Hefuna, Susan 364
Hein, Jeppe 570 **580–581**
Hellberg, Fatima **665**
Henrot, Camille 280
Herald St **357** 690
Herold, Georg 206
Heron, Patrick 750
Herzog & de Meuron 36 39
Hetzler, Max 206 362
Hetzler, Max (Galerie) 206 **357** **362**
High Line 124
Hiller, Susan 280
Hilliard, John 362
Hirakawa, Youki 280 364
Hirsch, Nikolaus 54
Hirschl & Adler (Modern) **358** 392
Hirst, Damien 7 36 **40** **462–463**
HistoryMiami 446
Hockney, David 79 254
Hoejsgaard, Hans-Kristian 151–153
Hoet, Jan 534 537 **539** 768
Hoffman, Rhona (Gallery) 338–**339** **358** 392 **677**
Höller, Carsten **667**
Holt, Nancy 534 543
Holzer, Jenny 440
Hominal, David 208
Hong Kong Arts Centre 71 280
Hong Kong Heritage Museum 316
Hong Kong Maritime Museum 316
Hong Kong Museum of Art 316
Hong Kong Museum of History 316
Hood, Alex Gregory 750
Hopf, Judith 169
Hopkins (Galerie) **358**–359
Hopkinson Mossman 208 359
Hoppen, Michael (Gallery) **359**
Hornig, Sabine 690
Hou Hanru 122 155 **156**–161
Houk, Edwynn (Gallery) **359**
Houldsworth, Pippy (Gallery) 264 **360**
Houseago, Thomas 690
Houshiary, Shirazeh **679**
Howey, Jaya 514
Hsu Yu-Jen 356
Hsu, Claire 661 **662–663**
Hu Xiaoyuan 514
Hubbard, Alex 690
Huber, Pierre 314
Hufkens, Xavier 360 **671** 690
Hui, Steve 63
Huot, Robert 600
Hur, Un Kyung 364
Hutchins, Jessica Jackson 570
Hutton, Leonard (Galleries) **360**–361
Huws, Bethan 690
Huyghe, Pierre 639
Hyber, Fabrice 542

I

i8 (Gallery) **376**
Iannone, Dorothy 514
Ibid **376**
Ignacio, Troy 364
IHN (Gallery) 364 **376**–377
Iles, Chrissie 724–725
Indieguerillas **330–331**
Ingleby (Gallery) **377**
Instagram **336–337**
ICA (Miami) 446
ICA (London) 665
Instituto de visión **190** **377** 514
Invernizzi (A arte) **378**
iPreciation 230 **324–325** 364 **374** **378** **663**
Ishida, Takashi 280
Ishida, Tetsuya 764
Ishii, Taka (Gallery) **379** **380**
Issa, Iman 550
Ito, Parker 280
Itten, Johannes 542
Iveković, Sanja 264 **278–279**
Izumi, Taro 208 280

J

Jablonka (Galerie) **386** **390** 690
Jablonka, Rafael 390
Jackson, Martha 440 600
Jacobson, Bernard (Gallery) **386**
Jacques, Alison (Gallery) **386** 690
Janda, Martin (Galerie) **387**
Janis, Sidney 600 604
Jankowski, Christian **191**
Jansen, Theo **454–455**
Janssen, Michael 364 **387**
Janssen, Rodolphe (Galerie) 264 **387**–388 570
Janssens, Ann Veronica 690 **716–717**
Jao, Chia-En 364
Jarpa, Voluspa 514
Jeffries, Catriona **388** 690
Jensen (Gallery) **388**
Jeppesen, Travis 748
Jetzer, Gianni 690
Jewish Museum of Florida 446
Ji Dachun 264
Jiang Zhi **665**
Jitrik, Magdalena 514
Johnen (Galerie) **388**–389 690
Johns, Jasper 539
Johnson, Larry 49
Johnson, Philip 682 724–725
Johnson, Rashid 280 415
Jonas, Joan 36 **41** **382–385** 512
Jones, Jennie C. 280
Jones, William E. 415
Jongma, Juliètte (Galerie) **389** 562
Joo, Eungie **125** 513
JPW3 514
Juda, Annely (Fine Art) **389** 690
Judd, Donald 537 600–601 682 730
Juliano-Villani, Jamian 514
Julier, Thomas 562

K

K11 Art Foundation 316 **665**
Kaabi-Linke, Nadia **208–213**
Kadel Willborn **274–275** **402**
Kaga, Atsushi 280
Kaikai Kiki (Gallery) **402**
Kalfayan (Galleries) **402**–403 562
Kander, Nadav 364
Kaneuji, Teppei **173** **252** **667**
Kantor, Tadeusz **293**
Kaplan, Casey **403**
Kaplan, Stephen 152
Kapoor, Anish **679** 688
Kargl, Georg (Fine Arts) **403**
Karilampi, Ilja 280
Karma (Gallery) **675**
Karma International 208 **404**
Kasmin, John 750
Kasmin, Paul (Gallery) **404** **458–459** 750
Kato, Tsubasa 280
Katrib, Ruba **562–569**
Katz, Alex **108–109**
kaufmann repetto **169** 392 **404**
Kaufmann, Craig 415
Kawaguchi, Tatsuo 364
Kawara, On 440 534 540–541
Keller, Walter 534 537 **540**
Kelley, Mike 79 362 390 415
Kelly, Leon 392
Kelly, Mary 264
Kelly, Sean **405**
Kempinas, Zilvinas 514
Keng, Tina (Gallery) **161** **405**
Kenyon, Gavin 690 **694–695**
Kepes, Gyorgy 539
Kerlin (Gallery) **116–117** **406**
Kern, Anton (Gallery) **406** 690
Kewenig **406**–407 690
Khan, Naiza 280
Khawaja, Nadia 208
Khoury, Bernard 658
Kicken (Berlin) 392 **407** **540**

Kicken, Rudolf 534 537 **540**
Kickstarter 8–11 **298–301**
Kiefer, Anselm 540
Kiesler, Frederick 598
Kil, Chosil 548
Kilchmann, Peter (Galerie) **407**–408
Kilimnik, Karen 49
Kim Tschang Yeul 364
Kimura, Yuki 380
Kippenberger, Martin 79 206 362
Kitchen (The) 124
Kitnick, Zak 562
Klabin, Maria 514
Klahr, Lewis 614
Klapheck, Konrad **178**
Kläs, Esther 562 **564–565**
Klee, Paul 126
Klein, Yves 542 658 688
Klimt, Gustav 531
Klingberg, Gunilla 570
Klosterfelde Edition 246 **408**
Klüser (Galerie) **408**
Knowles, Alison **182** 599 **627**
Knust , Sabine 246 **409**
Koether, Jutta **466–467**
Kogure (Gallery) 364 **409**
Kohn (Gallery) 409
König, Johann **410** 570
König, Kasper 390
Konishi, Toshiyuki 208
Koo Jeong-A **165**
Koolhaas, Rem 768
Koons, Jeff 49 143 362
Kordansky, David 415
Kordansky, David (Gallery) **410** **415** 690
Korot, Beryl 264
Koru (Contemporary Art) 364 **411**
KOW 264 **411**
Koyama, Tomio (Gallery) **166** 230 411 690
Koyanagi (Gallery) **412**
Krasiński, Edward 293
Kraupa-Tuskany Zeidler **412** 616
Kreps, Andrew (Gallery) 413
Krinzinger (Galerie) 230 392 **413** 550 690
Kristiansson, Joannis 151
Kruger, Barbara 415
Krugier, Jan 314 531
Krupp, Nicolas **413** 690
Kühn, Heinrich 538
Kuitca, Guillermo 392
Kukje/Kim, Tina (Gallery) 230 **414** **679** 690
Kunsthalle Basel 82 293
Kunsthalle Bern 540
Kunsthaus Baselland 82
Kunsthaus Zürich 658
Kunstmuseum Basel 82 601 673
Kurian, Ajay 514
kurimanzutto **104–105** **414** **671**
Kusama, Yayoi 6
Kwan Sheung Chi 280 **663**

L

L-Art (Gallery) 364 **430**
La Monte Young 598
Labor **189** **430** 514 616 **620–621**
Laet, Maria 582
Laffón, Carmen 79
Lahumière (Galerie) **430**–431 538
Lahumière, Jean-Claude 538 **541**
Lam, Pearl (Galleries) 230 **431**
Lamas, Nicolás 514
Lambert , Yvon **94–95** 431 **440** 690
Lamdark, Kesang **667**
Lamelas, David 690
Landau (Fine Art) **431**–432
Laric, Oliver 280 434
Larner, Liz 49
Lassnig, Maria 539 **541**
Laszlo, Carl 143
Latham, John 280 438
Laurens, Henri 750
Lavier, Bertrand 440 542
Lawson, Thomas 415
Layr, Emanuel (Galerie) **432** 514
Le Corbusier 54 212 542
Le Free Port 19
Le French May Arts Festival 316
Le Parc, Julio 264 538 690
Le Roy, Xavier 38
Lê, Dinh Q. 280
Leach, Sam 364
Leavitt, William 690
Leckey, Mark 280
Lee Kit 125 **667**
Lee Ufan 690
Lee Wen 230 **324–325** 364 **374** **663**
Lee, Patrick 548
Lee, Simon (Gallery) **432**–433 550 690
Leeahn (Gallery) 364 **433**
Léger, Fernand 314 750
Leguillon, Pierre 513
Lehman, Rachel 548
Lehmann Maupin 392 **433**–434 548 690
Lehmann, Gebrüder (Galerie) **434**
Leighton, Tanya 434 514 **520–521** **669**
Leite, Patricia 514
Lelong (Galerie) 392 **394–395** **434**–435 570 690
Lelong Editions **435**
Leme (Galeria) **435** 514
León de la Barra, Pablo **392–401**
Leon, Andres Basile 64
León, Cristobal 280
Leonard, Zoe 206
Leslie, Jolyon 172
Lett, Michael **435**–436
Leung Kui-Ting 358
Levine, Sherrie 390 540
Lévy, Dominique (Gallery) **436**
Lewis, Tony **671**
LeWitt, Sol 79 440 **464–465** 599 604 658 **736–737**
Lhote, André 538
Li Zhenhua 280
Liang Quan 364
Liao Li 280
Lichtenstein, Roy 309 682
Ligon, Glenn 510–513 **669**
Lima, Laura 36 38 68
Lin & Lin (Gallery) **436**
Lin, Michael 230 232–**233**
Linder, Gisèle (Galerie) **437**
Lipi, Tayeba Begum 364
Lippard, Lucy 600
Liprandi, Ignacio (Arte) **437** 514
Lisson (Gallery) **328–329** **437**–438 550 570 **679** 690
Liste 293 380 671 673
Liu Chuang 280
Liu Kuo Sung 364
Locust Projects **297** 298 **300** 446
Löhrl (Galerie) **438**
Lombard Freid (Gallery) **438** **667**
Long March Space 230 **439** 690 754 **756–757**
Long, Richard 440 690
Lonzi, Carla 541
López Hernández, Julio 79
López, Antonio 79
Louis, Morris 750
Lowe Art Museum 446
Lucebert 658
Ludwig, Peter 362
Luhring Augustine 206 362 **439** 550 690
Lund, Marie 616
Lunn, Harry 538
Lupo, Nancy 514
Lutker, Shana 512
Lutz-Kinoy, Matthew **673**
Luxembourg & Dayan 264 439
Lyon Biennale 122–123

M

m Bochum (Galerie) **488**
M+ 64
Maass, Jörg (Kunsthandel) **488**
Macao Museum of Art 316
Maccarone **118–119** **488**–489 690
Mack, Heinz 538
Mackie, Christina 514 690
Magazzino **489**
Maggiore (Galleria d'Arte) **489**–490
Magician Space **490**
Magritte, René 415 665
Mahinay, Erica 514
Mai 36 (Galerie) **490**

Maisterravalbuena **491** 514
Malevich, Kazimir 82 293 688
Malingue, Edouard (Gallery) **326–327** 364 **491**
MAMVP (Paris) 542 688
Manders, Mark 768
Mangolte, Babette 280
Manley, Dashiell 280
Mansfield, Andrew 614
Mansion, Gracie 593
Manzoni, Piero 688 730
Mara-La Ruche, Jorge 392 **491**
Marcelle, Cinthia 125
Marclay, Christian 56 **170** 690
Marconi, Gió **492** 690
Margolles, Teresa 514
Margulies Collection 446 **677**
Marks, Matthew (Gallery) 492
Marlborough London 143 **492**–493
Marlborough New York 143 **493**
Martin, Jean-Hubert 122 542
Martin, Mary-Anne (Fine Art) **493**
Martinat, José Carlos **187** 570
Martinez, Chus **616–625**
Mason, John 415
Mason, T. Kelly 264
Mater, Ahmed **158** 364 **368–369**
Matherly, Justin 570 **571** 601 **605**
Mathes, Barbara (Gallery) **494**
Matisse, Henri 309 750
Mauss, Nick **667** 690
MAXXI (Rome) 156
Mayer, Hans (Galerie) **464–465** **494** **740–741**
Mayor (Gallery) **494**–495 750
Mazzoleni (Galleria d'Arte) **495**
McAlpine, Alistair 750
McCaffrey, Fergus 495 690
McCarthy, Paul 415
McCollum, Allan **736–737**
McKee (Gallery) 495
McKenna, Noel 208
McMillian, Rodney 125 690
McNamara, Ryan 8–11 **474–487** **665** **675**
McQueen, Steve 614
MDC 446
Medina, Cuautémoc 513
Meert, Greta (Galerie) **496** 690
Meessen De Clercq **496** 514
Meier, Anthony (Fine Arts) **496**–497 **669** 690
Meile, Urs (Galerie) 230 392 **497**
Meireles, Cildo 131
Meisenberg, Florian 280
Mellor, Danie 364
Menconi + Schoelkopf **497** 626
Mendes, Pedro 508
Mendes Wood DM **498** **508** 514
Mendieta, Ana 264 690
Mendizabal, Asier 614
mennour, kamel **498** 690
Merz, Mario 362 537 690
Messager, Annette 293
Messen, Vincent 513
Metro Pictures **470–471** **499** 690
Metzel, Olaf 570 **675**
Meyer Riegger **499** **673** 690
Mezzanin (Galerie) **499**–500
Miami Children's Museum 446
Miami Grand Theater **475–487** **675**
Miao Xiaochun 280
Michael Jon (Gallery) **500** 514
Michael, Theo 280
Millan (Galeria) **500**
Milroy, Lisa 750
Ming (Art Gallery) 364 **500**–501
Ming Wong 64 **66–67** **663** 690
Minini , Francesca 208 **501** 514
Minini, Massimo (Galleria) **171** **501**–502
Minneapolis Institute of Arts 254
Miró, Joan 79 254 309 750
Miro, Victoria **502** 570 690
Mitchell-Innes & Nash **502** 570 690
Mitchell, Dane 208
Mitchell, Joan 254 362
Mizuma (Art Gallery) 230 **503** **667**
Mnuchin (Gallery) 314 **503**
MOCA (Los Angeles) 380
MOCA (Miami) 446
MOCA (Yinchuan) 759
Modern Art (Stuart Shave) **348–349** **503–504** 550
Modern Institute (The) **110–111** 504 550 690
Moeller (Fine Art) 504
Moholy-Nagy, László 407 538
Mohr, Manfred 280
Mokgosi, Meleko 562
Molzan, Dianna 392
MoMA (New York) 39 56 124 180 279 293 494 543 600 659 688
Monastyrski, Andrei 626
Monitor 208 **504**
mor charpentier **505** 514
Morandi, Giorgio 492 598 682 750
Morellet, François 538
Morgan, Jessica **162–167** 548
Morimura, Yasumasa 690
Moser, Claudio 690
MOT International 264 **272–273** 505 514 **669** 690
Mot, Jan **505** 550 690
mother's tankstation 208 **505** 514
Motherwell, Robert **673**
Moti, Melvin **673** 690
Motley, Archibald 513
Motta, Pedro 514
Mousawi, Aya **665**
Moyer, Sam 570
Mucha, Reinhard **679**
Muir, Gregor **664**–**665**
Mujin-to Production 208 506
Müller, Mark (Galerie) **506**
Mullican, Matt 227
Munch, Edvard 539
Muñoz, Oscar 514
Munro, Vera (Galerie) **506**–507
Muracciole, Marie 510–513
Murakami, Takashi 402 764
Murata, Takeshi 280
Muresan, Ciprian 208 280 392
Murphy, Jan (Gallery) 364 **507**
Murray White (Room) **507**
Museo Tamayo 513
Museum der Kulturen 82
Museum für Gegenwartskunst 82 **673**
Museum of Art (Fort Lauderdale) 446
Museum of Coastal Defense 316
Museum Tinguely 82
Musson, Jayson 280
Muzquiz, Milena 514 **518–519**
Mytkowska, Joanna 293

N

nächst St. Stephan (Galerie) **524**
Nada (Art Fair) 675 719
Nadi (Gallery) **524**
Nagare, Masayuki 526
Nagel Draxler (Galerie) **524**–525
Nagy, Richard (Ltd.) **177** **525** **531**
Nahem, Edward Tyler (Fine Art) **456–457** **525**–526
Nahmad, Helly (Gallery) 526
Nakamura, Kanzaburō 598
Nanzuka **526**
Nasar, Hammad 298
Nash, David 690
National Gallery of Art 512 513
Nauman, Bruce 36 690
Naumann, Francis M. 392 **526**–527
Navarro, Leandro (Galeria) **527**
Navarro, Miquel 79
Nazareth, Paulo 508
Nemours, Aurélie 143
Netjets **26**
Neto, Ernesto 68 570 **578**
Neu (Galerie) **527**
neugerriemschneider 230 **332–333** **460–461** **529**
New Museum (New York) 124 174 512
New World Center (Miami) 280
Newsome, Rashaad 280
Nguyen-Hatsushiba, Jun 280
Nicolai, Carsten 8–11 **52–59** 690
Nieto, Amalia 392
Ning, Anna (Fine Art) **528**
Nitsch, Carolina 246 **528** 669
Nkanga, Orobong 36 **43**
Noero, Franco (Galleria) **342–343** **528**–529 550 690
Nogueira, Lucia 614
Nolan, David (Gallery) 392 529
Noland, Cady 7 49 362
Nonas, Richard 690
Noonan, David **348–349**
Nordenhake (Galerie) **529** 570
Norris, Tameka 280
Norton Museum of Art 446
Nothelfer, Georg (Galerie) **530**

Novitskova, Katja 616
Novros, David 599
Nuoart 364 **530**
Nuur, Navid 362

O

O'Neill, Lorcan (Galleria) 264 **544**
O'Neill, Pat 280 284
O'Connell, Ruairiadh 514
O'hEocha, Mairead 514
Obadia, Nathalie (Galerie) **544**
Oberthaler, Nick 514
Obrist, Hans Ulrich 8 9 10 11 36 38 39 **44–45** 122 395
OCT Contemporary Art 316
Oehlen, Albert 79 206 362
Ohtake, Shinro 264 514 **522–523**
Oi! 316
Oiticica, Hélio 131 97 **665**
Oki, Hiroyuki 280
Okumura, Lydia 140 626 **630–631**
Oldenburg, Claes 309 539
Olitski, Jules 750
Olowska, Paulina **185** 293
Olsoff, Wendy 593
OMR 392 **545** 690
Ondák, Roman 36 38 **43**
One and J. (Gallery) **545** **548**
Onorato, Taiyo & Krebs, Nico 616
Ontani, Luigi 264
Op de Beeck, Hans 280
Oppenheim, Dennis 264 **272–273** 440
Ora-Ora (Galerie) 364 **546**
Ortega, Damián 125 **671**
Osage (Gallery) 230 **546**
Osage Art Foundation 316
Ota (Fine Arts) **546–547**
Otsuji, Kiyoji 380
Owens, Laura 206
Oxley9, Roslyn (Gallery) **547**
Ozawa, Tsuyoshi **160** 364 **667**

P

P.P.O.W **183** 264 **582** **593** **673** **675**
Pace **582** 601
Pace Prints 246 **583**
Pace/MacGill (Gallery) 583
Paglen, Trevor 690
Paik, Nam June **340–341** **740–741**
Pak Sheung Chuen **663**
Pakesch, Peter 206
Palacios Whitman, Sylvia 140
Paladino, Mimmo 750
Paley, Maureen **584** **671** 690
Panayiotou, Christodoulos & Wiegard, Philip **663**
Pane, Gina 140 626
Paolini, Giulio 658 687
Pape, Lygia 131
Para Site 316 364 365 **663** **665**
Paragon 246 **248–249** **584**
Paris Photo 538
Paris-Beijing (Galerie) 364 **584**–585
Park Ryu Sook (Gallery) 364 **585**
Parkett 168 445 537
Parra & Romero 514 **585**
Parrasch, Franklin (Gallery) **585**
Parreno, Philippe 38 **352** 639
Pasternak, Anne 661 **668–669**
Pauli, Alice (Galerie) **586**
Paviot, Alain 538
Pearlstein, Alix 570 **572–573**
Peel, Stephen & Yana 665
Pékin (Fine Arts) **586**
Penalva, João 550
Peng Wei 364
Pengyi, Jiang 364
Penone, Giuseppe **671** **679** 690
Pepper, Steve 598
Peres Projects 514 **586** **671**
Peress, Gilles 537
Péret, Benjamin 539
Pérez Art Museum (Miami) 446 512
Pérez Rubio, Agustín 510–513
Performa 8–11 124 482 675
Perilli, Achille 541 683
Perret, Mai-Thu 415
Perrotin (Galerie) **419** **428–429** **587**
Pessoli, Alessandro 264 **270–271**
Pestoni, Jon 514
Petzel, Friedrich 206
Petzel (Gallery) 550 **587**
Phillips, Glenn 298 299 301
Pi (Artworks) 364 588
Pia, Francesca (Galerie) 588
Piacentino, Gianni **675**
Piano, Renzo 123 513 682
Picabia, Francis 446 750
Picasso, Pablo 252 254 309 314 536 542 750
Piccinini, Patricia **422–423**
Piene, Otto 534 538 539 **542**
Pierson, Jack 590
Pilkington, Penny 593
Pimentel, Taiyana 155 **188–191**
Pinault, François 536
Pineda, Jorge **151**
Pistoletto, Michelangelo 658 690 **698–699**
Pivi, Paola 542 **671**
PKM (Gallery) **588**
Plan B (Galeria) 208 **589**
Planet Art 20–**23**
Platform China **589**
Platon 390
Podnar, Gregor (Galerija) **590**
Pohle, Sascha 208 **216–217**
Poitras, Laura 513
Polígrafa (Obra Gráfica) 246 **590**
Pomodoro, Arnaldo 698
Pompidou (Centre Georges) 293 537 538 539 543 658
Ponce de León, Rita **188** 514
Poons, Larry 750
Porter, Fairfield 392
Porter, Liliana 392
Pozanti, Hayal 280
Prager, Alex 280 690
Prasad, Srinivasa 514
Presenhuber, Eva (Galerie) **344–345** 550 570 **590**–591 **669** **671** 690
Price, Elizabeth 280
Price, Seth 206 550 587
Price, Tom & Ba, Omar 208
Prina, Stephen 206 362 415
Prince, Richard 49 390 537 540
Printed Matter 445 604 **675**
Project Fulfill (Art Space) 364 **372–373** **591**
ProjecteSD **591**
Protoplast **726–737**
Prouvost, Laure 280 514 **669** 690
Proyectos Monclova **191** 550 **592**
Przywara, Andrzej 293
PSM **592** 616
Ptaszkowska, Anka 293
Public Art Fund 570
Pulitzer, Sam 514

Q

Qingtai Hu 208
Qiu Jiongjiong 364
Qiu Zhijie 264 356
Quistrebert, Florian & Michael 562
Qureshi, Saad 208

R

Raad, Walid 614 658
Rabinowitch, David 362
Rae, Fiona 750
RaebervonStenglin 208 562 **606** 616 690
Rafman, Jon 280
Rainer, Arnulf 658 764
Rakowitz, Michael 392 **677**
Ramiken Crucible **176** 562 **606** 616 **671** 690
Randall Weeks, Ishmael 562
Rasdjarmrearnsook, Araya **301**
Rasgado, Pablo 616
Raspet, Sean 514
Rauschenberg, Robert 79 309 539 601
Raven, Lucy 38
Ray, Charles 82 415 **673**
Ray, Man 79 409 538

Razuk, Marilia (Galeria) 562 570 **606–607**
Real Fine Arts 514 607
Rech, Almine (Gallery) 570 **607**
Rechmaoui, Marwan 658
Reena Spaulings (Fine Art) 607–608
Regen Projects 608 **669** 690
Rehberger, Tobias 230 232 **244–245**
Reich, Steve 599
Reid, Clunie 280
Reid, Maeghan 208 **216–217**
Reinhart, George 537
René, Denise (Galerie) **608**–609
Revolver (Galería) **187** 562 570 **609**
Reyes, Pedro **189** 446 514
Reynolds, Anthony (Gallery) **609** **614** 690
Rhode, Robin 280
Richard, James **665**
Richardson, Charlie 280
Richter, Gerhard 82 148 **149** 525 **669**
Ricks, Jim 570
Rigg, Jean 599
Riis (Galleri) **609**–610 690
Riley, Bridget 362
Riley, Terry 599
Rinke, Klaus 362
Rist, Pipilotti **733**
Robak, Tabor **181** 280 **724–725**
Robbins, David 49
Roberts & Tilton **610**
Robertson, Bryan 750
Robinson, Walter 7
Rodchenko, Alexandre 407
Rodeo 264 550 **610**
Rodríguez, Alex 280
Roesler, Nara (Galeria) 392 **400–401** **610**–611
ROH (Projects) 364 611
Rokeby 208 **611**
Roldán, Ana 280
Rondinone, Ugo 570 **579** 590
Ropac, Thaddaeus (Galerie) 570 **611**–612 **669** **675** 690
Rose, Rachel 280 **722–723** 724–725
Rose, Tracey 562 **566–567**
Rosen, Andrea (Gallery) 612 **673**
Rosenfeld, Lotty **184** 626 **677** **679**
Rosenfeld, Michael (Gallery) **612**
Rosenkranz, Pamela 208
Rosenquist, James 254 539
Rosler, Martha 6 264
Rossi & Rossi **612** **667**
Rossi, Garcia 538
Rotella, Mimmo 682 688
Rothko, Mark 525
Rothschild, Eva 550 **554–555**
Rothschild, Judith 392
Rowan (Gallery) 750
Rowland, Cameron **673**
Rubell Family Collection 446
Rubins, Nancy 570 574–**575**
Ruby, Sterling 280 380 **671** 690 **704–705**
Rückriem, Ulrich 362 658
Ruff, Thomas 49
Rugoff, Ralph **122**–123
Ruilova, Aïda 280
Ruinart **33**
Rumma, Lia 392 **613**
Ruppersberg, Allen 49
Ruzicska, Nikolaus (Galerie) **613**
Ryman, Robert 600

S

S.M.A.K. 539
Sachs, Tom **675**
Sagri, Giorgia 614
Saint-Jean, Sébastien 63
Sakhai, Simon 665
Sakshi (Gallery) **638**
Sala de Arte Público 186
Salamé, Tony 661 **670–671**
Salon 94 **638**
Samore, Sam 206
Sàn Art 512
Sandback, Fred 730
Sanfilippo, Antonio 541
Santos III, José 364 **370–371**
Saouma, Samia 362 543
Sarkissian, Hrair 299 562
Sasnal, Wilhelm 293
SASSAS 299
Satorre, Jorge 616 **620–621**
Savu, Serban 208 392
Sawa, Hiraki 280 514
SCAD (Hong Kong) 316
SCAI (the Bathhouse) **638–639**
SCAPE (Public Art) 513
Schad, Christian **177**
Schaulager 82 390 **669**
Scheggi, Paolo **671** 688
Schiele, Egon 531
Schilling, Alfons 626
Schinwald, Markus 690
Schipper, Esther **96–97** **639**
Schipper, Otavio 514
Schmela, Alfred 506
Schneemann, Carolee 593
Schneider, Gregor 293
School of Creative Media 316
Schorr, Collier 49
Schöttle, Rüdiger (Galerie) **639**–640
Schulte, Thomas (Galerie) 392 570 **640**
Schwartz, Anita (Galeria de Arte) 514 **640**
Schwartz, Anna (Gallery) **641**
Scott-Douglas, Hugh 514
Scott, Kitty 513
SculptureCenter 298 301 562 563
Seal, Ivan 208
Sehgal, Tino 36 38
Semarang (Gallery) **641**
Semercioglu, Gulay 364
Senatore, Marinella 123
Serota, Nicholas 750
Seroussi, Natalie (Galerie) **641**–642
Serpa, Ivan 392 **396–397**
Seton, Alex 364
Seung Yui Oh 548
Sfeir-Semler, Andrée 658
Sfeir-Semler (Gallery) **642** **658**
SFMOMA 769
Shainman, Jack (Gallery) 570 **642**
Shanghai Gallery (of Art) **643**
ShanghART (Gallery) 230 254 **643** 690
Shaomin, Shen 230
Sharif, Hassan 125 **164** 364
Sharjah Art Foundation 125 513
Sharjah Biennal 12 125 513
Shaw-Town, Dan 514
Shaw, Jim 690 **708–709**
Sheikha Hoor Al Qasimi 125
Sherman, Cindy 6 **470–471**
Shetty, Sudarshan 514 690
SHIMURAbros 280
Shin, Misa (Gallery) **160** 364 **643** **667**
Shonibare, Yinka (MBE) 570
Shore, Stephen 49
Shrigley, David 280
ShugoArts **173** **644** **667**
Si-Qin, Timur & Ned Vena 514
Sicardi (Gallery) 392 **644**
Sicilia, José María 514
Side 2 (Gallery) 364 616 **644**
Siem, Wiebke 690
Sierra, Santiago 36 38 **42** 264
Sies + Höke **468–469** **645** 690
Signer, Roman **227** 280
Sikkema Jenkins (& Co.) **645** 690
Silverlens **645–646**
Silverman, Jessica (Gallery) 514 **646**
Silverstein, Bruce 646–647
Simmons, Laurie 6
Siributr, Jakkai 364
Skape (Gallery) **647**
Skarstedt **88–89** **647**
SKE (Gallery) 514 **648** 690
Skoog, John 616 **622–623**
Skopia (P.-H. Jaccaud) **648** 690
Slager, Henk 513
Slinger, Penny 140
Slominski, Andreas 690
SlyZmud 562 570 **648**
Smith, John 280
Snauwaert, Dirk 511–513
Snitzer, Fredric (Gallery) **649**
Sobrino, Francisco 534 538
Société 514 616 **624–625** **649**
Soka (Art) **649–650**
Sorayama, Hajime 526
Sosnowska, Monika 206 **293**
Soulages, Pierre 536
Spalletti, Ettore 392
SpazioA 562 **564–565** **650**
Spellman, Lisa 49
Spero, Nancy 614
Sperone Westwater 392 **650**
Spirito, Mari 298
Spong, Sriwhana 280

Spooner, Cally **147**
Spring Workshop **663**
Sprüth Magers (Berlin London) **175 650 671 679** 690
St Ives School 750
St. Etienne (Galerie) **651**
Stadtkino, Basel **281**
Stærk, Nils (Galerie) **651**
Stahel, Urs 537
Stahl, Lucie 562 **568–569**
STAMPA **652**
Standard (Oslo) **102–103** 652 **669** 690 **691**
Standing Pine 364 **652**
Star (Gallery) 364 **653**
Starkwhite 230 **653**
Starmach Gallery **653–654**
Stein, Christian **654** 690
Stella, Frank 79 254 513 539
Stevenson **654**
Stieglitz, Alfred 49
Stingel, Rudolf **596–597**
Stockholder, Jessica 570
Stolper, Paul (Gallery) 246 **462–463 654–655**
Storr, Marcel 626 **634–635**
STPI 230 246 **251**–**254 655**
Strina, Luisa (Galeria) **655 679**
Stuart, Michelle 626
Sturtevant 534 539 540 **543** 614 **675**
Suárez Londoño, José Antonio 392
Subal, Simone (Gallery) 562 570 **656**
Subotzky, Mikhael 690
Sudek, Josef 407 537
Suga, Kishio 230
Sugiyama, Hisako 364 764
Sulaiman, Shooshie **166** 690
Sullivan+Strumpf 364 656
Sultan, Donald 254
Sun Kim, Christine 208
Sun Xun 230 **234–235** 254 364
Sundaram, Vivan **167 663**
Sung Hwan Kim 280 **667**
Suntag, Noh 364
Superflex 280
Supportico Lopez 264 **266–267** 514 **656** 690
Sur (Galería) **657**
Sylvester, David 750
Szántó, András **148–153** 298 300
Szeemann, Harald 122 540 730
Szwajcer, Micheline (Galerie) 657 690
Szymczyk, Adam 293

T

T293 514 **680**
Taaffe, Philip 390
Taguchi, Yukihiro 208 280
Take Ninagawa 208 264 380 514 **522–523 680**
Tan, Eugene 513
Tanaami, Keiichi 526
Tanaka, Koki **157**
Tang (Contemporary Art) 230 680
tanzer, dianne (gallery + projects) 364 **680–681**
Tàpies, Antoni 79 392 750
Tate 7 **147** 148 543 658 688 750 768
Tatsuki, Masaru 364
Taylor, Timothy (Gallery) 392 **681** 750
Taylor, Zin 514
Tayou, Pascale Marthine 690 **706–707**
Tchorek, Mariusz 293
team (gallery inc.) **181 681**
TEFAF 531
Tega (Galleria) **682**
Templon, Daniel (Galerie) **682**–683 690
Tezuka, Aiko 364
The Frost Museum 446
The Mosaic Rooms 299
The Moving Museum 665
The Whitworth Art Gallery 285
Theater Basel 8 36 38 669 671
Thomas (Galerie) **683**
Thomas, Mickalene 392
Thompson, Bob 309 598
Thompson, Jon 614
Thornton, Sarah 5–7
Three Star (Books) 246 **255 683–684**
Tillmans, Wolfgang 661 **671 672–673**
Tilton (Gallery) **684**
Tinari, Philip 665
Tinguely, Jean 82 536 542
Tiravanija, Rirkrit 49 125 **251** 690
TKG+ 364 **684**
Toguo, Barthélémy 570
Tokyo + BTAP (Gallery) **684–685**
Tolarno (Galleries) **422–423 685**
Tom of Finland 415
Tompkins, Betty 264
Tonkonow, Leslie 626 **685–686**
Toren, Amikam 614
Tornabuoni (Art) 686 **688**
Toroni, Niele 440
Torres-García, Joaquín 223
Torres-García, Taller 626
Travesía Cuatro 514 **518–519 686**
Trecartin, Ryan 512
Triennial (New York) 512
Trockel, Rosemarie 690 **714–715**
Troika 690
Trouvé, Tatiana 570 **579**
Trung, Nguyen 364 **366–367**
Truth & Consequences **673**
Tschudi (Galerie) 686 690
Tseng, Rudy 61 **666–667**
Tsuchiya, Nobuko 614
Tucci Russo (Studio) **671 686** 690
Turcato, Giulio 541
Turnbull, William 750
Turner, Daniel 690
Turrell, James 392
Tuttle, Richard 388
Tuymans, Luc 293 768
Tweedy, Ian 208
Two Palms 246 **247** 392 **687**
Tyler, Kenneth 251 254
Tyson, Keith 614

U

UBS 20–**25** 392
UCLA (Los Angeles) 7 415
Uecker, Günther 538
Uklanski, Piotr 671
Ullens Center 754
Ultra Violet 534 540
Umbo (Otto Umbehr) 407
University Galleries (Florida) 446
University Museum (Hong Kong) 316
Upstream (Gallery) 208 **718 719**
Urabe, Fumito 364 616
Ursuta, Andra **176 675** 690
Usui, Ryohei 208
Utopian Slumps 208 **718**

V

Vadehra (Art Gallery) **726**
Valie Export 197 626
Vallois, Georges-Philippe & Nathalie (Galerie) 626 **636–637 726**
Van de Weghe (Fine Art) **424–425 677 727**
van den Eynde, Isabelle (Gallery) **164** 364 **727**
van der Stokker, Lily **169**
van der Werve, Guido 550 **556–557** 690
Van Doren Waxter 392 **727**
van Elk, Ger 534 540 **543** 719
van Orsouw, Bob (Galerie) **728**
van Roijen, Hester 750
Vance, Lesley 415
Vargas Lugo, Pablo 514
Vari, Sophia 682
Venice Biennale 122 127 128 314 512 513 539 540
Venosa, Angelo 514
Vermelho **728**
Verna, Annemarie (Galerie) **171** 728–729 **730**
Verna, Annemarie & Gianfranco 730
Videotage 316
Vielmetter, Susanne 264 **276–277** 690 **729**
Vilanova, Oriol 514
Viola, Bill **679**
Vitamin (Creative Space) **157 663 667 729**
Vitiello, Stephen 280
Vitra Design Museum 82
Vizcaya Museum & Gardens 446 **452–453**
Volpi, Alfredo 626 **633–634**
von Heyl, Charline 206
Voulkos, Peter 415

W

Wada, Yumie 764
Wadden, Brent **671**
Waddington Custot (Galleries) **744** **750**
Waddington, Leslie 593 750
Waddington, Victor 750
Walcheturm (Gallery) 590
Walker, Jake 208
Walker, Kara 690 **694–695**
Wallinger, Mark 280 614
Wallner, Nicolai (Galleri) **744**
Wallspace 514 **745**
Walsh, Dan 604
Wang Chung-Kun 364 **372–373**
Wang Fujui 364 **372–373**
Wang Guangle 514
Wang Haiyang 280
Wang Jianwei 230
Wang Qingsong 287 446
Wang Yi 364
Ward, Eleanor 600
Warhol, Andy 7 98 **99** 143 390 531 539 540 601
Warren, Rebecca **671**
Washburn (Gallery) **745**
Watanabe, Maya 280
Weber, John (Gallery) **736–737**
Weber, Marnie 280
Weems, Carrie Mae 593
Weerasethakul, Apichatpong 614
Wei-Ling (Gallery) 364 **745–746**
Weiner, Lawrence 293 440 508
Weingrüll 208 **216–217** 746
Weiss, Barbara (Galerie) **746**
Wentrup 570 **675** **746**
Werble, Kate (Gallery) 616 747
Werner, Michael 362 390 **675** **747**
West, Franz 79 293 542
Wheeler, Doug 690
White Cube 90 **747**
White Space (Beijing) **420–421** 748
Whitechapel Art Gallery 750
Whitman, Robert 598
Whitney Biennial 540
Whitney Museum of American Art 512 513
Whitten, Jack 768
Wiels 513
Wieser, Claudia **468–469**
Wigram, Max (Gallery) 748
Wilke, Hannah 386
Wilkes, Cathy 690
Wilkinson 264 **268–269** **667** **748**
Willard, Marian 600
Williams, Christopher 178 206 362
Williams, Sue 49
Wilson, Jane & Louise 280 282 **283–285**
Wilson, Martha 593
Wilson, Robert 392
Winter, Hubert (Galerie) **748–749**
Winters, Terry 392
Witz, Konrad **673**
Wojnarowicz, David 264 513 **593** **673** **675**
Wolbers, Saskia Olde 690
Wolff, Jocelyn (Galerie) 392 **749**
Wolfson, Jordan 36 **41**
Wolfsonian-FIU 446
Wolin, Ron 600
Won Jae Park 546
Wong, Adrian 63 **338–339**
Wong, Martin **183** 593 **675**
Wong, Morgan 230
Wong Ping 62
Wong Wai Yin **663**
Wood & Harrison 280
Wood, Jonas 415
Wood, Matthew 498 508
Woodman, Betty 415
Woodrow, Bill 750
Wool, Christopher 206 362
Woolfalk, Saya 280
Workplace (Gallery) 208 **214–215** **749**
World House (Gallery) 598 599
Wu Chang-Jung 280
Wu Dayu **161**
Wu Jian'an 364
Wu Shanzhuan 252 356
Wu, Robert 261
Wyss, Kurt **732–743**

X

Xiao Feng 364
Xiao Yu **665**
Xu Bacheng 364
Xu Qu 230 **242–243**
Xu Zhen 36 38 **41** 690 **752–757**
Xu, Leo (Projects) **159** **163** 208 **663** **758**
XVA (Gallery) 364 **758** **759**

Y

Y++ Wada (Fine Arts) 364 626 **762** **764**
Yabin Wang 364
Yamaki (Fine Art Gallery) 364 **762**
Yamamoto Gendai **763**
Yamamoto, Takahiro 364
Yamazaki, Tsuruko 514
Yan Xing 392
Yang (Gallery) 364 **763**
Yang, Haegue 125 **252** **667** 690
Yang Xinguang 230
Yang Yongliang 364
Yangjiang Group 300
Yassin, Raed 280
Yavuz (Gallery) 364 **763**
Ye Linghan 280
Yeats, Jack 750
Yeesookyung 230 232 **238–239**
Yeh Wei-li 356
Young At Art Museum 446
Yu Cheng-Ta 230
Yuan Jai 356
Yuan Yuan 364
Yuen, Nina 280
Yvaral, Jean-Pierre 538

Z

Zaatari, Akram 658
Zahedi, Morteza 759
Zander, Thomas (Galerie) 690 **766**
Zao Wou-Ki 71 161
Zazeela, Marian 598
Zen Foto (Gallery) 316
Zeng Fanzhi 287 550 **560–561**
Zeno X (Gallery) **766** **768**
ZERO 538
ZERO (Gallery) 690 766–767
Zhan Wang **261** 690
Zhang Guiming 71
Zhang Huan 690
Zhang Qing 513
Zhang Quan 364
Zhang, Enli 316 **665**
Zhao Liang **665**
Zilberman (Galeri) 364 **767**
Zink Yi, David **188** 514
Ziolkowski, Jakub Julian **179**
Zobernig, Heimo 79 206 690
Zwirner, David 767 690
Zwirner, Rudolf 362 390

Art Basel Team 2014

EXECUTIVE COMMITTEE

Marc Spiegler
Director

Marco Fazzone
Director Resources & Finance

Magnus Renfrew
Director Asia

Annette Schönholzer
Director of New Initiatives

MANAGEMENT BOARD

Andreas Bicker
Head of General Management

Laura Blagho
Head of Marketing & Communications

Maureen Bruckmayr
General Manager Miami Beach

Patrick Foret
Head of Sponsorship

Michèle Sandoz
Head of VIP & Visitor Services

Andrew Strachan
General Manager Hong Kong

Sven Tresp
Head of Operations & Logistics

Thomas Wüstenhagen/Daniel Lechner
Head of Gallery Relations

DIRECTORS' ASSISTANTS

Janett Schickler
Directors Assistant

Jenny Or
Director's Assistant Asia

Muriel Meidinger
Office and Project Coordinator

GALLERY RELATIONS

Isabelle Baume
Gallery & Project Assistant

Barbara Berli
Gallery & Project Assistant

François M. Croissant
Gallery & Project Manager

Lucy Crommelin
Gallery & Project Manager

Ursula Diehr
Gallery & Project Manager

Charlotte Draycott
Gallery & Project Manager

Jonas Egli
Gallery & Project Assistant

Dunja Gottweis
Gallery & Project Manager

Benjamin Grappin
Gallery & Project Manager

Markus Mäder
Gallery & Project Manager

Michael Müller
Gallery & Project Manager

Daniela Schimmel
Gallery & Project Manager

Angelle Siyang-Le
Gallery & Project Manager

Stefanie Wenger
Assistant Unlimited

OPERATIONS & LOGISTICS

Zenia Choy
Operations & Logistics Executive Asia

Nour El-Gourany
Operations & Logistics Assistant

Trevor Hyland
Operations & Logistics Manager Asia

Crystal Lai
Operations & Logistics Executive Asia

Suez Lui
Associate Operations & Logistics Manager Asia

Thibaud Schmitt
Operations Associate

MARKETING & COMMUNICATIONS

Kristi D'Arcy
Media Production Manager

Jessica Bourgoz
Talks Program Coordinator

Renata Catambas
Publishing Manager/Year 45 Book

Joey Chan
Marketing & Communications Assistant Asia

Janice Ching
Marketing & Communications Assistant Asia

Yoko Choy
Media Production Manager Asia

Dorothee Dines
Public Relations Manager

Magdalena Dysli
Event Manager

Marion Erard
Graphic Designer

Lucinda Evans
Associate Event Manager Asia

Camilla Hall
Marketing & Events Assistant

Myrta Holinger
Public Relations Assistant

Lucy Knight
Digital Manager

Ron Lux
Events Assistant

David Meier
Marketing Project Manager

Maxi Moshammer
Marketing Project Manager

Jennifer Pratt
Marketing & Communications Manager Asia

Caroline Sieg
Content & Channel Manager

Claudio Vogt
Associate Event Manager

SPONSORSHIP

Hanna Barber/Melissa Netecke
Sponsorship Manager Americas

Gerda van den Bergh
Sponsorship Manager Europe

Dovenia Chow
Sponsorship Manager Asia

Lucinda Evans
Associate Sponsorship Manager

Nadine Lopez
Sponsorship Manager

Lena Walter
Associate Sponsorship Manager

VIP & VISITOR SERVICES

Andrina Brunner
VIP Relations Assistant

Claudia Chan
VIP Relations Assistant Asia

Isabel Dombos
VIP Relations Assistant

Olivia Doppler
Visitor Services Manager

Deborah Ehrlich
VIP Relations Manager Asia

Naoki Fukushima
VIP Relations Assistant

Sarah Huber
CRM Development Coordinator

Nicola Hüll
VIP Relations Manager

Alena Lachmann
VIP Relations Assistant

Priscilla Lee
VIP Relations Assistant Asia

Oliver Lerch
VIP Relations Assistant

Marina Mottin
VIP Relations Manager

Sascha Nikitin
VIP Relations Manager Switzerland

Claudia Schachenmann
VIP Relations Project Manager

Mandy Shek
VIP Relations Assistant Asia

Philipp Voellmy
VIP Client Development & CRM Manager

Alison Weill
VIP Relations Assistant

Verona Zeng
VIP Relations Assistant Asia

VIP RELATIONS

Princess Alia Al-Senussi
Middle East

Mirta d'Argenzio
Italy

Charlotte Bancroft
USA, Canada

Stefanie Block Reed
USA/Florida

Bambi Blumberg
Australia, New Zealand

Karen Boros
Germany

Anjali Devidayal
India

Amanda Echeverria
Mexico

Deborah Ehrlich
Hong Kong

Luluc Huang
China/Beijing

Jenny Lee
Taiwan

Hélène Mairlot
Benelux

Marina Mottin
Africa

Adeline Ooi
Singapore, Malaysia, Indonesia, Philippines

Nikolay Palazhenko
Russia and CIS Countries

Iciar S-Mangas
Latin America, Spain, Portugal

Ricardo Sardenberg
Brazil

Selen Sarıoğlu
Turkey

Andreas Siegfried
United Kingdom

Natane Takeda
Japan

Denise Vilgrain
France, Greece

Euna Yoo
South Korea

Malena Zhang
China/Shanghai

REPRESENTATION

FITZ & CO, New York
USA

Garber + Goodman, Inc., Miami
Florida

Hong Kong

SELECTION COMMITTEE

Massimo De Carlo, Massimo De Carlo, Milan & London
Emi Eu, STPI – Singapore Tyler Print Institute, Singapore
Shireen Gandhy, Chemould Prescott Road, Mumbai
Suzie Kim, Kukje Gallery/Tina Kim Gallery, Seoul & New York
Maho Kubota, SCAI The Bathhouse, Tokyo
David Maupin, Lehmann Maupin, New York & Hong Kong
Urs Meile, Galerie Urs Meile, Beijing & Lucerne
Zhang Wei, Vitamin Creative Space, Guangzhou & Beijing

SECTOR EXPERTS

Discoveries
Finola Jones, mother's tankstation, Dublin
Atsuko Ninagawa, Take Ninagawa, Tokyo

Modern Art
Mathias Rastorfer, Galerie Gmurzynska, Zurich, St. Moritz & Zug

CURATOR

Encounters
Yuko Hasegawa, Tokyo

Basel

SELECTION COMMITTEE

Xavier Hufkens, Xavier Hufkens, Brussels
Jochen Meyer, Meyer Riegger Galerie,
Berlin & Karlsruhe
Lucy Mitchell-Innes, Mitchell-Innes & Nash, New York
Tim Neuger, neugerriemschneider, Berlin
Franco Noero, Galleria Franco Noero, Turin
Eva Presenhuber, Galerie Eva Presenhuber, Zurich

SECTOR EXPERTS

Statements and Feature
Miguel Abreu, Miguel Abreu Gallery, New York
Silvia Dauder, ProjecteSD, Barcelona
Sunitha Kumar Emmart, GallerySKE, Bangalore

Edition
Niels Borch Jensen, Niels Borch Jensen Gallery &
Edition, Berlin & Copenhagen

Classical Photography
Edwynn Houk, Edwynn Houk Gallery, New York

Appeals Board
Cyrill Häring, President, Basel
Christoph Degen, Basel
Christina Végh, Bonn

CURATORS

Film
This Brunner, Zurich
Marc Glöde, Berlin

Parcours
Florence Derieux, Reims

Unlimited
Gianni Jetzer, New York

HONORARY BOARD

Ernst Beyeler †
Trudi Bruckner
Felix Buchmann †
Pierre Huber
Gianfranco Verna
Annely Juda †
Denise René †
Lucio Amelio †

Miami Beach

SELECTION COMMITTEE

Chantal Crousel, Galerie Chantal Crousel, Paris
Peter Freeman, Peter Freeman, Inc., New York
Martin Klosterfelde, Galerie Klosterfelde, Berlin
José Kuri, kurimanzutto, Mexico City
Friedrich Petzel, Friedrich Petzel Gallery, New York
Jeff Poe, Blum & Poe, Los Angeles
Mary Sabbatino, Galerie Lelong, New York

SECTOR EXPERTS

Nova and Positions
Marcío Botner, A Gentil Carioca, Rio de Janeiro
Joanna Kamm, Galerie Kamm, Berlin
Andrew Kreps, Andrew Kreps Gallery, New York

Florida Galleries
Fredric Snitzer, Fredric Snitzer Gallery, Miami

CURATORS

Film
This Brunner, Zurich
David Gryn, London

Public
Nicholas Baume, New York

Editorial Committee
Laura Blagho
Lionel Bovier
Clément Dirié
Gilles Gavillet
Marc Spiegler

General Editorial Coordination
Lionel Bovier
Clément Dirié
Eléonor de Pesters

Art Direction
Gavillet & Rust/Gilles Gavillet

Gallery Data
Barbara Berli
Renata Catambas

Editing
Clément Dirié
Eléonor de Pesters
Clare Manchester

Copyediting and Proofreading
Clément Dirié
Clare Manchester
Karin Prätorius
Jennifer Pratt
Kevin Slide

Assistance
Amandine Roggeman
Naïma Saidi

Translations
Deke Dusinberre (von Bartha; Discoveries; Lambert; Ovations, Tornabuoni); Karin Prätorius (Curiger)

Design
Gavillet & Rust/Vincent Devaud

Assistance
Alice Franchetti, Noémie Gygax, Chi-Long Trieu

Typefaces
Plain, Genath Basel (François Rappo/www.optimo.ch)

Color Separation & Print
Musumeci S.p.A., Quart (Aosta)

Image Courtesies
All images in the Exhibitors Lists as well as in the Curators' Choices, Top Tens, and Galleries Focus are courtesy of the galleries unless otherwise mentioned.

Photo Credits & Courtesies
Unless otherwise noted here, the photographs, including portraits, of Art Basel in Hong Kong, in Basel, and in Miami Beach are by Julien Gremaud.

Additional photography of the three fairs by MCH Messe Schweiz (Basel) AG photographers: 40b, 43t, 53, 58–59, 84–85, 120, 187, 188, 216–217, 238–239, 242–243, 247, 248–249, 250, 255, 274–275, 281, 320–321, 327, 330–335, 340–341, 344–347, 380b, 420–421, 422–423, 428–429, 475–487 (Scott Rudd: 475–483; 486–487), 508, 554–557, 620–621, 624–625, 671–672, 675–677, 692–693, 755; as well as by Kevin Slide: 44–45, 58–59, 83, 90–91, 253, 322–323, 419, 448–449, 452–453.

303 Gallery: 282, 677-1; 4A Centre for Contemporary Asian Art: 300t; Absolut/Roberto Chamorro: 62, 65, 66–67, 663-8; Terry Adkins Estate and Salon 94: 537; Asia Art Archive: 663-3, 663-6; Everton Ballardin: 500t; Bruno Bani: 378l; Filipe Berndt: 435bl; Bernd Borchardt: 76l; Biennale de Lyon/Jasper Clarke: 122; Cosima von Bonin: 527r; Galerie Gisela Capitain: 206; Janni Chavakis (2004)/Harun Farocki Filmproduktion: 539l; Paula Cooper Gallery/Stefan Altenburger: 596–597, 605b; Pilar Corrias: 722–723; Oliver Cowling for Tate Photography: 147; Davidoff Art Initiative: 151, 152, 153; Massimo De Carlo: 227; Delfina Foundation: 301t; Claire Dorn/Takashi Murakami/Kaikai Kiki Co., Ltd., JR-ART.NET: 587l ; Sepp Dreissinger/Hauser & Wirth and Maria Lassnig Estate: 541r; East of Borneo: 299b; Foksal Gallery Foundation: 293t; Edouard Fraipont: 728tr; Saša Fuis: 310b; Marco Funke: 193l; Gasworks: 300m; Max Geuter: 126; Liam Gillick and Esther Schipper/Andrea Rossetti: 639l; Lucy Hensel/Galerie In Situ–Fabienne Leclerc: 538r; Maren Heyne: 542; Sheila Hicks & galerie franck elbaz/Zarko Vijatovic: 257tr; Pontus Hook: 647r; Mireille Hoster/Archivio Accardi: 536; Tom Huber: 168; Karma Gallery: 675-9; Kunstmuseum Basel (Geschenk von August La Roche-Burckhardt 1868)/Martin P. Bülher: 673-3; Galerie Lahumière, Paris: 541l; Tanya Leighton: 669-3; Magnum Collection/Magnum Photos: 538l; The Mosaic Rooms: 299m; Gregor Muir: 665-7, 665-9; Roberta Neiman/Joan Jonas Studio: 383; Michiel van Nieuwkerk: 543b; Eduardo Ortega: 288br; Dirk Pauwels: 539r; Performa/Patrick McMullan: 124; Sigmar Polke Estate: 540l; Reserved Rights: 667-7, 669-1; Anthony Reynolds Gallery: 614; SASSAS: 399t; SculptureCenter: 301b; Lisa Spellman: 47l; Wolfgang Stahr: 149; STPI: 251t, 252b, 254; Studio Olafur Eliasson © BMW Group/Olafur Eliasson: 150; Loren Sturtevant/Courtesy Air de Paris: 543t; Team (gallery, inc.): 725; Harald Thierlein/Gallery Kicken: 540r; Richard Tuttle: 684l; Upstream Gallery: 719b; Annemarie Verna Gallery: 730; Ben Westoby: 747t; Jane & Louise Wilson: 284–285; XVA Gallery: 758; Kurt Wyss: 599, 605t, 733, 734–735, 736–737, 738–739, 740–741, 742–743

Acknowledgments
We are grateful to all the authors, artists, and photographers who contributed to this book, to all those who have helped us gathering the information, in particular to Winka Angelrath, Charlotte Bancroft, Alexia Dehaene, Albertine Kopp, Michelle Kuo, Nawale Lacroix, Ellie Levitt, Ulrika Lövdahl, Rachel Patall-David, Job Piston, Paloma Szathmáry, Rebecca Taylor, Karine Verloren van Themaat (FEAGA), Abigail Varian, Annik Wetter, Tobias Wyss, and the Infocentric team for their kind support.

The information printed in this book is based on the three 2014 Art Basel online information (Hong Kong, Basel, Miami Beach) and questionnaire answered directly by the exhibitors: gallery name and list of artists, sectors' participations, etc. thus follow Art Basel's formatting and editorial guidelines. Every attempt has been made by the publisher to copyedit and correct this information within the constraints of these guidelines and the timeframe of the publication.

Printed in Europe

Published by
JRP|Ringier
Limmatstrasse 270
CH–8005 Zurich
T +41 (0) 43 311 27 50
F +41 (0) 43 311 27 51
E info@jrp-ringier.com
www.jrp-ringier.com

ISBN 978-3-03764-395-2

JRP|Ringier books are available internationally at selected bookstores and from the following distribution partners:

Switzerland
AVA Verlagsauslieferung AG
verlagsservice@ava.ch, www.ava.ch

France
Les presses du réel
www.lespressesdureel.com

Germany and Austria
Vice Versa Distribution GmbH
www.vice-versa-distribution.com

UK and other European countries
Cornerhouse Publications
www.cornerhouse.org/books

USA , Canada, Asia, and Australia
ARTBOOK|D.A.P.
orders@dapinc.com, www.artbook.com

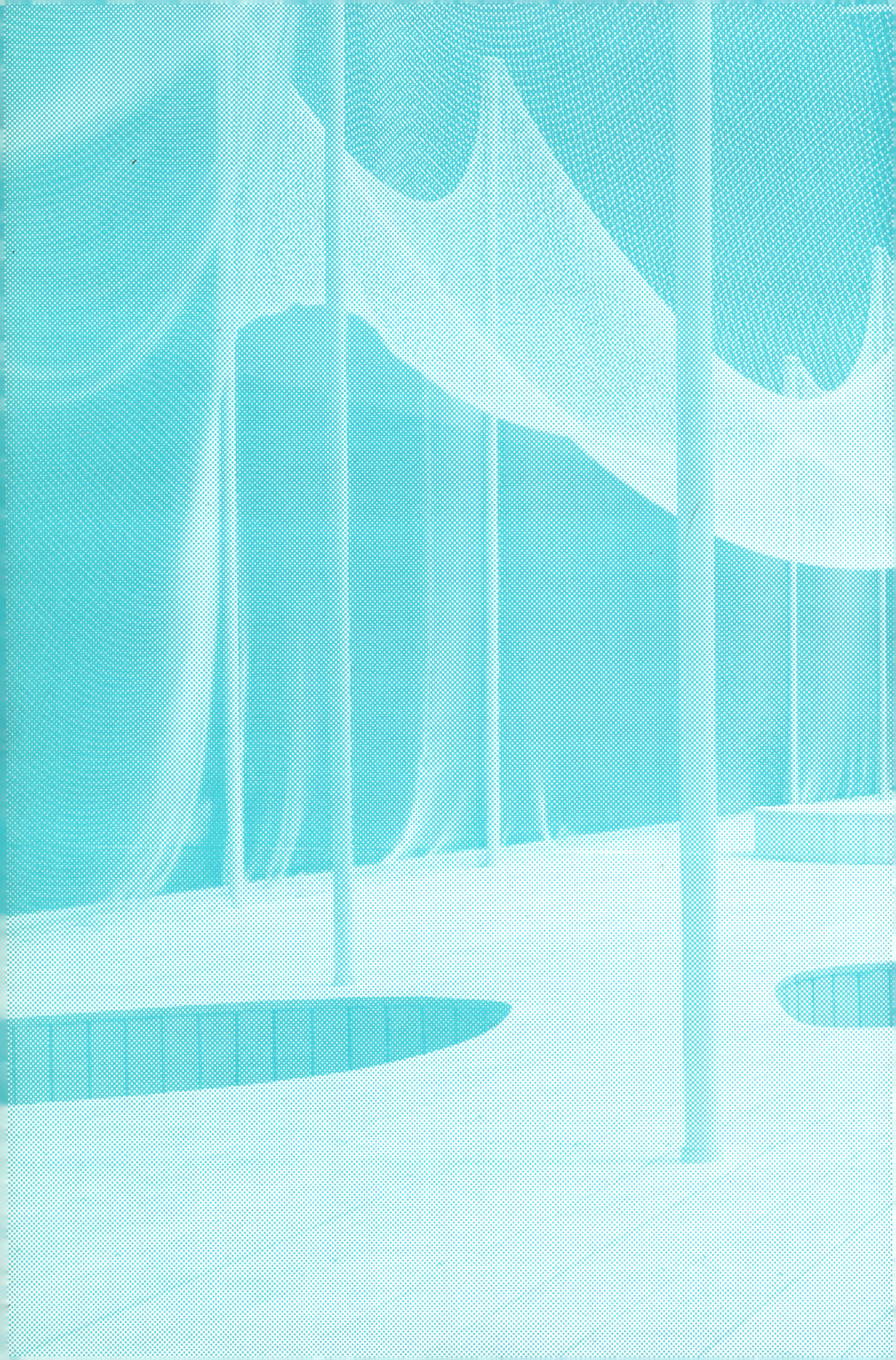